ISSUES
IN
PAKISTAN'S
ECONOMY

S. AKBAR ZAIDI

OXFORD
UNIVERSITY PRESS

OXFORD

UNIVERSITY PRESS

Great Clarendon Street, Oxford OX2 6DP

Oxford University Press is a department of the University of Oxford.
It furthers the University's objective of excellence in research, scholarship,
and education by publishing worldwide in

Oxford New York

Athens Auckland Bangkok Bogotá Buenos Aires Calcutta
Cape Town Chennai Dar es Salaam Delhi Florence Hong Kong Istanbul
Karachi Kuala Lumpur Madrid Melbourne Mexico City Mumbai
Nairobi Paris São Paulo Singapore Taipei Tokyo Toronto Warsaw
with associated companies in Berlin Ibadan

Oxford is a registered trade mark of Oxford University Press
in the UK and in certain other countries

ISBN 0 19 579052 9

Second Impression 2000

Printed in Pakistan at
New Sketch Graphics, Karachi.
Published by
Ameena Saiyid, Oxford University Press
5-Bangalore Town, Sharae Faisal
PO Box 13033, Karachi-75350, Pakistan.

Contents

Figures

Tables

Preface

Writing this book has been a challenging and often daunting task. The idea originated from the staff of Oxford University Press, who suggested that there was a need for a book on Pakistan's economy, which could be understood by graduate students, researchers, scholars, academicians, and the general public at large, even without having a sound grounding in economic theory. This has indeed been the focus of the book, targeting a wide spectrum of readers, in simple language, exploring processes, ideas, and trends. I hope that this book will provide new insight on numerous home truths and myths which abound in Pakistan, and allow the reader to question what is perceived to be conventional wisdom. The most ambitious of the many aspirations of this book is to stimulate the process of enquiry amongst readers. I do not expect all readers to agree with me, but I hope they will see and welcome the different interpretation that is presented here. This, I hope, will generate debate, which is, after all, the purpose of enquiry. Since there are no absolutes in social science, only interpretations and perspectives, let this book be a new, and one hopes fresh, perspective on the economy and society in Pakistan.

This project started when I was an Associate Professor/ Senior Research Economist at the Applied Economics Research Centre, University of Karachi, where I worked for almost fifteen years and taught a course called 'Issues in Pakistan's Economy'. All my professional life was spent at the University, and I owe a debt of gratitude to the institution, and my former colleagues and students, for shaping my way of thinking. I was forced to leave the Applied Economics Research Centre under rather sad and unfortunate circumstances. My departure was only partially voluntary, and was largely in disgust at the goings on at the University and the Centre at that time. However, the work on this book continued at home, and the end result of this endeavour, which has taken four and a half years, shows that research and scholarly pursuit are possible by 'independent' researchers not necessarily affiliated to any particular organization or institution.

Despite this 'independence', however, one cannot pursue intellectual and academic interests without interaction and exchange of ideas with other scholars and academics. A number of friends have been a constant source of pleasure and irritation, in the extended discussions that I have had with them over the years. Aly Ercelawn, Asad Sayeed, Anjum Altaf, Arif Hasan, Jaffer Ahmed, Rathin Roy, Talat Aslam, and Shahzad Amjad have all spent hours and days over the last few years, arguing with me over what I thought were important issues. We remain friends despite our severe disagreements. I often refused to accept their opinions, thinking that I was the one who was always right. However, I am now more willing to accept my numerous faults, shortcomings, and mistakes, and to give credit where it is due. To all these friends named above, who have inspired me at different times for different reasons, I give my heartfelt thanks for bearing with someone who has the reputation of being a difficult and stubborn person, prone to long bouts of brooding. Arif Hasan, in particular, deserves immense gratitude for taking the effort to read through the entire raw manuscript, and for his generous encouragement.

I acknowledge the persistence of Oxford University Press staff at Karachi, in making me accept and start this project. In particular, Yasmin Qureshi and Nighat Gaya were instrumental in my taking on this assignment. Zohrain Zafar, who later managed this project from OUP Karachi, is also acknowledged for directing my overly ambitious enthusiasm into concentrating on the task at hand. It is due to Zohrain that I completed this project on time. Although this has been an enormous undertaking, one which I may not have willingly accepted on my own, I now feel the wiser for having undertaken it.

After I submitted this manuscript to OUP Pakistan in August 1997, it was sent on to OUP in Oxford for the final production phase. Moreover, while the manuscript was being managed and edited at Oxford, I too was at the University of Oxford as a Visiting Scholar on the South Asian Visiting Scholars Programme. My presence in Oxford at a critical stage of the editing and management of the manuscript allowed me to interact closely and frequently with the editor of the manuscript and with the Oxford University Press staff handling the book. I must acknowledge the great help and understanding offered to me by Sally Rigg and Tony Dale of the International Education Unit at Oxford University Press in Oxford. The editor of the manuscript, Chris Bessant, has quite remarkably transformed the manuscript into a book; to Chris I acknowledge a huge debt for such a highly impressive achievement. I must also mention Aditya Nigam and Anandhi, two other scholars with me on the South Asian Visiting Scholars Programme at the University of Oxford, for making me reconsider numerous biases which I held under the guise of convictions. Had I met Aditya and Anandhi a few years earlier, this book would probably have taken on a different form.

The special contribution made by Qaisar Anjum and by Mukaram Farooqi, in typing and producing the manuscript, is beyond praise. They have produced work of exceptional quality, under unrelenting pressure from me to meet a constantly shifting deadline. To them, my wholehearted and sincere thanks.

Although it is customary to thank one's family for their inspiration and silent contribution, in my case things are a little more complicated. Both my sons Faiz and Amar still wonder why their father does not go to work: I hope when they are in a position to read this book, they will understand that one can 'go to work' sitting in the next room. Rabab, too, has often felt that I spend too much time doing academic work and not making lots of money; to her, thanks are due for being patient, supportive, and understanding, and for not complaining too much.

S. Akbar Zaidi
Karachi, August 1998

Introduction

Pakistan's economic performance over the last five decades has been, at times, quite spectacular, and at others, nothing but dismal. It failed to maintain the high growth in agriculture and manufacturing which it experienced in the 1960s, after a difficult start in the first decade following independence. The 1970s, for a host of reasons, most beyond the control of the incumbent government, were not even a patch on the 1960s, although surprisingly in the 1970s the economy performed better than it did in the 1950s. Towards the end of the 1970s, and for much of the 1980s, until at least 1988, the high-growth pattern re-emerged, though being qualitatively different from the growth performance of the 1960s. The economy in the 1980s seemed to be on a higher plain than that of the 1960s. There were murmurs that perhaps Pakistan had once again returned to the 'natural' growth rate path of 6 per cent plus, and would now continue where it had left off in 1968–9. However, just as the ten-year period after 1958 unravelled resulting in an appreciable slowing down of the economy, so too did the end of the ten or so years from about 1978–9 onwards.

With the return of democracy in 1988, the growth rates of the economy once again fell to levels reminiscent of the first democratic period of 1971–7. This trend gave rise to suggestions that, since growth rates in Pakistan were highest under military regimes, and also under democracy the economy had performed particularly poorly, perhaps one way of achieving high growth rates for the economy would be to maintain military regimes for some time to come. Once high growth rates had been achieved and the economy had been launched on a stable growth path, perhaps then politicians should be allowed a stake in running the government, and not before. The often-quoted examples of South Korea, Taiwan, Singapore, Malaysia, Thailand, and Indonesia seemed to fit the pattern, where authoritarian states had high-performing economies.

Yet much of the analysis examining the economic miracle of East Asia ignored specific factors, institutional arrangements, the nature of the state, and issues of governance and administration. There are as many similarities between the East Asian economies as there are differences, and a more detailed study of each country shows peculiarities which explain why and how they developed. In fact, Pakistan's growth pattern, at least in the 1960s, also offered some general and particular pointers on how to 'do development'.

The period after 1988 has brought about an extraordinary sea change in how the world thinks about economics, markets, growth, and development. In the 1960s the single focus was growth, with little concern for distribution, equality, or any other consequence of growth. As long as growth rates were high, the economy was doing well. Growth was supposed to trickle down from the high-income and rich savers and investors to the rest of the population. In the 1990s, growth is still important, but it is now subservient to a development which needs to be participatory, distributive, just, sustainable, and environmentally friendly. A growth rate of 7 or 8 per cent, while welcome, must be seen in the light of these other important indicators of development.

More importantly, the way growth is to take place now differs substantially from the way economic growth was supposed to take place prior to the mid-1980s. Now markets must be efficient and must determine the demand and supply of scarce resources. States and governments must stay out of the economy, and privatization, openness, liberalization, and globalization, according to conventional wisdom, must determine choices regarding how and where to invest and what to produce. Countries should get their prices right, and reduce subsidies and all other distortions in the economy. Even in the social sectors, the role of the state is supposed to be minimized, with private sector initiative leading the way.

One of the arguments made in this book is that after 1988, when a package of policy reform was introduced, the economy has performed less well than it did in the past. To a great extent, the structural adjustment programme, launched in Pakistan in 1988 under the guidance and direction of the IMF and the World Bank, has resulted in a visible slowing down in the economy, increasing income inequality, poverty, and unemployment, and hastening the process of deindustrialization. The post-1988 period may turn out to be the worst decade in terms of economic growth and development over the last fifty years.

Ironically, although the example of South Korea in particular, and that of other East Asian economies in general, is repeatedly cited for Pakistan to emulate, the conditions and policies that were essential for the growth of the East Asian economies *are quite the opposite* of those being propagated post-1988 under the structural adjustment programme. As an illustration, we can cite just a handful of policies pursued by South Korea which are believed to be the critical cause of high growth.

South Korea's was certainly what is called an 'authoritarian industrialization pattern', where the existence of a developmentalist bureaucracy and state, an *interventionist* bureaucracy and state, was fundamental to the process of growth that emerged. In Korea, landlordism was abolished and an extensive land reform undertaken. Cheap credit, i.e. directed credit, was made available to the private sector at subsidized rates, with certain sectors receiving priority treatment. Prices were continuously got 'wrong' rather than right, with numerous government-imposed controls and restrictions pushing the industrial pattern in a preferred direction. Essentially, it was the state, a particular kind of state, which intervened in the process of economic development, *and not the market*, which was responsible for the extraordinary rate of growth observed in South Korea and much of East Asia. In contrast, just the opposite to interventionist and statist policies are being recommended for Pakistan in the post-1988 structural adjustment period.

While a comparison of the Ayub and Zia years shows that both decades achieved high growth, it also suggests that at the end of the decades, the growth performance unravelled because the existing political settlement that permitted high growth came into conflict and contradiction with the very structures and system that it had created. The result was the emergence of popular movements and opposition to the military regimes, and the foundation of a kind of democratic order. However, while the democratic regime of Zulfiqar Ali Bhutto ended with a return to martial rule, the post-1988 democratic structure – although it has seen ten governments between May 1988 and February 1997 – is of a different nature. One of the more important contributions of this book is to highlight the essence of that new order.

This book, after developing a factual and interpretive story about economic growth and development in Pakistan over fifty years, ends with the observation that a new economic and political order has emerged in the country. For want of different terms, this new order is called the 'middle-class consolidation', if not revolution, after 1988. The reasons for it are to be found in the nineteen chapters of this book. We argue that, while as an economic category the middle class emerged and consolidated itself, first in the late 1960s, and then again in the 1980s, it is only now that it is consolidating itself as a political entity and force. Quite possibly it is too soon to 'announce' a middle-class revolution, but some signs indicate that it may be at some stage of development. Having said this, it is important to emphasize that nowhere do we glorify this class, if indeed it is *one* social class, for this is no pristine, revolutionary, and progressive class. This is Pakistan, and Pakistan's corrupted, rent-seeking, inefficient, pampered middle class which has, as yet, no understanding of the role it is expected to play. For example, it does not see the essential prerequisites of human capital formation and infrastructure development, for progress, for itself or for the nation in the years to come. Pakistan's middle class, like all other classes present, has evolved in the particular and specific conditions that define what Pakistan is. To expect otherwise, that we would necessarily have a modern, progressive, educated, forward-looking middle class, as did Europe some centuries ago, or Latin America many decades ago, is wishful thinking. In many ways, what we have is the result of what Pakistan is. That, perhaps, is the story of the process of economic development in Pakistan, not just over the last fifty years, but probably, for the next fifty as well.

About the Book

There is no denying the fact that this book has an ambitious agenda. Its purpose is to question some of the key myths that have been handed down by at least a couple of generations of social scientists. We question some of the most repeated, incorrect statements perpetuated by students of Pakistan's economy and society. While this is perhaps a key purpose of this book, we also provide new facts about, and interpretation of, areas of the economy and time periods that have not been evaluated by researchers or academicians. Hence, the purpose

is twofold: (1) to re-examine much of the perceived conventional wisdom about developments in Pakistan's society and economy, myths which have now assumed the scale of folklore; and (2) to provide facts, data and information about the economy, particular sectors, and recent years, which are not to be found in other books on the topic. While this is not another book in the Fifty Years of Pakistan series, by virtue of it covering the period 1947 up to and including the present, it does cover at least fifty years, if not a little more. An attempt is made to look at historical events and developments of the past, as well as more contemporary issues.

In this book we question some of the following assumptions, which not only students of economics, but even so-called experts on Pakistan repeat *ad nauseam*.

In the first chapter, we try to assess whether Pakistan's fifty years of development and growth have been a success or failure. However, this is an impossible task, and in many ways, the issue itself is redundant. The parameters of success or failure, the comparisons over space and time, the possibilities of what might have been, etc. are so imponderable and complex that it is best to leave such a debate inconclusive. Pakistan has performed far better than, say, Afghanistan; however, it has fared far worse than South Korea or any of the East Asian economies, which were at comparable levels of development forty or fifty years ago. We do look at some of Pakistan's achievements and failures in the last five decades, but leave it to readers to reach their own conclusions based on the arguments presented in the chapter and the rest of the book.

The most popular myth still prevalent in Pakistan is that Pakistan is a feudal country; in Part I of this book, which deals with agriculture, and especially in Chapters 2, 3, and 4, we show that this is certainly not the case – feudalism, as the dominant economic category, may have passed into history many decades ago. What we see now, and have seen for many years, is a capitalist agriculture in Pakistan. Another often-quoted statement by students studying Pakistan's economy – through no fault of their own, for one finds these statements in most textbooks on economics – is that Pakistan is an agricultural country. This too is no longer strictly true, since agriculture now constitutes less than one-quarter of the country's GDP. Although 47 per cent of those gainfully employed are said to work in agriculture, the trend is fast diminishing and more people are moving away from rural areas altogether, or are finding non-agricultural employment. The four chapters in Part I examine the nature of transition in Pakistan's agriculture over many decades, with Chapter 5 examining the salient problems that afflict agriculture at present. The current deep crisis in agriculture also, perhaps, bears witness to our claim that Pakistan is no longer an agricultural country, or at least, is moving away from agriculture.

In Part II, on industry and trade, the four chapters look at the process of industrialization in Pakistan over the last fifty years. Chapter 6 looks at the period 1947–77, evaluating and rejecting two important assumptions made by observers in the past. The first concerns the performance of the economy in Ayub Khan's Decade of Development. Unlike other interpretations, where the nature of growth has been criticized for being inequitable, we argue that this was an intrinsic and inherent consequence of the capitalist economic policy followed by the Ayub regime. Capitalist economic development manifests its own contradictions and there is no controversy over this form of development. This chapter also takes strong issue with the popular view that the Bhutto regime was a dismal failure on account of the policies it followed. This is found to be factually incorrect. The performance of the economy was understandably not as impressive as the phenomenal growth of the 1960s, but it was better than that of the 1950s. Moreover, it was not all the fault of Bhutto and his economic managers that the economy did not do as well as had been hoped – a multitude of extrinsic and foreign factors that were not in the control of the government affected the economy severely. It seems that political ideology and a dislike for Bhutto have perpetrated the myth of the disastrous 1970s. Certainly, there is more fiction than fact in this evaluation of the Bhutto period.

Chapter 7 looks at developments in industry after 1977, with particular emphasis on the post-1988 structural adjustment period and its consequences for industry. Chapter 8 analyses the state of industry at present, and the main problems that afflict it. This chapter and Chapter 9, in which we examine the development and changing nature of foreign trade in Pakistan, questions yet another key assertion about Pakistan's economy: that the process of industrialization, under highly protected tariff walls, has been inefficient, and hence has given rise to an industry that is inefficient. However, a large number of recent studies which examine the impact of trade policy on industrialization have concluded that, while there are problems in the pattern of industrialization in Pakistan, the assertion that it has been inefficient 'is grossly exaggerated'. Both Chapters 8 and 9, read together, may open to question the claim that industry in Pakistan has been highly inefficient.

From our examination of the more traditional sectors of the economy, agriculture and industry, we move in Part III to an analysis of monetary and fiscal policy, and its impact on and consequences for economic development. In Chapter 10, we examine in detail the nature of the taxation structure and resource mobilization by different tiers of government in Pakistan, and look at the reasons why expenditure tends to be larger than revenue. Chapter 11 looks at what is considered to be Pakistan's biggest economic problem: that of the large and increasing debt burden and the fiscal deficit, considered by many to be the single biggest cause of Pakistan's economic malaise. This latter assumption, however, is contested, and we show that blaming the fiscal deficit for all the economic ills of the country is utterly distorting the facts. Rather than being responsible for low growth, high inflation, a high current account deficit, crowding out, and low investment, we find that the fiscal deficit in Pakistan has, until very recently, been most benign. Moreover, the fact that government expenditure in Pakistan often crowds in private sector investment is conveniently ignored by mainstream economic evaluations of Pakistan. We find that government expenditure has quite a positive role to play in development, if this money is spent correctly and in the right areas. What is important when considering government revenue and expenditure is to evaluate who is paying taxes and who is not,

how much tax is being collected and how much evasion exists, where and how much government is spending, and the quality of that expenditure. Blanket statements like 'a budget must always be balanced' and 'government expenditure is always wasteful and inefficient' are, in fact, quite erroneous.

Chapters 12 and 13, which look at monetary policy, begin with a history of the banking sector in Pakistan, showing its close imprint on economic development and industrialization. Chapter 12 also looks at the equity market in Pakistan, and after examining the role that capital markets have played in other countries, notably South Korea, we argue that directed credit schemes, subsidized credit, and distorted credit markets may be better policy options than fostering and sustaining an equities market that resembles more a game of loaded dice than a mechanism to allocate and ration credit. Chapter 13 on money, savings, and inflation, shows that inflation in Pakistan, and probably elsewhere, is not 'always and everywhere a monetary phenomenon'. Inflation seems to depend more on government-administered prices of key commodities and utilities, and on devaluation, than on an increase in money supply, excessive or otherwise. The reasons for high inflation and low savings in Pakistan also need to be re-examined in the light of the facts rather than on the basis of preconceived notions.

With Part IV we come to the two chapters that describe Pakistan's economic programme since 1988. This is the structural adjustment programme, imposed upon Pakistan by the IMF and World Bank, and so willingly accepted and endorsed by Pakistan's élites. After explaining in Chapter 14 what constitutes the structural adjustment programme and the consequences it has for the countries that have endorsed and implemented it, in Chapter 15 we turn to its impact on Pakistan. The history of IMF and Government of Pakistan relations shows that the last two comprehensive programmes of 1988 and 1993–4 were both negotiated and enforced by unelected caretaker governments, and had to be ratified by the incoming democratically elected government – in both cases, interestingly, of Ms Benazir Bhutto. The chapter shows that, since the advent of the programme, the economy's performance has declined rather sharply, causing a significant loss in social welfare, especially for the poor social classes. We emphasize the point that in 1988 when the first major structural adjustment programme was implemented, Pakistan *did not really need* such a programme, which is usually reserved for those countries that, according to the IMF, are in deep economic crisis and stagnation. In 1988 Pakistan was actually booming, and one of the consequences of following the programme may have been to dampen the high growth performance of the 1980s. We suggest that, although restructuring of the economy is essential, it needs to be done on more friendly terms than those enforced by the IMF and World Bank. The reasons why Pakistan's governments run to the IMF to borrow on any pretext is that they, along with the ruling élite, are not willing to undertake the extensive reforms needed to restructure the economy, for those reforms will hurt the interests of this ruling élite. It is far safer to borrow, delay the inevitable, and pass on the debt burden to the unsuspecting general public.

Chapters 16, 17, and 18, which constitute Part V of the

book, try to understand Pakistan's development paradox. With impressive growth in different sectors of the economy, the performance of the social sectors has been visibly poor. The development paradox has a dual meaning here, since not only has economic development not translated into social sector development, but the fact that impressive economic development has taken place *without* an adequate social and human capital base is itself perplexing. Different subsectors in the social sector, such as health, education, housing, and population, are analysed in Chapters 16 and 17. We question the assertion that population, just like the fiscal deficit, is one of Pakistan's major problems, and we find that this is not necessarily the case. Moreover, the population rate seems to be falling now as economic austerity and hardships increase, and it is unafforable to have large families. There is also a section on gender and women, where we argue that, while cosmetic changes and positive discrimination may address some of the issues facing women in Pakistan, the deep-rooted structures that cause gender bias must be confronted if economic, social, cultural, and judicial emancipation for women is to take place.

The third chapter in the part on the social sectors, Chapter 18 on institutional issues, is perhaps the most interesting of the three, for it looks at institutional factors and constraints that have inhibited social development. Often finances are not the sole problem affecting a sector, but issues of management, administration, and delivery are equally important. Issues like community participation, the role of non-government organizations (NGOs), governance, and decentralization are also evaluated in the light of past experience and current propaganda. We find that, despite the attempt to have community participation as a key element of the delivery of social services, especially under the Social Action Programme, none really exists. We also question the belief that NGOs provide an efficient and productive development paradigm, since experience in Pakistan suggests that most of these institutions have been co-opted by members of the élite to further their own personal and financial goals. Devolution, decentralization, and local government seem to be emerging as the new liberal panacea in development theory. We argue that, while they are well meant, such concepts need to be placed in a context of power relations and there are numerous structural constraints, if not prerequisites, which must be addressed to make any of these ideas functional, productive, and successful.

The last chapter of the book, in Part VI, looks at the impact of the economy on political formations, the state, and classes. We argue that much of the evidence presented in this book suggests that Pakistan's middle classes are beginning to assert themselves collectively, not just in economic terms, but also as a political class. While Pakistan has a long way to go to become a modern, dynamic, educated, and vibrant society, we may see the beginning of such phenomena. However, we are still far from achieving any sustainable and stable order in the economy, in society, and particularly in politics.

This book offers no solutions and does not contain a programme or agenda for alternative paths of development to the ones that have been followed for the last few decades. There are no absolute answers to many of the questions it raises. The aim is different: to provide, analyse, and interpret something called 'facts'. There is usually, amongst students, a desire for prescriptions and definite answers. Unfortunately, this book does not provide them.

What the book does, however, is to reinterpret accepted dogma, home truths, and myths about the economy. It is important to emphasize that this is *one of many interpretations*, and readers are invited to contest the claims made in this book. By challenging preconceived notions, the book allows for alternative interpretations, which each reader can accept or reject after evaluating a range of theories, ideas, and interpretations.

The emphasis in this book is on *process*. We examine facts and issues and developments over time, placing them in their specific contexts. There are numerous stories embedded in these pages, all documenting and describing events, processes, and developments. It is not possible to understand the present without recourse to the past. Pakistan's economy and development today – the word 'development' implies transition and a process – need to be traced back in time; only then can we better understand the present and possibly attempt to look into the future.

A few words about the quality of data and about data availability are necessary when looking at Pakistan's economy. Data in Pakistan are notoriously poor, inadequate, of dubious quality, and often fabricated to suit the needs of the government in power. In 1996 the government of Benazir Bhutto was accused of distorting key macroeconomic data provided to the IMF; the official inflation rate in Pakistan, as anyone living in Pakistan knows, is always underreported by between five and seven percentage points, as is the unemployment rate. In this book we have tried to look at a very extensive literature on Pakistan, citing different sources of data and numerous references. While most of the data originate from official sources, researchers do manage to get around the numbers. For example, the growth rate of the small-scale manufacturing sector has been reported by government to be a constant 8.4 per cent for more than a decade; as any observer of the Pakistani scene knows, the growth rate has actually been almost twice or even three times this rate.

One of the features of this book is that it relies on, and uses, extensive quotations from numerous published articles and books. This, we feel, will represent the arguments made by the authors themselves, rather than our understanding and interpretation of what the author is actually trying to say. Moreover, one hopes that these quotations and the use of references will whet the appetite of the reader to go to the sources and read their works in the original.

The book has set out a tall and ambitious agenda, much for the purpose of self-enquiry. Rather than aiming to convince and convert, the book is meant to be a vehicle for looking at complex issues, phenomena, and processes in a somewhat different light. If this book can convince the reader that there are many ways of looking at what constitutes conventional wisdom, and if it stimulates the process of enquiry and questioning, it will achieve what is probably its greatest ambition.

1 Fifty Years of Development

How does one begin to evaluate the performance of a country over a period of half a century? Do we choose some key economic indicators of fifty years ago and today, and simply make comparisons, or are there other ways of looking at conditions and situations over fifty years? Does comparing a snapshot of 1947 with one of 1997 show anything of value, other than the obvious fact that over fifty years there has been extraordinary change? And, if it does, we must then ask the more important question: how has that change been brought about? What has been the *process* of development or growth or progress over the last fifty years? Perhaps in any evaluation, the story itself, the process and mechanism of change, the directions, developments, and dimensions of the process are the most interesting and relevant factors.

Related to the issue of *how* one looks at change and development is the critical issue of *what* one is looking at. How can we make the claim that Pakistan today is far better off, at least economically, than it was in 1947? Does one use some statistics and show that because they are higher/better, so is the country or its people? A snapshot comparison of 1947 with 1997 will certainly confirm the assertion that Pakistan is far better off at the end of the twentieth century than in 1947. However, it may be argued that over fifty years, *any* country should have become better off, and hence Pakistan is no exception.

The only suitable manner in which a country can be evaluated is to examine its history, and to look at how certain features have evolved through certain processes and the direction in which these developments have taken place. The *story of development* is more important than a mere comparison of the numbers at the beginning with those at the end. However, numbers do provide some insight into the process itself. For example, one can see in absolute and relative terms the *extent* of growth, development, and progress that has taken place in the economy. For example, the threefold increase in per capita income over the last fifty years may suggest that, at least according to one important indicator, the people of an area or community are better off and their standard of living in economic and material terms has trebled. If the literacy rate has also increased threefold over the same period, this too shows that the country is better off than previously.

It is, perhaps, more important to assess what the key numbers and indicators could have become, i.e. the potential – fulfilled or unfulfilled – of the country. While 6 per cent of GNP growth per annum may sound impressive, perhaps there are conditions that mean the country should have achieved 8 or 9 per cent growth and, hence, 6 per cent suggests

unfulfilled potential and expectations. Thus, figures need to be looked at with respect to a potential or trend rate as well. Another relative criterion which could measure success or achievement for a country is some comparison with other countries. If a number of countries were at a similar level of economic development, say, three decades ago, and all of them have now shown tremendous growth in absolute terms, it might be necessary to look at how relatively well these countries have progressed. The comparison between Korea and Pakistan is a much cited case, where both were considered to be at a similar level of development and growth in the 1960s. While both have shown impressive economic growth over the last four decades, today Korea's GNP per capita is *eighteen times* that of Pakistan. This is, indeed, an extremely telling statistic.

While there are a number of important issues that one needs to be aware of when evaluating the record of economic growth over fifty years, the story is incomplete, if not inadequate, unless one examines the *consequences* and *results* of economic growth. Does a country with high rates of economic growth measured by per capita income over fifty years, with a largely illiterate, uneducated, unhealthy population, reflect progress? And in contrast, does a poorer country with low income growth, but with higher social and human capital, with a literate, healthy, and educated population, represent progress? Or are both measures equally relevant? Pakistan's impressive economic record is always contrasted with its dismal performance in the social sectors, in absolute terms and also relative to comparable countries. In contrast, countries like Cuba and Vietnam have economic statistics that seem to be less impressive than those for Pakistan, but both countries have eradicated illiteracy and have statistics in the health sector that are comparable to most developed countries. One must then ask the question: economic development *how* and *for whom*? If economic growth, development, and prosperity are manifested mainly in buying arms, spending beyond one's means on defence, and propping up a large military establishment, all at the expense of expenditure in the social sector and on the people, then no matter how dynamic the economic growth, it is surely quite meaningless. Moreover, the question of equitable distribution of resources is important, where growth in GNP per capita may not be reflected in who or how many benefit from that growth.

It is important to emphasize that the historical moment in which one discusses and evaluates issues that have evolved over time also matters. For example, in the 1950s and 1960s, economic success was dependent almost exclusively upon growth rates, regardless of their composition, distribution, or impact. A high growth rate suggested success, while those countries that had different parameters or priorities and did not come up to some acceptable growth criterion were considered poor achievers, or outright failures. In the 1970s, redistribution with growth and social sector performance became important criteria for success, and now, in the 1990s, 'modernization', openness, and indices of involvement and participation of the private sector have emerged alongside growth as important indicators. There have also been important shifts in political ideology and in ways of achieving the targets set. When growth was the only thing that mattered for economists, conventional wisdom held that it did not matter how you achieve high growth, for it would eventually filter down to the people. These economic pundits went so far as to suggest that strong, often authoritarian, states were necessary to oversee high growth rates and adequate economic performance. Perhaps many of the military dictatorships that emerged in the Third World in the 1950s, 1960s, and 1970s found justification from this argument. The foreign policy and diplomatic manoeuvring of the two superpowers, the United States and the Soviet Union, in these decades reflected this thinking when both countries propped up and supported highly dictatorial and oppressive regimes.

Today, in the so-called neo-liberal era at the close of the millennium, progress and development incorporate many more qualities than they may perhaps have ever done in the past. Today, economic development must be *sustainable*, *participatory*, *environmentally responsible*, and *distributive*. The single-minded focus on growth has been replaced by a very large number of other, equally important criteria, just as the way of bringing about this growth and development has done. Hence, when we evaluate an economy or country, looking back a few decades, our evaluation is tainted by the times in which we write and by the new conventional wisdom that dominates at that historical moment. No abstract, purely scientific, universal methodology can help in evaluating a long-drawn historical process, and concepts and methods used are relative, contextual, and at times quite subjective.

The long preamble above has been made necessary to guard against the pitfalls that afflict us when we evaluate economies or societies, whether our own or someone else's. In the case of Pakistan, it is very easy to adopt a before-and-after approach, showing what was and what is. But an evaluation cannot be even half complete unless one studies the process of economic development, the process of change and transition, in order to understand where we were, where we are, and where we may possibly be heading. Two points in time do not provide that way of looking at society.

This book is about the *process* of economic development in Pakistan since at least 1947, if not a little earlier. This chapter presents a largely static picture of what was and what is. The details of what happened during the fifty years are to be found in later chapters of this book. The numbers, the information, and the analysis in this chapter, as in the rest of the book, should be studied with caution, and all the arguments listed above, about the dangers of studying and

evaluating societies and economies, must be kept in mind. While the rest of the book talks about the *process* of economic development, about change, about history, and about how these processes unfolded in a dynamic manner, with each specific period or era having different manifestations, this chapter, often simplistically and summarily, presents arguments that are extensively detailed in the rest of the book. The purpose of this chapter, then, is simply to highlight the *extent of change*, rather than the *manner of change* in Pakistan over the last fifty years. The eighteen other chapters of this book address the latter issue.

1.1 Structural Change

Probably the most striking factor that is manifested in a view of Pakistan in 1997 compared to 1947, a factor that finds few parallels in recent history, is that Pakistan today is less than half of the country it was in 1947. In 1949–50, 55 per cent of Pakistan's population lived in what was then East Pakistan, making it the majority province in terms of population. Despite this majority, the eastern wing was economically discriminated against and exploited. A section of the ruling élite of the western wing of Pakistan became the oppressors and exploiters of the East Pakistani people, leading to their eventual secession after a long and painful war of liberation ending in 1971.

The contribution made by East Pakistan to Pakistan's economy and society was huge, though never fully recognized or appreciated by West Pakistanis. This point is emphasized in the chapters of this book that look at economic development, industrialization, and trade in Pakistan during the 1950s and 1960s. No matter how significant this loss, post-1971 Pakistan seems to have moved on from the history of its first twenty-five years. However, the mid-point of Pakistan's history seems to constitute a conspicuous break with the past, after which a new country came into existence.

In 1947 Pakistan had every right to be called an 'agricultural' country. Unfortunately, most students of economics make the serious mistake of calling Pakistan an agricultural country fifty years later, when there is no justification for doing so. At the time of independence, the major share of (West) Pakistan's gross domestic product was from agriculture, which contributed around 53 per cent, compared to 7.8 per cent from manufacturing and 11.9 per cent from retail trade. More than 65 per cent of Pakistan's labour force worked in agriculture, and almost all of Pakistan's exports consisted of primary products, essentially agricultural commodities like jute and tea, which, not surprisingly, originated from East Pakistan (see Table 1.1 and Figure 1.1, and Chapters 6 and 9).

By 1997 the extent of change in Pakistan's economic structure can also be seen in Figure 1.1, and the cliché that Pakistan is basically an agricultural country is no longer true. Now, agriculture contributes a mere 24 per cent towards GDP, while manufacturing is up to 26.4 per cent. The services sector has replaced agriculture as the dominant sector of the economy, contributing almost half of total GDP. The population employed in agriculture has also fallen, although

Table 1.1
Pakistan: basic indicators, 1947–1997

Pakistan is the world's seventh most populous nation, and has the 44th biggest economy in terms of GDP, although in terms of purchasing power parity, Pakistan's economy is the 22nd biggest in the world. However, it is also the 32nd poorest nation out of 132 in terms of GNP per capita, and the 128th worst performer out of 174 countries, in terms of a composite United Nations Human Development Index.

I	Population (millions)	33.78	(1951)[1]	140	(1997) est.
	Urban (%)	17.8		40.0	
II	Contribution to gross domestic product, by sector (%)	1949/50[2]		1996/7[3]	
	1 Agriculture	53.2		24.2	
	2 Manufacturing	7.8		26.4	
	3 Others (mostly services and trade)	39.0		49.4	
	Labour force, by sector (%)	1950/1[2]		1994/5[3]	
	1 Agriculture	65.3		46.8	
	2 Manufacturing	9.5		18.52	
	3 Others (mostly services and trade)	25.2		34.69	
III	GNP per capita (US$)	170	(1976)[4]	430	(1993)[4]
	Per capital income (Rs) constant factor cost (1959/60)	350	(1949/50)[5]	915	(1992/3)[5]
	PPP real GDP per capita (US$)	820	(1960)[4]	2,160	(1993)[4]
IV	Composition of exports (%)	1951/2[2]		1995/6[3]	
	1 Primary commodities	99.2		16	
	2 Semi-manufactures			22	
	2 Manufactures			62	
V	Primary schools (number)	8,413	(1947/8)[1]	150,963	(1996/7)[3]
	Literacy (%)	15	(1951)[1]	36	(1993)[4]
	Female literacy (%)	12	(1951)[1]	23	(1993)[4]
VI	Life expectancy (years)	43	(1960)[4]	62	(1993)[4]
	Infant mortality rate	137	(1960)[4]	95	(1994)[4]
	Access to safe water (%)	29	(1975)[4]	50	(1993)[4]
	Access to sanitation (%)	14	(1980)[4]	33	(1995)[4]
	Total registered doctors	1,014	(1948)[1]	74,229	(1996)[3]
	Population per doctor	14,835	(1951)[1]	1,773	(1996)[3]

est.: estimate.
Sources: 1. Government of Pakistan, *Twenty Five Years of Statistics in Pakistan, 1947–72*, Karachi, 1972; 2. Ahmed, Viqar and Rashid Amjad, *The Management of Pakistan's Economy, 1947–82*, Oxford University Press, Karachi, 1984; 3. Government of Pakistan, *Pakistan Economic Survey, 1996–7*, Islamabad, 1997; 4. Haq, Mahbubul, *Human Development in South Asia, 1997*, Oxford University Press, Karachi, 1997; 5. Malik, Sohail, *et al., Pakistan's Economic Performance, 1947 to 1993: A Descriptive Analysis*, Sure Publishers, Lahore, 1994.

at around 47 per cent of the total labour force, agriculture is the biggest sector in terms of the employed labour force. More importantly, the nature of exports from Pakistan has also changed dramatically. From 99.2 per cent of total exports in 1947, primary commodities now constitute only around 16 per cent. However, one must emphasize the fact that, although 62 per cent of Pakistan's exports are now manufactured goods, with textiles, garments, and yarn making up most of them, these figures are less impressive when we realize that most of Pakistan's exports still depend critically on raw cotton.

These economic changes in structure are also manifested in where people live. In 1951 when the first census in independent Pakistan was held, only 17 per cent of West Pakistanis lived in areas designated as urban; today estimates suggest that perhaps 40 per cent live in cities and towns. This shift has major repercussions for the economy, society and the political process under way. In fact, in the context of Pakistan, perhaps the most important political factor over the last few decades has been the process and extent of urbanization and the emergence, and perhaps consolidation, of a middle class (see Part VI for further discussion of this issue). With around

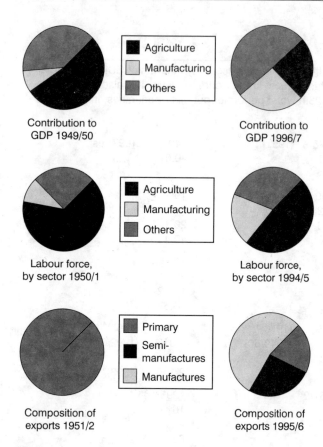

Figure 1.1
Structural change in Pakistan, 1947–1997

40 per cent of the country's population living in cities and towns, the economic profile, in terms of consumption and production patterns, has also changed quite drastically. Urbanization's impact on social and economic development is also very significant. The extent and process of urbanization used to be considered an indicator of progress and modernization. Although many latter-day modernizers and developmentalists may no longer hold that this assumption is true, one cannot overlook the significant structural change that has been brought about by the process of urbanization in the last fifty years, from only 6 million inhabitants out of a population of 33.8 million in 1947, to around 50 million who now reside in cities and towns. (The implications of this change are discussed in Chapter 19.)

Just as the cliché that 'Pakistan is an agricultural country' is repeated *ad nauseum* by students of Pakistan's economy, another myth that prevails and is related to the earlier one is that 'Pakistan is a feudal country'. No matter how one looks at the facts and observes the manner in which society has evolved, there is no justification for believing, let alone repeating, what is perhaps Pakistan's most popular myth. By any criteria, there is no evidence to support this illusion. The Green Revolution of the1960s, with its extraordinary impact on the rural areas, agriculture, the economy, and the social relations of production, put an end once and for all to the myth that Pakistan is a 'feudal' country. Chapters 2 to 5, on agriculture in Pakistan, re-emphasize this point using

different criteria. Chapter 19 re-examines the issue of feudalism, asserts once again that it is no longer of any consequence, and then goes on to examine the implications of this understanding. If in 1947 there were suggestions that Pakistan was a feudal country, long before the Golden Jubilee Celebrations took place, all the evidence pointed to the contrary. While feudalism in Pakistan died a very long time ago, modern-day Pakistan has also seen the demise of agriculturists as a powerful economic, social, and political force. The huge change in economic, social, and hence political power, from the agriculturist, so-called feudal, lobby towards an urban and rural middle class, is also one of the key indicators highlighting the extraordinary structural transformation of Pakistan in the last fifty years.

1.2 Five Decades and Five Epochs

The fifty years since 1947 can be distinguished by five specific epochs or eras, which represent different economic policies, and planning and management choices. The first eleven years, between 1947 and 1958, are the years when the country and economy were trying to settle down, but to no avail. This period was followed by what many still call the golden era of economic development (or at least economic growth) in the Decade of Development under Ayub Khan. The economy and the political scene had indeed stabilized and settled down, with the result that growth rates were unprecedented, and Pakistan was considered to be one of the few countries at that time which would achieve developed country status. With the war of liberation in East Pakistan, the majority wing left Pakistan to form Bangladesh and two new countries, not one, were born.

Post-1971 Pakistan was a new country in every respect, compared to the one that existed between 1947 and 1971. The third brief, albeit highly significant era in Pakistan's history, was the five-and-a-half years of Zulfiqar Ali Bhutto. His populism or Islamic Socialism, or just plain rhetoric, made him the most popular, and at that time the only elected, leader to emerge in what was left of Pakistan. His rule ended with the imposition of Pakistan's second martial law under General Zia ul Haq in 1977. There were some similarities between the first and the second martial laws (discussed in detail in later chapters), but the world was now a very different place compared with the 1960s. The opening up of the Middle East, the Afghan war (with its consequences of a drug and arms culture in Pakistan), attempts at the Islamization of the economy and society, and a praetorian sort of democracy between 1985 and 1988, were amongst the salient features of the Zia era.

The death of General Zia in many ways brought about the end of the old Pakistan, and 1988 signals the third birth of the nation after 1947 and 1971 (see Chapter 19 for far greater detail about the evolution of society after 1988). While political and social changes were fast to emerge, the post-1988 economic changes and programmes also represented a departure from the past, with very significant impacts on society, many of which were highly deleterious.

This section very briefly presents the main features, achievements, and consequences of the five epochs in the five decades since Pakistan's independence. As will become clear, especially with reference to the continuing fifth era, 'independence' and 'sovereignty' are words that have little meaning in a country that recently celebrated its Golden Jubilee of Independence.

1.2.1 Laying the Foundations: 1947–1958

In 1947 Pakistan was, indeed, a predominantly agrarian, undeveloped, newly independent nation, with little industry, few services, and no infrastructure. In the first few years, our main concern was one of survival, where adverse international conditions and a precarious domestic situation, with millions of refugees, made the provision of very basic necessities the primary task of the government. Attempts to restructure the economy and to ensure that it was on a strong footing could be undertaken only after the initial political and economic shocks had been dealt with.

The first decade of economic policy and planning witnessed the attempts of a bureaucracy to keep Pakistan on its feet. The herculean task of building an economic base was left to the state sector as the private sector was still in embryo and did not have the capital to lead an industrial revolution in the country. It was the windfall gain made by the mercantile class during and after the Korean War in 1952 that paved the way for the foundation of industry, an industry which the state sector helped develop and then handed over to the private sector.

1.2.2 The Decade of Development: 1958–1968

If one examines Pakistan's economic growth record, the 1960s stands out as the decade with the best performance. Table 1.2 gives a useful indication of the nature of the differences between the 1960s, 1970s, and 1980s. While the rates of growth for the 1960s and the 1980s seem to be quite close in most categories, there are important conceptual and ideological differences in the modes of development under the two military regimes.

Curiously, the 1960s has been termed a 'controversial' decade for the type of economic policy pursued, and the resulting economic and political effects. Dozens of economists and social scientists have written about Ayub Khan's era and they are generally agreed that considerable economic growth and development did indeed take place. They argue that significant leaps were made in industrial and agricultural production, where growth rates in excess of 20 per cent per annum were witnessed in the large-scale manufacturing sector. In the first five years of the Ayub rule, manufacturing grew by as much as 17 per cent, and in the second half of Ayub Khan's rule, agricultural growth increased by 6 per cent, while industry grew by 10 per cent. Table 1.2 shows that the economy in general, and the different individual sectors, grew by phenomenal rates, and Pakistan was considered to be a model capitalist economy in the 1960s.

The controversy surrounds the eventual effects and results of this phenomenal growth rate. Observers have pointed out that this aggressive capitalist development caused serious economic, social, and political tensions. They argue that there was increased disparity in incomes across different regions. This was manifest in the concentration of economic prosperity in both the industrial and agricultural sectors in central Punjab, and in industry in Karachi. Critics of Ayub Khan's model of development point out that these two regions were permitted to grow at the expense of the rest of the country, and the end result was the feeling on the part of East Pakistan of utter neglect and betrayal. Apart from the very obvious phenomenon of regional disparities, a number of scholars also took pains to show that there was a great deal of economic concentration amongst individuals and that numerous business empires were created. This, they said, resulted in increasing income inequality.

Of course, all this did happen. There was tremendous growth, but there was also increasing disparity across classes and regions. The social sectors were also neglected. There was little or no increase in the level of real wages, and social equity was of little concern. Functional inequality was the preferred philosophy of Mahbub-ul-Haq and Ayub Khan's Harvard Advisory Group, and their focus was on the rich, who were supposed to generate more savings, and thus were to be the motors of capitalist growth and development.

It is surprising that economists and social scientists were so surprised and upset at what had happened during Ayub Khan's rule. What would have been surprising is the *lack* of this 'controversial' and contradictory development. Capitalist development, especially in the manner in which it was implemented in Pakistan at that time, implied unequal development, and to have expected otherwise is *naïveté*. There is a need now to examine the Decade of Development afresh. The consequence of Ayub Khan's economic policies was that there was growth and development, the forces of production did expand, a proletariat was born, and compared to the earlier periods, this was indeed a very progressive era in the evolution of the economic and political process that is Pakistan. The 'controversial' repercussions were inherent, inbuilt, and inevitable.

However, what is most interesting about Ayub Khan's era is the fact that the economic package was thoroughly illiberal, and was almost the opposite of what is being termed economic liberalism today. It was capitalism, and the private sector did play a significant role, but it was a guided, bureaucratically governed, and directed capitalism. The bureaucracy played an active, influential, and constructive role in the establishment of private sector capital in Pakistan. Dozens of constraints on setting up industry, red tape, and numerous hurdles in financial and industrial policy did not stop the impressive growth in this period. The nature of the economy was precisely what it should not have been according to the doctrine of economic liberalism and liberalization. Trade was highly controlled and closed. The exchange rate was overvalued and it distorted local markets. Financial capital was rationed, and the stock market was a playground for a handful of people. The government's presence was everywhere, directing and encouraging the private sector and the market. The agricultural sector was consciously identified by the government as a vehicle for growth, and numerous (governmental) decisions were taken which resulted in growth at times in excess of 11 per cent per year. The transformation of the agricultural sector from a pre-capitalist to a capitalist one was accelerated by the active involvement and interference of the government. Even public sector projects commissioned by the Pakistan Industrial Development Corporation (PIDC) were gifted away to the private sector. The bureaucracy, in essence, gave birth to the private sector capitalist in Pakistan – indeed, a very illiberal process according to conventional wisdom.

1.2.3   The Bad Luck Years: 1971–1977

Ironically, while most intellectuals condemned Ayub Khan's policies, it was these policies which gave rise to populism and the brand of policies particular to Zulfiqar Ali Bhutto, who was supported by the same intellectuals. Without Ayub, Bhutto would not have been possible. Bhutto's economic policies were more illiberal than those of his predecessor, and his nationalization was said to be the major cause for a huge downward trend in growth. However, Table 1.2 shows that in the 1970s GDP grew by close to 5 per cent, which indicates the need, as in the case of Ayub, for a thorough re-examination of the economic programme of Bhutto.

Bhutto's economic programme has been labelled a failure by his critics, and even his supporters have, under the barrage of propaganda and the changed world situation, at best been apologetic and at worst joined the maligning chorus. In many ways he was an unlucky politician, and events beyond his control affected his economic programme. The economic loss of East Pakistan was strongly felt – West Pakistan 'exported' 50 per cent of its goods to the eastern wing and acquired a large amount of foreign exchange from its raw material exports. The devaluation of the Pakistani rupee by 120 per cent in May 1972 brought significant dividends in terms of export growth – in one year (1972–3) despite the loss of East Pakistan's exportable produce, West Pakistan doubled its foreign exchange earnings. However, the 1973 OPEC price increases played havoc with Pakistan's import bill and the balance of payments deteriorated. Also, the period after 1973 saw a serious worldwide recession affecting Pakistan's exports. Recurrent domestic cotton crop failures, and floods in 1973, 1974 (along with pest attacks), and 1976, affected Pakistan's main exports. The large nationalized units taken over by Bhutto were the most inefficient in the industrial sector, and despite this, industry experienced a reasonable

growth rate, with the nationalized sector doing better than most believe.

Bhutto's government also laid the foundations for future growth and development from which his successor benefited. Basic industries were set up and a base for a capital goods industry was established which resulted in subsequent growth. The Middle East boom which Bhutto initiated, another irony in Pakistan's history, helped keep Zia in power for some years. The illiberal economic policies of Zulfiqar Ali Bhutto were responsible for growth not only during his own tenure, but also in the period after 1977.

1.2.4   The Second Military Government: 1977–1988

General Zia's regime was more liberal in economic terms – though certainly not politically – than any of his predecessors. While the civilian-military bureaucracy played a prominent role in acquiring capital and in assuming the role of entrepreneur and financier, numerous individual capitalists emerged in the stable post-Bhutto era. High rates of industrial growth were led by the coming on stream of the earlier investment made by the public sector under Bhutto, especially in heavy industries, and also by a rapid expansion in domestic demand. While the trend to liberalize the economy was escalated consciously in the Zia period, the Soviet invasion of Afghanistan and the excessive involvement in Pakistan by the USA, helped ensure that steps were taken to increase growth. Remittances from the Middle East and aid from abroad helped launch Pakistan's second economic revolution, where the middle class emerged as a formidable economic and political category. By becoming the capitalist world's 'front line' state against all things Soviet, and especially against Soviet expansionism in the region, Pakistan's government gained in terms of financial aid and resources. However, General Zia's martial rule inflicted deep-rooted damage to Pakistani society.

1.2.5   The Era of Structural Adjustment: 1988 Onwards

The period after the death of General Zia in 1988 has resulted in the return of democracy to Pakistan. Between August 1988 and August 1997, Pakistan has had four general elections, with both Benazir Bhutto and Nawaz Sharif being returned to power twice. Since none of the elected governments has been able to complete its full term, there have also been more than

Table 1.2
Growth rates in Pakistan in main eras (average annual, %)

	1960s	1970s	1980s	1988–1997
GDP	6.77	4.84	6.45	4.70
Agriculture	5.07	2.37	5.44	4.09
Manufacturing	9.93	5.50	8.21	4.95
Commodity-producing sector	6.83	3.88	6.49	4.67
Service sector	6.74	6.26	6.65	4.75

Source: Government of Pakistan, *Pakistan Economic Survey, 1996–97*, Islamabad, 1997.

a few 'caretaker' governments, of which the last two in particular, headed by Moeen Qureishi (a retired World Bank Vice President) and by Meraj Khalid, who had Shahid Javed Burki (a serving World Bank Vice President) as Finance Advisor, have been very controversial. However, while the post-1988 period could be termed the 'Period of the Return to Democracy', we have chosen to call it the 'Era of Structural Adjustment'. We argue later in this book that, rather than the democratic process, it is a particular economic programme and process that has determined the course of Pakistan since 1988.

Since that date, Pakistan's economy has been under the tutelage of the international lending agencies, the IMF and the World Bank. The economic policies, labelled 'economic liberalization, stabilization and structural adjustment', evolved in Washington and have been imposed upon eighty countries worldwide, with Pakistan and its governments amongst the most enthusiastic adherents to the Washington Consensus. Moreover, Pakistan's governments have taken the art of subservience to new heights: an examination of World Bank and IMF documents since 1988 reveals that almost every decision of any consequence taken by the various governments that have been in power has been predetermined by the two Washington agencies, and that Pakistan has merely followed diktat. This is evidenced also by the fact that Pakistan has seldom found the need to appoint a full-time Finance Minister, as numerous advisers on loan from the World Bank and the IMF ensure that implementation is thorough. While this blind adherence to Washington has meant a loss of sovereignty for the Pakistani state and its people, the outcome of these policies has spelt unmitigated disaster for the economy overall, and for individuals – see Part IV of this book for more on the structural adjustment programme in Pakistan.

The main focus of the structural adjustment programmes has been on the fiscal deficit. In all the long- and short-term agreements with the IMF, the government of Pakistan has been told to lower its fiscal deficit to 4 per cent of GDP. Ways of achieving this have involved high taxation and a decrease in public expenditure. In the last three years alone (1994–7), additional taxes of Rs140 billion have been imposed on the people without a significant widening of the tax base. Those who were already paying taxes have had their tax burden increased through higher sales taxes and other indirect taxes, while the expansion in the number of new direct taxpayers has been negligible. Despite this surge in mainly indirect taxation, the government has been unable to meet the 4 per cent target, and has hence resorted to a reduction in public expenditure. Had the reduction been in the form of a cut in wasteful current and recurring expenditure, this step by the government would have been welcome. However, the largest cuts in public expenditure have come in the area of development. From 9.3 per cent of GDP in 1981, development expenditure fell to only about 3.5 per cent in 1996/7. In fiscal year 1996/7, the original allocation for development expenditure of a mere Rs105 billion was slashed to only Rs85 billion. Another key area of the adjustment programme has been a reduction in tariff rates, falling from 125 per cent in 1992 to 45 per cent today. Along with this, the government

has been continuously raising the administered prices of utilities such as electricity, gas and petroleum products. The selling-off of state-owned enterprises, or privatization, has also formed part of the adjustment package, as has the continuous devaluation of the Pakistani rupee.

The consequence of these policies has been a serious economic crisis at the macroeconomic and individual level. The imposition of higher taxes, the continuous escalation in administered prices, and the free fall of the Pakistani rupee have all been crucially responsible for the high inflation rate existing in Pakistan. The trade 'reforms' have been responsible for the deindustrialization of the economy, with a large number of goods that were previously produced locally now being imported, resulting in the closure of industrial units. By opening up the economy to foreign competition, without providing any benefits or protection to local industry, the latter has suffered, with closures and greater unemployment. Privatization, which has been hurried through, has also caused the attrition of a large chunk of the previously employed workforce.

Adherence to the adjustment package has affected different segments of the population differentially. While the escalating price rise has affected all consumers, the hardest hit have been the salaried and the low-income sections of society, who have not been able to negotiate wage increases commensurate with the price rise. The cut in the public sector development programme has also affected these sections of society far more than the well-to-do, as the main beneficiaries and consumers of public services tend to be the low-income groups. With fewer schools, health facilities, and other services in the public sector, it is fair to surmise that the state of our much lamented social sectors will get far worse, affecting the poor adversely. Administered prices are the single largest factor that affects inflation, and repeated price hikes in power, gas, and petrol have had a serious negative impact on the purchasing power of the poor. Added to this spiral of inflation has been the government's attempt to cut the fiscal deficit by the imposition of further indirect taxation, which causes a larger dent in the pocket of the salaried and low-income groups. With continuous and spiralling devaluation – the rupee lost as much as 17 per cent in 1996 alone – the imported component of inflation has made matters far worse.

There is extensive evidence, some even from studies conducted by the World Bank and the IMF, that the structural adjustment programme causes far more harm to the economy and to low-income groups than the benefits it supposedly brings forth. Pakistan is no exception, where this programme has been responsible for causing severe hardship to the people. Unfortunately, though, no government in Pakistan's recent past has had the ability or means to stand up to the powerful agencies in Washington. Moreover, Pakistan's severely chequered history and experience with democracy have made matters far worse. The last two major agreements with the IMF were both made by unelected, so-called caretaker governments, and the elected governments that followed were simply told to follow the programmes through. With the democratic process repeatedly sabotaged by the powers in the background, no elected government has been given the permission or the room to produce any independent programme. It is clear that the political process in Pakistan has been gagged and bound by the requirements and orders of the IMF, the World Bank, and the domestic élite. (Many of these arguments about the structural adjustment programme, and particularly its consequences, form an important part of this book – see Chapters 14, 15, and 19.)

1.3   The Balance Sheet

This book is about the process of economic development in Pakistan over the last fifty years, and is devoted to understanding how, why, and under what conditions that process has taken place. The summary presented in section 1.2 is an extremely brief condensation of a few of the ideas that constitute this book, and should not be seen as an alternative to the more detailed story that follows. Having presented an introduction to the five main epochs in the first five decades of Pakistan's existence, in this section we try to examine the issue of whether Pakistan's fifty years of economic growth and development can be called a success or a failure, or whether, as is often the case, the answer lies somewhere in between.

For most of Pakistan's fifty years, the economy has shown healthy growth around a trend rate of nearly 5.6 per cent per annum. There have been years where the rate rose to even more than the trend rate, and other years when it fell to less than even half, as it did in 1992/3 when it was a mere 2.27 per cent. If an evaluation of Pakistan's economy had taken place in 1968, for the most part, based on economic growth criteria, one would have called it a resounding success. Indeed, the government of Ayub Khan called its era the 'Decade of Development'. An evaluation of Pakistan's first quarter-century, in August 1972, would have looked at the country's history differently, Pakistan having lost its eastern wing and having suffered the consequences and contradictions of the Decade of Development, which were manifested in late 1968 just as the government of the day celebrated its pyrrhic victory. Success and failure are, clearly, highly relative terms.

Even if the growth rate of Pakistan has shown impressive trends, what has been the consequence of that growth? Does Pakistan produce most of its products, or is it now a highly import-dependent economy? Many countries of the world depend on trade and on imports. Is it of any consequence that Pakistan is a member of that group? The nature and quality of output and the conditions under which it is produced are also important. For example, if Pakistan's high growth rate takes place behind high protection walls, what is the consequence of such industrialization when tariffs fall, as they have over the last decade? Such questions must be confronted if any view is to be taken of the success or failure of economic growth over the last half century.

One also needs to compare Pakistan's performance with that of other countries, to see if Pakistan has done as well (or as badly) as its own data show. Six per cent per year, even in simple terms, sounds commendable. But countries with similar initial conditions to Pakistan experienced growth rates that were higher, more consistent, and longer lasting

than Pakistan's 6 per cent. Many of those countries now rank among the newly industrializing countries (NICs), while Pakistan is currently the 31st poorest nation out of 132 classified by the World Bank, using GNP per capita as the main criterion (see Chapter 16 for further discussion of this issue). In terms of human and social capital, the United Nations Development Programme ranks Pakistan 128 out of 174 countries, i.e. only 45 countries out of a possible 174 are worse off than Pakistan when it comes to non-economic indicators. Transparency International, a German research institution that analyses society and politics around the globe, ranks Pakistan as the second most corrupt country in the world after Nigeria. Hence, by what measure does one compare or classify success?

One can list tables of numerous indicators showing their trend over the last five decades. For example, in 1947 there were 8,413 primary schools in the country, of which 1,549 were for girls. By 1996 the number of primary schools had increased to 150,963, a rise of almost eighteenfold. Girls' schools had increased by a factor of twenty-five in this period. On paper these statistics indicate major achievements, but has the quality of education increased at all? Can one say that the eighteenfold increase in education facilities reflects at least a three- or fourfold improvement in the quality of education? The answer is probably in the negative. Indeed, many people would feel that, despite the increase in quantity, the *quality* of public sector education has made a noticeable downward shift. Perhaps the increase in the quantity of education has allowed a larger number of people to have access to whatever education is available. Quite possibly, children of poorer families and those in the lower income groups may have had the first opportunity ever to send their children to school. This change in the social and economic profile of schoolchildren must count as some measure of success. However, the fact that the quality ought to have been far better and the results of education literacy, scientific skills, etc. far more extensively spread amongst the population suggests that it may be only a small measure of success. While it is usual practice to show how numbers have increased over the years, one must look at such trends and 'evidence' with great caution.

Another measure of success is the extent of autonomy, sovereignty, or independence that a country faces. After fifty years, such criteria should be of less importance than when a country has been newly created and is trying to find its feet. Section 1.2 shows, however, that after 1988 any semblance of sovereignty and independence that Pakistan may once have had has been lost. Today, Pakistan is a highly aid-dependent economy with multilateral institutions playing a dominant role in both the political and economic affairs of the state, even after fifty years of political independence. While other countries have also made use of aid and loans, they have used that money for development purposes, unlike Pakistan, where much of the assistance has been squandered, often in dubious circumstances and in illegal and illicit channels.

Fifty years is a fairly long time for countries to change and transform their economic and social systems. Given even a semblance of sensibility in a nation, with an élite that has the desire to improve even only itself, in fifty years much can be expected to change. Pakistan has had much more than just a bare minimum of endowments and resources, and has achieved far more than a bare level of subsistence. Living standards have improved manifold over the last five decades, and more so during the latter half of this period. Numerous factors have been responsible for this growth, some fortuitous, most consciously sought after. In some ways the growth/development/progress that has taken place has been unremarkable, because it was almost inevitable, given initial conditions. Even without all the effort that was made to influence and direct policy, growth and development would have taken place. The only contentious issue is the degree, extent, and form of that growth and development, and the extent to which it fulfilled prospects and potential.

There are also economic and social costs and consequences of development and growth. Since growth has been the overriding aim of governments in the past, and as it is probably the statistic that most impresses politicians, planners and economists, any negative ramifications of this single mindedness have been ignored. Environmental degradation is now considered to be the most serious repercussion of this strategy, with pollution and the decay of natural resources quite rampant. Urbanization, which has a great many advantages, also brings with it greater demands on basic facilities and infrastructure, which cannot be provided to all. The result is squalor and poor and unhygienic living conditions for the large majority of people who live in cities, not always out of choice. For urban residents in Pakistan, rich and poor alike, the deteriorating law and order situation, with no protection for life or property, is possibly the most important and immediate negative consequence of inequitable growth. Many Pakistanis would question the claim made by statisticians and others, on the basis of high growth figures, that Pakistan has made huge progress; for these people, lower growth with more personal security and freedom is probably a preferred alternative.

Pakistan's economic development has been a capitalist development, where the private sector has played a key role. In the early days, the state played the critical role in establishing industry and assisted the private sector, but in more recent years as the role of the state has diminished, private sector-led growth has been the norm. However, Pakistan's capitalist path of development has been unusual for reasons which are discussed at different times in this book, and especially in Chapter 19. Pakistan's has been a very crude, peculiar capitalism, much influenced by the country's history and culture and the formation of social, economic, and political classes. The excessive amount of corruption, rent-seeking, and clientelism in Pakistani society is both responsible for and a product of the specific nature of Pakistan's development. It is not possible to speculate about what would have happened if we had had less corruption and had been more honest, for these are counterfactuals. Pakistan would not be what it is today – for better or worse – had it not evolved in the way it has; an evolution much determined by given material conditions, existing and past.

1.4 Conclusions

Pakistan's economic development over its first half century is spectacular, yet commonplace. Compared to what it was in 1947, the country seems like a modern, dynamic state – unlike, say, Afghanistan. Compared to other countries, such as the south-east Asian countries of Malaysia, Thailand, and Korea, Pakistan's achievements look minuscule. Pakistan would necessarily have grown from whatever existed in 1947, as the country had skilled labour and sufficient natural endowments. It could and should have grown more, given its own potential and the performance of other comparable nations. Although important directions can be given to the process of history governing nations, and critical decisions can have dramatic consequences, either positive or negative, there is a logic to history itself that governs and determines the course of society and of nations. Comparisons with other countries to deduce 'what could have been done' or how to go about development, often ignore elements of *specificity* and *contextuality* on the one hand, and chance and randomness on the other. Many events in history, outside the control of those whom they affect, have altered the course of nations. Hence, comparisons and evaluations need to be considered in relevant contexts, given specific histories.

Yet there are generalities as well. All nations belong to, and are part of, the global economy, and increasingly so. They cannot avoid the influences – both negative and positive – of this integration. Their destinies are often closely linked with

Table 1.3
Pakistan: indicators of failure

	%
Illiterate adults	64
Illiterate female adults	77
Population below poverty line	28
Without access to health services	45
Without access to safe water	50
Without access to sanitation	67
Malnourished children (under 5)	40

- 17 million children were out of school in 1995
- 60 million people do not have access to health facilities; 67 million are without safe drinking water; 89 million are without basic sanitation facilities.
- There are 740,000 child deaths a year, half of them linked to malnutrition.
- One-half of primary school children drop out before reaching grade five.
- Against 100 males, only 16 females are economically active.
- 36 million people live in absolute poverty.
- There are nine soldiers for every one doctor and three soldiers for every two teachers.

Note: All figures, unless otherwise stated, are for 1993.
Source: Haq, Mahbubul, *Human Development in South Asia; 1997*, Oxford University Press, Karachi, 1997.

those of others, and by being part of the world order, they have the ability to learn much more from each other, and at a greater pace. With the communications revolution, physical integration is no longer essential, and influence and trends cross political borders, bringing markets and people together. Comparisons and attempts to emulate become easier.

This first chapter has tried to answer the difficult question of whether Pakistan – as a people and as a nation – is better off today than in 1947. There is no definite answer to this question. In many ways Pakistanis are far better off than we could have even imagined; in other important areas, we have not even begun to address the issues that a country at the level of Pakistan's economic, social, and political maturity should have resolved (see Table 1.3 for Pakistan's 'indicators of failure'). Pakistan could have done far better than it has, as has been shown by the performance of other comparable countries. That it has not may imply a certain level of failure. But then again, given constraints and initial endowments and material conditions, and the interactions of different social and political classes and groups, perhaps this was unlikely.

We have presented here a 'before and after' picture without giving the 'how, what and where' of Pakistan's economic development. The rest of the book tries to paint the complete picture, and seeks to understand and explain Pakistan's particular story. The answer to whether Pakistan after fifty years has been a success or failure is to be found in the following pages.

Part 1

Agriculture

Agriculture has been the mainstay of the Pakistan economy for many years, although in recent years, its importance has somewhat declined. From a contribution to gross domestic product of more than half in the 1940s, today it accounts for less than a quarter. The share of employment in agriculture has also fallen, from more than 65 per cent of the labour force in 1950 to about 47 per cent today. The two most common perceptions held by students and observers of the Pakistan economy are that Pakistan is mainly an agricultural country and that Pakistan's agriculture is 'feudal'. The four chapters on the agricultural sector in Pakistan deal with these two commonly held myths. In Chapter 2, an attempt is made to trace the history of the development of agriculture in Pakistan, questioning the claim that agricultural production in the country is still of a feudal nature. Large landowning patterns are often confused with feudalism leading to misperceptions. Chapters 3 and 4 develop the theme of the transition of the agricultural sector, arguing that a more capitalistic and capital-intensive agriculture now dominates. Chapter 5 highlights the key issues that currently exist in the agricultural sector and, given the diminishing contribution of agriculture to the overall economy, suggests that perhaps Pakistan's economy is no longer mainly agricultural or 'feudal'.

2

Is Pakistan Feudal? A Historical Account of the Development of Agriculture in Pakistan

There is a general perception held by many within Pakistan that, even at the close of the twentieth century, Pakistan is a 'feudal' country. This view is endorsed by political scientists, observers and journalists, the electronic media, and lay people in general. It assumes that in the economic, political, and social arena, Pakistan and Pakistanis have 'feudal social relations' and are 'feudal in attitude'. The label 'feudal' is pasted on to anyone owning large tracts of agricultural land, and even on rich urban dwellers who seem to have no known or apparent source of income to support their ostentatious lifestyles. Essentially, the popular image from film and television is of a feudal as someone who lives in luxury, often, but not necessarily, having an agricultural background. Politicians especially are considered to be from feudal backgrounds, and even the more sensible magazines and newspapers endorse the impression that the national and provincial assemblies in Pakistan are predominantly full of 'feudals'.

This chapter, the first of four on the agricultural sector, will try to assess the claim that Pakistani agriculture, and hence Pakistan, is feudal. We will recount the history of agricultural development in Pakistan from the pre-colonial Mughal times and examine the consequences of British rule for the social and economic relations of production within agriculture. This narrative will summarize the changes that have taken place over three centuries and culminate with a picture of the agricultural sector at the time of independence in 1947. The next chapter will develop the story of agriculture in Pakistan, explaining how the process of the development of agriculture continued after Pakistan came into existence.

A recurrent underlying theme of this book is that one needs to examine the present as a continuum from the past. In other words, we need to see the present as a part of the historical process to which it belongs, and to which it is linked. To some readers it may seem a little irrelevant that in a book about economic issues in contemporary Pakistan we begin the first substantial chapter with a history that goes back four centuries. We have argued in the Introduction why this is the manner in which issues should be discussed, and that this is the pattern adopted in this book. In addition, the question of whether Pakistani agriculture is feudal or capitalist has important economic, social, and political ramifications. The nature of agriculture has important repercussions not only for agriculture, but also for numerous related and distant sectors within the economy. This point will become clearer as the narrative progresses, especially when we discuss the social, political, and economic

consequences of the Green Revolution. Suffice it to say that it is important to observe how societies change, especially when they are transformed from one major historical epoch (or mode of production), feudalism, to another, capitalism (see Boxes 2.1 and 2.2). This chapter will do precisely that.

2.1 The Development of Agriculture Before the Consolidation of British Rule

There is a belief amongst some social scientists that pre-colonial India was a stagnant society with little progress taking place and rigid economic and social structures. They have tended to believe that it was only British rule which awakened the Indian subcontinent from its slumber. They believe that, had it not been for the positive and modern impact of British colonialism, most of South Asia would still be backward and perhaps still stuck in the nineteenth century. On the other hand, there are other social scientists who believe just the opposite. For them, the modernizing impact of British colonialism was debilitating and cruel, and they feel that the underdevelopment that we see in the South Asian subcontinent today is a result of that colonial impact. These are different ways of reading into, understanding, and interpreting history, and each individual has the privilege to reach his or her own conclusions. Here, we briefly present an outline of the nature of agricultural production before the conquest of India by the British.

India was a pre-capitalist social formation when the British conquest came about. There is some evidence of development and change in a society that was essentially pre-capitalist, and some writers have suggested that this movement was towards capitalism.[1,2]

In the pre-British period, under the Mughal Emperor, all land was owned by the king alone. There was no private property in land, and permission for the use of land was granted by the king. In 1647 the ruling class comprised the Emperor and about 8,000 *mansabdars* or nobles who were supposed to maintain large armies to serve the Emperor whenever he requested them. These *mansabdars* were either paid salaries in cash or, as was more common, were given *jagirs* or large tracts of territory in which they were responsible for collecting revenue from peasants and then transferring it to the state. Such *jagirdars*, or revenue collectors, were transferred from one area assigned to them for the purposes of revenue collection to another, usually after three or four

BOX 2.1
What are 'modes of production'?

Doug McEachern writes:

For our purposes, it is sufficient to recognize that the term 'mode of production' refers to those relations that exist at the heart of a given society, identify the major classes of that society and indicate the inherent logic of the relations and conflicts between those classes. In all societies we may identify means of production, direct producers and a relevant class of non-producers that combine in a process of social production. Production is also surplus production and surplus extraction; that is, the process of production also constitutes a process of class exploitation. The relations generated in the production process assume a different character in societies dominated by different modes of production. The problem is to suggest the different character of these relevant direct producers and non-producers and the forms of the relationships between them.

The modes of production identified by Marx can be codified as follows: *Primitive Communism* is a mode of production in which means of production (low level means of hunting and agriculture) are dominated by some form of communal institutions which organize production and distribute the surplus. *Feudalism* is a mode of production in which there is a partial separation of the direct producers from the means of production (largely the basis of agricultural production, land and the means to work that land). *Capitalism* is a form of society in which the direct producers have been separated from the means of production. These now exist as the private property of a class of non-producers. These outlines do not indicate all the ingredients of the modes of production. It is also necessary to show the way in which the various classes relate to each other through their relations to the means of production in the processes of production and surplus extraction. In primitive communism the problem is less obvious. Through membership of the community one has access to the means of production and the production process. On that basis, means of survival are acquired. Under feudalism, the situation of divided ownership, but with a dominant position (especially over the ownership of land) going to the non-producers, production and surplus extraction is organized through rent and tax relations. (It is incorrect to see a division between the process of surplus extraction and the domination of the means of production. The direct producers do not control the production process and the surplus is not extracted by external, essentially non-economic relations.) Under capitalism, the form of association is through wage-labour and surplus is extracted through surplus value relations and based on the separation of the direct producer from the means of production. Further, each mode of production has a characteristic state form. Primitive communism is a society without classes and without a state as such, though state-like functions are performed by other means. In feudalism the state and the process of surplus extraction are closely interconnected; the state is involved both at a national level and in the local process of production and accumulation. Under capitalism, the state is formally separated from the economy, centralized, bureaucratic and concerned with relating (mediating?) the relations between the economic and political spheres of society. Though different state forms appear to coincide with different modes of production, it is open to dispute whether the form of state is part of what constitutes a mode of production.

Source: McEachern, Doug, 'Capitalism and Colonial Production: An Introduction', in Alavi, Hamza, *et al.*, *Capitalism and Colonial Production*, Croom Helm, London, 1982, pp. 5–6.

---

years, so that they did not have the opportunity to build an entrenched base for themselves. While *jagirdars* were essentially officials rather than feudal lords, another category of assignees, the *zamindars*, bore a closer resemblance to the concept of feudal lord. *Zamindars* were also responsible for collecting revenue on behalf of the king, and were usually amongst the influential individuals from the villages. The Mughals had established a strong and elaborate revenue system under Akbar in the 1570s. Besides these two mechanisms for collecting revenue, there were also *khalisa* lands, from which land revenue accrued to the state directly.

The *zamindar* was the local lord and (feudal) master and had an obligation to the state to collect revenue and turn it over to the Emperor. Although he did not own the land, in many ways he had the characteristics of a feudal lord (see Box 2.2). He was the supreme lord at the village level, the 'linchpin of the system'. He used coercive force and extra-legal methods to extract revenue. He also presided over all social and judicial matters at the village level. Although he was appointed by the Emperor, he exercised complete authority at the village level. Here, there was a fusion of economic and political power at the point of production.

Under the Mughals, as all land was owned by the king, there was no question of land being inherited by either the peasant's family or the *zamindar*'s. There were no occupancy rights that could be alienated or mortgaged, although some transfer within villages or families did take place. While *zamindars* and *jagirdars* were in a position to assert authority over assigned tracts of land, their position was dependent on the favour of the ruler. In many cases, the right to collect revenue after the death of a *zamindar* was passed on to his sons, but this too depended on how much the Emperor wished to retain the status quo.

Soon after the death of Aurangzeb in 1707, the Mughal empire began to decay and fall apart. As central authority weakened, there were contending claimants to power. The *zamindars* and *jagirdars* who were the intermediaries in the Mughal system became more entrenched where they could, and tried to strengthen their claims on the land and increase their hold on the peasants.

BOX 2.2
What is feudalism?

Most people, when they use the terms 'feudal' and 'feudalism', do so rather loosely. They forget, or do not know, that 'feudalism' is an economic concept and that, when we talk about feudal relations, we usually mean relations, whether social or economic, based on a number of economic criteria. There has been continuous debate about what exactly feudalism entails. A number of historians and scholars have examined the conditions mainly in Europe before the Industrial Revolution, and have identified certain economic features that define feudalism. We present below a list of components or properties of the feudal mode of production which gives us some flavour of what the concept of feudalism entails. Feudalism is a concept that relates specifically to the agricultural sector. Hamza Alavi has explained the five criteria that constitute feudalism as follows:

i) *Unfree labour* rendered not necessarily in the form of labour services but taking a variety of possible forms. That would be contrasted with free labour in CMP [capitalist mode of production], in a double sense (a) in that it has been separated from (or 'freed') from possession of means of production (land) and (b) that it is free from feudal obligations to serve a lord; the direct producer is now free to sell his labour power or starve.

ii) *Extra-economic coercion in the extraction of the surplus* from the direct producer, as against economic coercion as the basis of exploitation in CMP.

iii) *A fusion of economic and political power at the point of production and a localized structure of power*, as against

separation of economic (class) power and political (state) power within the framework of a bourgeois state in CMP. The power of the exploiting class, the bourgeoisie, over the exploited class is then exercised indirectly, through the state apparatus and subject to the rule of (bourgeois) law, and not arbitrarily and directly as in FMP [feudal mode of production].

iv) *Self-sufficient ('subsistence') economy* of the village (or the manor), commodity production being secondary for the direct producer; subject to the condition that he produces also a surplus that is appropriated by the exploiting class of which a significant proportion may enter into circulation as commodities. That contrasts with generalized commodity production in CMP where (a) production is primarily of commodities, i.e. to be sold for the value to be realized on the market and (b) labour power itself is a commodity.

v) *Simple reproduction* where the surplus is largely consumed by the exploiting class which acquires it, instead of being accumulated, so that the economy and society merely reproduce themselves on the existing level of productive resources and technology, whereas in CMP we have expanded reproduction of capital, where the surplus is primarily deployed towards capital accumulation (though not without supporting rising consumption levels of the exploiting classes) and consequent expansion of the forces of production and technological advance.

Source: Alavi, Hamza, 'India: Transition to Colonial Capitalism', in Alavi, Hamza, *et al.*, *Capitalism and Colonial Production*, Croom Helm, London, 1982, p. 29.

2.2   The Impact of British Colonialism

With the start of active colonial expansion in South Asia in the middle of the 18th century, the British established either direct or indirect control over the greater part of its territory by the end of the century. Spreading the sphere of their political influence in the direction from the east (out of Bengal) towards south-west and north-west, they stopped in the case of the latter direction at the lines that closely fit the present-day frontier between India and Pakistan. The north part of these lines coincided with the confines of the Punjabi Kingdom, and the south one with the boundary of Sind with the authority of feudal rulers from a Baluchi clan of Talpurs to be established there by that time. A distinctive feature of the north-west regions was predominance of Moslem population.[3]

There is little disagreement among social scientists about the proposition that profound changes were brought about in the character of Indian society following the imposition of British rule. For our immediate context, three institutional changes

introduced by the British had important consequences for landholding and agricultural production. The institution of private property, as the British understood it, was introduced in India in the late eighteenth and early nineteenth centuries. At the same time, a legal system was established that was closely related to the ownership of property. And thirdly, the British established an 'efficient government'.[4]

Hamza Alavi analyses the impact of these changes and says:

> The main impact of the change brought about by the colonial dispensation was the elimination of petty sovereignties of chieftains and *zamindars* who *ruled* the land, as much as they owned it. *Thus the 'fusion of economic and political power at the point of production', that we identified as a structural condition of feudalism, the power of the landlord over the peasant, was dissolved and was reconstituted in the form of bourgeois landed property, under the authority of the colonial state which marked a separation of economic and political power.* The most important turning point in the evolution of new system of landownership brought about by the colonial regime was the 'Permanent Settlement' in Bengal (of land revenue obligations) of 1793 which was instituted in conjunction with

fundamental changes in the rural social and economic structure. The peasant was dispossessed of the land which now became the 'property' of the *zamindar*. Concomitantly the direct coercive powers of the *zamindar* (and his private armies) were abolished.[5]

The multiple claims that had emerged following the decline of the Mughal empire were 'systematized and unified' under the British all over India. The Permanent Settlement in Bengal in 1793 conferred property rights in land on the revenue collectors who were found as intermediaries between the cultivator and ruler. With the decline of Mughal rule, *zamindars* took over *de facto* possession of land. 'The British in their first settlements then granted to this *zamindar* a property right that in their judgement would be stable and ensure the collection of their revenue demand through him.'[6] Essentially, then, we have the beginnings of the concept of private ownership of land and of private property, protected by a legal system that recognizes these property rights.

This imposition of the legal concept of private property and ownership of land was a major step forward in transforming the indigenous society in the direction of a bourgeois, capitalist society. The British introduced the institution of the alienation of property in land by virtue of bourgeois civil law proceedings. With this, the principles of inheritance, guaranteed rights, and the privilege of succession were implemented.

Sindh was annexed to the British empire in 1843. The British 'made their first settlements on the basis that land was held directly from the state on a tenancy basis but its security was guaranteed. Payment of land revenue was a condition for the usufruct of land. The occupant was given heritable and transferable rights of occupancy. The land system was called the *ryotwari* system in which the state was the landlord and the occupant was its *ryot* or tenant.'[7] At the other end of the spectrum, the British granted ownership rights on large tracts of land to the Mirs as *jagir* lands. Other influentials were also awarded similar grants, as long as they provided services of some sort to the new rulers of India. These owners of large tracts of land became the landlords of Sindh.

Apart from these important changes in the relationship between land and the intermediary or owner, the British were responsible for numerous other changes which resulted in agriculture developing on capitalist lines. The introduction of the monetary tax, and the fact that it had to be paid regularly and on strict terms, required producers to sell their crops in the market to pay the tax on land. A market for agricultural commodities emerged, and the previous self-sufficiency and remoteness of villages was shattered. A much greater integration of the rural economy with that of the rest of the Indian subcontinent – and, subsequently, with the economy of imperial Britain – followed, with desolate and far-flung places becoming part of the money and commodity exchange nexus.

These interventions in the agricultural economy caused the cropped area and the marketable agricultural produce to grow. No cotton was grown in Sindh at the time of the British conquest. However, in 1873–4, 4,000 tons were produced, while Punjab's production grew over sevenfold in less than ten years from the mid-1850s to the mid-1860s.[8] Thirty times more wheat was exported from the Punjab in the 1880s than in the 1860s. As the industrial revolution progressed in Great Britain, there was a dire need for raw materials. In the 1840s and 1850s a poor cotton crop in North America produced a shortage of raw cotton for industry in England. It was at this time that British industrial capital urged the imperial government to develop resources to extract further raw material from India. With increased production for the market, the local economy became more integrated with, and dependent upon, the requirements of imperial Britain.

As the commercialization of agriculture continued and as the tax burden began to be felt, many landowning peasants were unable to pay the taxes and had to seek loans from money-lenders and merchants. Some were even forced to sell or mortgage their lands. *Zamindars* and *jagirdars* were expected to pay taxes on fallow land as well as on cultivated land. As some of them were unable to pay the tax, they were forced to sell their lands. The land of the defaulters was bought up by usurers, tradesmen, and merchants, many of whom belonged to urban areas with little direct involvement in agricultural production.

While these tax laws were strictly enforced, they began to have serious negative repercussions as far as the British were concerned. The colonial authorities felt that the landed aristocracy was the mainstay of their power in Sindh and the Punjab, and the erosion of their economic and, hence, political power was undermining the political strategy of the British. Thus, in Sindh between 1870 and 1890, a series of acts and laws were passed to protect the rights of the *zamindars*. Earlier, from the mid-1860s in both the Punjab and Sindh, courts of civil justice had come into existence which ensured the compulsory alienation of land in the case of non-payment of debt. The 1870s saw the beginning of the replacement of the initial land taxation code with a revised version under which only cultivated areas were subject to taxation and there was no tax on fallow lands. However, despite this change, in the mid-1890s over 42 per cent of usable land in Sindh either had been appropriated by, or was in the possession of, usurers under mortgages.[9] In the Punjab, the British went one step further. They were quite disturbed about the fact that, due to a debt market emerging and with landlords unable to pay their taxes and loans, agricultural land was going to non-agricultural users. They felt that this would undermine the position of the 'agrarian castes' on whom the British relied. Thus, they implemented the 1900 Punjab Land Alienation Act, which prohibited the passing of land from agricultural to non-agricultural castes and permitted land transfers only within the related agricultural caste group in each district.[10]

From 1885 onwards, the economy of the Punjab began to be reshaped by the considerable extension in agricultural production which resulted from canal colonization after the late 1870s. While the process of building canals took place all over India, the coverage in the Punjab was particularly impressive.[11] In the early years of the twentieth century, a little over half of the entire irrigated area was watered from canals. Within a period of two decades, canals watered about

80 per cent of irrigated land. In the first half of the twentieth century, the rate of expansion in the area of irrigated lands in the territory that now constitutes Pakistan outstripped the Indian region. The area irrigated from water from state-owned canals in the Pakistani territory saw an almost sevenfold increase in the first half of the twentieth century.[12]

The British needed to expand the potential area of agricultural production in India so as to ensure the availability of raw materials for industry in Britain, and for food crops in the Indian subcontinent, where the population was increasing at an alarming rate and the threat of famine loomed large. While early British policy had broken the century-old shackles of rural Indian life, capitalist agriculture was only just emerging. Hence, to increase production, rather than use intensive means, a more expansive form was necessary to bring more land under cultivation. The canal colonization programme was the result of this policy. The British did not want to settle rentiers on the newly colonized lands, and instead were looking for small well-to-do agriculturalists of the yeoman type, who would cultivate their own holdings. Grants were given to peasants to cultivate land, the ownership of which the state had every intention of retaining. These peasant grantees were to remain as occupancy tenants of the state and were not allowed proprietary rights. However, this policy was changed when this landholding peasantry, essentially of the self-cultivator type, was given proprietary rights in 1912.

According to some scholars, the principal change to take place in the first half of the twentieth century in the rural areas of Sindh and the Punjab was the increase in landlordism, which occurred by increasing the number of landlords and the landlord ownership of land.[13] In the Punjab, land ownership became increasingly concentrated, with large landowners controlling 38 per cent of arable land by 1939 (see Table 2.1). In 1947 in the Punjab, the owner-cultivated arable land comprised about 42 per cent of the total, while the remaining 58 per cent was leased. In Sindh,

Table 2.1
Structure of land ownership in the Punjab province, 1924 and 1939 (%)

Plots, acres	1924		1939	
	Owners	Area owned	Owners	Area owned
Up to 5	58.3	11.2	63.7	12.2
5–10	18.0	15.1	16.9	13.1
10–15	8.6	12.5	7.3	9.1
15–20	4.3	8.4	3.6	7.2
20–25	2.7	6.8	2.2	5.6
25–50	4.8	20.4	3.9	14.8
Over 50	3.3	25.7	2.4	38.0

Source: Belokrenitsky, Vyacheslav, *Capitalism in Pakistan: A History of Socioeconomic Development*, Patriot Publishers, New Delhi, 1991, p. 99.

80 per cent of the land belonged to big and middle owners of the more traditional landlord type, and was let out to lease. In the Punjab, 51 per cent of the sown area was cultivated on conditions of non-occupancy tenancy. This percentage was much higher in Sindh, where landlord ownership and peasant land-use constituted the most typical pattern of the region.[14]

In Sindh and the Punjab, tillers of land were usually called *muzareen* or *haris*, whose rights to cultivate land under the British were not recognized in law or practice. In the Punjab, some tenants, *maurusi muzareen* (occupancy tenants), did have the law on their side regarding a hereditary right to cultivate land, but such rights were not always respected in practice. In Sindh, while the mirs were granted *jagirs*, the British had also recognized the rights of tenants who held land owned by the state, and their security was guaranteed as long as land revenue was paid to the state. The occupants of

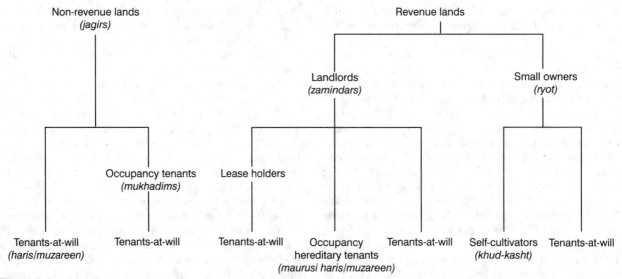

Figure 2.1
The land tenure system in Pakistan (circa 1947)
Source: Khan, Mahmood Hasan, *Underdevelopment and Agrarian Structure in Pakistan*, Westview Press, Boulder, 1981, p. 131.

these state lands had heritable and transferable rights of occupancy. This was the *ryotwari* system, where the tenant, *ryot*, worked on the land of which the state was the landlord (see Figure 2.1).

The *zamindar* and the *jagirdar* parcelled out land to the *haris* and *muzareen* in lots of 10–15 acres. A manager or *kamdar* used to oversee the work of the tenants. The *hari* was a landless sharecropper 'who traded his family's labour for a share in output which in theory was fifty per cent of the gross produce. He also supplied seeds, implements and oxen. In addition to the *batai* share, a *hari* paid levies, perquisites and free labour to the landlord. The landlord paid about one-third of his net rental share to the state as land revenue. He usually assigned to a *hari* each year a different block of land to prevent the *hari* from establishing any occupancy rights on a particular piece of land'.[15]

2.3 Feudal or Capitalist?

In the previous two sections, an attempt has been made to delineate the main features of the agricultural sector from the period of the Mughals to about the time of the independence of Pakistan. The direction of the discussion has been towards examining the issue of whether Pakistan's agriculture is, or was, feudal or capitalist. To do this, we need to show how the development of agriculture has matured from one historical form to another. If we reach the conclusion that until 1947 Pakistan's economy, particularly the dominant agricultural economy, was still overwhelmingly pre-capitalist, and that capitalist forms of agriculture had not established themselves, then Chapter 3, which examines the post-independence era, will need to evaluate the nature of this transition from one mode of production to another. On the other hand, if we conclude that the transition from feudalism to capitalism took place many decades ago, then we can take up the theme of the development of capitalism in agriculture in Pakistan since at least the early years of the twentieth century. This discussion is important because there are still many observers and students of Pakistan's economy who feel that Pakistan in general and its agriculture in particular are 'feudal'. Let us interpret the evidence.

There is great debate over the claim that British colonialism initiated capitalism in agriculture in the regions that constitute Pakistan. Imran Ali, who examines the impact of the British on the Punjab, especially with reference to the canal colonies of the province, writes that there was an absence of an agricultural revolution in the region. He accepts the fact that there 'was great economic growth' in the canal colonies, but 'agriculture did not experience any major transition from traditional modes. Quantitative increase was not accompanied by qualitative change.'[16] He argues that, if we look at conventional growth indices such as cultivated area, output, marketing, and trade, we see an 'impressive process of growth'. He adds that the process of agricultural colonization transformed the Punjab 'into one of the most important areas of commercial farming in Asia',[17] with agricultural produce being exported all over the world. Imran Ali also discusses the impact of the extended communications

network, especially railways, on increasing agricultural production, and how the monetization of the rural economy was responsible for the greater integration of the backward areas with the rest of the world. However, he concludes that 'capitalistic forms of agriculture ... did not emerge on any significant scale',[18] and that 'agricultural expansion did not produce a social base conducive to rapid change; indeed, the reinforcement of the existing class structure created, through the very process of economic growth, *a situation that was hostile to an economic transformation*'.[19]

So, for Imran Ali, the conclusion is clear: agriculture remained feudal or at least pre-capitalist under the British and, if anything, the old structures were *strengthened and reinforced* by colonial intervention. This interpretation, which is difficult to accept, is drawn into question by much of what Imran Ali himself describes. For example, he recognizes that 'the process of individualization [of property rights] created, probably for the first time, the prospect of alienation of land rights. With the increase in marketing of agricultural produce, aided by the development of road and rail transport, land came to have a monetary value',[20] and 'after 1880 there was a considerable increase in land sales in the Punjab ... Agriculturalists entered more into the money economy ...'.[21] Mahmood Hasan Khan, the great doyen of agricultural economists in Pakistan, shares views somewhat similar to Imran Ali's, writing as follows:

> With the recognition of absentee landlordism, and its protection by the British in the Indus basin as in other parts of India, *there emerged an agrarian system which could not have led to economic development*. The fusion of the feudal rural society and British administration decisively eliminated the chances for positive change in India. The economic surplus which peasants created was appropriated by those in the society who failed to invest in industrial growth. The relative abundance of land was fast disappearing and the peasant population was rising at unprecedented rates, with their consequent adverse effects on prospects of growth and on the condition of peasants. The problem of underdevelopment was intensified further by the growing imbalance between land and population. The British settlements gave birth to an economic and political system which could not get the Indian society in general and peasantry in particular out of the morass of backwardness. *This system reinforced feudal relations on land* which, though asymmetrical, provided a measure of stability for the colonial power to rule India.[22]

Let us now come to a different interpretation, where scholars believe that the colonial influence actually generated and speeded up the process of change in agriculture, from feudalism to capitalism. While there is some debate about the existence of capitalism and capitalist tendencies before the arrival of the British, many scholars believe that the impact of the British was both to destroy and to create.[23]

A critical element that would differentiate capitalist from pre-capitalist forms is the pattern of ownership. We have seen that in pre-colonial times land was owned by the supreme ruler of India, and that after the collapse of the Mughals contending claims surfaced, with ownership being determined by land-grabbing tactics. The British instituted the capitalist and bourgeois concept of private ownership of land, making it marketable and alienable, and introduced a legal system to protect owners and the market, guaranteeing the protection of bourgeois property and personal rights. We would argue that this step was such a radical and progressive departure from past practice that it alone would be responsible for the emergence and growth of capitalist, not feudal, development. Furthermore, the emergence of a land market in the 1860s; the imposition of a land tax which was in cash not in kind, as were other taxes; the establishment of official sources of credit, even long-term credit; the hugely expanded quantity of crops grown, much of them being exported, with cash crops taking an increasing share in production; the increasing polarization between landlords and the growing landless, with wage labour emerging; greater interaction and integration between town and country, breaking away from the self-sufficiency and isolation of the village community; and the advent of small-scale manufacturing, set up near agricultural zones to produce implements that could improve and expand agricultural output – *all point to a conclusive shift from a pre-capitalist to a capitalist type of agriculture*. Importantly, too there was a marked shift away from the fusion of economic and political power at the point of production, which was so central to feudal power relations, once bourgeois British law and political control over the Indian subcontinent was concretized.

In fact, Vyacheslav Belokrenitsky identifies approximate dates for specific events, highlighting the point that the roots of capitalism had been laid during the time of the British. For example, he points out that a land market had emerged during 1860–70 (p. 29); in the early 1860s, land tax was in cash rather than in kind (p. 42); in the mid-1860s, courts of civil justice came into existence, overseeing the compulsory alienation of land in the case of non-payment of debt (p. 44), and this could have happened only after private property in land had been established; after the 1880s, in Punjab and other areas, the export specialization of agricultural commodities took place, i.e. the agricultural economies joined the world and national capitalist markets, producing for exchange and profit (p. 108); and the first half of the twentieth century saw an increase in the number and share of landless agricultural labour in the countryside, especially in the Punjab, and a key feature of the capitalist form of economy in agriculture, the free worker, emerged and was a fact of life (p. 105).[24] All these factors cast doubt on the claim that feudalism continued to exist well after the establishment of British colonial rule.

A number of scholars recognize the fact that the British colonial influence affected the genesis of capitalism by creating a somewhat 'distinctive form of capitalism', and that the transformation of these non-capitalist societies took place by the domination of capitalism through a process of colonial rule.[25] Belokrenitsky, for example, argues that when in the nineteenth century British rule was established in the regions

that became Pakistan, it did not distort the evolution of capitalist relations there, for the latter had not started taking shape by that time. Capitalism that came into existence in that part of the world, under the direct and indirect impact of colonial conditions, was initially a kind of by-product of the policy pursued in India by colonial authorities, and of the influence they produced in direct and indirect ways on the local society.[26]

Moreover, Belokrenitsky argues that the 'development of capitalism as such (or rather of a western economic system familiar to the English) was not directly perceived as a goal of the colonial rule ... although it was stressed that the coming into existence of components of these practices would be desirable'.[27]

In dealing with the sort of conclusions reached by Imran Ali, discussed earlier, Doug McEachern argues that some researchers have assumed that if the surplus was extracted from the agrarian sector and not reinvested in technology and improved production in agriculture, then the mode of production would not be capitalist. He argues that this surplus can be accumulated in other spheres or even in other countries, as was the case in India, where surplus was transferred to Britain.[28] Moreover, he says that widespread commodity production and the sale of goods for the market (a fact observed in India even by Imran Ali) are 'incompatible with the designation of feudal or unchanged class and production relations ... such an occurrence is only possible on the basis of a reorganization of production and the generation of a new set of class relations'.[29] McEachern concludes that colonial domination and economic policy initiated the process of capitalist development in agriculture in India. Hamza Alavi elaborates on these themes in great detail and is also clear in his conclusions, arguing that a particular type of capitalism, one tainted by colonial rule, was observed to be emerging all over India. Without question, pre-capitalist forms of production were being replaced by capitalist forms under British colonialism. He argues that

> what we have in colonized India, therefore, is a capitalist mode of production, *but a capitalist mode of production that has a specifically colonial structure.* One thing is clear. *The feudal mode of production was dissolved* and there is no basis on which we can justify designation of relations of production in agriculture that resulted from the colonial transformation, any more as feudal.[30]

We conclude our analysis on the note that capitalism in agriculture was observed to emerge in the areas that constitute Pakistan as early as one hundred years ago. The seeds had been planted by British colonization in the early nineteenth century and bore fruit in the early twentieth century. Clearly, huge tracts of pre-capitalist or feudal landholdings, especially in Sindh, continued to exist. But the trend and process was *one conclusively of moving away from feudalism and dissolving pre-capitalist forms of production, replacing them with capitalist forms*. Hence, while feudal practices may have been extensive at the time of independence, and, in fact, may have even been dominant (see Table 2.2 and Appendix 2.1), capitalist agriculture has been the leading trend and it is

Table 2.2
Distribution of land ownership in Pakistan and provinces, 1950–1955

Farm size (acres)	Pakistan		Punjab		Sindh	
	Number of owners	Area owned (acres)	Number of owners	Area owned (acres)	Number of owners	Area owned (acres)
All sizes	5,068,376 (100.0)	48,642,530 (100.0)	3,555,457 (100.0)	28,309,744 (100.0)	337,665 (100.0)	10,285,021 (100.0)
5 or less	3,266,137 (64.4)	7,425,614 (15.3)	2,358,119 (66.3)	438,517 (15.7)	100,601 (29.8)	365,817 (3.6)
5–25	1,452,421 (28.7)	15,438,138 (31.7)	1,029,108 (28.9)	11,041,708 (39.0)	155,163 (46.0)	1,937,073 (18.8)
25–100	286,470 (5.7)	10,616,308 (21.8)	146,893 (4.1)	6,198,128 (21.9)	54,792 (16.2)	2,390,358 (23.2)
100–500	57,287 (1.1)	7,671,537 (15.8)	19,401 (0.6)	3,842,986 (13.6)	24,064 (7.1)	2,600,123 (25.3)
500 and above	6,061 (0.1)	7,490,933 (15.4)	1,936 (0.1)	2,788,405 (9.9)	3,045 (0.9)	2,991,650 (29.1)

Note: The data for the Punjab are for 1954/5; for Sindh for 1946/7. The data for Pakistan are the aggregate figures for all provinces. The Punjab includes the former State of Bahawalpur, and Sindh includes the former State of Khairpur.
Source: Khan, Mahmood Hasan, *Underdevelopment and Agrarian Structure in Pakistan*, Westview Press, Boulder, 1981, p. 68.

not possible to label Pakistan or Pakistani agriculture today as 'feudal'. As Appendix 2.2 shows, the myth of feudalism still prevails. However, our interpretation of the facts leads us to believe that, once the transition began and became more entrenched, capitalism soon asserted itself, removing pre-capitalist forms of production. The next two chapters develop this theme further.

2.4 Summary and Further Reading

2.4.1 Summary

This chapter has discussed the issue of the mode of production in agriculture in Pakistan. More specifically, it has tried to show that feudalism, despite popular perception, does not dominate production in the agricultural sector. A major reason why people believe that feudalism is prevalent in Pakistan is that they equate large landholdings with feudalism. This chapter has used a common and general definition of feudalism which has very specific characteristics, not dependent primarily on size of landholding. We have argued that, from the time of the British colonization of India, certain structural conditions were established by the imperial government which laid the foundations of capitalist development in agriculture. The rights of private property ownership and inheritance, defended by British civil law, brought forward this new form of production in agriculture.

Although 'feudal' enclaves existed at the time of independence, their trend was on the decline, being replaced by an altogether different and new order.

2.4.2 Further Reading

To understand the concept of feudalism, capitalist development in agriculture, and the process of transition, see: Hindness, Barry and Paul Hirst, *Pre-Capitalist Modes of Production*, Routledge and Kegan Paul, London, 1975; Hindness, Barry and Paul Hirst, *Modes of Production and Social Formation*, Macmillan, London, 1977; Hilton, Rodney (ed.), *The Transition from Feudalism to Capitalism*, Verso, London, 1976; Anderson, Perry, *Passages from Antiquity to Feudalism*, New Left Books, London, 1975; Marx, Karl, *Capital*, vol. 1, Penguin, London, 1975; Marx, Karl, *Grundrisse*, Penguin, London, 1973; and Lenin, V.I., *The Development of Capitalism in Russia*, Collected Works vol. 3, Progress Publishers, Moscow, 1977.

For material on Pakistan/South Asia, see: Habib, Irfan, *The Agrarian System of Mughal India*, Asia Publishing House, London, 1963; Habib, Irfan, *Essays in Indian History: Towards a Marxist Perspective*, Tulika, New Delhi, 1995; Alavi, Hamza, *et al.*, *Capitalism and Colonial Production*, Croom Helm, London, 1982; Belokrenitsky, Vyacheslav, *Capitalism in Pakistan: A History of Socioeconomic Development*, Patriot Publishers, New Delhi, 1991; Ali, Imran, *The Punjab Under Imperialism, 1885–1947*, Oxford University Press, Delhi, 1989; Vanguard Publishers, *Studies in the Development of Capitalism in India*, Vanguard, Lahore, 1978; Hamid, Navaid, 'The Process of Agricultural Development: A Case Study of the Punjab', unpublished Ph.D. dissertation, Stanford University, California; and Khan, Mahmood Hasan, *Underdevelopment and Agrarian Structure in Pakistan*, Westview Press, Boulder, 1981.

Appendix 2.1

The land systems of Pakistan in 1947

Mahmood Hasan Khan has given a graphic description of agrarian economic and social relations of production in Pakistan at the time of independence. He writes:

There were essentially two land systems in the Indus basin, with regional variations in tenurial arrangements, in layers of intermediaries on land and in the degree of land concentration. The dominant among these two was the landlord–tenant system. The other system was of peasant-proprietors or owner-cultivators.

While precise estimates on owners, tenants, etc., are not available for 1947, it is estimated that over 75 percent of the agricultural population was of peasant-proprietors and tenants in the Punjab and Sind. It is also estimated that most farms in Sind were operated by *haris* and they cultivated over 50 percent of the cultivable area. In the Punjab, over 58 percent of the cultivated area was farmed by *muzaraeen*. Landownership was highly concentrated in both provinces. Owners of holdings of over 100 acres constituted only 2 percent and 9 percent of all owners in the Punjab and Sind, but they owned 41 percent and 52 percent of area in the two provinces. The really large landowners, with holdings of over 500 acres, constituted 0.5 percent and 1 percent of all owners, but owned 25 and 30 percent of the area ... Peasant-proprietors, with holdings of 5 acres or less, were evidently more numerous in the Punjab than in Sind: 67 percent of all owners in the former and 30 percent in the latter. However, they owned only 30 and 4 percent of all area. Most of these peasant-proprietors were in the newly settled and irrigated areas (canal colonies and central districts) of the Punjab.

In the landlord–tenant system, the first group controlled most of the land, although it was small in number. The second group, though numerous, owned no land and enjoyed few if any permanent or recognized rights to its cultivation. The *zamindars* had rights of ownership which were heritable, partible and alienable. Only some *jagir* lands were not heritable. Most *zamindars* parcelled their lands out to tenants in small lots, usually of less than 15 acres. A *zamindar* used an *ahalkar* or a *kamdar* (supervisor) on tenants. He paid to the state as land revenue about 50 percent of his net rental share in the Punjab (and 33 percent in Sind) for each matured crop.

The tenants were mainly landless sharecroppers, who traded their labour and that of a pair of oxen for a return which in theory was about one-half of the crop output they produced on [the] *zamindar*'s land. The tenants supplied seeds and implements and paid water charges, but they did not pay land revenue to the state. The *haris* in Sind enjoyed no legal rights on tenancy: their contract with *zamindars* was verbal and annual. Similar terms existed for the ordinary *muzaraeen* in the Punjab. For *maurusi muzaraeen*, their tenancy rights and contract with *zamindar* were to be regulated by the Punjab Tenancy Act of 1887. The conditions of occupancy for these tenants were by no means easy to fulfil in practice, reducing their status to that of tenants-at-will.

There were then two basic features of the landlord–tenant relationship on land, namely (1) the *batai* system, and (2) the temporary tenure a tenant held at the pleasure of his landlord, who at least in Sind regulated the tenancy by a system of shifting cultivation. The *batai* system had two parts. First, there was the distribution of crop shares between landlord and tenant on a 50:50 or 40:60 basis. Second, a *zamindar* charged his tenant *abwab* or *huboob*, which ranged in number from five to twenty. Their number depended on tradition in a particular area. Their total bite on a tenant's share varied from about 5 to 30 percent. Many tenants-at-will were also required to provide *begar* to *zamindar* on demand. In Sind, a *zamindar* assigned to a tenant each year a different parcel of land, supposedly to rotate crops in a water-scarce agricultural system.

In disputes arising from the *batai* system, no legal protection existed for the landless tenants in any area. Even in the case of occupancy tenants in the Punjab, where such legal protection did exist, the political influence of *zamindar* with revenue officials at the local level determined the outcome of disputes. Like much else, the *batai* system was maintained by the power of *zamindars*. More significantly, this system of crop sharing militated against the development of agriculture as it was unjust to tenants in the extreme. There existed no incentive for the tenant to expand production. By the same token, it did not create any pressure on the landlord to undertake investment to make crop production more efficient. With the ownership of large landed estates concentrated in the hands of these *zamindars*, it encouraged absentee landlordism. The transfer of surplus from the tenant to *zamindar* was ensured by the social and political power enjoyed by landlords in the society, buttressed of course by the legal and administrative structure of the state.

Peasant-proprietors played an important role only in the newly settled areas of the Punjab. Many of these cultivators had lost their lands to moneylenders. Those who survived faced a new menace resulting from increased fragmentation of holdings. Fragmentation of holdings intensified because of rising population on land and operation of the customary law of inheritance among Muslims. In some areas, many of these small owners could not sustain their families entirely on their own holdings. They became progressively tenants as well. So their existence was only slightly less precarious than of the landless tenants.

Differences though there were between the Punjab and Sind provinces, the rural scene in the Indus basin was dominated by two factors. Most power resided in the hands of those who were small in number but whose economic contribution to agricultural output was that they owned and controlled large tracts of land. Most peasants, on the other hand, were landless tenants and small owners. The tenure of the landless tenant was tenuous and the existence of small owner was only slightly better. The asymmetrical relations in this predominantly landlord–tenant system were maintained and reinforced by the monopoly power of the absentee landlords and supported by the state. The characterization of tenants, no matter which source one cares to select among many, clearly established them as cultivators who had low economic and social status and whose surpluses were transferred to a dominant class of rulers, the *zamindars*.

Source: Khan, Mahmood Hasan, *Underdevelopment and Agrarian Structure in Pakistan*, Westview Press, Boulder, 1981, pp. 130-4.

Appendix 2.2

The myth of feudalism

This colourful recent article, written by Ayaz Amir in *DAWN*, re-emphasizes the point that feudalism still causes a great deal of concern to most people in Pakistan. Despite the considerable evidence presented to the contrary, the myth of feudalism prevails.

There can be little doubt that next to the great buzzwords of corruption, good governance and the environment, the most overworked concept in Pakistan today is that of feudalism. Commentators who have never spent a night in a village or ever set eyes on a patwari talk freely about waderas and feudal culture, ascribing all the country's political problems to these twin phenomena.

There is a gross misconception at work here because while there is nothing healthy about feudalism (except insofar as it led in Europe to the rise of the mercantile classes and in time to the establishment of democracy), feudalism proper, with its vast landholdings and tenant farmers, is certainly not as widespread or potent a circumstance in Pakistan today as it was, say, in the first two decades of the country's history or as it continues to be in the feverish imaginations of our deskbound political analysts.

About the only regions of Pakistan where we still find large landholdings is the province of Sindh and the Seraiki or the southern belt of Punjab. In the Frontier there were few large landholdings to begin with. If there are any today they must be few in number. In most districts of Punjab – a province which was once the centre of a thriving feudal tradition – large estates are a thing of the past. More than the imperfect land reforms of Ayub Khan and Zulfikar Ali Bhutto what has been responsible for this development are the laws of inheritance with what were once large estates becoming smaller holdings.

The result of this process is not hard to see. In pockets of Mianwali and Attock districts there are still a few large landholdings. But in the districts of Rawalpindi, Chakwal, Jhelum, Mandi Bahauddin, Gujrat, Wazirabad, Gujranwala, Sheikhupura, Lahore, Kasur, Sialkot, Narowal, Faisalabad and Toba Tek Singh (this by no means being an exhaustive list) there are no big zamindars, the norm in these districts being of small peasant proprietors or farmers with middle-size landholdings. It is true that citrus growers and mango and cotton farmers of central and southern Punjab make fat profits every year. But that is because of the cash crops they cultivate and not because all of them are sitting atop rolling vistas of farmland. In tehsil Bhalwal of Sargodha district, for example, even small farmers with citrus gardens of, say, 15 or 20 acres are able to get a good yearly return. But that scarcely turns them into feudals.

Not that feudalism as a form of land tenure has disappeared completely from Punjab. But it is confined to small pockets – Dera Ghazi Khan (courtesy the Legharis and Mazaris) and parts of Multan, Sargodha, Bahawalpur and Rahim Yar Khan.

The urban misconception of course is that anyone who looks like a hick, dresses like one, has a rural surname, curls his moustache and rides a Pajero (or as is the case nowadays, a Turbo Cooler) is necessarily a feudal. The Punjab provincial assembly certainly looks like a rural assemblage. But that is because most of its members are from rural backgrounds and represent rural constituencies and not because they are feudals. Just as every Memon, Gujrati or Chinioti is not a captain of industry, every Chattha and Warraich or Malik and Chaudry is not a feudal landlord.

The question raised in discussions about feudalism, however, is not about the size of landholdings but about the pernicious consequences of this phenomenon, with feudalism, in urban discourse, being considered almost synonymous with political power. The argument advanced is that parliamentary democracy has been unable to establish itself on a sound footing because feudals with their retrogressive ways, have a strangle-hold over the assemblies. This is a distorted view of Pakistani politics. Rural interests have a predominant influence in the assemblies simply because, reflecting the concentration of population, there are more rural constituencies in the country.

Feudal influence in politics received a major blow in the 1970 elections when big-name feudals in Punjab tasted defeat at the hands of less well known candidates from the Pakistan People's Party. Later, it is true, Zulfikar Ali Bhutto tried to reverse the process he himself had set in motion by admitting some of the same feudals into the PPP at the time of the 1977 elections. Even so, there was no going back to the politics of the forties and fifties when feudalism automatically meant political power.

Today in Pakistan few landholders, no matter how big, can make it into the assemblies if they are not supported by one or the other of the two major parties: the PPP and the PML(N). This is true even of Sindh where a PPP ticket counts far more than being a wadera. Jatoi needs PPP support to win in Nawabshah. After several defeats, Mumtaz Bhutto (no small landowner) made it to the Sindh assembly with some difficulty during the 1993 elections. The Pir of Pagaro has been trounced several times by PPP candidates. Indeed, it is a measure of the change in Pakistani politics that with the exception of the Bhuttos in Larkana, Nawaz Sharif in NA-95 Lahore, the Legharis and Mazaris in D.G. Khan and Khar in Muzaffargarh (and possibly Shaikh Rashid in Rawalpindi) few other politicos can claim to have safe constituencies. Even in this list it is only in D.G. Khan that feudal influence can be seen as the decisive factor for electoral success. The Bhuttos win in Larkana not because they are big landowners (there being other big landowners in the district as well) but because of their famous surname. Even Khar is not quite the big feudal that Tehmina Durrani has made him out to be. The clout that he enjoys in his district is because of his political standing which is quite independent of his landowning status.

The fact, however, remains that in Pakistan today, when political ideology has taken a back seat to the pursuit of power for its own sake, a party ticket alone is not a sufficient condition for election success. In order to produce the desired results it must be matched with local influence. So the question really is that if feudalism is a waning force, what are the other factors which make for rural influence in Pakistan today?

There is none more important in this respect than the ability to interact with the local bureaucracy: the police, the magistracy and the revenue department. The administrative system in Pakistan is riddled with corruption and inefficiency. If it responds to anything it is to graft and influence-peddling. In order to win the kind of influence which can later be translated into votes, a politico first has to be 'available' to his constituents, the days of absentee politics having long gone in Pakistan. But availability is of use only when the politico concerned is wise to the politics of thana, tehsil and katcheri. At one time it was mostly the feudal who performed this role. Nowadays his place has been taken by other representatives of the rural gentry: those who have disposable incomes because of their cash crops or those who have made money in other fields: transport, construction, light industry, the Gulf, etc.

So if anything has to be reformed or changed it is not just the remaining bastions of feudalism but the administrative system which still puts a premium on a feudal style of politics. As long as the administrative system continues to function in its present groove the rural population will understand local power-brokers better than candidates who may otherwise be better qualified to speak glibly on national and international issues.

This is not to say that with the breakdown of feudalism Pakistani politics have become more egalitarian. That is far from being the case. It is only in this that the nature of the Pakistani oligarchy has changed. It is no longer neatly divided into the bureaucracy, the military and the landowning class as it was for the first decade of the country's history. Today all these various segments (plus high finance and industry) have come closer to each other through inter-marriages and a commonality of economic and political interests. Retired generals and bureaucrats are landowners and captains of industry. Former landowners are industrial barons. The old industrial houses have married into the old feudal aristocracy. A new moneyed breed has entered politics. The old familiar societal distinctions, therefore, have lost much of their validity.

If the cause of egalitarianism has to be served then the enemy is not just feudalism (which in any case, as I have tried to show, has lost much of its traditional power) but an incestuous oligarchy which dominates social, political and economic life in the country. To keep the focus of public anger only on the Pajero-riding rural politico is to ignore the evolutionary complexity of this elite whose depredations have brought the country to its present sorry pass.

Source: Amir, Ayaz, 'The Myth of Feudalism', *DAWN*, 10 June 1996.

Notes

1. See Habib, Irfan, *The Agrarian System of Mughal India*, Asia Publishing House, London, 1963; and Habib, Irfan, 'Potentialities of Capitalist Development in Mughal India', *Journal of Economic History*, vol. 29, no. 1, 1969; and Habib, Irfan, *Essays in Indian History: Towards a Marxist Perspective*, Tulika, New Delhi, 1995.
2. The rest of this and the following section make liberal use of: Habib, Irfan, op. cit., 1963; Khan, Mahmood Hasan, *Underdevelopment and Agrarian Structure in Pakistan*, Westview Press, Boulder, 1981; Alavi, Hamza, *et al.*, *Capitalism and Colonial Production*, Croom Helm, London, 1982; and Belokrenitsky, Vyacheslav, *Capitalism in Pakistan: A History of Socioeconomic Development*, Patriot Publishers, New Delhi, 1991.
3. Belokrenitsky, Vyacheslav, op. cit., 1991, p. 8.
4. Alavi, Hamza, 'India: The Transition to Colonial Capitalism', in Alavi Hamza, *et al.*, op. cit., 1982, p. 38.
5. Ibid., p. 38, emphasis added.
6. Khan, Mahmood Hasan, op. cit., 1981, p. 126.
7. Ibid., p. 143.
8. Belokrenitsky, Vyacheslav, op. cit., 1991, p. 37.
9. Ibid., p. 42.
10. Ali, Imran, *The Punjab Under Imperialism, 1885–1947*, Oxford University Press, Delhi, 1989, p. 49
11. For detailed documentation and discussion, see Ali, Imran, op. cit., 1989.
12. Belokrenitsky, Vyacheslav, op. cit., 1991, p. 134.
13. Ibid, p. 89.
14. Ibid., p. 93.
15. Khan, Mahmood Hasan, op. cit., 1981, p. 143.
16. Ali, Imran, op. cit., 1989, p. 235.
17. Ibid., p. 237.
18. Ibid., p. 241.
19. Ibid., p. 242, emphasis added.
20. Ibid., p. 4.
21. Ibid., p. 4.
22. Khan, Mahmood Hasan, op. cit., 1981, p. 130, emphasis added.
23. See amongst many: Marx, Karl, *On Colonialism*, Foreign Language Publishing House, Moscow, 1960; Habib, Irfan, op. cit., 1963; Alavi, Hamza, op. cit., 1982; McEachern, Doug, 'Capitalism and Colonial Production: An Introduction', in Alavi Hamza, *et al.*, op. cit., 1982; and Belokrenitsky, Vyacheslav, op. cit., 1991.
24. Belokrenitsky, Vyacheslav, op. cit., 1991.
25. See Alavi, Hamza, op. cit., 1982; McEachern, Doug, op. cit., 1982; and Belokrenitsky, Vyacheslav, op. cit., 1991.
26. Belokrenitsky, Vyacheslav, op. cit., 1991, p. 16.
27. Ibid., p. 29.
28. See Alavi, Hamza, op. cit., 1982; McEachern, Doug, op. cit., 1982.
29. McEachern, Doug, op. cit., 1982, p. 12.
30. Alavi, Hamza, op. cit., 1982, p. 64, emphasis added.

3

The Green Revolution and Land Reforms

It would be fair to say that one of the most important events in Pakistan's agricultural history, with extensive repercussions on other sectors, has been the process called the Green Revolution, which occurred in the mid-1960s. The technology package associated with it generated major changes in the economic, social, and political structure of the country, transforming the agricultural and rural sectors irreversibly. Much of what we see today, in terms of economic groups and classes, political affiliation, and even culture, has its roots in, and is a consequence of, the Green Revolution. It forms a watershed between the old and new Pakistan. However, while the mid-1960s are in many ways an important juncture in our history, it is necessary to emphasize that change is a continuous process and events like the Green Revolution act only as an impetus to that change. While present-day Pakistan may have its roots in the Green Revolution, a lot more has happened since the mid-1960s to make Pakistan what it is today. This chapter will examine the nature and consequences of the major transformation that took place in the mid-1960s.

Land reforms are an important mechanism for changing ownership and wealth patterns, economic and social relations of production, political relations, and a host of other factors. Land reforms usually imply a redistribution of land away from those who own large chunks of it to those who are often landless (see Box 3.1). There have been two sets of land reforms in Pakistan, both of which will be analysed in this chapter.

The purpose of studying any sector or society is to see how it has changed over time and how it continues to evolve. In Chapter 2, we discussed the process of change in agriculture from the times of the Mughals until independence. This chapter discusses some important events resulting in the transformation of the agricultural sector, while the next chapter examines the overall process of agrarian transition. The events and issues discussed in the present chapter have an important bearing on how agrarian transition has taken place.

3.1   The Green Revolution

The annual growth rate in agriculture between 1949 and 1958 was a mere 1.43 per cent, less than half of the annual growth rate in population. Agriculture was allowed to stagnate in the 1950s because the ruling élite believed at that time that it was essential to industrialize at all costs and at great speed. Government policies were heavily biased against agriculture, and it was only towards the end of the 1950s – when it became clear that growth in agriculture was necessary for the survival of the country – that the importance of the agricultural sector was recognized.

BOX 3.1

Land reforms: need and constraints

Viqar Ahmed and Rashid Amjad examine the principle behind land reforms. They argue as follows:

In agrarian societies, land is the primary productive asset and the tangible expression of economic and political power. Therefore, the struggle for control of land and its fruits is a constant one. Throughout history, patterns of land ownership and tenure have played an important, and at times decisive, role in shaping the political and social system. It has, in most cases, also helped to determine the possibility and pace of economic change. It was thus inevitable as economic development became a major goal in these societies, and the principal concern of governments, that large concentrations of land ownership and the feudalistic pattern of social relationships came to be regarded as prime obstacles to sustained growth and development. Demands for radical changes in the land-

tenure systems became more and more persistent both on grounds of social justice as well as a pre-requisite for economic development …

… A decision to undertake land reforms often meets with strong resistance from landowners who constitute a powerful élite in agricultural societies. It is, therefore, preceded by political controversies and national debate. Even after a land reforms proposal passes through the legislative process, its implementation is a complicated task due to the lack of organization at the village level, a dearth of proper data, a faulty maintenance of land records, and lengthy and complex legal procedures. These obstacles can, of course, be overcome by a strong political will and the active support of the rural masses for the programme.

Source: Ahmed, Viqar and Rashid Amjad, *The Management of Pakistan's Economy, 1947–82*, Oxford University Press, Karachi, 1984, pp. 117–18.

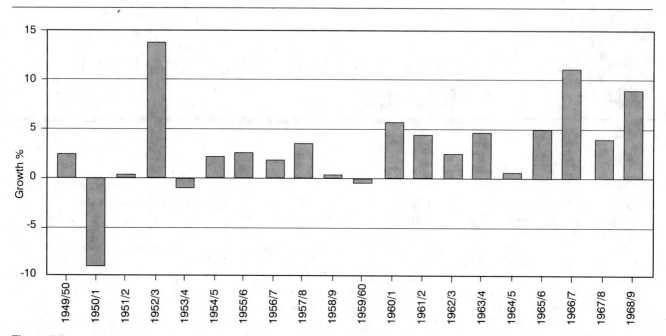

Figure 3.1
Growth rates in agriculture, 1949–1969

Figure 3.1 shows the growth rates in agriculture in the 1950s and 1960s, and indicates a marked change between the two decades. Between 1959 and 1964, agriculture grew at an overall rate of 3.7 per cent, but this impressive rate was overshadowed by the even greater 6.3 per cent between 1965 and 1970. Between 1966/7 and 1967/8, the years when the Green Revolution was at its peak, agricultural output grew by 11.7 per cent, and it maintained a high growth rate of 9.6 per cent in 1968/9 to 1969/70. How were these rates achieved?

The phenomenal increase in growth took place in two phases. In the first, 1960 to 1964/5, the main cause of the growth was the increase in irrigation facilities, mainly tubewells. The second phase, between 1965/6 and 1969/70, showed impressive growth when the expanded irrigation facilities were supplemented by the technology package of high yielding variety (HYV) seeds, chemical fertilizers, and pesticides. Essentially, then, it was the complete package of water, seed, fertilizer, and pesticides that caused the large growth in agricultural output and production.

Without any doubt, *the most important ingredient in the technology package was water,* and water which was guaranteed and available as and when required. It was the key variable that established the spread of Green Revolution technology, since the new HYV seeds and the fertilizer package were critically dependent on the timely availability of a sufficient quantity of water. The increase in the availability of water, either by tubewells or through canals, was estimated to be responsible for half of the total increase in output.[1]

In the first phase, where irrigation was the critical component of agricultural production, privately owned tubewells were the main factor responsible for the increase in water availability. Between 1960/1 and 1964/5 about 25,000 tubewells were installed, each costing Rs5,000–12,000, and

the farm area serviced by tubewells doubled.[2] In the second half of the 1960s, two HYV seeds, one for wheat, developed by the International Wheat and Maize Institute in Mexico, and the other for rice, developed by the International Rice Research Institute in the Philippines, were introduced in Pakistan. The Mexi-Pak wheat seed had been experimented upon in the early 1960s and, along with the IRRI rice seed, yielded higher output. These experimental results were soon reproduced across large areas of agricultural land. Since the HYV seeds required large sources of water, those areas that had better irrigation facilities and those that had installed tubewells were the first to adopt these seeds. Moreover, farmers who wanted to use the new seeds were also seen sinking tubewells and the number of tubewells in the country increased from 34,000 to 79,000 between 1964/5 and 1969/70. The area serviced by tubewells increased sixfold between 1959 and 1969. More than half of the irrigated area of the country (6 million acres) was cultivated with the improved seeds in 1969/70. Fertilizer consumption also saw a dramatic increase of 150 per cent between 1965/6 and 1970/1 and a rise of 235 per cent between 1965/6 and 1971/2.[3]

As Figure 3.1 shows, there were substantial increases in agricultural growth rates in each of the Green Revolution years. Moreover, the output of major crops between 1960 and 1970 increased substantially: wheat production by 91 per cent and rice by 141 per cent. Even other crops not directly related to the HYV seeds showed increases due to the extensive use of other non-seed factors in the package. So it seems that the Green Revolution, at least as far as production, growth, and output are concerned, was a resounding success. Nevertheless, we need to analyse the numerous issues and repercussions of this significant event in Pakistan's agricultural history.

3.1.1 The Issue of the Tubewells

While the growth in tubewells from a few hundred in 1960 to 75,000 in 1968 and 156,000 in 1975 was a key factor in providing irrigation, and hence in permitting the adoption of the technology package, there are a number of issues around the apparently 'simple', and supposedly mere technical, issue of sinking tubewells.

The first issue concerns the location of tubewells: they were highly concentrated regionally, mainly in the rich old settled districts and the canal colony districts of the Punjab; indeed as many as 91 per cent of the 76,000 tubewells in 1968 were in that province. Outside Punjab there was very little tubewell development. In the NWFP and Baluchistan, the shortage of accessible supplies of ground water, due to the hard stony mountainous terrain, made the depth of drilling required for tubewells prohibitively expensive. In Sindh, the fact that ground water is saline meant that this water could not be used for agricultural purposes, and thus very few tubewells were sunk. Thus, it was not the entire province of the Punjab, but only a handful of districts in the Punjab that were able to sink tubewells and gain all the benefits of the Green Revolution. This, some observers believe, caused interregional disparities to grow (see below).[4]

Secondly, given their size and cost, tubewells were mainly installed by landowners with over 25 acres of land. Mahmood Hasan Khan writes that 'given the indivisible and large capacity of diesel and electric tubewells, even the middle peasants cannot afford their fixed and variable costs. Therefore, there has been a high concentration of ownership of tubewells.'[5] Seventy per cent of tubewells were put in by farmers owning over 25 acres, and only 4 per cent by farmers owning fewer than 13 acres.[6]

Thirdly, inducement to invest in tubewells was given to farmers through large public subsidies on fuel, installation costs, and maintenance. Moreover, the Agricultural Development Bank of Pakistan (ADBP) followed a fairly liberal credit policy and made numerous loans to farmers so that they could set up private tubewells.

Essentially, then, the apparently 'neutral' effect of increasing irrigation through tubewells seems to have had a number of important repercussions on interregional concerns, economic status and the ability to borrow money. The extensive sinking of tubewells was far from scale neutral.

3.1.2 Tractorization

In Chapter 5 where we discuss the critical issues in agriculture, an important issue examined is tractorization and mechanization. Tractors are now an important part of the agricultural and rural scene, but their contribution during the Green Revolution had very important consequences. Akmal Hussain writes:

> tractor imports were systematically encouraged [after 1960] by the provision of cheap credit through institutions such as the ADBP. At the same time the overvalued exchange rate made tractors available in Pakistan at prices considerably below world market prices. Another factor stimulating tractorization was the greatly increased profitability of agricultural production, as the result of the availability of HYV of foodgrains, subsidized fertilizer, cheap electricity for tubewell installation as well as improved provision of canal water following massive public surface water projects.[7]

Hence, due to the technology being used, tractors became more useful on the farm.

In 1959 there were 2,000 tractors in the country, which increased by over 8,000 per cent to 18,909 in 1968. Most of these tractors were of the larger size, with 84 per cent above 35 horse power. A World Bank Study of 1966 and the Giles Report in 1967 recommended the use of the larger tractors.[8] Once these tractors were imported the pattern was set, and large tractors still dominate today (see Chapter 5). Not surprisingly, most tractors were owned by those with more than 100 acres of land.

In a study in the early 1970s, Carl Gotsch reported that over 38 per cent of all tractors in the country were located in the Multan Division in Central Punjab, while 58 per cent were in the three divisions of Lahore, Multan, and Bahawalpur.[9] There was also a very close link with tubewell ownership, where almost 75 per cent of privately owned tractors were on farms that had sunk tubewells.[10]

Clearly, tractorization took place in those areas which had 'complementary inputs, [was] carried out by the larger and more resourceful farmers and [was] associated with a proximity to urban markets and services'[11] – similar to those found with tubewells.

3.1.3 Regional and Income Disparities

If tubewells were the single most critical factor that was responsible for the Green Revolution, and if the sinking of tubewells had a close correlation with tractorization, which in itself would have helped production further, a pattern emerges. Moreover, if we discovered another close correlation, that between large farms, in specific regions, and tractors and tubewells, the impact on regional and income inequality would be self-evident. Let us examine the evidence.

Hamza Alavi writes that 'because private tubewell development is closely relative to concentration of land in large farms, the "Green Revolution" has tended not only to intensify already large disparities in income and wealth of the different strata of rural population but, by the same token, it has also widened disparities between different regions'.[12] He adds that the incomes of the rural élite increased, while the incomes of small farmers in the districts where the Green Revolution was most successful, and in other poorer regions, 'have failed to improve or have not improved in the same measure'.[13] These views are shared by most researchers on the Green Revolution. Moazam Mahmood argues that the inputs, especially the installation of tubewells and access to credit, were inaccessible to poorer farmers and, hence, that the latter did not share in the fruits of the Green Revolution, causing increases in relative poverty.[14]

Mahmood Hasan Khan says that, since the use of fertilizers and new seeds was premised on the availability of adequate water supply, the lack of water caused 'serious interregional and intra farm disparities'.[15] The NWFP and the south-eastern parts of Sindh had inadequate access to water and the HYV technology. The difference between the poor and rich peasants also increased due to the unequal access to inputs.

Carl Gotsch has argued that one should talk not of the increase in agricultural growth in Pakistan, but rather of growth in a relatively few districts. These districts in the Punjab–Lyalpur (Faisalabad), Montgomery (Sahiwal), and Multan – grew at 8.9 per cent per annum between 1959/60 and 1964/5, twice the 'national' rate. Thus, as Shahid Javed Burki has argued, it was the farmers who owned between 50 and 100 acres, almost all of them in the Punjab, who produced 'Pakistan's' Green Revolution.[16]

3.1.4 Élite Farmer Strategy and Capitalist Development

Some observers have argued that the Green Revolution was 'an élite farmer strategy because … it rest[ed] on the economic power of large landholders who [were] its principal beneficiaries'.[17] For them, this rural élite constitutes less than 5 per cent of the rural population of Pakistan and was the only real beneficiary of the Green Revolution. Akmal Hussain believes that

> The new technology made it possible to accelerate agricultural growth substantially through an 'élite-farmer strategy' which concentrated the new inputs on large farms. Now the crucial determinant in yield differences became not the labour input per acre in which small farms had been at an advantage, but the application of the seed–water–fertilizer package over which the large farmers with their greater financial power had superior access. Thus the technocrats felt that the Green Revolution had made it possible to accelerate agricultural growth without having to bring about any real change in the rural power structure.[18]

Despite (or possibly because of) these anomalies in the benefits of the Green Revolution, one outcome upon which all observers are agreed is that the Green Revolution resulted in the development and entrenchment of capitalist farming in the regions where the technology was adopted. However, there are some differences of opinion over who were the leaders of this change in the mode of production and in farming techniques.

Shahid Javed Burki and others believe that the rapid agricultural growth was led by a new breed of dynamic middle-class farmers who were capitalist to start with. These farmers had been created by the shift in political power under Ayub Khan, who, Burki argues, through his Basic Democracies scheme took away political power from the traditional big landlords and gave it to the middle-class landowners. It was these middle-class farmers, owning between 50 and 100 acres of land in the Punjab, who 'produced' the revolution in Pakistani agriculture. Ayub Khan's creation, the rural middle class, was considered a 'new powerful and independent factor in the political

system', which had been 'released from the political and rural control of the landed aristocracy' and emerged as the 'traditional profit maximizer'.[19]

This view has not been shared by the likes of Hamza Alavi and Akmal Hussain, who believe that it was the large landlord and not the middle class which was at the vanguard of this revolution.[20] They believe that farmers who had land over 100 acres were dominant in the adoption of the new technology and in reaping the fruits of the Green Revolution. Alavi feels that the new mechanized methods did not bring into existence a new class of capitalist farmers, but that it was 'mainly the big landowner who … made the greatest progress in the direction of farm mechanization'.[21] Nevertheless, they all agree that the impact was one of deepening capitalist relations.

There was increased leasing-in of land as large farmers were now willing to take back the land previously leased to sharecroppers. Due to the large scale of tubewells and tractors, more and more land was resumed for production under capitalist means. Not only that: owners of this technology began to lease-in their neighbours' land as well. These farmers began to evict tenants or send them to more marginal portions of the land, and began to hire wage labour instead. Self-cultivation was on the increase in areas where this technology was used. There was greater income in the hands of landowners, who began to purchase manufactured goods. As demand and consumption expanded, markets began to emerge around small towns. A number of attributes particular to capitalism (see Chapter 2) began to dominate in the agricultural sector, probably ending once and for all the debate on whether agriculture in Pakistan was feudal or capitalist. Capitalism had entrenched itself forcefully and permanently.

3.1.5 Social and Political Effects

Although the economic effects of the Green Revolution were easily observable, with growing overall output and increasing incomes for some, the social and political effects took a little longer to emerge. Amongst the economic factors that had social and political impacts were: the displacement of labour, both at the low end of the spectrum in the form of sharecroppers, and at the higher end, where those with land either sold it or rented it out to neighbours; increased rural–urban migration; an increase in consumerism; the emergence of small towns near agricultural areas that were using capitalist techniques, and hence required new and different services; and the awareness of disparities between farmers and regions.

There was also a change of attitude towards education, especially amongst the big farmers. Writing at that time, Hamza Alavi argued that 'the revolution in mechanical technology and chemical technology which is now employed in agriculture is making new demands upon the capabilities of the farmers. They are becoming increasingly aware of the values of education in terms of their own situation, namely for better farming and coping with new technologies.'[22] However, the emphasis upon the social sectors was not particularly impressive in the 1960s and education was not considered important by the Ayub Khan regime (see Chapter 16).

Before the Green Revolution there was a lot of talk about the small farmer and how efficient he used to be. However, as the new technology spread, the size–efficiency relationship was reversed: rich peasants and landlords made most and best use of the lumpy investments in a technology that, as we have seen, was not scale neutral and was biased in favour of the large landlord. Mahmood Hasan Khan argues that 'the structure of technology and the direction of credit flows themselves reflect the influence of large landowners and capitalist farmers on public policy'.[23] Moreover, it is important to emphasize the fact that, since Punjab and Sindh are the backbone of Pakistan's agricultural economy, with more than 75 per cent of the country's population, and 80 per cent of its cultivated and cropped area, the impact of the Green Revolution was restricted to these provinces. Moreover, because of the water and technology packages identified above, the NWFP and Baluchistan missed out on the Green Revolution of the 1960s. (However, Chapter 5 reveals some interesting recent trends regarding increases in output and production in these two provinces.)

Nirmal Sanderatne has been particularly observant about the political consequences of the Green Revolution and relates them to the rise and subsequent victory of the Pakistan People's Party in 1972. He argues that 'the overwhelming electoral victory of the PPP amply justified its strategy [of making promises to the peasantry on agrarian reform] and demonstrated the validity of the hypothesis advanced earlier that the nature of agricultural development in the past, while successful in terms of increasing aggregate production, had intensified existing economic disparities and dissatisfactions. In turn these had radicalized Pakistan's politics.'[24] The PPP won conclusively in the heartland of the Green Revolution and some observers found a 'high correlation between the voting for the PPP and the area under Mexi-Pak varieties of wheat. The PPP won in all but one of the constituencies in which more than 56 per cent of the wheat area was under the new varieties.'[25]

The emergence of the Pakistan People's Party on the Pakistani political scene and its subsequent victory in the 1970 general election were the result of the policies of Ayub Khan's decade. The election results from the rural areas were a direct consequence of the Green Revolution, and even urban areas were not spared the outcome of agrarian change as migrants from rural areas began to play some role in industrial and urban areas as well. With hindsight, one can say that the 1970 election, with the victory of the Awami League in East Pakistan and the People's Party in West Pakistan, may have been the only election held in Pakistan where economic conditions so directly influenced political outcomes. Perhaps it was the degree of turmoil and disparity that emerged after the Green Revolution of the 1960s, as it usually does after any revolution, which made such politics possible. Since then, development in Pakistan has probably been less disharmonious, and hence change has been more gradual and less disruptive. The Green Revolution was the first big shock that disrupted gradual growth, especially in agriculture, but also more generally across Pakistan. There is little doubt that it radically transformed the economic, political, and social direction of the country, establishing

deeper, more entrenched, capitalist relations of production than those that had existed earlier in agriculture.

Development and growth, especially of capitalist relations, is a disharmonious process, often creating but also destroying, and having negative consequences for some sections of the population. However, one needs to examine the overall nature of development and not lament the fate of a few. Hamza Alavi, for example, disappoints when he argues that 'the present course of the "Green Revolution" … has brought about a deterioration in the conditions of life of a majority of the population and further progress of farm mechanization is creating a situation when a very large number of the rural population is faced with the prospect of having no viable means of livelihood'.[26] At a micro level this scenario did happen, but this analysis ignores the impact of the greater dynamic of change (even progress) that resulted in the use of this technology. Moreover, Hamza Alavi's lament ignores his own analysis where he recognizes that the Green Revolution was geared to the needs of large landowners, and was even made by the bureaucracy in tandem with their class allies, and hence that the outcome was inevitable. Any other outcome, given the nature of the state, class alliances and the focus on large landowners, would have been unlikely.

Akmal Hussain, too, falls into such a trap. He realizes that the new technology did accelerate growth in agriculture substantially through an élite farmer strategy, and that the 'growth of capitalist farming accelerated considerably in the late '60s as large landowners began to resume rented out land to operate their own farms with hired labour and capital investment'.[27] But, for Akmal Hussain, 'it was this process of the development of capitalist farming which has generated new and potentially explosive contradictions in Pakistan's rural society'.[28] Again, any other outcome would have been unlikely. Given the existing contradictions, class alliances, and the role of the state, the result was a natural consequence of the policies followed.

3.2 Land Reforms[29]

Pakistan has had a long and varied history of land reform. Most attempts have been just that: attempts without any serious purpose. Table 3.1 gives details of many such attempts, most of which failed. From 1945 onwards there was talk of reform in the nature of tenancy and in the structure of landholding, but little came of it. The reasons for this are fairly clear and not surprising. In the Central Council of the Muslim League in 1947 there was a large representation from the (very) large landlords of the provinces of the Punjab and Sindh – these comprised 50 per cent of councilmen from Punjab and 60 per cent from Sindh. Furthermore, with quite exploitative conditions in rural areas in the 1940s, involving complete domination and control by landlords, it was a little unrealistic to assume that they themselves would be willing to put a dent in their source of power (see Chapter 2, Table 2.2 for landholding patterns in 1947). Landlords were the most significant class in the Muslim League, comprising 163 of the 503 Muslim League parliamentary members in 1942. From the time of independence, all Chief Ministers of the Punjab,

Table 3.1
Key dates and features of land and tenancy reforms in Pakistan

Year	Reform	Key features and recommendations
1945	Tenancy Laws Committee, Sindh	Occupancy rights should be granted to *haris* who had personally cultivated at least 4 acres of land annually for the same *zamindar* for 8 years.
1947	*Hari* Committee, Sindh	Defended the landlords; famous Note of Dissent from one member who argued for radical changes in the land tenure system.
1949	Muslim League Agrarian Committee Report	Abolition of *jagirs*; security of tenure for all tenants; share rents should replace rents-in-kind; ceiling on landholdings of 150 acres irrigated and 450 acres for unirrigated; land distribution to tenants and compensation to landlords (report shelved).
1950	Punjab Tenancy Act	No charge by landlords from tenants other than 50 per cent crop share.
1950	Sindh Tenancy Act	Permanent rights of tenancy to long-term tenants; eviction rights to landlords under certain conditions.
1950	Punjab Protection and Restoration of Tenancy Rights Act	Eviction of tenants allowed only under specified conditions.
1952	Punjab Tenancy (Amendment) Act	Abolition of occupancy tenancy; transfer of ownership rights to occupancy tenants; share of landlord reduced from 50 per cent to 40 per cent.
1955	Executive Order	Abolition of *jagirs* and other revenue-free grants; like other *zamindars*, now *jagirdars* required to pay land revenue. Landlordism remained intact, for no limit to ownership as long as all legal dues paid to the government.
1955	Challenge to the Executive Order	Challenge upheld by Sindh High Court.
1959	Land and Tenancy Reforms – Martial Law Regulations 64, 64A and 64B	Ceiling on landholdings: 500 acres irrigated, 1,000 acres unirrigated additional land allowed to bring landholding to equivalent 36,000 PIUs; resumed land to be sold first to tenants and then to small farmers; abolition of *jagirs*; occupancy tenants made owners; all tenants, *haris* and tenants-at-will given legal protection; rents to be paid in kind and all charges other than crop share abolished.
1972	Land and Tenancy Reforms – Martial Law Regulation 115 and amendments	Ceilings on landholdings: 150 acres irrigated, 300 acres unirrigated or equivalent of 12,000 PIUs + 2,000 PIUs for tractor and tubewell owners; no compensation to landowners, land redistributed without charge to landless tenants cultivating resumed land; untenanted resumed land redistributed without charge to small owners/tenants with holdings below subsistence; share system remains unchanged; land revenue, water rates, and seed costs borne by landlords and cost of fertilizers and pesticides to be shared equally; tenant eviction decided by revenue courts if tenant failed to pay rent, failed to cultivate land, sublet tenancy, or rendered land unfit for cultivation.
1977	Land Reforms Act	Landholdings: 100 acres irrigated, 200 acres unirrigated or 8,000 PIUs equivalent; compensation to landowners on resumed land at Rs30 per PIU; redistribution as in 1972. This Act was completely ignored by the military government after July 1977.

Sources: For 1945 and 1947, Khan, Mahmood Hasan, *Underdevelopment and Agrarian Structure in Pakistan*, Westview Press, Boulder, 1981. For the rest of the chart, Nabi, Ijaz, *et al.*, *The Agrarian Economy of Pakistan: Issues and Policies*, Oxford University Press, Karachi, 1986, p. 60.

Sindh and NWFP were big landlords. If the power of landlords prior to 1947 was substantial, the creation of Pakistan increased their power even further. Many of them were able to acquire large tracts of land from the fleeing Hindus, while others bought land from moneylenders at cheap rates in the mayhem that ensued. Others, because of their influence in the area, were able to get the revenue officials to sign over land to them, in excess of their due share. Hence, there was little scope for serious reform in agriculture at the time of partition.

The 1949 Muslim League Agrarian Committee proposed some measures that would have addressed the issues related to land, its distribution, and its use. The report was shelved soon after being finalized. The hold of large landlords on political power can be demonstrated by the provincial elections held in the Punjab in 1951, where they won 80 per cent of the seats, while in the provincial election in Sindh in 1953 large landowners won 90 per cent of seats.[30] Mahmood Hasan Khan writes that in the 1950s,

> the landed élite continued to exercise their traditional power without hindrance or opposition in the countryside. In this they were supported by the civilian bureaucracy, as was evidenced by the failure of tenancy reform measures legislated in the Punjab and Sindh. More significantly, as new irrigation and settlement schemes in the Punjab and Sindh were undertaken in the mid-fifties, civil and military bureaucracies were clearly given preferential treatment for irrigated land.[31]

Thus, the nexus of political power between the civil and military bureaucracy and the landlords ensured that the status quo would not be disturbed. As Mahmood Hasan Khan argues,

> it seems fair to conclude that the approach to land reforms depended on the class character of the power élite. As long as landlords occupied a central place in the balance of power, and their position remained without threat in rural areas, no land reforms could have been implemented. The political system created new pressures which the landed elite could not successfully resist.[32]

The first land reforms in Pakistan were undertaken by a military regime that was perceived to be modern and progressive. The Ayub Khan regime did not owe its allegiance to, and nor was it dependent on, the influence of the agrarian landed class, and thus it was in a position to undertake some sort of reform. However, although the reforms set out to break the power of the large landholding class and to make tenancy more humane, their impact was severely limited. What they did was to distribute power away from some landlords and include the civil and military élite in their strategy. While Shahid Javed Burki has implied that these land reforms were the precursor to the dynamic middle-class farmer of the Green Revolution, who emerged as the main beneficiary of the Basic Democracies system, most other

scholars disagree (see section 3.1). Hamza Alavi[33] and Mahmood Hasan Khan[34] argue that the Basic Democracies system maintained the hold of the landlord on the political system of Pakistan. Nirmal Sanderatne also argues that the 1959 land reforms were an eyewash, where the power of the ruling coalition of landowners, bureaucrats, and industrialists was left well intact.

3.2.1 The 1959 Land Reforms

Table 3.1 presents the salient features of the Ayub Khan land reforms of 1959. The reforms were meant to put ceilings on landholdings and were supposed to be an attempt to change tenancy regulations.

As we showed in the previous chapter (Table 2.2), before the land reforms of 1959 the distribution of land ownership was highly skewed in favour of a few large landlords who controlled large tracts of land. Approximately 6,000 owners owned more than the ceiling of 500 acres permitted in 1959. They constituted 0.1 per cent of the owners, but owned 7.5 million acres or 15.4 per cent of the total land. Table 3.2 shows that in all there were only 5,064 declarants, of which only 15 per cent or 763 were affected by the ceilings on individual holdings. The area of land owned by the affected declarants was 5.5 million acres, of which only 1.9 million (35 per cent) was resumed. The main portion of their land was retained by the landlords due to numerous provisions made in the law, such as for the transfer of land to dependants and other members of their families, and exemptions for numerous categories.

Not only was a small amount of land handed over, but of that land, more than half (57 per cent) was uncultivated. Of this, parts were hills or deserts – terrain which was not fit for cultivation – and some consisted of land that needed to be developed in order to be made fit for cultivation. Since a central feature of the 1959 land reforms was that owners were to be paid compensation for their lands, many benefited by handing over poor-quality lands to the government. As Mahmood Hasan Khan argues, 'given the high proportion of uncultivated land surrendered in certain districts, it is clear that landowners received payments for land which was producing nothing and most of it would require improvement after it was sold to new owners'.[35] Compensation was paid at rates of Rs1–5 per Produce Index Unit (PIU) (see Appendix 3.1) and in 'fifty half-yearly equated installments in transferable but non-negotiable bonds bearing 4 per cent per annum interest on unpaid balance'.[36]

Another feature of the 1959 reforms was that resumed land was to be sold to landless tenants. By 1967, only 50 per cent of the resumed land had been sold, with only 20 per cent of the resumed land sold to landless tenants. The remainder was auctioned to rich farmers and civil and military officials. According to one estimate, only 67,000 landless tenants and small owners could have bought the resumed land sold to them.[37] The land was sold at the rate of Rs8 per PIU, payable in fifty half-yearly instalments with a 4 per cent annual interest rate on the outstanding balance.

Due to the abolition of *jagirs* in 1959, 0.9 million acres were declared as *jagir* lands, of which one-third were resumed by

Table 3.2
Number of declarants and resumed area under the land reforms regulation of 1959

Province/division	Number of declarants			Area of affected declarants (acres)	Area retained (acres)	Area gifted (acres)	Area resumed (acres)
	All	Unaffected	Affected				
Punjab	2,152	1,844	308	3,637,648	2,306,657	288,715	1,044,276
Multan	838	720	118	2,838,325	1,934,664	225,411	672,250
Sargodha	606	504	102	412,213	165,033	28,701	218,479
Rawalpindi	249	227	22	148,827	53,019	9,947	85,861
Lahore	102	85	17	38,813	25,631	4,008	9,176
Bahawalpur	357	308	49	199,470	128,310	12,650	58,510
Sindh	2,388	1,993	395	1,487,253	655,384	169,803	662,066
Khairpur	1,006	870	136	637,029	368,154	67,903	200,972
Hyderabad	1,375	1,117	258	842,872	281,220	101,900	459,752
Karachi	7	6	1	7,352	6,010	–	1,342
Punjab and Sindh	4,540	3,837	703	5,124,901	2,962,041	456,518	1,706,342
Pakistan	5,064	4,301	763	5,478,945	3,077,738	497,419	1,903,788

Source: Khan, Mahmood Hasan, *Underdevelopment and Agrarian Structure in Pakistan*, Westview Press, Boulder, 1981, p. 163.

the government. The purpose of the abolition of revenue-free lands (*jagirs*) was to transform them into revenue-paying tracts. In 1960, the government realized about Rs3 million from this provision.[38]

The land reforms allowed farmers to have their lands valued in PIUs, up to a maximum of 36,000 PIUs. The PIU is 'estimated as a measure of the gross value per acre of land by type of soil and was, therefore, seen as a measure of land productivity'.[39] However, the measurement of the PIUs was based on pre-partition revenue settlements, which substantially under-reported the true value of the land. Thus, even if we take the 1959 PIU as the correct measure of productivity, the 36,000 limit was far greater than the allotted ceiling of 500 acres of irrigated land. For example, it has been calculated that in the irrigated areas of Sindh the PIU per acre would have been about 20. This meant that each individual could own at least 1,800 acres according to the law which limited holding to 500 acres.[40] (For a note on PIUs, see Appendix 3.1.)

Mahmood Hasan Khan sums up his evaluation of the reforms as follows:

It is now evident that the land reforms of 1959 could not have reduced the feudal power of landlords. For one thing, the generous ceiling on individual holdings, with transfers and exemptions, defined as they were in PIUs, left the concentration of land in the hands of landlords. If we accept that the average retained area by the so-called affected landlords was the *de facto* ceiling, then its limit was 7,489 acres in the Punjab, 1,659 acres in Sindh, and the average for the country was 4,033 acres. Further, almost three-quarters of resumed land, at least in the Punjab, was uncultivated and untenanted. This meant that the amount of land available for

redistribution (and remember by sale) was even more limited. Further, landlord–tenant relations were left unchanged, to be governed by the tenancy acts passed in the early fifties and to be supervised by the revenue service.[41]

3.2.2 The Bhutto Reforms of 1972

The 1972 reforms were different from those of 1959 in many respects. Firstly, the philosophy behind the Bhutto reforms was based on the social democratic leanings of the Pakistan People's Party. In March 1972, Bhutto gave a speech in which he said that his land reforms would 'effectively break up the iniquitous concentrations of landed wealth, reduce income disparities, increase production, reduce unemployment, streamline the administration of land revenue and agricultural taxation, and truly lay down the foundations of a relationship of honour and mutual benefit between the landowner and tenant'.[42] The Manifesto of the People's Party laid the premise for this action by stating that 'the break up of the large estates to destroy the feudal landowners is a national necessity that will have to be carried through by practical measures'.[43]

The main features of the reforms are shown in Table 3.1. A few features distinguished the 1972 reforms from the earlier ones. While ceilings had been further lowered in 1972 and a number of exemptions removed, possibly the most prominent feature of the reforms was that, unlike in 1959, land resumed from landowners would not receive any compensation, and this land was to be distributed free to landless tenants. In addition, all those peasants who had acquired land under the 1959 reforms and had dues outstanding, had their dues written off and were not required to make any further payments.

Of the land declared to be above the ceiling by the landowners, after they had made generous use of the possibilities for getting around the imposition, only 42 per cent was resumed in the Punjab, while the figure in the Sindh was 59 per cent. In all, 0.6 million acres were resumed, far less than the 1959 figure and constituting only 0.001 per cent of the total farm area in the country.[44]

The problem of the evaluation of the Produce Index Units arose once again. The ceiling of the land was defined both in area and PIUs, and the landowner could retain the larger. However, Mahmood Hasan Khan writes that

> the most serious problem of defining the ceiling in PIUs was that their values had remained unchanged, while almost everything affecting their value had changed drastically in most areas of the Indus Basin. The produce value of an area of land was being grossly underestimated in the Indus Basin, thanks to changes in prices, cropping intensities and patterns, irrigation, etc.[45]

The result was that with 12,000 PIUs one could get away with 400 acres in the Punjab and 480 in Sindh. Moreover, with other exemptions for tubewells and tractors, a family could have retained up to 932 irrigated acres in the Punjab and 1,120 in Sindh![46] (See also Appendix 3.1.)

Although a lot of propaganda was issued about the success of the 1972 reforms, as the resumed land was far less than in 1959, only 50,548 persons benefited from the redistribution of 308,390 acres during 1972–8. Only 1 per cent of the landless tenants and small owners benefited by these measures. Table 3.3 shows that, of the land resumed in 1959, 6 per cent still needs to be distributed even after 38 years, and 39 per cent of the area resumed under the 1972 reforms is still held by the government despite the presence of a large number of landless cultivators.

Table 3.3
Progress of implementation of land reforms up to June 1994 (hectares)

Province	Area resumed	Area disposed of	Balance	Persons benefiting
1959 reforms				
Punjab	511,244	505,082	6,162	109,889
Sindh	346,307	300,091	46,216	46,131
NWFP	112,108	97,287	14,821	24,314
Baluchistan	53,268	53,196	72	6,221
Total	1,022,927	955,656	67,271	186,555
1972 reforms				
Punjab	121,593	94,583	27,010	36,017
Sindh	112,920	72,477	40,442	17,167
NWFP	57,415	55,122	2,293	12,811
Baluchistan	189,316	73,755	115,562	5,506
Total	481,244	295,937	185,307	71,501

Source: Government of Pakistan, *Agricultural Statistics*, *1993–94*, Islamabad, 1995, p. 129.

3.3 Summary and Further Reading

3.3.1 Summary

It seems that the technological package that resulted in the Green Revolution in the mid-1960s was focused on the more well-to-do farmers in the more prosperous regions. This is factually correct, but fails to highlight the externalities and other repercussions of this important process. The demonstration effect of using the technological package was substantial, but more importantly, a supposedly simple technological intervention let loose many economic and social processes, resulting in migration, labour displacement, the formation of small towns, skilled labour power, and a host of other political outcomes. Our evaluation of the 1959 and 1972 land reforms, however, shows that they failed to make substantial changes in the landowning structure of the country. Shahid Javed Burki argues that the 1959 reforms created the enterprising middle farmers – a view that is contested by Hamza Alavi, who argues that landlordism became more established and entrenched. Of course, given the hold of the landowning class on government and its institutions, this is not very surprising. The huge loopholes that existed in the 1959 reforms to make intra-family and intra-household transfers meant that the landowning structure remained largely unaltered. Hence, effective land reform in Pakistan will continue to be a problem. Nevertheless, we show in the next two chapters that, even if formal land reforms are not undertaken in Pakistan, other social and economic processes can achieve similar results. Smaller landholdings and more capitalist lines of agricultural production have developed despite a lack of adequate land reform. Demographic and economic changes over the last twenty years have resulted in evolving a different pattern of ownership and production than in the past. While these processes are not a substitute for land reform, it is important to realize their contribution towards achieving somewhat similar ends.

3.3.2 Further Reading

Amongst the books on the two topics covered in this chapter, the following are recommended: Khan, Mahmood Hasan, *The Economics of the Green Revolution in Pakistan*, Praeger, New York, 1975; Khan, Mahmood Hasan, *Underdevelopment and Agrarian Structure in Pakistan*, Westview Press, Boulder, 1981; Stevens, Robert D., *et al.*, (eds.), *Rural Development in Bangladesh and Pakistan*, University Press of Hawaii, Honolulu, 1976; Ali, Karamat (ed.), *Pakistan: The Political Economy of Rural Development*, Vanguard, Lahore, 1986; Hussain, Akmal, *Strategic Issues in Pakistan's Economic Policy*, Progressive Publishers, Lahore, 1988; Ahmed, Viqar and Rashid Amjad, *The Management of Pakistan's Economy, 1947–82*, Oxford University Press, Karachi, 1984; and Nabi, Ijaz, *et al.*, *The Agrarian Economy of Pakistan: Issues and Policies*, Oxford University Press, Karachi, 1986.

Appendix 3.1

The measurement of Produce Index Units and a case for their revision

M. Shafi Niaz documents the history of Produce Index Units and how they are measured. He makes the strong case for their reappraisal as follows:

Before the partition of the Indian sub-continent, there was an obligation on the part of the governments to periodically carry out revenue assessment of land holdings. This period generally varied between 15 to 20 years. The last assessment that had taken place before partition in the undivided Punjab was in the mid-thirties. The main idea of such assessments was to revise the land revenue in accordance with the changed values of the land. For such valuation, each administrative district was divided into assessment circles. In each such circle, land was categorized whether it was *chahi* (well-irrigated), *chahinehri* (well-cum-canal irrigated), flood irrigated, or *barani* (rain-fed) and so on.

According to the information contained in the Report of the Land Reforms Commission for West Pakistan, 1958–59, the produce value per acre of each class of soil in the various assessment circles was worked out on the basis of average 'matured-acre-yields' and prices adopted by the Settlement Officer at the time of the last settlement of each district. The total produce value thus obtained for each class of soil in each assessment circle was, therefore, divided by the average matured area in order to arrive at the average productive value for one matured acre of land.

The Land Reforms Commission Report further states that for working out a reasonable formula, it was felt by both the governments that since the settlement operations were carried out at different times in different districts, 'suitable' multiples had to be applied to the produce values, as described above, for bringing them to uniform levels in both the Punjab and other agreed areas of India.

For this purpose, a basic period of three years (excluding unusually bad years) was selected for all the districts in both the Punjabs, and average value of the output per acre of sown area in the year in which actual prices corresponded, as far as possible, with the prices assumed by the Settlement Officer were ascertained. This period was called the 'settlement period'. Then the average value of the output per sown acre in this base period was calculated and figures of produce given by the Settlement Officers were multiplied by the ratio which the average value of the produce per acre of the base period, bore to that of the settlement period. This methodology can be explained, by an example of tehsil Lahore for the assessment circle 'Bet Chahi' having '*chahi*' (irrigated land) as the class of soil. In this case, the total area involved was 10,117 acres having a gross produce value of Rs409,104. The produce value for the 'matured' area comes to 40 (gross produce value divided by the total matured area). This is multiplied by 2.0, the worked out ratio for the Lahore district. The resultant figure of 80 is the produce index (or produce index unit) for the assessment circle referred to above.

The agreed formula was adopted by both the governments as a pressing need of the time with a view to settling the refugees without loss of time. It is no denying the fact that the objective in accepting the formula was to try to allot land holdings, as best as possible, of equal value to the immigrants so that they could quickly start to earn their livelihood for the upkeep of their uprooted families.

This formula served the purpose of the day despite the inherent weakness it had. According to the available information, the assessment of land was not carried out on an extensive and comprehensive scale in provinces other than the Punjab. So the exercise in the three provinces had to be carried out in haste so that the rehabilitation process was not held up and to let it go ahead without any undue hindrance. A close reading of the methodology as quoted above, would raise a number of questions about the validity of the produce index units and it would not serve a useful purpose to go into the details here. It is, however, generally believed that in the NWFP and the Punjab, the PIUs were worked out, inter alia, on the basis of 'total' production of land while in Sindh these were worked out on the basis of the shares of the produce which the landlord got and these varied generally between 50–60 per cent of the total produce. A disparity thereby seemed to have developed at the time of the formulation of the PIUs which has its implications at the implementation stage, whenever these were used as a basis for policy decision. The result has been that the farmers in the NWFP and the Punjab were bound to bear the inequalities in the allotment of land at the time of independence and in the future use of PIUs, particularly when a ceiling on individual ownership of land was determined as a result of land reforms in 1958-9, 1972 and 1977. The situation in Baluchistan was not much different. The province-wise details are given below.

For the Punjab, as mentioned above, the PIUs were worked out more systematically. The assessment circles, totalling 265, were made the basis, and each assessment circle was divided according to the status of the soil, irrigation facilities and other identical factors. In all, some 1363 areas were categorized. Of these areas, about 600 (or 44 per cent) were those where the PIUs were above 40. If agricultural tax is to be levied on lands having 40 PIUs or more, 40 per cent of the areas would be liable to land tax.

In Sindh, PIUs were worked out by each Taluka (tehsil) and the land in each Taluka (74 in all at that time) was, in general, categorized on the basis of the type of irrigation (flow, lift, combined) available for raising crops. The total number of such categorized areas (as one would call them) amounted to 480. It is very interesting to note that it was only in one out of the 480 areas where the PIUs were 42 and in all other areas these were much less than 40. So, if agricultural tax is to be levied on land having 40 PIUs or more, only one of 480 areas would be liable to tax; other areas should get exemption.

The basis for working out PIUs in the NWFP province is similar to that of the Punjab. The total assessment circles were about 100. These circles were divided into about 480 areas depending mainly on the mode of irrigation facilities, type of crop grown, and so on. Of these 480 areas, about 200 or 40 per cent have PIUs more than 40. If agricultural tax is levied on land having 40 PIUs or more, about 40 per cent of the areas would be liable to land tax. The PIUs in Balochistan province were prepared only for 4 tehsils divided into 16 assessment circles in which PIUs for 44 types of land were recorded. Only 17 out of these have PIUs above 40 which could be liable to agricultural tax if it is levied on areas having 40 PIUs or more.

The above facts and figures bring out not only the disparity that exists in the methodology used in working out PIUs in the various provinces but also show that these are by now far outdated and thus unrealistic and unequitable for use either in determining the ceiling on ownership or for using as the basis

for land tax. If PIUs have to be used in future for any useful purpose, these must be redetermined. And for this purpose, land assessment may have to be carried out as a prerequisite. Time and effort for the exercise will be well spent and will bring dividends in the form of, amongst other things, upward revision of the land revenue as the value of land must have gone up manifold since last assessment operations were carried many decades ago. This would undoubtedly also help the provincial governments to improve their resource base and all the provinces would get an equitable and uniform basis for future use of PIUs.

Source: Niaz, M. Shafi, *DAWN*, 7 October 1995.

Notes

1. Alavi, Hamza, 'The Rural Elite and Agricultural Development in Pakistan', in Ali, Karamat (ed.), *Pakistan: The Political Economy of Rural Development*, Vanguard, Lahore, 1986, p. 34.
2. Sanderatne, Nirmal, 'Landowners and Land Reforms in Pakistan', in Ali, Karamat, op. cit., 1986, p. 306.
3. Ibid., p. 317.
4. Khan, Mahmood Hasan, *Underdevelopment and Agrarian Structure in Pakistan*, Westview Press, Boulder, 1981; and Khan, Mahmood Hasan, 'Classes and Agrarian Transition in Pakistan', in Ali, Karamat, op. cit., 1986.
5. Khan, Mahmood Hasan, op. cit., 1986, p. 446.
6. Sanderatne, Nirmal, op. cit., 1986, p. 307.
7. Hussain, Akmal, 'Technical Change and Social Polarization in Rural Punjab', in Ali, Karamat, op. cit., 1986, p. 320.
8. Ibid., p. 322.
9. Gotsch, Carl H., 'Tractor Mechanization and Rural Development in Pakistan', in Ali, Karamat, op. cit., 1986, p. 65.
10. Ibid., p. 65.
11. Ibid., p. 67.
12. Alavi, Hamza, op. cit., 1986, p. 37.
13. Ibid., p. 53.
14. Mahmood, Moazam, 'The Pattern of Adoption of Green Revolution Technology and its Effect on Landholdings in the Punjab', in Ali, Karamat, op. cit., 1986, p. 191.
15. Khan, Mahmood Hasan, op. cit., 1986, p. 447.
16. Burki, Shahid Javed, 'The Development of Pakistan's Agriculture: An Interdisciplinary Explanation', in Stevens, Robert D., *et al.* (eds.), *Rural Development in Bangladesh and Pakistan*, University Press of Hawaii, Honolulu, 1976, p. 308.
17. Alavi, Hamza, op. cit., 1986, p. 21.
18. Hussain, Akmal, 'Land Reforms in Pakistan', in Hussain, Akmal, *Strategic Issues in Pakistan's Economic Policy*, Progressive Publishers, Lahore, 1988, p. 178.
19. Burki, Shahid Javed, op. cit., 1976.
20. Alavi, Hamza, op. cit., 1986; Hussain, Akmal, op. cit., 1986.
21. Alavi, Hamza, op. cit., 1986, p. 44.
22. Ibid., p. 31.
23. Khan, Mahmood Hasan, op. cit., 1981, p. 44.
24. Sanderatne, Nirmal, op. cit., p. 309.
25. Ibid., p. 309.
26. Alavi, Hamza, op. cit., p. 55.
27. Hussain, Akmal, op. cit., p. 187.
28. Ibid., p. 188.
29. This section is drawn from Khan, Mahmood Hasan, op. cit.; Sanderatne, Nirmal, op. cit.; and Ahmed, Viqar and Rashid Amjad, *The Management of Pakistan's Economy, 1947–82*, Oxford University Press, Karachi, 1984.
30. Khan, Mahmood Hasan, op. cit., p. 147.
31. Ibid., p. 143.
32. Ibid., p. 150.
33. Alavi, Hamza, op. cit.
34. Khan, Mahmood Hasan, op. cit.; Khan, Mahmood Hasan, op. cit., 1989.
35. Khan, Mahmood Hasan, op. cit., 1981, p. 164.
36. Ahmed, Viqar and Rashid Amjad, op. cit., 1984, p. 124.
37. Khan, Mahmood Hasan, op. cit., 1981, p. 166. This figure differs from that in our Table 3.3 as it is much older and is probably calculated differently.
38. Ahmed, Viqar and Rashid Amjad, op. cit., 1984, p. 121.
39. Hussain, Akmal, op. cit., 1988, p. 180.
40. Khan, Mahmood Hasan, op. cit., 1981, p. 159.
41. Ibid., pp.166–7.
42. Sanderatne, Nirmal, op. cit., 1986, p. 309.
43. Khan, Mahmood Hasan, op. cit., 1981, p. 171.
44. Hussain, Akmal, op. cit., 1988, p. 182.
45. Khan, Mahmood Hasan, op. cit., 1981, p. 176.
46. Ibid., p. 177.

4 The Nature and Direction of Agrarian Change

We have established the premise in the previous chapters, that capitalism in agriculture began to establish itself early in the twentieth century following a number of interventions made by the British colonialists in the region that constituted Pakistan. The feudal or pre-capitalist structures, while prevalent, were slowly being dismantled and dissolved. Pre-capitalist forms have shown a resilience in many parts of the world despite the development of capitalism. Notably, peasant forms of farming which should have been dissolved under capitalism, where two classes of owners are supposed to emerge and coexist, have shown persistence against all odds. Nevertheless, in Pakistan it would be fair to say that, once capitalism took root in agriculture, it began to eliminate pre-capitalist and feudal modes. Once established, capitalism became the dominant mode of production in agriculture and throughout the entire economy.

This, in many ways, is the most important theme in agriculture: that is, to examine how and why Pakistan's agricultural sector has been developing in a particular direction, and to assess what possible direction it will take. Agrarian transition or change, by definition, implies movement from one place or type to another. How have economic and social relationships changed over time in agriculture? Have there been significant changes in landholding and land ownership patterns? What has been the trend of sharecropping – is it on the rise, or falling? These are some of the questions that this chapter will discuss. We will also see the different patterns in the four provinces, and especially in the Punjab and Sindh, which form the backbone of Pakistan's economy and politics. Our main focus in this chapter will be on the change in agrarian structure and agrarian relations from the 1960s to the present.

The chapter contains numerous tables, which are extensive and cumbersome. However, these numbers are essential, for we can base our analysis only on the observation and interpretation of data. While making the tables available for those interested in examining the precise figures, we attempt to describe and summarize their salient features before discussing and interpreting them.

Things are further complicated by the problem of how one should classify and categorize the pattern of land ownership and other phenomena that we want to observe. However, we may not always be able to choose the categorization that we want, as data limitations – severe at times – may force us to accept and use only what is already available. For example, we may prefer to use the concept of *classes* to explain agricultural processes and change, and to show which class constitutes what share in the agricultural sector as landowners and as producers of labour power. The use of class helps us to observe important trends in the types of change taking place. For example, how is the process of capitalism being consolidated over time? Can one identify feudal remnants, and what has been their contribution over time? However, while we would like to use the concept of class to study agrarian transition, data of this nature are not easily obtained. Despite its numerous shortcomings we must make use of what is published (see Appendix 4.1).

What is published by the Government of Pakistan regarding agricultural landholding patterns is usually based on the nature of tenure: 'owners', 'owner-cum-tenants' and 'tenants'. Moreover, size usually plays an important role in the classification, where either small/medium/large is used, or some distribution by the size of holding, i.e. acreage categories, is made available. However, Mahmood Hasan Khan correctly points out that 'the concept of farm size by its very nature is quite arbitrary and therefore not universal. Secondly, division of farms into small and large does not reveal anything about who controls and cultivates these farms.'[1] Although there are problems with this sort of classification, we use these criteria in the tables that follow – not only because of the lack of alternative data, but also because they still offer useful insights into the nature and direction of change in Pakistani agriculture.

4.1 Explaining the Numbers

In this section we attempt to highlight the main features of the tables provided. The explanations given here are important in following the arguments in a later section. Those who can grasp the numbers and their meaning easily are advised to read the text and then explore further details in the tables.

There have been four agricultural censuses in Pakistan, in 1960, 1972, 1980, and 1990. We have taken the relevant data from the first three censuses together with some of the statistics from the 1990 census in summary form. Our method of presentation and explanation takes the following pattern. For each of the four census years, we will highlight, separately, the main features in the relevant table. We will try to standardize the format as far as possible so that the trends can be followed. After presenting a summary of each census, we present some tables which compare the trends over time, describing the salient features. In the next section, we try to interpret these tables and examine their implications.

Table 4.1
Distribution of land ownership in Pakistan and provinces, 1950–1955

Farm size (acres)	Pakistan		Punjab		Sindh	
	Number of owners	Area owned (acres)	Number of owners	Area owned (acres)	Number of owners	Area owned (acres)
All sizes	5,068,376 (100.0)	48,642,530 (100.0)	3,555,457 (100.0)	28,309,744 (100.0)	337,665 (100.0)	10,285,021 (100.0)
5 or less	3,266,137 (64.4)	7,425,614 (15.3)	2,358,119 (66.3)	438,517 (15.7)	100,601 (29.8)	365,817 (3.6)
5–25	1,452,421 (28.7)	15,438,138 (31.7)	1,029,108 (28.9)	11,041,708 (39.0)	155,163 (46.0)	1,937,073 (18.8)
25–100	286,470 (5.7)	10,616,308 (21.8)	146,893 (4.1)	6,198,128 (21.9)	54,792 (16.2)	2,390,358 (23.2)
100–500	57,287 (1.1)	7,671,537 (15.8)	19,401 (0.6)	3,842,986 (13.6)	24,064 (7.1)	2,600,123 (25.3)
500 and above	6,061 (0.1)	7,490,933 (15.4)	1,936 (0.1)	2,788,405 (9.9)	3,045 (0.9)	2,991,650 (29.1)

Note: The data for the Punjab are for 1954/5; for Sindh for 1946/7. The data for Pakistan are the aggregate figures for all provinces. The Punjab includes the former State of Bahawalpur, and Sindh includes the former State of Khairpur.

Source: Khan, Mahmood Hasan, *Underdevelopment and Agrarian Structure in Pakistan*, Westview Press, Boulder, 1981, p. 68.

4.1.1   Data from the Censuses

The 1960 Census (Table 4.2)

Table 4.1, which appeared in Chapter 2 and is repeated here, presents some basic data about landholding in the 1950s, and is a good starting point for our discussion.

The main feature of Table 4.1 is that ownership was highly concentrated: 64.4 per cent of the owners owned 15.3 per cent of land, while the 6,061 owners (0.1 per cent) with very large landholdings, owned more (15.4 per cent). In Sindh, land ownership was even more skewed, with 29.1 per cent of land owned by a little over 3,000 people. In the Punjab, fewer than 2,000 owners owned 2.78 million acres, or about 10 per cent of the total area. In Sindh, the 8 per cent of owners who had holdings above 100 acres owned 54 per cent of the total land in the province. Thus it seems that, while both provinces had a highly differentiated structure of land ownership, Sindh was far more inequitable than the Punjab.

For the 1960s, we can make the following observations from Table 4.2:

1. Block A shows that in Pakistan tenant farms were the largest in both number (column VII, 42 per cent) and acreage (column VIII, 39 per cent). Owner-cum-tenant farms were the smallest of the three categories on both counts (columns V and VI, only 17 and 23 per cent, respectively). In Sindh, almost half (49 per cent) of the farms were tenant farms (column VII), which were 56 per cent in terms of acreage of the total area cultivated (column VIII). In the Punjab, owner farms had both the largest number (43 per cent, column III) and the largest

area (38 per cent, column IV). We thus see a very different pattern of ownership and tenure in the two provinces in the 1960s, with more owner-operated farms in the Punjab, and greater tenant or sharecropper farms in Sindh.

2. In Pakistan, 49 per cent of all farms were in the under 5 acre category (Block B, column I). However, these 49 per cent had access to only 9 per cent of land. At the other extreme, those with more than 150 acres constituted only 0.29 per cent of owners, but owned 10 per cent of the total land (Block G). More than half of the total acreage in both Sindh and Punjab is in the two categories which constitute the 5–25 acre group (Blocks C and D), with 54 per cent in the Punjab and 51 per cent in Sindh between 5 and 25 acres.

3. Of all the owner farms in the Punjab, 61 per cent lie in the under 5 acre category (Block B, column III), while in the 'tenants' category, half the farms in the Punjab are less than 5 acres (column VII). In Sindh, since only 18 per cent of all farms are less than 5 acres (Block B, column I), the three categories columns III to VIII constitute a very small fraction of the under 5 acre category.

4. The owner-operated area constitutes more than 50 per cent in the Punjab and only 37 per cent in Sindh (Block A, column IX). Tenant farming was far greater in Sindh than in the Punjab (Block A, columns VII and VIII).

The 1972 Census (Table 4.3)

1. By 1972, owner farms had replaced tenant farms as the largest category in terms of both number (42 per cent) and acreage (40 per cent) in Pakistan (Block A, columns III

Table 4.2
Distribution of the operational holdings by size and tenure in Pakistan, 1960 (000 farms and acres)

Farm size (acres)	All farms Number (I)	All farms Acres (II)	Owner farms Number (III)	Owner farms Acres (IV)	Owner-cum-tenant farms Number (V)	Owner-cum-tenant farms Acres (VI)	Tenant farms Number (VII)	Tenant farms Acres (VIII)	Owner-operated area (IX)	Tenant-operated area Total (X)	Share cropped (XI)	Leased or rented (XII)	Others (XIII)
A All sizes													
Pakistan	4,860 (100%)	48,930 (100%)	1,998 (41%)(100%)	18,723 (36%)(100%)	834 (17%)(100%)	11,012 (23%)(100%)	2,028 (42%)(100%)	19,195 (39%)(100%)	24,595 (50%)(100%)	23,971 (100%)	21,271 (100%)	1,941 (100%)	759 (100%)
Punjab	3,326 (100%)	29,214 (100%)	1,422 (43%)(100%)	11,169 (38%)(100%)	623 (19%)(100%)	7,180 (25%)(100%)	1,282 (39%)(100%)	10,665 (37%)(100%)	15,252 (52%)(100%)	13,961 (100%)	12,114 (100%)	1,319 (100%)	528 (100%)
Sindh	979 (100%)	9,698 (100%)	137 (14%)(100%)	2,819 (29%)(100%)	60 (6%)(100%)	1,411 (15%)(100%)	483 (49%)(100%)	5,468 (56%)(100%)	3,559 (37%)(100%)	9,136 (100%)	5,864 (100%)	232 (100%)	40 (100%)
B Under 5.0													
Pakistan	2,404 (49%)	4,591 (9%)	1,203 (50%)(60%)	2,014 (44%)(11%)	276 (33%)(11%)	716 (16%)(7%)	925 (46%)(36%)	1,861 (41%)(10%)	2,406 (52%)(10%)	2,185 (9%)	1,903 (9%)	175 (9%)	106 (14%)
Punjab	1,717 (52%)	3,129 (11%)	866 (50%)(61%)	1,452 (45%)(13%)	208 (33%)(12%)	547 (17%)(8%)	644 (38%)(50%)	1,193 (37%)(11%)	1,752 (55%)(11%)	1,440 (10%)	1,266 (10%)	114 (9%)	60 (11%)
Sindh	174 (18%)	529 (5%)	38 (22%)(28%)	106 (20%)(4%)	5 (8%)(3%)	18 (3%)(1%)	130 (27%)(75%)	405 (77%)(7%)	113 (21%)(3%)	414 (7%)	402 (7%)	10 (4%)	2 (5%)
C 5.0–12.5													
Pakistan	1,340 (28%)	10,903 (22%)	434 (32%)(22%)	3,468 (32%)(19%)	293 (35%)(22%)	2,414 (22%)(22%)	613 (30%)(46%)	5,020 (46%)(26%)	4,784 (44%)(19%)	6,119 (26%)	5,383 (25%)	571 (29%)	165 (22%)
Punjab	894 (27%)	7,281 (25%)	313 (35%)(22%)	2,505 (34%)(22%)	231 (37%)(26%)	1,903 (26%)(26%)	350 (27%)(39%)	2,873 (39%)(26%)	3,552 (49%)(23%)	3,729 (27%)	3,199 (26%)	419 (32%)	110 (21%)
Sindh	265 (27%)	2,180 (22%)	44 (17%)(32%)	360 (17%)(13%)	18 (30%)(7%)	157 (7%)(11%)	203 (42%)(77%)	1,663 (76%)(30%)	432 (20%)(12%)	1,747 (28%)	1,696 (29%)	42 (18%)	9 (23%)
D 12.5–25.0													
Pakistan	729 (15%)	12,533 (26%)	220 (30%)(11%)	3,747 (30%)(20%)	169 (20%)(23%)	2,922 (23%)(27%)	340 (17%)(47%)	5,864 (47%)(31%)	5,323 (42%)(22%)	7,210 (30%)	6,480 (30%)	549 (28%)	182 (24%)
Punjab	488 (15%)	8,326 (29%)	160 (33%)(11%)	2,686 (32%)(24%)	127 (20%)(26%)	2,176 (26%)(30%)	202 (16%)(41%)	3,464 (42%)(32%)	3,877 (47%)(25%)	4,448 (32%)	3,908 (32%)	403 (31%)	137 (26%)
Sindh	159 (16%)	2,776 (29%)	28 (18%)(20%)	505 (18%)(18%)	19 (32%)(12%)	336 (12%)(24%)	112 (23%)(70%)	1,935 (70%)(35%)	666 (24%)(19%)	2,111 (34%)	2,041 (35%)	58 (25%)	12 (30%)
E 25.0–50.0													
Pakistan	286 (6%)	9,468 (19%)	94 (33%)(5%)	3,114 (33%)(17%)	71 (9%)(25%)	2,382 (25%)(22%)	121 (6%)(42%)	3,972 (42%)(21%)	4,417 (47%)(18%)	5,051 (21%)	4,570 (21%)	345 (18%)	136 (18%)
Punjab	180 (5%)	5,903 (20%)	61 (34%)(4%)	1,990 (34%)(18%)	46 (7%)(26%)	1,529 (26%)(21%)	74 (6%)(41%)	2,384 (40%)(22%)	2,853 (48%)(19%)	3,049 (22%)	2,695 (22%)	255 (19%)	100 (19%)
Sindh	61 (6%)	2,044 (21%)	16 (26%)(12%)	548 (27%)(19%)	12 (20%)(20%)	407 (20%)(29%)	33 (7%)(54%)	1,089 (53%)(20%)	753 (37%)(21%)	1,291 (21%)	1,233 (12%)	50 (22%)	9 (23%)
F 50.0–150.0													
Pakistan	88 (2%)	6,539 (13%)	39 (44%)(2%)	3,009 (46%)(16%)	23 (3%)(26%)	1,693 (26%)(15%)	26 (1%)(30%)	1,837 (28%)(10%)	4,007 (61%)(16%)	2,532 (11%)	2,251 (11%)	185 (10%)	96 (13%)
Punjab	42 (1%)	4,230 (14%)	19 (45%)(1%)	1,459 (34%)(13%)	11 (2%)(26%)	788 (19%)(11%)	12 (0.9%)(29%)	839 (20%)(8%)	1,961 (46%)(13%)	1,125 (8%)	955 (8%)	104 (8%)	64 (12%)
Sindh	18 (2%)	3,087 (32%)	9 (50%)(7%)	677 (22%)(24%)	5 (8%)(28%)	398 (13%)(28%)	4 (0.8%)(22%)	297 (10%)(5%)	904 (29%)(25%)	488 (8%)	419 (7%)	44 (19%)	5 (13%)
G 150.0 and over													
Pakistan	14 (0.29%)	4,896 (10%)	9 (64%)(0.45%)	3,372 (69%)(18%)	3 (0.36%)(21%)	884 (18%)(8.03%)	2 (0.10%)(14%)	640 (13%)(3%)	4,023 (82%)(16%)	874 (4%)	684 (3.22%)	115 (5.9%)	75 (10%)
Punjab	5 (0.15%)	1,426 (4.88%)	3 (60%)(0.21%)	1,078 (76%)(10%)	1 (0.16%)(20%)	237 (17%)(3.30%)	0 (0.03%)(8%)	111 (8%)(1%)	1,256 (86%)(8%)	170 (1%)	91 (0.75%)	25 (5.90%)	54 (10%)
Sindh	2 (0.20%)	797 (8.22%)	2 (100%)(1.46%)	623 (78%)(22%)	0 (0.67%)(20%)	95 (12%)(6.73%)	0 (0.06%)(15%)	79 (10%)(1%)	692 (87%)(19%)	105 (2%)	72 (1.23%)	29 (1.250%)	4 (10%)

Source: Khan, Mahmood Hasan, Underdevelopment and Agrarian Structure in Pakistan, Westview Press, Boulder, 1981.

Table 4.3
Distribution of the operational holdings by size and tenure in Pakistan, 1972 (000 farms and acres)

Column key:
- **All farms** — I Number, II Acres
- **Owner farms** — III Number, IV Acres
- **Owner-cum-tenant farms** — V Number, VI Acres
- **Tenant farms** — VII Number, VIII Acres
- **IX Owner-operated area**
- **Tenant-operated area** — X Total, XI Share cropped, XII Leased or rented, XIII Others
- **Area owner-cum-tenant farms** — XIV Owner operated, XV Share cropped, XVI Leased or rented, XVII Others
- **Area tenant farms** — XVIII Share cropped or rented, XIX Leased, XX Others

Farm size (acres)	I	II	III	IV	V	VI	VII	VIII	IX	X	XI	XII	XIII	XIV	XV	XVI	XVII	XVIII	XIX	XX
A — All sizes																				
Pakistan	3,762 (100%)	49,061 (100%)	1,569 (42%)	19,400 (40%)	897 (24%)	15,160 (31%)	1,296 (34%)	14,500 (30%)	26,388 (54%)	22,672 (100%)	18,915 (100%)	3,344 (100%)	413 (100%)	6,988 (100%)	6,351 (100%)	1,584 (100%)	237 (100%)	12,564 (100%)	1,760 (100%)	176 (100%)
Punjab	2,375 (100%)	31,030 (100%)	1,006 (42%)	11,951 (39%)	683 (29%)	11,050 (36%)	684 (29%)	8,029 (26%)	16,957 (55%)	14,073 (100%)	11,404 (100%)	2,440 (100%)	229 (100%)	5,006 (100%)	4,719 (100%)	1,204 (100%)	121 (100%)	6,885 (100%)	1,236 (100%)	108 (100%)
Sindh	748 (100%)	9,460 (100%)	178 (24%)	2,909 (31%)	97 (13%)	1,760 (19%)	472 (63%)	4,790 (51%)	3,700 (39%)	5,759 (100%)	5,047 (100%)	634 (100%)	78 (100%)	791 (100%)	648 (100%)	270 (100%)	51 (100%)	4,399 (100%)	364 (100%)	27 (100%)
B — Under 5.0																				
Pakistan	1,059 (28%)	2,563 (5%)	650 (41%)	1,423 (7%)	125 (14%)	402 (3%)	284 (22%)	731 (5%)	1,618 (6%)	947 (4%)	789 (4%)	126 (4%)	32 (8%)	186 (3%)	171 (3%)	36 (2%)	9 (4%)	618 (5%)	90 (5%)	23 (13%)
Punjab	619 (26%)	1,503 (5%)	397 (39%)	896 (7%)	81 (12%)	270 (2%)	141 (21%)	336 (4%)	1,020 (6%)	482 (3%)	387 (3%)	77 (3%)	18 (8%)	124 (2%)	119 (3%)	23 (2%)	4 (3%)	268 (4%)	54 (4%)	14 (13%)
Sindh	138 (18%)	424 (4%)	49 (28%)	129 (4%)	9 (9%)	30 (2%)	84 (18%)	264 (6%)	141 (4%)	262 (5%)	272 (5%)	32 (5%)	12 (15%)	12 (2%)	17 (3%)	1 (0.37%)	0 (0%)	255 (6%)	8 (2%)	1 (4%)
C — 5.0–12.5																				
Pakistan	1,501 (40%)	12,338 (25%)	449 (29%)	3,916 (20%)	381 (42%)	3,204 (21%)	621 (48%)	5,218 (36%)	5,288 (20%)	7,050 (31%)	6,282 (33%)	677 (20%)	91 (22%)	1,372 (20%)	1,553 (24%)	245 (15%)	34 (14%)	4,729 (38%)	432 (25%)	57 (32%)
Punjab	926 (39%)	7,619 (25%)	332 (33%)	2,604 (22%)	296 (43%)	2,502 (23%)	298 (44%)	2,513 (31%)	3,667 (22%)	3,942 (28%)	3,392 (30%)	497 (20%)	53 (23%)	1,072 (21%)	1,215 (26%)	195 (16%)	19 (16%)	2,177 (33%)	302 (24%)	34 (31%)
Sindh	387 (52%)	3,261 (34%)	65 (37%)	523 (18%)	44 (45%)	376 (21%)	278 (59%)	2,361 (49%)	689 (18%)	2,591 (45%)	2,495 (49%)	84 (13%)	12 (15%)	146 (18%)	210 (32%)	18 (7%)	2 (4%)	2,285 (52%)	66 (18%)	10 (37%)
D — 12.5–25.0																				
Pakistan	794 (21%)	13,061 (27%)	248 (16%)	4,065 (21%)	250 (28%)	4,269 (28%)	296 (23%)	4,708 (32%)	5,904 (22%)	7,158 (32%)	6,218 (33%)	857 (26%)	83 (20%)	1,819 (26%)	2,013 (32%)	391 (25%)	45 (19%)	4,205 (33%)	466 (26%)	37 (21%)
Punjab	549 (23%)	8,942 (29%)	169 (17%)	2,732 (23%)	201 (29%)	3,427 (31%)	179 (26%)	2,782 (35%)	4,172 (25%)	4,769 (34%)	4,031 (35%)	684 (28%)	54 (24%)	1,440 (29%)	1,626 (34%)	331 (7%)	30 (25%)	2,405 (35%)	353 (29%)	24 (22%)
Sindh	165 (22%)	2,766 (29%)	39 (22%)	689 (24%)	29 (30%)	505 (29%)	96 (20%)	1,573 (33%)	904 (24%)	1,853 (32%)	1,736 (34%)	114 (18%)	13 (17%)	215 (27%)	247 (38%)	38 (14%)	5 (10%)	1,489 (34%)	76 (21%)	8 (30%)
E — 25.0–50.0																				
Pakistan	289 (8%)	9,215 (19%)	111 (7%)	3,516 (18%)	99 (11%)	3,300 (22%)	79 (6%)	2,399 (17%)	5,024 (19%)	4,191 (18%)	3,372 (18%)	747 (22%)	72 (17%)	1,508 (5%)	1,374 (22%)	374 (24%)	44 (19%)	1,996 (16%)	373 (21%)	26 (16%)
Punjab	209 (9%)	5,606 (21%)	75 (7%)	2,349 (20%)	78 (11%)	2,571 (23%)	57 (8%)	1,687 (21%)	3,505 (21%)	3,102 (22%)	2,459 (22%)	595 (25%)	48 (21%)	1,156 (23%)	1,080 (23%)	307 (25%)	28 (23%)	1,379 (21%)	288 (23%)	20 (19%)
Sindh	39 (5%)	1,247 (13%)	16 (9%)	514 (18%)	10 (10%)	346 (20%)	12 (3%)	386 (8%)	680 (18%)	566 (10%)	439 (9%)	122 (19%)	5 (6%)	166 (21%)	125 (19%)	52 (19%)	3 (6%)	314 (7%)	70 (19%)	2 (7%)
F — 50.0–150.0																				
Pakistan	103 (3%)	7,402 (15%)	50 (3%)	3,652 (19%)	36 (4%)	2,666 (18%)	16 (1%)	1,085 (7%)	5,000 (19%)	2,403 (11%)	1,704 (9%)	629 (19%)	70 (17%)	1,348 (19%)	926 (15%)	344 (22%)	48 (20%)	778 (6%)	285 (15%)	22 (13%)
Punjab	65 (3%)	4,569 (15%)	30 (3%)	2,177 (18%)	25 (4%)	1,777 (16%)	10 (1%)	615 (8%)	3,074 (18%)	1,495 (11%)	1,022 (18%)	483 (18%)	40 (17%)	897 (18%)	605 (13%)	246 (20%)	29 (24%)	417 (6%)	187 (15%)	11 (10%)
Sindh	13 (2%)	1,013 (11%)	8 (4%)	605 (21%)	4 (4%)	257 (15%)	2 (0.42%)	140 (3%)	745 (20%)	257 (5%)	166 (3%)	91 (14%)	10 (13%)	140 (18%)	40 (6%)	81 (30%)	6 (12%)	51 (1%)	85 (23%)	4 (15%)
G — 150.0 and over																				
Pakistan	16 (0.43%)	4,482 (9.14%)	10 (0.64%)	2,796 (14.42%)	5 (0.56%)	1,324 (8.73%)	1 (0.8%)	359 (2.48%)	3,556 (13.48%)	925 (4.08%)	549 (2.90%)	310 (9.27%)	66 (16%)	758 (19%)	314 (5%)	195 (12%)	57 (24%)	235 (2%)	115 (7%)	9 (5%)
Punjab	7 (0.29%)	1,789 (5.77%)	5 (0.50%)	1,192 (9.97%)	1 (0.29%)	502 (4.54%)	0 (0.06%)	94 (1.17%)	1,508 (8.89%)	280 (1.99%)	111 (0.97%)	154 (6.31%)	15 (7%)	316 (8%)	73 (2%)	102 (8%)	11 (9%)	52 (1%)	38 (4%)	4 (4%)
Sindh	3 (0.40%)	748 (7.91%)	2 (1.12%)	448 (15.40%)	1 (1.03%)	235 (13.35%)	0 (0.06%)	66 (1.38%)	516 (15.61%)	188 (3.25%)	140 (2.77%)	12 (1.89%)	36 (14%)	113 (14%)	8 (1.23%)	80 (30%)	34 (67%)	4 (0.09%)	60 (16%)	2 (7%)

Source: Khan, Mahmood Hasan, *Underdevelopment and Agrarian Structure in Pakistan*, Westview Press, Boulder, 1981.

and IV). In fact, the shift in both tenant farms and owner farms in the period 1960 to 1972 is quite significant (compare Block A, columns VII and VIII in Tables 4.2 and 4.3; also compare Block A, columns III and IV in the two tables). Owner-cum-tenant farms remained the smallest category. In Sindh, tenant farms now comprised 63 per cent of farms with 51 per cent of the area (Block A, columns VII and VIII). In the Punjab, owner farms dominate in both number and area, and their proportion in each category is almost identical to the 1960 situation (compare Block A, columns III and IV in Tables 4.2 and 4.3 for the Punjab).

2. In the less than 5 acre category, Block B, now only 28 per cent of all of Pakistan's farms number can be observed (column I) with 5 per cent of total cultivated area. In the more than 150 acres category (Block G, columns I and II), 0.43 per cent of farms own 9.1 per cent of cultivated land.

3. The proportion of owner farms in the less than 5 acre category (Block B) has fallen to 41 per cent (column III) compared to 60 per cent in 1960, with a severe cut in the tenant farms category (Block B, column VII), which fell from 46 per cent in 1960 to only 22 per cent in 1972.

4. The owner-operated area in both provinces has increased somewhat over the period 1960–72.

The 1980 Census (Table 4.4)

1. Owner farms now constitute a simple majority in both number and area in Pakistan (55 and 52 per cent, respectively), and in the Punjab (54 and 50 per cent, respectively) (Block A, columns III and IV). In Sindh, tenant farms are the largest in number (49 per cent of all farms) (column VII), but owner farms have access to 47 per cent of total cultivated area in the province (column IV).

2. Thirty-four per cent of the number of farms in Pakistan are in the less than 5 acre category, and own 7 per cent of the land (Block B, columns I and II). Less than half a per cent, 0.34 per cent of the farms in Pakistan, own 8.5 per cent of the land (Block G, columns I and II).

3. Forty-two per cent of owner farms in the Punjab are less than 5 acres (Block B, column III), while of all tenant farms, almost half are in the 5–12.5 acre category (Block C, column VII). In Sindh, the largest number of farms (50 per cent) are in the 5–12.5 acre range, as they are in the Punjab (39 per cent) (Block C, column I).

4. Owner-operated farms are the predominant form in both provinces: 64 per cent in the Punjab, and 55 per cent in Sindh (Block A, column IX).

The 1990 Census (Table 4.5)

The data available from the 1990 Census is as yet somewhat limited and does not include the nature of tenure as in the earlier tables. Nevertheless, we can see that 35 per cent of farms in Pakistan are in the under 5 acre category and they own 11 per cent of the farm area, while 0.9 per cent own more than 150 acres with access to 10 per cent of acreage.

4.1.2 Changes Over Time

Having looked at some of the main characteristics in each of the four census years, we should now turn our attention to what has happened over time and see how certain categories have shifted in importance. Let us turn to tables 4.6 to 4.9.

Table 4.6 shows the *number of farms* with tenure classification across the four provinces. It shows how the shares of each tenure type have changed since 1960, and the share of farms in each province. Some highlights:

1. Owner farms increased from 41.1 per cent in 1960 to 68.8 per cent in 1990 for the whole country (Block A, column II to Block D, column II). Today, they dominate in each of the four provinces. Tenant farms fell in number from 41.7 per cent of the total in 1960 to only 18.6 in 1990 (Blocks A and D, column IV).

2. In 1960, 69.6 per cent of farms in Sindh were tenant farms; in 1990, they constituted 41.8 per cent (Blocks A and D, column IV). Owner farms increased substantially in these three decades in the Punjab (from 42.8 to 69.5 per cent), as well as in Sindh (21.6 per cent to 50.6 per cent).

3. Punjab had more than 68 per cent of all Pakistan's farms in 1960, which fell to 58 per cent in 1990 (Blocks A to D, column I). The largest rise has been in the NWFP's share, which was 13.9 per cent of the number of farms in all of Pakistan in 1960, but had risen to 21.1 per cent by 1990, overtaking Sindh.

4. The share of tenant farms has seen a consistent downward trend, just as owner farms have shown a consistent upward trend over the three decades. Owner-cum-tenant farms have always been the smallest category, but showed a substantial rise during the 1960s, after which they have shown a rapid downward trend.

5. Since we are here looking at the change in the *number* of farms across the three decades, we can return to Tables 4.2 to 4.5, and observe that the marginal (under 5 acres) and small (5–12.5 acres) farms continued to dominate in the Punjab in 1990 as they had in 1960. However, their share had fallen from 79 per cent of all farms to 68 per cent. Moreover, the pattern has been uneven; the share of 79 per cent in 1960 was followed by a sharp fall in 1972 to only 65 per cent, rising to 71 per cent in 1980, and finally falling again to 68. In Sindh, the distribution was as follows: 45 per cent in 1960, 70 per cent in 1972, 75 per cent in 1980, and 80 per cent in 1990. The patterns in the two provinces have followed a diametrically opposite trend, except in the 1972–80 period. The area of these groups as a proportion of total acreage in the Punjab in the four censuses has been 36, 30, 33, and most recently 40 per cent. In Sindh the acreage owned by these small farms was 27 per cent in 1960, 38 per cent in 1972, and 42 per cent in both 1980 and 1990.

Just as Table 4.6 showed the trend in the tenure and total number of farms, Table 4.7 shows the same tenure categories with *farm area*. Some features:

1. Like the number of farms, the area farmed fell consistently and systematically for the tenant farmer between 1960

Table 4.4
Distribution of the operational holdings by size and tenure in Pakistan, 1980 (000 farms and acres)

Farm size (acres)	All farms		Owner farms		Owner-cum-tenant farms		Tenant farms		Owner-operated area	Tenant-operated area				Area owner-cum-tenant farms				Area tenant farms		
	Number	Acres	Number	Acres	Number	Acres	Number	Acres		Total	Share cropped	Leased or rented	Others	Owner operated	Share cropped	Leased or rented	Others	Share cropped	Leased or rented	Others
	I	II	III	IV	V	VI	VII	VIII	IX	X	XI	XII	XIII	XIV	XV	XVI	XVII	XVIII	XIX	XX
A — All sizes																				
Pakistan	4,069 (100%)	47,095 (100%)	2,227 (55%)	24,533 (52%)	789 (19%)	12,396 (26%)	1,054 (26%)	10,165 (22%)	30,274 (64%)	16,821 (100%)	13,589 (100%)	2,900 (100%)	332 (100%)	5,741 (100%)	5,078 (100%)	1,584 (100%)	157 (100%)	8,511 (100%)	1,479 (100%)	175 (100%)
Punjab	2,544 (100%)	29,898 (100%)	1,385 (54%)	14,883 (50%)	618 (24%)	9,334 (31%)	542 (21%)	5,681 (19%)	19,199 (64%)	10,749 (100%)	8,456 (100%)	2,083 (100%)	209 (100%)	4,266 (100%)	3,912 (100%)	1,204 (100%)	93 (100%)	4,544 (100%)	1,020 (100%)	117 (100%)
Sindh	795 (100%)	9,207 (100%)	323 (41%)	4,350 (47%)	85 (11%)	1,528 (17%)	386 (49%)	3,328 (36%)	5,091 (55%)	4,116 (100%)	3,452 (100%)	617 (100%)	47 (100%)	741 (100%)	489 (100%)	270 (100%)	16 (100%)	2,963 (100%)	334 (100%)	31 (100%)
B — Under 5.0																				
Pakistan	1,386 (34%)(100%)	3,320 (7%)	920 (66%)(41%)	2,173 (65%)(9%)	124 (9%)(16%)	392 (12%)(3%)	283 (20%)(27%)	755 (23%)(7%)	2,345 (71%)(8%)	974 (6%)	826 (6%)	134 (5%)	14 (4%)	173 (3%)	181 (4%)	36 (2%)	9 (6%)	645 (8%)	96 (7%)	11 (6%)
Punjab	804 (32%)(100%)	1,938 (6%)	586 (73%)(42%)	1,327 (68%)(9%)	88 (11%)(14%)	289 (15%)(3%)	150 (19%)(28%)	326 (17%)(6%)	193 (10%)(1%)	483 (4%)	588 (7%)	86 (4%)	9 (4%)	127 (3%)	130 (3%)	23 (2%)	2 (2%)	257 (6%)	61 (6%)	7 (6%)
Sindh	202 (25%)(100%)	527 (6%)	98 (49%)(30%)	259 (49%)(6%)	9 (4%)(11%)	31 (6%)(2%)	94 (47%)(24%)	295 (56%)(9%)	272 (52%)(5%)	314 (8%)	306 (9%)	7 (1%)	1 (2%)	13 (2%)	17 (3%)	1 (0.37%)	0 (0%)	289 (10%)	6 (2%)	1 (3%)
C — 5.0–12.5																				
Pakistan	1,604 (39%)(100%)	12,855 (27%)	724 (45%)(33%)	5,646 (44%)(23%)	352 (22%)(45%)	2,907 (23%)(23%)	528 (33%)(50%)	4,301 (33%)(42%)	6,096 (54%)(23%)	5,947 (35%)	5,231 (38%)	662 (23%)	54 (16%)	1,261 (22%)	1,401 (28%)	245 (15%)	14 (9%)	3,829 (45%)	431 (29%)	41 (23%)
Punjab	996 (39%)(100%)	8,014 (27%)	463 (46%)(33%)	3,591 (45%)(24%)	285 (29%)(46%)	2,363 (25%)(29%)	249 (25%)(46%)	2,509 (26%)(36%)	8,014 (100%)(42%)	3,399 (32%)	2,857 (34%)	504 (24%)	37 (18%)	1,024 (24%)	1,131 (29%)	195 (16%)	10 (11%)	1,729 (38%)	306 (30%)	27 (23%)
Sindh	401 (50%)(100%)	3,297 (36%)	126 (39%)(31%)	1,008 (31%)(23%)	39 (46%)(10%)	325 (21%)(10%)	236 (59%)(61%)	1,902 (58%)(57%)	1,143 (35%)(22%)	2,093 (51%)(58%)	2,000 (58%)	80 (13%)	12 (26%)	135 (18%)	175 (33%)	18 (7%)	1 (6%)	1,824 (62%)	68 (20%)	11 (33%)
D — 12.5–25.0																				
Pakistan	705 (17%)(100%)	11,617 (25%)	323 (46%)(15%)	5,339 (46%)(22%)	198 (28%)(25%)	3,358 (29%)(27%)	185 (26%)(18%)	2,920 (25%)(29%)	6,824 (59%)(23%)	4,794 (29%)	3,970 (29%)	751 (26%)	73 (22%)	1,484 (26%)	1,524 (30%)	391 (25%)	28 (18%)	2,446 (29%)	429 (29%)	45 (26%)
Punjab	494 (19%)(100%)	7,981 (27%)	213 (43%)(15%)	3,427 (43%)(23%)	159 (32%)(26%)	2,390 (30%)(26%)	122 (25%)(23%)	1,864 (23%)(33%)	7,981 (100%)(35%)	3,387 (70%)	2,746 (32%)	587 (28%)	54 (26%)	1,167 (27%)	1,234 (32%)	331 (27%)	19 (20%)	1,512 (33%)	318 (31%)	34 (29%)
Sindh	132 (17%)(100%)	2,258 (25%)	62 (47%)(19%)	1,083 (48%)(25%)	22 (17%)(26%)	385 (17%)(25%)	48 (36%)(12%)	79 (35%)(24%)	1,266 (56%)(25%)	993 (24%)	850 (25%)	130 (21%)	13 (28%)	183 (25%)	157 (32%)	38 (14%)	4 (25%)	692 (23%)	89 (27%)	9 (29%)
E — 25.0–50.0																				
Pakistan	264 (6%)(100%)	8,386 (18%)	131 (50%)(6%)	4,169 (46%)(17%)	84 (32%)(11%)	2,770 (33%)(22%)	48 (18%)(5%)	1,448 (17%)(14%)	5,444 (65%)(18%)	2,942 (17%)	2,232 (16%)	636 (22%)	75 (23%)	1,275 (22%)	1,107 (22%)	374 (24%)	35 (22%)	1,125 (13%)	284 (19%)	39 (22%)
Punjab	184 (7%)(100%)	5,792 (19%)	84 (46%)(6%)	2,640 (46%)(18%)	64 (35%)(10%)	2,118 (37%)(23%)	35 (19%)(7%)	1,034 (18%)(18%)	5,792 (100%)(30%)	2,199 (20%)	1,673 (20%)	469 (23%)	57 (27%)	953 (22%)	871 (22%)	307 (25%)	27 (29%)	802 (18%)	201 (20%)	31 (26%)
Sindh	43 (5%)(100%)	1,393 (15%)	25 (58%)(8%)	827 (59%)(19%)	11 (26%)(13%)	358 (26%)(23%)	7 (16%)(2%)	209 (15%)(6%)	1,009 (72%)(20%)	384 (9%)	224 (6%)	150 (24%)	10 (21%)	182 (25%)	95 (19%)	52 (19%)	4 (25%)	129 (4%)	73 (22%)	6 (19%)
F — 50.0–150.0																				
Pakistan	96 (2%)(100%)	6,913 (15%)	59 (61%)(3%)	4,267 (62%)(17%)	28 (29%)(4%)	2,052 (30%)(17%)	9 (9%)(1%)	593 (9%)(6%)	5,319 (77%)(18%)	1,594 (9%)	1,057 (8%)	462 (16%)	74 (22%)	1,052 (18%)	689 (13%)	344 (22%)	45 (29%)	389 (5%)	175 (12%)	29 (17%)
Punjab	59 (2%)(100%)	4,230 (14%)	34 (58%)(2%)	2,468 (58%)(17%)	20 (34%)(3%)	1,417 (33%)(15%)	5 (9%)(1%)	345 (8%)(6%)	423 (2%)	1,034 (10%)	682 (8%)	310 (15%)	42 (20%)	729 (17%)	459 (12%)	246 (20%)	27 (29%)	223 (5%)	106 (10%)	16 (14%)
Sindh	15 (2%)(100%)	1,088 (12%)	10 (67%)(3%)	740 (68%)(17%)	3 (20%)(4%)	256 (24%)(17%)	1 (7%)(0.3%)	92 (8%)(3%)	883 (81%)(17%)	206 (5%)	62 (2%)	140 (23%)	4 (9%)	143 (19%)	37 (8%)	52 (19%)	4 (25%)	26 (1%)	73 (22%)	6 (19%)
G — 150.0 and over																				
Pakistan	14 (0.34%)(100%)	4,004 (8.50%)	10 (71%)(0.45%)	2,939 (73%)(11.96%)	3 (21%)(0.38%)	917 (23%)(7.40%)	1 (7%)(0.09%)	148 (4%)(1.46%)	3,434 (86%)(11.34%)	570 (3.39%)	273 (2.01%)	255 (8.79%)	42 (13%)	469 (9%)	196 (4%)	195 (12%)	32 (20%)	77 (1%)	62 (4%)	10 (6%)
Punjab	7 (0.28%)(100%)	1,943 (6.50%)	5 (71%)(0.36%)	1,430 (74%)(9.61%)	2 (29%)(0.32%)	460 (24%)(4.93%)	0 (3%)(0.04%)	53 (3%)(0.931%)	194 (1.01%)	247 (2.30%)	110 (1.30%)	127 (6.10%)	10 (5%)	266 (6%)	87 (2%)	102 (8%)	8 (9%)	24 (1%)	28 (3%)	2 (2%)
Sindh	2 (0.25%)(100%)	644 (6.99%)	1 (50%)(0.31%)	433 (67%)(9.95%)	1 (50%)(1.18%)	173 (27%)(11.32%)	0 (10%)(0.05%)	39 (6%)(1.17%)	518 (80%)(10.17%)	126 (3.06%)	10 (0.29%)	110 (7.83%)	7 (15%)	85 (11%)	85 (11%)	80 (30%)	5 (31%)	3 (0.10%)	33 (10%)	2 (6%)

Source: Khan, Mahmood Hasan, *Underdevelopment and Agrarian Structure in Pakistan*, Westview Press, Boulder, 1981.

Table 4.5
Number and area of farms by size of the farms, 1990

Farm size (acres)	All farms				Average size of farm (acres)
	Number	%	Acres	%	
All sizes					
Pakistan	5,071	(100)	47,575.3	(100)	9.38
Punjab	2,957.5	(100)	27,206.0	(100)	9.20
Sindh	802.0	(100)	8,631.7	(100)	10.76
NWFP	1,068.9	(100)	5,838.1	(100)	5.46
Baluchistan	242.8	(100)	5,899.5	(100)	24.30
Under 5.0					
Pakistan	1,784.1	(35)	5,313.7	(11)	2.98
Punjab	1,015.6	(34)	3,009.2	(11)	2.96
Sindh	266.4	(33)	768.0	(9)	2.88
NWFP	741.0	(69)	1,831.2	(31)	2.47
Baluchistan	54.0	(22)	133.4	(2)	2.47
5.0–12.5					
Pakistan	1,698.7	(33)	13,055.4	(27)	7.69
Punjab	1,005.8	(34)	7,774.2	(29)	7.73
Sindh	375.6	(47)	2,888.4	(33)	7.69
NWFP	233.0	(22)	1,702.5	(29)	7.31
Baluchistan	84.2	(35)	690.3	(12)	8.20
12.5–25.0					
Pakistan	623.1	(12)	10,216.4	(21)	16.40
Punjab	406.2	(14)	6,508.0	(24)	16.02
Sindh	108.5	(14)	1,860.2	(22)	17.15
NWFP	59.6	(6)	991.2	(17)	16.63
Baluchistan	48.9	(20)	857.0	(15)	17.54
25.0–50.0					
Pakistan	237.9	(4.7)	7,494.5	(16)	31.50
Punjab	147.4	(5)	4,560.6	(17)	30.94
Sindh	33.8	(4.2)	1,097.0	(13)	32.48
NWFP	25.2	(2.4)	813.1	(14)	32.30
Baluchistan	31.6	(13)	1,023.8	(17)	32.40
50.0–150.0					
Pakistan	91.8	(1.8)	6,458.9	(14)	70.33
Punjab	48.6	(1.6)	3,405.0	(13)	70.11
Sindh	14.6	(1.8)	1,054.4	(12)	72.16
NWFP	9.0	(0.8)	630.5	(11)	70.13
Baluchistan	19.7	(8.1)	1,368.9	(23)	69.62
150.0 and over					
Pakistan	15.4	(0.9)	4,781.8	(10)	311.4
Punjab	6.7	(0.7)	1,851.3	(7)	275.1
Sindh	3.1	(1.2)	936.4	(11)	302.7
NWFP	1.1	(0.1)	289.3	(5)	267.9
Baluchistan	4.5	(8.2)	1,704.8	(29)	383.0

Source: Government of Pakistan, *Agricultural Statistics of Pakistan, 1993–94*, Islamabad, 1995.

Table 4.6
Tenure classification of the farms by provinces

	Number of farms (m)						
Unit	Total	Owner		Owner-cum-tenant		Tenant	
	I	II		III		IV	
Census 1960							
Pakistan	4.859 (100%)	1.998 (100%)	(41.1%)	0.835 (100%)	(17.2%)	2.026 (100%)	(41.7%)
NWFP	0.674 (13.9%)	0.325 (16.3%)	(48.2%)	0.137 (16.4%)	(20.3%)	0.212 (10.5%)	(31.5%)
Punjab	3.326 (68.5%)	1.422 (71.2%)	(42.8%)	0.623 (74.6%)	(18.7%)	1.281 (63.2%)	(38.5%)
Sindh	0.694 (14.3%)	0.15 (7.5%)	(21.6%)	0.061 (7.3%)	(8.8%)	0.483 (23.8%)	(69.6%)
Baluchistan	0.165 (3.4%)	0.101 (5.1%)	(61.2%)	0.014 (1.7%)	(8.5%)	0.05 (2.5%)	(30.3%)
Census 1972							
Pakistan	3.76 (100%)	1.568 (100%)	(41.7%)	0.896 (100%)	(23.8%)	1.296 (100%)	(34.5%)
NWFP	0.466 (12.4%)	0.256 (16.3%)	(54.9%)	0.103 (11.5%)	(22.1%)	0.107 (8.3%)	(23%)
Punjab	2.375 (63.2%)	1.008 (64.3%)	(42.4%)	0.683 (76.2%)	(28.8%)	0.684 (52.8%)	(28.8%)
Sindh	0.747 (19.9%)	0.178 (11.4%)	(23.8%)	0.097 (10.8%)	(13.0%)	0.472 (36.4%)	(63.2%)
Baluchistan	0.172 (4.6%)	0.126 (8.0%)	(73.3%)	0.013 (1.5%)	(7.6%)	0.033 (2.5%)	(19.2%)
Census 1980							
Pakistan	4.07 (100%)	2.227 (100%)	(54.7%)	0.789 (100%)	(19.4%)	1.054 (100%)	(25.9%)
NWFP	0.528 (13.0%)	0.361 (16.2%)	(68.4%)	0.072 (9.1%)	(13.6%)	0.095 (9.0%)	(18%)
Punjab	2.545 (62.5)	1.385 (62.2%)	(54.4%)	0.618 (78.3%)	(24.3%)	0.542 (51.4%)	(21.3%)
Sindh	0.795 (19.5%)	0.323 (14.5%)	(40.6%)	0.085 (10.8%)	(10.7%)	0.387 (36.7%)	(48.7%)
Baluchistan	0.202 (5.0%)	0.158 (7.1%)	(78.2%)	0.014 (1.8%)	(6.9%)	0.03 (2.8%)	(14.9%)
Census 1990							
Pakistan	5.071 (100%)	3.491 (100%)	(68.8%)	0.626 (100%)	(12.3%)	0.954 (100%)	(18.7%)
NWFP	1.069 (21.1%)	0.835 (23.9%)	(78.1%)	0.0.89 (14.2%)	(8.3%)	0.145 (15.3%)	(13.6%)
Punjab	2.957 (58.3)	2.054 (58.8%)	(69.5%)	0.464 (74.1%)	(15.7%)	0.439 (46.4%)	(14.8%)
Sindh	0.802 (15.8%)	0.406 (11.6%)	(50.6%)	0.061 (9.7%)	(7.6%)	0.335 (35.4%)	(41.8%)
Baluchistan	0.243 (4.8%)	0.196 (5.6%)	(80.7%)	0.012 (1.9%)	(4.9%)	0.035 (3.7%)	(14.4%)

Source: Government of Pakistan, *Pakistan Economic Survey, 1994–95*, Islamabad, 1995.

Table 4.7
Tenure classification of the farms' area by provinces

Unit	Total		Owner			Owner-cum-tenant			Tenant		
	I		II			III			IV		
Census 1960											
Pakistan	48.926 (100%)		18.721 (100%)		(38.3%)	11.011 (100%)		(22.5%)	19.194 (100%)		(39.2%)
NWFP	5.463 (11.2%)		1.187 (6.3%)		(21.7%)	1.871 (17%)		(34.2%)	1.722 (9%)		(31.5%)
Punjab	29.212 (59.7%)		11.168 (59.7%)		(38.2%)	7.18 (65.2%)		(24.6%)	10.864 (56.6%)		(37.2%)
Sindh	10.19 (20.8%)		3.229 (17.2%)		(31.7%)	1.474 (13.4%)		(14.5%)	5.487 (28.6%)		(53.8%)
Baluchistan	4.061 (8.3%)		2.454 (13.1%)		(60.4%)	0.486 (4.4%)		(12%)	1.121 (5.8%)		(27.6%)
Census 1972											
Pakistan	49.058 (100%)		19.398 (100%)		(39.5%)	15.16 (100%)		(30.9%)	14.5 (100%)		(29.6%)
NWFP	4.251 (8.7%)		1.615 (8.3%)		(38%)	1.713 (11.3%)		(40.3%)	0.923 (6.4%)		(21.7%)
Punjab	31.029 (63.2%)		11.95 (61.6%)		(38.5%)	11.051 (72.9%)		(35.6%)	8.028 (55.4%)		(25.9%)
Sindh	9.459 (19.3%)		2.909 (15%)		(30.8%)	1.759 (11.6%)		(18.6%)	4.791 (33%)		(50.7%)
Baluchistan	4.319 (8.8%)		2.924 (15.1%)		(67.7%)	0.637 (4.2%)		(14.7%)	0.758 (5.2%)		(17.6%)
Census 1980											
Pakistan	47.094 (100%)		24.533 (100%)		(52.1%)	12.396 (100%)		(26.3%)	10.165 (100%)		(21.6%)
NWFP	4.099 (8.7%)		2.388 (9.7%)		(58.3%)	1.103 (8.9%)		(26.9%)	0.608 (6%)		(14.8%)
Punjab	28.898 (61.4%)		14.883 (60.7%)		(51.5%)	9.334 (75.3%)		(32.3%)	5.681 (55.9%)		(19.7%)
Sindh	9.206 (19.5%)		4.35 (17.7%)		(47.3%)	1.528 (12.3%)		(16.6%)	3.328 (32.7%)		(36.2%)
Baluchistan	3.891 (8.3%)		2.912 (11.9%)		(74.8%)	0.431 (3.5%)		(11.1%)	0.584 (5.7%)		(15%)
Census 1990											
Pakistan	47.319 (100%)		30.723 (100%)		(64.9%)	8.982 (100%)		(19%)	7.614 (100%)		(16.1%)
NWFP	5.828 (12.3%)		4.251 (13.8%)		(72.9%)	0.902 (10%)		(15.5%)	0.675 (8.9%)		(11.6%)
Punjab	27.107 (57.3%)		16.656 (54.2%)		(61.4%)	6.604 (73.5%)		(24.4%)	3.847 (50.5%)		(14.2%)
Sindh	8.604 (18.2%)		5.098 (16.6%)		(59.3%)	1.04 (11.6%)		(12.1%)	2.466 (32.4%)		(28.7%)
Baluchistan	5.78 (12.2%)		4.718 (15.4%)		(81.6%)	0.436 (4.6%)		(7.5%)	0.626 (8.2%)		(10.8%)

Farms area (m acres)

Source: Government of Pakistan, *Pakistan Economic Survey, 1994–95*, Islamabad, 1995.

and 1990, from 39.2 per cent to 16.1 per cent. In a mirror-image process, the farmed area of owner farms has risen considerably, most notably in the NWFP (column II). By 1990 owner farms dominated, by far, the total area farmed in all the provinces. Owner farms used to farm 38.3 per cent of total farm area in 1960; by 1990, this had risen to 64.9 per cent of total farm area (column II).

2. While owner-cum-tenant farms are fewer in number than tenant farms (Table 4.6, Block D, columns III and IV), they have more land to farm than tenant farms in the Punjab and NWFP (Table 4.7, Block D, columns III and IV).

3. Sindh, which used to have such a dominance of tenant farms (see Table 4.2) has seen a halving of the area farmed by tenants from 5.487 million acres in 1960, to 2.466 million in 1990 (Table 4.7, column IV). In all the four provinces, the area of tenant farms has fallen quite drastically.

4. Of the total farm area in the country, Punjab continues to hold the majority, but Baluchistan has made considerable progress in increasing its farm area and in 1990 constituted 12.2 per cent of the total farm area of the country (Block D, column I).

5. The total farm area in Pakistan has fallen from a high in 1972 to an all-time low in 1990. In fact, except for Baluchistan, all the three provinces have lost land on which farming takes place. Punjab has lost as much as 4 million acres since 1972 (Blocks B and D, column I).

Table 4.8 takes the data from Tables 4.6 and 4.7 and builds a series showing trends since 1960. The base year is taken to be 1960 = 100, and changes for each of the four provinces in the four censuses can easily be identified.

1. In the table, we see that in 1972 the index for the total number of farms fell in the NWFP and the Punjab, rising thereafter. The number of farms has declined in the Punjab, but it rose substantially in the other three provinces between 1960 and 1990.

2. There has been a huge upward movement in owner farms and an equally impressive downward movement in the number of tenant farms. Owner-cum-tenant farms, after rising, have fallen again.

3. With respect to farm area, owner farms have shown large increases, as tenant farms have lost considerable area, falling from an index of 100 in 1960 to 39.67 for Pakistan in 1990. Owner-cum-tenant farms, after increasing their farm area in 1972, continued to lose area in 1980 and 1990.

Table 4.9 shows how the average farm area has changed over time. We see that the area under 5 acres has gone up over time in the Punjab, and fallen in the 5–12.5 acre category in both Sindh and the Punjab. In the larger categories, between 50–150 acres, it fell a great deal in both the Punjab and Sindh between 1960 and 1990. In the extra-large category, after falling appreciably in 1972, presumably due to the land reforms of the Bhutto government, it rose again and has more or less stabilized.

Table 4.8
Tenure classification of the farms and area by provinces (index 1960=100)

Unit	Number of farms				Farms' area			
	Total	Owner	Owner-cum-tenant	Tenant	Total	Owner	Owner-cum-tenant	Tenant
Census 1972								
Pakistan	77.38	78.48	107.31	63.97	100.27	103.62	137.68	75.54
NWFP	69.14	78.77	75.18	50.47	77.81	136.06	91.56	53.60
Punjab	71.41	70.89	109.63	53.40	106.22	107.00	153.91	73.90
Sindh	107.64	118.67	159.02	97.72	92.83	90.09	119.34	87.62
Baluchistan	104.24	124.75	92.86	66.00	106.35	119.15	131.07	67.62
Census 1980								
Pakistan	83.76	111.46	94.49	52.02	96.26	131.05	112.58	52.96
NWFP	78.34	111.08	52.55	44.81	75.03	201.18	58.95	35.31
Punjab	76.52	97.40	99.20	42.31	98.93	133.26	130.00	52.29
Sindh	114.55	215.33	139.34	80.12	90.34	134.72	103.66	60.65
Baluchistan	122.42	156.44	100.00	60.00	95.81	118.66	88.68	52.10
Census 1990								
Pakistan	104.36	174.72	74.97	46.69	96.72	164.11	81.57	39.67
NWFP	158.61	256.92	64.96	68.40	106.68	358.13	48.21	39.20
Punjab	88.91	144.44	74.48	34.27	92.79	149.14	91.98	35.41
Sindh	115.56	270.67	100.00	69.36	84.44	157.88	70.56	44.94
Baluchistan	147.27	194.06	85.71	70.00	142.33	192.26	89.71	55.84

Source: This table is calculated from Tables 4.6 and 4.7.

Table 4.9
Average size of operational holding, 1960–1990

Farm size (acres)	1960	1972	1980	1990
All sizes				
Pakistan	10.07	13.04	11.57	9.38
Punjab	8.78	13.07	11.75	9.20
Sindh	9.91	12.65	11.58	10.76
Under 5.0				
Pakistan	1.91	2.42	2.40	2.98
Punjab	1.86	2.43	2.41	2.96
Sindh	3.04	3.07	2.61	2.88
5.0–12.5				
Pakistan	8.14	8.22	8.01	7.69
Punjab	8.14	8.23	8.05	7.73
Sindh	8.23	8.43	8.22	7.69
12.5–25.0				
Pakistan	17.19	16.45	16.48	16.40
Punjab	17.06	16.29	16.16	16.02
Sindh	17.46	16.76	17.11	17.15
25.0–50.0				
Pakistan	33.10	31.89	31.77	31.50
Punjab	32.79	31.62	31.48	30.94
Sindh	33.51	31.97	32.40	32.48
50.0–150.0				
Pakistan	74.31	71.86	72.01	70.33
Punjab	100.70	70.29	71.69	70.11
Sindh	171.50	77.92	72.53	72.22
150.0 and over				
Pakistan	349.70	280.10	286.00	311.44
Punjab	285.20	255.60	277.60	275.09
Sindh	398.50	249.30	322.00	302.74

Source: Government of Pakistan, *Agricultural Statistics of Pakistan, 1993–94*, Islamabad, 1995.

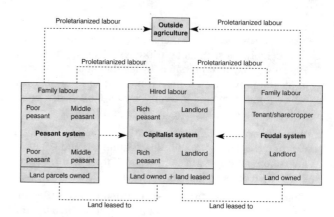

Figure 4.1
Agrarian transition in Pakistan

Source: Khan, Mahmood Hasan, *Lectures on Agrarian Transformation in Pakistan*, PIDE, Islamabad, 1985, p. 17.

4.2 What Do the Numbers Mean?

The overall nature of transition in agriculture can best be captured by Figure 4.1. While the three systems of agriculture – peasant, capitalist, and feudal – can and do coexist, the trend has been for feudalism to give way to capitalism, which emerges and consolidates itself, while a peasant system is able to survive its onslaught. Figure 4.1 shows these changes with particular reference to Pakistan, where both the feudal and peasant systems are feeding the capitalist system within and outside agriculture.

Possibly the single most important feature of the transition in agriculture depicted by the tables in this chapter is the marked fall in tenancy. Tenant farms have fallen sharply in both number and acreage across all sizes of holding in Pakistan. At the same time, there has been an impressive increase in owner farms and the area that they farm. In addition, the owner-operated area has shown a substantial increase in the 5–50 acre groups.

In the category of marginal farms that are less than 5 acres, we see a large decrease in their number and area between 1960 and 1972, but a considerable rise in both during 1972–80 and 1980–90. The fall in tenancy between 1960 and 1972 is reflected in the large decrease in the number and area farmed. The later rise in both is not reflected by an equivalent rise in tenancy. There has been a large rise in the number of owners in the marginal category.

The category of small, 5–12.5 acre farms shows a consistent increase in all the inter-census periods. The growth of this category is probably the result of the fall in the number and area farmed in both the 12.5–25, and 25–50 acre groups during the period 1972–80. Both size categories, medium and large, lost a number of farms and a large chunk of their area during the 1970s. Between 1980 and 1990, the small category grew in number, although there was a small drop in the area owned and farmed. There was a continuous fall in the number of farms and area owned in both the medium and large categories in both provinces between 1980 and 1990.

The category of very large 50–150 acre farms remained more or less the same in Sindh between 1980 and 1990, but continued to fall in the Punjab in this period, as it did in the 1972–80 period. In the category of extra-large farms, 150 acres and above, there was a sharp increase in both the number of farms and their area in Sindh, between 1980 and 1990, with a small decrease in the Punjab in the same period.

The increase in owners and the decline in tenancy suggests that more are more landowners are acquiring land from tenants and are going in for self-cultivation, probably hiring in agricultural wage labour. It is unlikely that many of the tenants are in a position to become owners, so most of them will probably have been changed into agricultural or rural wage labourers or have migrated to urban areas and towns as they have been displaced by owner-cultivators. The dramatic increase in the area farmed by owners over the last four decades may indicate that tenants have been displaced and land brought under self-cultivation, or that many owners have bought land from other landowners. The tables show that the number of farms in the Punjab increased by about the same proportion as the increase in farm area. In Sindh, the number of owners increased much faster than the increase in farm area between 1960 and 1990. However, over this period there has not been a very sharp decline in agricultural employment: the proportion of those employed in agriculture has fallen from 60 per cent of the labour force to 47 per cent in 1994/5. It is likely that more share croppers and tenants have become agricultural wage workers than have migrated. This implies greater marginalization.

The growth in small farms at the expense of the medium and large farms may be due to greater fragmentation of landholding caused by inheritance, where many heirs may become owners of a single property which was hitherto of a larger size.

In the Punjab, there was a fall in farm sizes 12.5–25 acres, 25–50 acres, and 50–150 acres between 1980 and 1990, and a rise in the number of farms in the 5–12.5 acre category, but with a small fall in area owned, causing the average size to fall. In Sindh, there has been a fall in the categories 5–12.5, 12.5–25, and 25–50 acres, with more or less no change in the 50–150 acre category. This seems to suggest that there is some consolidation of holding taking place on the high side (above 50 acres) in Sindh, with the hold of the extra-large Pakistani landowner (over 150 acres) slipping. However, the most phenomenal factor is the consistent rise of the small farm.

The method that we have been using to discuss the nature and direction of agrarian transition very clearly reveals how insufficient and handicapped it is. If we had access to data based on class, or more elaborate data as depicted in Appendix 4.1, we might have been able to get a better handle on the nature of change. Had we known about the relations of production, whether labour was hired or land rented in, we would have been in a position to elaborate on the nature of *capitalist* development and how *capitalist* relations have been further developed. At the moment, we can see that more small farms are being created and many more owner-farms are emerging. However, we do not know how, and under what type of relations of production, these self-cultivators produce. It would be reasonable to assume that they are either family farmers or peasants who, in all likelihood, hire in labour. At the other end of the spectrum, the increase in the extra-large category suggests that these are capitalist farmers who have resumed their land from sharecroppers and probably hire in a large number of agricultural wage labourers. It is also possible that these large landholders have bought land from the medium and large farmers of between 12.5 and 50 acres, who have found it less profitable to farm as competition has increased further.

Mahmood Hasan Khan, who has differentiated the data based not only on size of holding, but also on the categories shown in Appendix 4.1, has been able to show us a clearer picture of the nature of the agrarian transition.[2] He looks at data pertaining to land rented in and rented out by various sizes of farms in the 1970s and finds that 'farmers owning 5 acres or less were renting their area out but the area so rented out also increased substantially in the seventies ... Owners of middle-sized farms 5–25 acres, in the Punjab rented out land but in Sindh they rented in from others.'[3] This, he argues, is due to the very different nature of production in the two provinces: the middle-sized farmer in the Punjab is of the capitalist type of family farmer, while in Sindh this farmer employs sharecroppers. Furthermore, he says that in the Punjab the middle and poor peasants lease out increasing amounts of their land to others, while in Sindh sharecroppers rent in land from landlords. He also has evidence which supports our contention above, that in Sindh there was 'a shift towards capitalist farming through increased resumption of land by landlords from share-croppers for cultivation by their own selves',[4] which is one reason why the size of farm has increased over the years in the extra-large category of over 150 acres. For Mahmood Hasan Khan, capitalist farmers are increasing in the Punjab and Sindh 'at the expense of poor and even middle class peasants in the former and against landlords and their sharecroppers in Sind'.[5] Elsewhere he argues that 'capitalist farming is ... facilitated by the increased size of operational holding (farm)'.[6]

Finally, Table 4.10 shows quite dramatically how a number of important changes have taken place between 1960 and 1980. It would have been even more interesting to see the changes from the 1990 census, but data are not yet available in this form. Nevertheless, the table only amplifies and endorses the analysis presented above. It shows the following:

1. The number of pure owner farms has increased, as has their share of area, but not by as much.

2. Pure tenant farms are much fewer in 1980 than in 1960; their area has also fallen markedly, although their average size seems to have increased marginally.

3. Sharecropping has also seen a very marked decline in this period, although some 'pure' tenant farms may have become owner-cum-tenant farms.

5. Overall, the total number of farms has fallen and so has the total farm area, but at a slower pace, resulting in an increase in the average farm size.

4.3 Summary and Further Reading

4.3.1 Summary

This has not been an easy chapter to deal with. It has been made cumbersome by the huge array of numbers presented here, which are no doubt off-putting for many readers. Nevertheless, we could not avoid the reference to these very useful and essential numbers. They bring together very important data from the 1950s to the present, and allow the interested reader to expand on the simplified and brief analysis presented here.

The essential purpose of the data presented is to enable the observation and study of the pattern of agricultural transition. We observe that tenancy and sharecropping, essential cornerstones of feudalism, have fallen drastically,

Table 4.10
Summary data on number, size, area and operational status of farms by tenure based on agricultural census data, 1960–1980

Private farms		Pure owner farms	Owner-cum-tenant farms			Pure tenant farms	All private farms
			Owner	Tenant	Total		
Numbers (m)							
	1960	1.998	n.a.	n.a.	0.834	2.028	4.86
	1972	1.569	n.a.	n.a.	0.897	1.296	3.762
	1980	2.227	n.a.	n.a.	0.789	1.054	4.07
Ave. farm size (m acres)							
	1960	10.06	n.a.	n.a.	13.20	9.46	10.07
	1972	13.04	n.a.	n.a.	16.90	11.19	13.04
	1980	11.57	n.a.	n.a.	15.71	9.65	11.57
Farm area (m acres)							
	1960	18.723	6.235	6.107	12.342	17.864	48.929
	1972	19.399	6.988	8.172	15.16	14.5	49.059
	1980	24.533	5.741	6.655	12.396	10.166	47.095
Area operated by (m acres):							
Owner	1960	18.723	6.235	–	6.235	–	24.958
	1972	19.399	6.988	–	6.988	–	26.387
	1980	24.533	5.741	–	5.741	–	30.274
Share cropper	1960	–	–	7.776	4.776	16.495	21.271
	1972	–	–	6.351	6.351	12.564	18.915
	1980	–	–	5.078	5.078	8.511	13.589
Lease holder	1960	–	–	0.979	0.979	0.962	2.941
	1972	–	–	1.584	1.584	1.76	3.344
	1980	–	–	1.421	1.421	1.479	2.9
Other	1960	–	–	0.352	0.352	0.407	0.759
	1972	–	–	0.237	0.237	0.176	0.413
	1980	–	–	0.156	0.156	0.175	0.322

n.a. = not available.
Note: (1) 1 ha = 2.47 acres.
         (2) The 1960 Census, based on an extractive survey of the land revenue records, may not be comparable to the 1972 and 1980 Censuses, based on population surveys.
Source: Government of Pakistan, *Pakistan Economic Survey, 1994–95*, Islamabad, 1995.

both in the number of farms and in the area farmed. Tenancy farms and sharecroppers have been replaced by owner-operated farms. This is a major change in the pattern of agricultural production in Pakistan and shows the direction for the future. This chapter has also tried to show how different classes in agriculture coexist and the nature of their relationship with each other.

4.3.2   Further Reading

Although a number of books and papers have been contributed on the agricultural sector in Pakistan, most have presented a static analysis and have not been much concerned with change or transition over a period of time.

The *process* itself has not been observed, and analysis has often been restricted to one point in time. This is a major shortcoming of such work, for it does not allow us to see how the present situation and structure have evolved. One major exception has been the work by Prof. Mahmood Hasan Khan of the Simon Fraser University in Canada, whose *Underdevelopment and Agrarian Structure in Pakistan*, Westview Press, Boulder, 1981, and *Lectures on Agrarian Transformation in Pakistan*, PIDE, Islamabad, 1985, do present a historical analysis and allow us to see the process of development itself. Some of the references listed in Chapter 3, dealing with the Green Revolution, which itself was such an important impetus to the nature and direction of change discussed in this chapter, would also be useful to the reader.

Appendix 4.1

Classes in agriculture

Mahmood Hasan Khan in his *Lectures on Agrarian Transformation* writes:

There are at present five distinct classes in the agricultural sector of Pakistan.

First, there are landlords who own large areas of land and rent almost all of it in small parcels to landless share-croppers. Landlords do not rent or lease land from others. Labour is entirely provided by the share-cropper households. Landlords neither work for themselves nor provide their labour-power to others. Their overlordship on land is exercised mainly through their agents (*kamdars*). In Sindh, for instance, share-croppers play no role in production decisions. Profits and wages as economic rewards do not exist here; only rent exists. Primordial and traditional factors, and not economic considerations, play a central role in determining the nexus of landlords and tenants, including their shares in output.

Secondly, there are farmers. Contrary to the popular perception in Pakistan that there are 'farmers' with complete homogeneity of interests, I emphasize heterogeneity. The capitalist farmers, who can also be called rich peasants, may own most or some of the land they cultivate and rent or lease from others part of it. They do not normally rent or lease their lands to others. Others' labour is the basis of production and source of surplus value for capitalist farmers. Landless workers or the so-called free labour are hired for wages. Rich peasants do not sell their labour-power to others: they work on their

land as entrepreneurs *par excellence*. They organize production, supervise free labour and innovate. Profit and wages appear as basic economic categories for the first time in the distribution of output, although rent may still remain as an important component of income. Rent does not disappear.

Thirdly, there is the class of family farmers who could be called middle peasants. This class consists of farmers who may own, rent or lease part of the land they cultivate. They may even rent or lease out part of their land to others. However, these landowners depend almost entirely on family or household labour for production. They usually do not work for others, nor do they hire others to work on their farms. These farms are probably nearest to the classic peasant farm of Chayanov, the famous Russian economist who gave this idea and developed a theory of peasantry. Chayanovian peasants have shown great resilience in the face of capitalistic development of agriculture in history in Russia and other countries.

Fourthly, there is the class of share-croppers, or *haris* as they are called in Sindh. Landless share-croppers rent all the land they cultivate and share the output with landlords on some traditionally-determined basis, often in kind. This class may include some poor peasants, whom I call marginal landowners and who must supplement their meager income by share-cropping on small farms of land rented from the landlord or others. Share-croppers do not hire labour and depend almost entirely on their household labour. They may sell their labour-power to landowners to supplement their

Table 1
Agrarian class differentiation in Pakistan

	Class	Land			Labour		
1	Landlords	LO	$>$	0	SE	$=$	0
		LR_o	$>$	0	HL_i	$>$	0
		LR_i	$=$	0	HL_o	$=$	0
2	Capitalist farmers (rich peasants)	LO	$>$	0	SE	$>$	0
		LR_o	$=$	0	HL_i	$>$	0
		LR_i	$>$	0	HL_o	$=$	0
3	Family farmers (middle or poor peasants)	LO	$>$	0	SE	$>$	0
		LR_o	$>$	0	HL_i	$=$	0
		LR_i	$>$	0	HL_o	$>$	0
4	Share-croppers	LC	$=$	0	SE	$>$	0
		LR_o	$=$	0	HL_i	$=$	0
		LR_i	$>$	0	HL_o	$\geq$	0
5	Wage workers	LO	$=$	0	SE	$=$	0
		LR_o	$=$	0	HL_i	$>$	0
		LR_i	$=$	0	HL_o	$\geq$	0

Note: LO = land owned; LR_o = land rented out; LR_i = land rented in; SE = employment; HL_i = hiring in labour; HL_o = hiring out labour.

Source: Khan, Mahmood Hasan, *Lectures on Agrarian Transformation in Pakistan*, PIDE, Islamabad, 1985, pp. 10–13.

meager income. They are the linchpin in the feudal system which exists in parts of Pakistan even today.

The fifth and final class is that of wage workers. This class consists of what I call unattached (landless) workers, who must earn income by selling their labour-power. They work mainly for rich peasants or capitalist farmers. Their wage is partly in cash and partly in kind. They may work on a permanent basis but most of them find only seasonal work. They may supplement their incomes by working outside agriculture. These workers constitute the burgeoning proletariat for agriculture and industry.

I want to clarify here two or three points in [Table 1]. First, hiring of labour by landlords implies use of share-croppers, i.e. the labour power of others. It is a reference to the attached labour. Secondly, family farmers may work for others either in or outside agriculture. This, of course, depends on the requirement of the family farm and the level of income of the household to reproduce its labour power. Thirdly, share-croppers may also work for others outside the landlord–tenant nexus, either in or outside agriculture. Finally, leasing of land by capitalist farmers or rich peasants could be either from landlords to whom they pay the ground rent or from the middle to poor peasants on fixed payments.

Our typology cuts across the simplistic tenure categories of lessors and lessees. It also does not maintain a direct relationship to large and small holdings. Lessors could be landlords or even middle or poor peasants owning but not using land. Therefore, you may be lumping together in this category different sorts of people such as landlords and small owners. Lessees could be capitalist farmers or share-croppers and poor peasants supplementing their own holdings. So, you are putting together apples and oranges in one box. I am saying: get out of this box which is empty, nonsensical. A classification based on the arbitrary size and tenure categories does not reveal the true relations of production. They mystify the creation and appropriation of social surplus in agriculture. These groupings do not even assist in analysing the problems of farm organization in relation to the issues of efficiency and equity in Pakistan. Finally, and more importantly from the point of view of rural poverty, they do not reveal the impact of extraction of agricultural surplus for capitalist accumulation on each of the classes.

Source: Khan, Mahmood Hasan, *Lectures on Agrarian Transformation in Pakistan*, PIDE, Islamabad, 1985, pp. 10–13.

Notes

1. Khan, Mahmood Hasan, *Underdevelopment and Agrarian Structure in Pakistan*, Westview Press, Boulder, 1981, p. 2.
2. Khan, Mahmood Hasan, *Lectures on Agrarian Transformation in Pakistan*, PIDE, Islamabad, 1985.
3. Ibid., p. 24.
4. Ibid., p. 24.
5. Ibid., p. 24.
6. Khan, Mahmood Hasan, 'Classes and Agrarian Transition in Pakistan', in Ali, Karamat (ed.), *Pakistan: The Political Economy of Rural Development*, Vanguard, Lahore, 1986, p. 446.

5

Agriculture: Critical Issues

In the previous three chapters, a history of the development of agriculture in Pakistan has been presented, where the focus has been on the changes that have taken place since the times of the Mughal Empire. So far, we have discussed how the process of change was initiated and the nature of that change. We have seen how, from pre-capitalist or feudal modes of production in agriculture, capitalist forms emerged and how they then established themselves, becoming the dominant form of production. In all of this story of agriculture, we have seen how economic and social relations have changed over time. However, while we have learnt a great deal about this transformation in agriculture, we have learnt nothing about what is grown, what actually constitutes agricultural production, and so on. This chapter will fill that gap.

We will first introduce the nature of agricultural production itself – crops grown, yields, area under cultivation, etc. The purpose will be to inform the reader about Pakistani agriculture and how it has changed since 1947. After a broad overview, salient contemporary issues related to agriculture will be introduced and discussed before we close this part of the book on the agricultural sector.

5.1 An Overview and Major Trends

The agricultural sector in Pakistan is classified as containing five subsectors, comprising major crops, minor crops, livestock, fisheries and even forestry (see Figure 5.1). Not surprisingly, the major crops make the largest contribution to the GDP from the agricultural sector, although as Figure 5.1 shows, their contribution has fallen slightly in the last fifteen years. In fact the fall in the contribution from major crops has been made up by an increase in livestock farming and production.

The rabi (winter) and kharif (summer) seasons divide the agricultural calendar. In rabi the main food crop grown is wheat, with tobacco the largest cash crop. In kharif, cotton and sugar cane, both cash crops, are cultivated along with rice, the main food crop. Interestingly, it is the kharif season that provides Pakistan with its most important exports, cotton and rice, and hence floods due to excessive or prolonged monsoons can play havoc not just with agricultural production, but also with industry and exports. As we show in subsequent chapters, this has been the case many times in Pakistan's past.

The extent of change in Pakistan's overall economy and society over the last fifty years can best be summarized in a

Five subsectors: major crops, minor crops, livestock, fisheries, forestry.

Share in agriculture's contribution to GDP (%)

	1980/1	1995/6
Major crops	51.87	45.28
Minor crops	17.22	18.03
Livestock	26.36	32.03
Fisheries	3.53	3.87
Forestry	1.02	0.79

Rabi (winter) crops:
wheat, barley, gram, tobacco, rapeseed, mustard

Kharif (summer) crops:
cotton, rice, sugar cane, bajra, maize, sesame.

Food crops:
wheat, rice, bajra, jawar, maize, barley, gram.

Cash crops:
cotton, sugar cane, tobacco, rapeseed, mustard, sesame.

Figure 5.1
The agricultural sector

single figure which shows the extent of the contribution of agriculture to Pakistan's gross domestic product (GDP): in 1949/50, agriculture was by far the largest sector, contributing more than 53 per cent to GDP; in 1995/6, this share was down to only 24.8 per cent, i.e. less than even one-quarter. This is despite all the progress, growth, and development that was made in agriculture following the Green Revolution, and other salient milestones. While in 1949/50 agriculture contributed more than half of GDP, today the services sector contributes half, and is twice as large as agriculture. Another equally important statistic regarding agriculture is the fall in the share of the labour force employed in agriculture, from 65 per cent in 1950/1 to 47.5 per cent in 1995/6, although agriculture is still the largest sector in terms of employment.

The total geographic area of Pakistan is 79.61 million hectares (or 196.64 million acres), and the 'reported' area in 1995/6 was 73 per cent of the total area (Table 5.1). (The reported area is that amount of the total geographical area for which official records exist. It has risen to 73 per cent today from 58 per cent in 1947/8.)[1] The non-reported area (27 per cent of Pakistan) for which records do not exist 'is due to large tracts of unsettled lands in most parts of the northern

Table 5.1
Land utilization, 1947–1996 (m hectares)

Year[a]	Total area	Reported area	Not available for cultivation	Total area cultivation	Area sown more than once	Total cropped area
1947/8	79.61	46.70	20.82	14.69	0.95	11.63
1960–1965	79.61	50.52	18.94	17.78	1.68	15.08
1965–1970	79.61	52.98	19.08	19.19	1.99	16.28
1970–1975	79.61	53.53	20.50	19.21	2.54	17.04
1975–1980	79.61	54.27	20.62	19.84	3.30	18.44
1980–1985	79.61	56.29	21.29	20.32	4.09	19.68
1985–1990	79.61	57.87	23.97	20.78	4.79	20.49
1990–1995	79.61	58.04	24.49	21.17	5.70	21.86
1995/6	79.61	58.51	24.49	21.60	5.95	22.14

[a]Averages, except 1947/8 and 1995/6.

Note: 1 ha = 2.47 acres.

Sources: For 1947/8: Ahmed, Viqar and Rashmid Amjad, *The Management of Pakistan's Economy, 1947–82*, Oxford University Press, Karachi, 1984, p. 110. For other years: Government of Pakistan, *Pakistan Economic Survey, 1994–95*, Islamabad, 1995, p. 45.

tribal territories in the NWFP and in the north-western and western parts of Baluchistan; some south-eastern and eastern desert areas in the Punjab and Sindh are also included'.[2] The fact that there has been an increase of 15 per cent in reported area since 1947 shows that larger areas and tracts of the land have become 'officially' part of Pakistan and are accountable for. This process is important for revenue records, inheritance, and other purposes.

For agricultural purposes (and our analysis) the reported area is the relevant area. As one would expect, however, not all of the reported area is cultivable – in fact, in 1995/6 as much as 42 per cent of this area was not available for cultivation (Table 5.1). In 1948 this proportion was 48 per cent, while in 1980/1, only 37 per cent of the reported area was uncultivable (see Figure 5.2). This interesting trend is like a U-shaped curve, where the area not available for cultivation is very high in 1948, almost half of reported area, then falls, implying that more land as a percentage can be cultivated upon, and then rises again in the late 1990s. There are probably two very important reasons for this trend. Firstly, as we have seen in earlier chapters, following the commercialization of agriculture with Green Revolution technology, more land was brought into cultivation – this explains the increase in cultivable area. The fall in later years could be due to the faster increase in reported area compared to the colonization of new land. But since reported area has increased by only 20 per cent over the last five decades, compared to the 30 per cent increase in total area cultivated, this cannot be the case. The other reasons could be increasing urbanization, where urban land has been creeping on to agricultural land for the purposes of industry and residences, especially in the Punjab; or water logging and salinity, which is slowly eating away the land that was once cultivable.

Total cultivated area in Pakistan was 36.3 million acres in 1947[3] and 53.35 million acres in 1995/6. It was 32 per cent of reported area in 1947 and now constitutes 36.8 per cent. Table

5.1 provides basic data about land utilization in Pakistan. From the table we see that, as irrigation has expanded, so has multiple cropping (area sown more than once). In the period 1960–5 only 9 per cent of the total area cultivated was used for multiple cropping, while by 1995/6, this had risen to 27 per cent.

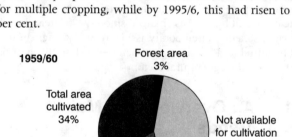

1959/60

Forest area 3%

Total area cultivated 34%

Not available for cultivation 42%

Cultivable waste 21%

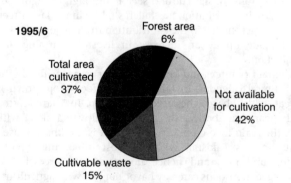

1995/6

Forest area 6%

Total area cultivated 37%

Not available for cultivation 42%

Cultivable waste 15%

Figure 5.2
Land utilization, 1959/60 and 1995/6 (% use of reported area)

Table 5.2
Index of agricultural production, 1959–1996

Years	All crops	Food crops	Fibre crops	Other crops
1959/60	100	100	100	100
1960/1	100	98	103	103
1961/2	109	105	111	122
1962/3	119	108	128	151
1963/4	118	108	144	124
1964/5	128	120	130	162
1965/6	127	107	142	181
1966/7	135	114	156	189
1967/8	157	150	171	170
1968/9	168	160	180	184
1969/70	186	177	185	214
1970/1	174	164	188	195
1971/2	183	170	245	169
1972/3	188	181	243	163
1973/4	196	190	228	188
1974/5	187	183	220	171
1975/6	199	207	176	193
1976/7	203	212	149	224
1977/8	209	208	197	223
1978/9	219	238	162	212
1979/80	239	245	250	210
1980/1	249	254	245	236
1981/2	258	257	247	261
1982/3	270	277	283	235
1983/4	237	253	170	248
1984/5	275	265	346	239
1985/6	298	290	418	212
1986/7	124	115	185	92
1987/8	127	109	206	100
1988/9	134	118	200	112
1989/90	134	119	204	108
1990/1	142	122	230	110
1991/2	161	126	306	120
1992/3	141	124	216	118
1993/4	142	127	192	134
1994/5	152	138	208	140
1995/6 (P)	167	147	253	140

(P) = Provisional.
Source: Government of Pakistan, *Pakistan Economic Survey, 1995–96*, Islamabad, 1996, p. 43.

If we examine the data in Tables 5.2 to 5.7 regarding agricultural output and production, a number of interesting features are observed.

1. Table 5.2 shows us that the indices of 'all crops', 'food crops', and 'other crops' peaked in the late 1970s and early 1980s. After rising from 1959/60 until 1984/5, the index for agricultural production has seen a sharp fall in more recent years. For the category 'all crops', the index was only 50 per cent higher in 1995/6 than in 1959/60, after touching an all-time high of 298 in 1985/6. Thus, in the nine years after 1985/6 the index was almost halved. In

the case of food crops, the index was 115 per cent lower in 1995/6 than in the peak of 1985/6. Fibre crops are the only ones that have shown a doubling of output in 1995/6 compared to 1959/60, but they have also been reduced to almost half compared to the exceptional year of 1985/6 (see Figure 5.3).

2. In Table 5.3 we see that the total area under food crops has increased by more than 50 per cent since 1959/60. Wheat is the largest sown crop and today constitutes 66 per cent of the total area of food grains, up from 60 per cent in 1959/60. For the four major crops of Pakistan, the area under wheat in this period is up 67 per cent, rice 75 per cent, cotton 93 per cent, and sugar cane, 125 per cent. In the 1960–5 period, the four major crops covered about 53 per cent of total cropped area, whereas by 1995/6 this had increased substantially to 64 per cent (see Figure 5.4 for changes in the relative positions of crops).

3. Total production shows the following trends between 1950–5 and 1995/6 (Table 5.4): wheat up by 542 per cent; rice 473 per cent; and sugar cane 628 per cent. Cotton increased by 530 per cent between 1960–5 and 1995/6. Thus we see that for all major as well as minor crops, there has been a very substantial increase in total output over the last fifty years.

4. While increases in total area sown and total quantity produced are important in their own right, yield per unit of land (per acre or hectare) is a better indicator of how agriculture is progressing. Table 5.5 shows the average yields for major crops. Comparing the period 1990–5 with the early 1950s, wheat's yield is up from 776 kg/hectare to 1,950; rice is up from 878 to 1,622, although much of this improvement came in the early years; sugar cane is up from 29,180 to 44,000; and cotton is up from 212 to 594. This table, perhaps, best exemplifies the huge impact of the Green Revolution, where due to the high yielding variety seeds for wheat and rice there was a marked increase in output. For example, between 1960–5 and 1974/5, the yield for wheat increased by 59 per cent, and for rice by 55 per cent. Between 1974/5 and 1995/6, the yield for rice increased by only 27 per cent, although the yields for wheat continued to show large increases, by as much as 59 per cent. However, it now took two decades to achieve what was achieved earlier in only one decade (see Figure 5.5).

5. Table 5.6 shows how the sources of irrigation in Pakistan have changed over the last forty years. In 1950/1 canals provided 81 per cent of all irrigation, while in 1992/3 they provided 71 per cent. Tubewells, which were almost non-existent in the 1950s, now provide as much as 25 per cent of irrigation.

6. Given the rise in output and production over the last few years, one might assume that the people of Pakistan are better fed now than they used to be. However, the high growth in population of around 3 per cent might indicate that on a per capita basis they are not any better off. Table 5.7 shows that, in fact, since 1986/7 the per capita availability of the most important foods has increased by at least 10 per cent for rice, and by as much as 22 per cent

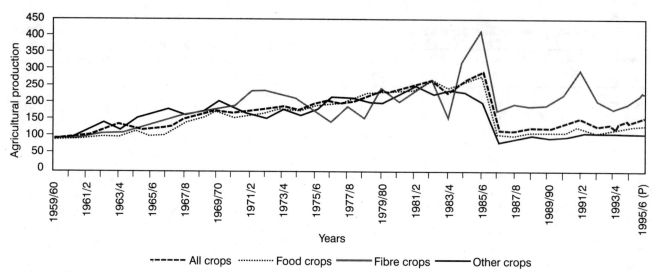

Figure 5.3
Index of agricultural production, 1959–1996

for meat. However, this table should be taken as indicative only, for it does not show either distribution or the amount actually consumed. Availability may suggest production, but it does not take account of exports, losses, or actual consumption (see Figure 5.6).

7. Figure 5.7 shows the overall annual growth rates in agriculture since 1949/50. We can see that growth in double figures took place in only three years, with negative growth in five. The highest growth achieved in any one year was 13.6 per cent in 1953/4–1954/5, with the lowest being -9.1 per cent, in the very early years. The trend seems to be more unsettled in the first fifteen years after 1949, and settles down in the mid-1960s. Despite a couple of very bad years in the 1980s and 1990s, the trend has

been fairly stable since the early 1970s, and more so since the early 1980s.

While agriculture was the dominant sector of the economy in 1947, having a substantial share of employment and being the main contributor to GDP until about 1958, agricultural output and production stagnated, with the growth rate between 1949 and 1958 being only 1.43 per cent, which was less than half the growth rate in population. This meant that even the per capita consumption of food grain declined in this period. Food had to be imported and there was a heavy dependence on foreign aid and other hand-outs, many of which came with strong political overtones and consequences. It was possibly the realization of the need to become somewhat less dependent on foreign money, and to

Table 5.3
Area under major crops, 1950–1996 (000 hectares)

Year[a]	Wheat	Rice	Sugar cane	Cotton	Percentage of total cropped area
1950–1955	4,154.0	947.0	245.6	1,275.8	–
1955–1960	4,736.6	1,078.8	365.4	1,393.2	–
1960–1965	4,896.2	1,214.2	447.6	1,375.4	52.59
1965–1970	5,591.8	1,426.6	559.0	1,635.6	56.58
1970–1975	6,017.4	1,514.6	597.6	1,860.2	58.62
1975–1980	6,272.0	1,797.6	747.0	1,916.4	58.20
1980–1985	7,174.4	1,984.2	859.8	2,177.7	61.96
1985–1990	7,418.2	1,986.6	833.0	2,459.6	62.26
1990–1995	8,058.6	2,099.0	927.4	2,758.0	63.32
1995/6 (P)	8,167.0	2,162.0	963.0	2,997.0	64.53

(P) = Provisional.
[a]Averages, except for 1995/6.
Note: 1 ha = 2.47 acres.
Source: For 1950–5 and 1955–60: Ahmed, Viqar and Rashid Amjad, *The Management of Pakistan's Economy, 1947–82*, Oxford University Press, Karachi, 1984, p. 110. For other years: Government of Pakistan, *Pakistan Economic Survey, 1995–6*, Islamabad, 1996, p. 47.

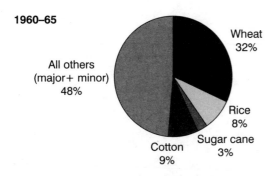

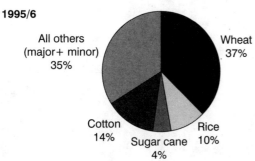

Figure 5.4
Total area sown, 1960–1965 and 1995/6 (%)

make agriculture more profitable, which led to a number of very important interventions in the agricultural sector in the 1960s.

The land reforms of 1959 may have been a failure in terms of land redistribution (see Chapter 4), but they caused a significant shock to a moribund system. The Green Revolution technology was a critical factor in the impressive growth rates in agriculture achieved in the 1960s. Viqar Ahmed and Rashid Amjad write:

> Growth rates in the agricultural sector were significantly high in both the first and second half of the sixties. During the first half, the years of high agricultural growth were between 1960–1 and 1962–3 and then between 1963–4 and 1964–5. There was a marked slowing down during 1965–6 and in 1966–7. There was a very slow recovery in food crops in 1966–7 although overall agricultural growth was positive from a very low base of the previous year. The first significant year of the so-called 'green revolution' is between 1966–7 and 1967–8 when agricultural growth increased by 11.7 per cent after which there were significant increases in the next two years especially between 1968–9 and 1969–70.[4]

The early 1970s also saw a second set of land reforms, which were much stricter in application, but did not produce the same results as the 1960s. Agriculture grew by a minimal 2.3 per cent between 1972 and 1977 – well below the growth rate in population. While political uncertainty in the country may have caused overall production to be below historical trends, three of the five years of the Bhutto government had floods and pest attacks in which crops were severely

damaged, resulting in low output. The government wanted to follow a pro-agricultural policy by devaluing the rupee, so as to increase agricultural exports, and by increasing the support prices of agricultural commodities. However, inclement weather ensured poor output.

The late 1970s and 1980s witnessed a return to an overall healthy growth rate in agriculture despite a few noticeably bad years. However, although the annual growth rates (Figure 5.7) seem to be somewhat higher than the growth in population, disturbing trends have emerged. Table 5.2 shows that, from a peak in the early 1980s, the index of agricultural production has fallen significantly, despite growth in output and production (Table 5.4), and nor has there been an appreciable increase in yield per hectare. The rest of this chapter will try to examine what the salient issues in agriculture are today. Perhaps the analysis will offer an insight into the falling trends and ways to reverse them.

Before we turn to specific issues, it is worth looking at one theory which examines how output and productivity in agriculture are affected over time. Rashid Faruqee of the World Bank, in a recent study, uses analysis developed by Derek Byerlee, who divides the growth in output due to technical change in countries like Pakistan into four stages. Rashid Faruqee describes these stages as follows:

> (1) the pre-Green Revolution phase, when growth is driven by (irrigated) area expansion, and productivity growth is modest, (2) the Green Revolution phase, when growth is driven by high yielding varieties with increased responsiveness to inputs, (3) the first post-Green Revolution phase, when growth is driven by intensification of input use, especially chemical fertilizer, and irrigation water (which facilitates multiple cropping), and (4) the second post-Green

Table 5.4
Production of major crops, 1950–1996 (000 tonnes)

Year[a]	Wheat	Rice	Sugar cane	Cotton (000 bales)
1950–1955	3,235.8	837.2	7,192.6	–
1955–1960	3,677.6	909.6	10,318.6	–
1960–1965	4,016.4	1,107.8	14,247.8	1,995.8
1965–1970	5,175.6	1,512.6	20,718.0	2,625.0
1970–1975	7,145.6	1,929.2	17,402.8	3,705.0
1975–1980	8,765.0	2,778.2	26,743.0	3.094.0
1980–1985	11,330.6	3,292.8	32,651.6	4,926.6
1985–1990	12,947.2	3,232.2	31,973.4	7,632.6
1990–1995	15,724.0	3,412.0	40,901.6	9,648.4
1995/6 (P)	17,570.0	3,966.0	45,230.0	10,587.0

(P) = Provisional.
[a]Averages, except for 1995/6.
Sources: For 1947–8: Ahmed, Viqar and Rashid Amjad, *The Management of Pakistan's Economy, 1947–82*, Oxford University Press, Karachi, 1984, p. 110; For other years: Government of Pakistan, *Pakistan Economic Survey, 1994–5*, Islamabad, 1995, p. 45.

Table 5.5
Yield of major agriculture crops, 1950–1996 (kg/hectare)

Years	Wheat	Rice	Sugar cane	Maize	Gram	Cotton
1950–1955	776.6	878.4	29,180	–	–	212.0
1955–1960	782.2	846.8	28,240	–	–	212.0
1960–1965	831.8	929.6	33,580	–	–	254.6
1965–1970	977.0	1,507.6	37,840	–	–	289.4
1971/2	1,189	1,554	36,100	1,114	529	364
1972/3	1,246	1,574	37,354	1,095	544	349
1973/4	1,248	1,624	37,014	1,212	551	357
1974/5	1,320	1,443	31,563	1,217	552	312
1975/6	1,422	1,531	36,496	1,294	563	277
1976/7	1,431	1,565	37,466	1,224	593	233
1977/8	1,361	1,553	36,590	1,251	558	312
1978/9	1,488	1,615	36,338	1,228	439	250
1979/80	1,568	1,581	38,298	1,248	278	350
1980/1	1,643	1,616	39,223	1,262	400	339
1981/2	1,565	1,736	38,627	1,259	326	338
1982/3	1,678	1,741	35,673	1,273	550	364
1983/4	1,482	1,671	38,224	1,270	588	223
1984/5	1,612	1,659	35,553	1,271	517	450
1985/6	1,881	1,567	35,713	1,256	567	515
1986/7	1,559	1,688	39,273	1,361	539	527
1987/8	1,734	1,651	39,227	1,320	453	572
1988/9	1,865	1,567	42,094	1,391	466	544
1989/90	1,825	1,528	41,562	1,367	543	560
1990/1	1,841	1,542	40,712	1,401	486	615
1991/2	1,990	1,546	43,376	1,414	514	769
1992/3	1,946	1,579	43,023	1,357	344	543
1993/4	1,893	1,826	46,143	1,380	393	488
1994/5	2,081	1,622	46,747	1,481	524	557
1995/6 (P)	2,100	1,834	46,943	1,457	585	601

Note: For the years 1950–5 to 1965–70, these are average yields over the period.
Sources: For 1950–5 and 1955–60: Ahmed, Viqar and Rashid Amjad, *The Management of Pakistan's Economy, 1947–82*, Oxford University Press, Karachi, 1984, p. 110. For other years: Government of Pakistan, *Agricultural Statistics of Pakistan, 1993–94*, Islamabad, 1995.

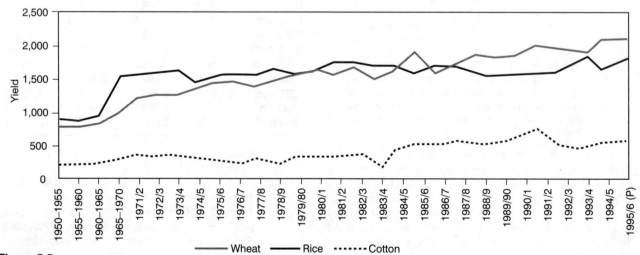

Figure 5.5
Yield per hectare of main crops, 1950–1996

Table 5.6
Area irrigated by different sources, 1950–1993
(m hectares)

Year[a]	Canals	Tubewells	Others	Total
1950–1955	7.77	0.03	1.81	9.42
1955–1960	8.64	0.09	1.51	10.25
1960–1965	9.03	0.39	1.63	11.05
1965–1970	8.92	1.02	2.31	12.25
1970–1975	9.24	2.27	1.22	12.72
1975–1980	10.29	2.82	1.08	14.18
1980–1985	11.42	3.07	0.96	15.53
1985–1990	11.48	3.88	0.82	16.18
1990–1993	12.05	4.29	0.56	16.90

[a]Averages.
Source: Government of Pakistan, *Pakistan Economic Survey, 1994–95*, Islamabad, 1995, p. 58.

Table 5.7
Per capita availability of main food items, 1986–1994

Year	Wheat	Rice	Meat	Milk
1986/7	112.11 (100)	20.22 (100)	12.15 (100)	56.86 (100)
1987/8	105.83 (94)	17.69 (87)	12.70 (104)	57.84 (102)
1988/9	127.38 (114)	20.13 (100)	13.10 (108.1)	58.89 (104)
1989/90	128.97 (115)	20.70 (102)	13.60 (112)	59.81 (105)
1990/1	115.18 (103)	16.36 (81)	13.90 (114)	60.93 (107)
1991/2	125.48 (112)	13.10 (65)	14.38 (118)	61.69 (108)
1992/3	127.90 (114)	15.70 (78)	15.48 (127)	62.63 (110)
1993/4	131.91 (118)	22.30 (110)	14.84 (122)	64.12 (113)

Source: Government of Pakistan, *Agricultural Statistics of Pakistan, 1993–94*, 1995.

Revolution phase, when input use begins to plateau, and the source of growth becomes increases in input efficiency, coupled with the ongoing release of new varieties. According to this framework, the Green Revolution shifted the production function upwards and raised the marginal responsiveness to inputs. Farmers did not operate initially on the production frontier. In the first post-Green Revolution phase, use of complementary inputs rose, and farmers improved allocative efficiency (equalizing marginal products and prices). In the second post-Green Revolution phase, farmers encountered diminishing returns to inputs, and moved towards the production frontier by raising their efficiency. Resource degradation is a form of technical regress which would shift the production function downward.[5]

This scenario seems to fit Pakistan, which is now, according to Rashid Faruqee, in a second post-Green

Revolution phase, where input efficiencies are seen to be the main sources of growth now that high yielding variety seeds have been extensively disseminated and use of irrigation and fertilizer is levelling off. While in the past, land expansion, multiple cropping, liberal availability of water, and a technical package were responsible for high growth in agriculture, for Rashid Faruqee, 'future growth must rely almost entirely on efficiency gains, the potential for which is considerable'.[6] For the World Bank, these efficiency gains arise through, amongst other mechanisms, output prices that are 'market determined', where the government does not 'distort prices', ends all forms of directed credit, and

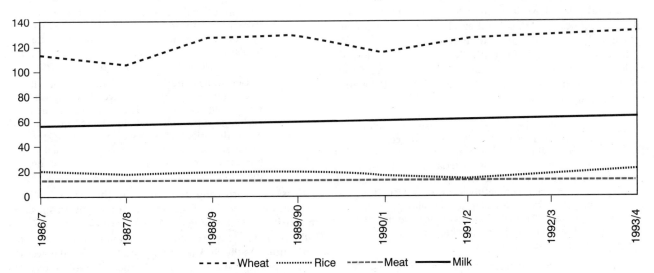

- - - - - Wheat   ········· Rice   - - - - -Meat   ——— Milk

Figure 5.6
Per capita availability of main food items, 1986–1994

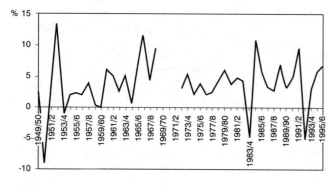

Figure 5.7
Average annual growth rates in agriculture, 1949–1996

introduces a large number of institutional reforms. See Appendix 5.1 for the World Bank's view on Pakistan's agriculture. Some other recommendations as part of the structural adjustment programme can be seen in Appendix 5.2 and Chapters 14 and 15. The next sections discuss some of these issues.

5.2 Agricultural Pricing Policy

A government can play a critical role in determining what, and how much, to produce through its pricing policy. Along with the right types of seeds, water, fertilizer and other inputs, as well as a package of technology and credit, the pricing policy of agricultural inputs and outputs can determine the direction of agricultural productivity and produce. Agricultural pricing policies can also impact significantly on income distribution, particularly of small farmers. They can also have a noticeable effect on industrial productivity, urban wage goods, exports, and the cost of living, determining the terms of trade between agriculture and other sectors. A good agricultural pricing policy can be defined as one where, *ceteris paribus*, price acts as an incentive to produce certain goods in required quantities (see Box 5.1). This, however, has not been the case in Pakistan, and agricultural prices have been used for various purposes by different regimes. Appendix 5.3 shows how support prices for agricultural commodities are determined.

The comprehensive report of the National Commission of Agriculture (NCA) in 1988 examined the issues around the agricultural pricing policy of the first two decades following 1947, and had this to say:

> In the beginning, Government's main concern in regulating agricultural prices was to keep the cost of food low for the urban industrial workers and provide cheap raw materials for domestic industries. The objective was to enhance international competitiveness of the infant industries by maximizing the so-called 'labour' advantage. The main features of the Government trade and pricing policies during the period up to the mid-sixties were as follows:
>
> a) Government fixed retail consumer prices of foodgrains at low levels which had the effect of

depressing market prices for producers. Studies show that during this period the domestic prices of foodgrains remained consistently below the international parity prices calculated at the equilibrium rate of exchange.

> b) Heavy export duties were levied on cotton which had the effect of reducing domestic prices of cotton for the benefit of the local textile industry.
>
> c) Monopoly procurement of wheat and rice was resorted to at fixed prices which were deliberately kept low in order to minimize subsidies to consumers. Producers often sold to merchants at lower than the Government prices in order to receive prompt cash payments.
>
> d) Inter-district and inter-province restrictions of movement were imposed with the result that producer prices were depressed in the surplus producing areas.
>
> e) Prices of vegetable ghee were controlled at an artificially low level which had a depressing effect on producer prices of seed cotton and oilseeds like rapeseed and mustard.
>
> f) Proceeds from the agricultural exports were converted at an overvalued fixed exchange rate. The implicit exchange tax on agricultural exports from 1960 to 1971 averaged 89 per cent. In contrast, the industrial sector benefited from the overvalued exchange rate which reduced the domestic cost of imported machinery and other inputs. When it came to the industrial exports, the exchange losses were offset by bonuses and subsidies. This heavy protection of the industrial sector at the cost of the agricultural sector failed to produce an efficient and viable industrial base for the economy. It rather became the cause of the dismal performance of the sector despite its highly privileged position.
>
> g) For nearly a decade after independence no systematic attempt for the development of agriculture was made. The first agricultural development programme in the country was launched in 1955.
>
> h) Barter deals were a common feature of Pakistan's international trade in which agricultural produce was exchanged for industrial machinery and inputs to the disadvantage of the agricultural producers.
>
> i) Government freely accepted the agricultural commodity imports at concessional prices which, when converted at the overvalued exchange rate, resulted in depressing the domestic prices. The adverse effect of the imported commodities was further intensified by budgeted subsidies given by the Government on their local sale prices.[7]

It is not surprising that, due to the above policies, agriculture suffered and was seen as a medium to subsidize industrial production and urban consumers – part of the pro-industrial strategy which was heavily biased against agriculture. As the NCA Report argues, 'the implied objectives of the pricing policies during the period 1960–5 were to provide low cost food to the urban consumers, to provide

BOX 5.1
The objectives of an agricultural pricing policy

The study by the National Commission of Agriculture argues as follows:

Pricing of agricultural inputs and outputs would be a major element of the dynamic agricultural policies necessary to achieve national targets of agricultural production. The Government should pursue an active price support policy seeking to consolidate the gains in four major commodities achieved in the last few years, making the policy fully effective for minor crops including oilseeds and extending the policy to cover more products as found necessary. The pricing of inputs and outputs should be closely coordinated keeping in view the following objectives:

i) Carefully devised price signals can promote a balanced increase in production of agricultural products so as to fulfil domestic consumption requirements; increase earnings of foreign exchange through exports of products like cotton, rice and horticultural products, and save foreign exchange expenditure by reducing dependence on imports of agricultural products, especially edible oils, milk and sugar.

ii) Gradually rising but stable prices can create a suitable economic and psychological framework for positive response from producers to production incentives and move to the desired cropping patterns.

iii) The Price Policy should help to achieve and maintain equitable terms of trade for agriculture and support the incomes of farmers.

iv) It should help maintain stable food prices for consumers.

v) It should keep domestic prices of export commodities and potential exports largely in line with the international prices to maintain competitiveness of agricultural commodities and minimize subsidies.

vi) It should encourage larger investment in agriculture, especially in production of the products in which the national targets call for major increases in production.

vii) It should encourage increase in agricultural productivity and reductions in production costs by promoting use of better technologies and other non-price measures.

Source: Government of Pakistan, Ministry of Food and Agriculture, *The Report of the National Commission on Agriculture*, Islamabad, 1988, pp. 490–1.

Viqar Ahmed and Rashid Amjad present a more holistic view of agricultural prices. They write:

The determination of the prices of agricultural crops by the government, along with other administrative and economic controls on their processing, distribution, and export, amount to the suppression of the market mechanism. But markets in Pakistan, as in other developing countries, are hardly perfect. Imperfections in the form of under-developed transport and communication facilities, a high degree of heterogeneity among both the buyers and the sellers, and the division of the market into small isolated sub-markets, make the market system incapable of generating a substantial degree of competition. The farmers belong to a highly differentiated structure of interests in land, ranging from sharecroppers and tenants to owner-cultivators and still further to capitalist farmers and absentee landlords. Most farmers have little contact with the market either because they are subsistence owners-cultivators without a marketable surplus or because they are sharecroppers whose surplus is taken away by a non-cultivating class.

State intervention under these circumstances is essential in order to create a mutually accommodating price-structure. This could allocate land and other resources among competing crops and also reconcile prices of agricultural output with the overall cost structure within agriculture. Inter-sectoral terms of trade between agriculture and other sectors also need to be maintained at levels which would eliminate causes of social frictions and distortions in development priorities.

It is quite obvious that in the foreseeable future the agricultural price policy will have to be framed in such a way so as to achieve conflicting objectives like incentives for the farmers, stability of the urban cost of living, easy domestic availability of food grain and industrial raw materials, and adequate exportable surplus. In addition, small cultivators, including subsistence farmers, have to be given access to new inputs and technology and also to the benefits of the subsidy programmes so that these large public outlays do not become the cause of widening social disparities ...

... What is required in this situation is to look beyond subsidies as a policy instrument, and to pay serious attention to such matters as improving the overall supply position of the inputs, particularly such divisible inputs as seeds, fertilizers, and pesticides, and to ensure their timely availability. Attention should also be paid to the extension of rural outlets, the encouragement of multiple market channels, and the improvement of the farmers' ability to make efficient use of the inputs. As the supply position improves, it would be easier to reduce the subsidy level and to allow prices to rise gradually. If the farmer has access to institutional credit and is able to increase his net returns, an increase in input prices may not inhibit his demand for them.

There is also a need to gradually raise output prices so that resources now tied to consumer subsidies are released for other purposes on the one hand and, on the other, the farmer can confidently look forward to larger cash flows and can plan his investments for a longer period than one or two crop seasons. It is imperative that the price signals sent to the farming community should be unambiguous and have a certain amount of continuity.

Finally, an agricultural price policy by itself cannot necessarily serve as a grand design for major institutional or technological changes. It can serve limited goals and its success will depend upon it being supplemented by coordinated efforts in other related areas. It can heighten the effectiveness of various other tools of economic policy rather than become a substitute for them. In other words, it can function as a 'fine tuner' and not as a 'prime move'.

Source: Ahmed, Viqar, and Rashid Amjad, *The Management of Pakistan's Economy, 1947–82*, Oxford University Press, Karachi, 1984, pp. 154–5.

cheap raw materials for the domestic agriculture-based industries, to keep wages of industrial workers low by supplying cheap food; and to transfer resources from agriculture to the urban sector for investment in industries and other non-farm activities'.[8] Clearly, these policies were not focused on improving and expanding agricultural output.

For some strange reason, it was assumed that farmers would not be price sensitive and would produce at their most efficient and best output regardless of the prices received by them. Policy makers assumed that 'low prices resulting from compulsory government procurement or high export duties on agricultural products would not affect the output level'.[9] However, the dismal conditions in agriculture prior to the Green Revolution forced the government to reconsider its approach to the agricultural sector, and along with the technical package, new pricing policies were also introduced so as to encourage agricultural output. Viqar Ahmed and Rashid Amjad argue that 'a recognition of the role of prices in agricultural development did provide much needed incentives to the growers, and may have partly contributed to the high growth rates in the late sixties'.[10]

The first steps that the government took in this direction to encourage agricultural production was to begin to subsidize inputs, and not to raise the support or procurement price of output. During the 1960s and 1970s an extensive structure of agricultural input subsidies was evolved which covered fertilizers, seeds, plant protection, tubewells, and agricultural machinery. Viqar Ahmed and Rashid Amjad believe that

> the objective of subsidizing inputs was to provide greater production incentives and to encourage the use of superior technology. It has been argued that while high output prices may or may not lead to greater investment in better technology, and may be diverted to higher consumption, subsidization of inputs, which comprises the new technology, would ensure its rapid adoption.[11]

The main beneficiaries of the subsidized inputs were those who most used these inputs, i.e. large farmers. As we saw in Chapter 3, the HYV technology and package were heavily biased towards the larger farmers. Hence they were the main beneficiaries, rather than the small and medium farmers who, due to numerous constraints did not make much use of modern inputs as well as water, credit, and agricultural extension services. For these reasons, some observers felt a need to 'look beyond subsidies as a policy instrument, and to pay serious attention to such matters as improving the overall supply position of the inputs ... such as seeds, fertilizers and pesticides and to ensure their timely availability'.[12] It was as late as 1981, when the Agricultural Prices Commission was established, that there was greater realization of the relevance of agricultural output prices.

The government introduced the concept of a minimum price support programme, which shielded the farmers from severe fluctuations in international prices and ensured a minimum return to producers. In the past, producers have received market prices well above the support price. The support price also acts as an incentive to produce more, as it is related to higher than average productivity. The National Commission on Agriculture (NCA) argues that 'the main role of the support prices is to protect the producers from a drop in the producer prices below the minimum level at which production remains profitable for good producers'.[13]

A theme that will recur in this book is the major changes that have taken place in Pakistan since 1988 when the government made the first of its three major agreements with the International Monetary Fund (IMF) and the World Bank. Pakistan has been actively following a Structural Adjustment Programme (SAP) since 1988 under agreements with both these organizations. While an entire section of this book (Part IV) has been set aside for this theme, in the present chapter we will only examine some of the issues that relate the Structural Adjustment Programme to agricultural issues, such as pricing policy and taxation (see Appendix 5.2 for a more detailed outline of the Structural Adjustment Programme).

In its 1988 report, which became the precursor to the actual Structural Adjustment Programme agreements (see Chapters 13–15), the World Bank's opinions regarding subsidies to the agricultural sector were expressed clearly. The World Bank stated that, 'fertilizer subsidies should be eliminated in line with government plans, wheat subsidies reduced further, and edible oil and sugar subsidies kept from reappearing'[14] (see Box 5.2 for an analysis of the problems with the wheat and fertilizer subsidies). In its evaluation of the first major Structural Adjustment Programme 1988–91, the World Bank report argued as follows:

> Over the adjustment period, Government has made progress in reducing price distortions by adjusting administered prices and in some cases liberalizing the markets in question. Output prices of agricultural commodities have generally been brought closer to farmgate export/import parity levels, thus reducing the implicit tax on the agriculture sector. However, movement in this area has been limited and the current situation still induces a misallocation of resources in the agricultural sector. For example, farm prices for rice remain below international prices, creating disincentives to grow a crop where Pakistan has a strong comparative advantage. The same applies to wheat where domestic prices remain below import parity. Moreover, the Government did not adjust the issue price in FY92 [1991/2] despite a sharp increase in the import price. As a result, the consumer price subsidy increased sharply, reversing the progress achieved in earlier years. On the other hand, Pakistan has no comparative advantage in sugarcane. An adjustment of sugarcane support prices would induce farmers to increase yields or to shift to cotton, rice or wheat production. With regard to agricultural inputs, subsidies on pesticides, seeds and agricultural machinery have been eliminated. During the last three years, formal control over the price of nitrogenous fertilizer (urea) has been lifted and prices of phosphatic and potash fertilizers have been adjusted upwards so as to bring them closer to the (declining) international prices.[15]

Hence, on the advice of the World Bank and the International

BOX 5.2

How the wheat and fertilizer subsidies work

The World Bank has been a strong and consistent supporter of the free market and opponent of government intervention. It has advocated the removal of subsidies in almost all cases. About Pakistan it writes:

The wheat subsidy in Pakistan, which dates back to independence in 1947, increased sharply in the 1980s. At its height (FY86), it reached Rs3.8 billion (4.2% of current revenue), compared to just over Rs1 billion (2.1%) in FY81. Following changes in the subsidy system in April 1987, the FY88 budget allocated about Rs3 billion for it, although the actual outcome may be higher.

Under the current system the Government continues to procure wheat at a fixed price (presently Rs2.15 per kg) and stands ready to sell at the same price to private mills and other intermediaries as much as they require. The distribution cost and other incidentals, which are met from the government budget, currently result in a subsidy of Rs0.60 per kg wheat compared to Rs0.80 per kg prior to de-rationing, but could increase depending on the wheat harvest and the volume of procurement by the Government. The Bank recommends a phase out of this general subsidy within five years, and the substitution of a wheat subsidy limited to the needy. The present system is available to rich and poor alike, and benefits the urban population more than rural population. Identifying the eligible population for a more targeted subsidy requires more administrative work. It could be achieved through specifically targeted compensatory programs for the poor and nutritionally vulnerable groups, such as food stamps; food distribution via health centers, clinics, schools and other welfare centers; and food-for-work schemes. At the same time, Government intervention in the wheat trade would be reduced. It would then regulate the market mainly through periodic interventions, via regulation of a strategic stock, and allow the private sector to perform the major market functions.

The fertilizer subsidy has been an important element in the Government's policy to promote agricultural production by providing the farmer with low-cost imports. It has fluctuated between Rs1.5 billion and Rs2.5 billion a year since FY81, depending on the volume and prices of fertilizer imports, domestic production, and the Government's fertilizer price adjustments, which have usually fallen short of the increases in world fertilizer prices. In FY87, the decline in world fertilizer prices and deregulation of nitrogenous fertilizer prices in May 1986 helped reduce the subsidy to Rs2 billion. The FY88 estimate is Rs1.6 billion for phosphate and potash fertilizer subsidies, which are almost entirely imported.

The Government has decided to phase out the current fertilizer subsidies through equal annual reductions of the current subsidy rate over a period of four years for phosphate (the principal type) and eight years for potash fertilizers. This is to be attained through annual price adjustments in line with international price trends; cost reduction measures in procurement, marketing and distribution; and possible substitution of low cost potash fertilizer imports. This program will be supported by emphasizing farm-level adaptive research and extension services to raise the efficiency of fertilizer use. This phase-out, which the Bank endorses, is desirable for more than budgetary reasons. The fertilizer subsidy has now served its objective of educating the farmer in its use and benefits. The subsidy benefits particularly the large farmers since they have greater access to the complementary inputs. In addition, the Government's policy of deregulating agricultural output prices, combined with the setting of floor procurement prices at or above world prices, should provide appropriate incentives to agriculture without the fertilizer subsidy.

Source: World Bank, *Pakistan: Growth Through Adjustment*, Report No. 7118-PAK, 1988.

Monetary Fund, under the terms of the Structural Adjustment Programme, many subsidies were eliminated and domestic prices were freed to come at par with international prices.

5.3 Rural Financial Markets and Agricultural Credit[16]

There have been five major studies and surveys conducted by different research institutes and by the State Bank of Pakistan which examine the nature and sources of rural credit. The main conclusions from these surveys are as follows:

 i) although there is a significant increase in the borrowing from formal sources in 1985 onwards when mark-up free loans were made available to farmers, these studies suggest that the principal source of farm credit continues to be informal sources, especially for small farmers. The 1985 survey shows that 68% of the credit to agriculture is provided by non-institutional sources while the 1972–73 survey had shown that 90% of borrowing by farm households was from non-institutional sources. [Another study] demonstrate[s] from the 1985 credit survey that 85% of the small farmers obtain their loan from non-institutional sources compared to 40% in the large farmers category;

 ii) a significant proportion of loans (over 30 per cent) disbursed by institutional sources are either proxy loans or roll over funds.[17]

A recent (1995) World Bank study examining the extent

and degree of rural finance in Pakistan has reached the following conclusions:

1. Credit does play an important role in agricultural productivity and output.

2. Rural credit reaches few rural households, and institutional sources provide credit to only a small proportion of rural households. Only 32 per cent of all rural households take loans, and of these a mere 10 per cent borrow from institutional sources. The main sources of institutional credit are: Agricultural Development Bank of Pakistan (ADBP) 76 per cent, commercial banks 17 per cent, and co-operative societies 6 per cent. Ninety per cent of the households that take loans do so from informal sources, mainly friends and relatives (67 per cent) and landlords (11 per cent). Not surprisingly, non-institutional or informal sources of credit dominate the rural sector.

3. Both sources of credit tend to be short term, but serve different needs. For example, 94 per cent of institutional or formal credit is meant for production and investment, while most (47 per cent) non-institutional credit is used for consumption purposes.

4. Not surprisingly, there is an inverse correlation between wealth and access to sources of credit. Richer households in the rural areas have better access to institutional sources, which are also cheaper, while poor households depend primarily on more expensive, non-institutional credit (see Table 5.8).

5. The access by poorer households to institutional sources of credit is constrained by complex procedures, and informal sources are much simpler and more flexible, often requiring little collateral. As much as 76 per cent of formal institutional credit was against the security of landed property and 21 per cent against personal surety. For informal sources of credit, as much as 96 per cent of loans were advanced on personal surety. This may help explain why there is differentiation between institutional/non-institutional credit based on size of farm, and by ownership pattern. One would expect smaller farmers to access informal sources of loans more easily and frequently than larger farms, which would have better access to institutional sources. Moreover, owners would take out greater loans than tenants from either source (see Table 5.9).[18]

5.3.1 Informal Sources of Credit

A study in the Punjab has shown that only 15 per cent of the small farmers had access to institutional credit, while a 1986 study in Sindh suggested that only 8 per cent of farmers had this source of credit available.[19] There were also numerous problems related to the availability of this meagre amount of credit. The need for credit at a particular time, like other inputs, can have a critical influence on whether a crop will succeed or fail. Studies have found that a disproportionate number of farmers (69 per cent in one study)[20] were given credit well after the deadlines had expired.

Although Table 5.10 shows the quantum jumps made in the amount of credit available to farmers through institutional sources, there is a very noticeable preference amongst users for credit from non-institutional or informal sources. The reasons given for this include: easier access; absence of cumbersome procedures; availability as and when required; the availability of credit even for consumption purposes or emergency loans, unlike official sources which have rather restricted uses of credit; the possibility of a deferred repayment of debt if crops fail; and often the availability of credit through informal sources without the need for any collateral.

A major complaint heard from farmers pertains to the high transaction costs that borrowers are forced to pay in order to acquire a loan. Transaction costs are said to comprise various components, including 'application fees, form filling fees, loan registration fees, borrower's travelling expenses, costs of entertaining people who assist the farmer in getting the loan,

Table 5.8
Sources of loans by asset quintile

Asset quintiles	Institutional		Non-institutional			
	Percentage credit	No. of loans	% credit from friends and relatives	No. of loans	% credit from other informal sources	No. of loans
Lowest	1.05	3	31.43	201	67.51	585
Second	4.83	13	49.53	249	45.63	396
Third	12.60	23	48.33	244	39.07	308
Fourth	29.62	52	35.44	174	34.95	285
Highest	58.36	116	20.10	139	21.54	263
All households	32.16	207	32.39	1,007	35.45	1,837

Source: World Bank, *Pakistan: Rural Finance for Growth and Poverty Alleviation*, Washington, 1995, p. 9.

Table 5.9
Distribution of institutional loans as a percentage of all loans by categories and size of farm, 1973 and 1985

Size (acres)	Owner		Owner-cum-tenant		Tenant		All cultivators	
	1973	1985	1973	1985	1973	1985	1973	1985
0–5	1.80	8.83	1.50	1.90	0.43	1.36	1.48	7.45
5–15	12.52	33.10	2.19	16.83	3.38	3.17	6.88	21.81
15–25	12.25	45.96	2.91	24.73	1.22	5.76	6.40	33.63
25–50	20.62	62.05	6.99	49.83	0.81	5.68	13.38	51.82
Over 50	31.15	65.18	24.92	57.20	21.02	16.24	29.00	61.31
All sizes	14.71	37.47	6.10	33.57	3.02	4.01	9.80	13.16

Source: World Bank, *Pakistan*: *Rural Finance for Growth and Poverty Alleviation*, Washington, 1995, p. 61.

and the opportunity cost of the borrower's time in negotiating the loan'.[21] In comparison, such non-mark-up costs are almost negligible when credit is borrowed from informal sources. Since many farmers feel that the difference in the total cost of borrowing from both sources is almost negligible, farmers prefer to acquire credit from informal, non-institutional, sources.

Official government figures in the 1970s revealed that as much as 80 per cent of rural credit was supplied by informal leaders, but with the huge increase in formal credit, the expansion of bank services and greater monetization, there was a fall in this proportion to about 55 per cent by the early 1980s.[22] Box 5.3 contains the arguments for and against informal loan markets.

There is a belief that moneylenders in the informal market charge 'usurious' rates of return, but it has been observed in Pakistan that they are a disappearing breed; the main actors in informal rural financial markets are now the commission agents or *arhtis*. One needs to examine how the rate of return is determined in informal lending and to what extent this rate differs from the formal sector. Amongst the mechanisms that determine this return is the

> most obvious and visible mechanism [which] is the statutorily fixed commission on the marketed value of output. However, a large component of the return may consist of less visible mechanisms like manipulation of output purchase and input supply prices, biases in weighing of output, charging of fictitious costs, payments in installments, etc. The issue is the extent to which reliance is placed on market imperfections and extortionary mechanisms to charge effectively high rates of return from borrowers.[23]

As Viqar Ahmed and Rashid Amjad argue, 'the very fact that a large number of farmers prefer to borrow from informal sources in spite of the high cost shows that the demand for agricultural credit is highly service elastic, a significant factor which is overlooked'.[24]

Table 5.10
Agricultural credit disbursed in Pakistan by agencies, 1955–1995 (Rs m)

Year[a]	ADBP	Taccavi	Co-operatives	Commercial banks	Total[b]
1955–1960	7.4	12.3	32.0	–	51.6
1960–1965	40.3	15.9	72.1	–	128.3
1965–1970	89.6	11.9	59.1	–	160.7
1970–1975	230.4	21.8	72.5	297.7	503.5
1975–1980	546.0	13.9	241.8	1,192.7	1,994.3
1980–1985	2,446.8	8.5	1,332.4	2,981.2	6,768.7
1985–1990	7,422.5	17.5	2,221.9	4,899.2	14,566.1
1990–1995	8,375.4	54.5	2,788.1	3,827.1	15,023.2

[a]Averages.
[b]These may not add up due to rounding.
Source: Government of Pakistan, *Pakistan Economic Survey, 1994–95*, Islamabad, 1995, p. 54.

5.3.2 Formal Sources of Credit

Formal rural financial institutions are of different types and include government departments and corporations, co-operatives, commercial banks, and specific agriculture-related development banks (see Figure 5.8 for the changes in sources of formal credit in agriculture). Specialized financial institutions in the rural areas, such as the Agricultural Deveopment Bank of Pakistan (ADBP) may be involved in the disbursement of medium- and long-term credit.

In a study conducted by IFPRI[25] it was observed that, in the case of formal sources, the success of a scheme requires proper financial intermediation to disburse credit of the right kind at the right time, along with specialized and decentralized management structures. The study found that 'supervised credit and development of access to inputs and marketing facilities have been the major responses to tackle the problem of efficient targeting, disbursement and recovery of credit'.[26] In the case of Pakistan it has been seen that the 'development of supervised credit operations by commercial banks has been constrained by the need to limit costs of lending'.[27] In the study conducted by the Applied Economics Research Centre based on field work in the different areas of Pakistan, four major issues concerning formal rural financial institutions were found to be critical. These were as follows:

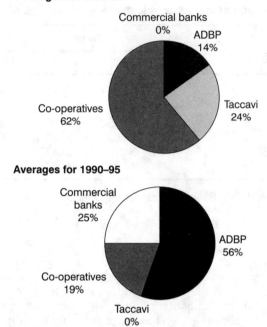

Averages for 1955–60

Commercial banks 0%
ADBP 14%
Taccavi 24%
Co-operatives 62%

Averages for 1990–95

Commercial banks 25%
ADBP 56%
Taccavi 0%
Co-operatives 19%

Figure 5.8
Agricultural credit disbursed in Pakistan by formal institutions, 1955–1995 (%)

BOX 5.3

Are informal financial markets always exploitative?

Different views exist about the nature of informal financial markets. Some are summarized here:

i) According to one view, informal lending is inherently 'exploitative' in character, with 'usurious' rates of return being charged from small farmers who find themselves in a state of perpetual indebtedness. In this view the informal credit market is fragmented, imperfect and characterized by local monopolies. Consequently, rates of return are high, ranging from 30% to 50%. Various mechanisms exist for extracting a high rate of return on loans which include lower prices for output marketed to the lender (commission agent), higher prices for inputs, biased weighing of output, charging of fictitious costs etc. Consistent with this view of informal lending is the policy prescription that institutional finance is essential to get the small farmer out of the clutches of these exploitative arrangements.

ii) Various authors have also highlighted the constraints of informal lending which have inhibited its growth. They have indicated that resources and activities of informal lenders are inadequate and ill-suited for modernization. This is largely due to their inability to lend for long enough periods for farmers to acquire productive assets. Hence, the growth of informal lenders has been slow.

Another failure has been the lack of mobilization of financial deposits because deposit facilities are inadequate, unsafe, untrustworthy or less remunerative.

iii) The other sharply contrasting view of informal lenders was first articulated by Michael Lipton. He argued that there should be greater reliance on informal sources which do indeed get to poor farmers, albeit at high rates of return. As opposed to this, concessionary institutional finance is largely siphoned off by large farmers. Also, informal lending has a number of inherent advantages. It is potentially more efficient, decentralized and accessible, loans can be obtained on time and scope exists for receiving consumption loans for financing emergency needs along with production loans. It has been shown that the difference between costs of borrowing from formal and informal sources is greatly diminished if transaction costs are included ... In Bangladesh effective costs [mark-up + borrower transaction costs] of small loans from informal sources are, in fact, lower than those from financial institutions. If informal lending is seen as performing a useful function, especially for small farmers, in a competitive environment then the policy stance would have to change towards greater integration of the rural financial markets with more role being assigned to informal lending.

Source: State Bank of Pakistan, *Rural Financial Markets Study: Phase 1*, Karachi, 1994, pp. 5.1–5.2.

a) *Targeting of Credit:* A major problem with lending practices by branches is the substantial diversion of credit away from the intended beneficiaries (small farmers). In particular, a high proportion of proxy loaning exists in the case of personal sureties type of collateral. An earlier study has also highlighted this problem. Given this misallocation, there may be a stronger case for bringing rates of return on agricultural loans closer to market rates in order to remove incentives for arbitrage by large landowners and the resulting adverse consequences on equity.

b) *Problems of Regulatory Policies:* The presence of mandatory targets for agricultural lending and the linkage between establishment of urban and rural branches has greatly reduced the emphasis on profitability of rural banking. This has increased the orientation towards loan disbursement and permitted sub-optimal location of branches. However, it appears that, in the face of high default rates, commercial banks are beginning to opt for a policy of paying penalties rather than achieve lending targets.

c) *Diversification of Lending Instruments:* Most banks have experimented with new types of lending instruments, including Islamic modes of financing like *musharaka*, mark up, hire purchase, buy back finance, etc. Mark up free loans have also been disbursed to small farmers. This has probably had a positive impact on the demand for credit as varying preferences of borrowers have been more effectively catered for. However, the mark up system may have created a greater incentive for default, as the penalty in the event of non-repayment of a loan is linked only to the amount of outstanding principal.

d) *Lack of Decentralization:* High rates of default appear to have created a centralization tendency in terms of loaning powers. Increasingly, branch managers and mobile credit officers (MCO) of commercial banks are being required to refer loan applications, of even relatively small amounts, to zonal offices for approval. This is affecting the speedy and timely disbursement of loans. In addition, growing risk aversion on the part of RFIs has led to institution of more elaborate documentation requirements. This has increased borrower transaction costs and contributed to delays.[28]

Co-operatives

In the area which is Pakistan today, co-operative societies began giving loans to associations on easy terms in 1904. The main reason for the growth and promotion of the co-operative societies by the government was an attempt to free farmers from the clutches of moneylenders. In 1990 there were 60,562 co-operative societies of all types, with 3.3 million members in the country. Agricultural credit societies constitute 65 per cent of the total, and have about 40 per cent of the membership. Of these, 93 per cent of the societies are in the Punjab, which has 92 per cent of the working capital and 95 per cent of the membership.

While co-operatives are provincial institutions, the Federal Bank for Co-operatives (FBC) is the principal funding institution and provides loans to co-operative societies via the provincial co-operative banks, which then distribute these loans. All five provincial co-operative banks (the four provinces and Azad Jammu and Kashmir) work out their credit requirements for production, development, and project loans, based on the expected demands of their affiliated co-operative societies. Once this happens, before June each year, the FBC is asked to examine these requests, which it does. The FBC looks at the disbursement and utilization of the previous year and then forwards the relevant requests to the State Bank of Pakistan, which distributes the loans after the National Credit Consultative Council has approved them.

The State Bank of Pakistan gives the FBC the funds and imposes a service charge of 0.5 per cent, which the FBC passes on to the provincial banks at a rate of 1.5 per cent. These provincial co-operative banks give loans to their societies at 14 per cent for short-term loans and 15 per cent for medium-term loans. Small farmers are given a special discount and receive the loans at 9.5 per cent. Since the concept of the 'rate of interest' is considered to be un-Islamic, the interest charged is not an annualized rate, but a fixed, one-time amount, payable on the principal.

Although co-operative societies were originally started to establish a collective means of production, marketing, saving, and working together on other farm and off-farm activities, in Pakistan today they operate only as a mechanism for providing loans to co-operative societies, and nothing more. The FBC has not made any loans in Baluchistan since 1980, or in Sindh since 1985, because these provinces have been constant defaulters and have not been able to collect any outstanding loans. Only Punjab's provincial co-operative bank has been getting new loans as it has been able to repay previous loans.

Since the provincial banks have not made any new loans, no new societies have been registered in the other provinces (hence the large share of the Punjab in the overall numbers). However, even in the Punjab, the loans by the provincial co-operative banks have been made available only to existing societies, and no new societies have been registered since 1992. In Sindh, no new agricultural co-operative society has been registered since 1990.

Five studies that have looked at the role of the co-operative movement in the agricultural sector agree that a very high percentage (opinions vary between 60 and 95 per cent) of all agricultural co-operative societies are bogus, fictitious, one-man 'paper' societies. These have usually been formed by influentials in the area, who bring in their relatives and farm workers. Although all the members of a co-operative are responsible for the loans advanced, the influential often absconds with the money advanced. It would be fair to say that the co-operative movement in Pakistan is an utter failure.

The Extent of Debt

A study in the early 1960s found that 45 per cent of the cultivators in Pakistan were in debt and received an average

Table 5.11
Agricultural credit advanced by ADBP, 1980–1994 (Rs m)

Year	Pakistan	Punjab	Sindh	NWFP	Baluchistan
1980/1	1,058.97 (100)	741.21 (100)	257.05 (100)	45.21 (100)	15.50 (100)
1985/6	5,217.11 (493)	3,169.74 (428)	1,422.10 (553)	468.89 (1,037)	156.41 (1,009)
1990/1	8,218.39 (776)	5,624.59 (759)	1,679.00 (653)	722.59 (1,598)	490.80 (3,166)
1993/4	8,877.91 (838)	6,282.40 (848)	1,964.60 (764)	376.25 (832)	254.60 (1,643)

Source: Government of Pakistan, *Agricultural Statistics of Pakistan, 1993–94,* Islamabad, 1995.

Table 5.12
Agricultural credit advanced by commercial banks, by size of holding, 1980–1994 (Rs m)

Year	Total		Up to 12.5 acres		12.5–50 acres		Over 50 acres	
	Amount	%	Amount	%	Amount	%	Amount	%
Pakistan								
1980/1	1,661.30 (100)	(100)	929.20 (100)	(55.90)	500.57	(30.10)	231.50 (100)	(24.90)
1985/6	4,913.47 (296)	(100)	3,923.81 (422)	(79.90)	822.70	(16.70)	167.00 (72)	(4.30)
1990/1	4,172.38 (251)	(100)	2,268.20 (244)	(54.40)	803.10 (160)	(19.20)	284.80 (123)	(12.60)
1993/4	3,920.70 (236)	(100)	2,351.20 (253)	(60.00)	1,219.10 (244)	(31.10)	350.40 (151)	(14.90)
Punjab								
1980/1	779.70		440.12		237.10		102.50	
1985/6	2,213.08		1,881.10		271.80		60.10	
1990/1	1,690.50		1,309.00		282.30		99.20	
1993/4	2,617.90		1,677.30		704.80		235.80	
Sindh								
1980/1	561.61		331.78		155.91		73.92	
1985/6	2,035.77		1,466.69		482.60		86.50	
1990/1	1,420.21		734.10		505.80		180.80	
1993/4	1,178.10		581.30		501.00		95.80	
NWFP								
1980/1	294.38		139.16		102.45		52.77	
1985/6	501.11		465.38		32.60		3.20	
1990/1	156.60		153.30		3.30		0.00	
1993/4	94.10		84.50		9.60		0.00	
Baluchistan								
1980/1	25.61		18.14		5.11		2.36	
1985/6	163.51		110.64		35.70		17.20	
1990/1	88.30		71.80		11.70		4.80	
1993/4	30.70		8.00		3.80		18.90	

Source: Government of Pakistan, *Agricultural Statistics of Pakistan, 1993–94,* Islamabad, 1995.

annual cash loan of Rs598. The loans were utilized mostly for household expenditure (45 per cent) and livestock (36 per cent). More productive activities, such as land development and storage facilities, received a very small share.[29] The 1972 Pakistan Census of Agriculture quoted a figure of 43 per cent for the total proportion of agricultural households that were in debt. While the distribution of households in debt by size of holding showed little variation, the households with 150 acres or more were relatively more indebted: 50 per cent of households in this category were in debt compared with around 43 per cent for all other households. Of the three categories, owner households, owner-cum-tenant households, and tenant households, the last named were the most indebted, while owner households were the least indebted: only 39 per cent of all owner households were in debt, while 49 per cent of tenant households were in debt. In all three categories, households above 150 acres were more indebted than smaller households.[30]

It is very interesting to observe that there was a major change by the time of the 1980 Census of Agriculture. Only 21 per cent of farm households (less than half the proportion in 1972) were in debt. Nevertheless, the pattern regarding type of household and size of landholding was similar to that for 1972. An interesting figure provided in the 1980 Census concerned the distribution of debt in terms of institutional and non-institutional (informal) sources, which stood at 32 per cent and 68 per cent, respectively. For smaller households, not surprisingly, informal sources provided much more credit than formal sources: 90 per cent of the credit for households under 5 acres came from informal sources. Compared to this, 60 per cent of the credit for households above 50 acres came from institutional sources. Owner households had 38 per cent of their credit supplied by institutional sources, while tenant households had only 8 per cent supplied from this source.[31] Clearly, access to agricultural credit from formal or informal sources was divided by type of household and by ownership patterns, with smaller households (in area) and tenant farms making greater use of informal sources, and large farms and owner-farms using formal institutional sources.

Bank Credit to Agriculture

ADBP is the largest source of institutionalized credit in the agriculture sector, on average providing more than 55 per cent of total credit between 1990 and 1995 (Table 5.10). Table 5.11 shows the huge jump in ADBP's loans since 1980/1, growing by over 800 per cent by 1993/4. Interestingly, the NWFP and Baluchistan have seen the largest growths, but still receive a minute share (7.1 per cent jointly in 1993/4). Most of the advances by the ADBP are for a long-term duration and a large percentage of the loans are used for the purchase of tractors (see Box 5.4 for different types of loan).

Commercial banks did not make any loans to agriculture prior to 1972 when they were nationalized, and at best provided loans for trade in agricultural products. In the 1990–5 period they constituted about 25 per cent of loans in the formal sector (Table 5.10). Table 5.12 shows recent trends in agricultural credit advanced by commercial banks by size of holding.

5.4   Mechanization

When we talk about mechanization, it is essentially tractorization that we have in mind, and other implements are often of a secondary nature. The reason for this synonymity is the huge impact of tractorization on output, employment, the nature of social relations of production, and so on. In our analysis of the Green Revolution we saw how the HYV package was supplemented by tractorization and how these tractors impacted on the agricultural process, changing agricultural production for ever. In this section we will discuss the effects and issues around tractorization/mechanization, and add some discussion of the use of tubewells and how this process of mechanization in the area of irrigation has affected agriculture over the years.

BOX 5.4
Different types of loan

The distinction between different types of loans of variable duration is important. Some salient features are as follows:

Rural credit is usually classified as short-term (up to one year), medium-term (one to five years), and long-term (exceeding five years). Short-term loans are needed for meeting annual production costs (for example, seeds, pesticides, fertilizers), and for the replacement of a portion of the farmer's fixed capital (for example bullocks, sheds, implements, and the cost of consumption needs up to harvesting). Thus these loans can be treated as part of the working capital requirements. Medium-term loans are needed for the purchase of livestock, implements, the construction/improvement of water courses, and for equipment not expected to last more than five years.

Long-term loans are needed for improvements of a more lasting character like the sinking of wells and tubewells, the purchase of additional land, or for repayment of old debts.

Loans can also be categorized into productive loans and unproductive loans. According to the conventional definition, a productive loan is a loan which is utilized in such a way that it leads directly to an increase in the income of the farmer and adds to his capacity to repay. These loans may finance current production, i.e. meeting current cultivation costs, and future development, i.e. increasing future returns. Unproductive loans are those which do not directly increase the efficiency of cultivation or the farmers' income. But ... it is sometimes difficult to separate productive loans from unproductive loans.

Source: Ahmed, Viqar and Rashid Amjad, *The Management of Pakistan's Economy, 1947–82*, Oxford University Press, Karachi, 1984, pp. 159–60.

The importance of mechanization can be judged by the attitude of the various governments of Pakistan in the early years. The Report of the National Commission on Agriculture evaluates the attitude of the government in the early years as follows:

> Mechanization in Pakistan had a late start and slow initial progress because of the Government policy of restricting mechanization based on the apprehension that it would displace farm labour and cause the problem of unemployment. Even the international agencies like the FAO and the World Bank advocated caution and recommended that small farmers should not be encouraged to purchase tractors. *In retrospect, it is now clear that it was a misguided concern.* Mechanization, to the extent it has taken place, has resulted in increased farm incomes and manpower productivity and the employment effect has, on the whole, been positive. Total employment in agriculture increased from 9.8 million in 1965 to 14.6 million in 1986. The value added per farm worker also went up from Rs946 in 1960 to Rs1357 in 1985 (constant 1959–60 prices). However, the most important development *was the generation of increased farm related off-farm employment in manufacture*, the supply and servicing of agricultural machinery, the supply of other inputs and the post harvest handling of increased agricultural production.[32]

Despite the early bias and recommendations against tractorization, there has been an astronomical increase in the number of tractors available in the country. In 1960 there were only 1,665 tractors on farms in Pakistan. In 1968 this went up to 16,583, and it had doubled again by 1975. The number of tractors increased by 400 per cent between 1975 and 1984, and in 1986, the latest year for which figures are available, there were reported to be 187,255 tractors on farms in Pakistan.[33] In the ten years since then, it would be fair to speculate that the number for 1986 has at least doubled, if not increased further. Thus, tractors have become a major ingredient in agricultural production in Pakistan.

An important feature of the tractorization process in Pakistan has been that most of the tractors available have been of the larger type. Table 5.13 shows that 80 per cent of tractors are in the 46–55 horsepower range, with 17 per cent in the 56–65 horsepower range. Also, the ownership of tractors (Table 5.14) is concentrated, not surprisingly, in the middle range of farm sizes. These are the dynamic capitalist farmers who played an important role in the Green Revolution. One consequence of the policies regarding tractor size and ownership, as pointed out by Mahmood Hasan Khan, was that tractor ownership 'gradually increased the size of landholdings, through both an increase in the land leased from the poor and middle peasants and cultivation by the landlords themselves at the expense of sharecroppers'.[34]

Just as there was a bias against tractorization in general, there have also been official recommendations in the past against providing tractors to small and medium farmers. The issue here was one of cost, since the government realized that these farmers would not be able to buy the imported tractors unless they were heavily subsidized. However, since the early 1980s, the small and medium farmers have bought tractors, many of them using loans, but more recently, a large number have probably financed their tractors from remittances from the Middle East. Since the tractors available have been of the larger variety, these small and medium farmers have had excess capacity on hand. They have made profitable use of the tractors by hiring out the excess capacity to do custom work for other farmers, by participating in the earth moving operations in construction of rural roads, by using the tractor to operate stationary threshers, chaff cutters, cane crushers and other specialized equipment and, above all, by the tractor drawn trolley for haulage of goods from villages to markets and agricultural inputs and non-farm requisites from towns to villages. Use of tractor for haulage is perhaps the

Table 5.13
Number of tractors by horsepower (000)

	Total		Tractors by horsepower													
	Tractors	%	Below 26	%	26–35	%	36–45	%	46–55	%	56–65	%	Above 65	%	Not reported	%
Pakistan	157,310 (100%)	(100%)	572 (100%)	(0.4%)	186 (100%)	(0.12%)	2,894 (100%)	(1.8%)	125,633 (100%)	(79.9%)	26,642 (100%)	(16.9%)	1,328 (100%)	(0.8%)	55 (100%)	(0.3%)
Punjab	127,589 (81%)		495 (87%)		182 (98%)		2,674 (92%)		103,523 (82%)		20,300 (76%)		363 (27%)		52 (95%)	
Sindh	16,542 (11%)		20 (3%)		1 (1%)		132 (5%)		11,676 (9%)		4,266 (16%)		444 (33%)		3 (5%)	
NWFP	10,105 (6%)		51 (9%)		3 (2%)		82 (3%)		7,858 (6%)		1,891 (7%)		220 (17%)		0 (0%)	
Baluchistan	3,074 (2%)		6 (1%)		0 (0%)		6 (0.2%)		2,576 (2%)		185 (1%)		301 (23%)		0 (0%)	

Source: Government of Pakistan, *Agricultural Statistics of Pakistan, 1993–94*, Islamabad, 1995.

Table 5.14
Farms reporting use of important agricultural machinery (by size of farm)

Farm size (acres)	All farms	Tractors		Tubewell/pump	
		Owned	Rented	Owned	Rented
All sizes	4,379 (100%)	285 (100%)	3,288 (100%)	479 (100%)	1,421 (100%)
Under 5.0	2,097 (48%)	31 (11%)	1,617 (49%)	113 (24%)	745 (52%)
5.0–12.5	1,521 (35%)	82 (29%)	1,151 (35%)	181 (38%)	485 (34%)
12.5–25.0	553 (13%)	77 (27%)	375 (11%)	101 (21%)	144 (10%)
25.0–50.0	198 (5%)	57 (20%)	112 (3%)	54 (11%)	38 (3%)
50.0–150.0	69 (2%)	31 (11%)	30 (1%)	25 (5%)	9 (1%)
150.0 and over	11 (0.25%)	7 (2.46%)	3 (0.09%)	5 (1.04%)	1 (0.07%)

Note: These data are for 1984.
Source: Government of Pakistan, *Agricultural Statistics of Pakistan, 1993–94*, Islamabad, 1995.

predominant feature of the utilization of tractors owned by the small and the medium farmers.[35]

Despite the ownership of the tractors by small and medium farm owners, as Table 5.14 shows, a much larger number of farmers in this category rent in tractors. This is also supported by the evidence that farmers are giving up bullocks at a rate higher than the rate of acquisition of tractors, implying that these farmers hire tractors from other owners.

Box 5.5 summarizes the main arguments for and against tractor/mechanization use. One study undertaken in 1982 in Pakistan,[36] based on field surveys, came up with the following findings:

1. Tractors were used mainly for land preparation.
2. Income of farmers, measured as the gross value of output per acre, *is not significantly different between tractor and non-tractor farms.*
3. The average yield levels of major crops *are not different on tractor and non-tractor farms.*
4. Cropping intensity is significantly higher on tractor farms.
5. Labour productivity is higher on tractor farms.
6. There is considerable displacement of animal labour by tractors.
7. While the use of labour falls on tractor farmers, the outcome is not as severe as often suspected. However, family labour is higher on non-tractor farms and also falls as farm size increases.

Overall, it seems that tractorization does not directly result in displacement of labour on the scale suspected, and nor are yields impressively enhanced. However, Viqar Ahmed and Rashid Amjad cite a number of studies which show that output does increase, quite dramatically. One study shows an increase of 20 per cent, another shows that maize and wheat increase by 30 per cent, and they quote yet another study by the World Bank (although conducted in 1969) that there is an increase of between 140 and 200 per cent in cropping intensity on irrigated farms due to mechanization in the Punjab.[37] Nevertheless, the *nature* of labour changes as a result of tractorization. If farm labour, and especially tenants, are displaced, they are often replaced by the short-term wage workers, which sometimes causes a problem of shortages at peak times. Tractorization also implies the resumption of previously unused land, or land let out to subsistence farmers, often displacing them. But the issue of tractorization, and especially mechanization, cannot be looked at in isolation. Numerous externalities need to be considered.

Once tractorization and mechanization commence, they give rise to numerous ancillary activities. A process of small-town urbanization begins, and technicians and skilled workers related to mechanization are created. Off-farm activities increase, and other avenues away from agriculture are opened up for employment purposes. Traditional methods, values, and traditions are confronted by inventions of the new age, and the slumber of old habits and times is broken. In essence, mechanization is a dynamic process that affects institutions and economic and social relations, and transforms entire regions. These impacts must not be underestimated for they can overwhelm societies. Many of these changes are irreversible: some presumed to be detrimental, others considered to be progressive. Nevertheless, the question is not *whether* technology in agriculture and elsewhere ought to be used, but *how*, and to whose benefit.

5.5 Agricultural Income Tax

The debate over whether agriculture should be taxed is a fascinating one, and many reasons are given for and against imposing taxes on agriculture (see Box 5.6 and Appendix 5.4). As much as taxation is an economic issue, where the government is concerned about increasing its revenue and dealing with the budget deficit (see Chapters 10, 11, 14, and 15), it is also a political issue, where some political lobbies have resisted, while others have demanded, such a tax. The politics of the taxation of agriculture issue is reflected not only in parliament and government, but also in reports and commissions set up to study the issues. The 1988 report of the National Commission on Agriculture is one such example.

The report of the NCA is one of the better and more comprehensive documents produced by the Government of Pakistan. Indeed, the present chapter has drawn a great many of its arguments from this source. However, the true colours of the Commission come through when it discusses the issue of agricultural taxation. The following, somewhat lengthy,

BOX 5.5

Should there be mechanization in agriculture?

Arguments for and against farm mechanization are raised by Viqar Ahmed and Rashid Amjad in their book *The Management of Pakistan's Economy, 1947–82*.

Against

1. Farm mechanization is basically capital-intensive. This has so far thrived in developing countries on the basis of direct subsidies and subsidized credit since scarcity of capital is not reflected in its price.
2. Mechanization of farming will divert capital and foreign exchange from non-agricultural sectors to agriculture where labour-intensive alternatives are available.
3. The argument that mechanization increases the productivity of land (except through multiple cropping) has not been conclusively proved.
4. Mechanization not only displaces labour but also induces landlords to cultivate land through hired hands, hence the social cost in terms of tenants converting into landless labourers.
5. Farm technology has a big-farmer bias and accentuates social disparity particularly in the case of assets having lumpy investments.

For

1. Mechanization encourages multiple cropping and greater intensity of cultivation and is thus land-saving.
2. It reduces the dependence upon draught animals whose number is not increasing as fast as the availability of water. One reason why the cropped area has not increased in proportion to the water supply is the inadequacy of farm power. Mechanization will free land from growing fodder for draught animals.
3. Mechanization will make dry-farming possible and will in this way counterbalance the regional bias of the package of modern inputs in favour of irrigated areas.
4. The new package of modern inputs and greater water supply can attain their highest potential yield only with the help of mechanization.
5. Mechanization lowers the cost of production by allowing more efficient utilization of land, labour, irrigation, and other inputs.

Source: Ahmed, Viqar and Rashid Amjad, *The Management of Pakistan's Economy, 1947–82*, Oxford University Press, Karachi, 1984, pp. 159–60.

excerpt from the report shows how the Commission floundered on an extremely important issue.

> A section of the business and industrial community has been pressing that there are excessive agricultural incomes that must be taxed [sic]. Their contention regarding the sector as a whole is unfounded as most of the agricultural holdings are too small to generate taxable surpluses of income. Even for the relatively large holdings there is no assurance of sustained incomes. Agriculture by nature is a risky business and incomes can fluctuate from negative returns in some years to very good incomes in others. Extreme dependence on natural factors creates a high degree of uncertainty for the final output which is not even insurable with insurance firms. A farmer can, for instance, lose all or most of his harvest due to some natural catastrophe and he may lose not only that year's income but also some of his capital like the livestock. The farmer acts as his own insurer in the absence of the commercial insurance facilities. In good years he pays his accumulated debts and then, if possible, generates some savings to supplement his capital stock to make up for losses in bad years. The replenishment and the building up of farm capital is an essential condition for sustained growth in agricultural production. Unlike industrial establishments with easy access to multiple sources of credit, the farmer has to finance capital replacement and additions largely from his own savings. If these savings are

> skimmed off, the farms gradually lose their capacity to produce and the whole country suffers.
>
> ... Although the incidence of direct taxes on agriculture is small relative to other sectors, the total proportion of income transfers out of agriculture is quite high. *There is no scope for further taxation of the sector without adverse impact on the sector's productive capacity. In the face of this situation the demand that agricultural incomes should be taxed as personal incomes in line with other income earners in the country must be rejected as counter productive.* However there are certain inadequacies and inequities in the present system which must be removed.[38]

In an earlier official report, the National Taxation Reforms Commission (NTRC) in 1986 evaluated the possibilities of imposing a tax on agriculture. Although there were some disagreements about how, and if, further taxes should be imposed, the members of the Commission on their analysis of the existing situation argued as follows:

> Although a vast majority of people engaged in agriculture are living below subsistence level, yet a number of persons in this sector are enjoying better incomes. This has been mainly due to two reasons. A number of bigger landowners managed to save their lands from the two land reforms by various devices and secondly, many agriculturists have set up orchards, fruit gardens, vegetable and horticultural estates etc. on their lands which yield higher incomes. The

BOX 5.6

The issue of agricultural taxation

Should agriculture be taxed? There are a number of arguments presented for and against a tax on agriculture, and Viqar Ahmed and Rashid Amjad summarize some of the main issues.

Arguments Against Income Tax on Agriculture

1. It would be inconvenient to both the tax-collectors and taxpayers since farming in Pakistan is generally of the subsistence type and not of the commercial type. Farmers do not maintain standardized accounts of their costs and returns and, therefore, it is difficult to assess their net incomes.
2. The number of farmers is very large and they are scattered all over the country, many in remote inaccessible areas. It would cause considerable loss of time and money to even contact the potential taxpayers.
3. Agricultural incomes being uncertain, depending upon the vagaries of nature, it is quite probable that a large number of farmers may frequently move across the tax exemption limit, thus making it difficult and laborious for tax authorities to keep tabs on them.

Arguments in Favour of Income Tax on Agriculture

1. It is unfair and illogical to make a distinction between agricultural and non-agricultural incomes for purposes of taxation. Just as incomes below a certain level are exempted from tax in case of non agricultural incomes, the same principle should be extended to agricultural income. This would take care of the large majority of subsistence farmers who would be automatically excluded.
2. There is considerable evasion of income tax by those having both agricultural and non-agricultural incomes. Part of their non-agricultural income is shown by them as accruing from agriculture, thus evading the tax. Extending income tax to agriculture would reduce tax evasion.
3. Agricultural income tax would be more income-elastic than land revenue. With a greater yield per acre, higher procurement prices, and mechanization, the benefits of which are mainly confined to large farmers, incomes in the agricultural sector have risen considerably but yield, in terms of direct taxes from agriculture, has not risen so fast. Between 1972–3 and 1978–9, the yield from direct taxation on agriculture (land revenue and irrigation charges) increased by 78 per cent (from Rs472 million to Rs762 million) while value-added in agriculture at current factor cost increased by 157 per cent (Rs21,907 million to Rs56,370 million).

Is Agriculture Already Over-taxed?

1. Agriculture is subject to a large number of direct, indirect, and hidden taxes. Indirect taxes constitute over 85 per cent of the total revenues of the federal government. Since these taxes are paid by all, it can be safely assumed that the agricultural population (being about three-fourths of the total population) bears a heavy burden. There are also hidden taxes in the form of low procurement prices paid by the government for many agricultural products, export duties on agricultural commodities, and the mechanism of terms of trade between industry and agriculture.
2. Increase in agricultural incomes has been off-set by a rise in population and higher expenditure on agricultural inputs and equipment.
3. Higher taxation on agriculture will adversely affect the motivation for savings and investments at a time when farmers must make larger investments in order to increase productivity.
4. Agricultural income has increased not only due to higher income per acre but also due to the increase in area under cultivation. Higher taxation will discourage farmers from bringing new land under the plough.

Further Capacity for Agricultural Taxation

1. Direct taxes on agriculture have risen at a slower pace than growth in agricultural incomes.

   But the introduction of subsidies to agricultural producers on inputs and to urban consumers on wheat, edible oil, and sugar provides further complications. Subsidy is a 'negative tax' and should be taken into account while calculating relative tax burdens. Gotsch and Brown have attempted the calculation of subsidy transfers between the agricultural producers, the urban consumers, and the government (which includes both the federal and provincial governments).

   The data supports the view that the rural sector has (a) received much less subsidy from the government than the urban sector, and (b) contributed a substantial share to the consumer subsidies. However, these figures do not show the full effect of the subsidy transfer due to, apart from other reasons, the fact that Gotsch and Brown did not include in their calculations such implicit subsidies to agriculture as canal water, power supply, institutional credit, and the benefits of extension services.
2. Any comparison of an aggregate tax burden on agriculture with another sector will have little meaning in terms of equity unless a large number of variables are considered and given due weightage. However, a simple comparison between direct taxes on agricultural and non-agricultural incomes will be instructive.
3. The population argument is weak because the urban population has increased even faster than the rural population due to both natural factors and migration from the rural sector.
4. The major benefits of a rise in incomes due to higher yield in agriculture went to larger farmers. This has intensified inequities in income distribution in the rural sector and would indicate additional taxable capacity.
5. The rise in incomes has not been accompanied by any corresponding increase in the level of domestic savings which has remained low. The failure of the government to expropriate this surplus has resulted in a considerable increase in consumption expenditure of the rich farmers. According to Alavi, even when there are adverse changes in terms of trade (for agriculture) the rural élite enjoy considerably enhanced real incomes.

Source: Ahmed, Viqar and Rashid Amjad, *The Management of Pakistan's Economy 1947–82*, Oxford University Press, Karachi, 1984, pp. 156–7.

green revolution and mechanized farming have also increased the income of a large number of agriculturists. There is now a class of landowners who reside in urban centres and have made substantial investments in real estate in the cities. Since they pay no income tax at all, they have created jealousies among the trading and industrial classes as well as the professional and the salaried class who have to pay income tax. This is why demands for levy of income tax on agricultural income keep constantly pouring from various trade associations and chambers of commerce and industry. Persons in the professions have also voiced their protests in the press against exemption to agricultural income. It has been stated that the existence of an exempted class among the taxpayers discourages tax compliance and provides strong incentive for tax evasion amongst businessmen and professional income tax payers.

Many traders and industrialists have purchased agricultural lands with the intent to whiten untaxed black income from business by showing it as agricultural income. Also many businessmen have entered into collusive arrangements with land owners; they obtain fictitious leases of lands from which they show enormous amounts of agricultural income which, in fact, is their business income and thus escape income tax.[39]

One argument that has been raised against imposing any further taxes on agriculture is that the agriculture sector bears the heaviest burden of indirect taxes, which according

to the NTRC were 42 per cent of all indirect taxes at a time when contribution by agriculture to GDP was only 26 per cent.[40] The NTRC report also cited figures which showed that as much as 20 per cent of the net income of the agricultural sector would be transferred out in 1986/7 through taxes, subsidies, and price transfers – equivalent to Rs30 billion, which in that year was more than three times the total collection of income tax.[41]

Anjum Nasim and Asya Akhlaque examine the need for an agricultural tax and say that it is justified on 'grounds of horizontal equity (individuals in equal economic position should be taxed equally)', and also due to the practical compulsions that ensue.[42] Exempting agricultural income usually has a disincentive effect on those who pay tax, and raises the 'possibility of evasion and fraud by attributing incomes from non-agricultural sources as agricultural incomes or by passing-off unexplained loans as loans from agriculturalists'.[43]

Tables 5.15–5.18 show the trends in agricultural taxation, in comparison with other sectors. Table 5.15 shows that in 1987/8, while income from agriculture was around 25 per cent of GDP, the taxes generated were a mere 4.6 per cent. In the non-agricultural sector, while income was less than that from agriculture, taxes as a percentage of income were around 15 per cent. Table 5.16 shows that while indirect taxes have increased as a proportion in agriculture, they have fallen in the non-agricultural sector. The fact that direct taxes in agriculture fell from 10.7 per cent in 1973/4 to 4.3 per cent in 1987/8 may suggest that the poor sections of the agricultural sector have to bear a disproportionately larger burden of the increase in indirect taxes. Almost a third of total indirect

Table 5.15
Revenue raised from agricultural and non-agricultural sources, 1973–1988 (Rs m)

	1973/4	1975/6	1977/8	1979/80	1985/6	1987/8
Agricultural						
Income from agriculture sources	45,851	64,354	83,300	112,668	294,620	373,376
Total taxes	2,233.35	3,701.25	5,066.51	7,635.55	13,679	17,331
Direct taxes	239	204	130	269	642	743
Indirect taxes	1,993	3,497	4,935	7,366	13,037	16,588
Total taxes as % of income	4.8	5.7	6.02	6.7	4.6	4.6
Direct taxes as % of income	0.52	0.31	0.15	0.23	0.21	0.19
Indirect taxes as % of income	4.3	5.4	5.9	6.5	4.4	4.4
Non-agricultural						
Income from non-agricultural sources	37,807	57,068	73,870	99,914	261,264	331,107
Total taxes	6,003	10,832	15,940	24,579	41,517	50,104
Direct taxes	1,200	1,925	2,727	5,111	5,950	12,480
Indirect taxes	4,862	8,907	13,212	19,468.4	31,927	37,624
Total taxes as % of income	15.8	18.9	21.5	24.6	15.9	15.1
Direct taxes as % of income	3.1	3.3	3.6	5.1	3.6	3.7
Indirect taxes as % of income	12.8	15.6	17.8	19.4	12.2	11.4

Sources: Kazi, Shahnaz, 'Inter-sectoral Tax Burden in Pakistan', *Pakistan Development Review*, Winter 1984, no. 4; *Public Finance Statistics*, 1987/8; Explanatory Memorandum of Budget, 1987/8.

Table 5.16
Share of direct and indirect taxes in agricultural and non-agricultural sector tax revenue, 1973–1988 (Rs m)

Years	Agricultural				Total	Non-agricultural				Total
	Direct tax		Indirect tax			Direct tax		Indirect tax		
	Amount	(%)	Amount	(%)		Amount	(%)	Amount	(%)	
1973/4	239.74	10.7	1,993.61	89.3	233.35	1,200.56	20.0	4,802.59	80.0	6,003.16
1975/6	204.15	5.5	3,497.10	94.5	3,701.25	1,925.15	17.8	8,907.40	82.2	10,832.55
1977/8	130.57	2.6	4,935.95	97.4	5,066.61	2,727.73	17.1	13,212.60	82.9	15,940.33
1979/80	269.04	3.5	7,366.51	96.5	7,635.55	5,111.46	20.8	19,468.40	79.2	24,579.86
1985/6	642.00	4.7	13,037.00	95.3	13,679.00	9,590.00	23.0	31,927.60	77.0	41,517.00
1987/8	743.00	4.3	16,588.00	95.7	17,331.00	12,480.00	25.0	37,624.40	75.0	50,104.00

Source: Kazi, Shahnaz, 'Inter-sectoral Tax Burden in Pakistan', *Pakistan Development Review*, Winter 1984, no. 4; *Public Finance Statistics*, 1987/8; Explanatory Memorandum of Budget, 1987/8.

Table 5.17
Distribution of direct, indirect, and total taxes between the agricultural and non-agricultural sector, 1973–1988 (Rs m)

Years	Direct taxes				Indirect taxes				Total taxes			
	Agricultural		Non-agricultural		Agricultural		Non-agricultural		Agricultural		Non-agricultural	
	Amount	(%)	Amount	(%)	Amount	(%)	Amount	(%)	Amount	(%)	Amount	%
1973/4	239	16.6	1,200	83.4	1,993.61	29.3	4,802.59	70.7	2,233.35	27.0	6,003.16	73.0
1975/6	204	9.6	1,925	90.4	3,497.10	28.2	8,907.40	71.8	3,701.25	25.5	10,832.55	74.5
1977/8	130	4.6	2,727	95.4	4,935.94	26.2	13,212.60	72.8	5,066.61	24.0	15,940.33	76.0
1979/80	269	5.0	5,111	95.0	7,633.51	27.5	19,468.40	72.5	7,635.55	23.7	24,579.86	76.3
1985/6	642	6.3	9,590	93.7	13,037	29.0	31,927.70	71.0	13,679	24.8	41,517	75.2
1987/8	743	5.7	12,480	94.3	16,580	30.6	37,624.40	69.4	17,331	25.7	50,104	74.3

Source: Kazi, Shahnaz, 'Inter-sectoral Tax Burden in Pakistan', *Pakistan Development Review*, Winter 1984, no. 4; *Public Finance Statistics*, 1987/8; Explanatory Memorandum of Budget, 1987/8.

Table 5.18
Sectoral incidence of budgetary taxes (Rs m)

	Value added (VA)		Direct taxes	Indirect taxes	Taxes as % of VA		
					Direct	Indirect	Total
Agriculture	92,165	(24.27%)	452	16,631	0.5	18.1	18.6
Manufacturing (public)	3,334	(0.9%)	418	367	12.5	11.0	23.5
Manufacturing (private)	64,141	(17.2%)	5,115	7,055	8.0	11.0	19.0
Rest of the public sector	11,793	(3.2%)	1,272	873	10.8	7.4	18.2
Rest of the private sector	201,315	(54.0%)	3,411	14,897	1.7	7.4	9.1
Total	372,748	(100%)	10,668	39,823	2.0	10.7	13.6

Source: Government of Pakistan, *National Taxation Reforms Committee: Final Report*, Islamabad, 1986, p. 155.

taxes are collected from agriculture (Table 5.17), but only 5.7 per cent of total direct taxes accrue from agriculture.

Those who support the proposal of imposing agricultural income tax show (Table 5.18) that, while the amount of indirect taxes paid by the agricultural sector in 1986 was higher than other sectors, the bulk of this taxation was borne by the low-income groups and poorer farmers.[44] This view supports the claim that indirect taxes are highly regressive and inequitable. An argument that the anti-taxation lobby continues to propound is that the agricultural sector is in bad economic shape as a whole, and thus should not have taxes imposed on it. The pro-tax lobby argues that, despite this poor shape, a number of individuals do earn very large incomes and there are no grounds for allowing them to go scot-free. Taxes are imposed on personal income and not on the sector as a whole. Moreover, other sectors of the economy are often also 'in bad economic shape', but must be accountable to the exchequer for any profit, or even production, that they undertake. Hence the argument that agriculture should be exempt from taxes does not hold on equity grounds, and given the financial and budgetary shortfall and constraints faced by the government, the need to tax agriculture gains greater urgency (see Appendix 5.4 and Chapters 10 and 11).

5.6 Summary and Further Reading

5.6.1 Summary

Having presented a history of agriculture in Pakistan in the previous three chapters, we have looked in this chapter at the agricultural sector today. We have examined the main trends in output, production, irrigation, etc., over the last five decades, and seen how this sector has evolved. From being the dominant contributor to GDP in the 1950s, the agricultural sector today contributes less than the services sector or even industry. Hence the often-repeated claim that 'Pakistan is mainly an agricultural country' is questionable on this evidence. While agricultural production has increased over the last five decades, there has been somewhat of a reversal in these trends in recent years, which should be cause for concern. From peak production years in the mid-1980s, the index of agricultural production for all crops has fallen quite dramatically. There is a growing belief that agriculture is in the throes of a serious crisis, and that drastic measures need to be undertaken to enhance output, arrest waterlogging and salinity, and bring forth another Green Revolution reminiscent of the agricultural changes in the mid-1960s.

A number of bad policies may have been responsible for creating this crisis. Economic incentives were not given to farmers, as they were expected to subsidize urban consumers and continue to increase output despite a lack of adequate pricing policies. Mechanization was heavily biased against the smaller farmers in favour of the large and very large producers. This was despite the fact, shown in Chapter 4, that the structure of ownership and mode and means of production had undergone a radical transformation, with smaller farms emerging at the expense of larger farms. Credit to farmers continues to be a weak link in the input–output chain, where higher rates from the informal sector affect the small farmers. Moreover, overall credit to farmers is insufficient, and far less than can be justified. While direct production-related issues like types of seeds and salinity may have affected agricultural output, some of the ancillary inputs such as credit, and guidelines such as pricing signals, may also be a cause of poor performance.

5.6.2 Further Reading

Many of the contemporary issues facing agriculture are discussed frequently in newspapers and magazines, and these are an important source for more information and understanding of the sector (see Appendix 5.5). With taxation taking on more importance lately, numerous articles, almost all in favour of agricultural taxation, appear in the press regularly. Other than newspapers and magazines, a few books and reports discuss the key issues facing agriculture in the past and today. Viqar Ahmed and Rashid Amjad's *The Management of Pakistan's Economy 1947–82*, Oxford University Press, Karachi, 1984, is a good reference, as is Nabi, Ijaz, *et al.*, *The Agrarian Economy of Pakistan: Issues and Policies*, Oxford University Press, Karachi, 1986. Two reports by the Government of Pakistan are also very useful: *Report of the National Commission on Agriculture, 1988*, and *National Taxation Reforms Commission: Final Report*, 1986.

Appendix 5.1

Problems in Pakistan's agriculture

In an article published in September 1996·in a local newspaper, Muhammad Ilyas presented the main arguments from a World Bank report on Pakistan's agriculture. This appendix is an edited version of Muhammad Ilyas's newspaper report.

The World Bank in a recent report on the grave environmental situation in Pakistan has recommended enforcement of genuine land reforms as an essential measure to ensure sustainable exploitation of the natural resources including land and water. The report 'Pakistan: Economic Policies, Institutions, and the Environment' prepared by Rashid Faruqee and Jonathan Coleman, said that giving ownership to farmers would help protect the environment. Land redistribution among cultivator farmers also eliminates chances of voter-exploitation by landlords. However, as Faruqee and Coleman have pointed out in the report, 'Because the laws in Pakistan were lax and easy to circumvent, past land reforms did not bring about the desired change in land tenure and did not have any effect on environmental protection.' 'Redistribution of income and wealth has an effect on the environment', they stress.

Poverty and population growth have contributed to the degradation of the environment in Pakistan, where they have caused soil degradation, deforestation, rangeland degradation, marine and coastal zone damage, and many forms of urban and industrial pollutions. 'Short time horizons are not innate characteristics, however, but are the outcome of policy and institutional and social failures', the report points out.

Poor farmers face very high production and financial risks that are often the result of misguided policy interventions in factor and product markets or insecure land tenure. Many poor farmers with below subsistence holdings are unable to afford the mechanism available for coping with risks, such as selling stored crops, credit, and crop insurance, and have limited access to extension and market information. In many cases, they have no choice but to over-exploit the available natural resources.

These misguided policies are at the roots of many serious environmental problems. Take salinity for example. Surveys have shown that three-fourths of tubewells provide brackish water that is unfit or only marginally fit for agriculture, resulting in salinity. Most of these tubewells are set up with subsidies and have been running these on subsidized electricity and selling the water at rates much higher than what is paid for canal water.

On the basis of farm-level data, it has been estimated that yield losses in wheat as a result of sodic irrigation water were 9 per cent and 20 per cent in two different locales in the central Punjab. Experts have also estimated that crop yields are reduced by about one-third for crops grown on slightly saline areas and that yields on moderately affected areas are reduced by about two-thirds. Crop production of any kind is difficult on highly saline soils, the report has pointed out.

Another instance of influential landlords laying their hands on government funds is the subsidy on application of gypsum. The government undertook a programme to popularize gypsum in order to combat the salinity that is caused by low-quality tubewell water. A similar programme was very successful in the Indian Punjab, where the problem of salinity has been drastically reduced through the use of subsidized gypsum. There are, however, no data on the effects of the Pakistani programme. Field experience indicates, however, that in most instances, influential landlords were the main beneficiaries of the subsidies. Moreover, the report observes, application of gypsum to fields has not always followed disbursement of subsidies, because of rent-seeking behaviour. In other words, the subsidy money was misappropriated.

Waterlogging is also a function of a faulty water rate system which the conglomeration of big landlords and the bureaucrats does not allow to be changed at all. As the report also remarks, underpricing of water and the complicated system of assessing water rate liability eliminates incentives to use water efficiently and has aggravated waterlogging and salinity.

The structure of water pricing provides no incentives for using canal water efficiently, and discourages investments in water conservation, such as drip or sprinkler irrigation systems. Capital intensive agricultural practices are other characteristics of absentee landlordism. Facilitated by factor price distortions, these lead to the adoption of production methods that do not reflect factor endowments. Subsidies or targeted credit for tractors and threshers, to which again only the big landlords have access, have displaced labour, for example.

The indiscriminate use of agricultural chemicals, such as fertilizer and pesticides – which small farmers with 93% of farms but representing only about 41% of the cultivated area cannot afford – has contaminated ground- and surface water. Their use in Pakistan's irrigated agriculture has expanded rapidly over the past twenty years. Excess nutrient loading as a result of fertilizer run-off can lead to uncontrolled algae growth.

The widespread use of often dangerous pesticides on the cotton crop is associated with several potential health hazards, including contamination of workers who apply it (three-quarters of producers use a back-pack sprayer and no protective clothing), harvesters (all of whom are women), soil and groundwater used for drinking, and consumers of agricultural products. Summarized evidence from blood tests shows that as many as one third of cotton workers in Pakistan have been exposed to dangerous levels of pesticides, according to the report.

Source: Ilyas, Muhammad, 'IBRD Proposes Land Reforms', *DAWN*, 12 September, 1996.

Appendix 5.2

Summary and timeframe for structural and policy reforms in agriculture

Policy area	Objectives	Measures	Proposed timing of initiating measures and expected implementation period
Incentives	Market-determined output prices	*End subsidy on wheat imports	1994/5, short run
		*Remove wheat and flour import restrictions	1994/5, short run
		*End support prices for sugar cane	1994/5, short run
		End support prices for all other crops	1995/6, medium to long run
		Initiate study into alternative means of reducing volatility of agricultural prices	1994/5, short to medium run
		*Build up enabling environment for private sector entry into storage and distribution	1995/6, medium run
		Regulation of processing industry where necessary	
	Trade policy reflecting comparative advantage	*Complete trade reform	1995/6, medium run
		Remove export taxes, import duties, and quantitative restrictions	1995/6, short to medium run
	Efficient and equitable tax system	Extend income and wealth tax to agriculture	1994/5, short run
		Eliminate all agricultural tax exemptions	1994/5, short run
		Update tax base in agriculture by review of Producer Index Units	1994/5, short run
		Installation of mechanism for periodic review of Producer Index Units	1995/6, short to medium run
Input markets	Private sector production and distribution of commercial inputs	*Privatize urea production and distribution	1994/5, short run
		Divest National Fertilizer Corporation, including plants operated by its subsidiaries	1994/5, short to medium run
		*Expedite privatization of phosphate imports	1994/5, short run
		*Level playing field between public and private sector in input markets	1995/6, short run
		*Commercialize seed corporations	1994/5, short run
		Privatize seed corporations	1995/6, medium run
		Strengthen seed certification process	1994/5, medium run
	Market-determined input prices	Remove subsidy on electricity	1995/6, medium run
	Reform the irrigation system	*Decentralize irrigation system based on water user associations, public utilities and market in water rights	1995/6, medium run
		*Raise irrigation charges	1994/5, short run
	Remove distortions in land markets and reform credit provision	Initiate a study of land reform	1994/5, short run
		*Improvement and computerization of land records	1994/5, medium run
		Clamp down on delinquent loans and end cheap loans for machinery purchase	1994/5, short run
		End directed credit	1994/5, short run

Appendix 5.2 continued

Policy area	Objectives	Measures	Proposed timing of initiating measures and expected implementation period
Government expenditure	Reorient public expenditure towards changing needs of agriculture and enhance efficiency of expenditure programme	Reduce burden of administrative expenses on research and extension budget and increase operational funding	1995/6, short run
		Introduce new research priorities including research on farming systems, growth-enhancing public goods, and the environment	1994/5, short run
		Induce private sector to undertake privately profitable research	1994/5, short to medium run
		Introduce patent protection for seed varieties	1994/5, short run
		Reduce duplication and increase co-ordination of research institutions to minimize wastage of resources	1995/6, short to medium run
		*Reduce the number of front-line extension workers and replace them with fewer, better trained workers, more responsive to the needs of farming *systems* and not just given crops	1995/6, medium run
		*Open consulting services by adaptive research institutes to better off farmers on a cost-sharing basis	1994/5, medium run
		*Extensive use of mass media and other group approaches for basic messages about available technology and better farming systems	1994/5, medium run
		Increase investment in education, including functional education of farmers	1995/6, medium to long run
		Remove subsidies on capital	1994/5, short to medium run
Poverty	Rural poverty alleviation	Target developmental expenditure towards poor and marginal farmers	1995/6, medium run
		Develop participatory community-based organizations	1995/6, medium run
		Ensure enforcement of tenancy protection	1995/6, short to medium run
Environment	Environmental protection and sustainable development	Price water at economic cost	1995/6, short to medium run
		Phase out sapling subsidy to encourage private sector participation in sapling market	1994/5, short to medium run
		Regulate pesticide use	1994/5, short run
		Provide incentives to use Integrated Pest Management	1995/6, medium run
		Create community institutions to manage local resources and common property	1995/6, medium to long run
		Encourage private and public sector investment in soil and water conservation	1995/6, short to medium run

*Element of high priority.
Note: For implementation periods, short run implies 1 to 2 years, medium run, 3 to 5 years, and long run, 5 to 7 years.

Source: Faruqee, Rashid, 'Pakistan's Agriculture Sector: Is 3 to 4 per cent Annual Growth Sustainable?', *Policy Research Working Paper no. 1407*, World Bank, Washington, 1995, pp. (iii–vi.)

Appendix 5.3

The determination of support prices of agricultural commodities

How should agricultural support prices be determined?

Support prices for agricultural commodities can be determined either on the basis of the cost of production or by what is termed as the 'parity approach'.

The cost of production approach aims at guaranteeing a fair return of a certain crop to the farmers and establishing a balance between a number of competing crops so that an optimum cropping pattern is achieved. Subject to soil, climatic, and other agronomic conditions influencing crop substitution in certain areas, cropping patterns can be moulded to correspond to planned production targets. For instance, wheat competes for area with both cotton and rice so a certain balance between the prices of the three commodities can help in attaining their required production levels.

However, there are certain problems in the cost of production approach. Agricultural production requires a number of inputs which are not marketed and whose valuation will, therefore, present difficulties. Such inputs include labour, management, and land. Labour and management costs, which should be the share of the entrepreneur, are difficult to assess. Similarly land rent, which may be the single largest cost item, is difficult to determine in a country where there is no organized land market.

The regional variations in physical resource endowments also have to be taken into account in the choice of samples for calculating cost. Moreover, with rise in prices, the cost of production has to be periodically adjusted.

The cost of production is also related to technology. For purposes of price support the cost of production may either pertain to old traditional technologies, which means a higher level of support price, or to the new technologies where costs may be low. A support price based on the new technology cost structure will have adverse equity effects particularly if the new inputs are subsidized or a large number of farmers have no access to the new technology. Large holdings with lower production costs may get higher net returns compared to small holdings. Thus the higher the support price, the greater the transfer of income to large holdings from the general revenues. It is now believed that the support price programme in Pakistan has operated in contradiction to the original intent of better income distribution among various segments of the rural farm sector since, mainly, the cost of production approach has been followed while determining the structure of support prices.

In addition to the problem of identifying the technology, and the cultivators using that technology, there is another question: which cost should be taken into consideration? Average or incremental? In a production system as varied as Pakistan's agriculture in technology as well as scale, both types of unit costs are bound to create complications.

The 'parity price' approach is used in order to correct imbalances in terms of trade between the agricultural and the non-agricultural sectors. The 'parity price' is an output price that will yield income which will buy the same quantity of other products as it would in some specified based period. Thus a balance can be maintained between the prices of commodities sold by the farmers and the commodities which they purchase. It can be calculated through a comparative index of agricultural and non-agricultural prices. In this approach, the effects of inflation which keep upsetting the income and expenditure structure of the farm household are accounted for. Although it is free from the usual objections of lack of scientific rigour and bias in favour of transfer of resources to a particular category of land holding, the choice of the base year for working out the parity ratio may introduce some distortion in the income distribution pattern of different tenure and size farm categories.

The choice between the two approaches depends upon the relative importance of various objectives of the price support programme. If the major objective is providing production incentives for particular crops or crop combinations, the cost of production approach may serve the purpose at least in the short run. Parity prices, on the other hand, provide a range within which prices may be located in order to reflect the influence of the forces of demand and supply as well as the long-run objective of equity between urban and rural sectors.

In addition to the two approaches mentioned above, three other criteria are sometimes used for determining support prices: (i) open market prices; (ii) inter-crop parity index; and (iii) world prices.

An assessment of the open market price, as determined by the supply–demand interaction, is essential and should be kept in mind while making decisions regarding the support price. It serves as a retraining factor since too much deviation from the open market price may make the price support programme unrealistic and ineffective. It is, however, difficult to make an accurate assessment of the open market price since the markets are highly imperfect, unstable, and dominated mostly by a few buyers (*arhtis*/sugar mills). In fact, an agricultural price policy itself represents an attempt to escape from the uncertainties and distortions of the so-called 'open market'.

The inter-crop parity index reflects the relative positions of various agricultural products and the rates at which these are exchanged. Their main utility lies in monitoring the use of scarce resources for competing crops and calculating optimal resource allocation.

World prices are relevant in the case of export commodities or those commodities which are partly supplied from abroad. But world markets are not equally competitive for all commodities. Their use is further restricted by the fact that while a certain product and some of the inputs (for example, pesticides and fertilizers) may have relevance to world market conditions, major elements in the cost structure (for example, canal water and labour) may have no linkage.

Source: Ahmed, Viqar and Rashid Amjad, *The Management of Pakistan's Economy, 1947–82*, Oxford University Press, Karachi, 1984, pp. 179–80.

Appendix 5.4

Taxes on land and farm income

Professor Mahmood Hasan Khan, in a recent article, assesses the taxation and land revenue structure in Pakistan.

The federal government has made no serious attempt so far to improve the structure of direct taxes in agriculture, which at present are mainly in the form of land revenue (tax) assessed and collected by the provincial governments. The modest yield from land revenue has no relation to the increase in agricultural incomes and the general rise in the value of land since at least the mid-1970s. Direct taxes contribute about 23 per cent of the total tax revenue of the federal and provincial governments. In 1994–95, the land revenue of Rs1.1 billion was around 1.9 per cent of all direct taxes collected in the country, falling from 4.7 per cent in 1980–81.

What is even more interesting is that the ratio of land revenue to the value-added by crops has declined from 3 per cent in the 1950s to 0.58 per cent in 1980–81 and 0.45 per cent in 1994–95. Put it differently and the direct tax (land revenue) paid by farmers works out to Rs51 per hectare of cultivated land in 1995. Using a conservative figure of Rs3,000 per hectare for net crop income (after cultivation expenses), the average land tax is around 1.7 per cent of a farmer's income. The contribution of land revenue to the provincial taxes and provincial revenue has fallen significantly: land revenue used to contribute 30–55 per cent of the provincial taxes during the first 25 years of Pakistan (1947–1972), but has contributed 8–14 per cent in the last 25 years. Likewise, its contribution to the provincial revenue has decreased from 13–16 per cent to 6–11 per cent in the two periods.

The agriculture sector has been taxed heavily by the government's pricing policies and taxes on exports of agricultural products. These policies have (i) transferred resources from agriculture to the rest of the economy; (ii) generated revenue for the governments; and (iii) distorted the allocation of resources. Price subsidies on agricultural inputs, though substantial over time, have not altogether offset the burden of hidden taxes on producers. While there is some doubt if these subsidies have contributed to increased farm productivity, it is certain that most of them have been appropriated by large and influential farmers (landlords).

It is absolutely essential to maintain a favourable macroeconomic environment for agricultural producers if we want additional resources for investment in physical and social infrastructure to help improve the living standards of those whose incomes and jobs depend on agriculture. One should strongly oppose policies that penalize agricultural productivity, including perverse policies on output and input prices, exchange rate, regulation and control of internal and international trade, farm credit, and investment in physical infrastructure, research and extension. In the last five years, the burden of implicit taxes on agriculture has fallen substantially as a result of significant changes in prices and structural reforms.

We should here distinguish clearly between two issues: (i) the tax burden on the agriculture sector and (ii) the tax on personal income and wealth, irrespective of the sector in which they are produced or created. The first issue has been addressed gradually in that there has been substantial reduction in the tax burden on agricultural producers. The second issue of taxing agricultural income has, however, remained unresolved because of the effective political power of the large farmers and landlords. All kinds of excuses and deceptive arguments have been used by this group or by others on its behalf.

The case for increased reliance on direct taxes on actual agricultural income, or on presumed agricultural income (based on land according to its productivity) is quite persuasive on several grounds: indirect and hidden taxes on agriculture adversely affect and hurt the wrong people and send wrong signals on the question of efficient allocation of resources; the government revenue from direct taxes is small and has declined relative to other tax revenue and agricultural income; interpersonal equity (fairness) in (direct) taxation is not well served by differentiating incomes for tax purposes by sector or activity which produces income; and the tax base has to be expanded and made more flexible in order to reduce the fiscal deficit.

At present there are only two forms in which the government taxes landowners directly and includes the revenue in its budget: (i) wealth tax on agricultural land as immovable property and (ii) land revenue as a tax on land that generates income. The former is assessed and collected by the federal government and the latter by the provincial governments. In 1982–83, the military government introduced the ushr levy on (Sunni Muslim) landowners in lieu of the land revenue, but the paltry ushr revenue has not been part of the government's budget. *Land revenue is still almost the only direct tax revenue collected from landowners.*

The tax on movable and immovable wealth was introduced in 1963, but agricultural land was exempted in 1970 from this tax for those landowners whose only source of income was agriculture. The value of land for wealth tax was set at Rs10 per Produce Index Unit (PIU), which was used as a relative measure of productivity of land parcels in different locations to set the land claims of Muslim refugees from East Punjab in the late 1940s and then in the implementation of the land reform acts of 1959, 1972 and 1977.

The federal government has raised the assessment value of land from Rs10 to Rs250 per PIU since 1990, although the PML Taxation Committee in 1990 was in favour of raising it to Rs400 per PIU which is the basis for acquiring loans from the banking system. In 1993, the second caretaker government removed the wealth tax exemption of 1970 for the landowners owing mainly to the pressure of donor agencies. However, following the recommendations of the Prime Minister's Task Force on Agriculture in 1994, the PPP-led government introduced several generous deductions to dilute the effect of wealth tax on large landowners. Further, the federal government has not accepted the suggestion by donors that the number of PIUs per hectare should be revised as a measure of the value (productive capacity) of land for wealth tax purposes. It is obvious that, without raising the assessment value of land to Rs400 per PIU and the upward revision of PIUs per hectare, the wealth tax receipts from agricultural land would remain inconsequential.

The land revenue system in Pakistan has a very long history, but in its present form it was concretised by the British colonial government in the Punjab Land Revenue Act of 1887. This system now has no redeeming feature: it is a relic of the past developed under the absolutist, authoritarian, feudal, and colonial regimes and maintained by the political influence of landlords and rich farmers since 1947.

The land tax has no merit now because of the ad hoc changes made in the rates and exemptions in the last 25 years after the West Pakistan Land Revenue Act of 1967 which replaced the Punjab Land Revenue Act of 1887 was extended on a uniform basis to all parts of Pakistan.

It is no longer linked to the presumptive (income) capacity of the land one owns, hence it is highly inequitable between landowners and between those who earn their income from agriculture and others whose income is earned from other activities. In addition, the land revenue produces very modest income for the provincial governments in spite of the ad hoc increases in the rates in 1983/84.

There is a long history of opposition to the idea of taxing agricultural incomes, going back to the times of the British rule in India. With the passage of the Income Tax Act of 1886 agriculture was to have only the land revenue system. The Income Tax Act of 1922 granted specific tax exemption to agricultural incomes, which is still available in Pakistan under the Income Tax Ordinance of 1979. In the decade after 1947, successive governments were able to avoid the issue of taxation on land and agricultural income. In the next fifteen years, in spite of the strong recommendations of the Taxation Enquiry Committee of 1959, Taxation and Tariffs Commission of 1964, and Agricultural Enquiry Commission of 1972–74, the federal government did not replace the land revenue system by a system of tax on agricultural income.

A major breakthrough on the issue of taxation of agricultural incomes was the enactment of the Finance (Supplementary) Act of 1977 by the PPP government. This act abolished the land revenue and replaced it by a uniform and universal income tax in the country in January 1977. However, before the PPP government could start the implementation of the Finance Act of 1977, the military government which took over power in July 1977 first suspended and then cancelled the act. The former tax exemption on agricultural income was restored in the Income Tax Ordinance of 1979.

In the 1980s, at least three 'expert' bodies – National Taxation Reform Commission in 1986, National Commission on Agriculture in 1988 and the Committee of Experts on Taxation of Agricultural Incomes in 1989 – examined the question of changes in direct taxes on agriculture, including land revenue, ushr and income tax. The majority view was against introducing a tax on agricultural income mainly on the ground that the federal government was not empowered to legislate on matters falling in the provincial jurisdiction, except in a State of Emergency under Article 232 of the Constitution. They emphasized the need to improve the assessment and collection of land revenue and ushr, but without specifying the measures for implementation.

A minor policy reform with respect to agricultural income was introduced by the federal government in the Finance Ordinance of 1988. It amended the Income Tax Ordinance of 1979 to include agricultural income (if any) in the 'chargeable income' for determining the tax rate for non-agricultural incomes. This so-called clubbing formula, introduced with the federal budget of 1988–89, has had no major impact on tax evasion and the income tax revenue. At the end of 1990, the PML government appointed a taxation committee, which was in favour of a tax on agricultural income, but it repeated the excuse earlier made by the three expert committees in 1986, 1988 and 1989. So the committee recommended that the federal government should redefine the concept of agricultural income by excluding the rental part received by landowners and incomes earned from orchards, livestock and poultry farms. However, the PML government took no action on this recommendation.

The persistently high fiscal deficit and the pressure of the international donor community since the early 1990s have moved up the issue of reforming the land revenue system on the government's policy agenda in Pakistan. The caretaker government after the dismissal of the PML government in July 1993 acted on two fronts in September–October 1993. First, it removed the 1970 exemption for agricultural land for wealth tax purposes. Second, it issued ordinances in all provinces to introduce a flat tax rate of Rs2 per PIU on all landholdings above 4,000 PIUs to replace the existing land revenue. In February 1994, the newly elected PPP government enacted a somewhat watered-down version of the Wealth Tax (Amendment) Ordinance to justify the changes in the original legislation.

The elected provincial governments, however, did not follow up on the provincial tax ordinances on presumed agricultural income (based on PIUs) issued by the caretaker government in September–October 1993. The provincial assemblies of the NWFP and Baluchistan have enacted the land tax legislation, introducing a graduated scale of tax on presumptive income expressed in rupees per PIU. However, the two provincial governments have apparently not started the implementation process. The provincial governments in Punjab and Sindh have been dragging their feet and taken no concrete action to legislate and implement the new tax system on presumed income based on even unrevised PIUs per hectare.

At least two major steps are required immediately: (i) abolition of the current system of land revenue assessment and (ii) revision of the number of PIUs per hectare in all provinces, based on the existing productive capacity of agricultural land. If the presumed income tax on land has to serve as a fair measure of taxation, a source of increased government revenue to meet the development needs of the rural people, then the provincial governments must consider increasing and graduating the flat tax rate of Rs2 per PIU and reducing the basic exemption for the individual landholding in terms of the revised number of PIUs per hectare equivalent to no more than five hectares irrigated.

Source: Khan, Mahmood Hasan, 'Taxes on Land and Farm Income', *DAWN*, 8 June 1996.

Appendix 5.5

Getting the policies right in Pakistan's agriculture

In another article, Prof. Mahmood Hasan Khan examines the key problems that face Pakistan's economy.

The economy's vulnerability to the performance of agriculture is based on its contribution to the supply of food and raw material, employment and export earnings. These facts are well documented and need no further comment. What is, perhaps, less obvious is the (increasing?) burden on agricultural imports on the economy. The annual import bill on account of wheat, edible oils, sugar, pulses, and milk and its products is between $1.2 and $1.8 billion or around 15–18 per cent of the value of all imports. A high proportion of the food import bill is for edible oils ($800–900 million) and the rest for wheat and sugar.

Pakistan is importing this year probably 2.5 million metric tons or about 15 per cent of its expected wheat output. Perhaps a more distressing aspect of food security is that a sizable part of the supply of edible oil products, wheat, wheat-flour, and sugar find their way into the markets of neighbouring countries, thanks largely to price differentials and the low cost of these transactions to participants.

It is also well-known that much of the progress in agricultural production has come from the increased quantity of resources (inputs) and not from their increased efficiency (productivity). For instance, crop yields in Pakistan are among the lowest in the world, but mercifully have potential for significant increase. There is considerable evidence of waste of the key production resources, water and land, in most agricultural areas. Experts tell us the deterioration in the physical integrity of the irrigation and drainage system and quality of soils has become perhaps the single most important threat to the sustainability of agricultural growth in Pakistan.

Inadequate public investment, high cost of maintenance and wrong-headed price policies have been rightly regarded as the major contributors to this problem.

A large part of the explanation for low productivity and waste of resources has to do with the rights to land and water and the state policies affecting incentives for a profitable agriculture. Successive governments have done either too little in areas that could significantly enhance agricultural production, or too much in others that have significantly debilitated the agriculture industry in Pakistan. Numerous committees/task forces/commissions – at least four since 1988 – have reported on the problems of agriculture and made policy recommendations.

Constraints on agriculture go beyond the issue of price adjustments; they include structural and institutional problems.

There are clearly four policy areas that have a direct impact on the productivity and profitability of agriculture in Pakistan: (1) control of and access to (good) agricultural land; (2) access to and (efficient) use of irrigation water; (3) market structures

for and prices of inputs and outputs; and (4) availability of public goods, including physical infrastructure and the support system of agricultural research and extension.

The idea of land reforms in Pakistan evokes little interest and much hostility, although it is at the heart of the problem of control and access to agricultural land. Property rights in land – or the responsibility to use it – need to be defined and protected to increase efficiency and check unfairness. The existing system of land titles is in a mess.

One has simply to look at the land records and the massive volume of intra-family and inter-family litigation for rights in land. The landlord–tenant contracts are more messy both in their written and verbal forms. In practice, they depend mainly on the power of one of the parties. The government's resources and efforts should focus on improving land titles and tenancy contracts with quick and fair dispensation of justice in disputes. The land revenue machinery, including revenue courts, is bloated in numbers but grossly inadequate in its effectiveness.

Prices

The access to water and its efficient use for agriculture is no less important in Pakistan. The existing irrigation system has almost no redeeming feature: rampant rent-seeking and neglect of the irrigation infrastructure are certainly its two most costly manifestations. An apparent paradox is that canal water is grossly underpriced from society's point of view and grossly overpriced from the viewpoint of the water user. It is, however, quickly resolved by looking at the rent-seeking system. On the surface, the case for an autonomous (private sector) irrigation authority is quite strong, but some of the underlying assumptions for its success seem dubious. The experience of the Water Users Association (WUAs) so far has not been encouraging, hence the problems associated with the On-Farm Water Management (OFWM) projects throughout the Indus Basin. The growth of genuine (participatory) organisations of farmers (water users) requires a socio-economic environment that the existing land system cannot provide. The proposed (autonomous) water utilities may turn out to be as serious a bottleneck to agricultural growth as the existing irrigation system has been. The water problem has to be resolved at the national level as well in terms of disputes between provinces on their 'fair' shares and 'leakages' experienced at critical times in each crop search.

Prices are (or can be) very strong signals for allocation of resources and profitability of the individual enterprise (farm). I am entirely in favour of price liberalisation for both outputs and inputs, but policy makers have to take into account some of the side-effects such as redistribution of welfare (income) in the society. We are told almost ad nauseam that farmers want and should get 'fair' prices for their outputs, which the present price support system does not allow. The trade-off is that they may have to accommodate greater seasonal variability in prices. Governments and financial institutions can assist the private sector in developing storage systems that can stabilize prices.

The existing price support and procurement system should be abolished and support should be extended to private marketing channels for greater competition and investment in the distribution network for commodities. Consumers can and should be protected by targeted (price or income) subsidies. Generalized consumer subsidies on wheat flour, sugar, and edible oils are a major source of cross-frontier trade or smuggling. In this regard, one should also seriously question the wisdom of maintaining the rent-seeking bureaucracy in the provincial Food Departments and a variety of parastatals at the federal and provincial levels. Is this really not a very costly way of providing subsidy to urban residents?

Subsidies

The case for price subsidy on agricultural inputs has never been too strong or persuasive since its co-called incentive effect is more than offset by (i) waste and (ii) unfair distribution of benefits. The experience of subsidised credit is by far the best case to make this point. Targeted subsidies combined with greater access to credit for smaller farmers and rural entrepreneurs are the answer. Public sector financial institutions have proved to be a disaster since their activities have been dominated by political and not market forces. Innovative credit arrangements between private financial institutions and small-scale borrowers have to be expanded, particularly in those areas in which viable farmers (water users) organisations can develop. In some of the NGO-supported rural development programmes, this has already happened. Imported inputs, particularly machinery, should neither be taxed too heavily nor subsidised. Reduced Customs duties on exports and imports seem to be the most reasonable approach to take.

There is finally the role of the government in building and strengthening the physical infrastructure and agricultural support services. Public investment in the irrigation, drainage, and road systems can have reasonably high rates of return provided the infrastructure (i) is based on good design and responds to the needs of people in different areas and (ii) has a reasonable cost recovery system. So far both of these aspects have been grossly neglected. Public investment in agricultural research and extension services can yield even higher returns.

However, the existing national and provincial systems must be restructured. The research system has to be brought closer to where the problems are and integrated with the delivery system to reach the intended beneficiaries. The army of front-line extension workers (field assistants and others) should be replaced by localised adaptive research outfits (establishments) to act as the meeting point for suppliers and recipients of technologies. In fact, a large part of the extension services can be done through these entities in collaboration with private sector companies and farmers (village) organisations. The cost saving from a significantly reduced size of the extension bureaucracy can be used to improve the research-based delivery system and rural education.

Governments are not being asked to do less but do things differently. Get your hands out where they tend to stifle economic activity and exacerbate income inequality and concentrate on policies – structural and institutional reforms included – and investment that contribute to economic growth and alleviate rural poverty.

May I add that a vibrant and productive agriculture will also (a) neutralise the oft-repeated arguments of the farm lobby against taxation of the incomes of the rich (large) farmers and landlords and (b) yield substantial tax revenue for public investment in the agriculture sector itself.

Source: Khan, Mahmood Hasan, 'Agriculture in Pakistan: Get the Policies Right', *DAWN*, Economic and Business Review, 31 March–6 April 1997.

Notes

1. Khan, Mahmood Hasan, *Underdevelopment and Agrarian Structure in Pakistan*, Westview Press, Boulder, 1981, p. 20.
2. Ibid., p. 21.
3. Ibid., p. 21.
4. Ahmed, Viqar and Rashid Amjad, *The Management of Pakistan's Economy, 1947–82*, Oxford University Press, Karachi, 1982, p. 79.
5. Faruqee, Rashid, 'Pakistan's Agricultural Sector: Is 3 to 4 per cent Annual Growth Sustainable?', *Policy Research Working Paper 1407*, World Bank, Washington, 1995, p. 6.
6. Ibid., p. 8.
7. Government of Pakistan, Ministry of Food and Agriculture, *Report of the National Commission on Agriculture*, Islamabad, 1988, pp. 486–7.
8. Ibid., p. 487.
9. Ahmed, Viqar and Rashid Amjad, op. cit., 1984, p. 147.
10. Ibid., p. 149.
11. Ibid., p. 151.
12. Ibid., p. 155.
13. Government of Pakistan, *Report of the National Commission on Agriculture*, op. cit., 1988, p. 489.
14. World Bank, *Pakistan: Growth Through Adjustment*, Report No. 7118-PAK, Washington, 1988, p. 37.
15. World Bank, *Pakistan: Country Economic Memorandum FY931*, Report No. 11590-PAK, Washington, 1993, pp. 7–8.
16. A large part of the discussion in this section draws from the seven extensive Rural Financial Market Studies preliminary report prepared by the Applied Economics Research Centre, University of Karachi, conducted for the State Bank of Pakistan in 1994. The large surveys and analysis of the studies were being undertaken at the time of our writing.
17. State Bank of Pakistan, *Rural Financial Market Studies: Phase 1*, Karachi, 1994, pp. 1–2.
18. World Bank, *Pakistan: Rural Finance for Growth and Poverty Alleviation*, Washington, August 1995.
19. State Bank of Pakistan, op. cit., pp. 1–2.
20. Ibid., p. 1.3.
21. Ibid., p. 2.1.
22. Ibid., p. 5.1.
23. Ibid., p. 5.4.
24. Ahmed, Viqar and Rashid Amjad, op. cit., 1984, p. 162.
25. State Bank of Pakistan, op. cit., 1994, p. 6.1.
26. Ibid., p. 6.2.
27. Ibid., p. 6.2.

28. Ibid., p. 6.3–6.4.
29. Ahmed, Viqar and Rashid Amjad, op. cit., 1984, p. 160.
30. Government of Pakistan, Agricultural Census Organization, *Pakistan Census of Agriculture, 1972*, Islamabad, 1976.
31. Government of Pakistan, Agricultural Census Organization, *Pakistan Census of Agriculture, 1980*, Islamabad, 1983.
32. Government of Pakistan, *Report of the National Commission on Agriculture*, op. cit., pp. 225–6, emphasis added.
33. Ibid., p. 226.
34. Khan, Mahmood Hasan, *Lectures on Agrarian Transformation in Pakistan*, PIDE, Islamabad, 1985, p. 48.
35. Government of Pakistan, *Report of the National Commission on Agriculture*, op. cit., 1988, p. 226.
36. Applied Economics Research Centre, *Impact of Tractors on Agricultural Production in Pakistan*, AERC, Research Report no. 20, Karachi, 1982.
37. Ahmed, Viqar and Rashid Amjad, op. cit., 1984, pp. 176–7.
38. Government of Pakistan, *Report of the National Commission on Agriculture*, op. cit., 1988, p. 536, emphasis added.
39. Government of Pakistan, National Taxation Reforms Commission, *Final Report*, Islamabad, 1986, p. 134.
40. Ibid., p. 137.
41. Ibid., p. 138.
42. Nasim, Anjum and Asya Akhlaque, 'Agriculture Taxation and Subsidies', in Nasim, Anjum, *Financing Pakistan's Development in the 1990s*, Oxford University Press, Karachi, 1992, p. 476.
43. Ibid., p. 476.
44. Government of Pakistan, National Taxation Reforms Commission, *Final Report*, op. cit., 1986, pp. 155–6.

Part 2

Industry and Trade

There is a general belief, amongst economists, policy makers and the general public, that industrialization implies economic growth and development. Unless countries industrialize, the assumption goes, countries will continue to remain un- or underdeveloped. The progress of countries like South Korea, Taiwan, and other East and South-East Asian countries, which have been called the Newly Industrialized Countries (NICs), only endorses that view. The first three chapters of this part of the book examine the process of development in industry in Pakistan, from the early days when very little existed. The extraordinary growth in industry in the 1950s and 1960s suggested that Pakistan might be one of the very few countries at that time which would join the developed world. However, much of the growth that had taken place in the first two decades soon unravelled, with growing income and regional inequalities, resulting in the separation of East Pakistan.

Pakistan after 1971 was a new country in many respects, not least because of the industrial and economic policies followed between 1972 and 1977. The role of the public sector was increased substantially and the economy, for numerous reasons, did not do as well as it had in the first two decades. However, as the discussion shows, most claims that the early 1970s were a disaster are factually incorrect. Just as much as there was a change in economic policy in the early 1970s, in the 1980s, too, there was another shift, in many ways similar to that of the earlier period, but also influenced by the new world order of globalization, privatization, openness and neo-liberal economic policy. The Structural Adjustment Programme sponsored by the IMF and the World Bank now determines much of what happens regarding industrial policy in Pakistan.

Chapter 8 evaluates the key issues in the industrial sector in Pakistan, and questions most of the myths that have been perpetuated over the last few decades. We find that the claims that Pakistan's industry has been severely inefficient are not supported by the evidence. Many of the accusations made about the trade regime causing inefficient import substituting industrialization are also found to be false. Moreover, the claim that the public sector, too, was wasteful and inefficient is not borne out by the facts. These chapters offer a reinterpretation of the industrial and trade process in Pakistan, arguing that although there are problems in the industrial and trade sectors, many of the allegations have been grossly exaggerated.

6

The Process of Industrialization in Pakistan I: 1947–1977

For a region that was considered to be the Indian subcontinent's economic backwater at the time of partition, Pakistan's industrial and economic growth performance, at least up to the late 1960s, was phenomenal. Pakistan was considered a model developing country in the 1960s and enjoyed growth rates of gross domestic product (GDP) of over 6.7 per cent during the decade. This in a country that was considered to be 'an economic wreck [with] serious social unrest rising'[1] by the influential *TIME* magazine in 1947. Gustav Papanek, a professor from Harvard University, who played an important role as adviser to the Pakistan Planning Commission between 1954 and 1960, summarized the perception most observers had of Pakistan:

> At independence, Pakistan – simultaneously created and disrupted by the partition of British India – was widely considered an economic monstrosity. The country was among the poorest in the world and had no industries to speak of, almost no industrial raw materials, no significant industrial or commercial groups. It was difficult to see how Pakistan's economy could grow more rapidly than its population. Economic chaos and political disintegration seemed more likely. The 1950s were a period of apparent stagnation and mounting economic problems, when early dire predictions seemed to be fulfilled.[2]

The metamorphosis over a few years confounded all the prophets of doom who had predicted total anarchy in, and annihilation of, the country. By the mid-1960s the tone of dismay had changed considerably, and the international media had this to say about Pakistan: 'Pakistan may be on its way toward an economic milestone that so far has been reached by only one other populous country, the United States',[3] and 'the survival and development of Pakistan is one of the most remarkable examples of state and nation building in the post-war period'.[4]

This is the first of two chapters in which we examine Pakistan's industrial performance since 1947. The thirty-year period covered in this chapter consists of three very distinct, albeit interconnected, phases in industrial and economic policy. The first phase is the period 1947–58, when the foundations for the future years were laid. This was a period of huge change in the demographic make-up of the country, as well as in the political sphere, where governments were changed frequently.

The mere fact that the government had to deal with a refugee/migrant influx of about 7 million into West Pakistan (about 20 per cent of the entire population) was itself a massive responsibility and task. Add to that the fear of being taken over by India, and the lack of an industrial base or a skilled labour force, and we do indeed have every reason to believe the prophets of doom. However, Pakistan, despite heavily weighted odds against it, did manage growth rates of GDP of more than 3 per cent per annum in the earlier years. In the first main section of this chapter we examine how commercial and foreign exchange policies helped guide the economy on its path. This phase was a classical, and fairly successful, implementation of import substituting industrialization (ISI).

There was a continuation of these economic policies, at least in general direction and principle, during the second period between 1958 and 1968, under the leadership of Ayub Khan. Growth rates continued to impress, and a substantial industrial and economic base was established. However, there were major differences between the two periods, not least regarding political control and stability. In contrast to the confusion and frequent changes in government in the first decade, the second decade represented a period of political stability, authoritarianism, and bureaucratic control. The political situation under Ayub Khan was probably a key determinant of the economic performance of the country, both positive and negative. When the Ayub Khan government was celebrating its ten years in office and calling it the 'Decade of Development', unrest in both West and East Pakistan was identifying the failure of the regime by the way it had contributed to income and regional disparities. Most observers have claimed that the overall assessment of the ten years of Ayub Khan must be mostly negative, and that this regime was more a failure than a success. Some have even called Ayub Khan's ten years the 'Controversial Sixties'. Unlike most analysts, we will argue that the Ayub Khan era was in fact highly progressive and dynamic, and that despite some negative consequences of its economic strategy, it was overall a resounding success.

The Zulfiqar Ali Bhutto regime, which largely emerged out of the contradictions and conflicts under Ayub, was very different from the regimes of the past. The circumstances of Pakistan itself were very different in December 1971 when Bhutto took over than they had been in the previous twenty-four years. A very clear break with the past was represented by the fact that the more populous eastern wing of the country had fought for its liberty and had emerged as an independent nation. Criticism of the performance of the

Bhutto regime has been particularly harsh and there is a general impression that this period was Pakistan's 'worst' period economically. However, here as in the case of the Ayub Khan period, we re-examine the evidence and the issues, and reach somewhat different conclusions. We argue that, while some of Bhutto's economic policies may have had negative repercussions on the economy, the five-and-a-half-year period probably also had Pakistan's worst share of luck. The 'bad luck' factor between 1972 and 1977, when Zulfiqar Ali Bhutto happened to be in power, contributed significantly to the poor performance of the economy.

The period since 1977, from the fall of Zulfiqar Ali Bhutto until the present, once again has a continuous theme, which is discussed separately in the next chapter. Just as a major break came about in the evolution and development of Pakistan in 1971, so the period from about 1977 to the early 1980s forms a different development pattern.

In this chapter, then, we take a look at the performance of Pakistan's economy, with particular emphasis on the industrial sector, in the period 1947–77. We examine data, look at events and discuss policy issues that were important in determining the success and failure of that performance. Although there is some discussion of the role of the state and of political and institutional factors in determining economic strategy, policy, and outcomes, for the most part, we reserve our comments on the role of the state and political and institutional factors for a later chapter. In Chapter 19, we synthesize the crucial link between these apparently independent and unique factors – the state, institutions, classes, strategy – and examine economic development in a more realistic and holistic context, distant from the factual and largely empirical nature of this chapter.

6.1   1947–1958: Exchange Rates, Trade Policies, and Import Substituting Industrialization[5]

Very soon after independence, the Pakistan government acknowledged the precarious nature of the base of Pakistan's economy and identified areas and strategies that would need to be given urgent consideration. In its Statement of Industrial Policy of April 1948, it stated:

> The most striking feature of Pakistan's present economy is the marked contrast between its vast natural resources and its extreme industrial backwardness. A country producing nearly 75 per cent of the world's production of jute does not possess a single jute mill. There is an annual production of over 15 lac [1.5 million] bales of good quality cotton, but very few textile mills to utilize it. There is an abundant production of hides and skins, wool, sugarcane and tobacco – to name a few of the important products – but Pakistan's considerable resources in minerals, petroleum and power remain as yet untapped. In laying down any policy of industrialization, note has to be taken of these deficiencies and handicaps, and a concerted effort made to overcome them.[6]

On the basis of this assessment, the government felt that Pakistan would need to

> seek, in the first place, to manufacture in its own territories, the products of its raw materials, in particular jute, cotton, hides and skins, etc. for which there is an assured market whether at home or abroad. At the same time, to meet the requirements of the home market, efforts will be made to develop consumer-goods industries for which Pakistan is at present dependent on outside sources.[7]

The result of these objectives was that between 1949 and 1958 the growth rate of industry in Pakistan was amongst the most rapid for any country in the world. In United Pakistan, large-scale manufacturing grew at a phenomenal 23.6 per cent between 1949 and 1954, and afterwards, by the still very impressive 9.3 per cent up to 1960. The investment rate more than doubled during the 1950s, even though there was no increase in per capita income in that decade – in United Pakistan, GNP per capita grew on average by only 0.2 per cent between 1949 and 1954, and at zero per cent in the next five years.[8,9] In West Pakistan the growth rates were even more impressive, with large-scale manufacturing growing at 19.1 per cent between 1949 and 1958, and per capita income increasing by 6.97 per cent in the same period.[10] The main feature of the 1950s was the establishment and expansion of the large-scale manufacturing sector, which ranged from a high annual growth rate of 28.7 per cent in 1953/4 to a (still high) low of 4.9 per cent in 1957/8. Although starting from a non-existent base, and against all odds, Pakistan achieved very impressive rates of growth in its first decade (see Table 6.1).

With industry growing at high rates, there was a reverse picture in the agricultural sector, which only once in this period achieved double-digit growth rates. This is also the period when agriculture suffered negative growth rates in some years. Agriculture stagnated to the extent that its growth was not even enough to cope with the growth in population, resulting in a fall in per capita consumption of food grain and the need to import food as well.[11] In the mid-1950s, as much as 65 per cent of the civilian labour force was employed in agriculture and more than 75 per cent of the population lived in rural areas. Hence, a low growth rate in agriculture meant that the potential market for the growing manufacturing sector was also stagnant, restricting further growth in the manufacturing sector. Gustav Papanek has argued that 'agriculture was the sick man of economic development in Pakistan during the 1950s. A stagnant agriculture in a predominantly agricultural, economy meant a slowly growing economy.'[12] As we will show, the policies that were adopted in this period had a marked anti-agricultural bias and the terms of trade between agriculture and industry were heavily biased against the former (see Table 6.2). In fact, Stephen R. Lewis argues that 'the major impact of economic policy in the 1950s was to transfer income away from agriculture and from urban consumers, and to the new and rapidly growing manufacturing sector'.[13] Let us now turn to some of the tools and mechanisms which influenced investment and economic development in the first decade.

Table 6.1
Annual growth rate, 1950–1958, at 1959/60 factor cost (% per annum)

Year[a]	Agriculture	Manufacturing		Wholesale and retail trade	Banking and insurance	Public administration and defence	Services	GDP
		Large scale	Small scale					
1950/1	2.6	23.5	2.3	6.1	9.1	2.5	4	3.9
1951/2	–9.1	18.7	2.4	0.5	10	4	4	–1.8
1952/3	0.2	23.6	2.2	0.6	7.6	–4.4	4	1.7
1953/4	13.6	28.7	2.3	6.3	8.5	–2.4	4	9.4
1954/5	–0.8	24.1	2.3	5.5	2.6	4.6	4	2.7
1955/6	2.1	17.5	2.3	2.3	21.5	1.6	4	3.4
1956/7	2.3	8.1	2.3	3.2	22.9	–2.6	4	3
1957/8	1.9	4.9	2.2	3.4	–1.7	–2.2	4	2.6
1950–1954 (ave.)	1.8	23.6	2.3	3.4	8.8	–0.1	4	3.3
1954–1958 (ave.)	1.4	13.6	2.3	3.6	11.3	0.4	4	2.9

[a]The annual growth rate for 1950/1 means the rate for the period 1949/50 to 1950/1.
Source: Government of Pakistan, *Pakistan Economic Survey, 1984–85*, Islamabad, 1985.

Table 6.2
Domestic terms of trade for West Pakistan (three-year moving averages), 1951–1964

Year	West Pakistan	
	Manufacturing sector	Agricultural sector
1951–1954	108.62	97.39
1952–1955	112.22	91.14
1953–1956	116.42	87.36
1954–1957	112.00	91.41
1955–1958	107.77	96.03
1956–1959	104.52	98.76
1957–1960	102.60	99.43
1958–1961	98.05	103.13
1959–1962	95.32	106.39
1960–1963	94.75	108.28
1961–1964	96.06	107.84

Source: Lewis, Stephen, *Economic Policy and Industrial Growth in Pakistan*, George Allen & Unwin Ltd, London, 1969, p. 60.

6.1.1 The Impact of the Exchange Rate

Before the partition of the subcontinent, the area constituting Pakistan was the bread-basket of India. The areas that became Pakistan were net importers of industrial goods from India and produced agricultural commodities, such as cotton, wheat, and jute. After independence, a customs union between India and Pakistan existed through the use of a common currency, but this was broken up in 1949. The same year also saw the government of Pakistan taking one of its most important decisions, which had a vital impact on industrial development in the country.

In September 1949, the pound sterling was devalued, as were the currencies of numerous countries including that of India, Pakistan's main trading partner. Viqar Ahmed and Rashid Amjad argue that 'the reason why the Pakistan government did not devalue its own currency at that moment is one of the most controversial questions of the period and the genesis of the pro-industrial bias in government policy in many ways can be traced back to this decision'.[14] One reason why this decision was taken was to announce to the world that Pakistan was an independent country and did not mimic Indian economic policy. Other reasons were to continue to sell raw jute to India (since Pakistan had no jute mills) at a now higher price, and to be able to import machinery and capital goods at a cheaper price. However, India punished the newly-born Pakistan by suspending trade between the two countries and refusing to accept Pakistan's independent stand. The Pakistani government imposed some controls on imports and exports in order to manage trade with countries that had devalued, as their imports were now cheaper. By not devaluing, the interests of Pakistan's exportable raw materials remained protected.

Pakistan was a monopoly exporter of jute, mainly to India, and hence gambled on the presumption that by not devaluing it would reap additional profits from the higher price of jute. In 1948/9, India imported 55.8 per cent of Pakistan's exports, but all such exports were suspended in September 1949. The consequences of the Indian retaliation could have been quite catastrophic for Pakistan's economy: either Pakistan would have been forced to devalue, as was the motive for India's trade suspension, or Pakistan would need to hurriedly find alternative markets for its exports. Neither decision was easy. However, Pakistan's luck changed for the better, as it has done on so many occasions, with positive effects for the economy.

The Korean War broke out in June 1950, and there was a fear that it might trigger off World War Three. Countries began stockpiling and storing raw materials, and as demand for them increased, so did their price. Jute and cotton were both in heavy demand, and Pakistan was able to make spectacular profits on its exports. Not only that, but demand was worldwide – Pakistan's traditional markets, India and Britain, now no longer reigned supreme as Pakistan was able to diversify into new areas. Import controls that had been imposed only a few months before were again liberalized after the Korean War began. India also recognized Pakistan's new exchange rate, and trade was resumed after a suspension of eighteen months, but on a smaller scale than earlier.[15] The decision not to devalue had paid off.

The Korean boom lasted from 1950 to 1952, but by mid-1951 world prices of raw materials began to decline and export earnings also saw a decrease. There were clear signs that the market was heading for a recession, but Pakistan was too slow to react, and policies continued as if nothing had changed. Since Pakistan's exchange rate was still high compared to its trading partners which had devalued in 1949, after the Korean boom in 1952 there were expectations of a devaluation. In 1952 jute and cotton prices fell, as did export earnings, and Pakistan was facing a serious balance of payments crisis and sharply falling reserves. As it did in 1949, the government decided not to devalue and instead imposed very strict exchange controls and a set of physical controls on imports and exports. As Lewis shows, 'tariffs were maintained, but they were not the major determinant of prices of import composition. Export taxes on jute and cotton were raised during the Korean war, and were lowered somewhat following the fall in prices. Exporters of such commodities received low rupee prices for their goods both because the currency was devalued and because of the export taxes'.[16] The probable reason for not devaluing in 1952 despite a deterioration in the balance of payments was that capital goods were now needed to start the process of industrialization and a devaluation would have raised their prices. Hence, the government resorted to the imposition of controls instead.

The decision not to devalue may, with hindsight, have been the critical decision that started Pakistan on the road to industrial and economic development. Since industry was non-existent in the earlier years, international trade was the main sector where large profits could have been made. The Korean War export boom resulted in traders and merchants amassing considerable amounts of wealth. Trading was much more profitable than industry during the Korean boom. Viqar Ahmed and Rashid Amjad make the pertinent point that 'the favourable conditions for the conversion of merchant capital into industrial capital were the result of another important economic event related to the Korean war: the collapsed prices of raw materials after the end of the war'.[17] With controls imposed on imports, especially on consumer goods, 'the prices of these goods increased sharply in the domestic market which changed the terms of trade in favour of industry and against agriculture. This led to a sharp increase in the profitability of the industrial sector, and in comparison with the other sectors including trading, industry now became the most attractive sector.'[18] Hence, traders with their amassed wealth converted merchant capital into industrial capital and so began the process of industrialization in Pakistan. Although one study has argued that it was 'practical exigencies rather than conscious policy [that] provided the initial diversion of investible resources

towards industry',[19] Stephen Lewis makes the essential point that 'government policy was not neutral, however, but decidedly favoured industrialization, particularly the decision not to devalue'.[20] Moreover, Lewis argues that, once the import licensing scheme was under way, here too conscious decisions were taken about the direction that the process of industrialization should take (see following sections).

6.1.2 The Trade Policy Regime[21]

Once the industrialization process had begun after merchant capital moved into industry, and after the collapse of the Korean boom in 1952, when falling export prices caused the balance of payments position to deteriorate, controls and restrictions were imposed on trade, having a substantial impact on the ensuing industrialization process. As Lewis argues, 'from 1953–64 virtually all imports into Pakistan were regulated by some form of quantitative controls'.[22] The trade policy adopted by Pakistan 'had three major aspects: (i) overvaluation of the rupee relative to other countries, (ii) use of quantitative controls on imports to regulate the level and composition of imported goods, and (iii) a highly differentiated structure of tariffs on imports, and export taxes on the two principal agricultural exports: jute and cotton'.[23]

The government began to favour tariff protection as a means to promote industrialization. It wanted a cascaded tariff structure, with lower tariffs on intermediate and capital goods, tight controls over the import of luxuries, controls on other consumer goods, and easier access to capital goods and industrial raw materials. Table 6.3 shows the cascading nature of tariffs imposed in the late 1950s. However, despite the high prevalence of tariffs, Lewis makes the point that 'while the tariff structure played some role in directing resources in Pakistan, *that role was a relatively minor one* ... The principal determinant of the structure of imports and the set of domestic relative prices was the import licensing system.'[24] Licensing was used explicitly as a protective or exchange-saving device.

In assessing the role of tariffs, compared to that of quantitative measures, Lewis's conclusions are clear:

> It is clear that tariffs and indirect taxes played relatively minor roles in directing resource allocation, even when compared with other policy variables. Direct quantitative controls were dominant in setting prices and incentives. Through their substantial impact on relative prices, these controls speeded the process of structural change both by imposing the inducements to invest in various industries and by transferring substantial amounts of income to industrialists who reinvested them in the profitable manufacturing sector. The *directions* that industrial growth took were probably the same as those that would have been taken in the absence of major policy decisions due to market size and domestic resource availabilities. The policies adopted increased the *speed* with which the transformation of industrial structure occurred, both by increasing incentives and by increasing incomes in the hands of the 'saving' sector of the economy.[25]

Table 6.3
Average rate of duty on imported goods by types of commodity, 1955–1964

Description	1955/6	1956/7	1957/8	1958/9	1959/60	1960/1	1961/2	1962/3	1963/4
Consumption goods									
Essentials	35	35	35	35	35	55	55	55	56
Semi-luxuries	54	99	99	99	99	111	111	111	116
Luxuries	99	99	99	99	99	140	140	140	142
Raw material for consumption goods									
Unprocessed	26	26	26	26	26	27	27	27	30
Processed	43	43	43	43	43	50	50	48	51
Raw material for capital goods									
Unprocessed	23	23	23	23	23	28	28	28	31
Processed	38	38	38	38	38	40	40	39	42
Capital goods									
Consumer durables	71	71	71	71	81	85	85	85	89
Machinery and equipment	14	14	14	14	14	17	17	17	17

Source: Lewis, Stephen, *Economic Policy and Industrial Growth in Pakistan*, George Allen & Unwin Ltd, London, 1969, p. 72.

6.1.3 The Consequences of Exchange Rate and Trade Policy for Industrialization

The consequences of the exchange rate and trade policies adopted by Pakistan should be fairly clear. Box 6.1 describes how such policies lead to a particular type of import substituting industrialization. The type of protective policy pursued in Pakistan can be put simply as follows: '(i) produce anything that can be reasonably produced domestically; (ii) once production has started domestically, ban imports of competing goods so as to save foreign exchange'.[26] More specifically,

> If the average tariffs were any guide to the differential incentive structure during the early years of industrialization, the very high incentives for domestic production were given to those items for which the domestic market was

BOX 6.1
How import substituting industrialization (ISI) works

The economic strategy that was in vogue in the 1950s and 1960s was import substituting industrialization. Stephen R. Lewis explains how it worked.

A country beginning with virtually no productive capacity in manufacturing, and facing present or potential balance of payments problems, will be tempted to follow a policy of placing restrictions on the imports of non-essential goods, usually consumer goods, for two reasons. First, given the scarcity of foreign exchange, it feels that essential needs of established industries, or potential industries, should have priority. Second, there is some appeal to the idea that restricting the flow of imported consumer goods will release more resources for saving, since consumption would be restricted by lack of physical availability. The difficulty with this approach, as has been noted by numerous writers, is that it encourages the domestic production of consumer goods only, and it does so both because there is a relatively protected market for consumer goods and there is a relatively cheap source of imported capital goods and raw materials on which to base the production of the consumer goods. Industries are established which have heavy dependence on imported supplies, and there is little incentive to develop local capital goods and intermediate goods industries to serve them. In addition, since this sort of policy is usually a concomitant of maintaining an overvalued currency, the export of the newly produced consumer-oriented goods is discouraged; domestic resources are valued more highly in saving than in earning foreign exchange. As a result, after the process has gone on for some time, the country finds itself with productive capacity heavily dependent on imported sources of supply and with no new means of earning foreign exchange.

Source: Lewis, Stephen, *Economic Policy and Industrial Growth in Pakistan*, George Allen and Unwin, London, 1969, pp. 38–9.

the smallest: luxury consumer goods and consumer durables. Imports of these goods were most heavily penalized, primarily as a measure to save foreign exchange. Essential and semi-luxury (or semi-essential) consumer goods, which included most of the basic mass-consumption items (food, cloth, kerosene, matches, soap, etc.) received more protection than raw materials for production of such goods. Only since 1959/60, after the first rush of industrialization was over, were the differential incentives given to broad-based consumption goods (particularly semi luxuries) widened sharply. It is true throughout, however, that producer durables had low tariffs, and, if the classification system is right, the duties on raw materials for producer durables exceeded the duties on the goods themselves.[27]

Import substitution progressed easily and very rapidly in those industries that had the highest protection, i.e. consumption goods, and those that had cheap and ready access to domestically produced, primarily agricultural, raw materials, such as cotton, jute, and leather. Another reason why consumer goods grew is provided by Lewis. He argues that 'the size of the domestic market at Partition and well into the 1950s was decidedly larger for consumer goods than for most intermediate and investment related goods'.[28] These were also those industries in which Indian imports made a significant contribution to Pakistan's domestic market.

There is a tendency for some observers to suggest that much of what happened in the industrial and economic sphere in Pakistan in the 1950s was erratic and not thought through. However, as we have shown above, even the decision not to devalue seems to have had a clear logic behind it, although good luck did endorse that decision further. Similarly, the import licensing scheme also seemed to be a thought-out policy measure which affected relative prices and hence patterns of industrialization. The pattern of investment and import substitution influenced the decisions of the licensing authorities about what sorts of imports and, hence, what sort of industrial development should take place. Lewis agrees that the 'licensing system was largely a mirror of the decisions to invest in different industries'.[29]

6.1.4 The End Result

Since almost all capital goods and most non-agricultural industrial goods were imported, the state played a major role in determining the nature and structure of industry through the licensing system and tariff structure, and through the incentives it provided. Stephen Lewis summarizes the impact of these measures on trade as follows:

> The exceedingly rapid growth of modern manufacturing during the 1950s, amid a relatively stagnant economy, particularly in agriculture, was reflected in the decline of imports of some manufactured goods, the rise of those imports related to investment activity, the emergence of certain manufactured exports, the conversion from an export surplus to an import surplus in food grains, and the decline of

agricultural exports that were used as raw materials by domestic industries. In the 1960s the changes in the structure of production were somewhat smaller, and in different directions due to the increased flows of aid-financed imports and the more rapid growth of such sectors as agriculture.[30]

The significant increase in exports was from the newly established manufacturing industries, mainly jute and cotton textiles, which replaced competing imports by the mid-1950s. Towards the end of the 1950s, Pakistan was in a position to produce export surpluses as well. In many ways, these results indicate the success of the first phase of the import substituting industrialization policy of the 1950s, where the emphasis was on consumer goods rather than on intermediate or capital goods. This strategy also rested on the government's preference for investment in those areas where foreign exchange could be saved regardless of cost, and its 'desire to produce domestically almost anything that technologically could be produced there'.[31]

Stephen R. Lewis estimates that the success of the import substituting strategy can be gauged by the fact that almost all the growth that took place in manufacturing between 1951 and 1955, and hence in overall growth, was due to import substitution. The increase in domestic demand was not a cause of growth up to 1954/5 and was only of consequence after 1960. The complete dominance of import substitution in the first half of the decade was reduced a little in the second half, but still accounted for over 20 per cent of growth of manufacturing output, with the newly established manufactured exports responsible for about 25 per cent.[32] Moreover, the trend in the first phase of import substituting industrialization was also showing a shift, as consumer goods industries, which accounted for about 70 per cent of manufacturing value added in 1954/5, contributed less than half of the growth after that period (Table 6.4).

While Pakistan's impressive growth rate in the 1950s was due to the fact that the country started with a low base in the first place, the other important factor was that, due to the restrictive measures enforced on the economy, profit rates in industry were very high. The government had very openly encouraged private sector initiative in economic growth, an encouragement to which the private sector responded enthusiastically. The annual returns on investment ranged from 50 to 100 per cent in the early 1950s, but dropped to between 20 and 50 per cent in the latter part of the decade. There were strong economic incentives to becoming an industrial entrepreneur, but Papanek notes that while 'high profits were strongly conducive to industrial investment ... perhaps even more important were the strong disincentives to alternative activities. With the end of the Korean boom, international trade, and especially importing, suddenly became unattractive',[33] and therefore industrial development became a natural choice. Thus it was the lure of extraordinary profits and a lack of good alternatives that induced the process of industrialization.

The pattern of industrial development resulted 'inevitably', as Papanek argues, in a high degree of concentration. Most of the nascent industrialists were traders who had made money

Table 6.4
Sources of growth in manufacturing value added, 1951–1964 (% distribution in three periods)

Percentage of total growth due to:	Domestic demand (1)	Export growth (2)	Import substitution (3)	Value added coefficient (4)	Total change (5)	Annual rate of growth of value added (6)
1951/2–1954/5						
Consumptions goods	–6.2	0.2	85.0	–	78.9	43.0
Intermediate goods	0.8	0.7	12.6	–	14.1	28.0
Investment and related goods	0.1	0.0	6.8	–	7.0	16.8
All industries	–5.3	0.9	104.4	–	100.0	38.8
1954/5–1959/60						
Consumptions goods	31.2	10.8	16.5	–5.8	52.6	15.6
Intermediate goods	8.7	15.3	2.2	0.5	26.7	27.0
Investment and related goods	12.5	0.2	5.6	2.4	20.7	28.0
All industries	52.4	26.3	24.3	–2.9	100.0	38.8
1959/60–1963/4						
Consumptions goods	45.1	–	–1.1	3.4	47.4	12.8
Intermediate goods	10.8	6.1	6.0	–3.7	19.2	13.7
Investment and related goods	30.6	0.4	–2.7	5.2	33.5	26.0
All industries	86.5	6.5	2.2	4.9	100.1	38.8

Source: Lewis, Stephen, *Economic Policy and Industrial Growth in Pakistan*, George Allen & Unwin Ltd, London, 1969, p. 49.

in the Korean boom and were already well established and well-off. However, they had better possibilities for making more money and amassing further wealth given the high-profit, near-monopoly markets that were developing. Papanek shows that in 1950 there were 3,000 individual firms in Pakistan, but the concentration of wealth was so high that only seven individuals, families, or foreign corporations constituted 25 per cent of all private industrial assets in United Pakistan. Twenty-four units constituted nearly 50 per cent of all private industrial assets.[34]

While the development of the economy and of industry was private sector oriented, the institutions of the state did play an important role too. In the field of credit, the government was particularly significant. The Pakistan Industrial Credit and Investment Corporation (PICIC) and the Pakistan Industrial Finance Corporation (PIFCO) provided funds to the larger, more established firms which had adequate security and a high profit rate. PICIC provided nearly 'half of all its loans to a tiny group of leading industrialists'.[35] However, the role of both institutions was more important after the 1960s, and the links they made with industry show how the network of industry and finance in the private and public sector interacted (these issues are discussed in Chapter 19). The institution that played a more important role at this time was the Pakistan Industrial Development Corporation (PIDC), which 'pioneered in industries and areas which were neglected by private investors during the early period of industrialization'[36] and 'fulfilled an extremely useful function in supplementing private enterprise'.[37]

Although East Pakistan seceded from United Pakistan in 1971, the seeds for this process were sown long before. While Ayub Khan's decade is held responsible for fostering the economic decay and underdevelopment of East Pakistan, leading to the formation of Bangladesh, this is only part of the picture. In fact, it would be very unfair to hold the policies of Ayub's regime solely responsible for Pakistan's break-up, as many observers do. Even in the 1950s, strong biases in economic development had emerged, which were blatantly tilted against the eastern wing. For example, state institutions in the 1950s, such as PICIC and PIFCO, concentrated on industries in West Pakistan, while in 1958 about 66 per cent of the government's investment through PIDC was based in West Pakistan, which also received 62 per cent of foreign loans compared to the eastern wing's 38 per cent[38]. The cessation of trade between India and Pakistan in 1949 also had greater negative consequences for East Pakistan, as about 50 per cent of West Pakistan's trade and 80 per cent of East Pakistan's was with India. Table 6.5 shows that, in fact, West Pakistan had a continuous deficit in trade throughout the 1950s, while East Pakistan had a consistent surplus. The overall trade figures for United Pakistan were in surplus due to East Pakistan's contribution, mainly by exporting jute. This evidence shows very clearly that East Pakistan was instrumental in supporting the process of industrialization in (West) Pakistan. West Pakistan's development was built on a transfer of resources from the eastern wing, which got very little in return, and this process was initiated as early as the late 1940s and early 1950s.

Table 6.5
Balance of payments of trade, 1949–1958

Balance of payments of trade (Rs m)	1949/50 to 1950/1	1950/1 to 1951/2	1951/2 to 1952/3	1952/3 to 1953/4	1953/4 to 1954/5	1954/5 to 1955/6	1955/6 to 1956/7	1956/7 to 1957/8
East Pakistan								
Exports	683	1,211	1,087	643	645	732	1,042	910
Imports	372	453	764	367	294	320	360	819
Balance of payments	311	758	323	276	351	412	682	91
West Pakistan								
Exports	535	1,343	922	867	641	491	742	698
Imports	912	1,167	1,473	1,017	824	783	965	1,516
Balance of payments	−377	176	−551	−150	−183	−292	−223	−818
Pakistan								
Exports	1,218	2,554	2,009	1,510	1,286	1,223	1,784	1,608
Imports	1,284	1,620	2,237	1,384	1,118	1,103	1,325	2,335
Balance of payments	−66	934	−228	126	168	120	459	−727

Source: Ahmed, Viqar and Rashid Amjad, *The Management of Pakistan's Economy, 1947–82*, Oxford University Press, Karachi, 1984, p. 65.

Just as East Pakistan was neglected, so was the agricultural sector: Table 6.2 shows how the terms of trade developed against agriculture and in favour of industry in the 1950s. Viqar Ahmed and Rashid Amjad write that 'the initial accumulation of industrial capital had taken place as a result of the large tribute paid by the agricultural sector to the industrial sector and by the urban consumers. The former had supplied agricultural raw materials at cheap prices and had paid high prices for manufactured consumer goods in return'.[39] The devaluation in 1955 was meant to redress the balance against agricultural exports and occurred simultaneously with a shift in giving some priority to agriculture.

Despite some negative consequences of the economic policies pursued by the governments in Pakistan in the first decade, it would be fair to say that they initiated an era of industrial growth and development which laid the foundation for the Decade of Development between 1958 and 1968. On the basis of the criteria that were considered important at that time – in the 1950s, when import substituting industrialization was the received wisdom – Pakistan did very well for itself. Much of the criticism made of those policies forty years later (see Chapter 8) is quite unwarranted.

6.2 1958–1968: The Decade of Development

There is little disagreement over the fact that the growth rates in agriculture, large-scale manufacturing, and GDP showed quite astonishing trends over the ten years between 1958 and 1968. The disagreements exist over the nature and consequences of those growth rates and over an interpretation of the economic policies that formed what the government of the time called the 'Decade of Development' and what its critics have very mildly termed the 'Controversial Sixties'.[40] Viqar Ahmed and Rashid Amjad argue that

this period of rapid economic growth, achieved mainly as a result of the policies pursued, generated a great deal of economic tensions ... Increasing disparities in regional income between the provinces, a concentration of industrial economic power, the failure of real wages to increase significantly, and a general belief of increasing income inequality, all contributed to the rejection of the Ayubian growth philosophy and strategy.[41]

We will examine the nature of these developments in the course of this section after looking at the facts regarding growth rates, the policies pursued, and the consequences of those policies.

The impressive performance of the main sectors of the economy can best be gauged from Table 6.6. The high growth rates in large-scale manufacturing continued in the first few years of the Ayub regime with the average for the period 1960–5 rising to a phenomenal 16.9 per cent. Even after 1965, when there was a marked slowdown, growth rates in manufacturing still remained above to 10 per cent. In industry, it seems that the previous trends maintained during the 1950s continued well into the 1960s. Agriculture presents a marked improvement in the 1960s compared with the dismal situation in the 1950s. The reasons for this growth were the recognition in the late 1950s that the excessive pro-industrial bias was affecting agriculture very negatively and that a redress was necessary. Some steps were taken, but it was the Green Revolution (see Chapter 3) that was responsible for the very high growth rates of the late 1960s. For Papanek, 'the spurt in agricultural production was the main difference between the Pakistan of the 1950s and of the 1960s, as well as between Pakistan and other countries'.[42] In the first half of the 1960s, overall investment had risen to

Table 6.6
Annual growth rate, 1958–1970, at 1959/60 factor cost (% per annum)

Year[a]	Agriculture	Manufacturing		Wholesale and insurance	Banking and insurance	Public administration and defence	Services	GDP
		Large scale	Small scale					
1958/9	4.0	5.6	2.3	2.5	12.9	9.8	4.0	5.5
1959/60	0.3	2.7	2.3	5.9	22.1	−2.7	3.8	0.9
1960/1	−0.2	20.3	2.9	6.9	10.0	1.3	4.7	4.9
1961/2	6.2	19.9	2.9	7.8	8.5	3.9	4.0	6.0
1962/3	5.2	15.7	2.9	9.8	11.5	2.8	4.2	7.2
1963/4	2.5	15.5	2.9	10.1	8.9	9.7	4.0	6.5
1964/5	5.2	13.0	2.9	7.9	37.9	17.8	7.0	9.4
1965/6	0.5	10.8	2.9	8.7	10.9	56.5	1.1	7.6
1966/7	5.5	6.7	2.9	5.3	12.7	−14.4	4.3	3.1
1967/8	11.7	7.6	2.9	3.7	11.8	−2.5	4.0	6.8
1968/9	4.5	10.6	2.9	7.1	8.5	5.0	3.9	6.5
1969/70	9.5	13.9	3.0	10.9	19.4	3.6	6.8	9.8
1958–1964 (ave.)	3.0	13.3	2.7	7.2	12.3	4.1	4.1	5.2
1965–1970 (ave.)	6.2	10.4	2.9	7.2	16.9	11.0	4.5	7.2

[a]The annual growth rate for 1958/9 means the rate for the period 1957/8 to 1958/9.
Source: Government of Pakistan, *Pakistan Economic Survey, 1984–85*, Islamabad, 1985.

over 18 per cent of the GNP, and savings had doubled between 1949 and 1965.

6.2.1 Trade Policy Directing Industrialization

Although there was a great deal of continuity between the 1950s and 1960s, hence the similar levels of growth and development, some critical steps were taken, especially in the trade and exchange rate policies that were the prime movers of the 1950s. The new regime of Ayub Khan disbanded many of the controls that had been imposed following the post-Korean War recession in 1952. In 1959 there was a fundamental reordering and change in the method of directing industrialization through trade policy, and a series of liberal policies were introduced which remained in effect till 1965.

The main emphasis of the new trade policy in 1959 shifted away from direct controls and towards indirect controls on imports and on domestic prices of other goods. As Lewis shows, 'a number of measures were taken in import licensing that made market forces more important in determining the commodity composition of imports and the distribution of ownerships of import licences'.[43] It was the Export Bonus Scheme (EBS) or the Bonus Voucher Scheme, launched in 1959, that was considered to be the key to the import liberalization process in Pakistan (see Box 6.2 for how the scheme worked). The scheme allowed a free market in the bonus vouchers for certain commodities. In addition, the earlier, closed and selective import licensing scheme of the 1950s, which was based on the importer's ability to import during the Korean boom of 1950–2, was replaced in 1961 by the Open General Licence (OGL), which allowed newcomers

to enter the trading sector. A large amount of foreign exchange was allocated to the OGL, and given the buoyant nature of trade and of the economy, the new traders made substantial profits and gains from possessing import licences. The most 'market friendly' change was the introduction of the 'Free List', which permitted the import of certain goods without any licence. The Free List was extended over time from four items to fifty in 1964. The tariff structure continued to be used as a signalling device, as it had been in the 1950s, but as Table 6.3 shows, the differentials in the tariff rate structure widened, with the rates for consumer goods rising much more than for other goods. The bias against producing machinery and equipment locally continued, as the import duty on these items was still the lowest, thus making it easier to import these goods rather than produce them at home.

The main reason why the government could be so generous in its import policy in the first half of the 1960s was critically linked to the availability of foreign aid, which increased from 2.5 per cent of GNP in the mid-1950s to 7 per cent of GNP in the mid-1960s.[44] In fact, according to an important Asian Development Bank study, the 'import liberalization which took place during the first half of the 1960s *would have been impossible without this large increase in aid*',[45] In 1965 the Free List suffered serious setbacks as foreign aid was curtailed, and due to the resulting foreign exchange squeeze, the import liberalization policies were abandoned and many new import controls were introduced. (See section 6.2.2 for more on the contribution of foreign aid in the 1960s.) As long as foreign exchange resources were available, largely through aid, the government was eager to follow a liberal import regime.

The government's import licensing scheme was supposed

BOX 6.2

The Bonus Voucher Scheme

One of the most controversial instruments adopted by Pakistan's managers of the economy was the Bonus Voucher or Export Bonus Scheme. Some writers have argued that this scheme was responsible for Pakistan going on the wrong industrialization track, while others believe that the scheme was largely responsible for Pakistan's high growth. This box explains how it worked.

The Export Bonus Scheme which was introduced in 1959 was a flexible and fascinating device which was used both to subsidize exports and to allow a safety valve on imports, while maintaining the basic structure of import controls on the vast majority of imports and while maintaining at the same time the official exchange rate at its existing level. Under the Export Bonus Scheme, an exporter received, in addition to the amount of rupees converted at the official exchange rate, Bonus Vouchers equivalent to some percentage of his export earnings (the percentage varied from time to time and from commodity to commodity). The Bonus Voucher could be used to import any item from a list of importables that changed from time to time. At some times during the last decade, goods on the Bonus Voucher importable list overlapped with goods importable under other types of licence, and sometimes there was no overlap. The exporter could import items himself, or he could sell the Bonus Vouchers in an organized market, at which the Bonus Vouchers have sold at a consistent premium above their face value. In most years of the Scheme the premium on Bonus Vouchers has been stabilized at around 150 per cent of face value, the stabilization having been accomplished by additions to and subtractions from the list of importables and the list of exports eligible for Bonus Vouchers or the rate at which Bonus Vouchers were awarded for those exports.

An example may be helpful at this point. An exporter sells $100 worth of Pakistani goods abroad, the Bonus rate on the goods being 20 per cent, and the premium on Bonus

Vouchers 150 per cent. The exporter receives Rs475 from the State Bank of Pakistan, as well as Bonus Vouchers with a face value of Rs95. The exporter then sells the Bonus Vouchers in the market for Rs142.50, which gives him total receipts for his exports of Rs617.50, or 30 per cent more than the official exchange rate. The rate of subsidy is easily computed on any item, since it is the rate at which Bonus Vouchers are awarded *times* the premium at which Bonus Vouchers are selling. For some items the extent of subsidy has reached 60 per cent of the f.o.b. value of exports. Bonus Vouchers were awarded to almost all manufacturing industries and to some non-traditional primary products such as fine rice and fish.

On the import side, Bonus Vouchers acted as import licences, and at times when Bonus Vouchers sold at 150 per cent of face value, the cost of foreign exchange to importers was 150 per cent above, or two-and-a-half times, the official exchange rate. Tariffs and sales taxes on imports were added to the cost to importers, but were computed at the official exchange rate, not the Bonus Voucher exchange rate. The advantage of Bonus Vouchers from the point of view of importers was that it was possible to import items immediately, and the waiting period until the next shipping period was announced in accordance with the regular licensing system could be by-passed through the use of Bonus Vouchers. Thus, the Bonus Voucher system provided an excellent safety valve for those firms who might have run short of a critical spare part or raw material during a licensing period. A number of items of machinery and transport equipment were also imported under Bonus Vouchers, so that the initial fears, which were that Bonus Vouchers would simply provide more luxury consumption goods, did not materialize to the extent that many people had expected at the time of the introduction of the scheme.

Source: Lewis, Stephen, *Pakistan: Industrialization and Trade Policies*, George Allen and Unwin, London, 1970, pp. 28–30.

---

to encourage the private sector to invest, just as the EBS was a means for exporters to acquire additional foreign exchange by exporting more. The exchange rate had been overvalued in the 1950s (and later as well), but the EBS compensated for that and boosted exports, especially of manufactured goods. The scheme transferred a subsidy to exports, and the exports of raw jute fell from 60 per cent of total exports in 1958 to 20 per cent in 1968/9, while the exports of cotton and jute textiles increased from 8.3 to 35 per cent in this period, and the exports of other manufactures increased tenfold from 2 to 20 per cent. The EBS also had a positive impact on imports, making raw materials and machinery imports easier and cheaper. The Export Bonus Scheme was considered to be an innovative device helping both import substituting and export growth.[46] In 1965 Pakistan's manufactured exports were greater than those of South Korea, Turkey, Thailand, and Indonesia *combined*.[47] The main feature of the foreign exchange regime in the 1960s was that, with an overvalued

exchange rate, it became cheaper to import industrial machinery, which resulted in low prices for agricultural inputs, while the EBS transferred subsidies to manufactured exports.

The impact of the EBS and the import licensing and liberalization strategy on industrial development was considered to be 'dramatic' by some observers. The Asian Development Bank study shows that large-scale manufacturing growth increased from 8 per cent per annum between 1955 and 1960, to 17 per cent between 1960 and 1965 in the Second Five-Year Plan. The controls reimposed following the foreign exchange and aid curtailment caused this growth to fall to about 10 per cent in the second half of the 1960s.[48]

An interesting outcome of these trade policies, as Stephen Lewis shows, is that in sharp contrast to the 1950s *none* of the growth in industry during the period of the Second Five-Year Plan was due to import substitution – a remarkable transformation, indeed.[49] Instead, domestic demand and absorption were the dominant factors. As foreign aid had increased, so had imports, and even though manufacturing output grew at impressive rates due to the import policies and foreign resources, imports increased at a faster pace. Both industrial production and investment responded well to the liberalization of imports. The nature of import substituting industrialization had also changed over the years, shifting away from almost wholly the consumer goods industry to intermediate and capital goods. Table 6.7 shows the differences in the three sectors in the 1960s, and also shows that the growth rate was much higher in the first half of the decade than in the second half. The most interesting observation that can be made from Table 6.7 is that the growth in investment goods was by far the fastest of all sectors during the early 1960s. The reason, according to the Asian Bank, was that since this sector was most dependent on imported raw materials, it benefited the most from import liberalization.[50] Another reason why import substitution slowed down was the EBS, which encouraged the export of manufactured goods. The share of exports in total consumer goods output rose from 15 per cent in 1959/60 to 45 per cent in 1969/70.[51] Meekal Ahmad evaluates the impact of the EBS on exports and argues that it 'compensated for the overvaluation of the domestic currency by introducing a series of multiple exchange rates depreciated in relation to the official exchange rate so that the profitability of exporting was brought more in line with the incentives for sales in the domestic market'.[52]

Asad Sayeed goes beyond looking at growth rates of industrial performance, as he feels these often hide the costs incurred in the process. Instead, he argues that 'productivity growth rates, especially total factor productivity growth (TFPG), is one measure which reveals the efficiency of factor use'[53] (see Box 6.3 for how to calculate TFPG). The growth rates in total factor productivity shown in Tables 6.8 and 6.9 reveal that Pakistan's growth rate of 5.06 per cent was far higher than many comparable countries, indicating 'both technological dynamism and dynamic allocative efficiency in a comparative perspective'.[54] This evidence only underlines the fact that growth in manufacturing was higher than in most other countries in the 1960s, and was highly efficient, as it came about due to improvements in the amount of output per unit input (see Box 6.3).

6.2.2 Foreign Aid, the Private Sector, and Inequalities

Gustav Papanek writes that 'foreign aid contributed *significantly* to Pakistan's growth, from the late 1950s; *without it, the rapid increase in development in the 1960s could not have been possible*'.[55] Keith Griffin felt that in the mid-1960s 'the entire social and economic system that had been built up, was heavily supported by and sustained through foreign assistance'.[56] Rashid Amjad argues that the 'explanation for the boom in private industrial investment in the first half of the sixties and its subsequent slowing down lies principally in the change in foreign aid inflows to the industrial sector in

---

BOX 6.3

How can productivity growth be measured?

What is the engine of growth? Is it education, technological improvement or hard work? Some answers:

Asia's growth performance has been so spectacular and so sustained that it has been dubbed the East Asian Miracle in a study by no less an authority than the World Bank. But as miracles have true believers, so too must they have debunkers. To challenge the received wisdom that Asia has a magic formula for success, we have Prof. Paul Krugman of Stanford University, who states flatly that the miracle is based on 'perspiration rather than inspiration'. Krugman's argument, in which he relies heavily on empirical work by Prof. Alwyn Young of MIT and others, is very simple. He says that Asian growth has been driven by growth in inputs like labour and capital rather than by gains in efficiency. In this sense, East Asia is no different from other economies at similar stages in their development, like the Soviet Union in the 1960s and 1970s. Hence, the miracle is no miracle at all.

Introducing 'Growth Accounting'

Krugman makes his case by using a basic equation of 'growth accounting'. This is a technique which uses regression analysis to isolate and quantify contributions to economic growth. The equation is as follows:

GDP growth = growth in labour input + growth in capital input + total factor productivity (TFP)

The rationale behind this is simple. Economic growth comes about either through the application of more inputs or through a rise in output per unit input, i.e. improvements in TFP. The labour input variable captures all the influences that increase either the quantity or quality of labor used in the production process. These include growth in population, rising participation rates, growth in employment and improving levels of education and skills. The capital input variable reflects changes in the stock of physical capital used in production and is measured by spending on plant, machinery, equipment, roads, telecommunications and so on. What is left is TFP which is a pure measure of efficiency, i.e. improvements in the amount of output per unit input. This comes from improvements in management and work organization and improvements and innovations in technology. Since it is very difficult to measure TFP directly, empirically it is derived as a residual in the growth equation. TFP is what is left after the contributions of labour and capital are determined and subtracted out.

Source: Jardine Fleming Securities Limited, 'Asian Economic Outlook', Hong Kong, 1996, p. 18.

Table 6.7
Rate of growth of manufacturing output, 1960–1970 (% per annum)

Industries	1960–1965	1965–1970	1960–1970
Total manufacturing	16.0	10.0	12.0
Consumer goods	10.6	9.0	10.0
Food	9.2	11.3	11.0
Beverages	16.5	6.1	11.0
Tobacco	17.3	10.4	15.0
Textile	5.9	8.7	7.0
Footwear	8.1	4.6	6.0
Woodwork	12.7	5.4	9.0
Furniture	17.0	4.0	11.0
Printing	9.4	8.1	9.0
Miscellaneous	19.3	7.0	13.0
Intermediate goods	12.0	8.0	9.0
Paper	7.2	11.2	8.0
Leather	15.7	9.6	12.0
Rubber	17.2	8.5	13.0
Chemicals	20.3	15.9	18.0
Petroleum	49.3	7.4	27.0
Investment goods	20.0	8.0	13.0
Non-metals	11.5	8.0	9.0
Basic metals	12.0	9.8	10.0
Metal products	21.8	7.0	14.0
Machinery	23.4	7.0	15.0
Electrical machinery	24.8	5.7	16.0
Transport equipment	26.9	7.5	19.0

Source: Ahmed, Meekal, in Sayeed, Asad, 'Political Alignments, the State and Industrial Policy in Pakistan: A Comparison of Performance in the 1960s and 1980s', unpublished Ph.D. thesis, University of Cambridge, 1995, p. 54.

Table 6.8
Growth rate of total factor productivity, 1960–1970

Industries	TFPG
Food processing	2.17
Tobacco manufacturing	8.19
Textile manufacturing	5.27
Footwear and wearing apparel	1.30
Paper and paper products	−8.71
Printing and publishing	5.68
Leather and leather products	9.60
Rubber and rubber products	12.64
Chemicals and chemical products	−2.31
Non-metallic minerals	−2.83
Basic metal industries	8.13
Metal products	1.52
Non-electrical machinery	2.81
Electrical machinery	5.65
Transport equipment	0.90
Miscellaneous	10.95
Total	5.06

Source: Sayeed, Asad, 'Political Alignments, the State and Industrial Policy in Pakistan: A Comparison of Performance in the 1960s and 1980s', unpublished Ph.D. thesis, University of Cambridge, 1995, p. 56.

the sixties'.[57] In fact, he goes even further and says that the entire

> economic system which operated in Pakistan in the sixties was quite different from that suggested by earlier writers. It bore little resemblance to classical nineteenth-century capitalism (portrayed by writers like Papanek). On the other hand, the system did not fail because the capitalist class were no longer prepared to 'play the game' or had lost the desire to invest (as, for example, Nulty would make us believe). The system which operated in Pakistan came very close to being what we can term a 'Foreign Aid Dependent Regime' in which the mechanics of industrial growth were in one way or another made dependent on foreign aid inflows. Once these aid flows slowed down, the system, not being able to replace foreign aid with other forms of external finance like direct foreign investment, and without the peculiar boost to profitability associated with the local system for dispensing aid, found it difficult to sustain the earlier growth it had generated.[58]

These extracts and the discussion in the earlier sections show that Pakistan's growth in the 1960s, and the policies pursued (import liberalization, for example), were contingent upon the country receiving a substantial amount of foreign aid. Once the aid stopped, so did growth in the economy. And while foreign inflows mattered, the (unwritten) conditions to the aid made the role of the private sector paramount. Papanek, a firm believer in the leading role of capitalism and the private sector, argues that 'for ideological reasons, the United States, Germany, the World Bank, and others have been strong advocates of private enterprise. A country that caters to this preference is bound to profit.'[59] He considers Pakistan's industrial experience from the 1950s to the mid-1960s to be a success story of private enterprise, but the incentives that foreign aid generated were critical. Rashid Amjad argues that 'foreign aid played a crucial role in the creation of ... favourable conditions and had a direct impact on the private sector'.[60] Thus, foreign aid in association with the private sector was the main instrument in Pakistan's economic growth in the 1960s. Interestingly enough, there was also an explanation of the economic development model of the 1960s which not only rested its premise on the leading role of the private sector, but also justified increasing inequalities. This was the Doctrine of Functional Inequality.

Ali Cheema explains the concept of Functional Inequality rather eloquently. He says that this philosophy was part of Ayub Khan's Martial Law government's policy, and

Table 6.9
Total factor productivity in manufacturing: selected countries

Country	Period	TFPG
Argentina	1960–1970	2.64
Brazil	1960–1970	0.75
Chile	1960–1970	0.33
Colombia	1960–1970	3.46
India	1959–1976	0.00
Korea	1960–1973	8.30
Mexico	1960–1970	3.01
Thailand	1963–1977	1.50
Turkey	1963–1976	1.50
Venezuela	1960–1970	1.92

Source: Sayeed, Asad, 'Political Alignments, the State and Industrial Policy in Pakistan: A Comparison of Performance in the 1960s and 1980s', unpublished Ph.D. thesis, University of Cambridge, 1995, p. 56.

was the central pillar of the advice given to the Pakistan government by the Harvard Advisory Group. In simple terms the doctrine suggested that resources should be directed towards the industrial sector which has a higher propensity to save, and that agriculture and wages should bear the brunt of this transfer. The idea was that profits in the industrial sector should be raised giving the push towards growth which will result in automatically positive distributional consequences as development proceeds.[61]

Essentially this doctrine propagated the pursuit of what Papanek calls 'the social utility of greed'. The outcome was the concentration of wealth and income in the industrial sector (see Box 6.4).

Rashid Amjad's excellent work on private industrial investment in Pakistan documents and highlights the extent of that concentration. A dominant small group of monopoly houses had begun to emerge in the 1950s in the industrial sector, a trend which was accentuated in the 1960s. In 1970 there were 44 monopoly houses, which controlled about 77 per cent of gross fixed assets of all manufacturing companies listed on the Karachi Stock Exchange. These firms controlled about 35 per cent of all assets of the entire large-scale manufacturing sector and at the same time had close links with the financial sector. Seven of the seventeen Pakistani banks were under the direct control of the monopoly houses, accounting for 60 per cent of total deposits and 50 per cent of loans and advances. They had an extended network of interlocking directorates, where the board of directors of one company sat on the board of directors of others. Moreover, there were strong links between private industry and government financial institutions: between 1958 and 1970, 65 per cent of total loans disbursed by PICIC went to thirty-seven monopoly houses, with the largest thirteen of these accounting for about 70 per cent of these loans. Dr Mahbubul Haq, a key supporter and architect of the Ayub government's Doctrine of Functional Inequality, revealed figures, as the Ayub regime was falling, of even greater concentration: he claimed that (the famous) twenty-two families controlled 66 per cent of industrial assets, 70 per cent of insurance, and 80 per cent of total banking assets. Rashid Amjad argues that, while this claim was never substantiated, it nevertheless had a great deal of truth in it, and his own research does show very high concentration.[62]

While there was certainly economic concentration at one end of the wealth spectrum, there was also a general belief that income inequalities had increased during the 1960s and that there was no substantial increase in the level of real wages. The labour movement of 1968/9 was a major factor in the fall of Ayub Khan's regime, as it was fuelled by the perception that the fruits of growth had not trickled down to sections of society other than the industrialists. The strategy of Functional Inequality also gave low priority to the social

BOX 6.4

The social utility of greed

Gustav Papanek argues that inequality leads to economic growth. He writes as follows:

The problem of inequality exists, but its importance must be put in perspective. First of all, the inequalities in income contribute to the growth of the economy, which makes possible a real improvement for the lower-income groups. The concentration of income in industry facilitates the high savings which finance development. Allowing the more enterprising and wealthy peasants to sink tube wells is a major factor in expanding agricultural output. In turn, growth of the economy means cheaper cloth, cheaper food, and more adequate supplies for the bulk of the population. Great inequalities were necessary in order to create industry and industrialists; but to maintain industrial growth after the first 5 to 10 years does not require the same high rate of profit and therefore does not imply the same inequities. Greater equality during the early period at the cost of growth would probably have left the poorer groups in a worse position absolutely, though they would have been better off relatively. This argument holds true, however, only because inequalities in income result substantially in inequalities in savings, not in consumption. High incomes are more acceptable, politically and morally, because they are used chiefly for investment, rather than for conspicuous consumption.

Source: Papanek, Gustav, *Pakistan's Development: Social Goals and Private Incentives*, Harvard University Press, Cambridge, Mass., 1967, pp. 242–3.

Table 6.10
Income distribution in Pakistan, 1963/4 and 1969/70

% of households	% of income	
	1963/4	1969/70
0–10	2.3	3.2
10–20	4.1	4.8
20–30	5.0	5.6
30–40	6.1	6.6
Lowest 40%	17.5	20.2
40–50	7.1	7.4
50–60	8.4	8.6
60–70	9.8	10.0
70–80	11.9	11.8
Middle 40%	37.2	38.0
80–90	15.1	14.7
90–100	30.2	27.1
Highest 20%	45.3	41.8
Gini coefficient		
National	0.386	0.336
Rural	0.362	0.304
Urban	0.433	0.367

Note: Income shares according to each decile of
          household have been estimated by fitting a
          (Lorenz) curve to the cumulative share of various
          income groups in total household and income
          derived from the Household Income and
          Expenditure Survey for the respective years.
Source: Government of Pakistan, *Pakistan Economic
          Survey, 1984–85*, Islamabad, 1985.

sectors such as education and health. Viqar Ahmed and
Rashid Amjad argue that, after the cut in foreign aid in 1965,
with foreign exchange down and defence spending up, the
ensuing economic crisis between 1965 and 1967 was a key
cause of Ayub Khan's downfall. The sugar crisis of 1967/8
acted as a major trigger to a smouldering feeling of
discontent. Prices had risen by 15 per cent in 1965/6 and 10
per cent in 1966/7, adding fuel to the fire. Along with these
factors, there was what Viqar Ahmed and Rashid Amjad call
a *popular feeling* that inequality had increased. They argue that

> A major factor responsible for this feeling was
> the considerable increase in the level of
> conspicuous consumption and wasteful
> expenditure on extravagant and lavish housing
> and other consumer durables by the richer
> classes in the country. Also, even if the actual
> level of income distribution had not worsened,
> the number of people living in abject poverty
> was still very significant and the display of
> conspicuous consumption in the face of this
> extreme poverty stirred considerable tension and
> finally led to an outbreak of unrest in the
> country.[63]

Table 6.11
**Per capita GDP in East and West Pakistan at 1959/60
constant prices**

Year	Per capita GDP East	Per capita GDP West	West–East disparity ratio	Index of disparity
1959/60	269	355	1.32	100
1964/5	293	426	1.45	141
1969/70	314	504	1.61	191

Source: Ahmed, Viqar and Rashid Amjad, *The
          Management of Pakistan's Economy, 1947–82*,
          Oxford University Press, Karachi, 1984, p. 89.

Interestingly though, Table 6.10, which shows income
inequality over the period, indicates that inequality actually
decreased in the 1960s.

While there are differences of opinion about the extent of
inequality as a result of the policies pursued under Ayub,
there is no denying the fact that interregional disparity
between West and East Pakistan did worsen. Even Gustav
Papanek accepted the presence of high inequality between
the two provinces, although he was able to justify this
through an argument that endorsed the social use of
inequality (see Box 6.4). Economists, especially in East
Pakistan, were great critics of this policy and argued that all
the growth or development that had taken place was in West
Pakistan and that there had been a transfer of resources from
East to West (Tables 6.11 and 6.12 give some indication of
this phenomenon).[64] Stephen Lewis shows that the level of
per capita income in West Pakistan was only 10 per cent
higher than in East Pakistan in 1949/50. This disparity had
risen to over 30 per cent in 1964/5. The 'East Pakistanis
complained that not only were they less well off at the time
of Partition, but they also had been exploited by the West
wing to provide resources for development in that richer
province.'[65] (Further discussion of regional inequality takes
place in Chapter 18.)

Table 6.12
**Index of disparity in per capita income (West minus
East, divided by West)**

Year	Index of disparity
1949/50	17.9
1954/5	19.5
1959/60	24.5
1964/5	31.1
1969/70	37.9

Source: Ahmed, Viqar and Rashid Amjad, *The
          Management of Pakistan's Economy, 1947–82*,
          Oxford University Press, Karachi, 1984, p. 89.

6.3 1972–1977: The Bhutto Years — Bad Luck or Bad Management?

If there was any economic continuity between the first and second decades, it seems to have all but evaporated between the Ayub and Yahya regimes and that of Zulfiqar Ali Bhutto. In many ways, there was a clear break from the past, as more than half of what was Pakistan from 1947 to 1971, had seceded to become an independent country, Bangladesh. Bhutto inherited a new Pakistan, defeated in war by India, and he came to power as Pakistan's first democratically elected leader. These differences from the past were sharp enough, but not only was the political set-up different, Bhutto's economic policies also made a sharp break from the pro-private sector strategies of the earlier years. Bhutto's regime has come in for a lot of criticism for 'destroying' the economy. Critics have argued that his strange concept of socialism was responsible for the dismal growth rates and for the highest rates of inflation ever seen in Pakistan. They have argued that it was poor policies and bad economics which caused the malaise. We examine these claims and also see how factors not in the control of the government affected economic performance. Our interpretation suggests that numerous 'bad luck' factors played a critical role in causing the economy to grow at below trend rates.

There is no doubt that the growth rates of the 1950s and 1960s were particularly impressive. It is also unlikely that those growth rates could have been sustained unless other institutional factors were also changed. Thus, it was inevitable, and more so after the independence of East Pakistan, that the rate of growth would decline. The performance of the Bhutto regime must be seen in the context of the circumstances in which it took over power and the problems that it inherited.

Table 6.13 shows the annual growth rates for GDP and its constituents for 1971/2 to 1976/7. A comparison with the 1950s shows that the growth rates for GDP overall were higher in this period than in the 1950s, although in manufacturing the 1950s had higher rates, while in agriculture the two periods were somewhat similar. For services, given the more developed economy in the 1970s, the growth rate was higher then, despite the fact that industry and agriculture, which form a close link with services, were not growing at the rates of the 1960s. Services grew by 5.7 per cent even when in 1974/5 growth rates in agriculture and manufacturing were both negative. In fact, in each of the three years from 1972 to 1975, the annual growth rate in all services considered together was actually above 10 per cent.

Table 6.14 shows the rates of inflation over the Bhutto period. By any standard, inflation was high in most years of the Bhutto government, especially compared with the very low 3.83 per cent average for the 1960s (however, see section 6.3.2 for an explanation).

Before we turn to an evaluation of the Bhutto government's policies, a word about the data is of particular interest. The Ayub Khan government fell in 1968 and Bhutto took over from General Yahya Khan in December 1971. However, some studies, when examining the performance of the Bhutto period, lump the post-Ayub three years with the Bhutto period, distorting the facts. One example is Nawab Haider Naqvi and Khwaja Sarmad's study, which in its evaluation of Pakistan's economy in the 1970, considers 1969/70 to 1976/7 as one homogenous period and produces average growth rates for the whole of it.[66] The Bhutto period was a distinct period, so clubbing it with the Yahya period does not reveal the true nature of the Bhutto regime. The Pakistan Economic Survey of 1984/5 makes the same mistake and provides average growth rates for the period 1970–7, calling it the 'Non Plan' period.[67] While there may have been no implementation of the Five-Year Plans produced between 1970 and 1977, to evaluate the performance of the Bhutto regime the correct time-frame needs to be kept in mind.

Table 6.13
Annual growth rate, 1971–1977, at 1959/60 factor cost (% per annum)

Year[a]	Agriculture	Manufacturing		Wholesale and retail trade	Banking and insurance	Public administration and defence	Services	GDP
		Large scale	Small scale					
1971/2	3.5	−6.8	7.2	−0.5	0.8	6.8	5.1	1.2
1972/3	1.7	11.9	7.3	6.7	29.1	14.1	5.2	7.2
1973/4	4.2	7.5	7.3	14.9	6.4	14.8	5.4	7.7
1974/5	−2.1	−1.7	7.3	3.2	14.4	33.2	5.7	3.9
1975/6	4.5	−0.5	7.3	1.8	3.3	−3.0	5.7	3.3
1976/7	2.5	−0.2	7.3	−0.3	8.2	7.3	3.2	2.9
1971–1977 (ave.)	2.4	1.7	7.3	4.3	10.4	12.2	5.1	4.4

[a]The annual growth rate for 1971/2 means the rate for the period 1970/1 to 1971/2.
Source: Government of Pakistan, *Pakistan Economic Survey, 1984–85*, Islamabad, 1985.

Table 6.14
Inflation rates in Pakistan, 1970–1980 (% per annum)

Year	Annual rates of change in the general price level
1970/1	5.71
1971/2	4.69
1972/3	9.7
1973/4	29.98
1974/5	26.73
1975/6	11.66
1976/7	9.24
1977/8	6.89
1978/9	8.33
1979/80	10.44
Growth rates for selected periods[a] (% per annum)	
1969/70 to 1976/7	13.96
1976/7 to 1979/80	8.55
1969/70 to 1979/80	12.34

[a] Growth rates are trend values significant at the 95 per cent confidence level.
Source: Naqvi, S.N.H. and Khwaja Sarmad, *Pakistan in the Seventies*, PIDE, Islamabad, 1993.

6.3.1 Economic Policies and Performance

In its election manifesto, the Pakistan People's Party had promised the nationalization of all basic industries and financial institutions. The manifesto had said that 'those means of production that are the generators of industrial advance or on which depend other industries must not be allowed to be vested in private hands; secondly, that all enterprises that constitute the infrastructure of the national economy must be in public ownership; thirdly, that institutions dealing with the medium of exchange, that is banking and insurance, must be nationalized'.[68] The economic policies of the Bhutto government rested on the premise that the control of the leading enterprises was to be in the hands of the state. Figure 6.1 highlights the salient features of the nationalization agenda of the Bhutto government.

The first phase of nationalization took place in the large-scale manufacturing sector, essentially in the capital and intermediate goods industry. This produced a small share of the total value added of the sector (less than 20 per cent) since much of the growth in this sector had taken place in the consumer goods industries. The nationalization programme was later extended to the vegetable oil sector and then to cotton ginning and rice milling. The nationalization of banks and insurance companies was a critical assault on the close link that had built up between industrial and financial capital since the mid-1950s. This link had been one of the causes of the economic concentration that became a political issue in the late 1960s. The party's promises to urban organized labour, as to rural peasants and agricultural workers, were

20 December 1971	Zulfiqar Ali Bhutto takes over as President of Pakistan.
January 1972	Public takeover of 31 large firms in 10 basic industries: iron and steel, basic metals, heavy engineering, motor-vehicle assembly and manufacture, tractor assembly and manufacture, heavy and basic chemicals, petrochemicals, cement and public utilities.
March 1972	Land reforms.
March 1972	Management and control of 32 life insurance companies.
May 1972	Banking reforms; State Bank of Pakistan extends controls over scheduled banks, reorientating credit policy towards small farmers and small industrial entrepreneurs.
May 1972	Devaluation of the rupee by 131 per cent.
June 1972	Comprehensive labour reforms.
August 1972	Comprehensive public health programme.
September 1972–September 1974	Nationalization of educational institutions.
June 1973	Trade in cotton and rice nationalized.
September 1973	Vegetable oil, petroleum marketing, and shipping nationalized.
January 1974	Nationalization of all private and domestically owned banks.
August 1976	Cotton ginning, rice husking, and flour milling nationalized.

Figure 6.1
Bhutto's nationalization programme, 1972–1977

fulfilled within six months of coming to power through the labour reforms and land reforms of 1972. The devaluation of the Pakistani rupee by 131 per cent had important repercussions as we show below, and 'removed at one stroke the subsidy the industrialists had received in the earlier period because of the overvalued exchange rate. This reform, together with the increase in procurement prices of agricultural goods (which went up by about 100 per cent in this period), made a deliberate attempt to alter the pro-industry anti-agriculture bias of the previous growth strategy.'[69] The Export Bonus Scheme, a key feature of the 1960s, was also abandoned.

The impact of the government's policies must be seen in the context of what the government had inherited. The loss of East Pakistan, if for no other reason, was important because 50 per cent of West Pakistan's products found a way into East Pakistan in 1969/70, and the loss of such a large market was cause for concern enough. Furthermore, 18 per cent of the West's imports came from East Pakistan. Hence,

Table 6.15
Trade pattern, 1970–1977

Year	Exports	Imports	Balance	Exports	Imports	Balance
	(Rs m)			($ m)		
1970/1	1,998	3,602	−1,604	420	757	−337
1971/2	3,371	3,495	−124	591	638	−47
1972/3	8,551	8,398	153	817	797	20
1973/4	10,161	13,479	−3,318	10,626	1,362	−336
1974/5	10,286	20,952	−10,666	1,039	2,114	−1,075
1975/6	11,253	20,465	−9,212	1,137	2,067	−930
1976/7	11,294	23,012	−11,718	1,141	2,325	−1,184

Source: Government of Pakistan, *Pakistan Economic Survey, 1995–96*, Islamabad, 1996.

new markets had to be found immediately to compensate for this loss of market. The success of the devaluation measure was apparent soon after, when new markets were found and

the value of export to areas other than the former East Pakistan rose by 41% in the financial year 1972 and 39% in the financial year 1973. This reflected both a sharp jump (about one-third) in the size of the cotton crop in the exports of cotton and cotton textiles, and the successful diversion of most of the flow of cotton, textiles, rice and other goods with which West Pakistan had previously reimbursed East Pakistan for its flow of jute and jute earnings to West Pakistan.[70]

Exports in 1972/3 increased by 153 per cent over the previous year,[71] and manufactured exports grew by 19 per cent in 1973/4, which, according to the Asian Development Bank, 'was due to favourable world demand conditions for cotton textiles, and the capacity available for production for exports following the loss of the East Wing market in 1971'.[72] The growth in exports was a key factor in the growth in industrial output between 1972 and 1974 (see Table 6.15). Agricultural output also rose, and this was attributed to 'the higher support prices for wheat, rice, sugar, and timely and adequate supply of essential inputs'.[73] Availability of credit also played a vital role in the improved performance, for after May 1972 when the government had tightened its control over the banking system, more credit was available to the export sector and to small farmers. The export refinance scheme was started by the State Bank of Pakistan in 1973, and its lending rate was lower than the nominal banking rate or the kerb market rate.

The economic boom of 1972/3 and 1973/4 seemed to be fairly short-lived and was attributed to the rebound of domestic demand following the disruption in the economy in the early 1970s and to the worldwide commodity boom. However, the world recession after 1974 considerably slowed the demand for Pakistani exports. After about two and a half years of impressive growth, the last three years of the Bhutto government saw the trend substantially reversed with dismal growth rates. Viqar Ahmed and Rashid Amjad argue that those last three years of the Bhutto regime also 'coincide with

the "big-push" in public sector investments in long gestation projects and show a dismal performance in both the agricultural and manufacturing sector'.[74]

Table 6.16
Investment and growth rates in the large-scale manufacturing sector, 1969–1980, at constant price level of 1969/70 (Rs m)

Years	Private sector	Public sector	Total	Relative share of public investment in total (%)
(1)	(2)	(3)	(4)	(5)
1969/70	1,208.2	177.1	1,385.3	12.8
1970/1	1,038.4	58.3	1,096.7	5.3
1971/2	699.9	63.8	763.7	8.4
1972/3	313.1	45.1	358.2	12.6
1973/4	230.8	113.7	344.5	33.0
1974/5	182.8	276.8	459.6	60.2
1975/6	344.5	831.5	1,176.0	70.7
1976/7	369.0	1,085.3	1,454.3	74.6
1977/8	482.3	1,922.1	2,404.4	79.9
1978/9	459.7	1,944.9	2,404.6	80.9
1979/80	544.6	1,644.0	2,188.6	75.1

Growth rates for selected periods[a] (% per annum)

1969/70 to 1976/7	−45.1	−[b]	−39.0	11.5
1976/7 to 1979/80	17.0	45.5	34.2	12.5
1969/70 to 1979/80	−[b]	39.8	11.7[c]	11.9

[a] Growth rates are trend values significant at the 95 per cent confidence level.
[b] Insignificant trend.
[c] Values significant at the 90 per cent confidence level.
Source: Naqvi, S.N.H. and Khwaja Sarmad, *Pakistan in the Seventies*, PIDE, Islamabad, 1993.

One outcome of the nationalization measures was the complete reversal of public and private investment. The substantial contribution by the private sector in the 1960s was cut by a stroke. In 1974/5, the height of the Bhutto regime's nationalization programme, private sector investment was only 15 per cent of its 1969/70 level (see Table 6.16). Public sector investment, which was 5 per cent of the total in 1970/1, rose to 75 per cent at the end of the Bhutto era. These figures may suggest that the Bhutto regime's nationalization programme alone was responsible for this trend, but it is important to realize that 'private investment had already started to climb down even before nationalization struck it down in 1972',[75] and that the decline in investment during the second half of the 1960s, which indicates that growth in large-scale manufacturing had slowed, was a trend which continued into the 1970s. However, there is no doubt that the anti-industrialist policies and great uncertainty of the 1972–7 period were also responsible for the lack of private sector investment. The private sector had lost all trust in the government, for Bhutto had broken his promises: 'his assurance of no further nationalization [prior to nationalizing the vegetable oil industry in September 1973] until the elections of 1977 no longer seemed meaningful and the little confidence that the businessmen had developed in the regime was now completely gone'.[76] Such promises were broken time and time again.

6.3.2 The Bad Luck Factor

The fact that the economy suffered after 1974 is clear. The reasons, for this, however, are open to some debate. Figure 6.2 shows that a number of events that took place outside the control of the government were largely responsible for the poor performance of the economy after 1974. There was a very large increase in the prices of imports following the oil price rise in 1973, which resulted in inflation at close to 30 per cent in 1973/4. The oil price rise had begun to affect the gains from devaluation and exports, and in one go wiped out the positive balance of trade from 1972/3. While export growth still showed some positive signs, albeit at a much slower pace, the import bill grew very significantly (see Table 6.15). In one year alone, oil imports rose from US$60 million in 1972/3 to $225 million in 1973/4; fertilizers increased from $40 million to $150 million in the same period.[77] The result of the huge rise in oil prices was an international recession that was not in the control of the Bhutto government.

Moreover, in the five years of the Bhutto government, floods and pest attacks damaged crops severely, putting pressure on prices and affecting industrial production.[78] The failure of the cotton crop in 1974/5 came at a time when there was a surge in international prices and hence Pakistan was not able to exploit the situation to its advantage. The year 1976/7 saw Pakistan's worst floods, devastating large areas of cultivated land.

Excessive inflation was seen as Bhutto's biggest failure, but a closer look at the management of the economy and of the growth in monetary assets suggests that much of the inflation was imported. Table 6.17 shows that excessive monetary growth took place only in the first and last of his five and a half years. The increase in 1971/2 was primarily

Figure 6.2
Bhutto: the bad luck factor?

20 December 1971	Zulfiqar Ali Bhutto takes over as President of Pakistan.
May 1972	Devaluation of the Pakistani rupee; initial outcome highly positive with exports growing by more than 100 per cent.
August 1973	Massive floods hit Pakistan; import of food grain.
October 1973	Fourfold increase in international petroleum prices; imports cost much more; prices of fertilizers, essential inputs, and oil jump; excessive inflation domestically.
1974–1977	World recession follows OPEC price rise; demand for Pakistani exports remains severely depressed and affects industrial output.
1974–1975	Huge failure of cotton crop by as much as 25 per cent at a time when international cotton prices had risen; affected industrial output.
1976–1977	Worst floods in Pakistan's history; agricultural crops destroyed; further import of food crops; excessive expenditure on public good measures, all affecting industrial output.

due to the adjustments necessitated by the loss of East Pakistan and to the increase in exports. Viqar Ahmed and Rashid Amjad write that the economy had been well managed in the early years without excessive deficit financing despite the costs incurred due to the floods, and monetary expansion had been kept well in line with GNP growth, and was 'almost entirely limited to the private sector. There had in fact been an overall contractionary effect in the government and foreign sector'.[79] A very negative perception seems to have become part of the literature on the Bhutto period, where, despite the facts, a number of observers believe that the economy under Bhutto was in a shambles. William McCleary, for example, argues that there was 'generally poor performance and relative stagnation in the 1970s', and that a 'lack of fiscal and monetary discipline led to high budget deficits, rapid monetary growth, and inflation'.[80]

Mohsin S. Khan of the IMF, however, has also made an important intervention in the debate over Bhutto's economy, and particularly about the rate of inflation. He writes that 'a good part of the increase in the earlier period [of the Bhutto era] was a result of the oil price shock in 1973/74. If these two years are dropped from the case, the average annual rate of inflation in the 1970s falls to less than 10 per cent ... Certainly, it is not obvious from the numbers that the 1970s

Table 6.17
Differential growth rates of money supply, GDP, and commodity-producing sectors, 1969–1980 (% per annum)

Years (1)	Growth of money supply[a] (2)	Growth of real GDP (3)	Growth of commodity producing sectors (4)	Excess of col. (2) over col. (3) (5)	Excess of col. (2) over col. (4) (6)
1969/70	10.69	9.78	10.07	0.19	0.62
1970/1	10.80	0.30	−1.42	10.50	12.20
1971/2	42.66	1.17	1.35	41.49	41.31
1972/3	14.21	7.21	4.25	7.00	9.96
1973/4	11.06	7.74	5.24	3.32	5.82
1974/5	12.44	3.94	−1.26	8.50	13.70
1975/6	11.14	3.32	3.48	7.82	7.66
1976/7	24.30	2.53	1.98	21.77	22.32
1977/8	22.97	7.38	4.63	15.59	18.34
1978/9	20.20	4.90	3.90	15.30	13.30
1979/80	18.51	7.28	7.88	11.23	10.63
Growth rates for selected periods[b] (% per annum)					
1969/70 to 1976/7	15.72	4.22	2.21	11.50	13.51
1976/7 to 1979/80	18.66	6.16	5.17	12.50	13.49
1969/70 to 1979/80	16.50	4.59	2.84	11.91	13.66

[a] Growth rate for 1969/70 means the rate for the period from 1968/9 to 1969/70.
[b] Growth rates are trend values significant at the 95 per cent confidence level.
Source: Naqvi, S.N.H. and Khwaja Sarmad, *Pakistan in the Seventies*, PIDE, Islamabad, 1993.

was characterized "by generally poor performance and relative stagnation" or that the 1980s were so much better on all fronts.'[81] Shahid Javed Burki, otherwise a critic of Bhutto's politics, also maintains that 'Pakistan's performance during the seventies appears unsatisfactory only when compared to that of the sixties. The seventies produced a better overall record compared to the fifties ...'.[82]

The key causes of low growth in the mid-1970s were possibly an extremely adverse weather cycle along with an international recession. Government policy did not help much either, where industrialists were eyed with suspicion, and in response to government fears and threats the industrialists created artificial crises. While organized labour felt that it had a greater right to the share of industrial produce, industrialists feared more lock-outs or outright nationalization. Entrepreneurs were demoralized and unwilling to invest. Capital and capitalists had fled overseas and it was clear that the economy and industry were faced with a severe crisis, no matter what the causes may originally have been. The Bhutto era has been considered one of Pakistan's worst economically. Nawab Haider Naqvi and Khwaja Sarmad have argued that this period was 'a period of domestic and international economic turmoil, significant external shocks and economic dislocation and disruption'.[83] We have tried to show that (1) things were not as bad as they seemed, given the conditions inherited and the odds against Bhutto, and (2) it was more bad luck than bad management which resulted in poor economic growth rates. The implications and consequences of the Bhutto regime for the social and political evolution of Pakistan are addressed in Part VI of this book.

6.4 Summary and Further Reading

6.4.1 Summary

This is an important chapter in many ways, because it examines the history of the industrialization process over the first three decades of Pakistan's existence, and examines specific policies persued by different regimes to further the goals of industrialization. In the first decade, the exchange rate and the trade regime played an important role in determining the direction of industrial development in Pakistan, laying the ground for later years. Starting from an almost non-existent industrial base, economic growth in the period 1947–58 was impressive. It became even more astonishing in the Decade of Development under Ayub Khan between 1958 and 1968.

Industrial development showed extraordinary growth rates under Ayub, and there was a perception that Pakistan would soon emerge as one of the few underdeveloped countries to join the ranks of the developed world. Moreover, while agriculture suffered severely during the 1950s, in the 1960s the Green Revolution brought about an equally impressive transformation, complementing industrial growth. Overall economic development was quite phenomenal in this period.

There was also a downside to this capitalist development, as is always the case. Inequalities between East and West Pakistan increased, as did those between different economic and social classes. However, despite these inherent contradictions in the mode of capitalist development under the Ayub regime, we argue that the economic programme and policies followed resulted in extremely impressive growth. Rather than being labelled as a failure, the Ayub regime was dynamic and a 'success' by whatever criteria were available at that time to measure success.

The Bhutto era represents a significant break with the past. With more than half the country now an independent nation, Bhutto assumed leadership of a war-torn Pakistan and inherited extremely difficult conditions. Despite this, the first two years of his five-and-a-half year rule showed exemplary growth by any standard. In the subsequent years, however, a large number of factors over which Bhutto had no control resulted in a slowing down of the growth rate and of economic development, especially after the high-growth 1960s. We argue that it was not bad management that caused economic deterioration in the Bhutto period, but bad luck.

This chapter makes an important contribution to the debate over economic growth and development during the first three decades, by contesting and arguing against some of the more popular myths that have emerged about this period in the literature.

Firstly, we argue that the import substituting industrialization policy pursued in the first decade was the right policy *for that time*, and that a careful and selective manipulation of key economic variables resulted in an industrial base being formed. Secondly, we argue that Ayub Khan's Decade of Development was indeed that –not a failure of development, as some observers contend – and that the contradictions that emerged were all inherent in the policies pursued. This was, probably, Pakistan's Golden Age. And lastly, we show that the Bhutto government suffered the consequences of bad luck, both domestic and international. Not only was Bhutto not wholly responsible for the poor performance, but the extent of that poor performance has, itself, been grossly exaggerated. Economic performance was not half as bad as we have generally been led to believe.

6.4.2 Further Reading

Some of the best academic work that has been done on Pakistan looks at the period 1960–70 and the growth model adopted in this period. Since industry was such a major component of growth, many of the best works on Pakistan examine industrial performance in the earlier years. The two books by Stephen R. Lewis, Jr, *Economic Policy and Industrial Growth in Pakistan*, George Allen and Unwin, London, 1969 and *Pakistan: Industrialization and Trade Policies*, George Allen and Unwin, London, 1970, are classics which examine in great detail the early period following Pakistan's independence. Gustav Papanek's *Pakistan's Development: Social Goals and Private Incentives*, Harvard University Press, Cambridge, Mass., 1967, also covers the early period, and is a first-hand account by someone who was involved in public policy. Other books on the early period include White, L.J., *Industrial Concentration and Economic Power in Pakistan*, Princeton, 1974; MacEwan, Arthur, *Development Alternatives in Pakistan*, Harvard University Press, Cambridge, Mass., 1971; and Madison, A., *Social Development in Pakistan, 1947–1970*, Harvard University Press, Cambridge, Mass., 1971.

On the industrial policy of the Ayub Khan era, good references are Rashid Amjad's *Private Industrial Investment in Pakistan, 1960–1970*, Cambridge University Press, Cambridge, 1982, and two Ph.D. dissertations, one by Meekal Ahmed, 'Productivity, Prices and Relative Income Shares in Pakistan's Large Scale Manufacturing Sector, 1958–70', University of Oxford, 1980, and A.R. Kemal, 'An Analysis of Industrial Efficiency in Pakistan, 1959–60 to 1969–70', University of Manchester, 1978. For the Bhutto period, see Shahid Javed Burki's *State and Society in Pakistan, 1971–77*, Macmillan, London, 1980; Adams, J. and Sabiha Iqbal, *Exports, Politics and Economic Development in Pakistan*, Vanguard, Lahore, 1987; and two doctoral dissertations, Maleeha Lodhi's, 'Bhutto, the Pakistan People's Party and Political Development in Pakistan', London School of Economics and Political Science, 1980, and Zareen F. Naqvi's 'Distributional Impact of Public Enterprise Operational Policies in Pakistan', Boston University, 1994.

Two texts worth studying in greater detail which look at all three of the periods covered in this chapter are Viqar Ahmed and Rashid Amjad's *The Management of Pakistan's Economy, 1947–82*, Oxford University Press, Karachi, 1984, and Asad Sayeed's excellent 'Political Alignments, the State and Industrial Policy in Pakistan: A Comparison of Performance in the 1960s and 1980s', Ph.D. dissertation, University of Cambridge, 1995.

Notes

1. Quoted in Papanek, Gustav, *Pakistan's Development: Social Goals and Private Incentives*, Harvard University Press, Cambridge, Mass., 1967, p. 1.
2. Ibid., pp. 1–2.
3. *The New York Times*, 18 January 1965, quoted in Papanek, op. cit., 1967, p. 1.
4. *The Times*, London, 26 February 1966, quoted in Papanek, op. cit., 1967, p. 1.
5. This section makes extensive use of Lewis, Stephen, *Economic Policy and Industrial Growth in Pakistan*, George Allen and Unwin, London, 1969; Lewis, Stephen, *Pakistan: Industrialization and Trade Policies*, George Allen and Unwin, London, 1970; and Papanek, Gustav, op. cit., 1967.
6. Lewis, Stephen, op. cit., 1969, pp. 67–68.
7. Ibid., p. 68.
8. Ibid., p. 3.
9. Unless otherwise stated, all figures in the text are for West Pakistan only.
10. Ahmed, Viqar and Rashid Amjad, *The Management of Pakistan's Economy, 1947–82*, Oxford University Press, Karachi, 1984, p. 65.
11. Ibid., p. 64.
12. Papanek, Gustav, op. cit., 1967, p. 145.
13. Lewis, Stephen, op. cit., 1969, p. 157.
14. Ahmed, Viqar and Rashid Amjad, op. cit., 1984, p. 68
15. Ibid., p. 243.
16. Lewis, Stephen, op. cit., 1969, p. 7.
17. Ahmed, Viqar and Rashid Amjad, op. cit., 1984, p. 66.
18. Ibid., p. 66; see also Papanek, Gustav, op. cit., 1967, on this point.
19. Institute of Developing Economies, *The Study on Japanese Cooperation in Industrial Policy for Developing Economies: Pakistan*, Tokyo, 1994, p. 123.
20. Lewis, Stephen, op. cit., 1969, p. 13.
21. This section makes liberal use of Lewis, Stephen, op. cit., 1969, and Lewis, Stephen, op. cit., 1970.
22. Lewis, Stephen, op. cit., 1969, p. 76.
23. Ibid., p. 40.
24. Ibid., p. 75, emphasis added.
25. Ibid., p. 111.
26. Ibid., p. 70.
27. Ibid., p. 73.
28. Ibid., p. 110.
29. Ibid., p. 106.
30. Ibid., pp. 7–8.
31. Ibid., p. 10.
32. Ibid., p. 46.
33. Papanek, Gustav, op. cit., 1967, p. 34.
34. Ibid., p. 67.
35. Ibid., p. 88.
36. Ibid., p. 92.
37. Ibid., p. 104.
38. Ibid., p. 101.
39. Ahmed, Viqar and Rashid Amjad, op. cit., 1984, p. 67.
40. Ibid., p. 77.
41. Ibid., p. 77.
42. Papanek, Gustav, op. cit., 1967.
43. Lewis, Stephen, op. cit., 1969, p. 10.
44. Amjad, Rashid, *Private Industrial Investment in Pakistan, 1960–1970*, Cambridge University Press, Cambridge, 1982, p. 5.
45. Asian Development Bank, *Strategies for Economic Growth and Development: The Bank's Role in Pakistan*, Manila, 1985, p. 359.
46. Institute of Developing Economies, op. cit., pp. 135–6.
47. Ibid.
48. Asian Development Bank, op. cit., p. 359.
49. Lewis, Stephen, op. cit., 1969, p. 46.
50. Asian Development Bank, op. cit., p. 366.
51. Ibid., p. 366.
52. Cited in Cheema, Ali, 'Pakistan's Textile Policy and Trade Performance: 1972–1990', mimeo, Sidney Sussex College, Cambridge, 1995, p. 3.
53. Sayeed, Asad, 'Political Alignments, the State and Industrial Policy in Pakistan: A Comparison of Performance in the 1960s and 1980s', unpublished Ph.D. dissertation, University of Cambridge, 1995, p. 55.
54. Ibid., p. 56.
55. Papanek, Gustav, op. cit., p. 225, emphasis added.
56. In Amjad, Rashid, op. cit., 1982, p. 11.
57. Ibid., p. 10.
58. Ibid., p. 166.
59. Papanek, Gustav, op. cit., p. 221.
60. Amjad, Rashid, op. cit., 1982, p. 12.
61. Cheema, Ali, op. cit., 1995, p. 7.
62. All figures are from Amjad, Rashid, op. cit., 1982.
63. Ahmed, Viqar and Rashid Amjad, op. cit., 1984, p. 90.
64. Ibid., p. 89.
65. Lewis, Stephen, op. cit., 1969, p. 4.
66. Naqvi, S.N.H. and Khwaja Sarmad, *Pakistan's Economy Through the Seventies*, PIDE, Islamabad, 1984, p. 12.
67. Government of *Pakistan, Pakistan Economic Survey, 1984–85*, Islamabad, 1985, p. 22.
68. Institute of Developing Economies, op. cit., p. 161.
69. Ahmed, Viqar and Rashid Amjad, op. cit., 1984, p. 3.
70. Institute of Developing Economies, op. cit., p. 185.
71. Government of Pakistan, op. cit., 1985, p. 195.
72. Asian Development Bank, op. cit., p. 380.
73. Ahmed, Viqar and Rashid Amjad, op. cit., 1984, p. 94.
74. Ibid., p. 95.
75. Naqvi, S.N.H. and Khwaja Sarmad, op. cit., 1984, p. 38.
76. Burki, Shahid Javed, *State and Society in Pakistan 1971–77*, Macmillan, London, 1980, p. 118.
77. Ahmed, Viqar and Rashid Amjad, op. cit., 1984, p. 94.
78. Ibid., p. 92.
79. Ibid., p. 94.
80. McCleary, William, 'Pakistan: Structural Adjustment and Economic Growth', in Thomas, V., *et al.*, *Restructuring Economies in Distress*, Oxford University Press, 1991, p. 414.
81. Khan, Mohsin S., 'Comments', in Thomas, V., *et al.*, *Restructuring Economies in Distress*, Oxford University Press, Oxford, 1991, p. 436.
82. Burki, Shahid Javed, 'A Historical Perspective on Development', in Burki, Shahid Javed and Robert Laporte, *Pakistan's Development Priorities: Choices for the Future*, Oxford University Press, Karachi, 1984, p. 19.
83. Naqvi, S.N.H. and Khwaja Sarmad, *External Shocks and Domestic Adjustment: Pakistan's Care 1970–1990*, General Monograph Series no. 1, University Grants Commission, Islamabad, 1993, p. 92.

The Process of Industrialization in Pakistan II: 1977–1997

After the fall of Zulfiqar Ali Bhutto in July 1977, Pakistan can easily be delineated by two specific eras or periods. From 1977 to August 1988 General Zia-ul-Haq ruled Pakistan, the longest rule ever by a single individual in Pakistan's fifty years of existence. Zia's military dictatorship varied from downright ruthlessness to a more benign form of praetorian democracy in 1985. Despite attempts to introduce participation, starting from the Local Bodies elections of 1979, General Zia never let go of the reins of power, a fact ably demonstrated in May 1988 when the elected government of Mohammad Khan Junejo was summarily dismissed. Zia-ul-Haq was killed in an air crash in August 1988 and we can only speculate about the nature of developments in Pakistan had Zia not met his death in this fashion. Nevertheless, with the death of Zia, we see the end of the Zia era, although much of his legacy still has a strong bearing on political and economic developments in Pakistan some years on.

In the Zia era, Pakistan witnessed the return of high growth rates and an increased role for the private sector, in many ways reminiscent of the Decade of Development of the Ayub regime. But much had changed, in the form of class structures, social and political alliances, and the nature of the development of society, and the comparison between the Ayub and Zia periods makes very interesting reading.[1] This chapter will examine the policy of the Zia government with special emphasis on the process of industrialization. A comparison between the Ayub and Zia regimes and an analysis of social and economic outcomes under Zia are given in Chapter 19. However, Appendix 7.1 provides a flavour of the extent and result of differences between the two regimes, regarding the type of entrepreneurs that emerged.

Just as much as the 1977–88 period is distinct in its form and manner, so the post-Zia period opens up a very different age in Pakistan's history, both politically and economically. There has been a return to democracy, with elections being held in Pakistan in 1988 after a lapse of eleven years. Moreover, there have been three general elections since then. Pakistan has seen ten governments between 28 May 1988 and February 1997, and despite this high turnover, the military, which is prone to interfere in national politics in Pakistan, has let the political process take its course.[2] More interestingly, despite the frequent changes in government, the economic programme of different governments in Pakistan has been more or less the same, and one finds a great deal of continuity in policy, especially since September 1988.

Much of what has happened in the economic arena in Pakistan since 1988 forms part of a series of comprehensive structural adjustment programmes undertaken under the close supervision of the International Monetary Fund (IMF) and the World Bank. Although Pakistan's adherence to IMF and World Bank policy began in earnest in 1980 when a large Extended Fund Facility programme was supported by the IMF, followed by many structural adjustment and sectoral loans from the World Bank, it would be fair to say that since 1988 Pakistan's economic programme has totally capitulated to the requirements of the IMF and the World Bank. Since then, Pakistan's numerous and varied governments have failed to come up with any independent economic or industrial development programme, and the very minutely detailed Policy Framework Papers of the IMF and World Bank determine the nature and direction of policy. Given the complete dominance by these two Washingtonian organizations of the economic life of the country, the whole of Part V deals with the consequences for Pakistan of adhering to these structural adjustment policies. In this chapter, we try to limit ourselves to industrial policy and related issues. However, for a more comprehensive understanding of the industrial policy after 1988, a concurrent reading of Part V is also highly recommended.

There are two broad sections to this chapter: we examine first the process of industrialization in the Zia period, and second, the post-1988 era of structural adjustment.

7.1 The Zia Years: 1977–1988[3]

7.1.1 The Nature and Extent of Growth

The phenomenal performance overall of the economy in this period can best be gauged from the following observation by Akbar Noman: 'according to *World Development Report 1990*, during 1980–88 Pakistan's GDP growth rate of 6.5% was exceeded only by that of Korea, China and Hong Kong ... The growth of real wages in Pakistani manufacturing during 1980–88 was just about the fastest in the world – at 6.2% a year surpassed only by Thailand (7.0%) and equalled only by Singapore.'[4] For the period 1978–86, S.N.H. Naqvi and Khwaja Sarmad show that GDP growth averaged 7 per cent per annum.[5] According to the World Bank, manufacturing GDP grew at an annual average rate of 9.5 per cent between 1977 and 1986, and investment in medium- and large-scale industry grew at an average of 18.2 per cent per annum,

Table 7.1
Growth rates of output, labour, capital stock, and total factor productivity, 1978–1988

Industry sector	Output	Labour	Capital stock	TFP output	TFP
Food manufacturing	8.8	7.4	7.3	1.5	−1.1
Beverages industries	6.5	9.2	12.8	−5.9	−6.7
Tobacco	9.1	1.6	10.9	−1.4	−3.4
Textiles	8.6	1.5	9.4	3.0	3.1
Wearing apparel	21.0	21.9	10.4	7.9	4.5
Leather products	7.3	10.7	13.7	−6.0	−19.8
Footwear	8.2	10.0	7.8	−0.3	2.2
Ginning, pressing and bailing	5.1	2.3	3.1	2.1	−2.7
Wood and cork products	13.7	14.5	13.7	−0.1	−0.9
Furniture	13.3	11.8	23.6	−7.0	−11.8
Paper and paper products	10.7	7.6	13.8	−1.2	−6.4
Printing and publishing	10.1	7.6	13.9	−1.3	−2.9
Drugs and pharmaceuticals	11.3	8.2	13.8	−1.4	−3.3
Industrial chemicals	11.2	7.1	8.5	3.0	3.2
Other chemicals	11.2	8.8	8.2	2.9	7.0
Rubber products	4.8	3.8	16.3	−5.0	−2.9
Plastic products	18.3	11.7	13.4	5.4	3.3
Glass products	14.1	8.7	16.1	0.8	−0.5
Other non-metallic minerals	11.7	9.8	14.5	−2.2	−3.1
Iron and steel	17.0	15.3	32.9	−11.0	−12.1
Non-ferrous metals	−8.6	−0.6	4.3	−10.4	−2.7
Metal products	−0.9	1.0	8.8	−6.0	−5.9
Non-electrical machinery	17.6	7.5	5.6	11.1	5.3
Electrical machinery	13.3	5.7	11.7	3.2	−0.6
Transport equipment	9.8	3.3	8.5	4.3	9.6
Total (weighted)	9.6	5.8	10.3	0.3	−0.9

Source: Sayeed, Asad, 'Political Alignments, the State and Industrial Policy in Pakistan: A Comparison of Performance in the 1960s and 1980s', unpublished Ph.D. thesis, University of Cambridge, 1995, p. 109.

while total private industrial investment expanded at 15.6 per cent per annum.[6] This is, indeed, a very impressive performance by any standard, whether in comparison with the performance of the Ayub regime or with the newly industrialized countries in the same period.

Table 7.1 shows the annual growth rate in value of output, labour and other indicators for a large number of manufacturing industries in the period 1978–88. The total average growth in this period was a very impressive 9.6 per cent, with the first half of the Zia era showing an even higher rate of 12.8 per cent.[7] In both the Fifth and Sixth Five-Year Plans (1978-83 and 1983-8), actual growth rates exceeded the targets of 12 per cent and 9 per cent, respectively,[8] a rare occurrence in Pakistan's economic record. Table 7.2 shows how the high growth rates were disaggregated over the Fifth and Sixth Five-Year Plans.

Although the growth figures are very impressive, Asad Sayeed writes that a significantly different, and much less rosy, picture emerges with productivity growth figures (fourth column in Table 7.1). Not only is the aggregate of 0.3 per cent per annum low compared to the 5 per cent growth in the 1960s, but also the variation across sectors is significant.[9]

Furthermore, if we aggregate the total factor productivity (TFP) growth rates, we can see that consumer goods have negative TFP growth, with the exception of the wearing apparel industry. A fairly mixed picture is presented by the intermediate goods industry. Table 7.3 highlights the low contribution of TFP growth to overall growth during the decade. As much as 82.3 per cent of the overall growth was due to the growth in the capital stock, 14.5 per cent to labour, and only 3.17 per cent to TFP growth – compare this to the figures presented in the previous chapter in Table 6.8. Asad Sayeed writes that in the case of Pakistan not only is the contribution of TFP significantly lower than that of the developing country average, but the contribution of capital is also inordinately high.[10]

Table 7.4 shows that there had been very little growth in employment in almost all industries between 1975 and 1986, and that the growth in labour productivity had also fallen in many industries. Interestingly, although the wearing apparel industry experienced the greatest increase in employment, it also saw output fall by nearly 19 per cent. A UNIDO report on the manufacturing sector gives the reasons for this low employment generation and says that an underlying feature of industrialization in Pakistan is the deteriorating performance of the manufacturing sector in generating new employment opportunities. Although the decade of the 1980s has been a period of relatively high growth in manufacturing value added, the growth in manufacturing employment has remained insignificant. This partly represents more an increase in capital industry than labour absorption during the period of accelerated expansion.[11]

Pakistan's manufacturing sector became more capital intensive between 1975 and 1986 and the share of wages and salaries in value added fell from 26.9 per cent in 1976 to 20.3 per cent in 1986.[12] A report published by the Institute of Developing Economies in Japan found it 'ironic' that

some of the public sector dominated industries, such as electrical machinery and chemicals, show a high rate of growth in labour productivity. Firstly, we would expect labour productivity to be higher in capital-intensive projects where the labour–output ratio is high. And secondly, as large firms attain a higher level of capacity utilization, labour productivity will be expected to increase.[13]

7.1.2 Industrial Policy

For Asad Sayeed, the 1978–88 period 'is the only epoch in the country's 48 year history when an industrial policy was formulated and executed for any length of time'.[14] S.N.H. Naqvi and Khwaja Sarmad see the Zia regime consisting of two sub-periods, 1978–81 and 1982–6,[15] while for the

Table 7.2
Average annual growth rates of value of output, 1978–1988
(constant prices 1976/7)

Industries (PSIC 3-digit)	1978–1988	5th Plan	6th Plan
Food	9.7	13.7	5.76
Beverages	10.1	16.5	5.08
Tobacco	8.2	11.5	5.63
Textiles	8.8	11.0	7.16
Wearing apparel except footwear	33.9	35.2	32.7
Leather products except footwear	14.2	−1.2	26.4
Footwear	48.5	38.0	71.0
Ginning, pressing and bailing	9.8	8.5	10.7
Wood and cork	21.2	23.8	19.0
Furniture	30.6	38.1	24.5
Paper and paper products	16.9	18.8	15.5
Printing, publishing and allied	10.6	15.2	7.0
Drugs and pharmaceuticals	11.8	12.0	11.6
Industrial chemicals	14.7	19.7	10.65
Other chemicals	13.3	13.4	13.3
Petroleum refining	10.3	22.8	0.3
Miscellaneous petroleum and coal	15.7	34.1	1.0
Rubber products	5.5	10.1	1.8
Plastic products	20.4	30.7	12.1
Pottery, china and earthenware	11.5	20.1	5.8
Glass and glass products	18.8	27.3	15.0
Other non-metallic minerals	18.2	22.5	14.8
Iron and steel basic	19.1	19.9	18.5
Non-ferrous metals	15.0	10.5	23.3
Fabricated metal except machinery	7.9	6.0	7.3
Machinery except electrical	15.3	15.0	20.3
Electrical machinery	13.2	10.6	14.5
Transport equipment	12.9	−3.8	25.6
Scientific equipment	16.0	10.1	16.4
Sports goods	22.1	22.6	18.6
Others	12.1	1.3	10.6
Average growth (total)	10.4	12.8	9.9

Source: Institute of Developing Economies, *The Study on Japanese Cooperation in Industrial Policy for Developing Economies: Pakistan*, Tokyo, 1994, pp. 257–8.

Table 7.3
Decomposition of manufacturing growth, 1978–1988

Industry sector	α	β	Share of labour %	Share of capital %	Share of TFP %
Food manufacturing	0.13	0.87	11.20	71.92	16.88
Beverages industries	0.11	0.89	16.02	176.25	−92.27
Tobacco	0.40	0.96	0.63	115.37	−16.00
Textiles	0.49	0.51	8.30	55.75	35.96
Wearing apparel	0.24	0.76	24.75	37.73	37.53
Leather products	0.13	0.87	19.69	161.75	−81.44
Footwear	0.29	0.71	35.86	67.34	−3.20
Ginning, pressing, and bailing	0.18	0.86	6.35	51.92	41.73
Wood and cork products	0.24	0.76	24.91	76.06	−0.97
Furniture	0.28	0.72	24.92	128.44	−53.36
Paper and paper products	0.30	0.70	21.50	89.81	−11.31
Printing and publishing	0.40	0.60	29.63	82.99	−12.62
Drugs and pharmaceuticals	0.20	0.80	14.59	97.61	−12.20
Industrial chemicals	0.23	0.77	14.26	58.59	27.16
Other chemicals	0.20	0.80	15.77	58.35	25.88
Rubber products	0.52	0.48	40.86	165.93	−106.80
Plastic products	0.34	0.66	21.75	48.36	29.89
Glass products	0.38	0.62	23.41	70.75	5.84
Other non-metallic minerals	0.13	0.87	10.63	108.69	−19.32
Iron and steel	0.28	0.72	25.66	138.61	−64.27
Non-ferrous metals	0.50	0.50	3.61	−25.20	121.59
Metal products	0.47	0.53	−56.54	−529.97	686.51
Non-electrical machinery	0.47	0.53	19.86	16.95	63.19
Electrical machinery	0.27	0.73	11.56	64.50	23.94
Transport equipment	0.58	0.42	19.71	36.12	44.17
Total (weighted)	0.24	0.76	14.50	82.33	3.17

Note: Alpha and beta refer to shares in values added for labour and capital in the year and capital in the base year respectively.

Source: Sayeed, Asad, 'Political Alignments, the State and Industrial Policy in Pakistan: A Comparison of Performance in the 1960s and 1980s', unpublished Ph.D. thesis, University of Cambridge, 1995, p. 111.

Institute of Developing Economies there were three such periods: 1977–81, which was the period of 'cautious attempts at dismantling existing government policies and restoring confidence in the private sector, while simultaneously trying to gain political legitimacy'; 1982–5, 'a more forceful drive towards Islamization which followed the regime's consolidation of power'; and 1985–8, the 'attempt to disengage the government from direct control of the economy'.[16]

One of the most important concerns of the new Zia regime in mid-1977 was the need to restore business confidence and, particularly, private sector confidence and motivation, in order to revive investment in industry and agriculture, so as to improve the economy's performance substantially compared to the less than impressive performance in the Bhutto period. The military government of General Zia-ul-Haq, like the military government of Field Marshal Ayub Khan, made the decision that the private sector was to play the leading role in the industrial sector.

Amongst the earliest steps taken by the Zia government to appease the private sector was the denationalization of a number of agro-based industries – rice husking, flour milling and cotton ginning – which were run inefficiently and were heavily 'in the red', in September 1977, along with the denationalization of some small engineering units as well.[17] In December 1977, a number of basic and heavy chemical and cement industries were opened up to the private sector, which was also given further incentives, such as tax holidays in March 1978, which were essentially aimed at encouraging industrial activity in the less developed regions of the country. Export rebates were also given priority, and in June 1978 the interest rate on fixed investment in agriculture and industry was also reduced. Some attempts were also made by the new military government to ease economic controls and regulations, including the procedures for the sanctioning of private sector investment.[18]

If the prominence given to the private sector brought back memories of the Ayub Khan era, so did the return to planning

Table 7.4
Growth and structure of manufacturing employment, 1975–1986

Industry sector	Growth of employment in manufacturing	Structure of manufacturing employment		Labour growth of Value-added per employee (% at 1980 prices)
	1975–86	1975	1986	1975–86
Food products	3.58	9.9	12.9	3.53
Beverages	5.07	0.7	1.0	11.32*
Tobacco	2.82	1.7	2.1	1.11
Textiles	–1.64	50.6	41.1	–4.31
Wearing apparel, except footwear	14.75	0.2	0.9	–18.63**
Leather products	2.81	0.8	0.9	–1.88**
Footwear, except rubber or plastic	–2.03	0.3	0.3	–3.55**
Wood products, except furniture	7.46	0.3	0.5	–4.11
Furniture, except metal	3.75	0.2	0.3	2.24**
Paper and paper products	0.03	1.9	1.6	12.28
Printing and publishing	4.52	1.4	2.1	5.79**
Industrial chemicals	3.33	2.5	3.1	6.91
Other chemicals	3.88	3.1	4.2	5.42
Petroleum refineries	1.63	0.5	0.6	1.41
Misc. petroleum and coal products	6.79	0.1	0.1	3.97**
Rubber products	0.11	2.2	2.0	1.75
Plastic products	11.26	0.3	0.6	–
Pottery, china, and earthenware	5.77	0.3	0.5	–6.39**
Glass products	3.37	0.5	0.8	–4.71**
Other non-metallic mineral products	1.90	2.6	2.9	3.25
Iron and steel	9.64	4.1	7.5	1.16**
Non-ferrous metals	–5.51	0.1	0.1	–5.19**
Fabricated metal products	–3.17	2.7	1.9	3.12**
Machinery, except electrical	1.41	3.3	3.3	0.17
Machinery, electric	0.60	3.5	3.6	8.34
Transport equipment	–1.04	4.7	3.9	6.3
Professional and scientific equipment	–3.55	0.8	0.5	14.22
Other manufactured products	–1.01	0.7	0.6	7.96**

* 1975–82
** 1975–80
*** 1975–85
Source: UNIDO, *Pakistan: Towards Industrial Liberalization and Revitalization*, Basil Blackwell, Oxford, 1990, pp. 19 and 22.

in the guise of the Five-Year Plans. As an Asian Development Report stated: 'with a change in government in 1977 came a change in industrial strategy. The new government reinstated the system of five-year plans, and the Fifth Five-Year Plan was launched in 1978/79.'[19] In fact, there had not been much planning after the very successful second Five-Year Plan of 1960–5, when the third was curtailed and handicapped by the cut in foreign aid and the political situation domestically. The Third Five-Year Plan was made redundant after the major part of Pakistan became an independent Bangladesh, and the Fourth Five-Year Plan was lost somewhere in Zulfiqar Ali Bhutto's rule of five years, a period better known as the Non-Plan Period.

The investment programme of the Fifth Five-Year Plan gave very high priority

to producer and investment goods industries with industry based on indigenous raw materials next in line. Apart from bringing back the private sector, the stress on the use of indigenous raw materials in industry was also seen as important to revive the sluggish performance of the agricultural sector ... The economic managers of the Zia regime were looking for short and medium term gains to accrue from a boost in textile exports.[20]

Growth in large-scale manufacturing was projected at the highly ambitious rate of 12 per cent per annum, a target which was, surprisingly, achieved.

The policy measure that distinguishes the Zia regime from all others before and after General Zia was that of Islamization. In fact, it became General Zia's government's and his own mission to purify Pakistani society from all the ills and evils that had become ingrained. Islamic laws were enacted and Commissions formed, and even the economy was brought under the influence of Islamic laws and principles. Writing in 1984, Viqar Ahmed and Rashid Amjad argue that

> The major hallmark of the current phase is the initiation of the process of Islamization of the country's economic structure. The cautious steps taken so far are few and the overall framework is yet to acquire an Islamic look. But this is a task of historic magnitude. Starting with a lag of many centuries during which little effort could be made to apply Islamic principles to the changing socio-economic conditions and institutional structure in Muslim countries, considerable homework needs to be done and this underlines the need for a slow but firm start. But, given the people's commitment to Islam and the Islamic principles of faith in God, social justice, and fair play, the process which has been started is not likely to be reversed.[21]

They continue:

> Currently most of the government's effort in long-term management is concentrated on the process of Islamization which, in terms of the long-run impact on the economy, may surpass the restructuring of the development strategy and the Plan priorities. The process involves a basic transformation of the entire society and intra-social relationships in conformity with the tenets of Islam. Social justice in every walk of life by following the Islamic principles, especially in the distribution of income and wealth in favour of the poor, and the elimination of interest (*sood*) charged by banks are viewed as key features of the Islamization process.[22]

Although much was made of the Islamization programme of the Zia regime at that time, most critics of the regime felt that it was a ploy on the part of the military government in order to legitimize and perpetuate its hold on power. Anita Weiss argues that 'attempts by the state to develop an Islamic economic system are not substantive departures from capitalist industrial culture, but are instead substitutes for specific aspects of it'.[23] Islam became the veil behind which Zia and his coterie hid and perpetuated their authoritarian form of government. Although all the Islamic laws passed by that government are still part of the law of the land, the fanfare has died and governments since Zia's have not (as yet) used Islam for propaganda purposes. Interestingly, while Viqar Ahmed and Rashid Amjad, writing at the height of the Islamization campaign and at the time of a strict military authoritarianism, like most other authors, gave the Islamization process extensive prominence, much of what has been written on the Zia period's economic programme after the death of the General does not give much importance to what was considered to be his key programme. While Islamic codes and regulations do prevail, they seem to exist mainly on paper (see Chapter 10 on banking).

7.1.3   The Public/Private Sector Divide

One would have thought that, with the Zia government's penchant for the private sector, the first step would have been large-scale denationalization and the return of assets seized and nationalized under the Bhutto regime. At the time when Bhutto was deposed, the public sector dominated industrial development and the private sector had been reduced to a much smaller role than under Ayub Khan. An immediate reversal was anticipated, but other than the small and insignificant measures mentioned above, very little denationalization took place. The major contribution by the Zia government in the early years was to give a 'clear signal to the private sector that the government expected future growth to come from its increased participation in industrial activity'.[24]

An Asian Development Bank report defends this action by the Zia regime on the following grounds:

> The military government made the decision that the private sector was to play the leading role in the industrial sector. However, the existing public industrial sector was quite large, employing over 50,000 persons, and a massive investment program of over Rs40 billion was underway. Thus it was not practical for the Government to undertake any large-scale denationalization. Original owners were only prepared to take the units back if the losses accumulated since nationalization in 1972 were written off and the surplus workers fired. The Government could not do that because of political and administrative reasons. Neither was it possible to abandon the industrial sector investment program because a large proportion of the funds had been either spent or committed in the form of international contracts. The Government therefore decided on a more gradual process of reorientation toward private sector-led industrial growth. To restore the confidence of the private sector, the agricultural processing industries taken over in 1976 were denationalized, and a number of industrial incentives similar to those existing during the 1960s were introduced. As for public sector industries, a program for improving efficiency and profitability was initiated, and the investment program was restricted to ongoing projects and to the balancing, modernization and replacement (BMR) of existing public sector units.[25]

However, the study by the Institute of Developing Economies in Japan makes the rather more pertinent point that 'in contrast to its [the Zia regime's] rhetoric against the Bhutto government's economic agenda, the Zia government was hoping to reap the rewards from investments made by the previous regime'.[26] This study continues that, even at the time of the Sixth Five-Year Plan, there were no clear moves towards privatization: 'In fact, public sector industry was seen as playing an instrumental role in industrialization in particular and development in general'.[27] Moreover, the study goes on to make the very astute point that

the political economy of the government's decision not to go on a large scale privatization drive was that it did not want to alienate those groups and classes which had benefited from nationalization by seeking employment in the sector. This group also comprised of the urban lower middle class, which had been the most potent political agitator in Pakistan's history.[28]

While there was no immediate reversal, there certainly was a marked slowing down. Table 7.5 shows that the public sector's share in total industrial investment fell from as much as 72 per cent in 1978–9 to less than 18 per cent ten years later. Although there was some increase in employment, this was mainly due to the projects originated earlier. The bulk of public sector investment during the first half of the Zia regime was going into ongoing projects. In the Fifth Five-Year Plan (1978–83) only 23 per cent of total public industrial outlay was on new projects.[29] In the early years of the Zia government, public sector output increased much more rapidly than private sector large-scale manufacturing output, but in the second half of the ten years, the growth of the private sector was faster.[30] The impetus of growth in the first three years of the Fifth Plan was the public sector, as many of the projects started earlier, especially in the fertilizer and cement sectors, came online.

Essentially then, while the Zia government was very favourably inclined towards the private sector and blamed much of the ills of the economy on Bhutto's economic policies, including nationalization, the Zia regime took a far more pragmatic and politically clever line by not denationalizing in haste. It encouraged the private sector by giving it greater incentives and removing controls, and by opening up sectors and areas previously exclusive to the public sector. Once the government realized that ownership and control of the public sector industries was an effective tool for granting political patronage and favour, there seemed little recourse to gift such a means away. The best example of this is the fact that the all powerful and important financial sector was retained by the government, and no denationalization or privatization of banks took place when General Zia was in power.

7.1.4 Deregulation and Liberalization

The Sixth Five-Year Plan (1983–8) marks the beginning of the process of deregulation and liberalization, which was carried out with much greater force after 1988 when Pakistan's economy became completely subservient to IMF and World Bank directives. The Sixth Five-Year Plan is seen as a departure from the government's earlier policies on industry, and 'it was for the first time that the emphasis moved from purely one of sectoral investment planning to one which also incorporated incentives and institutional reforms to enhance the efficiency of the industrial sector'.[31] Export-led industrialization was mentioned for the first time as a policy goal, and there was an emphasis on the broadening of manufactured exports towards higher value-added items.

Amongst the more important initiatives in pursuit of deregulation and liberalization in this period were the following:

An increase in the investment sanction limit; drastic reduction in the list of specified industries (which require government sanction); reduction of tariffs on a number of raw materials, intermediate and capital goods; introduction of a three-year liberal trade policy; and upgrading of an Industrial Incentives Reform Cell (IIRC) into a Tariff Commission in 1989 to make recommendations on fiscal anomalies and effective protection.

A series of measures ... introduced to de-regulate industrial operations in the cement, oil-seeds and fertilizer industries. Private investment ... permitted in cement production and State-owned enterprises ... allowed to vary their prices. Subsidies ... substantially reduced and cement imports permitted. A similar package of de-regulation and reform was adopted for the oil-seeds sector and a major divesture programme was initiated by the public ghee corporation.[32]

Table 7.5
Share of public industrial enterprise in total large-scale manufacturing, 1978–1988

Years	Employment share (%)	Value added (%)	Public sector share in total industrial investment (%)
1978/9	14.47	7.12	72.74
1979/80	14.34	14.55	65.25
1980/1	15.24	12.27	58.01
1981/2	16.15	13.28	52.03
1982/3	14.82	13.90	48.29
1983/4	16.36	11.81	44.56
1984/5	–	–	31.38
1985/6	–	–	30.68
1986/7	–	–	21.64
1987/8			17.85

Source: Sayeed, Asad, 'Political Alignments, the State and Industrial Policy in Pakistan: A Comparison of Performance in the 1960s and 1980s', unpublished Ph.D. thesis, University of Cambridge, 1995, p. 117.

Along with these measures, important steps were taken to liberalize and encourage foreign trade. Prior to 1983, imports were considered to be either 'free' or 'tied', and goods that were on neither of the two lists were banned. In 1983 this system was changed and a negative list was introduced, where everything not on that list was now importable. There was also a replacement of quantitative restrictions (non-tariff barriers) by tariffs, which according to the Asian Development Bank was a 'significant development since in Pakistan quantitative restrictions have been a more important source of protection than tariffs'.[33] To encourage exports, manufactured exports were given rebates, and exporters were given import facilities, income tax concessions, and finance at concessionary rates.

All the major works on the Zia period – Asad Sayeed, the Asian Development Bank, the Institute for Developing Economies and S.N.H. Naqvi and Khwaja Sarmad – are agreed that

> Perhaps the most important and far reaching economic decision taken by the government was to remove the fixed peg of the Rupee to the Dollar by introducing a managed float of the currency in 1982. As a result between 1982 and 1987–88 the Rupee was devalued by 38.5%, with an average devaluation of 7.7% per annum. While there were other macro considerations which dictated the decision to move away from the peg, its impact on industrial decisions to invest and produce was central. The biggest impact was expected to come in export performance. Conventional wisdom has it that Pakistan's export performance has been sluggish because of an overvalued exchange rate. The overvalued exchange rate, it is argued, discriminates against exports not only in capturing larger world market shares but [also in] the implicit protection it accords to manufactured goods at home which inhibits the direction of resources into export industries. Correcting for the exchange rate was seen as the [most] important step in devising an incentive structure geared towards exports.
>
> Devaluation was also expected to perform an important import substitutive function. Devaluation will enhance prices of imported capital and intermediate goods and will thus induce backward linkages for producer goods industries. Thus the decision was also consistent with the industrial policy priorities of the government as outlined above.[34]

The World Bank, not surprisingly, was particularly happy with the results of the deregulation and liberalization policies of the Sixth Plan. It calculated that the 'private sector's share in total fixed investment increased from 38 per cent in FY83 [1982/3] to 42 per cent in FY88 [1987/8] and in the manufacturing sector its share in investment rose from 51 per cent to 83 per cent'.[35] In a report published earlier, in 1988, the World Bank argues as follows:

> Industrial growth has been encouraged by an improvement in the industrial policy environment for private sector initiative, in accord with Sixth Plan objectives. The composition of industrial investment has shifted heavily toward the private sector. Private industrial investment expanded by almost 23% p.a. in real terms during the Plan period, as against a 7% annual increase in total industrial

investment. In total, over 72% of total industrial investment during FY84–87 was contributed by the private sector. The restriction that public manufacturing investment be limited to the completion of ongoing projects and to rehabilitation of existing plants contributed to this outcome.[36]

7.1.5 Causes of High Growth and the Success of the Zia Regime

The fact that General Zia ruled Pakistan for more than eleven years surprised almost all observers. In July 1977 when he took over from Bhutto, Zia came across as an inexperienced, bumbling General who, it seemed, either would not be able to hold on to power, or would willingly transfer power to politicians as he kept promising. No one at that time could have envisaged the fact that General Zia would emerge as Pakistan's longest ruler. Moreover, the only way power was transferred away from Zia to another head of state was through his death in an air crash. The political reasons why he managed to outlast and outwit the opposition have been documented by, amongst others, Omar Noman, Jonathan Addleton, and Asad Sayeed[37] (see also Chapter 19 of this book). This chapter only highlights the reasons why the economy performed as well as it did and how a booming economy helped neutralize all political opposition against the government. While there were many political and human rights grounds for the protests against Zia that continued all through his rule, there were few economic justifications for opposition.

Again, all the major authors cited in this chapter are agreed about the causes of a high-growth economy under Zia. The Institute of Developing Economies study summarizes these issues as follows:

> On the whole the manufacturing sector in Pakistan has recorded impressive growth rates during the 1977–88 period. As we have attempted to show the principle reason for this performance has been a result of two important phenomena:
>
> i) the coming on stream of the public sector provided the requisite diversity in the manufacturing sector. This resulted in both the once and for all gains that such large investments are expected to bring in and secondly in the linkage effects that it created.
> ii) the revival of confidence in the private sector to invest in industry once again after the brief interlude of the Bhutto regime. The spheres for private industrial investment that were charted out by the Bhutto regime, i.e. the consumer goods sector and the picking up of linkage effects that the public sector would create, reached fruition in the period under review.
>
> The underlying reason for high rates of growth and investment for growth in output was buoyant demand in the economy as a whole.

Because of the remittances from the Gulf and a growing agricultural and services sector consumption demand increased. Investment demand, on the other hand, was enhanced by high resource inflows from the international community, particularly the US, because of Pakistan's strategic role in the Afghan war.[38]

Nawab Haider Naqvi and Khwaja Sarmad believe that the high growth rate of GDP which averaged 7 per cent per annum between 1978 and 1986 was due to a strong expansion in manufacturing led by a booming domestic market (due to remittances and the income from illegal trade, which increased significantly following the Afghan crisis) and the utilization of excess capacity'.[39] Workers' remittances had peaked at $3 billion in 1982/3, and a steady flow of official capital such as long-term loans and grants, amounting to an 'annual average of more than one billion US dollars enabled the government to finance its way out of the difficult situation created by the deteriorating terms of trade',[40] and helped maintain macroeconomic stability as well as promoting a high growth rate of GDP. During the Fifth Five-Year Plan (1978–83), according to Robert Laporte and Muzaffar Ahmad, the *yearly average* of foreign aid committed to Pakistan was $1.45 billion, up from the yearly average of $871 million during the Non-Plan period 1970–78'.[41] This annual average of foreign aid committed to Pakistan during the Sixth Five-Year Plan (1983–8), rose to as much as $2.29 billion.[42]

Asad Sayeed shows that, while the contribution of foreign resource inflows was an important source of assistance to the Zia regime and helped finance industrial investment, interestingly, its share in total investment declined to almost half its share of 1965–70, and to one-sixth of the heyday of the Ayub period (1960–5) when foreign assistance was a critical factor, resulting in very high rates of growth.[43] Foreign resource inflows are yet another similarity between the Zia and Ayub eras, where external sources helped fund Pakistan's economic development programme. Under Ayub, it was US aid that played the most critical role, while under Zia both US aid, following the invasion of Afghanistan by the Soviet Union, and remittances by Pakistani workers contributed very significantly. In some ways, while the 'bad luck' factor may have contributed to the below-par performance of the Bhutto regime, a 'good luck' element, particularly the Soviet invasion of Afghanistan and high Gulf remittances, helped General Zia's economy considerably, and helped prolong his rule.

However, such a high dependence on external assistance and on extraneous sources meant that, when foreign inflows ceased, so would economic development. This was most noticeable under the Ayub regime, but also became a factor in the later period of General Zia's rule. S.N.H. Naqvi and Khwaja Sarmad write:

> The outstanding feature of this period [1978–81] is the rise in remittances, which pushed up the national saving rate. The average share of investment in the GDP rose to 20 per cent in 1977, and was high by historical standards. The

growth in investment was due to an increase in public investment in the social and economic infrastructure. The investment in public enterprise remained low, and so did private investment. Public investment increased to an average of 11.6 per cent of the GDP despite the relative decline in external capital to the public sector. This, however, did not alter the public sector's position as the largest recipient of foreign capital. The high level of public investment was financed mainly from household savings (net resource).[44]

While there seems to be agreement that the Zia regime produced high growth, two of the studies cited above have argued that much of what we have seen 'cloaked' the inefficiencies of the economic regime and that it is necessary to go beyond mere appearances and aggregated growth rates. The Institute of Developing Economies in its study argues as follows:

> The relevant question in the context of this study is the extent to which the government's industrial policy, as revealed in its Five Year Plans and the Industrial Policy Statement, contributed to this growth. The evidence suggests that growth occurred, not *because* of the specific incentives provided in the industrial policy of the government but *in spite* of it. The outline of industrial policy ... shows that the cornerstone of government policy was to move towards the higher stages of import substitution (through giving priority to technology-intensive and non-consumer goods manufactures), export enhancement (through increasing the value-added in manufacturing exports and export-led growth) and enhancing efficiency in the manufacturing sector. Given the evidence that we have presented in this section, the goal of import substitution in the intermediate and capital goods sector remained unfulfilled. Although, growth in exports increased the contribution of value-added exports and the composition of manufactured exports remained virtually unchanged through the decade. We also tentatively conclude that the productivity performance was also below par.
>
> *In that case the only achievement of the government was to lure the private sector back into industrial activity. Other than that, it was fortuitous circumstances* (the gestation of public sector projects and the international situation) which was responsible for the above average performance of Pakistan's manufacturing sector.[45]

Asad Sayeed is less charitable in his criticism of the cloaked inefficiencies, and concludes his evaluation of Zia's industrial policy in the following manner:

> The 1978–88 period is unique in Pakistan's economic history for exhibiting high output growth without corresponding improvements in

the efficiency of factor use in the manufacturing sector. We saw that much of this growth in output was financed by foreign remittances and aid flows coming into the country. The inefficient use of these resources meant that *the country squandered the windfall gains that it received as a result of favourable exogenous conditions.*

In general, the industrial policy structure of the period was not much different from that pursued in countries which performed markedly better than Pakistan, or for that matter from that which prevailed in the high productivity period of the 1960s. Yet, we also saw that in many cases industrial policy was either not implemented, or the policy structure in some cases was not amenable to productivity growth. The existence of smuggling, the precipitous increase in the number of sick industries, irregularities with the licensing procedures, etc., *pointed towards a failure in the implementation of policy during this time.* We also saw that policies were not altered even when it was abundantly clear that they were harmful for growth and productivity. In particular, the existence of negative ERPs [effective rates of protection] for certain industries, the regulatory regime of the period and the lack of incentives for value addition in the textile sector were identified as important policy errors.[46]

7.2 The Age of Structural Adjustment: 1988 Onwards

The history and political and economic background of the role that the IMF and World Bank began to play in Pakistan's economy after 1988 are discussed in Part V of this book. The present section only examines the relevance of the Structural Adjustment Programme (SAP) to the industrial sector.

The Seventh Five-Year Plan (1988–93) was commissioned at the same time as the IMF/World Bank induced conditionality was accepted by the government in the guise of a structural adjustment programme. The plan had set ambitious targets for overall reforms in the industrial sector, and included further deregulation, privatization, tariff reform, and regulation of foreign investment. As far as the three-year agreement (1988–91) with the IMF was concerned, the industrial policy outlined in the letter of interest committed the government of Pakistan to the following:

i)   limiting the list of specified industries;
ii) de-regulating business decisions;
iii) raising the investment sanctioning limit annually [it was to be raised from Rs700 million in 1988 to Rs1 billion in 1989];
iv) phasing out industrial location policies over a three-year period, and provision of infrastructural services at prices that reflect economic costs;
v)   divesting the shares of public sector companies to the private sector;

vi)   instituting a corporate rationalization programme to enhance efficiency in the remaining, i.e., non-divested, public enterprises;
vii) considering a realistic trade regime as a primary investment or structural adjustment effort;
viii) enhancing export incentives;
ix)   reducing the level of protection accorded to different industries;
x)   reducing the list of restricted import items as well as those subject to quantitative restrictions;
xi)   achieving a tariff range of 0 to 100 per cent by 1st July 1990; and
xii) phasing out all tariff exemptions by 1990/91 except duty drawback for exporters, exemptions for import of capital equipment in key industries and reasonable baggage allowances.

In addition to the above industry-specific recommendations, the following prescriptions of the IMF's macroeconomic recipe have a direct impact on industrial development in Pakistan.

i)   an increase in the level of indirect taxation (in the form of a generalized sales tax) by July 1990;
ii) withdrawal of subsidies on gas, electricity, telephones and fertilizers;
iii) an increase in producer prices of major crops (wheat, cotton, sugarcane, rice and oil seeds) and in the prices of petroleum products;
iv) a 12.5 per cent reduction in the public sector development programme during the agreement period (1989–1991); and
v)   restriction on government borrowing and credit allocation to the private sector.[47]

The World Bank, in its review of the programme of 1988–91, felt that the economy 'responded well to these policy reforms. Progress in implementing structural reforms to promote private sector activity has been exceptional during the last four years, despite three changes in government during this period.'[48] The large-scale manufacturing sector managed an impressive 7.4 per cent in 1991/2 due essentially to the rapid expansion of cotton manufacture. The World Bank considered Pakistan to have achieved an 'excellent growth performance'.

A major emphasis of the structural adjustment programme was on the enhancement of growth by encouraging the private sector, which was supposed to take a lead role. Amongst the investment and industrial policies followed was a 'forceful' programme of liberalizing the economy from government control. Furthermore,

Not only was sanctioning of private investment and import licensing abolished, but also a number of other regulatory restrictions (including registration of technical and foreign loan agreements, procedures for employment of

BOX 7.1

Credit allocation for industry and the new rules of the structural adjustment programmes

Credit plays a critical role in investment, as the Institute of Developing Economies study shows:

The allocation and cost of credit to industrial sectors is a key tool for implementing industrial policy. It has been used extensively in countries with active state interventionist policies, to ensure that targeted industries are provided with adequate input of capital to meet their investment and working capital requirements. Multi-lateral financial institutions, under the influence of neo-classical thinking, have been opposed to the use of targeted and concessional financing, on the grounds that it distorts capital allocation, and causes financial repression. Through their structural adjustment loans, they have brought considerable pressure to bear upon the Pakistani planners to phase out concessional credit. The planners, however, are concerned about the effect this would have on the local machinery manufacturing industry and the export sector, which rely heavily on concessional funding. However, to date, no comprehensive analysis of the costs and benefits of concessional financial has been carried out.

Opponents of the scheme point out that while access to export financing has been increasing substantially, it does not seem to have had a corresponding effect on the level of exports, which is primarily determined by competitiveness, quality standards, tariff policy and exchange rate policy. They point out that interest rate subsidies cannot compensate for a lack of competitiveness, poor quality, a discriminatory tariff regime and an overvalued exchange rate: it merely creates further distortions.

Nevertheless, in an economy where until the recent financial sector reforms, credit was allocated in a detailed manner, through an annual credit plan, access to credit is a vital lifeline. Pakistani industry has always been highly leveraged, relying on debt rather than equity financing for capital investment. First, because it was relatively cheaper on a real post-tax basis, and secondly because it avoided all the legal complications associated with equity flotation. Thus, the volume of credit made available to industrial sectors is a crucial determinant of its output growth.

Source: Institute of Developing Economies, *The Study on Japanese Cooperation in Industrial Policy for Developing Economies: Pakistan*, Tokyo, 1994, p. 340.

---

foreign workers, etc.) were also removed. Areas of investment previously reserved for the public sector were opened to the private sector, including power generation, commercial and development banking and air and sea transport. [Also], it initiated the privatization of some 105 manufacturing units and began to take steps to expand the privatization program to the energy and telecommunications subsectors. By November 1992, 67 manufacturing units had been sold and important preparatory steps to privatize the telecoms utility (PTC) and gas utilities are underway. Finally, the Government also provided investment incentives to the private sector. In particular, to promote investment in rural areas, an incentive package, including a five-year income tax holiday, exemptions from customs duty, sales tax and import surcharges, will be provided for all industries established in rural areas between Dec. 1, 1990 and June 30, 1995.[49]

According to the World Bank, the consequences of following these policies were as follows (see also Table 7.6):

Industrial value added grew by 6.3% p.a. during this period. Manufacturing, electricity and water, which explain most (86%) of this favorable result, expanded by 5.9% and 11.3% p.a. on average, respectively. Large investments in the energy sector led to significant increases in all major energy sources during this period: crude oil grew by 5% p.a., gas by 6% p.a., and electricity by 9% p.a., although power shortages continue to be a significant problem. Construction activity was relatively subdued perhaps reflecting the stagnation in public investment. In manufacturing, cotton industries ... once again dominated the subsector. However, the strong performance of small-scale manufacturing (which accounts for about one-third of total manufacturing value added) and non-traditional large scale industries is encouraging.[50]

According to the World Bank's analysis, 'the cornerstone of the government's adjustment programme is to increase the level and efficiency of private investment and activity by deregulating the economy and promoting competition'[51] (see Box 7.1 for the new rules of credit allocation). There is a very strong emphasis in most structural adjustment programmes on increasing foreign direct investment (FDI) and foreign portfolio investment (see Box 7.2). The government was urged in 1993 to continue pursuing the private sector agenda aggressively in the coming years, a demand that Pakistan's government was eager to pursue in the next three-year programme of 1993–6 (see Part V).

While the World Bank and the IMF have concluded that the three-year structural adjustment programmes launched in 1988 and 1993 went rather well – especially in the industrial sector, where the private sector has been the main protagonist of the new policies – it is worth ending this section with an evaluation by a neutral party. The Japanese Institute of Developing Economies, comparing actual industrial production with the targets between 1988 and

Table 7.6
Sectoral contributions to GDP growth, 1981–1992 (%)

Sectors	Sectoral contributions to GDP growth[a]					
	Average 1981/1988	1988/90	1989/90	1990/1	Prelim. 1991/2	Average 1988–1992
Agriculture	1.07	1.77	0.79	1.31	1.64	1.38
of which:						
Wheat	0.06	0.44	−0.04	0.10	0.01	0.13
Rice	0.00	0.02	0.02	0.05	−0.11	−0.01
Cotton	0.35	−0.06	0.04	0.52	1.23	0.41
Sugar cane	0.00	0.24	−0.10	0.04	−0.08	0.02
Livestock	0.41	0.44	0.46	0.38	0.45	0.44
Mining and quarrying	0.04	0.01	0.05	0.06	0.02	0.04
Manufacturing	1.44	0.67	1.00	1.11	1.36	1.03
Large-scale	1.09	0.29	0.60	0.70	0.94	0.63
Food and beverages	0.15	0.03	0.04	0.03	0.20	0.08
Cotton related	0.14	0.09	0.28	0.26	0.38	0.25
Fertilizers	0.09	0.02	0.03	−0.02	−0.04	−0.01
Petroleum products	0.04	−0.03	0.03	0.09	0.00	0.02
Cement	0.02	0.00	0.01	0.01	0.01	0.01
Pig-iron	0.05	−0.02	−0.01	0.03	0.01	0.00
Automobiles	0.05	0.03	0.04	0.00	0.03	0.02
Others	0.57	0.16	0.17	0.31	0.35	0.25
Small-scale	0.36	0.38	0.40	0.41	0.42	0.40
Construction	0.22	0.10	0.13	0.24	0.25	0.18
Electricity, gas and water	0.21	0.37	0.44	0.34	0.24	0.35
Transport and communication	0.73	−0.41	0.61	0.52	0.66	0.35
Commerce	1.26	0.87	0.58	0.91	1.25	0.90
Financial institutions and insurance	0.21	0.08	0.09	0.08	0.04	0.07
Public administration and defence	0.40	0.57	0.20	0.24	0.13	0.28
Other services	0.69	0.77	0.78	0.78	0.79	0.78
GDP (at factor cost)	6.51	4.79	4.67	5.59	6.38	5.35

[a] Sectoral contributions to growth rate are computed by weighing the sectoral growth rates by the previous year's sectoral share (in GDP).

Source: World Bank, *Pakistan: Country Economic Memorandum FY93: Progress Under the Adjustment Program*, Report No. 11590-Pak, Washington, 1993, p. 5.

1992, draws the following conclusions:

The first point revealed by an examination of the data is the extent of variation between targets and achievements, and the number of products that were subject to them. We note, for example, that the variations affect up to 30 products for which data were available and range from a deficit of 75% to an excess of 1013%. The corresponding growth rates also show large variations. The second fact that becomes immediately apparent is the degree to which variations match the difference between revised and original targets for the plan. *It appears that planning in Pakistan is really an ex-post exercise. In other words, as the planners realize that their original targets are not being met, they revise the targets to more closely approximate likely outcomes.* Thus, in 1992, the planners readjusted their targets, in light of the data on actual production as of that year, so that it could be said at the end of the plan period that targets were accomplished. This is really an exercise in self deception. No attempt, it appears, is made to find causes for variations, or solutions to overcome the problems identified. Objectives are outlined, targets set, and then the planners await, with bated breath, the ultimate outcome! The monitoring of plan outcomes is not done in a periodic and systematic manner.[52]

For further analysis of policies and their consequences under the Structural Adjustment Programme, see Part IV.

BOX 7.2

The recent policy initiative to attract foreign direct investment (FDI)

The World Bank documents Pakistan's recent attempts to attract FDI:

Since late 1990, the Government in Pakistan has initiated a number of policy and regulatory measures to improve the business environment in general and attract FDI in particular. The requirement for government approval of foreign investment has been removed and 100 per cent ownership is permitted, with the exception of projects in industries included in the Specified List, which are: (a) arms and ammunition, (b) security printing, currency and mint, (c) high explosives, and (d) radioactive substances. Foreign investment remains prohibited in the areas of agricultural land, forestry, irrigation, real estate, insurance, health and related services. In the petroleum subsector, the Government enacted a new Petroleum Policy which is significantly more conductive to foreign investment than previous policy guidelines. Foreign firms can now also engage in export trading activities. Previously, the Provincial Governments had to issue a No Objection Certificate and effectively controlled the physical location of the investment. Now, these governments limit their a-priori approval only to so-called negative areas. Furthermore, the elaborate controls that used to be imposed on the transfer of technology have been entirely removed. Technology buyers face no ceilings over the amount of royalties and technical fees they are allowed to pay.

One of the most important measures taken recently by the Government affecting FDI was the liberalization of the foreign exchange regime. Residents and non-resident Pakistanis and foreigners are now allowed to bring in, possess and take out foreign currency, and to open accounts and hold certificates in foreign currency. Foreigners using foreign exchange have now access to the capital market. For example, no permission is required to issue shares of Pakistani companies to foreign investors, unless they belong to industries included in the Specified List. Remittance of principal and dividends from FDI and from portfolio investment made by foreign and non-resident Pakistani investors are allowed without prior permission or clearance from the State Bank of Pakistan (exceptions: foreign airlines, foreign shipping companies, insurance companies).

Export incentives have been introduced or broadened. The highly cumbersome duty-drawback system is being replaced with a scheme whereby 80 per cent of the duty-drawback is paid automatically within three days to the firm, and the remaining 20 per cent is paid within one week after inquiry. Moreover, import policy has been partially liberalized: the average import duty on raw materials was lowered, a large number of quantitative restrictions and non-tariff barriers were removed, and the negative and prohibited lists of imports were reduced. Finally, the 55 per cent income tax rebate on export earnings was changed into a 75 per cent rebate for export of high value added products, and a 50 per cent rebate for all other products. As in the case of investment incentives, these rebates may not be cost-effective and generally lead to distortions in the incentive structure.

The Government has also enacted an extensive set of investment incentives including tax holidays for projects in rural and underdeveloped areas. Imported machinery not manufactured locally is fully or partially exempted from import duties, depending on whether a project is located in a rural area, underdeveloped areas, or industrial estates. A variety of other fiscal and monetary incentives are offered for projects in selected industries like electronics, tourism, pharmaceutical, dairy farming, mining, engineering, fertilizer and cement. Experience in other countries generally indicates, however, that these kind of incentives are not cost effective.

Source: World Bank, *Pakistan: Growth Through Adjustment*, Report No. 7118-Pak, Washington, p. 40.

7.3 Summary and Further Reading

7.3.1 Summary

During this period, industrial development regained the momentum lost between 1972 and 1977, and growth rates of industry and of the economy returned to the historically high levels of the pre-Bhutto era. For this reason, and also because both Ayub Khan and Zia-ul-Haq were military dictators, there are quite a few similarities in the process of development in the periods of their rule. The private sector returned to Pakistan after the Bhutto years and began to play a key role in industrialization.

Zia reaped many rewards that resulted from the initiative of his predecessor, and fortuitous circumstances, too, helped in establishing and maintaining an economy with very high growth. A number of public sector projects came online, and the Middle East boom in this period resulted in workers' remittances of as much as $3 billion in one year, easing any strain on the economy. The Soviet invasion of Afghanistan resulted in Pakistan acquiring the rather dubious title of 'frontline state', with military and financial aid, again reminiscent of the Ayub era, flowing into Pakistan. Not only did large-scale production play an increased role as it did under Ayub, but the small-scale sector, due to Bhutto's policies, showed dynamic growth in the Zia period.

After General Zia's death, the democratic transition was matched by a new economic order, and Pakistan entered the world of the structural adjustment programme, under the careful eye of the IMF and World Bank. Almost ten years into the programme, despite (or perhaps, due to) the extensive reforms undertaken in the economy, Pakistan's industry and economy are facing a serious crisis. Growth rates have plummeted to around 3 or 4 per cent per annum, and the economic revival seems far away. The eleven years of high growth under Zia now seem to be unravelling, and the high expectations of the Structural Adjustment Programme have not been fulfilled.

7.3.2 Further Reading

It is usually difficult to find books and manuscripts analysing recent eras, and there is usually a lag of a decade or so before interpretation and analysis begin and are made available to the general public. This is the case for the industrialization process discussed in this chapter, starting with the Zia period and followed by the reforms and interventions since 1988. Probably the most outstanding piece of work on the subject is by Asad Sayeed, 'Political Alignments, the State and Industrial Policy in Pakistan: A Comparison of Performance in the 1960s and 1980s', unpublished Ph.D. dissertation,

University of Cambridge, 1995. Other useful texts include Omar Noman's *The Political Economy of Pakistan, 1947–85*, KPI, London, 1988; Anjum Nasim's edited book entitled *Financing Pakistan's Development in the 1990s*, Oxford University Press, Oxford, 1992; UNIDO's *Pakistan: Towards `Industrial Liberalization and Revitalization*, Blackwell, Oxford, 1990; the Institute of Developing Economies' *Study on Japanese Cooperation in Industrial Policy for Developing Economies: Pakistan*, Tokyo, 1994; S.N.H. Naqvi and Khwaja Sarmad's manuscript, *External Shocks and Domestic Adjustment: Pakistan's Case, 1970–1990*, University Grants Commission, Monograph Series, 1994; and the three reports prepared by the World Bank on changes since 1988: *Pakistan, Growth Through Adjustment*, Report No. 7118-Pak, Washington, 1988; *Pakistan: Medium-term Economic Policy Adjustments*, Report No. 7591-Pak, Washington, 1989; and *Pakistan: Country Economic Memorandum FY93: Progress Under the Adjustment Program*, Report No. 11590-Pak, Washington, 1993.

Appendix 7.1

The emergence of a new breed of entrepreneur under Zia

This article by Asad Sayeed tries to compare the change in the nature of entrepreneurs from the time of Ayub Khan to the end of the Zia period.

If the Habibs, the Saigols, the Valikas, Ispahanis and Fancys were considered role models for budding businessmen during the 1950s and 1960s, today's corporate kingpins like the Lakhanis, the Sharifs and the Hashwanis have become the idols of aspiring yuppies at the business schools of Karachi and Lahore in the 1980s.

The last decade has seen a significant transformation in the country's industrial elite, as a result of the separation of East Pakistan and the nationalization policy of Zulfikar Ali Bhutto's regime. This is not to say that all the big names from the original '22' have literally gone under. In fact, if one goes by the financial assets listed on the stock exchange some of the industrial giants of the pre-nationalization phase – like the Habibs, the Dawoods, the Saigols, the Crescent group and the Wazir Alis – continue to occupy prime positions on top of Pakistan's corporate ladder.

But according to most observers of the country's corporate scene, the list of industrial giants would have been quite different if some of the new groups – like the ubiquitous Sharifs of Lahore, the FECTO group, Captain Athar's Schon group and a horde of other textile empires – had all their companies listed on the exchange. 'I believe that if one was to sum up all the net worth of say, the Ittefaq group, they would certainly be way up among the top 5 industrial giants of the country,' says a veteran observer of Pakistan's corporate scene. He goes on to say that 'the big groups in Pakistan have always

held way above the majority of shareholdings required for controlling the management, and with liberal credit available from DFIs, it does not make any real difference to them if they do not seek equity from the stock market.' It seems that the new industrialists have learnt from the tumultuous '70s when Zulfikar Ali Bhutto used the 'big 22' phenomenon as a major rallying point to come into power and subsequently nationalized many of the big industries.

However, there are some other important ways also in which the new guard is clearly distinct from the old. For one thing, almost all of the big entrepreneurs of the '80s have adopted aggressive marketing and advertising strategies. But while this high-profile corporate strategy may apply to their marketing activities, as mentioned earlier, the opposite is true about their financial standing. While it was a matter of pride for the older industrial giants to be listed on the exclusive club of the 'big 22', their lifestyles were conversely, far less ostentatious than the conspicuous consumption pattern that has become characteristic of the more nouveau brand of financial tycoons today. Financial savvy now amounts to carefully protecting all the particulars of one's financial worth, especially if some of the wealth has been fashionably fuelled through this decade's business obsession of under and over-invoicing.

Another legacy of the Bhutto years – the labour laws – have made the mode of operation of Pakistan's industrial sector in the 1980s different from that of their predecessors. The introduction of the old-age benefit scheme, social security, medical cover, and a limitation on the discretion of the employers to hire and fire, has increased the costs of the employers by considerable proportions.

While the corporate generation of the 1960s could happily amass fortunes without being saddled with such 'oppressive' legislation, the new lot has dealt with these laws in quite an ingenious manner. Instead of hiring their labour force on a permanent basis, the industrial sector of the 1980s has resorted to the now popular practice of hiring it on a contract basis. By doing this, they manage to sidestep another major impediment in the way of accumulating huge profits.

However, boasting palatial houses or gleaming limousines these days is not just the hallmark of the business magnates aspiring to become socially indispensable, or of the powder-kings with not enough places to spend their highly liquid drug money. These are also some of the crasser symbols of bourgeois bounty flashed around by a whole new breed of export-led trade magnates. Indeed, it might even be true to say that the 1980s has seen the proliferation of a new class of entrepreneurs who can match their big brothers in business in terms of conspicuous consumption. These 'businessmen' are mostly exporters of value-added goods like garments, leather products, rugs and other items which have an exotic appeal in the western world and Japan.

These exporters – with leading names like Ilyas Malik, Mohammed Saeed, Mohammed Hussain, Khalid Javaid, S. Mohammad Din, Aziz Brothers and Haji Abdul Latif – have grown and prospered partly as a result of changing governmental priorities, like the devaluation of the rupee. In particular, they have been quick to reap profits from concessions like the very liberal export policy with massive rebates for value-added exports and, like their counterparts in big industries, they have also extorted huge profits by cutting down on labour costs. Instead of relying on the traditional factory-oriented method of production, many exporters have gone for sub-contracting their production to the small power and hand looms, tanneries and weaving units in the informal sector.

While, on the one hand, this arrangement has made it possible for these exporters to keep their overhead costs low, on the other, it has effectively kept the workforce out of the ambit of labour laws. Thus, with their fixed assets working out as almost negligible on paper, they have been able to make an average profit, which ranges from 400 to 700 per cent per unit of exports.

But despite these differences in the two different generations of corporate élites, it is not entirely wrong to say that they have essentially made it big by riding on the back of the country's bureaucracy.

Most observers of the first industrial boom assert that the infamous 22 families of the 1960s were more a product of state patronage, rather than that of any intrinsic entrepreneurial genius. Which leads one to wonder if the new business brass has also made it big by accumulating a large share of their booty through the assiduous cultivation of the bureaucracy – who are notorious for not being averse to scratching others' backs if theirs are kept well groomed. Certainly, there can be no denying that the role of the country's establishment in the concentration of industrial assets has remained almost as significant as it was during the industrial boom of the 1960s. If at that point during the 'decade of development', the nascent industrial class of the country was provided easy capital through state-owned financial houses like the PIDC, PICIC and ICP, the new breed have not exactly been starved of liberal loan windows through nationalized banks and the many DFIs which have been created over the last 15 years (NDFC, BEL, etc.) Similarly, the famous bonus voucher scheme of the 1960s and the overvalued rupee – mechanisms for easing the import of raw materials and export of finished products have taken on the guise of excise and export tax rebates, and import of capital equipment at lower duties. Apart from obtaining these concessions which are general to the industrial sector, big business has essentially thrived by maintaining a close rapport with the top echelons of the bureaucracy – an arrangement which has occasionally been disturbed during the brief interludes of parliamentary democracy in the country.

Another similarity between the élites of the two different eras is that the big industrial conglomerates have backed their industrial and personal assets by floating insurance companies and banks. After the nationalization of all banks and the major insurance companies during the Bhutto era, it took some time for the new groups to commit so much capital to venture in the financial market. But despite memories of the Bhutto squeeze, over the last 10 years almost all the big groups – the Habibs, the Dawoods, the Adamjees from the old lot, and Hashwani, Lakhani, Shirazi and Firdous groups – have managed to set up insurance companies or modarrabas. The Crescent group is the first which has recently launched its own investment bank.

In terms of industries again, there seems to be little difference in the product mix of the two eras. Like in the past, most of the industries are essentially textile based. Some of the new names have, however, distinguished themselves by venturing heavily into areas like hoteliering (Hashwanis), steel (Sharifs), auto assembly and light engineering (the Atlas and Sony groups).

The picture that emerges out of the present set-up of corporate activity then, is that it continues to be essentially patronized by the state, which not only supports this group, but also turns a blind eye to its numerous illicit practices.

Since the onset of parliamentary democracy in 1985, however, many politicians have been going into industry in a big way – with some leading names like the Saifullahs, Zarri Sarfaraz, and the late Mohsin Siddiqi. And if the present trend continues, one wouldn't be too far off the mark in conjecturing if the '90s is going to see the new breed of politicians-turned-industrialists pushing out the present tycoons to gain a higher position near the top of the corporate ladder.

Certainly, if one is to go by the business community's recent protest marches and convention jamborees, which embodied its threat to boycott government revenues and withdraw advertisements from the electronic media, it is becoming increasingly clear that they are not exactly going to lie low while the feudal politicians sweep away the fruits of their financial standing. There is little doubt in any business observer's mind that, given the present aggressive posture of the business community, it seems that this time they will pre-empt the traditional politicians' move to keep the reins of power in their hands by carving out a political niche for themselves.

Source: *The Herald*, June 1990.

Notes

1. For one of the most outstanding recent works on Pakistan, a work that compares the political and economic similarities and differences of the Ayub era with that of the eleven years of General Zia-ul-Haq, see Sayeed, Asad, 'Political Alignments, the State and Industrial Policy in Pakistan: A Comparison of Performance in the 1960s and 1980s', Ph.D. dissertation, University of Cambridge, 1995.

2. However, the military has been an active player on the political scene both at the national level and, more overtly, in Karachi. See Zaidi, S. Akbar, 'The Roots of the Crisis', *The Herald*, Karachi, August 1992.

3. This section makes extensive use of Sayeed, Asad, op. cit., 1995.

4. Noman, Akbar, 'Industrialization in Pakistan: An Assessment and an Agenda', paper presented at the Seventh Annual General Meeting of the Pakistan Society of Development Economics, Islamabad, 1991, pp. 15–16.

5. Naqvi, S.N.H. and Khwaja Sarmad, *External Shocks and Domestic Adjustment: Pakistan's Case, 1970–1990*, General Monograph Series no. 1, University Grants Commission, Islamabad, 1993, p. 11.

6. World Bank, *Pakistan: Growth Through Adjustment*, Report No. 7118-Pak, Washington, 1988, p. 63.

7. Institute of Developing Economies, *The Study on Japanese Cooperation in Industrial Policy for Developing Economies: Pakistan*, Tokyo, 1994, pp. 257–8.

8. Ibid.

9. Sayeed, Asad, op. cit., 1995, p. 110.

10. Ibid.

11. UNIDO, *Pakistan: Towards Industrial Liberalization and Revitalization*, Blackwell, Oxford, 1990, p. 20.

12. Ibid., p. 23.

13. Institute of Developing Economies, op. cit., 1994, p. 264.

14. Sayeed, Asad, op. cit., 1995, p. 2.

15. Naqvi, S.N.H. and Khwaja Samad, op. cit., 1994, p. 7.

16. Institute of Developing Economies, op. cit., 1994, p. 53.

17. Ahmed, Viqar and Rashid Amjad, *The Management of Pakistan's Economy, 1947–82*, Oxford University Press, Karachi, 1984, p. 110.

18. Ibid.

19. Asian Development Bank, *Strategies for Economic Growth and Development: The Bank's Role in Pakistan*, Asian Development Bank, Manila, 1985, pp. 391–2.

20. Institute of Developing Economies, op. cit., 1994, p. 228.

21. Ahmed, Viqar and Rashid Amjad, op. cit., 1984, p. 100.

22. Ibid., p. 102.

23. Weiss, Anita, *Culture, Class and Development in Pakistan: The Emergence of an Indigenous Bourgeoisie in Punjab*, Vanguard, Lahore, 1991, p. 156.

24. Institute of Developing Economies, op. cit., 1994, p. 228.

25. Asian Development Bank, op. cit., 1985.

26. Institute of Developing Economies, op. cit., 1994, p. 228.

27. Ibid., p. 223.

28. Ibid., p. 229, footnote.

29. Sayeed, Asad, op. cit., 1995, p. 116.

30. Asian Development Bank, op. cit., 1985, p. 395.

31. Institute of Developing Economies, op. cit., 1994, p. 230.

32. UNIDO, op. cit., 1990, p. 73.

33. Asian Development Bank, op. cit., 1985, p. 390.

34. Institute of Developing Economies, op. cit., 1994, pp. 237–8.

35. World Bank, *Pakistan: Medium-term Economic Policy Adjustments*, Report No. 7591-Pak, Washington, 1989, p. (i).

36. World Bank, op. cit., 1988, p. 4.

37. See Noman, Omar, *The Political Economy of Pakistan, 1947–85*, KPI, London, 1988; Addleton, Jonathan, *Undermining the Centre: The Gulf Migration and Pakistan*, Oxford University Press, Karachi, 1992; and Sayeed, Asad, op. cit., 1995.

38. Institute of Developing Economies, op. cit., 1994, pp. 270–1.

39. Naqvi, S.N.H. and Khwaja Samad, op. cit., 1994, p. 11.

40. Ibid., p. 15.

41. Ahmad, Muzaffar and Robert Laporte, *Public Enterprise in Pakistan: The Hidden Crisis in Economic Development*, Westview Press, Boulder, 1989, p. 10.

42. Ibid.

43. Sayeed, Asad, op. cit., 1995.

44. Ibid., p. 45.

45. Institute of Developing Economies, op. cit., 1994, pp. 271–2, emphasis added.

46. Sayeed, Asad, op. cit., 1995.

47. UNIDO, op. cit., 1990, pp. 74–5.

48. World Bank, *Pakistan: Country Economy Memorandum FY93: Progress Under the Adjustment Program*, Report No. 11590-Pak, Washington, 1993, p. 3.

49. Ibid., pp. 3–4.

50. Ibid., pp. 4–5.

51. Ibid., p. 38.

52. Institute of Developing Economies, op. cit., 1994, p. 336, emphasis added.

The previous two chapters have given a chronological account of developments in the industrial sector in Pakistan, showing how perspectives of different regimes have influenced industrial and economic growth. This chapter looks at contemporary issues in the industrial sector, including privatization, the textile sector, and a host of others. Many of the issues in the industrial sector today have their roots in policies adopted many years ago; so much so, that some analysts and experts blame the problems of today on key decisions of yesteryear.

8.1 Numbers and Trends in Industry

The phenomenal growth rate experienced in the industrial sector in Pakistan in the early 1950s can best be captured by Figure 8.1, which shows how, from an almost non-existent base, the growth rate of the industrial sector was doubling itself every few years. The extraordinary growth rates of over 20 per cent between 1950 and 1955 in large-scale manufacturing were achieved primarily because very little existed to start with and, hence, any investment and production, no matter how little, would register impressive gains. Only in the early 1960s did large-scale manufacturing come close to the extraordinary period of the early and mid-1950s. Nevertheless, overall manufacturing did manage to

produce a growth rate of close to 10 per cent on average throughout the 1960s (Table 8.1), followed by a substantial reduction in the 1970s, the reasons for which were discussed in the previous chapters. The 1980s once again saw a return to a very impressive annual average growth in manufacturing of 8.21 per cent, a fact which received much recognition by international agencies and independent analysts and scholars (see Chapter 7).

A trend which is striking for its monotony in Figure 8.1 is that exhibited by the small-scale sector. The first few years, 1950 to 1962, show a consistent trend of 2.3 per cent annual growth, followed by a growth rate of 2.9 per cent over the next eight years, with the Bhutto period registering an annual growth rate of 7.3 per cent. From 1977 until the present, we again witness a consistent trend of 8.4 per cent. This trend seems too consistent for it to be of any real substance. In fact, the growth rate for the small-scale sector is not calculated, as it is for the large-scale sector, and is merely imputed or assumed. Every few years, as the graph indicates, a readjustment in the annual growth rate is made to reflect a more realistic trend. However, as discussed in section 8.2 the small-scale and informal sector is much more dynamic and productive than the government's upwardly adjusted figures show. Moreover, this estimate for the small-scale industrial sector implies that, because the estimate is on the low side, so too would be the figure for overall manufacturing, which is based on both large- and small-scale

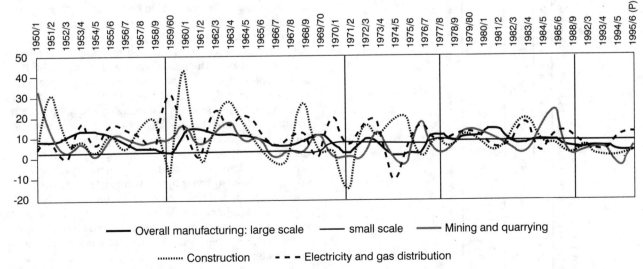

Figure 8.1
Growth rates in the industrial sector, 1950–1996, at constant factor prices of 1959/60 (annual % increase)

Table 8.1
Growth rates in manufacturing, 1980–1996 (% increase at constant factor cost)

	Average annual																					
	1950–1955	1955–1960	1960–1965	1965–1970	1970s	1980s	1980/1	1981/2	1982/3	1983/4	1984/5	1985/6	1986/7	1987/8	1988/9	1989/90	1990/1	1991/2	1992/3	1993/4	1994/5	1995/6 (P)
Total manufacturing	10.30	5.16	11.73	8.10	5.50	8.21	10.63	13.75	7.03	7.89	8.09	7.55	7.53	3.98	3.96	5.72	6.25	8.05	5.35	8.39	2.91	4.80
Large scale							11.50	15.70	6.60	7.70	7.98	7.25	7.22	10.60	2.40	4.70	5.40	7.90	4.10	4.10	0.54	3.13
Small scale							8.40	8.40	8.40	8.40	8.40	8.40	8.40	8.40	8.40	8.40	8.40	8.40	8.40	8.40	8.40	8.40

Source: Government of Pakistan, *Pakistan Economic Survey*, various issues, Islamabad.

industry. Furthermore, we argue in the next section that not only is the small-scale sector more dynamic on its own, but many activities previously undertaken in the large-scale sector have shifted to the small-scale sector – textiles in particular. The implications of this are that, unless a correct annual estimate of the small-scale sector is made, the growth rate reported for the overall manufacturing sector will always be on the low side. In fact, as the small-scale sector prospers, the extent of error in the sum for overall manufacturing will increase unless proper figures are made available.

A feature of Figure 8.1 is that, while manufacturing growth has been more or less stable in the last five decades, although there have been some important fluctuations, the growth rates of the other three sectors in the graph have been much more volatile. Construction, in particular, has experienced huge growth one year, followed by negative growth in the very next year. This fluctuation in construction could be due to the commissioning of large projects one year followed by fewer or no projects the next year. Dams, power plants, etc., and other large public (and now private) sector projects would show huge investments for one or two years in a row, followed, not surprisingly, by lower or even negative growth rates. For example, in 1960/1 the growth rate of construction over the previous year was an astronomical 43.3 per cent, followed by -2.6 per cent in the subsequent year. However, it is interesting to note that, once the economy began to develop and expand, the degree of fluctuation in construction became minimal. From 1977 onwards, and especially since the mid-1980s, not only has the annual growth in construction been positive, but the extent of fluctuation has been small. In fact, for all the sectors shown in Figure 8.1, the extent of fluctuation decreased after about the mid-1970s. This may suggest that the economy has been more stable and mature since the mid-1970s than in the earlier period.

Gross fixed capital formation (GFCF) is the value of capital stock at a particular time. In Table 8.2 although the GFCF is presented for a number of years, because they are in current prices, they are not strictly comparable. GFCF can double over a period of time, simply if inflation doubles. However, we can compare the distribution between the private, public, and government sectors. The table shows, as has been argued in previous chapters, that the private sector led growth in industry and the economy through much of the 1960s and again in the 1980s. The public sector dominated in the 1970s and the role of government also increased in the same period. The most recent figures available, for 1994/5, suggest that a pattern similar to the 1960s is once again emerging, with the possible difference that the share of government is greater. Once the role of government is allowed to balloon, as was the case in the 1970s, it is not easy to trim its share later on. Currently, despite the belief that less government is better, less is not easy to come by. It is probable that, with more privatization and the involvement of the private sector in areas which were earlier the exclusive terrain of the public sector, in future years the role and contribution of the private sector in the economy and in GFCF will grow at the expense of the public sector.

The lower panel of Table 8.2 shows the contribution of both the public and private sectors to GFCF. The shift towards the

Table 8.2
Gross fixed capital formation in private, public, and general government sectors at current market prices, 1963–1995

	1963/4		1971/2		1976/7		1980/1		1987/8		1994/5	
	Rs m	% of total	Rs m	% of total	Rs m	% of total	Rs m	% of total	Rs m	% of total	Rs m	% of total
Total	5,055		6,813		27,856		42,972		111,266		320,896	
Private sector	2,870	56.7	3,546	52.0	9,214	33.1	16,874	39.3	51,769	46.5	165,807	51.7
Public sector	1,523	30.1	2,350	34.5	12,637	45.4	17,131	39.9	34,886	31.4	96,556	30.0
General government	662	13.2	917	13.5	6,004	21.5	8,967	20.8	24,611	22.1	58,553	18.3

	1987/8		1994/5	
	Rs m	% of public sector	Rs m	% of public sector
Total manufacturing	19,605	15.6	75,950	3.2
Large scale	16,966	18.6	66,097	3.7
Small scale	2,639	1.0	9,853	0.0
Construction	4,592	89.0	16,991	34.1
Electricity and gas	13,226	100.0	52,711	93.8
Transport and communication	12,461	58.3	30,338	75.0

Source: Government of Pakistan, *Pakistan Economic Survey*, various issues, Islamabad.

private sector in most fields is quite noticeable, mainly for the reasons listed above. Large-scale manufacturing now takes place almost exclusively in the private sector, and with pro-private sector policies and denationalization, the private sector is playing a much greater role in construction and the electricity and gas sector.

Table 8.3 and Figure 8.2 show the index of production in manufacturing, while Table 8.4 shows the distribution of production by the main sectors since the early 1970s. Textiles, not surprisingly, dominate, with the food sector also contributing a fairly large share. The pattern since 1969/70 shows that a number of new industries have come online which did not exist in the early and mid-1970s. Most notably, petroleum refining, the ginning, pressing, and bailing of fibre, transport equipment, industrial chemicals, and a number of other products now contribute a great deal to production.

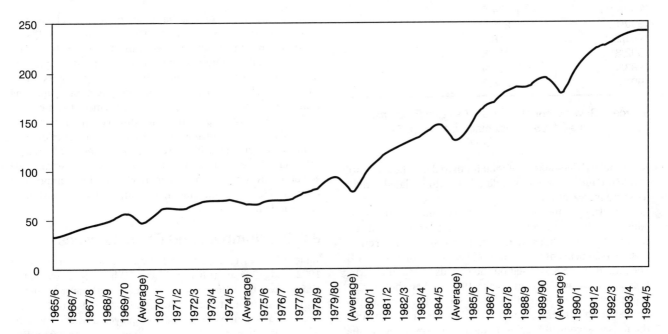

Figure 8.2
Production index of manufacturing, 1965–1995

Table 8.3
Production index of manufacturing, 1965–1995
(1980/1 = 100)

Year	Index
1965/6	39.1
1966/7	41.7
1967/8	44.9
1968/9	49.6
1969/70	56.5
(Average)	46.4
1970/1	60.0
1971/2	59.7
1972/3	65.2
1973/4	69.2
1974/5	68.1
(Average)	64.4
1975/6	67.7
1976/7	67.6
1977/8	74.9
1978/9	80.8
1979/80	89.7
(Average)	76.1
1980/1	100.0
1981/2	115.7
1982/3	123.3
1983/4	132.8
1984/5	143.4
(Average)	123.0
1985/6	153.8
1986/7	164.9
1987/8	179.1
1988/9	183.4
1989/90	192.1
(Average)	174.4
1990/1	202.5
1991/2	218.5
1992/3	227.5
1993/4	236.9
1994/5	238.3

Source: Government of Pakistan, *Pakistan Economic Survey, 1995–96*, Islamabad, 1996, p. 69.

Nevertheless, one-quarter of total industrial production is still textile production, and if we add other cotton-related activity, its share increases further.

A similar picture emerges when we consider the value added by industry, although Table 8.5 shows that the contribution of textiles increased from about 17 per cent in 1987/8 to 26 per cent of all value added by industry in 1990/1. The data in Table 8.5, based on the Census of Manufacturing Industries, are available only up to 1990/1 when the last CMI census was held, it is difficult to say what contribution textiles make currently, given the crisis which has engulfed them (see section 8.3 below). Table 8.6 shows the annual growth for some industrial items, and the most marked

feature of the table is the phenomenal growth of the 1950s. An equally interesting feature is the very high fluctuation in these items in the 1980s, where very impressive growth in one year is followed by negative growth in the next. One important exception is output of cotton yarn, which, although it has fluctuated, has shown impressive growth rates for most of the last decade. However, probably the most interesting and alarming set of figures in this table, if not in this chapter, are those for growth in 1994/5. Except for cotton yarn production, *all industries had registered negative growth rates.*

Table 8.7 concludes this section on facts and figures in industry with the average daily employment in major industrial sectors. The striking feature of this table is that, while the overall population of Pakistan almost doubled between 1969 and 1990, the number employed in industry went up by less than half. The reason for this could be that industry is becoming more capital intensive. But this is unlikely, given the output and production trends shown in earlier tables. Another reason could be that the figures listed in Table 8.7, which are for the formal sector only, do not show the trend towards the small-scale/informal sector that took place in the 1980s. Although there may not have been a complete shift of industry from the large scale to the small, larger growth in the small may have captured the increase in the labour force (see section 8.2). It is also possible that, to circumvent labour legislation, employers have preferred to hire part-time, non-unionized, contract workers, rather than formal employees. Nevertheless, whatever the cause of the slow growth in employment, all the figures presented in this section show somewhat alarming trends and are cause for serious concern and urgent redress.

8.2   The Small-Scale Manufacturing Sector

Much of the discussion that has taken place in this book with regard to the process of industrialization in Pakistan (Chapters 6 and 7) has revolved almost exclusively around the large-scale manufacturing sector. For most people, the image of industry is one where there are large plants either run by machines, robots, or the computer, or employing hundreds, if not thousands, of workers. Thus, it comes as a surprise to many people when they discover that it is not the large-scale manufacturing sector that provides employment to most workers in the industrial sector, but the small-scale or informal sector[1] that dominates our lives. The small-scale sector is, by far, the more dynamic, exhibiting impressive growth rates in employment, output, and contribution to value added.

8.2.1   Numbers and Characteristics

Table 8.8 gives us a picture of the informal sector between 1972 and 1986 in urban Pakistan. While there was little change over the fifteen years as a whole, and the share of the informal sector increased only slightly from 69.1 to 72.7 per cent, the actual numbers of those employed have increased by more than 72 per cent, from 2.8 million in 1972 to 4.9 million in 1985 (Table 8.9). This shows an annual increase of 4.3 per

Table 8.4
CMI value of production, selected dates (Rs m)

Industry sector	1969/70	1976/7	1980/1	1987/8	1990/1
All industries	11,801	30,674	84,288	230,886	374,858
Food	2,420	9,587	17,532	43,791	62,236
Beverages	55	419	994	2,379	3,092
Tobacco	652	2,207	4,850	9,074	8,767
Textiles	2,964	9,065	14,639	40,361	91,736
Wearing apparel	–	182	608	4,152	7,019
Leather and products	300	805	1,195	7,552	10,782
Ginning, pressing, and bailing	–	797	8,678	12,095	19,838
Wood and products	26	61	200	662	792
Furniture and fixtures	18	23	85	305	562
Paper and products	172	461	1,109	2,952	5,576
Printing and publishing	123	332	555	1,947	3,762
Drugs and pharmaceutical products	–	1,001	2,655	7,532	14,102
Industrial chemicals	–	1,614	3,290	11,484	20,186
Other chemical products	937	904	1,995	5,875	8,425
Petroleum refining	–	–	12,505	19,852	30,367
Petroleum and coal products	654	862	481	1,420	2,431
Rubber products	75	608	789	2,040	3,036
Plastic products	–	109	225	1,340	1,985
Non-metallic mineral products	401	1,000	2,738	11,723	16,034
Iron and steel basic industries	385	1,719	3,309	16,112	21,868
Fabricated metal products	252	637	924	2,109	3,326
Non-electrical goods	172	672	1,424	5,562	8,754
Electrical machinery	339	1,105	2,656	8,668	12,408
Transport equipment	247	1,383	2,419	10,195	14,529
Measuring, photographic, optical goods	–	4	57	706	1,056
Sports and athletic goods	–	40	89	518	1,489
Others	1,609	434	1,287	480	713
All other industries	–	3,043	–	–	–

Source: Government of Pakistan, *Pakistan Economic Survey, 1995–96*, Islamabad, 1996.

cent in employment over this period. During 1976–83, the peak growth of the small-scale sector (see below), the annual real growth rate in employment was as high as 10.3 per cent compared with the *negative 1.1 per cent* for the formal sector in the same period.

A look at Table 8.8 reveals that the informal or small-scale sector has dominated employment in the construction, wholesale and retail trading, hotels, transport, communications, and storage industries in urban Pakistan since at least 1972. However, probably the most interesting feature of the table is the fact that in 1972/3 the formal sector dominated urban employment in manufacturing, but by 1984/5 the informal sector had begun to dominate urban manufacturing in an unprecedented manner. Clearly, given the scale of the small-scale and informal sector, it can 'hardly be termed as marginal to the economy, provider of "employment of the last resort" or as a temporary sponge to absorb new migrants entering the urban labour market and seeking formal sector employment'.[2] The small-scale sector is not only here to stay, but will continue to play an increasing and critical role in a number of areas in the urban economy.

In the urban manufacturing sector, which mainly concerns us here, as many as 98 per cent of manufacturing units were small-scale unregistered firms, and in terms of urban manufacturing employment, 51.4 per cent worked in the informal/small-scale sector, while only 48.6 per cent worked in the formal sector. Tables 8.10 and 8.11 make other comparisons between the formal and small-scale sectors, from which it is clear that much of the capital stock and value added takes place in the large-scale formal manufacturing sector. The annual growth rates over the period 1976–84 (Table 8.12) reveal that in many important areas – employment generation, value added, and growth in capital stock – the small-scale sector has performed far better than the formal, large-scale, manufacturing sector. While the reasons for this growth are discussed below, these same reasons would very strongly suggest that, by most criteria, the small-scale informal sector has outperformed the formal sector in the last ten years.

Further characteristics of the formal (large) and informal (small-scale and household) sectors can be seen from Tables 8.13 and 8.14. In the formal manufacturing sector in urban

Table 8.5
CMI value of value added, 1987/8 and 1990/1 (Rs m)

Industry sector	1987/8	1990/1
All industries	**74,310**	**111,006**
Food	11,854	15,600
Beverages	1,333	1,568
Tobacco	7,488	7,050
Textiles	12,895	29,251
Wearing apparel	1,167	1,512
Leather and products	991	1,717
Ginning, pressing, and bailing	1,091	1,292
Wood and products	254	296
Furniture and fixtures	89	174
Paper and products	828	1,745
Printing and publishing	707	2,513
Drugs and pharmaceutical products	2,802	5,140
Industrial chemicals	5,185	8,713
Other chemical products	2,598	2,838
Petroleum refining	4,379	2,273
Petroleum and coal products	550	1,028
Rubber products	695	1,067
Plastic products	344	607
Non-metallic mineral products	6,480	8,416
Iron and steel basic industries	4,827	6,146
Fabricated metal products	770	956
Non-electrical goods	1,319	2,801
Electrical machinery	2,428	4,561
Transport equipment	2,706	2,875
Measuring, photographic, optical goods	202	262
Sports and athletic goods	141	421
Others	187	194

Source: Government of Pakistan, *Pakistan Economic Survey, 1995–96*, Islamabad, 1996.

areas, the largest number of employed workers are in textiles, as they are in the small-scale and household sector. Fabricated metals account for a substantial share in the small-scale urban manufacturing sector and is ranked second, while food and tobacco are the next largest sector in the formal sector. Table 8.14 shows the distribution of employment within major industries by sectors. The formal sector dominates in the heavier, capital-intensive large-scale industry, while the informal sector dominates in wood and furniture products and jewellery (see Table 8.15).

8.2.2 Emergence and Growth

The early development and emergence of the small-scale manufacturing sector in Pakistan, especially in the Punjab, is summarized by Asad Sayeed as follows:

> The tradition of small scale manufacturing in the Punjab goes back to the middle of the 19th century. But ... governmental bias against the small scale sector, low levels of absolute income, a stagnant agrarian economy through the 1950s and lack of linkages from consumer

goods-based import substitution, provided little impetus to small scale industry in the 1950s. The emergence of any significant growth in the sector can be traced back to the beginnings of mechanization in agriculture in the 1961–65 period and the subsequent giant leap experienced in the 1967–70 period with the introduction of green revolution technologies. A survey carried out in 1969 discovered specialized clusters of small scale industry that had mushroomed in various large and small towns of the Punjab since the beginning of the 1960s. [Others] also report that in 1968 there were 20,000 power looms producing cotton cloth in the non-mill sector in the Punjab.[3]

Khalid Aftab and Eric Rahim, writing about the Punjab, say that there was a sudden emergence of the small-scale sector, 'as if out of nowhere', in the early 1960s. Daska, a small town in central Punjab, had at best a few machine shops in 1961, but by 1965 more than 120 shops were engaged in diesel production. The small-scale agriculturally related engineering industry producing small diesel engines and water pumps,

Table 8.6
Growth of selected industrial items, 1980–1995 (%)

	Cotton yarn	Cotton cloth	Jute goods	Veg. ghee	Cigarettes	Fertilizers	Cement	Soda ash	Caustic soda	Sugar
1950s	32.89	27.96	n.a.	22.97	20.38	1.47	8.16	n.a.	n.a.	20.68
1960s	5.63	3.05	n.a.	16.88	10.73	27.49	10.68	12.00	24.35	34.26
1970s	3.37	−5.24	3.38	13.80	4.86	13.19	2.52	2.62	5.04	2.24
1980s	9.96	−1.07	9.48	4.46	−0.36	10.69	8.56	6.89	6.64	14.36
1980/1	3.33	−10.06	20.10	11.73	3.59	36.40	5.83	21.41	−3.51	45.22
1981/2	14.72	5.57	11.55	5.15	6.24	21.61	3.36	11.20	5.19	52.88
1082/3	4.25	3.24	18.57	−3.39	0.18	31.91	7.68	−11.94	1.48	−13.37
1983/4	−3.76	−11.61	26.51	15.98	4.97	3.91	14.35	12.92	−3.41	1.77
1984/5	0.03	8.35	−6.90	7.56	−2.93	1.44	5.09	14.54	15.87	13.86
1985/6	11.69	6.75	27.88	−4.38	1.73	0.73	22.00	5.16	19.13	−14.55
1986/7	21.61	−6.15	13.60	−0.49	0.85	7.11	12.73	1.48	0.18	15.23
1987/8	16.83	18.39	−1.85	14.45	1.92	−2.42	8.67	2.92	11.66	37.71
1988/9	10.64	−4.18	−6.82	−10.47	−22.43	2.49	0.75	7.61	8.48	4.91
1989/90	20.28	9.26	−7.80	9.45	2.26	3.74	5.09	3.60	11.28	−0.05
1990/1	14.22	−0.65	1.15	−3.95	−7.41	−2.66	3.66	−1.54	6.08	4.15
1991/2	12.44	5.13	4.13	−2.59	−0.72	−5.50	7.20	26.29	4.46	20.06
1992/3	4.12	5.67	−3.37	13.46	−0.92	14.63	2.76	0.16	0.71	3.23
1993/4	7.44	−3.22	−21.64	−7.45	19.86	20.96	−5.27	0.59	9.46	21.90
1994/5	3.04	−7.78	−11.42	−1.04	−3.05	−1.28	−3.24	−0.66	−4.38	−2.73

Notes: Figures from 1950s, 1960s, 1970s, and 1980s represent the average annual growth rate. Figures from 1980/1 onwards represent growth over previous years.
Source: Government of Pakistan, *Pakistan Economic Survey, 1995–96*, Islamabad, 1996, p. 78.

which 'hardly existed' in 1960, employed a labour force of 6,000 by 1965. They argue that 'this aspect of the development assumes even greater importance when it is realized that regular manufacture of these products was unknown in this region of the subcontinent before the 1950s'.[4] They add that 'the emergence of a completely new small-scale sector without any direct government assistance, employing over 6,000 workers in a short period is not, to put it mildly, an everyday occurrence in less developed countries'[5] (see also Appendix 8.1).

Clearly, agricultural growth and the Green Revolution played a critical role in the development of the small-scale industrial, especially agricultural engineering, sector in the Punjab in the 1960s (see Chapters 3–5). In fact, the Green Revolution and its consequences transformed the entire agricultural, industrial, social, and economic structure in major ways (see Chapter 19). One consequence of these developments was the phenomenal growth in the small-scale sector in that period.

Ijaz Nabi analyses the impact of the Green Revolution on the industrial process as follows:

> Demand for farm machinery resulted from the impressive growth of Pakistan's agriculture after the introduction of new dwarf wheat and rice varieties and chemical fertilizers in the 1960s. The agricultural sector grew between 3% and 6% per year, reaching a peak in the late 1960s, and this growth generated considerable demand for

agricultural machinery. The most important demand was for tubewell engines and water pumps, which ensure timely supply of water and thus facilitate the use of chemical fertilizers. During this period of rising farm incomes, other farm activities such as ploughing and threshing also started to be mechanized. By the late 1970s farmers began to complain about shortages of labour at peak periods of sowing and harvesting. As a result, there was a rapid increase in the use of tractors and tractor-driven threshers, which enabled early harvesting of the winter crop (wheat) and timely sowing of the summer crops (cotton and rice), and which contributed to an overall increase in cropping intensity. Agronomists have called this phenomenon the Thresher Revolution, following the earlier Green Revolution. Demand was also created for haulage machinery such as trolleys for marketing the increased agricultural produce.[6]

For Asad Sayeed, the growth impetus for the small-scale sector in the 1970s occurred as a 'consequence of the convulsions suffered by the large scale sector'[7] under Bhutto. For him, the most important policy in this regard was the pro-labour legislation introduced in 1972. However, for the Asian Development Bank,

> Possibly the single most important factor in the increase in the SSI [small-scale industrial]

Table 8.7
Average daily employment by major industry sectors (000)

Industry sector	1969/70	1976/7	1980/1	1987/8	1990/1
All industries	418	457	452	515	622
Food	34	48	52	67	84
Beverages	2	3	4	6	5
Tobacco	11	8	13	9	6
Textiles	198	220	187	171	238
Wearing apparel	–	2	4	12	20
Leather and products	5	4	5	12	15
Ginning, pressing, and bailing	13	10	10	–	4
Wood and products	1	2	2	3	3
Furniture and fixtures	2	1	1	2	2
Paper and products	6	8	8	8	8
Printing and publishing	9	9	8	8	8
Drugs and pharmaceutical products	–	7	11	18	18
Industrial chemicals	–	13	13	18	18
Other chemical products	22	7	9	9	9
Petroleum refining	–	2	4	2	2
Petroleum and coal products	2	–	1	2	2
Rubber products	3	10	6	8	8
Plastic products	–	1	2	5	5
Non-metallic mineral products	17	14	12	28	28
Iron and steel basic industries	14	17	18	44	44
Fabricated metal products	–	–	–	12	12
Non-electrical goods	13	15	14	25	25
Electrical machinery	16	17	17	19	19
Transport equipment	17	20	23	19	19
Measuring, photographic, optical goods	–	–	–	4	4
Sports and athletic goods	–	2	1	8	8
Others	21	11	15	2	2
	–	1	–		

Source: Government of Pakistan, *Pakistan Economic Survey, 1995–96*, Islamabad, 1996.

Table 8.8
Estimates of the share of the informal sector in urban employment by industry (%)

Industry	1972/3 (1)	1984/5 (2)	1985/6 (3)
Agriculture	100.0	100.0	100.0
Manufacturing	34.6	70.9	71.1
Construction	79.3	87.9	86.5
Wholesale and retail trade, hotels, etc.	98.9	98.8	98.8
Transport	61.5	74.1	68.0
Finance, insurance, and real estate	67.7	40.9	48.1
Community and social services	55.4	50.5	34.7
All	69.1	75.9	72.7

Source: Nadvi, Khalid, *Employment Creation in Urban Micro-Enterprises in the Manufacturing Sector in Pakistan*, ILO/ARTEP, Bangkok, 1990, p. 36.

Table 8.9
Estimates of the size of the informal sector in urban employment by industry (000 persons)

Industry	1972/3 (1)	1984/5 (2)	1985/6 (3)
Agriculture	376.9	457.2	467.3
Manufacturing	262.8	1,131.5	1,265.0
Construction	227.3	378.9	455.2
Wholesale and retail trade, hotels, etc.	936.1	1,534.0	1,785.9
Transport	212.4	463.9	380.8
Finance, insurance, and real estate	65.3	65.4	97.1
Community and social services	671.0	642.2	513.7
All	2,878.3	4,741.1	4,970.0

Source: Nadvi, Khalid, *Employment Creation in Urban Micro-Enterprises in the Manufacturing Sector in Pakistan*, ILO/ARTEP, Bangkok, 1990, p. 37.

Table 8.10
Formal and informal sector employment in urban Sindh and Punjab, 1984/5 (000 persons)

Industry	Formal	Informal	% distribution Formal	% distribution Informal	Sectoral employment as % of total
Agriculture	0.0	457.2	0.0	100.0	7.3
Mining	13.0	0.0	100.0	0.0	0.2
Manufacturing	465.1	1,131.5	29.1	70.9	25.6
Electricity, gas, and water	69.4	21.1	75.0	25.0	1.5
Construction	52.0	378.9	12.1	87.9	6.9
Wholesale and retail trade, and hotels	18.8	1,534.0	1.2	98.8	24.9
Transport, storage, and communication	162.2	463.9	25.9	74.1	10.0
Financing, insurance, real estate, and business services	94.4	65.4	59.1	40.9	2.6
Community, social, and personal services	630.6	642.2	49.5	50.5	20.4
Other activities	0.0	45.8	0.0	100.0	0.7
Total	1,505.2	4,741.1	24.1	75.9	100.0

Source: Nadvi, Khalid, *Employment Creation in Urban Micro-Enterprises in the Manufacturing Sector in Pakistan*,
ILO/ARTEP, Bangkok, 1990, p. 3.

growth rate during the 1970s was the massive devaluation of 1972 and the Government's abandoning the multiple exchange rate as a part of the Export Bonus Scheme. Since the Government allowed LSM [large-scale manufacturing] a subsidy on the import capital and raw materials via artificially cheapened foreign exchange while SSI had to pay the free market rate for foreign exchange to import these items, it was difficult for SSI to compete with LSM in the production of consumer goods or engineering industry products. Devaluation changed this by reducing LSM's cost advantage vis-à-vis imported capital and raw materials. Further, the increase in the effective exchange rate for machinery and equipment was much

greater than that for raw materials required for their local manufacture. Thus SSI's competitiveness vis-à-vis imports was also improved. Finally, since SSI goods (e.g., carpets, garments, surgical instruments, sporting goods, etc.) tend to be export-oriented and therefore face price-elastic external demand curves, these industries received a relatively larger boost from the devaluation than did the LSM industries which had become more oriented toward the protected domestic market.[8]

Asad Sayeed agrees with this analysis and argues that it helped the small-scale export-related industries such as cloth, surgical instruments, and sports goods. He also identifies the

Table 8.11
Characteristics of formal and informal manufacturing sectors in urban Pakistan, 1983/4

	Formal	Informal Small scale	Informal Household
No. of workers/unit	86.71	2.34	1.82
Capital stock/unit (Rs 000)	8,261.23	24.14	7.66
Capital–labour ratio	95.28	10.30	4.20
Employment cost/ waged worker (Rs)	19.25	7.47	5.82
Proportion of workforce unwaged (family workers)	0.30	60.65	87.01

Source: Nadvi, Khalid, *Employment Creation in Urban Micro-Enterprises in the Manufacturing Sector in Pakistan*, ILO/ARTEP, Bangkok, 1990, p. 47.

Table 8.12
Annual real growth rates in the formal and informal manufacturing sectors in urban Pakistan, 1976/7 to 1983/4 (%)

	Formal	Informal Small scale	Informal Household
Employment	–1.1	10.3	5.0
Capital stock	15.2	19.6	28.6
Value added	8.7	54.6	4.2
Capital–labour ratio	16.6	8.3	22.5
Labour productivity	49.4	39.7	67.8
Capital productivity	–6.0	–2.8	2.9
Real wages for waged workers	5.7	5.0	1.0

Source: Nadvi, Khalid, *Employment Creation in Urban Micro-Enterprises in the Manufacturing Sector in Pakistan*, ILO/ARTEP, Bangkok, 1990, p. 48.

Table 8.13
Major industries in terms of employment in the formal and informal manufacturing sectors in urban Pakistan, 1983/4 (%)

Industry sector	Formal	Informal	
		Small scale	Household
Food, tobacco	16.1	15.5	30.0
Textiles, leather, clothing	41.9	30.6	41.7
Wood, furniture	0.9	15.7	8.7
Paper and publishing	3.7	1.7	1.9
Chemicals	10.4	1.7	2.7
Mineral products	4.7	2.0	4.6
Basic metals	7.6	0.6	0.2
Fabricated metals, machinery and equipment	13.7	20.0	5.9
Others	1.0	12.3	4.4
Total	100.0	100.0	100.0

Source: Nadvi, Khalid, *Employment Creation in Urban Micro-Enterprises in the Manufacturing Sector in Pakistan*, ILO/ARTEP, Bangkok, 1990, p. 53.

Table 8.14
Distribution of employment within major industries by formal and informal manufacturing sectors, 1983/4 (%)

Industry sector	Formal	Informal	
		Small scale	Household
Food, tobacco	45.2	36.3	15.5
Textiles, leather, clothing	54.6	33.4	12.0
Wood, furniture	5.4	82.5	12.1
Paper and publishing	66.4	25.7	7.8
Chemicals	83.5	11.7	4.8
Mineral products	63.7	22.7	13.6
Basic metals	93.3	6.3	0.4
Fabricated metals, machinery, and equipment	43.1	52.8	4.1
Others	8.3	83.9	7.8

Source: Nadvi, Khalid, *Employment Creation in Urban Micro-Enterprises in the Manufacturing Sector in Pakistan*, ILO/ARTEP, Bangkok, 1990, p. 53.

Table 8.15
Industrial categorization: formal, informal, mixed

Purely formal	Purely informal	Mixed
Basic metals	Wood products/ furniture	Food/tobacco
Chemicals/rubber/ plastics	Others (jewellery)	Textiles/clothing/ leather
		Fabricated metals/ machinery/ equipment

Source: Nadvi, Khalid, *Employment Creation in Urban Micro-Enterprises in the Manufacturing Sector in Pakistan*, ILO/ARTEP, Bangkok, 1990, p. 54.

impact of the Suzuki car and motorcycle assembly plants on the small-scale engineering goods industry through backward linkages from subcontracting.[9]

The import liberalization that followed the 1970s and 1980s is identified as a positive development for the small-scale industrial sector compared with the 1960s, when this sector was faced with raw material constraints. Also, Bhutto's nationalization was addressed towards private, large-scale manufacturing investment, which declined later for fear of further reprisals, and it is possible that some of these investment funds were diverted towards the small-scale sectors. The Asian Development Bank study argues that 'this seems particularly likely in the textile industry where many looms were uprooted from large mills and set up as small independent production units by mill owners'.[10] Another boost to the small-scale sector following nationalization was that industrial capital from the large-scale manufacturing sector was diverted to trade and exports, possibly making it easier for the products of the small-scale sector to find domestic and foreign markets.

John Adams and Sabiha Iqbal have made a number of very important observations about the growth of the small-scale sector under Bhutto. They believe that there was actually a 'considerable bias' towards the small-scale sector, government credit to which increased by 122 per cent between 1972 and 1974, and was 'sharply higher' in 1976.[11] The devaluation of the Rupee also helped, and the new import policy of Bhutto allowed industrial plants costing less than Rs200,000 to be freely importable against cash.[12] Since the small-scale sector did not fear nationalization, it attracted more private investment, and labour laws were also not strictly applied to that sector. John Adams and Sabiha Iqbal argue that the small-scale sector expanded during the Bhutto

era, not because his government treated the sector in 'any exaggeratedly special fashion and it was more the absence of favoritism towards the big units that helped them'.[13]

Ali Cheema identifies yet another cause of the growth of the small-scale sector in the 1970s, which was the Cottage Industries Act of 1972.[14] The textile sector was the most affected by this, after which there was a major shift in textiles from the large-scale manufacturing sector to the small-scale and informal sector (see section 8.3).

A very pertinent point regarding the shift in the nature and composition of the small-scale sector is made by Asad Sayeed, who says that, due to the causes identified above, we see the 'emergence of the small scale sector in the engineering and capital goods industry and textile sector also. *The important qualitative change that the above developments during the Bhutto interregnum brought about was to move small scale manufacturing out of exclusively agrarian servicing activities to the terrain of broader manufacturing in the larger urban agglomerations.'*[15]

From the late 1970s and especially in the 1980s, Pakistan became a remittance economy, with large sums of money from the Gulf greasing the engines of industry and probably resulting in higher than average growth.[16] The large inflows of remittances and the increased purchasing power created a large demand for consumer goods, which was fulfilled by a small-scale sector eager to expand. This demand-led expansion had a multiplier effect as many of the locally produced goods had linkages with the capital goods industry, increasing demand and their production too. The construction boom of the 1980s, with increased demand for household items, was also an important catalyst, causing demand for local products to grow and having expansionary effects on the small-scale sector.

Since data regarding the actual size and trend rates related to the small-scale sector are particularly scarce, it is impossible to quantify its exact size. However, there is every indication that its growth rate is far higher than reported. It caters to a growing middle class and is being led by increased demand for goods consumed by this class. Hence, it would be interesting to know whether the sector is at all efficient compared to the formal large-scale sector, given the attitude of the government towards it in the past.

8.2.3 Issues Affecting the Small-Scale Sector

Khalid Nadvi, in his comprehensive study of the small-scale/informal sector, summarizes the main features of the sector as follows:

> The informal sector consisting of small enterprises and household units appears to be expanding more rapidly than the formal sector and already provides employment to the majority of those engaged in urban manufacturing in Pakistan. Informal sector units are characterized by extremely low levels of employment and a high incidence of unwaged family workers. As to capital intensity there appears to be a distinct technology hierarchy on the basis of which household units are the most labour intensive and formal sector concerns the most capital intensive. Furthermore, capital intensity is in real terms growing more rapidly in the formal sector leading to a net displacement of labour. As a result labour productivity is substantially greater in the formal sector while capital productivity is inversely related to unit size.[17]

He also argues that 'a focus on the informal small scale units would appear to lead to the most socially efficient allocation of capital and thereby have the greatest potential for generating productive employment'.[18]

Large productivity differences exist between the two sectors, as can be seen in Table 8.16. The labour productivity (O/L) for the large-scale sector is expected to be higher due to the higher capital–labour ratio in the sector, a trend which,

not surprisingly, can be seen amongst all industries in both periods in the table. An outcome that is taken for granted in much of the literature on the small-scale sector is that the small-scale sector is more efficient than the large-scale sector in the use of capital. However, the results provided by Asad Sayeed in Table 8.16 show that the ratio K/O presents a 'mixed picture', with some industries not subscribing to the norm. Nevertheless, the increase in the ratio K/O over time shows an 'increasing relative efficiency in capital use' for the small-scale sector. Moreover, a rising O/L ratio over time for the large-scale sector indicates increasing labour productivity in that sector. Asad Sayeed concludes his analysis by saying that 'the claim that higher labour intensity in the small scale sector leads to its higher capital efficiency is not borne out by the data'.[19]

One opinion expressed, without exception, by all scholars working on the small-scale sector is that the state or government has until very recently treated the sector usually with indifference, but often with contempt. As the previous two chapters also reveal, almost without exception – the exception possibly being the Bhutto regime – state policy has been very heavily biased in favour of the large-scale manufacturing sector.

Khalid Aftab and Eric Rahim, who have examined the phenomenal growth of the small-scale agricultural-engineering sector in the Punjab, argue that 'government policy in Pakistan during the period under consideration [the 1960s] did not assign any important developmental role to small scale enterprises. It was never thought that small scale producers were capable of exhibiting any dynamism. Government policies explicitly aimed at large scale industries and large scale enterprises received special privileges.'[20] All favourable policies were directed towards the large-scale sector and in fact, according to the Asian Development Bank study, discriminated against the small-scale sector. Asad Sayeed argues that, after the bias of the state towards the large-scale sector in the 1960s, in the 1970s and 1980s 'the only change in government attitude seems to be the acknowledgement of the existence of the small scale sector, though with no tangible policy thrust'.[21] While it is clear that the state plays no real role in explicitly promoting the small-scale sector, an interesting observation made by a scholar on the sector is worth quoting here: 'the fact that this sector is exempt from or evades any form of tax and generally free rides on utilities such as electricity, gas, water and sewerage, means that it enjoys an implicit "hands off" policy'.[22]

There is a clear consensus on the position that the state, given the formidable contribution and growth rates of the small-scale sector, must now explicitly address the issues confronted by it and actively promote the small-scale sector. Khalid Nadvi argues that 'if manufacturing is increasingly going to be dominated by small and informal units, a larger and more comprehensive policy framework for this sector, that goes further than employment generation issues, would be required'.[23]

One of the more interesting findings of the work on the small-scale sector has been its close links with the large-scale manufacturing sector. Khalid Aftab and Eric Rahim believe that one of the reasons for the success of the Punjab firms

Table 8.16
Labour productivity (O/L) and capital–output ratio, small scale and large scale, 1983/4 and 1987/8, for selected industries (Rs 000)

Industry sector	1983/4 Small scale		1983/4 Large scale		1987/8 Small scale		1987/8 Large scale	
	K/O	O/L	K/O	O/L	K/O	O/L	K/O	O/L
Food	0.31	85.78	0.22	399.51	0.31	64.65	0.28	454.53
Textiles	0.23	41.11	0.40	105.98	0.44	19.86	0.45	170.49
Footwear	0.08	21.60	0.16	100.87	0.09	24.23	0.18	441.20
Wood and cork	1.04	11.35	1.24	141.21	0.88	17.34	0.94	147.41
Furniture	0.28	15.27	0.29	85.67	0.32	18.97	0.78	125.82
Non-metallic minerals	0.10	86.53	0.65	303.30	0.23	51.98	0.80	387.72
Metal and metal working	0.33	19.98	0.27	113.38	0.30	28.40	0.28	173.60
Non-electrical machinery	0.97	15.86	0.24	209.50	0.57	29.88	0.35	210.17
Others	0.23	26.62	0.36	103.16	0.39	25.45	0.26	123.58
Total	0.23	49.33	0.36	265.90	0.39	29.86	0.41	280.50

Notes: Total is weighted by the three-digit share in value added for respective sectors for the respective periods. The above numbers for the small scale only include 'Small Manufacturing Establishments' to the exclusion of 'Household Units' which include 10 or fewer workers. A combined estimate of the two resulted in even lower labour productivity without affecting the capital–output ratio significantly.

Source: Sayeed, Asad, 'Political Alignments, the State and Industrial Policy in Pakistan: A Comparison of Performance in the 1960s and 1980s', unpublished Ph.D. thesis, University of Cambridge, 1995, p. 40.

was the overall environment of economic expansion along with the small firms' proximity to large enterprises. For the individual small producer, 'the external economies generated by the large were as important as those it obtained through the evolution of vertical specialization within the small scale sector'.[24] Asad Sayeed, examining the experience of the successful small-scale sector in Japan and Taiwan, argues that the

> large-scale capital goods sector can create the appropriate linkages for the embodiment of technical change in equipment, which can then enhance the productivity of the small sector accordingly. Secondly, because of economies of scale, the large scale sector can contribute towards reducing the cost of intermediate and capital goods for the small scale. Thirdly, with large firms subcontracting to the small, productivity enhancement and technical upgradation is further encouraged through user–producer interactions, quality standards, specification requirements, etc.[25]

This link with the large-scale sector can at times be critical, since the experience of countries where the small-scale sector has flourished shows that 'ultimately the fortunes of the small are intimately linked with those of the large'.[26] Hence, any strategy to improve the small-scale sector will also need to address the issue of developing an efficient large-scale intermediate and capital goods industry. Areas where linkages between the small- and large-scale manufacturing sectors already exist will need to be further strengthened so that both benefit.

The single most important constraint faced by the small-scale sector has been the availability of credit. All surveys consistently come up with this finding. Khalid Nadvi, in his survey of 328 small-scale enterprises, found that only two of them had been able to obtain credit from the formal banking sector and both the loans were of very small amounts. The constraints to borrowing from the formal sector were many:

> Formal credit from the banking sector had been obtained by only two of the sample of 328 enterprises, both cotton weaving units in Gujranwala. In both cases the volume of credit availed was low (Rs7,000 and Rs10,000) and used towards purchases of plant and equipment. All units were unregistered which technically restricted them from qualifying for credit from the formal banking sector. In addition collateral, guarantees, lengthy procedures and detailed paperwork (usually in English) necessary to obtain formal bank loans were major barriers to those operating unregulated units. Even if collateral was available, a large number of informal enterprise owners were either illiterate or had extremely low levels of formal education and were consciously alienated from the formal procedures required by commercial banks.
>
> Alongside the daunting procedures, respondents stated that the banking bureaucracy was actively unhelpful and discouraging to small scale informal units. Many respondents felt that the level of bribes, which they alleged had to be paid to bank officials in order to access formal bank loans, were prohibitively high for unregulated small scale units.[27]

The small-scale and informal sectors therefore have to find credit for working and fixed capital from other sources. The sources vary according to type of industry; in some, the most important source of credit is through the linkages which exist in that sector with wholesalers, large intermediaries, or capitalists. For example, most of the loans in the carpet weaving, transport, and fishing sectors are made in the form of advances with very high rates of interest, and the borrowers are almost bonded to the person making that loan. In other sectors, the nature of borrowing is less exploitative and relatives and friends, as well as family savings, provide loans for the sector. The committee system – or *bisee* – is also an important source of funds for enterprise.

Some recommendations have been made by various scholars on how to deal with this credit constraint. There is the mainstream neoclassical argument of working through the market and providing a 'level playing field', by removing the subsidy on the interest rate on capital, and by providing a 'credit package' (see also Box 8.1). However, as the Asian Development Bank study argues, 'it must be kept in mind that SSI [small-scale industry] comprises several hundred thousand units and any attempt to provide incentives directly to individual enterprises through bureaucratic channels would be futile'.[28]

There is no denying the fact that the small-scale sector plays, and is going to play, an increasingly important role in Pakistan's economy. Rashid Amjad, for example, argues that as much as 25 per cent of Pakistan's total export earnings are generated from the small-scale industrial sector.[29] Ironically, in many ways, the dynamic growth of this sector has taken place because the state has kept away from it and let it function largely on its own. Government interference or even 'help' may actually prove to cause a slowing down of this impressive growth.

8.3 The Textile Industry and its Crisis

When we think of manufacturing industry in Pakistan, it is the textile industry that immediately comes to mind, and for good reason too. The textile sector holds a very important position in Pakistan's economy in terms of employment and value added, but especially in the contribution the industry makes to exports. It has the highest manufacturing value added for any industry in the manufacturing sector, contributing 17.5 per cent, with the food sector next in line,

---

BOX 8.1

Credit availability to the small-scale sector

Asad Sayeed discusses the problem of the availability of credit to the small-scale sector:

Proponents of the level playing field argue that once interest rates truly reflect the scarcity value of capital, it will remove the implicit bias against the small scale producer. Given the prevalence of borrowing from the curb market in the small-scale sector, market-determined interest rates would increase the cost of capital for the largescale sector and lower them for the latter. However, the moral hazard of lending to a large and diverse number of borrowers still remains. As Anderson argues, in a situation where interest rates are market determined and the small scale sector is the recipient of credit, interest rates will rise to the level of the curb market, increasing the risk of default in the formal financial sector. Moreover, because the interest rate is above the actual opportunity cost of capital (because it has to cover the losses incurred by those who have defaulted), entrepreneurs in both the large and small scale sectors, facing interest rates above the opportunity cost of capital will be loath to borrow. Not only will there be a disequilibrium created from the demand side, but as Stiglitz and Weiss show, this will lead to adverse selection on the part of borrowers. Once the lenders decide on a more discriminatory lending policy, typically the axe will fall on the small scale borrower. Therefore, according to Anderson:

The practical effect, therefore, of simply removing administrative controls would be for institutions not to lend rather than charge high interest rates, on the one hand, or face significant short-run losses in the uncertain expectation of long-run profits on the other. The above mentioned externality then takes the form of potentially low risk projects and efficient investments in small scale industry being entirely excluded from access to institutional finance.

The question to ask is that given the above identified market failures in the credit market, how did the countries which have efficient and growing small scale industrial sectors overcome the problem of moral hazard? Particularly in the case of Taiwan, real interest rates – though state controlled – were high, yet significantly lower than the curb market rates. Amsden reports that small scale firms in Taiwan were also discriminated by the state-controlled financial sector, with the share of large firm borrowing being three times more than that of the small and even medium sized firms. The same study cites that start-up capital for small firms in Taiwan is either raised through family savings, the curb market or in many cases from windfall gains made through urban real estate. So far as working capital and at times equipment is concerned, 'big business appears to be an important source of finance for small business'. Other differences between the success stories and the failures is that small scale is provided with adequate infrastructure, which lowers their overall cost structure, thereby increasing their profitability to the extent that they can afford to borrow from the usurious curb markets.

Source: Sayeed, Asad, 'Political Alignments, the State and Industrial Policy in Pakistan: A Comparison of Performance in the 1960s and 1980s', unpublished Ph.D. dissertation, University of Cambridge, 1995.

Table 8.17
Cotton textile statistics, 1955–1995

Years[a]	Number of mills	Spindles (000)			Looms (000)		
		Installed	Working	% working	Installed	Working	% working
1955–1959	n.a.	1,537	1,434.2	93.3	25.1	22.2	88.4
1959–1964	74	1,674	1,629.6	97.3	28.2	26.4	93.6
1964–1969	92	2,058	1,923.4	93.5	30.4	27.6	90.8
1969–1974	131	2,877	2,711.8	94.3	29.8	26.6	89.3
1974–1979	139	3,536	2,700.8	76.4	28.0	19.2	68.6
1979–1984	156	4,077	3,008.6	73.8	24.8	13.6	54.8
1984–1989	184	4,446	3,467.0	78.0	18.4	9.2	50.0
1989–1994	271	6,356	5,150.0	81.0	14.8	7.2	48.6
1994–1995	334	8,307	5,991.0	72.1	14.0	5.0	35.7

[a] Averages for the years.
Source: Government of Pakistan, *Pakistan Economic Survey*, various years, Islamabad.

contributing 16 per cent in 1987/8. Similarly, about one-third of the entire manufactured employment is in the textile sector, with food a distant second, having only 13 per cent. In terms of exports, approximately 30 per cent of Pakistan's total exports came from cotton textiles in 1990/1, up from 20 per cent in 1982/3.[30] Cotton yarn's contribution to exports increased from 10 to 18 per cent between 1982 and 1990. These figures are only for cotton textiles, and if we included synthetics they would be even higher. According to UNIDO, textiles constituted 56 per cent of Pakistan's exports in 1985.[31] Tables 8.17 and 8.18 give an overview of the cotton textile industry.

Pakistan's textile industry has lost its relatively more prominent position of the 1960s and 1970s, and today holds a little over 2 per cent of the world market. Pakistan enjoyed a very dynamic performance in the 1960s, and was among the leading underdeveloped countries that were emerging in the world cotton textile market. In fact, Pakistan's record was quite envious, as between 1962 and 1970 it cornered over 11 per cent of the world market. By 1972 Pakistan held about 3.5 per cent of the world market in textiles, which fell to 1.5 per cent in just four years. It rose again to 2.5 per cent in 1983 and has since stabilized at around 2 per cent.[32]

More interestingly, the share of Hong Kong and Korea as a proportion of the world market tells a revealing story. In 1972 Hong Kong held less than Pakistan's share, with under 3.5 per cent of world output, while Korea's output constituted a mere 1.5 per cent. In 1988 Hong Kong held a little under 9 per cent, while Korea's share of the world market had risen to 6.5 per cent.[33] Some of the reasons for the relative fall in Pakistan's performance, and the rise in Korea's and Hong Kong's contribution to world output, are discussed below.

Many fortunes were made in the 1960s by leading Pakistani industrialists, almost all of whom had significant interests in the textile sector. In 1959 the nine largest industrial houses accounted for 50 per cent of total production, with the five biggest contributing as much as 37.3 per cent. The Saigol group alone controlled 15 per cent of the total production of cotton textiles in Pakistan (West

Pakistan). Of the thirteen largest industrial houses in (West) Pakistan, cotton textiles accounted for as much as 71 per cent of total production; engineering came second with only 7.9 per cent. By 1970 the top four industrial houses controlled almost 28 per cent of cotton textiles, being produced by a mere twenty-three industrial houses.[34] What is clear from the above is that the cotton textile industry was highly concentrated amongst a few houses and that it was located almost totally in the large-scale textile manufacturing sector.

Table 8.17 presents a rather unflattering picture of Pakistan's prime industrial sector, cotton textiles. Although the number of installed spindles has been growing steadily, and shows a rise of 440 per cent, the percentage of spindles actually working is substantially lower than during the 1950s and 1960s: currently, only 72 per cent of installed spindles are working. In the looms sector, the position is far worse, with only 35 per cent of installed capacity being utilized. Moreover, the number of installed looms has been cut by almost half and the number of working looms is currently less than one-fifth of that in the 1950s and 1960s. The main industry of Pakistan does not seem to be doing well at all, a fact confirmed by Table 8.18 and Figure 8.3. While yarn production may have increased tenfold since 1955, cloth production, having touched a peak in the early 1970s, has now fallen to well below 1950 rates.

However, as Table 8.19, and sections 8.1 and 8.2 show, much of manufacturing in general, and of textile manufacturing in particular, now takes place in the small-scale manufacturing sector. The dramatic shift that took place in the nature of manufacturing industry in Pakistan, for the reasons explained in section 8.2, also affected the textile industry in a major way. For example, cotton cloth production, which was 625.3 million square metres in 1970/1, fell to 123.5 million square metres by 1988/9 largely on account of this shift from the large-scale to the small-scale sector.[35] The cottage and small-scale segment of the textile industry employs more than double the number of workers in the large-scale textile sector (see Table 8.19). According to a study by the Institute of Developing Economies, the negative

Table 8.18
Indices for production of yarn and cloth, 1955–1995

Year	Total yarn produced	Total cloth produced
1955	100	100
1956	108	112
1957	112	121
1958	121	131
1958/9	130	138
1959/60	140	139
1960/1	143	157
1961/2	146	164
1962/3	153	172
1963/4	174	178
1964/5	180	183
1965/6	169	167
1966/7	181	175
1967/8	196	183
1968/9	209	182
1969/70	239	186
1970/1	265	202
1971/2	293	193
1972/3	329	180
1973/4	332	182
1974/5	307	170
1975/6	306	159
1976/7	247	125
1977/8	261	120
1978/9	287	104
1979/80	317	105
1980/1	328	94
1981/2	376	99
1982/3	392	103
1983/4	377	91
1984/5	377	83
1985/6	422	78
1986/7	513	73
1987/8	599	86
1988/9	663	83
1989/90	797	91
1990/1	911	90
1991/2	1,024	94
1992/3	1,066	100
1993/4	1,145	96
1994/5	1,198	98

Source: Government of Pakistan, *Pakistan Economic Survey*, various years, Islamabad.

productivity in the textile and garment sector is mainly the result of fragmentation of the industry, shifting from large-scale to smaller-scale units.[36]

Ali Cheema states that 'under the Bhutto government the textile sector lost the importance it held in the state policy regime in the '60s. This is because the emphasis of the state shifted towards the creation of public sector intermediate and capital goods industry and was no longer on the promotion of growth through manufacturing exports.'[37] Moreover, the Cottage Industries Act created a bias against large-scale production and according to Cheema, 'this act changed the structure of the industry in the textile sector', resulting in the fragmentation of firm size. Both output and employment in the small-scale sector grew significantly after the Act, with the number of power looms increasing from 20,000 in 1968 to 32,000 in 1972 and to 53,000 in 1978.[38] Moreover, the nationalization programme of the Bhutto government broke the hold of the large-scale manufacturing sector generally, but most importantly, the power of this group was significantly depleted as the critical link between the financial and industrial sectors was ruptured. John Adams and Sabiha Iqbal concur with this view, arguing that the policies that Bhutto's Finance Minister 'put into place were the single most important cause of the poor performance of the textile industry,'[39] since the nationalization of major industry, banks, and insurance companies, and the new labour laws enacted, were all against the interest of large industry, where the textile sector was located.

Table 8.20 shows how Pakistan's textile industry performed compared to Hong Kong's and Korea's between 1973 and 1987, and explains the reasons why Pakistan's share of the world market in textiles fell during this period and why those of Hong Kong and Korea increased. Asad Sayeed argues that

> both Hong Kong and Korea captured greater market shares as a result of a much larger component of their growth in exports coming from the competitive effect. This means that these countries were able to break into world markets on the basis of more dynamic production and marketing performance rather than merely relying on growth in the world market or product specialization at a given time.[40]

Further reasons given by Ali Cheema for this fall in world output share relate to the fact that both Hong Kong and Korea shifted into higher value-added subsectors like man-made cloth and bleached cotton cloth. He writes that 'Pakistani entrepreneurs on the other hand ignored up-gradation into either downstream higher value added processes and/or into higher value added products within each sub-sector.'[41] Essentially *Pakistan failed to diversify* into other products and lines at a critical juncture when the world textile industry was undergoing change. This conclusion is reinforced by the fact that, despite the imposition of import quotas by the advanced capitalist countries, Pakistan was even unable to meet the quotas. Moreover, both Hong Kong and Korea faced a stricter quota regime than that applicable to Pakistan. While both these South-East Asian countries were able to beat the quota constraint by diversifying and upgrading into higher value-added and quality products, Pakistan was not able to meet this challenge, and hence suffered.

Asad Sayeed argues that the 'loss in world market shares

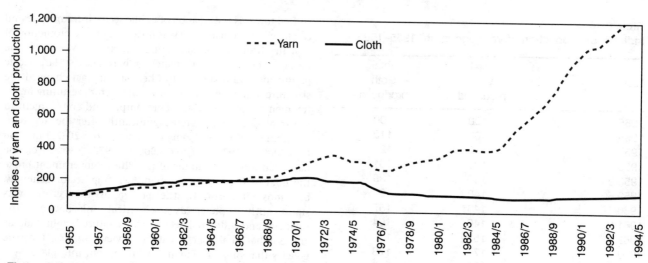

Figure 8.3
Indices for production of yarn and cloth, 1955–1995

Table 8.19
Overview of the cotton textile industry, 1988

	Number of units	Equipment	Direct employment (estimates)
Large-scale mill sector			
1 Spinning	186	4.72 million spindles including rotors	150,000
2 Composite mills	44	16,000 looms	
3 Finishing	10	. .	. .
4 Garments	50	3,000 sewing machines	1,000
Total			5,000
			156,000
Small-scale cottage sector			
1 Power looms	15–20,000	100,000 looms	150,000
2 Finishing	150	. .	6,000
3 Towels	160	2,500 looms	4,000
4 Garments	2,500	80,000 sewing machines	150,000
5 Hosiery	550	10,000 knitting machines	20,000
Total			330,000

Source: UNIDO, *Pakistan: Towards Industrialization and Revitalization*, Blackwell, Oxford, 1990, p. 54.

points to underlying inefficiencies in the textile sector, in spite of relatively high productivity growth in the sector',[42] and this is despite the fact, as pointed out by the World Bank, that 'the textile industry in Pakistan is the *most efficient industry within the manufacturing sector*'[43] (see Box 8.2). For UNIDO, the factors that will have to be addressed in order to increase the textile performance include problems presently related to 'a narrow production base, outdated technology, limited product range, [and] increase in quality consciousness in importing countries'.[44] Appendix 8.2 tries to identify some political and institutional factors that have resulted in the deterioration of the textile industry in recent years.

8.4   Has Public Sector Industry Been a Failure?

The public sector and the role of the government in general have been much maligned and discredited in recent years. There has been a wave of denationalization and privatization of state-owned enterprises not only in underdeveloped countries, but in advanced capitalist states such as the UK as well. Not only have publicly owned and managed industrial and non-industrial units been handed over to the private sector, but with the process of liberalization, deregulation, and so-called market-friendly policies adopted by underdeveloped countries, usually in the guise of a Structural

BOX 8.2
Efficiency in the textile sector

The World Bank in its evaluation of the textile sector has argued somewhat surprisingly as follows:

The textile industry in Pakistan is the most efficient industry (DRC = 0.92) [DRC: domestic resource cost] within the manufacturing sector. Efficiency is, however, far from uniform, with DRC estimates at the product group level varying from 0.72 for cotton spinners to 2.20 for woolen products. In general, the industry is more efficient in the spinning of locally sourced fiber (cotton) and the use of the same in made-up items (towels, canvas, knitwear and garments). It is relatively less efficient in the conversion of spun short staple and filament yarn into cloth (both finished and grey) and is least efficient in the conversion of imported fiber (wool) into both yarn and cloth. Internationally, the textile industry is characterized by large scale integrated operations employing very sophisticated technology to produce an increasingly more demanding product. Both the weaving and finishing industry and the woolen industry in Pakistan are characterized by small scale, non-integrated units employing very simple, relatively labor intensive technology to produce a product of questionable quality.

The industry as a whole operates within a largely neutral assistance regime (EPR=13%) [EPR: effective protection rate], earning average private financial returns of 17% which are approximately equal to the estimated public economic return of 18%. This picture is, however, highly misleading. Some 25% of domestic resources are employed in industries which are very efficient and are negatively protected. These industries are all characterized by the use of man-made fiber (MMF) and are unable to pass-on an average 24% distortion in input prices to their consumers because of competition from a close substitute – pure cotton textiles – which is generally priced domestically at or near the world price. Such a situation is hardly conducive to the growth of the MMF section of the industry which is necessary if Pakistan is to develop a more balanced profile relative to international demand trends.

The increased availability of imported fabric and garments after implementing the trade reform would induce a restructuring of parts of the textile industry. Such a restructuring will help Pakistan's textile sector to make better use of its competitive advantage in world markets. The trade reform would eliminate the bias against the use of man-made fiber. Cotton spinning (including mixed-fiber) would become more profitable despite the elimination of the export tax on raw cotton. In all other areas of the industry profits will suffer, unless the efficiency of production is increased, in particular the weaving and finishing and woolen yarn industries which are currently operating under high protection with low levels of efficiency.

Source: World Bank, *Pakistan: Country Economic Memorandum FY93: Progress Under the Adjustment Program*, Report No.11590-Pak, Washington, 1993, pp. 48–9.

Table 8.20
Constant market share analysis: Pakistan, Korea, and Hong Kong, 1973–1987

Country	World trade effect	Commodity composition effect	Competitive-ness residual
Pakistan	82.1	41.9	–24.1
Hong Kong	41.1	9.5	49.4
Korea	24.6	5.9	69.5

Sources: Compiled from: Cheema, Ali, 'Pakistan's Textile Policy and Trade Performance, 1972–90,' mimeo, Sidney Sussex College, Cambridge, 1995, and Sayeed, Asad, 'Political Alignments, the State and Industrial Policy in Pakistan: A Comparison of Performance in the 1960s and 1980s', unpublished Ph.D. thesis, University of Cambridge, 1995, p. 115.

'less is better'. So, in many ways, the existence of public sector industries is itself in question, and with the increased pace of privatization taking place in most countries, including Pakistan, one wonders if in a few years any state-owned enterprises will exist at all. One of the reasons why the privatization process is proceeding at such a pace is that there is a strong belief that public sector enterprises are inefficient, costly to run, poor performers, and a major drain on the exchequer. The argument goes that the state should no longer subsidize loss-making enterprises and they should be either sold to the private sector to run and manage, or closed down altogether. This section will evaluate the role, conditions, and performance of public sector enterprises in Pakistan.

Figure 8.4 gives a chronology of the main developments with respect to public sector enterprises in Pakistan. The main expansion of public enterprises took place under the government of Zulfiqar Ali Butto following his nationalization programme of 1972. The role of public sector industry in the 1950s and 1960s was mainly to supplement and assist the private sector, which was considered to be the leading vehicle of industrial development. The 1972 nationalization process reversed that trend, with the public sector taking the lead.

Prior to 1972 the main public sector industries were managed by the Pakistan Industrial Development

Adjustment Programme, the role of the state in the provision of basic social and infrastructural facilities has also diminished markedly. Today, the conventional wisdom is that, as far as intervention by the government is concerned,

Figure 8.4 Chronology of the main developments in the public enterprise sector

Event	Date
Establishment of the Karachi Port Trust as the first public enterprise in what is now Pakistan.	1886
Establishment of the Karachi Electric Supply Corporation (it became a public enterprise in 1952).	1913
Establishment of the Pakistan Refugees Rehabilitation Finance Corporation as one of the first public enterprises in independent Pakistan.	1948
Establishment of the National Bank of Pakistan as the first public enterprise in the finance sector.	1949
Establishment of Pakistan International Airline Corporation as a public enterprise and government monopoly in the air transport sector.	1955
Establishment of the Pakistan Industrial Credit and Investment Corporation as the first development finance institution.	1957
Establishment of the Water and Power Development Authority as a public enterprise and the major electrical power producer, transmitter, and distributor.	1958
Establishment of four development finance institutions to assist in the economic development of the country:	
Industrial Development Bank of Pakistan	1961
Agricultural Development Bank of Pakistan	1961
National Investment (Unit) Trust	1962
Investment Corporation of Pakistan	1966
Establishment of the Oil and Gas Development Corporation as a public enterprise in the fossil fuels energy sector.	1961
Establishment of the National Shipping Corporation as a public enterprise in the sea transport sector.	1963
Establishment of the Pakistan Steel Mills Corporation as a public enterprise in the heavy industries sector.	1968
Nationalization of 31 large firms in 10 'basic' industries. The private firms became public enterprises.	1972
Nationalization of the vegetable oil industry. The private firms became public enterprises.	1973
Nationalization of private, domestically owned banks and insurance companies. The private firms became public enterprises.	1974
Nationalization of 2,000 rice, flour, and cotton ginning mills. The private firms became public enterprises.	1974
Denationalization of 2,000 rice, flour, and cotton ginning mills.	1977
Efforts initiated in Ministry of Production through its Experts Advisory Cell to improve the performance of 56 of its public enterprises.	1981
Establishment of the National Disinvestment Authority.	1985
Junejo government agrees to permit the private sector to establish banks.	1986
Junejo government permits private sector firms to bid on construction contract for electrical power station.	1986
Benazir Bhutto pledges no more nationalization of industry in the election campaign of 1988.	1988

Source: Ahmad, M.B. and R. Laporte, *Public Enterprise in Pakistan: The Hidden Crisis in Economic Development*, Westview Press, Boulder, 1989, pp. 173–5.

Corporation (PIDC), which was created in 1952 with the aim of accelerating the rate of industrial development in the country. PIDC was 'to invest in fields in which private investment would be weak due either to technological complexity or the lack of immediate profit potential. It was also to transfer its projects to private entrepreneurs once they became profitable in order to promote and strengthen the private sector.'[45] It was also expected to promote some sense of regional balance between East and West Pakistan, developing industries in backward areas.

PIDC played a very important and effective role in fulfilling its mandate and initiated numerous projects in the jute, fertilizer, heavy engineering, and cement industries, some of which were later sold to the private sector. More importantly, however, it acted as an important 'catalyst in the subsequent development of these industries'[46] by training labour and creating important linkages with other sectors. In many ways, the role of PIDC was one of a pioneer, leading the way for the private sector in later years.

In the period 1972–7 the role of the public sector was considerably expanded, and by 1977 the government was 'heavily involved in finance and insurance, manufacture, transportation and communication, and energy. It had also entered the construction, trade and commerce, mining and agricultural sectors.'[47] The Zia-ul-Haq regime did not increase the role of the government by establishing new public enterprises, and much of the public sector investment during the early years of the Zia period went into ongoing projects. Although very little was privatized under the Zia government, the role of the public sector began to diminish as the private sector was unabashedly chosen as the leading vehicle to bring about economic and industrial development. After 1991 the contribution of public sector enterprises was further minimized with the launch of the privatization programme (see Table 8.21 for the share of the public sector in various activities, and see also Appendix 8.3).

Given the abhorrence of the regimes after Zulfiqar Ali Bhutto towards the public sector enterprises and the desire to

Table 8.21
Share of the public sector in various activities, 1960–1988 (%)

	1960/1	1965/6	1970/1	1974/5	1984/5	1987/8
Agriculture	–	–	–	–	–	–
Forestry	–	–	–	–	–	–
Fishing	0.0	0.0	0.0	0.2	–	–
Mining	3.7	19.1	24.9	10.1	93.0	93.0
Manufacturing	2.1	2.4	2.4	8.1	11.1	10.1
Electricity and power	85.0	98.2	65.0	77.5	100.0	100.0
Construction	0.0	0.0	0.0	0.0	0.5	0.4
Trade	0.0	0.1	0.4	7.9	1.3	30.2
Transport and communication	62.3	44.1	34.2	33.9	30.1	30.3
Finance	n.a.	n.a.	14.6	67.5	95.2	95.2
Others	0.0	0.0	0.0	0.0	0.1	1.6
Share in GDP	4.9	4.8	4.2	7.7	10.6	11.6
Share in non-agriculture GDP	9.3	7.9	6.6	11.5	14.3	13.7

Source: Kemal, S.N.H. and A.R. Kemal, 'The Privatization of the Public Industrial Enterprise in Pakistan', *Pakistan Development Review*, vol. 31, no. 2, 1991, p. 111.

get rid of these units by the different governments since 1991, one might have the impression that the state was burdened by these loss-making, inefficient units and wanted to rid itself of them as soon as possible and at any price. Interestingly, however, the evaluations undertaken of the public sector at different times since 1977 paint a very different picture.

It must be remembered that public sector enterprises not merely have to respond to pure market criteria, but also have social and political responsibilities and motives. Hence the 'inclusion of socio-political goals in the objective function of the existence and operations of public industrial enterprises can pull down productivity and profitability of these units'.[48] This means that the overall evaluation in financial or economic terms, as reported, will be less than the actual contribution and outcome of the public sector enterprises. Nevertheless, despite this proviso, their contribution has been very impressive.

Table 8.22 shows the important indices of the public sector industries compared to the overall manufacturing sector in the period 1972–82. There is little doubt that the public sector industries performed far better than the overall manufacturing sector, *even under the Bhutto government* (1972–7) when the nationalization and pro-public sector policies were severely criticized and considered to be a failure. By no stretch of the imagination, based on Table 8.21, can one reach that conclusion. While public sector industries did fairly well under the Bhutto government, they performed *even better* under the more open and liberal economic regime of Zia. There was a significant increase in profits and productivity by the state-owned enterprises in the early Zia period, possibly due to a pro-investment and growth-friendly, overall economic and political environment, encouraging economic growth. Moreover, under the Zia regime a number of new units, initiated earlier, came into production. Asad Sayeed shows that the *weighted average of*

Table 8.22
Output, employment, and productivity indices of public sector industries and the manufacturing sector, 1972–1982

	1972/3	1973/4	1974/5	1975/6	1976/7	1976/7	1977/8	1978/9	1979/80	1980/1	1981/2
Public sector industries											
Production value (constant 1972/3 prices)	100	131	160	167	162	100	117	126	166	169	192
Employment	100	119	136	14	158	100	100	102	109	121	126
Labour productivity	100	111	118	116	102	100	117	124	152	140	152
Productivity index[a]	100	120	123	120	n.a.						
Manufacturing sector in Pakistan											
Production index (includes SSI)	100	107	108	100	110	100	109	114	126	139	155
Employment index	100	103	115	120	128	100	105	115	114	119	122
Productivity index	100	104	94	92	86	100	104	103	111	117	127

Source: Federal Bureau of Statistics, *Annual Report on Public Sector Industries, 1981–82*, 1981–2, except [a] productivity index, which is from Ahmed, Viqar, and Rashid, Amjad, *Management of Pakistan's Economy, 1947–82*, Oxford University Press, Karachi, 1984.

productivity growth in the public sector was higher than that of the private sector once the numbers for the Steel Mill are removed from the sample. This, he argues is a 'surprising result', where apart from Pakistan Steel, 'the two sectors were equally (in)efficient'.[49] Sayeed's analysis clearly questions the biases perpetrated by the World Bank, which has played a central role in discrediting the contribution by the public sector. With reference to the late 1980s, a World Bank study argues that 'the private sector was confronted with pervasive regulatory controls in manufacturing and *burdened by large public enterprises suffering from poor performance and inefficiency*',[50] which clearly seems to be untrue.

A more detailed analysis than Asad Sayeed's has been conducted by Nawab Haider Naqvi and A.R. Kemal, who have extensively analysed the performance of public sector enterprises. The salient conclusions from this analysis are as follows:

1. Of the eight corporations which run the public enterprises, five of them, accounting for 71 per cent of output originating in public enterprises, have been *'reasonably profitable* even from a strictly commercial view'.[51]

2. It is presumed that the effective rates of protection are usually higher for the public sector than for private enterprises, but their results show that these rates are relatively *lower* in industries where public enterprises dominate.

3. The industries dominated by the public sector do not suffer from a higher level of inefficiency than that observed in the private sector, hence *'efficiency levels across industries are independent of the locus of ownership'.*[52]

4. *'The incidence of the worst kinds of allocative inefficiency is in the private sector rather than in the public sector.'*[53]

5. Of the 60 inefficient industries identified, only 9 were in the public sector.

6. Capacity utilization is high in public enterprises, where 39 of the 60 enterprises had capacity utilization rates exceeding 75 per cent.

The overall conclusions of Nawab Haider Naqvi and A.R. Kemal regarding the public sector are forcefully articulated as follows:

> The public sector's profitability is due not to the higher level of protection that it enjoys (indeed, the effective protection rates are lower for them) nor due to any restrictions placed on the entry of new firms, but to its better performance and superior productive efficiency; and the charge of the *inherent* inefficiency of the public industrial enterprises is based neither on good theory nor solid empirical evidence.
>
> The basic message that comes out clearly ... *is that changing the locus of ownership of industries is by itself neither a necessary nor a sufficient condition for an efficient operation of specific industrial enterprises.* Indeed, ... both the private and public sector firms have operated efficiently as well as inefficiently, depending on the type of industry to which they belong. These results suggest very

strongly that, in Pakistan, *there is nothing inherently good or bad about the public sector; or even about the private sector for that matter.*[54]

Finally, for them, 'where industrial inefficiency is the problem, steps should be taken to improve the situation regardless of the locus of ownership. The divestiture of public enterprises, mainly on ideological grounds or to secure dubious gains, or to satisfy the sensibilities of donors and creditors, is certainly not an optimal policy.'[55] And this leads us, quite naturally, to the theme of privatization.

8.5 The Privatization Process

One of the most controversial and interesting aspects of the Structural Adjustment Programme since 1988 has been the privatization programme begun in 1990. Six years later, in 1996, it was still provoking strong reactions by observers (see Box 8.3). While the government of the day may be pleased at privatizing a reported 65 per cent of the targeted industries, the way the process has been managed and the consequences of this programme have been subject to debate, controversy, and mainly criticism (see Appendix 8.3).

A large-scale privatization effort was launched in November 1990 by the Nawaz Sharif government when the Disinvestment and Deregulation Committee was established to identify the enterprises to be privatized and to make recommendations on how this process should take place. Earlier, the first of the Benazir Bhutto governments also paid lip-service to the concept, and said that it would privatize the state-owned sector, but no manufacturing industry was targeted for disinvestment and not much in the form of privatization actually took place. The reason that the government gave for the slow pace of privatization was 'that it wanted to conduct an exercise that was transparent, well-conceived and broad based'.[56] Most critics felt that the government was just dragging its feet and lacked the commitment and political will to carry the policy through.

The Disinvestment and Deregulation Committee established the principle that the government should completely retire from the production of industrial goods, and identified 109 industrial units that should be privatized at the earliest opportunity, and four of the five nationalized commercial banks, which had 88 per cent of total deposits with them (see Table 8.23). The Committee was dissolved and replaced by a Privatization Commission in January 1991, which was to supervise the privatization process. The mandate of the Commission included the valuation of public enterprises that were to be privatized, based on the assessments made by independent consultants, the implementation of the bidding process, and the supervision of the transfer of the units to the private sector.[57]

In the early phase of privatization, the programme was unsuccessful with few bidders for the targeted firms. Since privatization was a cornerstone of the government's economic policy, the government revised its strategy and accelerated the process. It improved the legal and administrative procedures, and while it had decided initially to adopt the policy of offering only a few units for sale at a

BOX 8.3

Privatization controversy reveals the unsavoury aspects

A number of articles in the press have criticized the government of Benazir Bhutto for its policy and manner of privatizing state-owned enterprises. Sultan Ahmed writes:

The controversy in respect of privatization of large public sector units is getting heated again, and is acquiring an increasing number of disturbing facets.

The disputes are over the timing of privatization of large public sector units, such as UBL, Bankers Equity and the selling of 26 per cent of the shares of the Pakistan Telecommunications Corporation (PTC) to a strategic buyer, over the specific use the large sale proceeds of what is often described as the family silver should be put, and about the methodology or transparency of the transactions which have not been found to be satisfactory.

The question of timing of the sale is very important. To begin with, share prices in Pakistan are low, and the Karachi Stock Exchange price index at 1,488 is about 44 per cent below the peak of 2,661 achieved 20 months ago, and has been in the doldrums for too long a time without a significant and sustained break. Worse still, the PTC shares sold abroad at Rs55 per share have swung between Rs28 and Rs30 making many foreign investors disinvest and move to greener pastures.

Foreign investors are usually ready to buy shares of bigger enterprises when the economy is booming, and not when it is stagnating and when they see that an economic break-through is imminent. That is not the case in Pakistan as the economic growth has been too low during the last three years – 2.3 per cent, 3.8 per cent and 4.7 per cent despite the high growth targets set for each year. The growth target set for the current year [1995/6] is 6.9 per cent, and expectations suggest that the performance this year will be better than earlier years, particularly as the cotton crop may be as much as 10 million bales or more.

For a number of reasons, not only former prime minister Nawaz Sharif and former finance minister Sartaj Aziz have cautioned against hasty privatization of large public sector units but President Farooq Leghari has also joined the chorus. Addressing the two-day Asia-Pacific Privatization Conference in Islamabad he said: 'We cannot allow distress sale of our national assets', and wanted the privatization to take place in the best possible financial and legal environment.

When it comes to the using of the sales proceeds of privatization there is a large national consensus that they should be used for reduction of the overwhelming national debt, domestic as well as foreign. During the days of Moeen Qureshi as caretaker Prime Minister, he set up the Debt Reduction Fund to which the sale proceeds of privatization were to be credited. Dr Mahbubul Haq is emphatic that the funds should be used for reducing the costly debt.

The government, however, has other ideas and it has talked of setting up a 'Future Generations Fund' and utilizing that for promoting education, employment, etc. And it has already used Rs11 billion for its Social Action Programme [SAP] and has budgeted for an outlay of Rs12 billion this year on the SAP.

How much is the money received so far from privatization? Various figures have been given, but not a clear well audited picture. We need a clear and complete picture now.

Makhdoom Shahabuddin, Minister of State for Finance, said recently that until June 1993 Rs5.467 billion was received from privatization and since then Rs30 billion, making a total of Rs35.47 billion. But then, through the sale of 6 million vouchers of PTC alone Rs30 billion was received. He also said the Privatization Commission had so far used Rs13.98 billion for reducing domestic debt to the extent of Rs6.13 billion and the balance for the SAP.

Commenting on the issue, President Leghari has said the cynicism about privatization must go, and it is for the Prime Minister, the cabinet and the Privatization Commission to ensure that the cynicism is replaced by enthusiasm at the national level. 'It is time the government came up with a categorical well-audited statement on the use of the privatization fund for debt reduction and gives complete details of the funds received, spent and the balance.'

The third controversy is over the methodology of the privatization and the extent of transparency. The latest controversy in this regard is around the sale of 266 Kanals of land belonging to the Pakistan Engineering Company (former Batta Engineering) at Badami Bagh, Lahore for just Rs362 million which will reduce its overwhelming liability of Rs709 million only to some extent, and the government and the company will be the loser for it.

The buyer is the big gainer as after buying it he got the stipulation, that the land should be used only for industrial purposes, deleted. If this condition had been deleted before the sale of the plot in the key market area with the Badami Auto-Market next door, the government might have got Rs900 to Rs1,200 million, and the liabilities of the company would have been wiped out altogether. It has also been argued that if instead of the 266 Kanal plot being sold as a single piece it had been split into three or four plots, even with the stipulation that it should have been used for industrial purposes only, it would have fetched about Rs100 million. Hence, the disappointed candidates for buying have appealed to the PM for cancelling the same and some are proposing to move the courts for its cancellation.

It is to prevent such controversies and deep suspicions that President Leghari called for the kind of privatization that is clear and transparent and done with full awareness that the family silver was not thrown away. He said 'we gave hell to the IJI government when we were in the opposition for its non-transparent methodologies of privatization. Criticism of these methodologies still persists.' And clean and transparent privatization was the answer to it.

A long catalogue of major enterprises awaits privatization, while the IMF is castigating the government for being slow or dragging its feet. Among them are the public sector banks and DFIs [Development Financial Institutions], power and gas enterprises, mining and engineering projects, while the canal system is not to be privatized in the immediate future.

According to the Chairman of the Planning Commission, the pace of privatization is purposely slow, so as to avoid allegations of impropriety. But being slow alone is not enough, as the case of PECO has shown, as too many persons were interested in that precious land which was finally sold so cheaply. The President's comprehensive advice in respect to privatization has to be taken seriously by the government and the Privatization Commission, if the controversy is not to get over-heated as more large projects are put on sale.

Source: *DAWN*, Economic and Business Review, Karachi, 20–6 January 1996. This is an edited version of the original article.

Table 8.23
Privatization of state-owned enterprises

	Number of units				Value of units sold (Rs m)	
	Total	of which:			Total	Received
		For sale	Sold	Management transferred		
Commercial banks	5	4	2	2	5,122	2,135
Industrial units	124	105	67	47	8,219	3,896
Automobiles	15	10	8	5	1,043	583
Cement	15	15	11	8	4,658	2,253
Chemicals and ceramics	14	12	5	5	1,030	431
Engineering	12	9	4	4	141	58
Fertilizer	7	5	2	1	457	183
Ghee and vegetable oil	23	23	15	9	626	250
Roti plants	17	17	13	11	99	60
Rice mills	8	8	7	4	165	78
Miscellaneous	13	6	2	0	0	0
Total	129	109	69	49	13,341	6,031

Source: World Bank, *Pakistan: Country Economic Memorandum FY93: Progress Under the Adjustment Program*, Report No. 11590-Pak, Washington, 1993, p. 51.

time, it reversed this policy in October 1991, and advertised all the 105 industrial units for immediate sale. Attempts were also made to make the entire privatization procedure more 'transparent' and effective.

One of the reasons for privatization has been the need to raise revenue. However, this measure is fraught with problems, as an important report on Pakistan's industrial sector identifies:

> Privatization is being undertaken partly to offset declining budgetary revenue and partly to compensate for government investment shortfalls. It is hoped that liberalizing the economy and opening it up to competitive pressures will encourage private investment. An option open to the government is to commercialize public enterprises. The commercialization of some of the public enterprises has enhanced their financial performance since 1983. While an improvement in the performance of public enterprises may be a catalyst for further industrial progress, progressive expansion of the private sector will depend on a number of far-reaching changes in the industrial investment environment, including an improvement in the law and order situation which has adversely affected industrial development in recent years.[58]

The result following the renewed vigour to privatize in October 1991 was that, by November 1992, 67 of the 109 units had been issued letters of interest to sell. Of these 67, the management of 49 units had been transferred to the private sector, and an amount of Rs6 billion (of the total Rs13.3 billion for the 67 units) had been received by the

government. One reason why the privatization programme did not develop on the lines that the government hoped it would was that most of the companies put on the 'for-sale' list 'were already technically bankrupt'[59] and hence interest from buyers was low.

The three most coveted sectors to be privatized were the energy sector, telecommunications, and the four commercial banks. By late 1995, the telephone and telegraph sector had been partially privatized (see Appendix 8.3) and of the two banks, the Allied Bank Limited was sold to its employees, and the Muslim Commercial Bank to a private business house. The balance sheets of the banks show that these 'newly privatized banks have rapidly improved their performance'.[60] Two commercial banks, the Habib Bank Limited and the United Bank Limited, and two industrial banks, the National Development Finance Corporation and the Industrial Development Bank of Pakistan, are still to be privatized. However, a report by the World Bank made the following interesting observations about the banking sector:

> It has been a problem for potential investors to gain access to sufficient information about the quality of the assets of banks. Whereas domestic investors seem to be able to overcome this, robust foreign investors that require the information be presented according to internationally recognized standards are believed to be unsatisfied with quality and quantity of the data. This obstacle will be especially important for Habib Bank, which as the largest financial institution to be privatized probably cannot be sold exclusively to domestic investors. However, the Government remains committed to privatize all state-owned banks (except the National Bank of Pakistan)[61]

BOX 8.4
UBL sale to foreigners

One of the key issues that has emerged regarding the privatization process is whether the 'family silver' should be sold to foreigners. Ashfaq Kadri writes:

United Bank Limited, one of the big nationalized banks is being put on sale. Only two foreign bidders have been qualified by the Privatization Commission for the purchase. Privatization of financial institutions is of course desirable on the same grounds as industry, transport and insurance. However the question currently being debated in business circles is, whether putting a large domestic bank under foreign ownership and control will be advisable?

The justifications for privatization are important and well understood. In the case of banks they carry a heavy weight in the face of official direct control on bank advances, lower level of bank's operational efficiency and the tendency for having large stuck-up loans. The experience of privatization of the Muslim Commercial Bank and Allied Bank Limited speaks eloquently in favour of moving ahead with the programme of privatization of commercial banks as well as Development Financial Institutions (DFIs).

But how far will it be a judicious decision to hand over such a large bank as UBL to foreign financiers? Let us briefly go into the history of our banking structure. In fact in the early days, just a rudimentary banking infrastructure existed in the country. With the rapid growth of industries and trade during the 1950s and 1960s, the requirement of varied services professionally rendered by a well structured bank system arose. Indeed, it goes to the credit of early pioneers of our banks that within less than two decades a wide network of the banking system was evolved.

Pakistan inherited the British system of branch banking and following this pattern quite a number of private banks with a highly extended branch banking structure started operating. They opened foreign branches to render services in foreign exchange dealings. Industry, trade, and financial institutions recorded exuberant growth under private ownership and management. In the 1970s, several banks were merged together and nationalized. Although quite a number of deficiencies appeared under public ownership of banks and DFIs, yet their business expanded in scope and content.

Now looking at the apparent deficiencies of public sector owned and operated banks, the decision to privatize them carries wide support of financiers and businessmen. Hence privatization of the United Bank Limited is fully justified. But in my view selling it to foreigners will not be a very wise decision.

First of all it is being stated in financial circles that the price at which the bank's shares are being sold to foreign bidders is extremely low. Selling such an important and large bank at highly depressed share prices can be termed as a poor decision. Besides this, there are other types of losses which the economy may likely suffer. UBL is believed to possess nearly 1700 branches spread over almost all the important 'mundi' towns as well as big business centres like Faisalabad, Multan and Karachi. After privatization, through judicious management of foreign would-be owners, the latter will emerge as powerful financial tycoons in the country. They will possess power to indirectly control domestic trade, small and big business activity and financing of large enterprises. Why should such a strong lever be handed over to foreign control?

If all this financial authority and leverage would have been in the hands of indigenous private bankers, it would have been most welcome. But placing it in foreign hands means allowing considerable dominance of domestic and foreign trade by foreigners. The foreigners can encourage foreign traders to operate in Pakistan and hence Pakistani exports and imports will start slipping into foreign hands.

Likewise, foreign controlled banks can financially support foreigners' entry in the country's small and medium enterprises. These enterprises contribute nearly 40 per cent to the national income. As such, foreigners' share in our small and medium enterprises will begin to increase. New ventures in engineering industries of Gujrat and Gujranwala and textiles of Karachi will be started by foreign enterprisers, backed by foreign owned commercial banks.

If foreign private owners succeed in efficiently running the bank, they will surely succeed in generating more deposits and controlling advances to trade and industry of their choice. In other words, they will have considerable influence in the direction and growth of Pakistan's trade and industry.

Moreover, UBL has a number of foreign branches, through which foreign remittances are received and foreign banking services are rendered to Pakistanis operating in foreign countries. This important segment of our financial earnings will also be handled by foreign operators.

The number of foreign banks is already increasing in Pakistan and most lucrative business is already in their hands. However, the number of these foreign bank's branches is rather limited. But placing a large bank with an extensive branch network will provide extensive opportunity to win over Pakistan's financial business operations.

Foreigners have already started creeping into Pakistan's Capital Market, and now they will get more opportunities to hold influence and sway in the Money Market as well. Infrastructure like energy, telecommunications and transportation is also being offered to big foreign multinationals. If this trend of privatization continues, perhaps we will end up with a large share of influence by foreigners in Pakistan's trade, industry, infra-structure and financial operations. Pakistanis will be turned into growers of grain and cutters of wood. The conclusion in straightforward terms is that UBL should not be handed over to foreigners. Some indigenous bidders must be found.

Source: *The News*, Business and Finance Review, 20 January 1996.

Interestingly, towards the end of 1995 the United Bank Limited was offered for sale and only foreign bidders remained in the final stages of the process, a move which came in for criticism from concerned economists (see Box 8.4).

All the evidence seems to suggest that the process of privatization has come in for a great deal of criticism in recent years and that as the government aggressively pursues its privatization programme, opposition will continue. The Institute of Developing Economies in Japan identified the following criticism of the process:

> The privatization process was severely criticized by several quarters for the lack of transparency, and the inadequate attention paid to the antecedents of the new management. It was

suggested that the bid evaluation procedures were incorrect, and furthermore, inconsistently applied from case to case. It was also alleged that the process suffered from favoritism, as some bidders had privileged access to information and competing bids. In a number of cases, units were transferred to management that had no previous record or experience of running an industrial unit at all; in others the new management had defaulted on its loans from the banking system even though the Commission had stipulated that previous loan defaults would invite an automatic disqualification. The government's response to these allegations, apart from a denial of any deliberate wrong doing, was that speed was of the essence, in order to overcome the inertia generated by vested interest groups.[62]

BOX 8.5

How does one measure protection and inefficiency?

Viqar Ahmed and Rashid Amjad discuss the methodology used in the calculation of effective rates of protection, and show how we come up with such concepts as a 'negative' value added by industry.

> Basically, these exercises calculate the cost of inputs and the value of outputs first at 'market' or 'domestic' prices, which include protection and other subsidies, and compare these with the costs of inputs and the value of outputs of similar (or nearly so) goods at what they would be in the 'world' market or 'trading prices', i.e., if they were bought and sold in the open world market. The rate of effective protection is then defined as the per cent of value added due to protection.
>
> A simple version of this concept may be shown as follows:
>
> Value added in industry 'i' at 'market' or 'domestic' prices
> $= w =$ sale value of output minus cost of inputs
>
> Value added in industry 'i' at 'world' or trading prices
> $= \hat{w} =$ sale value of output minus cost of inputs
>
> Effective rate of protection of value added due to protection $= \dfrac{w \stackrel{\frown}{-} w}{w}$
>
> Let us illustrate by taking three different cases. Suppose value added at 'domestic' prices is a hundred but at 'world' prices is only ten. Then value added due to protection or the effective rate of protection is 90 per cent. In the second case, suppose value added at 'domestic' prices is again a hundred but at world prices is negative, i.e., sale value of output is less than the cost of inputs (say minus ten). In this case then, as the rate of effective protection is > 100, it would imply *negative value added* by that industry. What this means is that rather than add value to the inputs it uses, it actually 'loses' value when we evaluate the inputs and outputs at world prices. Finally, suppose value added at 'world' prices is greater than value added at domestic

prices, then this would indicate that the protection system is discriminating against the output of that industry (for example, tariffs, on inputs exceed tariffs on output).

Arshad Zaman also measures EPR as follows:

> The concept of effective protection was designed to be a summary measure of the degree of incentive provided to an industry, and is usually measured in terms of Effective Protection Rate (EPR), defined as the difference between value added at domestic prices (VAD) and that in world prices (VAW), expressed as a ratio to the latter. Thus:
>
> $$EPR = \frac{VAD - VAW}{VAW} = \frac{VAD}{VAW} - 1$$
>
> In practice, a number of assumptions are made in calculating EPRs which should be borne in mind. First, the calculations assume that domestic producers are taking full advantage of the protection offered by the tariffs. Where there is significant smuggling, this is clearly not the case, and the degree of protection is overestimated, perhaps by a wide margin. Similarly, where prices are controlled, the producers are unable to exploit the potential advantages of protection. Second, survey data on which EPR estimates are based typically exhibit under-reporting of production, imparting again an upward bias to protection estimates. Third, price comparisons based on reported CIF import prices reflect underinvoicing of imports, and consequently lead to overestimates of implicit EPRs. Finally, the substantial variation in production coefficients across firms makes precise policy formulation difficult. Due to these problems of interpretation and estimation, the actual level of effective protection should not be taken too seriously, the ranking by industry is more relevant.

Sources: Ahmed, Viqar and Rashid Amjad, *The Management of Pakistan's Economy, 1947–82*, Oxford University Press, Karachi, 1984, p. 211; Zaman, Arshad, 'Effective Protection and Performance of Public Enterprises in Pakistan', *Public Enterprise*, 1986, vol. 7, no. 1, p. 43.

In another equally critical appraisal of the privatization process, Nawab Haider Naqvi and A.R. Kemal question the entire concept of privatization and show how the process may result in serious negative consequences.

> We share the view that public and private investments are essentially complementary in nature; and that while private investment holds the greatest promise in areas where productive efficiency matters, its success depends on a well-thought out programme of public investment which first provides an efficient infrastructure. Furthermore, public sector investment in those productive activities where the market 'fails' due to the externalities dominating there, or where no markets exist, is essential to maximize social output notwithstanding the contrary claims of the privatization enthusiasts who attribute every possible economic ill to the so-called phenomenon of 'government failure'. Also, recognizing that public sector investment – even in the productive activities – is a fact of economic life in Pakistan, it is essential that privatization should take place where it has the most promise of adding to productive efficiency and economic growth. Indeed, efficiency (and growth) considerations must be seen as the only valid grounds for privatization. And in this context, there is enough empirical evidence in Pakistan to show that changing the locus of ownership from public to private is neither a necessary nor a sufficient condition for achieving any of the avowed goals of privatization; even on theoretical grounds, other objectives for going private – e.g., mobilizing financial resources for the government – had better be achieved by other, more effective policy instruments. *Indeed, the real-world experience suggests that across-the-board privatization, taking place mostly on ideological grounds, may prove not only self-defeating but positively counter-productive.* Thus, profitable companies can as well be given over to their (not-too-worthy) competitors, exacerbating the degree of concentration in the economy; and the (apparently) defaulting enterprises may in fact be given away to friends of the regime, thus increasing the element of 'crony capitalism'.[63]

Given this extensive criticism, Aftab Ahmad Khan identifies some reasons why there has been so much criticism of the privatization programme:

> An imperative for the success of privatization is the transparency of the process to avoid people's suspicion and ensure their support. All aspects of the privatization exercise must be out in the open and there should be no suspicion of political patronage, corruption, favouritism or cronyism in implementing it. Unfortunately, this important dimension of privatization has not been given due attention in some privatization transactions and this has resulted in casting doubts on the integrity of those responsible for deciding the choice of parties in the cases. The privatization exercise in our country so far has been suffering from a lack of proper planning. There has been no systematic approach to timing, prioritization, sequencing, classification of units, valuation and modes of privatization. If one of the purposes of privatization is to broadbase share ownership and expand the equities market, then it is imperative that all sales are quickly followed by successful flotations. A significant proportion of the privatized firms have yet to float equity in the market.[64]

Past trends suggest, however, that little change is to be expected in the manner of the privatization process in the coming months and years, no matter how strong the criticisms made of a process fraught with serious problems and objections.

8.6 The Debate Over Efficiency in the Industrial Structure

Following the end of the boom in industrial development in the late 1960s, a number of books and papers were written on Pakistan's industrial performance, and the collective view was that the high growth had been achieved at very considerable costs, and that the entire industrial structure was severely inefficient.[65] The policy instruments that were held responsible for creating this inefficiency rested on the extent and degree of state intervention in distorting prices in the domestic market, which was said to affect the manufacturing sector adversely. As we saw in Chapter 6, much of Pakistan's early industrial and economic growth was predicated on an import substituting industrialization policy, which was the conventional wisdom of the times and was being followed by most young developing countries. The main tools for such a policy consisted of protecting domestic industry by building up trade barriers in the form of tariff and non-tariff restrictions, using multiple exchange rates, and import licensing.

The main work that sparked off the debate over the inefficient nature of Pakistan's industrial structure was undertaken by Ian Little, Tibor Scitovsky, and Maurice Scott,[66] and his work challenged the then premises of import substitution, protection, and the industrialization process. This study found that amongst the developing countries studied, Pakistan had the highest effective rates of protection (see Box 8.5) in manufacturing. Recalculating the manufacturing sector's contribution to value added, the authors found that the industrial value added actually grew at a *negative rate*, and not at 16 per cent as believed. The conclusions of the study were that too much emphasis had been given to the manufacturing sector and, hence, the agricultural sector and manufactured exports had suffered. The policy tools that caused these distortions did so in the following manner:

Table 8.24
Capital utilization in manufacturing industries of Pakistan (%)

	1960/1	1965	1965/6	1967/8
Rates of capital utilization				
0–20	60.98	18.57	36	16.67
20–40	29.97	71.43	44	36.67
40–60	4.88	2.86	8	23.33
60–80	4.88	4.26	12	18.33
80–100	0	4.26	0	5
Average capital utilization rates by end use				
Consumer goods	47.87	62.61	57.80	68.13
Intermediate goods	21.60	66.45	62.07	54.42
Capital goods	25.33	39.11	30.23	55.76
Average level of capital utilization				
Simple average	21.82	32.04	31.44	41.33
Weighted by capital stock	41.67	59.02	48.65	62.65

Source: Sayeed, Asad, 'Political Alignments, the State and Industrial Policy in Pakistan: A Comparison of Performance in the 1960s and 1980s', unpublished Ph.D. thesis, University of Cambridge, 1995, pp. 63–4.

> The policy tools which were deemed to be responsible for this distortion were the multiple exchange rates, the tariff structure and to some extent the system of import licensing. The multiple exchange rates meant that exporters imported their inputs at a below par exchange rate and then exported their goods at a higher rate. Also the existence of an export tax, in certain industries such as leather and cotton, meant that there was a disincentive for exports as compared to sale in the local market (where because of protection a preferential rate could be commanded). As for imports, the overvalued exchange rate meant that whereas raw materials and machinery was imported at the official exchange rate it was sold in the market at its full scarcity premium.[67]

Another study revealed that in 1964 about 75 per cent of actual value added was due to distortions in the industrial structure. Due to this protection, according to this study, the manufacturing cost of value added was increased by an average of nearly 300 per cent compared to what the cost would have been had there been no protection.[68]

The analysis from the work on protection, distortion, and inefficiency in the industrial sector in the 1960s suggests that the following principal distortions were created: the neglect of agriculture at the cost of industry; excessive emphasis on the manufacturing sector, resulting in poor export performance; a distorted sectoral distribution in industry (i.e. between the consumer, intermediate and capital goods industries); and a disincentive for technical change, as the existing structure would not have encouraged much development in technology because returns were already very high.[69]

However, all the evidence presented in the earlier chapters, particularly Chapter 6, shows that none of the alleged consequences followed. In fact, one sees the reverse, with agriculture showing very high rates of growth throughout the 1960s at a time when there was supposed to be considerable anti-agricultural bias in policy. We also see that, despite the import substituting strategy, there was actually no distortion of the sectoral distribution in industry, and although the consumer goods sector showed high growth, as it should have under these circumstances, the intermediate and capital goods sectors also showed very high rates of growth.

The evidence that total factor productivity growth and growth in labour productivity were considerable also confirms that there was substantial technological dynamism in the industrial sector. As Meekal Ahmed argues:

> There is little support for the arguments, that the rise in the productivity of labour in Pakistan is to be explained mainly in terms of a strong factor substitution effect combined with insufficient innovations, or that high effective rates of protection are symptomatic of high costs. On the contrary, the present analysis shows that manufacturing industry in Pakistan has, in general, demonstrated a high capacity for technological adaptation and innovational assimilation, a result which is substantiated by the important role that technical progress and increasing returns play in explaining the pattern of labour productivity advance. Cost reductions were, however, not adequately reflected in price reductions in oligopolistic markets. Hence the fact that prices remain relatively stable in the more dynamic sectors of production means that the potential for changing the pattern of production in response to the unequal incidence of productivity tends to operate much more weakly.[70]

Asad Sayeed concludes that 'there seems to be no conclusive evidence on the existence of technological ossification or other related inefficiencies in Pakistan's manufacturing sector during the decade'.[71] The reasons why the work by Little, Scilovsky, and Scott and by others consistently came up with the conclusion that Pakistan's industry was inefficient are discussed below.

Another criticism launched against the industrial policy of the 1960s in Pakistan relates to the hypothesis that, despite having scarce capital, the incentive structure was such that there was underutilization of capacity, and hence an expensive and scarce resource was being wasted. This argument ran as follows:

> Little et al. argue that in an environment where the relative cost of capital is artificially low, there will be a tendency towards over-capitalization.

Also, other government controls, primarily in the form of import licensing, further exacerbate the problem of capacity utilization as the import of raw materials is linked to the acquisition of these licences as well as the availability of foreign exchange. Particularly in the case of Pakistan, the argument goes, since import licences for raw materials were linked to installed capacity, this created a tendency to install new plants in order to avoid raw material bottlenecks. To the extent that this problem exists, as the evidence put forth by Hogan and Winston suggests, this is unfortunate as the primary problem of development is deemed to be scarcity of capital and here we have a situation where there is idle capital.[72]

Asad Sayeed, examining this proposition with respect to Pakistan in the 1960s, concedes that while the rate of utilization of capital was increasing over time, the absolute level was still low (see Table 8.24). However, examining the data, he concludes that it was structural constraints – such as the inadequacy of demand, infrastructural bottlenecks such as power and transport, scarcity of skilled labour and problems of assimilating foreign technologies – which were primarily responsible, rather than the constraints pertaining to the misallocation of resources as the neoclassical orthodoxy would have us believe.[73]

Akbar Noman has argued that the claims made by Little *et al.*, regarding inefficiency are 'highly misleading'. He argues that these authors 'derive their estimate of value added from the calculations of effective protection rates made for Pakistan. These suffer from the familiar problems of data and interpretation, *though quite possibly more acutely for Pakistan than most cases*'.[74] In the case of Pakistan, the calculation used to establish inefficiency employed figures for value added at world prices that were understated, and effective protection rates that were overstated. Akbar Noman also shows how effectively and pervasively underreporting of output by firms in Pakistan takes place by 'very considerable margins'.

Unfortunately, a number of important works on Pakistan have taken for granted the evidence and data provided by the numerous studies conducted after the 1960s, without questioning the methodology or data sources used. This has helped perpetuate the myth that Pakistan's industrial structure was very inefficient. Viqar Ahmed and Rashid Amjad also fall prey to this, arguing that

> The evidence put forward clearly showed the basic 'inefficiency' of the industrial structure, which had emerged by the mid-sixties, when compared to 'world prices'. Although it can be argued that any country starting the process of industrialization behind tariff barriers would show considerable 'inefficiency' in terms of 'world prices', there is still no doubt that the industrial structure in *Pakistan was extremely inefficient even after fifteen years* of industrialization. The reason for this was the incentive structure, created for the manufacturing sector, which put little or no

pressure on the producers to cut down on costs especially capital costs of production. Also, little attention was given to the question of whether it was really beneficial for the country to set up an industry which would never really ever become internationally competitive and whose value added would in the extreme case continue to be negative even after many years of production behind highly protective barriers.[75]

However, a number of leading scholars have critically evaluated the data and evidence, and have come up with a re-evaluation of the state of inefficiency in the 1960s. Akbar Noman argues that 'the inefficiencies of Pakistan's industrialization during the 1950s and 1960s *have been much exaggerated*. They were still considerable but not so great as to rule out any justification of them as the price of rapid growth, at that stage of Pakistan's industrial development'.[76] He believes that 'the argument that high protection in the early years affected mainly the rate rather than the pattern of industrialization would appear to be correct'.[77] The work by A.R. Kemal and Meekal Ahmed also substantiates much of these findings, as does the excellent recent work by Asad Sayeed.[78] Asad Sayeed concludes his evaluation of the efficiency debate by the very important observation that 'the allocative efficiency losses that might have occurred as a result of state intervention appear to have been compensated by dynamic efficiency gains that accrued'.[79]

Another line of argument that emerged regarding the efficiency/inefficiency issue was related to industrial concentration that was excessive, and which was considered responsible for the inefficiency and deceleration in Pakistan's growth in the late 1960s.[80] However, the report by the Institute of Developing Economies concludes that 'the argument of industrial concentration provides no economic reason *per se* for either falling investments or inefficiency in the manufacturing sector of Pakistan in the 1960s'.[81] A.R. Kemal also believes that by the end of the 1960s much of Pakistan's manufacturing industry could 'survive without protection. The protection has resulted in higher profits and is not a result of inefficiency.'[82] The evidence on growth of total factor productivity and labour productivity, as seen in Chapter 6, shows that even though the industrial structure was concentrated, it was able to use resources efficiently.[83]

Most of the work on the industrial sector of the 1960s has tended to argue that the industrial policy was protectionist and distortionary, giving rise to deep-rooted inefficiencies in the industrial structure, which later carried on into the 1970s and caused the industrial crisis. Interestingly, a recent World Bank (1993) study on Pakistan has argued that the three industrial subsectors of chemicals, engineering, and textiles face domestic resource costs that are 'close to international standards and are *thus not operating particularly inefficiently*'.[84]

Table 8.25 shows the effective rates of protection and the domestic resource costs (DRCs) of some industries – a DRC coefficient above 1 indicates inefficient production conditions. The DRCs show that the textile industry is the most efficient industry within the manufacturing sector, and chemicals and engineering are only slightly inefficient. The study also argues that the 'current average effective

Table 8.25
Impact of trade reform on effective protection and profitability

		Pre-reform			Post-reform	
		DRC	EPR	Private returns	EPR	Private returns
Chemical						
Paper and paper products		0.86	−8	12	24	26
Basic industrial chemicals		1.69	70	9	1	−5
Fertilizers		1.08	23	14	3	9
MMF		1.30	29	9	0	3
Other chemical products		0.76	10	27	19	32
Rubber and plastics		1.03	19	13	32	18
Glass and ceramics		1.03	6	11	20	15
	Subsector	1.04	20	14	13	12
Engineering						
Basic metals		1.32	25	7	48	14
Metal products		1.10	19	12	11	10
Mechanical machinery		1.25	58	19	24	9
Electrical machinery		0.76	−13	14	30	31
Electronics		0.92	−31	2	16	16
Transport equipment		1.07	−1	7	24	13
	Subsector	1.07	12	11	27	15
Textiles						
Cotton spinning		0.72	−5	20	12	26
Weaving and finishing		1.22	45	16	22	10
Cotton made-ups		0.87	9	18	3	16
Woollen products		2.20	93	6	17	−5
Jute products		1.07	38	16	21	12
	Subsector	0.92	13	17	12	16

Source: *Pakistan Country Economic Memorandum FY93: Progress Under the Adjustment Program*, Report No. 1590–Pak, Washington, 1993, p. 48.

protection levels *seem moderate*, but conceal vast differences among product groups'.[85] In the chemical subsector, industrial chemicals, fertilizers, and synthetic fibres are highly protected, while in engineering, basic metals and mechanical products enjoy high effective protection. The electrical and electronic products are negatively protected, and protection levels for cotton spinning and made-ups are low.

While much in terms of industrialization policy and strategy has changed in the 1990s compared with the 1960s, it is likely that, had the extreme extent of inefficiency identified by Little *et al.* actually existed, the more recent picture presented by the World Bank would have been less positive. Had Little *et al.* been correct, much more inefficiency would have carried over into the 1980s and 1990s than actually did. While the data, calculations, and methodology are fraught with numerous serious problems, one may nevertheless conclude that the claims of the extent of inefficiency in the industrial sector in Pakistan have been grossly exaggerated (see Appendix 8.4).

8.7 Summary and Further Reading

8.7.1 Summary

It would surprise most people to know that the small-scale industrial sector of Pakistan has been the backbone of the economic growth and development that has taken place, particularly in the 1980s. In the 1960s, large-scale manufacturing produced the high growth rates, but after the intervention in the economy by Bhutto, the small-scale sector grew to prominence. This sector, which has been consciously ignored and neglected by government – ironically, one possible reason for its success – is a major source of employment in the urban areas of Pakistan, and provides as much as 25 per cent of Pakistan's exports. In a situation where overall trends in industry show alarmingly worsening signs, the small-scale sector continues to thrive and show dynamism. However, it must be emphasized that the fortunes of the small-scale sector are closely tied to those of the rest of the economy: if growth falters, as has been the trend in recent years, so too must the small-scale sectors.

The crisis affecting the textile industry has resulted from political interference, poor policies, bad management, and the inability of the industry to adapt to changing world demands and needs. Today, much of the industry is considered 'sick', and thousands of industrial units remain closed.

This chapter, using numerous sources, has tried to show that the public sector has not been an out-and-out failure, as is conventionally believed, and that public sector enterprises have been efficient, productive, and even profitable. The public sector has been much maligned, as is the trend these days, and so there have been growing moves to privatize all things owned by the state. However, privatization is no panacea, as changing ownership need not automatically result in efficiency, or any of the other attributes assumed to be inherent to the private sector. Moreover, the privatization process in Pakistan has been seen as a means to offer political patronage, and for this reason may prove to be counterproductive.

There is a consensus amongst economists in Pakistan that Pakistan's industry has been inefficient, due to high protection and warped incentives. This myth is repeated *ad nauseam* by scholars who have commented on the industrial sector. However, as we have shown, there is now growing awareness amongst a small group of academics that this is not the case. The claim that industry is inefficient has been overstated, and the evidence presented is misleading, misunderstood, or distorted. Recent work shows that, while numerous problems and hindrances have hampered industrialization in Pakistan, most are of a structural nature, and the causes and claims that are popularly believed are in fact incorrect.

8.7.2 Further Reading

In addition to the texts mentioned in Chapters 6 and 7, which cover many of the general issues related to industrialization in Pakistan, including those covered in this chapter, other important and interesting books and papers include Khalid Nadvi's *Employment Creation in Urban Micro-Enterprises in the Manufacturing Sector in Pakistan*, ILO/ARTEP, Bangkok, 1990, which is a very useful piece of work on the informal/small-scale sector; Ijaz Nabi's *Entrepreneurs and Markets in Early Industrialization: A Case Study from Pakistan*, International Center for Economic Growth, San Francisco, 1988, should also be consulted, as well as Anita Weiss, *Culture, Class and Development in Pakistan: The Emergence of an Industrial Bourgeoisie in Pakistan*, Vanguard, Lahore, 1991. M.B. Ahmad and Robert Laporte's *Public Enterprise in Pakistan: The Hidden Crisis in Economic Development*, Westview Press, Boulder, 1989, gives a useful overview of the state-owned industries.

For more details on various aspects of industry, the references provided in the Notes should also be consulted. Newspapers, magazines, and various government publications that come out from time to time should also be studied to keep abreast of current issues.

Appendix 8.1

The history of the emergence of the small-scale engineering sector in the Punjab

The small-scale sector, particularly in the Punjab, has changed the face of industry in the province. Khalid Aftab and Eric Rahim tell us how it emerged.

At the time of its establishment in 1947, Pakistan inherited one large engineering enterprise (BECO) under a management with considerable experience in metal working. Besides this enterprise, there were less than ten medium-sized metal working and iron founding units (each employing about 20 workers) in Lahore, Sialkot, Gujranwala and Wazirabad. In addition, these towns were also centres of considerable small-scale activity in metal working. During the Second World War, Sialkot achieved renown as a centre of manufacture of high quality surgical instruments which were exported to various parts of the Empire. Much of this production of surgical instruments was carried out small scale with fairly extensive sub-contracting arrangements. (Sialkot was also famous for sports goods manufacture, again with a substantial small-scale sector.) Wazirabad, a centre of medium and small-scale cutlery manufacture, had the reputation of being West Punjab's Sheffield. Gujranwala was also a well known centre of medium and small-scale metal manufacturing. Finally, there were numerous artisan workshops in various towns catering to the farmer's needs for traditional agricultural implements and producing simple metal products for domestic use.

The indigenous labour force in the western Punjab was augmented at the time of the partition of the subcontinent by an influx from the eastern districts of workers with metal working experience. A majority of the united Punjab's blacksmiths was Muslim. A majority of the labour force in general metal work was also Muslim. Thus, with the 1947 cross-migration of Hindus and Sikhs and Muslims the Pakistan Punjab inherited more than its share of the blacksmith population and metal working labour of the united Punjab. The newcomers together with their indigenous counterparts formed a large reservoir of labour with a metal-working tradition going back many generations. Concentrated in a small number of towns they engaged in diverse metal-working activities either as labourers or as small workshop owners.

These resources formed a modest, but not negligible, base upon which future metal working in the Punjab was to be founded.

Demand from a variety of sources created markets for diesel

engines, electric motors, pipes and water pumps. The most important of these sources was irrigation in agriculture. The severe constraint imposed by water shortage on agricultural expansion was widely noted in the early 1950s. Continuing schemes launched before the partition to extend the use of tubewells, the Agriculture Department of the Punjab government, throughout the 1950s (and the 1960s), provided installation and other facilities to farmers. Although the volume of water delivered by the increasing number of tubewells during the 1950s was small, in absolute terms this development was of considerable importance in spreading the new water technology among farmers.

During the 1950s this expansion remained modest and it was confined to rich farmers in a small number of districts in the Punjab. The really spectacular expansion in demand for tubewells started from 1959–60 when the government of Pakistan's policy towards agriculture, which had suffered neglect during the 1950s, changed radically. The new policy relaxed controls and provided significant incentives for increased production. As a result, the terms of trade between agriculture and industry were improved from the point of view of the farmers who experienced a significant increase in real income. At the same time the volume of loans available to farmers for the purchase of tubewells and other inputs (for example, chemical fertilizers) increased markedly. The farmer thus had the resources to invest in improved means of water supply. He also had a strong incentive to invest because shortage of canal water, particularly at certain critical times in the year, presented a serious obstacle to increased production. After the shift in government policy towards agriculture the farmer's rate of return on investment in a tubewell was estimated by one researcher at 100 per cent. Another estimated that on a 50-acre farm in Gujranwala district the cost of a diesel engine tubewell was recovered in two years, and of an electric powered water pump in less than one year. Rural electrification in certain districts of the Punjab also exerted a highly favourable influence on the extension of tubewell installation. Thus, from 1959–60 there was an explosion in demand for tubewells from private agriculture. [From 750 tubewells installed on average annually between 1948 and 1960, to nearly 16,000 each year between 1960 and 1970.] This is also the period when small units in large numbers began to establish themselves in the industry.

... The small-scale sector – small production units, artisans and the reservoir of labour with tradition in metal working – did not initially (early and mid-1950s) have the technical and other resources to respond effectively to the challenge of the expanding tubewell market. However, expanding industrial activity during the period offered this sector opportunities appropriate to its resources and skills. For instance, a variety of activities (for example, electric fan making) enabled workshop owners not only to keep their skills alive but also to upgrade them. Expanding operations of large and medium-sized enterprises in metal working provided opportunities for employment and acquisition of new skills. Diffusion of skills was also assisted by a number of technical and vocational training centres set up by the central and provincial governments.

Slow-speed diesel engine and centrifugal water pump production was first established in the large-scale sector and it was only gradually that the small-scale obtained the skills, technical knowledge and physical inputs required to effect entry to the tubewell industry. Diffusion of the technology for production of tubewells proceeded simultaneously with the increasing use of tubewells in private agriculture ...

The initiative in producing slow-speed diesel engines and centrifugal pumps on a regular basis was taken by BECO in 1949. It obtained designs of slow-speed diesel engines from a British firm and at the same time imported equipment for their production. In 1952, it set up a joint company with KSB-AG, a West German firm specializing in pumps and turbines. (This partnership ended in 1959 when BECO purchased KSB's share in the joint company and KSB, in collaboration with a number of leading Pakistani business houses, set up a new company in the Punjab.) In the second half of the 1950s, BECO established technical collaboration with overseas – American (turbines), British (electric motors) and German (high-speed diesel engines) – firms. Thus over the decade all or much of the technical know-how required for the production of various types of diesel engines, water pumps, etc., was imported into the Punjab through the medium of BECO.

BECO and other large and medium-sized firms were able to draw on the reservoir of labour with metal-working experience for the manpower required for their expansion. The large and, subsequently, the medium-sized enterprises (in the course of their normal production and under apprenticeship schemes they were obliged by law to operate) trained a substantial number of workers in the production of diesel engines and pumps and, in this way, knowledge of this technology was more widely disseminated. Many of the new small units that entered the industry from 1959–60 were set up by (or in collaboration with) skilled workers who had obtained the necessary experience with one of the larger firms. Many tubewell components requiring advanced technology in their manufacture were initially imported, later being locally produced by the large firms. By the late 1950s small units had access to these and other inputs. Some of the medium-sized firms benefitted in a similar way from co-existence with the large firms, they also had access to labour trained, and components and equipment produced, by the large firms. In their turn, when markets began to expand rapidly in the late 1950s, the medium-size firms often found it necessary to give out part of their work to small workshops in the neighbourhood. In this way know-how was passed on to many workshops who later set up their own production.

Source: Aftab, Khalid and Eric Rahim, 'Emergence of a Small-Scale Engineering Sector', *Journal of Development Studies*, 1986, vol. 23, no. 1, pp. 61–6.

Appendix 8.2

Who is responsible for the textile industry crisis?

Ovais Subhani argues that it is not rains or pest attacks which have resulted in the deterioration of the textile industry, but the powerful spinners lobby. He writes:

After two successive cotton crop failures, the specter of an imminent crisis is once again haunting the Pakistani textile industry. But ironically, the industry's present woes are not simply the fallout of the expected shortfall in production this year. Instead, what is causing most of the problems is the back-door manipulation and speculation that precedes almost every cotton season and has of late become the hallmark of business and industry in Pakistan.

Initially convinced that this year's cotton crop would not fall short of the 9.5 million bales target, government officials have since scaled down their estimate to nine million bales in the wake of an unusually long monsoon season and the pest attack that followed it. Market experts and growers, meanwhile, feel that the total crop will be no more than between eight and 8.5 million bales. This uncertainty has spurred a flurry of speculative activity at the Karachi Cotton Exchange, with ginners and spinners trying to manipulate prices to their own advantage – the former exaggerating the extent of the supply shortage and the latter providing inflated requirement figures.

The textile industry, which accounts for nearly 65 per cent of our total export earnings, is notorious for influence peddling, tax evasion and defaulting on huge bank loans. At times, in fact, it seems that the government is virtually hostage to the immensely influential textile barons, who have over the last two decades never ceased to complain and dictate terms to the economic planners in Islamabad.

As if two decades of patronage were not enough, the country's spinners are again demanding additional concessions from the government, highlighting the fact that Pakistan's largest industrial sector has yet to mature and willingly accept the market realities of supply and demand. The government, for its part, has for all practical purposes succumbed to the textile lobby's latest pressure tactics. In a somewhat veiled move, it has asked the State Bank of Pakistan to relax the Prudential Regulations – the lending guidelines that banks and DFIs have to follow – for sick industrial units as well as loan defaulters.

Later the State Bank came out with a more explicit statement, making it clear that only those units hit by cotton crop failures after 1992 would be entitled to benefit from an easing of the Prudential Regulations. This move represents a major concession to the spinners, who had demanded the rescheduling of all their debts only a month earlier.

Financial analysts in Karachi feel that this relaxation of rules for the textile industry could cause serious credit constraints for the banking sector. By even the most conservative of estimates, sick spinning units owe more than five billion rupees to the country's banks and DFIs, and rescheduling such

a staggering volume of bad debt will obviously cause a lot of problems. Liquidity will also be adversely affected by having to extend credit to those already defaulting on their loans. On the other hand, a number of spinners with sick units on their hands will be entitled to yet another injection of hard cash to square off their losses – that is if they ever incurred them in the first place. Even the governor of the State Bank has said that most of the sick units belong to groups that are otherwise very healthy.

This relaxation in lending to spinners represents compensation of sorts by the government, which in August had come out with a cotton policy which the spinners lobby saw as slanted in favour of the growers.

The government had raised the support prices of lint cotton by almost 27 per cent while keeping raw cotton and cotton yarn import at nil tariff and, at the same time, barring the Cotton Export Corporation and private exporters from entering the market until December 1994. Earlier, in May, seed cotton support prices had also been raised – by announcing a proportional increase in lint support prices, the government had in effect guaranteed that cotton prices would remain above the 1,000 rupees per maund mark.

However, this still falls short of what growers and ginners – the ones hit worst by successive crop failures – would ideally like to see. Growers, for instance, have had to invest more in farm inputs in order to keep production at desired levels. To do this, they were forced to buy more pesticides and fertilizers as well as put in additional man-hours on account of the unusually long monsoon. The result is an expensive crop which growers say will be unprofitable if sold for under 600 rupees per mound. Ginners, on the other hand, are looking at a break-even price of 1,500 rupees per maund for lint cotton if they are to keep their ginneries running.

The powerful spinners, however, are predicting disaster for the textile industry as a whole if cotton is not available to them at less than 1,400 rupees per mound. At present, the price of ginned cotton is fluctuating between 1,700 and 1,800 rupees per mound, and is expected to rise if the crop falls short of the original target figure of 9.5 million bales.

Anwar Ahmed Tata, Chairman of the All Pakistan Textile Mills Association (APTMA), fears that high cotton prices might put several spinning units out of business. 'Nearly 133 out of a total of 477 textile mills have already closed down due to heavy losses accruing from high cotton prices in the domestic market and low yarn prices abroad,' says the APTMA chairman. This view is echoed by Maqsood Ismail, Chairman of the Pakistan Yarn Merchants Association. 'Pakistani 21-count cotton yarn presently gets 350 dollars for a 400-pound bale while raw cotton import at nil tariff costs 1.01 dollars per pound,' he says, adding that yarn production will be viable only if cotton is available for under 1,400 rupees per mound.

Market analysts, meanwhile, believe that the 1,400 mark could be a reality come November or December when ginners will be producing nearly 100,000 bales a day. Both growers and ginners have a limited holding capacity, and as such prices are bound to fall when fresh crop starts pouring in from the Punjab. At that point, the ginners will have little or no option but to increase supply.

The spinners, however, are not willing to wait that long. APTMA has already been successful in pressurizing the government into rescheduling the debts of textile units, and is now demanding duty-free import of all types of synthetic fibre. According to insiders, APTMA has not only asked the government to do away with indirect taxes such as sales tax and excise duty on yarn and cloth, but also wants a further devaluation of the rupee against the dollar in order to boost export earnings.

They may well get what they want, but the fact remains that the spinners are hiding from the harsh realities of the current global export environment. Demand for yarn has been sliding downwards because an increasing number of competitors with comparatively lower investment and production costs are flooding the market with low priced yarn of better quality. Pakistan has a huge spinning capacity but, unlike its competitors, lacks an integrated weaving and garment manufacturing industry. This obviously hampers value addition and reduces the flexibility of our export strategy, making it difficult to adjust to global changes in demand and supply.

The textile, or more precisely yarn, export boom in Pakistan was largely the result of a sharp rise in demand for textile goods in Japan and to a lesser extent, in other foreign markets starting in 1987. The boom produced a marginal improvement in yarn quality and weaving capability, but spinning capacity went through the roof in the early '90s after the government announced significant concessions for the import of textile machinery.

As a result, the production of cotton yarn increased dramatically, from 685 million kilograms in 1987–88 to 1,041 million in 1990–91, an average increase of 13 per cent per annum. There was a decrease, however, in exports in terms of value towards the fag end of the boom, from about 1,200 million dollars in 1990-91 to 1,100 million dollars in 1991–92. Pakistan produced a record 12 million bales in 1991–92, but an over-production crisis ensued as international yarn prices started slipping.

In 1993, APTMA came up with demands for more concessions, claiming that 120 million spindles, or 20 per cent of spinning capacity, were lying idle because of duties on export. Huge advertisements started appearing on the front pages of all leading newspapers, replete with an analysis of the balance sheets of 105 textile mills. Over a period of six months, APTMA claimed at the time, nearly a hundred of these mills had incurred losses. To counter this trend, APTMA demanded further devaluation, even though the rupee had already been devalued by 51 paisas within the relatively short period of two months. For this to happen APTMA had to wait until Moeen Qureshi became prime minister, but it did succeed in getting excise duty on yarn reduced from five rupees to two rupees per kilo. At the same time, import duties on synthetic fibres were also cut.

There appears to be a consensus among market analysts that the crisis facing the textile industry is the result of reckless expansion in spinning capacity. Pakistan imported 4.9 billion dollars worth of textile machinery – most of which went towards spinning units – from 1991 to 1993, in the process depriving the national exchequer of millions of rupees in waived taxes and duties. The number of textile mills, meanwhile, increased from 300 in 1992–93 to 477 in 1993–94. Little thought was given to the fact that competitors such as India and China were, in addition to expansion, also modernizing their textile sector as a whole with special emphasis on the weaving sector.

Experts also point to the case of South Korea, which was more or less absent from the export market when Pakistan was experiencing a boom in this area from 1987 to 1992. Unlike their Pakistani counterparts, the Korean textile barons had shrewdly diverted all of their spinning capacity to feed a growing cloth and garment manufacturing sector. Within a few years, Korea was importing yarn for its domestic integrated textile industry based on value-added cloth and garments, which are now in great demand all over the world for both their price and quality.

Pakistan, on the other hand, has relinquished its leading role in the export market. Most of the weaving industry is concentrated in the unorganized sector, while the organized power loom sector produces low value-added grey cloth. At the same time, garment exports, despite their steady growth over the last couple of years, are still grossly undervalued.

Keeping this track record in mind, most market analysts are convinced that even if the target of 9.5 million bales is somehow met, a crisis situation is still very much on the cards. But more than rains and pest attacks, it is the spinners lobby itself which is to blame for the deteriorating state of Pakistani textile industry. Nature is simply a convenient scapegoat.

Source: *The Herald*, November 1994.

Aftab Ahmad Khan writes about the serious crisis that has emerged in Pakistan's textile sector.

The textile sector has played a crucial role in Pakistan's economy. It employs about 40 per cent of the industrial labour force, accounts for around 60 per cent of merchandise export receipts and contributes 20 per cent to total value-added in the large-scale manufacturing sector.

The performance of Pakistan's economy is to a significant extent determined by the state of health of this important sector. Unfortunately, the sickness of this sector during the last two—three years has had an adverse impact on the domestic output growth, employment generation, export earnings and the performance of the financial sector.

At present, there are 463 textile units in the country of which 234 are listed. There are 8.8 million spindles, 139,960 rotors and 150,000 to 200,000 shuttleless and power looms. According to official estimates, 87 textile mills have remained closed as of April 1996.

The textile industry, at present, is in a crisis. Not only is a significant proportion of the industry closed, it is suffering from low productivity and escalating cost of production. In view of the liberalization and globalization of international trade under the World Trade Organization (WTO), the industry is confronted with a vast challenge which necessitates a massive improvement in its productivity.

Unfortunately, during the last 45 years the industry has been pampered a great deal. It grew under the protective shield of tariff and non-tariff barriers, massive fiscal incentives, highly subsidized cotton and generous rebates to enable it to compete in international markets. The banks and development finance institutions (DFIs) have also extended large loans to this sector.

The protective and concessionary environment in which the textile industry has grown blunted its appetite for achieving enhanced productivity and led to its unbalanced growth. At present, the spinning sector is suffering from over-capacity and the bulk of yarn produced by it is of low and medium counts and is exported. Only about three per cent of the yarn produced in the country is used for weaving by the mills. Aside from yarn, the textile exports primarily comprise coarse fabrics and low quality made ups of woven and knitted fabric. On account of our tax policy, the production of fabrics has shifted from mills to the power loom sector. Despite recent increases in the consumption of yarn on account of the growing demand stemming from the power loom sector and the knitters, the country still exports over 45 per cent of yarn.

In recent years, there has been a considerable shift from the production of purely cotton yarn to blended yarn in response to growing domestic and international demand for the latter.

Despite a strong yarn base, the industry has not significantly diversified its product mix and has not shown any worthwhile progress in the output and export of high value added textile items. Notwithstanding the fact that the Export Promotion Bureau projects Pakistan as the 'Cotton Country' Pakistan's share in world textile garment exports is a mere two per cent.

The country undoubtedly has prodigious potential to become a significant player in the international textile market provided it develops the capacity to produce high value-addition goods at competitive prices for which an essential precondition is the improvement in the quality of yarn. Pakistan can considerably increase it's export receipts from the textile sector by improving quality. Improvement in quality will also enable us to retain our market share once quotas are completely abolished by the year 2005. Unfortunately, the textile industry in Pakistan has paid scant attention to increasing productivity or innovating new products. Quality has also been ignored. There has been no focus on scientific management and very little amount of money has been spared for research and development. Again, only minimal amounts have been allocated for skill development.

In the past, despite low productivity and unbalanced growth the textile industry has been able to prosper because of the availability of cotton at lower than international prices, high protection provided by tariff and non-tariff barriers, availability of development loans, working capital at low rates and duty drawbacks. This favourable milieu is no longer available. The growers are now quite legitimately demanding international prices for raw cotton and no curbs on exports. The government is under pressure from the International Monetary Fund and World Trade Organization (WTO) to lower

tariff barriers. The cost of development loans and working capital has also escalated significantly in recent years. Again, the government policies for the regulation and development of this crucial sector have been ad-hoc and non-pragmatic aimed primarily at short term crisis management without a clear long term vision.

The current crisis of the industry primarily stems from the high prices of raw cotton. The price of Niab-785G, for example, has climbed from Rs815.76 per maund in 1990–91 to Rs1930.40 per maund in 1994–5. The increase in cotton prices during the last five years has on the average been around 100 per cent.

The All-Pakistan Textile Mills Association (APTMA) has been quite unjustifiably demanding a ban on the export of cotton which would result in cotton growers not getting their due price. The Karachi Cotton Association (KCA) has quite correctly pointed out that in 1995–96, despite all the hue and cry raised by them, the textile mills fully covered their requirements to the tune of 8.2 million bales, as compared with the total consumption of 77 million bales in 1994–95 and 7.6 million bales in 1993–94. In 1995–96, the mills not only fully met their own requirements of cotton, but exported 400,000 bales themselves.

The 1996–97 estimates of cotton crop are higher than the production achieved in 1995–96. It is expected that the cotton crop this year may be around 11 million bales. As such, there is no case at all for implicitly or explicitly banning cotton exports. Better return to cotton growers has not only helped the country in increasing cotton output but also significantly added to our foreign exchange earning to the tune of US$5000 million in 1995–96.

The APTMA spokesmen have also frequently complained about the inadequate availability of bank credit for the cotton sector. The State Bank of Pakistan, however, is of the view that it has always ensured adequate credit for this key sector of the economy. In the current year's credit plan, as indicated by the chief economist of the State Bank, a total allocation of Rs40 billion has been made for this sector and the major portion of this credit (Rs24.7 billion) has been allocated for the textile sector, while Rs9.3 billion would go to ginners and Rs7–8 billion would be earmarked for cotton exports. The APTMA, however, feels that the textile industry requires Rs48 billion credit in 1996–97. The banks, for understandable reasons, are hesitant to provide generous credit facilities to the textile sector because of its doubtful creditability. At present, this sector is the biggest defaulter of banks. The creditability of the cotton export sector, however, is excellent. The cotton exporters are also fully satisfied with the credit allocation of Rs7 billion for 1996–97.

The APTMA conveniently blames the government for its current woes. While the government could be criticized for the cumbersome system of refunds of duties and for not consistently pursuing policies aimed at value addition, the present crisis the textile industry is passing through is due to external factors as well as its unbalanced structure and low productivity. The government has always tried to help the industry whenever it was in distress. In 1995, for example, it provided a generous incentive package whose important features were: zero tariff for import of raw materials, removal of procedural bottlenecks hampering exports, re-scheduling of loans in appropriate cases, export rebates and duty drawbacks, freight concessions of up to 50 per cent, exemption of payment of export development surcharge.

This package unfortunately had only a limited and temporary impact. It has become abundantly clear now that the textile sector for its sustained growth in the new international trading environment requires restructuring with an accent on value addition and a quantum jump in its productivity.

Source : *DAWN*, Economic and Business Review, 31 August–6 September 1996.

Appendix 8.3

How the privatization of Pakistan Telecommunications Corporation was mishandled

Ahmed Rashid shows how the government mishandled the privatization of one of its most lucrative assets.

It's been a month long roller coaster ride for stock brokers and bankers with their hopes soaring and plummeting in quick succession as Islamabad initiated the long awaited privatization of the Pakistan Telecommunications Corporation (PTC). The government, for its part, has succeeded in raising huge revenues from the sale, but there appears to be a consensus that the hastiness it exhibited and the methodology it used simply cannot be repeated if international investors are to retain confidence in the Pakistan economy.

The government, though, tends to think otherwise. It's the largest ever placement of equity from South Asia, very open and completely transparent, so the criticism is unjustified, Shahid Hassan Khan, special advisor to the prime minister on economic policy, told the *Herald*. 'The international reaction has been phenomenal,' he added. On that count, at least, there is little room for argument.

On September 13, a three-day open book bidding began in London for an international offering of five million PTC vouchers, worth a minimum of 4,500 rupees each. Each voucher represented a hundred shares in the future PTCL, which is yet to be incorporated. Jardine Fleming International and Muslim Commercial Bank (MCB) were joint lead managers for the international placement, which was underwritten for 750 million dollars at 45 rupees a share.

When books closed, however, an overwhelming response had raised the share price to 55 rupees, which means that the government will generate 898 million dollars through the offer. 'Given the two primary aims – transparency and maximizing returns to the government – the offer has been hugely successful,' says a director of BMA Capital Management, advisors to MCB.

Earlier in mid-August, the government had offered one million vouchers at 3,000 rupees each (30 rupees a share), putting the total offer at a record three billion rupees which was oversubscribed seven-fold to the tune of 19.1 billion. Pakistanis accounted for 2.7 million rupees in shares, with 126 million coming from PTC employees. Foreign investors, meanwhile, subscribed to 16.46 billion rupees worth of shares. The offer also gave investors the option of selling their vouchers back to the government after two years, at a price of 3,840 rupees each, if PTC Limited (PTCL) fails to be listed by that time.

The stock market went crazy, with the 30-rupee share being quoted at 62 rupees in curbside trading immediately after the offer was announced. The first offering represented 1.96 per cent of the giant PTC, which the government initially valued at 10 billion dollars but this figure was later revised to five billion. Together, the two offerings represent a 12 per cent stake in PTC.

The confusion arose when the second offering was hastily ordered by Ms Bhutto, apparently to satisfy foreign investors and to ensure that the government could hold on to the money it had raised from the first tranche. Otherwise, the government would have had to return the oversubscribed, largely foreign, funds by September 13. Senior finance officials admit that there was a difference of opinion in the cabinet on this count, with most senior bureaucrats wanting to forgo the second placement and return the money. 'But the prime minister felt the country needed the money and ordered the placement,' says an official.

As a result, on September 2, the government made the foreign offering at 30 rupees a share, creating a furor in the Karachi Stock Exchange (KSE) because the share was thought to be undervalued at this price. But despite the hue and cry, the offering was still oversubscribed to the tune of 1.3 billion dollars.

The KSE and the press had been critical as it is, alleging that even the first offering was undervalued, and that the government had effectively devalued PTC's overall worth with a single stroke of the pen. Moreover, the memorandum on the first share offering had made no mention of a second subscription. The haste with which the second offering was pushed through created a state of near panic in the KSE, with fears abounding that the price of the original 30-rupee share would plummet.

Fearing another backlash and fervently hoping to raise more funds, the government canceled the second offering on September 5 and frantically looked round for new underwriters for the second placement. In this connection, the original lead managers for the international placement, Union Bank of Switzerland (UBS) – who were called in by Khadim Ali Shah Bukhari and Co. (KASB), the advisors to the Privatization Commission – had their deal canceled after MCB offered a better deal. Mian Mansha's bank promised to underwrite the new vouchers for 750 million dollars, or 45 rupees a share – 15 rupees higher than the original offer.

'The KSE said it would underwrite the new offering at 30 rupees a share and wanted more time to see if it could raise that bid, while UBS gave a confirmed offer of 30 rupees a share,' explains a senior official involved in the placement. 'We rang up all the banks and MCB came up with 45 rupees a share, overall worth 750 million dollars,' he adds. By then, the share price of the first offer had slid down to its face value of 30 rupees on curbside trading. The KSE index also plunged, recording a sudden drop of 26 points in a single day.

For a time there was a very real possibility of a KSE crash, a fear that appeared to be justified because the second issue was so large – equal to nearly one-twelfth of KSE's total capitalization, which stands at nearly 13 billion dollars. However, once the second offering had been well received by institutional investors, KSE confidence returned and curbside trading of the first offer shot back up to 60 rupees, double its original value.

The revenues generated were enormous by any standards but the questions raised by many investors went unanswered by the government. What, for instance, happened to the original strategy on privatization as announced in February by Privatization Commission chairman Naveed Qamar? The privatization supremo had declared at the time that regulatory bodies would be in place and that strategic investors would be awarded management interest in utility organizations before shares are off-loaded to the public. Moreover, he had promised an up to date revaluation of PTC prior to the sale of shares. Instead, the government offered shares first, even though there are still no strategic investors in mind. At the same time, PTC's balance sheet is in order only up to June 30, 1992, there is no regulatory body in operation and PTC still has to be turned into a limited company.

A presidential ordinance on July 13 had divided PTC into the National Telecommunications Corporation (NTC) and PTC Limited. NTC would provide services to the armed forces and the federal government – a move made necessary by the military's fear that foreign investors may come to control the national telecommunications network. The ordinance also authorized the setting up of two regulatory bodies, the Pakistan Telecommunications Authority and a Frequency Allocation Board. However, these steps have still to be implemented and PTCL is still not an operating company.

Placing a value on PTC proved to be an extremely testing task for the government. In fact, most of the criticism from institutional investors has focused on the government's tardiness in bringing in international assessors earlier on in the process and maintaining certain strict criteria. 'What will happen when even bigger and more diffuse utilities like WAPDA are privatized?' asks a foreign banker.

The government admits the difficulty involved, but says it wanted to get on with privatization. 'Valuing PTC is very difficult. A balance sheet had never been prepared in the corporate style,' says Shahid Hassan Khan. 'We also intentionally wanted to keep the share price low, unlike the Nawaz Sharif government which privatized at the highest premium,' he adds. Other officials maintain that if they had waited for all legal requirements to be in place, privatization of PTC would have been delayed by a year. At the same time, Ms Bhutto had hoped to follow her mentor Margaret Thatcher by offering shares to the more passive public. To some extent that has been achieved, even though 80 per cent of the domestic share applications came from Karachi alone.

The government needed to raise money, and seeing the public's positive reaction to the first offer, it jumped the gun with the second hoping to keep the money it had already made. In the global market, however, these actions showed up the government as ham-handed and naive. At home, it created a rumpus in the KSE. However, the overwhelmingly enthusiastic response from institutional investors, regardless of the methods adopted by Islamabad, demonstrates that there is considerable international confidence in the Pakistan economy. But to retain if not bolster this confidence, Ms Bhutto and her economic managers still need a lesson or two in the whys and wherefores of international finance.

Source : *The Herald*, September 1994.

Appendix 8.4

Performance and problems of public sector industries

The BIM (Board of Industrial Management) inherited from the private sector and PIDC a productive apparatus that was not, in general, economically efficient. This was because most of the PIDC projects were chosen for non-economic reasons (e.g., regional balance, promotion of capital goods industries, etc.), and the projects originally undertaken by the private sector were initiated under very high rates of effective protection and seriously distorted factor prices. However, the substantial profits enjoyed by the private sector under the latter regime during the 1960s gave rise to inflated expectations when these industries were nationalized. The public industrial sector was consequently burdened with multiple and conflicting tasks and objectives. The Government decided that the public manufacturing sector was to give 'a fair deal' to consumers, workers and shareholders, and to pay in full the taxes and duties that it owed. In addition, prices were to be reduced or held down despite overall inflation. Price controls were placed on basic chemicals, cement, fertilizers, bicycles, and a number of engineering products. These prices were based on production cost plus a margin for overhead and (in some cases) a specified return on investment. This pricing regime penalized efficient producers and allowed inefficient ones to pass on the cost of their inefficiency to consumers. At the same time, employment, wages, salaries and benefits increased rapidly. As a result, between 1972/73 and 1976/77

Table 1 Employment, profits, and taxes and duties of public sector industries, 1972–1977

	1972/3	1973/4	1974/5	1975/6	1976/7
Employment (000s)	40.8	48.4	55.4	58.8	64.6
Net profit before tax	18	174	278	192	59
Net sales (Rs m)	1,806	2,956	4,838	5,212	6,020
Profit margin (%)	1.0	5.9	5.7	3.7	1.0
Taxes and duties (Rs m)	198	667	1,214	1,156	1,408
Taxes and duties as % of net sales	11.0	22.6	25.1	22.2	23.4

Source: Federal Bureau of Statistics, *Annual Report on Public Sector Industries*, 1981–2.

employment increased by 58 per cent and the wage bill increased fourfold. Since public enterprises were at the same time expected to pay taxes and duties in full, BIM's total bill for the payment of the latter increased from Rs193 million (11 per cent of net sales in 1972/73) to Rs1,214 million (25 per cent of net sales in 1974/75) [see Table 1].

Thus the situation faced by these industries prior to nationalization was drastically different from that prevailing after 1972. Pre-nationalization private sector profits were made possible by a protection system that allowed it to charge high prices and to avoid paying taxes and duties. Since public sector industries were not allowed these privileges – and since higher wage levels and a substantial amount of employment expansion were forced on them – pre-nationalization profit levels were not possible for these public sector industries.

Productivity Performance

[Table 1] shows that while labour productivity grew faster in BIM units than in the manufacturing sector overall, the entire increase in this productivity took place during the first two years. It should be noted, however, that while productivity in BIM units declined after this initial period, the decline was largely due to employment expansion. Further, productivity in the manufacturing sector as a whole also declined during the same period.

Export Performance

In general, public sector industries mainly supply the domestic market and it is only disposable surpluses that are exported. Until 1974/75 cement was the most important sector with

regard to exports (60 per cent of total [$29 million] BIM export sales that year). As the cement surplus disappeared in subsequent years, however, export of cement ceased and Pakistan became an importer of cement. Since exports of petroleum products correspond to refinery surpluses which cannot be absorbed by the domestic market, the share of petroleum exports in total BIM export earnings (19 per cent during 1974/75) continued to expand throughout the 1970s. Other exports consisted of light engineering products (diesel engines, simple machine tools, etc.) and chemical products (soda ash, caustic soda, etc.).

Financial Performance

While it was argued above that under the circumstances, it would be unreasonable to have expected high profit levels in public sector enterprises, financial profitability is nevertheless an important indicator of performance, and the performance of public sector enterprises in Pakistan is mixed. Before tax profits of BIM operating units as a whole increased from Rs18 million in 1972/73 to Rs278 million in 1974/75 after which they declined to Rs59 million in 1976/77. [Table 2] shows that profit margins for the sector as a whole reached a peak in 1973/74 and then declined throughout the period, reaching their 1972/73 level again in 1976/77. There is, however, considerable variation in profit margins among corporations. In 1974/75 profit margins ranged from 14 per cent in the cement sector to 2 per cent in petroleum. The cement and fertilizer industries have, however, been consistently good performers. An additional measure of profitability is return (before interest and tax) on investment (total assets), or ROI.

Table 2 Output, employment, and productivity indices of public sector industries and the manufacturing sector, 1972–1977

	1972/3	1973/4	1974/5	1975/6	1976/7
Public sector industries					
Production value (constant 1972/3 prices)	100	131	160	167	162
Employment	100	19	136	144	158
Labour productivity	100	111	118	116	102
Manufacturing sector in Pakistan					
Production index (includes SSI)	100	107	108	100	110
Employment index	100	103	115	120	128
Productivity index	100	104	94	92	86

Source: Federal Bureau of Statistics, *Annual Report on Public Sector Industries*, 1981–2.

With regard to the latter, the data show that for BIM as whole, ROI increased from 6.3 per cent in 1973/74 to 7.4 per cent in 1974/75, but then declined to 5.9 per cent in 1975/76 and to 2.3 per cent in 1976/77. While this performance was clearly unsatisfactory, the private sector did not do much better during the same period. The average ROI (after interest but before tax) for 242 companies quoted on the Karachi Stock Exchange was 5.3 per cent and 4.1 per cent in the years 1973 and 1974 respectively, while BIM's ROI (similarly defined) was 3.3 per cent and 4.2 per cent in 1973/74 and 1974/75.

Source: Asian Development Bank, *Strategies for Economic Growth and Development: The Bank's Role in Pakistan*, Asian Development Bank, Manila, 1985, pp. 424–7.

Notes

1. There are definitional problems in trying to identify exactly what the informal sector really is and what sort of activity forms part of it. The small-scale sector is also a badly defined term, especially in Pakistan, where it constitutes units 'not registered' under the Industries Act. Size is also a factor, where the informal manufacturing sector consists of those unregistered manufacturing units that employ fewer than ten persons. Moreover, the informal sector and the small-scale sector are not the same thing, although they are used here interchangeably for our purposes. See Nadvi, Khalid, *Employment Creation in Urban Micro-Enterprises in the Manufacturing Sector in Pakistan*, ILO/ARTEP, Bangkok, 1990, and Alvi, Imtiaz, *The Informal Sector in Urban Economy: Low Income Housing in Lahore*, Oxford University Press, Karachi, 1997, for an extensive discussion of what the informal and small-scale sectors are.
2. Nadvi, Khalid, op. cit., 1990, p. 17.
3. Sayeed, Asad, 'Political Alignments, the State and Industrial Policy in Pakistan: A Comparison of Performance in the 1960s and 1980s unpublished Ph.D. dissertation, University of Cambridge, 1995, p. 138.
4. Aftab, Khalid and Eric Rahim, 'The Emergence of a Small Scale Engineering Sector: The Case of Tubewell Production in the Pakistan Punjab', *Journal of Development Studies*, vol. 23, no. 1, 1986, p. 61.
5. Ibid., p. 61.
6. Nabi, Ijaz, *Entrepreneurs and Markets in Early Industrialization: A Case Study From Pakistan*, International Center for Economic Growth, San Francisco, 1988, pp. 4–5.
7. Sayeed, Asad, op. cit., 1995, p. 138.
8. Asian Development Bank, *Strategies for Economic Growth and Development: The Bank's Role in Pakistan*, Asian Development Bank, Manila, 1985, p. 417.
9. Sayeed, Asad, op. cit., 1995, p. 138.
10. Asian Development Bank, op. cit., 1985, p. 419.
11. Adams, John and Sabiha Iqbal, *Exports, Politics and Economic Development in Pakistan*, Vanguard, Lahore, 1987, p. 26.
12. Ibid., p. 30.
13. Ibid., p. 84.
14. Cheema, Ali, 'Pakistan's Textile and Trade Performance: 1972–1990', mimeo, Sidney Sussex College, Cambridge, 1995.
15. Sayeed, Asad, op. cit., 1995, p. 138, emphasis added.
16. See the outstanding work of Jonathan Addleton: *Undermining the Centre: The Gulf Migration and Pakistan*, Oxford University Press, Karachi, 1992.
17. Nadvi, Khalid, op. cit., 1990, p. 58.
18. Ibid., p. 58.
19. Sayeed, Asad, op. cit., 1995, p. 141.
20. Aftab, Khalid and Eric Rahim, op. cit., 1986, p. 72.
21. Sayeed, Asad, op. cit., 1995, p. 143.
22. Ibid., p. 144.
23. Nadvi, Khalid, op. cit., 1990, p. 182.
24. Aftab, Khalid and Eric Rahim, op. cit., 1986, p. 73.
25. Sayeed, Asad, op. cit., 1995, pp. 144–5.
26. Ibid., p. 145.
27. Nadvi, Khalid, op. cit., 1990, p. 125.
28. Asian Development Bank, op. cit., 1985, p. 420.
29. Amjad, Rashid, 'The Employment Challenges for Pakistan in the 1990s', in Nasim, Anjum (ed.), *Financing Pakistan's Development in the 1990s*, Oxford University Press, Karachi, 1992, p. 63.
30. Government of Pakistan, *Pakistan Economic Survey*, 1995–96, Islamabad, 1995.
31. UNIDO, *Pakistan: Towards Industrial Liberalization and Revitalization*, Blackwell, Oxford, 1990, p. 53.
32. Cheema, Ali, op. cit., 1995.
33. Ibid.
34. Amjad, Rashid, 'Industrial Concentration and Economic Power in Pakistan', in Gardezi, H. and J. Rashid (ed.) *Pakistan: The Unstable State*, Zed Press, London, 1983, pp. 232–3.
35. UNIDO, op. cit., 1990, pp. 53–4.
36. Institute of Developing Economies, *The Study on Japanese Cooperation in Industrial Policy for Developing Economies: Pakistan*, Tokyo, 1994, p. 260.
37. Cheema, Ali, op. cit., 1995, p. 2.
38. Ibid., p. 13.
39. Adams, John and Sabiha Iqbal, op. cit., 1987, p. 83.
40. Sayeed, Asad, op. cit., 1995, p. 115.
41. Cheema, Ali, op. cit., 1995, p. 26.
42. Sayeed, Asad, op. cit., 1995, p. 114.
43. World Bank, *Pakistan: Country Economic Memorandum FY93: Progress Under the Adjustment Program*, Report No. 11590-Pak, Washington, 1993, p. 48.
44. UNIDO, op. cit., 1990, p. 55.
45. Asian Development Bank, op. cit., 1985, p. 422.
46. Ibid.
47. Ahmad, M.B. and R. Laporte, *Public Enterprise in Pakistan: The Hidden Crisis in Economic Development*, Westview Press, Boulder, 1989, p. 12.
48. Sayeed, Asad, op. cit., 1995, p. 116.
49. Ibid. p. 120.
50. World Bank, op. cit., 1993, p. 2, emphasis added.
51. Naqvi, S.N.H. and A.R. Kemal, 'The Privatization of the Public Industrial Enterprise in Pakistan', *Pakistan Development Review*, vol. 30, no. 2, 1991, p. 108, emphasis in original.
52. Ibid.
53. Ibid., p. 117.

54. Ibid., p. 131.

55. Ibid., pp. 132–3.

56. Institute of Developing Economies, op. cit., Tokyo, 1994, p. 303.

57. World Bank, op. cit., 1993, p. 49.

58. UNIDO, op. cit., 1990, p. 8.

59. Ibid., p. 51.

60. Ibid., p. 52.

61. Ibid., p. 52.

62. Institute of Developing Economies, op. cit., 1994, p. 324.

63. Naqvi, S.N.H. and A.R. Kemal, op. cit., 1991, pp. 106–7, emphasis added.

64. *The News*, Karachi, 20 January 1996.

65. See, for example, Lewis, Stephen, *Economic Policy and Industrial Growth in Pakistan*, London, 1969; Lewis, Stephen, *Pakistan: Industrialization and Trade Policies*, London, 1970; Papanek, Gustav, *Pakistan's Development: Social Goals and Private Incentives*, Harvard University Press, Cambridge, Mass., 1967; Little, I., T. Scitorsky, and M. Scott, *Industry and Trade in Some Developing Economies*, Oxford University Press, London, 1970; Ahmed, Viqar and Rashid Amjad, *The Management of Pakistan's Economy, 1947–82*, Oxford University Press, Karachi, 1984; Adams, John and Sabiha Iqbal, op. cit., 1987.

66. Little, I., T. Scitorsky, and M. Scott, op. cit., 1970.

67. Sayeed, Asad, op. cit., 1995, p. 60.

68. Quoted in ibid., p. 60.

69. Sayeed, Asad, op. cit., 1995, p. 60.

70. Ahmad, Meekal, cited in Noman, Akbar, 'Industrialization in Pakistan: An Assessment and an Agenda', paper presented at the Seventh Annual General Meeting of the Pakistan Society of Development Economists, Islamabad, 1991, p. 25.

71. Sayeed, Asad, op. cit., 1995, p. 61.

72. Ibid., p. 62.

73. Ibid., p. 64.

74. Noman, Akbar, op. cit., 1991, p. 18, emphasis added.

75. Ahmed, Viqar and Rashid Amjad, op. cit., 1984, p. 212, emphasis added.

76. Noman, Akbar, op. cit., 1991, p. 32, emphasis added.

77. Ibid., p. 23.

78. Kemal, A.R., 'An Analysis of Industrial Efficiency in Pakistan: 1959–60 to 1969–70', unpublished Ph.D. dissertation, University of Manchester, 1978, and Ahmed, Meekal, 'Productivity, Prices and Relative Income Shares in Pakistan's Large Scale Manufacturing Sector, 1958–70', unpublished D.Phil dissertation, University of Oxford, 1980; Sayeed, Asad, op. cit., 1995.

79. Sayeed, Asad, op. cit., 1995, p. 71.

80. See, for example: White, L., *Industrial Concentration and Economic Power in Pakistan*, Princeton University Press, Princeton, 1974; Amjad, Rashid, *Industrial Concentration and Economic Power in Pakistan*, South Asian Institute, Punjab University Press, Lahore, 1974; Ahmed, Viqar and Rashid Amjad, op. cit., 1984.

81. Institute of Developing Economies, op. cit., 1994, p. 151.

82. In Noman, Akbar, op. cit., 1991, p. 25.

83. See Sayeed, Asad, op. cit., 1995.

84. World Bank, op. cit., 1993, p. 45, emphasis added.

85. Ibid., p. 45, emphasis added.

9 Balance of Payments and Trade Regimes

The previous three chapters, on the industrialization process in Pakistan and on the issues which have subsequently emerged as a consequence, show that perhaps the most critical factor to affect industrialization has been the trade regime. The import substituting industrialization of the 1950s and 1960s, the non-devaluation decision in 1948, the export-led Korean War boom, the high tariffs and protection given to domestic industry in the 1960s, the devaluation decision of the Bhutto government in 1972 with its serious repercussions for the economy, the decision by the Zia regime to delink the rupee from the dollar, and all other issues related to trade and the exchange rate have had numerous consequences for the rest of the economy, and especially for the industrialization process. The trade regime in Pakistan was held responsible for gross inefficiencies in the industrial structure towards the end of the 1960s, allegations which later helped to develop a new liberal orthodoxy with respect to trade policy. The Structural Adjustment Programmes agreed to by the Pakistan governments since 1988 include trade sector reform as a major plank in the strategy. The trade regime since then has seen drastic changes in its composition and will continue to affect the way industry develops. Moreover, given the fact that the taxes raised from imports constitute more than half of total government revenue, recent changes in the tariff structure will also have a significant effect on revenue generated by the government. For all these reasons, the importance of trade policy must be realized as it plays a critical role in the nature of developments within the country.

This chapter will examine how trade policy and the changing trade regimes over the years have influenced the course of development, particularly industrialization, in Pakistan. It will also analyse how Pakistan's trade process and pattern have evolved over the last fifty years, where, from producing and exporting agricultural primary commodities in 1947, Pakistan today exports mainly manufactured and semi-manufactured goods. There have been many more changes in the direction of trade, the management of the exchange rate, tariffs, etc. All these factors are discussed in the sections that follow. The first section provides information about the basic structure and nature of different aspects of Pakistan's balance of payments and trade, as has been the practice in chapters which deal with large amounts of data. Subsequent sections in this chapter then, address specific issues and debates regarding trade and its impact on the economy.

9.1 Pakistan's Foreign Trade: Basic Facts

The pattern and nature of foreign trade gives a fairly good indication of the pattern and nature of the economies that enter into trade agreements. Those countries with comparative advantage in certain products are likely to produce and export those commodities. Often, they will need to import raw materials for their exports, establishing a strong link between the two. Countries that are dependent on climatic conditions for their exportable agricultural products may have to contend with output being determined by the vagaries of the weather. Single commodity exporting countries must frequently contend with changes in world demand, which can play havoc with any long-term strategy to industrialize or develop, based on foreign exchange earnings (see Box 9.1). Over time, the pattern of trade often changes, as countries move from exporting primary products to finished manufactured goods, and their imports change from consumer goods to machinery. Pakistan's foreign trade pattern follows such a sequence and this section examines that change.

In 1948/9, 99 per cent of Pakistan's export earnings were made up of just five primary commodities: raw jute, raw cotton, raw wool, hides, and tea. Pakistan fits the classical case of an unindustrialized undeveloped country, in the early years producing and exporting only primary products and mainly dependent on adequate climatic conditions. A change began to occur early in the pattern of exports, as Pakistan's economic policies shifted towards an emphasis on industrialization (see Chapter 6). By 1951/2, the five main primary commodities contributed 93 per cent of export earnings, which by 1958/9 had fallen to 75 per cent. Pakistan's main imports in the first decade were consumer goods, cotton textiles, and cotton yarn. In these years, the direction of trade also changed: in 1948/9 India's share in exports was close to 56 per cent, but this had fallen to only 4.1 per cent a decade later. Dependence on India for imports was also reduced in this period. The main trading partners of Pakistan in the early years, not surprisingly, were the developed countries of the West, mainly the UK, the USA, Germany, Belgium, Italy, and Japan.[1]

In the decade of development under Ayub Khan, as industry was further established and the nature of production changed, so did that of trade. In the first decade, most of Pakistan's trade had been with the developed, industrialized countries, since they produced commodities

BOX 9.1
The objectives and tools of commercial policy

Viqar Ahmed and Rashid Amjad show how commercial policy and the management of foreign trade take place:

Foreign trade management has a special significance for policy-makers in developing countries since it provides opportunities to stimulate the growth process. Even if production relations are given, foreign trade offers the policy-makers choices between import and local production, and export and domestic consumption, leading to a more efficient allocation of resources. Foreign trade can also transform the existing production relations by providing opportunities to remove domestic shortages of scarce factors of production, to overcome the diseconomies of the small size of the domestic market, and to exchange goods with less growth potential (for example, raw materials) with goods having more growth potential (for example, technical know-how and equipment). Commercial policy is the art of managing the exchange of goods and services between countries.

In a typical developing country, particularly in the early stages of development, the bulk of exports consists of primary commodities and export earnings, due to the relative inelasticity of supply, and production levels of primary goods are not only unpredictable but also vulnerable to a number of factors. The developing country also depends upon the advanced industrial countries for most of its developmental needs (technology, capital, and producer goods) and consumption requirements. The developing countries, therefore, find their external environment difficult as their terms of trade deteriorate, their access to the markets of the advanced countries is limited by tariff and non-tariff barriers, and the trade and payments gaps widen with the passage of time.

The only short-term solution available to them is to seek extensive external assistance which, in due course, creates its own complications.

Within the context of the compulsions of economic development, commercial policy in developing countries may pursue the following objectives:

i)   Maintaining equilibrium in the balance of payments and balance of trade, or at least limiting the extent of disequilibrium;

ii) Attaining favourable terms of trade so that, with the same quantity of exports, the country is able to import greater quantities of goods and services and thus achieve a net addition to real income;

iii) Promoting exports to derive the full benefits of comparative advantages and also to finance the country's import requirements;

iv) Import substitution to protect domestic production, accelerate the rate of capital formation, create employment opportunities, narrow trade and payments gaps, and seek a certain degree of national self-sufficiency;

v)   Ensuring adequate availability of imported goods for both development and other purposes;

vi) Keeping the internal and external values of the national currency at desired levels.

Governments usually have a wide range of instruments of commercial policy to achieve policy goals. The most commonly used tool is the tariff structure consisting of import and export duties. Import duties can be used to influence the relative profitability of importing various commodity groups (for example, taxing development imports at lower rates than non-development imports), and to restrict the access of certain commodities to the domestic market in order to encourage savings and investment. Export duties may be used to limit the export of commodities in short supply at home and also sometimes to fill the gap between low domestic prices and high world prices.

Non-tariff measures may be divided into direct and indirect trade restrictions. Direct measures comprise embargoes on the import or export of certain commodities or quota restrictions which are often specific to certain commodities, destinations, or currencies. The imposition of exchange control and the licensing of imports and exports, common in developing countries, also constitute direct trade restrictions. Licences may be issued for the import of certain commodities without much formality and with no restrictions on quantity or source. In Pakistan this is known as the Open General License (OGL) system. But for most imports, a proper licensing system is introduced which may restrict the importer to make purchases from a specific country or currency area.

Indirect trade restrictions include various incentives and disincentives designed to influence the flow of foreign trade or its composition, such as a) raising or lowering margin requirements for letters of credit to import certain commodities or categories, b) fiscal incentives for industries using domestic materials aimed at reducing the demand for imported substitutes, and c) subsidies and credit concessions or priorities of certain import-replacing goods or exportable. A special tool, often used by developing countries but regarded unfavourably by international monetary and lending institutions, is the multiple exchange rate system. This seeks to maintain a high external value of the national currency in order to export goods with greater competitive advantage in the world market while importing high-priority commodities, and to maintain a low external value to export goods with lesser advantage and to import low-priority commodities.

Source: Ahmed, Viqar and Rashid Amjad, *The Management of Pakistan's Economy, 1947–82*, Oxford University Press, Karachi, 1984, pp. 241–2.

Table 9.1
Balance of payments, selected dates (US$ m)

Items	1976/7	1980/1	1987/8	1994/5 (P)
Merchandise exports	1,132	2,799	4,362	7,884
Merchandise imports	−2,418	−5,563	−6,919	−10,137
Trade balance	−1,286	−2,764	−2,557	−2,253
Non-factor services (net)	−187	−254	−553	−817
Investment income (net)	−169	−261	−828	−1,729
Income	33	95	105	154
Payments	−202	−356	−933	−1,883
Private transfers (net)	590	2,242	2,256	2,397
(Workers remittances)	(578)	(2,116)	(2,013)	(1,866)
Current account balance	−1,052	−1,037	−1,682	−2,402
Private capital (net)	+161	261	330	1,911
Direct investment[a]	4	71	155	1,530
Other long-term	104	137	164	352
Short-term	53	53	11	29
Public capital (net)	+582	+811	1,242	871
Disbursements, long-term[b]	807	843	1,679	2,516
Less: repayments, long-term	−128	−270	−714	−1,584
Other (short- and long-term)[c]	−97	238	277	−61
Allocation of SDRs (net)	0	37	0	0
Change in reserves (− = increase)	252	−45	140	−242
Errors and omissions (net)	57	−25	−30	−138

P = Provisional
[a] Includes portfolio investment, except Foreign Exchange Bearer Certificates and Dollar Bearer Certificates.
[b] Includes net official transfers.
[c] Includes Foreign Exchange Bearer Certificates (introduced with effect from August 1985) and Dollar Bearer Certificates (introduced with effect from April 1991).
Source: Government of Pakistan, *Pakistan Economic Survey*, various issues, Islamabad.

that Pakistan needed at that time. As more and more countries began to develop and industrialize, their demands and needs for foreign goods also changed. For Pakistan this meant the diversification of both export and import markets. Pakistan began to sell its exports outside the developed countries, while the developed countries now also had a choice to buy goods from other sources.

The pattern of trade takes on a different story after 1971, when Bangladesh was created, for the contribution of East Pakistan in Pakistan's trade and foreign exchange had been quite substantial (see Box 9.2). Tables 9.1 to 9.3 give the basic features of the trade regime following 1971. Table 9.1 is a summary balance of payments table, showing the main categories of earnings and expenditure related to trade. The trade balance, which is the difference between exports and imports, has for the most part been in the negative, implying that imports have been greater than exports. The current account deficit is an important statistic composed of the balance of trade and the flow of income through invisibles, such as tourism, banking services, and insurance. In Pakistan's case, the most important contribution to the balance of payments has been workers' remittances, mainly from the Middle East. In fact, for many years Pakistan's trade and economy have been highly dependent on money from the Gulf. The rest of Table 9.1 shows the contribution of

foreign investment in Pakistan, and loans and aid made by donors to the country.

Table 9.2 is a more detailed table, showing Pakistan's exports and imports from 1950 to the most recent statistics. Pakistan's trade (exports plus imports) has expanded from US$759 million in 1950/1 to $18.5 billion in 1994/5, an increase of about 25 times. However, this figure can be a little misleading due to inflationary trends. If we examine the constant prices for trade, the 1950/1 figure was Rs2.9 billion, rising to Rs17.11 billion in 1994/5, a rise of less than sixfold. Hence in real terms, the expansion in Pakistan's trade has been less than what current prices may suggest.

One of the most interesting statistics from Table 9.2 is that for the balance of trade. Except for 1950/1 and 1972/3, the balance of trade has been negative, implying that Pakistan always imports more than it exports. Although in constant (rupee) prices, exports may show a positive trend and the balance of trade is positive, the more important column, due to the exchange rate and foreign exchange earned, is the last column of the table, where in constant US dollars the balance of trade continues to be negative and fairly high.

The growth rates in key balance of payments components are shown in Table 9.3. One can see a fairly haphazard pattern for exports and imports both from the table and from Figure 9.1. The current account deficit has shown some huge

BOX 9.2
East Pakistan's contribution to trade

In 1948/9, 99 per cent of United Pakistan's foreign trade comprised of five primary commodities: raw jute, raw cotton, raw wool, hides and skins, and tea.[1] All the raw jute and tea exported came from East Pakistan. In 1951/2, 51 per cent of United Pakistan's exports were constituted by tea and raw jute alone. In 1969/70, just raw jute and jute-related manufactured products originating from East Pakistan were providing more than 47 per cent of Pakistan's total exports.[2] In 1969/70, East Pakistan was a large market for West Pakistan, absorbing 50 per cent of the West's exports, while the East wing provided 18 per cent of (West) Pakistan's total inputs for that year.

[Table 1] shows that while East Pakistan was exporting goods worth more than West Pakistan, the western wing of the country was using these proceeds to import goods into West Pakistan, far in excess of its share in exports. As the table shows, East Pakistan usually had a surplus trade balance, while West Pakistan had a huge trade deficit in all the seven years between 1960 and 1967. Hence this evidence suggests that West Pakistan was living off the exports of East Pakistan.

[1] Ahmed, Viqar and Rashid Amjad, *The Management of Pakistan's Economy, 1947–82*, Oxford University Press, Karachi, 1984, p. 245.
[2] Government of Pakistan, *Twenty Five Years of Statistics of Pakistan*, Islamabad, 1972, pp. 407, 408, 442.

Table 1 Visible trade balance (merchandise) (Rs m)

	1960/1	1961/2	1962/3	1963/4	1964/5	1965/6	1966/7
Pakistan	−1,389	−1,266	−1,572	−2,131	−2,966	−1,490	−2,186
East Pakistan	244	427	230	−224	−434	186	101
West Pakistan	−1,633	−1,693	−1,802	−1,907	−2,532	−1,676	−2,287
Exports							
East Pakistan	1,259	1,300	1,249	1,224	1,268	1,514	1,668
West Pakistan	540	543	998	1,075	1,140	1,204	1,338
Imports							
East Pakistan	1,015	873	1,019	1,448	1,702	1,328	1,567
West Pakistan	2,173	2,236	2,800	2,982	3,672	2,880	3,625

Source: Institute of Developing Economies, *The Study on Japanese Cooperation in Industrial Policy for Developing Economies: Pakistan*, Tokyo, 1994, p. 12.

fluctuations over the last fifteen years, more than doubling from the previous year in 1983/4, 1987/8, and 1992/3. These variations from one year to another need to be seen in light of the whole economy. Hence, Table 9.4 shows how some of these constituents of the balance of payments have changed with respect to GDP. Exports have shown a healthy trend as their share of the GDP has increased since 1980/1, while that of imports has fallen (see Figure 9.2). The trade deficit has also been brought down to manageable levels, but workers' remittances have fallen by one-third compared to the huge contribution of 10 per cent of GDP they made in 1981/2. The current account deficit, one of the more important indicators for the whole of the economy, is shown in Figure 9.3, where one can see that it has stayed on the high side, at a level which is considered to be unsustainable. Less than 3 per cent of GDP, implying that there is not too great a difference between imports and exports of all kinds, is considered a reasonable level for a country developing in the direction and at the rate of Pakistan.

Table 9.5 shows how drastically the composition of exports and imports has changed. Even in a brief period of less than twenty-five years from 1971, the nature of Pakistan's trade has changed considerably (see Figure 9.4). Primary commodities, which were 99 per cent of exports in 1948/9, fell to 45 per cent in 1971/2, and were a mere 11 per cent in 1994/5. Similarly, manufactured goods now contribute as much as 66 per cent of Pakistan's exports. (However, these figures do not reveal a very important aspect of the nature of manufactured exports which is discussed below). Regarding imports, capital goods, such as machinery, and industrial raw materials have replaced consumer goods as the main imported item.

Tables 9.6 and 9.7, which look at the composition of trade in somewhat greater detail, reveal the brittle nature of Pakistan's exports. Although 66 per cent of exports are supposed to be manufactured items, in 1994/5 as much as 75 per cent of Pakistan's exports (Table 9.6) were dependent on a single commodity, i.e. cotton. Raw cotton, cotton yarn, textiles, fabrics, cotton made-ups, garments, etc., while at different stages of processing and value added, nevertheless have their source in cotton. Rice and vegetables and fruit, which formed about 8 per cent of exports in 1994/5 are also agricultural commodities. Hence, while in 1948/9 Pakistan exported mainly unprocessed raw primary products, fifty years later, exports continued to be dependent on agricultural commodities and on the weather, which can have serious effects on the level of exports.

The table for imports shows that not only does Pakistan import a great deal of machinery and capital goods; it also imports wheat and cotton, two products in which Pakistan

Table 9.2
Exports, imports, and trade balance, 1950–1995

| Year | Rs million | | | | | | US $ million | | | | | |
| | Current prices | | | Constant prices[a] | | | Current prices | | | Constant prices[b] | | |
	Exports	Imports	Balance	Exports	Imports	Balance	Exports	Imports	Balance	Exports	Imports	Balance
1950/1	1,343	1,676	176	1,038	1,869	−831	406	353	53	503	437	66
1951/2	922	1,474	−552	679	2,122	−1,433	279	445	−166	339	541	−202
1952/3	867	4,017	−150	1,083	1,773	−690	262	307	−45	312	365	−53
1953/4	641	824	−183	823	1,306	−483	194	249	−55	226	291	−65
1954/5	491	783	−292	601	1,307	−706	149	237	−88	169	368	99
1955/6	742	965	−223	808	1,153	−345	156	203	−47	171	222	−51
1956/7	698	1,516	−818	704	1,444	−740	147	319	−172	156	338	−182
1957/8	434	1,314	−880	379	1,176	−797	91	276	−185	95	287	−192
1958/9	444	1,025	−581	459	1,017	−558	93	215	−122	95	218	−123
1959/60	763	1,806	−1,043	763	1,806	−1,043	160	379	−219	160	379	−219
1960/1	540	2,173	−1,633	520	2,100	−1,580	114	457	−343	113	452	−339
1961/2	543	2,236	−1,693	510	1,956	−1,446	114	470	−356	110	455	−345
1962/3	998	2,800	−1,802	956	2,732	−1,416	210	588	−378	201	562	−361
1963/4	1,075	2,982	−1,907	1,030	2,432	−1,402	226	626	−400	213	589	−376
1964/5	1,140	3,672	−2,532	1,050	3,055	−2,005	239	772	−533	219	708	−489
1965/6	1,204	2,880	−1,676	1,069	2,465	−1,396	253	605	−352	224	536	−312
1966/7	1,297	3,626	−2,329	1,188	2,997	−1,809	273	762	−489	235	657	−422
1967/8	1,645	3,327	−1,682	1,459	2,793	−1,334	346	699	−353	284	574	−290
1968/9	1,700	3,047	−1,347	1,522	2,572	−1,050	357	640	−283	278	499	−221
1969/70	1,609	3,285	−1,676	1,460	2,600	−1,140	338	690	−352	249	508	−259
1970/1	1,998	3,602	−1,604	1,698	2,380	−682	420	757	−337	293	528	−235
1971/2	3,371	3,495	−124	2,370	1,774	596	591	638	−47	394	425	−31
1972/3	8,551	8,398	153	2,848	2,329	519	817	797	20	511	498	13
1973/4	10,161	13,479	−3,318	2,102	2,584	−482	1,026	1,362	−336	589	782	−193
1974/5	10,286	20,925	−10,639	2,279	2,693	−414	1,039	2,114	−1,075	543	1,104	−561
1975/6	11,253	20,465	−9,212	2,487	2,778	−291	1,137	2,067	−930	559	1,016	−457
1976/7	11,294	23,012	−11,718	2,128	2,901	−773	1,141	2,325	−1,184	526	1,071	−545
1977/8	12,980	27,815	−14,835	2,321	3,217	−896	1,311	2,810	−1,499	563	1,206	−643
1978/9	16,925	36,388	−19,463	2,431	4,049	−1,618	1,710	3,676	−1,966	675	1,450	−775
1979/80	23,410	46,929	−23,519	3,111	4,267	−1,156	2,365	4,740	−2,375	855	1,714	−859
1980/1	29,280	53,544	−24,264	3,675	4,005	−330	2,958	5,409	2,451	976	1,785	−809
1981/2	26,270	59,482	−33,212	3,351	4,016	−665	2,464	5,622	3,158	764	1,743	−979
1982/3	34,442	68,151	−33,709	4,072	4,270	−198	2,694	5,357	−2,663	804	1,599	−795
1983/4	37,339	76,707	−39,368	3,945	4,584	−639	2,768	5,685	−2,917	795	1,633	−838
1984/5	37,979	89,788	−51,799	3,834	5,049	−1,215	2,491	5,906	3,415	695	1,649	−954
1985/6	49,592	90,946	−41,354	5,243	5,154	98	3,070	5,634	−2,564	836	1,535	−699
1986/7	63,355	92,431	−29,076	6,021	5,051	970	3,686	5,380	−1,694	973	1,420	−447
1987/8	78,445	112,551	−34,106	6,007	4,948	1,059	4,455	6,391	−1,936	1,137	1,631	−494
1988/9	90,183	135,841	−45,658	6,737	5,418	1,319	4,661	7,034	−2,373	1,143	1,725	−528
1989/90	106,469	148,853	−42,384	6,926	5,179	1,747	4,954	6,935	−1,981	1,167	1,364	−467
1990/1	138,280	171,114	−32,832	8,807	5,063	3,744	6,131	7,619	−1,488	1,387	1,740	−337
1991/2	171,728	229,889	−58,161	10,283	6,788	3,495	6,904	9,252	−2,348	1,501	2,011	−510
1992/3	177,028	258,643	−81,685	10,337	7,253	3,084	6,813	9,941	−3,128			
1993/4	205,499	258,250	−52,751	10,581	6,501	4,080	6,803	8,564	−1,761			
1994/5	251,173	320,892	−69,719	10,219	6,890	3,329	8,137	10,394	−2,257			

[a] Deflated by unit value indices constructed from official data at different bases linked by 1959/60 base.
[b] Calculated through GNP deflator of USA, at 1959/60 base.
Source: Government of Pakistan, *Pakistan Economic Survey, 1995–96*, Islamabad, 1996, p. 161.

Table 9.3
Balance of payments growth rates, 1980–1995 (%)

	1970s	1980s	1980/1	1981/2	1982/3	1983/4	1984/5	1985/6	1986/7	1987/8	1988/9	1989/90	1990/1	1991/2	1992/3	1993/4	1994/5
Exports	13.5	7.7	19.6	-17.2	13.3	1.6	-7.9	19.7	18.9	24.7	6.2	6.3	19.8	14.6	0.3	-1.4	17.9
Imports	16.6	-4.3	14.5	3.7	-2.7	6.7	0.3	-0.4	-3.2	19.5	4.2	2.8	13.1	7.3	11.7	-13.6	16.7
Trade deficit	20.5	-0.1	9.9	24.8	-13.4	11.2	6.9	-14.4	-24.6	11.5	0.6	-3.4	-0.1	-9.9	46.1	-37.6	12.7
Private transfers		2.3	18.3	7.6	27.7	-1.2	-11.7	5.0	-9.4	-11.8	-6.9	5.2	-4.9	-48.1	-25.3	2.7	0.3
Workers' remittances		1.1	19.9	6.2	29.7	-5.2	-10.6	6.4	-12.2	-11.7	-5.8	2.4	-4.8	-20.6	6.5	-7.5	29.1
Current account deficit		21.2	-9.0	47.9	-66.3	92.8	68.5	-26.4	-41.8	133.9	15.0	-2.2	14.8	-38.0	174.0	-46.7	22.1

Source: Government of Pakistan, *Pakistan Economic Survey, 1995–96*, Islamabad, 1996, p. 4.

should have achieved self-sufficiency many years ago. Almost 4 per cent of Pakistan's imports were for wheat in 1994/5 when 2.6 million tons were imported. Animal and vegetable oils and fats used for making cooking oil contributed more than 10 per cent of Pakistan's imports in 1994/5.

Table 9.8 is revealing of the direction that Pakistan's trade has taken over the last twenty or so years. While the United States is still Pakistan's major trading partner, its share has fallen slightly since 1973/4. The rise of the Middle East as a major importer of Pakistani products in recent years and as a source for Pakistan's imports, mainly of petroleum, is also seen in the table. Kuwait, for example, provided almost 6 per cent of Pakistan's total imports in 1994/5, all of which is oil. However, Kuwait imports very little from Pakistan. This is also the case with Malaysia, where trade with Pakistan is mainly in one direction. Malaysia provides Pakistan primarily with palm oil for the manufacture of edible oil and ghee, but Pakistan exports next to nothing to Malaysia in comparison. This pattern is reversed for Hong Kong, which imports mostly cotton yarn, while Pakistan imports very little in return. Although there has been some diversification in the direction of Pakistan's trade since the 1970s, even by 1994/5 only four countries – the USA, the UK, Germany, and Japan – constituted more than 30 per cent of Pakistan's trade.

One of the most important features of Pakistan's economy in recent years has been the contribution made by workers' remittances. Rising to 10 per cent of GDP in 1982/3, at a peak value of about $3 billion, they have since decreased substantially, although they still contributed 3 per cent of GDP or $1.86 billion in 1994/5 (see Table 9.9). The main source of these remittances, by far, is Saudi Arabia, followed by the United Arab Emirates. Interestingly, as Table 9.10 reveals, in 1972/3 the United Kingdom was the source of more than half of Pakistan's remittances, which were then a total of only $136 million.

This section has shown that, although the nature of Pakistan's trade has changed considerably in fifty years, from producing and exporting primary products to exporting manufactured products, agricultural products, particularly cotton, still form the basis of those exports. However, for many years, Pakistan's main export has not been a tangible item, but the services provided by workers in the Middle East, again a source of income that fluctuates, as the 1991 Gulf War showed. Moreover, if the Middle Eastern countries decide to opt for non-Pakistani workers, or those that provide different skills (since most Pakistanis in the Middle East provide unskilled or low-skilled services), this source of foreign exchange will also be somewhat unstable. Since 1973/4, Pakistan's exports have grown by about eightfold. However, between 1973 and 1993, Malaysia's exports have increased twelvefold, South Korea's twenty-eight times over and Singapore's by almost fifty times, from a mere $1.8 billion (slightly above Pakistan's) in 1973 to a staggering $89 billion in 1993. Pakistan's export and trade performance by its own standards may have improved, but clearly, by any comparison, Pakistan has not been able to ride the wave of dynamic export-led growth which has become a key feature of the Asian Tigers. Some reasons for this can be found in the following sections of this chapter.

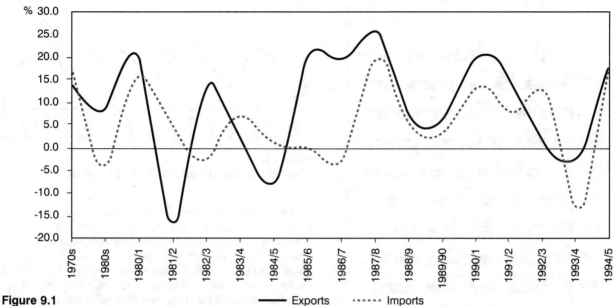

Figure 9.1
Balance of payments growth rates, 1980–1995
——— Exports   ······· Imports

9.2   Trade Policy and Trade Regimes: 1947–1997

9.2.1   The Early Years: 1947–1958[2]

In 1948/9, Pakistan's major trading partners were India and the UK, which together accounted for 67 per cent of Pakistan's trade, and Pakistan, along with both these countries, was a member of the sterling area. In September

1949, the pound sterling was devalued by 31 per cent, and most countries linked to sterling also devalued. Pakistan, however, decided to maintain its old exchange rate and did not devalue, making imports from the UK and India cheaper, while Pakistan's exports to these two countries became more expensive. According to Rashid Amjad and Viqar Ahmad, 'the main motivation behind the non-devaluation decision was to be able to sell raw jute to Indian industry'.[3] In 1949 more than 50 per cent of West Pakistan's trade and 80 per cent of

Table 9.4
Components of balance of payments, 1980–1995 (% of GDP)

Year	Exports[a]	Imports[a]	Trade deficit[a]	Workers' remittances[b]	Current account deficit[b]
1980/1	10.53	19.25	8.72	7.53	3.69
1981/2	8.02	18.3	10.28	7.24	4.99
1982/3	9.39	18.68	9.29	10.06	1.8
1983/4	8.89	18.26	9.37	8.79	3.2
1984/5	7.99	18.95	10.96	7.85	5.39
1985/6	9.63	17.67	8.04	8.14	3.88
1986/7	11.06	16.14	5.08	6.84	2.16
1987/8	11.61	16.65	5.04	5.24	4.38
1988/9	11.64	17.56	5.92	4.74	4.83
1989/90	12.41	17.38	4.96	4.87	4.74
1990/1	13.47	16.74	3.27	4.06	4.77
1991/2	14.16	18.97	4.82	3.01	2.76
1992/3	13.18	17.24	6.05	3.02	7.14
1993/4	13.05	16.42	3.39	2.77	3.77
1994/5	13.46	17.19	3.73	3.09	3.97

[a] Based on the data compiled by FBS.
[b] Based on the data compiled by SBP.
Source: Government of Pakistan, *Pakistan Economic Survey, 1995–96*, Islamabad, 1996, p. 160.

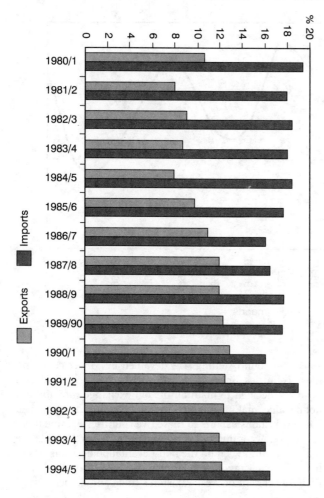

Figure 9.2
Components of balance of payments, 1980–1995 (% of GDP)

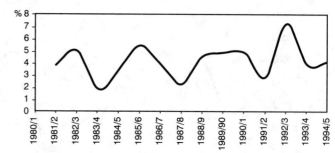

Figure 9.3
Current account deficit, 1980–1995 (% of GDP)

import policy and impose some 'rather loose' quantitative controls on imports and exports in September 1949.

However, the trade regime was again liberalized within one year after the Korean War broke out and demand for Pakistan's exports – which were mainly composed of jute and cotton – increased by 109 per cent. Not only was there increased demand for these raw materials, but their prices also increased appreciably. The balance of payments position improved substantially, and subsequently, trade with India was also restored, but not before Pakistan had found other trading partners as well. The Korean boom lasted about two years and, as the balance of payments situation was particularly good, the government liberalized trade to the extent that by June 1951 as much as 85 per cent of the imports were virtually without licence, importable on the Open General Licence System (OGL)[6] (see Box 9.1).

Following the collapse of the Korean boom, the government reimposed trade and foreign exchange controls in 1952, which according to an Asian Development Bank Study was 'probably the most important cause of the rapid rate of growth of manufacturing in Pakistan'[7] in the early years. The study continues:

> Probably the most important cause of the rapid rate of growth of manufacturing in Pakistan was the system of trade and foreign exchange controls it adopted. The country set off on this course in 1952 when it chose licensing and quantitative import controls over devaluation as a means of dealing with its balance-of-payments problems which emerged after the collapse of

East Pakistan's trade was with India, and raw jute and cotton accounted for about 65 per cent of exports to India.[4] India, however, was 'resentful and refused to recognize the new exchange rate of its currency in terms of the Pakistani Rupee',[5] and trade between the two countries came to a halt. The Pakistani government had to abandon its more liberal

Table 9.5
Economic classification of exports and imports (%)

	Imports				Exports		
Year	Capital goods	Industrial raw material for capital goods	Industrial raw material for consumer goods	Consumer goods	Primary commodities	Semi-manufactures	Manufactured goods
1971/2	42	11	24	23	45	27	28
1976/7	38	6	40	16	41	17	42
1980/1	28	8	50	15	44	11	45
1987/8	36	7	43	14	28	20	52
1994/5	34	5	47	14	11	23	66

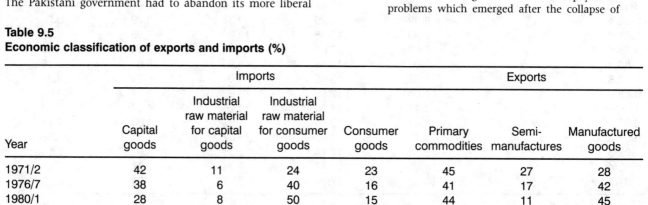

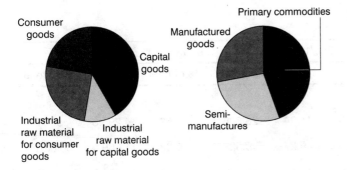

Imports, 1971/2   **Exports, 1971/2**

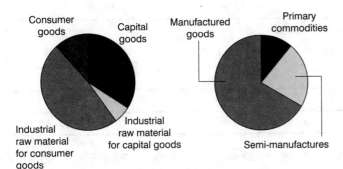

Imports, 1994/5   **Exports, 1994/5**

Figure 9.4
Economic classification of exports and imports, 1971/2 and 1994/5

the Korean War raw material boom.

Indeed, the import control system adopted in 1952 remained the sole basis of import licensing decisions up to 1959, and was dominant in these decisions throughout the 1960s. This system allowed the rupee to remain overvalued throughout the period, which in turn created excess demand for imports at duty-paid prices and made rationing of imports via quantitative controls necessary.[8]

This policy of 'high tariff walls and stringent quantitative controls on imports'[9] was responsible for the initiation of industrialization in general, and of the import substituting industrialization in particular, which took place in the 1950s. For Stephen Lewis, the decision by the government not to devalue in either 1949 or 1952, but instead to rely on exchange controls and quantitative restrictions to control imports, was one of the 'two major factors determining the course of industrial growth in Pakistan in the 1950s and into the early sixties'.[10] As high tariffs on consumer products raised their domestic prices, and industry became more profitable as an option than trade, it became profitable to shift into the production of these commodities domestically (see Table 9.11 for the rate of duty on imported goods). Also, there was no real export promotion policy at least until 1956, when the Export Promotion Scheme, which covered 67

primary commodities and 58 manufactured goods, was introduced, whereby exporters were entitled 'to be granted import licences for certain specific items to the extent of 25 per cent and 40 per cent on various categories of manufactured goods and 15 per cent on the export of raw materials'.[11]

The trade restrictions that were imposed determined both the extent and pattern of industrialization that was established in the 1950s and that set the trend for later developments. The trade restrictions affected industrialization in two ways:

(i) Because of the quantitative restrictions in place, the protection to domestic producers was far greater than that implied by a comparison between domestic and duty paid prices of competitive imports, and (ii) the general scarcity created by the licensing system meant that the incentives for investment were raised across the board rather than differentially between industries. The former points to the degree of channelling of investments that did take place and the latter [indicates] that any bias created by the differences in tariff rates across sectors was offset by the licensing system.[12]

Viqar Ahmed and Rashid Amjad argue that these

Import controls became a very powerful lever in the hands of the government to affect and influence resource allocation in the domestic economy. Firstly, the import control system after 1952 favoured mainly the establishment of consumer goods industries by restricting the import of consumer goods and hindered the establishment of capital goods and intermediate goods industries since imports were freely allowed. Secondly, the government gave import licence privileges mainly to those importers who had imported during the 1950–2 period. These importers were called 'category holders' and this policy was referred to as the 'category system'. It obviously bestowed considerable economic gain on those who were in this category as they had almost a virtual monopoly in the trade of the imported items.[13]

Their analysis of these controls is that, while the system was effective following the post-Korean recession between 1952 and 1955, the control mechanisms 'not only failed to keep pace with the basic economic changes, it also became a source of corruption and bribery'.[14] It further resulted in importers making monopoly profits, especially after the category system was introduced, and they argue, 'the licence system also became a source of economic disparity between East and West Pakistan',[15] as there were many more West Pakistani importers who received import licences.

The work by Stephen Lewis on trade policy and industrialization in Pakistan is of particular interest, for he has extensively analysed the relationship between the two and the effect of the former on the latter, for the 1950s and 1960s. He writes that after 1952 the salient features of the

Table 9.6
Pakistan: major exports

	1971/2		1980/1		1986/7		1994/5	
	Rs m	% of total	Rs m	% of total	Rs m	% of total	US$ m	% of total
Textile yarn, fabrics, made-up articles, and related products	993.0	29.45	4,170.0	14.24	26,306.3	41.52	4,295.6	52.76
Articles of clothing and clothing accessories	–	–	2,715.0	9.27	9,522.7	15.03	1,669.9	20.51
Leather manufacturers	–	–	–	–	–	–	–	–
Rice	274.1	8.13	5,601.6	19.13	5,139.2	8.11	454.6	5.58
Cotton	982.5	29.14	5,222.3	17.84	7,776.9	12.28	126.8	1.55
Vegetables and fruit	20.0	–	166.0	–	827.6	1.30	215.3	2.64
Fish	96.7	2.87	511.9	1.74	195.0	–	154.3	1.90
Others	1,005.1	29.81	10,892.8	37.20	9,433.5	14.89	943.6	11.60
Total	3,371.4		29,279.5		63,354.9		8,141.3	

Source: State Bank of Pakistan, *Annual Reports*, various issues, Karachi.

Table 9.7
Pakistan: major imports

	1971/2		1980/1		1986/7		1994/5	
	Rs m	% of total	Rs m	% of total	Rs m	% of total	US$ m	% of total
Machinery and transport equipment	1,048.6	30.00	11,590.0	21.65	27,543.5	29.80	2,989.6	28.74
Chemicals and related products	389.1	11.13	7,349.2	13.73	15,773.1	17.06	1,587.4	15.26
Petroleum and related products	294.4	8.42	15,354.0	28.68	13,976.8	15.12	1,587.5	15.26
Wheat	269.8	7.72	0.1	–	1,184.0	1.30	413.3	3.97
Animals and vegetable oil and fats	130.8	3.74	3,137.0	5.86	5,003.4	5.41	1,078.5	10.37
Cotton	9.4	–	23.0	–	–	–	307.2	2.95
Others	1,353.3	38.72	16,089.8	30.05	28,950.0	31.32	2,437.6	23.43
Total	3,495.4		53,543.0		92,430.8		10,401.1	

Source: State Bank of Pakistan, *Annual Reports*, various issues, Karachi.

Table 9.8
Pakistan: direction of trade (%)

	1973/4		1980/1		1986/7		1994/5	
	Exports to	Imports from	Exports to	Imports from	Exports to	Imports from	Exports to	Imports from
USA	5.32	25.61	6.05	10.92	10.12	11.02	16.16	9.38
UK	6.76	7.05	3.97	6.12	7.14	6.68	7.06	5.11
Germany	4.56	7.79	4.3	5.03	7.03	7.52	7.01	6.77
Kuwait	1.43	3.7	–	7.99	–	7.43	–	5.81
Dubai	1.8	–	3.5	3.6	2.8	2	3.95	1.8
Saudi Arabia	3.91	6.62	5.95	12.83	7.12	5.3	2.74	4.94
Other Middle Eastern countries	–	–	–	–	–	–	5.75	8.55
China	–	3.5	12.2	3.3	–	3.9	–	4.4
Hong Kong	10.98	–	3.9	–	2.8	–	6.6	–
Japan	6.2	9.35	6.4	11.56	10.86	16.4	6.67	9.56
Malaysia	–	–	–	2.81	–	3.02	–	8.77
South Korea	–	–	–	–	3.1	2.16	3.33	3.2
Bangladesh	–	–	2.2	1.3	1.7	–	2.08	–
Indonesia	9.48	–	–	–	–	–	–	–
Iran	3.23	1.64	7.8	–	1.5	1.08	–	–

Source: Government of Pakistan, *Pakistan Economic Survey*, various issues, Islamabad.

Table 9.9
Workers' remittances, 1972–1995 (US$ m)

Year	Total
1972/3	136.00
1973/4	139.14
1974/5	211.10
1975/6	339.02
1976/7	577.72
1977/8	1,156.33
1978/9	1,397.93
1979/80	1,744.14
1980/1	2,115.88
1981/2	2,224.89
1982/3	2,885.67
1983/4	2,737.44
1984/5	2,445.92
1985/6	2,595.31
1986/7	2,278.56
1987/8	2,012.60
1988/9	1,896.99
1989/90	1,942.35
1990/1	1,848.29
1991/2	1,467.48
1992/3	1,562.24
1993/4	1,445.56
1994/5	1,866.10

Source: State Bank of Pakistan.

Table 9.10
Main sources of workers' remittances (% of total)

	1972/3	1977/8	1980/1	1986/7	1995/6
United Kingdom	53.04	6.63	8.74	8.99	7.62
Saudi Arabia	5.79	40.14	46.52	41.50	44.12
Kuwait	5.18	4.67	6.30	9.14	4.15
Oman	8.97	5.53	4.36	5.88	5.54
UAE	3.41	26.17	14.55	14.46	17.35

Source: Government of Pakistan, *Pakistan Economic Survey, 1995–96*, Islamabad, 1996.

fully processed intermediate goods. Moreover, there was no duty levied on capital goods or on industrial raw materials.

However, Lewis makes the important point that 'while the tariff structure played some role in directing resources in Pakistan, *that role was a relatively minor one*. The principal determinant of the structure of imports and the set of domestic relative prices was the import licensing system.'[17]

Moreover, he makes the very interesting observation that, despite numerous interventions and distortions by the government in the 1950s, the structure of production would have been quite similar without them. He argues that

the differentiated effects of the tariff structure, the system of import licences, and the overvalued currency had little influence on the structure of production that began to emerge in the mid 50s since the scarcity of all manufactured goods in Pakistan made it profitable to produce almost any kind of manufacture. The restrictive trade policy *speeded the process* of industrial growth by transferring substantial amounts of income from the agricultural sector to manufactures, but it is *unlikely if the structure of production* would *have been any different* if, say, a floating exchange rate had been adopted to deal with the exchange crisis of 1952.[18]

trade policy adopted by Pakistan were: '(i) overvaluation of the rupee with respect to other countries, (ii) use of quantitative controls on imports to regulate the level and the composition of imported goods and (iii) a highly differentiated structure of tariffs on imports and export taxes on jute and cotton'.[16] The tariff structure favoured in the earlier years was of a cascading type, with lower tariffs on intermediate and capital goods than on final goods or more

Table 9.11
Rate of duty on imported goods by types of commodity, 1955–1960

Description	1955/6	1956/7	1957/8	1958/9	1959/60
Consumption goods					
Essentials	35	35	35	35	35
Semi-luxuries	54	54	54	54	54
Luxuries	99	99	99	99	99
Raw materials for consumption goods	26	26	26	26	26
Unprocessed	43	43	43	43	43
Raw materials for capital goods					
Unprocessed	23	23	23	23	23
Processed	38	38	38	38	38
Capital goods					
Consumer durables	71	71	71	71	71
Machinery and equipment	14	14	14	14	14

Source   Lewis, Stephen, *Economic Policy and Industrial Growth in Pakistan*, London, 1969.

Hence, for Lewis, unlike other observers, the trade policies and the trade regime were not the principal cause of the pattern of industrial production adopted in the first decade, but only acted as a catalyst. For Lewis, the main cause of the structure of industrial production was the imbalance between the supply and demand for manufactured goods.

9.2.2   Trade Policy and the Decade of Development

A key feature of the high growth rates in industry in the 1960s was the trade regime adopted by the military government of Ayub Khan. Possibly the single most important component of the trade policy was the Export Bonus or Bonus Voucher Scheme (see Box 9.3). A study by the Asian Development Bank summarizes the key features of the trade regime as follows:

> The martial law government which came to power in 1958 began to dismantle the system of direct controls on imports, prices, profit margins and investment. One important component of this program was the adoption of the Export Bonus Scheme in 1959. This scheme was essentially a floating multiple exchange rate for exports. The gradual liberalization of import controls continued with the Open General Licensing System and the Repeat and Automatic Licensing Schemes introduced in 1961, and reached a peak with the introduction of the Free List for selected raw materials in 1964 [see Table 9.12]. This liberalization process was unfortunately reversed in order to meet the foreign exchange shortages which arose after the war with India in 1965, the Government once again opting for direct controls.[19]

Stephen Lewis argues that after 1959 there were a number of changes in economic policy and a shift from direct to indirect controls on imports. In addition, a 'number of measures were taken in import licensing that made market forces more important in determining the commodity composition of imports and the distribution of ownership of import licences'.[20]

Unlike in the earlier years, during the 1960s there was a direct emphasis on the promotion of manufactured exports as special consideration was given to exporting industries through the Export Bonus Scheme, and additional licences were also made available to import raw materials and spare parts. Those industries that were export-oriented received a higher percentage of entitlement in licences.

The import liberalizing programme that started in 1959 along with the Bonus Voucher Scheme was responsible for the following:

> (i) over 1959–64 total imports increased much more rapidly than exports or GNP, and the composition of imports continued to shift towards the import of capital goods and processed intermediate goods (ii) market forces were increasingly relied upon to determine the commodity composition of imports (iii) a variety of new devices were introduced into the licensing scheme to increase the flexibility of entrance into the import trade (iv) substantial increases in the rates of duties on import goods which acted from the cost side, to reduce excess demand for imports.[21]

In addition, the Open General Licensing system was expanded to allow newcomers to enter the import trade 'particularly those from areas outside the major industrial and commercial centres. One of its principal effects was to give a wider distribution of the gains from processing an import licence',[22] with a large amount of foreign exchange allocated to the new OGL importers. Hence, the monopoly of the category holders of the 1950s was broken. In 1961 eleven commodities were on the OGL list, which was increased to fifty-one by 1964. Despite the numerous liberalizing measures taken in the early 1960s, Viqar Ahmed and Rashid Amjad argue that 'the import trade was still more or less controlled by the licence system which was strongly biased towards capital goods imports'.[23]

The Export Bonus Scheme undoubtedly had a positive effect on exports in the early 1960s. The scheme compensated for the overvalued exchange rate and increased exports, particularly of manufactured goods. The export of raw jute fell from 60 per cent of total exports in 1958/9 to 20 per cent in 1968/9, while exports of cotton and jute textiles increased from 8.3 to 35 per cent in the same period, and other exports increased from 2 to 20 per cent in the same ten years.[24] The Bonus Voucher Scheme also made the import of raw materials and machinery much easier when there was increased demand for such imports. For Asad Sayeed, the scheme 'was an ingenious incentive for both export expansion and import substitution'.[25] He quotes a study where it was shown that the Bonus Voucher Scheme accounted for 72 per cent of the effect of incentives on exports.

Although exports did increase due to the Bonus Voucher Scheme, the scheme has been criticized for giving wrong

Table 9.12
Change in import patterns from licences to bonus vouchers in the 1960s

Year	Licensed	Free List[a]	Bonus
1960/1	90.3	–	9.7
1961/2	89.6	–	9.4
1962/3	86.3	2.8	10.9
1963/4	75.3	14.9	9.8
1964/5	39.5	48.9	11.6
1965/6	32.6	40.0	27.4
1966/7	26.2	49.9	23.9

[a] After June 1965, the Free List was subject to varying and increasing degrees of administrative restriction.
Source: Amjad, Rashid, *Private Industrial Investment in Pakistan, 1960–1970*, Cambridge University Press, Cambridge, 1982, p. 40.

BOX 9.3
The Export Bonus Scheme

The Bonus Voucher or Export Bonus Scheme has been singled out as one of the most important instruments causing distortions in Pakistan's trade and industrialization process. However, a few studies have challenged that assertion and this excerpt from an Asian Development Bank Study reaches different conclusions.

Success in maintaining the momentum of growth in manufacturing during the 1960s was largely due to the Export Bonus Scheme which allowed Pakistan to avoid to some degree the inefficiencies of prolonged import substitution.

Introduced in 1959, this scheme provided exchange rates to exporters of manufactured goods more favourable than the official rate. Essentially, it allowed exporters of manufactured goods to receive a percentage of their export earnings in the form of transferable Bonus Vouchers in addition to the rupee equivalent of their export earnings converted at the official rate. These vouchers allowed the holder either: (i) to purchase an equivalent amount of foreign exchange at the official rate which can be used to import any item on the Bonus list, or (ii) to sell the voucher on an organized market. Since Bonus Vouchers were generally quoted on the stock exchange at 1.5 to 1.8 times their face value, the effective exchange rate for voucher recipients was Rs6.19 to Rs7.62 per dollar or even higher against the official rate of Rs4.76 per dollar. This compensated exporters of manufactured goods for the overvaluation of the rupee, allowing them to successfully compete in international markets, and helped to replace import-substitution-based growth with export expansion.

There is considerable evidence of the impact of the Export Bonus Scheme on promoting manufactured exports. [Meekal] Ahmad [had] found that 'empirical investigation shows that the introduction of the Export Bonus Scheme in 1959 rotated the entire export function upwards'. Nurul Islam also found a high elasticity of export supply with respect to the export incentive schemes. However, the correlation between the ranking of manufactured exports by effective exchange rates and domestic resource cost was low and insignificant, leading to the conclusion that changes in effective exchange rates brought about by the frequent variation in bonus entitlement during the post-1965 period tended to confuse private decision-makers.

The Export Bonus Scheme also functioned as a safety valve for imports of critical items by industry, thus providing some flexibility to the import licensing system. However, until the mid-1960s it was primarily used for importing luxury goods since the effective exchange rate on imports under the scheme was Rs11.90 per dollar or more. Because of declining foreign aid and the resulting foreign exchange shortages, a cash-cum-bonus list for most industrial raw materials was introduced in 1967 which provided an intermediate rate of Rs8.33 per dollar. Following this, the Export Bonus Scheme became something akin to a full fledged multiple exchange rate since it operated both on the import and export sides.

Source: Asian Development Bank, *Strategies for Economic Growth and Development: The Bank's Role in Pakistan*, Asian Development Bank, Manila, 1985, pp. 361–2.

signals and causing distortions (see Box 9.3). Viqar Ahmed and Rashid Amjad criticize the scheme on the following grounds:

The value of exports covered under the scheme did increase appreciably but the data does not tell the whole story. The rise in exports of processed goods was at the expense of the raw materials that would otherwise have been exported. Also, to the extent that the diversion of certain goods from the home to the foreign market releases domestic purchasing power to procure goods which could otherwise be exported, there is a presumed loss of earnings. Moreover, allowing for a trend factor, some rise in exports may have taken place even if this scheme had not been introduced. Finally, many exporters sold their goods in the foreign market at lower prices, sometimes even below cost, since they calculated their return in Rupees in which terms the loss could be made up by the sale of bonus vouchers.[26]

The early import liberalizing policy of the military government included the dismantling of the import controls of the 1950s, and the items importable on licences, which were 90.3 per cent of imports in 1960/1, fell to 39.5 per cent in 1964/5 (Table 9.12). Also, the Free List, where commodities could be imported without licences, was increased from four to fifty items in two years, and by 1964/5 about half of all imports were on the Free List.

One reason why the government was able to be so generous in its import policy was the large amount of foreign aid the military government received. More than 40 per cent of the imports of the government were financed by the foreign aid component, which was 6 per cent of GDP in 1964/5.[27] The Asian Development Bank study argues that 'clearly, the import liberalization that took place during the first half of the 1960s, would have been impossible without this large increase in aid'.[28] After the foreign exchange squeeze when aid was severely curtailed after June 1965, the government had to abandon its liberal import policy and felt it necessary to reimpose a number of import controls. The Free List, for example – 'the most important step in the decontrol of imports taken during the first half of the 60s – was subject to increasing administrative restrictions which negated its very purpose'.[29] The Free List was reduced from sixty-six items in 1964 to fourteen in 1968 and to eleven in 1971. There was also a cut in the licensable list, but the Bonus List expanded from 215 in 1966/7 to 277 in 1970.[30]

9.2.3 A New Country: 1972–1977

The Bhutto government took over a Pakistan in 1971 that was different from that of the 1950s and 1960s in almost every respect. Most importantly, the majority province had seceded after a bloody war of liberation and had become an independent Bangladesh. Not only was half the country no longer part of Pakistan, but most of the policies of the 1960s which were held responsible for the negative outcomes regarding income and regional inequality were also quickly done away with. The People's Party government in December 1971 took over a new country and this was particularly so with regard to the trade regime.

Almost half of West Pakistan's 'exports' went to East Pakistan in 1969/70, while 18 per cent of the western region's imports came from the east (see Box 9.2).[31] East Pakistan sold its jute, tea, and other products in international markets and earned over half of united Pakistan's exports, paying for its own imports through these export receipts. On account of East Pakistan's exports, West Pakistan was in a position to import much more than its own export earnings, since raw jute and jute textiles were Pakistan's main export earners. Thus, the loss of East Pakistan was a major structural break for what remained of Pakistan. In addition, many of the reforms that were identified with the Ayub Khan regime were perceived to be the causes of income concentration in the 1960s. Thus, in May 1972 the government took steps to abolish the import licensing system, as well as the multiple exchange rate system and the Export Bonus Scheme, and the import of all luxury items was banned. However, 'the most dramatic and perhaps the most crucial of the economic measures taken in the early months of PPP rule was the devaluation of the rupee. A criticism of the Ayub and Yahya governments had been their unwillingness to lower the value of the rupee, despite the exchange rate's patent unreality and distortive effects on exports and investment decisions.'[32]

In May 1972, along with the other measures listed above, the rupee was devalued by 56 per cent from Rs4.74 to one US dollar to Rs11, and after the US dollar was devalued in February 1973, the rupee found its new exchange value of Rs9.90 to one US dollar, a rate that remained fixed for about eight years (see Box 9.4).

After the devaluation, there were considerable changes in import policy. Viqar Ahmed and Rashid Amjad write that

> except for a few items reserved for industrial users, all registered importers could obtain licences for any number of importable items. The import trade was thus thrown wide open and imports were again liberalized after having gone through a restrictive phase. This was done in order to increase the availability of all types of goods so that industries could improve their capacity utilization and increase production in anticipation of a higher demand for exportable goods as a result of devaluation. The liberalization trend continued during the seventies and the Free List was extended to 407 items in 1976 and 438 in 1978–9.[33]

John Adams and Sabiha Iqbal write that 'a prominent feature of the Bhutto era was the absence of an explicit export policy. Between 1972 and 1977, and even beyond, Pakistan lacked a formal, organized export policy in which clear objectives and the means to realize them were laid out ... The government never issued a formal document, or sequence of documents, articulating an export policy.'[34] They argue that 'there was a lack of appreciation of the role of exports in the nation's development. Decisions that were made were often inconsistent with existing policy. The result was that economic incentives and disincentives for exports coexisted simultaneously.'[35]

Thus, the devaluation was seen as the main, if not the only, means of encouraging exports, and exports did indeed grow by 38.4 and 24.7 per cent in 1972/3 and 1973/4, respectively.[36] The government also collected additional revenue by imposing export taxes and was able to share in the windfall profits generated. However, the export boom was short lived due to the quadrupling of oil prices in 1974 – affecting oil and fertilizer imports, and worsening the balance of payments position – and the recession that followed in the developed

---

BOX 9.4

A pegged exchange rate

John Adams and Sabiha Iqbal explain how the crawling peg works:

> When a country decides to peg its currency to that of a major trading partner, the rate between the two is stabilized, but the two currencies then move jointly against others. Such a policy means that the pegged country abandons autonomous control of its exchange rate which then moves independently of its policies and conditions. An increase in the value of the currency, due to a rise in the value of the currency to which it is pegged, could damage exports by limiting growth and diversification of exports. Pakistan was in this situation during the 1970s when the rupee was pegged to the US dollar. The dollar and the rupee moved downwards between 1972 and 1975 and this encouraged Pakistan's exports, but with the appreciation of the dollar in 1976–77 there were complaints from exporters that their competitiveness was being damaged. In any case, neither the downward nor the upward movement in the value of the dollar, and of the linked rupee, reflected cost and price changes in Pakistan. Moreover, Pakistan's trade has become diversified enough to reduce the predominant importance of the US dollar in its external transactions.

Source: Adams, John and Sabiha Iqbal, *Exports, Politics and Economic Development in Pakistan*, Vanguard, Lahore, 1987, pp. 59–60.

countries. Moreover, a sequence of bad crops due to floods, pests, and other natural factors affected cotton and rice, Pakistan's two main export items. Hence all positive effects of the devaluation were very soon lost and the consequences on the rebound were particularly severe.

The one – probably the only – positive outcome for Pakistan of the developments on the international scene in the mid-1970s was a consequence of the oil price rise and boom in the Middle East. Pakistan was one of those countries that gained in various ways from the opening up of the new markets. In terms of labour and commodity exports, the new Middle East markets were able partially to compensate for the loss of East Pakistan's exports. Remittances touched about US$3 billion in the 1980s and in many ways transformed the social structure of the country, but the beneficiary of the opening up of the Middle East was not Bhutto, who was responsible for building close ties with the Islamic countries, but his detractor General Zia.

It is difficult to identify many positive export-promoting measures by the Bhutto government, with the possible exception of the concessionary credit facilities for exporters, where the rate of interest charged by commercial banks on export credits was lower than the normal bank lending rate. Other than that, the following verdict from John Adams and Sahiba Iqbal best summarizes the policies of the Bhutto government towards exports.

> Between 1972 and 1977 Pakistan did not devise an adequate policy to encourage exports. The various measures were complex and provided weak incentives, often inclined towards big exporters with established records. Emerging firms did not qualify for many programs. Exemptions from excise and sales taxes were not positive incentives but merely equalized Pakistan's external competitive position. The Bhutto government was absorbed in domestic reforms and connected exports and export concessions with the previous orientation towards fostering big industries. The bureaucracy was demoralized and not charged with formulating export policy. Policy first moved in the direction of diverting potential profits from the devaluation. Poor export performance, attributable to a weak international economy and to a lack of domestic push, engendered new incentive policies. These policies were devised slowly, in a patchwork way, with many changes. The direction of movement was to facilitate most kinds of exports but most programs were not heavily utilized and were not very effective.[37]

9.2.4 The Beginning of a Liberal Trade Regime: 1977–1988

Soon after coming into power, the Zia government began a series of steps to liberalize the trade regime, particularly imports, by reducing the number of banned goods and lifting other restrictions. Most non-tariff barriers, which had been imposed after the oil shock and foreign exchange stringency in the 1970s, were also removed. Between 1977 and 1983 the number of items on the Free List was increased and the procedure for importing commodities was streamlined and made much easier. In 1977 the Free List contained 438 items; by 1982/3 91 new items had been added, including some consumer items.[38]

Despite these early measures, the World Bank, in a report examining the trade policy regime of the 1980s, argues that in 1980, 'Pakistan's import regime reached its most restrictive stage, [and] about 41% of the domestic industrial value added was protected by import bans, and another 22% by various forms of import restrictions. By 1986, the equivalent percentages were 29% and 3.7%, respectively.'[39]

The government took the step of removing explicit import quotas on non-capital imports and the 'number of commodity categories subject to import licensing value ceilings was reduced from 406 in 1980/81 to 5 consumer goods in July 1983'.[40] In addition, previously banned and restricted imports were also liberalized. In July 1983, when the import policy for the fiscal year 1983/4 was announced, the classification of imports was changed:

> Whereas previously all items not specifically permitted were banned, now all items not specifically banned were importable. Under the present system there are two lists: a banned list and a restricted list, the latter having three parts: consumer goods subject to quantitative restrictions, items importable exclusively from a tied source, and items importable by the public sector only. Along with the above changes, a number of items were made freely importable: 148 previously banned items, 5 items previously importable only by the public sector, and 15 items, previous importable only from tied sources. In September 1983, 70 additional items were removed from the negative list, of which 14 were transferred to the tied list, 17 were placed on the list of items importable only by the public sector, and the remaining 39 items were made fully importable. Another significant feature of import liberalization was the virtual elimination of licensing ceilings for permitted imports, though import licensing remains in effect.[41]

While tariff and import duty adjustments were a repeated occurrence in the 1980s, some measures were also taken to boost exports. These measures included export rebates, concessionary credit for exports and income tax and import facilities for exporters. However, the most important policy reforms that affected exports were the delinking of the Pakistani rupee from the dollar and the introduction of a flexible exchange rate. Earlier, the rupee/dollar rate was fixed at Rs9.90 per dollar, and the strong dollar in 1980/1 also appreciated the Pakistani rupee vis-à-vis other currencies, reducing the competitiveness of Pakistan's exports on world markets.

Although there were frequent tariff reductions during the Zia regime, in 1986 Pakistan's nominal tariff rates for manufacturing industries were still among the highest in the world.[42] Table 9.13 shows the nominal tariffs faced by

Table 9.13
Unweighted average and frequency distribution of nominal tariffs in Pakistan, 1986/7

	Manufacturing	Consumer goods	Intermediate goods	Capital goods
Average tariff (%)	67.5	100.4	57.8	51.1
Standard deviation	54.2	52.9	53.8	43.6
Frequency distribution (% of goods)				
0–25	26.5	8.6	23.9	42.3
26–50	16.0	5.5	29.2	12.4
51–75	5.3	1.8	11.6	2.5
76–100	37.2	46.8	30.3	35.9
101–125	6.2	12.5	2.9	4.3
126–150	9.0	232.6	0.8	2.5
151–175	0.1	0	0.3	0
176–200	0.2	0	0.2	0
201–350	0.5	1.2	0.3	0.1

Source: Sayeed, Asad, 'Political Alignments, the State and Industrial Policy in Pakistan: A Comparison of Performance in the 1960s and 1980s', unpublished Ph.D. dissertation, University of Cambridge, 1995, p. 126.

Pakistan's imports in 1987. In June 1987, comprehensive changes were made in the trade regime, where tariff slabs were reduced from seventeen to ten. Other changes included the reduction of the economy-wide unweighted average tariff from 77 per cent to 66 per cent, while the dispersion of the tariffs remained the same. The largest proportionate decline was in capital goods, where the average tariff fell from 61 to 51 per cent.[43] Despite these changes, 'about 50% of all tariff categories, and 84% of consumer goods, carry customs duties in excess of 75%'.[44] By 1988 the World Bank felt that the trade regime that existed then 'still seems to be biased in favour of import substituting production. Domestic markets are insulated from foreign competition through non-tariff barriers and high tariffs.'[45]

9.2.5   Trade Liberalization Under Structural Adjustment: 1988 Onwards

In the budget announced in June 1988, a number of important and far-reaching measures were announced with regard to the trade policy.

> The main policy measures consisted of improving the tariff structure, reducing the number of items in the banned and restricted lists, creating a better set of export incentives and streamlining import licensing requirements. The maximum ad valorem duty rate on all imports, with the exception for luxury cars and alcoholic beverages, was reduced from a range of 150%–225% to 125%. This change affected close to 400 items, mostly consumer goods. In conjunction with this measure, the authorities reduced the average level and narrowed the dispersion of duty rates on imported raw materials, which now range from 20 to 50% ad valorem. Greater rationalization of the tariff

structure was also accomplished by consolidating the duty rates on all items with similar degree of processing within a narrow range and by adopting graduated rates on most imports according to the stage or processing. In all, tariff rates were decreased for a total of 1134 items and increased for 462 items, out of a total of more than 3200 tariff lines. The improvement in the dispersion of the duty rates, particularly for imported inputs not produced in Pakistan, should help to spur industrial activity and economic growth. Similar positive effects should result from the decision to reduce the number of commodities whose import were previously prohibited or restricted.[46]

Under the first major Structural Adjustment Programme begun in 1988, the government of Pakistan was committed to making extensive changes in its trade regime. The major components of the agreement with the IMF which related to foreign trade were as follows:

> The emphasis is on the removal of non-tariff barriers (NTBs) and their replacement by tariffs, with the objective of reducing the number of banned commodity categories from about 400 to 80 by FY91 [1990/1], leaving only those on account of religion, security, reciprocity, and international agreements. Also on the import side, the adjustment program contains tariff measures as well, including the reduction of the maximum tariff to 125% in FY89 and further to 100% by FY91, tariff alterations aimed at establishing some escalation with the degree of processing, and gradual removal of most tariff exemptions and concessions, except the duty drawbacks afforded to exports and exemptions granted to some key industries. Phasing out tariff exemptions will help the resource

mobilization effort and also constitute an important step in the process of streamlining the tariff structure. On the export side, the adjustment program continues to emphasize export promotion by replacing the previous uniform income tax rebate system with a graduated one that encourages higher valued exports, by permitting Export Houses to retain a small part (5%) of their foreign exchange earnings, and by allowing the private sector a greater involvement in exporting rice and cotton.[47]

By 1993 a number of important steps based on the Structural Adjustment Programme had been taken. The maximum tariff had been reduced from 225 per cent in 1988 to 90 per cent at the end of the adjustment programme. In March 1991, import licensing had been abolished except for commodities on the negative list, while this list of banned and restricted imports was cut down.

One of the more important policies undertaken by the government was initiated in February 1991, when resident Pakistanis were allowed to open foreign currency deposit (FCD) accounts, which were previously allowed only to foreigners and non-resident Pakistanis. The procedure for opening such FCD accounts was greatly liberalized and banks paid higher interest rates on these deposits than LIBOR.[48] Although the rupee was not fully convertible, no questions were asked about the source of funds. Foreign currency

deposits increased from $1.6 billion in June 1988 to $2.3 billion in February 1991, and to $3.7 billion in June 1992, rising to more than $8.5 billion in August 1996 (see Table 9.14). Of the last amount, 37 per cent was held by Pakistani residents.[49] The World Bank believes that since 1990 'the foreign exchange inflows into FCDs have significantly helped meet Pakistan's external financing requirements. In FY92 new inflows into FCDs were almost as large (about 75%) as Pakistan's total capital account balance. *However, the reliance on FCDs has increased Pakistan's vulnerability to external shocks*, in particular in view of the low reserve cover.'[50]

At the end of the 1988 Structural Adjustment Programme, the World Bank suggested that the government of Pakistan should take the trade policy measures further, especially with reference to the trade taxation regime. These measures included:

(i) removal of all remaining non-tariff barriers to imports, except those in force for health, safety, and religious reasons; (ii) removal of import tax exemptions and partial concessions, except to exporters; and conversion of specific duties into ad valorem duties; (iii) reduction of the range of customs duty rates with a maximum rate of 30% and a minimum rate of 10% (with only 3 rates, 10% for raw materials, 20% for intermediates, 30% for finished consumer goods); (iv) removal of Iqra and the license fee; (v) elimination of

Table 9.14
Foreign currency deposits, 1980–1996 (000$)

Month and year (end month)	Non-residents					Residents	Total
	Foreign banks (institutions)	Individuals	Total	NBFIs	Total		
June 1980	–	115.25	115.25	–	115.25	–	115.25
June 1981	–	201.85	201.85	–	201.85	–	201.85
June 1982	–	259.51	259.51	–	259.51	–	259.51
June 1983	–	550.71	550.71	–	550.71	–	550.71
June 1984	–	638.27	638.27	–	638.27	–	638.27
June 1985	–	597.63	597.63	–	597.63	–	597.63
June 1986	480.00	614.82	1,094.82	–	1,094.82	–	1,094.82
June 1987	839.42	654.38	1,493.80	–	1,493.80	–	1,493.80
June 1988	893.40	755,34	1,648.74	–	1,648.74	–	1,648.74
June 1989	911.70	938.00	1,849.70	–	1,849.70	–	1,849.70
June 1990	1,088.46	1,027.49	2,115.95	–	2,115.95	–	2,115.95
June 1991	950.78	1,251.95	2,202.73	–	2,202.73	389.46	2,592.19
June 1992	905.74	1,083.51	1,989.25	–	1,989.25	1,706.01	3,696.26
June 1993	864.45	1,186.04	2,050.49	177.00	2,227.49	2,050.49	4,477.90
June 1994	1,058.94	1,404.08	2,463.02	475.14	2,920.16	3,002.44	5,922.60
June 1995	1,198.82	1,324.81	2,523.63	667.54	3,191.17	3,383.82	6,574.99
Sept. 1995	1,135.06	1,279.99	2,415.05	679.17	3,094.22	3,517.01	6,611.23
Oct. 1995	1,037.59	1,311.89	2,349.48	669.65	3,019.13	3,604.53	6,623.66
Nov. 1995	933,38	1,311.20	2,244.58	656.32	2,900.90	3,427.65	6,328.55
Dec. 1995	1,514.57	1,398.59	2,913.16	683.69	3,596.85	3,536.59	7.133.44
Jan. 1996	1,591.94	1,457.83	3,049.77	1,108.41	4,158.18	4,146.98	8,305.16
June 1996	1,532.55	1,382.32	2,914.87	1,182.29	4,097.16	4,314.64	8,411.80
Aug. 1996	1,517.64	1,398.39	2,916.03	1,192.02	4,108.05	4,407.47	8,515.52

Source: State Bank of Pakistan.

export taxes; and (vi) extension of the coverage of the sales tax to imports of all manufactured goods, concurrently with the removal of exemptions from sales tax granted to domestically produced manufactures, and elimination of any inequality in the treatment of domestically produced and imported goods with regard to excise duties. Finally, further actions are also needed to reform the existing deletion programs (related to domestic content requirements) and to enhance the effectiveness of export promotion schemes aimed at putting exporters on a 'duty-free basis' while at the same time reviewing the cost effectiveness of other export incentives such as the income tax rebates. Such a program should be accompanied by continued active and timely use of the exchange rate policy.[51]

In light of these and other recommendations, the government in 1993 announced a new trade reform package, the main features of which were as follows:

1. Maximum tariff levels will be set at only 35 or 50 per cent with six slabs of 10, 15, 25, 35, 45 and 50 per cent. Existing tariff rates will apply to motor vehicles, alcoholic beverages, POL, wheat, fertilizers, pesticides and life-saving drugs.
2. Tariff reduction will be phased in gradually over a three-year period.
3. Many concessions and exemptions present in the existing tariff regime will be withdrawn gradually.
4. Tariff structure will represent a cascading of nominal tariffs with progressive stages of manufacturing. Locally produced goods will be subjected to higher tariff rates compared to goods not produced domestically.
5. Tariffs on machinery and equipment will be 10 per cent unless this machinery is produced locally.
6. High-priority domestic industries (such as engineering and chemicals) will receive

nominal protection of 50 per cent.
7. Raw materials and intermediate goods predominantly used in the production of exports would be subjected to zero rate of duty.
8. Existing import licence fee, iqra surcharge and flood relief surcharge will be merged with the statutory tariff rates.[52]

The importance of the trade regime, and imports in particular, can be gauged from the fact that 54 per cent of total federal government revenue in 1992/3 originated from import taxes. Hence, any attempt to change the tariff regime would also have significant effects on revenue generation.

Riaz Riazuddin evaluates this policy and in Table 9.15 shows the rate-wise value of imports and import duties for the fiscal year 1991/2. He shows that as much as 45 per cent of total imports are no longer subject to any duty. And although the statutory duty rates range from 0 to 435 per cent, 'the effective rate of duty which is the proportion of actual duty collection to the value of imports subjected to duty is only 33 per cent'.[53] The table also shows that as much as 61 per cent of collection is obtained from the statutory duty range of 40–90 per cent, while duty rates of below and above this range contribute only 16 per cent of the collection.

For Riazuddin, 'there is a likelihood that lower tariffs in the short run can cause balance of payment difficulties as well as displacement costs. The phased reduction of tariffs and gradual withdrawal of exemptions is likely to lessen these costs.'[54] These suggestions are quite different to those proposed by the World Bank, which believes that 'with regard to the phasing of the proposed reforms package, international experience *shows that a speedy process is feasible and has strong advantages*'.[55] The World Bank cites Mexico's trade reform programme of 1985–9 as a good example of this approach, where the maximum tariff rate was reduced from 100 per cent to just 20 per cent within two years. Given Mexico's geographical and political importance with respect to the USA, and the fact that it is one of the three states along with the USA and Canada which form the North American Free Trade Association (NAFTA), the comparison with Pakistan

Table 9.15
Rate-wise value of imports and duties, 1991/2

Statutory rate of duty	Total import value	Duty-free imports	Dutiable imports	Import duty	Effective rate of duty
Zero to 40%	44,843	32,391	12,425	2,600	21
40% to 90%	67,771	20,187	47,584	19,593	41
90% to 435%	4,023	813	3,210	2,307	72
Specific	54,955	23,977	30,978	6,220	20
	171,592	77,368	94,224	30,720	33
Share in total import value	100%	45%	55%	18%	–

Note: Figures are for Custom House Karachi, representing 85 per cent of Pakistan's total import duty collection.
Source: Central Board of Revenue, *Yearbook 1991–92*, Islamabad, 1992, p. 330; Riazuddin, Riaz, 'An Evaluation of Trade Policy', *Pakistan Journal of Applied Economics*, vol. X, nos 1 and 2, 1994, p. 119.

may seem a little irrelevant. Moreover, the crash of the Mexican economy in December 1994 has also been blamed on the liberalization programme followed by its government, and other countries would be wiser to learn from Mexico's mistakes rather than follow its example (see also Chapter 15). (The international trade environment has changed since the formation of the World Trade Organization in 1995. Repercussions for Pakistan are discussed in Appendix 9.1.)

9.3 The Debate Over Efficiency and the Trade Regime

Asad Sayeed writes that 'protection through tariffs, quotas and exchange rate distortions is deemed to distort allocative efficiency and hence reduce growth and productivity of the economy over time'.[56] We will now examine this claim with respect to trade policy in Pakistan, especially in the 1980s. (Although some of the discussion from section 8.6 is repeated here, this present section focuses more on trade-related inefficiencies and the impact on the effective exchange rate.)

With respect to the rapid industrialization and high growth of exports in the 1960s, John Adams and Sabiha Iqbal summarize the issues as follows: 'Pakistan followed a highly protective industrial policy to encourage import substitution. Incentives were provided in the form of a highly graduated tariff structure, import licensing and quantitative restrictions on imports. At the same time, elaborate stimuli were provided to encourage the export of manufactured goods.'[57] Asad Sayeed argues that 'the incentives provided by the tariff structure have been the central bone of contention in discussions about efficiency of the industrial sector in the 1960s'[58] And the result, for John Adams and Sabiha Iqbal as for so many others before them (see section 8.6 in the previous chapter), was as follows:

> Although the profusion of inducements encouraged the growth of the output and exports of the manufacturing sector, they generated inefficient resource use in industry and created a bias against exports of agricultural goods. Within the manufacturing sector resources were often attracted to high-cost industries dependent upon imported inputs. Guisinger and Lewis estimated effective rates of protection for thirty industries and found negative value-added for three cases, implying that the world market value of material inputs exceeded the value of output. Others were also critical of the import-substitution policy. Pakistan's industries were using processes which were economically inefficient, when judged by world market prices for inputs and output. Since domestic prices had become distorted by tariffs, quantitative restrictions, and multiple exchange rates, economically inefficient choices of processes and techniques by private businessmen became real possibilities. In effect, producers could purchase capital inputs at well below the opportunity cost to the economy since they were direct licensees

for imported goods. An incentive was thereby created to use excessively capital-intensive techniques. Khan found that the capital–labour ratio in many industries in Pakistan was higher than in countries where labour was far less abundant.[59]

We have argued in section 8.6 that almost all these allegations were proven to be incorrect by scholars once they studied the data in much greater detail. However, even today the same sort of criticism continues to be launched of the industrial policy pursued in Pakistan.

In recent years, the World Bank and the IMF have become the greatest champions of free trade in Pakistan and all across the globe. They castigate countries like Pakistan for maintaining tariffs, restrictions and non-tariff barriers, and, in general, an import-substituting regime. The World Bank and the IMF argue that such import-substituting policies have an anti-export bias and cause allocative inefficiencies. Their recommendations include a drastic cut in tariffs, the removal of all non-tariff barriers, and constant devaluation. They recommend a 'liberalized', 'neutral' trade regime based on the 'rationalization' of the tariff structure, with lower average tariff rates and the elimination of exemptions. For them, not to take these comprehensive steps would result in continued inefficiency.

The World Bank, in its analysis of the trade regime in Pakistan, argues that despite the very extensive and far-reaching changes that have been made since the early 1980s, 'the changes have not been substantial enough to establish a more neutral trade regime'.[60] The continued presence of non-tariff barriers is a problem because they 'generate more serious distortions, with greater resource allocation inefficiencies, than direct price protection obtained through tariffs'.[61] Moreover, they create a host of other inefficiencies, as follows:

> As is well known, import bans/restrictions break the link between domestic and international relative prices, pushing the economy further away from resource allocation patterns consistent with the country's comparative advantage. NTBs [non-tariff barriers] work to create monopolies and oligopolies through the elimination of foreign competition in industries where scale economies are important. Government attempts to regulate and control such markets rarely achieve the level of efficiency generated by the spur of foreign competition. In other industries where the domestic market is too small to support production at a minimum efficient scale, NTBs, combined with existing investment sanctioning procedures, allow several firms to operate profitably in the small domestic market with no pressure to improve their cost competitiveness. Examples of fragmentation of production are evident in some of Pakistan's manufacturing industries, such as transport equipment, polyester yarn, electrical machinery and household appliances.[62]

The World Bank very strongly recommends the replacement of non-tariff barriers by tariffs, as the latter form of protection for domestic industry is deemed to be much less inefficient. However, due to the high tariff rates and dispersion of the tariffs, the structure is still considered to be highly inefficient and protectionist. Summarizing the main features of the trade regime in the late 1980s, with its numerous faults and resulting distortions, the World Bank argues that

> Pakistan's import regime provides high and extremely uneven levels of protection afforded to various domestic industries, with many commodities benefiting from almost absolute protection (subject to the fact that smuggling restricts these levels). Due to exemptions, baggage allowances and extensive smuggling, some products enjoy lower nominal protection than those implied by the statutory tariff rates. This combination of heavy protection and extensive exemptions and import leakages (formal and informal) has fostered an inconsistent structure of protection with indeterminate and, perhaps, continuously changing effects on the incentives for industrial investments. As a result, socially suboptimal production and investment decisions in terms of production mix, diversification and plant scale are being undertaken while other economic opportunities are foregone. Finally, as a result of the complexity and diverse effects of various elements of the protective structure, it is very difficult for the Government to determine the effects of the present import regime and thus administer the protective system in a way that supports Pakistan's economic objectives.[63]

While the above quote finds faults with the trade regime on the import side, the export side is also not spared. The World Bank believes that the trade regime has a strong anti-export bias: 'The fundamental problem is that Pakistan's export growth prospects are being adversely affected by the remaining import-substituting bias of the trade regime.'[64] This anti-export bias is shown using estimates for effective exchange rates for imports and exports and their ratios (Table 9.16). The EER (effective exchange rate) ratios in the table indicates neutrality if the ratio is 1, and a bias towards import substitution and against export promotion, as is actually revealed by the table, when the ratio is greater than 1. The table shows that the import substitution bias has increased over time (row 4A), and that there is a bias against primary agricultural exports (row 4C). The final conclusion: 'both the qualitative and quantitative evidence suggests that Pakistan's trade regime is still biased in favour of import-substituting production',[65] and hence is inefficient.

Just as in the 1970s there was a strong bombardment of 'evidence' and analysis that the government in the 1960s had got its industrial and trade policies all wrong, with the result that it was claimed that there was huge inefficiency in the industrial sector, so in the 1980s and 1990s the World Bank and the IMF have taken it upon themselves to expose the persistent perceived inefficiencies in Pakistan's trade and industrial regime. However, unlike the scholars who examined Pakistan's trade and industrial structure in the 1960s and found inefficiencies, the World Bank and the IMF in the 1980s and 1990s are in a position where they can not just recommend, but impose, alternatives. Clearly, the Structural Adjustment Programmes since 1988 are evidence of that. However, even in the 1970s and later, there were a group of scholars who showed that much of what was considered to be conventional wisdom was, in fact, pure myth, and that the extent of inefficiency in the industrial structure in the 1960s was grossly exaggerated (see section 8.6 in Chapter 8). It is possible, then, that as further independent research is conducted on the trade and industrial regime of the 1980s, much of the evidence, 'both qualitative and quantitative', will be exposed as incorrect and biased. One recent study has done just that.

The work by Asad Sayeed has shown that virtually every study and analysis conducted on the manufacturing sector in Pakistan in the 1980s argues that protection through tariffs, quotas, or exchange rate distortions affects allocative efficiency negatively and, consequently, reduces growth over time. There seems to be almost an identical repeat of the situation prevalent in the 1970s at the end of the Ayub regime, when virtually every study and analysis conducted on the manufacturing sector argued that the Ayub regime was highly inefficient. Just as the high-growth regime of Ayub Khan was labelled as inefficient, so the high-growth Zia regime been put in the same category.[66]

Asad Sayeed has taken great pains to show that much of what has been suggested about the consequences of the trade regime under Zia is incorrect. Although Pakistan had the highest average tariff rates compared with other developing countries in 1986, *there was no direct relationship with the growth performance of the manufacturing sector* – in other words, countries with low tariffs do not necessarily have high growth, and vice versa.[67] The World Bank has also held Pakistan's high tariff dispersion to be a cause of inefficiency in the industrial sector, yet it has been shown that 'a high dispersion of tariffs was central to Taiwan's successful trade regime'.[68] Moreover, it has been seen that countries with the highest dispersion in tariffs may actually have high growth rates in manufacturing.

Sayeed's study also questions the overemphasis on showing the causality between tariffs and growth, and shows that actually 'productivity growth, or any other measure of efficiency, therefore, is more critically determined by other policies and the political economy of the sector'[69] and tariffs cannot be singled out as the causal factor. The empirical and conceptual problems that effective rates of protection (a central component of perceived inefficiency in the industrial sector) had in the scholarship of researchers in the 1970s still persist, and Asad Sayeed finds that there are serious difficulties in their calculation and use. He very strongly rejects the claims made by the World Bank that Pakistan's import policy has resulted in inefficiency in industrial production. He says 'that the excessive importance given to the tariff and non-tariff barriers is unwarranted. Firstly, there is no definite conclusion that can be drawn about efficiency reducing elements from the import regime. Secondly, no

Table 9.16
Effective exchange rates for exports and imports, and their ratio

	1980/1	1984/5	1986/7[ad]
1 **Nominal exchange rate (Rs/$) – period averages**	9.90	15.15	17.00
2 **EERs for imports**[a]			
A All imports			
a) Based on statutory import levies (EERm)	19.27	30.25	33.35
b) Based on actual import taxes (EERm2)	15.74	25.90	n.a.
B Import EER by commodity categories:			
a) Consumer goods			
EERm1	25.74	40.15	40.03
EERm2	19.01	27.30	n.a.
b) Raw materials for consumer goods			
EERm1			
EERm2	15.92	30.75	n.a.
c) Raw materials for capital goods			
EERm1			
EERm2	15.25	23.76	n.a.
d) Capital goods			
EERm1	18.13	28.50	30.60
EERm2	14.81	24.09	n.a.
e) Textile products			
EERm1	24.95	38.94	38.76
EERm2	n.a.	n.a.	n.a.
3 **EERs for exports**[b]			
A All exports (EERx)	11.02	17.18	17.92
B Export EERs by commodity categories[c]			
a) Raw cotton	8.91	13.64	15.50
b) Rice	9.90	15.15	17.00
c) Cotton yarn	11.66	16.45	17.19
d) Cotton cloth	11.75	17.75	18.22
e) Leather products	10.49	16.66	18.69
f) Carpets	10.99	18.50	18.63
g) Ready-made garments	16.25	23.79	25.00
4 **EER ratios**			
A EERm1/EERx	1.75	1.76	1.86
B EERm2/EERx	1.43	1.51	n.a.
C (EERx for manufactured exports/EERx for primary agr. exports)	1.25	1.27	1.21

[a] Customs duties, sales tax, and surcharges are included in the calculations. Due to unavailability of information on domestic and international prices, no attempt was made to take scarcity premiums resulting from non-tariff barriers into account.
[b] Duty and tax drawbacks, compensatory rebates (until mid-1986), and the subsidy components of concessionary export credited and included in the calculations.
[c] Further disaggregation was not possible because of lack of detailed data.
[d] July–November period.
Source: World Bank, *Pakistan: Growth Through Adjustment*, Report No. 7118-Pak, Washington, 1988, p. 74.

major inconsistency between the tariff regime and the structure of tariff exemptions and non-tariff barriers was identified.'[70]

One of the major allegations against the Ayub regime was that, since there were inefficiencies in the nature of protection, there was too much emphasis on import substitution at the expense of exports. This was seen to be incorrect, for there was ample growth and diversification of exports under Ayub, despite inefficiencies and an anti-export bias. The same allegations that the trade regime of the 1980s

was anti-export based are equally untrue, for Pakistan's aggregate export growth in this period was a healthy 9 per cent per annum. While there are numerous problems with Pakistan's export structure, especially that it has such a narrow base, that it is dependent on one commodity – cotton – and that the textile sector has been in a crisis in recent years, the annual growth of exports has, nevertheless, been quite impressive. Clearly, there is a need to diversify into more value-added products within the textile sector, and in other sectors, but it would seem to be a little harsh to draw the conclusion, as the World Bank does, that Pakistan has had an anti-export bias.

The barrage of criticism of the industrial and trade policies of the Ayub regime was never articulated into policy, for Ayub was thrown out and replaced by a regime which had different priorities. Moreover, those who found fault with the policies were not in a position to implement alternatives. It was another matter that much of the analysis was itself found to be faulty later on. The difference is that the analysis and evidence that is currently invoked to identify the extent of inefficiency in the trade regime also makes recommendations that can actually be translated into policy. It is too soon for studies to emerge, as they did earlier, to examine in detail the claims made that industry was indeed inefficient. However, even if such evidence does emerge, it may be a little late to reverse the policies currently being advocated and implemented.

9.4   The Exchange Rate

The exchange rate has played a critical role in the trade regime and the process of industrialization in Pakistan on more than a few occasions. As early as 1949, a conscious decision by the government of the day not to revise its exchange rate downwards, i.e. devalue, in line with the devaluation of the pound sterling by about 37 per cent, caused a great deal of uproar and eventually had serious, albeit positive, repercussions for the economy of the country (see Chapter 6 and section 9.2 above). The decision taken by the government was so important that it has become known as the 'Non-Devaluation' decision. While the young government of Pakistan faced a serious crisis on the exchange rate front so early in its tenure, which added to numerous other crises of that era, the role that the exchange rate has played throughout the nearly fifty years of Pakistan's existence is very significant indeed. This section will highlight some of the features of the foreign exchange regime in Pakistan.

For nearly thirty-five years, Pakistan maintained a fixed-peg regime for its exchange rate. The rupee was first linked to the pound sterling in the early years after 1947, and Pakistan was a member of the sterling area. Later, as the USA became more dominant across the globe, and as Pakistan's political fortunes became more aligned with those of the USA, the US dollar became the key currency with respect to the Pakistani rupee, as it did with most other currencies.

Pakistan did not devalue in 1949 when other countries linked to the pound sterling followed the fate of the pound and devalued; nor did it devalue in 1952, following the Korean War boom, once the post-boom recession had set in and foreign exchange was scarce. Instead, Pakistan pursued import controls so that imports could be regulated and the foreign exchange crisis managed. The government was criticized on both counts: for not devaluing and for imposing controls and tariffs on the free import of goods. Such controls were considered to be inefficient in attracting scarce resources, and a more market-friendly mechanism was considered to be more efficient. Finally, the first devaluation

took place in June 1955, when the rupee was devalued by 30 per cent with respect to the pound sterling in order to bring it in line with other trading countries.

For the next seventeen years, the official, nominal exchange rate of the rupee was fixed at Rs4.76 to one US dollar. However, as far as almost all analysts are concerned, the rupee was, for most of those seventeen years, grossly overvalued (see sections 8.6 and 9.3). Not only was the rupee overvalued, but a system of multiple exchange rates is said to have undermined all semblance of efficiency normally attributed to a reliable and correct exchange rate value. Gustav Papanek shows how the official Pakistani exchange rate was, in a real sense, a multiple exchange rate:

> Some exporters faced an effective rate of 8 rupees to the dollar, if their commodities had been assigned 40 per cent vouchers, all of which could be sold in the open market. At the other extreme, exporters who received no vouchers and export duties faced an effective rate of less than 4.7 rupees to the dollar ...[71]

> ... The importer who could get a regular import license paid the official exchange rate (4.7 rupees to the dollar). The importer who had to buy a bonus voucher paid more than twice that amount (as much as 12 rupees to the dollar). Finally the importer who bought a voucher restricted to the import of raw materials or investment goods, could pay yet a third rate, somewhere between the other two.[72]

The entire Ayub period, despite the substantial success related to the growth rate and exports, was criticized for maintaining multiple exchange rates and an overvalued rupee. When Zulfiqar Ali Bhutto took over after the elections, much of the old order was drastically changed and the rupee was devalued by 58 per cent.

Not only did the rupee find a new value of Rs11 to the US dollar, but the entire system of multiple exchange rates and the Bonus Voucher Scheme was done away with. Viqar Ahmed and Rashid Amjad argue that 'the substantial net devaluation of the rupee removed at one stroke the subsidy the industrialists had received in the earlier period because of the overvalued exchange rate'.[73] While earlier in 1949, 1952, and 1967 the governments had been criticized for *not* devaluing, in 1972 the government was criticized *for* devaluation and for the extent of the devaluation. The arguments which criticized the devaluation decision were as follows:

a) devaluation on such a high scale could have been justified if domestic production of exportable goods could also be increased rapidly which was doubtful at that particular time due to the unsettled environment created by the loss of East Pakistan;

b) devaluation increased the cost of investment [involving foreign exchange] by about 131 per cent (which was the increase in the value of the dollar in terms of the Pakistan Rupee);

c) the internal price structure was adversely

affected since devaluation raised the overall cost structure and thus accelerated the inflationary pressures on the economy.[74]

Hence, the nominal exchange rate of the Pakistani rupee was changed by the government only twice during the period 1947–82, once by 30 per cent in 1956, and then by 58 per cent in 1972. In February 1973, the US dollar was devalued by 10 per cent and hence the Pakistani rupee was revalued by 10 per cent to Rs9.90 per dollar, the official rate which continued until January 1982. Until then, the government had maintained a fixed-peg exchange rate, needing to intervene only twice. The rupee/dollar exchange rate was fixed, and the Pakistani rupee's fortunes were inextricably linked to those of the dollar (see Box 9.4). When the dollar appreciated, so did Pakistan's currency with respect to its numerous other trading partners. Hence, Pakistan's economy was tied to the prospects of an economy sixty times its size. While alignment in the political sphere between Pakistan and the USA had progressed a great deal, this linking of the currencies was perhaps taking things a bit too far.

On the recommendations of the IMF, the old system of pegging the rupee was replaced by a flexible exchange rate mechanism, whereby the government of Pakistan – actually the State Bank of Pakistan, to be more precise – sets a rate for the Pakistani rupee based on a weighted average of the currencies of Pakistan's major trading partners. After 1982, the US dollar no longer retained its unique status as the determinant of the rate of the Pakistani rupee, but became one of many in the basket of currencies that collectively determine that rate. This mechanism of determining the exchange rate for the Pakistani rupee vis-à-vis other currencies, established in 1982, is still followed today. However, the very controlled nature of the exchange rate market in the 1980s has given way to a more open market in the 1990s (see Box 9.5). Nevertheless, what needs to be emphasized is that the official value of the rupee is determined not by the market, but by State Bank directive. The 'market' rate, which is indeed determined by the supply and demand for currencies, is an unofficial kerb rate and not the official exchange rate.

From Rs4.76 to one dollar in April 1972 to Rs9.90 for a period of nine years, once the rupee was allowed a managed float, its value depreciated by more than 230 per cent between January 1982 and June 1996 (see Table 9.17). Figure 9.5 shows the annual depreciation for each year, ranging from a minimum of 2.3 per cent in 1994/5 to 28.28 per cent in the very first year. Table 9.18 gives recent trends of the rupee/dollar rate, where since 1993, three interventions (devaluations) have taken place. For much of the 1980s the fall in the value of the rupee was caused by the crawling peg or floating exchange rate, under which the State Bank of Pakistan nominally depreciated the rupee by a few paisas whenever needed. Since 1993 these depreciations – or technical adjustments as the State Bank calls them – have been supplemented by direct devaluation.

How much devaluation is enough? What should be the 'correct' rate for the rupee/dollar? Many analysts feel that the Pakistani rupee has always been and continues to be overvalued, and hence Pakistan's exports are overpriced and

Table 9.17
Value and depreciation of the rupee since April 1972

	April 1972	May 1972	Feb. 1973–Jan. 1982	1982/3	1983/4	1984/5	1985/6	1986/7	1987/8	1988/9	1989/90	1990/1	1991/2	1992/3	1993/4	1994/5	1995/6
Rupees to one dollar	4.76	11.0	9.90	12.70	13.48	15.15	16.14	17.18	17.60	19.22	21.45	22.42	24.84	25.96	30.16	30.85	33.25
% change each year	–	–	–	28.28	6.10	12.39	6.50	6.40	2.40	9.20	11.60	4.50	10.80	4.50	16.20	2.30	7.80
% change since 1982 when managed float began	–	–	–	28.28	36.20	53.00	63.00	73.50	77.80	94.10	116.70	126.50	150.90	162.20	204.60	211.60	235.90

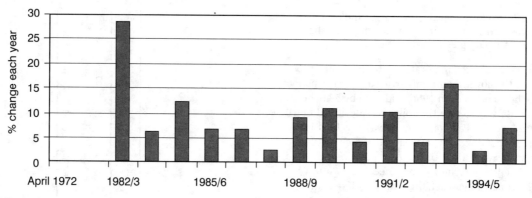

Figure 9.5
Annual depreciation of the rupee (w.r.t. US dollar) (%)

Table 9.18
Recent government interventions in the rupee-dollar rate

	7.1.93	After the devaluation on 15.7.93 and 22.7.93 by 9.5%	6.1.94	5.1.95	After the 26.10.95 devaluation by 7.5%	4.1.96	After the 10.9.96 devaluation by 3.79%
Rupees to one dollar	25.85	29.85	30.19	30.80	34.25	35.25	36.97
Annual change (%)	–	–	16.79	2.00	–	14.40	–

uncompetitive compared to its competitors. They would prefer to see a substantial devaluation of the rupee at frequent intervals. Different reasons are given for this constant adjustment, some quite irresponsible (see Appendix 9.3). Nevertheless, despite the argument made repeatedly that Pakistan's exports are inelastic (i.e. their quantity will not rise substantially even if there were some devaluation: see the first article in Appendix 9.3), it is probable that the rupee will continuously lose value against foreign currencies. This may not be the best way to increase exports. Structural factors, including better-quality products, credit, and infrastructure, may be the key with which Pakistan can open the door to more and better exports. The net result of a falling rupee is likely to be highly negative.

9.5 Summary and Further Reading

9.5.1 Summary

Pakistan's trade pattern has changed dramatically since 1947. From being a primary goods exporter, Pakistan now exports primarily manufactured and semi-manufactured commodities. However, its exports are still critically dependent on cotton, which contributes as much as 60 per cent to exports. From about 11 per cent of GDP in 1947, exports and imports together now amount to around 35 per cent of GDP. Remittances have played an important role in Pakistan's economy since the late 1970s, and once provided as much as 10 per cent of GDP; their role has since diminished, and they now account for around 3 per cent of GDP.

The rupee has depreciated markedly in the last seventeen years, since the exchange rate was Rs9.9 to one US dollar. Since it was allowed a managed float, the annual devaluation of the rupee has been, on average, 8 per cent a year, fluctuating between 2 per cent in one year, and as much as 16 or 17 per cent in another year. Given the nature of Pakistan's macro economy, its inflation rate, fiscal deficit, and adherence to the Structural Adjustment Programme, one can expect a continuous drift in the value of the Pakistani rupee.

Just as the industrial policy of the early years was maligned for causing inefficiencies in the economy, so too was the trade policy. The same reasons were given for distortions being caused in the structure of the economy by trade policy, as were alleged to have resulted from industrial policy. However, this chapter, looking at the work of some scholars, has argued that many of the so-called distortions had export-enhancing impacts, and that these measures were productive. The Bonus Voucher Scheme of the 1960s, in particular, was singled out as a mechanism that caused serious distortions in the economy. However, as this chapter has shown, the scheme was conducive to promoting industrialization and exports.

Pakistan's trade pattern and trade policy have continuously been moving towards fewer and fewer controls, lower tariffs, and more openness. Non-tariff barriers have been replaced by tariffs, and tariff rates have come tumbling down. More

BOX 9.5
The foreign exchange market

In previous years, there was no foreign exchange 'market', and the State Bank of Pakistan rationed foreign currency. All that has now changed, and foreign currency can now be purchased openly in the market.

Foreign exchange is bought and sold in Pakistan in two markets – the official market and the parallel market. In the official market, the State Bank of Pakistan (SBP) announces every morning rates at which it stands ready to buy or sell foreign currency to authorized dealers, which, in turn, transact with customers at a specified spread. Purchases and sales of foreign currency for trade transactions are required to take place through the official market. Some capital account transactions, such as repatriable foreign currency portfolio flows, also go through the official market. In addition, banks are required to turn over foreign exchange held in foreign currency accounts to SBP at the official exchange rate, and may buy the foreign currency back when the deposit matures or is withdrawn.

All other transactions take place on the parallel market, which consists of money changers licensed by the SBP. Transactions on this market are not taxed, nor are identities of the transactors recorded. The money changers set exchange rates to equilibrate market supply and demand, thereby determining the size of the premium that foreign exchange on the parallel market commands over the official rate.

The parallel foreign exchange market in Pakistan can provide potentially useful information about the likely course of future official exchange rate adjustments by the SBP. In principle, an increase in the parallel market premium should reflect market expectations that the rupee is misaligned, presumably because reserves have dwindled or because inflation has eroded external competitiveness. In either event, a devaluation would be required to ease the economy's external adjustment.

Actual daily data from the parallel market, however, suggest that, at least in recent months, the premium does not generally anticipate changes in the official rate. Indeed, the premium tends to widen immediately *after* official exchange rate adjustments by the SBP. If, following some adjustments, the official rate is held fixed for some time, the premium tends to return to its trend level. Thus, it appears that rather than responding to economic fundamentals, the parallel foreign exchange market premium responds to exchange rate moves by the SBP in the short run.

As an alternative to selling foreign exchange on the parallel market, individuals may purchase Foreign Exchange Bearer Certificates (FEBCs) from commercial banks. FEBCs, though purchased with foreign exchange, are rupee-denominated obligations of the Government of Pakistan, and pay a rupee return. The certificates, the face value of which is determined at the official spot rate when purchased, may be encashed at any time in either rupees or foreign currency. If the bearer of the FEBC chooses to encash in foreign currency, the official spot exchange rate prevailing at the time of encashment is applied. The FEBC is a bearer certificate, and the purchaser is not required to declare the source of foreign exchange at the time of purchase.

There also exists a secondary market for FEBCs, in which the certificates are bought and sold for a premium over their face value. Arbitrage between the parallel foreign exchange market and this secondary market equates the premia associated with foreign exchange and FEBCs.

Finally, there also exists a forward market for foreign exchange. Authorized commercial banks are allowed to quote forward buy and sell rates of foreign currency in rupees for transactions that would go through the official market. While these rates are set to equate supply and demand at the various maturities, they do not necessarily reflect true market forces since market players are not allowed to take positions except to offset foreign currency receipts or payments for trade transactions.

Source: ABN AMRO Economic Bulletin, *The Exchange Rate*, vol. 1, no. 7, Special Issue, Economics Department, ABN AMRO Bank NV – Pakistan, 1995, September/October.

recently, as per the agreement with the IMF and the World Bank under the Structural Adjustment Programme, a 'liberal' import policy has been pursued, with lower tariff rates and fewer tariff slabs, along with a persistent 'readjustment' of the Pakistani rupee. Despite the substantial devaluation that has taken place, Pakistan's exports have not responded as one would have hoped.

Export-led growth is considered to be a key ingredient in economic development as the much-cited East Asian Miracle suggests. However, the important factor overlooked by Pakistan's policy makers is that supply-side incentives – prices, inputs, tax incentives, etc. – do not help exports as much as removing structural weaknesses. Quality control, the provision of infrastructure like communications and energy, and direct incentives to exporters, are all necessary to ensure that exports increase to an extent where they contribute extensively to economic development. To do that, Pakistan requires an export bias in policy, a fact that has been ignored for most years.

9.5.2   Further Reading

Since industrialization and trade are so closely linked, many of the references given in Chapters 6–8 should also be studied to understand how trade influenced industrialization in Pakistan. The one book in recent years on Pakistan's trade is that by John Adams and Sabiha Iqbal, *Export Politics and Economic Development in Pakistan*, Vanguard, Lahore, 1987; see also Viqar Ahmed and Rashid Amjad's *The Management of Pakistan's Economy, 1947–82*, Oxford University Press, Karachi, 1984. Some references in the Notes will also be useful for additional reading on trade.

Appendix 9.1

The World Trade Organization

The following is an edited extract from a report by the Export Promotion Bureau in 1995.

It all began in the Latin American resort town of Punta del Este, Uruguay. And it seemingly ended in Marrakesh in April 1994. *Seemingly*, because now is the real beginning of the outcome of the talks that commenced in Uruguay in 1986.

On January 1 1995, a new organization came into existence – the World Trade Organization (WTO). This new organization replaces the General Agreement on Tariffs and Trade (GATT) and will supervise and oversee the most ambitious global trade accord ever.

What is this GATT accord and how is this likely to affect Pakistan's exports?

The Uruguay round of trade talks ended with the signing of an accord that is about 500 pages long which contains resolutions that affect a wide variety of subjects both directly and indirectly.

The signing of this accord could allow Citibank to open more branches in Pakistan. It could result in the closing up of thousands of factories across the country because of accusations of environmental pollution. It could reverse our efforts to make Pakistanis computer literate. It could threaten our carpet exports because of social dumping. It could rake in profits for our garment and footwear exporters. The list goes on.

But like all agreements, the WTO Agreement has its loopholes and provisos, its qualifications and conditions and its *Schedule* of *Commitment* which can help protect infant industries and restrict market access.

So, did the Marrakesh agreement achieve nothing more than a 'new and improved' label? The answer depends on how the world implements the accord.

Objectives of the WTO Agreement

Recognizing that their relations in the field of trade and economic endeavour should be conducted with a view to raising standards of living, ensuring full employment and a large and steadily growing volume of real income and effective demand, and expanding the production of and trade in goods and services, while allowing for the optimal use of the world's resources in accordance with the objective of sustainable development, seeking both to protect and preserve the environment and to enhance the means for doing so in a manner consistent with their respective needs and concerns at different levels of economic development,

Recognizing further that there is need for positive efforts designed to ensure that developing countries, and especially the least developed among them, secure a share in the growth in international trade commensurate with the needs of their economic development,

Being desirous of contributing to these objectives by entering into reciprocal and mutually advantageous arrangements directed to the substantial reduction of tariffs and other barriers to trade and to the elimination of discriminatory treatment in international trade relations ...

A group of 117 countries agreed on 15 April 1994 to set up a World Trade Organization to implement, administer, operate and further the objectives of the multilateral trade accord.

The basis of the WTO Agreement is the premise that free trade is good for all. By lowering tariffs and quotas the playing field will be levelled and everyone will have the opportunity to compete in a free world market.

Studies have estimated that by removing restrictions, world income is likely to grow by over $200 billion a year by the year 2002. This growth will be shared by all countries, albeit disproportionately – the developing countries are likely to experience slower growth in their income.

Salient Features of WTO Agreement

The GATT accord is expected to reduce tariffs around the world by an average of about 40%. This will make consumers happy because prices of imported goods will decrease. It will make exporters glad because reduced prices will stimulate increased demand for their exports. However, developing country industrialists with large excess capacity or inefficient plant and management who were previously protected by prohibitive import duties will have to face price as well as quality competition.

According to the WTO agreement, developed nations which were restricting the import of textiles and clothing have to phase out the Multi-Fibre Arrangement (MFA) – quantitative restrictions on the import of fibre, textiles and apparel. Quotas are to be totally lifted over a staggered period of ten years. This will mean that Pakistani apparel exporters can sell as many T-shirts in America as US buyers want. However, restrictions on importing T-shirts from India, Bangladesh and Hong Kong will also be removed and Pakistani shirt exporters will have to be competitively priced.

This agreement has also introduced new patent and copyright protection laws for intellectual property. We will now have to pay top dollars for computer software. Pirated software will be confiscated and destroyed. The computer revolution that is sweeping across developing countries may come to a grinding halt – unless software manufacturers in the West adopt LDC user-friendly pricing policies.

While pirate shops will have to go underground, authorized dealers of computer software and vendors of audio and video cassettes and CDs will experience a massive growth in their sales. The recent introduction of Time-Warner videos in Pakistan shows the tremendous market opportunities available. Even though Time-Warner video rental rates are over 100% higher than those of pirate videos, the introduction of a quality product has been well accepted in the market. Appropriately priced computer software can also take off.

The WTO agreement also addresses the problems of trade in services – including banking and insurance. A country cannot indefinitely limit market access to foreign firms in the service sector based on quantitative restrictions on the number of service suppliers or the total value of service transactions, or the number of service operations. For example, if a foreign bank which already exists in a country applies to open an additional branch, it is seeking market access. If the procedure for licensing of new branches is less onerous for domestic banks than it is for foreign banks, then the country can be accused of discriminatory restrictions.

WTO and Tariff Reductions

The results of the market access negotiations of the Uruguay round of talks has been the agreement to reduce tariff rates on non-agricultural goods by about 40%. These rates have been annexed to the agreement in the form of national schedules of concessions.

The tariff reduction programme agreed upon is to be implemented in five equal rate reductions unless otherwise specified by a country. The first such reduction has come into effect on January 1, 1995 and the final rate is to become effective within a period of four years.

Pakistan has been very liberal in its tariff reduction and market access programme and has already announced the reduction in tariffs on several important product categories. On January 1, 1995 Pakistan slashed by 50% the tariff on an item of interest to both the US and Europe – cotton and silk fabrics. Our textile mills will now have to compete with European and US fabrics under protectionist fences that have been lowered from about 70% (plus 15% sales tax) to 35% (plus sales tax).

The government has also committed itself to reducing average tariffs from the current 70% to 45% in 1995–96 and 35% in 1996–97. Used to working under a regime of import restrictions and licensing, Pakistan's industrial sector has numerous inefficient and obsolete factories. The tariff reductions that will come into effect will result in a shake out and inefficient producers will have to shape up or close down.

Tariff Reductions and Government Revenue

Pakistan relies heavily on indirect taxation for government revenue. Import duties and sales tax on imports account for over 40% of total government revenue and a reduction in tariffs is expected to cut heavily into this source of funds. This may exacerbate the budget deficit.

However, the government is banking on the success of its taxation reforms to bridge the gap. First, reduction in import tariffs compounded with restrictions and monitoring of Afghan Transit Trade may result in a reduction in smuggling. More imports will come in through the legal channel thereby generating import duty income for the government. Secondly, introduction of VAT - a broad based General Sales Tax – is likely to increase revenues. And, finally, greater sectoral coverage of income tax through the inclusion of agricultural income in the tax net is expected to yield sufficient revenues to bring down the budget deficit to 3% of GDP by 1996–97. If the political will to enforce all aspects of the tax reforms programme is lacking, we may end up with lower import duty collections and a yawning deficit.

The WTO Agreement and Agriculture

The Uruguay round of talks have deliberated on various aspects of the agricultural sector. This sector is heavily protected not only in developing countries but also in developed countries. Tariffs on agricultural products are to be reduced by 36% in developed countries, 24% in developing countries. This reduction is to be undertaken over a period of 6 years for the developed countries but over 10 years for developing nations. Least developed countries are not required to reduce their tariffs.

The Japanese rice growers have a powerful lobby that almost managed to disrupt the Uruguay accords by preventing the opening up of the Japanese rice market to foreign competition. However, they later agreed to minimal market access – between 3% to 8% of domestic consumption over a ten-year period.

European Community farmers also work under heavy farm subsidies. Their subsidized output is sold in the domestic market as well as to foreign buyers. Reduction of these farm subsidies may lead to higher international food prices as subsidizers reduce the surplus that they dump overseas. Developing countries that import such food grains will suffer.

Domestic farm support policies that have a limited impact on trade are excluded from reduction commitments. Such policies include government support for research, disease control, food security and environmental programmes. Other farm support policies which are not exempted will have to be reduced by 20% by developed countries and 13.3% by developing countries (excluding the least developed).

Direct export subsidies on farm products have to be reduced and the total quantity of subsidized exports also has to be limited. However, subsidies to reduce the cost of marketing exports of agricultural exports or inland transport and export freight charges have not been subjected to reduction. This is of significance to Pakistan as we are currently providing a 25% freight subsidy to encourage the export of fresh fruits and vegetables.

Circumvention of the agreement through food aid donations and export credits is to be controlled through certain provisions in the agreement.

As protectionist farm policies supported by strong political lobbying are expected to threaten the accord, the WTO agreement includes an agreement on Sanitary and Phytosanitary Measures. This gives governments the right to control food safety and plant protection but has to be limited to the extent necessary to protect human, animal or plant life.

Japan's recent removal of the ban on the import of Washington apples from the United States is an example of how this policy could open up markets. What is important is that the countries which have signed up should apply these rules across the board. Succumbing to US pressure, Japan could selectively open its market for agricultural imports but phytosanitary regulations could be enforced to ward off rice imports from Pakistan.

The EC has recently stiffened its import regulations for fruit and vegetables, introducing packaging as well as quality standards. Pesticides and fungicides imported from developed countries are used in the production of fruit and vegetables in developing countries and at times residues of such products constitute grounds for barring entry. With good intentions, the WTO agreement can help resolve these problems. But if nations so desire, they can wield the quality card for discriminating against foreign imports.

An important issue related to agriculture is the protection given to intellectual property rights insofar as they apply to patents for plant varieties and 'breeder's rights'. This could mean that farmers would have to pay royalties for growing crops of a particular type even if they used their own seeds. Such royalty payments could affect the profitability of farmers in developing countries. Indigenous research into plant varieties – especially rice and cotton in Pakistan – should be speeded up to avoid heavy royalty payments.

The WTO Agreement and Textile Exports

World trade in textiles and clothing is heavily restricted and subjected to quantitative restrictions. The United States and Canada as well as most of Western Europe have shuttered out suppliers of clothing and textiles from Asia, Latin America and several other regions to protect their own overpaid workers.

One of the major achievements of the Uruguay round of trade talks is the agreement to phase out the Multi-Fibre Arrangement and put an end to quotas on textiles and clothing. The phasing out of quotas is scheduled to take place over a ten-year period in three phases. The first phase began on January 1, 1995 when the quota imposing countries lifted quotas on several items allowing the free import of a number of textile and clothing products from Pakistan.

According to the agreement, 16% of total 1990 imports of textiles were integrated into the GATT – freed from quotas – on January 1, 1995. These products are from a specific list in the agreement and have to include items from each of the following categories: fibres and yarn, fabrics, textile madeups, and clothing.

On January 1, 1998, in the second phase, an additional 17% of 1990 imports would be integrated followed by a further 18% of 1990 imports on January 1, 2002. All remaining products would be integrated on January 1, 2005.

Between each phase, the level of quotas imposed on the products that remain under restraint is to be reduced by a speedy enhancement of quota limits. According to the MFA, annual growth levels accepted for most categories are about 5–7%. These are to be increased by 16% in Phase I, by 25% during Phase II and by 27% in Phase III. This means that a product that remains under quotas for the entire duration of the ten-year phasing out period will have its quota level enhanced by 5.8% every year between 1995–98 from the existing level of 5%. In Phase II (1998–2002) the annual growth level will be enhanced to 7.25% and in Phase III (2002–2005) this will increase to 9.2%.

During the initial three years there will be a marginal opening up of the textile and clothing sector. Between 1998–2002 the level of integration will be only 33%. It is only after the seventh year of the accord begins in 2002 that 51% of the textile products under quotas will be freed. The developed countries have, therefore, delayed the opening up of their textile sector to unhindered foreign competition but they have negotiated with developing countries like Pakistan

and India to lower tariff levels on imported fabrics and textile products. In fact, Pakistan has already agreed to allow the import of foreign fabrics and children's garments at a nominal tariff level of 35%. This lowering of the tariff level took effect on January 1, 1995.

Impact of the WTO Agreement on Pakistan's Textile Exports

Cotton Yarn

Pakistan's most significant textile export is cotton yarn which accounts for about a third of all textile exports. Selling yarn has never posed a major problem and greater market access for our yarn will not lead to any significant trade gains. It is the availability of cotton which will determine growth in this sector. If cotton is available in abundant quantity, our textile spinners can convert it into yarn for both domestic sale and export.

The declining cotton crop may lead to increased usage of man-made fibres and poly-cotton yarn. Spinning mills have to be flexible enough to make both types of yarn. Besides, finer counts of yarn will be spun when cotton is not readily available. Both these point towards quality upgradation as a means of increasing export earnings.

Increased exports of textiles and apparel in a quota-free world will increase the demand for cotton yarn and push up prices which have already climbed up from an average of about $1.5 per kg to $2.75 per kg within the last two years.

In 1992–93 and in 1991–92 we doubled our textile spinning machinery imports each successive year and we now have sufficient capacity in our spinning sector to meet our domestic needs and export over $2 billion worth of yarn in 1996–97 (from the current $1.2bn) provided we have a good cotton crop.

The WTO accord may help keep yarn prices up but removal of supply constraints is important to keep our yarn exports going. In six years our yarn exports jumped up in value from $260 million in 1984–85 to $1,183 million in 1990–91. They have only remained stagnant during the last few years due to lack of cotton.

Cotton Fabrics and Synthetic Textiles

Some cotton fabrics and synthetic fabrics are subjected to quota restrictions and it is expected that as soon as quotas are lifted, their exports will grow.

About 30% of our cotton fabrics and 50% of our synthetic textiles go to developed countries and the WTO accord may lead to an initial spurt in exports to these countries. However, increased competition from the Far East may reduce US and European apparel and textile madeup manufacturing and the fabrics being exported by Pakistan may find a bigger and growing market in the Far East or Latin America rather than in Europe or North America.

Quality improvements in the processing of fabrics will be needed to meet competition from the Far East. Colour fast printing and dyeing as well as a quantum leap in the designing of motifs and patterns will be essential for upgrading the quality of our fabric exports. Flawless weaving and strict quality control will also ensure growth of this sector.

Textile Madeups

Bedsheets, towels and other textile madeups supplied by Pakistan are among the cheapest in the world – barring China. Exports of most of these items are affected by quotas. The WTO agreement will provide greater market access to our exporters and we should be able to increase our exports of such products.

The current cotton crisis has pushed up the cost of raw material – yarn – for madeups manufacturers and they are experiencing difficulties in export at their traditional low prices. What is required is that exporters of madeups should invest in upgrading their marketing skills and cater to the higher level of the market.

Providing institutional linen in bulk – plain white towels and bedlinen – may generate export sales but dyed, embroidered and appliqued towels fetch prices that are several times greater. Admittedly, they require more marketing efforts but they are the long term saviours. A shipment of cheap towels from China can immediately displace exports from Pakistan but a well-designed and packaged product from Pakistan will not be easily dislodged by foreign competition.

Garments and Knitwear

The clothing sector possesses the biggest promise for delivering Pakistan out of the under $10 billion exporters club. Our knitted T-shirts are in great demand in the US and Europe and quotas on the export of T-shirts have been stifling growth in this sector. Once the quotas are removed we should experience a tremendous growth in the demand for a large number of our clothing goods.

However, it is unclear as to when quotas on these items will be reduced. It seems most likely that quotas on major clothing exports will only be lifted in 2005. This will mean that there will be no significant change in our exports of garments and knitwear for the next ten years.

As the phasing out of the MFA involves the lifting of restrictions of different categories during different periods, it is likely that Pakistan's exports of, for example, trousers, will become quota free while export of trousers from India and Hong Kong will continue to remain under quotas. These opportunities have to be seized and efforts have to be made to get our foot in the door as soon as possible.

There will be continued resistance from the West to our clothing exports as is evident from the following statement made by the President of the US Amalgamated Clothing and Textile Workers Union:

> [By signing] the accord without toughening its labor standards, Congress and the administration are putting millions of US jobs at risk by linking the American economy to those of countries that lag dramatically behind America in wages and work standards.
>
> [Supporting this agreement is to] rob children and young adults of their youth. The [WTO] should include mechanisms to enforce internationally recognized workers' rights, including outlawing child labor, and set environmental standards.

If such 'social dumping' or 'environmental dumping' objections are given weightage, the West will continue to have a ploy for limiting our clothing exports.

As it is, the first phase of abolishing quotas has shown that the West is planning to take the harder decisions later. By only abolishing quotas on items such as 'umbrellas' and 'fabrics for making parachutes', it is obvious that apparel exporters need not celebrate just yet.

Long term prospects for growth in Pakistan's garment and knitwear exports, however, are quite positive. In the last five years, garment exports have grown from $394 million to $613 million while hosiery (knitwear) exports have grown from $274 million to $509 million.

The textile export sector – aided by the Export Promotion Bureau – is making investments in improving fashion designing and upgrading skills in manufacturing by setting up a dozen textile training institutes and a fashion design school. By the time quotas on the export of apparel are lifted, these institutes should have turned out enough trained professionals to meet the quality requirements of an unfettered world of competition.

Leather and Leather Goods Exports

After textiles, leather is the most important sector of Pakistan's exports. Every year, we have been supplying over 15 million sq. metres of leather to the world, of which 3 million sq. metres goes to Italy alone – Italy's famous Gucci shoes may be made of Pakistani leather!

During the last ten years we have also developed our leather garments industry which is now generating exports of $376 million. Our footwear industry is, however, still in its infancy and is expected to take off in the next few years.

The entire leather group today contributes about 4600 million in export earnings. With some marketing and training efforts leather garments exports can grow substantially. Footwear exports can also grow dramatically if import regulations for raw material used in the footwear industry are relaxed. The leather industry has the potential to become a $2 billion export industry within five years if we continue to upgrade skills and also ensure adequate supplies of hides and skins by tapping the Central Asian markets.

Central Asia presents a very large export market for our leather products and is currently catered for by 'tourist-businessmen'. Streamlining the financial and banking arrangements between the region and Pakistan will help boost exports there.

One major problem that looms large for the leather sector is the environmental rules that infiltrate into the WTO. The WTO agreement incorporates an Agreement on Technical Barriers to Trade which covers processing and production methods related to the characteristics of the product itself. If the leather that is being exported by Pakistan is being manufactured in tanneries that spew untreated effluent into the environment, countries can restrict our leather exports.

The leather industry of Pakistan has taken cognizance of this and is already undertaking efforts to minimize ecological damage.

Food Exports – Rice, Fruit and Vegetables and Seafood

Last year, when the Japanese government opened up its rice market due to a bad rice crop it was very selective in its policy. Pakistan was unable to get a share of its market. Although we do not produce the glutinous rice that is eaten by the Japanese, we do produce rice which can be used for industrial purposes (making sake and rice noodles). 'Quality considerations' prevented the import of our rice.

The opening up of the rice market in Japan is unlikely to create any major new opportunities for us.

We should be watchful of conditions on 'quality' safeguards that will need to be taken on the export of fruits and vegetables. Traces of pesticides and chemicals – that were sold to Pakistan by the West – are posing as hurdles in our export of produce.

We have to educate our farmers on the proper usage of chemicals and a back-to-basics approach is ideal for green vegetable exports. Proper packaging and temperature controls are also needed to increase our exports of fruits and vegetables.

Fish and seafood exports are also affected by quality standards. Untreated sewage flows into the sea and is polluting our marine environment. Industrial effluents are also being dumped untreated into the sea. These, along with overfishing, have affected our fish catch. Indiscriminate use of fine mesh nets and fishing during the breeding season is reducing our fish population.

These problems need to be addressed if our fish exports are to grow. But what is more important is the quality upgradation that we have to undertake to ensure that we are not subjected to restrictive trade practices.

In early 1994, French fishermen protested against the cheap import of fish from abroad by destroying containers of imported fish. Within weeks of this incident, the French authorities asked the Pakistani government to supply them with a list of exporters of seafood whose fishing and packaging practices conform to the health and hygiene requirements of the EC.

An attempt was apparently made to bow down to domestic pressure by using the subterfuge of quality.

Our seafood exporters generally work in extremely unhygienic conditions. They have to upgrade their facilities to conform to internationally acceptable standards as the sword of quality will be used more and more aggressively in the new, liberated world of trade.

WTO and ISO 9000

When quotas on our textile exports are removed, the world will have another instrument to restrict our exports. This is the ISO 9000 rule. ISO 9000 is a new quality standard that is being espoused by the world to foster good manufacturing practices and quality safeguards in all processes both in the manufacturing and service sectors.

In Pakistan one company has so far been certified to be conforming to ISO 9000 standard – AEG. Unless other manufacturers and exporters join the bandwagon and begin standardization and quality controls, Pakistan's exports will perpetually remain under the ominous threat of quality sanctions.

Source: The Export Promotion Bureau, *Uruguay Round of Trade Talks: Impact on Pakistan's Exports*, Export Promotion Bureau, Karachi, 1995.

Appendix 9.2

Problems posed by Afghan transit trade

R.M.U. Suleman has highlighted how smuggling affects Pakistan's trade, through lost revenue and its effects on industry in the country.

Afghanistan, a land-locked country bordering Pakistan, has been using Karachi as the port for its sea-borne trade and Pakistan territory for transit of its foreign trade from, and to, Karachi since before the independence of Pakistan. Such use of a neighbour's territory and ports by a land-locked country has the sanction of international usage as well as laws. These privileges were also duly endorsed under GATT.

In 1965 Pakistan concluded a bilateral agreement that has come to be known as Afghan Transit Trade Agreement (ATTA). This agreement, valid for 30 years, expired on March 2, 1995, and could not be renegotiated in time due to the current hostilities and disturbed conditions in Afghanistan. But on March 1 this year, the Rabbani Government did offer to start

renegotiation of ATTA with Pakistan.

The ATTA has been used as a means of smuggling high-duty goods into Pakistan and in earlier years, for bringing in goods liable to stringent import licensing and foreign exchange control restrictions. The volume of smuggling was rather low to begin with, but has gone on expanding with the passage of time.

The procedures prescribed were quite foolproof. On importation at Karachi, the transit goods loaded on wagons or trucks were sealed by the Customs authorities at Karachi. Consignment documents were prepared to accompany the goods up to the land Customs stations (Torkham or Chaman) and their copies were separately sent to the land Customs station concerned to return them to the Karachi Custom House to confirm the crossing of the Pak–Afghan border by the transit goods through the authorized route.

Complications started arising due to the Pakistan Customs having jurisdiction only on the authorized routes and not on the adjoining tribal hills and dales. The first malpractice adopted was to unload the transit goods trucks just a few miles across the border from where they were brought back into Pakistan as head loads or on animal transport. High-dutied goods could thus enter Pakistan without the payment of any Customs duties and other charges.

As the smugglers became bolder and more resourceful, the transit goods trucks stopped crossing the border to avoid bribing the Afghan Customs. Pakistan Land Customs officers started returning fake documents to the Karachi Customs House to confirm the transit truck's crossing of the border. The managers of the transit goods had, of course, to grease the palms of the Customs Officers at Karachi as well as the Land Customs station.

The next stage was that of the transit goods trucks leaving the Karachi port never reaching the relevant Land Customs Stations. The fake documentary confirmation of their border crossing kept coming back to the Karachi Custom House.

All the three methods of ATTA goods reaching Pakistan markets thus became operative at different times and places. Bara markets of smuggled goods thus sprouted all over the country, being regularly replenished.

Interest in the abuses of transit trade was much heightened in recent months as the search started for the causative factors of the sharp shortfall in the collections of import levies relative to the budget estimates for 1994–5. Based on the performance of the first seven or eight months, the total revenue shortfall for the year was estimated at Rs46 billion. Of this, Rs18 billion was contributed by the Customs import collections and Rs17 billion by sales tax, mostly at the import stage.

The Vice-Chairman of the Central Board of Revenue has recently estimated that misuse of ATT facility has already caused a short-fall of Rs3 billions in revenue collection. Out of this short-fall, Rs1 billion was attributable to black tea alone, for which there is little demand in Afghanistan due to decisive taste preference for green tea there.

The misuse of ATT is also seen as having brought the domestic industry to the verge of collapse. According to the Federal Commerce Minister, foreign goods which have no market in Afghanistan are being imported under ATT and items like piece goods, yarn, auto parts, crockery etc. are finding their way to the Pakistani markets instead of reaching their Afghan border destination.

During the first half of the current year ATT volume is reported to have escalated to Rs11 billion as compared with Rs3 billion in the corresponding period of 1993–94. The Government has striven in vain to discourage such smuggling through measures like reduced import levies on items such as textile dyes and chemicals.

Jeopardized Industry

Some industries have been particularly hard hit by such smuggling. Tyre manufacturing is one such industry. The Sony TV assembling factory had to be closed down after going into huge losses. At the same time, there are reports of 50,000 to 60,000 TV sets being smuggled into Pakistan through ATT. It was also intriguing how in a country like Afghanistan, where supply of electricity, if any, is very meagre and irregular, huge imports of air conditioners, refrigerators, TV sets and all other types of electric gadgetry could be absorbed.

The CBR [Central Board of Revenue] made a strong statistical case for misuse of ATT facilities by smugglers. Pakistan has a population of 120 million and Afghanistan of 15 million with much lower per-capita income and a war-ravaged economy. There was thus no sense in import values being Rs0.83 billion for Pakistan and Rs1.1 billion for Afghanistan in TV sets, Rs0.1 billion for Pakistan and Rs0.2 billion for Afghanistan in soap and shampoo, Rs0.7 billion for Pakistan and Rs1.4 billion for Afghanistan in art silk fabrics.

This was the justification for 15 items being excluded from ATT list. In mid-February this year eight new items were included in the ATT negative list – airconditioners, art silk fabrics, auto parts (all sorts), ball bearings, refrigerators, soaps and shampoos, television sets and parts thereof and timers/capacitors.

Out of 15 items which now stand excluded from ATT, seven were declared contraband for purposes of ATT in January 1995. These included: black tea, cigarettes, dyes and chemicals, polyester, metallised films, poly vinyl chloride/plastic moulding compound, tyres and tubes and yarn (all sorts). The 15 banned items cover 85 per cent of the total ATT.

A total of 800 railway wagons carrying consignments of the banned goods were immediately impounded at various railway stations of the country. Goods on board these wagons were confiscated. The government also unearthed a network of smugglers who had master-minded misuse of the facility. The financiers of transit trade were not the Afghans or tribal chieftains but residents of Karachi, Faisalabad, and Gujranwala, who were earning huge profits from ATT misuse. The imports were made through bogus Letters of Credit (LC). According to the CBR, the consignments confiscated could be released after the parties concerned paid duty and taxes.

Nationalist as well as commercial opinion in Afghanistan has not taken kindly to Pakistan's unilateral interference in a transit trade arrangement that has been operating for the last 70 years in unofficial or official form. They wondered why the government did not take such action against cross-border smuggling with India and Iran. They maintained that the government should have taken stringent border-security measures and purged its Customs of corrupt officials instead of putting restrictions on the transit trade. ATT, they held, had been used just as a scapegoat.

The CBR in collaboration with the Frontier Constabulary is planning to beef up vigilance actively along the Pak–Afghan border to check the influx of smuggled goods from Afghanistan. Time alone will show what success is achieved by these border control measures. Even if these measures succeed, the problem of fully documented ATT goods leaving Karachi and not at all reaching the Customs posts on the Afghan border, will still remain.

Unfair

Even if the exact Afghan demand is only a tenth of what moves under the cover of ATT, they have a right to receive this one-tenth without any unilateral interference from Pakistan. This facility is misused by Pakistanis and they alone, according to Afghans, should receive the punishment. If Pakistan takes any arbitrary measures, Afghans can easily retaliate by disrupting Pakistan's crucial trade links with the Central Asian

States.

In all the controversy about the ATT misuse, little has been heard of the causative factor of corruption of Customs officials not only at Karachi but also at the Land Customs stations on the Afghan border. Postings on these stations are treated as gold mines allotted to persons with the highest clout at the political or the administrative levels. Unless the patronage in these postings is given up, Pakistan can forget all about handling transit trade with a modicum of efficiency and honesty. The ambition of becoming a gateway to Central Asia will also remain a pipe-dream. Border control has also to be put on something approaching sound footing.

Source: Suleman, R.M.U., 'Problems Posed by Afghan Transit Trade', *DAWN*, Economic and Business Review, 18–24 March 1995.

Appendix 9.3

Devaluation – arguments for and against

The following three articles, two written a few days prior to the 28 October 1995 devaluation, one immediately following the 12 September 1996 devaluation, examine the arguments for and against devaluation in Pakistan.

The devaluation dilemma

Business and banking circles in Karachi are abuzz these days with the prospects of an imminent devaluation. Exporters and importers, understandably alert, are hedging their bets as they believe that the Government of Pakistan is about to devalue the rupee substantially. Leading currency analysts in the city, for their part, are also predicting a massive devaluation of the rupee against the US dollar before the end of the year.

These devaluation rumours have been sweeping the market for many weeks and have intensified of late, resulting in a near panic buying of dollars. At the same time, importers have stepped up business considerably in a bid to capitalise on the higher existing exchange rate before imports become more expensive. Even the federal commerce minister, Chaudhry Ahmed Mukhtar, joined the fray a few days ago, revealing that the government intends to devalue the rupee by three per cent by the end of the year. In all this ruckus, the only quarter which has consistently taken a different stance is, in fact, the very institution that is supposed to announce changes in the value of the rupee, the State Bank of Pakistan.

State Bank Governor Yaqub has repeatedly and strongly denied all the rumours and speculation about devaluation, massive or otherwise. With statements ranging from 'no devaluation in the offing' and reports that he has 'ruled out devaluation', to the stronger 'dismissal' of the commerce minister's statement, Governor Yaqub has consistently clung to his claim that devaluation will not take place. Furthermore, he has warned those 'gambling' on a probable devaluation of the rupee to do so 'at their own risk', in the process reminding them of a similar warning issued by him when the government decided to make the rupee convertible in June 1994.

At the time, currency analysts and market players were, as is the case now, expecting a massive downward movement in the rupee and had consequently indulged in 'a pre-1994 budget buying spree to make windfall profits'. In the event, however, the rupee depreciated and adjusted by only 9.3 per cent after the partial convertibility on July 1, 1994. But despite the claims and warnings by the governor that devaluation is nowhere in sight, the fact remains that the rupee has seen as many as nine downward adjustments since the budget was announced on June 14.

The spot buying rate of the rupee was pegged to the US dollar at 30.97 prior to the budget. The first post-budget downward movement occurred on June 28, when it lost four paisas and settled at 31.01 rupees. In the 14 weeks from the mid-June budget to the end of September, the nine downward adjustments have resulted in a 58 paisa, or 1.87 per cent, depreciation in the value of the rupee. At the end of September, the spot buying rate of the rupee with respect to the dollar was 31.55. The Governor of the State Bank, for his part, has called this drop a 'corrective adjustment' and not a devaluation.

Bankers and currency analysts, however, are forecasting a substantial devaluation before the end of the year. They predict that the December rupee–dollar parity will be 32 rupees to the dollar at the very minimum, but will most likely be closer to the 33 rupee mark. One analyst believes that the 'most real value for the rupee before the year is out' is a massive 35 rupees to the dollar. Another view, that of a senior banker in a leading US bank, is that the rupee will depreciate by 10–15 per cent by early November. This means that his bank is advising its clients that the dollar will be worth 36.2 rupees in a few weeks, well before the end of the year.

Most analysts give four reasons for the impending devaluation, three of which relate to what are called 'fundamentals'. They believe that there is a need for devaluation because of the continued widening of the trade gap, the fall in foreign exchange reserves and mounting inflationary pressures. The fourth reason is said to be the recent adjustment in the Indian rupee. Not all of these claims are valid.

The trade and current account deficits, for instance, have both been falling over the last few years, not widening. The trade deficit in the last financial year 1994–95 as a percentage of GDP was the lowest since 1980. The current account deficit (as a percentage of GDP) for the last year, meanwhile, was the lowest since 1987 with the exception of 1991–92. The trend for the two deficits, which are very closely related to the exchange rate, has, therefore, been downward. On the other hand, foreign exchange reserves have been rising consistently since 1990, and at the end of the last financial year stood at 2.74 billion dollars, the highest level ever. On these two counts, which reveal important trends related to the exchange rate, currency analysts have got the direction of the movement wrong.

Inflation is the only fundamental on which the analysts are right, but for the wrong reasons. Inflation has been on the rise and has affected what is known as the real exchange rate, which compares the inflation rate in exporting and importing countries. High inflation in one trading country vis-à-vis the other implies a deteriorating real exchange rate, and hence the need to devalue the nominal exchange rate to make our goods more competitive. It is true that Pakistan's inflation rate is higher than that of its trading partners, but a devaluation on these grounds would only add fuel to the fire. Devaluation for Pakistan would prove to be inflationary and further worsen an already explosive price situation.

The main reason extended in favour of devaluation is that it will make exports more competitive – that is, cheaper – and thereby increase the volume of exports and foreign exchange earnings. However, even at a theoretical level this is a questionable proposition. Firstly, exports may not be price sensitive and they may respond to non-price factors; as such, lowering the price of exports may not affect volume and lead to an increase in demand. This very phenomenon was observed in Pakistan after Moeen Qureshi's devaluation two years ago. Often, a J-curve effect is seen, where the balance of trade – the value of exports minus the value of imports – first deteriorates before any improvement is seen. This often produces the knee-jerk reaction of further devaluation and only adds to existing problems.

Also, even if exports do indeed increase, the price of imports will also rise at the same time, and under numerous conditions the effect of a devaluation may substantially worsen the balance of trade and negate the entire exercise. Furthermore, after the utter devastation of the Mexican economy following a bungled devaluation nine months ago, foreign investors have become more cautious about such interventions in emerging markets, and local governments are aware of these concerns.

The fourth argument for devaluation is the weakest. The justification in fashion these days is that since the value of the Indian rupee has fallen, or depreciated, to be precise, Pakistan must devalue immediately. Newspaper articles are clamouring that the 'Indian move is an economic invasion to knock out Pakistani exports in the world market'. There are numerous inconsistencies in this claim.

Firstly, Indian goods are not strictly comparable to Pakistani exports and nor are all of them perfect substitutes. Secondly, export orders and contracts are usually signed well in advance, and are based on numerous non-price considerations such as political factors, long term dealings, practices and ties, institutional factors, tradition, culture and a host of other influences. Thirdly, Indian exports generate almost four times the foreign exchange that Pakistani exports are able to bring in, implying that the Indian market is already more established than Pakistan's. Fourthly, the devaluation seen in the Indian rupee actually took place in the kerb market, where the rupee fell to 35 per dollar for a short while, but then stabilized at around 33.80. The official value of the Indian rupee did not change.

Finally, Indian exports have surged this year, rising by as much as 29 per cent which is a very healthy trend indeed. Essentially, then, a devaluation in the Indian rupee by a few percentage points should not cause concern to our exporters. What matters for us is the US dollar.

Strangely enough, while all currency analysts and traders have been arguing in favour of devaluation, they have not given enough weight to what happens to the US dollar. Pakistan follows a managed float and although there is a basket of currencies to which the rupee is linked, the US dollar is still the key currency. This April the dollar fell to an all time low of one dollar to 80 Japanese yen, and after a 15-month high is now hovering around 100 yen. The US dollar started its upward movement in July and the changes in the dollar–Pakistani rupee rate need to be seen in that context. A stronger US dollar would put pressure on the Pakistani rupee, and hence the need for the 'technical adjustments'.

The key determinant in the next few months for the Pakistani rupee will be the value of the US dollar, not the Indian rupee. Once the dollar stabilizes, so should the rupee. Furthermore, there has been very little adjustment so far this year, mainly because the dollar was weaker, and based on past trends, there is considerable room to manoeuvre.

At the moment the government's most immediate task is to deal with rising inflation, which was 14.8 per cent in August on a year-on-year basis. Devaluation at this point will only fuel inflation without necessarily improving the balance of trade position. Exports showed a healthy trend last year growing by 15.7 per cent with a total value of 7.8 billion dollars. The target for the current fiscal year 1995–96 is 9.2 billion dollars, and if the cotton crop is good, as is very probable, one can expect an increase in exports. The stumbling block for high exports is not the rupee–dollar parity rate, but the anarchic and devastating political situation in Karachi. All attempts at improving the economy and expanding exports must be predicated on finding a quick and just solution to the politics of Karachi.

To this end, the business community should be pressurizing the government to come to terms with the real concerns of the people of this city. In comparison, the whole hype about devaluation as the key to our economic problems will soon fall into perspective.

Source: Zaidi, S. Akbar, 'The Devaluation Dilemma', *The Herald*, Karachi, October 1995.

Walking the Exchange Rate Tightrope

Most governments hate to devalue because in the short run there are more losers from devaluation than there are gainers. The reason is simple. Imports and locally produced import substitutes become more expensive after devaluation and this affects the consumption basket of a large number of voters. On the other hand, exporters who benefit from devaluation are relatively few and the benefits of export-led income and employment growth come with a lag. So, why did the Governor of the State Bank of Pakistan devalue the rupee last week by 3.65 per cent?

Prudent exchange rate management is a delicate balancing act. Ours is a managed float, whereby the Governor of the

State Bank sets the value of the rupee in view of the supply and demand for other currencies. In so doing, he weighs in the fact that the evidence on supply and demand is made murky by speculators. If he misreads the signals, and devalues excessively, the result is inflation and extra debt burden. If he over-values the currency, he risks out-pricing Pakistani exports and under-pricing imports, resulting in a trade deficit.

What should the Governor be guided by? The bazaar value of the rupee–dollar exchange rate and the FEBC premium are usually contaminated by speculation. More reliable guides are domestic and international inflation rates and the fiscal and trade deficits. Inflation in Pakistan, currently running at 13–14 per cent, is considerably higher than the trading partners' inflation of around 4 per cent. This suggests an appreciation of the real exchange rate, which requires a devaluation of the nominal exchange rate (real exchange rate is the nominal exchange rate times relative inflation; if the latter goes up, the nominal exchange rate has to be adjusted to maintain the value of the real exchange rate).

The other guide is the fiscal and the trade deficit, which together affect the current account in the balance of payments. A large current account deficit means that we are spending more than we are earning. The fiscal deficit is unsustainable at over 4 per cent (post-budgetary shenanigans render the government's fiscal target for this year less credible) and the trade deficit has shot up to $3.5 billion. If these deficits were temporary, due to crop failure or other calamities, and if we had the reserves, we could have run those down to tide over the emergency. Alternatively, we could borrow short term in the international commercial capital market to cushion the economic shock. But if the problem is endemic and if reserves are already low, the international capital market demands a heavy premium, which increases the debt burden. In any case, such quick fixes are unlikely to get to the root cause of the problem, which is that as a nation we spend more than we earn.

What the Governor needs is a policy measure that reduces our expenditures and increases our earnings. Given the current macroeconomic picture, a sizeable devaluation of the currency is precisely such a policy measure. It sends a strong signal to domestic spenders that imports are expensive, so avoid them. Simultaneously, a message is sent to foreign consumers that Pakistani goods are cheaper, come and get them. This brings down the trade deficit and checks the pressure on reserves. Having arrived at this conclusion without any arm twisting, we may now approach the concessionary international lenders, i.e., the IMF and the World Bank, borrow at low rates and be rewarded for our wisdom!

It is often argued that neither Pakistani imports nor exports respond to price changes and therefore devaluation is an ineffective instrument. This is nonsense. In the aggregate, responsiveness to price signals is rational human behaviour. When imports become expensive, we postpone purchases and that reduces aggregate demand. Similarly, why should foreigners not buy more Pakistani goods when they become cheaper?

But let us ask ourselves what would happen if we did not devalue. An increasing number of people would take a position against the Pak rupee, confident that the value of the rupee cannot be sustained. This would put greater pressure on the rupee and the needed devaluation to correct the imbalance later would have to be much larger.

Another woolly argument is that we do not have 'exportable surpluses' and therefore exports do not increase when we devalue. This notion of exportable surpluses is a perplexing one. Does Lahore export knitwear because T-shirts are left over after the Lahoris have bought what they need? Does Sialkot export soccer balls because it has some to spare after meeting the needs of Sialkoti soccer players? Countries don't export because they have surpluses, but because they have a comparative advantage based on their abundant factor, which in our case is labour, raw cotton and leather. If we price these factors correctly via the exchange rate, we will export, surplus or no surplus.

Finally, we must begin to address the fundamental problems faced by the economy to avoid devaluations, which may sometimes be necessary but are always disruptive. We must tame the impulses that result in fiscal deficits and address the perverse incentive structure that retards export-led growth. Otherwise, we shall find ourselves running frequently to the tailor to loosen our belts when the real culprit is obesity. Only by fighting obesity at both the aggregate and the individual level, will we achieve a stable and realistic exchange rate, which is the corner stone of sound macroeconomic management.

Source: Nabi, Ijaz, *The Friday Times*, Lahore, 19–25 September 1996.

Is There a Case for Devaluation?

The answer to this question is pretty straightforward. There is no evidence at all that the Pakistani rupee is over-valued and, therefore, there is little reason to believe that a devaluation is on the cards. Neither movements in the balance of payments and the capital account nor in the real exchange rate vis-à-vis our major trading partners and competitors suggest that the rupee is misaligned. Indeed, a devaluation, when none is called for, may actually retard our principal policy objective of reining-in inflation.

First, the balance of payments. A sudden surge of imports or a sharp fall in exports or in factor payments registers as a balance of payments deficit. If it is not funded by movements on the capital account, reserves begin to be depleted. This shows that we want the rest of the world's goods and therefore its currencies more than the world wants ours. This is a clear signal that we must adjust downwards the value of our currency.

However, the evidence on recent movements in balance of payments does not show any sudden deterioration. The balance of trade is a negative $2.3 billion, which is in keeping with the medium-term trend. The services account is also in the negative at around $2.5 billion, again fairly close to the trend. Remittances, on the other hand, have registered an increase of around $500 million over the previous year. All of this adds up to a current account deficit of $2 billion, which is a little worse than last year's but is a substantial improvement over the year before that, when we went on a spending binge (the yellow cabs scheme).

A current account deficit is consistent with the fact that being a developing country, we are a net importer of capital. The capital account shows that direct foreign investment and concessionary official flows have financed most of the current account deficit – in fact, our reserves actually improved by $242 million in 1994–95 as a result of such transfers. All of this adds up to the conclusion that there is absolutely no untoward development in the balance of payments or in capital movements that calls for a devaluation of the rupee.

The second argument for devaluation is that, as a result of high inflation relative to our trading partners, the real exchange rate (which is simply the nominal exchange rate adjusted for the change in relative prices) has appreciated. This has raised the price of our exports and lowered the price of imports. This loss of international competitiveness, it is argued, must be remedied by a devaluation of the rupee.

Installation Triggered

This is a sophisticated argument and requires a careful look at the evidence on movements in the nominal exchange rate and relative prices vis-à-vis our trading partners. I have done this for our five major partners, the US, Japan, Germany, UK and France who together account for nearly half of our foreign trade (imports plus exports).

Table 1 gives the movement in the nominal effective exchange rate, or NEER, (which is simply an index of the nominal exchange rates of the five major trading partners weighted by their shares in trade) between 1980–81 and September 1995. The calculations show that NEER depreciated from 100 to 405. In other words, the same unit of major trading partners' currency now costs nearly four times as much as in 1980–81. This is a substantial nominal devaluation of the rupee. The question is: is it enough given that inflation in Pakistan is considerably higher than in the major trading partners?

To answer this, we have to look at how the relative prices have moved between Pakistan and the major trading partners. Table 2 traces the movement of prices in Pakistan and its five major trading partners. The last column of the table shows that the trade weighted consumer price index of our trading partners has increased from 100 to 168, while the index for Pakistan has increased from 100 to 323. It is this relative increase that exporters bemoan when they ask for a devaluation.

In other words, what the exporters want is a depreciation of the real effective exchange rate (REER), which is simply the relative price index (calculated in Table 2) divided by NEER

Table 1
Nominal effective exchange rate

	1980/1 (R0)	Sept. 1995 (R1)	(R1–R0)/ Rol	Trade weight	NEER
USA	9.91	31.55	2.2	35	111.4
France	2.11	6.46	2.1	8	24.5
Germany	4.92	22.29	3.5	19	86.1
UK	22.68	50.4	1.2	17	37.8
Japan	0.0463	0.32	5.9	21	145.1
Total					404.9

Table 2
Trade-weighted relative price index

	1980/1 (P0)	Sept. 1995 (P1)	(P1–P0)/ Rol	Trade weight	Trade-weighted consumer price index
USA	100	172	0.72	35	60.2
France	100	204	1.04	8	16.3
Germany	100	148	0.48	19	28.1
UK	100	218	1.18	17	37.1
Japan	100	125	0.25	21	26.3
Pakistan	100	323	2.23		
Relative price index					167.95
					242

(calculated in Table 1). Notice that NEER is 405 and the relative price index 241. Thus the depreciation in the nominal exchange rate has more than compensated for the higher price level in Pakistan relative to the major trading partners. In fact, there has been a substantial depreciation of the real effective exchange rate, so that Pakistani exports have become even more price competitive than in the past. Thus there is no justification at present for a devaluation of the nominal exchange rate to restore price competitiveness.

The recent adjustment of the Indian rupee is being cited as the third argument for devaluation. The evidence does not support this either. Between 1974 and 1975, India's CPI index increased from 100 to 488.5, while the nominal exchange rate index fell from 100 to 24.23. Meanwhile, Pakistan's CPI increased from 100 to 379 and the nominal exchange rate fell from 100 to 31.36. Thus the ratio of the two indices in the countries has moved fairly close together over the years and Pakistan has not suffered any loss of price competitiveness vis-à-vis India. India's exchange rate is now market determined and short run fluctuations in it do not call for an immediate response from us.

It is interesting that the market has read the evidence correctly and is not signalling a lack of confidence in the nominal value of the exchange rate. There is virtually no premium, other than the small margin to cover transaction costs, either in the curb market or the FEBC rate of exchange.

It is worth bearing in mind that exchange rate policy can influence only the nominal exchange and not the real exchange rate. The latter, which is the proper measure of competitiveness, is determined by relative price movements. Indeed, it may well be that a short term devaluation, when it is not called for, may buy a lot of long term inflation, resulting in an appreciation of the real exchange rate, thus producing results contrary to those intended.

Furthermore, a devaluation always has some short run costs such as an increase in the international debt burden and a general reduction in the standard of living. If there is a crisis in the balance of payments or a substantial appreciation of the real exchange rate, it might be worthwhile to bear the short run pain. But when such misalignments are not indicated, it seems unnecessary to add to the difficulties of the ordinary citizen already suffering under the ongoing structural adjustment.

Having said all this, we must recognize that exporters indeed are hurting. But the real culprit is high domestic inflation, which has raised the costs of production, including the high interest rates. To control inflation, our principal policy target must continue to be a reduction in the fiscal deficit. This is the best way to restore competitiveness in the long run to put the economy on the path of exported growth.

Source: Nabi, Ijaz, *DAWN*, Economic and Business Review, Karachi, 11–17 November 1995.

Notes

1. All these numbers are from Ahmed, Viqar and Rashid Amjad, *The Management of Pakistan's Economy, 1947–82*, Oxford University Press, Karachi, 1984, p. 245.
2. See Ahmed, Viqar and Rashid Amjad, op. cit., 1984; Lewis, Stephen, *Economic Policy and Industrial Growth in Pakistan*, George Allen and Unwin, London, 1969; and Lewis, Stephen, *Pakistan: Industrialization and Trade Policies*, George Allen and Unwin, London, 1970, for more extensive commentary on the trade pattern in the early years.
3. Ahmed, Viqar and Rashid Amjad, op. cit., p. 65.
4. Lewis, Stephen, op. cit., 1969, p. 59
5. Ahmed, Viqar and Rashid Amjad, op. cit., p. 243
6. Ibid., p. 243.
7. Asian Development Bank, *Strategies for Economic Growth and Development: The Bank's Role in Pakistan*, Manila, 1985, p. 357.
8. Ibid., pp. 357–8.
9. Ibid., p. 358.
10. Lewis, Stephen, op. cit., 1969, p. 12.
11. Ahmed, Viqar and Rashid Amjad, op. cit., 1984, pp. 244–5.
12. Institute of Developing Economies, *The Study on Japanese Cooperation in Industrial Policy for Developing Economies*, Tokyo, 1994, p. 129.
13. Ahmed, Viqar and Rashid Amjad, op. cit., 1984, p. 74.
14. Ibid., p. 246.
15. Ibid., p. 246.
16. Lewis, Stephen, op. cit., 1969, p. 40.
17. Ibid., p. 75, emphasis added.
18. Ibid., p. 161, emphasis added.
19. Asian Development Bank, op. cit., 1985, p. 359.
20. Lewis, Stephen, op. cit., 1969, p. 80.
21. Ibid., p. 69.
22. Ibid., p. 80.
23. Ahmed, Viqar and Rashid Amjad, op. cit., 1984, p. 24.
24. Institute of Developing Economies, op. cit., 1994, p. 21.
25. Sayeed, Asad, 'Political Alignments, the State and Industrial Policy in Pakistan: A Comparison of Performance in the 1960s and 1980s', unpublished Ph.D. dissertation, University of Cambridge, 1995, p. 49.
26. Ahmed, Viqar and Rashid Amjad, op. cit., 1984, pp. 247–8.
27. Asian Development Bank, op. cit., 1985, p. 359.
28. Ibid.
29. Ibid.
30. Ahmed, Viqar and Rashid Amjad, op. cit., 1984, p. 249.
31. Ibid., p. 250.
32. Adams, John and Sabiha Iqbal, *Exports, Politics and Economic Development in Pakistan*, Vanguard, Lahore, 1987, pp. 29–30.
33. Ahmed, Viqar and Rashid Amjad, op. cit., 1984, pp. 252–3.
34. Adams, John and Sabiha Iqbal, op. cit., 1987, p. 91.
35. Ibid., p. 92

36. Ahmed, Viqar and Rashid Amjad, op. cit., 1984, p. 252.
37. Adams, John and Sabiha Iqbal, op. cit., 1987, p. 105.
38. Asian Development Bank, op. cit., 1985, p. 390.
39. World Bank, *Pakistan: Growth Through Adjustment*, Report No. 7118-Pak, Washington, 1988, p. 64.
40. Ibid., p. 64.
41. Asian Development Bank, op. cit., 1985, p. 390.
42. Sayeed, Asad, op. cit., 1995, p. 125.
43. World Bank, op. cit., 1988, p. 68.
44. Ibid., p. 68
45. Ibid., p. 63.
46. Ibid., pp. 32–3.
47. World Bank, *Pakistan: Medium-term Economic Policy Adjustments*, Report No. 7591-Pak, Washington, 1989, p. 49.
48. LIBOR is the London Inter Bank Offered Rate; this is an important international money market rate, showing the going rate for short-term loans among depositary institutions in England.
49. World Bank, *Pakistan: Country Economic Memorandum FY93: Progress Under the Adjustment Programs*, Report No. 11590-Pak, Washington, 1993, p. 25.
50. Ibid., p. 37, emphasis added.
51. Ibid., p. 44.
52. Riazuddin, Riaz, 'An Evaluation of Trade Policy', *Pakistan Journal of Applied Economics*, vol. 10, nos. 1 and 2, 1994, p. 117.
53. Ibid., p. 118.
54. Ibid., p. 125.
55. World Bank, op. cit., 1993, p. 45, emphasis added.
56. Sayeed, Asad, op. cit., 1995, p. 124.
57. Adams, John and Sabiha Iqbal, op. cit., 1987, p. 11.
58. Sayeed, Asad, op. cit., 1995, p. 51.
59. Adams, John and Sabiha Iqbal, op. cit., pp. 11–13.
60. World Bank, op. cit., 1998, p. 64.
61. Ibid., p. 67.
62. Ibid., p. 67.
63. Ibid., p. 71.
64. Ibid., p. 72.
65. Ibid., p. 75.
66. Sayeed, Asad, op. cit., 1995, p. 124.
67. Ibid., p. 125.
68. Ibid., p. 126.
69. Ibid., p. 127.
70. Ibid., p. 130.
71. Papanek, Gustav, *Pakistan's Development: Social Goals and Private Incentives*, Harvard University Press, Cambridge, Mass., 1967, pp. 128–9.
72. Ibid., pp. 130–1.
73. Ahmed, Viqar and Rashid Amjad, op. cit., 1984, p. 93.
74. Ibid., p. 251.

Part 3

Fiscal and Monetary Policy

Of the four chapters that constitute this part of the book, the first two are devoted to issues of taxation and expenditure, debt and deficit (i.e. fiscal policy), while the remaining two deal with the financial sector – banks, the equity market – and monetary policy, savings, and inflation. We examine the tax structure prevalent in Pakistan and the relationship between the three tiers of government. Pakistan's perennial fiscal deficit, and hence the ever-increasing debt burden, is considered to be the most severe of the economy's problems, affecting a number of other variables as well. However, we question the claim that the fiscal deficit causes most of the problems in the economy that are attributed to it. We find that while government expenditure in excess of revenue is a problem, the more conventional attributes of a fiscal deficit are found wanting in the case of Pakistan. Our analysis suggests that issues of politics, governance, and quality of public expenditure should perhaps form the focus of informed debate about the fiscal deficit. The two chapters on money and monetary policy examine the changing nature of the financial sector over the last few years, and we see to what extent monetary policy has become market oriented following the financial sector reforms. The causes of persistent inflation and low savings are also analysed. We show that the cause of inflation in Pakistan is not excessive money creation, as is commonly believed, and that the reasons for low savings can be found in arguments which suggest financial repression, insufficient financial structures, cultural factors, and the presence of a huge illicit or black economy.

10 Public Finance I: Resource Mobilization and the Structure of Taxation

One of the major functions of government is to tax its people. This revenue is then supposed to be used for a number of purposes, which include the running of government itself, the provision of law and order, the defence of the country, and for infrastructure and social development. Governments build roads, schools, hospitals, and dams, and provide a host of other services. For all these purposes, governments raise revenue from those who make profit, from one source or another, within that country. Even though the role and extent of government involvement in the economy and in the lives of the people has been in debate, with growing concerns that there may be 'too much government', taxes, like death, are one of the two certainties that affect our existence.

Taxation structures and the extent of taxation vary from country to country, and often, governments within a country may suggest taxation reform based on their particular political dispensation. In Pakistan, a well-defined constitutional framework determines the nature of resource mobilization and the responsibilities of each of the three tiers of government. This chapter discusses the structure, nature, and extent of taxation in Pakistan, focusing on the issues at each level of government. From the constitutionally ordained legislative functions of government to the relationship between different levels of government, and to the extent of revenue collected from different sources, this chapter examines the salient features of Pakistan's taxation structure.

10.1 The Structure of Government and Taxation[1]

10.1.1 Legislative Functions

The Federation of Pakistan is governed by the Constitution of Pakistan of 1973 and all amendments to it since then. The Constitution specifies the functions of the federal government and of the provincial governments. The federal government has exclusive responsibility for undertaking functions under the Federal Legislative, which is contained in the Fourth Schedule [Article 70(4)] of the 1973 Constitution.

The Federal Legislative List includes functions of a regulatory and service nature. Service functions include defence, external affairs, currency, stock exchanges, national highways, and strategic roads, railways, etc. (see Figure 10.1). In addition to these functions, which are the exclusive responsibility of the federal government, there is a Concurrent Legislative List which contains functions that can

be performed by either the federal or provincial governments, or both. These service functions include population planning and social welfare, tourism, and education. Residual functions not specifically contained in either the Federal Legislative List or the Concurrent Legislative List are the responsibility, primarily, of the provincial governments – functions such as agricultural extension, irrigation, justice, and police. While the specific roles and functions of the federal and provincial governments are part of the 1973 Constitution, *the existence of local governments is not a formal part of the constitution*. Many of the residual functions that are not part of either of the Legislative Lists, and which are supposed to be performed by the provincial governments, have been delegated to the local governments by the promulgation of ordinances. The 1979 Local Government Ordinance, which defines and allocates the responsibility of local government, is operative in the Punjab, Sindh, and the NWFP, while the 1980 Ordinance applies to Baluchistan. These ordinances define the functions and roles of the local government as delegated to them by the provincial governments (for a more extensive discussion of local governments, see section 10.4 below).[2]

Of the functions allocated to local government by the provincial governments, there are a set of *compulsory* functions that urban councils, in particular, are expected to perform, in addition to an *optional* set of functions, which, as the name suggests, may or may not be performed by the local governments.

Figure 10.1 presents the services and functions that each of the three tiers of government are *expected* to perform, and those that they *actually* perform. As the diagram shows, the federal government's role is of a more macro nature, while the provincial and local governments perform the key role in the provision of basic social and physical services and infrastructure. Moreover, an important observation from the way the responsibilities of the three governments are structured is that the type and number of functions that can be performed is 'very exhaustive and provides potentially for a high degree of decentralization of functions to local governments even in the rural areas'.[3]

While the potential of the role of different, especially lower, tiers of government may be extensive, Figure 10.1 shows that most of the functions which are on the Concurrent List, and hence are the functional responsibility of both the provincial and federal governments, are actually being performed by the federal government. Similarly, a large number of responsibilities that are technically in the jurisdiction of local governments, are being performed by the provincial

Legislative responsibilities	Services	Actual allocations of functions
Federal government	Defence External affairs and foreign aid Post, telegraph, telephone, radio, and TV Currency and foreign exchange Institutes for research Nuclear energy Parts and aerodromes Shipping, air service, railways, and national highways Stock exchanges Geographical and meteorological survey Censuses Mineral oil and natural gas Industries	Federal government
Federal/provincial governments	Population planning Electricity (except KESC) Curriculum development, syllabus planning, and centres of excellence Tourism	
	Social welfare and employment exchanges Vocational/Technical training Historical sites and monuments	Federal/ provincial governments
Provincial governments	Law and order, justice Highways and urban transport Agricultural extension and distribution of inputs Irrigation and land reclamation Secondary and higher education	Provincial governments
Local governments	Curative health Land development Primary education	
	Preventive health Farm-to-market roads Water supply, drainage, and sewerage	Provincial/local governments
	Link roads Intra-urban roads Street lighting Solid waste management Fire fighting Parks, playgrounds	Local governments

Source: Hanif, Naveed, 'The Structure of Government in Pakistan', *News on Friday*, Karachi, 25 August, 1996.

Figure 10.1
Legislative and actual allocation of functions among different levels of government in Pakistan

governments. This is more marked in smaller cities and the rural areas. Hence, it seems that some of the responsibilities of the lower tiers of government are being undertaken by a higher tier: the federal government in the case of the provincial governments, and the provincial government in the case of the local governments. Whether it is the higher tier that infringes on the jurisdiction of the lower tier, or the lower tier's inability – in terms of limited financial resources and/or inadequate institutional capacity – to cope with its designated responsibilities that is the cause of the encroachment will be discussed in subsequent sections of this chapter.

10.1.2 The Structure of Taxation

The 1973 Constitution outlines the taxes and duties that the federal government can collect based on the Federal Legislative List. These are as follows:

> Duties of customs, including export duties; duties of excise, including duties on salt, but not including duties on alcoholic liquors, opium and other narcotics; duties in respect of succession to property; estate duty in respect of property; taxes on income other than agricultural income; taxes on corporations; taxes on the sales and purchases of goods imported, exported, produced, manufactured or consumed; taxes on the capital value of the assets, not including taxes on capital gains on immovable property; taxes on mineral oil, natural gas and minerals for use in generation of nuclear energy; taxes and duties on the production capacity of any plant, machinery, undertaking, establishment or installation in lieu of any one or more of them; terminal taxes on goods or passengers carried by railway, sea or air; taxes on their fares and freights; and fees in respect of any of the matters enumerated in the Fourth Schedule, but not including fees taken in any court.[4]

The provincial governments have the powers to make laws with respect to any matter other than those reserved for the federal government as described above. Just as the provincial governments have delegated some of their legislative functions to local government, they have also allowed local governments to collect some taxes that the provincial government does not itself collect. Hence, the provincial governments collect taxes that the federal government does not collect, and the local governments collect the residual taxes that the provincial governments do not collect. The distinction between direct and indirect taxes is also important, as discussed later. Table 10.1 gives a breakdown of the two types of tax at the provincial and federal level.

The revenue sources, based on rates and taxes that the provincial governments collect, include the following: tax on agricultural income; water rate; tax on trade professions, callings, and employment; capital gains tax on immovable property; excise duties on alcoholic liquor, opium, and other narcotics; tax on immovable property; land revenue; motor vehicle tax; stamp duties; electricity duties; entertainment duty; tolls on roads and bridges; betterment tax; taxes on cinemas and hotels; arms licence fee; court fee; cotton fee; and various other fees and taxes.

The provincial governments do not have the authority to assess and collect the entertainment duty or the urban immovable property tax in the Cantonment Areas in the provinces. Nevertheless, the collecting and assessing authority in these areas, the Cantonment Board, does collect and pass on a certain percentage of this tax to the provincial governments.

The fiscal powers granted by the provincial governments to the local governments are specified separately for urban and rural local councils, as specified in the Local Government Ordinances. Essentially, local bodies such as municipalities, and district and local councils, can levy any of the taxes that the provincial governments have been authorized to levy under the Constitution, subject to the prior approval of the provincial governments.

The major revenue sources for urban local councils include the following:

> Octroi; tax on annual rental value of buildings and land (except Sindh); tax on transfer of immovable property; rates for water supply, conservancy, drainage (except for Sindh), fire protection (only in Sindh); street lighting; tax on vehicles; fees for erection of buildings, licences and sanctions, markets, parking (except Sindh), schools (only in Sindh), slaughter of animals; tax on advertisements; tax on entertainments and feasts; tolls on roads; and so on. Additional taxation powers granted to the KMC include a development tax (valorization charge) for a

Table 10.1
Direct and indirect taxes at different tiers of government

	Direct taxes	Indirect taxes
Federal government	Income tax Corporation tax Wealth tax Property taxes	Sales tax Excise duty Import duty Exports duty Gas, petroleum surcharge Foreign travel tax
Provincial government	Land revenue Urban immovable property tax Tax on transfer of property Agriculture income tax Capital gains tax Tax on professions, trades, and callings	Stamp duty Motor vehicle tax Entertainment tax Excise duty Cotton fee Electricity duty

specific period on works of public utility and rates for bulk supply of water and for drainage.[5]

For rural areas, district councils levy their own taxes, and the inter-provincial differences in fiscal powers of district councils are more pronounced than those of urban councils, where there is greater uniformity. The tax and non-tax revenue sources of rural councils include the following:

tax on transfer of immovable property; tax for export of goods and animals; fees for licences and sanctions, markets, fairs; rates on services like water supply, drainage and lighting and tolls on roads. Additional major sources available are tax on non-motorized vehicles (except Baluchistan), tax on professions, trades, callings and employment (in Punjab and Sindh), fees on sale of cattle at cattle fairs (only in Punjab), tax on the annual rental value of buildings and lands (in Sindh and NWFP).[6]

While the fiscal powers of the federal and provincial governments are better defined and well demarcated, there is a considerable overlap in the fiscal powers of provincial and local governments. For example, both local and provincial governments can

levy a tax on the rental value of immovable property, tax on motor vehicles (in urban areas, except for Sindh), tax on entertainments and a tax on professions, trades, callings and employment. In addition, urban local councils can levy any tax of the provincial government in Sindh and NWFP or introduce a cess/surcharge on provincial taxes in Sindh and Baluchistan. The latter option is also available to district councils in Baluchistan.[7]

However, it must be remembered that, since the existence of local governments is not constitutionally ordained or protected, their position is somewhat tenuous. This is also reflected in the nature of fiscal powers that provincial governments have granted local governments. A recent report highlights that 'although separate fiscal powers have been specified for local councils, the Provincial government has the overriding power to direct any local council within the province either to levy any tax or to increase or reduce any such tax by the specified extent or to suspend or abolish the levy of any such tax'.[8]

10.1.3 Inter-Governmental Fiscal Relations[9]

Provincial and Local Governments

Local governments are extensions of provincial governments and the former act on behalf of the latter. We would therefore expect a great deal of overlap between these tiers of government. The structure of taxes discussed above demonstrates this.

The provincial tax machinery collects some taxes which are then returned to the local councils. The Excise and Taxation Department and the Registrar of Stamp Duties, both of the provincial government, are responsible for collecting the local property tax and the tax on the transfer of property (see Table 10.2). The reasons given for this are as follows:

The justifications generally offered for provincial collection (with revenue sharing) of municipal taxes are, first, that sophisticated procedures are involved in the assessment of liabilities of some taxes. These procedures are perhaps beyond the capabilities of local taxation departments, especially in the smaller jurisdictions. This is the justification given for assumption of the responsibility for property tax collection by the provincial governments. Second, that it is possible to realize significant economies of scale and/or avoid double taxation. This is the case particularly with a local tax which is levied on a similar tax base as a provincial tax. For example, the base for the tax on transfer of property is analogous to that for stamp duty and that for the local rate is identical to that for land revenue. As such, it is efficient for the provincial tax agency to collect both taxes at the same time and hand over the local component of revenue to the councils.[10]

In 1985/6, provincial governments, on behalf of local governments, had collected about 12 per cent of the total revenue receipts of urban local governments, and 5 per cent of the receipt of rural councils.[11]

There is a revenue-sharing arrangement between provincial and local governments which consists mainly of the property tax and betterment tax, where a major portion of these taxes are transferred to the relevant local councils. In the case of the property tax, 85 per cent is returned to the local governments in the Punjab, Sindh, and Baluchistan, while in the NWFP, as much as 95 per cent of total receipts of this head (net of collection costs) is made available to the local councils. It is important to point out that, while provincial governments receive revenues from the federal government on the basis of population, the local governments receive revenue on the basis of *collection*. Hence, there is no cross-subsidization and the larger the amount of revenue collected from a particular urban local council, the more it receives, irrespective of its size. (There are no revenue-sharing arrangements between the provincial and rural local governments.)

We show below that provincial governments have access to revenue-deficit grants from federal governments that bail them out when they fall short of funds. Surprisingly, no such general grant-in-aid from provincial to local governments exists. The grants-in-aid from provincial government to local councils are specific in nature and used to finance recurring expenditure on education and health. Local governments have to take care of their recurring deficits themselves.

Moreover, local governments make further payments and transfers to provincial governments in the form of revenue from a surcharge on local taxes, especially in the NWFP and the Punjab. For example, an education cess of 12 per cent on octroi is charged in the NWFP, which is transferred totally to

Table 10.2
Modes of collection of different taxes

	Octroi	Export	Property tax	Tax on property transfer	Licence	Toll	Professional tax	Education cess	Local rate	Cattle fair	Marriage
Metropolitan corporation	C* D	–	P**	P D	D**	D**	–	–	–	–	–
Municipal corporation	C**	–	P**	P D	D**	D**	D**	–	D**	–	–
Municipal committee	C**	–	P**	P D	D**	D**	D**	–	–	–	–
Town committee	C**	–	P** D	P D	D**	D* C	D**	–	P**–	–	–
District council	–	C**	P**	D* C	D* C	D* C	D**	C**	P**	C** D	–
Union council	–	–	–	D**	D**	–	D**	–	–	–	D**
Development authority	–	–	–	D**	D**	–	–	–	–	–	–
Water and sanitation	–	–	P**	D**	D**	–	–	–	–	–	–
Cantonment board	–	–	–	LCB	LCB	–	–	–	–	–	–

P = Provincial government.
C = Contractor.
D = Department.
* Implies dominantly collected by.
** Implies exclusively collected by.
Source: Applied Economics Research Centre (AERC), *Resource Mobilization by Provincial and Local Governments in Pakistan*, Research Report No. 93, 1992, p. 113.

the provincial government. As an important and detailed report argues, 'this tendency of the provincial governments to ride on the back of the Local Government is a unique feature of the public finance structure of Pakistan'.[12]

Federal and Provincial Governments

It is somewhat surprising that local governments have been expected to keep their revenues and resources in check and maintain a significant ability to self-finance their expenditures, while provincial governments have, until recently, been given a somewhat freer hand by the federal government. There exists an elaborate mechanism by which fiscal transfers from the federal to the provincial governments take place from taxes collected by the former. In fact, this mechanism is sanctified by the Constitution, where 'the Federal Government is required to transfer revenues from taxes, as may be specified from time to time, to the provincial governments. Taxes to be included in the divisible pool and the share to be given to each province is determined by various awards/commissions.'[13]

The National Finance Commission (NFC) is a body constituted by the President of Pakistan which is meant to divide the revenue-sharing formula for the divisible pool of resources to be made available from the federal to the provincial governments. The NFC is supposed to announce an award every five years, on which basis the divisible pool is determined. However, as Table 10.3 shows, the NFC has not been constituted every five years and there was a gap of seventeen years between the 1991 award and the previous award of 1974. Attempts were made in 1979 and 1985 to form the NFC, but all such initiatives failed.The next award was to be made in June 1996, but was delayed by a few months and was finally announced by one of Pakistan's numerous unelected, so-called caretaker governments in late 1996. However, numerous objections to the award have been raised by members of parliament elected to the provincial and federal governments following the 1997 general elections (see Appendix 10.1 on the 1991 award).

Table 10.3 shows how the composition and size of the divisible pool from the federal to the provincial governments has changed over time. After an increase in the number and the amount of taxes between 1951 and 1970, there was a contraction in both in 1974, reducing the size of the divisible pool. The NFC award of 1991 distributes 80 per cent of the revenues from the federal to the provincial governments in

Table 10.3
Formula for federal tax sharing with provinces (%)

Tax category	Niemyer award 1937	Raismon award 1951	NFC 1962	NFC 1964	NFC 1970	NFC 1974	NFC 1991
Income tax	50	50	50	65	80	80	80
Sales tax	–	50	60	65	80	80	80
Central excise on tea, tobacco, and betel nut	–	50	60	65	80	–	80
Export duty on jute and cotton	62.5	62.2	100	65	80	80	80
Royalty on excise duty on gas							*
Development surcharge on gas							*
Royalty on crude oil							*
Profit from hydro-electricity							*

*On collection basis.
Source: Applied Economics Research Centre (AERC), *Resource Mobilization by Federal Government in Pakistan*, Research Report No. 91, 1992, p. 67.

the case of income tax, export duty on cotton, excise duty on tobacco and sales tax. 'In addition, the Federal Government has taken over the responsibility of financing any residual deficits of the Provincial governments in their recurring budgets. These ad-hoc subventions and grants have grown very rapidly in recent years.'[14] Hence, the provincial governments got a far better deal through this revenue-sharing arrangement in 1991 than ever before. This is most noticeable from the fact that the total revenue accruing to the four provincial governments more than doubled from Rs7.1 billion in 1990/1 to Rs15.9 billion the next year after the award in 1991/2. While provincial governments' tax revenue in these two years increased by 40 per cent, non-tax revenues increased by 370 per cent![15] The 1991 NFC award gave a much needed boost to provincial government finances, which ended up in surplus for a change, but in subsequent years, they again ran into the perennial problem of huge deficits (see Appendix 10.1).

In the case of revenue transfers from provincial to local governments, it was revenue raised from each council that determined the amount transferred to the urban local councils. In case of the NFC award and transfers from the federal to the provincial governments, it is essentially a single factor, population, that determines which province will get what share from the divisible pool. Hence, cross-subsidization will take place from a province that provides a greater share to the exchequer, to a province that does not contribute as much, simply because it is to receive a certain amount based on its population share (see also Appendix 10.1).

Despite an elaborate mechanism of resource transfers from the federal to the provincial governments, provincial

governments have very frequently been in deficit. Whenever this has happened, the federal government has given ad hoc subventions and grants. Moreover, the Annual Development Programmes of the provinces have also been financed, at times totally, by resources transferred from the federal to the provincial governments. Another important difference between provincial and local governments is that provincial governments have recourse to interest-bearing loans from the federal government, which local governments do not.

The salient features of the nature of inter-governmental fiscal transfers can thus be summarized as follows:

i)   Revenue sharing between provincial and local governments is very limited, and restricted to the property tax in urban areas.

ii) While provincial governments have generally had access to federal grants to cover their recurring deficits, no such access exists in the case of local governments.

iii) The entire ADP of the provincial governments is financed by the federal government. In contrast to this, the ADP of local councils (except the UCs [union councils]) is largely self-financed.

iv) Wherever there is an overlap in fiscal powers, provincial governments have pre-empted the common taxes. This includes the tax on professions, trades and callings, the motor vehicle tax, and the entertainment tax.

v)   The deteriorating financial position of provincial governments has meant that these government have not only encroached on local fiscal powers over time but also the flow of funds in real per capita terms to the local governments has tended to decrease.

vi) The dependence of local governments on provincial governments has decreased over time while that of provincial governments on the federal government has increased.

vii) The province of Baluchistan has more developed revenue-sharing arrangements with MVT [motor vehicle tax] being shared with the urban councils along with the property tax.

viii) While revenue sharing between the federal government and the provincial governments is largely on the basis of population, that between a provincial government and local governments is on the basis of collection.

xi) Unlike the federal government, provincial governments have shown a tendency to ride on the back of a lower level of government. For example, the provincial government of NWFP levies surcharge (education cess) on octroi.

x) A large proportion of the revenues from taxes of local origin is, in fact, taken away by higher levels of government, especially the provincial governments. Contrary to expectations, the share of resources transferred from the rural areas is greater.

xi) In recent years, some revenue-sharing arrangements have been established among the local governments, especially in the rural areas. For example, district councils have started giving a share of the local rate or export tax to the UCs.[16]

10.2 Public Finance: The Basic Facts

As has been the pattern in much of this book, having introduced the subject of public finance in Pakistan, we now present some data. This section is made cumbersome by the extensive nature of public finance statistics covering three tiers of government: federal, provincial, and local. Nevertheless, in order to appreciate the issues involved, a study of hard data is unavoidable.

Of the tables that follow, Tables 10.4 to 10.9 provide basic and historical information and data about the nature of Pakistan's public finances. Table 10.4 presents the expenditure and revenue pattern in Pakistan prior to the independence of Bangladesh. It shows that the main source of revenue has historically been from customs duties, i.e. taxation on trade. This should not be very surprising if Part II of this book has been studied, where the contribution of trade has been shown to be substantial in economic development. With high tariff barriers and import substituting industrialization, this is a logical outcome. However, taxes from imports are, even today, the main source of revenue for the exchequer. Another interesting figure on the revenue side in Table 10.4 is the contribution of income and corporation

Table 10.4
Principal sources of revenue and expenditure for United Pakistan (Rs m)

Year	Revenue					Expenditure						
	Customs	Central excise duty	Income tax and corporation tax	Sales tax	Total revenue receipts	General administration	Social sectors	Defence	Total expenditure	Surplus/deficit	Total development expenditure	Total non-development expenditure
1947/8	113.7	13.8	27.0		198.9	8.2	7.2	153.8	236.0	–37.1	98.1	22.4
1957/8	420.5	193.7	240.4	142.7	1,525.0	68.3	86.4	854.2	1,521.8	3.2	1,457.2	125.3
1964/5	1,030.2	697.0	342.3	268.6	3,301.0	111.1	132.3	1,262.3	2,736.2	564.8	2,426.0	254.5
1970/1	1,700.0	2,159.7	385.0	247.6	6,461.3	188.4	301.2	3,200.0	6,002.6	458.7	4,725.8	941.0

Source: Government of Pakistan, *Pakistan Economic Survey, 1972–73*, Islamabad, 1973, pp. 170–1.

taxes. Despite the impressive industrialization and dynamic economic growth that took place in the 1960s, the contribution of income and corporate taxes actually *declined* as a percentage of total revenue receipts for United Pakistan. From 15.7 per cent in 1957/8, they fell to less than 6 per cent in 1970/1. The issue of income tax is discussed in subsequent sections of this book, but it seems that the pattern of tax evasion and underreporting may have been established very early in Pakistan.

On the expenditure side, it seems that Pakistan's was an economy of defence, with more than half of total expenditure being spent on defence from 1947 to at least 1970/1. In 1970/1, 53 per cent of total expenditure was on defence, a figure astronomically high by any standards. Because Pakistan's economy, up to the 1970s, was highly dependent on external resources in the form of aid, grants, and foreign debt, development expenditure was higher than non-development expenditure. In 1962/3, for example, of the total resources available to spend in Pakistan, as much as 73 per cent were external funds; in 1966/7, this figure was 74 per cent. As soon as the military government of Ayub Khan took control of Pakistan in 1958, the share of external funds in total resources jumped to over half. The arguments made in Chapter 6, that Pakistan's economy was highly dependent on aid and that much of the industrialization boom of the Decade of Development was foreign funded, are re-emphasized on the basis of public finance data for those years.[17]

To understand the nature of public finance statistics, Tables 10.5 to 10.9 provide a good introduction. Table 10.5 gives a basic overview of how the Government of Pakistan presents its consolidated provincial and federal government expenditure and revenue, and includes figures on development expenditure and on the extent of the fiscal deficit and its funding for each year. Tables 10.6 and 10.7 then break down the revenue and expenditure statements of the government in greater detail.

In Table 10.6, we see that revenue from taxation is far greater than that from non-tax revenue, and that indirect taxes are many times as large as direct taxes. Within the category of indirect taxes, import duties dominate by far, and still provide the largest source of income to the government. On the expenditure side (Table 10.7), development expenditure is far less than current or non-development expenditure, and in 1994/5 was less than 25 per cent of total provincial and federal current expenditure. This pattern contrasts sharply with that seen in the period prior to 1971. The data for 1994/5 also show that defence and interest payments account for nearly half of all government expenditure. This issue is of key importance to the economy and politics, and is discussed in greater detail in this chapter and the next.

Since the figures in Tables 10.5 to 10.7 are in current market prices, a more useful indication of trend is a measurement of these figures with respect to a constant, say GDP. Table 10.8 shows how total revenue has not grown substantially over the last decade and ranges around 17 or 18 per cent of GDP. Tax revenue is only around 13 per cent and is cause for serious concern, as is discussed in section 10.3.1

Table 10.5
Summary of public finances, 1987/8 and 1994/5

	1987/8		1994/5	
	Rs m	% of GDP	Rs m	% of GDP
Total revenues	117,021	17.3	319,875	17.1
Federal	110,949		302,499	
Provincial	6,072		17,376	
A Tax revenues	93,456	14.3	256,780	13.8
Federal	88,958		247,376	
Provincial	4,498		9,404	
B Non-tax revenues	23,565	3.7	63,095	3.4
Federal	21,991		55,123	
Provincial	1,574		7,972	
Surplus of autonomous bodies and SAP[c]	5,789		5,000	
Expenditures	180,373	26.7	428,281	23.0
Federal	136,151		318,057	
Provincial	44,222		110,224	
Current[a]	133,645		346,381	
Federal	104,200		257,957	
Provincial	29,445		88,424	
Development	46,728		81,900	
Federal	31,951		60,100	
Provincial	14,777		21,800	
Overall deficit	57,563	8.5	103,405	5.5
Financing (net)	57,563		103,405	
External (net)	12,691		31,229	
Domestic (non-bank)	30,931		47,626	
Banking system[b]	13,941		18,551	
Memorandum items				
GDP at market prices	675,389		1,865,595[d]	

[a] Current subsidies are included in current expenditure and development subsidies in development expenditure.
[b] Differs from monetary statistics due to coverage and timing.
[c] SAP from 1992/3.
[d] Provisional estimate.
Source: Government of Pakistan, *Pakistan Economic Survey, 1995–96*, Islamabad, 1996, p. 138.

below. Figure 10.2 shows the almost unchanging trend and relationship between tax and non-tax revenue since 1986/7.

Table 10.9 shows how government expenditures have grown over time and the extent of allocation to different expenditure heads. Figure 10.3, based on the table, shows that while defence and interest payments have shown only positive, at times dramatic, increases over the previous year, development expenditure has even been cut, by equally dramatic amounts, in some years. What is more alarming from the lower panel in Table 10.9 is that proportion of development expenditure in total expenditure, while very

Table 10.6
Consolidated federal and provincial government revenues, 1987/8 and 1994/5 (Rs m)

	1987/8	1994/5
Total revenues (I + II)	117,021	319,875
Federal[a]	110,949	302,499
Provincial[a]	6,072	17,376
I Tax revenues (A + B)	93,456	256,780
Federal	88,958	247,376
Provincial	4,498	9,404
A Direct taxes (1 + 2)	12,441	59,376
1 Income and corp. tax[b]	11,528	54,300
2 Taxes on property	913	5,076
Federal	313	3,700
Provincial	600	1,376
B Indirect taxes		
(3 + 4 + 5 + 6 + 7)	81,015	197,405
3 Excise duty	17,560	43,607
Federal	17,399	43,000
Provincial	161	607
4 Sales tax [b]	8,743	43,000
4.1 On imports[b]	5,176	–
4.2 On domestic products[b]	3,567	–
5 Taxes on international trade	38,001	81,000
5.1 Import duties[b]	34,711	–
5.2 Export duties[b]	3,290	–
6 Surcharges[b]	12,974	21,526
6.1 Gas[b]	3,075	8,526
6.2 Petroleum[b]	9,899	13,000
7 Other taxes[c]	3,737	8,272
7.1 Stamp duties[c]	1,671	3,556
7.2 Motor vehicle taxes[c]	856	1,804
7.3 Foreign travel tax	–	850
7.4 Others[c]	1,210	2,261
II Non-tax revenues		
(8 + 9 + 10 + 11 + 12)	23,565	63,095
Federal	21,991	55,123
Provincial	1,574	7,972
8 Interest and dividend		
+ Federal	6,382	22,808
Federal	3,157	22,465
Provincial	225	343
9 Trading profits[b]	613	–
10 Post Office and T & T	4,103	–
11 Receipt from civil admin.	9,216	27,412
12 Others	3,251	12,876
Federal	1,902	5,246
Provincial	1,349	7,629

[a] Since consolidated revenues are invariant to 'Transfers to provinces', adjustment for such transfers has not been made in the federal and provincial figures.
[b] Revenues under these heads are exclusively federal.
[c] Revenues under these heads are exclusively provincial.
Source: Government of Pakistan, *Pakistan Economic Survey, 1995–96*, Islamabad, 1996, p. 139.

Table 10.7
Consolidated federal and provincial government expenditure, 1987/8 and 1994/5 (Rs m)

	1987/8	1994/5 BE
Current expenditure[a]	133,645	346,380
Federal	104,200	257,956
Provincial	29,445	88,424
Defence[b]	47,015	100,221
Interest	33,238	101,846
Federal	31,702	99,195
Provincial	1,536	2,661
Current subsidies	7,950	9,458
Federal	4,332	3,691
Provincial	3,618	2,767
General administration	8,642	32,627
Federal	5,098	18,480
Provincial	3,444	14,147
Social/ECO/community services	17,325	70,772
Federal	4,898	16,178
Provincial	12,427	44,594
All others	19,575	34,457
Federal	11,155	20,192
Provincial	8,420	14,265
Development expenditure	46,728	81,900
Federal	31,951	60,100
Provincial	14,777	21,800
Total expenditure	180,373	428,280
Federal	136,151	318,056
Provincial	44,222	110,224

[a] Current subsidies are included in current expenditure and development expenditure.
[b] Expenditures under these heads are exclusively federal.
BE = Budget estimates.
Source: Government of Pakistan, *Pakistan Economic Survey, 1995–96*, Islamabad, 1996, p. 140.

low, has continued to fall over the last decade. Table 10.10 looks at these expenditure figures as a proportion of GDP. Figure 10.4 shows that interest payments and defence consume almost half of total expenditure.

Having provided an overview of public finance statistics, we can now examine some of the key public finance ratios in Pakistan over a period of about thirty years, as shown in Table 10.11. While there has been some change in tax revenue as a proportion of total revenue in the last thirty years, the change has not been very substantial. Moreover, most other ratios – those for direct taxes, indirect taxes, customs duties, etc. – have not shown much change, although the nature and structure of the economy has changed considerably in thirty years. One should have expected changes in the revenue structure along with structural changes in the economy. The significant changes are, however, on the expenditure side, where debt servicing has increased quite substantially over the three decades. The dependence on external resources, if

Table 10.8
Summary of public finance: consolidated federal and provincial governments, 1978–1995 (% of GDP at market prices)

	1978/9	1979/80	1980/1	1981/2	1982/3	1983/4	1984/5	1985/6	1986/7	1987/8	1988/9	1989/90	1990/1	1991/2	1992/3	1993/4	1994/5
Total revenues	15.7	16.4	16.9	16.0	16.3	17.2	16.4	17.5	18.1	17.3	18.0	18.6	16.1	19.1	18.0	18.6	17.1
Tax revenues	12.9	13.9	14.0	13.3	13.5	12.8	11.9	12.3	14.5	13.8	14.3	14.6	12.7	13.6	13.3	13.9	13.7
Non-tax revenues	2.8	2.5	2.9	2.8	2.8	4.4	4.5	5.2	3.7	3.5	3.7	4.6	3.4	4.3	4.6	4.6	3.4
Expenditures	25.1	23.3	22.9	21.9	23.9	23.8	24.7	26.1	26.6	26.7	26.1	25.9	25.6	26.5	26.0	24.5	23.0
Overall deficit	8.9	6.3	5.3	5.3	7.0	6.0	7.8	8.1	8.2	8.5	7.4	6.5	8.7	7.4	7.9	5.8	5.5

Source: Government of Pakistan, *Pakistan Economic Survey*, various issues, Islamabad.

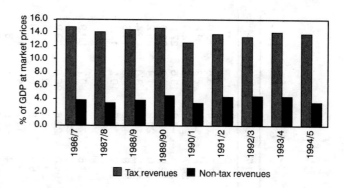

Figure 10.2
Tax and non-tax revenue, 1986–1995 (% of GDP)

high in the 1960s and 1970s, was even higher at the end of the 1980s.

So far we have been discussing largely consolidated figures. Before we turn to a disaggregation of revenue and expenditure patterns at different levels of government, Table 10.12 shows us the degree and role of each level of government in revenue and expenditure. The federal government collects about 88 per cent of total revenue and of tax receipts, while local government does as well as provincial government, despite numerous constraints and obstacles in raising revenue. Since the federal government provides provincial government's funds, the provinces' share of development expenditure is greater than the revenue they raise. In 1990/1, while provincial governments collected 6 per cent of total revenue receipts, they spent almost 28 per cent of total government expenditure. On the other hand, local government's share of total expenditure is far less than the revenue it raises (see Figure 10.5), an issue discussed in section 10.3 below.

Tables 10.13 to 10.15 show in greater detail the federal government's revenue receipts over the last few years and provide a far more relevant comparison of the different types of tax and their shares. While the share of income tax has increased since 1983, as has that of the sales tax, indirect taxes still constituted almost three-quarters of the total taxes collected in 1994/5. Figures 10.6 and 10.7 depict these changes over time quite starkly. While the issue of income tax, the sales tax, and the proportion of direct to indirect taxes is discussed in greater detail in later sections of this chapter, it is interesting to see how Pakistan performs compared to similar underdeveloped countries. Table 10.16 provides such a comparison.

From the table it seems that, as GDP rises, the share of total taxes should also rise, and direct taxes, in particular, should play a greater role in the overall taxation structure of the country. At the moment, though, Pakistan's tax effort is quite poor compared even with countries with similar levels of income, especially in the case of direct taxes. At 3.91 per cent of GDP, even poorer countries have a better tax effort than Pakistan. Indirect taxes do not vary all that much, although, not surprisingly, as income grows, foreign indirect taxes are also expected to increase. Hence, while a growth

Table 10.9
Consolidated federal and provincial government expenditure, 1971–1995

	1971/2	1976/7	1977/8	1980/1	1984/5	1986/7	1987/8	1988/9	1989/90	1990/1	1991/2	1992/3	1993/4	1994/5
Growth rate over preceding period (%)														
Current expenditure	–	–	–	–	–	22.8	15.0	14.5	8.2	18.2	17.6	18.4	13.8	18.0
Defence	–	–	–	–	–	16.1	13.7	8.6	15.0	10.1	17.2	15.5	7.2	9.2
Interest	–	–	–	–	–	21.4	38.7	14.7	22.5	7.1	24.7	26.3	30.7	12.0
Current subsidies	–	–	–	–	–	1.8	36.7	67.0	–31.9	18.4	–26.4	–7.8	13.5	27.6
General administration	–	–	–	–	–	40.8	–17.8	19.3	17.0	13.1	32.9	13.3	22.2	28.0
Social services	–	–	–	–	–	24.9	12.1	11.4	4.9	38.0	14.0	20.2	1.4	25.2
Others	–	–	–	–	–	39.0	1.4	7.8	–10.2	51.2	–18.5	15.9	3.0	45.4
Development expenditures	–	–	–	–	–	–9.1	29.2	3.0	16.5	16.5	39.9	–16.6	–2.8	14.6
Total expenditure	–	–	–	–	–	13.3	18.4	11.5	10.2	17.7	23.2	8.5	10.2	17.4
As percentage of total expenditure														
Current expenditure	68.1	45.6	52.3	62.7	71.7	76.3	74.1	76.1	74.7	75.0	71.6	78.1	80.7	80.9
Defence	44.5	26.1	26.6	24.5	27.3	27.1	26.1	25.4	26.5	24.8	23.6	25.0	24.1	23.4
Interest	11.9	6.0	8.2	9.3	14.1	15.7	18.4	18.9	21.1	19.2	194.0	22.6	26.8	23.8
Current subsidies	–	–	–	–	–	3.8	4.4	6.6	4.1	4.1	2.5	2.1	2.1	1.5
General administration	–	–	–	–	–	6.8	4.7	5.1	5.4	5.2	5.6	5.8	6.5	7.6
Social/ECO/community services	–	–	–	–	–	10.1	9.6	9.6	9.1	18.2	14.1	15.7	14.4	16.5
Others	–	–	–	–	–	12.8	10.9	10.5	8.9	11.0	6.4	6.9	6.5	8.0
Development expenditures	31.9	54.4	47.7	37.7	28.3	23.7	25.9	23.9	25.3	25.0	28.1	21.9	19.3	19.1

Source: Government of Pakistan, *Pakistan Economic Survey*, various issues, Islamabad.

Table 10.10
Composition of government's total expenditure, 1971–1995 (% of GDP)

	1971/2	1972/3	1973/4	1974/5	1975/6	1976/7	1977/8	1978/9	1979/80	1980/1	1981/2	1982/3	1983/4	1984/5	1985/6	1986/7	1987/8	1988/9	1989/90	1990/1	1991/2	1992/3	1993/4	1994/5
Current expenditure	10.4	10.4	9.8	10.3	10.3	9.5	10.8	15.6	15.1	13.6	13.7	15.8	17.1	17.7	18.4	20.3	19.8	19.9	19.2	19.2	19.1	20.3	18.8	18.4
Development expenditure	4.9	6.3	7.2	10.2	10.8	11.3	9.9	9.5	8.2	9.3	8.2	8.1	6.7	7.0	7.7	6.3	6.9	6.3	6.5	6.4	7.6	5.7	4.6	4.4
Defence expenditure	6.8	6.6	5.6	6.2	6.2	5.4	5.5	–	–	5.0	5.7	6.4	6.4	6.7	6.9	7.2	7.0	6.6	6.8	6.3	6.3	6.5	5.8	5.6
Interest payments	1.8	2.2	1.7	1.2	1.2	1.3	1.7	–	–	2.1	2.4	3.1	3.4	3.5	3.8	4.2	4.9	5.0	5.4	4.9	5.2	5.9	5.8	5.2

Source: Government of Pakistan, *Pakistan Economic Survey*, various issues, Islamabad.

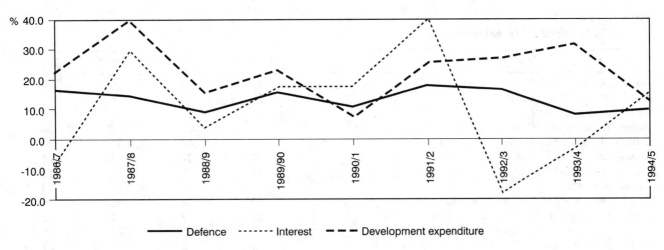

Figure 10.3
Government expenditure, 1986–1995 (% growth over previous year)

factor is important, tax effort and special effort also play an important role.

Like Table 10.10, Table 10.17 provides a similar comparison across three decades. Direct taxes have not shown much change, although indirect taxes and in particular import duties have increased substantially. There is also an increase in excise duties and the sales tax. Indirect taxes are often consumption taxes, which means that, as the economy grows and as the demand for and consumption of goods also increases, so does the revenue collected from the taxes on those goods. This is clearly visible from the table in the case of Pakistan, which corroborates the international evidence shown in Table 10.16 above.

Box 10.1 explains the measures of elasticity and buoyancy in the tax structure, and Tables 10.18 and 10.19 show the extent of both for some important taxes. The elasticity coefficient of a tax measures the built-in response of tax revenue to growth in income, without any change in the tax rate, while the buoyancy coefficient measures the total responsiveness in the tax revenue to the growth of income, inclusive of changes in tax revenue. Table 10.18 shows that except for the sales tax, and for income tax during 1972/3 to

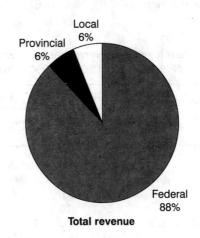

Total revenue

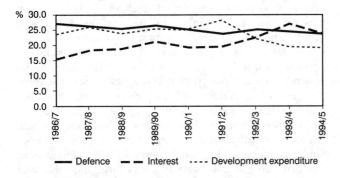

Figure 10.4
Defence, interest payments, and development expenditure, 1986–1995 (% of total expenditure)

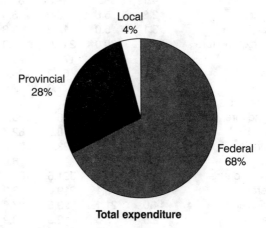

Total expenditure

Figure 10.5
Total revenue receipts and expenditure, 1990/1

Table 10.11
Key public financial ratios, selected dates

Revenue receipt of federal government	1964/5	1972/3	1985/6	1989/90
Tax revenue as % of TR	73	75	80	76
Non-tax revenue as % of TR	27	25	20	24
Direct tax as % of TXR	14	13	14	14
Indirect tax as % of TXR	83	87	86	86
Custom duties as % of TXR	43	44	41	46
Excise duties as % of TXR	23	37	22	21
Sales duties as % of TXR	11	5	7	18
TAX to GDP ratio	9	9	14	14
External resources as % of total capital exp.	49	48	58	73
Internal resources as % of total capital exp.	20	52	42	45
Debt servicing as % of total exp. of fed. govt.	3	6	27	39
Internal debt servicing as % of total recurring exp.	5	3	6	21
Ratio of development exp. to non-development exp.	1:3	1:2.8	1:2.3	1:2.6
Federal tax assignment as % of provincial receipts	16	14	31	39
Federal govt's recurring exp. in total recurring exp.	72	68	76	80
Prov. govt's recurring exp. in total recurring exp.	28	22	24	20
Budget deficit as % of GDP	–	–	8.1	6.5

Source: Applied Economics Research Centre (AERC), *Resource Mobilization by Federal Government in Pakistan*, Research Report No. 91, 1992, p. 67.

Table 10.12
Share of different levels of government in revenues and expenditure[a] in Pakistan, 1979/80 and 1990/1 (Rs m)

Revenue/expenditure category	1979/80 Level	1979/80 Share (%)	1990/1 Level	1990/1 Share (%)
Tax receipts	41.3	100.0	136.2	100.0
Federal	36.5	88.4	120.6	88.5
Provincial	2.3	5.6	6.8	5.0
Local	2.5	6.0	8.8	6.5
Total revenue receipts	50.0	100.0	214.7	100.0
Federal	44.1	88.2	189.5	88.2
Provincial	2.8	5.6	13.0	6.0
Local	3.1	6.0	12.2	5.8
Current expenditure	39.6	100.0	241.9	100.0
Federal	28.8	72.7	171.6	70.9
Provincial	9.1	23.0	63.3	26.2
Local	1.7	4.3	7.0	2.9
Development expenditure	26.6	100.0	76.6	100.0
Federal	20.9	78.6	48.0	62.7
Provincial	4.9	18.4	23.3	30.4
Local	0.8	3.0	5.3	6.9
Total expenditure	66.2	100.0	321.6	100.0
Federal	49.7	75.1	219.6	68.3
Provincial	14.0	21.1	89.5	27.8
Local	2.5	3.8	12.5	3.9

[a] For the country as a whole, in view of the difficulty in allocating federal expenditure to each province.
Source: Hanif, Naveed, 'The Structure of Government in Pakistan, *News on Friday,* 25 August, 1995.

1980/1, the elasticity figures are less than 1, implying that a 1 per cent increase in income increases tax revenue by less than 1 per cent. Customs duties and the sales tax have a buoyancy of more than 1, while excise duties and income tax have a less-than-1 buoyancy, implying that inclusive of all the discretionary measures, a 1 per cent increase in income, would result in less than 1 per cent change in tax revenue. The reasons for the low elasticity include the presence of a large black economy and tax evasion, the presence of a wide array of exemptions, and a poor and corrupt tax administration system.

We can now move from federal taxes to the provincial tax structure. As explained earlier, the NFC award of 1991 suddenly put all four provinces into a surplus position, as seen in Table 10.20. However, what the table reveals is that provinces' own revenue effort has fallen appreciably since 1990/1, and development expenditures, which are mainly the responsibility of the provinces (see Table 10.21) have either decreased, as in the case of the Punjab, or not shown much improvement, in the other three provinces. Education, health, and water supply and sanitation are the main sectors where the provincial governments dominate, and overall 64 per cent of expenditure on the social sectors is incurred at the provincial level. Table 10.22 nevertheless shows that there has been considerable effort to increase revenue. All the provinces have made considerable progress, especially Sindh, which has registered double-digit growth in almost all taxes. Karachi's contribution in raising revenue for the whole of Sindh is likely to be quite substantial. The increase in electricity duty, due to Karachi's very large industrial and population base, that for hotels due to Karachi's dominance of larger hotels, and other duties, such as on stamps and on property mainly from Karachi, have in all likelihood resulted in this increase for Sindh overall.

Table 10.13
Federal tax receipts (net), 1983–1995 (Rs m)

Year	Indirect taxes				Direct taxes							Total federal taxes
	Customs	Central excise	Sales tax	Total	Income tax	Wealth tax	Gift tax	Capital value tax	Estate duty	W.W. fund	Total	
(1)	(2)	(3)	(4)	(5)	(6)	(7)	(8)	(9)	(10)	(11)	(12)	(13)
1983/4	21,532	15,652	4,624	41,808	8,573	163	17	–	1	34	8,788	50,596
1984/5	23,371	15,313	4,674	43,358	9,071	177	15	–	–	49	9,312	52,670
1985/6	29,343	15,515	4,928	49,786	9,592	124	5	–	–	61	9,782	59,568
1986/7	33,364	15,361	6,409	55,134	10,354	152	3	–	1	58	10,568	65,702
1987/8	38,001	17,398	8,743	64,142	11,528	193	4	–	–	116	11,841	75,983
1988/9	42,362	20,038	14,700	77,100	13,407	326	1	–	–	186	13,920	91,020
1989/90	48,584	22,341	18,574	89,499	15,000	419	–	54	–	164	15,637	105,136
1990/1	50,528	23,239	17,008	90,775	19,079	496	–	105	–	188	19,868	110,643
1991/2	61,821	27,607	20,799	110,227	27,913	632	–	140	–	166	28,851	139,078
1992/3	61,400	31,545	23,516	116,461	35,018	1,196	–	313	–	244	36,771	153,223
1993/4	64,240	34,520	30,379	129,139	41,466	1,216	–	420	–	349	43,451	172,590
1994/5	77,653	43,691	43,574	164,918	59,064	1,644	–	546	–	406	61,660	226,578

Source: Central Board of Revenue, *CBR Year Book,* various issues, Islamabad.

Table 10.14
Taxes and their distribution, 1983–1995
(% share in total tax)

Year	Income tax	Other direct taxes	Customs	Central excise	Sales tax
(1)	(2)	(3)	(4)	(5)	(6)
1983/4	17.00	0.40	42.60	30.90	9.10
1984/5	17.20	0.50	44.40	29.10	8.80
1985/6	16.10	0.30	49.30	26.00	8.30
1986/7	15.80	0.30	50.80	23.40	9.70
1987/8	15.20	0.40	50.00	22.90	11.50
1988/9	14.70	0.60	46.50	22.00	16.20
1989/90	14.30	0.60	46.20	21.20	17.70
1990/1	17.30	0.70	45.60	21.00	15.40
1991/2	20.10	0.60	44.50	19.90	149.0
1992/3	22.90	1.10	40.10	20.60	15.30
1993/4	24.00	1.20	37.20	20.00	17.60
1994/5	26.10	1.10	34.30	19.30	19.20

Source: Central Board of Revenue, *CBR Year Book,* various issues, Islamabad.

Table 10.15
Distribution of direct and indirect taxes, 1983–1995
(% share in total taxes)

Year	Direct tax	Indirect tax
1983/4	17.40	82.60
1984/5	17.70	82.30
1985/6	16.40	83.60
1986/7	16.10	83.90
1987/8	15.60	84.40
1988/9	15.30	84.70
1989/90	14.90	85.10
1990/1	18.00	82.00
1991/2	20.70	79.30
1992/3	24.00	76.00
1993/4	24.20	74.80
1994/5	27.20	72.80

Source: Central Board of Revenue, *CBR Year Book,* various issues, Islamabad.

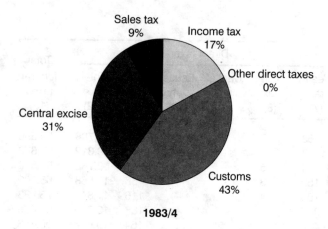

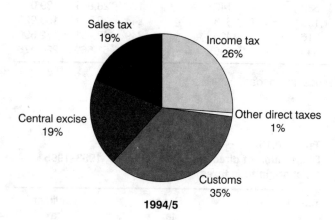

Figure 10.6
Percentage share of main taxes in total tax, 1983/4 and 1994/5

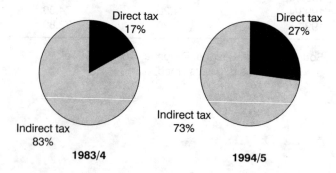

Figure 10.7
Percentage share of direct and indirect taxes in total tax, 1983/4 and 1994/5

Let us now turn to the more substantive issues in the taxation debate and examine the causes of many of the ratios and the consequences of some of the trends discussed in this section.

10.3 Important Issues in Public Finance and Revenue Mobilization

10.3.1 Federal Taxes

Hafiz Pasha summarizes the key features and problems of the (federal) tax system as follows:

> Pakistan's tax system is characterized by a number of structural problems. First, the overall level of fiscal effort is low and the tax-to-GDP ratio has remained, more or less, stagnant at between 12 to 13 per cent. This is one major explanation why budget deficits have been high, generally in excess of six per cent of the GDP. Second, there is overdependence on indirect taxes, which until recently accounted for a share in revenues of over 80 per cent. This has increased the regressivity of the tax system and imposed a higher excess burden of taxation. Third, within indirect taxes there is domination of taxes on international trade, which has promoted inefficiency, distorted the allocation of resources and encouraged illicit trade. Fourth, the effective tax bases of most taxes is narrow due to wide ranging exemptions and concessions and rampant tax evasion. For example, there is less than one income tax assessee per 100 persons and less than 60 per cent of imports actually pay duty. Consequently, tax rates have had to be pitched at high levels which has created a vicious circle of more tax base erosion and higher tax rates. Fifthly, tax administration is characterized by primitive and out-moded procedures, complex laws and considerable arbitrariness and discretion. The common perception is one of high levels of corruption and inefficiency.[18]

The World Bank, in its extensive evaluation of the economy prior to the commencement of the first major structural adjustment programme of 1988,[19] identified the issues of resource mobilization and the budget deficit as amongst the most important. Revenue generation was to be given special emphasis in any sort of adjustment programme, as the World Bank argued that, unless this area of the economy was put in order, much of the rest of the efforts would also fail (see Chapter 11 and Part IV of this book).

The World Bank report argues that the budget potential of an increase in resource mobilization comes from strengthening Pakistan's tax base, since tax revenues accounted for only 13–14 per cent of GDP, a figure far less than that of other countries at similar levels of development. The income elasticity of the tax system is low because of the very narrow tax base and the large number of exemptions

Table 10.16
Level and composition of tax revenues in developing countries and in Pakistan (% of GDP)

| Tax | Developing countries | | | Pakistan | |
	With per capita income of less than $360	With per capita income of $360 to $750	All	1989/90	1992/3
Direct taxes	**3.91**	**6.84**	**7.26**	**1.83**	**2.71**
Income tax	3.27	5.53	5.11	1.75	2.58
Wealth and property tax	0.24	0.31	0.45	0.08	0.13
Social security taxes	0.21	0.79	1.30	–	–
Others	0.19	0.21	0.40	–	–
Indirect taxes (domestic)	**4.55**	**4.74**	**5.21**	**4.81**	**4.33**
Sales, turnover, VAT	2.44	2.30	2.46	2.17	1.74
Excises	1.55	1.95	2.07	2.64	2.59
Others	0.46	0.49	0.68	–	–
Indirect taxes (foreign)	**5.30**	**7.58**	**5.13**	**5.68**	**4.52**
Import duties	4.05	6.70	4.32	5.11	4.46
Export duties	1.09	0.64	0.62	0.57	0.06
Others	0.16	0.22	0.20	–	–
Others	**0.26**	**0.41**	**0.45**	**0.51**	**0.70**
Total taxes	**14.02**	**19.66**	**18.05**	**12.83**	**12.26**

Sources: Pasha, Hafiz and M. Asif Iqbal, 'Taxation Reforms in Pakistan', *Pakistan Journal of Applied Economics,* vol. 10, nos. 1 and 2, 1994, p. 50.

given in sales tax, excise duty, income tax, and customs duties. The pre-Structural Adjustment Programme report emphasized that there was a need to 'broaden the tax base and increase the elasticity of the tax system by shifting the emphasis in indirect taxes towards domestic consumption (of both domestic and foreign products) and raising the contribution of the income tax'.[20] An extension of the sales tax to transform it into a consumption-type value added tax (VAT) needed to be imposed at the manufacturers' level. A theme which continues to be repeated in most analysis of the taxation structure, the need to subject agricultural income to taxation, was also identified by the World Bank.

Table 10.17
Tax/GDP ratios of individual taxes in Pakistan

| Nature of tax | Tax/GDP ratio (%) | | | | |
	1960/1	1971/2	1977/8	1987/8	1989/90
A Direct taxes	1.64	2.30	1.60	1.81	1.85
1 Income taxes	1.60	2.20	1.60	1.68	1.70
2 Others	–	0.10	0.00	0.13	0.15
B Indirect taxes	5.50	7.70	9.20	11.80	12.40
1 Customs duties	2.20	2.40	4.70	5.50	5.70
a) Import duties	2.10	2.10	4.50	5.10	5.20
b) Export duties	0.13	0.26	0.20	0.50	0.58
2 Excise duties	1.40	3.80	3.50	2.50	2.60
3 Sales tax	1.84	0.88	1.00	2.00	2.20
C Total taxes	7.20	10.00	11.00	13.60	14.30

Source: Applied Economies Research Centre (AERC), *Resource Mobilization by Federal Government in Pakistan,* Research Report No. 91, 1992, p. 67.

BOX 10.1

The elasticity and buoyancy of taxes

The elasticity and buoyancy of taxes helps determine how changes in the economy will impact on revenue.

The measure of *elasticity* of a tax system gives the automatic or natural responsiveness of tax yields to changes in national income. It is defined as a percentage change in total yield (or yields of individual taxes) associated with a given percentage change in GDP (or the relevant GDP component) without any change in the statutory rate of existing tax(es), in administrative efficiency or due to the introduction of new taxes.

Buoyancy measures the total response of revenue from a tax or taxes due to a change in income. It shows the growth that results from automatic growth of the base caused by the increase in GDP and from discretionary tax changes. The buoyancy of a tax system or individual tax is usually greater than or equal to the elasticity because tax rates are usually increased over time.

The magnitude of the elasticity depends on the level of tax rates, the progressivity of the rate structure, whether tax rates are specific or *ad valorem* in character and the change in the tax base due to changes in income. For the purpose of analysis, it is usually possible to break up the coefficient of elasticity into tax-to-base and base-to-income components. The first gives the responsiveness of tax yield to a change in tax base and the latter encompasses the effect of changes in base due to change in income.

The value of the tax-to-base elasticity depends on tax rates and the progressivity of the tax structure. If the rate structure is progressive or if there is an improvement in tax administration then the tax-to-base elasticity is likely to be high, thereby implying a higher overall elasticity. However, if high marginal tax rates induce higher evasion and corruption in tax payment then the tax-to-base elasticity is likely to be lower. Alternatively, if tax rates are specific rather than *ad valorem* then revenues may not rise proportionately with the increase in tax base and the elasticity in this case would be less than unity.

The base-to-income elasticity primarily depends upon the nature of the relationship between changes in income and changes in the tax base. This elasticity can be assumed to be largely exogenous and beyond the control of the tax collecting agency. In contrast to this, the magnitude of the tax-to-base elasticity can be influenced by policy action.

The elasticity of the entire tax system at any particular time is the weighted sum of the elasticities of the individual taxes, with the weights corresponding to the revenue shares. If the share of elastic taxes is higher, then the overall tax system will be more elastic.

Source: Applied Economics Research Centre (AERC), *Resource Mobilization by Provincial and Local Governments in Pakistan*, Research Report No. 93, 1992, pp. 56–8.

Table 10.18
Elasticity and buoyancy of major taxes w.r.t. income (GDP)

Federal taxes		Coefficient		
		1972/3 to 1989/90	1972/3 to 1980/1	1981/2 to 1989/90
Custom duty	Elasticity	0.692	0.943	0.696
	Buoyancy	1.063	1.177	1.065
Excise duty	Elasticity	0.658	0.916	0.526
	Buoyancy	0.894	1.148	0.532
Sales tax	Elasticity	1.010	1.082	1.446
	Buoyancy	1.259	1.256	1.713
Income tax	Elasticity	0.946	1.377	0.294
	Buoyancy	1.098	1.347	0.643
Total tax	Elasticity	0.800	1.064	0.800
	Buoyancy	1.070	1.206	0.983

Source: Applied Economics Research Centre (AERC), *Resource Mobilization by Federal Government in Pakistan*, Research Report No. 91, 1992, p. 67.

While the need to increase direct taxes as a share of total tax revenue has been an important realization, attempts to change the structure of indirect taxes have found equal emphasis. With trade taxes by far the key feature of Pakistan's taxation regime, Pakistan's resource mobilization efforts have been subject to impacts not necessarily of Pakistan's own doing. Hence, the need to develop another sort of tax that is consumption based and domestic. The World Bank report identified the need for a sales tax and highlighted various problems prior to attempts to remedy them in the structural adjustment programme of 1988:

> The objective for indirect taxation is to shift the emphasis from imports toward a broad-based tax on domestic consumption that is neutral between products made in Pakistan and imports. This would involve a modification of Pakistan's present *sales and excise taxes*. In principle, all goods produced/manufactured in Pakistan and sold wholesale are now subject to a sales tax, but practice has differed from principle. So many products have been granted exemptions that the sales tax now resembles a special consumption or excise tax rather than a broad-based consumption tax. In addition, differential coverage and differential rates between domestic products and imports (with higher rates for imports) have meant that the tax has 'protective effects' in addition to those generated by the tariff system. In the FY87

Table 10.19
Decomposition of buoyancy of major taxes

Federal taxes	Tax base	1972/3 to 1989/90			1972/3 to 1980/81			1981/2 to 1989/90		
		Tax to tax base buoyancy	Tax base to income buoyancy	Tax to income buoyancy	Tax to tax base buoyancy	Tax base to income buoyancy	Tax to income buoyancy	Tax to tax base buoyancy	Tax base to income buoyancy	Tax to income buoyancy
Import duty	Value of imports	1.002	1.061	1.063	0.920	1.271	1.177	1.208	0.881	1.065
Excise duty	Value added in large-scale manufacturing	0.776	1.152	0.894	0.675	1.701	1.148	0.563	0.945	0.532
Sales tax	Value of imports + Value of industrial production + Custom duty	1.203	1.047	1.259	1.188	1.057	1.256	1.561	1.097	1.173
Income tax	Non-agriculture GDP	1.024	1.072	1.098	1.260	1.069	1.347	0.596	1.079	0.643

Source: Applied Economics Research Centre (AERC), *Resource Mobilization by Federal Government in Pakistan,* Research Report No. 91, 1992, p. 67.

Table 10.20
Key financial ratios of the provinces, 1990–1995

Year	As percentage of recurring expenditure			As percentage of total expenditure[a]		
	Federal tax assignment[b]	Provincial own revenue	Revenue surplus/ deficit	Debt servicing	Development expenditures	Total federal transfer[c]
Punjab						
1990/1	59.5	25.7	−6.3	25.3	24.8	75.9
1991/2	77.8	23.8	4.7	24.9	23.5	81.8
1994/5	89.7	17.8	7.6	22.0	18.7	87.4
Sindh						
1990/1	48.6	20.6	−20.7	21.7	28.1	65.5
1991/2	78.4	19.0	1.1	24.1	23.5	87.1
1994/5	79.7	15.9	2.3	21.5	29.9	99.0
NWFP						
1990/1	41.8	11.6	−0.7	28.4	27.2	93.7
1991/2	97.6	10.2	11.0	30.8	33.6	87.6
1994/5	99.2	10.3	9.6	28.8	28.8	90.5
Baluchistan						
1990/1	49.5	6.3	−15.5	23.5	33.9	85.5
1991/2	119.8	4.8	26.5	22.0	39.5	96.5
1994/5	112.5	5.4	18.1	20.5	33.0	96.6
Four combined						
1990/1	53.0	20.5	−9.9	24.7	26.9	77.0
1991/2	84.9	18.6	6.7	25.4	27.1	85.7
1994/5	90.6	15.0	7.4	22.9	25.0	92.4

[a] Total expenditure = Development expenditure + Current expenditure.
[b] Including profit from hydro-electricity.
[c] Federal transfer = Federal tax assignment + Development grants + Federal loans + Development revenue receipts.
Source: Ghaus, Rafia and Andul Rauf Khan, 'Fiscal Status of the Provincial Government in Pakistan', *News on Friday,* 25 August, 1993.

Table 10.21
Share of different levels of government in expenditure on social sectors in Pakistan, 1990/1[a] (%)

	Federal	Provincial	Local
Education and training	13	83	4
Health and nutrition	16	62	22
Population welfare	97	3	0
Social welfare	73	27	0
Physical planning and housing[b]	5	50	45
Manpower and employment	74	26	0
Others	37	32	31
Total	20	64	16

[a] Latest year for which local government figures are available.
[b] Mostly water supply and sanitation.
Source: Hanif, Naveed, 'The Structure of Government in Pakistan', *News on Friday*, 25 August, 1996.

budget, the rates for domestic products and imports were made equal, but unequal coverage still leaves some protective effects intact. Cascading of the sales tax through several stages of production has been avoided in Pakistan by making taxes on inputs deductible from taxes on outputs, similar to the procedures under a value-added tax (VAT).

The simplest way, administratively, to develop a broad-based consumption tax would be to expand the coverage of the existing sales tax by drastically curtailing the number of exempted manufactured products. The present sales tax taxes domestic products and imports at the same rate (except for the differential coverage), covers

imported goods extensively, and allows taxes paid on inputs to be credited against taxes paid on outputs. Cutting the excessive number of exemptions would serve the objective of increasing the tax burden on domestic consumption.[21]

A key feature of the change in the taxation structure suggested was to cut the excessive number of exemptions under the existing taxation regime, which would then fulfil the objective of increasing the tax burden on consumption. The emphasis was on implementing VAT – a 'manufacturer's level consumption-type VAT'. This shift from a sales tax to a value added tax would require the extension of the coverage of taxation to almost all products at the manufacturers' level and would tax domestic and imported products at the same rate (see Appendices 10.2 and 10.3).

In the structural adjustment programme of 1988, a number of measures regarding the sales tax were undertaken (see Table 10.23). A gradual extension of the coverage of the sales tax on imported and domestically produced goods began. More and more commodities came under the sales tax and items previously exempted were now taxed. The adjustment programme envisaged a fully-fledged general sales tax (GST) – very much like a value added tax – by the end of the programme in 1991. The tax was extended quite substantially from the manufacturer/importer level to wholesalers and retailers for some products. However, the evaluation at the end of the structural adjustment programme revealed that 'the expansion in the tax base ... remained significantly less than what was initially envisaged, both in terms of the sectoral coverage and the number of taxpayers'.[22] There were many political considerations and constraints which continue to make the GST or VAT a very difficult tax to impose (see also Appendices 10.2 and 10.3). Moreover, Hafiz Pasha has identified a number of problems with the large-scale introduction of a full scale VAT in Pakistan. He argues that

Table 10.22
Annual compound growth rate in tax revenue by province, 1990/1 to 1994/5 (%)

Tax	Punjab	Sindh	NWFP	Baluchistan	Pakistan
Stamp duty	0.1	23.9	25.1	10.0	7.5
Urban immovable property tax	15.5	–	7.0	12.2	33.0
Tax on transfer of property	–2.6	19.6	7.5	21.5	6.1
Land revenue	17.6	13.3	3.9	28.2	16.3
Tax on professions, trades, and callings	11.4	21.3	–	0.0	18.1
Provincial excise	28.7	14.3	7.5	179.1	19.5
Motor vehicle tax	13.0	15.5	7.1	0.0	12.2
Entertainment tax	2.3	–7.8	0.0	2.6	0.3
Cotton fees	–0.1	4.9	–	–	0.5
Hotel tax	19.1	47.0	9.8	–	34.1
Electricity duty	–12.3	80.7	20.9	10.8	0.0
Other taxes	–6.0	37.2	–10.0	–	22.4
Total	3.8	23.8	13.9	6.3	9.5

Source: Ghaus, Rafia and Abdul Rauf Khan, 'Fiscal Status of the Provincial Governments in Pakistan', *News on Friday*, 25 August, 1993.

Table 10.23
Taxation and expenditure proposals according to the Structural Adjustment Programmes, 1988–1991 and 1993–1996

Policy areas	Objectives and targets	Strategies and measures
Structural Adjustment Programme, 1988–1991		
Overall deficit	Achieve a reduction in the overall fiscal deficit/ GDP ratio to 4.8 per cent by the end of the programme period; reduce budget's dependence on private savings and domestic bank borrowing.	Major improvements in overall revenue performance and tight control of expenditure growth.
Revenue	Foster domestic resource mobilization in order to achieve a sustainable level of development and essential current expenditures aimed at maintaining high economic growth in the context of economic and financial stability. Achieve an increase in the revenue/GDP ratio to about 20 per cent by the end of the programme period.	Begin to implement a tax reform directed at expanding the tax base and at increasing tax elasticity; continue the strengthening of tax administration. Extension of sales tax on about 22 per cent of domestic industrial production. Extension of sales tax on 30 per cent of domestic industrial production. Increases in telephone charges. Extension of ad valorem excise on certain services such as travel. Annual revision in those excises which are at specific rates so that there is revenue elasticity. Initiate a programme of action to prepare for the introduction of a general sales tax (GST) by 1 July 1990. Proceed with the implementation programme of action. Effective implementation of the general sales tax. Guidelines issued to income tax panels to set criteria for initiating prosecution against tax evaders. Maintain income and profit tax exemption limits at current levels. Review experience of self-assessment procedure for taxpayers earning less than Rs 100,000. Removal of most exemptions from the standard customs 1989/9 duties, except for duty drawbacks for exports and incentives for industries as given in the 1988/9 budget. It is the authorities' intention that these exemptions will not be extended beyond 1990/1, except for backward areas as defined in the 1988/9 budget. Continue implementation of tax reform.
Structural Adjustment Programme, 1993–1996		
Budget	Improve structure of the budget and revenue elasticity.	In GST following measures are to be implemented by 1 July 1994:
Direct taxes	Reduce the wide-ranging exemptions and concessions. Extend coverage to agricultural sector 1993/4; further expand the base 1994/5. Simplify the rate structure for direct taxation. Contain basic personal exemptions and provisions concerning employee benefits. Unification of corporate profit tax rate. Reduction of tax holiday provisions. Transfer the current presumptive tax provisions relating to supplies, contract, imports, and exports into an advance payment for regular income tax.	Removal of exemptions for mostly locally produced goods and imports (except basic foodstuff, medicines, fertilizers, and pesticides). Elimination of capacity scheme within the framework of GST. Introduction of turnover threshold for registration as taxpayer. All specific rates and assessments based on official prices and lower rates for manufacturers that do not claim tax credit to be eliminated. Evaluation of VAT to firms in trading and services sector by 1 July 1994. Excise regime will be rationalized.
Indirect taxes	Reduce maximum tariffs. Import licence fee requirement to be eliminated by 30 June 1994. Eliminate export taxes by 30 June 1994. Conversion of GST into modern broad-based VAT through significant expansion in the number of registered taxpayers, extension of horizontal and vertical coverage, and removal of exemptions.	

Sources: World Bank, *Pakistan: Medium-term Economic Policy Adjustments,* Report No. 7591-Pak, Washington, 1989, p. 159; Karachi Chamber of Commerce and Industry, *Proceedings of a Seminar on Reducing Fiscal Deficit – Key to Salvage Economy*, Karachi, 1994, p. 41.

there are some basic problems with the large scale introduction of VAT in Pakistan. First, in the absence of proper accounting and documentation of transactions, especially by smaller manufacturing and trading entities, enforcement of the tax becomes difficult. Also, there appears to be some reluctance on the part of large-scale units to accept tax invoicing of inputs and outputs because of the fear that furnishing of this information will also enable better determination of income tax liabilities and thereby limit possibilities of evasion. Second, there is a degree of political reluctance to levy GST on the consumption of goods like tea, vegetable ghee, etc. Third, there is a constitutional restriction on the extension of sales taxes to services by the federal government in Pakistan. This implies that the GST cannot be levied on major service inputs like power, gas, transport, etc., and as such it is impossible to make GST correspond to a true value added tax in the absence of an appropriate constitutional amendment.[23]

Direct taxes form a small part of the total revenue collected by the federal government, and income tax constitutes as much as 95 per cent of direct taxes, yet it suffers from numerous deficiencies. There is a very poor coverage of taxpayers, a narrow tax base is riddled with exceptions and exemptions, and the income tax procedure is badly integrated with company law. The large number of exemptions have 'traditionally been justified as incentives for investment, saving, exports, regional development, etc.'.[24] Only 800,000 income taxpayers in a population of 140 million exemplifies the extent of tax evasion in the country, and according to one observer, as many as three-quarters of potential taxpayers in Pakistan do not pay taxes.[25] According to another estimate, it is estimated that the evasion of income tax is almost five times the collected amount.[26] Hence, the 'collection of income tax has remained restricted largely to the industrial and financial sectors, to public limited companies and multinationals, to corporate profits and salary income and to the metropolitan cities of Pakistan'.[27]

To be able to have a more broad-based income tax, it would be necessary to have proper documentation of the economy and to do away with the numerous exemptions, as well as to streamline the taxation structure so as to make it easier to catch tax offenders. However, given the fact that the tax administration is highly corrupt and often in collusion with tax evaders, even if an effective income tax structure were imposed, it is likely that the real culprits would be able to get away, and only the smaller offenders would be caught. Nevertheless, the reform of tax administration, irrespective of cultural and structural problems such as pervasive and excessive corruption, is a minimum condition that must be fulfilled if any worthwhile measures towards better tax effort and resource mobilization are to take place (see Appendix 10.4). At the same time, it is important to emphasize that there are numerous vested interests in maintaining the status quo who may be unwilling to permit any sort of change (see Box 10.2).

10.3.2 Resource Mobilization at the Provincial Level

Although almost 90 per cent of revenue is collected at the federal level and the remaining 10 per cent distributed between the two lower tiers of government, the role that both provincial and local governments play in the delivery of services is often critical. Social services, in particular, such as education, health, and water supply and sanitation, are provided by provincial and local governments, hence the need to examine issues particular to resource mobilization (see Table 10.21).

Provincial governments have access to resources from a divisible pool of federal taxes for their recurring account, at least until June 1997, as per the prescribed formula of the National Finance Commission award of 1991. In this award, 80 per cent of revenues of the federal government income tax, export duty on cotton, excise duty on tobacco, and the sales tax are given to the provincial governments on the basis of their population share. Prior to the 1991 award, the federal government used to fulfil the deficit financing component of the provincial governments in the form of grants-in-aid or loans. At their peak, in 1987/8, these grants were worth Rs17 billion or 2 per cent of GDP. However, the 1991 award has stopped such payments from the federal government to the provincial governments, and there is greater pressure on the provincial governments to put their house in order and to self-finance their revenue deficits.

Aisha Ghaus and Asif Iqbal identify the following problems in the provincial resource mobilization structure:

1 Limited scope of resource mobilization as the large and relatively buoyant taxes, such as import duties, income and corporate tax, excise duties and sales tax, have been 'pre-empted by the federal government. The taking over of the sales tax, in particular, by the federation soon after partition has been cited as a major encroachment on provincial fiscal power.'[28]

2 The Islamization process has caused loss of revenue from provincial excises, entertainment tax and land revenue.

3 Provincial governments have not been able to exploit the agricultural income tax, tax on value added in the services sector and capital gains on immovable properties.

4 The elasticity of provincial taxes is low, which means low growth in tax revenue.

5 'The incentive environment prevalent in the country has not been conducive to greater fiscal effort by the provinces. Automatic access to ad hoc revenue deficit grants provided an opportunity to the provincial governments to declare higher revenue deficits (by lowering own revenue effort and by raising expenditure) and thereby receiving a higher grant from the federal government.'[29]

6 Poor tax administrators.

With pressure on them, surprisingly, provincial governments have tried to deal with having to raise revenue and meet their deficit requirements. The provinces, since the

BOX 10.2

Vested interests and the taxation structure

Hafiz Pasha argues that the taxation structure needs to be seen in the context of different interest groups active in the economy. He writes:

Behind each major tax exemption or concession there is a strong, entrenched vested interest group in Pakistan. Each group has organized itself as an effective lobbying entity, which has not only blatantly demonstrated its power in political terms, but in more subtle terms also has played the game of patronage seeking through party donations, supporting influential politicians, etc., and developed credible arguments for the retention of these exemptions and fiscal incentives in the greater national interest.

Perhaps the best example of this is the agricultural lobby. It is extremely well organized and enjoys enormous political power. Over 80 per cent of the elected members of the parliament either represent the feudal class or are sympathetic to the interests of this group. It is not surprising, therefore, that any legislation to change the status quo is effectively blocked. A number of arguments have also been developed to justify the exemption of agricultural income tax [including] the fact that the sector is already 'overtaxed' through the pricing mechanism (domestic prices below world prices), that food production is vital for national security and that the high costs of collection of the tax on agricultural income will not be justified because of the likely low revenue yield [see also Chapter 5].

Tax holidays have been aggressively supported by industrial interests who have formed an alliance with the provincial governments of backward areas. They have been successful in playing up the sensitive issue of large and widening regional disparities in the country. The Ministry of Finance (a key agent of the state itself) has justified the exemption of interest income on government savings instruments on the ground that this actually improves the income distribution because the bulk of participation in such savings schemes is by lower and middle income households, and that this incentive reduces the need to resort to inflationary mechanisms for financing the budget deficit.

The need for retention of the capital gains on financial assets has been successfully argued by representatives of stock exchanges in the country. Various associations of members of stock exchanges have portrayed the share market as a barometer of the performance of the government and the economy. They have stressed the need for fiscal incentives to attract foreign private portfolio investment and thereby improve the balance of payments position, and so on.

Altogether, tax reform involving broad-basing of direct taxes through the removal of major exemptions and concessions has been effectively frustrated by entrenched, powerful, well-organized and articulate interest groups. The government has had to retreat in the face of opposition from such groups. It has been left with the worst possible outcome. Tax rates have come down, while the multitude of tax expenditures continues.

The failure of government to broaden the base of direct taxes by reducing tax expenditures leads to the identification of a number of factors which mitigate against success of reform initiatives as follows:

i) Lack of commitment to the reform by agents of the state, arising from a perception that the reform may damage vital national interests like food production, savings, exports, etc.

ii) 'State capture' by special interest groups like the traditional feudal élite, bureaucracy and the emerging corporate business interests which extract substantial rent from the existing tax–expenditure system and are unwilling to give up their privileges.

iii) Wrong strategy of implementation of reforms. By first reducing tax rates the opportunity which existed for bargaining with (and compensating) losers was lost.

Source: Pasha, Hafiz, 'Political Economy of Tax Reforms: The Pakistan Experience', *Pakistan Journal of Applied Economics*, vol. II, nos. 1 and 2, 1995, pp. 143–4.

1991 NFC award, have 'adopted a diversified resource mobilization strategy focusing on most of the existing taxes like stamp duties, property tax, motor vehicle tax, hotel tax, tax on professions, trading and callings, electricity duty, paddy development fee, cotton fee and land revenue'.[30] This has been done by removing exemptions and by expanding the tax net. Those tax rates which were very low have been enhanced, such as stamp duties, motor vehicle tax, paddy fees, cotton duty and electricity duty. Also, there has been a switch from specific to ad valorem taxes. The consequence of these measures had been a considerable increase in the growth rate in provincial tax revenues between 1990 and 1995, especially in Sindh and the NWFP (see Table 10.22).

Aisha Ghaus and Asif Iqbal conclude their evaluation of the substantial changes in the provincial governments' resource mobilization strategy since the 1991 NFC award on a positive note. Although they add that these reforms constitute only a 'small step in the right direction' and much more needs to be done, their overall analysis is as follows:

On the whole, it appears that the tax reforms introduced by the provincial governments in the last few years will broaden somewhat that provincial tax base, introduce an element of buoyancy in tax revenues and reduce revenue leakages. On top of this, given the nature of provincial taxes like stamp duties, property tax, etc. with a heavy concentration on physical and financial assets the incremental burden of most of the reforms is likely to be on the upper income groups and, therefore, the reforms will increase the progressivity of the provincial tax system. Also, the reforms are unlikely to have had a significant impact on the price level of basic goods.[31]

These recent efforts at reform and improvement notwithstanding, there are numerous problems and issues regarding provincial resource mobilization measures which have still not been addressed. The urban immovable property tax is a case in point.

This tax is dependent and based on the gross annual rental values (GARVs) of properties, with assessment by the provincial governments due every five years. None of the provincial governments has regularly been revising its assessment every five years, and the last actual assessment in the province of Sindh was made almost thirty years ago, in 1968! There can be no denying the fact that there is a very strong case for immediate reassessment of the rental value of properties in urban areas. According to a report:

> The case, therefore, for a more or less immediate reassessment of GARVs is very strong. The longer this process continues to be delayed on the grounds of political expediency or otherwise, the less will be the degree of exploitation of the revenue potential of this tax. This is of particular significance to the local governments in the country who generally get the dominant share of revenues collected. Municipal revenues have tended to be constrained by the low level of revenues from the property tax which is internationally one of the principal sources of local revenue.[32]

This particular tax, which has immense potential as far as revenue from provincial governments is concerned, is one of the most underdeveloped sources of revenue for the provincial governments. Moreover, since most of the revenue from this tax (85 to 95 per cent) is given to the local governments at the lower tier, the underdevelopment of this tax and low effort on the part of provincial governments have had a serious negative impact at the local level as well. The constraint on developing and expanding this tax on the basis of new assessments and at enhanced rates has been political. Although the Ordinances require reassessment of property value every five years, there are parliamentary requirements that reassessed rental values cannot exceed 10 per cent of the previous value. This continues to lead to an underassessment of the true property value. Even if the rates are reassessed as frequently as they are supposed to be, the market values of urban property have increased by as much as eight or ten times in recent years. Thus the assessed values would only capture a very small percentage of the real market rental values.

10.3.3 Local Government Revenues[33]

The common perception is that local governments are nonentities when it comes to resource generation, expenditure, or the provision of services. Provincial governments are perceived to be the main providers of

benefits to the people, and it is assumed that they are also better at raising revenues. However, the surprising evidence is that local governments, especially in large cities, have been successful in increasing their contribution to total revenues and there has been an improvement in the revenue mobilization efforts of local governments. In the 1980s, local taxes grew by an annual rate of 18 per cent, far higher than the growth in revenues at the federal or provincial level. Moreover, in 1990/1, prior to the latest NFC award, local governments contributed Rs8.8 billion in tax receipts compared to the Rs6.8 billion contributed by the four provincial governments. Hence, 6.5 per cent of total tax receipts came from the lowest tier compared to 5 per cent from provincial governments. But this figure should not detract from the very serious problems faced by local governments, some of which are discussed in this section and in section 10.4.

Much of the credit for the good fiscal effort of local councils has been due to a handful of large urban local governments and some districts. There are very large variations between the levels of effort and results in resource mobilization among urban and rural, and between small and large, councils. With just one tax – octroi – accounting for more than half of the revenue of nearly all urban councils, there can be little disagreement with the urgent need to broaden the tax base of local councils.

One area of reform that has been identified is the way local taxes are collected. The provincial tax machinery collects the property tax and the tax on the transfer of property in urban areas, and the local rate in rural areas. The justifications given for provincial collection followed by revenue sharing of municipal taxes have been discussed earlier in section 10.1.3.

However, the problem is that the buoyancy and revenue-raising potential of, say, the property taxes, depend on the reassessment frequency and value, as discussed in the previous section, where the provincial government plays the only role. Since 85 to 95 per cent of the revenue is handed over to the local councils, provincial governments have few incentives to collect higher revenues as 'the net gain to them is very small in relation to the high political costs'.[34] Hence, arguments are given in favour of decentralizing the property tax to municipal governments. It is believed that local governments will have more incentive to mobilize revenues so as to diminish their complete dependence on octroi, and that people may also be willing to pay higher taxes because they see a closer link between payment and the provision of municipal services. The most important point, however, is that 'provincial governments have preempted a number of taxes which fall within the fiscal powers of local government',[35] which means that they have encroached on the revenue-generating avenues of local governments. Taxes such as the tax on the rental value of land and property, the motor vehicle tax, the tax on professions, trades and callings, and the entertainment tax could all have been collected by local governments.

Aisha Ghaus has argued that the 'current pattern of intergovernmental fiscal relations between the provincial and local governments in the country is such that the former *is instrumental in retarding the development*, in terms of expenditure growth, of the latter. This is the case because the provincial governments substitute for local governments in the provision of some important local services.'[36]

Interestingly, there is also evidence from an analysis of the sharing of revenues from taxes of local origin, where there are

> sizeable transfers of resources in Pakistan from local jurisdictions to higher levels of government, especially provincial. This would seem to *justify some reallocation of fiscal powers* in favour of municipal governments and/or the establishment of more elaborate revenue sharing arrangements with provincial governments. The case for this becomes even stronger if a further devolution of functions to local governments takes place in Pakistan.[37]

This argument for decentralization to local government has recently been gaining much currency.

The extensive and detailed Applied Economics Research Centre (AERC) reports on local government[38] have been arguing for decentralization, which they believe is 'justified on both economic and political' grounds. The economic justification rests on the premise that there would be an increase in efficiency in the provision of services, 'either by cost reductions or by enhancements in the quality of service (by more effective administration)', and that if local governments are included in the provision of services, then the quality of such services is also likely to be higher.[39] The main justification for decentralization based on political grounds is that decentralization would 'induce a sense of participation at the grass roots level of people in the provision and management of basic services that are of vital importance in influencing their quality of life. This process of involvement not only creates a sense of greater control and self-reliance but also provides for a clearer articulation of local needs and preferences.'[40] The presence of elected representatives from smaller communities is said to be 'beneficial' as local representatives have greater knowledge of local problems and priorities, and are supposed to be more accessible and involved in local issues. This view is also shared by Aisha Ghaus, who argues that

> decentralization of local services along with higher flows of funds to local governments is likely to improve the overall level of provision of local services in the country. Therefore, from a pure service delivery point of view a case exists for decentralizing delivery of local services to local governments. This strengthens the traditional arguments that have been made in favour of decentralization on economic, institutional and political grounds.[41]

With local governments emerging as the panacea for many revenue and developmental ills and shortcomings, we evaluate the role of urban local governments in Pakistan and conclude that the present emphasis on local government, while necessary, is too ambitious to deliver any meaningful results. See also Chapter 18, where issues of decentralization are discussed in a broader framework.

10.4   Is Local Government the Answer?[42]

Before we briefly examine the role of local governments in Pakistan, it is important to emphasize the point that presently, as of 1997, no elected local governments exist in Pakistan. All local governments at present stand dissolved. In the NWFP, all local bodies were dissolved in 1991, in Sindh in 1992, and in the Punjab in August 1993; in Baluchistan their term expired in 1997, and new elections have not been held. Different reasons exist as to why the provincial governments dissolved the local governments in their own provinces. In the case of the NWFP, mismanagement and corruption were cited as reasons, while the Punjab provincial government dissolved its local governments in order to ensure that national elections, held in October 1993, were not influenced by incumbent local government officials. Thus, in the absence of democratically elected local government, officials in the rural and urban areas, town committees, municipal committees, and municipal corporations, are all being run by administrators who are members of either the federal or provincial public (civil) service cadre. Administrators are appointed by the provincial government and are transferred between different posts for unspecified durations of tenure.

10.4.1   The Contribution of Municipal Government in Development

The overall analysis of municipal, i.e. urban, local governments regarding the provision of services suggests a number of conclusions. Firstly, almost all councils in the larger urban centres have more or less restricted their role exclusively to the performance of some (or all) compulsory functions. In smaller towns and cities, the financial and institutional capabilities of the councils restrict even the performance of compulsory functions, leave alone those of an optional nature as well. In these cases, the provincial government intervenes to help these governments make ends meet – both financially and technically. In larger cities, water and sewerage authorities and development agencies play a critical ancillary role to the municipal governments. Without this assistance, it is unlikely that local governments, even in big cities, could have managed. Some of the optional functions of these governments are also performed by such specialized agencies.[43]

Education and health are still the primary responsibility of the provincial governments, which continue to play an extremely important role in the provision of services in cities. In larger cities, the provincial government plays a minimal role, as a large number of schools and medical facilities are either private or have been developed, administered, and financed by the local municipal government. However, even large cities such as Peshawar (pop. 1.5 million), lack the capability to run and develop their own schools, hospitals, and dispensaries.[44] In smaller towns, the provincial governments play a formidable role, not only in education and health, but in almost all other sectors as well. The reason for this is clear, that smaller urban centres lack technical and administrative capabilities and do not have adequate staff to undertake substantial development works. In many cases, large schemes (water supply, sanitation, drainage) which can only be undertaken by the provincial department in the case of smaller towns and cities are, after completion, handed over to the local council. The local council is then responsible for operation and maintenance costs, which many are unable to meet.[45]

Essentially, then, local municipal governments, given the existing structure, especially that which comes with a smaller size, do not have the capability to provide essential services which could have positive effects on development in terms of water supply, drainage and sanitation, primary education, and hospitals and dispensaries. While many governments lack technical capabilities, financial constraints are even more severe.

A very large share of municipal government expenditure is recurring expenditure, a trend which is more pronounced in large cities. This expenditure goes towards maintaining and operating water supply schemes, public health, education, and curative care. The highest per capita expenditure in the urban councils of the two biggest provinces, Sindh and Punjab, is incurred on roads. In Baluchistan and the NWFP it is on drainage. In urban areas in the country, the high-priority sectors for development are water supply, sewerage and drainage, and roads, collectively accounting for 50 per cent of development expenditure.[46]

The picture regarding development provided and undertaken by municipal governments is therefore particularly dismal. Urban local governments, with the possible exception of the larger metropolitan corporations in Karachi and Lahore, along with a handful of the bigger cities, do not provide either services or facilities which would have a positive developmental effect.

10.4.2 Potential for Development by Local Governments

Urban local governments have been specified a large and varied number of tasks and functions which they have to perform, and some which they may themselves choose to perform. The scope of the statutes regarding the provision of services and facilities is broad enough to encourage major projects in the social sector which could benefit underprivileged and vulnerable groups, especially women and children. Almost all major areas are covered in the statutes and very few more could be added. Technically, provincial governments can delegate further responsibilities to the local governments as they deem fit.

The problem, then, is not one of statutory limitations, but of financial and technical, and possibly conceptual and motivational, constraints to developing facilities affecting social welfare for the general public. There is a clear relationship with size of city as far as the possibilities are concerned. The larger cities are usually in a position to raise funds and provide facilities and services for their population. Smaller towns and cities just do not have the resources – of any kind – to provide other than the very basic facilities, such as roads and drainage. To expect anything else would be very unrealistic. However, even the relatively large Peshawar

municipal corporation spends as much 86 per cent of its budget on salaries and on electricity bills.[47] While Lahore metropolitan corporation does have a large number of health and medical facilities, it spends in all less than one-half of a per cent on health care, or ten paisa per inhabitant.[48] Thus, while the larger corporations do have access to more funds, their budgets, too, are quite small. The low fiscal outlay of the municipal councils necessarily makes the salary and administrative costs look excessive. Thus, where revenue and expenditure are limited, as is the case in almost all councils, the costs of administration will remain high until the municipal revenue base is restructured and substantially enhanced.

While financial constraints are the biggest hindrance to the provision of services and facilities in cities, there are some others as well. In the larger cities, the establishment of development authorities and of specialized organizations like the water and sanitation agencies under the provincial government has played an important role in delivering services.[49] In small cities, the provision of local infrastructure is usually carried out by provincial line departments, in particular the Public Health and Engineering Department, in the case of water supply and sanitation. This has meant that local bodies have been left in the role of having to provide for solid waste management, cleansing services, drains, etc. This implies that, while services and facilities have been provided to the inhabitants, local governments have had their role further marginalized. It has been relegated to that of operating and maintaining services which have been developed and created by other agencies, a role that they have often been reluctant to play as they feel they were not involved in the planning and implementation process at an earlier stage. Furthermore, the link between service provision and local taxation has been weakened, and hence local government resource provision has been less than its potential.

The provision of services and facilities by other agencies has meant that local governments have not been willing or eager to develop their own organizational and technical capability. It has been seen that many communities are willing to pay local taxes and user charges if they feel that adequate services will be delivered. However, local bodies will have little incentive to generate additional sources of income if they are not in a position or under compulsion to provide municipal services because such provision is under the control of other agencies. Thus, on the one hand, while specialist agencies do provide facilities, their presence undermines the role that local governments ought to play.[50]

An overview of municipal local government reveals that even basic services and facilities are not provided by local governments because they do not have the funds to do so. Furthermore, even if there is expenditure on sanitation, water, etc., there is no guarantee that the projects envisaged by local governments will deliver to the more needy segment of the population. In most cities, it is the well-to-do who have access to better facilities. Poorer neighbourhoods, often on unregularized lands, where the most vulnerable and underprivileged people live, do not have access to the most basic of facilities. The population which needs facilities most for its development is often neglected the most by all tiers of government.

Furthermore, in recent years it has been observed that a large amount of local government funds have been embezzled by elected members of the councils, a fact which has only helped discredit the role and potential of local government. In the Punjab recently, 263 councillors and chairmen were accused of misappropriating close to Rs500 million.[51] A summary by the recently constituted Task Force on the New Social Contract states that

> since the 1980s, financial discipline in local bodies has been on the decline. They have learnt to live beyond their means and rules of financial proprietary are not followed and local funds are largely misappropriated. Some of these violations include that [sic] expenditure on personal privileges has risen out of proportion. Sale of assets is uncontrolled and pre-determined criteria are absent. Annual audits are often avoided with impunity although the Local Bodies Ordinance require such audits and publication of audited accounts.[52]

Thus, local governments have come into disrepute and the people have lost their trust and faith in this tier of government. However, it would be fair to say that the higher levels of government are also not exempt from extensive misappropriation and embezzlement, and if any faith has been lost in local government, much more faith has been lost in the higher levels of government.

10.4.3 Is Local Government the Answer?

While there has recently been growing lip-service paid to the role that local governments are expected to play in development, it seems quite clear that the existing structure of government in Pakistan does not permit any meaningful role to this important tier in the hierarchy. Local government has been reduced to an institution that pays recurring costs incurred by schemes often developed by other levels of government. Furthermore, most, if not all, local governments face severe financial constraints and are not even in a position to pay the (growing and excessive) salaries of their employees.

In the early 1980s, local governments seemed set to play a productive role in development, but ironically, the return to democracy at the national and provincial levels has helped to subvert that possibility. Today, local government in Pakistan is the least likely, given existing administrative and financial structures, to be able to play any positive role in development. Unless substantial steps are taken to redefine the context and nature of local development, local government will continue to be ineffective.

It would also be fair to say that local governments are not solely responsible for the dire straits they are in. Unless provincial and national governments practise better governance at all levels of the hierarchical structure, the status quo is unlikely to be changed. Local governments are ineffective not so much due to their own faults, but due to the way they have been treated by the higher echelons of government. For local governments to work more effectively, higher tiers of government must have more confidence in

them and must relinquish effective control. Good governance for urban local government necessarily implies good governance at the provincial and national levels as well. Lip-service alone will simply not do. (See Chapter 18 for a discussion of governance and decentralization.)[53]

10.5 The Nature of Public Debt and the Fiscal Deficit: A Preliminary Introduction[54]

If one single factor were to be identified on which the entire structural adjustment programmes of 1988 and 1993 were based, it would have to be the fiscal deficit (see Chapters 11, 14, and 15). The reduction of the fiscal deficit is, without doubt, the key component of the adjustment programmes, and most other measures seem to revolve around this theme.

The World Bank in its three reports on Pakistan's structural adjustment programmes, has consistently emphasized the importance of debt reduction.[55] For the World Bank, Pakistan's long-term growth path and the government's attempts to make development sustainable would have been severely jeopardized if the large deficits had not been reduced in the mid-1980s, when they were more than 8 per cent of GDP. Following the first of the major adjustment programmes in 1988, the World Bank concluded that 'the implementation of the adjustment program was weakest in the area of fiscal policy'[56] and that the high fiscal deficit would *ultimately undermine growth and inflation objectives*, and put pressure on imports, worsening the current account deficit position.

The level of domestic debt outstanding between 1981 and 1994 is shown in Table 10.24. This budget deficit has been funded by borrowing from both external and domestic sources (see Figure 10.8), with greater reliance on domestic borrowing, particularly non-bank borrowing. By relying on non-bank borrowing, Pakistan has avoided the inflationary effects seen especially in Latin America. The government has been able to avoid printing too much money to fund the deficit, and has kept external debt 'manageable'. However, the World Bank has argued that

> this borrowing strategy [i.e. non-bank borrowing] is not the most efficient, from the point of view of cost-effectiveness of debt finance and flexible monetary management. Furthermore, it has negative consequences on the development of financial markets, because of the size of the debt, its large array of instruments and interest rates, and the credit ceilings imposed on commercial banks, to avoid inflationary consequences.[57]

The government has also been held responsible for relying on the 'high-cost' non-bank borrowing source, causing an increase in interest rates and hence crowding out domestic investment. On the one hand, the World Bank compliments Pakistan for avoiding the inflationary impact of the deficit, but on the other, it castigates it for having done so. Some of the presumed negative consequences of the fiscal deficit, as

Table 10.24
Domestic debt outstanding, 1981–1994

	1981/2	1982/3	1983/4	1984/5	1985/6	1986/7	1987/8	1988/9	1989/90	1990/1	1991/2	1992/3	1993/4
Total debt (Rs m)					203,119	284,477	290,097	333,210	381,111	448,162	521,817	602,364	687,685
Total debt	20.9				39.5	43.4	43.0	43.4	44.6	43.9	43.4	44.9	44.2

Sources: For 1980–91, *Pakistan Economic Survey*, various issues. For 1991–4, State Bank of Pakistan, *Annual Report, 1993–94*, Karachi, 1994.

highlighted by the World Bank and the IMF, are discussed in the next chapter.

There are essentially three types of domestic debt (see Tables 10.25 and 10.26). Floating debt is of a *short-term* nature; it includes cash credit by commercialized banks to the government for its working capital needs and is constituted of ad hoc and regular Treasury Bills held by the State Bank of Pakistan and commercialized banks. In 1995/6 it constituted 35.1 per cent of the debt. All banks are required to keep 30 per cent of their deposits in government paper (the liquid assets requirement), most of which are in the form of Treasury Bills that are available on tap. *Medium-term* borrowings constitute *unfunded* debt, which is made up of voluntary savings schemes aimed at the general public, including Defence Saving Schemes and Khas Deposit Certificates. This part of the government debt accounts for 30.1 per cent of total debt and has high, usually tax-free, yields. The *permanent* debt of the government is the *long-term* debt; it is constituted of long-term market loans with maturities of between seven and twenty years and is usually held by institutions such as insurance companies and commercial banks. Table 10.25 shows how permanent debt has risen over the last few years, with floating debt falling. Total debt as a percentage of GDP has almost doubled since 1980/1. Table 10.26 gives a greater breakdown of the nature of debt and the debt instruments available to the government. After the introduction of open market operations, six-month Treasury Bills constitute the largest instrument of government debt, followed by Federal Investment Bonds, both of which are usually held by banks and other financial institutions.

One of the problems identified with the reliance on non-bank borrowing to finance the debt has been that the debt's maturity structure is short term, and since much of this debt can be cashed on demand, it is very liquid. The private sector prefers these investments because of easy liquidity and also because the tax-free rates are usually higher than the alternative saving instruments available. Moreover, the return on this form of debt is not particularly lower than for long-term debt. The problem for the government, given the liquidity and maturity structure of the national saving schemes, is that it has to take large refunding operations on a continuous basis.

> More importantly, these features make it difficult to plan precisely the refunding levels needed. Under such conditions, unforeseen circumstances, such as the recent political and economic uncertainties that led investors to accelerate the withdrawal of funds from the National Saving Schemes, can also undermine the Government's ability to manage monetary policy. In those instances, when the Government cannot cover the public's demand by issuing additional debt, the authorities may be compelled to monetize part of the debt temporarily. Such policy would require allowing monetary financing to exceed its targets for a period of time, possibly without significant consequences. But potential problems could arise if the outflows are sustained or if they are very large.[58]

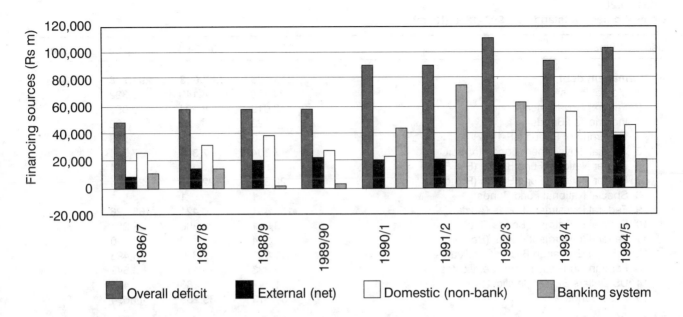

Figure 10.8
Sources for the financing of the budget deficit, 1986–1995

The World Bank and the IMF believe that, if Pakistan is to build longer-term foundations for economic development, 'the fiscal deficit must be brought down to a sustainable level. A sustainable deficit is one which permits an acceptable level of economic expansion within a framework of price stability and debt accumulation comparable with reasonable domestic and debt servicing ratios.'[59] The figure for the budget deficit which is supposed to be sustainable and which does not cause the numerous ills – inflation, low growth, current account deficits, etc. – is believed to be 4 per cent of GDP. Table 10.27, does, indeed, show how debt servicing has been eating up a substantial and growing part of the economy, while Table 10.28 shows how the fiscal deficit continues to be funded, causing domestic and foreign debt to grow, which eventually needs to be serviced. Interest payments are now the largest component of the annual budget announced by government each year. Some reasons why interest payments have been rising and why Pakistan continues to live on a high debt path, and its implications, are discussed in Chapters 11, 14, and 15. In the following chapter, we examine in detail the 'problem' of the fiscal deficit and how it impacts on the rest of the economy.

Table 10.25
Domestic debt outstanding at end of period, 1980–1996 (Rs m)

Type of debt	1980/1	1987/8	1988/9	1989/90	1990/1	1991/2	1992/3	1993/4	1994/5	1995/6
Permanent debt	13,758	63,791	78,827	98,703	157,012	185,070	245,470	264,205	289,460	298,610
Floating debt	31,688	127,524	135,238	144,978	150,929	197,252	215,819	257,638	279,139	301,639
Unfunded debt	12,641	98,782	119,145	137,630	140,220	142,754	146,738	180,197	245,395	258,995
Total	58,087	290,097	333,210	381,311	448,162	525,076	608,027	702,040	783,994	859,244
Memorandum items										
% share in total debt										
Permanent debt	23.7	27.6	22.0	23.7	25.9	35.4	40.4	37.6	36.9	34.8
Floating debt	54.5	42.2	44.0	40.6	38.0	33.5	35.5	36.8	35.6	35.1
Unfunded debt	21.8	30.2	34.0	35.7	36.1	31.1	24.1	25.6	27.5	30.1
As % of GDP										
Total debt	20.9	43.4	43.0	43.3	44.6	43.6	45.3	44.6	42.0	39.5

Note: The figures in this table may vary from those in Table 10.24 as the sources of data vary.
Source: Government of Pakistan, *Pakistan Economic Survey, 1995–96*, Islamabad, 1996, p. 143.

Table 10.26
Domestic debt outstanding, 1993–1995 (Rs m)

Debt instruments	30-06-93	30-06-94	30-06-95	% share
A Permanent debt	**249,486**	**267,633**	**291,788**	**36.68**
1 Market loans[a]	24,688	24,149	23,322	
2 Federal Government Bonds	8,619	8,604	9,056	
3 Income Tax Bonds	22	22	22	
4 Government Bonds (LR-1977)	3	53	53	
5 Special Government Bonds for SLIC	7,304	7,304	7,304	
6 Bearer National Fund Bonds (BNFB)[b]	22	16	14	
7 Bearer National Fund Bonds (Roll over)	22,309	22,309	20,694	
8 Special National Fund Bonds	1	1	1	
9 Federal Investment Bonds (Auction)	133,491	146,421	165,526	
10 Federal Investment Bonds (Tap)	3,311	3,300	3,281	
11 Federal Investment Bonds (Bearer)	214	0	0	
12 Foreign Exchange Bearer Certificates	11,009	11,815	13,493	
13 Foreign Currency Bearer Certificates	2,283	3,114	3,542	
14 US Dollars Bearer Certificates	1,547	1,266	486	
15 Prize Bonds	34,613	39,259	44,694	
B Floating debt	**215,819**	**257,637**	**294,232**	**36.9**
1 Ad hoc Treasury Bills	61,417	61,436	61,456	
2 6 Months Treasury Bills (Auction)	38,889	78,688	57,171	
3 6 Months Treasury Bills (SBP)	115,500	117,500	175,592	
4 Treasury Bills (3 months)	13	13	13	
C Unfunded debt	**137,059**	**169,240**	**210,819**	**26.5**
1 Defence Savings Certificates	52,995	64,365	85,019	
2 National Deposit Certificates/Accounts	1,679	969	2,193	
3 Khas Deposit Certificates/Accounts	−2,813	−3,654	1,376	
4 Special Savings Certificates (Registered)	58,451	64,101	71,524	
5 Special Savings Certificates (Bearer)	3,721	4,303	5,367	
6 Regular Income Certificates	1,120	5,364	9,387	
7 Special Savings Accounts	15,650	16,743	18,845	
8 Mahana Amdani Accounts	1,052	1,262	1,467	
9 Savings Accounts	58,208	15,787	15,640	
Total (A + B + C)	**602,364**	**694,510**	**796,839**	

[a] Including provincial government loans.
[b] Provisional.
Source: State Bank of Pakistan, *Annual Report 1994–95*, Karachi, 1995, p. 87.

10.6 Summary and Further Reading

10.6.1 Summary

Government expenditures arise from the revenue that government can raise through taxation, or the money that it can borrow from domestic or external sources, or the money that it can print. In this chapter, we have looked at the taxation and revenue side of government and at the overall taxation structure that exists in Pakistan. The three tiers of government – federal, provincial, and local – all raise revenue and all make expenditures. The largest share, in both revenue and expenditure, is made by federal government. With less than 1 per cent of Pakistan's population paying any income tax, indirect taxes provide about three-quarters of total tax, with customs duties the largest single contributor.

This chapter has identified and discussed the problems that exist between the three tiers of government, and has shown that each higher tier of government trespasses on the jurisdiction and functions of the lower tier. The arguments for more decentralization to the provincial and local level were also made, and the numerous problems in the structure and administration of the taxation systems were highlighted. There has been a growing awareness amongst policy makers and academicians that local government should be promoted as an effective means to deliver development to the community. The arguments for local government reform on

Table 10.27
Debt servicing, 1979–1992

	1979/80	1980/1	1981/2	1982/3	1983/4	1984/5	1985/6	1986/7	1987/8	1988/9	1989/90	1990/1	1991/2
Million rupees													
1 Interest on both domestic and foreign debt	—	—	—	—	14,128	16,538	19,734	24,163	32,315	39,132	48,505	50,017	67,475
Federal	4,870	5,631	7,260	10,624	13,591	16,045	19,019	23,190	30,779	37,525	47,367	48,710	64,930
Interest on domestic debt	2,494	3,531	4,489	6,249	8,443	10,182	12,642	15,817	22,549	28,093	35,497	35,710	50,307
Interest on foreign debt	2,375	2,280	2,270	4,374	5,148	5,863	6,377	7,373	8,230	9,432	11,416	13,000	14,623
Interest on provincial debt	n.a.	n.a.	n.a.	n.a.	537	493	715	973	1,536	1,607	1,138	1,307	2,545
2 Repayments/amortization of foreign debt	5,604	3,633	5,918	8,733	8,618	9,031	10,762	11,787	13,460	18,336	13,938	23,515	29,007
3 Total debt servicing (1 + 2)	10,474	9,264	13,178	19,357	22,746	25,569	30,496	35,950	45,775	57,468	67,897	73,532	96,482
As percentage of GDP													
Interest on domestic federal debt					2.0	2.2	2.5	2.8	3.3	4.3	4.2	3.5	4.2
Interest on foreign debt					1.2	1.2	1.2	1.3	1.2	1.2	1.3	1.4	1.2
Repayment of foreign debt					2.1	1.9	2.1	2.1	2.0	2.4	2.2	2.1	2.4
Total debt servicing					n.a.	n.a.	3.8	4.2	4.8	5.1	5.7	4.9	5.6

Source: Government of Pakistan, *Pakistan Economic Survey*, various issues, Islamabad; State Bank of Pakistan, *Annual Report*, various issues, Karachi.

Table 10.28
Sources of financing the fiscal deficit, 1978–1995

	1978/9	1979/80	1980/1	1981/2	1982/3	1983/4	1984/5	1985/6	1986/7	1987/8	1988/9	1989/90	1990/1	1991/2	1992/3	1993/4	1994/5
Million rupees																	
Financing (net)	17,315	14,663	14,618	20,992	25,654	25,147	36,777	41,644	46,710	57,563	56,879	56,060	89,193	89,970	107,525	92,179	103,405
External (net)	6,711	6,951	6,977	5,345	5,162	5,001	5,169	8,584	8,424	12,691	18,195	22,945	22,101	18,022	24,334	24,624	37,229
Domestic non-bank	2,108	1,407	5,286	6,313	14,368	12,280	12,873	29,962	27,371	30,931	37,865	29,581	23,724	−515	19,972	55,048	47,626
Banking system	8,502	6,305	2,355	5,516	6,124	7,866	18,735	6,098	10,915	13,941	819	3,534	43,368	72,464	63,219	12,507	18,551
Distribution by source (%)																	
External	38.7	47.4	47.7	25.5	20.1	19.9	14.1	20.6	18.0	22.0	31.9	40.9	24.8	20.0	23.0	27.0	36.0
Domestic	61.3	52.6	52.3	74.0	79.8	80.1	85.9	79.4	82.0	78.0	68.1	59.1	75.2	80.0	77.0	73.0	64.0
Non-bank	12.1	9.6	36.2	30.0	56.0	48.8	35.0	71.9	58.6	53.7	66.6	52.8	26.6	—	19.0	60.0	46.0
Banking system	49.2	43.0	16.1	44.5	23.8	31.3	50.9	7.5	23.4	24.3	1.5	6.3	48.6	80.0	58.0	13.0	18.0
Banking system's budgetary support as % of GDP	4.4	2.7	0.8	1.7	1.7	1.9	4.0	1.2	1.9	2.1	0.1	0.4	4.3	6.0	4.7	0.8	1.4

Source: Government of Pakistan, *Pakistan Economic Survey*, various issues, Islamabad.

the financial side have also been discussed in this chapter, and the main constraints to such measures identified.

The fiscal deficit is considered by many to be the single most troubling factor for Pakistan's economy. We have introduced the extent, nature, and scale of domestic debt, which is about 45 per cent of GDP. An evaluation of the role of the fiscal deficit, and the controversy around it, takes place in the next chapter.

10.6.2 Further Reading

The main sources cited in this chapter all deserve a thorough look. The large number of reports completed by the Applied Economics Research Centre of the University of Karachi, in particular, deserve special mention, for this is still the most comprehensive literature on the subject. The following reports published by the AERC should be studied for a greater understanding of the taxation structure in Pakistan: *Local Government Finances and Administration in Pakistan* (in two volumes), Research Report No. 72, 1990; *Resource Mobilization and Institutional Capacity* (in seven volumes), Research Report No. 85, 1991; *Resource Mobilization by Federal Government*, Research Report No. 91, 1992; *Resource Mobilization by Provincial and Local Governments in Pakistan*, Research Report No. 93, 1992; and *Metropolitan Resource Generation Study*, Research Report No. 97, 1993.

On the taxation structure, see Pasha, Hafiz, 'Political Economy of Tax Reforms: The Pakistan Experience', *Pakistan Journal of Applied Economics*, vol. 11, nos. 1 and 2, 1995; and Pasha, Hafiz and M. Asif Iqbal, 'Taxation Reforms in Pakistan', *Pakistan Journal of Applied Economics*, vol. 10, nos. 1

and 2, 1994. In addition, because there have been numerous changes in the taxation structure in recent years, the Central Board of Revenue *Yearbooks* and the annual *Pakistan Economic Survey* should be consulted. The following World Bank publications are also useful: *Pakistan: Growth Through Adjustment*, Report No. 7118-Pak, Washington, 1988; and *Pakistan: Country Economic Memorandum FY93: Progress Under the Adjustment Program*, Report No. 11590-Pak, Washington, 1993.

For local government and related issues, see the following publications by S. Akbar Zaidi: 'Effective Local Level Delivery of Human Resources: Development Related Programmes – The Case of Pakistan', mimeo, UNESCAP, Bangkok, 1991; 'A Study on Making Optional Use of Municipal Budgets to Finance Child Development (Pakistan)', mimeo, UNICEF, Karachi, 1994; 'Urban Local Government in Pakistan: Expecting Too Much From Too Little', *Economic and Political Weekly*, vol. 31, no. 44, 1996; 'Urban Local Governance in Pakistan', in Islam, Nazrul and M.M. Khan, *Urban Governance in Bangladesh and Pakistan*, Centre for Urban Studies, University of Dhaka, Dhaka, 1997; 'Politics, Poverty, Institutions: The Case of Karachi', *Economic and Political Weekly*, vol. 32, no. 51, 1997; 'Karachi: Prospects for the Future', in Khuhro, Hameeda (ed.), *Karachi: Megacity of Our Times*, Oxford University Press, Karachi, 1997; and the papers in *The New Development Paradigm: Papers on institutions, NGOs, Gender and Local Government*, Oxford University Press, Karachi, forthcoming, 1999.

A small selection of references on the fiscal deficit are given in the Notes; a more detailed reading list is provided in the next chapter.

Appendix 10.1

Impact of the NFC award on provincial finances

The financial relationship between provinces and the centre is supposed to be addressed through the National Finance Commission award. This analysis of the 1991 NFC award examines the consequences and implications of the award.

Introduction

The much awaited NFC award has come after a gap of many years (due since 1979) and some abortive attempts earlier. Meanwhile, the provinces had run into large, chronic deficits on the current account, indicating the growing inadequacy of divisible pool transfers as per the provisions of the 1974 award. Consequently, as an ad hoc provision, deficit grants and subventions had been sued increasingly to support the on-going operations of the provinces. At their peak in 1987–8, these grants were Rs12 billion, financing over one-fourth of the provincial current expenditure.

There had, however, been growing dissatisfaction with the existing pattern of inter-governmental fiscal relations in the country. On the one hand, the high and growing dependence

on fiscal transfers had mitigated against financial autonomy and, on the other hand, the implied residual access to grants had left provinces with little incentive either to mobilize their own resources or to economize on their expenditure. Consequently, it had become essential to review the relationship between the federation and the provinces to promote the process of decentralization, to expand the availability of resources of lower levels of government and to improve generally the efficiency in the mobilization and utilization of resources. This has become specially important in the current context when the country has embarked on the path of self-reliance and higher resource mobilization by all levels of government has assumed vital importance.

Description of the Award

The NFC award of 1991 expands the size of the divisible pool of taxes to include two additional taxes, excise duties on tobacco and tobacco manufacturers and sugar. These taxes are to be shared between the federation and the provinces on a 20:80 basis and distributed among the provinces on the basis of population. The award also transfers proceeds from a development surcharge on natural gas, a royalty on crude oil and net profits on hydel power generation to the province of collection. This large increase in the quantum of revenues to be distributed on the basis of collection makes the 1991 award unique in the history of inter-governmental fiscal relations in the country.

On top of this, special annual grants of Rs700 million for five years to Sindh, one billion to Punjab, Rs200 million to NWFP and Rs100 million to Baluchistan for three years each have also been announced.

On the whole, the special feature of the 1991 award is the large increase in total federal transfers to the provinces. In terms of distribution, however, the NFC has essentially opted for the same formula as contained in the 1974 award. Divisible pool taxes are to be shared on the same basis of 20:80 between the federation and the provinces, while the latter share will continue to be distributed on the basis of population. Revenues from depletable natural resources, in the form of the development surcharge on gas and royalty on oil, will be given on the basis of collection. This is an extension of the principles embodied in Article 161. In addition, the discretionary element in grants has been eliminated and a system of fixed, special grants to each province has been instituted.

Pros and Cons for each Province

The lack of innovation in the revenue-sharing formula, discussed earlier, has different implications for each province. Sindh has argued that a certain percentage of revenues be distributed on the basis of collection, given the high share of revenues accruing from this province. While there are serious problems in the apportionment of the effective incidence of taxes like the sales tax on imports and the corporate income tax, the need to preserve horizontal equity in the distribution of resources did imply that a province which contributed more to the exchequer should receive a somewhat higher share. The lack of inclusion of this criterion in the revenue-sharing formula is, therefore, to the detriment of Sindh and to the advantage of the other three provinces, especially Punjab.

NWFP and Baluchistan had both argued for inclusion of backwardness also as a criterion. This is essential if regional differentials in poverty are to narrowed over time. On top of this, Baluchistan had made the plea for higher allocations on grounds of its relatively large land area, which tends to increase significantly the unit costs of provision of services. The NFC's choice of the population basis as the sole criterion and total lack of recognition of other criteria implies that federal transfers will play only a limited equalizing role. As expected, this will benefit the two relatively developed provinces, Sindh and Punjab, to the disadvantage of the two smaller provinces. Altogether, the decision not to use multiple criteria for revenue sharing and to continue with the population based formula is unambiguously to the benefit of the largest province, Punjab.

The development surcharge on gas and the royalty on crude oil could also have been included in the divisible pool. Instead, revenues will be given to the provinces on the basis of collection. This decision, of course, does not work to the interest of Punjab and NWFP. Instead, it increases substantially the share of Baluchistan in the development

surcharge on gas and that of Sindh in the royalty from crude oil. Alternatively, excise duties on tobacco and sugar could have been shared on the basis of collection. Inclusion of these sources in the divisible pool implies a higher share for Punjab and Baluchistan and a much lower share in the revenues from excise duty on tobacco to NWFP and in excise duty on sugar to Sindh.

The inclusion of special grants in federal transfers reverses the earlier practice. Previously, only Baluchsitan and NWFP were entitled to special subventions, largely in recognition of their relative backwardness. Now the largest grants will go to the high provinces, Punjab and Sindh. The consequence is that there will be an increase in the flow of grants to these two provinces in relation to the 1990–91 budgeted level and a large decline in such grants, especially to NWFP. The rationale behind the determination of the level of grants remains largely unclear.

Altogether, the pros and cons of the award with respect to each province are given in [Table 1]. For Punjab the positive aspects are that the population sharing formula for the divisible pool has been retained, new taxes like excise duties on tobacco and sugar will also be shared on the basis of population, revenues will be enhanced by the profits from Mangla Dam and by the relatively large special grants of Rs1000 million. The only area where Punjab has lost out is in the development surcharge on gas, revenues from which will largely accrue on the basis of collection to Baluchistan and Sindh.

Sindh has lost on some fronts and gained on others. The biggest failure is its inability to convince the NFC that a premium be given to its high revenue contribution in the sharing from the divisible pool. There is some solace, however, in the decision of the NFC to hand over collection responsibilities of retail sales tax to provinces as and when the tax is extended to this stage. However, given the integrated nature of the GST it will be difficult to bifurcate this tax. Also, it is the only province which has been given a special grant for the full five-year period of operation of the NFC award.

NWFP perhaps perceives its biggest gain as the access to hydro-electric profits of over Rs5 billion, largely from Tarbela Dam. Against this, it has had to concede on its demand for inclusion of backwardness as a criterion, it will suffer a big drop in grants, and it will not get the full benefit of its high share in tobacco cultivation and manufacture. Baluchistan again can be satisfied that it will get the bulk of revenues from the development surcharge on gas and some share in revenues from tobacco and sugar. But it will also have to trade off these gains against the lack of inclusion of backwardness and land area as criteria for revenue sharing and the decrease in the level of federal non-development grants.

Altogether, the NFC award of 1991 is an ingeniously crafted set of arrangements for federal transfers. Each province has gained on some fronts and lost on others. The net quantitative implications of the bargaining process on each province are highlighted in the subsequent sections.

Size of the Federal Transfers

A number of important conclusions emerge from an analysis of the total federal transfers to the provinces under the 1974

Table 1
Positive and negative aspects of the award for each province

	Positive	Negative
Punjab	Sharing of revenue from excise duty on tobacco and sugar on the basis of population, not collection. Profits from hydro-electricity generated by Mangla Dam. Retention of sharing of population-based formula for divisible pool taxes. Increase in grants for three years.	Sharing of revenues from development surcharge on gas and royalty on crude oil on the basis of collection, not population.
Sindh	Sharing of revenue from development surcharge on gas and royalty on oil on the basis of collection, not population. Increase in grants for five years. Long-run transfer of retail sales tax to provinces.	Sharing of revenues from excise duty on sugar on basis of population, not collection. Lack of inclusion of criteria such as collection, and rate of urbanization in sharing formula for divisible pool taxes.
NWFP	Sharing of revenue from excise duty on sugar on the basis of population, not collection. Profits from hydro-electricity generated by Tarbela Dam.	Sharing of revenues from excise duty on tobacco on the basis of population, not collection. Sharing of development surcharge on gas and royalty on oil on the basis of collection, not population. Lack of inclusion of criteria such as backwardness in and divisible pool sharing formula. Decrease in grants.
Baluchistan	Sharing of excise duty on tobacco and sugar on the basis of population, not collection. Sharing of development surcharge on gas on the basis of collection, not population.	Sharing of royalty on crude oil on the basis of collection, not population. Decrease in grants. Lack of inclusion of criteria such as land area and backwardness in the divisible pool sharing formula.

and 1991 NFC awards. First, as highlighted earlier, the 1991 NFC award has considerably enhanced the transfer of revenues to the provinces. The overall increase for the four provinces is about 58 per cent implying a revenue gain of about Rs24 billion in 1991–2 over the previous year. As such the NFC award promises considerable improvement in the financial status of the provinces. Second, the award has significantly changed the pattern of inter-government fiscal relations in Pakistan. Initially, the bulk (83%) of the transfers were through the divisible pool, distributed on the basis of population, while ad hoc grants/subventions (mostly revenue deficit grants) constituted 13 per cent of the transfers. According to the new award more than one-fifth of the transfers are on the basis of collection, while ad hoc grants will form a marginal proportion of total transfers.

Third, even though all the provinces have gained from the award, the extent of immediate gain is different for the four provinces. The province which has gained the most is Baluchistan followed by Sindh. The immediate gain in revenues for the two respective provinces is 85 and 62 per cent.

Interestingly, and perhaps in contradiction to the popular claim, NWFP and not Punjab is the province which has gained the least. This is primarily because of the cessation of the revenue-deficit grant received by NWFP. In recent years, NWFP had received the highest revenue deficit grant in the country, budgeted to be Rs3.6 billion in 1990–1. As such, the overall share of NWFP in total federal transfers will be reduced from 20 to 18 per cent.

Policy Implications

Regional Imbalances
Though the NFC award has benefited all the four provincial governments in Pakistan, the extent of benefit varies significantly across provinces. For example, the biggest province, Punjab, is among the major beneficiaries while a less developed, backward province, NWFP, has gained the least. This anomaly is perhaps a consequence of the lack of innovation in the revenue-sharing formula and the exclusion of important considerations like backwardness, urbanization, land area, etc. This situation has been exacerbated by the special grant structure announced which reverses the earlier

practice when special grants were given to the two smaller provinces largely in recognition of their relative backwardness.

If this imbalance on the recurring side is to be removed and horizontal equity across provinces ensured, it is important that development transfers to the provinces through the ADP should be based on an improved formula which takes into account regional imbalances so that the improvement in provincial finances can be sustained over time.

Decentralization

An highlighted earlier the NFC award represents a big step forward in the process of decentralization in Pakistan. However, for the process of decentralization to be meaningful, along with the purse strings, regulatory controls will also have to be released by the federal government. As such, there is a strong case for winding up of federal ministries in areas like education, health, housing, agriculture, local government and rural development, etc., which essentially relate to provincial functions. Instead, inter-provincial coordination functions could largely be performed by the Planning Commission.

Simultaneously, all functions in the concurrent list of the Constitution which had been taken over by the federal government should be transferred back to the provinces. This includes university education, fertilizer subsidy, flood control, SCARP projects, highways, etc. Not only will this strengthen the provincial governments but it will also relieve the federal budget of the burden of expenditure on these functions. Given the improved financial position of the former they should be in a position to take on all functions constitutionally allocated to them.

On top of all this, we believe that the process of decentralization and devolution of functions will be incomplete if simultaneously the relationship between the provincial and local governments is also not altered. Hitherto, the former have not only encroached on the functions of the latter but they have also preempted their fiscal powers. Now that the provinces are better off financially, they should be willing to establish a system of grants and revenue-sharing arrangements with local governments in taxes like motor vehicle tax, professions and callings tax, etc., and involve them increasingly in the provision of local services like primary education, curative health, law and order, etc. Strengthening of local governments is the last remaining step in the process of decentralization. Without this, the goal of involving people in the management of their affairs will remain largely unfulfilled.

Fiscal Effort

Despite the change in the pattern of inter-governmental fiscal relations (with no access to deficit grants) brought about by the NFC, there is the danger that the provinces may slacken further their fiscal effort and increase their current expenditure more rapidly to absorb the short run surpluses that they will enjoy following the award. Given the macro resource constraints that the country faces it is important that the provinces also economize on resources and play a role in the mobilization of additional resources.

The NFC award has made reference to the recommendations of the Tax Reforms Committee regarding generation of higher revenues from provincial source. The Committee has demonstrated that provincial own revenues can be almost trebled in the next few years by exploration of the revenue potential that currently exists in sources like the property tax, motor vehicle tax, irrigation charges, stamp duties, etc. This recommendation is substantiated by our quantification of proposals for the provinces presented earlier.

We have indicated that even in the absence of discretionary changes in divisible pool taxes by the federal government, the overall surplus on the revenue account of the four provinces combined in 1991-2 will approach Rs7 billion. In addition, taxation proposals in the forthcoming federal budget in income tax, sales tax, etc., will further increase this surplus. It is essential that the additional revenues transferred be used primarily for development by the provinces. As such, we recommend that provincial ADP allocations in 1991-2 be reduced by an amount equal to the additional transfer from the divisible pool due to taxation proposals in the federal budget.

Also, an incentive mechanism may be instituted in the ADP allocations to the provinces whereby matching development grants are given to provinces equal to the additional revenues generated by them from their respective taxation proposals. This will ensure that the higher taxation is translated into higher level or better provision of services. The provinces will then find it politically more attractive to develop their own sources.

In conclusion, it can be said that the NFC award of 1991 represents a big step forward in the process of decentralization in the country. It rationalizes inter-governmental fiscal relations and not only improves the financial position of the provinces but also gives them considerably more autonomy. However, if the full benefits are to be reaped, then the provinces must be motivated to mobilize their own resources and the process of decentralization must be carried down to the level of the local governments.

Source: Applied Economics Research Centre, *Resource Mobilization by Provincial and Local Governments in Pakistan*, Research Report No. 93, 1992, pp. 90-101.

Appendix 10.2

Value added tax though necessary needs extensive preparation

Shadab Fariduddin presents some of the important issues surrounding the debate over the imposition of a value added tax.

The most important proposal in the 1996–7 budget is the development of the general sales tax, a value added tax (VAT), in Pakistan. Through broad-basing and enhancement in tax rate it is proposed to mobilize an additional Rs26 billion from the GST.

Despite the growth of GST, not much is known about the value added tax system in Pakistan. The objective of this article is to describe what VAT is, the case for and against VAT and its impact on the economy, and the problems associated with its implementation.

What is VAT?

Value added is the value that a producer adds to his raw materials or purchases (other than labour) before selling the new or improved product or service. Hence it is an increase in the value of a good in each stage of its production. As the inputs are bought, people are paid wages to work on these inputs to convert them into outputs which when sold leave some profit for the seller. So value added can be looked at from the additive aspect (wage plus profit) or from the subtractive aspect (outputs–inputs).

Value added = Wages + Profit = Output – Input

A tax rate (t) can be levied on this value added in four basic forms with identical results.

1) t (wages + profit): called the additive–direct or accounts method;
2) t (wages) + t(capital): the additive–indirect method;
3) t (output–input): the subtractive-direct method, sometimes called the business transfer tax; and
4) t (output)–t (input): the subtractive-indirect (the invoice or input credit) method.

Of these four possible ways of levying a value added tax (VAT) method 4 been most popular because of these principal reasons:

i) The invoice method attaches the tax liability to the 'transaction', making it legally and technically superior to other forms.
ii) The invoice method creates a good audit trail. As output of one producer becomes the input of the other, the whole chain of transactions can be traced back from retailer to manufacturer through all the middlemen.
iii) Unlike accounts-based methods (1 and 2), the invoice method eliminates the need for profit identification. It also allows for multiple rate VAT which methods 1, 2 and 3 can not accommodate.

Thus to date, method 4 is the only practical one. The tax liability can be calculated week by week, monthly, quarterly or annually. It also allows more than single rate to be used with

most uptodate assessments. This has led most countries to use the invoice or credit method whenever they opt for the VAT.

Why VAT?

The case for VAT can be made on the following grounds:

1) *Unsatisfactory existing sales taxes.* The simplest sales tax takes a certain fixed percentage of all business turnover. This causes 'cascading' of taxes as taxable goods are produced using taxed inputs. This tax-on-tax characteristic has caused most countries using it to switch to VAT. So sales tax levied on manufacturers and wholesaler multiplies and the product reaches the final consumer at very high price. Can only the retail sales tax be the solution? When compared with VAT the retail sales tax has some problems because the incentive for tax evasion is higher as compared to VAT. Given the nature of the VAT, it promotes the process of documentation in the economy.
2) *Abolition of border taxes.* Countries within regional economic groups like EC or NAFTA want to have neutrality and uniformity of the tax burden across borders to promote trade and industrialization through easy-to-implement customs rules. The VAT is, to date, the only sales tax in a customs union that fulfils the obligations of tax neutrality on traded goods and services under WTO.
3) *Buoyant source of new revenue.* Some countries go for a VAT not only to replace existing sales taxes, but also to increase revenue. Still some have viewed it as a new source of revenue which will enable other taxes to be reduced or abolished.
4) *Tax evolution and efficiency.* Industrial growth requires countries to move from traditional to modern tax structures and from systems that distort resource allocation to those that are more neutral. Relying on selective sales taxes with narrow bases is distortionary. Hence a broad-based tax like VAT is socially and economically desirable for government revenues. VAT has become a popular tax, accounting for important shares of revenue and GDP for a large number of developed and developing countries.

Problems with VAT

The adoption and implementation of VAT as a system involves many hurdles which can be categorized into 'pre-adoption' and 'transitional' problems.

The Pre-adoption Stage

First, a country must decide who to tax, who to exempt, and at what rates. A VAT rate can be as high as 25 per cent in Singapore or as low as 2 per cent in Korea. However, the fewer the rates the better. But the rates should be levied on full unadjusted prices, and inclusive of customs duties and excises (different rates can be used for different categories of goods and services). To grant exemption 'zero rating' can and should be used.

Otherwise an 'exemption' under a true VAT system actually means that the exempt trader has to pay VAT on his inputs without getting any credit for this tax paid on his inputs as he cannot impose VAT on his exempt sales. He, in effect, is treated as a final purchaser. On the other hand a zero-rated trader can make a full return of VAT in the normal way, and he is liable to pay a 'zero' rate of VAT. So when this trader applies the tax rate to his sales it adds up as a zero VAT liability but from this he can deduct the entire VAT paid on his inputs, generating a repayment of tax from the government. Zero rating of exporting, in particular, is the practice in most countries.

Second, designers of a new VAT system must decide about the goods and services to be included in the system. VAT as a system cannot bring into its fold certain goods and services because of their nature and also because of social considerations. Hence zero rating and exemptions are therefore called for and justified. Construction, catering, and financial services are examples of difficult-to-tax sectors mainly because exact transaction is difficult to document. Food, public transport, low cost housing, medical services, children's clothing, government purchases and sales might be exempted or zero rated by a country to improve the progressivity of VAT.

Third, the extent of the VAT net needs be decided. More specifically, the issue of whether the retail stage be included or not must be addressed. Ideally, it should be covered because:

i) Clear-cut definition for wholesalers and retailers hardly exists and many taxpayers perform both type of operations.
ii) It removes the incentive to split firms into retail sections to avoid the tax net.
iii) It will broaden the tax base to allow a lower rate to be used to collect a given revenue.
iv) It would complete the audit trail to facilitate the cross checking feature built into the VAT system.

But extension to the retail stage creates certain problems which must be considered. These include lack of records, tendency to deal in case transactions, costs of compliance, and self consumption.

Transitional Problems

Problems of the pre-adoption phase when overcome help erect the VAT system which initially runs parallel with the existing tax system. Before it becomes fully operational the new VAT system should handle some transitional problems like:

  i) How to harmonize VAT with the existing system of sales tax.
 ii) How to create public awareness and acceptance.
iii) How to go about registration of taxpayers.
 iv) How to train tax officials to administer the new tax.
  v) What treatment to be given to capital goods.
 vi) What type or organizational structure to use with how many people to staff.
vii) How to monitor costs of administration.
viii) How to decide and calculate relief.

ix) What control measures to devise to prevent tax-related corruption.

Economic Impact of VAT

VAT when efficiently administered by the taxmen and complied with by the taxpayers results in certain impacts on the economy.

- Most people think that prices would continuously rise once VAT is introduced. However, empirical evidence shows that the introduction of VAT may lead to a one-time shift in prices but it does not accelerate the rate of inflation.

- Another common charge against VAT is that it reduces the real consumption of low-income households more than that of high-income households; hence it is regressive. This accusation is based on assumptions about the taxes replaced, the exemptions and zero ratings and any special compensatory features. It should be noted that regressivity in an economy does not depend on one particular tax but on the entire tax and expenditure system. Moreover through wage supplement and changes in social security, desired progressiveness can be brought in without impairing the essence of VAT system.

- In the case of savings and investment, the effect of a broad-based VAT is neutral between consumption and saving as it metes out the same treatment to both present and future consumptions. The net effect of VAT on saving and investment hinges on the exact form of tax that VAT replaces.

- Finally, the main advantage of VAT is that international trade takes place on a transparent basis thus reducing trade disputes and resulting political frictions, though the monetary benefit is likely to be small and temporary.

Adoption of VAT in Pakistan

During the 90s Pakistan has made a transition form a conventional sales tax to a value added tax in the form of GST. Initially, the import and manufacturing stage has been covered. The rate originally was 12.5% which was enhanced to 15% in 1993–4 and has now been increased to 18%. In the budget of 1996–7 it is also proposed to expand the tax net to cover sectors like textiles, pharmaceuticals, etc. A multiple tax rate system has been adopted with rates ranging from 5% to 23%. Extension of the tax net to the wholesale and retail stage has been postponed but small scale manufacturers (with turnover exceeding Rs1 million) have been brought into the tax net.

The next few years will determine whether this new system of taxation is successful in promoting the process of documentation and raising additional revenues. This will not only hinge on the degree of voluntary compliance by Pakistani taxpayers but also on the quality of tax administration by the CBR.

Source: Fariduddin, Shadab, *The News*, 29 June 1996.

Appendix 10.3

Is the GST an unfair tax?

Farrukh Saleem discusses the equity concerns associated with the general sales tax.

The Finance Bill, 1996, is expected to broaden the General Sales Tax (GST) down to the retail level. Premier Bhutto while addressing the inaugural ceremony of the Allama Iqbal Medical College Complex in Lahore said: 'As you know, Pakistan, with the help of the IMF, is progressing towards a documented economy; through this documentation all commodities and services will become taxable. The time of the retail tax will come soon and every service will be taxed.'

Upon the approval of the Finance Bill by the National Assembly in its annual budgetary session sometime in June of this year almost every purchase in this country shall become subject to a consumption tax of say, 5 to 15 per cent (a specific percentage has not yet been identified). A number of developed, Western countries have developed comprehensive regimes of consumption taxes. France has perhaps been one of the oldest practitioners of consumption taxes. Britons have long been paying a gradually escalating Value-Added Tax (VAT) and Canada has also introduced its own version of VAT that it calls the Goods & Services Tax (G&ST). The Americans, on the other hand, haven't seen a nationally administered consumption tax but individual states in the Union impose their own State Sales Tax (SST) that vary from around 3 per cent in Wyoming to over 8 per cent in New York and California.

All consumption taxes, including VAT and GST, are indirect taxes that are highly regressive in nature. A regressive tax regime is one in which the ratio of taxes to income increases as the income level of the taxpayers decreases or in other words, a regressive tax is 'one in which the average tax rate falls as income rises'. A retail level VAT or GST, therefore, exacts a disproportionately higher burden of taxation on the segment of population that falls in the lower-income category; the poorer you are the higher shall be your average tax rate. What really happens is that lower-income taxpayers end up consuming a much higher percentage of their total incomes merely to acquire essentials, whereby, their entire consumption becomes subject to taxation. Upper-income categories, on the contrary, need to spend a much smaller percentage of their income and that smaller percentage is thus subjected to a consumption tax. Technically speaking, the incidence of consumption taxes is heavier on people who just about make enough, merely to make the two ends meet.

The justification of VAT or GST in France, Britain, Canada or other prosperous nations may be that a very large percentage of their population lives way above the internationally recognized level of poverty. Most residents of the developed world have discretionary incomes (discretionary income is the part of income left over after meeting the bare minimum, non-discretionary expenditure on food, shelter and clothing) and are taxed at a few percentage points. Such a system of regressive taxation, when most of the affecters are well be able to afford a few additional percentage points at the point-of-sale, may have some justification. In our part of the developing world, however, close to three-quarters of the population continues to live at, or below, the internationally acceptable level of poverty.

As a very large majority of our population must spend 100 per cent of its meagre income merely to support the basic necessities of life, 100 per cent of the income may thus be subjected to consumption taxes. A very small upper-income class, on the other hand, may only need to spend a mere 10 per cent to 20 per cent of their income to cover all their primary requirements, and 80 to 90 per cent of their income, thus, may very well remain outside the bounds of a consumption tax by their very nature. The tax will, therefore, snatch away a larger percentage of earnings of individuals with lower incomes. The poorer one is, the higher is the percentage of his income that is taken away by the retail tax collector, and the richer one is the better-off he becomes as he has to pay a smaller percentage of his income to the tax collector.

Any policy of fair taxation must take into consideration the three core concepts of taxation, that of equity, ability-to-pay and the benefit principle. The concept of 'equity or fairness' is measured by the presence (or lack) of horizontal and vertical equity. Horizontal equity is the 'notion that equally situated citizens should be taxed equally. And vertical equity is the notion that differently situated citizens be taxed'. The ability-to-pay principle of taxation dictates that an individual who can afford to pay a higher tax by virtue of his higher earnings, should be made to do so.

The third is the benefit principle, according to which, the class of citizens that directly benefits from government spending and reaps the rewards of public services ought to pay proportionate taxes. Any indirect, retail-level consumption tax that our government may be contemplating on imposing, shall indeed be violating the equity, the ability-to-pay, and the benefit principles of fair taxation. Most principled governments around the world attempt to derive a majority of their revenues in the form of direct taxes – individual income taxes, corporate income taxes and entertainment taxes.

The simple reason behind this heavy dependence on direct taxes is that they are equitable and are most likely to fulfil the ability-to-pay and the benefit principles of taxation. Our government, on the other hand, somehow remains adamant in relying almost exclusively on indirect taxation. In the 1995–96 Budget out of an accumulated tax revenue target of Rs259 billion our government is projecting to collect a full 73 per cent in the form of indirect taxes – customs, sales and federal excise.

All the three categories of indirect taxes – customs, sales and excise – are also highly regressive and unjustly inequitable. While the government already collects a majority of its revenue through indirect taxation why does it want to burden the distressed classes of this country with more of the same? The existing tax collecting machinery remains so corrupt and rotten that most of the taxes collected in the form of direct taxes are really the withholding of salaries at source. What is needed is a thoroughly revamped tax collecting organization that is capable of transferring the true burden of taxation from the poor, underprivileged classes, on to where it rightfully belongs, through the proper implementation of a fool-proof arrangement of direct taxation.

Has the government really thought of a mechanism through which to collect a massive, widespread retail tax? Does the government really know how many retail outlets there are? Is there a central regulatory authority which has managed to get all the retailers registered with it? We don't even know just how many people really inhabit this country of ours, or how many of them live in urban areas since the last census is 15 years old. It is possible that half of the retailers (small, large, urban and rural put together) may very well be illiterate, while the other half may not want to maintain books or may indeed be maintaining dual books. The government has not even attempted to educate the retailers about the pros and cons of a retail tax. What concrete steps has the government really taken towards encouraging the documentation of the economy? Is the increase in the stamp duty on cheques or the introduction of withholding on bank transfers going to increase documentation?

The government, at the same time, must also understand that each and every inspiration of Western economics cannot blindly be transplanted to Eastern economies. It is claimed that IMF conditionalities somehow oblige the current government to raise additional revenue. That may indeed be a half-truth. What the IMF really wants to see is a lower budgetary deficit, whether it be through the raising of additional revenue or via a drastic reduction in the government's excessively wasteful expenditures. Has anyone even tried to persuade the IMF that a retail consumption tax is not a good idea for this country. Are Western economics once again going to victimize 120 million poor, Eastern, consumers?

Source: Saleem, Farrukh, *DAWN*, Economic and Business Review, 17–23 February 1996.

Appendix 10.4

Issues in tax administration

Two reports on taxation and the need for reform in administration, present the following analyses:

The quality of tax administration and the politics of taxation are perhaps the two most important constraints to changes in a country's tax regime. The total environment surrounding the overall taxation policy determines whether the tax system of a country responds to its needs for resources. Because of a general lack of awareness on the issues surrounding tax policy, both the politicians and the government officials tend to avoid a public debate.

This therefore results in, first, the politician announcing an ill-conceived policy without discussions with the tax administrator, and second, the tax administrator translating this policy into administrative measures without taking into consideration either the spirit of the policy announced or the benefits to be granted to the particular target groups. Therefore the cardinal rule of the tax policy is violated, namely that the legislative (political) and executive (tax administration) arms of government must work in collaboration with each other to produce a viable tax system.

For this to occur, it is necessary that the system should be relatively simple and must be generally understood by the taxpayer. This would therefore require that legislation be simplified and codified and that a tax education system be in place.

Much of the effort today in reforming fiscal policy is geared to the generation of additional revenues either through rate enhancements on existing sources or through new sources. Even though it is a well recognized fact that the successful administration of some of the more buoyant and elastic tax sources could yield a considerable part of the additional sources required, little attention is paid to improvement in tax administration. This multiplicity of taxes results not only in dispersing the administrative machinery, but also in diluting its efficiency and perhaps also increasing its size (and therefore the resources required to pay for it) and thereby weakens the overall tax regime.

Before a policy of reform in tax administration can be brought about the critical question that needs to be answered is: can the administrative machinery absorb the change? It might well be that there may be a need to strengthen the existing machinery through a two pronged effort. The first should be geared to the development of human resources. The issues that would require attention in this field are staff training and motivation, review of terms and conditions of service to ensure efficiency and equity, and the establishment of pay and allowances to match minimum needs. The second could address the issue of existing procedures, particularly with respect to identifying and quantifying the tax base. The tax system can only be effective if it has accurate and up to date information on potential taxpayers and their ability to pay. This requires firstly, the existence of data, and secondly, coordination between the various tax agencies with access to each other's records and data. In addition compliance by the taxpayer plays a critical role in the success of the tax system. This can best be achieved through tax education programmes and a simplification of procedures coupled by a reduction in the multiplicity of taxes.

Another major issue which needs rectification is the lack of knowledge about the tax system itself. It is generally recognized that while, on the one hand, only a few taxes levied yield a considerable part of revenue occurring to government, yet on the other hand, the majority of taxes yield very little. In some instances, the exemptions available are so extensive that the tax is leviable only on a few people. In addition, the wordings of legislations themselves create confusion. Different meanings are used for the same terms, or no definitions are given thus providing an avenue for confusion and the use of discretionary powers. This arises primarily because of government's reliance on using non-specialist lawyers for drafting the legal provisions governing tax policy. Therefore, in the process of beginning the change, the whole tax system needs to be codified and rationalized, somewhere at the very start of the tax reform process with the help of a team of tax administrators, tax lawyers and specialist legal draftsmen.

Yet another series of issues which are ordinarily the bane of contention between administrators and payers are the procedures of assessment, collection, redressal of grievance and refunds. The laxity in drafting the basic legislation provides ample opportunity for the misuse of powers by the tax administrator. Counter to this is the legal right of the taxpayer to avoid the payment of taxes within the fullest advantages provided to him through this same laxity in legal drafting. The administrative procedures laid down by the issue of 'statutory rules and orders' from time to time makes an already difficult process even more difficult. It has been argued that the powers to make or modify rules should rest with the legislative arm of governments and not with the administrative arm. Unless the procedures laid down for each of the four areas of contention are clear and precise, are fair and just and are not open to abuse and arbitrariness, compliance and collection will always be poor.

Source: Applied Economics Research Centre, *Resource Mobilization by Provincial and Local Governments in Pakistan*, Research Report No. 93, Karachi, 1992, pp. 80–2.

In addition to the need to change tax rates and structure, improvements in tax administration could also realize substantial net gains in revenue. Some of the recommendations made to broaden definitions, end exemptions, and eliminate distinctions between different types of income or transactions, should simplify the tax code and ease problems of tax administration. However, it is clear that there are still a number of problems, that are clearly reflected in taxpayer dissatisfaction with the system and in the poor coverage and widespread evasion. Improvements in administration should involve (a) tax procedures; (b) taxpayer identification; (c) assessment; (d) audits; and (e) analysis.

In Pakistan, there is no general tax procedure law that specifies the rights and duties of taxpayers and tax administrators, the steps involved in assessment and collection, and the means by which disputes are resolved. Lack of transparency in the system has created substantial mistrust between taxpayers and administrators. A number of countries have passed laws which cover tax procedures, assessment methods, evidence, bookkeeping rules, and the settlement of disputes. While the number of taxpayers doubled between FY80 and FY84, the fraction of the population covered is still low and the large proportion of revenues collected from large firms is indicative of poor coverage of small and medium-sized establishments. Improved coverage will involve intensified use of field surveys, coordination between income and sales taxation collection information, the introduction of unique taxpayer identification numbers, and computerization of registers and information.

Self-assessment has made an important contribution to the increase in the number of income taxpayers, but its success has been marred by excessive examination of declared incomes and resulting disputes. It would be simpler for the Central Board of Revenue to accept and finalize all self-assessments (with supporting documentation) and then proceed to detailed scrutiny and possible audit of returns on a random sample basis according to an annual program. At the same time, granting immunity from scrutiny and audit to taxpayers whose self-assessments are 20% or more higher than last year should be dropped. Tax evasion is too high for Pakistan to be able to afford such easy escape from possible audit. To improve coverage of small businesses, increased use of lump-sum presumptive (income and/or sales) taxes based on set criteria would be desirable; such businesses could be given the option of choosing to be taxed on the basis of actual incomes. To reduce the potential for taxpayer harassment, it would also be desirable to make procedures more transparent, make the authority of individual tax officers clear, and limit the right of administrative assessment to higher level commissions. At present the Central Board of Revenue has no capacity for the analysis of tax policy and reform. A cell should be set up, staffed with experienced economists and tax administrators, and charged with responsibility of analyzing the equity, efficiency and revenue impacts of potential tax changes.

Source: World Bank, *Pakistan: Growth Through Adjustment*, Report No. 7118-Pak, Washington, 1988, p. 52.

Notes

1. See the following reports prepared by the Applied Economics Research Centre (AERC), Karachi: *Local Government Finances and Administration in Pakistan* (in two volumes), Research Report No. 72, 1990; *Resource Mobilization and Institutional Capacity*, (in seven volumes), Research Report No. 85, 1991; *Resource Mobilization by Federal Government*, Research Report No. 91, 1992(a); *Resource Mobilization by Provincial and Local Governments in Pakistan*, Research Report No. 93, 1992(b); *Metropolitan Resource Generation Study*, Research Report No. 97, 1993.

2. Although the 1979 and 1980 Ordinances are supposed to be operative, in effect, all local governments were dismissed in the 1990s and at present (August 1997) local bodies are run by federal and provincial government-appointed Administrators. See also section 10.4, below.

3. AERC, op. cit., 1990, p. (iii).

4. From ibid.

5. Ibid., pp. 53–7.

6. Ibid., pp. 57–8.

7. Ibid., p. 53.

8. Ibid., p. 58.
9. See AERC, op. cit., 1990, and AERC, op. cit., 1992(b).
10. AERC, op. cit., 1992(b), p. 112.
11. Ibid., p. 115.
12. AERC, op. cit., 1990, p. 78.
13. Ibid., p. 66.
14. AERC, op. cit., 1992(a), p. 5.
15. Government of Pakistan, *Pakistan Economic Survey*, 1995–96, Islamabad, 1996, p. 130.
16. AERC, op. cit., 1990, pp. 15, 29–30.
17. See Government of Pakistan, *Pakistan Economic Survey*, *1972–73*, Islamabad, 1973, pp. 172–5, for these figures.
18. Pasha, Hafiz, 'Political Economy of Tax Reforms: The Pakistan Experience', *Pakistan Journal of Applied Economics*, vol. 11, nos. 1 and 2, 1995, p. 129.
19. World Bank, *Pakistan: Growth Through Adjustment*, Report No. 7118-Pak, Washington, 1988.
20. Ibid., p. (vii).
21. Ibid., p. 47.
22. World Bank, *Pakistan: Country Economic Memorandum FY93: Progress Under the Adjustment Program*, Report No. 11590-Pak, Washington, 1993, p. 11.
23. Pasha, Hafiz and M. Asif Iqba, 'Taxation Reforms in Pakistan', *Pakistan Journal of Applied Economics*, vol. 10, nos. 1 and 2, 1994, p. 70.
24. Ibid., p. 49.
25. Khan, Mohsin, 'Comments', in Thomas, V., *et al.*, *Restructuring Economies in Distress*, Oxford University Press, Oxford, 1991.
26. AERC, op. cit., 1992(a), p. 20.
27. Pasha, Hafiz and M. Asif Iqbal, op. cit., 1994, p. 49.
28. Ghaus, Aisha and Mohammad Asif Iqbal, 'Resource Mobilization by Provincial Governments', *News on Friday*, 25 August 1996.
29. Ibid.
30. Ibid.
31. Ibid.
32. Applied Economics Research Centre, *An Analysis of Provincial Finances in Pakistan*, Research Report No. 55, Karachi, 1986, p. 55.
33. For a more detailed analysis of local government and its finances, see Zaidi, S. Akbar, 'Urban Local Government in Pakistan: Expecting Too Much From Too Little?', *Economic and Political Weekly*, vol. 31, no. 44, 1996; Zaidi, S. Akbar 'Urban Local Governance in Pakistan', in Islam, Nazrul and M.M. Khan (eds.), *Urban Governance in Bangladesh and Pakistan*, Centre for Urban Studies, University of Dhaka, 1997(a); Zaidi, S. Akbar, 'Poverty, Politics, Institutions: The Case of Karachi', *Economic and Political Weekly*, vol. 32, no. 51, 1997(b); and Zaidi, S. Akbar, *The New Development Paradigm: Papers on Institutions, NGOs, Gender and Local Government*, Oxford University Press, Karachi, forthcoming, 1999.
34. AERC, op. cit., 1992(b), p. 120.
35. AERC, op. cit., 1992(b), p. 120.
36. Ghaus, Aisha, 'Local Government Finances: Efficiency, Equity and Optimality', unpublished, Ph.D. dissertation, University of Leeds, 1994.
37. AERC, op. cit., 1990, pp. 14–16.
38. See AERC, op. cit., 1990; AERC, op. cit., 1991; AERC, op. cit., 1992(a).
39. AERC, op. cit., 1990, pp. 16–17.
40. Ibid.
41. Ghaus, Aisha, op. cit., 1994, p. 89.
42. This section is a summarized extract from my paper, 'Urban Local Government in Pakistan', op. cit., 1996. See also Zaidi, S. Akbar, op. cit., 1997(a); Zaidi, S. Akbar, op. cit., 1997(b); and Zaidi, S. Akbar, op. cit., 1999.
43. See AERC, op. cit., 1990; AERC, op. cit., 1993; Zaidi, S. Akbar, 'Effective Local Level Delivery of Human Resources: Development Related Programmes – the Case of Pakistan', mimeo, UNESCAP, Bangkok, 1991; Zaidi, S. Akbar, 'A Study on Making Optimal Use of Municipal Budgets to Finance Child Development (Pakistan)', mimeo, UNICEF, Karachi, 1994; Zaidi, S. Akbar, op. cit., 1996; Zaidi, S. Akbar, op. cit., 1997(a); Zaidi, S. Akbar, op. cit., 1997(b); and Zaidi, S. Akbar, op. cit., 1999.
44. Zaidi, S. Akbar, op. cit., 1994; Zaidi, S. Akbar, op. cit., 1996; and Zaidi, S. Akbar, op. cit., 1997(a).
45. AERC, op. cit., 1991; AERC, op. cit., 1993; Zaidi, S. Akbar, op. cit., 1994; Zaidi, S. Akbar, op. cit., 1996; Zaidi, S. Akbar, op. cit., 1997(a); Zaidi, S. Akbar, op. cit., 1997(b); and Zaidi, S. Akbar, op. cit., 1999.
46. AERC, op. cit., 1990; AERC, op. cit., 1991.
47. Zaidi, S. Akbar, op. cit., 1994.
48. Ibid.
49. AERC, op. cit., 1993; Zaidi, S. Akbar, op. cit., 1996; Zaidi, S. Akbar, op. cit., 1997(a); Zaidi, S, Akbar, op. cit., 1997(b); and Zaidi, S. Akbar, op. cit., 1999.
50. AERC, op. cit., 1991; AERC, op. cit., 1992(a); AERC, op. cit., 1993; Zaidi, S. Akbar, op. cit., 1996; and Zaidi, S. Akbar, op. cit., 1997(a).
51. *The Friday Times*, 27 January–2 February 1994.
52. *The Nation*, 19 and 21 January 1994.
53. See Zaidi, S. Akbar, op. cit., 1996; Zaidi, S. Akbar, op. cit., 1997(a); Zaidi, S. Akbar, op. cit., 1997(b); Zaidi, S. Akbar, 'Karachi: Prospects for the Future', in Khuhro, Hameeda (ed.), *Karachi: Megacity of Our Times*, Oxford University Press, Karachi, 1997(c); Zaidi, S. Akbar, op. cit., 1999.
54. The discussion on the fiscal deficit in this chapter only introduces the reader to this concept. Many of the issues and much of the controversy related to it are discussed in Chapter 11. See also Zaidi, S. Akbar, 'The Structural Adjustment Programme and Pakistan: External Influence or Internal Acquiescnce?', *Pakistan Journal of Applied Economics*, vol. 10, nos. 1 and 2, 1994; and Zaidi, S. Akbar, 'Locating the Budget Deficit in Context: The Case of Pakistan', *Pakistan Journal of Applied Economics*, vol. 11, nos. 1 and 2, 1995.
55. World Bank, op. cit., 1988; World Bank, op. cit., 1993; and World Bank, *Pakistan: Medium Term Economic Policy Adjustments*, Report No. 7591-Pak, Washington, 1989.
56. World Bank, op. cit., 1993, p. 11.
57. World Bank, op. cit., 1988, p. 98.
58. World Bank, op. cit., 1989, p. 47.
59. Ibid.

11

Public Finance II: Pakistan's Fiscal Deficit – The Mother of All Evils?

In recent years, the role that the fiscal deficit plays in the economy of any country – whether developing or developed – has probably become the most talked about topic around which other economic issues revolve. Academicians, policy makers and politicians have spent extensive time and written numerous papers and reports regarding the problem of public debt and of the fiscal deficit. In the western developed countries, and especially in the United States, political campaigns, including the US presidential campaign, had the growing fiscal deficit as one of the most important issues on which candidates were expected to have a clear policy position. Ross Perot, the independent candidate in the elections, made the deficit his principal issue and came up with a number of somewhat extreme 'solutions' to what is considered to be the USA's major 'problem', which included an amendment to the US constitution making it obligatory to balance the budget each year, which was subsequently approved by the Congress in 1995. In Europe, too, the Maastricht Treaty for European unity includes a clause that requires fiscal 'discipline' by its members.

The general concern is that the existing levels of budgetary deficit are abnormal and undesirable, and many OECD countries have felt the need to follow budgetary strategies that attempt to reduce, and if possible eliminate, the entire deficit as soon as possible. The general consensus seems to be that these large current deficits are not sustainable, and that unless some forceful and direct action is taken, the deficits are likely to continue growing until they swamp the entire economy.

In the case of underdeveloped countries, the importance attached to fiscal deficits is even greater. The World Bank and the IMF believe that the fiscal deficit is the single most important policy variable that affects the rest of the economy, and they are able to express this belief through the implementation of their structural adjustment programmes. As Willem Buiter, a leading academician who has carried out extensive work on the fiscal deficit writes, 'the International Monetary Fund lectures finance ministers and heads of central banks ... as follows: public sector deficits, and especially increases in public sector deficits, are bad always and everywhere, regardless of circumstances, and discretionary spending cuts and/or tax increases should be implemented to reduce these deficits always and everywhere regardless of circumstances'.[1] In the case of Pakistan, the fiscal deficit is seen to be the cause of almost all the ills facing the economy. Mr Shahid Hasan Khan, Special Assistant on Economic Affairs to the Prime Minister of Pakistan under the second Benazir Bhutto government, has said that 'the fiscal deficit is the primary cause of all major ills of the economy. Consequently, any effort aimed at rehabilitating the economy would have the elimination of fiscal deficit as the number one item in its agenda.'[2] Every single IMF and World Bank document on Pakistan, especially since the structural adjustment programmes of 1988 and 1993, says exactly the same (see Chapters 14 and 15).

Given the substantial importance of the fiscal deficit, this chapter will try to identify the issues involved. We will first highlight some of the more general and standard theoretical arguments, and then examine the claim that fiscal deficits are always bad, regardless of the consequences. This chapter will also address the issue of the fiscal deficit in Pakistan, and will analyse whether it really is the primary cause of 'all majors ills of the economy'.

11.1 Does the Fiscal Deficit Matter?

Despite, or because of, the growing awareness and concern regarding budget deficits and public debt, there is a great deal of confusion about what the implications and consequences of large and/or increasing budget deficits really are. Do government deficits absorb private savings? Does public debt diminish private demand for stocks of productive capital assets? Can the burden of current government expenditure be shifted to future generations? Are inflations caused by deficits and public debt? Will government borrowing continue to raise interest rates? And will a tax cut mean bigger deficits while it stimulates aggregate demand, employment, and output, or will it have no real consequences whatsoever? These are some of the numerous themes and questions that reappear in the debate concerning public debt, which has been singled out as causing most of the serious problems faced by the economy. As James Tobin, an economist who won the Nobel prize in 1978, argues: 'few issues of economic theory and fact evoke such polar disagreement. The contesting views carry radically divergent implications for public fiscal and financial policy.'[3] Willem Buiter goes even further: 'probably more uninformed statements have been made on the issue of public sector debt and deficits than on any other topic in macroeconomics. Proof by repeated assertion has frequently appeared to be an acceptable substitute for the more conventional methods of proof by deduction or by induction.'[4]

Given the extensive literature that has been generated over the last decade, it is not possible in our brief review to examine all the effects and consequences of large public debt and deficits. We are forced to present only a few themes which we feel are important, and attempt to do justice to them. We examine the issue of balanced budgets, and the problem of measuring the deficit itself. We then look at themes related to the effect of the deficit on future generations and on issues regarding intertemporal equity and distribution. The macroeconomic concerns of fiscal deficits – inflation, crowding out, etc. – are discussed very briefly in section 11.1.4, and in more detail with reference to Pakistan, below.

11.1.1   Should Budgets Always be Balanced?

Possibly, the converse of public debt and deficit is no debt and no deficit, i.e. a surplus, or at least a balanced budget. The argument is that, like households and firms, governments should also live within their means and not go into indefinite and extensive debt. But as Tobin argues, 'central government is different from other economic agents. It is entrusted with the ultimate taxing and monetary powers and responsibilities of society. Its horizon spans the generations.'[5] Hence, the analogy between households and nations living beyond their means does not really hold.

Alan Blinder and Robert Solow writing two decades ago, before public debt in the United States had accumulated to the present levels, argued that 'at the crudest level, the desire for a steady government policy translates into a plea for an annually balanced budget ... The belief that government deficits (but not surpluses) are somehow wrong lingers in the mind of many politicians.'[6] At the time they wrote, balanced budgets were not in vogue, but since then, there has been a demand by politicians in the USA, that an appropriate way to maintain fiscal 'discipline' without stabilizing the economy would be 'to determine the level of government spending on its own merits, independent of the requirements of stabilization policy, and to set tax rates so as to produce a balance (or a small surplus) at full employment'.[7] The demand to legislate for balanced budgets constraining government activity was approved by the US Congress in 1995.

James Tobin, arguing against the balanced budget and tax limitation amendment which were first proposed in the USA in the 1980s, takes a very clear stance. His focus was on the US Senate's resolution which would force future Congresses to balance every year's federal budget, and would limit the growth of federal revenues and outlays. In no uncertain terms, he says: 'to me it seems incredibly ironic that anyone would take this proposal seriously at this time ... The effects on the economy would be disastrous, converting the present depression into a great depression.'[8]

Unlike a school of thought which insists that deficits are *always* bad, Tobin argues that federal deficits may even be economically *desirable* in specific circumstances, *and what is really important is appropriate public policy*, which may or may not produce a balanced budget. However, he argues that making deficits unconstitutional would increase economic instability. It would force ill-timed expenditure cuts or tax increases, which would then make recessions much worse. 'To force Congress to decrease expenditure or increase taxes to offset cyclical deficits would further depress the economy. The deficits perform a useful function in absorbing saving that would otherwise be wasted in unemployment, excess capacity or lower production.'[9] Tobin argues that there are built-in stabilizers in the fiscal system which give it a sense of balance, but if there were a compulsion to balance the budget every year, these stabilizers would lose their efficacy. However, *the main focus for Tobin is sensible and appropriate public policy, rather than a fixation with the balanced budget*. This view is shared by Willem Buiter, who argues that 'optimal, or merely sensible, budgetary policy is bound to be characterized by systematic, predictable, and sometimes persistent departures from budget balance. Even in long run equilibrium, zero is not a uniquely interesting figure for the budget deficit.'[10]

11.1.2   The Problem of Measuring the Deficit

While concern about the deficit and the growing public debt has invoked substantial debate, there has also been a fair amount of discussion around the measurement of the debt and the deficit, and about which items constitute government assets and/or liabilities.

Robert Eisner and P.J. Piepper argue that conventional measures of fiscal deficit and debt are 'fundamentally flawed'. In their analysis they correct the figures for debt for changes in the market value of government debt due to changes in interest rates and changes in the real value due to inflation. They find these adjustments in measurement critical to their findings: 'failure to measure deficits correctly has not only contributed to a false view of fiscal impotence, but has possibly lead to an overestimate of the importance of money'.[11]

M.J. Boskins also questions the figure quoted for the officially reported deficit, which for him is a very poor indicator of the underlying public debt policies. He feels that there are 'very significant if not overwhelming difficulties of gauging the extent of true debt policies from official reports'.[12] For Boskins, the particular view of the federal financial picture depends critically on *what one chooses to include as a measure of debt and the deficit*. By making certain assumptions and adjustments, one can end up with very different figures for the deficit and debt, and thus one can make use of them to suit one's own particular goal. Despite the apparent cynicism in the context of measuring deficit and debt, there is a built-in warning which urges one to look beyond the very obvious, and examine the data and assumptions on which claims are being made. As Buiter argues, 'none of the (doctored or undoctored) deficit measures are reliable indicators of the magnitude or even sign of the effects of fiscal policy on interest rates, capital formation, or the capital account of the balance of payments'.[13] Food for thought, indeed! See Box 11.1 for definitions of the deficit.

BOX 11.1

Different budget deficits

Different figures for the budget deficit are quoted by different people due to the different definitions in use and also because of problems of measurement. Here we show how three different figures can be generated and used, depending on expediency.

Revenue Budget Surplus/Deficit

A revenue surplus or deficit of the budget is equal to the difference between net revenue receipts and current expenditure minus the repayment of foreign debt. Net revenue receipts are equal to the gross revenues of the federal government minus the transfer to the provinces. The revenue surplus shows the extent of public sector saving, where a surplus implies positive saving by the government, and a deficit negative saving. This revenue surplus or deficit is the bridge between the revenue and capital account of the government. In the case of Pakistan, public saving has been negative for many years, thus a revenue deficit of the budget. An increase in the revenue budget deficit shows that the government is using its borrowings increasingly to meet current expenditure, especially the salaries of government employees.

Overall Budget Deficit

This is the most commonly used indicator to refer to the state of a country's public finances, and measures the difference between the total expenditure of the government and its resources. It measures current expenditure plus development expenditure minus repayment of foreign debt minus net revenue receipts minus the contribution by autonomous bodies minus the amount earned by disinvestment of shares.

The Primary Budget Deficit

Usually budget deficits measure impacts of discretionary government policy. However, one important variable of the budget, i.e. debt servicing, is non-discretionary and is predetermined by the size and terms of previous budgeting decisions and loans. The primary budget deficit, by excluding the debt service, measures the impact of all discretionary changes of the government in any year. It is calculated by subtracting the interest payments on domestic and foreign debt from the overall budget deficit. [Table 9.7 shows this deficit in Pakistan's case.]

Source: Qazi Masood Ahmed and Hafiz Pasha, 'Definition, Measurement and Implications of Different Deficits in the Budget', unpublished manuscript, n/d.

Debt or Deficit?

Few people seem to know the difference between debt and deficit, and use the terms interchangeably. The deficit is the amount by which expenditures exceed tax revenues in a given period or, in the more comprehensive official jargon, 'outlays' exceed 'receipts', and hence the amount that must be borrowed or added to the debt over the period. The debt is the amount owed at any point in time – what has been borrowed and not paid back. In the case of any country which has accumulated a large debt, even a dramatic decrease in the deficit over a few years will not decrease the nominal debt – it will, in fact, increase the debt. Only if there were a budget surplus would there be some decrease in the debt.

Source: Eisner, R., 'Sense and Nonsense about Budget Deficits', *Harvard Business Review*, May–June 1993.

11.1.3 Fiscal Deficits, Intertemporal Equity, and Distribution

I. Ihori asks the important question of whether increasing debt finance is adding an increasingly unfair burden on future generations. If the answer is in the affirmative, then one may conclude that present generations are benefiting by consuming services provided currently, while future generations will have to foot the bill; hence, one should not borrow. On the other hand, one may be able to argue that, by borrowing now, there will be greater intergenerational equity, since part of the cost of capital outlays will be passed on to the future. He feels that the answer to the question of whether debt is passed on to future generations depends critically on the definition of the burden of debt. Modigliani's definition rests on the assumption that a permanent increase in government debt would crowd out private investment in the long run, causing a net decrease in the capital stock. He calls this negative effect on the capital stock a burden of the public debt – that is, 'each generation "burdens" the next one by bequeathing them a smaller aggregate stock of capital'.[14]

Even though some arguments suggest that a growing debt that must be financed by increasing interest payments is unfair to future generations, it could, in fact, be argued that future generations are better off because of the manner in which the public debt is spent. If governments invest in improving the quality of life of present and future generations by investing in social goods like health, education, and infrastructure, future generations may actually be better off in real (and human capital) terms. However, if deficits grow due to massive increases in military spending (as in the case of Pakistan, discussed below) and large tax cuts, one could argue that the burden of debt on future generations (and on the present one) may not be very fair. Thus the nature of spending public money and who actually decides where it should be spent is a critical factor often ignored in a debate that has become obsessed by the *amount* of public expenditure.

11.1.4 Macroeconomic Implications[15]

The IMF and the World Bank are agreed on one point, that dealing with budget deficits is one of the most 'vexing problems' for the majority of underdeveloped countries, and hence fiscal policy is now an essential component of adjustment programmes, where fiscal 'discipline' and 'restraint' are viewed as prerequisites for macroeconomic stabilization (see, for example, the issues in Chapters 14 and 15). Many observers argue that the fiscal deficit is a useful indicator of overall economic performance, and have found 'a significant statistical relationship between the deficit and many, though not all, macroeconomic performance variables'.[16]

The budget deficit is held responsible for high inflation, low growth, a current account deficit, and the crowding out of private investment and consumption. The relationship between deficits and other macroeconomic variables is said to depend on how the deficits are financed. Simply put, this view holds that

> money creation leads to inflation. Domestic borrowing leads to a credit squeeze – through higher interest rates or, when interest rates are fixed, through credit allocation and ever more stringent financial repression – and the crowding out of private investment and consumption. External borrowing leads to a current account deficit and appreciation of the real exchange rate and sometimes to a balance of payments crisis (if foreign resources are run down) or an external debt crisis (if debt is too high).[17]

Researchers also find 'strong evidence' from empirical studies examining the role of underdeveloped countries which supports the claims made above.

Professor Robert Eisner, a leading proponent of the minority Keynesian view regarding budget deficits, argues that budget deficits do matter and their effects can be substantial, but 'the current size of the federal deficit [in the USA] is not "our number one economic problem", if indeed it is a problem at all'.[18] He cites data from the USA 'the world's largest debtor nation' – and shows that, despite a large and growing deficit in the 1980s, inflation, thought to be one of the key victims of large budget deficits, has declined sharply. In fact, he argues, 'the time-series relation between deficits and inflation in the United States has generally been negative; bigger deficits have come with less inflation and smaller deficits with more inflation'.[19] What is more surprising, and what contradicts conventional wisdom, is the relationship between the deficit and growth: empirical evidence shows how US deficits 'have over the last several decades proved stimulatory to the economy'[20] – the greater the deficit between 1955 and 1983, the greater was the next year's increase in GNP; and the less the deficit, the less was the subsequent increase in GNP. Budget deficits are seen to be related not only to the growth of GNP as a whole, but also positively to consumption and investment. Furthermore, there is evidence that 'deficits have not crowded out

investment [but] there has rather been crowding in'.[21]

For the purposes of our analysis of Pakistan's fiscal deficit, we will be concerned mainly with the macroeconomic effects of the deficits. As the arguments above show, there is some disagreement over the macroeconomic implications of a large fiscal deficit. However, almost all conventional economists, especially those who work in and advise international agencies, particularly the World Bank and the IMF, argue that the fiscal deficit is bad and unwanted. They claim that the economy will suffer appreciably if the deficit is not removed, and for them, it is probably the single most critical statistic that determines the health of the economy. Let us now examine this role in the context of Pakistan.

11.2 Critical Concerns Regarding Pakistan's Fiscal Deficit[22]

Based on the large number of tables on the public finance structure presented in the previous chapter, and particularly those related to key variables, such as total expenditure, defence and development expenditure, interest payments, and the extent and trend of the public debt, we can summarize the main features of Pakistan's public finances and fiscal deficit as follows:

1 Total expenditure exceeds total revenue, and the growth in expenditure is greater than that in revenue.

2 Current expenditure alone exceeds total revenue.

3 Development expenditure has been falling, while current expenditure has grown.

4 Defence expenditure has been very high, and is now much higher than even development expenditure.

5 Interest payments along with defence expenditure constitute more than half of annual expenditure.

6 The main source for financing the fiscal deficit has been non-bank borrowing, rather than bank borrowing.

7 Domestic debt is greater than foreign debt.

8 The financing of the deficit is very substantially from domestic sources rather than from foreign sources.

9 The fiscal deficit of the government of Pakistan has been around 8 per cent of GDP for much of the 1980s.

Apparently, there is complete agreement over the claim that the federal budget deficit is the most important threat facing Pakistan's economy.[23]

Fiscal policy has been identified as a 'critical failure' in the context of Pakistan, and as one of Pakistan's key macroeconomic problems, threatening price stability, balance of payments, 'constraining essential government investment in economic and social infrastructure, and thereby, endangering growth prospects'.[24] See Appendix 11.1 for a particularly forceful presentation of this view.

The persistent reference to the 'high and unsustainable' fiscal deficit by the IMF and World Bank (and sundry other commentators) – 'the fiscal deficit has been perceived as a continuing problem in Pakistan'[25] – since at least the early

1980s, when the first Structural Adjustment Programme was initiated on the recommendations of the IMF, must rest on the premise that the budget deficit is responsible for most of the macroeconomic ills in the country, and thus, needs redress. The IMF, following the conventional wisdom which it has helped frame, would, in all likelihood, hold the deficit in Pakistan responsible for some, if not all, of the following consequences: growing inflation, crowding out of private investment, a falling growth rate, and the twin of the budget deficit, the continuing deterioration of the current account deficit. We must assume that, unless it was seen as a primary cause of the problems in the economy, it would not form the central tenet of policy statements and adjustment programmes that Pakistan continuously undertakes (also see Chapters 14 and 15). Let us examine some of the evidence.

Table 11.1 presents a summary picture of Pakistan's key macroeconomic variables since 1980. The budget deficit as a percentage of GDP is presented alongside other variables which it is supposed to affect. Let us consider growth. The 'very high', 'escalating' budget deficit, according to the IMF theory of causality, should have had severe repercussions on the growth of the economy. This is clearly not the case. Pakistan has experienced very high growth rates compared to other developing countries and averaged well over 6.5 per cent per annum in the 1980s. This is no mean achievement given the huge budget deficit, which has averaged 7 per cent in the same period. Surely, the numbers must give pause for thought.

The inflation rate is another key variable that should have exploded given the high budget deficit. An average of only 7 per cent inflation over a decade is quite creditable. Moreover, fewer than half the thirteen years since 1980 have seen double-digit inflation, with a maximum of 13.9 per cent. According to estimates, Pakistan's inflation rate should have averaged in excess of 50 per cent, given the high and unsustainable budget deficit.[26] With Latin American deficits, Pakistan has continued to have South Asian rates of inflation. Interestingly, however, since 1990 when the budget deficit was 8.7 per cent, the deficit has been falling, but inflation has actually *risen* in this period. It seems that there is an inverse relationship between the two, at least in the case of Pakistan.

The crowding-out phenomenon is a key favourite of orthodoxy and neoclassicists, given their penchant for the private sector. The theory suggests that the government, in its financing of the deficit, would have pushed up interest rates to such an extent that the private sector would have found it unaffordable to invest, and thus would have been crowded out (see also section 10.5 in the previous chapter). This would have implied a growth rate of far less than the hugely impressive 15 per cent per annum experienced by the private sector in the 1980s. Moreover, with the even greater 'burgeoning of the budget deficit' in 1990/1 (8.7 per cent), 1991/2 (7.5), and 1992/3 (7.9), one would not have expected the 19, 30, and 13 per cent growth in the private sector over the same years. Clearly, there seems to be little truth in the claim that the private sector has been crowded out due to government policies or the budget deficit. The evidence, no matter how superficial, points to utterly different

conclusions. Moreover, in the period since 1988 when the deficit has been particularly high, so much so that the structural adjustment programme of 1988 emphasized the need to cut the deficit drastically, the economy has behaved even more unconventionally with respect to IMF theory: real per capita GDP rose by 10.4 per cent between 1988 and 1992; merchandise exports have expanded by an average of 14 per cent per annum in volume; private sector gross fixed capital formation has gradually expanded from 7.7 to 9.4 per cent of GDP; and even domestic savings have risen from 10.5 to 12.2 per cent[27] (see Chapter 7 for why growth was so high in this period). Furthermore, even the current account deficit behaves quite contrary to IMF theory. With this evidence, one is forced to re-examine the questions: does the budget deficit matter in the context of Pakistan and how does the IMF/World Bank feel about this issue?[28]

11.3.1 The IMF/World Bank View of Pakistan's Fiscal Deficit

Given its repeated concern over the issue of the budget deficit, one is led to believe that the IMF has views on Pakistan's budget deficit consistent with its theoretical construct. Not so. The IMF/World Bank admit that

> the macro consequences of fiscal deficits in Pakistan have apparently been quite dissimilar from those in other developing countries with fiscal deficits of comparable magnitude. *Specifically, Pakistan has experienced neither hyperinflation nor debt rescheduling ... Growth has remained quite strong through the last two decades, inflation has not been high, and the current account deficit has averaged about 2 per cent of GNP, remaining largely financeable and not posing debt servicing problems for the country.*[29]

These institutions, despite their insistence on the need to lower the deficit, admit that the deficits have been 'quite benign' and that, despite the presence of fiscal deficits 'that are *very high* by international standards, the country's macroeconomic performance has been relatively good ... *There is no evidence in Pakistan of the chronic acute macroeconomic crises* – manifest in extended periods of negative per capita income growth, hyperinflation, and inability to service external debt – that have characterized many other developing countries with comparable fiscal performance.'[30]

The institutions that insist on cutting down the deficit admit that 'inflation performance in Pakistan appears to have been remarkably good ... At the same time economic growth has been robust',[31] and real GNP per capita between 1972 and 1987 has shown a cumulative increase of more than 60 per cent. Additionally, even the crowding-out argument seems to have been rejected, albeit reluctantly, with the IMF/World Bank admitting that public and private investment seem to be positively correlated and 'the infrastructural build up that results from government investment appears to facilitate private investment'.[32]

A recent study conducted by the IMF on determinants of private investment in Pakistan argues that aggregate

Table 11.1
Gross domestic product, inflation, current account deficit, and budget deficit, 1980–1995

Years	Growth rate (%)					As % of GDP							
		Investment		CPI	CAD		Investment	CAD	Defence exp.	Develop. exp.	Interest payments	Budget deficit	PBD
	GDP	Public	Private				Public	Private						
	(1)	(2)	(3)	(4)	(5)		(6)	(7)	(8)	(9)	(10)	(11)	(12)	(13)
1960s	6.8	14.0	20.9	3.8	–		–	–	–	–	–	–	–	–
1970s	4.8	25.3	17.0	12.3	–		9.2	7.2	–	–	–	–	7.0	–
1980s	6.5	10.6	15.0	7.3	21.2		8.6	7.3	3.7	6.5	7.2	3.8	7.0	–
1980/1	6.4	-1.2	13.1	13.9	-9.0		8.7	7.2	3.4	5.5	9.3	2.1	5.3	3.2
1981/2	7.6	19.8	8.0	11.1	47.9		8.9	6.7	4.6	5.7	8.2	2.4	5.3	2.9
1982/3	6.8	12.0	14.7	4.7	-66.3		8.7	6.6	1.6	6.4	8.1	3.1	7.0	3.9
1983/4	4.0	8.0	17.4	7.3	92.8		8.2	6.8	2.9	6.4	6.7	3.4	6.0	2.6
1984/5	8.7	11.4	14.0	5.7	68.5		8.2	7.0	5.0	6.7	7.0	3.4	7.8	4.4
1985/6	6.4	13.1	11.5	4.4	-26.4		8.6	7.2	3.6	6.9	7.7	3.8	8.1	4.3
1986/7	5.8	17.3	11.0	3.6	-41.8		9.2	7.3	2.0	7.2	6.3	4.2	8.2	4.0
1987/8	6.4	6.8	16.7	6.3	133.9		8.5	7.4	4.4	7.0	6.9	4.9	8.5	3.6
1988/9	4.8	16.0	23.9	10.4	15.0		8.7	8.0	4.8	6.6	6.3	5.0	7.4	2.4
1989/90	4.6	3.6	19.3	6.0	-2.2		8.0	8.6	4.7	6.8	6.5	5.4	6.5	1.1
1990/1	5.6	20.9	19.2	12.7	14.8		8.3	8.7	4.8	6.3	6.4	4.9	8.7	3.8
1991/2	7.7	23.2	30.3	10.6	-38.0		8.6	9.7	2.8	6.3	7.5	5.2	7.5	2.3
1992/3	2.3	14.5	13.4	9.8	174.0		9.0	9.9	7.1	6.5	5.7	5.9	7.9	2.0
1993/4	4.5	7.1	11.6	11.3	-46.7		8.3	9.5	3.8	5.9	4.6	5.8	5.9	0.1
1994/5	4.4	18.9	10.2	13.0	22.2		8.3	8.8	4.0	5.4	4.3	5.5	5.6	0.1

CAD = Current account deficit.
PBD = Primary budget deficit (budget deficit minus interest payments).
Source: Government of Pakistan, *Pakistan Economic Survey*, various years, Islamabad.

government investment has a significant positive impact on private investment, implying 'that the crowding out effect was not strong enough to balance the crowding-in effect in the period covered [1972–88] and is consistent with the view, inter alia, as to the importance of upgrading the country's roads and transportation networks, and improving the drainage system'.[33] This government investment in infrastructure was 'estimated to be *the most important positive determinant*' of private investment in the period covered. The investment in infrastructure is expected to continue to have a '*significant* crowding-in effect' in the future. Interestingly, similar conclusions have been reached for India as well, based on an evaluation of past trends.

The IMF believes that the deficit has not behaved in Pakistan as it should have, for several reasons:

1   There was a very high rate of growth of real output (6 per cent per annum) which permitted a fairly rapid expansion of both interest-bearing and non-interest-bearing debt without recourse to inflationary finance.

2   The equilibrium deficit is quite high – 5.5 per cent of GNP – despite a low inflation rate because of a very high underlying rate of growth of real output.

3   The government of Pakistan was able to borrow, both domestically and externally, at rates below the marginal cost of funds in the international private capital markets.[34]

In addition, throughout the 1980s, the budget deficit was not monetized, and external funds and non-bank borrowing were the main sources of funds to finance the deficit, so inflation remained low. It was only after 1990/1, when bank borrowing contributed a very large share of the financing of the budget deficit, that inflationary pressures emerged. However, after 1993/4 bank borrowing returned to the low, pre-1990 level (see section 10.5 in the previous chapter).

Our own observations regarding the impact of the budget deficit on key macroeconomic variables question the economic orthodoxy with respect to Pakistan, as do the observations and findings of IMF staff and IMF-sponsored studies. While the monetarist neoclassical assumptions and predictions regarding the behaviour of the budget deficit are clearly spurious, if not outrightly rejected, the Keynesian interpretations, where public spending causes an increase in aggregate demand and, subsequently, growth, given the less than full capacity of the economy, seem somewhat closer to reality. The greater the public expenditure, the greater the rate of growth of GDP and the greater the private investment. Moreover, since there is no crowding out through the mechanism of the interest rate as predicted by theory, one is led to believe that there are ample loanable funds available at a given interest rate. Easterly and Schmidt-Hebbel, in their review of developing countries, found that private investment does not respond much to interest rates.[35] As has been argued extensively elsewhere,[36] the evidence suggests that Pakistan's economy has been in far better shape for the duration of the structural adjustment programmes than the IMF/World Bank believes. Whether this is due to the huge underreported informal economy or to any other factor is open to debate. In fact, it is interesting to note that, if indeed it is true that Pakistan's GDP is underreported by as much as 40 per cent,[37] then the size of the budget deficit as a percentage of the true GDP would be much less than the reported official figure of 8 per cent and the present figure may even be 'sustainable'. Although this is a debatable and controversial point, it may nevertheless be the key in answering the question of why the deficit has, until recently, continued to remain 'benign', and has not disrupted the positive trends in the economy as it should have. Given the nature and robustness of the economy, a fact conceded even by the IMF, it seems quite clear that, in the conventional orthodox framework, *the budget deficit in Pakistan does not matter*.

11.3.2   Re-examining Critical Concerns

Having just argued that the budget deficit, in the conventional orthodox neoclassical framework, does not matter with regard to Pakistan, we will now argue that it is perhaps the most important statistic around which debate *ought* to take place. However, we take this view for very different reasons from the IMF and World Bank.

The obsession that policy makers in Pakistan have with the budget deficit detracts attention from the really important issues. The focus should not be on asking the question: how high is the budget deficit, and is it sustainable? The real concern regarding the deficit is the issue of *spending and redistribution*. It is more important to ask the questions: What use is being made of public money? Who is funding government expenditure, i.e. who is being taxed? How is public expenditure managed? And so on.

Table 11.1 again provides a very brief overview of what we feel is the central issue regarding the budget deficit. The contrast in the patterns of defence expenditure and development expenditure is the key concern regarding the budget deficit and public spending. In fact, Pakistan might well be the only underdeveloped country where defence spending outweighs development expenditure. Since 1980, as the table shows, there has been a relative increase in defence expenditure as a share of GDP compared to a relative decrease in development spending. Moreover, since 1985 defence spending has increased by 150 per cent, compared to an 89 per cent increase in development expenditure. Ironically, prior to 1985/6 when there was a military government in power and Pakistan was under martial law for most of the time, defence expenditure was considerably less than development expenditure. Following the advent of democracy in Pakistan, defence spending was higher than development expenditure in five of the next seven years. There are two possible explanations for this pattern: according to one view, during military rule, not only was the military making direct use of the defence budget, but also, due to its status as 'the government' and due to various privileges, it acquired a large share in the civilian side of the economy. Thus, in real terms, defence expenditure was just a fraction of the extent to which the military really benefited.[38] This also explains why the primary budget deficit was higher in the 1980–6 period (averaging 3.6 per cent) than in the 1986–93 period when it averaged 1.9 per cent.

BOX 11.2
Fixing targets for the budget deficit

In this excerpt, we examine whether having a fixed target for the budget deficit for Pakistan is a wise policy move or not.

If the government's deficit is used for stepping up public capital formation, then not only does it stimulate the economy from the demand side, but also it keeps relaxing the economy from the supply side, both through its direct effect on the magnitude of capital stock and through its indirect effect via stimulating private investment. On the other hand, if the increase in the government's deficit is confined to non-capital expenditure then revival of the economy would necessarily be brief and evanescent, since such a revival would fairly soon run into an inflationary barrier.

This consideration is particularly important for an economy where agriculture accounts for a major part of the consumer goods sector. It may, for instance, be argued that *any* government expenditure (even non-capital expenditure), by stimulating the economy, would call forth private investment via accelerator effects, so that the inflationary barrier would keep getting pushed back: this argument, however, would certainly not hold in the case of agriculture. Private investment in agriculture is not governed by any version of the acceleration (or capacity utilization or even profit) principle. It depends essentially upon the availability of complementary inputs like supra-individual irrigation facilities, power, extension facilities, seed-fertilizer packages, etc. whose provision is contingent upon public investment effort. In short, in an India-type economy it is not just any expansion in the government's deficit which can trigger off a sustained boom, but an expansion that takes the form of a larger investment effort. And this is precisely what the last two years' deficit expansion has not been used for.

It seems that Budget '96 is going to revolve around one single figure – 4 per cent. All indications about the deliberations underway at different levels of government in the build-up to the new budget suggest that Islamabad is going to do its utmost to bring the deficit down to 4 per cent of GDP. One of the key indicators which the government has specifically tried to control, the budget deficit, seems to have grown in importance over the last few years. In the coming financial year 1996/7, it will probably become the government's obsession, having extensive ramifications on a number of areas of the economy.

As far as raising revenue is concerned, despite the numerous tax measures taken each year to increase overall revenue – essentially by imposing a heavier burden on those who already pay taxes – in real terms very little has been achieved in the form of additional revenue. Moreover, there is growing resentment amongst those who currently pay taxes, for they believe that the tax system is riddled with glaring inequities with a large and wealthy section of society remaining exempt. Add to that the fact that for each increase in the tax rate and in tax collection, the quantity and quality of public services – from law and order to education and health – has deteriorated sharply. With additional taxes worth 25–30 billion expected in the next budget, with agricultural incomes still exempt, each taxpayer does indeed have the right to complain and question the government's logic of trying to raise more revenue to cut the budget deficit so that it could get yet another IMF loan.

One obvious way to raise additional revenue, and thereby cut the deficit, would be to tax agricultural income. But for purely political reasons, the present government is loath to tax its ally, the wealthy agricultural lobby. And herein lies the dilemma. The agriculturists cannot be taxed, but to remain in the good books of the IMF the budget deficit has to be cut. The government's solution: additional taxes on those who have no option but to pay, and fewer government schools and hospitals. In essence then, what the IMF loans do is that they allow the wealthy – whether rural or urban – to continue with their lifestyles without having to pay the consequences of living well beyond their private as well as collective means. As such, the continued access to and availability of IMF and World Bank loans has become an excuse to postpone structural reforms, such as land reforms and levying agricultural income tax.

By propping up regimes which do not have the ability or inclination to take sensitive or tough decisions, organizations such as the World Bank and the IMF ensure their longevity. By lowering the budget deficit to 4 per cent of GDP, as per IMF instructions for the coming year, the present government in Islamabad can be assured of another large IMF loan, and at the same time will ensure its survival by not disturbing the powerful agricultural lobby. For this government at least, 4 per cent is indeed sacrosanct.

Source: This is an edited version of Zaidi, S. Akbar, 'Is Four Per Cent Sacrosanct?', *The Herald*, June 1996.

A second explanation for this trend is that in the post-martial law period, while the military has not been *in government*, there is little disagreement that the military continues to be *in power*. Furthermore, given democracy's inability to deal with political problems in Pakistan, the military has had to play a more overt policing role. Ergo, a high share is given to defence expenditure – and a smaller residual share to development – under democracy.[39] Given Pakistan's political history and structure and the newly found policing role of the military, it is unlikely that any real cut in military expenditure will take place in the near future, possibly resulting in a clearer trade-off between defence and development expenditures. Nevertheless, one can simulate models to examine such an effect statistically. Ayub Mehar has shown that a one-time decrease of a mere Rs5 billion in defence expenditure in 1991/2 (when it was about Rs80 billion) would have resulted in a fall in net domestic borrowing and in the budget deficit in subsequent years, at least until the year 2000.[40]

Thus, if the budget deficit is 'the number one problem of

Pakistan's economy', as most observers believe, it is for reasons connected with the role and distribution of public expenditure, and is not dependent on the fetish of an abstract, arbitrary, badly calculated statistic. The question of governance, or how public money is utilized, allocated, managed, and siphoned off, is of critical importance. With corruption rampant at all levels of government, and with political power being bought and sold in different provincial and national governments over the last few years, it is clear that the taxpayer's money continues to be used to buy off opposition and keep dissent under control. Unquestionably, the specific context of fiscal policy and budgetary deficits is all important (see also Box 11.2 and Appendix 11.2).

11.4 Summary and Further Reading

11.4.1 Summary

This chapter makes the simple, though important point that fiscal deficits, and expenditure by government in excess of its revenue, are not always and everywhere 'a bad thing'. What matters is the type of expenditure and the context of the fiscal deficit. We have looked at the conventional wisdom which states that numerous ills that afflict the economy are said to originate from high fiscal deficits. After looking at the more general arguments, in which we showed that it is not always such a good idea to reduce public spending or to have a fiscal surplus or balanced budget, we then examined the specific case of Pakistan.

In the case of Pakistan, it seems that conventional wisdom regarding the fiscal deficit has been turned on its head. The high fiscal deficit does not do all the things it is supposed to, and until more recently has been rather 'benign', yet, at 6 per cent plus, the fiscal deficit in Pakistan is an important issue.

We have emphasized the point that, in itself, the fiscal deficit should not be of concern. What is critical is the use to which public money is being put (Box 11.2 and Appendix 11.2). If government spends more on the military and on interest payments, as opposed to the social sectors and development, causing the deficit to increase, that is a worrying sign. It is important to have some accountability about where the domestic and foreign debt has gone. Has it been used productively, or has it been squandered away? Hence, the question of public expenditure and fiscal deficits may be better answered by recourse to issues and ideas of governance, rather than according to the rather limited concerns of accountancy. Schemes like Nawaz Sharif's

'National Debt Retirement Programme' are meaningless given the huge size of the debt, and avoid issues of accountability. For this reason, we also suggest that debt retirement from privatization proceeds is improbable and would be a waste of money, which could be put to better use in social and infrastructure development (Appendix 11.3).

One problem that the debt raises is the high interest rate which government must pay on domestic debt, currently close to 20 per cent per annum. The financial sector liberalization reforms under the structural adjustment programme are partly responsible for these high interest rates, and are discussed along with the fiscal deficit issue in Part IV of this book.

11.4.2 Further Reading

There is no book which examines the issue of the fiscal deficit; some academic journal articles are all that is available. For the case of Pakistan, see: Zaidi, S. Akbar, 'The Structural Adjustment Programme and Pakistan: External Influence or Internal Acquiescence?', *Pakistan Journal of Applied Economics*, vol. 10, nos. 1 and 2, 1994; Zaidi, S. Akbar, 'Locating the Budget Deficit in Context: The Case of Pakistan', *Pakistan Journal of Applied Economics*, vol. 11, nos. 1 and 2, 1995; Haque, Nadeemul and Peter J. Montiel, 'Fiscal Policy Choices and Macroeconomic Performance in the Nineties', in Nasim, Anjum (ed.), *Financing Pakistan's Development in the 1990s*, Oxford University Press, Karachi, 1992; Haque, Nadeemul and Peter J. Montiel, 'The Macroeconomics of Public Sector Deficits: The Case of Pakistan', Working Paper no. 673, World Bank, Washington, 1991; and Haque, Nadeemul and Peter J. Montiel, 'Fiscal Adjustment in Pakistan', *IMF Staff Papers*, vol. 40, no. 2, 1993. See also the references cited in note 23 – in particular, the World Bank publications.

For a more general treatment of fiscal deficits, see: Buiter, Willem, *Principles of Budgetary and Financial Policy*, Harvester, Brighton, 1990; Blinder, A.S. and Robert Solow, *The Economics of Public Finance*, Brookings Institute, Washington, 1974; Arrow, Kenneth and M.J. Boskins, (eds.), *The Economics of Public Debt*, Macmillan, London, 1988; Easterly, W. and K. Schmidth-Hebbel, 'Fiscal Deficits and Macroeconomic Performance in Developing Countries', *World Bank Research Observer*, vol. 8, no. 2, 1993; Easterly, W. and K. Schmidt-Hebbel, 'The Macroeconomics of Public Sector Deficits: A Synthesis', Working Paper no. 775, World Bank, Washington, 1992; and Eisner, Robert, 'Budget Deficits: Rhetoric and Reality', *Journal of Economic Perspectives*, vol. 3, no. 2, 1989.

Appendix 11.1

The Budgetary Deficit and the Economy

Aftab Ahmad Khan presents his considered opinion on the budget deficit and argues, like many others, that the large budgetary deficit is the most serious issue confronting the economy.

It is a well known fact that Pakistan has experienced large fiscal deficits over the last two decades and currently budgetary imbalance is the most serious macro problem confronting the economy, requiring bold structural policy actions with long lasting effects on financial stability. Repeated attempts by the government, including the implementation of structural adjustment programmes with assistance from the International Monetary Fund (IMF), have only achieved partial success. The consolidated fiscal deficit during the period 1980/81–1991/92 averaged around 7.2 per cent of Gross Domestic Product (GDP) annually. In 1992/93 this deficit was Rs107.7 billion or 8 per cent of the GDP. In 1993/94 it was brought down to Rs907 billion or 5.8 per cent of the GDP. In the current fiscal year (1994/95) while the budget estimated it at Rs71.9 billion (4 per cent of the projected GDP), the current indications are that it would be around Rs105 billion or 5.7 per cent of the revised projected GDP of Rs1846 billion.

It is crystal clear that Pakistan has to reduce the dimensions of the overall fiscal deficit, otherwise there would be further deterioration of the already weak budgetary position with profound de-stabilizing consequences for the economy. It would intensify pressures on the already strained balance of payments with consequent financial instability, thus undermining Pakistan's international credit worthiness, crowd out private investment by pushing real interest rates upward and/or fuel inflationary expectations as increasing monetization of the deficit becomes unavoidable. With large and growing deficits the economy could easily enter into a trap where an upward spiralling cycle of inflation–devaluation–rising interest rates–rising wages and salaries–rising inflation could disrupt production and investment activity and could lead to large scale capital flight.

The deficit has remained high because of the political and administrative inability of the Government of Pakistan to mobilize adequate resources or to restrain expenditures. The present tax structure of Pakistan falls short in all major functions of a modern tax system: revenue generation, efficient resource allocation and equity. The system is characterized by the dominance of indirect taxes (nearly 78 per cent of total tax proceeds).

At the same time the system has many exemptions and concessions. Several income categories including agricultural are excluded from income taxation and those subject to taxation, with the exception of wage and salary earners, are known to pay only a fraction of their share. Despite considerable wealth concentration and sharp increases in asset values, especially real estate, Government revenue from taxation of wealth and capital gains is small. Tax administration is weak, resulting in a high level of tax evasion, corruption and harassment of taxpayers. In order to maintain the present low tax/GDP ratio (13.3 per cent in 1993/94), the tax system needs to be supplemented with frequent ad-hoc measures. In other words it is inelastic. Perhaps more importantly the tax system has haphazard effect on resource allocations as a large number of concessions result in widely different effective rates within the same industry. Moreover tax evasion has encouraged the growth of the 'black' or 'parallel' economy, which in turn results in cumulative revenue loss to the public exchequer.

On the expenditure front, defence spending accounts for 23.4 per cent of consolidated government expenditures and interest payments constitute 24.5 per cent. The share of general administration in total governmental expenditures is 6.7 per cent while social, economic and community services account for 15.4 per cent. With this pattern of current expenditures, it has not been possible to impose large cuts. The burden of expenditure reduction, accordingly, has fallen and continues to fall on development expenditure at the cost of renovating and expanding the much needed infrastructure facilities.

Pakistan, like most developing countries, makes use of three methods to finance the budget deficit: domestic borrowing from non-bank sources, external borrowing and borrowing from the banking system. The magnitude of the deficit and the sources and amounts of financing since 1981/82 are depicted in [Table 1].

Each method of covering the deficit carries different costs and benefits for the economy. Besides the direct budgetary cost, domestic borrowing from non-bank sources can lead to crowding out of investment by raising the interest rates or as a result of non-price credit rationing. However, it has the benefit of avoiding or postponing the inflationary impact of the given deficit.

External financing helps to preserve domestic investment rates, but at the cost of crowding out future domestic consumption/investment when the foreign debt must be serviced or repaid through higher exports and lower imports.

Bank borrowing for budgetary support can be either from commercial banks or the central bank. When a commercial bank subscribes to a government loan, its cash (including deposits with the State Bank of Pakistan) is reduced. This act by itself involves a withdrawal of private purchasing power at the same time as there is an addition to public purchasing power. The expenditure of Government thus financed is, therefore, non-inflationary. But the crucial point is, how did the bank acquire the cash to subscribe to the government loan and how are the bank's future operations affected as a result of the subscription to the government loan? Assuming that the bank had no surplus cash when it made the investment in government securities, the cash needed for the loan subscription could be acquired out of the proceeds of maturing loans or maturing investments in government securities. In such a case, the new asset replaces the old asset, and the bank does not add to the aggregate volume of its

Table 1 Sources and amounts of financing the consolidated budget deficit of federal and provincial governments, 1980–1995 (Rs bn)

	Consolidated budget deficit	Deficit as % of GDP	Banking system		Non-banking		External (net)	
			Amount	%	Amount	%	Amount	%
1980/1	14.6	5.3	2.4	16.1	4.5	30.9	7.7	52.9
1981/2	17.2	5.3	5.5	32.1	6.3	36.8	5.3	31.1
1982/3	25.7	7.1	6.1	23.9	14.4	56.0	5.2	20.1
1983/4	25.1	6.3	7.9	31.3	12.3	48.8	5.0	19.9
1984/5	36.8	7.7	18.7	50.9	12.9	35.0	5.2	14.1
1985/6	41.6	8.1	6.1	14.6	27.0	64.7	8.6	20.6
1986/7	16.7	8.2	10.9	23.4	27.4	58.6	8.4	18.0
1987/8	57.6	8.5	13.9	24.2	30.9	53.7	12.7	22.0
1988/9	56.9	7.4	0.8	1.4	37.9	66.6	18.2	32.0
1989/90	56.1	6.5	3.5	6.3	29.6	52.8	22.9	40.9
1990/1	89.2	8.7	43.4	48.6	23.7	26.6	22.1	24.8
1991/2	90.0	7.4	70.5	78.3	–3.1	–3.4	22.6	25.1
1992/3	107.7	8.0	62.6	58.1	19.7	18.3	25.4	23.6
1993/4 (PA)	90.7	5.8	12.9	14.2	55.0	60.0	22.8	25.1
1994/5 (BE)	71.9	4.0	15.0	20.9	26.3	36.6	30.6	42.6

PA = Provisional actuals.
BE = Budget estimates.
Source: State Bank of Pakistan, *Annual Report 1994–95,* Karachi, 1995.

assets (and liabilities). If this description were to apply to the banking system as a whole, the process of financing a government deficit through subscriptions to government loans would be non-inflationary. Suppose, however, the banking system acquires cash for the purpose of subscription to government loans not out of maturing loans and investments, but through fresh deposits which it receives in consequence of depositors receiving additional incomes (which is liable to happen when disbursements exceed revenues raised by the government); the subscription to government loans will have taken place without reducing the existing investment in government securities (i.e. it would be net addition to resources lent to the government) and without reducing the existing volume of loans. In this situation, the process is inflationary, for the proceeds of loans when spent constitute a net addition to the amount of private purchasing power.

In the case of borrowing from the State Bank of Pakistan for financing the budgetary deficit, the process is clearly inflationary because the proceeds of borrowing when spent go directly to enlarge the cash basis (including deposits with SBP) of the commercial banks. Not only has the initial step of meeting the deficit through central bank borrowing increased the volume of private purchasing power, but the direct expansion of the cash of the commercial banks enlarges their ability to contribute to additional government loans or to make further advances.

In order to understand fiscal choices for the coming years, there has to be a clear understanding of the connotation of 'sustainable deficit'. This can be defined simply as the deficit level that can be financed without adding to the country's overall debt burden as a proportion of GDP, and without violating the government's macro objectives such as low

inflation and real economic growth at the socially warranted rate, which in our case is at least 6.5 per cent per annum.

On the basis of studies conducted by the International Monetary Fund and the Ministry of Finance it appears that a fiscal deficit in excess of 4 per cent of GDP could have adverse macro-economic consequences including the danger of the economy sliding into the delirium of high inflation.

It has to be appreciated that the government's ability to create additional debt for financing the budgetary deficit is considerably constrained by the existing high level of indebtedness which at the end of 1993/94 constituted 88.4 per cent of GDP. The demand for Government debt could decline, if as a result of Government debt burden, the lender's confidence in the ability of the Government to faithfully fulfil its obligations in this regard is shaken or there is a fear of sharp erosion in the purchasing power of the Rupee. In such a situation, the Government would also be forced to sharply raise its interest rates or further crowd out private investment.

In case the Government finds itself unable to increase its non-bank borrowing or cut its spending or enhance revenues by means of taxation, there is only one option: to monetize the deficit and collect a higher inflation tax. The scope of mobilizing additional revenues through inflation, however, is significantly reduced on account of the removal of restrictions on capital flows from Pakistan as well as foreign currency holdings by domestic residents. Expectations of an increase in the rate of inflation in the future would lead to acceleration in the pace of currency substitution, thus shrinking the Government's inflation tax base.

The need for reducing fiscal deficit to a sustainable level is thus clearly indicated.

Source : *The News,* Business and Finance Review, 6 May 1995.

Appendix 11.2

Public debt reconsidered

After the Nawaz Sharif government was returned to power in February 1997, it launched the 'National Debt Retirement Programme', and emphasis returned to the recurrent problem of public debt. Here we present a different view of the issue.

The issue of Pakistan's public debt has returned to the top of the economic agenda yet again. The country's two leading monthly magazines have devoted their cover stories to the problem of the 'exploding debt bomb', and a number of articles, many by eminent economists, have appeared in the press reiterating the claim that the problem of Pakistan's debt burden is the single biggest economic problem facing the country today. Moreover, the Prime Minister's National Debt Retirement Programme, an attempt to involve the public and capitalise on their patriotism and enthusiasm, is part of the same scheme of things, where it is hoped that the public will help ease the burden of debt upon the government, by reaching well into their own pockets and contributing to the government's coffers.

If ever there was consensus on one single issue of importance amongst economists, bureaucrats, and politicians, then it must be over the agreement about the huge and growing debt and upon its consequences. However, I will argue that this focus is misplaced. In the light of such sentiment which constitutes much of conventional wisdom, it is necessary to consider the importance of the debt and expose a number of myths which constitute this feeling.

The facts regarding Pakistan's debt, however, are indeed quite startling. Pakistan's domestic debt has accumulated to more than Rs900 billion, or 42 percent of GDP, with debt servicing accounting for more than 5 percent of GNP each year. The rate at which this debt has been raised is on the high side, with interest rates in nominal terms around 16 to 18 percent, or between 4 to 6 percent if we assume a (very conservative and undervalued) rate of inflation of around 12 percent. Foreign debt accounts for about US$30 billion (46 percent of GDP), but for the most part, carries a far lower, single digit, rate of interest. Much of this is longer term debt, and despite Pakistan's immediate needs to meet some repayments which come due over the next nine months, the more serious and chronic problem is considered to be that of domestic debt.

Because of the large domestic debt, interest payments are high, and due to this, we end up having a large fiscal deficit each year. Interest payments and defence take up almost all of the budgeted annual expenditure, leaving very little for development and the social sectors. Given the excessive debt that has accumulated over the last few years, it is not likely that any recourse to patriotism will result in more than a minuscule amount being pocketed and the debt 'burden' or 'problem' is unlikely to go away for a long time to come. Given this fact, it is important to consider the other 'villain' of the piece, the fiscal deficit, and see what sort of impact that has on the economy.

Although many analysts frequently talk about Pakistan's annual fiscal deficit, and the IMF insists that it be reduced from the currently estimated 6.3 percent of the GDP to 4 percent by June this year (an irrational and ridiculous imposition, to say the least, and an impossibility, no doubt), what is often overlooked is the fact that the Primary Budget Deficit has been negative for the last few years. What this means is that in terms of the simple revenue/expenditure divide, if we exclude interest payments accumulated on past debt, then revenue, for the last three years, has been greater than expenditure. However, lest this fact result in an immediate cheer, it is necessary to point out that this positive balance over the last few years is not simply due to additions in revenue, but also due to larger cuts in expenditure.

In the current fiscal year alone, the original allocation for the annual development programme was reduced by 19 percent from a mere Rs105 billion to a dismal Rs85 billion, by the caretaker government of Shahid Javed Burki. As Burki in a much cited article himself confessed, 'if this figure is finally realized, Pakistan would have scored another low in its economic history in terms of the proportion of gross domestic product committed to development'. In order to cut the fiscal deficit and be as close to the 4 percent target proposed by the IMF and endorsed by the caretaker government between November 1996–February 1997, this year 1996–97, Pakistan's development expenditure will be no more than 3.4 percent of GDP, down from a peak of 9.3 percent a little over a decade ago. More interesting, however, has been the contrast in the pattern of expenditure on development with that on defence since 1980. Over the period 1980–90 when a military dictator ruled Pakistan for much of the decade, defence expenditure averaged around 6.5 percent of GDP, with development getting 7.3 percent. Currently, development receives less than half of what it got in the eighties, and receives only 3.4 percent, while defence receives almost 6 percent. Hence the composition of government expenditure is a critical factor overlooked by those who advocate its reduction.

If the question of the debt burden is to be considered, the fiscal deficit forms an important part of the equation. And, if the fiscal deficit is of importance, then we must examine the nature and the productivity of government expenditure, not simply its level or even the size of the deficit. This is the first factor ignored when issues of public debt are debated. To reemphasise the point, we argue that it is not borrowing as such which is the problem, but the use made of borrowed money. The argument is valid both for domestic and foreign loans.

The problem then, is not to tell government to reduce its spending, as the IMF insists all governments should do at all times, under all circumstances, nor even the matter that government's try their utmost to raise taxes, as has been the case with ever increasing taxation in Pakistan in the recent past, but what is imperative is that government expenditure be productive. The essential and minimum requirement is the need to hold government accountable for spending productively. One of the many reasons why Pakistanis refuse to pay taxes is that they feel cheated by government, in that they feel that their contribution to the exchequer is being squandered away. People may agree to pay more taxes only if they felt that their money was being used productively.

Another important caveat to the debt burden issue, linked to the efficient and productive use of expenditure, is the relationship between borrowing and growth. If the real rate of growth of the economy is greater than the real rate of interest at which government borrows, the problem is not a serious one at all. If economic growth can be sustained at around 7 to 9 percent, a number of problems which persist in the economy and are related to the debt/deficit issue will cease to exist. Firstly, a higher growth rate should generate a higher level of revenue to the government, both from direct and indirect sources. In fact, this is one of the assumptions which are inbuilt into the economic revival package of Prime Minister Nawaz Sharif announced last week. Secondly, the government can continue to borrow as long as the differential between the rate of growth and the rate of borrowing remains positive. Finally, higher growth may generate more investable funds for the economy, possibly also lowering the interest rate. In all this, a check by government on prices and on interest rates would be extremely useful as well.

It is unlikely that all of Pakistan's debt will ever be retired, and what needs to be put in focus is the current fiscal deficit, and particularly, the use made of government spending each year. Nevertheless, the large amount of accumulated debt in the past cannot be ignored, and it is essential that an evaluation be made of the use to which loans taken in the past have been put. Much of fiscal policy in Pakistan, which has resulted in the high debt in the first place, has been ill-conceived, impractical and downright irresponsible. Current proposals for reducing part of the debt, such as debt-for-equity swap, privatisation proceeds set aside for this specific purpose, and the use of the begging bowl, may make a small dent in the amount of debt outstanding. However, so as not to make the same mistakes again in the future, those responsible for creating the problem in the first place must be held accountable. This is the bare minimum for the success of any long term viable economic reforms package. The rest is mere window dressing.

Source : Zaidi, S. Akbar, 'Focus on Debt Misplaced', *DAWN*, Economic and Business Review, 7–13 April 1997.

Appendix 11.3

Debt retirement is a waste of money

What should the use of privatization proceeds be? Debt retirement or social sector development? Here we present one view.

There is an argument which has been floating around for a few months which has been propagated in the press by many learned and well-reputed journalists. The argument is based on the following facts: Pakistan's domestic debt has grown to gargantuan proportions and was Rs744 billion or 44.2 per cent of GDP at the beginning of the current fiscal year 1994–95, and is equal to our foreign debt. Thus, total debt was equal to 88.4 per cent of GDP. At the end of the current fiscal year 1994–95, domestic debt outstanding is expected to rise by a further Rs102 billion, taking the total domestic debt outstanding to Rs846 billion on 1 July 1995. Debt servicing in the current fiscal year was supposed to be Rs136 billion, of which Rs82.7 billion (60 per cent) was meant for interest payments on domestic debt alone and the remainder was distributed between foreign debt repayment and interest on foreign debt. It is believed that domestic debt and interest on it each year are serious problems facing our economy which lead to high inflation, low savings, and other sundry problems. These proponents believe that the high interest payments each year are causing a huge drain on our economic resources and should thus be reduced.

On the basis of the evidence presented above, the argument which is being made is that Pakistan must retire some of its debt if is to deal with the problem of high deficits and low growth and other repercussions. In this regard, it has been suggested that the proceeds from privatization should be earmarked for debt retirement. In the current fiscal year, in excess of Rs40 billion were accumulated by the government through its privatization programme, and next year, the government hopes to acquire Rs100 billion from the privatization of 26 per cent shares of PTC alone. If UBL and Habib Bank are also privatized over the next couple of years, the government can hope to receive considerably more. Proponents of the debt retirement view believe that by using these privatization proceeds, the problem of domestic debt and its annual interest bearing component can be dealt with. However, this view is highly fallacious for reasons that I make clear below.

Some facts other than those presented above will help make things clear. Each year based on the trend since 1990 on average, Rs74 billion is added to our domestic debt. This year Rs102 billion will be added. In fiscal year 1994–95, Rs82.7 billion contributed towards interest payments on the domestic debt of Rs744 billion, which was 11 per cent of the total domestic debt outstanding. For the sake of argument, let us assume that the government of Pakistan, by some sleight of a magic wand is able to bring down the fiscal deficit to 4 per cent of GDP (from the likely 5.6 per cent this current fiscal year) and is able to maintain this level for the next three years. The critical point which most observers have missed is that even if the fiscal deficit is a mere 1 per cent of GDP – an impossible happening, no doubt – *the debt will still grow and accumulate.*

Let us construct a highly favourable scenario to illustrate our point. By using the proceeds from privatization for debt retirement, the following scenario takes place: First, let us assume that GDP is Rs1,847 billion at the end of this year and grows at a constant high rate of 6 per cent over the next three years. Along with this favourable growth rate, we also assume

Table 1
(All in billion rupees)

	1995/6	1996/7	1997/8
Gross domestic product (with an annual growth of 6% per annum)	1,847	1,957	2,075
Fiscal deficit (at 4% of GDP)	73	78	83
Domestic debt outstanding	846	919	998
Interest payment without retirement (at 11% of domestic debt)	93	101	109
Domestic debt after debt retirement	846–100=746	819–100=719	797–100=697
Interest payments after debt retirement (at 11%)	82	79	77
Domestic debt for next year	746+73=819	719+78=797	697+83=780

Total interest payments without debt repayment of Rs100 bn for three consecutive years:
   93 + 101 + 109 = 303 bn
With debt repayment of 300 bn:
   82 + 79 + 77 = 238 bn
Net difference = Rs65 bn
By spending RS300 bn, the government saves Rs65 bn.

that the government achieves its target of a fiscal deficit of 4 per cent of GDP over the next three years. This means that GDP will grow from Rs1,847 billion at the end of this fiscal year to Rs1,957 billion next year and to Rs2,075 billion for our third year of analysis. Similarly, the fiscal deficit in these three years at the rate of 4 per cent of GDP will be Rs73.9 billion, Rs78.3 billion, and Rs83.0 billion [see Table 1].

What is important here is that each year a considerable amount (4 per cent of GDP which accrues in the form of the annual fiscal deficit) is being accumulated as part of the domestic debt and is being added to it. Now let us examine the repercussion on interest payments each year. The total debt in our scenario increases from the present Rs744 billion, to Rs846 billion at the start of the next fiscal year, and then to Rs919.88 billion and finally to Rs998 billion at the end of three years. If we take the current rate of repayment of domestic interest, which is 11 per cent of domestic debt outstanding, we have the following figures for interest payments for the next three years: Rs93.06 billion, Rs101.18 billion and Rs109.8 billion in the third year when our domestic debt should have grown to Rs998 billion.

Although we have not introduced the possibility of debt retirement in our argument as yet, based on the above highly positive economic growth and management scenario, the following picture emerges: despite excellent management and control of the economy, total domestic debt increases by more than Rs73 billion each year, and interest payments on domestic debt alone will exceed Rs100 billion. Let us now bring debt retirement into the picture.

Let us also take a highly favourable scenario regarding debt retirement and assume that in each of the next three years, the government will amass' the considerable amount of Rs100 billion from the sale of state owned enterprises and will use this amount exclusively for debt retirement. As can be seen from the table, despite such an extensive amount being retired each year, the net difference in interest repayment on the domestic debt would only be Rs11 billion each year, and we would still be paying more than Rs80 billion in interest on the earlier accumulated domestic debt alone.

The proponents of the debt retirement view have failed to distinguish between the concept of debt (which is a stock) and deficit (which is a flow and is added each year to the debt). They have also overlooked the fact that debt retirement of a huge amount of Rs100 billion each year will only make a very small, negligible net contribution at the margin. By giving up Rs100 billion, we will be left with a gain of Rs11 billion only. The privatization proceeds should be used for direct development projects rather than debt retirement, which will be a total waste of money.

Source: Zaidi, S. Akbar, 'Debt Retirement is a Waste of Money', *The News*, 28 June 1995.

Notes

1. Buiter, Willem, *Principles of Budgetary and Financial Policy*, Harvester, Brighton, 1990, p. 25.
2. Karachi Chamber of Commerce and Industry (KCCI) *Proceedings of the Seminar on Reducing Fiscal Deficit – Key to Salvage Economy*, Karachi, 1994.
3. Tobin, James, *Asset Accumulation and Economic Activity*, Blackwell, Oxford, 1980, p. 49.
4. Buiter, Willem, op. cit., 1990, p. 90.
5. Tobin, James, *Policies for Prosperity: Essays in a Keynesian Mode*, Wheatsheaf, Brighton, 1987, p. 221.
6. Blinder, A.S. and Robert Solow, *The Economics of Public Finance*, Brookings Institute, Washington, 1974, p. 37.
7. Ibid.
8. Tobin, James, op. cit., 1987, p. 219.
9. Ibid., p. 222.
10. Buiter, Willem, op. cit., 1990, p. 42.
11. Eisner, Robert and P.J. Piepper, 'Deficits, Monetary Policy and Real Economic Activity', in Arrow, Kenneth and M.J. Boskins (eds.), *The Economics of Public Debt*, Macmillan, London, 1988, p. 28.
12. Boskins, M.J., 'Concepts and Measures of Federal Deficits and Debt and their Impact on Economic Activity', in Arrow, Kenneth and M.J. Boskins, op. cit., 1988, p. 84.
13. Buiter, Willem, op. cit., 1990, p. 9.
14. Ihori, I., 'Debt Burden and Intergeneration Equity', in Arrow, Kenneth and M.J. Boskins, op. cit., 1988, p. 149.
15. This section is drawn from my paper, Zaidi, S. Akbar, 'Locating the Budget Deficit in Context: The Case of Pakistan', *Pakistan Journal of Applied Economics*, vol. 11, nos. 1 and 2, 1995.
16. Easterly, W. and K. Schmidt-Hebbel, 'The Macroeconomics of Public Sector Deficits: A Synthesis', Working Paper No. 775, World Bank, Washington, 1992, p. 2.
17. Easterly, W. and K. Schmidt-Hebbel, 'Fiscal Deficits and Macroeconomic Performance in Developing Countries', *World Bank Research Observer*, vol. 8, no. 2, 1993, p. 213.
18. Eisner, Robert, 'Budget Deficits: Rhetoric and Reality', *Journal of Economic Perspectives*, vol. 3, no. 2, 1989, p. 74.
19. Eisner, Robert, 'Sense and Nonsense about Budget Deficits', *Harvard Business Review*, May–June 1993, p. 104.
20. Eisner, Robert op. cit., 1989, p. 81.
21. Ibid, p. 83.
22. This section is drawn from Zaidi, S. Akbar, op. cit., 1995.
23. See, for example: World Bank, *Pakistan: Growth Through Adjustment*, Report No. 7118-Pak, Washington, 1988; World Bank, *Pakistan: Medium-term Economic Policy Adjustments*, Report No. 7591-Pak, Washington, 1989; World Bank, *Changes in Trade and Domestic Taxation for Reform of the Incentive Regime and Fiscal Adjustment*, Report No. 9828-Pak, Washington, 1992; World Bank, *Pakistan: Country Economic Memorandum FY93*, Report No. 11590-Pak, Washington, 1993; Haque, Nadeem-ul and Peter Montiel, 'The Macroeconomics of Public Sector Deficits: The Case of Pakistan', World Bank Working Paper No. 673, Washington, 1991; Khan, Mohsin S., 'Comments', in Thomas, V., *et al.*, (eds.), *Restructuring Economies in Distress*, Oxford University Press, New York, 1991; Mclearly, W.A., 'Pakistan: Structural Adjustment and Economic Growth', in Thomas, V., *et al.*, op. cit., 1991; Applied Economics Research Centre, *Resource Mobilization by the Federal Government*, Karachi, 1992; Pasha, Hafiz and Mohammad Akbar, 'IMF Conditionalities and Structural Adjustments in Public Finances', *Pakistan Economic and Social Review*, 1993; Pasha, Hafiz and Mohammad Iqbal, 'Taxation Reforms in Pakistan', *Pakistan Journal of Applied Economics*, vol. 10, nos. 1 and 2, 1994; and Karachi Chamber of Commerce and Industry, op. cit., 1994.
24. World Bank, op. cit., 1992, p. 2.
25. Haque, Nadeem-ul and Peter Montiel, op. cit., 1991.
26. Ibid.
27. World Bank, op. cit., 1993, p. 36.
28. Before anyone uses the 1992/3 data from Table 11.1 and scores a point arguing that finally, with a 7.9 per cent deficit, the IMF-predicted scenario of disaster has hit Pakistan's economy, it is best to put things in perspective. The World Bank (1993) report has explained this as follows: The economy was severely affected by the 1992 floods, the worst in 50 years, which hit the country in August/September. There was extensive damage to crops and livestock, 15 percent of cotton and rice was lost, and 10 percent of sugar cane was ruined. Subsequently, there was a loss of exports from cotton and rice, an increase in the import of wheat, relief items, fertilizers and reconstruction material and equipment. On the revenue side, there was a loss of Rs10 billion due to exemption from loan repayment, relief packages, and flood effectees were given exemptions from a number of taxes. There was also an additional expenditure of Rs13 billion on reconstruction and relief goods (World Bank, op. cit., 1993, p. 9).
29. Haque, Nadeem-ul and Peter Montiel, op. cit., 1991, p. 1, emphasis added.
30. Ibid., p. 2. emphasis added.
31. Ibid., p. 39.
32. Ibid., p. 39.
33. Sakr, Khalid, 'Developments of Private Investment in Pakistan', IMF Working Paper, 1993, p. 16.
34. See Haque, Nadeem-ul and Peter Montiel, op. cit., 1991.
35. Easterly, W. and K. Schmidt-Hebbel, op. cit., 1993.
36. See Zaidi, S. Akbar, 'The Structural Adjustment Programme and Pakistan: External Influence or Internal Acquiescence?', *Pakistan Journal of Applied Economics*, vol. 10, nos. 1 and 2, 1994(a).
37. Ibid.
38. See Zaidi, S. Akbar, 'How the Bourgeoisie View Pakistan', *Economic and Political Weekly*, vol. 23, no. 48, 1988; and Zaidi, S. Akbar, 'Sindhi vs Mohajir: Contradiction, Conflict, Compromise', *Economic and Political Weekly*, vol. 26, no. 28, 1991.
39. See Zaidi, S. Akbar, 'The Roots of the Crisis', *The Herald*, August 1992; Zaidi, S. Akbar, op. cit., 1994(a); Zaidi, S. Akbar, 'Pakistan's Economy in Deep Crisis', *Economic and Political Weekly*, vol. 29, no. 28, 1994(b).
40. Mehar, M.A.K., 'A Forecasting Model of Public Finance: An Experience from the Pakistani Economy', Unpublished M.Phil thesis, Applied Economics Research Centre, Karachi, 1992.

12

Financial and Capital Markets

Financial and capital markets in Pakistan have evolved from a state of near nothingness in 1947, to a situation today where Pakistan's banking and financial sector plays a formidable role in economic development and is integrated with the rest of the world. From a handful of bank branches at the time of partition, the financial sector has expanded exponentially, now having branches in every nook and corner of the country. Along with banks, development finance institutions and other non-bank financial institutions now play a leading role in providing credit to industry, agriculture, housing, and other sectors (see Box 12.1 and Figure 12.1). A growing securities market has also emerged in recent years as a conduit for investment funds. A modern and growing developing country requires a modern and advanced financial sector. Similarly, a modern and advanced financial sector works best in an economy that is money and market oriented. Moreover, conventional wisdom holds that 'the development of a vigorous domestic financial sector to channel domestic savings into high return investment has been recognized as an important element of economic policy that seeks to generate economic growth ... In the development literature, considerable emphasis has been placed on the development of a sound commercial banking system based on a system of market determined credit allocation'[1] (see Appendix 12.1 on the importance of the capital markets and the financial sector in Pakistan). The liberalization and deregulation taking place

in the economy since November 1990 has had particular significance for the financial sector. These reforms have been aimed at removing the constraints within the financial sectors so as to make financial capital more easily accessible. This chapter gives an account of the evolution of the financial and capital markets in Pakistan and then examines some key issues that affect the financial sector and, hence, the economy (see also Chapter 13 on the money market).

12.1 The Development of the Banking Sector[2]

12.1.1 The First Phase: 1947–1974

Although Pakistan gained political independence in August 1947, it would be fair to say that the country's economic and financial independence took many more years to acquire (even today there is some debate over whether Pakistan's economic and financial sectors are at all independent – see Chapter 15). The nature of industrial development outlined in earlier chapters shows how little developed industry was at the time of partition. The banking and financial sector suffered a similar fate due to partition, and the areas which became Pakistan were severely underrepresented in terms of banking and financial services.

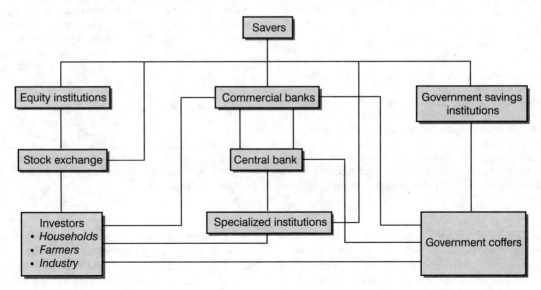

Figure 12.1
The system of financial intermediation in Pakistan

BOX 12.1

Pakistan's financial sector: main actors

There have been many changes in Pakistan's financial sector in recent years. Here we look at the role of the main players.

Pakistan's financial sector is comprised of the State Bank of Pakistan (SBP), commercial banks, non-bank financial institutions (NBFIs), and insurance companies.

The commercial banking sector consists of five nationalized commercial banks (NCBs), two state-owned provincial banks, two privatized commercial banks, 14 local private banks, and 19 foreign banks. The commercial banks offer short- to medium-term financing facilities, trade finance services, and retail banking facilities. In terms of assets and holdings of government securities, banks account for about 85 per cent of the financial sector. However, their share in total financial sector loans and investments is less than two thirds (Table 1).

Table 1
Financial institutions' assets, June 1993 (Rs bn)[a]

	Assets	Government securities	Loans/ investments
Banks[b]	1,604.4	203.9	395.6
DFIs[c]	196.9	11.1	187.7
Leasing companies	10.5	0.0	6.6
Modarabas	10.0	0.1	4.4
Investment banks	20.3	2.3	13.4
Gen. ins. cos.	4.1	0.1	1.6
SLIC	30.9	22.1	5.5

Gen. ins. cos. = general insurance companies.
SLIC = State Life Insurance Company.
[a] June 1994 for banks and DFIs.
[b] Includes ADBP, IDBP, FBC, and PPCBL.
[c] ADBP, IDBP, BEL, ICP, NDFC, PICIC, and NIT.

Aside from banks, NBFIs comprise an important part of Pakistan's financial sector. The NBFIs consist of 18 development finance institutions (DFIs) and specialized banks, 27 leasing companies, 52 mudarabas, and 12 investment banks.

DFIs and specialized banks focus on long-term institutional and term finance lending. While these institutions used to rely mainly on government and multilateral funding, this practice has changed in recent years. With the introduction of new schemes to attract saving, over one third of DFIs' assets now consist of funds that have been mobilized through local deposits.

Among the various DFIs are industrial DFIs, financial DFIs,

and specialized banks. The industrial DFIs provide long-term project financing for industrial and development projects in the private as well as the public sectors. The financial DFIs, consisting of the National Investment Trust (NIT) and the Investment Corporation of Pakistan (ICP), invest in publicly traded stocks. In addition, they offer mutual fund services and time deposit accounts. The ICP also underwrites public flotations.

Specialized banks include the Agricultural Development Bank of Pakistan (ADBP), the Industrial Development Bank of Pakistan (IDBP), the Federal Bank for Cooperatives (FBC), and the Punjab Provincial Cooperatives Bank Limited (PPCBL). The banks are also involved in financing development projects.

Leasing companies, introduced in Pakistan in the late 1980s, constitute another part of the NBFI sector. These companies are allowed to borrow funds from banks and other financial institutions to meet their capital investments, and may raise funds through equity issues, offshore and rupee credit lines, and the issuance of certificates of investment.

Mudarabas, a closed-end limited partnership where the modaribs (management) provide the expertise and the investors provide the capital, are an Islamic form of financing. Mudarabas may engage in any form of business as long as they do not pay out or receive interest. Modaribs are required to provide at least 10 per cent of the modaraba's total equity, while the rest is funded by investors. While mudarabas also deal in equity trading and investment, over 70 per cent of their income derives from leasing activity.

Investment banks differ from commercial banks in that they are not allowed to raise demand deposits nor engage in consumer banking activities. They are, however, allowed to issue time deposits. Although in principle investment banks are geared toward financing long-term investments by mobilizing long-term time deposits, their success so far in this area has been limited. Indeed, much of investment banks' present lending activity is short-term. Investment banks also engage in equity trading, though their emphasis has gradually shifted toward investment advisory services, underwriting, placement, and structured finance.

Finally, insurance companies constitute the rest of Pakistan's financial sector. The insurance sector is divided into general and life insurance. General insurance companies must hold 20 per cent of their locally generated business funds with the Pakistan Insurance Corporation in the form of reinsurance. While there are 35 general insurance companies, the market is dominated by three or four firms.

Source: ABN AMRO Economic Bulletin, *The Financial Sector*, vol. 1, no. 9, 1995, Economics Department, ABN AMRO Bank NV Pakistan, Karachi.

Pakistan had no central bank or banking system worth the name. The Reserve Bank of India, which was legally a common property of both India and Pakistan, continued to operate as a currency and banking authority for Pakistan, and had its operations directed and controlled from New Delhi until June 1948.[3]

Prior to partition, of the ninety-nine scheduled banks listed on the Second Schedule of the Reserve Bank, only one had its office in Pakistan.[4] United India had 3,496 branches of scheduled banks, but only 631 were located in the areas that were to become Pakistan (East and West). The paid-up capital and reserves of these banks amounted to no more than 10 per cent of the total paid-up capital and revenues of undivided India. These banks were small compared to their counterparts in India, and their share of deposits, advances, and bills discounted was just one-tenth of the total. The areas that were to become Pakistan had very few branches as it was, but once Pakistan came into being, the number of branches fell further. Of the 631 branches before partition, only 213 were functioning when Pakistan came into being. The paid-up capital and reserves decreased from 10 per cent of undivided India to a mere 1.5 per cent after partition.[5] A year later, when the State Bank of Pakistan was established, the number of branches of scheduled banks had dwindled to only 195, of which only 65 existed in Pakistan.[6]

The communal violence and subsequent migration that followed partition had major repercussions for the financial sector. In the financial sector as well as in trade and commerce, it was the Hindus who controlled a large part of the industry in the areas that became Pakistan, especially in the more developed region of the Punjab. The Hindus migrated to India *en masse* with all economic activity coming to a standstill. With a large number of commercial banks ceasing to function, sources of all types of credit for trade, commerce, and agriculture dried up. While informal moneylenders began to migrate to India, the closure of branches in the formal sector also implied the exodus of managerial and administrative staff, who were mainly Hindu. Most banks were controlled and owned by Hindus, and the services they rendered were no longer available after their head offices were transferred to India. The only scheduled bank that remained in Pakistan was the Muslim-owned Australasia Bank, which was just too small and ill-equipped to handle the business that used to be transacted by the migrating Indian bankers. The acute shortage of skilled staff was a key factor in inhibiting the evolution of even a basic system of banking.[7]

The State Bank of Pakistan began operations on 1 July 1948 and became the sole note-issuing authority, but the government of Pakistan at that time had no note printing press to print them on. The State Bank of Pakistan was faced with the huge task of establishing a banking system after the collapse at the time of partition.

Despite the exodus of banks and the closure of Indian banks at the time of partition, the number of Indian bank branches functioning after partition was greater than the number of non-Indian branches. The non-Indian (i.e. foreign) banks were mainly confined to financing import and export trade. These banks were subject to control and guidance from their head offices in almost all matters related to financing. However, their impact can be seen from the fact that on 1 July 1948, of the total bank deposits of Rs1.1081 billion held in Pakistan, as much as 73 per cent was held by foreign banks whose activities were largely confined to foreign trade.[8]

In the first eighteen months of the operation of the State Bank of Pakistan, 51 new branches were opened in both East and West Pakistan, of which 28 were Pakistani banks, 12 were Indian, 4 were Exchange (i.e. foreign) banks, and 7 were opened by the newly formed National Bank of Pakistan, of which 6 were in East Pakistan. By December 1949, there were 35 scheduled banks in Pakistan, of which 4 were Pakistani, 23 Indian, and 8 Exchange banks. These banks had 109 branches in West Pakistan and 83 in East Pakistan. Interestingly, though, of the 59 branches of Pakistani banks, only 7 were in East Pakistan. Exchange banks were confined to the port towns of Chittagong and Karachi, while some were granted permission to open branches at provincial headquarters if there were European or other foreign firms that required banking services, or had trade with foreign countries. The role of the National Bank of Pakistan until June 1950 was restricted to financing jute operations.[9]

As the number of branches of the commercial banks expanded in the 1950s, these banks continued to mobilize increasing domestic savings, which were then channelled into the demand for credit in the economy. While most credit was used to finance foreign trade and commerce in the late 1950s, commercial banks started playing an important role in supplying credit to domestic industries as well. Moreover, as time went on, Pakistani banks began to play an increasing role in financing economic development. In 1952 of the total advances made to different sectors, 38 per cent were by Pakistani banks, 22 per cent by Indian banks and 40 per cent by foreign banks. In 1955 Pakistani banks supplied 59 per cent of credit advanced,[10] and by 1970 this had risen to as much as 89 per cent.[11]

Over the years, as the number of branches of banks began to grow, the State Bank of Pakistan decided to set up a system of new branches under which a certain quota had to be opened in regions designated by the State Bank. Commercial banks were asked to extend their areas of operation to regions that were not particularly economically viable. As most industry and commerce, as well as agriculture production, was taking place in West Pakistan, it is not surprising that most of the new branches were opened in the western province. In 1963 there were 957 branches in both wings, with the more populous eastern wing having less then 35 per cent of bank branches.[12] The State Bank of Pakistan ordered commercial banks to open one branch in East Pakistan for each branch they had in West Pakistan. The fears that the State Bank's policy of opening new branches in unbanked places would be quite unsound proved to be misplaced. Within a year of their establishment, most of the branches had become viable. According to the State Bank of Pakistan,

> the branches licensing policy was not meant to obstruct the growth of the banking system but to foster it in the best national interest. In 1966 the State Bank of Pakistan fixed quotas for new branches for each bank every year, and prescribing the ratios for city and urban and rural branches. The quota of each bank was determined on the basis of its financial position, availability of trained personnel, soundness of its management and its capacity to open and operate the new branches without an adverse effect on its financiers.[13]

In the early 1960s, licences were given to known business magnates and parties which were deemed to be financially sound. This posed an interesting dilemma. Known business magnates and sound parties were, by definition, those who already had wealth and were able to invest it. There was a risk, then, that a further concentration of economic power would take place and a close nexus between industry and banking would emerge. The official history of the State Bank of Pakistan examines this issue as follows:

> The distribution of bank credit was a function of various government policies including those covering the grant of permission for setting up industry and import licensing. There was no denying the fact that though emphasis seemed to be gradually shifting in favour of the smaller parties, the bigger parties still enjoyed, by far, a predominant position. Bank credit had necessarily to follow the overall pattern of public policy which had permitted the establishment of such undertakings ... It was also agreed that big business was already placed in favourable positions in the matter of credit availability. Since banking business had become a highly lucrative enterprise, big businesses were naturally motivated to exploit this opening. They also evinced interest in this activity as a great deal of influence went with the control of banking institutions.[14]

12.1.2 The Relationship Between Economic Growth and the Development of Banking

There is a very close relationship between the nature and extent of economic growth and the growth of the banking sector. The pattern and size of deposits, the type of credit available, the location of bank branches, etc. all influence the pattern of economic development in a country. This is more marked when a country is underdeveloped and in the earlier stages of development. Some observations regarding Pakistan's banking sector until the 1960s allow ample reflection on the nature of Pakistan's economy and society in the earlier years.

Not surprisingly, the demand for industrial credit in the early years was quite low. There was very little industry to begin with, and hence little demand for credit. 'The demand for credit in the early years was not very large ... The affluent class during this period was more interested in commerce than in industry, as it could more quickly multiply its riches in trade rather than in any other branch of economic activity.'[15] These facts have been confirmed by our analysis in Part II of this book, particularly in Chapters 6 and 9.

In the period 1948–54 bank deposits grew by 61 per cent, a very high rate by any standard. It is interesting to observe that this growth was very closely linked with that of the overall economy. Five broad reasons are given by the State Bank of Pakistan for this growth:

1   The revival of economic activity across the country, which had come to a sudden halt immediately following partition.

2   The rehabilitation and consolidation of the banking sector.

3   The inflow of Muslim capital from other countries following the birth of Muslim Pakistan.

4   The increase in development activity, especially in the industrial sector, which resulted in the growth of money incomes – especially in urban areas where banking facilities were better developed.

5   A generally favourable balance of payments on the private account.[16]

Within this six-year period, bank deposits showed a trend closely in line with economic activity. For example, they increased in 1951 due to enhanced export earnings following the Korean War boom and the favourable balance of payments position on the foreign account. The next year, 1952, deposits fell, as there was a reversal in the terms of trade, a fall in export incomes, and an increasing amount spent on imports. Between 1952 and 1954, deposits increased again, mainly due to the reduced scale of commercial activity and the beginning of the flotation of share capital of a number of companies.[17]

In 1953 the financing of economic activity by banks was highly focused on commercial activity, which received 48 per cent of all advances made by banks in that year. This shows that commerce must have been quite profitable to consume such a large share of funds. The bulk of loans for commerce were utilized in financing the wholesale and retail trade of the country. The dearth of industrial activity is reflected in Table 12.1 and Figure 12.2, which shows that in 1953

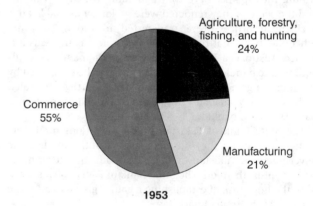

1953

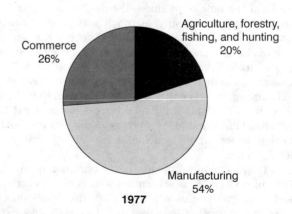

1977

Figure 12.2
Scheduled banks' advances by economic group (% share)

Table 12.1
Scheduled banks' advances by economic group (Rs m; percentages in parentheses)

Economic groups	June 1953	June 1963	June 1972	June 1977
Agriculture, forestry, fishing, and hunting	94.8	232.7	1,156.8	4,632.5
	(18.4)	(7)	(9)	(15.8)
Mining and quarrying	0.3	11.6	62.5	381.9
Manufacturing	82.4	1,236.5	6,124.3	12,576.9
	(16)	(37.4)	(49.3)	(42.9)
Construction	7.9	90.5	149.9	698.7
Electricity, gas, water, and sanitary services	1.1	7.3	68.6	101.3
Commerce	217.0	1,315.7	3,182.8	6,146.1
	(42)	(39.8)	(25.6)	(21.0)
Wholesale and retail trade		1,228.6	2,981.0	5,723.4
Transport, storage, and communication	12.3	76.3	305.5	391.4
Services	67.5	257.6	924.8	2,633.6
Employees and activities not adequately described	31.3	79.9	457.6	1,720.3
Total	514.7	3,308.0	12,432.8	29,282.7

Source: State Bank of Pakistan, *Banking Statistics*, various issues.

manufacturing received only 16 per cent of advances made; of this, one-third went for metal products and one-fifth for textiles. Not surprisingly, a greater share of credit was extended to West Pakistan than to East Pakistan (see also Chapters 6 and 9).

In the 1960s and 1970s, much of the pattern of credit disbursement changed, following the changes in the economy. As manufacturing progressed from the 1950s, through the boom of the 1960s, so did the credit available to the sector. In 1963 manufacturing received 37 per cent of credit, while in 1972 it received almost half, with textiles gaining the largest single share. Advances for commerce, in relative terms, declined from 42 per cent of the total in 1953 to 26 per cent in 1972. Essentially, as the economy grew throughout the 1960s, so did banks. Moreover, the pattern of economic concentration that had emerged in industry was soon reflected in the ownership of banks and in the distribution of bank credit. For example, on 31 March 1959, 63 per cent of the total bank credit was locked up in only 222 bank accounts of Rs1 million and above.[18] On the other hand, advances under Rs25,000 accounted for only 6 per cent of the total credit. On the face of it, this pattern would seem inequitable to most. However, given the distribution of wealth in industry and the type of industry being implanted in the 1950s and 1960s – essentially large scale – the pattern of the disbursement of credit should not come as a surprise. It is unlikely that economic growth of the level prevalent in the 1960s could have taken place without the active role and participation of the banking sector. This relationship was, moreover, mutually beneficial.

12.1.3 Nationalization in the 1970s

On the first day of 1974, the Bank Nationalization Ordinance was promulgated, according to which the federal government had exclusive rights of ownership, management, and control

of all banks in Pakistan. The shareholders of banks were compensated for their holdings in the form of Federal Bonds repayable on par at any time within a period of fifteen years. Although the banks were nationalized by the Z.A. Bhutto government in accord with the People's Party's manifesto when the party had been in office for more than two years, the roots of nationalization actually rest in the developments in the economy and the banking sector in the 1960s, a fact not very well known to most people.

A number of malpractices in the banking sector had begun to be identified, despite the success of the sector, as early as 1962. The State Bank was concerned that there was a maldistribution of credit amongst the different segments of the economy. The concentration of credit in a small class of big borrowers was observed, and given the role of the private sector in industry and banking, the State Bank was not legally empowered to bring about any change in the ownership structure of commercial banks. Furthermore, there was no legal obligation to earmark a percentage of bank advances for the development of businesses other than big businesses. The private sector, particularly those with greater wealth and capital, flourished in the 1950s and 1960s, and given the nature of developments, the close connection between industry and banking was an inevitable outcome.

In July 1969, fourteen major banks in India were taken into state ownership. This influenced the thinking amongst planners in Pakistan. Leading Pakistani economists in the Planning Commission were impressed by the performance of the Indian banks, and so also favoured the nationalization of banks in Pakistan as well. They argued that a reform of the banking system was needed to carry out any meaningful improvement in the structure of industry and the distribution of income to achieve some measure of social justice. Even foreign experts had begun to argue that the economy was in bad shape and identified the banking system as being responsible for many ills.[19]

Of the four largest banks in Pakistan, only one was state controlled, while the other three were owned by industrial families such as the Habibs, Saigols, and Adamjees. These four banks monopolized 75 per cent of total deposits and two-thirds of earning assets. The three private sector banks between them had half of the total deposits and earning assets. Apart from the top three private banks, there were four others owned by the Dawoods, Fancys, Sheikhs, and Haji Habib. These seven private banks were owned by business houses and accounted for as much as 92 per cent of deposits held by all local banks.[20] It is not at all surprising, then, that these family-owned banks promoted and patronized companies owned by them in the provision of credit. This sort of collusion gave rise to a further concentration of wealth.

However, the State Bank of Pakistan was quite realistic about these developments, stating quite rightly:

> If import licences and industrial sanctions were mainly restricted to a few big parties, banks could not possibly refuse accommodation to them. In fact, under the circumstances, banks' failure to provide necessary credit to them would have been detrimental to investment and economic growth. Similarly, concentration of credit in a few industries and commercial cities was a corollary of the location of trade and industry that developed within the broad policy framework of the government. *Given this background, credit disbursement would have followed the same pattern irrespective of the type of ownership of banks.*[21]

The discussions taking place at that time concerned remedial measures to deal with the issues related to the banking system and were, incidentally, quite independent of whether banks remained in private hands or were nationalized. The attitude of the State Bank of Pakistan towards nationalization was completely neutral.

In September 1970, a State Bank report revealed that only eighty-eight accounts in Pakistani banks had access to as much as 25 per cent of total bank credit. Most of these account holders were directors of the banks themselves.[22] Nevertheless the State Bank was unambiguously clear about such issues and argued that it was 'not correct to assume that the nationalization of banks per se could ensure a more equitable distribution of banks' resources between people and regions. Some people held the view that bank credit was not the cause of concentration of economic power but the result.'[23] In light of this background, banking reforms were undertaken in 1972 and were so wide ranging in their scope that people began to believe that the nationalization of banks in the country, which had appeared imminent, had been pushed into the background. However, this was not to be the case.

Fourteen banks were nationalized, of which thirteen were merged into five banks. The State Bank of Pakistan was also nationalized; the official history of the State Bank of Pakistan writes that 'this was perhaps the unique case in the banking world where the Central Bank of the country was simultaneously nationalized along with the commercial banks'.[24] Twenty years after the event, of the five banks, two had been privatized and two of the remaining three, UBL and Habib Bank, were scheduled to be returned to the private sector some time in 1998/9. Although some of the more salient traits and consequences of nationalization are presented in more detail in other sections, some early developments provide an insight into the concerns that were emerging very soon after nationalization.

There was concern that, now that the powerful and lucrative banking sector was in government hands, it was open to political pressure and to misuse. In a number of cases in the early years following nationalization, loans and advances were made on considerations not conforming to professional standards. The high-risk (classified) advances of the banks grew disproportionately in the total loans portfolio. The performance of banks came under severe criticism for growing inefficiency and deteriorating service standards, and for holding monopoly power which permitted them to charge very high interest rates. Some socioeconomic objectives were met when nationalized banks were ordered to open branches all across the country in every township that had a population of over 2,000 inhabitants. While this played a key role in bringing the extensive non-monetized economy into the more formal sector and may possibly have encouraged savings, there were some drawbacks too. Banks became overcrowded and overstaffed for political reasons. They now had their branches in streets and *mohallas* of residential areas regardless of their deposit potential, and there were cases where branches of nationalized banks were located next to each other. (Some more issues regarding the role and performance of nationalized banks are discussed in subsequent sections of this chapter.)

12.1.4 Islamic Banking

In 1979 Pakistan embarked on an extensive process of Islamization, with the financial sector undergoing substantial changes in the process. Two months after coming to power, in September 1977, General Zia-ul Haq had asked the Council of Islamic Ideology (CII) to prepare a blue print on an interest-free economic system in the light of Islamic teachings. In its two main reports, the CII recommended the immediate removal of interest from some financial institutions, with the intention of doing away with interest from all domestic financial transactions.

In February 1979 the government announced that it intended to remove interest from the economy in three years, and it began with the elimination of interest from the House Building Finance Corporation, the National Investment Trust, and the mutual funds of the Investment Corporation of Pakistan. From July that year, the government ordered the nationalized commercial banks to provide interest-free loans to small farmers for meeting their seasonal agricultural financial requirements. This scheme was expanded to fishermen and co-operative societies in 1980.

In January 1981 all five nationalized commercial banks set up separate counters to accept non-interest-bearing profit and loss sharing deposits. From 1985 onwards, no bank was allowed to accept any interest-bearing deposits, except foreign currency deposits, which continued to earn fixed interest rates, while all other accounts shared in the profit or loss earned by that bank.

In addition to these steps, three Islamic modes of financing were launched: *musharaka*, *murabeha*, and *mudaraba*. *Musharaka* means decreasing participation: a bank participates as a financial partner in a profitable project, on the basis of an agreement by the other partner that the bank will receive a certain part of the net profit actually realized, and is entitled to retain the remaining part as may be agreed upon, to be offset against the funds advanced by the bank to finance the project. A *murabeha* is a purchase for others on a prearranged profit basis. A bank buys on behalf of a contracting party and pays the price in full, while the other party repurchases the same commodities at a profit agreed upon in advance. The most popular form of Islamic financing in Pakistan is the *mudaraba*, which is an advance by the bank of the necessary funds, fully or partially, to finance a specific operation administered by another person, on the basis of participation in the profits or losses arising from such an operation.[25]

The Mudaraba Ordinance was promulgated in 1980 and was one of the earlier steps in taking Pakistan towards an 'Islamic' economy. However, there was little response by the public towards this Islamic financial instrument until 1985, when two multipurpose *mudarabas* were floated for public subscription and their share certificates were quoted on the Karachi Stock Exchange. These *mudarabas* were in the leasing business and in the early stages were being observed to see their utility and profitability. The leasing business was new in Pakistan and the concept of a *mudaraba* was not fully understood, hence there was little enthusiasm to establish more *mudarabas*. Nevertheless, these *mudarabas* were considered quite satisfactory and paid reasonable returns to their shareholders. The government of Pakistan encouraged the formation of *mudarabas* by giving them many tax exemptions.

Despite these attempts to Islamicize the economy, the truth is that Pakistan's financial sector has no real element of Islamic banking or finance, except in name only. For example, despite the presence of profit and loss sharing (PLS) deposit accounts, government securities quote a return in terms of a fixed rate of interest. Banks make loans with a variable rate of interest depending on their client's standing and the nature of the project. Moreover, despite their name, the return on PLS deposits contains a substantial element of interest, as banks are allowed to invest their PLS deposits in interest-bearing government securities. It would be fair to conclude that the Islamic mode of financing plays an insignificant role in Pakistan's economy, and what passes for Islamic financing is also often based on instruments with interest as a central feature in their interest-free 'profits'.

12.1.5 Developments since 1988

A major theme running throughout this book is that the economic system of Pakistan was transformed quite radically after 1988 (see Part IV). The structural adjustment programme that began actively in 1988 was a key element in this transformation, as were world events following the collapse of the Berlin Wall in 1989. The financial system in Pakistan came under scrutiny prior to the structural adjustment programme of 1988 and has become a target for reform since. There have been numerous dramatic changes in the financial sector in the last eight years and the trend of liberalization and the opening up of the sector has only just begun.

A major break from the past was the decision to allow new private sector commercial banks to function. In the past, the banking system consisted of the five main nationalized commercial banks (NCBs) and over two dozen foreign-owned banks. In 1991 the government issued licences to ten new banks in the private sector. However, a more important development was the denationalization of two of the five NCBs, the Muslim Commercial Bank (MCB) and the Allied Bank Limited (ABL). While these two were the smallest of the five NCBs, the experiment of handing the public sector banks to the private sector seems to have succeeded, as these two banks have been amongst the best performers in the entire industry. While both these privatized banks had previously high administrative costs compared to the other nationalized banks, following privatization both have significantly improved their cost control procedures. Spurred by the success of the privatization of these two banks, the government has committed itself to privatize all state-owned banks (commercial and development banks) with the exception of the National Bank of Pakistan. The two NCBs which are to be privatized, United Bank Limited and Habib Bank, are far bigger than ABL and MCB, and their privatization may prove to be somewhat more difficult than those of the smaller banks. Information about the quality of assets and about loans advanced may prove to be one of the many stumbling blocks. Nevertheless, given the economic atmosphere prevailing, it is inevitable that these two banks will also be privatized (see Chapter 8 on privatization, and especially Box 8.4).

12.1.6 Banking Trends: 1964–1991

Table 12.2 gives a fascinating picture of the role of banks over three decades, and reveals a great deal about the nature of developments taking place in Pakistan, not only in banking, but in the economy as a whole. It shows that in the 1960s, the number of branches increased almost threefold, reaching 3,418 by 1971. Due to the separation of East Pakistan, not surprisingly the number fell. The single biggest annual increase was in 1974/5, the year of bank nationalization, when the number of branches increased by almost a third. What is most interesting is that in the era of General Zia between 1978 and 1988, the number of branches increased only very marginally, showing, in fact, negative trends in many years. In this ten-year span, the number of branches increased by less than 130. There seems to be a consistent trend between number of branches and number of accounts, with accounts growing quite enthusiastically in the 1960s and early 1970s, and growing very slowly in the Zia era.

However, deposits, whether in nominal or real terms, have been showing a trend which is not as marked as in the case

Table 12.2
Branches and deposits in Pakistani banks, 1964–1991

Year	No. of branches	% change	Total no. of accounts	% change	Nominal deposits (Rs m)	% change	Real deposits[a] (Rs m)	% change	Savings accounts as % of total accounts	Savings deposits as % of nominal deposits
1964	1,298	–	1,907,011	–	6,501.9	–	6,052.0	–	–	–
1965	1,591	22.57	2,390,574	25.36	7,308.3	12.40	6,516.5	7.68	–	–
1966	1,967	23.63	3,133,264	31.07	8,965.9	22.68	7,776.8	19.34	68.11	21.39
1967	2,285	16.17	3,877,197	24.74	10,099.6	12.64	8,018.7	3.11	70.05	23.17
1968	2,536	10.98	4,686,116	20.86	11,557.7	14.44	8,904.2	11.04	73.30	26.23
1969	2,842	12.07	5,546,757	18.37	12,605.6	9.07	9,774.8	9.78	75.98	28.92
1970	3,170	11.54	6,380,959	15.04	14,131.3	12.10	10,555.2	7.98	77.06	29.92
1971	3,418	7.82	7,275,719	140.20	15,593.2	10.35	11,120.0	5.35	78.06	35.32
1972	2,600	–23.93	7,836,207	7.70	18,865.4	20.98	126,801.0	14.03	78.69	34.27
1973	3,195	22.88	8,694,269	10.95	21,957.4	16.39	12,738.5	0.46	78.72	36.13
1974	3,875	21.28	7,221,384	–16.94	22,142.6	0.84	10,364.4	–18.64	80.22	37.35
1975	5,066	30.74	8,745,774	21.11	27,933.7	26.15	10,694.9	3.19	79.82	37.61
1976	5,726	13.03	10,708,367	22.44	37,222.4	33.25	12,714.7	18.89	80.84	37.57
1977	6,737	17.66	11,970,966	11.79	42,494.5	14.16	13,116.8	3.16	80.46	40.39
1978	7,077	5.05	13,246,637	10.66	53,114.2	24.99	15,043.0	14.68	79.89	41.43
1979	6,960	–1.65	14,356,206	8.38	61,600.1	15.98	16,535.0	9.92	80.97	41.09
1980	7,076	1.67	15,374,410	7.09	69,975.3	13.60	17,000.4	2.81	80.58	40.93
1981	7,365	4.08	16,990,763	10.51	80,705.6	15.33	17,693.0	4.07	81.06	42.41
1982	7,375	0.14	18,251,389	7.42	95,977.6	18.92	19,238.0	8.73	81.41	43.51
1983	7,335	–0.54	19,563,836	7.19	122,355.9	27.48	23,297.0	21.10	80.46	42.99
1984	7,189	–1.99	20,488,157	4.72	129,660.0	5.97	22,513.0	–3.37	81.01	44.17
1985	7,120	–0.96	21,215,465	3.55	151,194.5	16.61	25,112.5	11.55	79.25	42.46
1986	7,097	–0.32	21,720,814	2.38	177,959.1	17.70	28,617.0	13.96	80.30	43.65
1987	7,163	0.93	22,578,568	3.95	206,134.5	15.83	31,714.5	10.82	81.15	42.99
1988	7,206	0.60	23,947,814	6.06	218,701.5	6.10	30,696.7	–3.21	81.15	42.99
1989	7,254	0.67	25,140,525	4.98	245,722.5	12.36	31,764.0	3.48	81:15	42.99
1990	7,404	2.07	24,323,793	–3.25	279,254.3	13.65	34,527.0	8.70	89.72	44.75
1991	7,405	0.01	30,993,837	27.42	377,924.0	35.33	40,554.0	17.46		

[a] Real deposits are in terms of 1960 prices.
Source: State Bank of Pakistan, *Banking Statistics of Pakistan, 1990–91*, Karachi, 1992.

of branches or accounts. In nominal terms, deposits have increased consistently, even in the 1978–88 period when the number of branches of banks diminished. In real terms, in the mid-1980s, there were substantial increases in deposits. This is attributed to the increase in money supply in the economy and money flowing in from the informal sector. The trend depicted in Table 12.1 is now re-examined in Table 12.3, in which we can see the substantial growth in advances made to the private sector in 1991, compared to 1985. As Chapters 7 and 8 showed, there was a continuous shift away from government and public sector enterprises in the 1980s. As the policies of privatization and denationalization were implemented, the private sector began to play a bigger role in development. The large shift in emphasis in favour of the private sector is also reflected in the allocation of bank advances to the private sector. Not surprisingly, textiles claimed about one-eighth of all advances in 1991. However, see Appendix 8.2 on the state of the textile sector, and Box 12.2 on non-performing loans.

12.1.7 Development Finance Institutions (DFIs) and Non-Bank Financial Institutions (NBFIs)

DFIs provide long-term debt, and in 1993/4 sanctioned loans worth Rs26 billion. The practice until recently was that DFIs acted as conduits for government funding, which was then made available to users. In addition, credit from multilateral agencies, guaranteed by the government, was utilized by DFIs. There has been a positive development of late, where locally mobilized deposits now make up about one-third of the assets of DFIs, a development which has brought DFIs under the regulatory control of the State Bank. Since DFIs are also highly controlled by the government, like nationalized banks, DFIs have not been able to maintain institutional autonomy. Political pressures, rather than economic and financial expediency, have been responsible for advancing loans, which has resulted in a significant loan arrears problem. Furthermore, given the nature of the changes in

BOX 12.2

The burden of non-performing loans

In 1997 non-performing loans are estimated to be worth Rs140 billion, raising significant problems for the portfolio of banks.

Over the years the capital base of NCBs has been severely affected by the poor quality of bank loans made primarily on political and uneconomic grounds. As a result the single most formidable problem facing the banks is the heavy burden of non-performing loans. Although rescheduling of loans is common, the total advances of NCBs categorized as bad and doubtful debts are Rs56 billion; Rs45.9 billion of these classified advances relate to the private sector. Just under 23% of the private sector's classified debt pertain to advances under mandatory targets and concessional credit schemes. In 1989 SBP estimated that around 14.2% of the lending portfolio of NCBs needed to be provided against.

The position of DFIs is even more delicate than that of commercial banks. Provisions against bad loans have increased from 0.1% of assets in 1980 to 0.9% in 1991. It is estimated that about Rs13 billion was stuck up in non-performing loans, representing 30% of the portfolio, Rs6 billion of which was in respect of cases that had been in litigation for more than one year.

The problem of debt recovery is not simply a technical issue. Not only have political pressures affected the quality of the loan portfolio of banks, they have also been instrumental in preventing banks to proceed against persistent defaulters and have resisted attempts to improve the enforcement mechanisms.

Source: Haque, Nadeemul and Shahid Kardar, 'The Development of Financial Markets in Pakistan', unpublished mimeo, 1993, pp. 14–15.

Pakistan's economy, with deregulation and liberalization on the one hand, and with changes in the financial structure on the other, it is probable that DFIs will become more like banks, or banks will begin to make longer-term loans, thus eroding the present protected position of DFIs.

NBFIs have a small, though growing, share of the market at the moment and may begin to play an increased role as financial liberalization continues. The main constituents of the non-bank financial sector are leasing companies, *mudarabas*, investment banks, and housing finance companies. Leasing companies are a relatively new phenomenon in Pakistan. However, leasing has grown at a rate of about 70 per cent over the last five years. Despite the competition in leasing, the sector is dominated by four large players: NDLC (National Development Leasing Corporation) (30 per cent of the leasing business), First Grindlays Mudaraba (17 per cent), Orix leasing (14 per cent), and First BRR Capital Mudaraba (about 11 per cent). *Mudarabas* have also grown rapidly in the last few years and their total value of paid-up capital is over Rs5 billion. They compete with

Table 12.3
Scheduled banks' advances, June 1985 and June 1991

	Million rupees		% share	
	June 1985	June 1991	June 1985	June 1991
Government	14,050.8	18,674.3	12.5	7.9
Public sector enterprises	18,058.8	16,434.9	16.1	7.0
Private sector	69,637.3	178,899.5	62.4	76.1
Agriculture, forestry, hunting, and fishing	14,029.1	51,301.8		
Mining and quarrying	464.9	942.7	30.2	30.9
Manufacturing	33,765.2	72,769.0	11.9	12.8
Textiles	13,266.6	30,195.5		
Construction	2,155.1	3,896.6		
Electricity, gas, water, and sanitary services	115.5	963.3	13.3	14.3
Commerce	14,896.6	33,710.0		
Wholesale and retail trade	5,269.7	13,251.3		
Transport, storage, and communication	648.3	1,239.5		
Services	709.9	2,144.1		
Other private business	2,852.6	11,932.6		
Trust funds and non-profit organizations	100.4	336.6		
Personal	8,806.2	20,473.0		
Other activities not adequately described	1,001.8	156.4		
Total	111,655.3	235,074.9		

Source: State Bank of Pakistan, *Banking Statistics*, various issues.

National Investment Trust (NJI) and the Investment Corporation of Pakistan (ICP) in portfolio management. Investment banks have yet to demonstrate their potential as they constitute less than 1 per cent of financial assets.

12.1.8 Some Salient Issues in the Banking Sector

Although most commercial banks have large asset bases, and for this reason there is great potential for them to explore further possibilities to develop medium- and long-term lending facilities, constraints in the present structure impede this potential. While the asset base may be large, the large holdings by banks of government securities cannot be lent or borrowed against. Thus, banks could provide capital by subscribing to corporate convertible commercial bonds/papers, and be more involved with DFIs in consortium financing for projects, only if they had a freer hand in determining their own portfolios unhindered by government directives.

However, the constraints that banks face in term lending include their ability to mobilize medium- and long-term resources. At the moment, given the structure of the banking system, banks do not have large long-term resources. It is also believed, often incorrectly, that many commercial banks, unlike DFIs, do not have the expertise for making medium- and long-term loans on the basis of economic viability, technical feasibility, and financial profitability. Furthermore, the nationalized commercial banks (NCBs), which constitute about 85 per cent of the banking system in Pakistan, are constrained by a management regime that is very bureaucratic, and like all government departments, the banks are highly centralized and initiative by middle and lower-level executives is not particularly encouraged or appreciated.

Pakistani banks, since they form a major part of the public sector, are not immune from political pressures to make loans for projects that do not satisfy the basic criteria of financial soundness or viability. Local banks and DFIs are very often used to provide financial favours to politically well connected individuals, thus often undermining all basic banking principles (see Box 12.2). It is estimated that in 1997 'non-performing' loans made by the banking sector accounted for around Rs140 billion, or almost 6 per cent of GDP. This problem, which has its roots in political patronage and corruption, is one of the main impediments to the further privatization of banks. Unless this 'infected portfolio' of banks is removed, the privatization process will be slow.

In a study conducted by the National Development Finance Corporation (NDFC) in May 1993, a comparison of foreign and private sector banks was made with NCBs. (In 1996 there were twenty-five Pakistani Scheduled Banks and twenty-two foreign banks operating in Pakistan.) It was found that between 1986 and 1991 the proportion of commercial banking assets owned by foreign banks grew from 6 per cent to 14 per cent. In 1991 the three largest NCBs accounted for 72 per cent of loans, 73 per cent of deposits, and only 33 per cent of pre tax profits. The three largest foreign banks used 5.4 per cent of the sector's assets, 4.6 per cent of loans, and 5.5 per cent of deposits to generate over 24 per cent of profits.

Total pre-tax profits earned by NCBs amounted to Rs2.2 billion on a paid-up capital of Rs6.4 billion, while foreign banks earned higher profits of Rs3.5 billion on a lower paid-up capital of Rs3.3 billion.[26]

There is a noticeable difference in efficiency and performance between state-owned nationalized commercial banks and foreign banks. Foreign banks have shown the highest growth rate in terms of deposits in the last three years, with an annual growth of 31.4 per cent, as compared to 12.7 per cent for NCBs and 18.2 per cent for the privatized banks. Furthermore, foreign banks have been able to control administrative costs, restricting their growth to 17.6 per cent, compared to 19.7 for nationalized and 18.3 per cent for privatized banks. The gross revenues of foreign banks have also grown at a much faster rate than the increase in costs. In the case of some domestic banks, the costs have exceeded growth in revenue. Administrative costs for NCBs have been 2 per cent of total assets, compared with 0.85 per cent for foreign banks, while the rate of return on total assets for foreign banks ranges from 1 to 2.4 per cent, compared with only 0.1 to 0.3 per cent for local banks.[27]

Although the above comparisons clearly show that foreign banks outperform local, particularly nationalized banks, it is important to emphasize the difference in how they function. Foreign banks neither compete in the same markets nor are subjected to the same degree of political pressure to hire staff and advance/reschedule loans, as is the case for nationalized banks. Furthermore, NCBs are forced to make advances to the agricultural sector, which often results in an increase in the number of bad loans. Also, it is not surprising that foreign banks are more profitable in terms of shareholders' equity, assets, and net spread on funds. Efficiency ratios reveal that the NCBs are the least efficient. The maintenance of a large number of unprofitable branches in order to provide banking services to rural areas necessitates the incurring of fixed operating costs that may not be particularly helpful in generating revenues for the NCBs. Furthermore, other than the numerous problems and hindrances highlighted above, which affect the emergence and functioning of an efficient banking system, the issue of direct credit has been of particular concern to nationalized banks. These banks are directed by the government of Pakistan to provide credit to specific sectors and at specific times, irrespective of economic and financial considerations. It is quite possible that the majority of these loans are bad loans with a low probability of being returned (see Chapters 14 and 15 on the structural adjustment programme and its implications for the financial sector).

12.2 The Equities Market

Of the three stock exchanges in Pakistan, Karachi dominates, with more than 80 per cent of trading. Stock market activity has grown substantially over the last three or four years and the number of listed companies in Karachi rose from 300 in 1986 to 775 in September 1996. The State Bank of Pakistan General Index of Share Prices, which was 100 in 1990/1, was 290 in June 1994, registering a rise of 80 per cent since

BOX 12.3
Factors behind the fall in the KSE index

The following extract is an analysis of the peaks and valleys of the KSE 100 index since 1991.

The KSE 100 index came into existence in November 1991 and the amount of foreign money entering the market increased sharply in June 1991 after the enactment of the Foreign Exchange Controls Act and other financial reforms and liberalization programmes. If we take a look back at the previous peaks and valleys of the KSE 100 index and the stock prices of selective index and blue-chip stocks, the poor conditions of the current market can be rationalized.

The first peak was on January 6, 1992 when the index reached 1714. The market in 1991 was small and relatively inactive and thus many blue-chip stocks were undervalued. However, with increasing activity from both local and foreign investors because of the reforms, the stock prices rose across the board, especially in the textile and modaraba sectors. The average daily turnover at this time was around 2.5 million and the market PE rose from 10x in November, 1991 to 15x. The boom of January 6, 1992 reflects the results of the introduction of financial reforms and liberalization policies. With any boom, there is always a correction.

After reaching 1714 in early 1992, the index dipped to 1084 on April 24, 1993, a correction of 37% within 15 months of the last peak. The circumstances surrounding this fall are mostly political due to the dismissal of the sitting government at that time. The reaction to the dismissal amongst investors and the business community was negative and thus reflected in most of the share prices. The market PE fell to below 10x and the average daily turnover was 3.2 million shares. Share prices of banks, synthetics and rayon and fuel and energy stocks reacted negatively while chemicals and pharmaceutical stocks felt little or no effect from the slide in the index.

One of the reasons why the chemical and pharmaceutical sector may have been immune to the bearish sentiments at that time could be because of the nature of the shareholding and history of good dividend payouts. The shares of multinational pharmaceuticals are closely held by the parent or by strong holders and, thus, are not the most active scrips on the market while other stocks are more widely held and may be in the possession of weak holders ready to sell in a panic in the face of adverse conditions instead of holding on to the shares.

The next important point is March 22, 1994 when the index had reached the historic apex of 2661, a rise of 145% from the previous low of April 24, 1993. In the aftermath of elections held during October 1993 and the formation of a new government, there was an euphoria in the market as investors breathed a sigh of relief as political stability was achieved. There was fresh capital injected into the market as both local and foreign investors entered the market in a big way. The gains were phenomenal as most stocks rose 3 to 4 times their prices as of April 24, 1993.

Also, many sectors such as synthetic and rayon and cement had positive fundamentals which were looked upon favourably by most investors. The market PEx more than doubled from the low point of 1993 to over 20. Also, average daily turnover doubled to 7.7 million shares. However, since March 22, 1994, the index has been continuously declining and has not surpassed the historic peak of 2661.

Source: Sheikh Humayun Saghir, 'Factors Behind the Fall in the KSE Index', *DAWN*, Advertising Supplement, 30 September 1996.

1992/3. The capitalized value of shares increased by 88 per cent in 1994 compared with 1992/3, and was Rs404 billion in June 1994. The value of shares traded more than doubled during the year, while the value in turnover of shares increased threefold between July 1993 and June 1994. When it came into existence in September 1947, the Karachi Stock Exchange had 90 members, but only 5 companies listed, and it had a paid-up capital of Rs37 million. By September 1996, it had 200 members of which 150 were active, and the 775 listed companies had a listed capital of Rs138.7 billion and a market capitalization of some Rs341.84 billion.

Although the equity market seems to show phenomenal growth, a number of particularities need to be pointed out. While the Karachi Stock Exchange ranks amongst the top Asian exchanges in terms of the number of listed companies, Pakistan has one of the smallest markets in terms of market capitalization and trading volumes. Pakistani equities are a mere 1.6 per cent of the total for emerging markets. Although the daily turnover of shares has touched 7.5 million, and about 300 equities are traded on an average day, trading in most shares is usually in insignificant volumes. Furthermore, trading in shares of only the ten best blue-chip companies is estimated to account for over 30 per cent of turnover in terms of value.[28]

Figure 12.3 shows the performance of the Karachi Stock Exchange (KSE) 100 index over a brief period of five years, and the huge variation is clearly evident. Having risen to a very high 2661 in March 1994 when the market experienced a boom, the valuation of companies has since been halved to a little over 1300. Moreover, for over a year since November 1995, the index has shown little movement. Some of the reasons for this trend are given in Box 12.3. Table 12.4 shows the rather dramatic rise and fall in price of some of the more popular shares in the stock exchange. The variations in most cases are extreme.

Essentially a number of factors explain this trend. It is believed that, despite having the right 'fundamentals' in sectors such as synthetics and rayons and cement, these sectors became weak as the rapid expansion of existing units and the construction of new plants caused an oversupply position. Moreover, the increase in the sales tax and excise duty, and the reduction in import tariffs, had negative

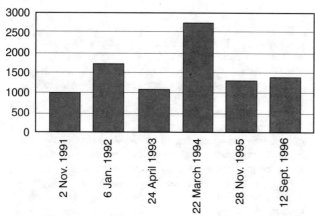

Figure 12.3
The KSE index, November 1991 to September 1996

consequences for production, leading to a loss in value on the Stock Exchange.

The boom of March 1994 was caused by the large public offerings made around that time, including key companies such as Pakistan Telecommunications Corporation (PTC), Hub Power, Faysal Bank, Lucky Cement, Dhan Fibres, and Ibrahim Fibres. Consequently, no fresh capital was left for

secondary markets. Another factor that undoubtedly affected the performance of the stock market was the law and order situation in Karachi. Furthermore, despite attempts to make the stock market an effective institution so as to raise funds for industry, much of the activity on the Karachi Stock Exchange has been speculative (see John Maynard Keynes' somewhat cynical views on the stock market in Appendix 12.3).

Although efforts are under way to reform it, the stock market is not perceived by most investors to be either efficient or fair. Insider trading, front running, cornering of shares, and excessive speculation are perceived to be endemic. A Securities and Exchange Commission is essential to provide a better regulatory framework for overseeing the workings of the markets. If the market is expected to work more efficiently, speedier implementation and efficient and timely information need to be provided to investors, particularly foreign investors. Better disclosure rules about the activities of corporations are also essential. Other concerns relate to the fact that investors do not have access to preference shares, a procedure discontinued in 1984. Aftab Ahmed Khan presents a large number of reasons why the stock market has not grown as many expected it to (see Box 12.4).

BOX 12.4

The weakness of the stock market

Pakistan's stock markets suffer from numerous problems. Some are identified here.

The retarded growth of equities markets in the past has been due to a variety of factors, of which the following are significant:

(a) Public companies and public sector enterprises were not encouraged to list on the stock exchange because government interest rate and credit allocation policies distorted the price structure of equity finance relative to loans from financial institutions and other sources. This stimulated excessive reliance on debt financing and led to high debt–equity ratios.

(b) Public enterprises received funding directly from the government either through appropriations from the national budget or at relative low interest rates from state-controlled financial institutions.

(c) The majority of private sector firms have tended to be relatively small and consequently their needs have tended to be modest, mainly confined to meeting working capital requirements. The firms have been able to generate the required finances from personal loans and their own contributions and retained earnings as well as short-term loan facilities from commercial banks.

(d) There is a strong concern among private company owners regarding the dilution of ownership and control of their firms. Most owners wish to keep the benefits of their entrepreneurship and control over the future of their enterprises within a limited circle of relatives and

friends. Even when a company is listed on the stock exchange, most of the shares are not available for public trading.

(e) A number of companies are reluctant to disclose information about their financial status. The disclosure requirement has been instituted to protect the interests of the investors.

However, since most of the private companies do not have to submit externally audited financial statements, they are better able to evade taxes in some way. The public listed company is placed at a disadvantage relative to its competitors.

(f) As a result of factors such as after-tax returns, risk and liquidity, other instruments offered higher yields and less risk than securities.

(g) Investors have generally felt that the market can be rigged against anyone but the largest investors. There is trading on the basis of privileged information involving considerable unacceptable risk for the small investors.

(h) Institutional investors such as investment companies, unit trusts, pension funds and insurance companies have played a limited role in the development of the share market. The active participation of institutional investors is critically important for the development of the quities market.

(i) There is a lack of appropriate financial information regarding the stock market. Of all the financial markets, the stock market is the most difficult to comprehend.

Source: Khan, Aftab Ahmad, *DAWN*, Economic and Business Review, November 1994.

Table 12.4
Fluctuations in the KSE and some scrips (Rs m)

KSE index	6 Jan. 92	24 Apr. 93	22 Mar. 94	28 Nov. 95	12 Sept. 96
Index	1,714	1,084	2,661	1,320	1,363
Paid-up capital	37,275,500	62,003,789	71,015,937	132,114,887	197,102,915
Market cap.	199,468,650	188,652,465	451,505,662	301,267,819	458,773,990
No. of companies	549	649	686	786	808

Scrip	6 Jan. 92 (1)	24 Apr. 93 (2)	% change (2)-(1)	22 Mar. 94 (3)	% change (3)-(2)	28 Nov. 95 (4)	% change (4)-(3)	12 Sept. 96 (5)	% change (5)-(4)	4-year return (5)-(1)	5 years High	5 years Low
Banks												
Al-Faysal Inv. Bank	NL	NL	n.a.	42.71	n.a.	19.75	-53.76	11.00	-44.30	n.a.	84.75	15.00
Askari Bank	NL	9.63	n.a.	36.91	283.28	24.00	-34.98	21.00	-12.50	n.a.	52.39	7.43
Crescent Inv. Bank	45.61	15.01	-67.09	59.38	295.60	21.00	-64.43	11.25	-46.43	-75.33	69.08	12.50
MCB	NL	16.97	n.a.	67.01	294.87	22.99	-65.69	31.60	37.45	n.a.	69.61	16.42
Synthetic												
Dewan Salman	98.81	34.96	-64.62	130.30	272.71	57.56	-55.83	23.25	-59.61	-76.47	150.75	25.50
Gatron Industries	NL	51.00	n.a.	75.00	47.06	26.50	-64.67	31.60	19.25	n.a.	88.50	25.25
Pak Synthetic	28.82	9.53	-66.93	41.15	331.79	20.50	-50.18	9.50	-53.66	-67.04	64.00	7.65
Rupali Polyester	114.84	71.34	-37.88	87.00	21.95	46.90	-42.99	25.00	-49.60	-78.23	123.54	22.75
Cement												
Cherat Cement	17.61	21.65	22.94	91.70	323.56	38.00	-58.56	18.25	-51.97	3.63	91.70	7.90
D.G. Khan	NL	19.81	n.a.	72.73	267.14	25.44	-65.02	9.50	-62.66	n.a.	84.00	12.75
Dandot Cement	13.78	24.19	75.54	127.42	426.75	15.00	-88.23	4.70	-68.67	-65.89	137.28	4.25
Maple Leaf Cement	NL	NL	n.a.	NL	n.a.	18.79	n.a.	10.00	-46.78	n.a.	133.87	10.53
Pakland Cement	28.75	11.00	-61.74	45.45	313.18	24.26	-46.62	13.25	-45.38	-53.91	66.88	3.38
Fuel energy												
KESC	34.39	14.22	-58.65	50.61	255.91	20.45	-59.59	21.75	6.36	-36.75	50.61	13.56
National Refinery	86.50	60.25	-30.35	140.00	132.37	42.00	-70.00	30.00	-28.57	-65.32	140.00	31.50
Pakistan Refinery	105.00	62.50	-40.48	145.00	132.00	99.00	-31.72	54.00	-45.45	-48.57	210.00	54.00
PSO	52.94	65.08	22.93	234.08	259.68	222.97	-4.75	320.00	43.52	504.46	424.00	21.27
Shell	64.28	50.34	-21.69	175.87	249.36	156.61	-10.95	125.00	-20.18	94.46	193.47	35.33
Sui Northern Gas	35.16	17.70	-49.66	44.25	150.00	23.53	-46.82	35.00	48.75	-0.46	47.00	7.62
Sui Southern Gas	26.10	13.63	-47.78	38.66	183.64	22.84	-40.92	29.75	30.25	13.98	42.63	5.52
Chemical and Pharmaceutical												
BOC	33.57	139.16	16.65	95.50	143.87	94.66	-0.88	120.00	26.77	257.46	550.00	12.19
Ciba Geigy	31.90	72.05	125.86	106.00	47.12	88.00	-16.98	56.50	-32.39	86.52	148.00	18.74
Engro	39.52	48.94	23.84	185.82	279.69	104.13	-43.96	135.00	29.65	241.60	194.29	19.57
Fauji Fertilizer	NL	47.00	n.a.	104.00	121.28	52.50	-49.52	64.25	22.38	n.a.	125.25	44.25
ICI	13.47	9.78	-27.39	28.03	186.61	20.05	-28.47	14.50	-27.68	7.65	39.04	7.36
Reckitt & Colman	49.22	50.65	2.91	141.10	178.58	82.56	-41.49	68.50	-17.03	39.17	144.71	33.40
Welcome	90.05	76.71	-14.81	173.42	126.07	125.00	-27.92	100.00	-20.00	11.05	197.10	42.15
Wyeth	105.00	125.00	19.05	250.00	100.00	200.00	-20.00	181.50	-9.25	72.86	271.00	63.00
Others												
Adamjee Insurance	35.31	59.50	68.51	174.86	193.88	68.00	-61.11	87.50	28.68	147.81	245.23	15.54
Lever Brothers	874.58	810.00	-7.38	1,500.00	85.19	640.00	-57.33	650.00	1.56	-25.68	1,650.00	367.96
Packages	94.60	90.40	-4.44	195.30	116.04	104.00	-46.75	70.00	-32.69	-26.00	204.60	40.72

Note: The above stock prices are fully adjusted for rights issues and bonus shares.
Source: Sheikh, Humayun Saghir, 'Factors Behind the Fall in the KSE Index', *DAWN*, Advertising Supplement, Karachi, 30 September, 1996.

As far as sources of equity are concerned, the bulk of the shareholding is by the sponsors themselves (60–65 per cent), individuals hold about 15–20 per cent, foreigners hold 3 per cent, and the balance is held by institutions. On the other hand, institutions such as NIT, ICP and mudarabas account for as much as 50 per cent of market volume, with individual investors and brokers accounting for almost all the rest.

The stock market is also affected by the fact that the settlement of shares involves a cumbersome procedure for share transfers and registration, and the physical handling of shares seriously affects trading volumes. Antiquated stock practices favour the informed investor and are biased against the small investor. The risk of non-delivery and non-payment and the high cost per transaction also restrict the access of small investors to the market. The lack of transparency and credibility of information affects the development of a modern financial system. It is also believed that a central depository system is needed to eliminate the numerous problems caused by the physical handling of securities.

Conventional wisdom in Pakistan, in line with the extensive liberalization, deregulation, and privatization that have taken place in the financial sector and other areas of the economy, believes strongly that the stock exchange has a role to play in industrialization and development (see, for example, Appendix 12.2). However, not only does this view ignore the experience from other countries, as shown in Appendix 12.4, but it also does not adequately examine the recent trends in the securities market in Pakistan. With only a handful of companies' shares being traded regularly and despite the large number of shares ostensibly changing hands each day, the role of the stock market is currently very limited in the context of Pakistan's growth strategies. Its role is almost entirely of a speculative nature, with many individuals making and losing fortunes. However, given the worldwide wave of interest in emerging markets and the mushrooming on the fund-managers' map of potential and new stock markets, it is probable that Pakistan's stock exchanges will continue to be of interest to local and international investors.

Given the distorted nature of the Pakistan stock market, not reflecting in any way changes in 'fundamentals', it is a far cry from the efficient markets hypothesis. The belief that the stock market in Pakistan is an indicator of economic development and progress, and reflects government policy and initiative, is quite erroneous. For this reason, despite the enthusiasm for 'investing' in the stock market, the contribution that this investment will make to real economic growth is largely cosmetic.

12.3 Summary and Further Reading

12.3.1 Summary

The banking sector and the stock market form the focus of this chapter, the first of two chapters on the financial and monetary sector of the economy. We have shown how, from a non-existent banking sector, the financial sector has emerged as a key component of the economy. The history of banking shows that industrialization and economic development are closely linked with the development of the banking sector. We have highlighted the numerous problems that afflict public sector banks. The fact that nationalized commercial banks have an infected portfolio equivalent to 6 per cent of GDP affects their performance, and also has negative impacts on the rest of the financial sector and on the economy.

Although there has been a scramble to establish stock markets in most developing countries, the positive impact of such investment is, for Pakistan, still a long way off. The stock market is not seen as a mechanism to raise capital and we find no reflection in stock market behaviour of changes in 'fundamentals'. Rather, the stock market in Pakistan is more like a small club, where just a handful of companies dominate the market, and just a few players call the shots. The claim that underdeveloped countries should develop stock markets at the expense of other sectors is questionable. Experience from other countries has shown that other means of raising revenue for economic development are perhaps better suited to the current needs of Pakistan.

12.3.2 Further Reading

Unfortunately, there is very little reading to recommend on either the banking sector or the equities market in Pakistan, because very little published material exists. On the financial sector, there is the excellent and informative history of the State Bank of Pakistan, published so far in two volumes by the Bank, and the book written by S.A. Meenai, *Money and Banking in Pakistan*, Oxford University Press, Karachi, 1984. The *Journal of the Institute of Bankers in Pakistan* contains analysis of and articles on recent developments in the financial sector. The State Bank's *Annual Report* is also a good source about yearly developments. Newspapers often carry reports and analysis on a regular basis, and should be consulted frequently.

Appendix 12.1

The nature and significance of capital markets and commercial banks' role in their development

Some salient issues in the capital market and financial sector in Pakistan are described in the following extract.

The capital market includes the portion of the financial system involved in (i) mobilization and intermediation of private savings, and (ii) allocation of medium and long term financial resources through a variety of debt and equity instruments of both private and public sector investment.

Capital markets play a crucial role in mobilizing domestic resources and channelling them efficiently to the most productive investments. The level of capital market development is thus an important determinant of a country's level of savings, efficiency of investment and ultimately of its rate of economic growth. An efficient capital market can also provide a range of attractive opportunities to both domestic and foreign individual and institutional investors.

A developed capital market usually comprises savings facilities, banking system, financial institutions for industry, primary and secondary markets where bonds and equities are traded and issued, an underwriting system and an official regulatory authority to supervise the market and protect the investors.

It should, however, be emphasized that an efficient capital market is not an end in itself, as the primary purpose of capital market development is to strengthen the economy and then thereby improve the standard of living of the people. Therefore, efficient capital markets complement and support the productive activities of the economy.

In Pakistan the capital market consists of (i) a dominant non-securities market with well established commercial banks, development finance institutions (DFI) and specialized banks/institutions for industry, agriculture, housing and small business, as well as a variety of other smaller, younger and marginally important non-bank financial institutions; and (ii) a rapidly developing securities market, with three organized stock exchanges but which in terms of total funds raised is less significant as compared to the non-securities market.

The non-securities market provides medium and long term equity and debt funds in negotiable form which are issued by corporations and governments or through financial institutions, directly to individual and institutional investors and then traded among different holders.

The securities market for negotiable equity shares and long term debt securities is typically divided into two parts. One is the 'primary' market in which new issues of securities are made by companies and are bought by investors. The other is the 'secondary' market in which the existing securities are traded through financial intermediaries, such as investment banks, brokers, dealers and individual investors. These institutions quite often provide or arrange for a commitment to the issuing company that the entire new issue will be sold at a set price, thus assuring the company of a fixed amount of total proceeds from the new issue. In addition to liquidity, the secondary market provides a pool of investors to whom new issues may be sold. Thus, while the primary market is necessary to provide issues of securities to be traded in the secondary market, the latter is essential for allowing the new issues to be sold. Thus both markets are mutually re-enforcing.

Need for Capital Market Development in Pakistan

So far Pakistan has raised a large portion of its investment funds from national savings, which are routed through national financial institutions such as commercial banks and non-bank financial institutions (NBFIs) as well as through national savings schemes (NSSs). These funds are supplemented by foreign savings in the form of ordinary and concessional loans from multilateral financial institutions and bilateral agencies as well as commercial loans from foreign banks. A limited but growing amount of total national investment is funded through direct foreign investment.

Furthermore funds are government guaranteed loans from development finance institutions (DFIs) or domestic commercial banks to government indicated/sanctioned projects to private sector and large scale public enterprises. Consequently, most enterprises have an excessive dependence on debt financing and have minimized equity financing. Excessive reliance on debt finance to fund capital intensive projects with low returns has in many cases caused debt servicing problems. Over-reliance on debt has also resulted in unbalanced capital structures, high debt/equity ratios and financial vulnerability to downturns in world and domestic economies.

Government policy makers and planners are aware that over the next decade it will become difficult to (i) fund public development expenditure, especially for public enterprises, through government budgetary allocations because of fiscal constraints; (ii) expect an increase in the flow of foreign commercial loans, because of mounting external debt servicing problems; (iii) rely on increasing supply of external aid funds because of budgetary pressures in developed industrial countries. In the foreseeable future, only foreign investment can fill a portion of the gap left by reduced external flows.

In the light of these structural, financial and attitudinal changes, the achievement of a high rate of growth by Pakistan will significantly depend on the development of domestic capital markets (i) to mobilize increased domestic resources to bridge the projected investment savings gap; and (ii) to efficiently allocate scare capital resources to the most productive investment projects. Moreover, without fully developed equity markets, Pakistan will not be able to increase the availability of equity funding and move towards more balanced capital structures. The development of capital market in Pakistan aside from easing the burden on government funds and mobilizing savings for productive investment would also establish a platform for raising tax revenues in the future.

Role of Commercial Banks in Capital Market

Commercial banks are the dominant financial institutions in the country. They are also playing an important capital market role by providing medium and long term loans for the purpose of financing fixed investment. During 1994–95 the gross disbursement of funds by commercial banks for this purpose amounted to Rs9,392 million.

Because of their large asset base, there is still considerable scope for commercial banks to develop medium and long term funding facilities. In particular, commercial banks could assist the corporate sector by subscribing to convertible commercial bonds paper as well as guaranteeing these for reputable and experienced entrepreneurs. They could also increase their participatory activities with DFIs in consortium financing for projects which have been professionally studied and found to be economically and technically feasible.

Commercial banks' involvement in term lending is, however, a complex issue and its dimensions depend, among other things, on the ability of commercial banks to mobilize medium and long term resources, as well as on 'term transformation', i.e. the acquisition of long term liabilities on the basis of short term deposits. At present, commercial banks do not have large long term resources and the practice of borrowing short term funds and lending a substantial portion of these on a long term basis carries the risk of liquidity.

Commercial banks also generally do not have adequate institutional expertise for making medium and long term loans on the basis of projects' economic and financial viability and technical feasibility. Moreover, since major commercial banks (except foreign banks) till recently have been government owned, their management tends to be bureaucratic in style, with an emphasis on centralized decision making which discourages management initiative. The commercial banks have also been extensively exposed to political pressures for making loans to projects that do not satisfy the criterion of financial soundness or viability. Unfortunately, commercial banks (and DFIs) have been quite often used for conferring unjustified favours on certain influential individuals.

Source: *The News*, 31 August 1996.

Appendix 12.2

The role of capital markets

Capital markets can play an important role in economic development.

Industrial development is commonly believed to be the engine of economic growth. If that is so, then its fuel must come from the capital markets. Significant economic development is not possible without the sustained availability of long-term funds and long-term funds are really only available through the capital markets. We know that most people save. How much they save and how these savings get re-deployed determines the size and nature of a country's capital markets. The capital markets, therefore, are simply a mechanism for repackaging financial flows. This repackaging can occur in the form of debt or equity. Debt is repackaged as fixed income instruments which offer a guaranteed return to the holder and promise the return of principal at maturity. Equity is a much more fundamental form of investment where the investor shares, to a greater degree, in the fortunes of the issuing company.

It is no coincidence that economies which are more developed than ours also have more sophisticated capital markets. It is also no coincidence that the savings rate in such economies tends to be much higher than the savings rate in Pakistan. Given that our savings rate is pretty poor, are we to conclude that our capital markets are doomed forever? The answer is obviously no, but the daily transactions, the level of the index, etc. have shown tremendous growth since 1989 and credit for this must go to the implementation of sensible, liberal policies. There is also no denying that foreign investment beginning in 1991 activated and propelled the local equity market. This allowed local companies and their sponsors to finally extract embedded values. It also allowed companies to raise money relatively quickly and encouraged issues to realize the benefits of public listing.

That's the good news. The bad news is that the equity market still remains fairly illiquid when compared to other countries in Asia. For instance, Pakistan has approximately 1.5 million investors which compares rather poorly with 25 million in India; and of the 1.5 million less than 5% are really active. The ability of this small number of investors to move the market is therefore significant. In addition, only 20 companies represent approximately 45% of the KSE's market capitalization and only about 15% of issued shares are actively traded. These facts notwithstanding, the trends are positive as more investors are entering the market and large equity holdings are being diluted.

The debt market is a different story. Effectively, the only debt instruments are government bonds and treasury bills and, together with the national saving schemes, they swamp the debt securities market. Until recently, private sector debt securities were severely victimized by discriminatory tax treatment and other disincentives. The net result is that Pakistan's financial backdrop is dominated by commercial lending, either through commercial banks or development finance institutions.

This situation has prevented the development of a private sector debt securities market in which individuals and institutions normally invest. Our system forces most investors to keep their money in bank deposits and other instruments which may yield substantially less than the inflation rate. Given the opportunity, perhaps these investors would rather invest in securities of top quality private sector companies where the yield for 5-year paper could be substantially more rewarding. Until our capital markets allow such instruments to develop, we cannot place any significant reliance on them.

It is inconceivable that Pakistan can achieve its ambitious economic objectives without the growth of its capital markets not only in size but also in depth. When a company cannot raise even US$50 million from its domestic capital markets in local currency, at affordable rates, then we have a problem. Pakistan has begun to access the global capital markets for both equity and debt, but we cannot rely heavily on these markets as they have limited appetite and are driven by profit opportunities in a stable environment that offers liquidity. Although we are moving towards improved stability and liquidity, we are not there yet.

Gloom and doom aside, it is our belief that there is a commitment on the part of all governments, past and present, to support the growth of our capital markets. Recent changes in regulations support this belief. The psyche of our people implies that the equity market will probably remain larger than the debt market for the foreseeable future. New products will be introduced and the investor base is expected to broaden, especially through the additional of mutual funds which will allow smaller investors a greater degree of protection. The equity market should continue to grow given privatization, the inherent growth in companies' earnings and the changed attitude of issuers. With a debt market that is awakening, economic reforms that are irreversible and consistent between governments, exciting developments are expected in the capital markets.

Source: *DAWN*, Advertising Supplement, 28 December 1994.

Appendix 12.3

Keynes on the stock market

John Maynard Keynes questions the logic of the stock market and how stocks are priced.

A conventional valuation which is established as the outcome of the mass psychology of a large number of ignorant individuals is liable to change violently as the result of a sudden fluctuation of opinion due to factors which do not really make much difference to the prospective yield; since there will be no strong roots of conviction to hold it steady. In abnormal times in particular, when the hypothesis of an indefinite continuance of the existing state of affairs is less plausible than usual even though there are no express grounds to anticipate a definite change, the market will be subject to waves of optimistic and pessimistic sentiment, which are unreasoning and yet in a sense legitimate where no solid basis exists for a reasonable calculation.

But there is one feature in particular which deserves our attention. It might have been supposed that competition between expert professionals, possessing judgment and knowledge beyond that of the average private investor, would correct the vagaries of the ignorant individual left to himself. It happens, however, that the energies and skill of the professional investor and speculator are mainly occupied otherwise. For most of these persons are, in fact, largely concerned, not with making superior long-term forecasts of the probable yield of an investment over its whole life, but with foreseeing changes in the conventional basis of valuation a short time ahead of the general public. They are concerned, not with what an investment is really worth to a man who buys it 'for keeps', but with what the market will value it at, under the influence of mass psychology, three months or a year hence. Moreover, this behaviour is not the outcome of a wrong-headed propensity. It is an inevitable result of an investment market organised along the lines described. For it is not sensible to pay 25 for an investment of which you believe the prospective yield to justify a value of 30, if you also believe that the market will value it at 20 three months hence.

Thus the professional investor is forced to concern himself with the anticipation of impending changes, in the news or in the atmosphere, of the kind by which experience shows that the mass psychology of the market is most influenced. This is the inevitable result of investment markets organised with a view to so-called 'liquidity'. Of the maxims of orthodox finance none, surely, is more anti-social than the fetish of liquidity, the doctrine that it is a positive virtue on the part of investment institutions to concentrate their resources upon the holding of 'liquid' securities. It forgets that there is no such thing as liquidity of investment for the community as a whole. The social object of skilled investment should be to defeat the dark forces of time and ignorance which envelop our future. The actual, private object of the most skilled investment to-day is 'to beat the gun', as the Americans so well express it, to outwit the crowd, and to pass the bad, or depreciating, half-crown to the other fellow.

This battle of wits to anticipate the basis of conventional valuation a few months hence, rather than the prospective yield of an investment over a long term of years, does not even require gulls amongst the public to feed the maws of the professional – it can be played by professionals amongst themselves. Nor is it necessary that anyone should keep his simple faith in the conventional basis of valuation having any genuine long-term validity. For it is, so to speak, a game of Snap, of Old Maid, of Musical Chairs – a pastime in which he is victor who says Snap neither too soon nor too late, who passes the Old Maid to his neighbour before the game is over, who secures a chair for himself when the music stops. These games can be played with zest and enjoyment, though all the players know that it is the Old Maid which is circulating, or that when the music stops some of the players will find themselves unseated.

Or, to change the metaphor slightly, professional investment may be likened to those newspaper competitions in which the competitors have to pick out the six prettiest faces from a hundred photographs, the prize being awarded to the competitor whose choice most nearly corresponds to the average preferences of the competitors as a whole; so that each competitor has to pick, not those faces which he himself finds prettiest, but those which he thinks likeliest to catch the fancy of the other competitors, all of whom are looking at the problem from the same point of view. It is not a case of choosing those which, to the best of one's judgement, are really the prettiest, nor even those which average opinion genuinely thinks the prettiest. We have reached the third degree where we devote our intelligences to anticipating what average opinion expects the average opinion to be. And there are some, I believe, who practise the fourth, fifth and higher degrees.

If the reader interjects that there must surely be large profits to be gained from the other players in the long run by a skilled individual who, unperturbed by the prevailing pastime, continues to purchase investments on the best genuine long-term expectations he can frame, he must be answered, first of all, that there are, indeed, such serious-minded individuals and that it makes a vast difference to an investment market whether or not they predominate in their influence over the game-players. But we must also add that there are several factors which jeopardise the predominance of such individuals in modern investment markets. Investment based on genuine long-term expectation is so difficult to-day as to be scarcely practicable. He who attempts it must surely lead much more laborious days and run greater risks than he who tries to guess better than the crowd how the crowd will behave; and, given equal intelligence, he may make more disastrous mistakes. There is no clear evidence from experience that the investment policy which is socially advantageous coincides with that which is most profitable. It needs *more* intelligence to defeat the forces of time and our ignorance of the future than to beat the gun. Moreover, life is not long enough; – human nature desires quick results, there is a peculiar zest in making money quickly, and remoter gains are discounted by the average man at a very high rate. The game of professional investment is intolerably boring and over-exacting to anyone who is entirely exempt from the gambling instinct; whilst he who has it must pay to this propensity the appropriate toll. Furthermore, an investor who proposes to ignore near-term market fluctuations needs greater resources for safety and must not operate on so large a scale, if at all, with borrowed money – a further reason for the higher return from the pastime to a given stock of intelligence and resources. Finally it is the long-term investor, he who most promotes the public interest, who will in practice come in for most criticism, wherever investment funds are managed by committees or boards or banks. For it is in the essence of his behaviour that he should be eccentric, unconventional and rash in the eyes of average opinion. If he is successful, that will only confirm the general belief in his rashness; and if in the short run he is unsuccessful, which is very likely, he will not receive much mercy. Worldly wisdom teaches that it is better for reputation to fail conventionally than to succeed unconventionally.

So far we have had chiefly in mind the state of confidence of the speculator or speculative investor himself and may have seemed to be tacitly assuming that, if he himself is satisfied with the prospects, he has unlimited command over money at the market rate of interest. This is, of course, not the case. Thus we must also take account of the other facet of the state of confidence, namely, the confidence of the lending institutions towards those who seek to borrow from them, sometimes described as the state of credit. A collapse in the price of equities, which has had disastrous reactions on the marginal efficiency of capital, may have been due to the weakening either of speculative confidence or of the state of credit. But whereas the weakening of either is enough to cause a collapse, recovery requires the revival of *both*. For whilst the weakening of credit is sufficient to bring about a collapse, its strengthening, though a necessary condition of recovery, is not a sufficient condition.

These considerations should not lie beyond the purview of the economist. But they must be relegated to their right perspective. If I may be allowed to appropriate the term *speculation* for the activity of forecasting the psychology of the market, and the term *enterprise* for the activity of forecasting the prospective yield of assets over their whole life, it is by no means always the case that speculation predominates over enterprise. As the organisation of investment markets improves, the risk of the predominance of speculation does, however, increase. In one of the greatest investment markets in the world, namely, New York, the influence of speculation (in the above sense) is enormous. Even outside the field of finance, Americans are apt to be unduly interested in discovering what average opinion believes average opinion to be; and this national weakness finds its nemesis in the stock market. It is rare, one is told, for an American to invest, as many Englishmen still do, 'for income'; and he will not readily purchase an investment except in the hope of capital appreciation. This is only another way of saying that, when he purchases an investment, the American is attaching his hopes, not so much to its prospective yield, as to a favourable change in the conventional basis of valuation, *i.e.* that he is, in the above sense, a speculator. Speculators may do no harm as bubbles on a steady stream of enterprise. But the position is serious when enterprise becomes the bubble on a whirlpool of speculation. When the capital development of a country becomes a by-product of the activities of a casino, the job is likely to be ill-done. The measure of success attained by Wall Street, regarded as an institution of which the proper social purpose is to direct new investment into the most profitable channels in terms of future yield, cannot be claimed as one of the outstanding triumphs of *laissez-faire* capitalism – which is not surprising, if I am right in thinking that the best brains of Wall Street have been in fact directed towards a different object.

These tendencies are a scarcely avoidable outcome of our having successfully organised 'liquid' investment markets. It is usually agreed that casinos should, in the public interest, be inaccessible and expensive. And perhaps the same is true of Stock Exchanges. That the sins of the London Stock Exchange are less than those of Wall Street may be due, not so much to differences in national character, as to the fact that to the average Englishman Throgmorton Street is, compared with Wall Street to the average American, inaccessible and very expensive. The jobber's 'turn', the high brokerage charges and the heavy transfer tax payable to the Exchequer, which attend dealings on the London Stock Exchange, sufficiently diminish the liquidity of the market (although the practice of fortnightly accounts operates the other way) to rule out a large proportion of the transactions characteristic of Wall Street. The introduction of a substantial Government transfer tax on all transactions might prove the most serviceable reform available, with a view to mitigating the predominance of speculation over enterprise in the United States.

The spectacle of modern investment markets has sometimes moved me towards the conclusion that to make the purchase of an investment permanent and indissoluble, like marriage, except by reason of death or other grave cause, might be a useful remedy for our contemporary evils. For this would force the investor to direct his mind to the long-term prospects and to those only. But a little consideration of this expedient brings us up against a dilemma, and shows us how the liquidity of investment markets often facilitates, though it sometimes impedes, the course of new investment. For the fact that each individual investor flatters himself that his commitment is 'liquid' (though this cannot be true for all investors collectively) calms his nerves and makes him much more willing to run a risk. If individual purchases of investments were rendered illiquid, this might seriously impede new investment, so long as *alternative ways* in which to hold his savings are available to the individual. This is the dilemma. So long as it is open to the individual to employ his wealth in hoarding or lending *money*, the alternative of purchasing actual capital assets cannot be rendered sufficiently attractive (especially to the man who does not

manage the capital assets and knows very little about them), except by organising markets wherein these assets can be easily realised for money.

The only radical cure for the crises of confidence which afflict the economic life of the modern world would be to allow the individual no choice between consuming his income and ordering the production of the specific capital-asset which, even though it be on precarious evidence, impresses him as the most promising investment available to him. It might be that, at times when he was more than usually assailed by doubts concerning the future, he would turn in his perplexity towards more consumption and less new investment. But that would avoid the disastrous, cumulative and far-reaching repercussions of its being open to him, when thus assailed by doubts, to spend his income neither on the one nor on the other.

Those who have emphasized the social dangers of the hoarding of money have, of course, had something similar to the above in mind. But they have overlooked the possibility that the phenomenon can occur without any change, or at least any commensurate change, in the hoarding of money.

Source: Keynes, John Maynard, *The General Theory*, Harbinger Books, New York, 1964, pp. 154–61.

Appendix 12.4

Should developing countries encourage stock markets?

Conventional wisdom suggests that all countries must have active equity markets if they are to develop. It is argued that these stock markets will provide scarce capital which can be used for development. However, Professor Ajit Singh questions these assumptions.

Today, however, as a part of a general trend towards liberalization, deregulation, privatization, the diminution of the role of the state and enhancement of that of the market, which for various reasons is sweeping the globe – the North and the South, and what remains of the East as well as the West – an important feature of the development of the financial sector in a large number of developing economies is the very fast growth of stock-markets in these countries. The establishment and expansion of these markets is favoured not just by the Bretton Woods institutions, as one would expect, but also by many heterodox economists as well as those from the centrally planned economies.

The World Bank, particularly through its affiliate the International Finance Corporation (IFC), is actively involved in fostering stock-market development in third world countries and in assisting and encouraging them to open up to foreign portfolio investment. Specifically, the IFC provides technical assistance to a large number of countries on the legal, regulatory and fiscal issues involved, as well as on other aspects of the institutional framework for the development of

these markets. According to Sudweeks, from 1971 to June 1988, 73 countries requested and received capital-market assistance in various forms from the IFC's Capital Markets Department. In 50 of these countries assistance has been provided especially for the development of security markets. Moreover, IFC's pioneering work in establishing the emerging markets Data Base (EMDB), which since 1975 has been analyzing records of a large number of third world companies and providing basic information on many 'emerging'. stock-markets, has been widely acknowledged to be instrumental in stimulating foreign investors' interest in these markets. The IFC in addition has assisted several countries with the launching of the so-called 'country funds' to attract foreign portfolio investment to developing-country stock-markets.

The Bretton Woods institutions justify their encouragement of third world stock-markets not on ideological grounds but on the ground that stock-market expansion is partly a natural progression of the development of a country's financial sector as long-term economic growth proceeds. More importantly, it is argued that the existing financial systems, which in many countries have invariably involved government-directed and often subsidized credit to priority industries or firms, have proved to be unsuccessful. The Development Finance Institutes (DFI) have been the main vehicles for providing long-term finance for industrial development in a number of countries. The DFIs have been facing acute financial difficulties since the economic crisis of the third world began at the end of the 1970s and in the early 1980s. *The World Development Report* for 1989, which focused on the financial sector, reported that in a sample of eighteen industrial DFIs worldwide, on average nearly 50 per cent of their loans (by value) were in arrears, and accumulated arrears were equivalent to 17 per cent of the portfolio value. For three of these institutions, loans accounting for between 70 and 90 per cent of the portfolio values were in arrears. The situation may be worse than the numbers show, because the rescheduling of overdue loans and growing loan portfolios reduce arrears ratios. The Report goes on to observe: The performance of agricultural DFIs has also been poor. Studies show default rates ranging from 30 to 95 per cent for subsidized agricultural credit programmes. In general, the Report argued strongly against the myriad inefficiencies of these DFIs and the bank-based interventionist financial systems; instead, it favoured a restructuring of these systems to make them more 'voluntary', fiscally neutral and to bring them as far as practicable under private ownership ...

... *Essentially, this paper suggests that it is arguable that even in advanced countries with well functioning markets the stock-markets are more likely do more harm than good to the real economy.* The supposed positive contributions of the stock-markets (encouragement of savings, more efficient allocation of investment resources, the discipline of corporate managements through competitive selection in the market for corporate control), ... do not materialize in practice. The market for corporate control encourages large companies to expand through takeovers rather than to seek organic growth which promotes economic development. Moreover, it is not at all clear that the take-over selection process leads to the survival of firms which are efficient at creating real wealth, rather than being simply skilled in financial engineering.

There is evidence as well as strong analytical grounds for believing that these and related negative features of the stock-markets (speculation, lack of long-term investor commitment to corporations, short-termism) may play a significant role in putting the stock-market dominated economies of the United States and the United Kingdom at a competitive disadvantage in relation to countries such as the Federal Republic of Germany and Japan. These unfavourable aspects of the stock-market are likely to be particularly important in third world countries with undeveloped stock-markets and high volatility of share prices.

To the extent that developing countries today have a choice, they should attempt to foster bank-based financial systems more along the lines of the 'follower' countries (Japan, the Federal Republic and France) rather than to establish and encourage stock-markets. Historically, these bank-based systems have a proven record of successfully promoting industrial development in these countries. Moreover, as we have seen earlier, the modern theory of information provides strong theoretical reasons for banks to be on the whole more suitable vehicles for achieving these ends than the stock-market. The ordinary shareholder of a larger corporation has neither the ability nor the incentive to obtain the necessary information (which is costly) to monitor management activities, thus leading him or her to eschew 'commitment' to the organization and to prefer liquidity. The banks, on the other hand, have both the means and the incentive to collect such information and to take a long-term

view of firms' prospects – a perspective which is vital for industrialization in developing economies.

Notwithstanding these extremely important advantages of bank-based financial systems, it would be a mistake not to learn from the experience of the last two decades during which, in many developing countries, such systems have performed far from adequately. In a number of developing countries experiencing a high degree of macro-economic instability bank-based finance has tended to degenerate into inflationary/inefficient finance. Experience suggests the following to be the most serious shortcomings of such systems in the developing-country context:

a) 'crony capitalism', which finances schemes for particular individuals and families with political connections, rather than promoting long-term industrial development;

b) industry–finance links of the bank-based type can in principle, and sometimes in practice, lead to monopolistic positions in product markets and thwart entry by new firms, thereby hindering efficient industrial development;

c) imprudent or inadequate government regulation of banks has sometimes jeopardized the integrity of the financial system as a whole (for example Chile, following financial liberalization in the early 1980s).

Thus, although bank-based systems are much to be preferred in principle to the stock-market-based systems, developing countries should pay particular attention to questions of proper regulation and to the prevention of monopolistic abuse by banks.

However, to be realistic, it must be recognized that stock-markets in developing countries are today a part of the new economic landscape and, notwithstanding their dubious merits in relation to economic development, they are there to stay. The question, therefore, arises how, if at all, can their negative features be contained? The analysis suggests that, from the perspective of economic development, an important general policy principle for the least developed countries should be to attempt to insulate as far as possible the real industrial economy from the influence of the stock-market. In this context, the following kinds of policy proposals require careful consideration by developing-country governments. First, they should examine schemes of taxation to reduce share turnover as was mooted by Keynes and has more recently been proposed by Tobin in relation to transactions on the international currency markets.

Secondly, the developing countries should be seriously concerned about the effects of a prospective market for corporate control. Since stock-markets in these countries are still in their infancy, most of them do not yet have an active market for corporate control (although some take-over bids on the Indian stock-markets have been reported in the most recent period). However, as the stock-markets become more mature and more firmly established, left to itself the development of a corporate control market is an inevitable evolution ... such a market greatly accentuates the negative features of a stock-market for economic development (e.g. by encouraging short-termism). The developing countries should, therefore, if at all possible, adopt the German-Japanese type institutional arrangements to pre-empt the development of a market for corporate control of the kind which exists in the Anglo-Saxon countries. However, if that is not feasible, these countries would be wise to take steps to restrict the operations of the market for corporate control. This may involve, for example, major changes in company law, reducing the role of shareholders and enhancing that of the stakeholders or the government in take-over situations.

Thirdly, to the extent that institutional investors, such as pension funds, are public agencies, which appears to be the case in many developing countries, the governments could use them to maintain more orderly markets. Fourthly, and importantly, the governments should encourage product market competition to discipline corporations rather than rely on the stock-market for this purpose. If a developing country possesses or is able to establish a German-Japanese-type financial system, such discipline would be supplemented by bank-monitoring of corporations.

Reducing the negative aspects of the role of the stock-market would require a full exploration of the policy areas outlined above in relation to the specific circumstances of a particular country. Many of these policy issues are currently subjects of considerable debate in the advanced countries. Their application and analysis in relation to developing-country stock-markets requires a separate paper in its own right.

Source: From Singh, Ajit, 'The Stock Market and Economic Development: Should Developing Countries Encourage Stock Markets?', UNCTAD Discussion Paper No. 49, October 1992, pp. 1, 43–5.

Notes

1. Haque, Nadeemul and Shahid Kardar, 'The Development of Financial Markets in Pakistan', mimeo, 1993, p. 3.
2. For an extensive and comprehensive history of banking in Pakistan, see State Bank of Pakistan, *History of the State Bank of Pakistan, 1948–60*, State Bank of Pakistan, Karachi, 1992; and State Bank of Pakistan, *History of the State Bank of Pakistan, 1961–77*, State Bank of Pakistan, Karachi, 1994. This section and much of this chapter draw extensively from both the *SBP* volumes.
3. State Bank of Pakistan, *History of the State Bank of Pakistan, 1948–60*, State Bank of Pakistan, Karachi, 1992, p. 3.
4. Ibid., p. 10.
5. Ibid., p. 118.
6. Ibid.
7. Ibid., p. 127.
8. Ibid., p. 130.
9. Ibid., pp. 136–9.
10. Ibid., p. 174.
11. State Bank of Pakistan, *History of the State Bank of Pakistan, 1961–77*, State Bank of Pakistan, Karachi, 1994, p. 39.
12. Ibid., p. 40.
13. Ibid., p. 43.
14. Ibid., p. 53.
15. State Bank of Pakistan, op. cit., 1992, p. 160.
16. Ibid., p. 168.
17. Ibid., p. 170.
18. Ibid., p. 187.
19. State Bank of Pakistan, op. cit., 1994, p. 127.
20. Ibid., p. 127.
21. Ibid., p. 129, emphasis added.
22. Ibid., p. 137.
23. Ibid., p. 135.
24. Ibid., p. 143.
25. Meenai, S.A., *Money and Banking in Pakistan*, Oxford University Press, Karachi, 1984, p. 251.
26. National Development Finance Corporation, *Financial Liberalisation Series*, Research Report, Karachi, 1993.
27. Ibid.
28. Haque, Nadeemul and Shahid Kardar, op. cit., 1993, p. 22.

13 Monetary Policy, Savings, and Inflation

Monetary policy is concerned with the regulation of the quantity, cost, and allocation of money and credit in the economy. It is a mechanism that has serious implications for economic development, as it helps determine how and where resources are to be allocated in the different sectors. Monetary policy establishes how much can, and should, be invested and where it should be invested; and by determining the cost of money, monetary policy helps individuals to decide how much they want to save and how much to spend at a particular moment of time. For many economists, inflation is always and everywhere a monetary phenomenon, where excessive monetary growth beyond the rate commensurate with a particular growth rate of the economy will result in inflation. Hence, monetary policy, like fiscal policy, is a key determinant of the course an economy can take.

In Pakistan as elsewhere, by definition, fiscal policy has been the purview of the government, which has determined who it is going to tax, how much tax it is going to impose, and how much and where it intends to spend. Monetary policy in many countries has been kept distant from the direct arena of government, and governments have only established the basic rules and eventual targets of monetary policy. The outcome and consequences of these rules and targets are then left to the market to determine. However, in Pakistan, monetary policy has been a much more government-controlled and influenced tool than in many other countries. Interest rates have been predetermined and strict sectoral credit targets defined, and the market has, until recently, not played an influential role. All this has been changing in the last few years, and the government has begun to allow the market to determine some key variables. This chapter will highlight those changes and will show just how much the market now influences monetary policy and where this is all leading to. Figure 13.1 provides a chronology of reforms in the financial sector since 1990.

Pakistan's savings rate has always been very low and attempts at increasing it have always failed. This chapter will try to examine the reasons why the savings rate is so low and what, if anything, can and should be done to increase that rate. Is inflation always and everywhere a monetary phenomenon? What does the evidence from Pakistan suggest? With double-digit inflation now recurring on a regular basis, this chapter will assess the possible reasons for high inflation, and examine some of the theories presented by researchers which may help explain why the inflation rate has been rising.

13.1 Monetary Policy and Monetary Management in Pakistan[1]

From 1991 until the time of writing (June 1997) the financial sector has been in the throes of a major transformation. Much, in fact almost all, of the pre-1991 measures that constituted monetary policy and the way monetary matters were managed have now been replaced by a different regime of management and policy. While much has already changed, many more changes are anticipated in the next few years, the direction and nature of which seem to have been well established.

The impetus to the drastic reforms in the financial sector, like much else in Pakistan in recent years, is the World Bank and the IMF. Just as the structural adjustment programmes (SAPs) since 1988 have dramatically transformed the nature of Pakistan's economy, especially at a macro level, similar reforms under the Financial Sector Adjustment Loan (FSAL) and those under the various structural adjustment programmes have dramatically transformed the nature of Pakistan's financial, fiscal, and monetary sectors. Essentially, there has been a marked transformation in the way monetary policy is conducted, from one that used to be heavily dependent on direct (government) involvement and controls, to one that has now increasingly become based on indirect (market-based) methods. This has been done, as one observer argues, 'at the urging of the IMF which now is the architect of our economic, fiscal and monetary policies. The IMF has been recommending for some years now a shift to market based management of monetary policy, as it views management through quantitative methods with distaste; these, in its judgement, result in inefficiency and the misallocation of resources.'[2] Before we analyse the nature of these changes, we need to look briefly at the way monetary policy was managed in the pre-1991 period.

Before the 1991 financial sector reforms, the government's debt management programme was considered to be a 'loosely managed, highly unorganized system of tap and ad hoc treasury bills, and readily refinanced non-marketable long term papers'.[3] In 1972, when the banking sector reforms were undertaken, a National Credit Consultative Council (NCCC) was established to determine the distribution of credit in the economy and to improve and make credit available to those areas that had, prior to the nationalization of banks, not been

---

Figure 13.1
Financial sector reforms, 1990–1995

Dec. 1990	Amendment made in the banks (Nationalization) Act 1974, to permit the establishment of banks in the private sector.
19 Dec. 1990	State Bank of Pakistan invites applications for Primary Dealers of Government securities.
22 Jan. 1991	Privatization Commission established.
26 Feb. 1991	'On-tap' issuance of three-month Treasury Bills stopped, stage set for debt auctioning.
03 Mar. 1991	Multinational banks and corporations allowed to invest in Treasury Bills.
13 Mar. 1991	Multinational banks and corporations allowed to invest in Federal Investment Bonds (FIBs).
25 Mar. 1991	Issuance of on-tap FIBs curtailed. Rediscounting of GTDRs (all maturities) raised to 12%.
08 Apr. 1991	Management of Muslim Commercial Bank handed over to the private sector.
26 Mar. 1991	Banks informed that FIBs count towards statutory liquidity requirements.
02 Apr. 1991	First FIB auction.
16 May 1991	SBP directive that henceforth banks will not hold more than 15% of their demand and time liabilities in paper of more than one year maturity. Banks to comply by 15 August.
15 Aug. 1991	SBP directs banks to give extra information in their weekly returns regarding holdings of government paper – specifically, the amount of paper (with terms to maturity) held by each bank.
26 Aug. 1991	Permission granted to ten new banks in the private sector. Banking Companies Ordinance 1962 amended to extend supervisory jurisdiction of SBP to 'non-bank financial institutions'.
10 Sept. 1991	Allied Bank Limited handed over to private sector management (buy-out by employees).
10 Oct. 1991	Discount rate raised to 13%. Concessionary financing schemes pared down, with termination of cotton financing.
09 June 1992	Prudential regulations amended, with compliance mandatory, with effect from 1 July 1992.
01 Feb. 1992	SBP discontinues rediscounting facility and replaces it with a three-day repo window. It also enhances rate to 14%. SBP proposes non-pecuniary cost on repo window access.
15 Mar. 1992	Foreign Currency Bearer Certificates to go on sale in Pakistan. FCBCs to be offered for sale abroad from 23 March 1992.
15 Apr. 1992	SBP allows FIB repo facility at 1% over coupon of security repoed. Facility for convenience of NCBs.
20 May 1992	SBP supervision of NBFIs to start with effect from 1 July 1992.
14 July 1992	Credit ceiling discontinued with effect from 1 August 1992. Credit–deposit ratio introduced. Rates of return structure rationalized and banks freed to offer loans to all feasible projects subject only to a ceiling of 65% of their deposits.
02 Aug. 1992	Liquid asset requirements of scheduled banks raised from 35% to 40% with effect from 13 August 1992. Cash reserve ratio remains unchanged.
09 Dec. 1992	Statutory liquidity ratio raised to 45% with effect from 19 December 1992. Nationalized commercial banks required to include details of written-off loans (those greater than RS0.5 million) in balance sheets.
29 Aug. 1993	List of loan defaulters published.
21 Sept. 1993	Banks, DFIs asked to provide details of bad debts and loans written off.
27 Oct. 1993	SBP lowers statutory liquidity ratio from 45% to 35%.
04 Dec. 1993	Banks and financial institutions asked to consult Credit Information Bureau of State Bank of Pakistan prior to financial accommodation of RS0.5 million or above.

Figure 13.1 continued

01 Mar. 1994	Maximum cap on lending rates reduced from 22% to 19%. Rates for concessional loans raised from 11% to 12%. Statutory liquidity ratio further reduced from 35% to 30%.
01 July 1994	Rupee made convertible on current account.
	State Bank declines to provide forward cover for foreign exchange transactions and invites commercial banks to take over this function.
	No free float for rupee.
05 July 1994	Nostro limits for banks doubled.
03 Nov. 1994	Interest rate cap reduced from 19% to 17.5%. Concessional finance rates raised from 12% to 13%.
26 Dec. 1994	Changes in CDR (goes up from 31.5% to 34%). Restriction on FIB holdings (restricted to higher of (a) current holdings and (b) 15% of deposits). SBP to set cut-offs for Govt Paper auctions (instead of Ministry of Finance).
Jan. 1995	Open market operations become major instrument of market-based monetary management.

---

given appropriate amounts of credit. The NCCC became the government's main, if not the only, source of managing monetary policy. An Annual Credit Plan was (and still is – see Box 13.1) devised each year, according to which the government used to determine the extent of monetary expansion for the year, and allocated credit to the various sectors of the economy. All rates of return were administered by the government and all institutions and players in the money market and in the rest of the economy had to accept the given rates and amounts of monetary expansion and credit.

A captive market for Treasury Bills existed on 'tap' (on demand) and these bills were issued on an ad hoc basis as and when the government required. Commercial banks, most of which were nationalized and government owned – hence

---

BOX 13.1

The Annual Credit Plan and monetary policy

Aftab Ahmad Khan explains how monetary expansion is determined each year.

In Pakistan the framework of regulatory monetary policy is provided by the Annual Credit Plan which is recommended by the National Credit Consultative Council (NCCC), a body set up under the aegis of the State Bank of Pakistan with the following functions: (i) to review the overall credit situation in the country with specific reference to its region-wise and sector-wise distribution and concentration; (ii) to make recommendations to the government with regard to monetary and credit expansion within safe limits and distribution of credit among various sectors and regions in conformity with the socioeconomic objectives and priorities and targets set out in the Annual Plan; (iii) to set out specific targets for (a) agricultural loans, and (b) small loans to be provided by commercial banks; and (iv) to periodically review the progress made in the implementation of its recommendations and, if necessary, modify or amend its previous recommendations in the light of the emerging situation.

In determining the safe limits of monetary expansion during a particular year, NCCC takes into account: (i) projected growth rate of Gross Domestic Product (GDP) for the year; (ii) the estimated rate of monetization of the economy; (iii) likely changes in the demand for cash balances; (iv) likely changes in prices including those originating in the external sector; and (v) expected changes in net foreign assets. The State Bank, after the legislation passed in February 1994, has been endowed with exclusive powers to regulate the monetary and banking system. It now provides quantitative guidelines about the safe limits of government borrowing and promptly advises the government when these limits are exceeded. It also reminds the provincial governments to stay within the limits of their ways and means advances. Notwithstanding these additional powers, the State Bank cannot pursue a sound monetary policy without the exercise of fiscal responsibility by the Government. Fiscal operations of the government are a dominant factor in determining the monetary outcome in the country. It is not only through borrowing from the banking system for budgetary support that government impacts on money supply but also indirectly through the utilization of privatization proceeds, short term borrowings from abroad and credit creation for specialized schemes. Pakistan's experience indicates that large fiscal deficits lead to excessive monetary expansion and often result in crowding out the private sector. In such situations the room for manoeuvre for the central bank tends to be restricted to attempting to offset its inflationary impact by limiting the secondary expansion of credit. Fiscal and monetary policies have not only to be appropriate but mutually supportive.

Source: Khan, Aftab Ahmad, 'Recent Monetary Trends and Revised Credit Plan', *The News*, Business and Finance Review, 16 March 1996.

the 'captive' market – were required to use their liquidity to buy these bills at fixed rates of return. Unlike in the period after 1991, the bills were redeemable at any time, making this aspect of the money market 'inflexible and unstructured'.[4] Moreover, the government utilized the National Savings Schemes to raise its debt from instruments that had high rates of return, causing funds to be moved out of the financial sector to these savings schemes.

The main mechanisms of monetary policy and management between 1972 and 1991 were the control of the volume, cost, and allocation of credit

> through the techniques of credit budgeting and credit ceilings rather than having recourse to traditional indirect methods of control, like changes in the bank rate and open market operations. Aside from global and sectoral credit ceilings, the instruments used by this policy of directed credit control included budget subsidies, credit floors, refinancing facilities, together with the imposition of cash reserves and liquidity requirements.[5]

The fiscal requirements of the government, as elaborated in the budget each year, used to determine how the government would manage its credit and debt policy for the year. The government used to borrow from the State Bank of Pakistan by selling its ad hoc (on tap) Treasury Bills at a rate of return of 0.5 per cent per annum. Commercial banks 'had to invest at least 30 per cent of their demand and time deposits in GOP [Government of Pakistan] paper. The paper that they invested in was also available "on tap" and carried a low rate of return of 6 per cent per annum.'[6]

If the role and objective of monetary policy is to maintain a relatively stable economic environment such that investment and growth take place at a regular pace, and there is price stability, it would be fair to say that the *dirigiste* policies prior to 1991 worked fairly well. The government had pursued an economic growth strategy by controlling interest rates, directing credit to priority sectors, and obtaining cheap credit from the banking sector for budgetary support. The growth rate in GDP averaged 4.8 per cent annually during the 1970s, rising to 6.5 per cent across the 1980s. The inflation rate was more than 12 per cent on average in the 1970s, but was due not to monetary mismanagement or excessive monetary expansion, but largely to factors not in the control of the government, such as the quadrupling of the oil price and numerous crop failures (see Chapter 7 on the Bhutto period). During the 1980s, the inflation rate – despite very high budget deficits, often in excess of 8 per cent of GDP – remained quite low, at an annual average of only 7.3 per cent. Nevertheless, conventional wisdom in the 1990s has gone out of its way to deride almost all the policies prior to the reforms, and the financial sector and monetary policy are no exceptions (see Chapters 14 and 15).

Ashfaque Hasan Khan, in particular, has been one of the harshest critics of government financial and monetary policy as it existed prior to the financial sector reforms. He has also been one of the leaders of the movement to reform the financial sector much further. About the structure of the financial sector and the way it functioned between 1972 and 1991, he writes:

> Prior to undertaking financial sector reforms the hallmark of Pakistan's financial sector has been the direct controls on interest rate movements, domestic credit controls (bank specific credit ceilings and selective credit allocations), high reserve requirements, segmented financial markets, the absence of well-developed securities markets, underdeveloped banking system, and commercial banks serving as captive institutions. In particular, the policies of imposing ceilings on interest rates accompanied by directed and rational allocation of credit to 'priority' sectors at low rates have led to widespread 'financial repression' in Pakistan. These policies are seen to impede financial 'deepening' which, in turn, weakens an important set of impulses to faster economic growth.[7]

Ashfaque Khan[8] and Javed Mahmood identify the following adverse effects of the policies that were adopted.

1 There was an excess liquidity problem as banks, while accepting as many deposits as came their way, were not able to lend them due to the credit ceilings imposed on them. Of the amount that banks lent, a large proportion went in the form of directed credit to subsidized sectors at unprofitable, low rates. Thirty per cent of the deposit base of banks was to be invested in low-yielding government debt as part of the liquidity ratio and a minimum of 5 per cent was to be kept in the form of a cash reserve requirement, which earned no interest. 'Given these "captive" sources of funds, the government could repress the interest rates payable on its borrowing from the commercial banks. Thus, the combination of credit ceilings and low return on government debt reduced the returns on asset portfolios. Furthermore, after meeting the credit ceilings a certain proportion of funds remained unutilized and were not earning any return which led to the emergence of an excess liquidity problem. Consequently the banks were discouraged to mobilize domestic savings through their vast network of branches.'[9]

2 Non-performing loans on political and uneconomic grounds affected the profitability of commercial (mainly nationalized) banks as they could not offer a high rate of return on deposits, hence discouraging these deposits (see Chapter 12).

3 Non-bank financial institutions (NBFIs), which were not under the supervision of the SBP, were able to mobilize a larger amount of financial savings than banks and were also able to override the credit ceilings, thus undermining the SBP's targets and plans.

4 Since interest rates on government savings instruments were higher than that offered by commercial banks, 'segmentation' of the financial market took place. This disparity also created an anomaly in the interest rate structure.

5 A disintermediation of the financial sector took place due to 4 above, as investors and savers shifted from banks to the higher-interest National Savings Schemes.

6 The government of Pakistan's debt structure was of a short-term maturity, requiring regular outflows and heavy refunding (see Chapter 10).

7 As a result of the above structure, the government did not have much control over the issuance of debt, since new issues were mainly demand driven. Moreover, since the Treasury Bills were redeemable at any time, the debt management programme became inflexible and unstructured.

8 'There was a lack of cash management control deriving from the encashments feature on government of Pakistan debt. This led to an unpredictable and volatile pattern of encashment which complicated cash forecasting and reduced the government's ability to manage this cash balances.'[10]

It was this old structure with its numerous problems and consequences that came under attack by the IMF and the World Bank. These two organizations suggested a drastic restructuring and reorientation of the financial system, to replace it with a more market-oriented structure. The reforms were to:

> (i) remove distortions and segmentation of the financial markets by creating a homogeneous market for government debt instruments in which all individuals and institutions can participate; (ii) switch from an administered interest rate setting to market based interest rate determination by indicating a regular auction programme of government debt; (iii) allocate credit in response to market forces by gradually eliminating the directed credit schemes and abolishing the subsidized credit schemes; (iv) create and encourage the development of secondary market for government securities – absolutely essential for the success for the auction programme of government debt; (v) strengthen the health and competitiveness of the banking system by recapitalizing and restructuring the nationalized commercial banks, increasing their autonomy and accountability and allowing private banks to enter the market; and (vi) improve prudential regulations and supervision of all financial institutions.[11]

One of the earlier measures taken as part of the reforms was the discontinuation of the system of credit ceilings after 1 July 1992. Bank credit was then regulated by changes in the bank rate and the liquidity ratio, by setting a credit–deposit ratio (CDR) – see below – by setting maximum and minimum lending rates, and most importantly, by a system of open market operations.

One of the principal aims of the government on the advice of the IMF and World Bank has been to establish a market-determined money market, where instruments in primary and secondary markets are traded so as to regulate money, credit, and the interest rate (see Box 13.2). The government started the auctioning of Treasury Bills in April 1988, but the amounts were very small and commercial banks with excess liquidity were ready buyers of the bills. The programme did not really have much of an impact on any of the important variables in the money market. With a very low rate of return on Treasury Bills not reflecting the market rate, and a higher return on National Savings Scheme instruments, it is not surprising that there were no takers of the Treasury Bills.

In 1991 the government started a full-fledged system of auctioning of government debt and allowed the rate of return on Treasury Bills to rise from the unrealistic 6 per cent where it was earlier, to a more realistic 13 per cent. Other, longer-term instruments in the shape of Federal Investment Bonds (FIBs) with a maturity of three, five, and ten years were introduced (see Box 13.3). With the removal of the credit ceilings and with higher rates of return, banks became interested in these instruments. They also began to encourage deposits as their ability to lend and invest was now dependent on the amount of deposits they were able to generate. Appendix 13.1 describes the main features of the money market in Pakistan.

From the initial attempts of auctioning Treasury Bills in 1991 onwards, the State Bank of Pakistan now feels that the auctioning of Treasury Bills is fully integrated with open market operations. From January 1995, according to the State Bank 'open market operations became the major instrument of market based monetary management in the context of a liberal CDR'.[12] Instead of regulating the volume of money through the allocation of credit and the manipulation and limitation on how much banks should lend, the State Bank has gradually moved towards an increasing use of the market mechanism. The direction is one in which open market buying and selling of government securities, along with the determination of the interest rate, becomes the main instrument of monetary policy. Henceforth, the federal

---

BOX 13.2

The primary and secondary markets

The financial sector is composed of the money market and capital markets, with primary and secondary dealers.

The *primary market* consists of investment banks, brokers, dealers, the State Bank of Pakistan, commercial banks and individual investors who conduct sales of new issues. The *secondary market* has brokers, dealers and banks which buy the securities and then sell them to investors. The *secondary market* is meant to provide liquidity and a pool of investors to whom new issues are re-sold.

Both markets are mutually reinforcing, as the primary market is necessary to provide new issues of securities, and the secondary market is essential for issues to be sold and to provide liquidity to the holders of the securities.

BOX 13.3
Money market instruments

The following extract describes the nature of two money market instruments: Treasury Bills and Federal Investment Bonds.

Treasury Bills

More familiarly known as T. Bills, these are negotiable, non-interest bearing securities, with an original maturity of one year or less. In Pakistan, presently, the maturity is six months. They are issued by the SBP with a face value of Rs100 and in minimum denominations of Rs1000 with multiples thereafter. SBP now also can hold the bills in Book Entry Form known as the Subsidiary General Ledger Account (SGLA).

The SBP invites bids for the sale of treasury bills every fortnight. Bidders are required to indicate a price at which they will buy the bills along with the quantity wanted. The auction is open to individuals, institutions and corporations including banks and DFIs and the bids must be made to the SBP through one of the primary dealers. Successful bidders are required to deposit the requisite amount, for the settlement of the accepted tender, through their primary dealers. Scheduled commercial banks are allowed to invest in treasury bills and these may be counted towards their liquid asset requirements. T. Bills can be held in the form of stock certificates, or as uncertificated bonds at the SBP. Technically, T. Bills can also be traded on the stock exchange. T. Bills are always issued at a discount from face value, and the amount of the discounts is determined in T. Bills auctions held by the SBP each time it issues new bills. At maturity, bills are redeemed by SBP for full face value. The investors thus earn a return because they receive more for the bills at maturity than they paid for them at issue. This return is treated as ordinary interest income and is taxable.

Federal Investment Bonds

These bonds are negotiable long term Government of Pakistan debt instruments of 3, 5 and 10 year maturities. The purpose of their introduction was three-fold. Firstly, it was to provide an outlet for provident funds which were not allowed to invest in Defence Savings Scheme and National Savings Certificates. Secondly, it would establish a yield curve for Government of Pakistan debt which would reflect market risks, and, thirdly, it would provide the Government of Pakistan with a sizeable stock of permanent debt. FIBs pay 13, 14 and 15% p.a. on bills maturing in 3, 5 and 10 years, respectively. Since returns on FIBs are taxable, this sort of rate structure reduces the net debt servicing burden to the Government of Pakistan without sharply reducing the posted rate of return. The rate structure also allows provident funds to be invested in securities with returns similar to those from NSS [National Saving Schemes] and DSC [Defence Saving Certificates], as well as establishes a positively sloped yield curve which should encourage the term extension of debt. FIBs are auctioned every two months. These bills are issued at a face value of Rs100 and in multiples of Rs1000. As in the case of T. Bills, investors are required to quote a price at which they will be willing to buy the bonds. Separate bids are made for the purchase of bonds of different maturities and prices. (Upon the introduction of FIBs, SBP did not accept tenders at a discount. The banks, especially the NCBs, were quite willing to accept a cut in their rates of return since FIBs presented an excellent opportunity through which they could mop up their excess liquidity. Shortly after, SBP imposed a maximum limit upon holdings of FIBs regarding the NCBs. This resulted in subsequent bids being placed at a discount or at par). Profit on FIBs is paid bi-annually from the date of issue, and a withholding tax is levied on any profits which might accrue from such an investment. Nevertheless, profits earned on investment in FIBs by charitable trusts are exempt from payment of income tax. FIBs can also be traded on the stock exchange.

Source: Mahmood, Javed, 'Money Markets in Pakistan: Concepts, Instruments and Operations', *Journal of the Institute of Bankers in Pakistan*, vol. 58, no. 1, 1992, pp. 39–42.

government is supposed to raise funds at the market rates of return through the auctioning of government securities. See Appendix 13.2 for a good account of the changes implemented.

Another important measure taken under the aegis of the reforms was the removal of the maximum lending rate which banks used to charge their clients. Before 1995, the maximum lending rate had been imposed by the State Bank of Pakistan and ranged between 17.5 and 22 per cent between 1993 and 1995. The State Bank decided not to impose any limit and removed the cap entirely in March 1995. This step is considered to be an important move towards making monetary and credit policy more market oriented as commercial banks can now charge any rate they want and their clients agree to. The State Bank, however, still controls the lending rate for concessionary finance for exports, the sale and purchase of locally manufactured machinery, and agricultural loans to small farmers. In all other areas, each bank can charge its own lending rate. The rationale for this move on the part of the State Bank, as it has been with almost all steps since 1992, is to allow the rate of return to be determined by the supply and demand of loanable funds. However, see the very interesting excerpt from the paper by Joseph Sliglitz and Andrew Weiss, on credit and the law of supply and demand (Box 13.4) and Box 13.5.

As has been shown above, the system of credit ceilings was discontinued after July 1992 and replaced by a credit–deposit ratio (CDR), a ratio that the government has changed and liberalized over time. While the government claimed that this was an important step towards indirect methods, Ashfaque Khan argues correctly that 'qualitatively, a shift from credit ceilings to CDR does not make any difference, with the exception that the extension of credit is now linked with the deposit mobilization efforts of the commercial banks'.[13] The

BOX 13.4
Credit and the law of supply and demand

With the growing desire to let the market determine the price for credit, i.e. the interest rate, it is believed that the forces of supply and demand would allocate credit at an appropriate price. However, a path-breaking article by Joseph Sliglitz and Andrew Weiss argues that, despite excess supply or demand for credit, the interest rate will not automatically fall/rise to clear the market, and credit may in fact be rationed.

Why is credit rationed? Perhaps the most basic tenet of economics is that market equilibrium entails supply equalling demand; that if demand should exceed supply, prices will rise, decreasing demand and/or increasing supply until demand and supply are equated at the new equilibrium price. So if prices do their job, rationing should not exist. However, credit rationing and unemployment do in fact. They seem to imply an excess demand for loanable funds or an excess supply of workers.

One method of 'explaining' these conditions associates them with short- or long-term disequilibrium. In the short term they are viewed as *temporary disequilibrium* phenomena; that is, the economy has incurred an exogenous shock, and for reasons not fully explained, there is some stickiness in the prices of labor or capital (wages and interest rates) so that there is a transitional period during which rationing of jobs or credit occurs. On the other hand, long-term unemployment (above some 'natural rate') or credit rationing is explained by governmental constraints such as usury laws or minimum wage legislation.

In *equilibrium* a loan market may be characterized by credit rationing. Banks making loans are concerned about the interest rate they receive on the loan, and the riskiness of the loan. However, the interest rate a bank charges may itself affect the riskiness of the pool of loans by either: 1) sorting potential borrowers (the adverse selection effect); or 2) affecting the actions of borrowers (the incentive effect). Both effects derive directly from the residual imperfect information which is present in loan markets after banks have evaluated loan applications. When the price (interest rate) affects the nature of the transaction, it may not also clear the market.

The adverse selection aspect of interest rates is a consequence of different borrowers having different probabilities of repaying their loan. The expected return to the bank obviously depends on the probability of repayment, so the bank would like to be able to identify borrowers who are more likely to repay. It is difficult to identify 'good borrowers', and to do so requires the bank to use a variety of *screening devices*. The interest rate which an individual is willing to pay may act as one such screening device: those who are willing to pay high interest rates may, on average, be worse risks; they are willing to borrow at high interest rates because they perceive their probability of repaying the loan to be low. As the interest rate rises, the average 'riskiness' of those who borrow increases, possibly lowering the bank's profits.

Similarly, as the interest rate and other terms of the contract change, the behavior of the borrower is likely to change. For instance, raising the interest rate decreases the return on projects which succeed. We show that higher interest rates induce firms to undertake projects with lower probabilities of success but higher payoffs when successful.

In a world with perfect and costless information, the bank would stipulate precisely all the actions which the borrower could undertake (which might affect the return to the loan). However, the bank is not able to directly control all the actions of the borrower; therefore, it will formulate the terms of the loan contract in a manner designed to induce the borrower to take actions which are in the interest of the bank, as well as to attract low-risk borrowers.

For both these reasons, the expected return by the bank may increase less rapidly than the interest rate; and, beyond a point, may actually decrease.

But the interest rate is not the only term of the contract which is important. The amount of the loan, and the amount of collateral or equity the bank demands of loan applicants, will also affect both the behavior of borrowers and the distribution of borrowers. We show that increasing the collateral requirements of lenders (beyond some point) may decrease the returns to the bank, by either decreasing the average degree of risk aversion of the pool of borrowers; or in a multiperiod model inducing individual investors to undertake riskier projects.

Consequently, it may not be profitable to raise the interest rate or collateral requirements when a bank has an excess demand for credit; instead, banks deny loans to borrowers who are observationally indistinguishable from those who receive loans.

It is not our argument that credit rationing will always characterize capital markets, but rather that it may occur under not implausible assumptions concerning borrower and lender behavior …

We reserve the term credit rationing for circumstances in which either (a) among loan applicants who appear to be identical some receive a loan and others do not, and the rejected applications would not receive a loan even if they offered to pay a higher interest rate; or (b) there are identifiable groups of individuals in the population who, with a given supply of credit, are unable to obtain loans at any interest rate, even though with a larger supply of credit, they would.

The Law of Supply and Demand is not in fact a law, nor should it be viewed as an assumption needed for competitive analysis. It is rather a result generated by the underlying assumptions that prices have neither sorting nor incentive effects. The usual result of economic theorizing: that prices clear markets, is model specific and is not a general property of markets – unemployment and credit rationing are not phantasms.

Source: Sliglitz, J.E. and Andrew Weiss, 'Credit Rationing in Markets with Imperfect Information', *American Economic Review*, June 1981.

BOX 13.5

Financial liberalization and some possible consequences

The United Nations Economic and Social Commission for Asia and the Pacific (UNESCAP) has criticized the imposition of structural adjustment programmes in the region.

Increased reliance on the market mechanism has not led to a complete resolution of market failures in the developing countries, their zeal for financial sector reforms notwithstanding, remarks the United Nations Economic and Social Commission for Asia and the Pacific (UNESCAP) in its recent report.

Such zeal might land them in greater macroeconomic instability particularly through the opening up of capital markets, UNESCAP has warned, while characterizing these as the 'new battlegrounds for savings' where market players 'will become a new class of stateless legislators' and with the power of the purse, they will check governments' ability to tax, spend, borrow or depreciate their debts through inflation.

The degree to which the financial sector in a country actually performs its functions is directly related to its level of development. Giving an example of market failure, the report points out that banking industry in the Third World is generally characterized by oligopolistic structure. Thus, for example, the share of the four largest banks in the total assets of the banking system was as high as 60 to 65% in 1987 in Indonesia, Malaysia, Taiwan and Thailand.

While discussing motivations behind designed and directed credit programmes, controlled interests rates etc., the UN agency recalls that the existing or emerging banking and financial institutions in the private sector catered mostly for the needs of the urban sector, whereas most of economies of the region were traditionally rural-agricultural with small urban sectors. (In Pakistan, a big foreign bank with newly established branches in Pakistan persistently refuses to accept agricultural assets as collateral and encourages opening of foreign currency accounts by offering credit at the concessional rate of 14%!) Hence the establishment of specialized financial institutions and, in some cases, the nationalization of commercial banks.

As the financial sector is closely interrelated with the real economy of a country (and with the conduct of its monetary and fiscal policies), the report has stressed, 'its reform should ultimately have a positive impact on the real economy influencing, inter alia, the growth and structure of production and of trade'.

The mobilization and allocation of savings through the financial systems are intermediate processes: Their role is ideally to keep the costs of borrowing financial resources low while encouraging, or at least not discouraging, savings.

It is contended that this balancing act is best performed through a competitive market mechanism. However, the report argues, this mechanism 'has limitations' as market failures are not unusual in the finance area.

Apart from this, it adds, 'some new concerns have arisen connected with increased inherent instability, more demanding forms of transparency, accountability and supervision and a more indirect and difficult conduct of monetary and exchange rate policies'.

Citing 'contradictory experiences' of Japan, Korea, China as well as South Asian countries, it wonders whether financial liberalization 'is either a necessary or sufficient condition for successful economic growth and development'. Rather the experiences of the countries that have undertaken financial reforms show that a stable macroeconomic environment is an essential condition for the reforms to function, as 'reforms carried out against an unstable macroeconomic background can make that instability worse'.

A liberalized system may lead to a socially unacceptable distribution of credit. Disadvantaged groups may not have access to credits through regular channels for the following reasons: (a) Remote physical location; (b) Rules on collateral which they cannot meet; (c) The small amount of credit they apply for being inefficient for banks to handle; or (d) Interest rates beyond their means.

These constraints have direct implications for the achievement of social goals and for income distribution, UNESCAP points out.

One consequence of a more market-based system is an increased exposure to various forms of instability. For example, the new easier entry for financial institutions, including banks, provided for in the liberalization process can lead to a proliferation of financial institutions. They may accumulate unbalanced portfolios of assets and liabilities, an unsustainable set of non-performing loans and so may collapse – as in the Philippines.

Then there is the instability generated through the capital markets. These markets are, however, well known for booms and busts largely unrelated to market fundamentals. Such movements are often caused by speculative runs and recently have tended to be exaggerated by the activities of investment funds which make decisions based on computer programme signals.

In Thailand, for example, the sharp decline in December 1994 was imputed to have been started by sales by foreign institutional investors but exaggerated by sales by local funds.

UNESCAP has, in this context, drawn the member countries' attention to two issues of very grave nature:

(a) Increasing recourse to currency substitution, whereby the debts and savings in local currency in some developing countries are being replaced by debts and savings in foreign currency. This reduces the control of a Government on its own money supply and the effectiveness of any changes it tries to induce; and

(b) How much of the expanded activity on stock markets actually relates to new physical investment, rather than a churning of funds or a refinancing of existing debts.

'While this may be a temporary phenomenon as enterprises and investors adapt to their new freedom and expanded menu of opportunities, it does call into question the impact of financial reforms on the performance of the real economy and the need to encourage direct foreign investment when possible,' the report remarks.

In the process of globalization of financial sectors, it further observes that the degrees of freedom of smaller countries to make independent policy decisions are becoming severely restricted as both domestic and foreign concerns will react quickly to the signals given. Moreover, it adds, changing circumstances or policies of the major economies can create large reactions in small economies irrespective of their own policies and position.

Source: *DAWN*, 21 May 1995.

CDR was not applicable to a number of sectors related to the government's directed credit programme, and moreover, it applied only to commercial banks and not to NBFIs. Ashfaque Khan considered the shift from credit ceilings to CDR to be 'not in the spirit of financial liberalization, and therefore needs to be gradually phased out'.[14] The credit deposit ratio was subsequently abolished on 30 September 1995.

The abolition of the CDR was another important step on the road towards a fully market-based structure of credit availability in the economy. According to one analyst, by taking this measure, the 'State Bank of Pakistan has made a decisive beginning towards lessening its dependence on quantitative credit controls and placing reliance on market based instruments of monetary policy. [The] abolishment ... will release an additional large bulk of amount for lending to the private sector ...'.[15] Instead of regulating the volume of money through, amongst other mechanisms, the CDR, the State Bank will, in the future, have to make more use of the market mechanism. As far as commercial banks are concerned, they will (at least technically) be allowed to invest their entire portfolio after allowing for the liquidity ratio and other reserve requirements imposed by the State Bank. This measure should inject a large amount of credit into the market, possibly (if the market is allowed to function) having a downward impact on the interest rate structure. While a lower rate of interest may have positive impacts on loans and investment, it may also result in an excessive expansion of credit, possibly affecting inflation.

A large number of reforms have taken place in the financial sector since 1992 and include the opening up of the banking sector to the private sector; the decontrol of interest rates from government intervention; much greater reliance on market forces to determine monetary policy; an improvement in the quality of financial intermediation and an expansion of the financial sector; and an increase in financial institutions. The reforms have helped banks to increase their profits, and a great deal of financial deepening has also taken place. Nevertheless, there are at least two areas where expected reforms have not taken place. Interest rates, for all practical purposes, are still controlled by the government, and a secondary market, supposedly a key factor in a well-functioning, market-oriented money market, has not developed.

Although the auctioning system for Treasury Bills and FIBs has come a long way since its inception in 1988 and a primary market for government debt has developed, the lack of a well-functioning secondary market has been a cause for concern. Since Treasury Bills and FIBs are non-redeemable before maturity, the secondary market should provide a market-based avenue of liquidity for holders of these government securities. Moreover, 'if the period between the subsequent primary auctions is long enough, the secondary market also provides a channel through which the buyers can have access to securities at all times. In other words, the secondary market enables investors to exchange securities for cash at any time they wish.'[16]

Ashfaque Khan[17] and Aftab Ahmad Khan[18] identify a number of reasons why the secondary market has not developed:

1 A lack of trust between financial institutions and the Ministry of Finance. The Ministry of Finance (MOF), acting on behalf of the State Bank, 'is perceived to be fixing prices of securities in an arbitrary fashion in order to keep debt servicing costs low, thereby hindering the functioning of the markets, whereby the MOF suspects that Primary Dealers are colluding and "fixing" the interest rates'.[19]

2 The government has taken arbitrary and inconsistent actions in accepting and rejecting bids, and it is believed that fiscal considerations, rather than monetary policy, have been determining the debt management strategy.

3 There are a few very large and a number of small players in the secondary market, who trade in a limited number of securities.

4 Other government paper, which is vastly superior to Treasury Bills and FIBs, in terms of rate of return and tax exemptions, has reduced the attractiveness of the latter two, and hence of the secondary market.

Banks are the main holders of Treasury Bills and FIBs (see Table 13.1) for the following reasons:

> Firstly, to fulfil the statutory requirements under the Banking Companies Rules to keep in their own portfolio Approved Government Securities for maintaining the Statutory Liquidity Ratio which is at present 35 per cent of demand and time liabilities of each banking company. Secondly, to earn a regular interest income on their investment in these two securities which accrue to them after every six months. Thirdly, to raise short-term funds against their T-Bills and FIBs holdings under Repo Contract from other Approved Dealers and also sometimes from their non-bank clients. Fourthly, when the funds are not available in Inter-bank Call Money Market and Repo Market, the banks avail cash accommodation against their auctioned securities holdings from SBP under the prescribed 3-Days Repo Facility.[20]

The rate of return structure is as yet not truly reflective of market conditions. Directed and concessionary credit still form a considerable part of the total credit available each year. This is despite the fact that the government of Pakistan, in its *Economic Survey* for 1994/5, claimed that 'the interest rate structure underwent changes so that it is ultimately determined by free market forces'.[21] According to conventional wisdom, all sorts of direct controls on interest rate movements *must* be removed, and the market, left to itself, is supposed to set the right price of borrowing money. However, because of government intervention in the credit market, different sets of rates of return exist, which do affect the functioning of a (free) money market. In 1991, when the government started its open market operations by issuing debt in the form of Treasury Bills and FIBs, banks found FIBs very lucrative compared to other investment instruments. (See Box 13.4, which presents an extract from one of the most quoted papers on credit rationing, and argues that the free

Table 13.1
Holder-wise analysis of total domestic public debts, 1990–1993 (outstanding amount in million rupees, as of end-June)

Group of domestic public debt instruments	1990/1			1991/2			1992/3		
	Banking sector	Non-bank sector	Total	Banking sector	Non-bank sector	Total	Banking sector	Non-bank sector	Total
Auction debts	101,466	9,528	110,994	189,753	25,962	215,715	247,715	39,890	287,880
Bearer public debts	–	9,861	9,861	–	18,071	18,071	–	37,148	37,148
NSS instruments (incl. prize bonds)	–	108,474	108,474	–	141,473	141,473	–	172,810	172,810
Other public debts (which are not marketable)	104,790	110,979	215,769	103,832	51,079	154,911	95,991	18,439	114,430
Total amount of domestic public debt	206,256	238,842	445,098	293,585	236,595	530,170	343,981	268,287	612,268

Source: *Journal of the Institute of Bankers*, March 1994, p. 18.

market may not automatically determine the best price for credit, i.e. interest rate.)

As shown above, banks had accumulated a great deal of excess liquidity, and a remunerative government-guaranteed investment in the form of the FIBs gave banks somewhere to put their idle funds. Also, after the end of the credit ceilings, banks were motivated to mobilize more deposits in order to be able to lend/invest more, as allowed by the CDR.

One of the reasons why banks were encouraged to invest in FIBs was to replace the government's short-term debt by a longer- and medium-term debt instrument. The government also believed that these banks would develop a secondary market and sell the instruments to the non-banking sector. This did not happen for the reasons listed above, but also because 'banks were building up FIB inventories simply for the purpose of earning a fixed interest income which was payable every six months'.[22] The government was then forced to intervene and impose a ceiling on banks investing more than 15 per cent of their liabilities in government paper of more than one year's maturity.

There has been a continuous differentiation in the rates of return on government debt instruments, and ironically, the nominal and effective rates of return on short-term government debt instruments have often been much higher than on longer-term debt (see Table 13.2). This is a serious anomaly in the debt structure which should be based on long-term debt rather than on short-term six-month Treasury Bills (see Chapters 10 and 11).

13.2 Money Supply and Monetary Expansion

In section 13.1 above, we saw how monetary policy and monetary management work in Pakistan, and how they have evolved over the years, especially since the early 1990s

following the financial sector reform programme. In this section, we will briefly look at the numbers and trends in monetary expansion and credit. This section will also help identify the link between money supply and inflation, a theme discussed below. Tables 13.3–13.8 show different features and growth rates of important variables related to the monetary sector.

Total monetary assets in an economy consist of currency in circulation, which is the currency issued by the State Bank of Pakistan, minus the amount held as cash by the banking sector. Adding demand deposits and other deposits with the State Bank, we get the measure of money supply, or M1. Table 13.3 shows the trends in the basic components of M1 over the last decade, as well as that for total monetary assets, M2. M1 is constituted almost equally of currency in circulation and demand deposits. M3, or broad money, includes M2 (and therefore M1 as well), in addition to NDFC Bearer Certificates, deposits in National Saving Schemes and the deposits of the Federal Bank of Cooperatives.

Table 13.4 provides a clearer picture of the trends depicted in Table 13.3, showing growth rates in monetary assets over the last few years. Monetary assets, M2, have shown a growth of around 16 per cent over the last two or three years, down from the very substantial increase of 30 per cent in 1991/2. One reason for this increase, however, was also the large increase in residents' foreign currency deposits in the same year.

In order to see the causes of the increase in monetary assets, we turn to Table 13.5. In 1994/5, domestic credit expanded by 12 per cent, a little more than in the previous year, but net foreign assets expanded by 170 per cent, due mainly to receipts from the sale of the Pakistan Telecommunications Corporation (PTC) vouchers. Government sector borrowing for budgetary support from the banking sector has grown in leaps and bounds, although the growth of 3.9 per cent in 1993/4 and of 8.1 per cent in 1994/5

Table 13.2
Pakistan: selected financial instruments

Description	Rate of return	Tax advantage	Source limits	Comments
Foreign exchange instruments				
Foreign Currency Accounts (FCAs): Time (3, 6, 24, and 36 months) and demand deposits denominated in foreign exchange in domestic banks. Practically no limitations on who can own these accounts. No restrictions on transfer of interest and capital overseas.	Not more than LIBOR plus $\frac{3}{4}$, $\frac{7}{8}$, $1\frac{5}{8}$ points for time deposits with maturities equal to/less than 1, 2, and 3 years, respectively.	Exempt from wealth and income taxes.	No questions asked about source of foreign exchange.	Banks are obliged to turn over foreign exchange to SBP in exchange for PRs at rate prevailing that day. SBP provides partial exchange risk cover.
Foreign Exchange Bearer Certificates (FEBCs): Three-year rupee obligations of the federal government that can only be purchased with foreign exchange. Can be encashed at any time in either PRs or foreign exchange at the prevailing official rate. Practically no restrictions on overseas transfers. Similar to a zero-coupon bond in the sense that interest is paid at maturity or at time of encashment for each completed one-year period.	The amount payable in PR is 114.5%, 131% and 152% of the face value after one, two, and three years. Interest not prorated within a year.	Exempt from wealth and income taxes.	No questions asked about source of foreign exchange.	Traded in secondary market at a premium (recently at 6.5%) as a result of remaining foreign exchange restrictions. Both residents and non-residents can use secondary market.
Dollar Bearer Certificates and Foreign Currency Bearer Certificates (DBCs and FCBCs). One-year dollar and other currency (DM, yen, and sterling) obligation of the federal government. Can be encashed in PRs and foreign exchange at prevailing official exchange rate. No restrictions on overseas transfers.	LIBOR plus $\frac{1}{4}$.	Exempt from wealth and income taxes.	No questions asked about source of foreign exchange.	
Selected rupee denominated instruments				
Special Savings Certificates (SSCs): Three-year obligations (registered as well as bearer) of the federal government introduced in February 1990. They were introduced to replace the Khas Deposits Certificates/accounts that were discontinued by the authorities on the same date. The certificates are issued under the auspices of the Central Directorate of National Savings and marketed by scheduled banks, National Savings Centres, and post offices. There are many other types of savings scheme with characteristics similar to the SSCs.	Interest on these instruments is paid semi-annually and must be drawn on due dates. Interest rates are 11.5% and 12.5% p.a. for first four payments and 14% and 15% p.a. for last two payments for Bearer and Registered Certificates, respectively.	Income from both Registered and Bearer Certificates is free of income tax. Bearer Certificates are also free of Zakat, while for Registered Certificates Zakat is deductible for the encashment year.	Registered Certificates are only open to purchase by individuals and local bodies, but there is no upper limit on investment.	Until discontinued, Khaas Savings Certificates constituted the most important source of non-bank budgetary financing. However, the Special Savings Certificates have not proven as popular, since their return is somewhat lower and corporate bodies are excluded.
Market Treasury Bills (TBs): Six-month obligations of the federal government introduced in March 1991 to replace (together with FIBs (see below)) other instruments for bank financing (e.g. ad-hoc and on-tap Treasury Bills) and non-bank financing of the budget. The rate of return is determined at an auction held approximately every 25 days.	Rate of return of most recent auctions was in the order of 12% p.a.	For personal income tax purposes, income from TBs is taxed at a flat 10% withheld at source. TBs are exempt from Zakat.	No restrictions. However, secondary market in TBs is still underdeveloped.	Despite recent moves to make rates more flexible, these rates are controlled by the government via the binding credit/deposit ratio.
Federal Investment Bonds (FIBs) are long-term (3–10 years) obligations of the federal government introduced to replace instruments that were being discontinued. As for TBs, rates of return were to be determined at regularly scheduled auctions.	Rates of return have more or less remained at their coupon rate, which is 13% and 15% for three- and ten-year bonds, respectively.	Same as TBs.	Same as TBs.	

Source: World Bank, *Pakistan: Country Economic Memorandum FY93*, Report No. 11590-Pak, Washington, 1993.

Table 13.3
Monetary assets, 1985–1995 (Rs m)

As at the end of	Currency issued (1)	Currency held by SBP (2)	Currency in tills of scheduled banks (3)	Currency in circulation (1)–(2)–(3) (4)	Scheduled banks' demand deposits[a] (5)	Other deposits with SBP[b] (6)	Money supply (M1) (4)+(5)+(6) (7)	Scheduled banks' time deposits[a] (8)	Residents' foreign currency deposits[c] (9)	Total monetary assets (M2) (7)+(8)+(9) (10)
June 1985	60,799	265	4,087	56,477	61,799	742	118,968	64,937	–	183,905
June 1986	67,804	427	4,101	63,276	70,677	878	134,831	76,280	–	211,111
June 1987	79,991	665	4,623	74,703	83,821	1,101	159,625	80,398	–	240,023
June 1988	93,437	517	5,125	87,785	95,967	1,218	184,970	84,374	–	269,344
June 1989	103,238	746	4,984	97,508	103,893	3,132	204,533	77,105	–	281,638
June 1990	120,817	399	5,351	115,067	119,704	2,209	236,980	80,241	–	317,221
June 1991	144,916	610	7,339	136,967	121,252	3,114	261,333	97,963	9,487	368,783
June 1992	161,433	652	38,962	151,819	145,136	3,322	300,277	137,263	43,004	480,544
June 1993	178,933	768	11,301	166,864	154,902	4,449	326,215	179,680	61,274	567,169
June 1994(RP)	199,070	624	13,738	184,708	167,231	5,506	357,445	213,226	92,134	662,805
June 1995(P)	232,589	647	16,363	215,579	201,097	5,055	421,731	246,194	105,073	772,998

(P) Provisional.
(RP) Revised provisional.
[a] Excluding inter-bank deposits and deposits of federal and provincial governments and of foreign constituents.
[b] Excluding IMF A/c Nos. 1 & 2, counterpart funds, deposits of foreign central banks, foreign governments, international organizations, and deposit money banks.
[c] The deposits under residents' foreign currency accounts (allowed to be opened by resident Pakistanis as from 23 February 1991) have been included as part of monetary assets instead of as foreign liability.
Source: State Bank of Pakistan, *Annual Report 1994–95,* Karachi, 1995, p. 87.

is lower than that of the three years prior. However, the bank borrowing of Rs27.5 billion in 1994/5 was higher than the Rs20 billion envisaged in the Annual Credit Plan for that year. Moreover, the borrowing for budgetary support in 1994/5 of about Rs25 billion, was higher by Rs10 billion than the plan for that year, and three times the expansion of Rs7.5 billion in the previous year.

In the case of commodity operations, the outstanding level of borrowing rose from Rs18.7 billion in 1992 to Rs41.5 billion in 1995, 'despite the fact that lending for commodity operations is essentially a short term accommodation'.[23] The State Bank of Pakistan *Annual Report, 1994–95* argues that 'this short term borrowing by the Government has assumed the character of long term borrowing and has become a source of monetary expansion. If the recovery rate of loans provided under commodity operations could be improved upon, there would be a considerable dampening, if not reversal, of this expansionary influence on monetary assets.'[24] The borrowings by the public sector corporations reflect their financial weaknesses, and if they had not incurred a large number of debts in the past, which they must retire, 'these bodies should be generating enough revenue to retire their bank borrowings rather than building liabilities to the banking sector'.[25]

Tables 13.6 and 13.7 give us the key money supply variables over a longer period of time. As is to be expected, the income velocities of money supply and monetary assets have shown only small fluctuations over fifteen years. The annual changes in different definitions of money are shown in Table 13.7 and make an important contribution to the

debate about whether 'inflation is always and everywhere a monetary phenomenon' discussed later in this chapter.

Table 13.8 gives us some evidence about the process of financial intermediation/disintermediation in the financial sector. In the 1980s, there was a shift away from time deposits and towards National Saving Schemes as they offered a far better rate of return. Consequently, there was a decline in the ratio of bank deposits to GDP, with demand and time deposits falling from 28.7 per cent of GDP in 1986/7 to 21.5 per cent in 1990/1. Time deposits (TD) fell from 36.1 per cent of monetary assets (M2) in 1985/6 to 25.3 per cent in 1989/90, as people started shifting their deposits from banks to higher-interest-earning sources (Table 13.8). In this period the rise in the M1/M2 ratio also shows the presence of high liquidity in the system, rising from 63.9 per cent in 1983/4 to 74.7 per cent in 1989/90.[26]

13.3 Inflation and its Causes

Pakistan's inflation rate over the years has been an enigma to most analysts. It has historically been rather low (see Table 13.9). A mere 3.3 per cent across the 1960s, it rose to 11.9 per cent on average in the 1970s, and fell again to an average of only 7.5 per cent in the 1980s. Only since the early 1990s has inflation become a matter of concern. Different theories of inflation (see Appendix 13.3) give different reasons for why inflation exists, but even though Pakistan's case does cause perplexity, there has been insufficient work on the reasons why prices rise as they do.

Table 13.4
Growth in monetary assets, 1990–1995 (Rs m)

Year	Currency in circulation	Demand deposits[a]	Other deposits with SBP[b]	Money supply (M1) (1)+(2)+(3)	Time deposits[a]	Residents' foreign currency deposits[c]	Monetary assets including RFCD (M2) (1)+(2)+(3)	Annual growth rates (%)	
								(M1)	(M2)
	(1)	(2)	(3)	(4)	(5)	(6)	(7)	(8)	(9)
1990/1	21,900 (42.5)	1,548 (3.0)	905 (1.8)	24,353 (47.2)	17,722 (34.4)	9,487 (18.4)	51,562	10.3	16.3
1991/2	14,852 (13.3)	23,884 (21.4)	208 (0.2)	38,944 (34.8)	39,300 (35.2)	33,517 (30.0)	111,761	14.9	30.3
1992/3	15,045 (17.4)	9,766 (11.3)	1,127 (1.3)	25,938 (29.9)	42,417 (49.0)	18,270 (21.1)	86,625	8.6	18.0
1993/4 (RP)	17,844 (18.7)	12,329 (12.9)	1,057 (1.1)	31,230 (32.7)	33,546 (35.1)	30,860 (32.3)	95,636	9.6	16.9
1994/5 (P)	30.871 (28.0)	33,866 (30.7)	−451 (−0.4)	64,286 (58.3)	32,968 (29.9)	12,939 (11.7)	110,193	18.0	16.6
Outstanding on 30 June 1995	215,579	201,097	5,055	421,731	246,194	105,073	772,998		

(P) Provisional.
(RP) Revised provisional.
[a] Excluding inter-bank deposits and deposits of federal governments and of foreign constituents.
[b] Excluding IMF A/c Nos. 1 & 2, counterpart funds, deposits of foreign central banks, foreign governments, international organizations, and deposit money banks.
[c] The deposits under residents' foreign currency accounts (allowed to be opened by resident Pakistanis as from 23 February 1991) have been included as part of monetary assets instead of as foreign liability.
Note: Figures in parentheses show percentage share in total growth in monetary assets (M2).
Source: State Bank of Pakistan, *Annual Report 1994–95*, Karachi, 1995, p. 48.

Akhtar Hossain, examining historical trends, concludes that 'in Pakistan, real money balances are found to contribute to an acceleration of inflation, while the bond-financed government expenditure is found to have a negative effect on the acceleration of inflation for 1961–88'.[27] After the high fiscal deficits of the late 1980s, however, high inflation was considered to be a key consequence of the irresponsible policies of the government.

While Akhtar Hossain's analysis shows how money affects inflation, the work by Jones and Khilji[28] and by Navqi *et al.*[29] argues that this is not the case. According to Naqvi *et al.*, 'money supply does not exert changes in the price level. The very small size of the coefficient of the money supply variable and its statistical insignificance contradict the simplistic notion held by some people in Pakistan that inflation is a purely monetarist (or monetary!) phenomenon.'[30] So what is responsible for the double-digit inflation of the 1990s? Recent work by Hafiz Pasha, Aynul Hasan, and Ashfaque Khan[31] attempts to answer this question, as does the publication by ABN AMRO Bank, partially reproduced in Appendix 13.3.

Pasha *et al.*, first examine all the reasons that have been advanced by other scholars for the high inflation in recent years. These include the following:

1　Increases in the price of food, raw materials, fuels, and manufactured goods.

2　Inflationary expectations.

3　The growth of money supply in relation to GDP.

4　Increases in sales and excise taxes.

5　Currency depreciation and devaluation.

6　Supply shocks like virus-induced reductions in cotton output and weather-induced lower wheat crops.

7　Higher agricultural support prices.

8　Increases in the prices of utilities.

9　Production losses due to power and infrastructural bottlenecks.

10　Increases in wages and salaries.

11　Insufficiently tight financial policies, with high budget-deficit financing.

Their work takes all these factors into consideration and they then classify the key policy variables in their empirical investigation into six demand management policies, as follows:

1　*Supply shocks.* Wherever the total availability of a commodity falls short of its long-run trend due to crop failure, viruses, floods, etc., the price of this sector should rise. The government usually has no control over such matters, especially in the short run.

Table 13.5
Causative factors for changes in monetary assets, 1990–1995 (Rs m)

	1990/1	1991/2	1992/3	1993/4 (RP)	1994/5 (P)	30 June 1995 (outstanding)
1 Government sector (net)	21,788	76,694	72,934	12,638	27,505	366,385
of which:	(19.3)	(43.4)	(28.8)	(3.9)	(8.1)	
Budgetary support	32,682	70,276	63,630	7,517	24,967	336,331
	(25.2)	(41.4)	(26.5)	(2.5)	(8.0)	
Commodity operations	–5,315	4,194	7,335	6,582	4,733	41,519
	(–22.2)	(22.5)	(32.1)	(21.8)	(12.9)	
2 Credit to WAPDA, OGDC, NFC PTC, and PTV	–416	1,007	6,162	2,400	3,701	13,410
	(–74.8)	(719.3)	(537.2)	(32.8)	(38.1)	
3 Non-government sector	21,110	30,132	56,640	40,716	66,326	445,402
(A + B)	(9.2)	(12.0)	(20.1)	(12.0)	(17.5)	
A Public sector enterprises	–3,986	–117	–1,644	–2,052	–1,361	25,352
	(–11.5)	(–0.4)	(–5.4)	(–7.1)	(–5.1)	
B Private sector	25,096	30,249	58,284	42,768	67,687	420,050
	(12.8)	(13.7)	(23.2)	(13.8)	(19.2)	
4 Other items (net)	3,368	–5,051	–15,098	6,473	–14,296	–64,226
	(8.7)	(–14.3)	(–37.5)	(11.7)	(–29.2)	
5 Domestic credit	45,580	102,782	120,638	62,227	83,236	761,971
(1) + (2) + (3) + (4)	(13.5)	(26.1)	(24.3)	(10.1)	(12.3)	
6 Foreign assets (net)	5,712	8,979	–34,013	33,402	26,957	11,027
	(25.2)	(36.9)	(–221.9)	(67.7)	(169.2)	
7 Monetary assets	51,562	111,761	86,625	95,636	110,193	772,998
(5) + (6)	(16.3)	(30.3)	(18.0)	(16.9)	(16.6)	

(P) Provisional.
(RP) Revised provisional.
Note: Figures in parentheses show percentage share in total growth in monetary assets (M2).
Source: State Bank of Pakistan, *Annual Report 1994–95*, Karachi, 1995, p. 48.

2 *Monetary policy.* The classic 'quantity theory of money' states that as money increases, so will prices; also, a monetized budget deficit will put further pressure on price (also see Appendix 13.3).

3 *Tax policy.* A rise in, for example, sales taxes and excise duties is usually passed on to the consumers by producers.

4 *External shocks.* As prices abroad rise and as goods are imported into the country, inflation is often imported as well, as these prices are usually a given for a small open economy like Pakistan. Moreover, devaluation and high tariffs also raise the domestic price of commodities.

5 *Pricing policy.* Procurement prices for agricultural products – the prices at which the government buys wheat, cotton, and sugar – are often different from market prices, as the government may want to encourage the growing of certain crops and offer higher prices to farmers and subsidize the cost to (mainly urban) consumers. Higher procurement prices and/or lower subsidies will cause prices to increase. In addition, prices of utilities such as gas, electricity, and fuel are regulated by the government, and may rise, as they have done in Pakistan, in order to be brought in line with world prices under IMF and World Bank pressure.

6 *Expectations.* How people expect the inflation rate to

Table 13.6
Income velocity of money, 1980–1995

End June	Money supply (M1) (Rs m)	Income velocity of money supply	Monetary asset (M2) (Rs m)	Income velocity of monetary assets
1980/1	73,560	3.7	104,621	2.7
1981/2	80,926	3.9	116,510	2.7
1982/3	96,542	3.8	146,025	2.7
1983/4	103,445	4.0	163,267	2.7
1984/5	118,968	3.9	183,905	2.7
1985/6	134,831	3.8	211,111	2.6
1986/7	159,625	3.5	240,023	2.5
1987/8	184,970	3.4	269,344	2.6
1988/9	204,533	3.5	281,638	2.8
1989/90	236,980	3.4	317,221	2.8
1990/1	261,333	3.6	368,783	2.9
1991/2	300,279	3.6	480,544	2.8
1992/3	326,214	3.7	567,169	2.5
1993/4	357,445	4.0	662,805	2.5
1994/5	421,731	4.3	772,998	2.6

Source: Government of Pakistan, *Pakistan Economic Survey, 1995–96,* Islamabad, 1996, p. 116.

Table 13.7
Money supply (M1, M2, M3), 1979–1995

End-period stocks (last working day basis)	Narrow money (M1)	% change	Monetary assets (M2)	% change	Broad money (M3)	% change
1972/3	18.05	–	27.07	–	30.94	–
1979/80	61.90	23.2[a]	92.42	22.7[a]	103.14	22.2[a]
1980/1	73.56	18.7	104.62	13.2	116.80	13.2
1981/2	80.93	10.0	116.51	11.4	133.87	14.4
1982/3	96.54	19.3	146.03	25.3	176.68	32.0
1983/4	103.45	7.2	163.27	11.8	206.90	17.1
1984/5	118.97	15.0	183.91	12.6	238.87	15.5
1985/6	134.83	13.3	211.11	14.8	277.63	16.2
1986/7	159.63	18.4	240.02	13.7	330.87	19.2
1987/8	184.97	15.9	269.34	12.2	392.50	18.6
1988/9	204.53	10.5	281.64	4.6	423.37	7.9
1989/90	236.98	16.0	317.22	12.6	480.13	13.7
1990/1	261.33	10.3	368.78	16.3[b]	537.54	12.0
1991/2	300.28	14.9	480.54	30.3[b]	654.15	21.7
1992/3	326.21	8.9	567.17	18.0[b]	749.15	14.5
1993/4	357.45	9.6	662.81	16.9[b]	881.63	17.7
1994/5 (P)	421.73	18.0	773.00	16.6	1,032.00	17.1

(P) Provisional.
[a] Annual compound growth during 1972/3 to 1979/80.
[b] The percentage changes have been worked out after adding resident foreign currency deposits.
Source: Government of Pakistan, *Pakistan Economic Survey, 1995–96,* Islamabad, 1996, p. 117.

Table 13.8
Key indicators of Pakistan's financial development, 1980–1994 (%)

Year	M2/GDP	M1/M2	DD + TD/M2	TD/M2
1980/1	37.6	70.3	66.2	29.7
1981/2	35.9	69.5	67.2	30.5
1982/3	40.1	66.1	68.3	33.9
1983/4	38.9	63.4	67.7	36.6
1984/5	39.0	64.7	68.9	35.3
1985/6	41.0	63.9	69.6	36.1
1986/7	41.9	66.5	68.4	33.5
1987/8	39.9	68.7	67.0	31.3
1988/9	36.6	72.6	64.3	27.4
1989/90	37.1	74.7	63.0	25.3
1990/1	36.1	70.9	60.2	26.9
1991/2	39.7	69.0	59.9	29.1
1992/3	42.3	57.3	59.8	32.1
1993/4	42.3	53.7	55.7	32.5

TD = Time Deposits.
DD = Demand Deposits.
Source: Khan, Ashfaque H., 'Need and Scope for Further Reforms in the Financial Sector in Pakistan', *Journal of the Institute of Bankers in Pakistan,* June, 1995, p. 45.

behave in the future will have key consequences for how it actually behaves. Once the expectations of a price rise are built into the mind-set of consumers, these expectations are often realized as consumers and producers build in a price rise in their future formulations. It is also more difficult for individuals to revise their expectations downwards; this takes a much longer time than adjusting expectations upwards.

The mechanism through which inflation is reflected in the wholesale price index (WPI) can be seen in Figure 13.2. The empirical simulation conducted by Hafiz Pasha *et al.* produced the following results: the supply shock has the greatest negative effect on food prices (84.8 per cent), and procurement prices for wheat are also highly significant; sales taxes and excise duties affect manufactured products, and imported commodities influence raw material prices by 50 per cent and manufactured prices by 30 per cent; the role of inflationary expectations is also very significant, causing prices to rise. More interestingly, the study found that monetary supply, contrary to the conventional view, is not translated into increasing overall inflation, essentially because monetary expansion does not have a significant impact on food prices, which form 51 per cent of the wholesale price index. This finding contradicts the view popularized by the IMF and World Bank, and repeated verbatim by the government of Pakistan. In addition, another popularly held view, that the floods and commodity shortages of cotton and wheat in 1992/3 may have caused double-digit inflation, was not borne out by their study.

Table 13.9
Historical WPI, CPI, and sectoral inflation rates

Years	WPI General	CPI General	WPI Food	WPI Raw materials	WPI Manufac-turing	WPI Fuel lube
1960–1969	2.6	3.3	2.6	2.0	3.4	3.3
1970–1979	13.5	11.9	13.4	12.9	11.7	17.8
1980–1989	7.1	7.5	7.2	6.9	7.0	7.2
1990/1	11.7	12.6	9.0	7.1	17.7	16.8
1991/2	9.3	9.6	10.2	11.0	9.5	4.9
1992/3	7.1	9.3	10.6	8.4	3.3	1.2
1993/4	15.0	11.1	14.1	24.6	10.7	22.4
July to Jan. 1994/5	18.9	n.a	n.a	n.a	n.a	n.a

In summary then, for Hafiz Pasha *et al.*, the key factor explaining the overall current inflation rate in Pakistan is neither demand management policy nor supply shocks, but interestingly enough, procurement prices, particularly that of wheat, and the administered prices of fuel, gas, and electricity.[32] In addition, an increase in indirect taxes helps to aggravate the situation. The authors argue that many of these measures which have caused the relatively high inflation of recent years are a key constituent of the IMF and World Bank structural adjustment programmes. However, Part IV of this book in which the structural adjustment programme is discussed in detail, shows that one of the key targets of the programme was a fall in the inflation rate, not its *increase*.

13.4   The Low Savings Rate

Table 13.10 shows that Pakistan's national savings rate during the 1970s was a mere 11.74 per cent, rising slightly, to 13.81 per cent, during the 1980s. This is considered to be a

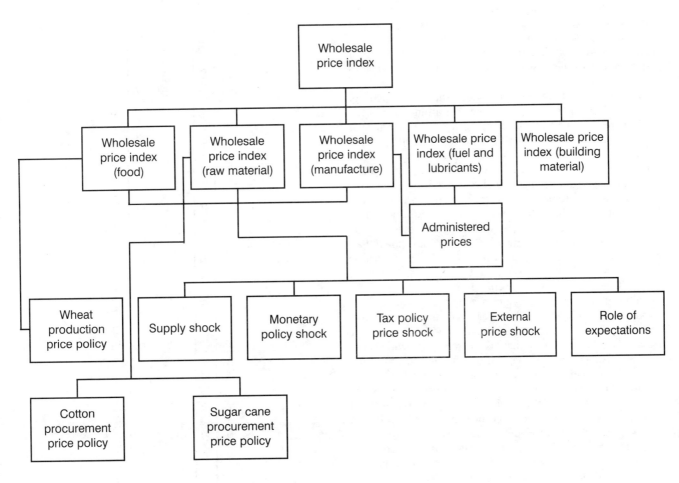

Figure 13.2
Schematic diagram explaining causes of inflation in Pakistan

Source: Pasha, Hafiz, *et al.*, 'What Explains the Current High Rate of Inflation in Pakistan?', *Pakistan Development Review*, vol. 34, no. 4, 1995.

very low rate by the standards of comparable economies, where a rate of around 20 per cent is common. This lack of savings is supposed to be 'one of the basic structural macroeconomic problems'[33] faced by the country. As Table 13.11 shows, savings are generated mainly in the household and unincorporated private enterprises sector, and government savings have been, for the most part, either very low or negative.

There are essentially two major schools of thought which explain why low levels of savings exist. The financial repression school argues that low or negative real interest rates, which are often caused by arbitrarily set government ceilings on nominal interest rates, along with high and variable inflation rates 'are the major impediments to savings, financial deepening, capital formation and growth'.[34] This view seems to be the one favoured by the authorities in Pakistan, as much of section 13.1 shows. The solution, as has been also implemented in Pakistan, is to place interest rates in a free market environment, so that they can find their own 'equilibrium' levels. The financial structure school believes that, especially in underdeveloped countries, low savings, investment, and growth exist because of the lack of depth and breadth in the financial sector, since financial assets, markets, and institutions are few and not well developed. Not surprisingly, according to this view, an extended network of financial institutions and the availability of different types of assets and instruments will have a positive impact on savings and investment.

Some evidence from Pakistan[35] shows that both schools of thought are supported. It is believed that an increase in the real interest rate will stimulate aggregate savings in Pakistan as people move out of non-financial assets and into the financial sector. Moreover, as financial development takes place and more institutions and instruments are made available, aggregate savings will also increase.

A number of studies have been conducted in Pakistan to investigate why the savings rate is so low. Appendix 13.4 shows the effects of fourteen different variables on the savings rate. Work by Siddiqui and Siddiqui[36] has shown that, as income increases, savings will also increase – this was found to be a positive and significant relationship. The effect of the dependency ratio was seen to be negative, but not very significant, implying that an increase in the dependency ratio would cause savings to fall, but not by very much. Zafar Iqbal, however, finds a strong negative effect of the dependency ratio on savings, showing that 'as the rapidly growing share of dependants in the total population tends to consume more than they produce, there is a consequent reduction in household savings'.[37] However, he also confirms the positive relationship between the domestic real interest rate and household savings. Inflation and the expectation of inflation in the future are negatively related to household savings: the expectation of higher inflation in the future means that households will substitute future consumption by present consumption, lowering the savings rate.

At a more macro level, Zafar Iqbal's results show that private capital outflows and the foreign interest rate have a 'strong negative' effect on household savings, 'which suggests that unfavourable circumstances, political unrest, and financial repression in Pakistan provoke people to

Table 13.10
Savings as a percentage of GDP, 1980–1995

Indicators	1960s	1970s	1980s	1980/1	1981/2	1982/3	1983/4	1984/5	1985/6	1986/7	1987/8	1988/9	1989/90	1990/1	1991/2	1992/3	1993/4	1994/5
National savings		11.74	13.81	13.98	13.23	15.34	13.76	11.96	13.78	15.96	13.07	13.59	13.61	13.86	16.90	13.47	15.56	14.77
Foreign savings		5.67	3.65	3.37	4.63	1.61	2.93	4.99	3.59	2.03	4.20	4.66	4.54	4.66	3.04	7.08	3.88	4.26

Source: Government of Pakistan, *Pakistan Economic Survey, 1995–96*, Islamabad, 1996, p. 2.

Table 13.11
Capital accounts of the public and private sectors (period averages, % of GDP)

	1970–1990	1970–1977	1978–1981	1982–1986	1987–1990
National savings	13.12	10.43	15.17	14.83	14.31
Public saving	1.12	0.42	2.30	1.74	0.55
Government saving	0.46	0.88	1.90	0.18	−1.46
Public enterprise saving	0.55	0.40	0.54	0.75	13.08
Private saving	12.00	10.01	12.87	13.09	13.75
Corporate saving	0.50	0.60	0.32	0.36	0.68
Household saving	11.50	9.41	12.55	12.73	13.08
Gross domestic investment	18.28	17.28	19.39	18.68	18.67
Public investment	9.94	9.10	11.33	10.30	9.79
Government investment	3.15	2.78	3.18	3.50	3.41
Household investment	0.73	0.64	0.90	0.90	0.49
Private investment	8.34	8.18	8.06	8.38	8.88
Corporate investment	0.74	0.86	0.46	0.48	1.11
Household investment	7.60	7.33	7.61	7.90	7.77
Saving – Investment (S–I)	−5.16	−6.85	−4.23	−3.85	−4.37
Foreign capital inflow	5.16	6.85	4.23	3.85	4.37
Public sector	2.67	4.30	2.67	0.93	1.51
Private sector	2.49	2.50	1.56	2.92	2.86
Recorded	0.94	0.56	0.80	1.51	1.11
Unrecorded	1.55	1.94	0.76	1.41	1.75
Resource transfer to the public sector	6.15	4.32	6.36	7.63	7.73

Source: Naqvi, S.N.H. and Khwaja Sarmad, 'External Shocks and Domestic Adjustments: Pakistan's Case 1970–1990', mimeo, University Grants Commission, Islamabad, p. 47.

transfer their resources abroad to a safer place'.[38] Export earnings, interestingly, have a strong positive effect on national savings, as exports increase the propensity to save compared to other sectors.

One of the more interesting findings related to savings is that of Shabbir and Mahmood, who show that 'foreign financial inflows may discourage domestic public and/or private saving behaviour and resource mobilization effects'.[39] The theory suggests that, if savings are low in a country and there is a resource gap between investment and savings, foreign capital inflows can fill that gap, ostensibly increasing growth. In the case of Pakistan, we see that foreign aid impedes domestic savings growth and mobilization. Foreign capital seems to *substitute rather than augment* domestic savings on two accounts: '(a) foreign capital inflows would lead to government being less enthusiastic about its resource generation efforts, the nation could increase its consumption expenditure and/or liberalize imports and (b) to the extent that saving is determined by available investment opportunities, by crowding out domestic investment, foreign portfolio investment could cause savings to fall'.[40] At a household level, Zafar Iqbal[41] found that easily available credit from banks discourages the efforts of households to generate their own savings, a result also confirmed by N.H. Naqvi and Khwaja Sarmad.[42] Khan *et al.* support Shabbir and Mahmood's findings by showing that a 1 per cent increase in foreign capital inflows cuts national savings by 0.21 per cent. 'The negative impact

of foreign capital inflows suggests that for the most part, external assistance has been used for consumption purposes and that it has discouraged savings efforts by both the private and public sector, in Pakistan.'[43] These findings have also been supported by the work of Nawab Haider Naqvi and Khwaja Sarmad.

Just to emphasize how complicated the reasons are for persistent low savings, and the extent to which the conclusions of each researcher vary, we cite some of the results of Ashfaque Khan *et al.* For them, the most important factors affecting national savings were per capita income, the dependency ratio, the real interest rate, and foreign capital inflows. They found that as per capita income increased, due to either a slowdown in the population growth rate or a higher real GNP growth rate, savings would rise. However, unlike the other studies cited, for Khan *et al.* 'the high dependency ratio caused by the rapid increase in population has been the most important factor causing the savings rate to remain depressed'.[44]

While there is some debate over why the savings rate in Pakistan is so low, the consensus rests on a few points:

1 There is a strong correlation between household savings and the real rate of return on financial assets, which means that the government's policy of keeping real interest rates low – financial repression – has helped reduce the level of domestic savings.

2 The greater availability and ease of access to financial

institutions, markets, and instruments should cause the savings rate to increase.

3 Foreign capital inflows – foreign aid – which were supposed to fill the savings–investment gap, have actually had a negative impact on domestic savings and have not acted as a catalyst to increase national savings.

4 Similar results regarding household savings and the availability of bank credit have been observed

5 Inflation and uncertainty about the future – as has been common in Pakistan – has been responsible for capital flight and greater consumption than is perhaps warranted.

Other factors that may be responsible include cultural factors, such as where savings in the form of assets, particularly gold and jewellery, substitute for financial savings. Due to the lack of awareness and use of banks, and with greater emphasis on savings in real assets, the real (as opposed to financial) savings rate in Pakistan is probably higher. Moreover, the presence of a very large informal financial sector suggests that the official savings rate does not capture the entire amount of money actually saved.

13.5 Summary and Further Reading

13.5.1 Summary

For some economists, money and monetary policy are the key determinants of economic activity. In Pakistan, until recently, monetary policy was closely controlled by the government and the market was almost non-existent when it came to determining the cost and allocation of money in the economy. Since 1991 a more market-based approach has been followed,

with the regular auction of Treasury Bills influencing, if not determining, the rate of interest. However, by all standards, the money market is still extremely underdeveloped in Pakistan, and for some economists, this is one reason why the economy has not functioned well.

Money supply and its annual expansion are supposed to be one of the key determinants of the price level in the economy. We have examined a large literature with respect to Pakistan and find that this is not the case. Inflation in Pakistan occurs for numerous structural reasons, and because of the frequent escalation in administered prices by government. In fact, there is almost no relationship between price levels and the growth of money in the economy.

Pakistan's savings rate, of around 14 per cent, is also considered to be a key deterrent to economic expansion, especially since most East Asian economies have savings rates almost double Pakistan's. One school of thought argues tht savings are low due to financial repression, i.e. the market does not play the dominant role in the financial system, while another view argues that savings stay low because the financial structure is undeveloped. We have examined a large number of causative factors for the low savings rate, and find that neither the financial repression nor the financial structure school provides an adequate explanation. Cultural factors, too, may suggest why the financial savings rate is low.

13.5.2 Further Reading

The works listed in the Notes should provide sufficient sources for those who want to examine the monetary sector and monetary policy in Pakistan. In addition, the *Journal of the Institute of Bankers in Pakistan* and articles in the press should be consulted regularly for recent changes, along with the State Bank of Pakistan's *Annual Reports*.

Appendix 13.1

The money market in Pakistan

This excerpt introduces the money market in Pakistan.

The money market in Pakistan can be divided into two broad segments. Firstly, there is the call money market where the banks lend cash to each other for very short periods of time. Secondly, there is the market in which the credit ceiling is traded. This is a peculiar feature of the Pakistani money market, and any explanation of it must be preceded by an understanding of credit ceilings and their implications.

Overnight Funds

The call market is basically an overnight market though seven-day call money trades are also conducted. Fund managers faced with a shortage, or surplus, of cash can borrow, or lend, at a market rate of return. Call money is literally 'on call'. This means that, technically, a lending institution can terminate a contract at any time and 'call' its money back. The debtor bank would be obliged to comply immediately with such a

request. The operative word here is 'technically' since generally no institution would withdraw from a lending agreement on ethical grounds. There would also be a cost involved in such a move.

The price of funds is set by market demand and supply. For example, if there is a dearth of money in the market, that is, the majority of financial institutions need funds, then lenders can get a high rate of interest on any loanable funds that they may have; of course, if most institutions have excess liquidity, then call money rates would fall. The major source of call market funds are the NCBs [nationalized commercial banks]. Excess liquidity created by a vast deposit base leads them to place substantial sums of money on the short term market very profitably. The major borrowers are the foreign commercial banks. There are two reasons for this. First, they have a small deposit base and must fund their everyday activities in some manner, and, secondly, the call market is a cheap source of funds for them. Surrounded by SBP regulations, the foreign banks borrow short on the call market and lend long, keeping a spread for themselves. They continuously roll over their short money to finance their long term assets. Call money transactions are normally conducted directly between banks, though, sometimes, intermediaries such as brokers are used. Settlement of trades is done in the following manner: Interest payments are made every month end, while principal is paid at the end of the specified period contained in the call agreement. For example, if bank A lends 48-hour money to bank B, then B will repay the principal after 48 hours, and the interest incurred will be settled at the end of the month. It can happen, however, that bank A does not call in its loan after 48 hours but, by mutual consent, allows B to retain the funds under the existing terms. B will of course be liable to render the additional interest accrued.

The SBP has a certain indirect regulatory role in the call market. It does this by restricting the number of players. The only non-bank to participate in the market was NDLC [National Development Leasing Company]. Although IDBP, PICIC and BEL are DFIs, they are not allowed to play the call market. This way, SBP keeps the amount of short term funds floating around to a manageable level. There are also reserve requirements and credit ceilings imposed upon the NCBs and other foreign banks, while the majority of the DFIs have no such restrictions. Hence, indirectly, the DFIs such as NDFC and NIT play quite an important role in providing much needed short term liquidity to the banking sector.

Trading in Credit Ceiling

The second segment of the money market is that of trading in credit ceiling. The *raison d'être* of trading in credit ceiling is the direct ceiling controls enforced by the SBP on the banking sector ...

... In order to ensure that the aggregate credit expansion by commercial banks does not exceed the overall limit determined in the credit plan, the SBP allocates the private sector projections between all commercial banks in the form of individual ceilings. The ceiling for each bank is calculated by a formula based on the bank's share of total deposits in the system in the previous year, size of the capital fund, foreign currency deposits and the previous year's utilization. To promote the flow of credit to priority sectors, SBP sets mandatory targets for the commercial banks in respect of loans to agriculture, business and industry, low cost housing and fixed investment. Should any bank fail to reach the targets set for it, it becomes liable to penalty in the form of an interest free deposit with SBP to the extent of the shortfall ...

... Ceiling trading takes place when banks market their under or over utilization of ceilings amongst themselves. At the end of the week, a bank may find that it has not utilized its full credit ceiling. SBP allows it to then sell that under-utilized amount to a bank which may have over-extended its credit limit. Trades are normally conducted on Thursday when each bank must submit its weekly report to the SBP. Each bank keeps a daily check on its credit disbursements, and, barring any unforeseen withdrawals or infusions of funds, can safely forecast its closing position. Consequently, a bank reasonably secure in the knowledge that it will not exceed its credit limit can conclude forward deals well before the end of the week. Bids and offers are made on the basis of the credit situation that week, and the rates charged depend upon

demand and supply. Just as in the call market, tight credit will result in higher interest rates charged on loans, while ready availability of funds implies the opposite. Ceiling trading agreements are usually for anywhere from 15 to 90 days. As a result, the rates prevailing in the market will obviously be higher than those for call money. (One way to look at it is that call money rates are the bottom line, and money market rates will never fall below call money rates). Just like the call market, funds are exchanged between banks by means of a promissory note. Similarly, settlement is also in two parts. Interest is paid monthly, and the principal is settled at the end of the contractual term through cheques drawn on the SBP. Hence, settlement is basically an accounting procedure for the State Bank ...

Other Short Term Financing (Repo Market)

Call money and ceiling trading are then the two main components of the Pakistan money market. There are, however, certain other short term financing methods that fall somewhere between these two, but are still, none the less, within the confines of the money market. The majority of DFIs are not allowed to participate in the call market but they do, however, play in the ceiling trading market. Since ceilings are not imposed on them, DFIs, like NDFC, are in a position to assist scheduled banks in meeting their ceiling requirements. What happens is that the DFI lends to the scheduled bank's customers against the scheduled bank's guarantee. In effect, the DFI takes on to its book for a certain period of time, assets belonging to the scheduled bank and charges a commission for the service. In this way, the bank records the transaction as an off balance sheet item and its credit ceiling requirements remain undisturbed. Shortly after the introduction of the system for auctioning public debt, on February 26, 1991, SBP decided that the scheduled banks may only hold 15% of their 30% liquid asset requirement in the form of government issued Federal Investment Bonds and Government of Pakistan Loans. Since both these securities offered very attractive rates of return, banks were understandably disappointed. One way of getting around this restriction presented itself in the form of Repo transactions. Say, for example, that Bank A bought more FIBs than it ought to have. However, it cannot show on its books any holdings of securities in excess of the prescribed 15% for fear of being penalized by the SBP. It can avoid such a penalty by engaging in a Repo transaction with a DFI (say NDFC) for the excess amount. This would be a Sale and Repurchase Agreement (SRA) whereby the bank would sell the FIBs to the DFI and then buy them back after the contractually agreed period of time. The interest component would be built into the agreement. It is important to note that during the Repo transaction the DFI does not actually own the FIBs and has no right to sell them. It is, in fact, taking the FIBs onto its books and holding them in safe keeping and charging a fee for this service. The bank meanwhile has a clear slate, avoiding SBP penalties as well as earning the interest accrued on these securities.

Source: Mahmood, Javed, 'Money Markets in Pakistan: Concepts, Instruments and Operations', *Journal of the Institute of Bankers in Pakistan*, vol. 58, no. 1, 1992, p. 27–32.

Appendix 13.2

Recent changes in monetary management

Ihtasham-ul-Haque writes about some of the changes that have been undertaken by the government under agreements with the IMF and the World Bank.

The State Bank of Pakistan will no longer introduce new concessional lending schemes, and the rates of return will be liberalized, according to the latest Policy Framework Paper (PFP) of the Federal Government.

The latest PFP has been prepared by the high government authorities in collaboration with the World Bank and the IMF, elaborating various new measures to be taken during 1994-5, 1995-6 and 1996-7.

It has been decided that the State Bank's lending rate to specialized financial institutions will be reviewed in order to reduce concessional elements of such lending. All necessary steps will be taken to reduce concessional schemes and mandatory credit. The State Bank has already eliminated mandatory credit target for tobacco marketing; the share of mandatory credit in total credit will be reduced, consistent with the objective of decreasing the concentration of credit. In this regard, the target for small business and industry will be eliminated in 1995-96.

The rates on concessional credits were increased from 8 per cent in August 1993 to 13 per cent in November 1994. But now the decision has been taken, and the World Bank and the IMF assured, that there would not be any new concessional lending schemes to be introduced.

The issue was reportedly discussed thoroughly in the light of the donors' pressure, about which the President and the Prime Minister also held detailed consultations and gave the go-ahead signal for the new programme keeping in view the position of the economy.

The decision might spark criticism by businessmen but officials said that the government had no option but to close down the chapter of concessional lending schemes introduced by the State Bank from time to time in the past.

Liquidity Ratio

The financial sector reform agenda of the updated Policy Framework Paper provides for strengthening prudential regulation and supervision. Efforts will focus on greater implementation and expansion of the prudential guidelines introduced in August 1992 and on harmonization of conditions facing market participants with regard to permissible activities and capital adequacy with a view to reaching international standards.

In addition, the level and appropriateness of the liquidity ratio will be reviewed with the objectives of turning it fully into a prudential regulation. Steps will also be taken to improve the legal environment for loan recovery, minimize differential taxation of financial instruments and institutions and enhance the prudential regulations of securities and insurance markets through institution-building.

The government has held out the assurance through the PFP that financial sector reforms would continue to be at the forefront of the policy programme and will be facilitated by the gains already achieved in the fiscal reform area.

The State Bank will continue to implement policies for the consolidation of the credit market, rationalization of the rate structure, reduction in impediments to a fully market-based allocation of credit, and completion of the move towards indirect methods of monetary control. Progress towards indirect monetary control will be pursued by increasing the credit–deposit ratio and integration of the treasury bill auctions into the SBP's open market operations. Specifically, the credit–deposit ratio will be increased in quarterly steps with a view to phasing it out completely by 1995-96.

The decision has also been taken to strengthen operational modalities of the open market operations through better coordination between the Ministry of Finance and the State Bank so that auction volumes for determining the basis of monetary policy considerations could be worked out.

Moreover, the government will take steps to enlarge and deepen the market for government securities with a view to enhancing the transmission mechanism of the monetary policy.

About foreign exchange and trade system reform, PFP says that the medium term adjustment and reform programme will include further liberalization of the trade regime. Concurrently, with the tariff reform, this will be pursued in four areas between 1994-95 and 1996-97. First, the government will review and consolidate the existing Statutory Regulation Orders (SROs) with a view to reducing exemptions from customs tariffs and rate dispersion of imports subject to exemptions under SROs will be reduced in two steps and exemptions will be limited to essential items (basic foodstuffs, medicines, fertilizer, and pesticides) by 1996-97 with the exception of existing contractual obligations and for exemption with the tariff band for a limited number of industries which need time for adjustment.

No Concessional Schemes

There will be no addition to the concessional schemes approved already nor any extension in their timeframe. The timeframe for eligibility will not go beyond June 1997 and the concessions will not be for more than five years. In this context, the existing deletion programme will be time-bound without prolongation and no new deletion schemes will be introduced. The reduction in the scope for SROs as well as streamlining of the procedures for introducing new SROs related to the tariff and tax concessions will be undertaken.

Second, the government will review customs valuation procedures based on the Import Trade Prices (Valuation manual) with a view to moving towards an invoice-based system in accordance with GATT norms over a five-year period; barriers to imports will be liberalized further in 1995-96 by eliminating the procedural limits. Third, after the removal of a number of textile items in the context of agreement with key trading partners, the Negative List will be reduced further in 1995–96 by eliminating items unrelated to health, safety, religious, and security reasons. Fourth, the export regime will be further liberalized through the reduction in the number of items subject to export quotas, the elimination of the export development cess, and the progressive reduction in the number of export bans.

Also the government will continue to manage Pakistan's exchange rate flexibility, with a view to maintaining the external competitiveness of Pakistan's tradable goods sector consistent while containing inflationary pressures. The introduction of an upper limit on reverse money will facilitate striking a more appropriate balance between these two objectives. The government will keep under review the operation and transparency of the exchange system and will discuss this issue further with the IMF during the next review under the ESAF and EFF arrangements.

The SBP has withdrawn from forward foreign exchange cover operation on the trade account and private banks have taken up this business. In this regard, the State Bank has also increased the limit on commercial banks' foreign exchange holdings to facilitate their forward operations. As regards the forward cover fee for foreign currency accounts, the SBP recently increased it again from $4\frac{1}{2}$ per cent to $4\frac{3}{4}$ per cent. The SBP intends to continue to review the scheme in view of the BOP development and changes in national and international rates of return. The Bank's withdrawal from the scheme, which is the ultimate objective, will depend on the speed of adjustment of the private market for forward exchange coverage and balance of payments developments.

Source: *DAWN*, Economic and Business Review, 21–7 January 1995.

Appendix 13.3

Theories of inflation

Two different publications look at what causes inflation in Pakistan.

Earlier theories on inflation relied heavily on cost-push and demand-pull factors as the key components in explaining the behaviour of prices. However, in recent years, particularly during the decades of the seventies and eighties, when acceleration of high inflation was observed, three other competing models became popular in the literature in interpreting inflation, namely: a) Monetarist Inflation Model; b) Phillips Curve Model; and c) Structural Model of Inflation.

The monetarist model developed by Milton Friedman and empirically tested by Anna Schwartz simply asserted that the prime factor explaining the current rate of secular price change is the past behaviour of money to output ratio. This is also the dictum of the popular 'Quantity Theory of Money' which, in Friedman's words, purports that 'inflation everywhere is a monetary phenomenon'.

On the other hand, the Phillips curve model, which started as an empirical investigation by A.W. Phillips and was subsequently formalized by Richard Lipsey, simply postulated that there exists a trade-off between price inflation and unemployment in the economy, at least in the short to medium run. In other words, an economy cannot simultaneously achieve lower inflation and unemployment rates.

Paul Streeten, Julio Olivera, William Baumol and Geoffrey Maynard and Willy van Rijckeghem promoted a 'structural' approach to model inflation. Essentially, these authors argued that it is the differential rates in productivity growth, wages and elasticities of income and prices between the industrial and services sectors that determine the long-run trend of rising prices.

Although the above three theories made important contributions in understanding the underlying behaviour of inflation, these models were, nevertheless, inadequate in

explaining the complex dynamic phenomenon of rising inflation particularly for third world countries. This is due to the fact that many of the underlying assumptions in the above models may not hold for those economies. For instance, the instantaneously market (money and labour) clearing assumptions made in developing 'monetarist' and 'Phillips curve' models may be too restrictive for third world economies because of the existence of structural rigidities and a large sparsely distributed monetized sector. Furthermore, because of surplus labour, particularly in the agricultural sector, the so-called 'trade-off' between inflation and unemployment may not be pronounced. Therefore, in developing economies, neither rapid monetary growth nor persistence of high unemployment independently is sufficient to explain the phenomenon of chronic high inflation.

In addition, it has also been argued that third world economies with rapidly growing manufacturing sectors when encountered with supply rigidities, especially from the agriculture sector, can produce an incessant rise in relative prices in the absence of corresponding matching increases in agricultural products. Such sectoral increases in relative prices due to ensuing 'structural rigidities' may easily be translated into a rising general price level thus producing high inflation.

Criticizing the existing theories of inflation in third world economies which attempt to explain the aggregate 'general price level' in terms of other broad macro economic monetary and demand and supply factors, Sukhamoy Chakravarty *et al.*, noted:

Efforts have been thwarted so far by undue reliance on analysis at the aggregate levels. It must ... be recognized that price increases cannot be readily attributed to factors, influencing only supply, or only demand. Empirical investigation of the issues ... therefore, [is] not easy at the aggregate level. At a disaggregated (micro) level there is perhaps more room for agreement as to policy actions.

In order to comprehend the factors explaining the behaviour of prices in third world countries it is, therefore, imperative to construct a framework which should not only be a hybrid of the above theories of inflation but, more importantly, the analysis must be undertaken at much disaggregated sectoral level.

Source: Pasha, Hafiz, *et al.*, 'What Explains the Current High Rate of Inflation in Pakistan?', *Pakistan Development Review*, vol. 34, no. 4, 1995, pp. 930–1.

Economic Policies and Inflation

Macroeconomic policies play a critical role in determining the rate of inflation. For example, growth of the money supply in excess of the increase in real output results in an increase in the price level in order to clear the goods market. Similarly, lax fiscal policy contributes to demand pressure, thereby fuelling inflation. Finally, exchange rate depreciation, by inducing a shift in expenditure away from internationally traded goods that become more expensive relative to nontraded goods, increases demand for domestic goods and factors of production. This, too, can have a significant impact on inflation.

Of course, monetary, fiscal, and exchange rate policies are interrelated. An expansionary fiscal stance, if financed through government borrowing from the banking system, will be reflected in an acceleration in the domestic credit and monetary aggregates. Moreover, lax monetary and fiscal policies fuel demand, part of which will be reflected in increased imports. Unless met with exchange rate depreciation, such polices can lead to lead to balance of payments (foreign exchange) difficulties.

Recent monetary developments suggest that there is a close relationship between key monetary aggregates and nonfood price inflation. While overall monetary assets growth fluctuated, movements in domestic credit were considerably more pronounced. Following a decline in 1993/94, domestic credit growth picked up sharply in late 1994 and continued to rise throughout 1995 and early 1996. Much of the acceleration in credit was accounted for by the increase in government borrowing for budgetary support. In other words, fiscal policy had a strong impact on credit expansion.

Reflecting developments in the credit aggregate, nonfood inflation moderated in 1994 but picked up in 1995 and early 1996. Since lax fiscal discipline accounted for much of the pick up in credit growth, the acceleration of nonfood prices can be attributed to fiscal policy. Moreover, the tightening of credit policy in 1993/94 took far longer to impact inflation than the subsequent expansion in domestic credit growth, lending support to the view that inflation is considerably easier to spark than to stamp out.

As regards exchange rate policy, changes in the rate of depreciation of Pakistan's nominal effective exchange rate (NEER), a trade-weighted basket of currencies, were closely linked to movements in nonfood price inflation during the 1993/94 and 1994/95 fiscal years.

Since mid 1995, however, movements in the two variables have diverged. The pace of depreciation slowed while nonfood prices accelerated. Although the devaluation of the rupee in October temporarily restored the link between the two variables, the pace of depreciation of the rupee in nominal effective terms has since slowed, mainly on account of the strength of the dollar against other major currencies. Over the same period, nonfood prices have continued to accelerate.

Other Determinants of Inflation

Aside from macroeconomic policies, several other factors can potentially impact the overall price level in the economy. These include supply shocks, such as sharp swings in agricultural production; adjustments in government-administered prices; movements in international prices; and the cyclical position of the economy.

Of these factors, fluctuations in agricultural output appear to be the most important determinant of overall inflation. The acceleration of prices in 1994/95 followed two consecutive years of sluggish agricultural sector performance, and the moderation in inflation starting in late 1995 came after a strong recovery in agricultural output.

However, this correlation is due entirely to the large weight of food prices in the overall consumption basket. Indeed, the observed correlation between nonfood prices and agricultural sector performance in recent years suggests that the impact of such supply shocks was limited to food prices. For example, nonfood prices decelerated in 1994/95, despite weak agricultural output, and accelerated in 1995/96 when agricultural production rebounded.

The impact of adjustments in government-administered prices on overall inflation is difficult to interpret from the data. To a large extent, such adjustments are unavoidable because, in the absence of the adjustments, the subsidy associated with the prevailing administered prices would give rise to an unsustainable financial imbalance for the Government.

Hence correlations between overall and administered price inflation can potentially be associated with a common underlying cause – the stance of macroeconomic policies. Lax financial discipline, for example, intensifies demand pressure and raises inflation. At the same time, inflation magnifies the extent to which administered prices diverge from their true market levels, necessitating the need for adjustments in the prices of administered goods.

In Pakistan, aside from some food items, most of the goods for which prices are administered by the Government are in the fuel and transport categories of the consumption basket. A comparison of changes in the fuel and transport sub-indices of the CPI with other nonfood goods sheds light on the relation between administered-price and overall inflation. While movements in prices of administered goods have been reflected in changes in overall nonfood inflation in recent years, prices of nonfood items other than fuel and transport have also moved in line with overall nonfood inflation. Hence, even if administered price adjustments entirely account for changes in fuel and transport prices, the deceleration of other nonfood prices in 1993/94 and the subsequent acceleration is still left unexplained.

Movements in world market prices, unless offset by exchange rate changes, can also impact the domestic price level. In Pakistan, however, movements in international prices have generally not been related to changes in nonfood price inflation in recent years. Throughout 1994, for example, import unit values accelerated sharply in dollar terms at a time when nonfood inflation was declining. After remaining at a high level for the first half of 1995, the increase in import unit values moderated during late 1995, just as nonfood prices started to accelerate.

Finally, the cyclical position of the economy can affect inflation. If, for example, growth is in excess of the economy's potential, factors of production would have to be utilized intensively, putting pressure on wages and prices. The recent acceleration in nonfood prices in Pakistan, however, appears not to be related to cyclical factors. After three years of growth well below the economy's long-run trend level of 6–6.5 per cent, present rates of employment and capacity utilization are likely to be well below those consistent with full-employment.

Source: ABN AMRO, *Economic Bulletin: Inflation*, vol. 2, no. 4, Karachi, 1996.

Appendix 13.4

What determines savings?

Here are fourteen factors that are supposed to affect savings.

Income Variable

Following both the Keynesian approach and the permanent income hypothesis it is hypothesized that the savings rate is positively related to the growth in national income because more surplus income means a higher savings rate in the economy. The GDP growth rate and per capita income are used alternatively as income variables in all the savings functions.

Domestic Real Interest Rate

The impact of the domestic real interest rate on domestic savings is a controversial issue among economists. On the one hand, it is argued that an increase in the real interest rate tends to encourage domestic savings through the substitution effect. On the other hand, current consumption is derived from current income through the income effect, resulting in less savings. But the empirical evidence suggests that the real interest rate is positively related with the savings rate. This study hypothesizes that an increase in the real interest rate provides an incentive to the household sector to save more. With a relatively higher interest rate, the corporate sector also generates its own savings due to the higher cost of borrowing loans from domestic banking and non-banking institutions.

Domestic Credits

Bank credits to the private sector are expected to have a negative impact both on household and corporate savings. Instead of domestic bank credits to the public sector, total domestic transfers to the public sector from banking and non-banking institutions are used in the analysis, assuming a negative relationship between domestic transfers and public savings. In fact, the availability of bank credits discourages the efforts of institutional agents to enhance their own savings.

Inflation Rate

It is assumed that the expected inflation rate has a negative impact on household and corporate savings. Because of the anticipation of a higher inflation rate in the future, people substitute their future consumption for present consumption, consequently saving less.

Foreign Interest Rate

A higher foreign interest rate may encourage people to transfer their savings abroad, thereby reducing household and corporate savings. As regards public savings, a higher interest rate on foreign debt means that the burden of debt servicing increases. Thus, foreign interest pushes the government to raise its domestic resources, resulting in increased public savings. The US prime rate is considered to be an appropriate measure of the foreign interest rate.

Export Earnings

The export sector is presumed to have an independent impact on the propensity to save and is a critical source of both private savings and government revenues. Export earnings allow the gross domestic product to rise by relieving the foreign exchange constraints, consequently increasing domestic savings. It is also argued that the export sector provides greater profits due to relatively higher prices in international markets. Therefore, the savings propensity for export earnings may be higher than in the other sectors of the economy.

Terms of Trade

Harberger, and Laursen and Metzler, postulate that savings out of any given income falls with deterioration in the terms of trade because a decline in export earnings means a fall of current income and consequently reduction in domestic savings. On the other hand, Obstfeld argues that savings may increase with deterioration in the terms of trade because the economy is forced to spend less on imported goods to maintain a target level of real wealth, thereby saving more. In this study, changes in the terms of trade are included in all the saving functions to facilitate empirical examination of these controversial arguments.

Private Capital Outflows

Private sector capital is like a migratory bird because when the weather is not favourable, it simply moves on to safer pastures. In Pakistan, nationalization measures and political unrest in the country during the 1970s and 1980s discouraged private sector economic activities, resulting in huge capital outflows from Pakistan. Moreover, capital flight resulted in a reduction of available resources to finance domestic investment, eventually leading to a decline in the rate of capital formation. This phenomenon has adversely affected the country's current and future growth and savings rates. Capital outflows hurt not only private savings but also public savings in Pakistan. Government revenue collections have declined as a result of private capital outflows, and so have, consequently, public savings.

Workers' Remittances

Workers' remittances are expected to have a positive impact on household savings because a large part of remittances are saved by the families of emigrants in Pakistan. A survey done by Gillani and Amjad revealed that 35 to 40 per cent of remittances were saved/invested by the families of emigrants in Pakistan.

Dependency Ratio

A well-known demographic variable, the dependency ratio, is also included in the household saving function. The influence of the dependency ratio on household savings in developing countries has remained a controversial issue in the literature. [A number of scholars] have found a strong negative relationship between the dependency ratio and the saving rate. Counter to this, [others] have found no significant influence of the dependency ratio on domestic savings.

Net Foreign Capital Inflows

In the economic literature, the relationship between foreign capital inflows and domestic savings has received considerable attention during the last three decades. Initially, the complementary approach was adopted. More recently, the hypothesis has been put forward that an increase in the foreign capital inflow exercises a depressing effect on domestic savings. [In our work we] focus on how the net foreign capital inflow impacts on the private sector with reference to corporate savings. The justification of not including the foreign capital inflow in the household saving function is that Pakistan is an official borrower and most of its foreign loans come through official sources. The impact of net foreign capital to the public sector is also analyzed in the public saving function.

Profitability

Profit is considered as a primary determinant of private corporate savings. Therefore, a positive impact of profitability on corporate savings is expected.

Real Wage Rate

It is hypothesized that a higher bias towards labour may be detrimental to corporate savings because an increase in real wages in the large-scale manufacturing sector raises the cost of production, consequently reducing profits. Thus, a negative correlation is expected between the real wage rate and the corporate saving rate.

Debt Servicing

A negative relationship between public savings and debt servicing is expected, as every year 17 to 20 per cent of total revenues are spent on debt servicing in Pakistan, which is expected to be saved by the public sector.

Source: Iqbal, Zafar, 'Institutional Variations in Saving Behaviour in Pakistan', *Pakistan Development Review*, vol. 32, no. 4, 1993, pp. 1296–9.

Notes

1. This section is based on Khan, Ashfaque H. 'Need and Scope for Further Reforms in the Financial Sector in Pakistan', *Journal of the Institute of Bankers in Pakistan*, June 1995; and on articles written in the press on monetary policy, in particular those by Aftab Ahmad Khan and M. Imtiaz Ali. Other articles in the *Journal of the Institute of Bankers in Pakistan* have also been a useful source.
2. Khan, Aftab Ahmad, *DAWN*, Economic and Business Review, 1–7 April 1995.
3. Mahmood, Javed, *Journal of the Institute of Bankers in Pakistan*, August 1993, p. 147.
4. Ibid.
5. Khan, Aftab Ahmad, 'New Monetary Policy Designed to Regulate Economy Through Market Based Instruments', *The News*, Business and Finance Review, 5 August 1995.
6. Ibid.
7. Khan, Ashfaque H., op. cit., 1995, p. 43.
8. Ibid., pp. 43–6.
9. Ibid., p. 44.
10. Mahmood, Javed, op. cit., 1993, p. 147.
11. Khan, Ashfaque, H., op. cit., 1995, p. 46.
12. State Bank of Pakistan, *Annual Report, 1994–95*, Karachi, 1995.
13. Khan, Ashfaque, H., op. cit., 1995, p. 49.
14. Ibid.
15. Ali, M. Imtiaz, *The News*, Business and Finance Review, 21 October 1995.
16. Khan, Ashfaque, H., op. cit., 1995, p. 51.
17. Khan, Ashfaque, H., op. cit., 1995.
18. Khan, Aftab Ahmad, *The News*, Business and Finance Review, 5 August 1995.
19. Ibid., p. 52.
20. Ilyas, Muhammad, 'Auctioning of Government Securities', *Journal of the Institute of Bankers in Pakistan*, vol. 60, no. 1, 1994, pp. 22–3.
21. Government of Pakistan, *Pakistan Economic Survey, 1994–95*, Islamabad, 1995, p. 61.
22. Ilyas, M., op. cit., 1994, p. 20.
23. State Bank of Pakistan, *Annual Report, 1994–95*, p. 49.
24. Ibid., pp. 49–50.
25. Ibid., p. 50.
26. This table and these arguments are drawn from Khan, Ashfaque Hasan, op. cit., 1995.
27. Hossain, Akhtar, 'The Monetarist versus the Neo-Keynesian Views on the Acceleration of Inflation: Some Evidence from South Asian Countries (with Special Emphasis on Pakistan)', *Pakistan Development Review*, vol. 29, no. 1, 1990, p. 25.
28. Jones, J.D. and N.M. Khilji, 'Money, Growth, Inflation and

Causality (Empirical Evidence for Pakistan 1973–1985)', *Pakistan Development Review*, vol. 27, no. 1, 1988.

29. Cited in Hossain, Akhtar, op. cit., 1990.
30. Ibid., p. 27.
31. Pasha, Hafiz, *et al.*, 'What Explains the Current High Rate of Inflation in Pakistan? *Pakistan Development Review*, vol. 34, no. 4, 1995.
32. Ibid.
33. Naqvi, S.N.H. and Khwaja Sarmad, *External Shocks and Domestic Adjustment: Pakistan's Case 1970–1990*, mimeo, University Grants Commission, Islamabad, 1993, p. 46.
34. Khan, Ashfaque Hasan *et al.*, 'Financial Repression, Financial Development and Structure of Savings in Pakistan', *Pakistan Development Review*, vol. 27, no. 4, 1988, p. 701.
35. Ibid.
36. Siddiqui, Rehana and Rizwsana Siddiqui, 'Household

Saving in Pakistan', *Pakistan Development Review*, vol. 32, no. 4, 1993, pp. 1281–92.
37. Iqbal, Zafar, 'Institutional Variations in Saving Behaviour in Pakistan', *Pakistan Development Review*, vol. 32, no. 4, 1993, p. 1300.
38. Ibid.
39. Shabbir, Tayeb and Azhar Mahmood, 'The Effects of Foreign Private Investment on Economic Growth in Pakistan', *Pakistan Development Review*, vol. 31, no. 4, 1992, p. 837.
40. Ibid., p. 832.
41. Iqbal, Zafar, op. cit., 1993.
42. Naqvi, S.N.H. and Khwaja Sarmad, op. cit., 1993.
43. Khan, Ashfaque Hasan, Lubna Hasan, and Afia Malik, 'Dependency Ratios, Foreign Capital Inflows and the Rate of Savings in Pakistan', *Pakistan Development Review*, vol. 31, no. 4, 1992, pp. 848–9.
44. Ibid., p. 849.

Part 4

The Era of Structural Adjustment Programmes: 1988 to the Present

The global processes of liberalization, privatization, and openness have also swept Pakistan into their fold, and the structural adjustment programme, now implemented in more than eighty countries, has become the mechanism through which these policies are followed. The structural adjustment programmes involved extensive changes in almost all sections of the economy, including issues of 'getting prices right', lower fiscal deficits, more open trade, and a freer financial sector. Despite the continued adherence of countries to structural adjustment programmes, there is now extensive evidence that most countries have suffered severely due to the programmes, while many are far worse off now than they were before the programmes began. Similarly, in Pakistan research has shown that poverty, inequality, and unemployment have all increased on account of the structural adjustment programmes since 1988, and low growth and high inflation persist. The reasons for the Pakistani government's continued recourse to IMF/World Bank 'assistance' lie in the fact that the ruling clique is unwilling to make essential and urgent reforms which are needed to redress critical shortcomings in the economy; they find it far easier to borrow. The period since 1988 has changed much of the geopolitical balance around the globe. In the case of Pakistan, the post-1988 period is one of structural adjustment rather than fledgling democracy. This period is expected to last for some years yet, leaving a profound imprint on Pakistan's economy and society.

14 Structural Adjustment Programmes: Composition and Effects

There is a general belief amongst students of, and within, underdeveloped countries (UDCs) that the International Monetary Fund (IMF) and the World Bank, or the Washington consensus as their ideology is called, have suddenly taken over the world and are influencing it to suit their own interests. In UDCs, politicians, academics, journalists, and numerous other concerned segments of society have come to believe that their own governments have lost all sense of autonomy and now merely follow dictation from the IMF and the World Bank. Many believe, in fact, that their own ministries of finance are now quite redundant, having been replaced by the International Ministry of Finance. Although it is true that these two agencies in Washington today exert the strongest external influence on underdeveloped countries and their governments, it is important to realize that this sort of outside influence is not something new. While political pressure in its more covert forms has existed for many decades – in fact, one can argue that since the time of colonialism it has *always* existed and has never quite gone away – economic ideas and packages have been exported from Washington at least since the formation of the World Bank and the IMF.

14.1 The Development and Export of Development Thinking[1]

In the 1950s and 1960s, the model that was suggested and developed by academics and government officials in the USA focused almost entirely on growth. This model, where the general aim was to increase growth in the economies of the relatively advanced underdeveloped countries – Latin America and some Asian countries – rested on the premise that increased growth should be the fundamental focus of all policy, and eventually the fruits of growth would 'trickle down' to the population at large. The doctrine of 'functional inequality' was promoted, where the general aim of the policy was to focus on the already well-to-do and to increase their wealth, assuming that they had high saving rates and would thus reinvest their incremental wealth (see Chapter 6 for the application of this philosophy to Pakistan in the 1960s). Industrialization was the mechanism for this enhanced growth, and underdeveloped countries began to produce goods, particularly consumer and intermediate goods, which they had imported earlier – this was the import substituting industrialization phase, popular everywhere. During this phase of development, agriculture was neglected and the internal terms of trade were biased against it (again,

Pakistan's experience, as shown in Chapters 6 and 8, is most revealing). Urbanization increased and the process of 'modernization' of the underdeveloped countries is said to have begun.

Soon after, the detrimental policies towards agriculture were corrected and, with the discovery of higher-yielding varieties of grain, an agricultural Green Revolution began in countries as diverse as Mexico, Pakistan, and the Philippines – often at the insistence of US officials, where the Ford Foundation and other agencies played a distinctive role.

Towards the end of the 1960s, Washington discovered that these policies of growth had caused as many problems as they had sought to solve. Economic growth had indeed taken place, but development was not assuming a particularly pleasant trend. All the countries that were being praised as high achievers in terms of growth were castigated for being poor performers on human indicators. This gave rise to other World Bank packages, such as Basic Needs, and Redistribution With Growth. Growth was still important, but countries were advised to look after their poor and provide basic facilities for them as well. The 1970s also saw huge amounts of dollars being loaned to (mostly) Latin American countries, which were intended to supplement their own efforts at raising capital for investment.

After the debt crisis of the 1980s, and with deteriorating balance of payments positions and inflation in excess of 10,000 per cent in many countries, the Washington agencies stepped in again to offer programmes and loans for stabilization and structural adjustment. While the Washingtonian view in the past may have been more advisory and suggestive, and somewhat covert in the era before the 1980s, with the structural adjustment programme it became much more involved, direct, aggressive, and overt than ever before. In the 1980s, the IMF and World Bank became the driving force at the global level, and facilitated and guided economic restructuring in dozens of countries. Structural adjustment has become the leading vehicle by which the official financial institutions have gained access to policy makers and, through conditionality, have been able to induce profound changes in development policy and economic structures.

In important ways, the 1960s and 1980s have many parallels. Most important were the broad overall macroeconomic perspectives, where growth mattered most, and issues of equity and welfare were somewhat secondary. Trickle down and functional inequality were revived under the structural adjustment programmes. It came to be believed as it had been in the past, that 'economic growth, unencumbered by ancillary concerns, remains the unquestioned imperative of development strategy and that the benefits derived from economic growth can best provide the means for addressing ancillary concerns, whatever they may be'.[2] However, unlike in the 1960s state intervention was to be minimized and protectionism became impermissible, though only for underdeveloped countries.[3] The market was the new institution that was to distribute the benefits of growth and/or development.

Strangely enough, while there are similarities between the 1960s and 1980s, the 1990s also seem to resemble a stage in the 1970s. The incomplete success of the 1960s led to the Basic Needs approach, while in the 1990s, following the structural adjustment programmes of the 1980s, concepts like social action programmes, sustainable development, adjustment with a human face, and sustainable poverty reduction have been introduced to address the incomplete success of the adjustment programmes of the 1980s. History does seem to follow a strange sort of repetitive logic, albeit with significant innovations.

While Washington's economic policies have influenced, if not dominated, much of what has happened in the underdeveloped countries since most of them acquired (a misnomer called) 'independence', the last dozen years have seen an active and much more involved presence. For this reason we now turn to an examination of what constitutes a stabilization and structural adjustment programme, and then examine its subsequent effects. Before that, however, it will be helpful to examine the genesis of the structural adjustment programmes (see Appendix 14.1 for the role of the IMF and World Bank over the last few decades).

14.2 From Structural Adjustment Loans to Structural Adjustment Programmes[4]

In the 1970s, the IMF and World Bank used to play a smaller, though important, role in the economic development of many UDCs. They used to provide loans which were based on careful country analysis and had stringent conditions attached to them. The focus of the IMF was essentially on improving the balance of payments problem, while the World Bank was more focused on specific projects and sectors. World Bank loans were usually made with projects in mind, rather than issues related to the more general workings of the macroeconomy. By the mid-1970s, commercial banks offering easy credit terms, often on few or no preconditions, replaced the IMF as the main source of credit. The rise of western banks as credit providers took place following the huge oil price rises in 1972 and 1979, when oil-rich countries deposited their petrodollars in international banks. These dollars were then recycled to UDCs, particularly to Latin American countries. The extent of this transformation was enormous: in 1971, 60 per cent of UDC debt was owed to official lenders, while in 1981 commercial banks constituted as much as 70 per cent.

This foreign money was lent on easy terms and had a negative real rate of interest. It fuelled extensive, often luxury consumption in most UDCs, where the élite benefited most. These UDCs had meanwhile accumulated substantial amounts of foreign debt. While interest rates were low and commercial banks were ready to lend, governments in UDCs and in the advanced countries were not very concerned about the accumulating debt. However, when US interest rates rose to 18 per cent to finance Ronald Reagan's largest peace-time military build-up, Third World countries were forced to increase their budgetary allocations to service the US dollar-denominated debt. While the cost of servicing outstanding debt increased, commercial credit to the Third World became much tighter. In a matter of a few years, commercial loans were no longer available to finance development projects, or to refinance the existing short-term debt obligations that countries had incurred.

By the early 1980s, the picture was very clear: almost without exception, UDCs were struggling to repay the debts that they had so eagerly acquired during the 1970s. At the same time, these countries had to absorb the financial losses caused by deteriorating terms of trade and high import prices for oil. In order to repay part of their debts or, more importantly, the huge interest, government spending priorities had to change. As a consequence, internal investment and social expenditures began to fall. In order to avert political unrest, many governments were compelled to maintain current spending, especially for public sector employment, at the same time as having to cut capital spending dramatically, particularly for infrastructure maintenance and improvement.

The results of such a policy were obvious at the outset: social expenditure fell in almost all those countries that had accumulated debts. The results were noticeably harsh on the poorer sections of society, who were, possibly, the main beneficiaries of public spending in the social sector. It is important to point out that defence spending suffered significantly smaller cuts than did social expenditure and investments. One reason for this was that, at least till the early and mid-1980s, many governments in the Third World were ruled by military dictators or juntas, and any cut in defence would have implied cuts in the privileges of the rulers themselves.

The IMF's initial approach to loans under the structural adjustment umbrella had two essential components. Along with the World Bank, it emphasized the stabilization of a country's macroeconomic situation by focusing on the balance of payments. Loans were meant to minimize short-term pressure on capital. There was also some insistence on measures to cut domestic aggregate demand. Demand reduction was to be undertaken by drastic cutbacks in public spending and, with the help of monetary policies, the expansion of the money supply was to be restrained. There was also a need to realign the domestic currency with international markets. It was believed that in the era of import substituting industrialization, the exchange rate was overvalued, since this made imports of machinery somewhat cheaper. Many countries also had two exchange rates – one for capital goods and the other for consumer goods. The cure for this was seen to be devaluation, after which it was believed that the country's exports would become more competitive and, since the prices of its imports would rise, the volume of imports would decline. These changes were meant to reduce the pressure on foreign reserves, hopefully improving the balance of payments position.

The second component of the policy was designed to improve overall economic efficiency and promote growth objectives by reforming macroeconomic policy and strengthening local institutions. This was the main difference between stabilization and adjustment. Stabilization, in order to deal with the contractionary repercussions of adjustment, required policy and institutional reforms on both a macroeconomic and sectoral level. The IMF continued to give priority to short-term loan support to economies where the primary focus was demand constraint measures and currency valuation. The World Bank focused on sectoral loans and on restructuring economies through institutional and policy reform in the medium term to stimulate the medium-term supply response.

There was a major change from the mid-1980s, when the programmes of the World Bank and IMF began to become more fused. Also, the distinction between stabilization and adjustment became narrower, and the structural adjustment programmes of the late 1980s onwards had elements of both. There were also differences in the time-span of loans. Earlier, structural adjustment loans were for twelve to eighteen months, but as institutional and policy reform became an increasingly important concern, the period of the loans increased to between three and five years. Now, more complex and stringent conditions were also being attached to loans, which were much bigger in money terms than ever before. The number of conditions attached to a structural adjustment loan increased from an average of twenty-seven in 1985, to fifty-six in 1989.

Since the 1980s, dozens of countries have made use of IMF and World Bank structural adjustment loans (see Figure 14.1). In the 1980s, as much as $41 billion was made available to finance 258 loans, and although Africa received almost half of those loans, it was the Latin American countries as a whole which received the largest amount in this period (see Table 14.1). Since the economies of Latin America are larger, they may have had recourse to fewer, but much larger loans (see Box 14.1 on the IMF's finances).

14.3 Structural Adjustment Programmes: Composition

A structural adjustment programme seems to be fairly general, in the sense that its basic principles are applied to countries irrespective of their differences – and this is one of the major criticisms of the approach, as we discuss in section 14.5.1. The timing of the programme and the specific rates may vary, but the general formula can be summarized as below.

The focus of a structural adjustment programme is on improving the balance of payments position, cutting the fiscal deficit, lowering inflation, and increasing growth. The different arenas around which these and other policies revolve are as follows:[5]

1 *Trade policy.* Countries are advised to adopt competitive real exchange rates, and the mechanism for doing this is devaluation. A consistently depreciating currency is recommended to keep real exchange rates competitive. The lifting of restrictions on exports is advised so as to encourage exports. A decrease in quantitative restrictions

---

BOX 14.1
The IMF's finances

Can the IMF help all the countries of the world facing an imminent economic collapse?

After committing $17.8 billion to rescue Mexico, how much money does the International Monetary Fund (IMF) have left in its coffers? The question sounds simple. But the answer is not, for the IMF's financial structure is fiendishly complex.

For a start, its internal accounts are calculated in terms of special drawing rights (SDRs) – artificial assets created by the IMF and made up of a weighted basket of the world's five top currencies. At present, one SDR is worth $1.47.

The IMF's main source of capital is the subscriptions, or 'quotas', that all its members pay. A country's quota depends on the size of its economy. The total amount of IMF quotas is 145 billion SDRs. But since countries pay part of their quota in their own currencies, and many of these are not freely convertible, the IMF's liquid resources stand at only 62.5 billion SDRs after its efforts to help the Mexicans. As some of these liquid resources have already been committed to countries in trouble, the IMF has an adjusted

measure for what it calls 'uncommitted usable resources'. These total 48 billion SDRs.

The usual way to top-up the IMF's resources is to increase members' quotas, but this takes time. So in emergencies there are other potential sources of cash. Under a special agreement, the IMF can borrow up to 17 billion SDRs from industrialized countries and another 1.5 billion SDRs from Saudi Arabia. In extremis, it could sell some of its 104m ounces of gold, which are probably worth around $39 billion.

The IMF has some liabilities too. Every one of its members is entitled to receive a portion of its quota (the so-called 'reserve tranche') with no questions asked. The IMF must always be in a position to honour these tranches, which add up to around 29 billion SDRs.

The reality, then, is that it is almost impossible to calculate how much the Fund could safely lend to a troubled country. Nonetheless, Lamberto Dino, the Italian prime minister and an old IMF hand, says that its resources are not suited to dealing with the stabilizing capital flows. One thing is sure: it could not cope with many more Mexicos.

Source: *The Economist*, 11 February 1995.

Table 14.1
Adjustment loans and lending commitments by region, 1980–1991

	1980–1982[a]	1983–1985[a]	1986–1988[a]	1989	1990	1991	Total 1980–1991
Africa[b] ($ m)	190	468	1,241	1,235	1,361	1,732	10,025
% of total adjustment loans	23	21	28	20	23	25	24
No. of loans	3	8	13	14	17	15	117
Asia ($ m)	200	383	380	1,130	700	914	5,934
% of total adjustment loans	25	18	11	19	12	13	14
No. of loans	1	2	2	6	5	4	29
Europe, Middle East, and North Africa ($ m)	357	657	981	1,064	900	2,593	10,540
% of total adjustment loans	44	30	22	17	15	37	25
No. of loans	2	3	5	6	3	9	46
Latin America ($ m)	62	675	1,777	2,665	2,996	1,791	14,993
% of total adjustment loans	8	31	40	44	50	25	36
No. of loans	1	4	8	7	7	11	66
Total ($ m)	809	2,183	4,379	6,094	5,957	7,029	41,491
No. of loans	7	17	28	33	32	39	258

[a] Average annual rates.
[b] Includes Special Facility for Africa (for dollar amounts but not number of operations).
Note: All figures are based on calendar years.
Source: World Bank, *Adjustment Lending and Mobilization of Private and Public Resources for Growth*, Policy and Research Studies, No. 22, 1992, p. 69.

on imports, i.e. quotas, and a reduction in tariffs are recommended to strengthen the international competitiveness of domestic industry. Essentially, the principle is that the economy should follow an outward-oriented export-led path, and domestic and international prices should be brought in line with each other.

2 *Fiscal policy.* The reduction and elimination of fiscal deficits by curtailing public expenditure is a high priority, and an increase in prices in the public sector so as to meet costs and increase revenues is also recommended. The tax system is supposed to be reformed and rationalized, essentially to improve the revenue-raising ability of the government. Subsidies to the energy and agricultural sectors are supposed to be either substantially cut or eliminated altogether.

3 *Public enterprises.* The preferential financial treatment to state economic enterprises is to be stopped and their performance is to be brought in line with the private sector. Public enterprises are to be reformed to improve efficiency and profitability. Unprofitable public enterprises are to be closed down or privatized in order to reduce the government's fiscal burden.

4 *Financial sector.* Improving the regulatory framework to facilitate better and smoother functioning and to restore public confidence is top of the list. Institutions are to be restructured so as to facilitate resource mobilization and to

reflect costs. Interest rate ceilings are to be relaxed. Time deposit rates and lending rates are to be liberalized.

5 *Industrial policy.* Protection is to be removed from the industrial sector so as to make it more competitive internationally, and price controls over goods are to be removed so as to improve resource allocation. Those industries that produce for export are to be encouraged and promoted.

6 *Agriculture.* The bias against agriculture is to be eliminated by adjusting the exchange rate and by removing the protection offered to industry. Agricultural prices are to be liberalized and subsidies discontinued.

To summarize, then, the structural adjustment programme is meant to improve the balance of payments position with the help of devaluation, which is supposed to encourage exports; it should cut the fiscal deficit by increasing some prices and cutting subsidies, and by decreasing government expenditure; and it should cut inflation and foster growth. As far as possible, intervention in the market should be eliminated and an attempt should be made to 'get prices right' (see Box 14.2). Balanced budgets, production, and trade liberalization are everywhere the buzzwords. For a self-assessment by the World Bank of structural adjustment programmes across the globe in the 1980s, see Table 14.2.

Figure 14.1
Structural adjustment loans to countries, 1986–1990

Intensive adjustment lending countries (27)

Bolivia	Mauritania
Brazil	Mauritius
Chile	Mexico
Colombia	Morocco
Costa Rica	Nigeria
Côte d'Ivoire	Pakistan
Ghana	Philippines
Guinea-Bissau	Senegal
Jamaica	Tanzania
Kenya	Thailand
Korea, Republic of	Togo
Madagascar	Turkey
Malawi	Zambia

Other adjustment lending countries(30)

Algeria	Hungary
Argentina	Indonesia
Bangladesh	Mali
Benin	Niger
Burkina Faso	Panama
Burundi	Sierra Leone
Cameroon	Somalia
Central African Republic	Sri Lanka
China	Sudan
Congo, People's Republic	Trinidad and Tobago
Ecuador	Tunisia
Gabon	Venezuela
Gambia	Yugoslavia
Guyana	Zaire
Honduras	Zimbabwe

Non-adjustment lending countries (20)

Botswana	Liberia
Dominican Republic	Malaysia
Egypt	Myanmar
El Salvador, Arab Republic of	Nicaragua
Ethiopia	Papua New Guinea
Greece	Paraguay
Guatemala	Peru
Haiti	Portugal
India	Rwanda
Lesotho	Syrian Arab Republic

Notes: Intensive adjustment lending countries are those that have received two structural adjustment loans or three or more adjustment operations effective by June 1990, with the first adjustment operation effective in June 1986 or before. Other adjustment lending countries are those that have received at least one adjustment loan effective by June 1990. Non-adjustment lending countries are those that did not receive adjustment lending by June 1990.

Source: World Bank, *Adjustment Lending and Mobilization of Private and Public Resources for Growth*, Policy and Research Studies No. 22, 1992, p. 15.

14.4 Structural Adjustment Programmes: Implementation and Effects

Since numerous countries have had recourse to IMF and World Bank loans in the course of their structural adjustment programmes, and many of these countries have had repeated access to these loans, a number of studies have examined the consequences of such programmes. Furthermore, many cross-country studies compare the performance of those countries which followed structural adjustment programmes and those that did not.[6]

Summarizing a large number of studies which look at the macroeconomic effects of Fund-supported adjustment programmes, Mohsin Khan of the IMF concludes that in some cases the balance of payments improves, but not in all; inflation is usually not brought down by the programme; and growth falls in the first year, but may then rise. He concludes his review by saying that 'on the basis of existing studies, we certainly cannot say whether the adoption of programmes supported by the Fund led to an improvement in inflation and growth performance. In fact, *it is often found that programmes are associated with a rise in inflation and a fall in the growth rate*.'[7]

World Bank studies argue that those countries 'that have carried out major adjustments have performed better on average in terms of their aggregate economic activity than those that have not ... There is a general and positive connection between adjustment lending and this relative improvement, but the connection is not a tight one and performance varies substantially among loan recipients.'[8] Regarding a cut in fiscal deficits, the World Bank itself concludes that 'the short-term impact of budgeting retrenchment has generally been recessionary, with a fall in investment and growth'.[9] This stringent fiscal adjustment which is central to the structural adjustment programme has led 'to sharp decline in public investment [which] may be leading to serious infrastructure bottlenecks to development'.[10] A cut in the budget deficit was almost always achieved by a cut in expenditure because 'deep seated institutional weaknesses' did not permit an expansion of revenue. In those countries that attempted to cut the deficit, debt service payments rose sharply because of the increase in interest rates and the devaluation of the domestic currency, as a result of which 'a widening gap between the fiscal deficit and current account deficit put increasing pressure on the private sector to generate a net surplus. This led to cuts in private investment and growth, often accompanied by higher inflation.'[11]

Critics of the programme challenge the significance of adjustment lending in restoring growth. If the adjustment effect on growth is weak, adjustment lending creates a negative investment effect: 'The influence of structural adjustment programmes on aggregate investment *is almost everywhere negative*'[12] and 'this negative impact on investment runs counter to one of the basic objectives of adjustment and thereby questions the assumptions on which policy lending was predicated'.[13] The United Nations Economic Commission

BOX 14.2

Is 'getting prices right' the answer? Is it possible and feasible for UDCs?

Professor Sir Hans Singer argues:

A key objective of the structural adjustment programmes inspired by the Washington Consensus is to extend the role of the market and reduce the role of government intervention by way of planning and regulation as well as direct production. This emphasis on 'market friendliness' has both international and domestic aspects. It is based on the assumption that the market is right: there are no market failures or if there are they are less serious or can be more easily rectified than government failures. This is perceived to be in contrast to the bad old ways of the 1950s when the reverse assumption was made, i.e. that government failures could be disregarded in comparison with market failures. The international aspect of market friendliness consists in the acceptance of international prices as the benchmark of comparative advantages and measures of competitiveness; this places emphasis on the selection of the correct exchange rate so that the assumedly correct market incentives of international prices can feed through into the national economy, resulting in proper emphasis on the production of tradeables as against non-tradeables. Tradeables of course include not only exports and potential exports but also import substitutes and potential import substitutes. This is recognized in theory although in practice the emphasis tends to be on exports rather than on import substitution. Similarly, allocation of resources, non-tradeables as well as tradeables, must be governed by the market prices. 'Getting prices right', in the sense of having prices as close as possible to what a free market would produce, are held to be the key to sustainable growth.

Critics might question this model on various grounds. First of all, international prices are not always free market prices and as such suitable benchmarks for countries undergoing structural adjustment. For example, international cereal prices can hardly be said to be the result of free market forces; rather they are artificially low as a result of agricultural subsidies to farmers in Europe and the US resulting in large surpluses overhanging the market and putting downward pressure on prices. Thus countries deciding their domestic priorities for domestic food production *versus* imports on the basis of international prices would allocate less to domestic production and rely more on food imports than true free market principles would suggest. This is sometimes acknowledged by accepting food security as a desirable objective in itself, apart from market friendliness, but this is really an acknowledgement that there are important market failures in this area.

Secondly, critics would point out that in developing countries, and especially in the poorer developing countries, the institutions and qualifications necessary for the operation of domestic markets are simply not there. This lack refers to essential infrastructure such as roads, telecommunications, etc. and also to the lack of an entrepreneurial and business class with the necessary information, access to credit, etc. to organize production in response to price incentives. The structural adjustment programmes are based on the assumption that the first and most essential step is to get the macroeconomic fundamentals right and that supply will respond to the right environment and proper price incentives and thus lead to sustainable growth. This seems to neglect some of the structural obstacles to supply response.

Source: Singer, Hans, 'Are the Structural Adjustment Programmes Successful?', *Pakistan Journal of Applied Economics*, vol. XI, nos. 1 and 2, 1995.

Professor Prabhat Patnaik has this to say about export performance and 'getting prices right':

Getting prices right (it is not worth talking about efficiency of resource use) as a condition for becoming a successful exporter, and for achieving high rates of viable growth, is belied consistently by actual experience. Virtually every instance of noticeable export dynamism, whether it is Germany in the late-19th century, or Japan and South Korea in the post-war period, has been characterized not only by not getting prices right in the neoclassical sense, but by having differential prices for the same commodity between the domestic and foreign markets. Indeed, such differential prices are what precisely have helped the export drive: capitalists have made up through profitable domestic sales what they have lost in foreign markets by keeping prices low for the sake of export expansion. Such differential pricing of course has been made possible by having a protectionist regime where the rates of protection have varied across commodities, a phenomenon which is diametrically opposite to what trade reforms being currently pursued ... under Fund-Bank advice, seek to achieve ... The proposition that a pre-condition for successful exporting is to 'get prices right' can hardly be sustained in the light of historical experience.

Source: Patnaik, Prabhat, 'International Capital and National Economic Policy: A Critique of India's Reforms' *Economic and Political Weekly*, vol. 20, no. 12, 1994, p. 684.

for Africa has accused the World Bank of 'stark manipulation of data' to prove that its programmes work. There is also evidence that 'many resource-poor countries experience severe economic contraction and social dislocations in the short term, [and] draconian austerity measures had a serious negative impact on the ability of many countries to improve economic efficiency and rekindle growth in the medium and long term'.[14] Furthermore, the attempt to correct the balance of payments position with the help of devaluation and an immediate and undifferentiated reduction in import tariffs has not given national industries adequate time to improve their competitiveness with foreign firms. 'Consequently, deindustrialization in many countries resulted from sudden trade liberalization and further eroded the industrial base of

Table 14.2
The World Bank's assessment of reforms in the major policy areas affected by adjustment programmes, 1981–1988

Policy area	Extent of reform	Assessment
Overall reforms	External adjustment rapid, internal adjustment often unsustained, institutional reforms slow.	Policies have mattered a great deal, but constraints include conflicts in design (for example, between fiscal and trade policies).
Fiscal	Initial deficit reductions not sustained. Some success in rationalization of public investment (as in Pakistan and Turkey). Tax reform not comprehensive and with limited success. Indonesia, Mexico, and Turkey are exceptions.	Expenditure cuts could not be maintained. More careful scrutiny of current expenditure needed. Short-run revenue concerns have dominated.
Trade	Progress in exchange rate flexibility and export incentives. Progress in replacement of quantitative restrictions by tariffs and in tariff reform, but import liberalization slower.	Strong responses in export volume, but non-price factors need greater emphasis (as in East Asia). Greater liberalization constrained by stabilization requirements and internal opposition; export response assists in import liberalization (as in Korea and Turkey).
Financial	Reforms initiated in only a few cases, but receiving greater attention.	Reforms often protracted and require sound macro framework (as in Chile and Turkey).
Public sector management	Institutional reforms and divestiture slow, particularly in sub-Saharan Africa. Some reduction in enterprise losses.	Introduced in almost every adjustment programme. Gains more from price increases than from improvements in efficiency.
Agriculture	Visible improvements in price policy. Reform of parastatals slower.	Improvements especially strong in sub-Saharan Africa. Supply response to price constrained by institutional factors.
Industry	Focus on trade policy and its impact on industry.	Reforms specific to industrial sector not given sufficient attention.

Source: Thomas, V., *et. al.*, *Restructuring Economies in Distress*, Oxford University Press, Oxford, 1991, p. 15.

many fragile economies.'[15] A major reason for this, which is more noticeable in low-income countries, is that industrial firms usually do not have the managerial or technical capacity to be able to stand up to increasing imports and greater openness. If domestic firms are inefficient and therefore protected, opening them up to more efficient foreign competition will not usually make them efficient; it will close them down.

Severe criticism of the IMF/World Bank structural adjustment programmes has been directed at their welfare consequences. Political unrest in countries as diverse as the Dominican Republic, where many people were killed in the early 1980s in a wave of protest against the severe economic austerity measures, or in Egypt, Morocco, Tunisia, and Zambia, following attempts to reduce food subsidies sharply, must suggest that these programmes do have some negative effects on the poor. 'Social unrest has often followed the implementation of stabilization and adjustment policies which severely curtail the purchasing power of the poor as well as their access to basic services.'[16]

In a UNICEF report written in 1984, which was the first of its kind and examined the effect of the structural adjustment programme on the human condition, the authors concluded that in many countries 'the declines in child welfare appear to be *closely associated* with stabilization and adjustment programmes'.[17]

Moreover, a study by Van der Hoeven found that it was mostly the extreme poor who were affected by the programme, since 'the economic environment in which they live is often more closely related to the external sector, and their principal source of income – wages – has often decreased drastically as part of structural adjustment policies'.[18] These findings have been supported by Veltmeyer, who argues that between 1973 and 1985, 'in almost every country in Latin America where the structural adjustment programme has been imposed, the share of labour in income derived from value added in manufacture has fallen'.[19] In the case of Chile, which is considered an 'economic miracle' by Washington, Veltmeyer found that there was a widening and deepening of various social inequalities in the distribution of income and other economic resources, as 'well as a dramatic decline in the purchasing power of wages and an associated deterioration in living standards'.[20] In 1969 those living below the poverty line in Chile were 29 per cent of the population; this figure had increased to 42 per cent by 1990. Increasing income concentration and inequality was also found in the other success story, Turkey, where studies indicate a 'significant worsening in both the size and functional distribution of income in the 1980s'.[21] There was a sharp decline in the share of both agricultural incomes, and wages and salaries. The worsening income distribution arose from the 'removal of subsidies following price decontrol in the public sector, a neglect of essential public services in health and education, as well as a sharp fall in real wages and agricultural terms of trade',[22] all which were implemented due to the structural adjustment programme.[23] The effect of structural adjustment programmes on the natural environment has also been seen to be harmful.[24]

Prabhat Patnaik and C.P. Chandrasekhar, in an excellent evaluation of the impact of the structural adjustment programme in India, have shown that 'the most palpable impact of structural adjustment has been an increase in rural poverty'.[25] They explain this phenomenon on the following grounds:

> Structural adjustment in other words has necessarily entailed costly food for the working people. And there is nothing to be surprised about it because it is part of the logic of structural adjustment: by insisting on a reduction in the magnitude of food subsidy, by insisting on an elimination of all input subsidies into agriculture (of which the fertilizer subsidy was the most important element in India), and at the same time by insisting that the prosperous farmers should not only get *remunerative* prices but in fact *international* prices in a regime largely of unfettered producer choices in matters of production and exchange of agricultural commodities, it necessarily ensures that the price of food in terms of the wage-unit, especially in the unorganized sector, goes up. A rise in rural poverty is an inevitable consequence of this phenomenon.[26]

Francis Stewart has offered an extensive critique of the structural adjustment programme on the grounds that it has affected welfare negatively. She argues that, in Africa and Latin America during the 1980s, the 'balance on the whole was *undoubtedly negative*'.[27] Per capita income declined as did investment, while inflation 'accelerated'; the budget deficit 'showed no improvement in Sub-Saharan Africa and a *considerable worsening* in Latin America'.[28] The real income of the low-income population was particularly affected by rising food prices where specific conditions in the adjustment programme required subsidies to be removed and producer prices to be raised, and where a devaluation of the local currency affected imported food.

Stewart's work also substantiates that of others, indicating that cuts in real per capita government expenditure following

IMF advice to decrease the budget deficit affected the resources available for health and education. She shows that, in the majority of countries following Fund/Bank programmes, health and education expenditure per capita was cut in the 1980s. Zuckerman finds that in *non-adjusting countries*, the majority of countries *increased* their expenditure on health and education. David Reed also argues that 'it is worth noting that defense spending suffered significantly smaller reductions than social expenditure and investments'.[29] In addition, 'draconian cut backs in government expenditure have frequently led to dramatic and often extended reduction in public investment in infrastructure. Deteriorating and inadequate infrastructure, in turn, has become a major bottleneck to economic expansion and often in terms of developing domestic markets.'[30]

Even World Bank staff admit that the social cost in adjusting countries has been high, with higher unemployment, lower real wages, and worse social welfare. They even admit that their policies have given birth to a new breed of people whom they call 'the new poor' – who, they concede, are the direct victims of adjustment. The removal of subsidies on food, public transport, energy, water, and fertilizers – all standard structural adjustment programme requirements – has a severe impact on the poor.

However, the IMF continues to reiterate that it is not in the business of solving the poverty problem. As its Managing Director has said, its programme involves 'first and foremost, macroeconomic discipline, beginning with the reductions of fiscal deficits and monetary measures aimed at achieving price stability and realistic exchange rates'.[31] These policies are said to 'serve the poor'.

Other World Bank staff go to the extent of arguing that 'it is debatable ... whether reducing structural poverty *ought to* figure prominently in a discussion of adjustment programmes'.[32] They continue that 'countries under adjustment are often short of resources and of the capacity to implement programmes. Asking them to add to the already large demands on their economic systems the task of developing programmes to reduce poverty permanently *may be very dangerous indeed*'.[33] The Bank repeatedly emphasizes the point that adjustments 'necessarily carried transitional costs (mostly for the poor) that had to be accepted before economic growth and enhanced efficiency would generate broader economic improvements'.[34] Today, the 'World Bank approach limits itself to the hope that efficient pricing and outward orientation usually suffice, in due course, to raise incomes and hence diminish the levels – or reduce the growth – of poverty'.[35] There seems to be a return to the thinking of the 1970s when the trickle down approach was in vogue. But Veltmeyer argues: 'medium or long term benefits of economic reform do not automatically trickle downwards or spread, and that the most vulnerable groups, particularly those in dire poverty, need to be protected and compensated with target policy measures'.[36] World Bank/IMF thinking has failed to learn its lessons from the experience of the 1960s and 1970s, and today for them 'the preferred approach to poverty reductions is to let markets work'.[37]

14.5 Economic Liberalization and Openness: Some Questionable Assertions[38]

In the 1980s, there was a noticeable rise of right-wing politics and supply-side economics in the advanced countries of the West. In particular, the elections of Ronald Reagan, George Bush, Margaret Thatcher, and Helmut Kohl represented a return to, and the ascendancy of, neo-classical thinking, particularly in economics. This rise was complemented by the demise of the Soviet Union as a country, and of socialism as an economic and political alternative. Capitalism, with its free markets and private sector, reigned supreme. In the advanced nations of the West, this philosophy was given vent by a dismantling and withering away of the state, by privatization, and by a curtailment of public expenditure programmes.

The UDCs did not escape the ascendancy of this global neo-classical thinking. Economists, politicians, and policy makers from the developed countries, particularly the USA, pressed financial liberalization upon those in the UDCs. The Baker Plan, devised in the USA to deal with the huge debt problem that had afflicted Latin American countries, offered relief for debt that had accumulated over the 1970s. However, the USA agreed to provide funds only if these countries agreed to deregulate and make major changes in their economies. The IMF conformed to the US position, and neo-liberal orthodoxy in economics became the only paradigm of any consequence. The structural adjustment programmes discussed above are an important policy tool in the broader framework of economic liberalism, and thus it is important to place them in their proper context.

Even a cursory examination of what constitutes economic liberalization will show its close parallels with the structural adjustment programme. For example, liberalization requires trade openness, where there is an exposure of the domestic goods market to the international economy. Financial openness requires exposure of the domestic financial system to world capital markets. Liberalization implies an outward orientation in which imports are to be liberalized and tariffs cut, devaluation of the local currency ought to take place, and production should switch from import substituting to exportable goods and commodities. A central feature of the liberal orthodoxy is a reduction in the role of the government, with minimal government restrictions and involvement in international trade in goods and asset markets, as well as in domestic financial, commodity, and labour markets. In essence, then, economic liberalization requires a policy package to take the economy away from illiberalism towards liberalism or, what is the same thing, towards *laissez-faire*, or a free-market, pro-private sector economy. The case for economic liberalization has rested upon the claim that all the above policy reforms contribute towards higher growth and reduced dependence of the economy.

The neoclassical position holds the view that financial activity is necessary not only for the mobilization and efficient allocation of resources, but also as a stabilizing force in the economy. Hence, the recommendation to deregulate and privatize the financial sector. Furthermore, this logic holds that the greater the openness of any country, the less its vulnerability to international economic fluctuations. However, see Box 14.3 for a very different view.

However, evidence from countries which have had more liberal and open economies shows that they have not performed as well as those which are considered closed and more controlled. For example, it has been seen, contrary to the ideology which advocates openness, that open financial markets are more vulnerable to exogenous shocks. In a comparison of India and China (closed) with Brazil and Mexico (open) there is evidence that the closed countries performed better during the world economic slowdown of the 1980s than the ones more closely integrated with the world economy.[39] India and China had long followed the path of self-reliance and import substituting industrialization and depended far less on foreign debt. Until a few years ago they were not very open to foreign interests and they were able to cope with the world economic recession precisely for this reason. By integrating with the international financial markets, most countries of Latin America have suffered as their dependence for foreign funds has always been quite substantial.

The neo-liberal thinking, and that accepted by the IMF in its stabilization and structural adjustment programmes, makes the strong claim that openness and trade liberalization have a positive outcome for growth. However, cross-sectional and time series evidence does not support this claim and these empirical linkages are not observed. In fact, a study by Alan Hughes and Ajit Singh suggests that the most successful countries in the 1970s and 1980s stayed far from the path of *laissez-faire* and openness.[40]

The structural adjustment programme finds its intellectual and policy roots in economic liberalization. We saw earlier how the programmes have been unable to address many of the issues they have targeted, and the supposed beneficial results from liberalization have also been found to be questionable. Open economies with greater degrees of liberalization are not necessarily better performers than closed economies. In fact, if anything, closed economies seem better suited to deal with slumps and crises in the world markets. These observations lead to an important criticism of neo-classical thinking, economic liberalization, and especially structural adjustment programmes, which is discussed in the next section.

14.5.1 The Contextuality of Policy[41]

A major criticism of economic liberalization and structural adjustment progrmmes is that they are being offered as a complete cure for a country's ills, *regardless of the particular institutional arrangements or the historical background which may exist*. A 'general' theory and a 'general' prescription is applied unilaterally to any 'typical' Third World country. What is required, however, is a deeper understanding of the *specific* historical conditions and *specific* institutional contexts of *specific* countries. Policy must take into account the historical and institutional contexts in which particular policies will operate. Neglect and misunderstanding of the particular

BOX 14.3
Hot money and its consequences

What happens when money is highly mobile? Some answers:

When hot money flows occur, the recipient country has two choices: either to maintain the exchange rate by adding to reserves or to prevent a swelling of reserves by letting the exchange rate appreciate. Any government wishing to prevent a gratuitous 'deindustrialization' of the economy (and hence a gratuitous 'manufacture' of a current account deficit to accommodate hot money inflows) would of course prefer to prevent an exchange rate appreciation by adding to exchange reserves. And since these enhanced reserves represent after all an additional command over resources, even hot money flows, it may be thought, can add to the pace of capital formation if properly utilized.

The problem however is two-fold: the minor problem relates to the fact that using reserves built up with hot money for undertaking investment implies in essence that the country is 'borrowing short to invest long' which exposes it to potential crises. But even if this is tackled by choosing short-gestation, foreign-exchange-earning investment projects, there remains a major problem, namely, there has to be an *agency* that must take the lead in stepping up capital formation: and an economy under Fund-Bank thraldom lacks such an agency. Since the state is increasingly forced to withdraw from its investment role it cannot step up investment directly. Since the state cannot order private investment, it can stimulate the latter only indirectly: but the obvious indirect instrument, namely, the interest rate, can scarcely be used for fear of frightening international rentiers. And portfolio investment which typically stimulates stock market booms makes speculation more attractive than productive investment for the domestic capitalists. Finally, since 'market-friendliness' takes the form *inter alia* of trade liberalization which brings in MNC products to the local market, this fact tends to dampen the inducement to invest of domestic capitalists.

The upshot is that foreign exchange reserves accumulate even as productive investment languishes. The reserve accumulation, it may be thought, would give rise to a *consumption-led boom*. But, for reasons already discussed, credit to finance such a boom is expensive. And even if it does play a role, the boom would be a brief and evanescent one, unit of domestic supply constraints begin to appear (at which point reserves would start getting used up to augment supplies and the domestic multiplier effects of higher consumption would disappear). What is even more likely, however, is that such consumption growth as occurs owing to the effects of hot money inflows would, in a 'liberalized trade' regime, leak out abroad without generating any domestic growth.

On the other hand, when hot money flows out, the very fact that the reserves have shrunk in the event of higher domestic consumption (or if the outflow is larger than the extant reserves can sustain), the economy has to be deflated, and a whole lot of measures, including handing over the country's natural resources 'for a song' to international creditors, have to be adopted, to cope with the foreign exchange crunch. The net result is a process of gradual economic atrophy together with 'denationalization' of assets and resources.

Source: Patnaik, Prabhat and C.P. Chandrasekhar, 'Indian Economy Under "Structural Adjustment"', *Economic and Political Weekly*, vol. 30, no. 47, 1995, pp. 3009-10.

Mexico is an old hand at IMF/World Bank structural adjustment programmes and began restructuring its economy under IMF guidelines from as early as 1976. The IMF and World Bank have evaluated the performance of Mexico quite favourably, for it closely followed the policy outlines, which are quite standard. There was considerable progress, as per conditions, on the trade front with imports liberalized and tariffs reduced. The real exchange rate was depreciated substantially, some state-owned enterprises were privatized, and food subsidies were removed. There was some progress in the financial sector with reductions in directed credit, in credit subsidies, and importantly, in controls on foreign direct and portfolio investment. On 20 December 1994, the bubble burst and the Mexican bond and equity market collapsed, having serious negative consequences for other Latin American and emerging markets.

The reasons why the bond and equity market collapsed in Mexico are now very clear. The government bungled a devaluation strategy which had been recommended and was necessary. The inability of the government of Mexico to uphold its promise of allowing the peso to devalue by a maximum of 13 per cent resulted in an exodus by foreign investors from the stock market. The immediate response to this exit was a knee-jerk flotation which ended up with a devaluation of more than 35 per cent. The reason for the first-announced devaluation was an attempt to come to grips with the burgeoning current account deficit, then at 8 per cent of GDP, which was believed to be due to an overvalued exchange rate.

The essential characteristics of the Mexican economy during 1994 were as follows: an overvalued peso, an overdependence on short-term flows of foreign money, and an over-expansionary monetary policy. Foreign investors held 70 per cent of Mexican peso-dominated bonds, and around 80 per cent of outstanding dollar-denominated bonds, most of which were held by short-term investors. The involvement of foreign investors in Mexico since 1990 has been substantial and they have snapped up more than $55 billion worth of Mexican shares in the last four years. Last June, the exposure of US banks in Mexico alone was $17.2 billion.

The key issue here is Mexico's vulnerability and exposure to hot money from abroad. Literally overnight, foreign portfolio investors withdrew from the Mexican markets, leaving the economy in potential ruin. The possible consequences of this move for Mexico are: very high inflation, low growth due to poor domestic demand and more expensive imports, growing unemployment and poverty, and a severe lack of confidence on the part of foreign investors. Despite the neo-classical doctrine supported by the IMF/World Bank of opening one's markets to international capital, there may be some wisdom in proceeding cautiously and very carefully, rather than adhering to every demand made by Washington.

Source: Zaidi, S. Akbar, own research.

circumstances of particular countries, and thus of which policies are most feasible, are responsible for the failure of many standard and conventional adjustment programmes that emphasize economic liberalization. The recognition of historical and institutional factors specific to a country would help us to examine more closely the special circumstances of each country and region, so that we can discover its particular strengths and weaknesses and chart a desirable direction for social change.

Whether a policy can be implemented at all, whether if implanted it will have the desired effect, and whether some policies will result in undesirable consequences may depend critically on the nature of economic institutions and the balance of political forces which exist in that country. As specific institutional arrangements and the nature of political involvement and organization are likely to differ from country to country, it is likely that an abstract generalist framework, such as that suggested by a structural adjustment programme, may be less effective than a precise and country-specific policy.

In sub-Saharan Africa, where the IMF/World Bank package of stabilization and structural adjustment has been most ambitiously imposed, the severely underdeveloped nature of property rights has caused problems in identifying and working with the 'market'.[42] The emphasis on 'getting prices right', and on letting the market determine resource allocation, may not be feasible in countries where the market is small, does not exist, or is distorted by numerous imperfections. Even the World Bank, in one of its more candid moments, 'has openly accepted the fact that the scores of conditions attached to structural adjustment loans may contribute little to the ultimate success of individual adjustment packages simply because they are too complex and *do not correspond to institutional conditions* and managerial capacities in an adjusting country'.[43] The Bank has recently realized that 'frequently, the necessary markets or other institutions are not there, or they do not work well or as expected. Failure to take into account institutional characteristics specific to the country can lead to poor advice ... *The blanket recommendation of generally accepted policies can be disastrous in particular circumstances*.'[44]

Economic theory and observations from across countries show that the nature of current economic, social, and political relationships is affected by the past economic history of that country and by its political and institutional arrangements. There is a 'path dependence' of economic variables and they are conditioned by their own past behaviour. The effect of government policies in macroeconomic variables is determined, somewhat, by the past behaviour of economic variables themselves, by economic policies, and by the past and ingrained behaviour of economic institutions. Governments cannot introduce successful institutional arrangements, a key factor in economic liberalization and in the structural adjustment programmes, unless the social and political conditions conducive to such change exist.

14.5.2 International Capital and the Loss of National Autonomy

The major consequence of economic liberalization, openness, and globalization has been the extension, or incorporation, of countries into the world economy. Under closed and less liberal economic policies, the unit of analysis used to be one's own nation, where economic policies and reform within a country affected economic, political, and social arrangements domestically. This has changed dramatically with the 'opening up' of the underdeveloped countries, where events in different geographical and economic regions now affect national economic performance. Countries have become more dependent on factors to which they are not related or for which they are not responsible. The economic 'meltdown' of the Asian Tigers following the currency mayhem in June 1997 is probably the most recent, and best, illustration of how financial openness and exposure to outside influences can, in one stroke, liquidate the gains made over a number of decades.

Financial openness or globalization as a factor in economic policy means that there is international substitutability of assets. When domestic financial assets are close, or perfect, substitutes for foreign financial assets, domestic policy makers can exert influence over the effective stock or price of those assets only to the extent that the domestic share is large compared to the world share. A large country that dominates financial markets has control over its own prices, and other relevant targets. For a relatively small country, as are most underdeveloped countries, control over domestic interest rates or money supply might be way off target, having serious negative consequences for real targets such as investment, growth, and inflation.[45] In the case of floating and 'free' exchange rates, weaker countries may even become more subject to the ill effects of international capital flows or the judgements of investors, despite the fact that domestic policies are sound.

Three important strands of the international economy have become quite predominant in the economic world of the 1990s.[46] There is a huge internationalization of capital, where wealth holders of any one country are now holding, directly or indirectly, much larger financial claims upon financial assets of other countries than in the past. Secondly, the average maturity of these claims has tended to decline over time. Finally, the shortening of the maturity of these claims is matched by a tremendous mobility of capital internationally. Essentially then, there is a huge amount of 'hot' or 'near-hot' money which can move in enormous quantities from one country to another at very short notice (see Box 14.3). Conditions in one country can result in the flight of capital from another, even when the latter is doing well in economic terms. A rise in interest rates in the West can cause large sums of money to shift overnight, causing havoc in smaller, more exposed markets. Thus, attempts to control the domestic economy can be made quite powerless due to factors well beyond a country's control. Clearly, the internationalization of capital undermines the autonomy of national economic planning. Economic liberalization and structural adjustment programmes emphasize more openness and globalization of economies. Beyond doubt, there are numerous contradictions inherent in such a policy, many of which have been identified in this chapter.

14.6 Summary and Further Reading

14.6.1 Summary

In this chapter we have taken a critical look at the structural adjustment programme and at the way the IMF and World Bank have evolved into the most influential organizations in the world, determining economic policy and programmes in dozens of countries across the globe. The chapter began with a brief historical look at how economic development has evolved over the last fifty years, and at how economic policy is now determined. A detailed section on the composition of the structural adjustment programme examined the different sectors and issues that such programmes address.

Since structural adjustment programmes have been in operation for almost a quarter of a century, there is enough evidence to examine their consequences and implications. A vast literature does that, and the general consensus seems to be that such programmes have very serious negative impacts on growth, inflation, income distribution, the social sectors, and poverty. In general, structural adjustment programmes have made matters far worse for countries that have followed them. We have examined the philosophy that governs such adjustment programmes, which is essentially one of liberalization, openness, and greater integration with the new economic world order, and we have found that not just the adjustment programmes themselves, but also the thinking behind them does not take acount of specific factors and the context of specific countries. With different sets of political and institutional arrangements governing economic and policy choices, the general policy rules of such programmes often fail to take root in many countries. The

prevalence of highly liquid, hot money, which disappears from a country literally overnight, has serious consequences for an economy that are beyond its control.

14.6.2 Further Reading

This is an area where one can find a very large number of books and articles, and cite endless references. With structural adjustment being propagated by both the IMF and the World Bank, both organizations publish numerous reports and publications, looking at policies, offering prescriptions, and examining case studies. Some of the references listed in this chapter are also very useful. The two special issues of the *Pakistan Journal of Applied Economics*, vols. 10 and 11, published in 1994 and 1995, respectively, have some excellent articles on the subject which provide a general analysis as well as specific case studies with reference to Pakistan.

David Reed's *Structural Adjustment and the Environment*, Westview Press, Boulder, 1992, is an excellent source, as is the World Bank's *Restructuring Economies in Distress*, edited by V. Thomas, *et al.*, published by Oxford University Press in 1991. The special volume 19, no. 12, of *World Development*, 1993, has some very good articles which look at the consequences of structural adjustment programmes across the globe. Tariq Banuri's edited *Economic Liberalization: No Panacea*, Clarendon Press, Oxford, 1991, is an outstanding book which looks at the policies of liberalization and openness and contains some excellent articles. The *Economic and Political Weekly*, a journal produced in India, continues to publish some good and well-researched articles on structural adjustment and should be scanned regularly. Two articles published by Prabhat Patnaik deserve special mention: 'International Capital and National Economic Policy: A Critique of India's Reforms', *Economic and Political Weekly*, vol. 29, no. 12, 1994, and with C.P. Chandrasekhar, 'Indian Economy Under "Structural Adjustment"', *Economic and Political Weekly*, vol. 30, no. 47, 1995.

Appendix 14.1

The role of the IMF and the World Bank

Professor Prabhat Patnaik and C.P. Chandrasekhar look at how the IMF and World Bank have come to influence our economies in such a major way.

Among radical economists there is a tendency to lump the Fund and the Bank together as entities indistinguishable from one another, and to think of them as having remained more or less immutable over time. Nothing however could be further from the truth. There were significant differences between the Fund and the Bank which have *narrowed over time*, and the reasons for this narrowing constitute an important element of contemporary political economy. And each of these institutions has changed in crucial ways through time.

The Bank of course has always been opposed to any attempts on the part of the third world countries to break away through conscious design (which necessarily means conscious state intervention) from the pattern of international division of labour inherited from the days of colonialism and semi-colonialism. If such a break is to be achieved then it must be achieved, according to its perception, entirely through the mediation of the market forces, which means in particular through the medilections of direct foreign investment. The Bank has remained absolutely faithful to this position of opposing state-intervention-sponsored industrialization, despite the fact that historical evidence marshalled earlier by Gerschenkron and subsequently by many others shows overwhelmingly that successful industrialization by late-industrializers has invariably depended upon active state intervention. What has changed in the case of the Bank over time is: first, the specific argument on the basis of which it has expressed its opposition to state-sponsored industrialization; secondly, the precise tactics it has brought to bear in order to undermine state-sponsored industrialization in third world countries; and thirdly, the precise package of programmes around this basic objective, reflecting as we shall see the changing nature of world capitalism.

The arguments, which of course were not mutually exclusive, though different ones received emphasis at different points of time, kept altering in the following manner: in the late-1950s and the early 1960s there was a macro-argument that substantial unutilized capacity in the industrial sector existed because of a scarcity of foreign exchange so that a combination of import liberalization and exchange rate devaluation would set up a virtuous circle of 'more imports–more capacity utilization–more exports–still more imports' and so on, which would unshackle the economy from the clutches of *dirigisme* (which was predicated *inter alia* upon a recognition of demand constraints both in the external and in the internal markets). This was the argument on the basis of which the World Bank pushed the Indian government into adopting an import-liberalization-cum-devaluation package in 1966 with disastrous consequences.

In the McNamara years the emphasis shifted to poverty. But *the concern for poverty did not express itself in terms of any argument in favour of an egalitarian alteration in asset or land distribution*; it expressed itself in the argument that the domestic intersectoral terms of trade were more unfavourable for agriculture *vis-à-vis* industry than the terms of trade prevailing in the world market, so that removing trade restrictions and thereby preventing state-sponsored industrialization would benefit the agricultural sector which is the repository of mass poverty. This argument was backed up by another one, namely, since the inequality in urban income distribution was larger than that in rural income distribution, a shift in income distribution from the urban to the rural sector, which means in effect from industry to agriculture, would have the effect of lowering overall income inequalities. This argument amounted yet again to an attack on state-sponsored industrialization; the vacuousness of this argument lay *inter alia* in the fact that nearly 60 per cent of the *agriculture-dependent* population in a country like India, being net buyers of food grains in the market and belonging to the poorest segment of society, would be actually harmed by a rise in food prices in terms of their wage-unit.

More recently the Bank has shifted to the well known micro-theoretic 'marketist' argument which focuses on the allegedly interrelated phenomena of 'onward orientation', 'price-distortion', and 'inefficiency'. Much has been written on the vacuousness of this critique: 'outward orientation' as manifested for example in successful export performance has been accompanied by highly state-interventionist neo-merchantilist policies rather than any attempt to 'get prices right' in the conventional sense; the alleged 'inefficiency' of *dirigiste* industrialization is established through dubious statistical exercises involving dubious concepts such as 'total factor productivity' (which is predicated upon the perennial

absence of any demand constraint); there is complete silence on the role of the domestic investment effort in explaining growth performance, notwithstanding the overwhelming evidence which exists on its importance, and so on. We shall not dilate on this critique here; the point to note is that the policy-package following from this critique is exactly the same as before, namely, to roll back state-sponsored industrialization.

Where the Bank did change was in two respects; the first relates to its tactics. In the beginning, up until the end of the 1950s in the case of India, the Bank studiously avoided giving any loans for government programmes. In the early 1960s it modified its stance to give loans for social infrastructure projects, but not for any public sector industrial undertakings. It is only when the policy of boycott of public sector undertakings appeared to be counterproductive from its point of view that it started financing investment in such undertakings but with its own conditionalities, such as global tendering, specifying technological details and the scale of plants, etc. This shift from 'boycotting' to 'infiltrating' the public sector enabled it to exercise great leverage, to induct multinational corporations (MNCs) directly into the public sector as collaborators, to undermine domestic technological self-reliance and indigenous technological capabilities, to dictate pricing policies and acquire an indirect say on the government budget, and to set up 'networks' with bureaucrats and managerial personnel of the public sector. Together with this began the process of World Bank employees shifting to key government positions, especially in the ministry of finance, even as they were drawing pensions from the Bank, or even as they kept open the option of moving back to the Bank. They provided a powerful lobby working in concert towards 'liberalization-cum-structural adjustment' (arguably, as mentioned earlier, pushing the country into a trap where these policies became inevitable).

The other respect in which the Bank did change was in its new insistence upon a range of financial sector reforms whose overall objective again was to detach the domestic financial institutions and the financial markets from their integration into the domestic development effort (through, for example, low long-term interest rates, subsidized credit, and minimum percentage, credit disbursements for 'priority sectors' such as agriculture, etc.) and to integrate them more closely instead with global financial markets. Together with this went the Bank's demand for privatization not only of the financial domain where the public institutions held sway, but of public sector assets including of natural resources. The economic, as opposed to the ideological, argument for privatization was again utterly dubious: as a means of closing the fiscal deficit it was no different from money created directly for the government's use; as a means of reducing the government's interest burden it could work only under the palpably impossible condition that the rate of return sacrificed on the sold government assets was lower than the interest rate on public debt (which is impossible because the market would never buy assets at such low rates of return, and in practice of course has insisted on obtaining public assets only at virtually throw-away prices); and as a means of introducing 'entrepreneurship' it was of no use because the buyers were either 'fly-by-night-operators', or, if reputable MNCs, had more complex objectives (on which more later).

This widening of the Bank's package, from simply rolling back state-sponsored industrialization through a removal of trade restrictions, government controls and the pre-eminence of the public sector, to an integration of the domestic economy to the operations of global finance, reflected a fundamental change that was taking place within world capitalism itself, namely, a tendency towards greatly increased fluidity of finance across national boundaries, a tendency in short towards a globalization of *finance*, which is very different from, though often confused with, globalization of *production facilities*.

This very tendency also explains the shift which was taking place in the position of the IMF as well. Earlier the IMF was exclusively concerned with 'stabilization'. The Polak model for example which provided the basis for the IMF's policy-prescriptions concentrated on a few macro-level identities and made no attempts at modelling 'structural adjustment'. Its assumptions were questionable (e.g. the absence of any recognition of a demand constraint, the attribution of external payments problems exclusively to the government sector's deficit, and the general monetarist bias) but it provided the tool-kit for a highly conservative financial institution whose sole concern, especially *vis-à-vis* third world countries, was to recover its loans by imposing fiscal discipline upon the latter. This ruthless conservatism drew the ire of the third world, and indeed of radicals everywhere. But it was the conservatism of a narrow-minded financier, not that of an ideologue of development frowning overtly upon any attempt to alter forcibly the colonial pattern of international division of labour. The latter role was left by and large to the World Bank.

A major change took place between the two oil-shocks. While the recycling of resources to the third world, such as it was, was organized in the wake of the first oil-shock by the IMF itself, the tremendous growth which took place in the role of the banks in the interim meant that by the time of the second oil-shock it was the banks which were doing whatever recycling was to be done, and the IMF was called upon only to provide 'security cover' to the banks. This was the beginning of a process; from being a leading financier the IMF had got reduced to being a 'gendarme' of international rentier interests. As a 'gendarme' then it had to insist that the countries, which were caught under its 'conditionalities' and thereby became possible candidates for receiving funds from international rentiers, adopted a host of measures that were to the liking of the rentiers, such as privatization of public assets, 'opening up' of financial markets, removal of exchange restrictions, convertibility of the currency on the current and capital accounts, and so on, all of which amounted to an espousal of the kind of 'structural adjustment' which the World Bank had also come around to.

To sum up then, while the conservatism of the Bretton Woods institutions has continued unabated, there have been major changes in the precise texture of this conservatism reflecting changes which have been occurring in world capitalism. Not only have the Fund and the Bank come closer together in terms of outlook, breaking down their earlier separateness, but this coming together has itself been promoted to a significant extent by the vastly enhanced role of globalized finance. On might even add that this ascendancy of globalized finance has been responsible, *inter alia*, for keeping down willy-nilly what Lenin would have called 'inter-imperialist rivalry': certainly as far as the third world is concerned, the governments of the advanced capitalist countries present a remarkably common front and give more or less unanimous support to the structural adjustment measures being imposed by the Bretton Woods institutions.

Source: Patnaik, Prabhat and C.P. Chandrasekhar, 'Indian Economy Under "Structural Adjustment"', *Economic and Political Weekly*, vol. 30, no. 47, 1995, pp. 3002-4.

Notes

1. This section and sections 14.2, 14.3, and 14.4 are drawn from my paper, Zaidi, S. Akbar, 'The Structural Adjustment Programme and Pakistan: External Influence or Internal Acquiescence?', *Pakistan Journal of Applied Economics*, vol. 10, nos. 1 and 2, 1994.

2. Reed, David, *Structural Adjustment and the Environment*, Westview Press, Boulder Colorado, 1992, p. 4.

3. While the emphasis of this new thinking has been on removing protectionism and making economies more open, most underdeveloped countries still face severe restrictions. Some 51 per cent of Pakistan's exports to the USA, 53 per cent to the EU, and 11 per cent to Japan are subject to quota restrictions: see Nabi Ijaz and Naved Hamid, 'Partnership in Pakistan', in Lele, M. and Ijaz Nabi (eds.), *Transitions in Development: The Role of Aid and Commercial Flows*, ICEG, San Francisco, 1991. However, one must add that, with the end of GATT and the birth of the World Trade Organization, international quotas are going to become minimal.

4. This section is drawn from Zaidi, S. Akbar, op. cit., 1994 and from Reed, David, op. cit., 1992. See Reed, David, op. cit., 1992, for a more detailed historical account.

5. For more details see: Thomas, V., *et al.*, 1991; *Restructuring Economies in Distress*, Oxford University Press, New York, 1991; Ferreira, F., 'The World Bank and the Study of Stabilization and Structural Adjustment in LDCs', DEP No. 41, *Development Economics Research Programme*, STICERD, London School of Economics, 1992; Reed, David, op. cit., 1992; World Bank, *Pakistan: Growth Through Adjustment*, Report No. 7118-Pak, Washington, 1988; World Bank, *Pakistan: Medium-Term Economic Policy Adjustments*, Report No. 7591-Pak, Washington, 1989; World Bank, *Adjustment Lending Policies for Sustainable Growth*, Policy and Research Studies No. 14, Washington, 1990; and World Bank, *Adjustment Lending and Mobilization of Private and Public Resources for Growth*, Policy and Research Studies No. 22, Washington, 1992.

6. Khan, Mohsin S., 'The Macroeconomic Effects of Fund-Supported Adjustment Programmes', *IMF Staff Papers*, vol. 37, no. 2, 1990; Thomas, V., *et al.*, op. cit., 1991; World Bank, op. cit., 1990; World Bank, op. cit., 1992.

7. Khan, Mohsin, S., op. cit., 1990, p. 222, emphasis added.

8. Thomas, V., *et al.*, op. cit., 1991, p. 544.

9. Ibid., p. 39.

10. Reed, David, op. cit., 1992, p. 24.

11. Thomas, V., *et al.*, op. cit., 1991, p. 14.

12. Reed, David, op. cit., 1992, p. 32, emphasis added.

13. Ibid., p. 32.

14. Ibid., p. 32.

15. Ibid., p. 37.

16. Helleiner, G.K., *et al.*, 'IMF Adjustment Policies and Approaches and the Needs of Children', *World Development*, vol. 19, no. 12, 1991, p. 1825.

17. Ibid., p. 1826; see also Stewart, Francis, 'The Many Faces of Adjustment', *World Development*, vol. 19, no. 12, 1991.

18. Hoeven, R. Van der, 'Adjustment with a Human Face: Still Relevant or Overtaken by Events?', *World Development*, vol. 19, no. 12, 1991, p. 1835.

19. Veltmeyer, V., 'Liberalization and Structural Adjustment in Latin America: In Search of an Alternative', *Economic and Political Weekly*, vol. 28, no. 39, 1993, p. 2082.

20. Ibid., p. 2083.

21. Senses, F., 'Turkey's Stabilization and Structural Adjustment Programme in Retrospect and Prospect', *The Developing Economies*, vol. 29, no. 3, 1991, p. 26.

22. Ibid., p. 226.

23. See also Stewart, Francis, op. cit., 1991; and Zuckerman, E., 'The Social Cost of Adjustment', in Thomas, V., *et al.*, op. cit., 1991.

24. See Reed, David, op. cit., 1992.

25. Patnaik, Prabhat and C.P. Chandrasekhar, 'Indian Economy Under "Structural Adjustment"', *Economic and Political Weekly*, vol. 30, no. 47, 1995, p. 3007.

26. Ibid., p. 3008.

27. Stewart, Francis, op. cit., 1991, p. 1848, emphasis added.

28. Ibid., p. 1848, emphasis added.

29. Reed, David, op. cit., 1992, p. 9.

30. Ibid., p. 36.

31. Quoted in Stewart, Francis, op. cit., 1991, p. 1858.

32. de Tray, D., 'Comments', in Thomas, V., *et al.*, op. cit., 1991, p. 72, emphasis added.

33. Ibid., p. 273, emphasis added.

34. Reed, David, op. cit., 1992, p. 17.

35. Ferreira, F., op. cit., 1992, p. 53.

36. Veltmeyer, V., op. cit., 1993, p. 2080.

37. Salop, J., 'Reducing Poverty; Spreading the Word', *Finance and Development*, December, 1992, p. 3.

38. Parts of this section are drawn from Banuri, Tariq, *Economic Liberalization: No Panacea*, Clarendon Press, Oxford, 1991, which should be consulted for a more extensive elaboration.

39. See Hughes, Alan and Ajit Singh, 'The World Economic Showdown and the Asian and Latin American Economies: A Comparative Analysis of Economic Structure, Policy and Performance', in Banuri, Tariq, op. cit., 1991.

40. Ibid.

41. See Banuri, Tariq, op. cit., 1991, especially chapters 1, 2, and 6.

42. Platteau, J.-Ph., 'Formalization and Privatization of Land Rights in Sub-Saharan Africa: A Critique of Current Orthodoxies and Structural Adjustment Programmes', DEP No. 34, *Development Economics Research Programme*, STICERD, London School of Economics, 1992; and Institute of Development Economics, 'The Political Analysis of Markets', *IDS Bulletin*, vol. 24, no. 3, 1993.

43. Reed, David, op. cit., 1992, p. 34, emphasis added.

44. Thomas, V., *et al.*, op. cit., 1991, p. 524, emphasis added.

45. See Zevin in Banuri, Tariq and Juliet Schor, *Financial Openness and National Autonomy*, Oxford University Press, Delhi, 1992.

46. See Patnaik, Prabhat, 'International Capital and National Economic Policy: A Critique of India's Reforms', *Economic and Political Weekly*, vol. 29, no. 12, 1994.

15 Structural Adjustment Programmes in Pakistan: History and Implementation

It would be fair to say that since 1988 Pakistan's economic policies, management, and performance, have been almost totally determined by the country's adherence to IMF/World Bank-sponsored structural adjustment programmes, and Pakistan's various governments have had no independent or original economic programme of their own. Almost without exception, the policy measures undertaken by the various governments in power since the implementation of the 1988 programme follow very closely the details in the Policy Framework Papers, which outline steps that the government is to undertake after signing the structural adjustment programme document. The programmes are so minutely detailed that the government has little need to be innovative, and merely follows steps that are incorporated in the programme document. While the period since 1988 can be termed 'economic management under structural adjustment programmes', Pakistan has had recourse to earlier programmes as well. However, there is a very marked difference in the constitution and application of the programmes prior to, and post, 1988. The purpose of this chapter is to document and highlight the role that structural adjustment programmes have played in Pakistan. As will become clear, profound and substantial changes have had to be made in Pakistan's economy over the last few years in order to have more IMF/World Bank loans released. The chapter also includes an evaluation based on the perceptions of the donors and implementors (the IMF and the World Bank) themselves, and tries to assess the impact of the structural adjustment programmes on Pakistan's economy and society.

15.1 History[1]

Pakistan has had a long association with the IMF, and the first time that the government of Pakistan asked for a loan was in 1958 (see Table 15.1). This was a standby arrangement worth SDR25 million[2] over a period of about ten months. However, the loan was cancelled prior to the expiration date and the entire amount of the loan went unused. Two more standby arrangements, both of a duration of one year, were made in 1965 and 1968 by the Ayub Khan government, worth more than SDR125 million. The Z.A. Bhutto government was granted four standby loans collectively worth SDR330 million. However, as was argued in the previous chapter, stabilization and structural adjustment programmes funded by the IMF did not play a critical role in the management of the economies of the Third World before the mid-1970s.

Pakistan's experience also follows the same general trend, where in twenty years since 1958 it had recourse to less than SDR460 million. In the case of Pakistan, as in other UDCs, the nature and extent of the IMF involvement changed drastically in the 1980s.

As the IMF's funding amount and pattern changed over the late 1970s and 1980s, Pakistan entered into a long-term Extended Fund Facility (EFF) in November 1980, for a period of three years under General Zia. It was worth SDR1.27 billion, three times the entire amount lent between 1947 and 1980. This three-year agreement was cancelled after one year, and a new agreement worth the undrawn amount for two years was signed the very next day. The second recourse to a long-term agreement with the IMF, following which the various governments in Pakistan have very closely followed the programme, was signed by the interim government after the death of General Zia-ul-Haq. In fact, it was literally the last day of the government when the agreement was signed, and the subsequently elected Prime Minister, Benazir Bhutto, took office the following day. Her (first) government then ratified the already agreed programme, which ran from 28 December 1988 to 27 December 1991. Analysts argued at the time of Ms Bhutto taking office that her selection as Prime Minister was preconditioned on, amongst other things, the ratification of the programme. Following her ouster after twenty months in office, the Nawaz Sharif government elected in 1990 was bound by the covenants of the agreement, and had to follow it through.

There was a gap of almost two years before another agreement was signed in September 1993. Although this was a one-year standby agreement, it is considered to be a forerunner to the more extensive subsequent agreement, worth almost SDR1 billion, signed in February 1994. However, Pakistan's political history since 1993 will help put the present structural adjustment programme in proper context.

The Nawaz Sharif government was dismissed on 18 July 1993, and another interim government was put together in Islamabad. It was headed by Moeen Qureshi, a former World Bank staff member who had been settled in the United States for the previous thirty years. The enhanced structural adjustment programme was prepared by his interim government, and by 30 August 1993, IMF and World Bank staff, which represented both the IMF and the government of Pakistan, had agreed to a Policy Framework Paper, which laid the basis of the more comprehensive three-year programme of 1994. A number of improprieties were recorded in the process of forming the programme. As Arshad Zaman argues,

Table 15.1

IMF arrangements with Pakistan (standby, extended, structural adjustment, and enhanced structural adjustment arrangements)

Date of arrangement	Type of arrangement	Date of expiration or cancellation	Amount agreed (SDRm)	Amount drawn (SDRm)	Undrawn balance (SDRm)
8 Dec. 1958	Standby	22 Sept. 1969[a]	25.00	–	25.00[a]
16 Mar. 1965	Standby	16 Mar. 1966	37.50	37.50	–
17 Oct. 1968	Standby	16 Oct. 1969	75.00	75.00	–
18 May 1972	Standby	17 May 1973	100.00	84.00	16.00
11 Aug. 1973	Standby	10 Aug. 1974	75.00	75.00	–
11 Nov. 1974	Standby	10 Nov. 1975	75.00	75.00	–
9 Mar. 1977	Standby	8 Mar. 1978	80.00	80.00	–
24 Nov. 1980	EFF	1 Dec. 1981[a]	1,268.00	349.00	919.00[a]
2 Dec. 1981	EFF	23 Nov. 1983	919.00	730.00	189.00
28 Dec. 1988	Standby	30 Nov. 1990[b]	273.15	194.48	78.67
28 Dec. 1988	SAF	27 Dec. 1991	382.41[c]	273.15	109.26
16 Sept. 1993	Standby	15 Sept. 1994	265.40	88.00	177.40
22 Feb. 1994	EFF	21 Feb. 1997	379.10	80.55	298.55[d]
22 Feb. 1994	ESAF	21 Feb. 1997	606.60	101.10	505.50[d]

[a] Cancelled prior to expiration date.
[b] Extended from 27 March 1990 to 30 June 1990, and again to 30 November 1990.
[c] Approved amount increased from SDR346.9m in March 1989.
[d] As of 31 July 1994.
Source: Zaman, Arshad, 'The Government's Present Agreement with the IMF: Misgovernment or Folly?', *Pakistan Journal of Applied Economics*, vol. 11, nos. 1 and 2, 1995, p. 81.

since Moeen Qureshi was a World Bank member who had recently retired, his government's position was explained by his IMF and World Bank colleagues, who acted in an informal capacity as advisers to the government officials themselves. This, Arshad Zaman argues, 'is not only contrary to conflict of interest rules of the IMF/WB, but also raises important legal questions about the validity of the letter of intent signed by the subsequent government, if it can be established that the letter was drafted not by government officials [as per procedure] but by staff members of IMF/WB'.[3] There was so much overlapping of interest over the content of the programme that it became difficult to see whether the government of Pakistan was initiating the programme based on its own particular needs and priorities, or whether the IMF and World Bank members, in their official and non-official capacities, were imposing the programme. In the Board meeting of the IMF held in February 1994, when Pakistan's loan came up for discussion and was approved, one of the Executive Directors was quite pleased that the proposed programme initiated by the Moeen Qureshi caretaker government was prepared with such 'close cooperation of the Fund'.[4]

The Moeen Qureshi government was given a standby loan of SDR265.4 million in record time by the IMF on 16 September 1993. For the second time, after she was re-elected, Ms Benazir Bhutto's government was handed a pre-prepared, detailed programme, which she was expected to endorse. Not only did her government endorse the 1993 programme, but also, within four months, signed the three-year loan under the Extended Fund Facility and the Enhanced Structural Adjustment Fund (ESAF). Although this programme was signed by the elected government of Benazir Bhutto, there is little doubt that the unelected Moeen Qureshi interim government was responsible for framing the programme and getting it approved. Ms Bhutto's government rubber-stamped an agreement in which, quite probably, her political future was at stake.[5]

It should be clear from the above account that there are major political connotations to structural adjustment programmes in the context of Pakistan. A number of domestic and foreign interests and forces are also at work, and one wonders how much autonomy the government of Pakistan has in the first place. The 1988 and 1993 agreements, which have quite drastically changed the course of Pakistan's economy, were agreed by (or, some believe, imposed on) unelected, interim governments. It seems that the elected governments that followed the SAPs may have been asked to give guarantees that they would not contest a programme designed by someone else. A more detailed analysis of the political and other consequences is reserved for later, and we now turn to some details about Pakistan's 1988 and 1994 programmes.[6]

15.2 Implementation of the Structural Adjustment Programmes in Pakistan

The very extensive table in Appendix 15.1 details the main features of the structural adjustment programme of 1988, signed between the government of Pakistan and the IMF. The reason why the table is presented in such detail is to show how particular and specific a structural adjustment programme really is. It goes into minute details on almost every account – the table here is actually a summary! For example, there are references to as mundane and apparently trivial concerns as telephone charges. It mentions and requires the deregulation of bus fares and the adjustment of power tariffs, gas prices charged to domestic household consumers, water and sewerage tariffs, taxes, fees, and user charges for roads, rail, ports, and aviation. There are dozens of very precise clinical interventions that a structural adjustment programme is meant to undertake.

Given the extensive detail in the table, one might lose sight of the larger issues and objectives of the 1988 programme. The programme is supposed to improve financial internal and external balances, increase average savings rates – particularly in the public and government sectors – and promote and encourage private sector investment and activity. In particular, the key objectives of the 1988 structural adjustment programme over the three-year period, with their annual targets were as follows:

a) Reduce the overall budgetary deficit to 6.5 per cent of the GDP in 1988–9, to 5.5 per cent in 1989–90, and further to 4.8 per cent in 1990–1, a level that is sustainable over the medium term;

b) contain the rate of inflation to 10 per cent in 1988–9 and reduce it gradually to 7 per cent in 1989–90 and to 6.5 per cent in 1990–1;

c) reduce the external current account deficit to 3.4 per cent of GDP in 1988–9, and further to 2.8 per cent in 1989–90 and 2.6 per cent in 1990–1, a level judged sustainable over the longer term;

d) reduce the civilian external debt-service ratio from 27–28 per cent in 1986–8 to the sustainable level of less than 22 per cent by 1990–1;

e) increase gross official foreign exchange reserves from the equivalent of about three weeks of merchandise imports at end-1987–8 to a safer level of about seven weeks of imports by 1990–1;

f) contain the growth of domestic credit and money supply in line with the growth of nominal GDP at the target rate of inflation, with sufficient allowance for the desired increase in net foreign assets; and

g) consistent with the macroeconomic adjustments, sustain real GDP growth at about 5.2 per cent in 1988–9 and at 5.5 per cent in 1989–91.[7]

There are three key areas under which the reforms detailed in Appendix 15.1 were to take place: fiscal policy, foreign trade policy, and the financial sector. Since these three broad areas were meant to help determine the impact on, say, agriculture, energy, or even transportation, a little more detail of how the IMF and World Bank wanted to achieve their objectives, is warranted.

15.2.1 Fiscal Policy

With an attempt to decrease the fiscal deficit/GDP ratio in three years from 8 per cent to 4.8 per cent, major emphasis had been put on resource mobilization, with major tax measures that were intended to increase the tax revenue elasticity. The purpose here was to raise the total revenue/GDP ratio from 17.6 per cent in 1988 to 20 per cent by 1991/2. The salient features of the tax effort included the gradual extension of the sales tax on imports and domestically produced goods, such that a general sales tax (GST) could have been implemented by the end of the three-year programme. The income tax system was also to be restructured so that there was greater vertical equity. To increase revenues, steps were outlined to increase prices and user charges for utilities such as electricity, natural gas, and water. The programme also suggested increases in the charges for higher education and health. While these attempts at raising revenue were identified, it was also decided to take measures that would strengthen the tax administration and implementation of these reforms.

Excessive government expenditure, particularly current expenditure, was also to be reduced from 26.2 per cent of GDP to 24.8 per cent in the three-year programme. This was to be achieved by reducing the growth of current expenditures, as well as by lowering and eliminating subsidies on fertilizers and revising the procurement prices of wheat. At the same time, since emphasis had also been placed on providing and increasing funds to the social sector, the structural adjustment programme of 1988 envisaged an increase of 0.4 per cent of GDP (from 7 to 7.4) for development expenditure. There was also a major attempt to tighten the control over provincial expenditures, with a new federal/provincial revenue-sharing agreement being worked out so that provincial government would make greater efforts to raise revenues.

15.2.2 Trade

Very significant reforms were earmarked for the trade sector, where it was hoped that all the non-tariff barriers would be replaced by tariffs. At the same time it was planned to reduce the number of banned commodities from 400 to about 80, leaving only those that were banned for religious and security reasons, or under reciprocal or international agreements. In essence, this step would have allowed the import of a very large number of items that were previously banned. While non-tariff barriers were to be reduced, there was also to be a drastic reduction in the maximum tariff rate to 125 per cent in 1989/90 and to 100 per cent at the end of the three-year programme. Tariffs were to be imposed on a discriminatory basis depending on the degree and stage of processing. Most tariff exemptions and concessions were to be removed, streamlining the entire tariff structure on imports. It is clear that the emphasis of the structural adjustment programme of 1988, in the trade sector, was on extensively reducing tariffs so that imports could be made cheaper. However, there was also an attempt to increase exports, particularly higher-valued exports. In addition, with deregulation and privatization being promoted, the private sector was to be permitted greater involvement in the export of rice and cotton, both of which were previously solely under government control.

15.2.3 Financial Sector

With the opening up of the economy, as controls were removed, the financial sector was expected to play an important role in allocating resources, and in providing guidelines for other macroeconomic targets. The structural adjustment programme of 1988 highlighted measures to improve the efficiency and profitability of the banking system and to increase the autonomy and accountability of public sector financial institutions, particularly nationalized commercial banks. Attempts were made in the programme to tighten prudential regulations and the supervision system of the banking system. Debt recovery has been woefully inadequate in the past, and it was recognized in the structural adjustment programme document that the legal framework for debt recovery needed to be strengthened. Since state-controlled nationalized banks have been very dependent on state patronage, attempts were also made to increase the banks' own capital resources. The programme also proposed the establishment of a credit information bureau within the State Bank, allowing access to the private sector about priority areas. On the monetary policy side, policies were to be undertaken to abolish negative real interest rates on concessional credit programmes, and efforts were to be made to free interest rates in the market for medium- and long-term credit, making the interest rate more responsive to market conditions rather than being under the control of the government. Directed credit schemes, which have been used extensively by the government to suit its needs, were to be limited under the proposals in the structural adjustment programme of 1988. It was believed that the deregulation of controls in the banking sector would provide competition, which should then allow the establishment of private banks unencumbered by government controls and priorities. Capital markets were also to be encouraged to act as another source of capital/credit for firms. In this regard, the government was expected to promote private venture capital firms and eliminate the official setting of share prices.

In addition to these steps, the structural adjustment programme of 1988 proposed policies in the monetary sector, where the government was expected to pursue cautious domestic credit policies so that inflationary pressures were curtailed and perceived improvements in the balance of payments were not jeopardized. Monetary expansion was to be kept in line with nominal GDP growth.

15.3 Was the 1988 Structural Adjustment Programme a Success? Achievements and Failures

One can determine the success or failure of a programme in conventional terms by identifying programme targets and then examining whether those targets were met. This method implies that there was sufficient information, knowledge, and understanding at the time the original targets and objectives were set, to highlight the problem areas and their possible solutions. If the problems were identified correctly and the programmes targeted them, we can determine success or failure by the extent and degree of the deviation from their targets. This is the methodology adopted by the IMF/World Bank, believing that its original framework, the identification of issues, and the priority attached to them were correct. In this section we reproduce and summarize the assessment of the structural adjustment programme of 1988 by the donor's themselves. In section 15.5 we question the entire basis of the structural adjustment programme with respect to Pakistan.[8]

The structural adjustment programme was expected to maintain a strong growth performance over the three-year period, of above 5.5 per cent GDP growth each year, relying mainly on increasing investment and improving efficiency in investment. The deregulation of the economy, increased competition from liberalized imports, the adjustment in administered prices, along with substantially better fiscal effort were all cornerstones of the 1988 programme. A summary of the extent of the reforms actually implemented is presented below.

15.3.1 Fiscal Policy

The implementation of the adjustment programme as evaluated by the IMF/World Bank was weakest in the area of fiscal policy. Most quantitative targets were not met (see Table 15.2). Tax revenues as a percentage of GDP remained stagnant. On the taxation front, the following steps were taken: numerous income and wealth tax exemptions were eliminated; there was a simplification and rationalization of the tax structure; major steps to improve tax administration were attempted; despite a general sales tax, the number of taxpayers and sectoral coverage was low, with over 121 commodity categories exempt from the GST; the maximum duty rate for imports was reduced from 225 per cent in 1988 to 90 per cent in 1992; progress in reducing exemptions and tax concessions was somewhat limited; and revenues from trade taxes declined from 5.9 per cent of GDP to 5.1 per cent. Furthermore, debt GDP ratios failed to improve despite rapid growth in GDP, and external debt increased from 44 per cent to 46.5 per cent of GDP.

15.3.2 Trade and balance of payments

There was a stepwise reduction in maximum tariff rates and an elimination of many non-tariff barriers (see Table 15.3).

Import licences were abolished except for products that were prohibited. Improved incentives for exports were given, but it was also observed that trade liberalization encouraged the import of goods and services. Exports increased sharply by 11.6 per cent per annum in US dollar terms, and by 14.4 per cent by volume, mainly due to increased exports in cotton manufactured products, synthetic textiles, leather products, sports goods and other non-traditional manufactured goods; and the trade balance improved significantly from -6.6 per cent of GDP to –4.6 per cent. There was deterioration in the services balance (from –3.6 per cent of GDP to -4.6), and a sharp decline in workers' remittances. Large foreign exchange inflows due to liberalization of foreign currency deposits took place, increasing by US$1.2 billion (2.4 per cent of GDP); the current account deficit declined. Gross external reserves increased due to large private capital inflows into foreign currency deposits. There were noticeable increases in foreign direct and foreign portfolio investment.

15.3.3 Financial Sector

Resident Pakistanis were allowed to operate foreign currency deposits; banking procedures were liberalized and banks were authorized to increase interest rates on these deposits above LIBOR. Two state-owned banks, Muslim Commercial Bank and Allied Bank Limited, were sold to the private sector. Ten new private sector commercial banks as well as eight new investment banks were sanctioned. In the *stock market*, there was a liberalization of regulations for domestic and foreign investment generally, and foreign portfolio investment in particular, resulting in increased activity and capitalization in the stock market; and a liberalization of rules regarding the pricing of new issues. In the *monetary sector*, a fully fledged auction of government debt was initiated; the rate of return on six-month Treasury Bills rose gradually from 6 per cent to 13 per cent; rates of return on concessional lending schemes increased so as to remove the negative real interest rate in this area; bank deposits increased; and there was a gradual narrowing of interest rate differentials between various financial instruments. Credit ceilings for individual banks were replaced by credit–deposit ratios: 35 per cent credit to the private sector was permissible on rupee deposits, and 40 per cent on foreign currency deposits.

15.3.4 Liberalization and Privatization

A forceful programme for liberalizing the economy from government control was undertaken. The sanctioning of private investment and import licensing was abolished. Other regulatory restrictions, including registration of technical and foreign loan agreements, and procedures for employment of foreign workers were also abolished. Areas where previously only the government sector could invest, such as power generation, commercial and investment banking, and air and sea transport were opened to the private sector. One-hundred-and-five manufacturing units were put up for privatization. By November 1992, sixty-seven had been sold, with further steps taken to privatize the telecommunication and gas sectors.

15.3.5 Other Areas

Performance of the agricultural sector improved significantly during the programme. Cotton, due to improved technology and attractive incentives grew markedly, at 10.2 per cent per annum in volume terms. The performance of other sectors in the agricultural sector was not particularly strong. Subsidies on pesticides, seeds, and agricultural machinery were eliminated. Formal control over the price of urea was lifted, and prices of phosphatic and potash fertilizers were adjusted upwards.

Industrial value added grew by 6.3 per cent during the structural adjustment programme of 1988. Large investments were undertaken in all major energy sources. Cotton industries dominated, with output of cotton yarn increasing at an average annual rate of 15 per cent.

Private sector gross fixed capital formation expanded from 7.7 per cent to 9.4 per cent of GDP. Domestic savings grew from 10.5 per cent to 12.5 per cent of GDP. There was a sharp rise in savings held overseas by Pakistanis, which were then transferred and deposited in foreign currency deposits in the domestic banking sector.

Energy prices increased by an average of 4 per cent in real terms. Telephone calls were subject to excise duty, earning substantial revenue.

15.4 The World Bank/IMF's Overall Evaluation of the 1988 Structural Adjustment Programme

The above sections have presented a list of reforms and targets that the structural adjustment programme of 1988 hoped to achieve. As we have seen, the government of Pakistan has implemented a large number of reforms in different sectors of the economy. Table 15.4 presents a detailed summary list of the key indicators and programme targets for the structural adjustment programme of 1988.

The World Bank's own opinion about the programme is as follows:

> while performance during the adjustment period has been strong in GDP and export growth and in structural reforms to encourage private sector economic activity, it has been weaker in achieving a sustained reduction in the fiscal deficit and in improving external sector balances. The financial imbalances, especially persistently large fiscal deficits, raise concern about their potential adverse effects on growth performance. Similar concerns are also raised by the lack of significant improvement in poverty and social sector indicators.[9]

These conclusions, however, seem somewhat at odds with the data available in Table 15.4. Four key indicators are believed to reflect the state of the economy: GDP growth rates, the budget deficit as a percentage of GDP, the current

Table 15.2
Summary of public finance,[a] 1988/9 to 1990/1 (% of GDP)

Item	1987/8 actual	1988/9 actual	1989/90 actual	1990/1 actual	SAP target
Total revenues	18.4	18.9	19.5	16.5	20.8
Tax and non-tax revenues	17.3	18.1	18.5	15.5	19.7
Tax revenues	13.8	14.3	13.9	12.8	14.9
Direct	1.8	1.9	1.8	2.0	2.4
Indirect	12.0	12.4	12.1	10.8	12.5
Domestic	5.8	6.4	5.7	5.3	6.6
Excise	2.6	2.6	2.7	2.5	2.8
Sales tax	1.3	1.9	1.8	1.7	2.1
Surcharges	1.9	1.9	1.1	1.2	1.8
Custom duties	5.6	5.5	5.9	4.9	5.4
Import duties	5.1	4.9	5.3	4.5	5.0
Export duties	0.5	0.6	0.6	0.4	0.4
Others[b]	0.6	0.5	0.5	0.5	0.5
Non-tax revenues	3.5	3.7	4.6	2.7	4.8
Surplus autonomous bodies	1.1	0.9	1.0	1.0	1.1
Total expenditures	26.9	26.6	26.1	25.2	25.6
Current	20.1	20.4	19.5	18.7	18.8
Federal	15.7	16.2	15.3	14.7	14.7
Defence	7.0	6.6	6.9	6.4	6.1
Interest payments	4.7	4.7	5.3	4.2	5.4
Subsidies	1.0	1.6	1.0	0.9	0.7
Other[c]	3.1	3.2	2.2	3.2	2.5
Provincial	4.4	4.2	4.2	4.0	4.1
Development	6.8	6.3	6.6	6.5	6.8
Deficit	−8.5	−7.7	−6.5	−8.7	−4.8
Deficit financing	8.5	7.7	6.5	8.7	4.8
External resources (net)	1.9	2.4	2.7	2.5	1.9
Domestic non-bank financing	4.6	4.9	4.5	2.0	2.5
Domestic bank financing	2.1	0.4	0.4	4.2	0.4
Borrowing outside budget	0.0	0.0	0.0	0.0	0.0
For memorandum					
Public savings	−1.7	−1.4	0.1	−2.3	2.0
Primary balance	−3.8	−3.0	−1.2	−4.5	0.6

[a] Of the federal and provincial governments and certain autonomous bodies (WAPDA, OGDC, PTC, NHA, PTV, and NFCP).
[b] Including additional revenue measures to be implemented in 1992/3.
[c] Includes unidentified expenditures.
Source: World Bank, *Pakistan: Country Economic Memorandum FY93*, Report No. 11590–Pak, Washington, 1993, p. 14.

account deficit/GDP ratio, and the inflation rate. Thus, even though extensive reforms have taken place in most sectors, including trade, liberalization, and the financial sector, if the above four indicators do not show a significant improvement, it would be difficult to conclude that the programme has been a success. Let us re-examine the case for the structural adjustment programme of 1988 with respect to the key indicators identified above.

Based on Table 15.4, it seems that GDP growth, the World Bank claim notwithstanding, has managed just a 5.5 per cent annual increase at the end of the structural adjustment programme of 1988. Gross domestic investment as a percentage of GDP, which was supposed to increase, has increased only marginally, mainly because public gross fixed capital formation has fallen. Gross domestic and gross national savings have, however, shown a substantial increase. Inflation, a key variable, is way off target in the final year of the programme, as are all fiscal indicators, a fact even acknowledged by the World Bank. The fourth key indicator, the current account deficit, is also substantially off target.

Table 15.3
Changes in trade policy, 1987/8 to 1992/3: non-tariff barriers

Year	Items removed from:					
	Negative List	Restricted List	Maximum tarriff[b] (%)	Import surcharges (%)	Iqra surcharge (%)	Licence fee (%)
1987/8	136	10	225	5	5	4
1988/9	169	51	125	6	5	5
1989/90	70	20	125	7	5	5
1990/1	97	43	95	10	5	6
1991/2	23	17	90	10	5	6
	21	11	90	0	5	6

[a] Items removed are a mixture of numbers and categories and therefore are only a broad indication.
[b] Automobiles and alcohol continue to carry tariffs up to 425%.
Source: World Bank, *Pakistan: Country Economic Memorandum FY93*, Report No. 11590–Pak, Washington, 1993, p. 20.

Thus, three of the four indicators that would provide a summary position of the achievements of the structural adjustment programme are *far from the targeted figures*. Clearly, on the conventional criteria laid down by the IMF and the World Bank, the structural adjustment programme of 1988, despite all the propaganda and fanfare, *has not been much of a success*.

The overall perception by the World Bank and IMF of their policies in Pakistan seems to be mixed. They feel that some positive developments have taken place, especially in the case of pricing policies, trade liberalization, export promotion and some public sector reform. Where governments have failed is in lowering the budget deficit to preferred levels, diversifying exports, cutting inflation, etc. William McCleary of the World Bank argues that in the mid to late 1980s Pakistan experienced 'a period of rapid growth and inflows of migrant workers' remittances [which] had raised standards of living broadly across the population. Private investment played a leading role in this expansion, and no longer was public investment in large scale industry viewed as the engine of growth ... The economy became more outward looking, flexible and market oriented.'[10] He continues that 'reforms in Pakistan have been sustained because of the government's incremental and flexible approach and because continued strong economic performance has obviated the need for reversals'.[11] His overall view is that Pakistan's economy was doing well for itself, and then the IMF intervened, after which it did somewhat better for a few years. McCleary argues that, when Pakistan's economy was doing well, it was because the conditions imposed on Pakistan were being followed and because the government of Pakistan was thinking like the IMF and the World Bank. He argues that the IMF/World Bank policies were sound and that when and if things went wrong, it was because of poor management on the part of the government.

William McCleary argues that the Fund and the Bank played a significant and positive role in the development of the economy during the 1980s. A leading exponent of structural adjustment programmes, and a director at the IMF, Mohsin Khan, seems to disagree. Khan argues that 'although

there have been some attempts at liberalization, the evidence is far too tenuous to argue, as McCleary does, that the economy has become more open and more outward oriented in the 1980s ... The changes that have been made have been marginal, and it is doubtful whether those made in the 1980s have been any greater than those of the previous decade.'[12]

Recognizing that some targets had not been met – for example, the savings/investment balances are significantly less than those targeted under the 1988 programme; large fiscal deficits persist and are a source of financial instability; efforts at resource mobilization have not been successful; the structure of government expenditures has not improved significantly; and the balance of payments, despite government reform, has not shown particular progress – the IMF and World Bank came up with yet another extended structural adjustment programme for Pakistan. This new structural adjustment programme which began in 1993 initially for one year, and then subsequently ran from 1994 to 1997, has features that are quite similar in principle to the 1988 programme (see Appendix 15.2). The government of Pakistan based each of its policy decisions and managed the economy almost precisely according to the 1994 programme.

Much of the analysis by the World Bank and the IMF of its 1988 structural adjustment programme has been done at a macro level, and they have not really looked at many of the more critical micro issues. Now that Pakistan has undergone two extensive programmes, some Pakistani scholars are beginning to evaluate the impacts of the programmes at a somewhat disaggregated level. However, because the impact of such programmes at the micro level takes place with a time lag, and studies that evaluate such impacts take even longer to be produced, the literature currently available is somewhat limited; it is probable that over the next few years, more research will be undertaken.

One very recent work has been undertaken by Shahrukh Rafi Khan, who has tested a number of hypotheses regarding the impact of the structural adjustment programme as applied to Pakistan. His results show that, particularly on labour and the poor, the impact is severe. The general sales

Table 15.4
Summary key indicators and programme targets, 1987/8 to 1991/2

Item	1987/8	1988/9	1989/90	Provisional 1990/1	Preliminary 1991/2
Growth and savings indicators					
GDP (market price – growth rate)	7.6	5.0	4.5	5.5	7.8
GDI/GDP	18.0	19.0	18.9	18.7	18.7
of which:					
Private GFCF	7.7	8.3	8.9	8.9	9.4
Public GFCF[a]	8.8	9.0	8.3	8.2	7.7
GDS/GDP	10.5	11.6	11.7	12.4	12.2
GNS/GNP	13.6	14.1	14.2	14.3	15.7
Inflation indicators					
CPI (% change)	6.3	10.4	6.1	12.7	9.6
Fiscal indicators					
Total revenue/GDP	18.4	19.0	19.5	16.5	19.4
Tax revenue/GDP	13.8	14.4	13.9	12.8	13.7
Public savings/GDP	–1.7	–1.4	0.1	–2.3	–0.3
Overall balance/GDP	–8.5	–7.7	–6.5	–8.7	–7.5
Bank financing/GDP	20	0.4	0.4	4.2	
Competitiveness indicators					
REER (% change)	–	–1.8	–8.2	–2.3	–2.7
Merchandise exports (growth in US$)	24.7	6.2	6.3	19.8	16.6
External indicators					
Current account[b]/GDP	–4.4	–4.8	–4.7	–4.3	–3.1
Gross external reserves (weeks of imports)	3.0	3.0	4.0	3.3	5.6
Total public debt[c]/GDP	44.4	47.4	49.4	45.5	46.5
Public debt service ratio[d]	26.9	24.0	24.5	21.5	22.5

GDI = Gross Domestic Investment.
GFCF = Gross Fixed Capital Formations.
GDS = Gross Domestic Savings.
GNS = Gross National Savings.
REER = Real Effective Exchange Rate.
[a] Based on a wider coverage than the fiscal accounts.
[b] Net of official transfers.
[c] Includes deposit liabilities of the banking system but excludes military debt.
[d] Includes debt service payments of medium- to long-term debt and interest payments on short-term guaranteed debt and deposit liabilities of the banking system. As a percentage of exports of goods and services and remittances.
Source: World Bank, *Pakistan: Country Economic Memorandum FY93*, Report No. 11590–Pak, Washington, 1993, p. 35.

tax and subsequent inflation hurt the poor, and cuts in government hiring in order to release pressure on government expenditure is likely to increase unemployment. The withdrawal of large subsidies also has similar deleterious consequences. For S.R. Khan, following the 1988 programme, 'the socioeconomic conditions of labour and the poor seem to have deteriorated'.[13]

Similar results have also been found by Asad Sayeed and Aisha Ghaus, who show that poverty, after having decreased in the 1970s and 1980s, has returned to Pakistan following the IMF programmes.[14] Low GDP growth, its sectoral distribution, lower employment and real wages, and fiscal policy designed to cut public expenditures and social

development are seen as the key causes of a return to poverty in the 1990s. Similarly, A.R. Kemal found that unemployment has increased, as have poverty and income inequality, on account of the 1988 structural adjustment programme.[15] The little research published so far on the impact of the structural adjustment programme in Pakistan seems to support the general conclusions from studies from across the globe.

The current situation (July 1997) regarding Pakistan's relationship with the IMF is a little ambiguous. The 1994–7 programme was halted by the second Benazir Bhutto government in 1995 (see Box 15.1), but her government was forced to go back some months later and agree to a standby loan, on stricter terms. The standby loan, too, was

BOX 15.1

The IMF shows its displeasure

Attempts by Pakistan's government to show independence were not received well by the IMF.

It was in September 1993 that Moeen Qureshi's caretaker government signed a standby agreement with the IMF, and this served as a precursor to the very large agreement signed later by the Benazir Bhutto government. Things went rather well for the first two years of the programme where, while targets went unmet, the general direction and pace of the so-called 'reforms' seemed acceptable to the IMF. The fiscal deficit was brought down substantially, as were tariffs, but again not by as much as the IMF had wanted. The deregulation, liberalisation and privatisation agendas set by the IMF were also closely followed, and frequently renegotiated when any hitch seemed to occur. Pakistan, in fact, was cited as a very good example of a country successfully following the structural adjustment programmes devised by the IMF.

But then came the 1995–6 budget in June last year. Analysts, economists and businessmen were surprised by the fact that the government had, very unexpectedly, offered a mild budget far removed from the very strict one that was widely anticipated. The tariff rate, for example, was cut by only five per cent, and not twenty as was expected, reducing the maximum tariff rate to 65 per cent. New taxes to the tune of only 16.3 million rupees were announced, and the target for the budget deficit was set at five per cent of GDP. The IMF,

for its part, had insisted on a 4.5 per cent target.

All in all, the 1995–6 budget was perceived to be pro-industry and growth enhancing, encouraging the belief that a number of the targets would be met for a change. Most of all, many analysts perceived the budget to represent the interests of Pakistan, rather than the demands of the IMF.

The IMF was not at all pleased with this attempt by the government to assert its independence, and the Fund froze the remaining tranche of the ESAF [Extended Structural Adjustment Facility] in its last year of operation. It took less than four months, however, for the government to make a quick U-turn. It imposed more taxes, devalued the rupee, promised the IMF that it would agree to its earlier conditions and begged the Fund to resume the aborted ESAF. Between October and December 1995, top officials of the Government of Pakistan made numerous trips to Washington trying to appease the IMF and to convince it of the sincerity of their intentions in carrying out the rest of the programme. IMF officials also visited Islamabad and finally, towards the end of last year, yet another agreement was signed.

The government immediately claimed victory and informed the public that the IMF, by agreeing to the new loan, had endorsed the policies of the Benazir Bhutto government and had confirmed that the economy was doing well enough to warrant a loan from the Fund.

Moral of the tale: the government simply cannot defy the IMF. And for that, it has only itself to blame.

Source: Zaidi, S. Akbar, *The Herald*, March 1996.

discontinued as the government failed to fulfil important conditions imposed by the IMF. After the dismissal of the second Benazir Bhutto government in November 1996, the second Nawaz Sharif government in March 1997 announced a large number of supply-side measures, such as cuts in income tax and a huge reduction in the maximum tariff rate from 65 to 45 per cent, with a reduction in tariff slabs. Although the government insisted that it was undertaking these measures 'on its own initiative', rather than on any advice or compulsion from the IMF, the measures seemed to be from an IMF manual, and were very well received by the IMF and World Bank. In October 1997, the Nawaz Sharif government signed yet another agreement with the IMF, the first in recent years by an elected government. This third major agreement since 1988, worth US$ 1.6 billion, was composed of an Extended Fund Facility (EFF) and an Enhanced Structural Adjustment Facility (ESAF). It is clear that the IMF and the World Bank will continue to influence government economic policy in Pakistan for some time to come.

15.5 The Political Economy of Structural Adjustment Programmes in Pakistan[16]

This section will examine the political nature, background, and consequences of Pakistan's acceptance of the Washington

consensus in the most recent guise of adherence to the structural adjustment programmes. Before that, however, we present a brief history of Pakistan's dependence on 'external forces' and on programmes and policies exported from abroad. This section also makes the strong case that perhaps Pakistan did not really need an IMF-sponsored structural adjustment programme, and that the economic and structural conditions that existed prior to the onslaught of the 1988 programme did not really warrant such a programme. This section then tries to answer the perplexing question why, if the structural adjustment programme was not really essential, it was accepted in the first place.

15.5.1 Pakistan's Dependence on Washington, or Are Governments Autonomous?

To state that governments, particularly in underdeveloped countries, are dependent on and pressurized by events, factors, agencies, and institutions outside the realm of the government itself is to state the obvious. Governments are affected by happenings within their own geographical domain, as well as by factors determined by outside interests many thousands of miles away. Foreign patronage of Third World governments has often been the norm, where local and indigenous sensitivities have been trampled upon and ignored by governments whose existence has depended on approval from abroad. The 1960s, 1970s, and 1980s, with the likes of Pinochet, Somoza, the Shah of Iran, Zia, and Marcos, provide ample proof that most governments in the Third World were imposed by, and dependent on, 'external influences'. And to be fair, nor was Washington responsible for this alone: puppets of the now extinct Soviet empire were also ruling their own countries with a severity that wrecked their societies.

Pakistan must count itself lucky to be amongst those countries in the world that have always supported the Washington consensus, whatever that may happen to be at a particular time. An examination of the political processes from the early years of Pakistan's existence shows that numerous important political and governmental decisions were influenced, if not directed, by the relationship with Washington. While Washington may not actually have manoeuvred the process of history as it has evolved in the political arena in Pakistan, it has had a serious influence, for geopolitical and other reasons, over the outcome of events. Subtle pressure and suggestive decisions have changed the course of history in Pakistan on more than one occasion.

As earlier chapters have shown, foreign aid, particularly from the US or sanctioned by it, has been one of the sources of its growth and development. In the early Ayub period, aid was considered to be an essential cause of the high rates of growth of the economy, and after 1979 aid, both bilateral and multilateral, provided large funds for the economy. From the time of the India–Pakistan war in 1965 until the Soviet invasion of Afghanistan, 'Pakistan remained in the United States' political disfavour'.[17] This meant that other multilateral agencies, too, were not enthusiastic about providing aid to Pakistan in this period. The first structural adjustment loan under the IMF Extended Fund Facility was made available to Pakistan in November 1980. Pakistan was advised to delink the rupee from the dollar, 'focus on efficient import substitution, reduce government expenditures, establish tax reforms to increase domestic resource mobilization, encourage savings, institute price reforms, and push for export led growth and privatization'.[18] The Zia regime, unlike those that have followed it, was selective in its choice of policy options: the rupee was delinked and devalued against the US dollar, farmgate prices were raised, and some import liberalization took place. To attract capital, a general assurance was also given to the private sector. On the other fronts, the government was not particularly pushed to reform immediately. As Nabi and Hamid[19] argue, Zia was in a position to, and did, resist external pressure from the IMF and World Bank: 'when the government can clearly see the value of particular economic policy changes, it is willing to implement reforms ... Reforms that adversely affect established interest groups or have broad negative political consequences are generally not undertaken despite external pressure.'[20] In more recent times, it seems that governments are willing to do anything to adhere to the Washington consensus (see below, and Boxes 15.2 and 15.3).

15.5.2 Did Pakistan Need to Go to the IMF?

The general proposition put forward by Fund/Bank staff in order to convince governments that they ought to apply for structural adjustment loans is that their countries are in a bad economic state. They are told that there are major structural problems, the balance of payments is in critical deficit, the budget deficit is high, inflation is rampant, and the growth rate of the economy is too low and unsustainable in the long run.

We have shown repeatedly in previous chapters that the overall growth performance of Pakistan has been good, if not quite remarkable. Even when the first major structural adjustment programme was started in the early 1980s, the main economic indicators showed very decent trends (see Table 15.5). Even after the onslaught of the 1988 programme, the economy continued to do quite well. Estimates show that GDP grew by 5 per cent during 1988–90, while in 1991/2 it grew by as much as 7.7 per cent. The growth rate in new (officially accounted) private investment has been in excess of 20 per cent per annum since 1988, and was as high as 30 per cent in 1991/2. Exports, meanwhile, grew by 20 per cent in 1990/1 compared to the previous year, and by 15 per cent in 1991/2. All these indicators very strongly suggest that there has been impressive growth, money is being generated and even the recorded official economy (not counting the buoyant unofficial economy) has shown signs of immense prosperity. Since the mid-1970s, the trend has been upwards, and most important indicators showed very healthy and positive signs even before the first structural adjustment programme in 1980 (see Table 15.5).

It would therefore seem that Pakistan's economy was in fairly good shape when the structural adjustment programmes were initiated, and while it could have been better, it had been functioning adequately without any so-called assistance. A comparison with Bolivia, which agreed to accept a wide-ranging orthodox stabilization programme in 1985, may highlight the extent of the differences in trends between the two countries. In 1985 Bolivia had an inflation rate of 11,000 per cent, a fiscal deficit in excess of 30 per cent of GDP, and a GDP per capita that was 20 per cent *less* than in 1980. Bolivia is an excellent example of a country which ought to qualify for an IMF/World Bank structural adjustment programme. Numerous other countries, especially in Latin America, also suffered the fall-out from the debt crisis and were forced to go to Washington. Pakistan did not need to go.

The arguments in this section rest on the assertion that Pakistan's economy, at the time of the initiation of the 1988 programme, was in relatively good shape and did not suffer from the problems faced by most African and Latin American countries, with rampant inflation, low or negative growth, large external debts, etc. Stabilization was usually meant for these countries, most of which were on 'the brink of economic crisis'.[21] Pakistan had never been in such a critical position. Furthermore, some of the outcomes and effects of structural adjustment programmes that have affected other countries have not taken place in Pakistan. The World Bank accepts that an 'investment lag' exists in countries following adjustment programmes, and that quite often investment shows *markedly negative* trends. In Pakistan this has not been the case, suggesting either that the adjustment programme has been particularly successful or, as we have argued, that

BOX 15.2
Aid linked to fulfilling IMF commitment

The message from the World Bank's latest aid to Pakistan consortium meeting held in Paris on April 23 and 24 [1996] couldn't have been clearer: Islamabad will only get the $2.7 billion in fresh funds it wants and needs if the 1996–7 national budget to be published in June reflects the International Monetary Fund's prescriptions for structural reform. Any deviation from the path set out by the IMF, warned donors, would prompt a cutback in foreign aid.

The bank and other donors are looking for specific action on a number of fronts: the government is being asked to restructure expenditures, to continue restraint on defence spending, to use privatization proceeds to retire high-cost government debt and to take measures to broaden the tax base. Further trade reform is also viewed as a key aspect of the fiscal adjustment required.

A slowdown in implementing these reforms will mean less or perhaps even no aid. Unusually, the World Bank's final communiqué does not mention Pakistan's request for $2.7 billion in aid. And in fact, for the first time, donors have established a firm link between the government's implementation of the IMF programme and the amount of money that will be made available during the coming year.

Donors are learning from experience. A total of $2.2 billion was pledged in foreign aid at the meeting in Paris last year. But Pakistan's decision to slow the pace of key trade and tax reforms and the subsequent cancellation of the IMF's Enhanced Structural Adjustment Facility clearly jolted foreign governments. To make up for lost time, disbursement from donors in 1996-7 will be approximately $2.4 billion.

But not surprisingly, this time around foreign assistance is conditional on the contents of Pakistan's next budget and its implementation. 'The government's request for aid can be met if the policy reforms are adequate,' a World Bank official stressed. 'If we are satisfied with what we see in the budget, there will be support for Pakistan. It could be $2.7 billion or it could be less.'

Pakistan has told donors that it is working on a new structural adjustment programme with the IMF, using the recent $600 million standby arrangement as a 'stepping stone' to secure the wider-ranging deal. It has also cautioned against 'exaggerated expectations' of how rapidly the fiscal changes can be accomplished.

'We are confident that the IMF agenda can be met,' V.A. Jafrey, the Prime Minister's Advisor on Finance, told *Dawn*. 'After last year's experience donors are making an explicit link. They are saying that if you do as planned, you will get the funds; if you deviate, the commitment might be lower. If the reform process is slowed, then there will be a reduction in commitment.'

'The key features donors will be looking for include a reduction in the overall budget deficit, tax reform, a lowering of import tariffs and an extension of the sales tax. They will also be looking at our development spending. Donors do not want the financial readjustment to be at the expense of the important social service programmes,' V.A. Jafrey said.

Source: *DAWN*, 25 April 1996.

Table 15.5
Growth rates in Pakistan, 1980–1992

Year	GDP	Budget deficit as % of GDP	Total investment	Private investment	Current account deficit as % of GDP	Consumer price index
1960s	6.7		n.a.	20.85		3.83
1970s	4.84		21.76	16.97		12.33
1980s	6.45	7.0	13.01	14.97		7.34
1980/1	6.40	5.3	9.83	13.06	3.69	13.85
1981/2	7.56	5.3	19.62	7.97	4.99	11.10
1982/3	6.79	7.0	9.63	14.69	1.80	4.70
1983/4	3.97	6.0	12.04	17.42	3.20	7.30
1984/5	8.71	7.8	12.81	14.07	5.39	5.70
1985/6	6.36	8.1	11.58	11.49	3.88	4.40
1986/7	5.81	8.2	13.46	10.99	2.16	3.60
1987/8	6.44	8.5	11.07	16.73	4.38	6.30
1988/9	4.81	7.4	19.65	23.94	4.83	10.40
1989/90	4.58	6.5	11.35	19.33	4.74	6.00
1990/1	5.57	8.7	19.35	19.15	4.77	12.70
1991/2	7.67	7.4	25.62	30.05	2.76	9.60

Source: Government of Pakistan, *Pakistan Economic Survey, 1994–95*, Islamabad, 1995.

BOX 15.3

High cost of IMF vigilance

Details of the new agreement between Pakistan and the World Bank and IMF signed in January, as published, show that soon their advisers and consultants will be sitting in the State Bank of Pakistan and many other official financial institutions and regulatory bodies to enforce financial discipline.

This Financial Sector Deepening and Intermediation Project (FSDIP) is to cost us 1.01 billion dollars. Some of that money will come as loans from the World Bank and Asian Development Bank, and the balance will be provided in local currency by public sector banks and other financial institutions to pay for these watchdogs in unspecified numbers in each institution. And they will ensure that we faithfully conform to the Extended Structural Adjustment Facility's dictates under which Pakistan is to receive 1.4 billion dollars during a three-year period 1993–96.

Evidently, the vigilance of the World Bank and IMF will now be total. They are not content with their independent offices in Islamabad monitoring our fiscal and monetary behaviour from there and their officers sitting in the Finance Ministry and some other departments in Islamabad and their representatives visiting the State Bank in Karachi from time to time on inspection missions. The new agreement has come 18 months after the ESAF came into effect. The IMF has noted with grave concern Pakistan's setback in the areas of reducing the large budget deficit and arresting the soaring inflation, contrary to its major conditionalities. Failure on both the fronts threatens the government's other achievements in the macro-economic sector, and hence wants adequate and sustained remedies in both areas.

If the new agreement is good for the country and essential for its economic well-being, why did not the government publish it? Instead the country came to know of that only through a report published in *Dawn* last week. Details of the agreement, as published, give rise to several major questions, and the government has not come forward to clarify them. Some amount of secrecy may be warranted at the time of negotiating such deals, but surely they should be published after formal agreements have been signed and before a large number of IMF advisers and consultants descend on the State Bank and many other financial institutions, including Corporate Law Authority, Privatization Commission, Controller of Insurance and public sector banks and DFIs, particularly Bankers Equity.

According to the agreement, as reported, the State Bank will spend 800 million dollars on advisers and the Corporate Law Authority 500 million dollars on consultants for hardware and software for computers. Is it a case of Pakistan getting a large amount of money from the World Bank or Asian Bank by one hand and spending the same on their men by the other without adequate results?

These advisers and consultants are to help consolidate and further expand the financial reforms under way for five years or until the year 2000. There are certainly areas like the Corporate Law Authority, insurance or privatization where the advice or guidance of competent experts is welcome but should the overall cost be so high and should their vigilance be so all-pervasive?

Source: *DAWN*, 13 April 1995.

---

the economy was strong enough to deal with such setbacks and did not need Fund-assisted programmes.

Finally, two interlinked issues need to be addressed. The IMF and World Bank agree that those countries that have done well on their economic agendas have had their own programmes *before* IMF or World Bank involvement.[22] Thailand and Korea are two such cases where governments had devised their own programmes and implemented them, and only then went to the Fund. Pakistan also falls into this category: 'improvements in policies affecting stabilization and efficiency *had already begun to accelerate growth before the 1979 shock*, and policy reforms adopted since then helped to reconfirm the process'.[23]

Reforms take place due to *internal structural changes*, which begin to change economic, institutional, and political alliances and arrangements. The development of productive forces in the economy influence the political and social structure of that country. To accommodate such changes, reforms are made to alleviate the transition. There is a logic in this dialectic, in which the economy, politics, society, culture, etc., are consistently transforming themselves independently and each other collectively. In this chapter we argue that the structural changes that have facilitated growth, development, and the private sector in Pakistan have evolved out of this internal logic. See also Chapter 19, in which we argue that developments in the 1980s, with the emergence of a middle class, have brought about changes in the economic structure of the country.

Even the IMF and World Bank accept the premise that their structural adjustment programmes restructure a country's political economy. 'The implicit purpose of adjustment is to diminish the influence of some social sectors or interest groups whose political and economic control has blocked efficient use of a country's resources. At the same time, adjustment programs stimulate the political and economic ascendance of other groups that can improve the country's competitiveness on international markets.'[24] Here we argue that these changes have also taken place in Pakistan, *without* adherence to an IMF/World Bank-sponsored structural adjustment programme. A major purpose of the structural adjustment programme is to create structural conditions that provide the impetus for enhanced growth. Institutions change, policies and politics take on a particular direction, and then certain specific programmes and policies follow. On the basis of the discussion presented here, we suggest that Pakistan has evolved these structural conditions without a structural adjustment programme. For this reason, too, it did not need a structural adjustment programme.

While Pakistan's economy needs better management, reform, alignment, etc., the critical question is whether it needs to run to the IMF every three years and accept the consequences of conditionality. Is it possible that the country can deal with its internal problems by itself? And if so, *why* does each government of Pakistan run to the IMF for more stringent conditions, more loans, and much more debt?

15.5.3 Why Does Pakistan Accept the Structural Adjustment Programme?

There seems to be very little or no debate about why certain policies are being implemented in Pakistan. Why we have to subscribe to an IMF/World Bank-sponsored programme is not discussed, at least not amongst academics, who one would think are equipped to do so. Pakistan is told to follow certain guidelines, policies, and packages, and it complies, trying to show how it is possible to change an indicator here or there. Pakistani academics and economic managers seldom question either the intentions of the programmes or the basic theory and philosophy behind the policies; they simply do what they are asked to. This has been the experience of the structural adjustment programme in Pakistan. It is difficult to find academic articles that actually *question the need for a programme in the first place*. There is no political debate either. There are, at best, a handful of scholars and journalists who question the repercussions of a structural adjustment programme on the economic and human condition of the populace, and who say that, if we accept the programme, the 'people' will suffer, but they too do not question the reasoning behind or the content of the programmes. One critic writes: 'we argue not against the necessity of structural adjustment, but against the adverse entailments of such adjustment'.[25] The question is: why *not* argue against structural adjustment? Does the author accept the need for such a programme and does he merely want to improve on it? Moreover, even the ultra-conservative *Economist* recognizes that 'many of its [the World Bank's] programmes designed to help the poor – called things like "social dimensions of adjustment" – are safety nets, not ways of lifting people out of poverty'.[26] In countries where there has been protest against IMF-sponsored programmes, academics, NGOs, popular groups, and unions have played critical roles. In Pakistan there seems to be very limited opposition to such programmes (see Box 15.4).

Studies are commissioned by the international financial institutions on issues that tend to justify the policies of the World Bank and the IMF. Resource mobilization, trade and tariff reform, agricultural credit, studies on the informal sector, the need for capital markets, etc., are areas that have recently been interesting Washington. Hence a large number of scholars and institutes are mobilized on these studies where the general guidelines have already been put down, and all that the researchers are asked to do is to supplement and justify the general arguments being recommended. Pakistan does not have its own agenda, nor do we think for ourselves and devise our own arenas of research. Not only that, we fail to question the more general principles behind the research agendas set from afar.[27]

But that still does not answer the question: *why do we think this way?* Why are we unable to study our own particular problems in our own way and find our own specific remedies?

One Pakistani social scientist argues that 'the major reason for [the Pakistani intelligentsia's] failure is that its source of inspiration and point of reference was not the objective study of its own society, with whom it has progressively lost contact to become part of the first world'.[28] Another argues that:

> Post-colonial governments continue with the cultural agenda of colonialism (modernization and development). They also serve as economic agents of their principals. In this role, they ensure, through 'liberal' economic policies, that their charges do not compete with their principals in global markets. They provide familiar and hospitable institutional arrangements to foreign investments. Above all, they ensure that the unsustainably large flows of interest payments on foreign debt are remitted abroad, while managing the levels of local discontent.[29]

While this may be true in the case of some countries, it does not explain how other post-colonial states have managed to avoid problems of this nature. However, Pakistan would fit this general model, since it has always been closely aligned with the West. Maybe it is its colonial hangover that has made it dependent on the decree from elsewhere, when political and economic managers only do what is good for the country when they are told. Or it may be due to the fact that military rule has taken away the Pakistani intelligentsia's ability to create new ideas, and hence, Pakistan's academics and professionals are only good at following orders. These are questions that must be addressed.

Although much of the criticism launched by academics against the imposition of structural adjustment policies has been directed against both the IMF and the World Bank, we argue that it is quite unfair to blame the IMF for the ills that plague the Pakistan economy. The IMF is justified in imposing any condition when extending a loan. It must ensure that the money is returned, and for that purpose it must also make sure that the money lent is used for a purpose which, in the Fund's view, will improve the economy so that the country is in a position to return the loan. As such, to castigate the IMF for imposing 'harsh' conditionalities is futile, for the problem lies elsewhere.

It is Pakistan's governments, past and present, that are responsible for the state of its economy. It is they who have signed agreements with the IMF, accepting the latter's conditionalities and promising to take measures that are not always beneficial or popular. If a government is forced to go to the IMF, the lender of last resort, it is only because it has not been able or unwilling to take immediate and important steps itself.

Take, for instance, two areas of critical concern: low resource mobilization and excessively high expenditure. Clearly, it is not the IMF that is responsible for either of these shortcomings, but rather the inability of various governments to tackle these structural concerns.

BOX 15.4

Pakistani non-governmental organizations (NGOs) assess Pakistan's experience with structural adjustment programmes

In March 1995, the World Summit for Social Development was held in Copenhagen, Denmark. The United Nations was the convenor and asked each member country participating to produce its Country Report. A group of NGOs in Pakistan felt that Pakistan's Country Report failed to analyse critically the domestic impact of World Bank/IMF policies and, instead, unquestioningly promoted a market-based economy and growth model. In response to the Country Report, these NGOs prepared 'An alternative NGO statement' which, in particular, criticized the government's adherence to the structural adjustment programme. An excerpt from the alternative statement is presented below:

Since the onset of the medium term Structural Adjustment Programme (SAP) in 1987–88, the socio-economic conditions of the poor, particularly women, have markedly deteriorated. There appears to be a direct association between the implementation of the SAP under the supervision of the IMF and the World Bank and a deterioration in the standard of living of the lower income classes.

The withdrawal of subsidies has hit the poor through price increases of essential commodities. Prior to the implementation of the SAP package, the bulk of subsidies were on wheat, sugar and edible oil which are important components of the total consumption of the poor. Not only have total subsidies declined but the share of wheat, sugar and edible oil in these subsidies has also declined sharply. This decline in subsidies was accompanied by an increase in the support price of wheat. In addition, the price of kerosene and petrol rose by about fifty per cent between 1987–88 and 1990–91. Since food constitutes a much larger share of the consumption basket of the poor than the rich, the dramatic increase in food prices has meant that Structural Adjustment has hit the poor much more than the rich. Similarly, the increase in energy prices has placed a disproportionate burden on the poor.

The burden of taxation over the period between 1987-88 and 1990-91 has also been borne largely by the poor. Taxes on the poor increased by 10.3 per cent while those on the richest group declined by 4.3 per cent between 1987-88 and 1990–91.

As a part of Structural Adjustment, trade liberalization and exchange rate flexibility have been followed. The rupee devaluation, recommended by the IMF to promote exports and reduce the trade deficit, has brought no change in the balance of trade. In fact it has resulted in inflation since imports are now more costly.

As part of Structural Adjustment, interest rates are now to be market determined. Despite high interest rates, the saving rate has remained low. Moreover, high rates of interest have had a negative impact on the growth rate. The rich who are able to save are obviously benefited by high interest rates. Moreover high interest rates are likely to result in a ballooning of the fiscal deficit. Interest payments amounted to one-fifth of total federal government expenditure in 1991–92 or about four-fifths of the overall deficit of 78.65 billion in 1991–92.

Accepting SAP means conceding autonomy in economic policy and a failure of leadership. Instead of living within our means, it has extended the begging bowl. Those who have put the poor in this predicament are immune from the negative repercussions of SAP. It is paradoxical that the poor must count on the same leadership for humane social and economic policies.

Responding to calls by the IMF and the World Bank for financial discipline, the government froze wages while jobs in the public sector were restricted as a result of a ban on recruitment and the encouragement of an early retirement via the government's 'golden hand shake' scheme. There has been no significant increase in jobs through investment in the private sector. Even the much doubted official unemployment statistics show a marked increase in unemployment between 1987–88 and 1990-91 in various categories of the work force. Amongst the clerical, sales, services, agriculture, production and related workers categories, unemployment increased dramatically over the period between 1987–88 and 1991. Unemployment has been accompanied by increasing inequality and poverty.

The impact of Structural Adjustment is particularly adverse for women since this economic model relies on the devaluation of labour in the formal and informal sectors so as to lower production costs. Women workers are the most harshly affected by these programmes, as they constitute the majority of home-based workers and are the least protected by statutory wage, security, and safety standards.

Major investment is needed in the productive sectors and infrastructure, with affirmative biases towards those areas which need to be nurtured for achieving equitable development. At the same time there needs to be a reduction in budgetary allocations to the defence establishment and civil administration. Their share of the budget, along with the cost of overall debt servicing, are a huge and unacceptable burden on the nation's resources.

Source: *The Nation*, 7 March 1995.

The taxation structure in Pakistan is wrought with numerous loopholes and exemptions, not to mention rampant corruption, ensuring that a large part of taxable income goes untaxed. Various quarters act to preserve their vested interests by demanding and usually acquiring exemptions in taxation. For example, there is as yet no agricultural income tax in Pakistan, even though 25 per cent of GDP is contributed by the agricultural sector. Most influential people, agriculturists as well as others, do not pay any tax at all, and only 800,000 individuals out of a population of 130 million pay income tax. Surely, many more than this 1 per cent of the population earn the minimum taxable 4,000 rupees per month. The inability or unwillingness of the government to ensure an equitable, just, and extensive taxation structure ensures low resource mobilization. This in turn results in a high fiscal deficit, with its numerous repercussions. Another area where successive governments have chosen not to express concern is defence expenditure. With close to 6 per cent of GDP being spent on defence, little remains for development. In fact, Pakistan must be one of the very few countries in the world where annual defence spending exceeds development expenditure. Although the political economy of the state does not permit the government to tackle the issue of military spending, it is perhaps time to do so.

Just these two examples highlight the fact that whatever mess Pakistan's economy finds itself in is due not to the meddling and interference of the IMF (although that does exacerbate the problem), but is largely of our own creation. In order to ensure their extended survival, governments do not touch controversial issues such as agricultural income tax and military spending. Instead, they rush to the IMF for financial assistance, continuing to delay the day of reckoning. They acquire loans to meet their revenue gap, so that unpleasant measures can be avoided. In all this, if the people of Pakistan have a voice, it must be directed at criticizing the wrongdoings of their elected representatives, not the officials of an international bureaucracy. By blaming the IMF, we are simply letting our governments off the hook.

It is the government that is responsible for the state of Pakistan's economy and it should be accountable to its people. Popular pressure should be directed towards demanding reforms that will improve the structure of the economy so that there is no need to borrow under harsh conditionalities. Whether it be agricultural income tax or land reforms, military spending or development expenditure, the government should be forced by public opinion to undertake the extensive reforms that are long overdue. Instead of blaming the IMF, there is need to examine the role of academics, the intelligentsia, and government (see Appendix 15.3 for different ways of looking at the problems in the economy and for alternative solutions).

15.6 Summary and Further Reading

15.6.1 Summary

Having presented in Chapter 14 a general overview of the structural adjustment programme and its impact on and consequences for those countries that have adhered to it, this chapter has examined the specific case of Pakistan and its experience. We started with an extensive and detailed overview of what the programme involves in the case of Pakistan and with a history of the IMF's involvement. It seems that Pakistan has been rather eager to seek IMF assistance in recent years, and some writers have argued that the way these loans have been agreed to gives rise to speculation that some non-economic factors may also have been involved.

We examined the analysis made of the structural adjustment programmes by the World Bank and the IMF themselves, and found that these two organizations were not totally satisfied with the outcomes, as many targets were missed. More importantly, the little independent research that has been done on the impact of the programme shows, very clearly, that the repercussions have been severe for poverty, employment, wages, and inequality. Moreover, some of the outcomes of a structural adjustment programme, like higher growth and lower inflation, have not manifested themselves in Pakistan, with growth being considerably lower and inflation higher than trend levels.

We also analysed the political economy of the structural adjustment programme and tried to examine why, if the repercussions of the programmes are so negative, the government of Pakistan runs to the IMF on the smallest pretext. The answer, we suggest, lies in the way our élites and the political settlement works. Pakistan has not even needed a structural adjustment programme sponsored by the IMF and the World Bank, yet finds recourse to their assistance. Because it is easier to acquire loans from such organizations than to implement far-reaching changes in the economy, such as an agricultural income tax, a cut in defence expenditure, and the elimination of conspicuous consumption, the rulers in Pakistan make use of so-called 'aid and assistance', having very serious repercussions for the economy overall.

15.6.2 Further Reading

The reading list provided in the previous chapter should be consulted, since it contains a good general overview of the structural adjustment programmes. For Pakistan, the four World Bank reports are essential.: *Pakistan: Growth Through Adjustment*, Report No. 7118-Pak, Washington, 1988; *Pakistan: Medium-term Economic Policy Adjustments*, Report No. 7591-Pak, Washington, 1989; *Changes in Trade and Domestic Taxation for Reform of the Incentive and Fiscal Adjustment*, Report No. 9828-Pak, Washington, 1992; and *Pakistan: Country Economic Memorandum FY93*, Report No. 11590-Pak, Washington, 1993.

In addition, the special issues of the *Pakistan Journal of Applied Economics*, vols. 10 and 11, 1994, 1995, contain some very useful articles In particular, see: Zaman, Arshad, 'The Government's Present Agreement with the IMF: Misgovernment or Folly?', *Pakistan Journal of Applied Economics*, vol. 11, nos. 1 and 2, 1995; Zaidi, S. Akbar, 'The Structural Adjustment Programme and Pakistan: External Influence or Internal Acquiescence?', *Pakistan Journal of Applied Economics*, vol. 10, nos. 1 and 2, 1994; and Zaidi, S. Akbar, 'Locating the Budget Deficit in Context: The Case of Pakistan', *Pakistan Journal of Applied Economics*, vol. 11, nos. 1 and 2, 1995. Shahrukh Rafi Khan's 'Do IMF and World Bank Policies Work?', Sustainable Development Policy Institute Monograph No. 6, Islamabad, 1997, is also a useful recent addition to the literature.

Appendix 15.1

Summary and time-frame for structural adjustment policies, 1988–1991

Policy areas	Strategies and measures	Timing of measures	Year of implementation[a]
FISCAL POLICY			
Overall deficit	Major improvements in overall revenue performance and tight control of expenditure growth.	1988/9–1990/1	–
Revenue	Begin to implement a tax reform directed at expanding the tax base and at increasing tax elasticity; continue the strengthening of tax administration.	By 1 July 1988	1989/90
	Extension of sales tax on about 22 per cent of domestic industrial production.	By 1 July 1988	1989/90
	Extension of sales tax on 30 per cent of domestic industrial production.	By 1 July 1989	1990/1
	Increases in telephone charges.	1 October 1988	–
	Extension of ad valorem excise on certain services such as travel.	By 1 July 1989	1990/1
	Annual revision in those excises which are at specific rates so that there is revenue elasticity.	1989/90–1990/1	1991/2
	Initiate a programme of action to prepare for the introduction of a general sales tax by 1 July 1990.	September 1988	–
	Proceed with the implementation of the programme of action.	1988/9–1989/90	1990/1
	Effective implementation of the general sales tax.	1 July 1990	–
	Guidelines issued to income tax panels to set criteria for initiating prosecution against tax evaders.	By 31 October 1988	1989/90
	Maintain income and profit tax exemption limits at current levels.	1989/90–1990/1	–
	Review experience of self-assessment procedure for taxpayers earning less than Rs100,000.	By 1 July 1989	1990/1
	Removal of most exemptions from the standard customs duties, except for duty drawbacks for exports and incentives for industries as given in the 1988/9 budget. It is the authorities intention that these exemptions will not be extended beyond 1990/1, except for backward areas as defined in the 1988/9 budget.	1988/9–1990/1	1990/1
	Continue implementation of tax reform.	1989/90–1990/1	1990/1
Expenditure	Contain the growth rate of non-subsidy recurrent expenditures to less than nominal GDP growth rate; target development expenditures to grow slightly faster than the expansion of nominal GDP, contingent on available concessional external financing and available bank and non-bank domestic resources.	1988/9–1990/1	
MONETARY POLICY AND FINANCIAL REFORM	Substantially reduce cash and economic subsidies through price adjustments, rationalize government expenditures for certain major commodities; implement tightened expenditure control procedure, including a quarterly expenditure reporting and control system.	1988/9–1990/1	–
	Tightening of control over provincial expenditures through containing federal transfers to and borrowing by provincial governments within the agreed target.	1988/9–1990/1	
	Continue to strengthen expenditure control procedures regarding spending by ministries.	1988/9–1990/1	–

Appendix 15.1 continued

Policy areas	Strategies and measures	Timing of measures	Year of implementation[a]
	Limit the rate of domestic credit expansion to significantly less than the growth of nominal GDP at the targeted inflation rate in 1988/9 and to the growth of nominal GDP, at the targeted inflation rate, in 1989/90–1990/1.	1988/9–1990/1	1990/1
	Continue to maintain global ceilings on the annual rate of expansion of domestic credit.	1988/9–1990/1	1990/1
	Eliminate mandatory margin requirements for opening import letters of credit.	1 July 1990	–
	Start to implement policy by rationalizing rate structure of the National Savings Schemes (NSS) and issuing auctioned debt instruments, beginning with pilot auction of Treasury Bills.	1988/9–1990/1	–
	Establish appropriate public debt management organization in State Bank of Pakistan (SBP) and establish co-ordination mechanism with Ministry of Finance (MOF).	1989/90	1990/1
	Maintain maximum ceiling of 20 per cent on rates of return (ROR) on non-investment financing by commercial banks.	1988/9–1990/1	1989/90
	Move toward market-oriented rates of return for concessional credit schemes.	1988/9–1990/1	1989/90
	Within the credit budget, the rate of mandatory allocations (to agriculture, fixed investment to industry, small businesses and industries, and tobacco marketing, excluding special credit programmes from foreign lending institutions) to the total allocation for private sector credit in respect of commercial banks will be limited to the level fixed in the excluding budget for 1988/9 on a net basis, excluding special credit programme for foreign lending institutions.	1989/90–1990/1	1990/1
	Prepare strategy statement and programme to introduce open market operations.	By November 1988	1989/90
	Prepare a draft programme and a timetable aimed at reducing automatic SBP refinance for special lending programmes and substituting it with other resources.	By November 1988	1989/90
	Prepare improved prudential regulations for supervision of banks and other financial institutions, including improved procedures for accounting and auditing.	1988/9	–
	Initiate legislation in order to unify supervision of financial institutions under SBP.	1988/89	–
	Establish credit information bureau within the SBP.	1989/90	1989/90
	Completion of comprehensive portfolio audit.	By January 1989	–
	Formulation of a programme for capital build-up.	June 1989	1990/1
	Sanction private investment banks which satisfy criteria of the government of Pakistan.	1988/9	1989/90
	Initiate legal amendments and prepare implementation circulars with regard to performance evaluation and restructuring of Pakistan Banking Council and NCBs.	By January 1989	1990/1
	Eliminate official setting of share prices.	1988/9	1989/90
	Prepare measures to strengthen supervisory role of Corporate Law Authority (CLA) over stock exchange to increase public confidence.	1988/9	–

Appendix 15.1 continued

Policy areas	Strategies and measures	Timing of measures	Year of implementation[a]
EXCHANGE SYSTEM **Exchange rate policy**	Continue pursuit of a flexible policy consistent with maintaining external competitiveness and facilitating trade liberalization. Policy to be guided by quantitative assessments of specified indicators, including growth in export receipts and net international reserves.	1988/9–1990/1	1990/1
	Take measures to narrow the premium between the market price of Foreign Exchange Bearer Certificates and the official exchange rate by increasing allowance for invisible transactions and unifying related procedure.	1988/9	–
Forward cover rates	Continue to implement flexible market rates for forward cover, with exchange rate premium that distinguishes between different currencies; annual review to ensure flexibility is maintained.	1988/9–1990/1	–
Bilateral payments	Accelerate phasing out of existing agreements with Fund members in order to terminate bilateral agreements during programme period.	Phasing down during 1988/9. Modify arrangements for China, Hungary, Poland, and Islamic Republic of Iran by July 1990 with a view to achieving convertibility of foreign exchange balance at the end of specified period.	–
EXTERNAL DEBT MANAGEMENT	Limit contracting of loans of 1–12 years' and 1–5 years' maturity.	1988/9–1990/1	–
	Limit public and publicly guaranteed debt of 1 year or less, including debt of domestic banking system.	1988/9–1990/1	–
	Computerize the collection of information on public and publicly guaranteed debt by Economic Affairs Division (Ministry of Finance and Economic Affairs) and private debt by the State Bank of Pakistan. Greater co-ordination between agencies collecting debt data to facilitate analysis and policy formulation.	Debt information data on computer by 1 July 1989.	–
AGRICULTURE **Investment**	Assure adequate funding for a three-year core investment programme covering high-priority projects in agriculture/irrigation.	1989/90–1990/1	–
	Complete study of water sector to refine investment priorities and improve sectoral planning capability.	September 1989	–
	Implementation of this programme.	1988/9–1990/1	–
Agricultural output prices	Review and adjust prices *annually* for key crops to keep these prices in line with trends and levels in world prices and exchange rate changes.	1988/9–1990/1 (at beginning of each crop year)	1989/90
	Implementation of *annually* agreed work programme for APCOM, including training and technical assistance requirements.	1988/9–1990/1 (by 1 October of each fiscal year)	–
	Complete study of the cost structure of RECP to provide basis for recommendations for efficiency improvements.	By end-February 1989	–

Appendix 15.1 continued

Policy areas	Strategies and measures	Timing of measures	Year of implementation[a]
Agricultural input pricing	Assure that the economic subsidy for nitrogenous fertilizer will not reappear.	1 July 1988	–
	Implement an agreed schedule of reductions of economic subsidies, with a view to eliminating the subsidy for phosphatic fertilizers by 1 October 1991 and the subsidy for potash fertilizer by 1995.	1988/9–1990/1 (price adjustment by 1 July or in the course of each fiscal year)	–
Irrigations operations and maintenance	*Annually* identify and establish a programme of optimum O & M allocations for various types of irrigation facility.	1988/9–1990/91 (by 1 July of each fiscal year)	1989/90
	Improve assessment and collection of water charges, on the basis of the implementation plan.	1988/9–1990/1	–
	Begin phasing out of all public tubewells in fresh groundwater areas, except South Rohri and Ghotki, and refrain from installing or replacing public tubewells for public operators in these areas.	1988/9–1990/1	–
INDUSTRY AND TRADE			
Deregulation	Complete the implementation of the remaining recommendations of the Deregulation Commission.	By 1 July 1989	1990/1
	Government will not expand the list of specified industries.	1988/9–1990/1	1990/1
	Annual inflation adjustments to the investment sanctioning limit of Rs700 million as of 1 July 1988.	1989/90–1990/1	–
Public enterprises	Divest partially or fully certain identified public enterprises. Develop corporate rationalization/restructuring programme for the remaining enterprises. Meanwhile, continue application of 'signalling system', institute complete autonomy and accountability, and introduce medium-term corporate planning.	1989/90–1990/1	–
Import policy	Replace non-tariff barriers (except for well-specified reasons such as religion, and security, reciprocity, and international agreements) by tariffs; and rationalize the tariff structure with a view to reducing the average level and dispersion of the rates.	1988/9–1990/1	1989/90
	Lowering of the maximum tariff rate from 150 per cent to 125 per cent, and rationalization of the tariff rate structure.	1 July 1988	–
	Removal of 162 categories of items (on the 1987/8 IPO basis) from the negative list thereby reducing the number of banned items to 216, 55 categories of items (on the 1987/8 IPO basis) from the restricted lists, and elimination of the list of items importable by specific industries.	1 July 1988	1989/90
	20 per cent increase in value ceilings on imports of machinery and millwork against cash licences, and a doubling of the ceiling imports by actual users to Rs10,000.	1 July 1988	1989/90
	Imposition of customs duty on items (i.e., air conditioners and refrigerators) covered under Transfer of Residence Allowance.	1 July 1988	–
	Further rationalization of the tariff rate structure.	1 July 1989	–
	Further removal of approximately 70 categories of items from the Negative List (on the 1987/88 IPO basis) and further reduction in the rationalization of the Restricted List.	1 July 1989	–
	Significantly increase the real value of ceilings on imports of machinery and millwork against cash licences and on imports by actual users.	1 July 1989	–

Appendix 15.1 continued

Policy areas	Strategies and measures	Timing of measures	Year of implementation[a]
	Further removal of approximately 70 additional items(on the 1987/8 IPO basis) from the Negative List, with a view to limiting the remaining items to about 80 categories of items banned on account of religion, security, and reciprocity considerations and because of international agreements; and further reduction in the rationalization of the remaining items on the Restricted List.	1 July 1990	–
	Further reduction in the maximum tariff rate to 100 per cent and rationalization of the tariff structure, with a view to rationalizing and lowering the import duty structure further in subsequent years.	1 July 1990	–
	All tariff exemptions – except duty drawbacks for exporters, newly established exemptions for imports of capital equipment and machinery by 'key' industries and industries established in backward areas, and reasonable baggage allowances – will be phased out during 1989/90–1990/1.	1 July 1990	–
	Introduction of special excise taxes on luxury consumer goods to be levied equally on imported and domestically produced goods.	1 July 1990	–
	Continue to increase significantly the real value of ceiling on imports of machinery and millwork against cash licences on imports by actual users.	1989/90–1990/1	–
ENERGY			
Investment and institutional framework	In the context of the Seventh Plan, formulation and implementation of medium-term energy investment programme based on least-cost principles.	1 July 1988	–
	Continued reliance on core investment programme and supporting financing arrangements to assure appropriate levels of investment.	1988/9–1990/1	–
	Implementation of programme to separate WAPDA's distribution function from its generation and transmission functions.	1990/1	–
	Agreement on a framework for allowing private generation of power and sales to the national grid.	1 July 1988	–
	Implementation of this programme.	1988/9–1990/1	–
Pricing, resource mobilization, and demand management			
Power tariffs	*Annually* adust power tariffs as required to achieve 40 per cent self-financing of agreed WAPDA investment programme. Investment programme for determining self-financing requirements has been changed from a retrospective to a prospective basis.	1988/9–1990/1 (adjustment at the beginning of each fiscal year)	1988/9
	Completion of load research and management study and implementation of main recommendations of the study.	By 1 July 1989	–
Petroleum	Shift away from cost-plus formula to increase incentive for efficiency and to encourage new private sector investments in the refinery subsector.	1988/9–1990/1	1989/90

Appendix 15.1 continued

Policy areas	Strategies and measures	Timing of measures	Year of implementation[a]
	Pass through to consumers increases in the cost of domestic and imported petroleum above the average level assumed for the budget as well as effects of the depreciation of rupee. Review domestic product prices if international oil prices should decline.	1988/9–1990/1 (by 1 July or in the course of each fiscal year, as required)	–
Gas consumer prices	*Annually* adjust the prices for gas supplied to domestic household consumers, with a view to reaching 100 per cent of the border price of fuel oil by 1992/3.	1988/9–1990/1 (adjustment at the beginning of each fiscal year)	–
Gas producer prices	Implement agreed gas producer pricing formula and discount for new concessions as necessary if low world prices inhibit exploration and development.	1988/9–1990/1 (price adjustment by 1 July or in the course of each fiscal year, as required)	–
Resource department	Agreement of programme for restructuring public sector Pakistan Mineral Development Corporation and for encouraging greater private sector participation.	By July 1989	1990/1
	Implementation of this programme.	1989/90–1990/1	–
PUBLIC SECTOR INVESTMENT PROGRAM	Review of *annual* public expenditure programme.	1988/9–1989/90 (by 1 July of each fiscal year)	–
	Implementation of *annual* public expenditure programme, in line with available resources and with Seventh Plan objectives.	1988/9–1989/90 (in connection with budget for each fiscal year)	–
INFRA-STRUCTURE			
Urban infrastructure	Formulation and implementation of *annual* priority investment programme to ensure appropriate levels of investment, in the context of the Seventh Plan.	1988/9–1990/1 (by 1 July of each fiscal year)	–
	Adjust water and sewerage tariffs *annually*.	1988/9–1990/1 (by 1 July of each fiscal year)	–
	Implementation of the improved system in Lahore.	1988/9	–
	Training of local government staff and introduction of monitoring system as well as accounting services through training of staff and provision of technical assistance to augment local administration.	1988/9–1990/1	1989/90
Transportation	In the context of the Seventh Plan, implementation of a public expenditure programme for transport sector.	1988/9–1990/1	1990/1
	Begin implementation of an investment programme for the modernization of container facilities, with a view to improving efficiency of freight handling and movements.	1988/9	1989/90
	Continue implementation of this investment programme.	1989/90–1990/1	1990/1
	Phased adjustments in taxes, fees, user charges for road, rail, ports, and aviation.	1988/9–1990/1 (by 1 July of each fiscal year)	–

Appendix 15.1 continued

Policy areas	Strategies and measures	Timing of measures	Year of implementation[a]
	Start implementation of a programme for restructuring Pakistan Railways.	1989/90–1990/1	1991/2
	Amend rules/regulations to permit resident companies to engage in international freight facilities.	1989/90	–
	Deregulate bus fares; permit import of range of truck types and sizes.	1988/9	–
	Improve balance between new investment, maintenance and rehabilitation; introduce modern planning and construction methods.	1988/9–1990/1	1989/90
HUMAN RESOURCES			
Investment Programme		1988/9–1990/1	1989/90
	Expand primary school places for girls.	1988/9–1990/1	1989/90
	Increase basic health care facilities.	1988/9	1989/90
	Review utilization/staffing/procedures of operation and draw up plans for improvements.	1988/9–1990/1	1989/90
Institutional changes	Phased expansion of network.	1988/89	1989/90
	Complete review of current organization and management procedures and develop strategy for private sector participation.	July 1989	–
	Begin to implement recommendations.	1989/90–1990/1	–
	Continue implementation of recommendations.		

[a] Information on the year of implementation has been obtained from various issues of *Pakistan Economic Surveys* and *Annual Report* of the State Bank of Pakistan.

Source: Applied Economics Research Centre, *Economic Reforms and the Environment in Pakistan*, Karachi, 1994.

Appendix 15.2

Summary of policy framework paper for Extended Structural Adjustment Facility, 1994–1997

Policy areas	Objective, strategies, and measures
FISCAL POLICY	
Overall deficit	Prudent demand management, higher budgetary revenues and expenditure curtailment.
Revenues	
Direct taxes	Reform of direct taxation will focus on reducing the wide-ranging exemptions and concessions.
	Extend coverage to the agriculture sector, through the imposition of the wealth tax; and provincial income taxation.
	Containment of the basic personal exemption and provisions concerning employee benefits.
	Unification of the corporate profit tax.
	Reduction of the tax-holiday provisions.
	Transforming the current mechanism of taxation on supplies, contracts, imports, and exports from final discharge of the tax liability into an advance payment of the regular income tax.
Tariffs	Trade taxes will continue to be rationalized through (1) adoption of a simplified structure based on a maximum of 4–5 bands with products allocated according to efficiency

Appendix 15.2 continued

Policy areas	Objective, strategies, and measures
	considerations, (2) a simultaneous reduction in the value of imports subject to exemptions and concessions, and (3) a consolidation of the various import taxation elements through their incorporation in the basic rates.
	Lower the maximum tariff rate to 80 per cent excluding Iqra surcharge and import licence fee.
	Removing exemption from Iqra surcharge.
	Elimination of import licence fee.
	Elimination of export taxes.
	Initiate an import inspection programme to strengthen revenue performance.
Indirect taxes	Converting GST into a modern broadly based VAT, through a significant expansion in the number of registered firms, and extension of horizontal and vertical coverage. To this end, the number of items subject to GST will be increased.
	Increasing the GST rate from 12.5 per cent to 15 per cent.
	Removal of exemptions for most locally produced goods and imports.
	Elimination of the capacity schemes and small excise duties within the framework of the GST.
	All specific rates and assessment based on official prices and the lower rates of manufactures that do not claim tax credit will be eliminated.
	Extension of GST to trading and services sector by July 1995.
Federal non-tax revenue	Administered prices of petroleum, gas, and electricity will be targeted to improve non-tax revenues.
	Petroleum prices to be adjusted with international prices and exchange rate. Replacement of surcharge with ad valorem excise and sales tax.
Provincial non-tax revenue	Higher water-user charges.
	User charges on social services.
Expenditures	
Federal current expenditure	Redirect the structure of expenditure to ensure the effective delivery of key public services.
	Contain defence expenditure consistent with the security needs of the country, i.e. to reduce it below the 1993/4 share of GDP.
	Reduce non-development expenditure to below the 1993/4 share of GDP.
	Fund operations and maintenance expenditures of roads, railways, irrigation and drainage, water supply and sanitation.
	Increasing provincial expenditure on social services including ensuring funds for full staffing of schools and health facilities.
	Reducing overstaffing and administrative inefficiences in the federal ministries.
Development expenditure	Increase in development expenditure on energy, irrigation and drainage, transport infrastructure, and population at the federal level. Basic social services in the context of SAP will be emphasized at the provincial level.
	Continue formulating annually a 'core' investment programme composed of projects of high priority.
	Reduce the share of block allocations in development expenditure in order to strengthen the investment screening process.
MONETARY POLICY AND FINANCIAL REFORMS	Increasing reliance on instruments of monetary control.
	Reduction in the scope of mandatory concessional credit facilities.
	• Increasing concessional rates to 11% with full market levels by 1994/5.
	• Freeing rate of return on deposits and loans on trade and investment related modes of financing.

Appendix 15.2 continued

Policy areas	Objective, strategies, and measures
	• Adjusting the premia on foreign exchange cover.
	• Eliminating differential taxation of financial instruments and institutions.
	Widening and deepening the market for government debt.
	• Market determination of yields at government auctions.
	Enhancing institutional capabilities of SBP.
	• Undertake liquidity programming.
	• Strengthening prudential regulations.
EXCHANGE AND TRADE REGULATIONS	Eliminate the restricted list. Ensuring that the negative list covers only items subject to religious, security, health, and reciprocity considerations.
	Consolidating and reducing, consistent with GATT obligations, the maximum rate, average rate, and dispersion of import duties, with corresponding adjustments in intermediate rates.
	Removing restrictions on the provision of foreign exchange for certain invisible payments and machinery goods.
	Replacing non-tariff barriers by tariffs.
	Greater nominal rate stability in the context of tighter financial stability, leading to current account convertibility and higher inflow of foreign private investment.
DEREGULATION AND PRIVATIZATION	Continue to deregulate investment and prices and encourage private investment.
	Progress further in privatizing industrial units and expanding the process to new areas such as services and infrastructure.
	Expand privatization effort to Pakistan Telecommunication Corporation (PTC) and Water and Power Development Authority (WAPDA), and establish regulatory framework for these bodies.
INVESTMENT POLICIES	Review the effectiveness of tax incentives granted to promote investment.
	Further simplify and clarify investment approval procedures and regulations, especially at the provincial and local level.
POVERTY REDUCTION AND SOCIAL SERVICES	In the context of Social Action Plan (SAP), expand the coverage and quality of primary education, primary health care, and rural water supply.
	Allocate at least 10 per cent of total recurrent education expenditures to education materials and other non-salary inputs.
	Increase school participation rate of females.
	• Permitting mixed primary education.
	• Construction of girls' schools.
	• Expanding the recruitment of female teachers.
	Providing better health care for mothers and children.
	• Decentralizing and strengthening management.
	• Reallocating recurrent budget expenditures towards non-salary items.
	Controlling population growth rate.
	• Integration of family planning into basic health services.
	• Launching of a more explicit population information campaign.
ENVIRONMENT	Programmes and projects to tackle waterlogging and salinity and undertake reforestation.
	Further progress in improving regulations and standards for air, water, and waste contamination.

Appendix 15.2 continued

Policy areas	Objective, strategies, and measures
SECTORAL POLICIES	
Agriculture	Concentrate on water resource management, input and output pricing and agricultural support services. • Privatize public tubewells in groundwater areas. • Move towards full cost recovering for on-farm irrigation works and drainage systems through higher user charges. • Promote private sector participation in rice and cotton exports and wheat imports. • Eliminate subsidy on potash fertilizer by October 1995.
Infrastructure investment	Increase the role of the private sector in the provision of infrastructure through privatization of state-owned companies, e.g. WAPDA, PTC. Fund operations and maintenance activities adequately. Increase tariffs and fees charged for public services and improve assessment and collection procedures to achieve gradually full cost recovery. Strengthen institutions and reduce their operating costs.
Energy	Restrain energy demand growth through demand management measures including pricing policies. Accelerate the development of domestic energy resources as part of least-cost energy investment programme. Strengthen the operations and management of the sector institutions, including building up their environmental managerial capability. Accelerate the process of restructuring and privatization of the energy sector. Rationalize energy prices. Petroleum to be priced at equivalent border prices. Electricity and gas to be priced at their economic cost of production. Adjust gas tariff as appropriate. Rehabilitate the transmission and distribution systems that contribute to power losses and load shedding.
EXTERNAL FINANCING REQUIREMENTS	Encourage non-debt creating flows (foreign direct and portfolio investments) and improve the maturity profile of existing foreign liabilities. Consider the possibility of placing a sovereign risk bond issue on the euro-market.

Source: Applied Economics Research Centre, *Economic Reforms and the Environment in Pakistan*, Karachi, 1994.

Appendix 15.3

The alternative to the IMF/World Bank policies

Do underdeveloped countries like Pakistan and India have any alternative to IMF/World Bank dependence? Professor Prabhat Patnaik and C.P. Chandrasekhar examine the possibilities:

What comes through clearly from the Indian experience with structural adjustment is the dominant role of the process of globalization of finance. We have suggested earlier that indeed the very design of the current package of structural adjustment bears the imprint of this process; and the sequel to the introduction of this package shows that the real mobility witnessed is that of finance rather than that of capital-in-production. But then if globalization of finance restricts the possibility of intervention within a 'national' (or for that matter any supra-national but restricted) space by undermining the concept of a 'control area', the question naturally arises: can there be any sort of an alternative to the current set of policies? To say that an alternative presupposes *international* co-ordination, and can no longer be based on a national, or any kind of a spatially-restricted, response, a proposition which some radicals advance, is inadequate: it amounts *de facto* to conceding that a feasible alternative to the current set of policies does not exist.

It is our contentional however that a feasible alternative, not just a desirable one, to the existing policies exists. We should draw a distinction here: obviously the East Asian and the South-East Asian cases underscore the possibility of a successful, neomercantilist (and in that sense nationalist) policy response in the contemporary environment. But those cases are also marked by economies where the development of financial institutions and hence the possibility of integration with global finance are limited to start with. China's stock exchange is very recent in origin. Vietnam does not even have one to date, and even in avowedly capitalist East Asia financial interests have generally played second fiddle (except briefly in Japan). One cannot of course recreate those initial conditions (and other conditions conducive to neo-mercantilism) in India: apart from being unhistorical that is not even necessarily desirable, since neo-mercantilist strategies have been associated with politically authoritarian structures. So, in discussing an alternative we have to talk of a *sui generis* alternative. And the question is: is it feasible?

The fallacy in our view lies in believing that an undermining of the 'control area' of the nation-state is tantamount to an impossibility of intervention. What such undermining does is to impose an important additional constraint upon the nation-state; the nation-state cannot certainly intervene in the *old* way. It can now intervene with some degree of success *only* if it takes this constraint into account.

Specifically for economies like India this involves that the volatility of financial flows has to be kept under check through a combination of: (i) direct regulations; (ii) an overall sound balance of payments (in relative terms, which is not synonymous with neomercantilism); (iii) and, above all, through a development strategy which ensures economic advance with social stability.

(i) The main form of direct regulation that we have in mind is of course a mix of capital flow controls with a non-convertible currency. External pressures against such regulation would be strong; but a country the size of India can, if she so chooses, show sufficient resilience to stand up to such pressures. After all even the current government, committed as it is to structural adjustment, has not moved towards full convertibility despite external pressures.

The real problem, it may be thought however, would be of a different kind; globalization of finance is such a strong process that direct regulation may prove ineffective in stemming illicit flows. But to believe that the existence of regulations makes *no* difference to the behaviour of economic agents is fallacious. And the effectiveness of regulations depends upon the character, and hence the social basis, of the state (a proposition which must not be confused with the view that an authoritarian state regulates more effectively; indeed we argue the contrary). The alternative we have in mind is not confined to merely having regulations by the extent state, but encompasses, as well shall see, a change in the character of the state.

(ii) Regulations, however, have to be backed by a sound balance of payments position through a sound *trade performance*. A part of the key to such a sound trade performance lies in the imposition of intelligently-devised import controls; at the same time, however, a sound export performance is essential. While the importance of boosting exports is stressed by neo-classical economists, they never distinguish between primary commodity and manufacturing exports. In agriculture, as already mentioned, private

investment is predicated upon public investment; and if the latter cannot be augmented, either because the system is already agricultural-supply-constrained *pace* Kalecki (and hence up against the inflationary barrier), or because the state is being made to withdraw from its inventing role, then an increase in agricultural *exports* necessarily means a lower profile of domestic availability, which has the effect of *both* impoverishing the domestic working masses, *as well as* contracting the home market for manufactured goods.

Manufacturing exports, however, as Kaldor had argued long ago, are in an altogether different category. To the extent that investment decisions here are induced by larger capacity utilization, larger exports provide both the inducement as well as the material wherewithal (from the supply-side) for larger investment. Manufacturing exports in other words can provide the basis for a self-sustaining growth-process in a way that agricultural exports (except under special circumstances) cannot. The history of colonial India provides ample evidence for this proposition: the last half-century of colonial rule saw both a stagnant per capita agricultural output and a rise in the proportion of exports out of it, resulting in a sharp decline in the per capita availability of foodgrains, from about 200 kg per year at the turn of the century to about 150 kg at independence.

An alternative development strategy therefore must specifically aim at increasing the exports of manufactured goods. And this requires not 'getting prices right' in some neo-classical sense, but above all high rates of investment which increase the flexibility of the economy's response to the changing international environment. The correlation between high investment ratios and high export growth rates in cross-country data relating to a host of underdeveloped countries is strong. The direction of causation is always seen to lie from exports to investment; but a mutuality of causation is much more plausible in which case it is not exports which need be the initial intervention variable but the investment ratio itself.

(iii) This brings us to the main issue, namely, the alternative development trajectory. *Any* meaningful development strategy for India, it seems to us, must aim to bring about an *immediate* improvement in the living conditions of the working masses, especially in the rural sector, i.e., the *modus operandi* of the development strategy itself must be such an improvement in their living standards. This is not merely an ethical proposition, but a practical necessity, both for the preservation of meaningful democratic structures, as well as for arousing the kind of enthusiasm and participation among the masses on the basis of which alone the structures of a more accountable state, a state capable of imposing discipline upon the rich and the capitalists, can be built. Such an immediate improvement must have as its cornerstone an accelerated agricultural growth based on egalitarian land reforms. The East Asian example has shown the importance of land reforms even for a neo-mercantilist strategy of economic nationalism: indeed it is important for *any* national economic programme. The Chinese example has shown the vigour of an industrialization drive based on an expansion of mass markets deriving from an accelerated agricultural growth. In their specific context, at the present conjuncture, this growth has been achieved through a break-up of communes though on the basis of the groundwork, e.g. the destruction of landlordism and the erection of water-management systems, prepared earlier. In India at the present conjuncture accelerated and dispersed, i.e. not regionally concentrated, agricultural growth requires the institution of land reforms.

Together with land reforms of course a number of complementary areas have to be dealt with such as irrigation and water management, rural infrastructure, literacy, sanitation and drinking water, etc. All these would require considerable investment, but investment that is best undertaken under the aegis of elected local-level bodies. The requirement therefore is also for a devolution of resources and decentralization of planning. But the resources themselves have got to be raised and there is no escape from heavier doses of direct taxation, of property at any rate if not of incomes (though tax evasion in the latter case has to be stopped through punitive action). It is here that the conflict between the strategy just advocated and 'marketism' becomes apparent. It is often argued by 'marketists' that they are all for rural development. But if tax concessions have to be doled out to entice capital to stay in the country, if food prices have to be raised for the surplus food producers (who happen to be the rural rich) while food subsidies are cut, if all talk of land reforms is eschewed, if financial reforms do away with any stem and earmarking of credit, and if even infrastructural development like power becomes the responsibility of the private sector, especially foreign capital, with profitability being the main consideration, then there is no scope left for an improvement in the conditions of the rural poor, or for rural development generally.

It is not enough, however, that an alternative programme exists; it is not even enough that one can identify in the abstract the class forces that are potentially capable of providing the social support for the implementation of such an alternative programme. These forces must be concretely ready for mobilization behind such an alternative. The concrete conditions for praxis in other words must exist; and in our view these conditions are rapidly ripening in the Indian context.

The early euphoria generated by tack of a 7–8 per cent growth rate after the 'marketist' economic reforms has vanished; the belief that the so-called withdrawal of the state would be followed by a less corrupt, less arbitrary, more rule-governed order has also vanished. In short the credibility of the new policy-regime in the civil society at large has suffered greatly. At the same time there are very strong and unmistakable pressures from below for a betterment in living conditions, pressures that sometimes find outlets in the refracted form of 'lower caste' demands, and are often contained through so-called 'populist' measures. The fact, however, that even the ruling party which is committed to structural adjustment is forced to undertake these very 'populist' measures frowned upon by the Fund and the Bank,

is indicative of the pressures from below for an improvement in living conditions (which does not of course nullify the observations about increasing poverty made earlier).

The only way these pressures can be met is if the basic classes, viz. the workers, both organized and unorganized, and the bulk of the peasantry, make the alternative programme into their own. If large DFI inflows are precluded, then the only means of improving the living conditions of the mass of the people is by tapping the existing reserves of the economy, i.e. by taking up the slack in agriculture through egalitarian land reforms as well as by more investment in rural infrastructure, and by raising the domestic savings ratio as the East Asians and South-East Asians have done. True, this appropriation of an alternative programme would take time, but the conditions for it are ripening.

We shall end with two comments. An essential component of any alternative programme over and above the mere nitty-gritty of an economic strategy must be a strengthening of democratic institutions and structures. Only then would its appropriation by the basic classes be a productive and more durable one. In other words what is essential is not a new bout of social engineering, but a genuine process of social transformation which expands the direct political intervention capacity of the basic classes. Much has been written on the state-versus-market dichotomy, and much of it, as we have seen, is facile. If the state is not sufficiently accountable to civil society, then it has to be made accountable; but this cannot be ensured merely by a *formal* change in its character. Such a formal change has to be accompanied by a substantive expansion in the capacity for direct intervention on the part of the very classes in whose favour the formal change in the character of the state is supposed to have occurred. Putting it differently, the state-versus-market debate is a red herring which sidetracks the real debate – greater or lesser democracy for the broad masses of the people.

The second comment is the following: the fact that globalization of finance has made the pursuit of progressive economic policies more difficult is obviously undeniable. But, in focusing upon this phenomenon exclusively, we run the risk of missing the dialectics between the external and the internal, of completely ignoring the possibility of domestic mobilization, of ignoring the effect of this mobilization upon the ability to tackle the external constraints, in short of ignoring the 'totality' of the situation which defines the scope for praxis. Into the constitution of this 'totality' what enters is not only the changes occurring at the level of world capitalism, but also the level of political mobilization of the masses domestically.

Source: Patnaik, Prabhat and C.P. Chandrasekhar, 'Indian Economy Under "Structural Adjustment"', *Economic and Political Weekly*, vol. 30, no. 47, 1995, pp. 3010–12.

Notes

1. This section draws heavily on the paper by Arshad Zaman, 'The Government's Present Agreement with the IMF: Misgovernment or Folly?', *Pakistan Journal of Applied Economics*, vol. 11, nos. 1 and 2, 1995.

2. SDRs, or special drawing rights, are the IMF's 'currency', based upon a weighted basket of the main currencies in world trade. This basket is supposed to ease the volatility in any single currency.

3. Zaman, Arshad, op. cit., p. 82, footnote 8.

4. Ibid.

5. Ibid., and Zaidi, S. Akbar, 'The Structural Adjustment Programme and Pakistan: External Influence or Internal Acquiescence?', *Pakistan Journal of Applied Economics*, vol. 10, nos. 1 and 2, 1994.

6. The 1993 loan, as has been argued, was a precursor to the extensive EFF/ESAF loans of 1994. For our analysis we refer only to the 1994–7 period.

7. See World Bank, *Pakistan: Medium-term Economic Policy Adjustments*, Report No. 7591-Pak, Washington, 1989, p. 31.

8. This section is based on the World Bank's analysis of the 1988 structural adjustment programme. See World Bank, *Pakistan: Country Economic Memorandum FY93*, Report No. 11590-Pak, Washington, 1993.

9. Ibid., p. 35.

10. McCleary, William, 'Pakistan: Structural Adjustment and Economic Growth', in Thomas V., *et al.*, *Restructuring Economies in Distress*, Oxford University Press, New York 1991, p. 432.

11. Ibid., p. 433

12. Khan, Mohsin, S., 'Comments', in Thomas, V., *et al.*, op. cit., 1991, p. 439.

13. Khan, Shahrukh Rafi, 'Testing Hypotheses and Assessing Impact of Structural Adjustment: The Case of Pakistan', Sustainable Development Policy Institute, Monograph No. 6, Islamabad, 1997, p. 144.

14. Sayeed, Asad and Aisha Ghaus, 'Has Poverty Returned to Pakistan?', mimeo, Social Policy and Development Centre, Karachi, 1996.

15. Kemal, A.R., 'Structural Adjustment, Employment, Income Distribution and Poverty,' *Pakistan Development Review*, vol. 33, no. 4, 1994.

16. See, Zaidi, S. Akbar, op. cit., 1994.

17. Nabi, Ijaz and Naved Hamid, 'The Aid Partnership in Pakistan', in Lele, M. and Ijaz Nabi, *Transition in Development: The Role of Aid and Commercial Flows*, ICEG, San Francisco, 1991, p. 53.

18. Ibid., p. 55.

19. Ibid.

20. Ibid., p. 64.

21. Tybout, J.R., 'Industrial Performance: Some Stylized Facts', in Thomas, V., *et al.*, op. cit., 1991, p. 157.

22. Thomas, V., *et al.*, op. cit., 1991.

23. McCleary, op. cit., 1991, p. 421, emphasis added.

24. Reed, David, *Structural Adjustment and the Environment*, Westview Press, Boulder, 1992, p. 39.

25. Banuri, Tariq, 'Just Adjustment: Protecting the Vulnerable and Promoting Growth', *Pakistan Development Review*, vol. 31, no. 4, 1992, p. 681.

26. *The Economist*, London, 30 October 1993, p. 48.

27. See, Hasan, Arif, 'The Unresolved Conflict', *DAWN*, Magazine, 13 March 1992.

28. Ibid.

29. Zaman, Arshad, 'Sustainable Development, Poverty and Policy Adjustments: Linkages and Levers of Change', mimeo, International Institute of Sustainable Development, Toronto, Canada, 1993, p. 7.

Part 5

The Social Sector, Institutions, and Governance

Pakistan presents a development paradox: it has had enviable rates of economic growth for most of the last fifty years, yet its social sector development is particularly abysmal. In many ways, this is a dual paradox, for Pakistan has achieved high rates of economic growth without adequate support from the social sectors, and nor has the economic growth trickled down in the form of increased social sector development. This part of the book looks at a large number of subsectors within the social sector, and evaluates their performance over time. A large array of facts and figures are presented, and we see how the numbers all suggest positive trends. Nevertheless, the emphasis on quantity seems to have compromised standards of quality, whether in health care or education. The general feeling is that the state and public sector have failed to provide adequate services to the population of Pakistan. The result has been an ever increasing private sector, with the informal sector playing a critical role in the delivery of social services, filling the void created by the state.

More than half of the population of Pakistan is composed of women, and one probable reason why Pakistan suffers from low social development is the poor status of women in the country. In order for development to be more equitable and productive, it is essential that women play a greater role in society, a role that is currently constrained by economic, political, and social forces. These same forces, moreover, are an impediment to participation in development and politics. While there is a growing need to deliver development via more localized channels, with decentralization and local government – the current buzz words in development circles – there are structural constraints that limit useful participation and decentralization. However, without social development, whether of a participatory kind or in some other guise, it seems unlikely that Pakistan's historically high standard of growth of economic development can be sustained. Already, there are signs that it is unravelling.

16

The Social Sector I

Almost without exception, every publication, whether by the government or by scholars and social scientists, laments the state of the social sectors in Pakistan. The high growth performance of nearly 6 per cent per annum for more than forty years is acknowledged, but at the same time, the rather dismal state of the social sectors is also highlighted. The arguments usually presented state that most governments and the public sector have ignored the social sector and not given it enough importance or resources. We will argue that, despite the lip-service paid to the need to develop the social sector, this situation continues even at the end of the twentieth century, with resources not substantially increased to different components of the social sector. Nevertheless, the more interesting question is not how the social sector has continued to remain underdeveloped, but how, with such an underdeveloped social sector, and extremely low literacy rates, for example, the economy has shown such resilient growth. If the social sector is in as bad a state as almost all observers believe, how has the economy continued to grow at very impressive rates? Moreover, this leads to another question: can a less developed social sector continue to produce high growth, or has a time now arisen when growth will be highly dependent on human capital formation, as the New Growth theories suggest?

Indeed, these are interesting and important questions, the answers to which may be difficult to find. While not being able to explain how high economic growth has coexisted with very low social sector development, there is now a growing consensus that this pattern may have been one of the past, and that now there is an urgent need for a highly skilled, educated, and healthy workforce and population to deal with open trade barriers, new technology, and the maximization of all human potential. This view examines the record of countries like Korea and Taiwan, and more recently of Malaysia and Thailand, and argues that, without social development, economic growth and development can no longer take place. While there is growing evidence that this may be the case, one must ask whether Pakistan's élite, bureaucrats, and leaders have learnt any lessons from the Pacific Rim and South-East Asian countries. Has there been any shift at all in approach towards the social sectors? Or has the old, tired rhetoric merely been repeated *ad nauseam*?

This and the next two chapters will try to examine the existing conditions – the facts – and the issues in a number of important constituents of the social sector. We will provide figures and show trends over time, examining the nature and impact of those trends. Some attempt will be made to examine the nature of issues, problems, and successes in different areas. A new effort in the guise of the Social Action Programme has been initiated in Pakistan, and while instigated by foreign donors, it follows the interesting and novel approach of dealing with social development in the Pakistani context. The numerous issues emanating from the approach of the Social Action Programme, and the new approaches to the delivery of social services and the role of the community, constitute the last of the three chapters in this part of the book. Chapters 16 and 17 present data and information about a number of social areas, followed by discussion of the salient features of these subsectors. This chapter begins with a comparison of Pakistan's social sector with those of other countries, many of which are in the South Asian region or have similar levels of development.

16.1 Some International Comparisons

It is probably not very wise to compare countries. There are too many specific factors – history, culture, governments, institutions – which may influence events and consequences in very special and specific ways. The context of each event or development must be recognized and appreciated. Often, standards of a very alien kind are imposed across a general universe, which may result in numbers or results that are not comparable. Even so-called scientific criteria are not insensitive to their social environment, and even simply counting and comparing 'obvious facts' can be hazardous. Hence, there are numerous problems in taking a set of indicators showing the state of the health of the economy and comparing them across countries. Nevertheless, this continues to be done, and there is a huge industry which churns out Ph.Ds and tomes on indicators comparing diverse nations and countries. We too, despite our criticism and concerns, continue that tradition in order to indicate some salient trends.

In this section, we examine the performance of Pakistan in the social sector in light of that of other developing countries. All seven of the countries we have chosen (see Table 16.1) belong to the World Bank's classification of Low Income Countries, i.e. those with a per capita GNP of less than US$730. There are forty-five such countries, with Mozambique being the poorest in the list with $90 per capita, and Myanmar (Burma) and the Yemen Republic the richest, with per capita GNP in the range of $660–730. Comparable economic status has to be the single most important criterion if some sense is to be made of international comparisons. It is quite futile, in fact nonsensical, to compare Pakistan with, say, the United States of America (per capita GNP $25,000), Singapore ($20,000), or even Korea ($7,660).

While low income status may be the first criterion for our selection of countries, there are some others. India, Bangladesh, and Sri Lanka share similar histories and belong to South Asia, and are also grouped together in the South Asian Association of Regional Co-operation (SAARC); hence they can have some valid grounds for comparison. China is included because it is a key player in the region, has a GNP per capita close to that of Pakistan, and is cited by many as a country where communist-led growth and development in the past have resulted in an egalitarian social structure with extensive social development. The liberal and open economic programme of the new China also makes it worth observing. Ghana and Nigeria, while very different from the Asian countries, are included because one has a large population (Nigeria) and the other a GNP per capita close to or equal to Pakistan's (Ghana). Also, like the four South Asian countries, they have both been under British colonialism, and hence some comparison is probably permissible. The outlier is Vietnam, which is included because it is still a socialist state (like China), but has not had as many years of capitalism as China; and despite having a per capita GNP of only 40 per cent of Pakistan's, it has some very interesting and revealing social indicators. GNP per capita need not, in fact, be the sole, or even the key, criterion for social development. Political commitment, structure, and involvement may be equally, if not more, important.

Table 16.1 is not easy to interpret – if, indeed, there were any interpretations that could be made from it. No conclusions or hard overriding truths emerge from the table; simply observations open to conjecture.

The first column gives the GNP per capita in US dollars for 1993 for each of the eight countries, while the second column shows the growth rates in GNP per capita over the period 1980–93. These growth rates indicate the rate at which countries have grown over the last decade or so. China's example is significant, since in just a few years it has increased its comparative and absolute position: in 1980 China had a GNP per capita of $206 compared to Pakistan's $285, and was one of the poorest countries in the world. With a phenomenal 8.2 per cent average annual growth rate for over a decade, it has improved its position markedly. Pakistan and India have also done well, maintaining a consistent growth rate of over 3 per cent. (In the 1980–93 period only South Asia with 3 per cent and East Asia and the Pacific with 6.4 per cent had positive growth rates in GNP per capita amongst the low and middle economies group; both Africa and Latin America had negative rates. The high income economies, with GNP per capita of $13,000–36,000, had growth rates of only 2.2 per cent.)[1]

The 'GNP per capita rank' lists the position of these countries on the basis of GNP per capita, Vietnam being the 5th poorest country in the world with a GNP per capita of only $170, and Pakistan, with a GNP per capita of $430, the 31st poorest country out of the 132 classified by the World

Table 16.1
International comparisons of the social sectors

	GDP and GNP					Population						Education				Health							Urbanization			Women				
	GNP pc 1993	GNP av. annual growth rate 1980-83	GDP pc rank	HDI rank	1993 population millions	Average annual growth rate % 1980-83	CBR 1963	CDR 1983	1993 TFR	Contraceptive usage % 1980-83	Adult literacy rate %	Primary enrolment rate 1970	Primary enrolment rate 1992	Secondary enrolment rate 1970	Secondary enrolment rate 1992	Life expectancy	Access to health facilities % of population	Access to water % of population	Access to sanitation % of population	Calorie intake per day	Infant mortality rate 1970	Infant mortality rate 1983	1993 % urban	1980-83 Average annual growth rate %	Female literacy 1992	Enrolment as a % of age of ratio Primary	Secondary	Life expectancy	Labour force partici-pation %	Maternal mortality 1980-82
Pakistan	430	3.1	31	128	122.8	2.8	40	9	6.1	14	35.7	40	46	13	21	61.5	55	68	38	2,316	142	88	34	4.2	22.3	55	44	62.6	13	500
Vietnam	170	–	5	120	71.3	2.2	30	8	3.8	53	91.9	–	108	–	33	65.2	90	24	17	2,250	111	41	20	2.7	88.7	96	95	67.3	47	120
Bangladesh	220	2.1	12	146	115.2	2.1	35	11	4.3	40	36.4	54	77	19	19	55.6	45	64	31	2,019	140	106	17	5.3	24.4	86	50	55.6	8	800
India	300	3.0	20	134	898.2	2.0	29	10	3.7	43	49.9	73	102	26	44	60.4	65	78	27	2,395	137	80	26	3.0	35.2	74	60	60.4	25	460
Nigeria	300	0.1	21	141	105.3	2.9	45	15	6.4	6	52.5	37	76	4	20	50.4	66	36	35	2,125	114	83	38	5.5	42.1	78	72	52.0	34	800
Ghana	430	0.1	30	129	16.4	3.3	41	11	5.9	13	60.7	64	74	14	38	56.0	60	52	42	2,206	111	79	35	4.2	49.0	87	71	57.8	39	1,000
China	490	8.2	33	111	1,176.4	1.4	19	8	2.0	83	79.3	89	121	24	51	68.5	90	69	16	2,729	69	30	29	4.3	69.8	95	78	70.4	43	95
Sri Lanka	600	2.7	39	97	17.9	1.5	20	6	2.4	–	89.3	99	107	47	74	71.9	93	60	50	2,275	58	17	22	1.6	85.8	100	108	74.2	27	80

Source: World Bank, *World Development Report, 1996*, and UNDP, *Human Development Report, 1996*.

Bank. Switzerland, with a GNP per capita of $35,760, is the richest, and has a GNP per capita *400 times* that of the poorest country, Mozambique. In the World Bank classification, 45 countries are considered to be low income economies (GNP per capita $90–730), 41 are middle income ($730–2,840), 22 are upper-middle income ($2,840–12,600), and 24 are the rich, high income economies, beginning with New Zealand with $12,600 GNP per capita, and ending with Switzerland.[2]

While GNP per capita is a very simplistic and crude (yet indicative) measure of social development, the Human Development Index (HDI) is a larger and broader composite indicator which captures much more than just per capita income. The United Nations Development Programme (UNDP), which created the HDI, says that this composite index contains three indicators: 'life expectancy, representing a long and healthy life; educational attainment, representing knowledge; and real GDP (in purchasing power parity dollars), representing a decent standard of living'.[3] The Human Development Index shows:

> How far a country has to travel to provide these essential choices to all its people. It is not a measure of well-being. Nor is it a measure of happiness. Instead, it is a measure of empowerment. It indicates that if people have these three basic choices, they may be able to gain access to other opportunities as well. The HDI, imperfect though it may be, is thus a viable alternative to GNP per capita, and it is increasingly being used to monitor the progress of nations and of global society.[4]

Thus, the HDI in Table 16.1 for our selected countries, unlike the GNP per capita, shows a reverse order: the higher the number, the worse the nature and extent of social development. Using the HDI, Pakistan's rank is 128th out of 174 countries, showing a lack of social development. In our sample, Sri Lanka is the best of the eight countries selected (97th) and Bangladesh (146th) the worst. Of the 174 countries, the best five performers are Canada, the USA, Japan, the Netherlands, and Finland. It is interesting to compare this ranking with the GNP per capita criterion. Canada, which is first on the HDI, is the 14th richest country in terms of GNP per capita, the USA 6th, Japan 2nd, the Netherlands 13th, and Finland 18th. Similarly, Switzerland, the richest country in terms of GNP, ranks 13th on the HDI. Of the seven worst performers on the HDI, six are African countries: Guinea (at number 168), Burkina Faso (169), Ethiopia (171), Mali (172), Sierra Leone (173), and the worst performer, Niger (174). Afghanistan ranks 170th. While Niger is the last on the HDI, it is not the poorest country economically, and with a GNP per capita of $270 it ranks 17th in the world. Interestingly, in our sample Vietnam, which is the 5th poorest country in the world on the basis of GNP per capita, is at the 120th position in the HDI, and out-performs 54 countries by this ranking.[5]

The next set of statistics in Table 16.1 deal with population. Our sample consists of five of the world's ten most populous countries, and includes China and India, the two most populous. Pakistan is the eighth most populous country in the world, and is followed by Bangladesh and Nigeria.

However, while absolute size may be important today, the growth rates in population reveal what lies ahead. For highly populous countries like Pakistan this is more important. While India and China have very low population growth rates at 2.8 per cent, Pakistan's position is not particularly good. In fact, a few years ago Bangladesh had more people than Pakistan, but with a slower population growth rate it has now halted the expansion in its population, while Pakistan has not been able to do so. Contraceptive use may be one factor; others will be discussed in further detail in section 16.4.

The total fertility rate (TFR), which is higher in Pakistan than any other country in our sample except Nigeria, is also a reason for high population growth. The TFR 'shows the number of children that would be born to a woman if she were to live to the end of her childbearing years and bear children at each age in accordance with prevailing age-specific fertility rates'.[6] Hence, we expect women in Pakistan, on average, to bear 6.1 children, while those in China will bear only 2. The crude birth rate (CBR) and crude death rate (CDR) indicate, respectively, the number of live births and deaths occurring per thousand population in a year. Hence, 40 live births per 1,000 population took place in Pakistan in 1993, compared to 29 in India, showing a sharp deviation. The deviations in the CDR across our sample are smaller and, for almost all the countries in our sample, the CDR compares favourably with the overall average of 9 for high income economies.

The next segment in Table 16.1, on education, contains one of the most important statistics cited for social development, that of literacy. Overall adult literacy (and importantly, female literacy, which is included separately) is considered to be a fairly good indicator of social development in any country. In 'new growth theories', where human capital formation is a prerequisite for growth, literacy acts as an important proxy for many key ingredients. In addition, with the need for more skills in the present electronic and computer age, in which there is increasing emphasis on competition and quality, education and literacy become even more important.

The table reveals that, among our sample, Pakistan's record is by far the poorest, for all the education statistics shown here. Vietnam, with a GNP per capita only 40 per cent that of Pakistan, has education statistics that would put many developed high-income economies to shame, as has Sri Lanka. The four poorest countries in our sample outperform Pakistan very markedly. Even Bangladesh, which many see as a country with few prospects, has done far better than much wealthier Pakistan. Not only is the current, absolute picture for Pakistan much worse, but the progress between 1970 and 1993 with regard to primary and secondary enrolment rates in the country has been particularly unimpressive.

While Pakistan has increased the primary enrolment rate from 40 to 46 in twenty-two years, Nigeria has more than doubled its rate (despite a negative economic growth rate between 1980 and 1993), and even Bangladesh has made impressive strides. Nigeria's secondary enrolment rate has increased fivefold, while Ghana's and China's has more than doubled, whereas for Pakistan in 1992, only 21 per cent of secondary school-age children were actually in school as compared to India's 44 per cent.

Pakistan's health statistics, compared to the other seven countries, show a mixed trend. With some exceptions, there seem to be fewer deviations amongst our chosen group. The daily calorie intake, with the exception of China and Bangladesh, does not reveal significant variation, and Pakistan's performance in this category is adequate. However, Pakistan's record of access to health services is very poor compared to that of other countries, notably Vietnam and India. While the relative access to water supply for Pakistan is remarkably good, it is, nevertheless, still worse than India's. The same sort of picture emerges for sanitation and sewerage facilities. These figures for Pakistan, while looking good, may be misleading. Since the numbers presented here for access to health services, sanitation and water are *for the whole country*, the higher level of urbanization in Pakistan may distort the picture. Higher urbanization means more facilities and more access. A better picture would emerge if we had an urban/rural differentiation of access to facilities.

The infant mortality rate (IMR) gives the annual number of deaths of infants under one year of age per thousand live births. This means that if 1,000 children were born in Pakistan in 1993, 88 of these would die before they reached their first birthday. The maternal mortality rate (MMR) shows the annual number of deaths of women from pregnancy-related causes per 100,000 live births. Hence, 500 women died of pregnancy-related causes in Pakistan, compared to 1,000 in Ghana and only 80 in Sri Lanka.

Many of the figures on health and education presented in Table 16.1 are for both men and women, and hence, do not reveal the extent of gender inequality and the far worse state of affairs faced by women. In this category too, Pakistan and Bangladesh are the worst performers.

Some 88 per cent of Vietnamese and 86 per cent of Sri Lankan women are literate, while only 22 per cent of Pakistani women can read or write. All Sri Lankan girls aged 5–9 are in school, but only half of Pakistani girls; even Bangladesh has a more impressive record in this area. Bangladesh and Pakistan are also the worst performers when it comes to labour force participation by women: only 8 per cent of Bangladeshi and 13 per cent of Pakistani women are in the labour force, compared to 47 per cent for the very poor Vietnam.

It is difficult to reach any definite conclusions from the myriad of data presented in Table 16.1. However, some general observations can be made:

1 Although Pakistan has the third highest GNP per capita in our sample of eight, its performance on most social development indicators is certainly not as good.

2 Vietnam with the lowest GNP per capita – 40 per cent less than that of Pakistan – outperforms most of the sample, and certainly outperforms Pakistan, when it comes to social development.

3 Pakistan's literacy rate is abysmally low. All other countries in our sample, including those much poorer than Pakistan, do much better.

4 The rate of change in the primary and secondary school enrolment rates over the period 1970–92 has been the lowest in Pakistan, and Pakistan is also the worst performer when it comes to literacy.

5 Pakistan's performance seems to be somewhat better in the health sector than in the other sectors, and better than that of other countries.

6 All indicators regarding women for our sample of eight countries show Pakistan as the worst performer, revealing excessive gender discrimination.

It seems, then, that despite having a high economic growth performance for many years, and outperforming other countries in the economic field, Pakistan's social development has been particularly poor. Even less developed and poorer countries measured on an economic scale have developed their social sector well ahead of Pakistan. From our evidence, one may surmise that economic growth, or GNP per capita, may not be the most important ingredient for social development, and that political will and commitment may be equally important. Pakistan's economic prosperity is contrasted sharply with its poor social development. Some facts, trends and issues are elaborated in the following sections.

16.2 Planning for the Social Sectors

This section is meant to be a brief introduction to two of the appendices to this chapter. It provides a brief history of the planning mechanism in Pakistan, as well as outlining some of the new arguments being circulated at a time when the role of the state and of government is expected to diminish, with current wisdom emphasizing the need for involvement from the private sector and non-governmental organizations (see also Chapter 18). Appendix 16.1 and Box 16.1 give different perspectives on the more general practical and theoretical aspects of planning.

Pakistan has implemented eight Five-Year Plans and is currently in the process of preparing and launching its Ninth Five-Year Plan (1998–2003). There have also been longer, twenty- and fifteen-year Perspective Plans, which were meant to give broader direction to the economy for a longer time. The reason why planning is introduced in this chapter on the social sectors is that it is in the social sectors that the role of the government has been most noticeable. Although the government has laid the ground rules for the establishment of industry and has announced, for example, agricultural procurement prices, much of the endeavour, especially in agriculture, has come from private individuals and entrepreneurs acting in response to the guidelines and rules issued by government. Farmers will decide how and what to grow once government prices and policies have been announced. The Green Revolution that took place in Pakistan is a clear example of how private producers in the agricultural sector responded to government incentives and priorities. The government gave the directions and made the policies, and individuals responded in a certain manner.

In the social sector, the government has until very recently not only laid out policy, but also been the implementor as well. It has both announced an education or health policy and also determined how and where facilities and services are to be provided. Hence, an evaluation of the social sector is also an evaluation of government policy and planning mechanisms. Much of Chapter 18 examines the methods employed by the government in the past, and looks at the new ways of implementing policies and plans under new guidelines and mechanisms. Appendix 16.1 and Box 16.1 in this chapter also provide a re-examination, and probably a justification, of the planning process and mechanism in Pakistan.

16.3 The Health Sector[7]

16.3.1 Statistics

The life expectancy of both males and females has continued to increase over the years. Whereas in 1965 women in Pakistan lived to an age of 44.5 years, in 1992 women were expected to live 17 years longer, till the age of about 62 (see Tables 16.1 and 16.2). The overall life expectancy rate also increased in this period from 45.8 years to 61.5. In the thirty years between 1965 and 1995, the infant mortality rate fell by about 37 per cent, from 149 to 95 per thousand (Table 16.2).

Most of the diseases in Pakistan are caused by inadequate and contaminated sources of water. The most widespread diseases, such as typhoid, cholera, and most intestinal infections, are the result of poor water and sanitation availability. Infant mortality usually falls when adequate water supply is made available, and making sure that internal piped water is provided to the household is one of the most effective means of lowering infant mortality and diarrhoeal disorders in children. In households with internal piped water, there is a decline of as much as 20 per cent in child morbidity. Hence the need for more and cleaner water and sanitation facilities if ill-health is to be reduced. Table 16.3 shows that, while there has been much improvement in drinking water availability in both rural and urban areas since the 1970s, even now only 45 per cent of the 60 per cent of Pakistan's population who live in rural areas have what is considered to be 'safe' drinking water. Sanitation conditions are even now almost non-existent in rural areas. Table 16.4 shows the prevalence of disease in Pakistan and the main causes of death, and indicates clearly that most of the diseases are a result of inadequate water and sanitation facilities.

Tables 16.5 and 16.6 show the curative side of the health sector, where the number of health facilities and medical personnel are given. The number of hospitals has increased by two-and-a-half times since 1955, while the number of hospital beds has increased fourfold, and the population-per-bed has fallen by about a quarter. Facilities such as Basic Health Units and Rural Health Centres, which are the primary source of contact, especially for the rural community, have increased substantially. Due to a concerted effort by the government to increase access to rural health facilities, Basic Health Units (BHUs) increased from 249 in 1971 to 4,843 in 1994, an increase of about twenty times. Likewise, Rural Health Centres (RHCs) have increased fivefold in the last twenty-five years. The desire by the government to provide a health facility in every Union Council in the country, at least on paper, may be close to being satisfied.

Just as health facilities have grown, so have medical providers: from only 127 doctors in 1955, there are more than 66,000 doctors registered today. There were only two dentists in the country in 1962, while there are more than 2,500 now. Secondary- and tertiary-level medical staff, such as nurses, lady health visitors, (LHVs) and midwives, are extremely important in the delivery of health and medical care. The number of nurses has increased by 87 times in twenty years, midwives by 37 times, and LHVs by 80 times. The population per doctor ratio fell from 75,000 people to one doctor in 1962, to only 1,880 per doctor in 1994. All these trends seem to suggest positive developments and show concerted government effort at providing health for all the people of Pakistan. But is that really the case?

16.3.2 The Issues[8]

This section will try to examine what the issues in the health sector have been in the past, what they are currently, and what emerging trends exist. We will try to see what the structure of health care in Pakistan looks like and whose interests it serves. We will try to see what sort of doctors are being produced, and whether Pakistan will be able to achieve Health For All by the year 2000, as it has promised to do. The role and contribution of the private sector in more recent times will also be examined, as will other recent developments in the health sector.

The History of Health Services in Pakistan

Until 1947, when Pakistan achieved independence, both India and Pakistan were ruled as one country by the British. The history of the two countries until then, despite regional

Table 16.2
Key indicators of life expectancy, 1965–1995

	1965	1970	1975	1980	1985	1990	1995
Life expectancy at birth (overall)	45.8	48.1	50.2	52.8	54.6	55.8	–
Life expectancy at birth (female)	44.5	47	49.2	52.7	54.5	55.3	–
Infant mortality rate (per thousand)	149	142	134	124	112	103	95

Source: World Bank, *Staff Appraisal Report: Pakistan Population Welfare Program*, Report No. 13611-Pak, 1996, p. 56.

Table 16.3

Access to drinking water and sanitation facilities, 1976–1990 (%)

Year	Drinking water			Sanitation		
	Total	Rural	Urban	Total	Rural	Urban
1976	22	11	54	–	–	22
1980	31	17	68	–	–	37
1985	44	25	79	20	–	53
1990	52	45	80	22	10	55

Source: Banuri, Tariq, *et. al.*, 'Human Resources Development', in Banuri, Tariq (ed.), *Just Adjustment: Protecting the Vulnerable and Promoting Growth*, UNICEF, Islamabad, 1992, p. 39.

specifics, followed similar trends and conformed to the dictates of colonialism. This was largely true of health services as well, except that the areas that comprise Pakistan today had a greater influence of Muslim and Arab medical tradition.

Before the arrival of the British rulers in India, there existed indigenous forms of health care in the subcontinent. Debabar Banerji writes that in the ancient civilizations of Moenjo Daro and the Indus Valley, there was 'a great emphasis on the preventive aspects of disease indicating a fairly mature attitude of the society towards the health problems ... of that time'.[9] As India was invaded by nations with foreign cultures, new social and political mechanisms evolved, as did methods of health care and medicine. The Arabs and the Mughals brought with them techniques that even today retain some influence on medical practice in Pakistan. When the British came to India, the indigenous system of health care was highly advanced and could compare quite favourably with that imported by the westerners.

With the arrival of the British, 'every facet of Indian life, including the medical and public health services, was subordinated to the commercial, political and administrative interests of the Imperial government in London'.[10] The western medicine brought to India by the British was

Table 16.4

Main causes of death in Pakistan

Name of disease	Pakistan	Urban areas	Rural areas
All causes	100	100	100
1 Infectious and parasitic diseases	53.84	67.64	63.07
2 Malaria	10.54	7.86	10.96
3 Congenital anomalies, birth injury and causes of perinatal mortality	7.36	5.64	7.71
4 Tuberculosis of all forms	5.55	2.86	6.09
5 Bacillary dysentery and amoebiasis	2.51	2.88	2.44
6 Accidents, poisoning, and violence	1.88	1.05	3.03
7 Diseases of heart and circulatory system	1.79	3.92	1.35
8 Peptic ulcer, appendicitis, intestinal obstruction and hernia	1.2	1.09	1.22
9 Diabetes mellitus	1.14	0.75	1.22
10 Complications of pregnancy and child birth	1.13	1.39	1.08
11 Tumours	0.34	0	0.41
12 Unknown causes	2.85	4.91	2.44

Source: Zaidi, S. Akbar, *The Political Economy of Health Care in Pakistan*, Vanguard, Lahore, 1988, p. 55.

primarily meant to suit the needs of their own administrative and military personnel. Along with their own people, the British also permitted the native Indian élite to consume this modern medical care, and this trend continued even after independence, when only the affluent and ruling classes had access to adequate medical facilities. At the same time, the British allowed a select few from this élite to become administrators, bureaucrats, and doctors, and to work alongside the colonists. Thus, when they left India and Pakistan, the British 'retained considerable influence on the entire health service system of the country by ensuring that

Table 16.5

Medical and health establishments, 1955–1994 (calendar-year basis)

Year	Hospitals	Dispensaries	BHUS sub-health centres	Maternity and child-health centres	Rural health centres	TB centres	Total beds	Population per bed
1955	333	984	–	198	–	–	19,197	2,077
1961	345	1,251	3	422	1	18	22,394	2,063
1971	495	2,136	249	668	87	79	34,077	1,804
1981	600	3,478	774	823	243	99	48,441	1,731
1991	776	3,993	4,414	1,057	465	219	75,805	1,500
1994	814	4,280	4,843	820	488	242	80,908	1,538

Source: Government of Pakistan, *Pakistan Economic Survey, 1994–95*, Islamabad, 1995, p. 212.

Table 16.6
Registered medical and paramedical personnel and expenditure on health, 1955–1994 (calendar-year basis)

Year	Registered doctors	Registered dentists	Registered nurses	Registered midwives	Registered lady health visitors	Population per doctor	Expenditure (Rs m) Dentists	Development	Non-development
1955	127	–	–	–	–	–	–	–	–
1961	612	–	–	–	–	75,470	–	21	69
1971	4,287	446	–	–	–	14,343	137,870	58	141
1981	13,910	1,018	6,110	4,846	718	6,027	82,357	1,037	993
1991	51,883	2,077	16,948	15,009	3,106	2,127	53,134	2,741	4,997
1994	66,199	2,590	21,419	19,759	4,107	1,880	48,046	4,282	8,501

Source: Government of Pakistan, *Pakistan Economic Survey, 1994–95*, Islamabad, 1995, p. 212.

the top of the medical profession in India remained heavily dependent on them'.[11] It was not only medicine, however, but the entire civil, military, and administrative services which were handed over by the British to the 'Brown Englishmen' of India and Pakistan.

British imperialism exploited the economic and cultural wealth of India, and built institutions (including those that delivered health care) to further its broader interests. What is worth noting is that the rulers of 'independent' Pakistan continued those policies which were designed to serve imperialism, and did not devise any measures to deal with the real problems of the people of Pakistan. At the time of independence, it was only the élite who had easy access to the best hospitals and doctors in the country. The masses had to make do with exceptionally poor government facilities. This is largely the situation even now.

In Pakistan, the health care system can very simply be described as follows: it is a highly inequitable, western-oriented curative care model, which certainly does not fulfil the requirements of a very great majority of the people of Pakistan. Let us now turn to the salient features and problems of the health care system in Pakistan today.

Two Biases: Urban and Class

A cursory glance at the distribution of health facilities in Pakistan gives a startling picture: despite the fact that nearly 60 per cent of the population lives in rural areas, most of the medical personnel and health facilities are found in the cities. For example, 85 per cent of all practising doctors work in the cities, which comes to a (theoretically) favourable doctor–population ratio of 1:1801 for the urban areas of Pakistan. The rural doctor–population ratio, on the other hand, is 1 doctor to 25,829 inhabitants (see Table 16.7). In Sindh, the second most populated province of the country, the rural doctor–population ratio in 1982 was 1:57,964. If that figure comes as a surprise, the nurse–population ratio in Sindh would astonish most people: in 1982 there was only one nurse to a population of 568,050 (see Table 16.8). Similarly, 23 per cent of the hospitals in the country were located in rural areas and only 8,574 beds (18 per cent) were available to a population of 80 million (Table 16.7).[12]

The phenomenon described above has been called an 'urban bias' by Michael Lipton. Although we have rejected the ideological underpinnings of the Liptonian thesis (he believes that there is a conspiracy of sorts by the urban populace against the rural inhabitants, and sees the struggle for the allocation of resources as being between urban and rural *areas*), the term can help in illustrating a phenomenon. It is quite clear that, whether it is in the field of education or health, an 'urban bias' does exist in the form of a lack of facilities in rural areas and discrimination against rural inhabitants.

The reasons for such an 'urban bias' in Third World countries are numerous. Firstly, the ruling class resides in cities. This applies to agricultural societies too, where, despite

Table 16.7
Population per medical facility in Pakistan, by urban and rural areas, 1988

Facility	Total Number	Total Population per facility	Urban Number	Urban Population per facility	Rural Number	Rural Population per faciity
Hospitals	602	139,172	467	58,011	135	444,837
All beds	47,412	1,767	38,838	610	8,574	7,004
Doctors	15,500	5,405	13,175	1,801	2,325	25,829
Nurses	5,100	16,427	–	–	–	–

Source: Zaidi, S. Akbar, *The Political Economy of Health Care in Pakistan,* Vanguard, Lahore, 1988, p. 19.

BOX 16.1

Government intervention, planning, and the market

J.R. Behrman discusses the reasons why, in a neoclassical world, planning may still be necessary and why government intervention, rather than determination by the market, may be necessary.

Efficiency reasons for policies include market failures due to externalities (that work other than through markets so private incentives differ from social marginal costs), increasing returns to scale/public goods (for which private incentives are to produce less than socially desirable, with information a particularly important example), local monopolies, and missing and incomplete markets (including capital and insurance markets for human resource investments). If there are efficiency reasons for considering policy interventions, alternative policies can be ordered in a 'policy hierarchy' in descending order of the number of distortions that the policies introduce. If policy makers had perfect and costless information both for policy design and for subsequent monitoring and enforcement, often there is a range of 'price' (tax, subsidy) or 'quantitative' (regulations, central directives) that could illicit the 'correct' outcomes. But in fact information is quite imperfect for policy makers and implementers. That implies that there is a premium on more transparent policies and policies that create incentives for efficient behaviour and accountability, particularly if they cannot be closely monitored in a timely fashion. A major problem in the provision of social services in Pakistan, for example, is thought to be the lack of client orientation and low accountability, which in considerable part reflects information problems in monitoring service delivery and in assessing client demands. In an uncertain world with asymmetrical information, there is a presumption that price policies are likely to be more effective in many cases on these grounds than quantitative policies or the direct provision of government services. There also is a presumption that more decentralized decisions are more likely to be responsive to the nature of local conditions than more centralized decisions, and that a broader sense of 'ownership' of activities is likely to increase efficiency. At issue is not a question of ideology regarding some general conclusion of whether market failures are pervasive, so that

strong government interventions are warranted, or policy failures predominate, so that almost all activities should be privatized and left to the market. The question pertains to specific activities, in some of which the government may have comparative advantage and in others of which the private sector may have comparative advantage. Responsible governmental stewardship must recognize the differing comparative advantages of public versus private fulfillment of various activities, and not blindly reserve certain activities to one or the other.

If there are *distributional reasons* for governmental interventions, two points merit emphasis. First, if a certain group is to be favoured by policies, there remains the question of what policies to utilize. Comparisons of the expected costs and benefits need to be made, which generally tends to point to policies that are higher in the efficiency policy hierarchy. For example, because society has a commitment to improve the human resources of the poor does *not* mean that direct public provision of education and health services is the best way to pursue that goal. In some circumstances (but certainly not in all circumstances), it may be more effective in terms of this commitment to provide subsidies directly to the poor (perhaps tied to specific uses, such as schooling) and let them choose their provider from among the private and public alternatives rather than channelling all such subsidies directly to public sector providers and thereby limiting the pressures on public sector providers to be more effective and limiting the possible choices for the poor. Second, almost all policies have distributional impacts, favouring some group or other, and not necessarily the poor by any means (in fact often not the poor). Often among the groups that have the strongest vested interests in particular policies, moreover, may be government employees. Therefore it is all the more important that policies, whatever their rationale, be as transparent as possible and subject to periodical review so that they do not continue long after the problem to which they originally were addressed has passed simply because they have created a strong vested interest in the public or private sectors.

Source: Behrman, J.R., 'Pakistan: Human Resource Development and Economic Growth into the Next Century', mimeo, 8 May 1995, p. 3.

---

a feudal structure, a very large proportion of the landlords are of an 'absentee' type and live in cities alongside the industrial and mercantile élite, enjoying the fruits of 'development'. Secondly, the cities are also the seat of government in Third World countries. Along with the ruling class, the members of government, the bureaucracy, and the military have made the urban areas their homes and power bases, and thus infrastructure has been developed to support them. Thirdly, organized, articulate, and politically active groups such as trade unions, students, and professionals have also made their presence felt in urban areas, and have acted as pressure groups to secure their demands.

In short, since the dominant classes in the Third World live in cities, the best facilities are also located here. Similarly, certain sections of society can put pressure on government, and thus the government must try to appease these groups by allowing them some access to health and other basic facilities.

These power groups have been living in the cities of Pakistan since long before partition. Thus when one looks at the health programmes of the British, we find this 'urban bias' even at that time, as we do now in post-partition Pakistan. The government, whether of imperial Britain or independent Pakistan, works under numerous constraints,

Table 16.8
Availability of health manpower in Sindh, 1982

	Population		Doctors		Nurses		Lady health visitors		Auxiliaries		Population per doctor	Population per nurse
	No. (000s)	%	No.	%	No.	%	No.	%	No.	%		
Sindh (inc. Karachi)	18,966		4,756		1,632		239		8,622		3,988	11,621
Urban	7,605	40	4,560	96	1,612	99	196	82	7,483	87	1,667	4,718
Rural	11,361	60	196	4	20	1	43	18	1,139	13	57,964	568,050
Karachi District	5,353		3,605		1,278		136		5,770		1,485	4,189
Urban	5,103	95	3,603	100	1,278	100	135	99	5,768	100	1,416	3,993
Rural	250	4	2	0	–		1	1	2	0	1,750	–
Sindh (exc. Karachi)	13,613		1,151		354		103		2,852		11,827	38,454
Urban	2,502	18	957	83	334	94	63	61	1,715	60	2,614	7,491
Rural	11,111	82	194	17	20	6	40	39	1,137	40	57,273	555,550

Source: Zaidi, S. Akbar, *The Political Economy of Health Care in Pakistan*, Vanguard, Lahore, 1988, p. 20.

one of which is to please the ruling classes and other vociferous sections living in the cities. Thus, all governments to date have, either overtly or covertly, shown an 'urban bias' in their programmes. For example, despite repeatedly stated attempts to 'redress the balance of facilities between rural and urban areas' (a common theme in most Plan documents), no real change has been made over the fifty years since independence. Despite the rhetoric, in the end, over 80 per cent of the already minuscule health budget (less than 1 per cent of GNP) gets allocated to urban-based, curative health facilities at the expense of rural health programmes. An important reason for a lack of trained medical manpower in rural areas is this dismal lack of facilities. Even if some well-intentioned doctors wanted to serve in rural areas, the abysmal conditions would force them to change their minds. Further, the government seems rather naive when it urges doctors to go to rural areas yet pays them *less* than their colleagues at equivalent positions in urban hospitals and health centres.

Our criticism of the Liptonian 'urban bias' thesis is that, although this bias is apparent, there exists a deeper, more fundamental bias, which is the main determinant of access to health facilities. This is the *class* bias. The facts reveal that not all urban inhabitants have equal access to health facilities, nor are all ruralites equally discriminated against. It may be much easier for a landlord to have access to good health care than it is for a slum dweller in a large city. A *basti* dweller may have 'apparent' access, in the sense that he may know of existing facilities, but it is not likely that he will be able to afford the high cost of quality private care. At the same time, the quality of care at a government hospital outpatient department, where a doctor has less than 60 seconds for each patient, is questionable. Similarly, for residents *within* cities, great differences of access exist. Those with money can afford the best and latest technology and have immediate access to facilities, while the majority, like our slum dweller mentioned above, face innumerable hurdles.

Thus despite the apparent urban bias, we can conclude that irrespective of *geographical* location, it is *social*, *economic*, and *class* location which determines access to health facilities.

Is the Medical Education and Training Model Appropriate?

The purpose of medical education is to produce medical personnel who can work effectively in the existing model of health care in a country. Thus, the doctors produced after six or seven years of training in Pakistan are those who work best in the setting described above: one that is urban care oriented, and works in the interests of the richer inhabitants of the country.

Medical students in Pakistan are taught from books written in and for the developed countries. Thus the diseases our students learn about are more specific to developed capitalist nations than to underdeveloped ones. For example, they learn from their books that cardiovascular disease and cancer are the main killers, while the real situation in Pakistan is that parasitic and infectious diseases are responsible for 54 per cent of all deaths, while diseases of the rich and of western countries (heart disease and cancer) account for less than 2 per cent of deaths. The teaching methods and books leave such a profound influence on the students that they begin to believe that one of the main causes of death in Pakistan is indeed cardiovascular problems.

Not only does the diagnosis of the disease come from western sources, but so does the approach to care and cure. The developed country, curative care approach is copied in underdeveloped countries where the emphasis is on urban-based hospitals. The teaching faculty plays a contributory role in accentuating this 'cultural imperialism'. Professors go to the West for training and urge their students to do the same to acquire skills in disciplines such as neurosurgery and plastic surgery. When (if ever) these doctors return, they become even more alienated from the masses of their country who live in urban slums and rural areas, and are unable or unwilling to work with 'poor and inadequate' facilities. Moreover, on their return, they lose touch with common ailments that afflict the poor, such as gastroenteritis, tuberculosis, malaria, and typhoid, and can deal best with the diseases of the rich. Secondly, and more importantly, the western-trained doctors are available to only a select few who can afford their high fees.

In underdeveloped countries like Pakistan, where most diseases are of a communicable and preventable nature, the emphasis should be on training doctors who are well versed in primary health care techniques. Yet, the course in Community Medicine in medical school is not taken very seriously by the students and teachers, who have no real community experience. Often, qualified doctors are unable to cope with simple and common problems like snake-bite. The training and practical experiences of medical students are solely dependent on their interaction with patients who come to their urban hospital – again, a curative approach, when a preventive one may be preferable.

The explanation for this inappropriate medical education is quite straightforward. Since it is the ruling class which essentially determines the dynamics of the health sector, it is also responsible for the production of a specific kind of doctor. This ruling class requires a doctor who works best in a hospital-based curative care setting, and who can deal effectively with the diseases of the rich of Pakistan, which are similar to those common in the developed countries. Consequently, the curriculum in medical college is designed to produce the desired product.

An important outcome of this type of education and training is the 'westernization' of doctors. Since doctors in Pakistan are taught about 'western diseases', most doctors can, after some acclimatization, work easily in hospitals in the developed countries. Pakistan's system of medical education has been a major reason for the medical 'brain drain' from Pakistan, with nearly 50 per cent of its doctors practising outside the country. Had the curriculum been designed to suit the needs of the poor of Pakistan, with more emphasis on conditions in rural areas and urban slums, this problem would not exist. At present, given the levels of medical education and doctor migration, the underdeveloped countries are subsidizing the West!

Health for All by the Year 2000?

In 1978 a revolution took place in the field of health care. More than 130 countries signed a declaration in which they promised to give their people adequate health care by the turn of the century. Pakistan was one of the signatories to the Alma-Ata declaration.

Twenty years have gone by since the signing, and only a couple of years are left before the twentieth century comes to an end, yet any impartial observer would be distressed by the health of the people in Pakistan. Not only have no significant changes been made in the last twenty years, but given the present trend, none can be expected in the next few. At best, one can expect some small cosmetic changes within the warped health care structure in Pakistan, but no real indications exist for overhauling the structure itself.

We have argued repeatedly that health care is a reflection of the social, economic, and political structure prevalent in a country. If a small ruling clique controls the resources of a country and little or no participation by the people is tolerated, then the health sector will reflect this pattern, with health for a few and not for all. To bring about a major change in the system and structure of health care, it becomes necessary to bring about an equally significant change in society. The experience of socialist-oriented countries is that, once they have changed the pattern of the distribution of resources within *society*, they have been able to change the pattern of *health care*, making access more equitable. This may be one reason why countries like China and Vietnam in our sample in Table 16.1 have better social indicators than many other countries. Apart from socialist countries, some social democratic nations with a long history of participation by the masses have also provided adequate health facilities to their people, and the resulting improvement in their health status is quite enviable – Sri Lanka, from our sample in Table 16.1, fits this description. Thus one cannot expect significant improvement in the health sector in Pakistan without substantial participation of the masses in the workings of society, and without substantial changes in the power structures as they exist today (more on this in Chapter 18).

The Private Sector in Health Care

The data given in Table 16.5, showing the number of health facilities, do not take account of the numerous private sector hospitals, clinics, and other facilities that go unaccounted for in government statistics. For example, the total number of hospitals listed in the table is only 814, but the number quoted by the government is a gross underrepresentation of the true situation. In a city as large as Karachi, one can find numerous facilities which call themselves 'hospitals'. Even in smaller towns, doctors have transformed their clinics into hospitals, offering a different quality of service. It is not possible to estimate the number of medical facilities in the private sector, for no survey of such facilities has been conducted. Nevertheless, one can be sure that they would be much more numerous than those in the government sector.

As long ago as 1982, the private sector was the largest source of funds for the health sector. Of the total health expenditure that year, 58 per cent was contributed by the private sector, while 27 per cent came from the government – the rest was contributed by welfare organizations and charities. If one considers the operating and maintenance expenditures on health alone, in 1982 private payments accounted for 71 per cent of the total, and the government for only 18 per cent.[13] Government expenditure on the health sector has seldom been above 1 per cent of GNP (see Table 16.9), while private consumption expenditure on health has been double, or even three times as much. Hence, the contribution by the private sector, in terms of expenditure and resources, is quite substantial.

Summarizing the Issues in the Health Sector

Over the last fifty years, there has been a considerable improvement in the distribution and availability of health services and facilities. Coverage has improved substantially, and the doctors and nurses per population ratios have also increased, and are now comparable to many middle-income economies. However, this high and growing coverage is not reflected in indicators of health and longevity, and many

Table 16.9
Estimates of private consumption expenditure and total public sector expenditure on medical care and education, 1985–1994

Medical care	1985	1988	1991	1994
As % of GNP				
Private consumption expenditure	1.8	2	2.1	n.a.
Total public sector expenditure	0.7	1	0.7	0.8
Combined	2.5	3	2.8	n.a.
Share of private consumption	72	67	75	n.a.

	% per annum during:		
	1985-1988	1988–1991	1985–1991
Expenditure in real terms			
Aggregate expenditure	9.3	4.9	7.1
Per capita expenditure	6.5	1.7	4.1

Education	1985	1988	1991	1994
As % of GNP				
Private consumption expenditure	0.9	0.9	1.1	n.a.
Total public sector expenditure	1.8	2.4	2.1	2.2
Combined	2.7	3.5	3.2	n.a.
Share of private consumption	33	28	34	n.a.

	% per annum during:		
	1985-1988	1988–1991	1985–1991
Expenditure in real terms			
Aggregate expenditure	3.8	10	6.9
Per capita expenditure	neg.	6.7	3.8

Source: Government of Pakistan, Planning Commission, *Pakistan Country Paper: World Summit for Social Development*, Islamabad, 1995, p. 26.

poorer countries have been able to develop better facilities, reflected in the better health status of their population. While the administrative and delivery issues in the social sector are dealt with extensively in Chapter 18, some key issues in the health sector can be summarized as follows:

1 Poor quality and the irrelevance of the available health services in the public and private sector.

2 A very high focus on curative, rather than preventive, health and medical care.

3 Inequitable access by geographical location, with most facilities located in urban areas.

4 Access to health facilities determined by wealth and income, with the rich having easy access to the best facilities.

5 Doctors being trained who are not aware of, or functional in, the local environment.

6 A huge private sector, but mainly in curative care, with little involvement in preventive health.

7 Poor delivery of health services and, like the rest of the public sector, no accountability.

The emphasis of governments in the past, as reflected in the Five-Year Plans, has been to increase the *quantity of health-related services* – numbers of doctors, Rural Health Centres, Basic Health Units, etc. Often the zeal to meet numerical targets has compromised the quality and type of facility provided. The end result has been unmanned and unsupervised health services. For example, Rural Health Centres and Basic Health Units, while available now in most of the rural areas of the country, have merely become a source of increasing employment in the public sector and not a source of adequate, efficient, and cheap health care. With fiscal constraints evident at all tiers of government, and with different levels of government having to be more discretionary in their use of resources, it is time now that the government focused on quality and performance, rather than on quantity.

There is a growing need felt by many to democratize, devolve, and decentralize all avenues of civil society. The

BOX 16.2
Health care in Pakistan: some observations

Samina Choonara examines some of the salient issues in the health sector.

The issue of health care in a country like Pakistan cannot be looked at in isolation ... The problem here is not one of illness but of well-being, and the government cannot abdicate all responsibility by making health a service whereby doctors and drugs are made available in the market as though anyone could purchase them.

What is needed instead is preventive medicine which includes good food, clean water and adequate sanitation. But this would mean bringing poverty and the unequal distribution of wealth back on the agenda. That is the reality for 80 per cent of the population of a country which has the highest per capita income in the region but the lowest quality of life indicators.

According to a UNIDO survey, 60 per cent of all people in Pakistan have no access to modern medicine, only 30 per cent have access to adequate sanitation, 79 per cent have clean drinking water (a figure that is disputed daily in the newspapers), and poorer households regularly spend 80 per cent of their monthly income on food. In addition, water borne diseases like cholera, typhoid and malaria still rule the lives of the poor. Simple diarrhoea kills one out of every 12 children born into such households before they are five years old. Similarly, so-called 'eradicated' diseases like tuberculosis remain fatal in Pakistan because those affected cannot afford the available treatment.

Under the circumstances, even if the government were to improve upon the doctor–patient ratio in the country, this would do little more than alleviate the symptoms because local medics are raised on curricula that do not address the diseases of the poor or deal with typically third world emergencies like snake bite and diarrhoea. Most doctors do little more than charge fat fees and prescribe often needless, expensive drugs instead of probing the cause of diseases that may well respond to simple home remedies and rest, or prescribe lower priced medicines, keeping in mind the spending power of the patient.

People are generally too much in awe of the doctor to question his or her prescription, and tend to purchase medicine as if the gods had ordained them to do so. What they don't see is the mercenary in many doctors whose loyalties have probably been bought by medical reps from multinational companies who offer the doctors freebies and free samples.

When governments medicalize the issue of health and privatize health services, policy very much part of the current regime's agenda, they are in fact abandoning the people to the sharks in the market. Other than doctors with private practices, it is the manufacturers and retailers of medicines that stand to benefit from such reckless management.

The pharmaceutical industry, for one, which is monopolized by 31 multinational companies in Pakistan, does not only sell medicines at arbitrary prices but has also flooded the market with several useless and sometimes harmful formulations. These companies are now marketing about 19,000 drugs in Pakistan when the overwhelming need is for little more than 200 essential medicines.

Other countries in the region with a far lower per capita income, such as Sri Lanka and Bangladesh, came up in 1976 with the uniquely simple and effective idea of 'essential' drugs. According to this policy, governments could limit the manufacture and sale of safe, efficacious and appropriate drugs which were no longer patented but produced in large quantities at reasonable cost. The lists were drawn up with the participation of the WHO but varied according to regional requirements. However, even though Pakistan was a signatory to the agreement, to date, this simple solution has not been enforced as part of the drugs act.

Weak governments in developing countries need not fear that taking this step would alienate foreign investors. Instead of aiming for third world élites, multinational pharmaceutical companies could simply be directed to change their marketing strategies to target the larger base of a society, and still rake in the profits. However, under fire from international donor agencies like the World Bank and the IMF to remove subsidies and deregulate the economy or else be choked for foreign funds, a party in power that was once known for its socialist ideals is now busy looking the other way as these economic bullies make more and more incursions into our everyday life, dictating everything from the user charges for electricity, gas, drinking water, irrigation, and now health services.

But it does not take a global revolution to limit the powers of these invaders and improve conditions at home. What it does take is the political will and a real commitment on the part of third world governments to improve the quality of life of the majority of their people. Considering that such governments are formed by self-serving local élites, however, there is no reason to believe that they will act out of the goodness of their hearts. Pressure needs to be exerted by renegades from their own class or educated polemicists and iconoclasts from the middle classes – those who are fighting to deny that market forces and the profit motive is all that rules human lives, and who believe that even Marxism, despite vehement denials, was a value system before it was an economic or a political one, a system that addressed what ancient traditions have always addressed as the human problem of greed.

For it is the greed of the few that releases toxic substances in the market and calls them medicine, which kills and maims the children of the more vulnerable members of society. This is what killed the four-year-old son of a gardener because the urban doctor he went to did not know how to treat dog bites; this is what killed 56 children from poor households who were prescribed a toxic anti diarrhoeal, because the mammoth multinational pharmaceutical companies that operated in their country had no commitment to the local population, had profits and not service on their minds.

Healing, at least in this part of the world, has always been a holistic discipline that emphasizes wisdom, concern for people and the spiritual commitment of the healer to his art. Unless these values are brought back, health will remain a commodity on the market that only the rich and powerful can afford.

Source: *The Herald*, July 1996.

structure by which the delivery of health care is administered can also have important bearings on the quality of health delivery and, hence, on health outcomes. If reforms in government take place, and if local governments are given a greater say, in terms of finances and skills, in running the lives of their cohort population, accountability and control of the smallest health facilities could be brought under the supervision of union and district councils. While facilities have been provided in most areas, the absence of medical staff allocated to those facilities has made them ineffective. With supervision, control, and accountability at the local level, the users of those facilities may, over time, develop the methods to ensure adequate delivery. In addition, managerial, administrative, and co-ordinating systems need to be strengthened to ensure the efficiency of the health delivery mechanism.

Given the need to promote social development and health care, the government should continue to own its large asset base in the health sector. The transfer of essential and basic services like health from the public to the private sector may put such services out of the reach of a very large number of users, many of whom may have no choice but to use the existing government facilities. The emphasis in the next few years should be on the better use of limited existing resources.

While the privatization of existing health facilities is not recommended, this is not to say that the private sector is to be discouraged. On the contrary, the private sector plays an increasingly critical if not a dominant role in the delivery of health care, especially in urban areas, but also, increasingly, in rural areas as well. The government is not in a position to provide health for all without assistance from the private sector.

The private sector should be encouraged to grow, but it should also be made aware of its social responsibilities. While the profit motive drives much of the health industry, some sort of taxation or cross-subsidization will have to be introduced into the health industry to support the efforts of the government in providing health care to those who cannot afford the higher private sector prices. The public–private partnership philosophy can be made very productive in the health sector (see Box 16.2).

16.4 Education

16.4.1 Statistics

One of the most important statistics in the social sector is the literacy rate, which acts as a proxy for a number of other indicators as well, and is therefore also one of the three indicators that form the Human Development Index. Pakistan's literacy rate is one of the lowest in the world, and is worse than countries which have per capita GNP equal to or close to Pakistan's level. While the literacy rate has nearly trebled since 1951 (Table 16.10), that for females is still particularly poor. The repercussions of this are discussed in the section on women in Chapter 17. Moreover, there is such a marked regional and provincial differentiation that, just as in the case of doctors and the availability of health services, it is futile to talk about a single literacy rate for the country.

Table 16.10
Literacy rates in Pakistan, 1951–1990

Year	Total	Male	Female
1951	13.2	17.0	8.6
1961	18.4	26.9	8.2
1972	21.7	30.2	11.6
1981	26.2	35.0	16.0
1985	29.4	–	–
1988	32.1	–	–
1990	34.9	45.1	20.9

Source: Banuri, Tariq, *et. al.*, 'Human Resources Development', in Banuri, Tariq (ed.), *Just Adjustment: Protecting the Vulnerable and Promoting Growth*, UNICEF, Islamabad, 1992, p. 34.

Table 16.11 shows the literacy rates from the 1972 and 1981 censuses, and indicates extensive regional disparity. While in Karachi the literacy rate was 55 per cent in 1981, it was only 8.2 per cent in Baluchistan. The rural literacy rate for women in Baluchistan was less than 1 per cent, possibly the lowest in the world. In all the provinces in the rural areas, the literacy rate for women was extremely low. Although it is probable that there has been considerable improvement in literary rates, possibly having doubled or tripled in the last fifteen years, they are still extremely low. Table 16.12 gives recent estimates of the literacy rates and a provincial profile of enrolment rates. The continuing low performance in literacy in the rural areas is evident.

Table 16.13 shows the participation or enrolment rates at the three levels of education. Despite commitments by the government that education is a priority and is still provided free of charge, less than three-quarters of the school-age population in Pakistan attends primary school. The regional differences here are also important (Table 16.12), with urban areas doing better than the rural, Punjab the best performer of the four provinces, and Baluchistan the worst. While enrolment rates give one side of the picture, the drop-out rates show that, of those enrolled at the appropriate tier of education, a very large number, especially in Baluchistan and the NWFP, fail to complete their education (Table 16.14).

Table 16.15, on the other hand, shows a phenomenal growth in the number of educational institutions at all levels since 1959/60, and a similar trend in the number of students enrolled. Primary schools have increased by nearly seven times in the last thirty-five years, while primary school enrolment has gone up by almost nine times. In the case of professional colleges, while the number of colleges has increased two-and-a-half times, the increase in the number of students has been sixfold. The biggest increase in enrolment is in the universities, where the number of students has increased by twenty-one times since 1959, with only a sixfold increase in the number of universities. Hence, the pattern observable seems to suggest that at all levels, while there has been an increase in the number of

Table 16.11
Literacy rates in Pakistan, 1972, 1981 (%)

Unit	Total			Urban			Rural		
	Both sexes	Male	Female	Both sexes	Male	Female	Both sexes	Male	Female
Pakistan									
1981	23.3	31.8	13.7	43.4	51.5	33.7	14.8	23.1	5.5
1972	21.7	30.2	11.6	41.5	49.9	30.9	15.3	22.6	4.7
NWFP									
1981	14.3	22.7	4.9	32.1	42.8	18.8	10.9	18.7	2.5
1972	14.5	23.1	4.7	33.7	44.7	19.9	11.0	19.0	2.2
Punjab									
1981	24.5	33.5	14.4	43.1	51.5	33.2	17.3	26.4	7.4
1972	20.7	29.1	10.7	38.9	47.8	28.0	14.7	22.9	5.2
Rest of Sindh									
1981	21.0	30.0	10.0	–	–	–	12.7	20.8	3.4
1972	22.5	32.6	10.0	–	–	–	17.6	27.5	5.8
Baluchistan									
1981	8.2	12.5	2.9	27.9	37.7	14.3	4.4	7.3	0.8
1972	10.1	14.8	4.2	32.3	42.4	19.2	5.6	9.2	1.2
Karachi									
1981	55.0	60.0	48.8	–	–	–	–	–	–
1972	51.2	55.8	45.0	–	–	–	–	–	–

Source: Zaidi, S. Akbar, 'The Economic Bases of the National Question in Pakistan: An Indication,' in Zaidi, S. Akbar, *Regional Imbalances and the National Question in Pakistan,* Vanguard, Lahore, 1992, p. 116.

institutions, there has been an even greater increase in enrolment. If this is due to the fact that many facilities run more than one school shift, then these ratios show positive trends; if this is not the case, then what is happening is that classrooms and schools are becoming congested, which may be affecting standards.

Government expenditure on education has increased from around 1.4 per cent in the 1970s, to about 2.3 per cent in the 1990s (Table 16.16). For the three-year period 1987–9, it was as high as 2.4 per cent of GNP.[14] The estimated private consumption expenditure on education between 1985 and 1991 increased at a cumulative rate of 6.9 per cent in real terms, or 3.8 per cent on a per capita basis.

Table 16.12
Regional differences in primary schooling enrolment rates and literacy rates, 1991 (%)

	Net primary school enrolment rates		Literacy rates	
	Male	Female	Male	Female
Punjab				
Urban	81.1	78.5	62.9	36.8
Rural North	70.8	52.9	44.6	13.6
Rural South	61.0	31.2	34.5	8.9
Sindh				
Urban	63.3	63.3	61.5	41.3
Rural	51.5	24.1	43.2	6.6
NWFP				
Urban	81.3	53.5	53.8	20.9
Rural	47.3	19.8	29.1	3.2
Baluchistan				
Urban	44.9	34.0	52.0	16.5
Rural	47.3	19.8	29.1	3.2

Source: Behrman, J.R., 'Pakistan: Human Resource Development and Economic Growth in the Next Century', mimeo, 1995, p. 12.

Table 16.13
Participation rates in education, 1983–1991 (%)

Year	Primary	Middle	High
1983/4	52.8	24.7	16.4
1984/5	56.1	24.8	16.6
1985/6	56.1	25.8	16.8
1986/7	60.5	27.2	17.0
1987/8	63.0	20.7	17.2
1989/90	68.5	33.9	21.1
1990/1	71.3	36.0	22.5

Source: Banuri, Tariq, *et. al.*, 'Human Resources Development', in Banuri, Tariq (ed.), *Just Adjustment: Protecting the Vulnerable and Promoting Growth,* UNICEF, Islamabad, 1992, p. 35.

Table 16.14
Provincial drop-out rates (%), 1986/7

	Punjab	Sindh	NWFP	Baluchistan
Primary level				
Urban	18	43	63	68
Male	12	40	60	56
Female	24	50	70	80
Rural	49	79	71	79
Male	18	77	70	68
Female	56	89	78	53
Secondary level				
Total	52	49	64	70
Male	53	47	58	64
Female	49	52	70	76

Source: Banuri, Tariq, *et. al.*, 'Human Resources Development', in Banuri, Tariq (ed.), *Just Adjustment: Protecting the Vulnerable and Promoting Growth*, UNICEF, Islamabad, 1992, p. 36.

16.4.2 The Issues

Viqar Ahmad and Rashid Amjad write:

> Before Independence, the main objectives of the education system as designed by the British were to train sufficient numbers of lower level government employees and to shape the mores and attitudes of the future élite by westernizing their cultural pattern. These objectives were well served by separating local-language-medium schools for the masses from exclusive English-medium educational institutions for the élite and by a disproportionate emphasis on a liberal arts education. After Independence, compulsions of economic and social development have changed the pattern of employment opportunities available in the country. The economy's requirements for a large variety of skills and knowledge at various levels are continuously rising. At the same time, attainment of greater equity in income and access to income-earning opportunities are now major social goals.[15]

Although the structure of education, with its clear divide along class and linguistic lines, continues to persist (see Box 16.3), and in fact is reinforced in contemporary Pakistan, some attempts were made in the 1970s to change the nature and orientation of the education system. In 1972 the Bhutto government nationalized all private schools, prior to which much of the country's secondary and higher level education was in the hands of the private sector, especially in the urban areas. While exact figures do not exist, in 1968 it was estimated that 11 per cent of schools and as many as 35 per cent of colleges were in the private sector. In 1972 the government nationalized 3,067 schools, 155 colleges, and 5

Table 16.15
Number of educational institutions and enrolment by kind, level, and sex, selected years

	Institutions													Enrolment					
	Primary schools		Middle schools		High schools		Secondary/ vocational institutes		Arts and science colleges		Professional colleges		Universities	Primary stage/ (I–V) (00s)		Secondary/ vocational (000s)		Universities	
Year	Total	Female	Total	Female	Total	Female	Total	Female	Total	Female	Total	Female	Total	Total	Female	Total	Female	Total	Female
1959/60	17,901	3,260	1,974	281	1,069	203	100	35	126	32	40	5	4	1,890	370	149	23	4,092	778
1971/2	45,854	12,290	4,110	1,038	2,247	571	284	134	339	93	73	6	8	4,210	1,110	366	71	17,507	3,878
1980/1	59,168	18,595	5,295	1,412	3,479	967	231	88	433	119	99	8	19	5,474	1,782	509	130	42,688	7,113
1990/1	114,580	30,422	8,539	3,345	8,011	2,039	725	344	612	218	99	8	22	11,487	3,693	1,068	317	80,354	10,600
1994/5	123,119	41,085	13,615	5,045	12,513	4,638	724	330	702	255	100	8	24	16,722	5,130	1,470	550	87,403	11,683

Source: Government of Pakistan, *Pakistan Economic Survey, 1994–95*, Islamabad, 1995, p. 212.

Table 16.16
Expenditure on education, 1972–1990

Years	Public expenditure (% of GNP)	Household expenditure (% of consumption
1972–1975	1.4	1.19
1975–1980	1.5	0.92
1980–1985	1.5	1.04
1985–1990	2.3	1.22

Source: Banuri, Tariq, *et. al.*, 'Human Resources Development', in Banuri, Tariq (ed.), *Just Adjustment: Protecting the Vulnerable and Promoting Growth,* UNICEF, Islamabad, 1992, p. 36.

technical institutes. A number of prestigious English-medium schools were exempted from privatization, as were schools owned by missionaries and charitable trusts.[16]

The impact of nationalization was severe, as between 1972 and 1979 the share of private schools fell. In 1976/7, only 1.5 per cent of all schools and 4.1 per cent of the colleges remained in private hands.[17] After the ouster of the Bhutto government, the Zia-ul-Haq government reversed the policy of nationalizing schools. In 1979 it once again allowed the private sector to open new schools, and also permitted the denationalization of some of the previously nationalized schools.

At present, while numbers are hard to come by, it is estimated that almost half of schools, especially in urban areas, are in the private sector (see Table 16.17). It is important to point out that the private sector caters not only to the élite or English-speaking population of Pakistan, but also to the middle and lower middle classes, who appreciate the need for good quality education. Even low income areas and *katchi abadis* in urban areas have their fair share of private

---

BOX 16.3
What should the medium of education be?

What medium of instruction should be used for education? Does English suit certain social groups better than others? Some observations from medical education.

The medium of instruction in all medical colleges in Pakistan is English. Pakistan, like India, is a country with different nationalities and cultures, each region having its own corresponding language. Although the official languages are English and Urdu, the entire population cannot speak Urdu, leave alone English. The regional languages have preference over the official ones, especially in the interior of all the four provinces. Further, only 26 per cent of the population is literate (in any language). Thus, of those 26 per cent, one can presume that very few would be able to read and write English. Even fewer would have English as a mother tongue. Moreover, although medical education is in English, schooling can be in any regional or national language. A student may speak his mother tongue at home, he may use another language for primary and secondary education, and yet a third for professional education. That means that although a student has spent 12 years of school life in a language other than English, he or she will be confronted with a 'foreign' language once they enter medical college. This foreign medium of education means that very few students from pre-medical schools will actually be able to learn much in medical colleges. This preference for English shows a bias towards the élite and westernized urban based minority who are accustomed to English in their homes and educational institutions. Members of this élite, apart from being able to learn more, and with much more ease, claim the best House Jobs, followed by the most lucrative job offers. Thus, discrimination on a 'class' basis is reinforced through the medium of instruction in medical colleges. Further, if medicine were taught in either the regional or national language, the international mobility of

doctors would fall dramatically. This is a situation which the élite, whether doctors or laymen, will not readily accept.

The problem of language is not restricted to the lecture halls alone. Students have to take histories from patients, if not in the mother tongue of the patient, then in the local or regional language. A student who does not even know the names of the most basic diseases in the national language will have substantial difficulty in finding out what is bothering the patient. There will be very little communication between the two, if at all. Language, however, is only a minor barrier compared to the cultural barrier that exists between the patient and doctor. In most post-colonial societies, a separate 'culture' exists for the élite, and even a mastery of the language will not necessarily close the cultural gap between the two.

The books that are used in medical colleges in Pakistan are in most cases written by foreign authors – mostly American and British. These books cater, primarily, to a western audience in medical schools in developed countries. They are written in, and for, a specific socio-economic culture and environment dealing with a particular health and disease pattern. The fact that they are used in UDCs without any changes, causes a few problems. Since the authors have the DC student in mind, quite naturally they talk more of diseases found in the West than in Pakistan or other UDCs. The main diseases in Pakistan which are caused by infections and are communicable have more or less been wiped out in the West. Further, a great number of diseases in UDCs have their roots in social and economic conditions which are far removed from the hygienic western hospitals in the countries of the authors. Thus, some diseases which are very common in Pakistan, such as typhoid and diphtheria, would be treated as 'interesting and rare' cases in the West, and would not be given the importance they deserve in the texts.

Source: Zaidi, S. Akbar, *The Political Economy of Health Care in Pakistan*, Vanguard, Lahore, 1988, pp. 107–8.

Table 16.17
Distribution of enrolment by school type (%)

Region	Government	Private
Rural Sindh	96.5	3.5
Rural NWFP	97.4	2.6
Rural Baluchistan	89.8	10.2
Rural North Punjab	92.3	7.7
Rural South Punjab	93.1	6.9
Small cities, towns	75.0	25.0
Major cities	57.3	42.7

Source: Behrman, J.R., 'Pakistan: Human Resource Development and Economic Growth in the Next Century', mimeo, 1995, p. 12.

schools, simply because there is a demand for a minimum standard of quality, which most government schools are unable to provide. However, it must also be recognized that not all private schools are of particularly good quality: one report argues that the 'bulk of private schools provide a quality which is only marginally better than the average public school. The major reason for the shortcomings of the majority of the private sector is the lack of any regulations and controls of entry into the sector.'[18] The very poor quality of education in both the private and public sectors has been blamed upon: inappropriate curricula, poor quality of teachers and textbooks, improper teaching methods and techniques, and the absence of a link between market demand and output from the sector.[19]

J.R. Behrman argues that issues of governance, limited accountability and responsiveness to clients, and particularly over-urbanization are key causes of the poor status of the education sector in Pakistan. Moreover, political interference only makes matters worse. He writes:

> Anecdotes suggest that there have been serious problems in these dimensions of governance: schooling quality often has been low; primary teacher appointments in a number of cases have been made by provincial Chief Ministers or Secretaries or by Members of Parliament (all of whom have heavy demands on them so this patronage has diverted them from more important activities as well as having delayed appointments and resulted often in poor fits between the appointments and the positions being filled); teacher absenteeism often has been high in part because of the difficulty of monitoring what is happening in the villages; physical capacities have been underused instead of having multiple shifts; curriculum decisions have been very centralized; centralized payment systems sometimes have had substantial arrears (e.g., reportedly 46,000 teachers in the Punjab recently have had five-month lags in remunerations); 'bricks and mortar' orientation has dominated even though staff and non-salary current expenses often have been the apparent

bottlenecks; focus has been on formal public schooling, with little attention and at times disincentives or strong regulations that do not seem related to education (e.g., provincial salary regulations for private schools) for informal education and private education; new girls schools have been delayed in becoming operational because of 'lengthy procedural requirements for sanctioning of new expenditures and teachers' posts'; monitoring and evaluation activities have not been carried out despite commitments to do so. Changes in a number of these dimensions of governance are underway or are being explored in various experiments underway, including some in SAP [Social Action Programme]. For example, reportedly under SAP, at least at the higher levels of the governmental educational hierarchy, some accountability for funds received is replacing the prior sense of entitlement without any need to account for use of resources. But substantial governance problems remain.[20]

Among the most distressing observations from the education sector are the statistics that show the dismal state of education amongst women. There are large gender gaps in schooling, where the primary enrolment rate for girls was 15 per cent below total enrolment rates in 1991, and 8 per cent below the total rates for secondary enrolment. Girls moving from primary to secondary schools in 1987 were 9 per cent less than boys, implying higher drop-out rates for girls.[21] One reason for this has been lower school availability and accessibility for girls. Whether or not a school is available in the same or nearby village is claimed to account for one-third of the large gender gap in schools.[22] While distance to a school may not be critical for boys, for girls, and especially girls in rural areas, it makes the difference whether they attend school or not. Travelling time to school is a significant variable, especially for girls: the longer the time involved, the less likely it is that the girls will attend school.

The high drop-out rates (Table 16.14) are a serious problem affecting the availability of an educated population. Drop-outs take place for a number of reasons: a low overall level of economic development; extensive and widespread poverty; the existence of child labour, which means that the opportunity cost of being in school is high; costly reading material and stationery; poor motivation among parents to retain their children in school; a persistent (albeit declining) negative attitude towards formal education; and a general lack of decent, cheap, and high-quality education.

Many of these issues, such as high drop-out rates, the imbalance between boys' and girls' education, and the poor quality of teachers and schools, exist in other underdeveloped countries. The medium of instruction is also a matter of concern among educationalists, planners, and politicians. Should schooling be in English, Urdu, or the native tongue, and how should the differences be marked? The case of education in Pakistan's medical schools is elaborated in Box 16.3. Rashid Amjad and Viqar Ahmad write:

The existence of élite English-medium schools side by side with national and regional-languages-medium schools also creates equity problems. Since command over the English language is still an asset in getting prized government and non-government jobs, entry to such jobs becomes restricted to those lucky enough to have access to the limited seats in English-medium schools. It is interesting to note that these schools were not nationalized in 1972.[23]

16.4.3 Summarizing the Issues in Education

As government facilities have not been able to keep pace with growing demand for educational services, especially at the lower levels, the private sector and non-governmental organizations have begun to play a critical role. Primary and secondary education has now developed into a large market where demand has outstripped supply, hence the increasing role of the private sector. Moreover, as consumers have become more quality conscious, the choice of type of education has burgeoned. The private sector will continue to grow over the next few years. Recognizing this fact, the government should encourage the growth of the private sector, but should also develop checks and balances to ensure an adequate standard of facilities. Some components of the private sector in education, while fulfilling an urgent need, have compromised on standards, relevance, and quality. The government will have to ensure, through a well-devised monitoring process, that minimal acceptable standards are maintained and enforced. However, this task, while important, cannot be left to the government alone, and the private sector, community groups, and government will need to work jointly towards common goals.

Although the government's role in the provision of educational facilities in the recent past has been eclipsed by the private sector, the government continues to own and run a vast network of schools. The increase in numbers has often meant falling standards and inadequate services provided to users. To ensure better quality from existing resources, local community groups need to be involved in supervising the educational facilities. Participation, even control, by lower tiers of government and concerned actors must also become part of the educational strategy (see Chapter 18).

One area where the government must continue its efforts at an increasing pace is that of girls' education. With very low and inadequate female literacy and school participation rates, the development of facilities for girls cannot be left to the private sector alone. If the government is to undertake one major task in social development over the next few years, it must be the expansion of facilities for girls. This will involve not just opening more schools for girls, but attempts to increase the availability and quality of female teachers. Since the mobility of females is restricted by social norms, potential teachers will have to be found from local communities. If adequate financial incentives are given to train such girls, it is likely that such schemes will be successful. In the informal sector, the phenomenon of home schools should also be encouraged.

Data from studies on education show that the number of primary schools has increased over the last few years, as has enrolment. The quality notwithstanding, the government should be complimented for its efforts at increasing these numbers. Perhaps now the time has come to provide for these primary school leavers at the next level. The strategy in the immediate future should shift from an emphasis on primary schooling to one where secondary schools form an increasing component of the education programme. Moreover, there is an urgent need to reform the curriculum in secondary schools and to add subjects with a vocational angle.

16.5 Population Welfare and Family Planning

16.5.1 The Evolution of the Population Welfare Programme

Pakistan, with a population of around 140 million, is the eighth most populous country in the world. Its annual population growth rate of around 3 per cent is amongst the highest in the world. This high growth rate is surprising, considering that before 1950 Pakistan's annual population growth rate was less than 2 per cent. The total fertility rate, 'the average number of children that would be born alive to a women during her lifetime, if she were to bear children at each age in accord with prevailing age-specific fertility rates',[24] fell from between 6.3 and 6.5 in the 1970s, to 6.0 in 1984/5 and 5.4 in 1990/1,[25] which is still on the high side. Table 16.18 gives some essential indicators regarding the demographic transition of the country.

Pakistan was one of the first countries in the world to initiate a national family and population planning programme, and did so as early as the 1950s. However, given the current situation, it seems clear that the many population programmes that have been initiated have had a limited impact on fertility, and that Pakistan's success rate has been poor compared with other countries that started later. For the most part, demographic targets have seldom been met, and the lack of political commitment is considered to be a key factor. Added to this has been a lack of funding for the programmes, as well as weak management to oversee and implement them. Moreover, changes in leadership, management, and focus have been frequent, thus failing to give the programmes a secure footing.

Given the changing approaches of the political and technocratic leadership, population policy has also undergone frequent change. In the period 1965–73, the population programme relied 'mainly on the use of traditional midwives (*dais*) to motivate the population, distribute contraceptives, and refer clients for IUD insertions and sterilization'.[26] The Bhutto government in 1973 introduced a novel mechanism called the 'continuous motivation system', which was meant to be implemented by well-trained couples rather than *dais*. The population programme suffered its worst setback in 1977, under the banner of the Islamization programme of General Zia-ul-Haq, when it was discontinued for three years. In these three years, no motivational campaigns or field

Table 16.18
Trends in demographic and health indicators, 1965–1995

	1965	1970	1975	1980	1985	1990	1995
Total population (millions)	52.6	60.6	71.0	82.6	96.2	112.4	129.7
Population growth rate (%)	2.7	3.0	3.1	3.0	3.1	3.1	2.7
Crude birth rate (per thousand)	48.0	47.6	47.4	47.1	45.1	41.6	–
Crude death rate (per thousand)	20.9	19.1	16.9	14.7	13.1	11.9	–
Total fertility rate (birth per woman)	7.0	7.0	7.0	7.0	6.5	5.8	5.6
Contraceptive prevalence rate (% of females 15–49)	n.a.	n.a.	11.0	5.0	9.1	10.7	–

Source: World Bank, *Staff Appraisal Report: Pakistan Population Welfare Program*, Report No. 13611-Pak, 1995, p. 56.

activities were undertaken. After 1985, when democratic forces began to re-emerge and share power in government, the population welfare progammes – essentially a pseudonym for family planning – were once again restarted.

In 1990, with the return to a more meaningful democratic order, and with the lame excuse that 'Islam is against family planning' finally out of the gamut of mainstream politics and out of issues of social development, the population programme was strengthened substantially when a separate Ministry of Welfare was created and given the responsibility for all population matters. There was such a sea-change that 'during 1991, government undertook an accelerated program and political support for family planning was now more open. Government programs included steps to expand service delivery and improve efficiency. The number of fixed and mobile sterilization units was expanded. Population education programs were enlarged and targeted better. Field supervision was strengthened and community involvement was sought.'[27]

Because the focus of the population planning organizations in the past had been primarily on the supply of contraceptives irrespective of the demand for these products, the impact on fertility was low, and the population growth rate remained high. By the time the Seventh Five-Year Plan was launched in 1988, a multi-sector population programme approach had been divided, consisting of three major components:

i) establishment of Family Welfare Centers to provide family planning services jointly with mother–child health care, motivation/ education and community development activities;

ii) provision of gynecological and obstetric services and contraceptive surgery through reproductive health service centers established in government and private sector hospitals; and

iii) implementation of a Major Information, Education and Communication Program, which through mass media, personal and group communication promotes breast feeding, maternal and child care practices, nutrition of the growing child, responsible upbringing of the child, late marriages and the status of women.[28]

Just as the philosophy and emphasis have changed, so has the amount of funds allocated to population welfare projects. During the 1980s, expenditure on the population sector averaged 0.06 per cent of GNP and never exceeded 0.07 per cent. As a share of total public expenditure, expenditure on population averaged 0.24 per cent during 1983–92, which was less than 10 per cent of the total expenditure on health.[29] This, by any stretch of the imagination, is on the very low side. As a World Bank report on population planning in Pakistan concludes, 'chronic underfunding of the population program has constrained its prospects for expanding outreach and improving service delivery'.[30]

With the change in emphasis prior to the Seventh Five-Year Plan, the government was, for once, willing to put its money into an area that it felt needed priority. The actual expenditure on the population sector during the Seventh Plan actually exceeded the Plan allocations, reflecting the renewed and growing priority given to the population sector. The Eighth Five-Year Plan has placed an even stronger emphasis on the government's population programme, aiming to spend 0.15 per cent of GNP between 1995/6 and 1997/8. Although a small figure in absolute terms, this is, nevertheless, double what the government has spent of late and is three times the amount allocated under the Seventh Plan.[31] The World Bank has observed that 'over the last few years, a consensus has been growing in Pakistan on the need to address the population issue seriously'.[32] While discussing the funding aspects of the population programme, it is also important to emphasize that a large amount of the funds have often come from abroad as foreign aid, a component that has varied considerably. Foreign aid contributed 19 per cent of funding to the population programme during the Fifth Five-Year Plan (1978–83), rising to 53 per cent during the Sixth Plan when the government itself cut its own initiative, and was 40 per cent of the allocation in the Seventh Five-Year Plan (1988–93). The main source of funding has been USAID, which provided as much as 87 per cent of total assistance during the Seventh Five-Year Plan. After the departure of USAID from Pakistan in 1993, foreign assistance covers about 25 per cent of the population programme expenditure.[33]

16.5.2 Knowledge and Usage

There are 1,296 Family Welfare Clinics (FWCs) in the country, whose function is to deliver non-surgical contraceptive services. Surgical contraception is provided through the 218 Reproductive Health Service Centres, which are located in government and private hospitals. Of these, 79 are run by the Ministry of Population Welfare or Provincial Population Welfare Department. There are 2,619 health outlets of the Ministry of Health, and 153 facilities of other provincial line departments (see Table 16.19).[34]

The World Bank report on population in Pakistan argues that 'taken altogether, all of Pakistan's family planning effects make services available to less than a quarter of the population. The Ministry of Population Welfare covers about 10–12 per cent of the population and other organizations another 13–15 per cent. *Such low coverage is partly responsible for the low contraceptive use.* The number of clients per facility, however, varies widely across and within provinces and between urban and rural areas.'[35] According to the estimates of the Ministry of Population Welfare, the coverage is about 54 per cent in urban areas, while it is only 5 per cent in rural areas. Although some facilities do exist, they are widely spread and most offer very limited services. It has been calculated that the average walking distance to a Family Welfare Clinic in the Punjab is about 9.3 km, while it is more than 100 km in parts of Baluchistan where, for all practical purposes, supply seems quite restricted, especially since visits to the clinics involve considerable time and travel costs. Evidence shows that few clients, rural or urban, are willing to travel more than 5 km to a clinic and very few actual users travel more than 10 km. In Pakistan, 'in both rural and urban areas, awareness and use of Family Welfare Clinics declines sharply with increasing distance from a Family Welfare Clinic'.[36]

Evidence about knowledge and use of family planning techniques in Pakistan has shown that a very high percentage of married urban women (91 per cent), and an impressive 71 per cent of rural women are aware of some form of modern birth control (Table 16.20). Education plays an important role: as the level of education among women rises, so does their knowledge about contraception. This is hardly a surprising result, since it is likely that women with more education have greater access to the media, which is a major source of information on family planning, and have access to a wider social network in which information about family planning is likely to be available. Moreover, since better-educated women are likely to marry better-educated men as well, there are possibilities of more information being available. One of the more surprising results from a large survey conducted in Pakistan was that it was the NWFP, rather than Punjab as one would have expected, where the largest number of married women were aware of modern contraceptive methods: 83.3 per cent of married women in NWFP knew about contraceptives, compared with 79.9 per cent in the Punjab, 73.9 per cent in Sindh, and 36.5 per cent in Baluchistan.[37]

The total fertility rate (TFR), which has fallen over the last few decades, depends upon: the incidence of marriage, the age at marriage, the practice of breast feeding, use of contraception, and a number of socioeconomic variables, especially those affecting women, such as female education, female labour force participation, and the infant mortality rate. Poverty, illiteracy, and women's low status in society all combine to sustain the high levels of population growth in Pakistan. Moreover, features such as location of residence – urban, large city, small town, rural, etc. – also affect the TFR (see Table 16.21). There is a marked fall in the TFR in large cities compared with the rural areas. Similarly, there is an even more appreciable decline when one considers levels of education: with no education, the total fertility rate is 5.7 and higher than the overall average of 5.4, while for those women who have secondary education, the total fertility rate falls sharply to only 3.6.

Table 16.19
Availability and access to family planning outlets, 1994

	Estimated no. of MWRA (000s)	FWC	RHC(A)	RHC(B)	MWRA/FWC (000s)	MWRA/RHC (A) + (B) (000s)	Average walking distance (km) to	
							FWC	RHC (A or B)
Punjab	13,301	775	44	77	17	107	9	71
Sindh	5,230	245	20	20	21	131	14	57
NWFP	3,006	203	8	31	15	77	11	69
Baluchisten	1,052	53	5	7	20	8	48	235
Federal programme	1,543	20	2	4	77	257	26	25
NGO (CC)	–	322	0	0	–	–	–	–
Total	22,658	1,618	79	139	14	104	–	–

MWRA = Married women of reproductive age (1991).
FWC = Family welfare clinics.
RHC(A) = Reproductive health centres, run by Provincial Welfare Departments (PWD).
RHC(B) = Reproductive health centres, run by Department of Health and Private Sector.
Source: World Bank, *Staff Appraisal Report: Pakistan Population Welfare Program*, Report No. 13611-Pak, 1995, p. 60.

Table 16.20
Fertility rates and contraceptive knowledge, attitude, and practice

	Total fertility rate 15–49	Knowledge of modern contraception (%)	Both husband and wife approve (%)	Current use of any method (%)
Residence				
Urban	4.9	91	53	26
Rural	5.6	71	24	6
Education				
None	5.7	73	27	8
Primary	4.9	92	43	18
Secondary	3.6	95	70	38
Overall	5.4	77	34	12

Source: World Bank, *Staff Appraisal Report: Pakistan Population Welfare Program*, Report No. 13611-Pak, 1995, p. 33.

16.5.3 Some Issues

Delivery and Quality

The quality of services available for family planning is considered to be uneven, and often poor. Many Family Welfare Clinics, like much of the public sector, work intermittently, are frequently closed, and have staff that are often absent or inadequately trained. A study found that about one-fifth 'of these centers lacked examination facilities, and many did not offer adequate privacy in examination and counselling areas'.[38] It is not surprising, then, that the poor quality of service in government clinics deters and discourages users. This is despite the fact that the demand for family planning services in the country is quite high and continues to go unmet. In rural areas where only 5 per cent of married women have access to family planning services, virtually no outreach has been provided for women who may want to use family planning services and who 'have to cover too great a cultural and physical distance to obtain them'.[39]

Economic Factors and Fewer Children

Much of the discussion in the earlier sections has focused on the technical side of family planning – number of facilities, demand for services, etc. One of the most important determinants of having fewer children is the household's economic constraints. It is becoming more and more difficult to afford large families nowadays, where the quality of human resources matters as much as the quantity. Many families are forced to opt for smaller families due to economic imperatives, which also cause larger families in the first place. People will begin to have smaller families once they realize that larger families are no longer feasible. In addition,

Table 16.21
Fertility by background characteristics

Background characteristics	Total fertility rate	Mean no. of CEB (women 40–49)
Residence		
Total urban	4.9	6.3
Major city	4.7	6.3
Other urban	5.2	6.4
Rural	5.6	6.4
Province		
Punjab	5.4	6.3
Sindh	5.1	6.6
Karachi	5.0	7.1
NWFP	5.5	6.1
Baluchistan	5.8	5.7
Education level attended		
No education	5.7	6.5
Primary	4.9	6.1
Middle	4.5	5.3
Secondary	3.6	4.3
Total	5.4	6.4

CEB = Children ever born.
Source: NIPS, *Pakistan Demographic and Health Survey, 1990/1991*, Islamabad, 1992, p. 41.

as much of the available information and data suggest, more education results in lower fertility rates and greater use of birth control methods. Greater migration to urban areas is another factor that results in smaller families, essentially because in larger cities, given the problems with employment, housing, and access to services, it is no longer economically viable to have large families.

The status of women – their education, labour force participation, etc. – is a critical factor that affects family planning. As we argue in Chapter 17, the status of women is also linked to economic development. Hence, as growth or development takes place, women's contribution to the economy increases and their status improves. The likely result is a fall in the population growth rate.

While cultural and social factors are also influenced by economic and social development, most changes in the population growth rate will come about once individuals and households recognize, or are forced to accept, the need for smaller families, essentially on economic grounds. Smaller families mean better-educated and healthier families, and for most people, given the increasing cost of living, there may be few choices regarding family size. In such circumstances, the role of family planning should be to improve the provision of information and the supply of services and facilities. The evidence suggests that there is growing knowledge and awareness of family planning techniques and a recognition of the need for such services. What is lacking is adequate supply.

16.6   Urbanization and Housing

16.6.1   The Extent of Urbanization

In a country that did not have a census for more than sixteen years, estimating the size of the population, its growth rate, and the urban–rural divide is a precarious, speculative activity. The census that was to be held in 1991 should have given us a fairly precise indication of a number of very important statistics. Now, all we have are educated guesses and estimates based on different ways of reasoning. Small surveys have helped provide further indications that may reflect part of the true nature of development, but again, an element of speculation is always involved. Hence, when we talk about population growth rates, the percentage of the population living in cities, or the extent of migration from the rural areas since 1981, we should bear in mind the incompleteness of the statistics. Nevertheless, a number of observations are valid.

There has been considerable growth in the urban population of the country over the last fifty years. In 1951, when the first census was held, only 17.6 per cent of Pakistan's population lived in urban areas; by 1981, at the time of the last census, this had increased to 28.3 per cent. Estimates now put Pakistan's urban population at about 40 per cent, more than double the proportion in 1951.

Urban population growth results mainly from three factors. Firstly, there is the 'natural' population increase, which is the growth in urban families themselves; then, urban areas grow as areas previously considered rural are transformed into urban areas; finally, there is net rural to urban migration, adding to the existing stock of residents in towns and cities.

Rural areas become urban as areas adjacent to urban centres, over a period of time, assume urban characteristics '(i) as a result of the overspill of urban activities and increases in population density resulting from natural population growth and migrants settling in these peri-urban areas; and (ii) the growth of small rural centres which through increases in population density and broadening of functions gradually assume more urban characteristics, allowing them to be reclassified as urban over time'.[40] This last is essentially an administrative criterion that 'creates' urbanization.

The urban sector has grown considerably since 1981, and the growth and dynamism in urban population and of the urban economy was substantial in the 1980s compared with the relative stagnation of the 1970s. By the administrative criterion alone, between 1983 and 1991, 114 additional rural settlements became urban as their population increased and they acquired the status of town committees. This growth can be contrasted with that of the period 1972–81, when only 24 new administrative urban areas were created.

In the period 1972–81, the urban population growth rate was 4.4 per cent per annum, which had increased to a growth rate of 4.8 per cent per annum between 1981 and 1993. Interestingly, the urban population growth rate had been declining in the intercensal periods between 1951 and 1981, and the rise since 1981 is distinguished by being against the trend. The reasons for this are discussed later in this section.

Between 1972 and 1981, of the intercensal urban population growth rate of 4.4 per cent per annum, the contribution of rural transformation to annual urban population growth was about 8 per cent, while during 1981–92, about one-third of urban population growth was attributed to rural–urban migration and spatial amalgamation.[41]

The provincial urban population growth rates in Table 16.22 reveal that the Punjab had the fastest growth of 4.9 per cent between 1981 and 1993, while Sindh and Baluchistan grew fastest in the 1970s. By 1993, about half the population of Sindh lived in areas designated as urban, while 35 per cent of the Punjab and 18 per cent each of Baluchistan and the NWFP were considered urban populations. Some 56 per cent of the entire urban population of Pakistan lives in the Punjab, 34 per cent in Sindh, 7 per cent in the NWFP, and 3 per cent in Baluchistan. The rise in the urban population during the 1980s has also meant that five more cities – Gunjranwala, Multan, Rawalpindi, Peshawar, and Hyderabad – have joined Karachi, Lahore, and Faisalabad in the group of cities with more than one million inhabitants. (See Appendix 16.2 on the problems of urban growth in Gunjranwala.)

Urban growth and particularly rural–urban migration are normally attributed to push and pull factors. Push factors are those which cause inhabitants to leave the rural areas, such as declining agricultural growth and production, tractorization causing the displacement and eviction of

Table 16.22
Urban and rural population by province, 1981 and 1993 (estimated)

	Land area (% of Pakistan)	1981		1993 (estimated)		Urban population as % of provincial population	
		Urban	Total	Urban	Total	1981	1993
Punjab	26	55	56	56	56	22.7	34.9
Sindh	18	35	23	34	24	42.3	50.3
NWFP	9	7	13	7	13	15.3	18.2
Baluchistan	44	3	5	3	4	16.3	18.0
FATA, Islamabad, etc.	3	1	3	1	3	11.4	11.4
Pakistan	100	100	100	100	100	28.8	35.0

Source: Asian Development Bank, *Pakistan Urban Sector Profile*, Manila, 1993.

farmers, and floods and natural calamities. The lure to urban areas depends on the availability of jobs in industry and services, the desire for better schooling and health facilities, aspirations to an urban culture, and the 'bright lights' phenomenon.

In the 1980s in Pakistan, some of the reasons listed above played an important role in the 4.8 per cent urban growth, most of which was due to rural immigration. Food production did not grow significantly in the 1980s, and the more than 3 per cent population increase in rural areas was now facing slower output growth. There has been increasing fragmentation of land holdings as population has grown, and mechanization has also affected rural migrants, displacing them from the agricultural land. In the cities, the 1980s were a boom period, with a growing and dynamic manufacturing sector, and the construction and service industries also showing very positive trends. Not only is migration affected by actual conditions, but even perceived and expected conditions may cause migration to grow. For instance, for each individual who actually finds an urban sector job, many more wait in line and follow him, hoping to find a job at a later date. Although figures are not readily available, urban unemployment is still not at the critical stage where migration from rural areas would be halted. As long as there is a belief that better jobs can be found in cities, rural–urban migration will continue.

It is not just the very large cities that have grown over the last decade; the most dynamic have been the intermediate cities, especially in the Punjab. As in the 1960s following the Green Revolution, so in the 1980s, due to linkages with the agricultural hinterland, but particularly due to remittances received from the Middle East, investment in industry, construction, and services has been noticeable in the smaller towns and intermediate cities. It is inevitable that the growth of cities will continue in Pakistan for many years to come, and by the turn of the century, close to 40 per cent of the country's population will be living in areas designated as urban.

16.6.2 Housing in Cities

While cities may be growing at unprecedented rates in Pakistan, social facilities and services have not been able to keep pace with the growth of natural and migratory populations in cities. While Table 16.23 shows that conditions and access to facilities are far better in urban areas than rural areas, which in fact is one of the reasons why people move in the first place, Table 16.24 shows that slums and squatter settlements (*katchi abadis*) constitute a large part of the living conditions of the urban population. While health, sanitation, and sewerage facilities in such areas are particularly poor, we examine the reasons for the failure of housing programmes initiated by the government, and how the government's role has been replaced by a dynamic and efficient informal sector.

Arif Hasan, in his *Seven Reports on Housing*,[42] evaluates the causes for the failure of government housing policies, and explains why an alternative, informal market emerges and how it plays a significant role in providing housing to low-income groups (see also Appendices 16.3 and 16.4).

Table 16.23
Housing accessibility to municipality services in urban areas of Pakistan by province, selected years (%)

	Electricity			Inside piped water			Gas piped			Kitchen			Latrine		
	1973	1980	1989	1973	1980	1989	1973	1980	1989	1973	1980	1989	1973	1980	1989
Punjab	16	29	58	7	11	16	1	5	7	20	n.a.	34	19	n.a.	25
Urban	58	73	92	27	36	55	6	17	34	32	35	51	68	57	78
Sindh	21	36	58	13	21	27	5	15	20	17	n.a.	45	48	n.a.	56
Urban	47	68	93	30	43	68	11	33	54	25	60	82	83	74	93
NWFP	24	39	68	5	8	22	0.1	2	4	22	n.a.	46	48	n.a.	58
Urban	66	81	97	23	34	54	1	10	30	35	31	63	76	60	37
Baluchistan	5	14	38	5	7	11	0.1	1	3	29	n.a.	37	19	n.a.	29
Urban	27	55	86	28	37	67	1	4	34	53	57	82	66	64	87
Pakistan	18	31	59	8	13	18	2	6	9	20	n.a.	38	29	n.a.	35
Urban	54	71	93	28	38	60	7	20	41	30	44	63	55	63	84

Source: Asian Government Bank, *Pakistan Urban Sector Profile*, Asian Development Bank, Manila, 1993.

Table 16.24
Urban population and population in slums and *katchi abadis* **in major cities, mid-1990**

Province /city	Total population	Katchi abadis Population	%	Slums Population	%	Katchi abadis and slums Population	%
Baluchistan							
Quetta	455,222	133,286	29	48,803	11	182,089	40
Others	626,130	166,714	27	83,738	13	250,452	40
Subtotal	1,081,351	300,000	28	132,541	12	432,541	40
NWFP							
Peshawar	849,200	212,301	25	127,382	15	339,683	40
Mardan	178,000	40,699	23	30,501	17	17,200	40
Others	1,459,332	0	0	583,733	40	583,733	40
Subtotal	2,486,540	253,000	10	741,616	30	994,616	40
Punjab							
Lahore	4,470,965	458,000	10	1,240,967	28	1,698,967	38
Faisalabad	1,600,284	240,739	15	367,369	23	608,108	38
Rawalpindi	1,171,162	19,636	2	429,206	36	448,842	38
Multan	1,069,787	40,300	4	366,219	34	406,519	38
Gujranwala	1,137,640	38,899	4	383,404	34	432,303	38
Sialkot	464,748	7,979	2	168,625	36	176,604	38
Sargodha	469,697	36,402	8	142,045	30	178,447	38
Islamabad	396,777	10,000	3	140,775	35	150,775	38
Jhang	311,468	17,758	6	100,600	32	188,358	38
Bahawalpur	254,158	78,204	31	18,376	7	96,580	38
Kasur	258,392	21,815	8	76,374	7	96,580	38
Gujrat	256,725	10,316	4	87,239	34	97,555	38
Okara	256,725	71,818	28	25,737	10	97,555	38
Sahiwal	253,390	76,422	30	19,866	8	96,288	38
Sheikhupura	255,882	73,173	29	24,062	38	56,046	38
Wah Cantt	147,491		0	54,046	38	56,046	38
R.Y. Khan	198,378	75,000	38	384	0	75,384	38
Jehlum	184,388	1,242	1	68,826	37	70,068	38
Chiniot	175,205		0	66,578	38	66,578	38
D.G. Khan	160,336	4,199	3	56,729	35	66,928	38
Others	6,940,169	458,098	7	2,179,166	31	2,637,264	38
Subtotal	20,443,668	1,750,000	9	6,018,594	29	7,768,594	38
Sindh							
Karachi	7,808,123	2,967,087	38	156,162	2	3,123,249	40
Hyderabad	1,077,382	104,828	10	326,125	30	430,953	40
Sukkur	2,525,613	17,806	7	83,128	33	101,024	40
Mirpurkhas	2,032,133	15,000	7	66,285	33	81,285	40
Larkana	201,574	5,328	3	75,302	37	80,630	40
Nawabshah	138,230	5,000	4	50,292	36	55,292	40
Others	2,735,109	584,951	21	509,093	19	1,094,044	40
Subtotal	12,416,192	3,700,000	30	1,266,477	10	4,966,477	40
Pakistan total	36,427,751	6,003,000	16	8,159,227	22	14,162,227	39

Source: Asian Development Bank, *Pakistan Urban Sector Profile*, Manila, 1993.

With reference to Karachi, where many of the problems faced by planners are similar to other cities, except that they are amplified here on a much larger scale, Arif Hasan highlights the causes of the failure of the Karachi Master Plan programmes. A number of factors are identified:

1 *An affluent middle class.* This class regularly invests in land and considers it a very safe investment. Most official schemes developed by the government and its agencies are purchased by this class for speculation purposes, and the intended beneficiaries are often sidelined.

BOX 16.4

Is education the key to development?

Experience from East Asia suggests that education is perhaps the key to development. What can the rest of the world learn from the classrooms of East Asia?

Many theories about East Asian economic success are controversial. Economists argue about the importance of industrial policy, cultural critics debate the existence of 'Asian values'. But one explanation commands almost universal assent: an emphasis on education.

The success that countries like South Korea and Taiwan make of educating their children is often held up as an example for poorer countries in South Asia and Africa. But international comparisons also regularly show that East Asian children outperform their western counterparts when tested on their knowledge of maths and science [see Figure 1]. In the 1995 World Competitiveness Report, Singapore and Taiwan were rated first and third on the ability of their educational systems to meet 'the needs of a competitive economy'.

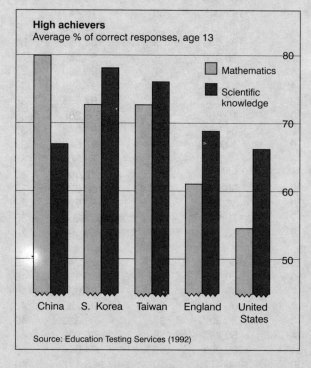

High achievers
Average % of correct responses, age 13

Source: Education Testing Services (1992)

One of the most striking characteristics of countries like Taiwan, Singapore and South Korea has been their emphasis on raising the educational standards of the whole population rather than an élite. Moreover, those developing countries that invested heavily in primary education have done much better economically than those that concentrated more on university education. In 1960, Pakistanis and South Koreans were about as rich as each other. But whereas just 30% of Pakistani children were enrolled in primary schools, 94% of South Koreans were. By the mid-1980s, South Korea's GDP per person was three times Pakistan's. Hard as it is to prove a direct connection, the figures are certainly suggestive.

But it is not just developing countries that are looking to the East Asian tigers. In America and Britain in particular, education debates have recently been shaped by arguments about what Asians are doing right and westerners are doing wrong. Tests of schoolchildren seem to show that the best of the West match the achievements of successful Asian schoolchildren. The great weakness of the rich nations and one of the reasons their test scores look so bad compared with the East Asians is that many more western children fail at school. These, the failures, end up on the periphery of the labour market and often on the welfare rolls. That the wages of the unskilled in the West are falling steadily suggests that the social and budgetary costs of educational failure are certain to increase.

Unlike South Asians and Latin Americans, Americans and Britons cannot blame their relative failure on a lack of universal primary education. So some westerners are inclined to shrug their shoulders and say that East Asian children are naturally more diligent or even more intelligent (a conclusion many Asian may quietly agree with). In any event, the achievements of Asian children brought up in the West suggest that cultural explanations, such as family support, may have a part to play. The success of Asian-Americans in gaining admission to élite universities like Harvard and the University of California has been so marked that it has provoked rows about discrimination against Asians, as the universities attempt to maintain an ethnic balance among their students.

Simply copying teaching methods may not compensate for cultural advantages like a deep commitment by parents to education. In South Korea, Taiwan and Japan, many children are sent to cramming schools in the evening to supplement their daily lessons. Examinations dominate the lives of the young far more than in the West. This may not make adolescence much fun, but it probably raises test scores.

The West is unlikely suddenly to acquire Asians' cultural traits, but it may still be able to learn from the tigers. The most impressive characteristic of their education systems is the belief that everyone can and should succeed. It is expected in Taiwan, for example, that every child will achieve a basic level of attainment by the age of 12. Classes in the first three or four years are of mixed ability. Those who fall behind are given special tuition in one-to-one catch-up classes. Primary schools tend to be much more alike in terms of the money spent on them, class sizes and exam results than in the West. The 'sink school' is not something that exists in Taiwanese.

Other factors may also contribute to the tigers' success. Their children work harder, with more days in the school year and more hours in the school day. Educational objectives are kept to a minimum and there is little debate about the nature of subjects and much concentration on the absorption of facts. A daily report on each child's progress is supplied to parents and the head teacher randomly inspects

BOX 16.4 continued

children's homework to monitor their progress and the form teacher's performance. Teachers enjoy considerable respect and prestige and are relatively well paid, compared with their counterparts in the West.

East Looks West

The Asian example is beginning to influence educational policy in the West. It has helped, for example, to bring regular tests and whole-class teaching back into fashion in Britain. Ironically, though, some Asian educationalists are beginning to voice doubts about their own methods. The strength of their educational system, with its emphasis on discipline, facts and learning by rote, may also be its weakness.

Some more advanced Asian countries, like Japan and Taiwan, are worried that current ways of doing things are stifling creativity and inventiveness among their students and that this may eventually carry an economic price. Manufacturing, with its emphasis on systems and teamwork, rewards the kind of disciplined and factfilled students produced in the tigers. But what about the more creative service industries in which Asian countries currently lag behind America – like software design or entertainment?

Yuan-Tseh Lee, who chairs a commission currently looking into education reform in Taiwan, is brutally critical of the exam system and its inability to identify and encourage original talent. Similarly, Professor Hiroyaki Yoshikawa, the president of Tokyo University, says that Japanese employers are increasingly complaining that new graduates are unable to think for themselves. He laments that students returning from the West are at first full of enthusiasm and ideas, but that this tends to be soon crushed by the Japanese system. Creativity and independence, however, are not qualities that can be readily manufactured. A big shift may take decades.

Meanwhile, educational priorities in the more-established tigers are now moving towards higher education. Over 10% of American doctoral degrees in science and engineering in 1990 went to students from Taiwan, China and South Korea – a legitimate source of Asian pride, but also a comment on the state of universities back home. In 1991, in a league table comparing the proportions of 20–24-year-olds in higher education, South Korea was tenth, Singapore 11th and Taiwan 20th, with Canada and the United States leading the ways. But change is on the way. Taiwan hopes to raise the share of its young who go to university from 18% now, to 30% by 2000. As in the West, a huge university expansion is under way. As both East and West revamp their education systems, lessons will flow in both directions.

Source: *The Economist*, 21 September 1996, pp. 29–30.

2 *Development on too small a scale.* The development programmes of the government and the development authorities (like the Karachi Development Authority, the Lahore Development Authority, and the Hyderabad Development Authority) involve schemes that either are too small in scale or take many years to materialize; thus very large amounts of government money are tied up in them unproductively.

3 *The developers' lobby.* There is often a large and powerful political lobby formed by developers, who have a major say in policy formulation, and whose priorities determine many programmes and plans; other political pressures also play a role.

4 *The socioeconomics of the poor.* One of the most important reasons for the failure of government programmes is that government planning is often incompatible with, and does not take cognizance of, the economics and sociology of the poor; hence, there is also a 'cultural gap' between the government and the poor.

5 *The high cost of development and/or lease.* Targeting and affordability are major issues.

6 *People want land immediately.* The lower income groups have a particularly urgent and often desperate need for land and housing, and cannot wait for the development process to be completed.

7 *Framing and implementation of government policies.* Since the urban poor have no representation in the framing of national policies, most policies – not only those related to housing – cater to the needs of the middle and upper classes at the expense of the poor. Moreover, technocrats and policy makers belong to the upper sections of society, and do not have or wish to have a proper understanding of the issues of the urban poor.

8 *Powerless municipal corporations.* Development authorities work in parallel to elected bodies like municipal corporations, and are not answerable to the corporation and hence to the people. The technocrats who constitute these authorities have to give in repeatedly to political pressures and modify their programmes, making a mockery of the planning process.

Because of the failure of government programmes and policies regarding land and housing, the informal sector has emerged and consolidated itself over the years and has built numerous institutions. It has been estimated that as much as 63 per cent of Karachi's annual housing needs are fulfilled by the informal sector.[43] The informal sector does everything that the formal and government sectors do not. It 'provides land, with immediate possession, at affordable prices; arranges for water supply to the townships it develops, and successfully lobbies with government agencies for acquiring electricity and transport. In addition, the building component yards in these areas provide materials on credit to the poor and give technical advice on house building. All this is done in defiance of government regulations.'[44] Moreover, the informal sector has, unlike the formal sector, a great deal of appropriateness for low-income groups. For example, the locations selected and developed by the informal sector are often closer to the workplaces of the urban poor, or have adequate access through roads and transport. The allotment procedure for plots is also simple, unlike the cumbersome red tape of the formal sector: 'there is no catering to corruption, no visiting banks and fulfilling other formalities'.[45]

Arif Hasan, in his evaluation of the role of the formal and informal sector in housing, concludes that attempts should not be made to formalize the informal sector. He writes that

> it must be clearly understood that the formal sector planning and delivery mechanisms as they are structured today cannot serve the urban poor. It must also be understood that the formalizing of the informal sector on the formal sector terms, can adversely affect the informal sector operations and make it all the more difficult for the poor to acquire land for housing.[46]

The inability and unwillingness of the formal public sector in housing, as in other social sectors, has resulted in people having to turn to the informal or private sector.

16.7 Summary and Further Reading

16.7.1 Summary

Despite high growth in the economy, the social sectors have shown poor performance over the last fifty years. This, the first of the three chapters on the social sectors, has tried to explain the factual position in health, education, population welfare, and housing. The chapter began by comparing other countries in the South Asia region, along with other underdeveloped countries at similar levels of development. The evidence very clearly suggests that, while Pakistan's economic growth performance has been far better than these countries, its social development has been equally unimpressive. It seems that the high rate of growth in the economy has not been translated into better social indicators, suggesting perhaps that political will, commitment, and priorities of government and the ruling élite may be equally important if social development is to take place.

Although planning for the social sector is not now in vogue, we have examined the issues around which planning takes place and how governments can influence social development.

A detailed evaluation of the health, education, population, and housing sectors suggests a large number of common threads. In health, we see that most of the health facilities are located in cities, and that the government's desire to achieve Health For All by the year 2000 is now a distant dream. The focus of health care in Pakistan has been curative rather than preventive, and suffers from a value system in which highly skilled doctors are trained, but many of them are incapable of working in Pakistan's local environment. Due to the failure of the public health sector, the private

sector has begun to play an increasing role in the provision of, mainly, medical care.

A similar situation exists in education, with private sector schools now dominating. Although there has been a secular increase in government facilities, their quality has noticeably deteriorated, and a private sector in education, even one which addresses the needs of low-income consumers, is thriving. Female literacy, probably the most important of all social sector indicators, is still extremely poor, and fewer girls go to school than boys, with the former having higher drop-out rates than the latter. Education is now increasingly being seen as the key to economic development, as the experience from East Asia suggests (see Box 16.4). Hence, this sector must receive high priority in years to come, and schools for girls must be at the top of the list.

Pakistan was one of the first countries to launch a population welfare programme, yet it has had the highest population growth rates in the world. Fortunately, though, this rate has fallen over the last few years. We argue that economic factors might be the key to smaller families, as it becomes more difficult to afford larger ones. In addition, as the status of women improves and as more are educated and join the labour force, we are likely to see lower population growth.

The proportion of the population in urban areas has doubled from 18 per cent in 1951 to anywhere between 36 and 40 per cent today. Since no census has been held since 1981, one only has guesstimates about the population size of the country. However, the urbanization phenomenon is visually evident, and the number and size of small and large towns have been growing. We have shown how the urban population has adjusted to its situation, turning to the informal and private sectors at an increasing rate.

16.7.2 Further Reading

For a general overview of the social sectors and in order to make comparisons over time and across countries, the World Bank's annual *World Development Reports* and UNDP's *Human Development Report* are essential references. For the health sector see Zaidi, S. Akbar, *The Political Economy of Health Care in Pakistan*, Vanguard, Lahore, 1988, which, while a little dated, presents an historical overview of key issues in the health sector. Ajaz Aslam Qureishi's *Development Planning in Pakistan*, Ferozsons, Lahore, 1991, also has a number of articles on different aspects of the social sector. Tariq Banuri's edited *Just Adjustment: Protecting the Vulnerable and Promoting Growth*, Oxford University Press, Karachi, 1998, is an excellent book covering a large number of issues that affect the economy – in particular, the social sectors. To understand issues on housing, see Arif Hasan's *Seven Reports on Housing*, OPP-RTI, Karachi, 1992. See also Imtiaz Alvi's *The Informal Sector in Urban Economy: Low Income Housing in Lahore*, Oxford University Press, Karachi, 1997; Hameeda Khuhro's edited *Karachi: Megacity of Our Times*, Oxford University Press, Karachi, 1997; and S. Akbar Zaidi's, *The New Development Paradigm: Papers on Institutions, NGOs, Gender and Local Government*, Oxford University Press, Karachi, forthcoming, 1999.

Appendix 16.1

The changing role of planning in Pakistan

Professor S.M. Naseem presents an evaluation and history of the planning process in Pakistan, and identifies the changing role of government and the private sector over the years.

During the past four decades, Pakistan has had a succession of seven Development Plans. The political and administrative environment in which the various plans were implemented have, however, changed considerably over time. The first three five-year plans were undertaken in the context of a larger territorial boundary, which included the present day Bangladesh. The second and third plans coincided with the regime of President Ayub Khan in which a strong central government, assisted by a well organized bureaucracy and with minimal democratic support but strong Western foreign aid programmes, laid the foundation of a planning machinery that was then considered all-powerful. The superstructure of planning inherited from the 1960s continued into the 1970s and 1980s, but with considerably reduced influence and eroded authority.

The erosion in the credibility and effectiveness of the planning machinery inherited from the second and third five-year Plan period has been the result of many factors. The separation of East Pakistan and the dissolution of One Unit gave a new dimension to the regional problem in Pakistan, which during the first two decades was primarily focused on the disparity between East and West Pakistan. The minority provinces, especially those of Baluchistan and NWFP, which had been relatively underdeveloped and where political parties opposed to that in the centre were voted into office, brought the regional issues to the forefront. In any event, planning itself was relegated to a relatively less important role as political and ad hoc decision making became more important. Many of the economic decisions taken by the People's Party's government were outside the planning framework and were motivated by its own ideological considerations and were reversed soon after the imposition of Martial Law in 1977. These domestic factors greatly weakened the planning machinery established in the late 1950s and strengthened in the 1960.

The planning machinery inherited from the Ayub era has also been under pressure from the changing importance of foreign aid, the channelling of which was one of the principal objectives it was geared to achieve, if not its real *raison d'être*. The second and third five-year plans were largely financed through foreign aid. Aid financed investment in water, power and transport and strengthened the infrastructural base – Tarbela and Mangla dams being the prime examples. Industrial development also received a high priority and was the largest recipient of project aid. In addition, programme aid was used to liberalize imports and augment the supply of needed industrial inputs, which had a favourable effect on industrial growth, through better utilization of industrial capacity.

Indeed, during the Third Plan period the essentiality of foreign aid to Pakistan's development was highlighted when the country's foreign assistance programme was suddenly brought to a halt in 1965 as a result of the war with India. Import liberalization schemes had to be reversed and import substitution in consumer goods became the main vehicle of growth. When aid was resumed, attention was shifted to agriculture and since the mid-1960s, industrial progress has failed to gain the momentum it achieved in the early 1960s. The suspension of, or interruption in, aid, based on political considerations, was again repeated, albeit in different contexts, in the 1970s and 1900s. This has rendered foreign aid as a considerably less reliable basis for planning than in the earlier phases of long- and medium-term planning in the country. Foreign assistance for structural adjustment reasons, however, has become more important since the 1970s in the wake of the oil price shocks and terms of trade deterioration.

The emerging geopolitical changes in the world economy have also dampened the climate for aid on which past successes in Pakistan's economic development were based. Both the increasing demands for concessional assistance, and its reduced supply, will force the country to choose either a deceleration of its growth rate or an increasing reliance on commercial borrowings, or increased efforts for domestic resource mobilization. The first two options, clearly, are unacceptable in view of their implications for poverty alleviation and debt servicing, and therefore, the only real option is the last one. This is an option which planners and policy makers have tried to their utmost to shy away from, partly because they have lost the authority to make such decisions. But if the option becomes unavoidable, as seems likely, it would require changes in the structure, as well as the policy thrust, of the present planning machinery.

While the main achievement of the planning machinery in Pakistan has been its considerable success in maintaining relatively high growth rates of GDP, largely through attracting large amounts of foreign resources, its record in attaining a balanced development, especially in the social sectors, and in mobilizing domestic resources, has been generally considered deficient. Pakistan's development has been highly dependent on the inflow of foreign resources, which have varied from about half the level of total gross investment in the 1960s, to a quarter in more recent times. The quantum of net aid flows in recent years has fallen – largely as a result of increasing requirements of debt servicing – but the dependence on gross aid inflows remains high. Much of the aid flows in recent years has been accompanied by a high degree of conditionality or of external policy advice, decreasing the need for a strong planning machinery capable of taking autonomous and innovative initiatives at planned development. Not all policy advice given by aid donors is necessarily bad and some has the distinct advantage of being otherwise disregarded as impractical or unpalatable, even when considered necessary. Such advice can, to a limited extent, be considered a blessing in disguise as it enables the planners to take unpleasant decisions. However, in general, external policy advice does deprive the planners of making autonomous decisions about the long-term and medium-term objectives of the economy. To what extent it is necessary or desirable to restore this autonomy in a period in which the relative roles of domestic and foreign resource mobilization must undergo a sea change in favour of the former, is clearly a question that needs to be addressed in all earnestness in the Eighth Five-Year Plan.

Another consideration which has affected the role of planning in Pakistan is the growing emphasis being laid on increasing the role of the private sector, in both productive and infrastructure sectors. Pakistan's early industrialization was based on the heavy involvement of the public sector in both industry and infrastructure. Lack of entrepreneurship, the low capital base of domestic enterprises and their inability to undertake large and risky projects, as well as the need for providing essential infrastructural support for the nascent industrial sector, provided a powerful argument for such a positive role of the public sector. Over time, however, the private sector overcame its 'shyness' and some of the public sector industries were handed over to the private sector. Import controls, tariffs, and an overvalued exchange rate encouraged the development of a private sector, which became increasingly powerful and oligopolistic in nature. By the end of the 1960s, fears of over-concentration of industrial power gave rise to the phobia of twenty families. These perceived fears later led to large-scale nationalization of industries, banks and financial institutions, causing panic and fear in the private sector. Many industrialists were tempted away to the Gulf region where business opportunities were plentiful in the wake of the oil boom of the mid-1970s. Others found real estate and other rent seeking endeavours, often obtained through political patronage in an unstable environment, as a profitable avenue for investment. The underground economy flourished and adversely affected the economy's productive potential, adding to the growing list of social problems such as drug abuse, urban crime, and ethnic strife.

The reversal of the nationalization policies undertaken in the 1970s has not been easy and despite the government's best efforts, private investment in the Fifth and Sixth Plans has not grown rapidly or in the desired directions. During the Fifth Plan, the result of the government's efforts to reduce the role of the public sector was manifested not in any crowding-in of private investment, but in the decline of the investment ratio from 16 per cent to 13.4 per cent. Private investment grew at 6.3 per cent per annum during the period. In the Sixth Plan period, the growth rate of private investment accelerated to 16.6 per cent through a variety of policy initiatives to provide incentives to private investment, which included deregulation, disinvestment, improved credit facilities, rationalization of sanctioning procedures, as well as a reduction in tariff rates. However, private investment did not move into priority sectors identified by the Plan, such as production of capital goods, export-oriented industries, and investment in backward regions. It moved largely into highly protected consumer goods and other import substituting sectors, as well as into rent seeking non-productive activities.

A major problem facing the planners in the Eighth Plan will be a clear delineation of the functions of the public sector and

devising policies which would aim at increasing and channelling private sector investment into priority areas of the economy, including physical and human infrastructure. Public policies, including public sector investment policies, will have to be reoriented in order to create a supportive environment for the private sector, and for acting as a catalyst for the country's industrial restructuring. At the same time, it would be necessary to keep in mind that the market does not always pursue activities which may be considered socially desirable. Can the private sector, for example, be relied upon to undertake investment to promote primary education or in rural health projects? The market mechanism is good at producing things efficiently, but it does not always help in building the economy's productive base. Does the encouragement of the private sector necessarily imply the abandonment of the government's role of redirecting resources according to plan objectives? In the Pakistani context, has the private sector broadly fulfilled the role that the planners had hoped it would achieve? What policy measures, if any, need to be taken to ensure a more coordinated role between the private and public sectors?

This is where the complementarity between planning and the market mechanism needs to be brought about. Planning is a useful tool – and can still remain so – to identify to achieve socially desirable goals. But it has to be supplemented by enabling economic agents – both private and public – to achieve these goals. In the past Plans, while much attention was paid to achieving the goals and even in fixing the targets to be achieved by public and private sectors, there was relatively little attention paid to incentives to induce the private sector to invest in priority sectors. A strategic role of the government and the planning machinery would be to correct, or avoid, the likelihood of information failure by the public sector, i.e. the inability to assess the social value of any particular piece of information of consequence to the country's development.

Source: S.M. Naseem, 'Major Issues for Consideration in Formulating Pakistan's Eighth Development Plan: A Preliminary Appraisal', mimeo, July 1990.

What is the role of planning in an era when the role of government has been much maligned and the concept of planning seems to be pushed off the agenda?

The Ninth Five-Year Plan is being envisaged, and is to be launched at a juncture, when a virtual consensus has developed in favour of the market mechanism as a fundamental tool to achieve efficient resource allocation across sectors, agents and regions. This consensus has roots in the general disillusionment with Plan outcomes involving a substantial role of the public sector, both nationally and globally.

With this heavy reliance on markets to allocate resources, it may legitimately be asked, whether a development planning exercise has any role in the first place? It is argued that planning does have a role, albeit in a different form than has been conceived in the past, simply because the gap between market determined results and socially desirable outcomes may still remain substantial. Desirable outcomes such as sustained growth and distributive justice are results which the market may not necessarily deliver. At best, allocation of resources through the market takes an economy up to its production possibilities frontier, but who the beneficiaries of growth are will depend on relative resource endowments and prior distribution of income and assets. Thus, distributional outcomes of the market mechanism may serve to reinforce the status quo or even accentuate inequalities. Apart from its ethical implications, such a strategy is politically infeasible as was provided in Pakistan in the 1960s. Moreover, reaching the production possibilities frontier also does not say anything about the sustainability of long term growth, because long term growth entails pushing this frontier further outwards. As much of the recent literature in new growth theory has highlighted, this frontier can best be moved through allocating resources to sectors which generate positive externalities that can be captured at a subsequent date.

From the above statement it stands to reason that planning still has a significant role to play in the development process. Since planning through direct controls and severe distortions of prices has not worked because of unfavourable implications

on efficiency, new mechanisms for allocating resources into economically desirable sectors and to specially desirable groups will have to be sought. Thus the theme for future planning will have to be strategic intervention in areas and sectors which have the potential to generate positive externalities, and greater growth, and where the benefits of growth are more widely dispersed.

Whether such externalities are captured and resources are actually diverted to intended beneficiaries will also depend critically on institutional reform. While planning mitigates perceived market failures, effective governance structures are a necessary condition for reducing the scope of government failure. Thus, for effective development planning, economic interventions have to be accompanied by institutional reform. The need for such reforms has never been as obvious and critical as it will be in the Ninth Plan Period as we turn the century.

Source: Social Policy and Development Centre, Ninth Five-Year Plan (1998–2003) Issues Paper, Karachi, 1996.

Appendix 16.2

Urban growth in Gujranwala

This piece from Salim Alimuddin provides an excellent example of how cities grow and the problems that emerge due to urban growth.

Dust clouds from unpaved roads, diesel fumes, blaring horns, the rattle of auto rickshaws, tangles of tongas, donkey carts and cars, raised voices of the roadside vendors and shoppers, crowds thronging the countless roadside eating houses and hovering by the heaps of second hand clothing on sale ... this is Gujranwala today. Only 20 years ago it presented a different picture altogether. A small sleepy town, pleasant to live in with just a few shops, some horse drawn carriages and a handful of cars, beautiful old houses, graceful trees, and open spaces.

The name Gujranwala comes from the word Gujjar or cattle graziers and the town was named after one Chaudhry Gujar, the owner of the Persian well supplying water to the region. In Mughal times, Gujranwala was of little importance. It later came under Sikh rule, before being virtually rebuilt by the British. The city still has large houses, some of them dating back to the Sikh days. The mausoleum of Mahan Singh, and the garden he laid out still remain. Today Gujranwala is the third largest industrial centre of the Punjab with the dubious honour of being dubbed the dirtiest city in Asia. How did this happen and why has Gujranwala paid such a high price for 'progress'?

In 1941 Gujranwala's population was only 884,545. By 1994 it was estimated to be 1.2 million. The initial increase was due to migration. The initial increase was due to migration at Partition. The good quality of the water and the agricultural produce of the area attracted many migrants, mainly from the Indian Punjab. In the 1960s when the green

revolution with its mechanization of agriculture, drove many agricultural labourers off the land, they came to Gujranwala and found work in its traditional industry, producing agricultural tools and implements. Many of these immigrants began to establish their own workshops and production units and this rapid growth in the small industrial sector tempted farmers and land owners on the city boundaries to sell their own lands and invest in industry instead. This process provided the basis for industrialization and urbanization on what had hitherto been prime agricultural land.

The city limits expanded as the population grew. Lahore, only 63 km away, was easily reached by road or rail and this proved useful for Gujranwala's industry. However, this also meant that when policy initiatives to contain Lahore's growth came into being, Gujranwala received even more immigrants. As engineering goods became a growing sub-sector in the national economy the city expanded rapidly. In the period between the last two censuses (1972 and 1981) Gujranwala grew at an annual rate of 7.4 per cent, making it probably the fastest growing city in Pakistan. By comparison, Karachi and Lahore grew at rates of 4.8 per cent and 3.7 per cent respectively over this same period.

Although an outline development plan for Gujranwala was prepared in 1971 in order to guide its growth, the plan was so out of touch with reality that most of its proposals could not be implemented. A bypass and a bridge over the main railway line (that cuts the entire city into half) are the sole remaining legacy of this particular plan. The plan was revised and updated in 1986 but even this was not implementable. The reasons for its failure, as described in the latest 1995 master plan report, were financial limitations, institutional infancy, inadequate legislation and the lack of coordination between public agencies and communities for infrastructure development. This monumental failure in city planning has meant countless everyday problems for the average person: traffic congestion, poor sanitation, paucity of civil services, lack of access across the railway line and lack of open spaces. In effect unimplemented and ineffective planning to handle Gujranwala's growth have progressively lowered the standards of living for its citizens.

The original city was walled with eleven gates, but has long since spilled out of these. Government led development has included some planned residential schemes like Satellite Town, Model Town and the Cantonment areas, developed in the 1970s and 1980s. But the private sector has developed most of Gujranwala's housing schemes many of which tend to be located along main roads. Housing settlements have generally followed the division of agricultural land into small parcels and have expanded on their own without proper planning, without the consideration of open spaces, facilities for the provision of basic services or space for utility buildings.

Informal sector housing settlements consist of approximately 27 katchi abadis, spread over an area of 429 acres, within the city. These lack civic services but are not worse off than the city as a whole: the net residential density in katchi abadis is much lower (65 persons per acre) compared to the rest of the city (175 persons per acre). Regularized katchi abadis have electricity, water, drainage and paved streets as well as relatively better housing and living conditions.

The Gujranwala Development Authority and the Municipal Corporation who are responsible for the development and maintenance of basic services do not coordinate their activities with each other. There is a gap between government institutions and people which is increasing day by day. Any municipal work that is undertaken is not monitored or evaluated or properly documented, which results in the duplication and wastage of meagre resources. Work is carried out on an ad hoc basis rather than in the context of any urban plan.

Municipal services are woefully inadequate: 543 tons of waste, 82 per cent of which is domestic and organic, is collected manually every day and disposed of in open dumps and ponds in and outside the city, creating air and water pollution and considerable health hazards. This is in addition to industrial waste, 10 per cent of which is hazardous. There are about 20 communal waste storage units catering for only 10 per cent of the total need. Sewers and drains are often clogged with uncollected refuse.

Urban sanitation has deteriorated both in terms of the extent of its converge as well as its effectiveness. The city's sewerage network has developed in a highly unsystematic and unplanned manner. The present system is run by 12 pumping stations serving 40 per cent of the population while the rest of the populace have access to individual septic tanks or soak pits. The installation of sewage treatment plants has lagged far behind in network development, with the result that substantial amounts of raw or partially treated sewage has been discharged in irrigation channels and rivers. The present sewage discharge is 90 million gallons per day, for which the 1994 draft master plan proposes four waste water treatment plants. The current drainage system is unable to prevent periodic flooding during the monsoon season; the effluent

from human settlements and industrial wastes mixes with flood wastes and is a growing menace.

Gujranwala's water distribution system was laid out in 1967. The water pipes are now contaminated due to infrequent water supply and low pressure. Leakages are responsible for the shallow pools of stagnant water around the city. The water supply system is based on groundwater sources, tapped through 36 tube wells providing 63 million gallons per day excluding 30 per cent losses and serves only half of the city's inhabitants. The other half pumps water from the shallow pollution-prone aquifer. A water supply scheme initiated at a cost of Rs60 million in 1986 remains unimplemented due to the lack of funds.

Gujranwala comprises seven radial roads, all of which have numerous commercial encroachments, poor accessibility and (apart from the Grand Trunk Road) are in an appalling condition. The pattern and pace of urban development has led to increasing traffic congestion in the inner city areas. Development of the road network and the public transport system has lagged way behind population growth. Tongas (horse drawn carriages) are the main feature of the transport system, performing the function of buses. The variety of such carts on the road, horse driven, donkey driven and ox driven, along with cars and trucks ensure constant traffic congestion.

Gujranwala is now an industrial city, with 45 per cent of its labour force employed in the manufacturing sector, but the government has done little to develop it as a proper industrial centre. Official efforts have included laying out two industrial estates (first in 1978 and then in the early 1990s), so that at present, 12.5 per cent of the total area of the city, (including the earmarked estates) has been taken over by various industrial units.

Gujranwala's dominating and best known industry is electrical appliances: fans, washing machines, motors and so on. The area is also known for sanitary ware, ceramics and steel utensils. The largest industrial units include chemicals, food products, textiles and engineering. Other industries are sugar manufacturing, paper and paper board, tannery, steel re-rolling, pipes, electric wire/ropes, edible oils and ghee, synthetic fibres, engines, turbines and steel containers, small industrial units including lighting and scientific equipment, utensils, hosiery and non-metallic work.

The industries too are victims of the lack of planning. As one industrialist, Mr Shafaqatullah points out, the government's unstable industrial policies and the taxation system have ensured that 90 per cent of the large industrial units are classifiable as sick. Owners of smaller units, unable to withstand government taxes, have split their production at different locations even though this raises their production costs. The impact on Gujranwala has been a mushrooming of cottage or small scale industries in the city; small production units constitute over 40 per cent of the city's industry. The absence of any landuse policy or effective legislative machinery has meant that industrial establishments are scattered throughout the city, often even located along main roads. Many manufacturing units function in narrow residential streets, where they cause environmental problems and put added pressure on the meagre infrastructural services in these residential areas. The impression is of a makeshift city.

If Gujranwala continues to expand without adequate planning, the forecast for it is complete chaos. Gujranwala may continue to grow economically and attract even more migrants but it will offer increasingly lower standards of living. Land prices have already skyrocketed, making many residential housing developments unaffordable for the majority of the people. Factory owner Alim Shaikh says 20 years ago 5 marlas of land cost Rs50,000; now it costs Rs200,000, i.e. 40 times as much. Compounding the pressure on housing is the lack of state land available, constraining the expansion of katchi abadis, the traditional pressure valve for those unable to afford formal private sector housing. The city will face acute water problems such as the other big cities are now facing. Due to insufficient piped water more and more people will probably turn to the aquifer which will eventually be depleted. The quantity of sewage generated will reach unmanageable proportions and its untreated disposal into the canal/river will cause unbridled water pollution. This, along with the fact that solid waste is rarely collected, will create massive health and environmental problems. Atmospheric and water pollution by the untreated sewage and unmanaged solid waste will breed diseases like malaria, diarrhoea and typhoid.

As commercial activity expands in the old city, the affluent class will tend to move further out to the suburbs, taking over precious agricultural land for housing and leaving behind beautiful historic architecture to be used as warehouses, or to be demolished. This phenomenon has already been experienced in Karachi and Lahore.

The unplanned usage of agricultural land for affluent suburban residents means less land for food crops. The land around Gujranwala is lush and fertile and for a country with a food deficit, using this land for urban housing makes no sense at all.

The above scenario of Gujranwala in 10 maybe 20 years hence, or perhaps even sooner, is likely to result in increasing levels of frustration among Gujranwala's residents, especially amongst the second and third generation immigrants who would tend to have higher aspirations and demands than their parents and will be less likely to passively accept the continual decline in their living standards. This increasing frustration could explode into increases in crime and violence or class, ethnic or political conflict, tearing apart the moral and social fabric of Gujranwala's urban society.

Planning documents exist, studies and surveys have been carried out and recommendations have been made, so why has the implementation of planning been such a miserable failure and why is Gujranwala such an unlivable city? The common perception is that local and municipal governments lack funds. But the real stumbling block is the void that exists between reality and planning. For example, the urban services standards used by the authorities, for estimating the financial requirements for a plan, are very high and similar to those applied in western countries. As such they are not appropriate for the local setting. The solution is to try to provide urban services at an acceptable standard in the right locations at an affordable cost. Similarly, in most cases, people require neither imported technology, nor finance, which is usually all they get offered in grandiose planning schemes. What they require is the right technical support, training and guidance to enable themselves to improve their own living environments. The failure of planning in Gujranwala has more to do with a flawed strategy rather than a lack of funds.

Source: Alimuddin, Salim, 'An Accidental City', *The Way Ahead*, IUCN, Karachi, December 1995, pp. 10–14.

Appendix 16.3

The development of the informal sector in Karachi

Arif Hasan explains how the informal sector in housing has developed in Karachi.

The Informal Sector: An Introduction

The inadequate and inappropriate response of government policies to the problem of housing the poor has led to the development of what is termed an 'informal sector' in housing. This sector has consolidated itself over the years and built up its own institutions. It manages to supply land, with immediate possession, to the poor of Karachi, at a price that they can afford. It arranges for the supply of water to the townships it develops, and lobbies successfully with government agencies for acquiring electricity and transport. In addition, the building component yards in these areas provide materials on credit to the poor and give technical advice on house building. All this is done in defiance of government regulations.

The informal sector has often been persecuted by the government and has had to deal increasingly with a clientele that is conscious of its needs. As a result, it has had to constantly adjust the manner of its operation to meet the challenges thrown at it by both the people and the state. Thus three types of informal sector developments have emerged in Karachi, each as a response to the politics of the age in which they developed. These three systems of development are: squatting by unorganized invasion, by illegal sub-division, and by organized invasion. In the following sections the three systems are discussed.

Unorganized Invasion

Origins and Growth

When the refugees moved into Karachi in the early 1950s they spontaneously occupied all open land in the city centre. The government did not discourage this process as it could offer no alternative habitation to the refugee population. However, with the passage of time this system of unorganized invasions spread to what was then the periphery of the city as well, and land along railway tracks, river beds and near government developed townships was occupied. Small settlements also developed near industrial complexes. The industrialists gave protection to these settlements as they were a source of cheap labour for their industries. However, in the 1960s the government launched a crusade against the squatter colonies and a large number of them were bulldozed. The inhabitants were shifted to new townships outside the city. Due to government persecution, lack of land in the city centre and an understanding of the value of land both by the people and the market forces, squatting by unorganized invasion became more and more difficult and is today an almost unknown phenomenon. The decline in the number of settlements formed by invasion is shown.

The Nature of the Settlements

Social. In most unorganized invasions, a clan or an ethnic group moving into the city identified a piece of land and settled there. Other clan members were then encouraged to settle in the vicinity. Thus, most settlements of this nature are ethnically homogenous. Very often, the residents formed clan-based organizations and lobbied through them for facilities such as water. This lobbying, in the initial stages, was done by petitioning the local government followed by processions and demonstrations. With the passage of time a political relationship was established between the leaders of these organizations and the government, and lobbying became a matter of negotiations for votes in exchange for services.

Physical. Most settlement through unorganized invasions is haphazardly planned. There is no fixed size of a plot and the lanes may be as narrow as three to four feet. Playgrounds, schools and other urban facilities have not been planned for. Houses are of poor quality and neighbourhoods are congested. If they have improved, it has been over a long period of time, and many of these settlements are stagnating in their development.

The reason for the physical nature of the settlements is that they were not laid out according to a plan and no assistance in the shape of technical advice or loans of cash or materials was available to the residents for building their houses. The continuing stagnation of most of these settlements is due to a low degree of security of tenure.

Tenure. The majority of settlements through unorganized invasions are near the city centre. Even those that were on the periphery are now part of the inner city. Thus the value of the land on which they are situated is very high and there is constant pressure from commercial interests to expel the residents. This is one of the major reasons for the stagnation of a large number of these settlements. In this context it is important to note that the majority of settlements not marked for regularization through the KAIRP [Katchi Abadi Improvement and Regularization Programme] have been established by unorganized invasion. A large number of residents of these settlements have now acquired property in *katchi abadis* created through illegal subdivisions.

Future directions. Due to the development of informal market forces it is no longer possible for people to settle themselves through unorganized invasion. It seems that many of the inner city settlements will also be cleared through 're-development projects'. In these projects, the settlement is bulldozed in stages; the commercially valuable land is sold to developers and finances the development of a site and services scheme on the remainder of the site for the residents. In the only settlement which has met this fate, the majority of the residents have sold their plots to commercial interests or people from a higher income group and moved out – many to a plot in an illegal subdivision.

Illegal Subdivisions (ISDs)

Origins and Growth

Illegal subdivision of state land took place as early as 1950 in Karachi. However, this system really expanded in the 1960s as a result of the government's action against squatter colonies and the increasing shortage of land in the city. Almost all informal sector development now takes place through this system and in spite of all government attempts to curb it, it continues to grow. The fact that Karachi is surrounded by unproductive state land helps in its growth ...

Mode of Operation

Involvement of government officials and influential people. The first ISDs took place without the involvement of state officials. However, by the 1960s it was well-placed state officials who were promoting and protecting this system and making large sums of money in the process. Other agencies such as the police and the district commissioner's office also got involved in the development process, and now a well-established relationship between them, the developer and the buyer has been established.

Illegal subdividers are now well known to government officials and they are established in the business. Therefore, there is no problem of mistrust between them and the state officials. Normally they occupy a piece of government land and wait for someone to come and challenge their occupation. When that occupation is challenged, negotiations between the parties take place and it is agreed that the government officials will receive a share of the profits from the sale. In addition, a number of plots, sometimes up to 30 per cent of the development, are set aside for speculation for government officials. If there are any other claimants to the land, and if they have the muscle power to press their claim, a share may also be set aside for them. The local police does not receive a share from the sale, but the construction of a house cannot begin unless a set sum of money is first paid to the police by the owner. In most cases the system has developed to such an extent that the KMC [Karachi Metropolitan Corporation], district and police officials now have regular agents who deal with the subdividers and collect money from them on their behalf.

In the period of the People's Party government (1972–7), the leaders of the ruling party, as well as government officials, gave protection to the subdividers and received their political support in return. As a matter of fact, a large number of subdividers joined the ruling party. During the years of democracy in Pakistan, development through illegal subdivision increased considerably.

The development process. After having negotiated the occupation of the land, the subdivider lays out the township in keeping with a plan he has 'in his head'. Planning is done as far as possible as per KDA [Karachi Development Authority] regulations. Thus, commercial areas are laid out along with residential plots on a grid-iron plan. A standard width of primary, secondary and main roads is maintained and plots for schools, mosques and playgrounds may be set aside.

Initially, plots are sold at a low price and sometimes even given away free, so that habitation may begin. Using his contacts with the state agencies, the subdivider arranges for bowzers from the KMC to supply water to the new residents and advises them to build ground tanks for storage. In some cases he may even construct a water tank in each lane or block. In the same way he 'hires' government machinery, such as tractors and bulldozers, to clear the land and level the roads he has laid out. There are cases when subdividers in the initial stages of development have even supplied people with free mats and bamboo poles to build their shacks.

The formation of an organization. In almost all cases, when there are a sufficient number of inhabitants, the subdivider forms a social welfare association of the residents and gets it registered with the relevant authorities. He appoints himself the leader of the organization and his trusted people the other office bearers. Through this organization he pressurizes the authorities to commence transport services and supplies electricity to the area. Subdividers have been known to hire journalists (the payment is in plots) to highlight the problems of their development schemes in the media so that the KMC may be forced to take some action.

Speculation and tenure security. It is in the interest of the subdivider and the officials who have acquired plots in the settlement that development take place as quickly as possible, so that the value of property increases. Consequently, people are pressurized into building at once. If a plot lies empty for more than a month or so, it is resold to someone else and the money paid for it is confiscated. Due to these reasons, development takes place fast, and apart from a sewerage system, most other services are acquired by the settlement (depending on the connections of its sub-divider) in a two to four year time period.

Land values in fully developed subdivisions are almost the same as of KDA developed townships in the vicinity. This shows how strong the security of tenure is in the ISDs. This tenure security is prevalent because of the large number of residents that form the subdivision, the good quality of housing in the area, and the presence of services such as water, paved roads and electricity. All these have been made possible because of the financial involvement of state officials in this form of development. Once land in an ISD becomes unaffordable to the poor, adjacent land is occupied and developed.

Construction of houses. Houses in ISDs are of good quality as compared to those in settlements which have developed through unorganized invasions. This is because of the institution of the *thalla*, or building component manufacturing yard. Wherever subdivisions take place an entrepreneur establishes such a yard and supplies the residents with concrete blocks, cement, aggregates and galvanized iron roofing sheets. He also gives technical guidance, and sometimes takes on the contract for partially constructing the house. In addition, he arranges to supply building materials on credit to the owner and sometimes cash credit as well. He relies on social pressure to recover his debts and becomes an important man of the new community. Once business becomes slack in a settlement, the *thalla* move to an area which is in the process of being developed.

In the same manner, other entrepreneurs cater to the needs of the settlement. Someone establishes an electricity generator and sells electricity to the residents. VCR halls are built where films are screened, and video football and caram clubs come into being. All this activity is strictly against state laws but it flourishes because of police protection.

The Government's Attitudes to ISDs and its Consequences

Reasons for government failure to control ISDs. The government has always expressed its resolve at containing the growth of ISDs and in demolishing the non-regularized ones. However, it has never really succeeded in doing so for a variety of reasons. The government administrative machinery is too weak to deal with the mafia involved in ISDs and the cost of controlling this form of development would be exceptionally high. In addition, government officials who are in charge of implementing policy decisions are actively involved in promoting ISDs. Also, ISDs effectively solve the housing problem faced by the city of Karachi, something the government cannot do as its development costs are far too high for the poor to afford. Therefore, this illegal system is convenient for the government. Again, by tolerating this form of development 'the state acts as an instrument of the capitalist class'.

The government's IRP [Improvement and Regularization Programme] and its consequences on ISDs. The government's IRP has had a major effect on the land and rent values of ISDs which have been marked for regularization. The prospect of regularization and development has converted these low income areas into potential middle income ones. Hence, there is already a movement of the poor out of these areas into new non-regularized ISDs. Again, as a large number of inner city colonies have not been marked for regularization, there is bound to be an exodus from them to the ISDs on the fringes of the city.

The April 7, 1986 announcement by the Prime Minister has made it possible for all *katchi abadis* established before March 23, 1983 to be regularized. The cut-off date before this announcement was January 1, 1978. This change in date is seen by the people and the subdividers as an acceptance of their political power and there is now a feeling that the demolition or prevention of further ISDs will just not be possible.

Organized Invasion

Organized invasion is a new phenomenon in Karachi. In this form of development, a number of households, mostly families living in rented houses, get together, select a piece of land, and then move into it and build their houses overnight. The occupation of the land is followed by litigation with the government authorities and the squatters usually manage to get a stay order, pending judgement, from a court of law. After this they invite other people to join them in the settlement, seeking security in numbers.

The main reasons for the development of organized invasions are: one, that the very poor living in rented houses cannot afford to continue to pay rent; two, that the cost of buying a piece of land in an ISD near to work has become far too high for the very poor to afford; and three, buying a plot in an ISD on the fringe means considerable expense on transportation to and from work. A study of a settlement

development through organized invasion reveals that 85 per cent of its residents previously lived in rented houses and wished to escape from paying rent, and 70 per cent of them had no fixed jobs. As compared to this, a study of three ISDs shows that 48 per cent of the residents lived previously in rented homes and only 5 per cent had moved to avoid paying rent. In addition, 69 per cent of them had fixed jobs.

A number of organized invasions attempted in the past three years have been successfully squashed by the government. As such, what new directions this form of development will take in the future remain to be seen.

Source: Hasan, Arif, *Seven Reports on Housing*, OPP-RTI, Karachi, 1992, pp. 24–30.

Appendix 16.4

The dallal as urban planner

In this extract, Arif Hasan shows how the *dallal* (or middleman) is the key in providing housing for the poor.

The *dallal* is the planner of the ISD settlements. He chooses the location for the settlement; locates the prospective buyers; establishes the relationships with the other actors so as make the project possible; conceptualizes the plan in his head and then physically implements it. Later on he struggles to get the settlement recognized, acquires services for it and often emerges as its leader. To do all this, he has to understand the social and economic aspects of his clients; maintain contacts with key persons in other settlements and *deras*; move around in government planning, development and administration offices; and to constantly update his knowledge regarding the 'market'. All this calls for exceptional skills.

The Choice of a Location

The Dallal Conceives Main Circulation Ways
The earlier subdivisions were near the main arteries of the city, whereas the newer ones are on major roads, or the continuation of these major roads taking off from the main arteries, that the *dallal* has established through his settlements. Often these roads are continued by other *dallals* through the new settlements that they establish. The direction of these roads is always towards some major government-built or proposed highway. For example, the road through the Yakoobabad settlement is supposed to continue till the RCD highway, which is about five miles away. All *dallals* working in the area are respecting this decision. Once the link with the RCD highway has been established, the value of land in the *abadis* on it will increase manifold and the land at the junction of the road and the RCD highway will become prime commercial property. It now belongs to a Balochi tribe.

ISD's Relation to Government Development Plans
The *dallals* keep in touch with KDA and other government plans for road and land development as this determines the areas in which a demand for housing or commercial activity

will be generated. For instance, all *dallals* in west Karachi are well acquainted with the proposals for a southern and a northern by-pass for Karachi and for the Port Qasim-Super Highway link road. Contacts with locals in possession of land in the area have already been established and so have contacts with relevant government agencies.

Physical Planning

The Plan Concept
The plan of the settlement is in the *dallal*'s head. He stands on high ground and decides the direction of his main road. In his head again, he sees the relationship of this settlement with other areas of Karachi. This makes him understand the nature of activity that may develop here in the future, in addition to residential activity. He has to cater to these possibilities and they decide certain road widths, plot sizes and the areas where plots for speculation have to be located. Sometimes, this is put down on a piece of paper in the form of a rough unscaled sketch. Some *dallals* have had plans made by their KDA collaborators in the town planning section, but complain that they were inappropriate for the 'market'. All planning, irrespective of contours, is usually on a grid iron.

Planning Criteria and Standards
The planning criteria and the standards developed by the *dallal* respond to what he terms as the 'market requirements'. He has no independent view on this issue. The standards that have emerged are:

a) *Plot sizes.* People, especially those moving from congested city settlement, prefer 120 square yard plots to 80 or 60 square yard ones and are willing to pay extra for them. The common dimensions of these plots are 30' x 36' or 27' x 40', with the smaller dimension facing the road. The squarer plot is preferred because in 30 feet one can build two rooms plus toilet facilities opening onto the street.

b) *Road widths.* Main roads, which are likely to house commercial or industrial activities in the future, are usually 50 feet wide. Those that are likely to link major KDA planned arteries are known to be over 100 feet wide. Link roads within the settlement are 30 feet wide while the lanes are 20 feet. If economics permit, then no more than 12 plots are put in the length of a lane. This is to increase the number of corner plots on which there is an initial premium of 25 per cent and a subsequent premium, after the houses have been built, of up to 100 per cent. Road widths of less than these standards are said to create a bad environment and plots in such settlements do not fetch a good price.

c) *Shop sizes*. Shop sizes are almost always 12' x 10'. On a 27 feet wide plot two shops of 10 feet frontage are possible, with space left over for a staircase to the floors above, and a passage to the ground floor flat at the back of the plot. In a 30 feet wide plot, two shops of 12 feet wide frontage are possible, with space left over for a staircase to the floor above and a passage to the back.

d) *Amenities*. The *dallal* provides no amenity plots except for a mosque. For this, he makes no charge and nor do the other actors receive any financial benefit from it. However, at a fairly early stage, residents do often take over some vacant land in the neighbourhood and use it as a playground. This space is fiercely protected by the residents, often with the help of the councillor. Many such spaces are over an acre in area, and when regularization takes place they are officially converted into parks and playgrounds.

Changes Over Time

All *dallals* feel that major changes have taken place in the 'market' over time, and this has led to changes in their planning. These changes are listed below.

a) When the first ISD settlements were created, the *dallals* did not fully understand the future relationship between these settlements, official planning proposals, and the other areas of Karachi. As such the potential of these settlements as future commercial areas and sub-markets was not understood nor catered to in their layouts. This is no longer the case.

b) As the *dallal* used to see the settlement in isolation from the rest of Karachi, he was unable to think of creating arteries and links between existing and/or proposed KDA communication networks. Nor did he have the confidence of interfering in or effecting change in official planning. This is no longer the case.

c) In the earlier stages the *dallal* tried to carve out as many plots as possible from a given piece of land. However, when the leasing process began it was noticed that regularization was easier if the plan corresponded to KDA regulations. This created a premium on land developed according to local body by-laws. Thus, regulations were followed as far as possible. Now, however, the *dallal* responds to the market and the market needs a pleasant open environment, wide roads, not too long lanes and lots of corner plots.

d) Until recently, the *dallal* used only a measuring tape and stones for laying out the settlement. Today, he uses string and chalk as well, and feels that a surveyor would lay a more accurate rectangle than him. However, the cost of hiring such a surveyor would either cut into his profits or increase the price of the plots. The former option is unacceptable to him and the latter to his clients. The drawing up of plans is seldom done for this reason. His *shahgirds* assist him in laying out the settlements. In Karachi, there are now three generations of *dallals*.

Source: Hasan, Arif, *Seven Reports on Housing*, OPP-RTI, Karachi, 1992, pp. 67–70.

Notes

1. World Bank, *World Development Report, 1995*, Oxford University Press, Washington, 1995(a), p. 163.
2. Ibid.
3. UNDP, *Human Development Report, 1995*, Oxford University Press, New York, 1995, p. 12.
4. Ibid.
5. Ibid., pp. 155–7.
6. World Bank, op. cit., 1995(a), p. 240.
7. For a comprehensive analysis of the health sector in Pakistan, see Zaidi, S. Akbar, *The Political Economy of Health Care in Pakistan*, Vanguard, Lahore, 1988.
8. See Zaidi, S. Akbar, op. cit., 1988, especially chapter 1, from where this section is drawn.
9. Banerji, D., 'Social and Cultural Foundations of Health Services Systems', *Economic and Political Weekly*, vol. 9, 1974, p. 1333.
10. Ibid., p. 1334.
11. Ibid.
12. The data for Table 16.7 are from 1985. Although outdated, they do show a trend that still continues.
13. World Bank, *Pakistan: Health Sector Report*, Washington, 1983.
14. Government of Pakistan, Planning Commission, *Pakistan Country Paper: World Summit for Social Development*, 1995, p. 30.
15. Ahmed, Viqar and Rashid Amjad, *The Management of Pakistan's Economy, 1947–82*, Oxford University Press, Karachi, 1984, p. 33.
16. Social Policy and Development Centre, *User Charges in Education*, Karachi, 1994, p. 12.
17. Ibid.
18. Ibid., p. 14.
19. Ibid.
20. Behrman, J.R., 'Pakistan: Human Resource Development and Economic Growth into the Next Century', mimeo, 1995, pp. 8–9.
21. Ibid., p. 8.
22. Ibid., p. 13.
23. Ahmed, Viqar and Rashid Amjad, op. cit., 1984, p. 34.
24. UNDP, op. cit., 1995, p. 221.
25. Government of Pakistan, op. cit., 1995, p. 32.
26. World Bank, *Staff Appraisal Report: Pakistan Population Welfare Program Project*, Report No. 13611-Pak, 1995(b), p. 11.
27. Ibid.
28. Banuri, Tariq, *et al.*, 'Human Resource Development', in Banuri, Tariq (ed.), *Just Adjustment: Protecting the Vulnerable and Promoting Growth*, UNICEF, Islamabad, 1992, p. 44.
29. World Bank, op. cit., 1995(b), p. 11.

30. Ibid.
31. Ibid., p. 12.
32. Ibid., p. 14.
33. Ibid., p. 11.
34. Ibid., p. 8.
35. Ibid., emphasis added.
36. Ibid., p. 9.
37. National Institute of Population Studies, *Pakistan Demography and Health Survey 1990/1991*, Islamabad, 1992, p. 56.

38. World Bank, op. cit., 1995(b), p. 9.
39. Ibid., p. 14.
40. Asian Development Report, *Pakistan Urban Sector Profile, 1993*, Manila, 1993, p. 8.
41. Ibid., p. 9.
42. Hasan, Arif, *Seven Reports on Housing*, OPP-RTI, Karachi, 1992.
43. Ibid., p. 183.
44. Ibid., p. 24.
45. Ibid., p. 70.
46. Ibid., p. 75.

17

The Social Sector II

This chapter continues the discussion on the social sectors initiated in Chapter 16. We looked there at what are considered to be the more traditional components of the social sector: education, health, and population welfare. Here we examine the development and role of some non-traditional aspects of the social sector, such as poverty and the environment. Chapter 18 examines issues of deliverability, and management, and other issues related to a more macro perspective on the social sector.

17.1 Gender Inequality and Women

Strictly speaking, women do not constitute part of the social sector, for if they did, so should the other gender, men. However, it has become convention – a convention established by men, no doubt – that women be relegated to the softer, social sector. One never finds a chapter on men, for it is assumed that it is they who constitute the real economy, working in construction or industry, while women are left to do the more menial chores, such as looking after the home and children. Essentially, their non-remunerative role distinguishes them from men, a classification which seriously undermines their role in the economy. While in underdeveloped societies this patriarchal dominance and male bias can more readily be understood, even in the developed western societies, women are considered less than equal to men. Moreover, while western developed societies and aid agencies have only recently discovered the role of women-in-development (WID), little do they know that in underdeveloped countries, women are never 'outside' development, for their very existence and survival, and that of their family and often of the entire country, depends very much on their being 'in' development. This section will try to show the discrepancies between Pakistani men and women using social sector statistics, and will look at how the role of women has been changing over the years (see also Appendix 17.1).

17.1.1 Statistics

A 1989 World Bank report on women in Pakistan argues that 'a major obstacle to Pakistan's transformation into a dynamic, middle income economy is underdevelopment in its people, particularly women ... Increasing opportunities for women will be essential to improve economic performance,

promote equity, and slow Pakistan's rapid population growth,'[1] Giovanni Cornia, agreeing with this general statement, elaborates on it a little further:

> To a very large extent the unsatisfactory social and economic development record in Pakistan depends on the low status of women in society, on their low level of literacy, on their restricted access to basic services, and on a pervasive gender bias in the access to economic resources which is the source of a severe intra-sex and intra-household income inequality. Women are married at an early age, have shorter lives, work longer hours, remain mostly illiterate, and have minimal opportunities for schooling, training and gainful employment. Their low/secondary status precludes any significant decision-making even in fertility control.[2]

Tables 17.1 and 17.2 highlight the problem and reinforce the evidence that 'on virtually every socio-economic indicator, Pakistani women fare worse than their South Asian counterparts and worse than women in other low income countries'.[3] The following observations can be made about the status of women in Pakistan.[4]

1 Pakistan has the lowest sex ratio in the world: in 1985 there were 91 women for every 100 men, down from 93 in 1965.

2 Life expectancy at birth for women has only just risen above that for men; until 1989, Pakistan was one of only four countries in the world where men lived longer than women.

3 Primary school enrolment rates for girls are among the ten lowest in the world.

4 While the incidence of ill-health and premature death among the poor of both sexes is very high in Pakistan, women and girls are worst affected.

5 Pakistan's maternal mortality rate is the highest in South Asia and greater than that in other Muslim countries, essentially due to birth-related problems. This is compounded by the very high prevalence of babies with low birth-weight – only three countries in the world have a higher percentage of such babies than Pakistan.

6 Only 13 per cent of the labour force is constituted of women, substantially below the 36 per cent average for all low-income countries.

Table 17.1
Male–female disparities in health, education, and work

	Females as % of males
Population	
0–4 years	103
0–14 years	94
15–49 years	91
50–59 years	83
60 years and above	73
Desire for more children	32
Health	
Infant mortality	84
Child mortality, 1–4 years	166
Under-5 mortality	98
Under-5 malnutrition	98
Under-5 full immunization	80
Life expectancy	99
Education	
Literacy	56
Primary school enrolment	57
Secondary school enrolment	43
Work	
Labour force	–
Administrators and managers	2
Professional and related workers	18

Source: Government of Pakistan, Planning Commission, *Pakistan Country Paper: World Summit for Social Development*, Karachi, 1995, p. 24.

17.1.2 Some Issues[5]

The social and economic benefits of educating girls and women are very significant, and there is a plethora of evidence that supports this finding.[6] Mothers' education favourably impacts on children; educated mothers increase the effectiveness of public health services and substitute for them when they are not available. There are higher survival rates amongst children of educated mothers, and such children are better nourished and often better educated as well. Moreover, educated women want to have fewer children and are more likely to use contraceptives than uneducated women.[7] The cliché that if you educate a woman, you educate not just her family but the entire nation is indeed very true.

There are supply and demand factors why female education is low in underdeveloped countries and Pakistan is no exception. The 'prevailing culture which values women's reproductive capacities much more than their productive ones, inhibits investments in education'.[8] Early marriages, lack of opportunity for women in the labour force, segregation between the sexes, and travelling long distances to schools also hamper girls' education. Moreover, girls provide critical household help in assisting mothers in childcare, cooking, and fetching water and fuelwood, and hence the opportunity cost of going to school may at times be very high.

Despite these numerous constraints on demand for education amongst girls and women, it is clear that much has been changing in Pakistan and that, due to greater urbanization and modernization, demand for education is growing. Incomes have gone up, and with higher incomes, the desire and affordability of education, even for girls, rises. There is a perceived need to educate girls, as it is recognized, especially in urban areas, that there are financial returns to education. Not only can educated girls get a job and supplement the household's income, but the family realizes that educated girls fetch better suitors, and hence can marry into a better social class. In addition, better transport and communications have made it easier for girls to go to school, and mass media campaigns have also been helpful. Stereotypes on television, which is now widely viewed even across remote areas, show girls and women as educated. Traditional values and mores have also undergone considerable change, and female seclusion, while still practised, has decreased.

While demand may have increased, supply constraints have adversely affected female education. The World Bank study correctly identifies a key cause of low female literacy and education: 'a shortage of female teachers is the single most important constraint to raising enrollments at the

Table 17.2
School enrolment ratios in Pakistan, 1960–1985

	1960	1965	1970	1975	1976	1980	1985
Primary							
Total primary	30	40	40	46	51	52	47
Female	13	20	22	28	30	30	32
Male	47	59	58	64	71	73	61
Secondary							
Total secondary	11	12	13	15	16	15	17
Female	3	5	5	7	8	8	9
Male	19	18	21	23	24	22	24

Source: World Bank, *Women in Pakistan: An Economic and Social Strategy*, Washington, 1989, pp. xv–xvii.

primary level, especially in rural areas. Apart from the low public expenditure which has created a shortage of girls schools and female teachers, hiring and retaining female teachers in rural areas is difficult.'[9] While there has been greater emphasis in recent years on girls' education, essentially due to the Social Action Programme (see Chapter 18), the situation is still far from satisfactory.

In the cause of health care, high fertility rates and closely spaced and frequent pregnancies are the most serious cause of high maternal mortality and morbidity. Furthermore, according to the World Bank report on Pakistani women,

> these are compounded by inadequate nutrition (especially during pregnancy and breast feeding), lack of clean water and sanitation facilities, women's economic and domestic workload and the health care system's inability to meet women's health needs. Poverty and *purdah* prevent many women from getting access to the few health facilities that cater to them. Cultural norms often prevent consultation with male doctors and health staff when female staff are not available, which further compounds problems.[10]

Since educating women has beneficial effects on the household, by training and educating women about basic health and medical issues, the rest of the family, particularly children, benefit. Better hygiene, sanitation, and nutritional practices may emerge if women are taught about basic diseases – by any means a very cost effective method of reducing health problems.

17.1.3 Finding Some Options

Although Appendix 17.1 provides a very different (in fact, radical) examination of the causes and implications of discrimination against women, some standard suggestions that may help on the margin can also be made. In terms of involvement in unremunerated work, paid employment, education, and in numerous other ways, the key to well-being rests on the development of the potential of women, as part of the family and as individuals. While there have been attempts at affirmative action to redress the balance in the past, much has been left wanting. Indeed, one of the reasons why social development has been poor is the lack of development specific to women.

The recent attempt on the part of the government to inform men and women about the rights of women is a very positive first step towards empowering women. Publicity campaigns about domestic violence and the rights of women, and on gender discrimination, along with measures such as the initiation of separate police stations for women, will help not only in building awareness, but also in rectifying injustices. Other programmes, such as the Prime Minister's programme of employment for women, especially in the health and education sectors, are welcome developments. Moreover, continued legislation to eliminate social injustices towards women, and to enhance their status, should be encouraged.

In rural areas, women do not have many independent opportunities to find paid work, and their role revolves around doing unpaid work for the family. This includes tending to livestock, getting wood for fuel, collecting water, working on the agricultural land, and a host of other economic and household-related activities. However, experiences from rural areas as diverse as those in Bangladesh and the northern areas of Pakistan have shown that, given the right opportunities and incentives, women can set up income-earning projects and supplement the family's income. Moreover, this small step of independence will become a big step towards empowerment and emancipation.

A critical factor in promoting enterprise by women is the availability of credit. In rural areas, women avail of credit to buy livestock or poultry, which often produce a small marketable surplus. In urban areas, the use of credit by women is more diverse, as the money can be used to develop home schools or some other sort of small enterprise based in the home. So far, most of the credit available to women to set up small-scale projects has came from non-governmental organizations (NGOs) or from international donors, while the government has not been an active player in this area. It is necessary to focus on means by which credit can be made readily available to women in rural and urban areas. Different mechanisms for delivery and accountability can be developed to ensure repayment. NGOs and the government can work closely together to achieve these goals. In order to expand the outreach of credit availability, the First Women's Bank should expand and enlarge its branches across the nation. Moreover, attempts should be made to develop a system of Mobile Field Officers, who can provide credit to women who are unable to come to the larger cities.

One of the most consistent and least controversial findings from the social sciences relates to the huge benefits that accrue from female education and literacy. No efforts should be spared in developing opportunities and facilities that help in promoting these aims. While school-going girls can acquire some formal literacy and education, an older generation has not been able to make use of the recently expanding opportunities to acquire formal education. Here, local, community-based organizations can fulfil an important role and teach the non-school-going female population basic education, nutrition, and health skills, by setting up classes at a mohalla level for women who stay at, or near, their homes. Nevertheless, one must emphasize the fact that the issues of discrimination which confront women in all spheres of the economy are based on structural, historical, and ingrained factors in society. One cannot achieve much success, no matter how well intentioned, unless the structural causes of discrimination are addressed (see Appendix 17.1).

17.2 Infrastructure

If the inclusion of women in this chapter on the social sector seems a little out of place, then this section on infrastructure, likewise, does not seem to belong. It is included here mainly because most of the areas covered in this chapter and the previous one are strongly influenced by the government's planning machinery. Until very recently, almost all infrastructure investment and development in Pakistan was government built, operated, and owned. Now, with the new pro-private sector policies, the emphasis has shifted on to initiatives from the private sector. We will concentrate here on the power sector, mainly because recent attempts by the government to woo foreign private investors have resulted in highly attractive policies for the private power sector. With the possibility of some, if not many, power plants coming on line, there has been considerable debate about the government's power policy and its possible effects on the social structure and the environment.

The provision of an extensive and adequate infrastructural network is a prerequisite for sustainable economic development. It is unlikely that a country can progress unless it is able to deal with the demand for, and provision of, electric power, telecommunications, roads, railways, ports, and other forms of transport. Infrastructure of both adequate quantity and appropriate quality is required to lay the foundations for fast-paced growth. The lack of infrastructure acts as a major hurdle to further growth.

A descriptive account of the essential components of infrastructure in Pakistan will help to highlight their status: only 40 per cent of all households have access to electricity, a figure much lower than in India (60), Nigeria (85), and Nicaragua (45), all of which have lower GNP per capita. The per capita consumption of electricity in Pakistan is only 392 kWh, compared to 550 in China, 825 in Thailand, 1,373 in Malaysia, and 2,761 in Korea.[11] One reason for these low per capita ratios is the very high system losses between electricity production and use: in Pakistan, the power system incurs a loss of at least 30 per cent, which is much higher than comparable countries. As in power, so in telecommunications. With 8 phones per 1,000, Pakistan fairs only marginally better than other underdeveloped countries. However, with 120 faults per 100 phone lines, Pakistan's telephone system has one of the highest fault rates in the world.[12]

Compared to other underdeveloped countries, Pakistan's road density of 229 km per million persons is very low, and even countries with half Pakistan's GNP per capita, have a greater density. With 165,000 km of roads, Pakistan's density of 0.21 km per sq. km is much lower than the 0.51 km suggested for underdeveloped countries. Moreover, only 18 per cent of paved roads are said to be in good condition, again, a very poor figure by any standard.

Having accepted the fact that Pakistan's infrastructure is in particularly poor state, the government has launched an ambitious policy package for the three most important ingredients of the infrastructure network: power, telecommunications, and roads. While specific policy statements have been spelt out for each of the three sectors, they form part of the pro-private sector deregulation, liberalization, and privatization policy prevalent in Pakistan today. While infrastructure has historically been in the domain of the public sector, towards the end of the twentieth century there is a growing belief that public enterprises have proven to be inefficient, corrupt, and costly. The balance has tilted towards the private sector in the hope that it can deliver

quality products. For the first time in most developing countries, private sector participation is being actively sought in infrastructure-related activities, such as power, telephones, and even roads. Public sector enterprises are being denationalized, and public–private participation is being encouraged.

The Eighth Five-Year Plan gives substantial emphasis to the need to develop the road network, and is directed at upgrading the existing network with a view to utilizing the system for speedy economic growth. The priorities of the Eighth Plan focus on improvement and maintenance of the existing road network to prevent deterioration, and on building new roads so as to extend coverage to isolated and far flung areas. The Eighth Plan also hopes to see the completion of the Lahore–Islamabad motorway. The government believes that all new and renovated highways that will offer improved services should levy tolls on the users which can then be used for their maintenance. Policies that attract private investment in the highways sector focus on the Build Operate and Transfer types of investment.

The privatization of the Pakistan Telecommunication Corporation (PTC), undertaken by the government in 1995, has brought mixed reactions: many detractors believe that a national asset has been sold at throw-away prices, while the government maintains that it has been able to raise revenue of $1 billion which will help satisfy its dire need for cash. The international placement, which accounted for $900 million of that amount, was the largest ever equity offer in Asia outside Japan. PTC was valued at a market capitalization of $9 billion, which made it nominally South Asia's largest company (see also Box 8.3 and Chapter 8).

17.2.1 The Power Sector

The total installed capacity in the power sector is approximately 11,000 MW, which is insufficient to meet demand on a year-round basis. In addition, a shortfall of 2,000 MW exists during peak hours due to low river flows at different times in the year. Although a policy for setting up private sector BOO (Build-Own-Operate) power plants has been in effect in Pakistan since 1986, the pace of progress has remained slow. Major factors that have discouraged prospective investors include the following:

1 There were protracted and detailed negotiations on technical and financial aspects of the projects leading to Power Purchase and Implementation Agreements, based on 18 per cent internal rate of return on equity.

2 The sale price of electricity was not internationally competitive.

3 There was a lack of clarity about facilities and concessions available to investors in private power plants.

4 The regime of import charges was often subject to misinterpretation, and at the same time required the potential investor to arrange large sums of money upfront to meet the demands of custom duties and other taxes.

There is a projected annual increase in demand of 8 per cent per annum for the next twenty-five years, which means that approximately 50,000 MW will be needed by the year

2018. To meet this demand, the government has offered lucrative incentives to the private, particularly foreign, sector in the production of electricity and the exploration of oil and gas. The main characteristics of the package to attract foreign investors are: internationally competitive terms, reduction in local currency investment requirements, simplification of procedures, and steps to create and encourage a domestic corporate debt securities market.

The financial incentives given to companies include the following:

1 The private power companies are exempt from corporate income tax.

2 The companies are allowed to import plant and equipment without payment of customs duties, sales tax, Iqra, flood relief, and other surcharges, as well as the import licence fee.

3 The companies have been allowed to register anywhere in Pakistan to avail of the reduction in stamp tax and registration fee for registration of loan documents by the federal government.

4 Repatriation of equity along with dividends is allowed freely.

5 There is exemption from income tax in Pakistan for foreign lenders to such companies.

6 Although the government of Pakistan encourages participation of local investors in the power sector, it is not mandatory, and foreign companies/investors are free to set up projects without local partners.

7 The companies can obtain foreign exchange risk insurance (FERI) on standard terms from the State Bank on the foreign currency loans contracted by them. The current premium rates of FERI are included in the bulk tariff, but any change in FERI will be considered as a 'pass-through' item.

8 The companies have been exempted from the requirements for obtaining insurance only from the National Insurance Corporation (NIC) under the NIC Act of 1976, if they are funded by multilateral lending agencies such as the World Bank and ADB. Now private power companies can get insurance as per the requirements of lenders and utilities.

9 Power generation has been declared an industry, and the companies are eligible for all other concessions that are available to industrial projects.

10 The private parties may raise local and foreign finance in accordance with regulations applicable to industry in general.

11 For local engineering and manufacturing companies, the present Statutory Revisionary Order (SRO) 555(1)/90 has been made applicable to private power plants.

12 Orders received by local engineering and manufacturing companies from private power companies will be treated as an export for refinance under the State Bank of Pakistan Finance Scheme for exports.

The response to the government's power policy has been unprecedented for underdeveloped countries, and foreign investors have shown keen interest (see Table 17.3). Over 300 parties have registered themselves for setting up private power projects, while 91 have submitted proposals. Performance guarantees by 25 projects have been filed to produce 6,500 MW. The Sindh Local Board has signed memoranda of understanding with a number of organizations which would be interested in integrated projects of coal mining and coal-based power generation. In all, about $12 billion worth of projects seem to be in the pipeline. In addition to the projects to attract *new* private sector investment, the government has taken measures to increase the pace of restructuring and privatization of public sector enterprises in the power and gas sectors. However, there are serious objections to the government's enthusiasm over the power sector, which has given rise to grave economic and environmental fears (see Box 17.1 and Appendix 17.2).

17.3 The Environment[13]

While Pakistan's population is a little over 2 per cent of the entire world's population, its energy consumption is a mere 0.29 per cent, i.e. less than even half of one per cent. This is not a surprising statistic, as much of the energy consumption takes place in the developed western nations of the globe, and while the majority of the population lives in underdeveloped countries, it is the minority, developed countries, that consume much more energy. The low-income countries use energy of about 353 kg (oil equivalent) per capita, while the corresponding figure for high-income economies is 5,245 kg per capita. Pakistan's energy use of 209 kg per capita is well below the low-income country average, and lower than that for India (242). While Pakistan's energy use is lower than that of comparable countries, its average annual growth rate of 6.8 per cent between 1980 and 1993 is higher than the average for low-income economies (5.4 per cent growth), and amongst the highest for this category.[14]

Table 17.4 shows that Pakistan's energy consumption per capita of 7.42 gigajoules is about one-eighth as much energy as is used globally per capita. Each Pakistani contributes 0.1 tonnes of carbon to the atmosphere, which is about one-twentieth of the per capita average contribution globally. Carbon monoxide emissions per capita are one-third of the global average, with the entire country providing less than 1 per cent of the globe's share.

Pakistan's deforestation is a minuscule proportion of the deforestation taking place at a global level, and the rate at which it is taking place in Pakistan is much slower than the world rate of deforestation (see also Box 17.2). The rate of loss of tropical forests is one-third as rapid as the global rate. Similarly, the loss of topsoil is also far slower than the world average. The IUCN report, in its evaluation of Pakistan's contribution to environmental problems, argues that 'it is clear that Pakistan is neither a major global polluter nor a large consumer of resources. In fact, it has a considerable unutilized quota of both the productive and assimilative

Table 17.3
Prospective power projects to be built in Pakistan

Project	Partners	Size	Fuel	Value ($m)
AES Lal Pir	AES	360 MW	Oil fired	350
AES Sidnai	AES	360 MW	Oil fired	350
Agrilectric	Agrilectric Power (US)	2 x 5 MW	Pilot project biomass from rice hulks	10
Armstrong	Greaves Cotton (Pak) and Armstrong (US)		Steam traps for industrial steam efficiency	1
Badin-II	Government of Pakistan and Union Taxes (US)		Oil and gas exploration and production licence	175
Chenab River	Enron Bechtel and GE Capital	760 MW	Natural gas combined cycle	740
Jamshoro	Sepco (Pak), Intrag (US), and Scepter (US)	310 MW	Natural gas combined cycle	174
Kabirwala	Fauji (Pak), Intrag (US), and Scepter (US)	144 MW	Low Btu natural gas combined cycle	175
Quetta	Habibullah Energy Ltd (Pak), Ogden Power Systems (US), and GE (US)	104 MW	Natural gas combined cycle	105
Ratana	Government of Pakistan and Occidental Petroleum (US)		Gas and pet. dev. and production lease	100
SUI Northern	SUI Northern Gas Pipeline (Pak) and Solar Turbines		High-efficiency gas compressor stations	7
Power Gencorp	Power Gencorp Ltd (Pak), Synergics Energy Dev. Inc. (US), and ENTECH (US)	75 MW	Hydro-power at three sites (Synergics)	150
			Solar power projects (ENTECH)	40
Uch	Tenaska, Energy GE Capital, and GE Capital (all US)	585	Low Btu natural gas combined cycle	660
Wakgas	WAK (Pvt) Ltd (Pak), Orient Point, and Caterpillar (US)	800 MW (16 x 50 MW)	Barge mounted, diesel fired	800
Thar	Hangpak United Power Generation (Pvt) Ltd. A joint venture of American United Machinery Corporation, USA, and Tunson Development Ltd, Hong Kong	1320 MW	Coal mined in Sindh	1700
Lakhra, Dadu	BBI Power Incorporated USA	200 MW	Coal mined in Sindh	200
Sonda, Thatta	Sindh Coal Electric Power Co. and the Leesburg Financial Group	100 MW	Coal mined in Sindh	100

capacities of global systems, insofar as such utilization is sustainable.'[15]

Table 17.5 and Figure 17.1 show the distribution of Pakistan's nine land capability classes. Cultivable land of different grades capable of growing crops (classes I–IV) constitute only 21 per cent of total area; about a quarter of the available land is considered to be of 'very good' quality, while poor quality available land, fit for a few crops only, constitutes about 15 per cent. Good-quality forests and farmland are a minuscule proportion of all the land in Pakistan. Class VIII is 'not capable of growing trees, shrubs or grasses either because of a total absence of soils or because the soils that do exist cannot support productive plant growth'.[16]

Overall, agricultural land that is being used in Pakistan is being used at below its productive capacity, resulting in less than potential output. The factors that affect land productivity include water erosion, wind erosion, salinity/sodicity, waterlogging, flooding, and loss of organic matter. The greatest effect is by water erosion (17 per cent) followed by salinity (8.6) and wind erosion (7.6 per cent).

In the industrial sector, air and water pollution result from industrial processes, and with extensive urban growth resulting in an increase in mechanized vehicles, pollution levels in cities have reached critical levels, especially in the more industrialized sectors of urban areas. To these environmental effects of industrialization one can add the extent of 'encroachment by industrial units on farmland and on the habitats of various plants and animal life'.[17] A survey that examined industrial waste pollution in Karachi, Multan, Faisalabad, Nowshera, and Peshawar found that a number of industries were 'discharging effluents with high concentrations of pollutants varying from toxic metals and metal salts to bacteria, acids and salts'.[18] In Karachi, contaminated and heated sea water is sent back into the creek after industrial use, affecting sea life and the marine ecological balance. Contamination by petroleum hydrocarbon residues, chlorinated hydrocarbons, is also common on the

Table 17.4
Resource base and degradation, world and Pakistan, late 1980s

Resource	World	Pakistan	Pakistan's share of global (%)	Ratio of Pakistan to global
Land area (million hectares)	13,079	88.2	0.67	–
Population (millions)	51,624	109.7	2.12	–
Population density, 1989 (per 1000 hectares)	389	1,541	–	4
Projected population increase, 1990–2000 (millions)	1,000	40	4	–
GNP per capita, 1987 (US$)	3,100	350		1/9
Energy consumption (petajoules)	282,924	814	0.29	
Energy per capita (gigajoules/capita)	55	7.42		2/15
Increase in atmospheric concentrations of greenhouse gases (million tonnes of carbon)	5,900	15	0.25	
Per capita addition to CO_2 flux (tonnes)	1.7	0.1	–	1/7
Carbon monoxide emissions (million tonnes/year)	193.5	1.53	0.79	1/3
Per capita	0.037	0.013		
SO_2 emissions (million tonnes/year)	155	0.632	0.4	1/5
Per capita	0.03	0.0058		1/5
Per capita additions to methane flux (tonnes)	0.05	0.03	–	2/3
CFC production per capita, 1986 (kilograms)	0.2	0	–	–
Forest area (million hectares)	4,081.50	4.58	0.11	
Deforestation (hectares/year)	20 million	7,000–9,000	0.082	
Annual rate of deforestation (%)	0.48	0.15–0.197		1/3
Topsoil loss (million tonnes)	26,000	47	0.181	
Soil loss (tonnes/hectares)	1.988	0.53		1/4
Crop land (million hectares)	1.475	20.4	1.4	
Expenditure on pesticides (US$m/year)	18,500	100	0.54	–
Annual pesticide expenditure per hectare crop land (US$/hectare)	12.54	4.9	–	2/5
Average annual marine catch (thousand tonnes)	–	78,955.2	333.7	0.42
Per capita annual catch (kilograms/capita/year)	14	2.8	–	1/5

Source: IUCN, *The Pakistan National Conservation Strategy*, Karachi, 1992, pp. 10–11.

sea coast in Karachi. Along with industrial emissions, pollution from automobiles is also a major and growing problem in cities (see Box 17.2).

Unlike many other countries, in Pakistan environmental degradation and excessive rural and urban pollution are not yet a critically serious problem. While the trend is one of substantially increasing energy consumption, the negative impact on the environment is selective. Deforestation is destroying parts of the Potohar region where timber is being cut at a far faster rate than new trees are being planted.

Salinity in much of Sindh is destroying potentially good-quality agricultural land, and is also affecting rural housing. Both deforestation and salinity are, and will continue to be, a serious potential threat to the rural sector. Industrial waste and emissions and pollution from cars and other vehicles in cities will exacerbate the problem, especially since urban growth is going to continue and industrial and manufacturing output is likely to expand.

In 1992 the government of Pakistan adopted the National Conservation Strategy as an official policy document. The

BOX 17.1

The costs of the energy policy

In January 1995, when the government's policy of attracting foreign investment for its energy and power programme was at its height, four non-governmental organizations, the Human Rights Commission of Pakistan, Shehri, Sungi Development Foundation, and the Sustainable Development Policy Institute, came out with a full-page advertisement in the national press, warning people about the possible consequences of the government's policy.

1 By 1997, an estimated 16 power plants generating 7,260 mega watts sanctioned by the Government of Pakistan will be functioning in the Karachi region and its coastal waters. Experts fear that these plants constitute the single most significant threat, posed to the environment and habitat of any South Asian city by a government in this century.

2 Why are 13 new plants being located in Karachi? Does the city need the extra power? No. Karachi will continue to generate more electricity than its needs. Breakdowns in the metropolis are largely attributable to a faulty transmission system. The truth is that more than three fourths of the extra mega watts generated will be transmitted upcountry to WAPDA's customers in other provinces. Karachi's abundant sea water, due to the absence of effective regulation, constitutes a cheap and pollutable input in the running of power plants. Whilst transport costs are thus reduced to increase power profits, the cost to the health of Karachi's citizens is ignored – or even more conveniently, forgotten.

3 Can the major pollutants that threaten Karachi be estimated? A leading pollutant from thermal power plants are the noxious gases and chemicals emitted, especially deadly sulphur oxides. At present, between the three existing KESC power plants, refineries, cement plant, steel mill, factories, trains, ships and aircraft – not to mention 830,000 registered automobiles in the city of Karachi – a total of 1,500 tons of sulphur oxides and other pollutants are being hurled daily into Karachi's atmosphere. By 1997, the emissions from the sanctioned thermal power plants will add on an incredible estimated 2,300 tons of deadly sulphur oxides making a grand daily total 3,800 tons of corrosive chemicals. To eventually pour down upon the citizens of Karachi in the form of acid rain.

4 Can Karachi's ecosystem absorb these new levels of emission? Not exactly, 3,800 tons of toxic sulphur oxides a day spread over 591 sq. km of Karachi and its suburbs, will play havoc with the welfare of 18,000 people residing on every sq. km of the city. An emission approximately equivalent to that from the entire Federal Republic of Germany – with an area 700 times that of Karachi, and a population density at only 3% of that of the city. Coupled with emissions of nitrogen oxides, the highly toxic carbon monoxide, various metals and hundreds of tons of ash, the city has been provided with a sure recipe for ecological disaster.

5 But that's not all. The rising prevalence of electromagnetic radiation through the proliferation of high tension wires; a marked increase in the noise level and ground vibrations; a warming of sea waters accompanied by sharply rising salt concentrations posing drastic implications for marine life and fisheries, the extinction of several species of flora and fauna in the coastal wetlands and mangroves; all this is forecast for Karachi at the turn of the century. With more fog, more smog. And, yet, more dirt.

6 The total degradation of Karachi's ecosystem – of its air and water – will lead to the destruction of life support systems. The increased incidence of respiratory, eye and skin diseases will presage a sharp rise in the prevalence of several types of cancer. The eventual displacement of offices and residences would imply population shifts, designed to exacerbate Karachi's ongoing urban crisis – with grim consequences.

7 Who can stop this madness? You can by taking a stand. By making your feelings known. And by being counted. By mobilizing both individuals and small support groups. By making your indignation at the fate of Karachi known to those in power. You can write to President Farooq Leghari or to Prime Minister Benazir Bhutto expressing your feelings. You can petition the Chief Minister of Sindh, Syed Abdullah Shah, highlighting the disastrous effects of the federation's energy plant location policy in the Karachi region. Or you can demand from Mr Asif Zardari, MNA and Chairman of the Environmental Protection Council, the restitution and enforcement of your environmental rights – rights that he has sworn to uphold and protect by virtue of the offices he occupies.

8 And what are these environmental rights? Put simply, your right to breathe clean air and access clean water. For yourself and your children. And their children. Do not let the mere promise of a few jobs barter away their right to a better future.

policy has three explicit objectives: (1) conservation of natural resources, (2) sustainable development, and (3) improved efficiency in the use and management of resources. Fourteen programme areas have been identified for priority treatment:

1 Maintaining soils in croplands.
2 Increasing irrigation efficiency.
3 Protecting watersheds.
4 Supporting forestry and plantations.
5 Restoring rangelands and improving livestock.
6 Protecting water bodies and sustaining fisheries.
7 Conserving biodiversity.
8 Increasing energy efficiency.
9 Developing and employing renewable resources.

Table 17.5
Land capability classifications

Land class		Soil limitations	Production potential
I	Very good agricultural land	None for general agriculture	Very high
II	Good agricultural land	Minor	High for general agriculture
III	Moderate agricultural land	Moderate	Moderate for general crops
IV	Poor (marginal) agricultural land	Severe	Low for a few crops only
V	Good forest or rangeland	None/minor for forestry/ rangeland	High for forestry/ range development
VI	Moderate forest or rangeland	Moderate	Moderate for forestry/range development
VII	Poor forest or rangeland	Severe	Low for forestry/ range development
VIII	Non-agricultural land	Severe	None for any type of economic agriculture

Source: IUCN, *The Pakistan National Conservation Strategy*, Karachi, 1992, p. 22.

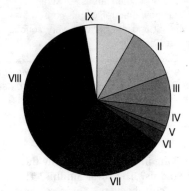

Land class	Land capability
I	Very good agricultural land
II	Good agricultural land
III	Moderate agricultural land
IV	Marginal agricultural land
V	Good forest or rangeland
VI	Moderate forest or rangeland
VII	Poor forest or rangeland
VIII	Non-agricultural land
IX	Unclassified

Total area: 61.82 million hectares

Figure 17.1
Land capability by classes

10 Preventing/abating pollution.

11 Managing urban wastes.

12 Supporting institutions for common resources.

13 Integrating population and environmental programmes.

14 Preserving the cultural heritage.

17.4 Regional Inequalities[19]

For a country that has 'lost' more than half its people, who have chosen to become independent on the grounds that they have been seriously discriminated against, we would suggest that economic, social, and political imbalances between regions are a serious issue. It is believed that the economic policies that favoured West Pakistan at the expense of East Pakistan resulted in the western wing of pre-1971 Pakistan developing at a much faster pace than the eastern half of the country. Economists and politicians in the 1960s argued that much of the development in West Pakistan was due to the extraction of surplus from East Pakistan, a surplus that benefited and was reinvested in the western half of Pakistan. East Pakistanis were discriminated against socially, economically, and politically, and hence were forced to express their rights of collective identity, leading towards greater autonomy and subsequently, after a cruel and bloody war, to independence.

Since the greater part of pre-1971 Pakistan broke away and became Bangladesh, there have been a number of political movements based on the perception that their unit (province), language, people, or nationality has been discriminated against. The consequence of this perception has been protest against the federal structure and federal government in various ways. In the early 1970s, some Baluch leaders fought a 'war of independence' against Islamabad under Bhutto. In the early 1980s, political parties from Sindh agitated against the dictatorship of General Zia-ul-Haq under the banner of the MRD (Movement for the Restoration of Democracy), a movement which eventually acquired a Sindhi nationalist colour. For much of the 1970s, the people of the NWFP, the Pakhtuns, were considered to be outside mainstream politics, with supposed designs of a Greater Pakhtunistan which included much of Afghanistan. Most recently, the late 1980s and early 1990s saw the emergence of possibly the worst and most brutal forms of protest and subsequent repression since the independence of East Pakistan: in Karachi, after the Mohajir Qaumi Movement (MQM) emerged demanding rights for the Urdu-speaking people of Sindh, mainly Karachi and Hyderabad.[20] Other than the Punjab, all major linguistic and ethnic groups have, at some time or other, protested against and confronted the federal structure.

With such a recent and continuing history of protest, which usually involves the loss of hundreds, possibly thousands, of lives, one cannot ignore the importance of regional, linguistic, and ethnic issues in Pakistan. We need to assess whether the fears of discrimination are indeed real or mere perception, or worse still, are issues created purely to gain political advantage. Political scientists and historians have their own

BOX 17.2

Environmental degradation

Arif Hasan and Ameneh Azam Ali look at the reasons for environmental degradation, the repercussions of deforestation, and industrial pollution.

The increase in the price of building timber is already adversely affecting the quality of housing in the country and the scarcity and cost of fuelwood is becoming a major economic burden on low-income communities. As a result, gas cylinders are in great demand, even in rural areas, as their monthly cost is less than half that of fuelwood.

One of the most visible, and perhaps the most significant, impacts of deforestation is soil erosion. The mountain regions where the majority of natural forests are located are characterized by steep slopes, fragile and thin topsoil, and unstable geological conditions. When tree cover is removed, there is nothing to stop the soil from being washed away by even mild rainfall. In addition, landslides and rockfalls, which occur frequently in spring as a result of melting snow and ice, are exacerbated by the absence of tree cover. Vast areas of the Karakorams and Hindu Kush are naturally arid and barren, and little can be done to prevent or control soil erosion in these areas. But the historically heavy silt load of the Indus, which flows through these mountains, is being augmented now by large quantities of valuable topsoil swept off the slopes of the foothills and lower mountains in the monsoon zone. This erosion has a dual impact on the environment: it leads to desertification of once-productive upland areas, and silting-up of waterways in the plains, making them more prone to flooding. In addition, there is increased silting-up of irrigation and hydro-electric systems, lowering their efficiency and shortening their lifespans. The building of roads is probably the single biggest factor contributing to rapid deforestation. Previously inaccessible mountain areas, like the Kohistan district of NWFP, have in the last twenty years been connected to the plains by major roads. Transportation facilities have made the logging of these rich and ancient natural forests a viable commercial proposition. The extreme poverty and hardship of life in these remote areas has meant that the local communities have seized this opportunity to earn a substantial income in a short space of time, by selling their trees to down-country contractors …

… Studies on Karachi have established that effluent from tanneries contains a higher pollution load of oil than the oil industry itself. In addition, it contains chromium and other toxic metal salts that are used in the tanning process, such as chlorides and sulphates of sodium and potassium. There is no on-site treatment of this effluent, not even the removal of suspended solids. The effluent from the cotton industry, though high in organic contents, is less noxious but does contain traces of chromium and copper. The cotton industries and tanneries are the most widespread industrial activity in Pakistan and are carried on through small, often informal units, in both the urban and rural areas …

… Apart from small industrial units which pollute water bodies, most cities also have larger formal sector units that do the same. In Multan, the Pak-Arab Fertilizer factory releases highly polluted waste into the Multan canal, a major irrigation and drinking water source for animals. The effluent of 235 industries in Faisalabad is carried untreated to the river by the main drain of the city. At Kala Shah Kaku industrial estate in Lahore, the industrial effluent is also carried untreated to the river Ravi through the Deg nullah …

… In addition to industrial emissions, a major source of pollution is from automobiles. Their number in Pakistan had increased from 575,558 in 1975 to over 1.654 million in 1984. Since then, it is estimated that they have increased overall by 30 per cent and are concentrated in about 8 major cities of the country. Studies carried out on traffic policemen working in the more polluted areas of Karachi and other studies on Lahore show that traffic emissions in these cities have become critical and are creating very serious health problems for the residents.

Source: Hasan, Arif and Ameneh Azam Ali, *Environmental Repercussions of Development in Pakistan*, OPP-RTI, Karachi, 1993, pp. 40–9.

way of looking at the evolution of specific societies, languages, and ethnic groups, while economists can perhaps identify economic factors that differentiate amongst regions. Economic factors are usually, if not always, the main cause of protest, and instigate the perception that a particular region, province, or people is consciously being discriminated against. Even if such claims are justified, there are very serious methodological issues in determining biases and imbalances.

The first issue concerns the size, composition, and extent (area) of the region or people who feel that there is economic and social imbalance against them. Does one choose a province, city, or collection of similar types of people? For example, if we were to agree that Sindh was being discriminated against, how would we determine who in Sindh was being discriminated against and to what extent? Is it all the people living in the province? Only those who speak Sindhi, i.e. the Sindhis? The rural Sindhis? The non-Sindhi rural settlers? The city dwellers? Some sections of the city dwellers, e.g. the Urdu-speaking mohajirs, or the migrant Seraikis? And if it is at all possible to isolate the area/region/group which claims that it is being discriminated against, how does one measure discrimination? Is it share of employment in government jobs with respect to share of population in the country? Is it lack of private sector investment in a certain area? Does greater contribution to the government's exchequer in the form of taxes, with lower return in the form of government expenditure, qualify as discrimination? How important is cultural indifference? Furthermore, even if we do isolate and distinguish a region or an ethnic group in order to examine the extent of perceived or real discrimination, another important question arises:

which social group in that ethnic group is discriminated against? How important are class and social differentiation? Is it the élite or the middle class demanding its 'national' rights, or the workers or peasants who want deliverance from discrimination and 'oppression' by a dominant national group? And what about exploitation by members of one's own community? Is that any better/different from 'national' exploitation? Clearly, the questions are endless.

Moreover, while some of the issues of identification highlighted above are difficult, even if we do isolate a region for the purposes of analysis, we are faced with a set of other problems. What do we select in identifying imbalances? Do we look at industrialization, income, schooling, the extent to which women are part of the labour force, or some or all of these indicators? There is an even more fundamental question: what constitutes development? Is development more income, or is it a non-material quality of life, as some observers feel? The attempt to compare countries in section 16.1 shows how difficult, and often contradictory, comparisons can be. Besides, looking at a set of indicators at any one point in time is quite meaningless, unless one considers trends over a period of time and examines where these unfolding trends are taking us. The *process* is the key to deciphering and understanding what development, absolute or relative, really is.

However, having set these rather high ideals for regional comparisons, in this chapter we will limit ourselves to some preliminary quantitative analysis which does not take sufficient cognizance of historical processes and phenomena.[21] We now present some of the more basic and conventional methods that attempt to compare districts, followed by some results that this methodology generates.

17.4.1 Methodology and Results

Table 17.6 has become a fairly standard table showing the 46 districts of Pakistan, ranked by five different and independent studies, using different criteria. The fact that when the first study was done in the 1960s there were 46 districts, while now there are more than 110, means that all attempts to interpret the table must be made with considerable caution. Add to this the problem that each of the studies uses different sets of indicators and different methodologies in composing its indices and rankings, and we have reason for even more caution.

Nevertheless, many 'results' shown in the table are probably intuitive in the first instance, and despite problems with methodology and choice of indicators, it is probable that Karachi would still top anyone's list as the most developed district, with the four provincial headquarters following behind. Moreover, large and dynamic cities like Faisalabad, Gujranwala, and Hyderabad would also have a high ranking. Not surprisingly, one would expect most of the districts of Baluchistan to be on the lower rungs of the development ranking ladder.

The third column of Table 17.6 is based on an evaluation by Hafiz Pasha and Tariq Hasan for the 1970s, while the fifth column uses similar indicators employed by Hafiz Pasha and his colleagues in the 1980s. Hence, despite our criticism

above, some intertemporal comparisons are possible. Those districts that the authors feel have shown dynamism in the 1980s compared to the 1970s are Dadu, Larkana, and Jacobabad, as well as Sanghar, Nawabshah, and Khairpur. The north-western districts of the Punjab, especially Rawalpindi, Cambellpur, Jhelum, and Gujrat, have improved their rank, as have Peshawar, Mardan, Hazara, and Kohat. The main feature of the two columns is the decline of the south of Punjab, where districts such as Multan, Muzaffargarh, Dera Ghazi Khan, Bahawalnagar and Rahim Yar Khan have all fallen over time. Baluchistan's backwardness continues unabated.

At a provincial level, the two studies by Hafiz Pasha and his colleagues show how the share of the populations have shifted over time. Table 17.7 indicates that in the 1980s, of the total percentage of the population in the top quartile by development level, 53.2 per cent was in the Punjab, 34.6 per cent in Sindh, 10.5 per cent in the NWFP, and only 1.8 per cent in Baluchistan. The comparison with the 1970s shows that the Punjab's share has increased significantly. The authors believe that 'while some of this change can be attributed to changes in district boundaries, it testified to the buoyancy in some of the larger cities of the Punjab and an enhancement, in particular, in the share of industrial value added'.[22] The reason for the dominance of the Punjab in the second quartile is the 'dynamism of the small-scale industrial sector in the province and the establishment of stronger urban–rural linkages'.[23] The significant jump of the NWFP in this category is due to the presence of Abbotabad, Mardan, and Kohat. In the bottom quartile there were 29 districts (of the 62 surveyed), 14 of which were in Baluchistan and 5 each in the three other provinces. However, the share of the Punjab in the lowest population quartile was close to 41 per cent, Sindh 23 per cent, NWFP 18 per cent and Baluchistan 18 per cent. For the authors of these two studies, this result indicates that 'even the relatively developed provinces like Sindh and Punjab have large underdeveloped pockets. Comparison with the shares in the early 1970s reveals that the share of Baluchistan [in the bottom quartile] has increased, while that of the other provinces has declined somewhat. This points to the possibility that the gap between Baluchistan and the rest of the country has widened even further.'[24]

Table 17.7 shows that in the 1970s, of all the population in Pakistan in the top quartile by level of development, 41.8 per cent was in the Punjab; similarly, while the next quartile was distributed between the NWFP and Punjab, almost all were in the latter province; likewise, Punjab contained 45.4 per cent of Pakistan's poor. Table 17.8 looks at the same data in a different manner. Here we see an even clearer result: as much as 91 per cent of Baluchistan's population was in the bottom quartile, while only 18 per cent of Punjab's population was in the bottom quartile. Similarly, while 41.8 per cent of the entire country's population in the top quartile was in the Punjab, this constituted only 18 per cent of the Punjab's population. What is more interesting is that, while the NWFP and the Rest of Sindh (i.e. the province of Sindh minus Karachi) have 27 and 21 per cent of their population in the relatively better districts, unlike the Punjab, both have only

Table 17.6
Comparative ranking of districts in Pakistan

	Infrastructure of social development (Heblock and Naqvi, 1960)	Infrastructure and production indices (Hamid and Hussain, 1970)	Infrastructure and social development (Pasha and Hasan, 1970s)	Infrastructure (Qutub, 1980s)	Infrastructure and social development (Pasha et. al., 1980s)
Punjab					
Lahore	2	2	2	4	2
Rawalpindi	4	3	3	2	3
Faisalabad	7	4	7	10	7
Multan	8	5	9	11	13
Jhelum	9	7	16	9	15
Rahimyar Khan	12	10	15	27	19
Gujrat	13	8	23	19	16
Gujranwala	14	9	8	15	8
Sargodha	16	16	20	14	23
Sahiwal	17	6	14	21	25
Bahawalnagar	18	17	28	30	30
Sheikhupura	21	12	12	6	21
Mianwali	23	20	34	25	33
Dera Ghazi Khan	25	21	35	35	36
Sialkot	26	11	10	12	12
Muzaffargarh	31	25	31	31	37
Jhang	33	26	24	23	28
Attock	27	22	33	13	32
Sindh					
Karachi	1	1	1	1	1
Hyderabad	6	15	6	7	4
Sanghar	10	15	18	32	10
Sukkur	19	18	21	8	9
Nawabshah	22	24	22	29	18
Jacobabad	24	37	37	38	35
Khairpur	28	23	26	33	22
Dadu	30	31	25	24	24
Larkana	32	27	27	20	17
Tharparkar	34	37	19	40	27
Thatta	37	32	30	39	31
NWFP					
Peshawar	3	13	5	5	5
Bannu	11	36	29	18	29
Mardan	15	14	13	26	11
Kohat	29	35	32	22	26
Dera Ismail Khan	35	33	11	16	20
Hazara	36	34	36	17	34
Baluchistan					
Quetta	5	30	4	3	6
Chagai	38	38	40	34	38
Kharan	39	46	44	45	45
Sibbi	40	42	41	37	40
Zhob	41	41	38	36	41
Kalat	42	44	43	42	43
Loralai	43	43	39	41	42
Mekran	44	45	42	44	46
Katchi	45	39	46	43	44
Lasbela	46	40	45	46	39

Sources: Kardar, Shahid, 'Polarization in the Regions and Prospects for Integration', in Zaidi, S. Akbar, *Regional Imbalances and the National Question in Pakistan,* Vanguard, Lahore, 1992, pp. 322–3; Pasha, Hafiz A., *et. al.*, 'The Changing Profile of Regional Development in Pakistan', *Pakistan Journal of Applied Economics*, vol. 9, no. 1, 1990, p. 21.

Table 17.7
Share of provinces in population quartiles by level of development (%)

	Punjab	Sindh	NWFP	Baluchistan
Early 1980s				
Top quartile	53.2	34.6	10.5	1.8
Second quartile	76.6	5.5	17.2	0.7
Third quartile	62.1	29.7	8.3	0
Bottom quartile	40.8	22.6	18.1	18.4
Total	56.1	22.6	13.1	5.1
Early 1970s				
Top quartile	41.8	42.1	12.4	3.6
Second quartile	96.8	0	3.2	0
Third quartile	64.9	27.6	7.5	0
Bottom quartile	45.4	23.5	19.4	11.7
Total	57.9	21.2	12.8	3.7

Source: Pasha, Hafiz, *et. al.*, 'The Changing Profile of Regional Development in Pakistan', *Pakistan Journal of Applied Economics*, vol. 9, no. 1, 1990, p. 15.

one district each in this category. Peshawar for the NWFP, and Hyderabad for the Rest of Sindh, constitute a large share of the population of their regions, both in the top quartile, while Punjab's 18 per cent, though less in population terms, had two districts in the top quartile. This shows that, at least in the 1970s (and possibly even today), the Punjab had a more even spread of population and development than the other provinces.[25]

As we have argued earlier, social infrastructure, especially the levels of literacy and education attained by a population, have important consequences for levels of development. Hence it would be useful to examine the level of regional disparities in social infrastructure. Table 17.9, which also appeared in Chapter 16, shows a huge variation in literacy rates across the provinces in Pakistan. Punjab's overall literacy rate is three times that of Baluchistan, which is close to one-seventh that of Karachi. The female literacy rate, a key ingredient in health care and family planning, is particularly poor in rural areas, with the Punjab showing the highest, albeit dismal, literacy rates for rural women. Table 17.10 introduces some more recent statistics, seeming to indicate that rural NWFP performs very well compared to the other rural areas in the provinces. The maldistribution within rural Punjab, where the growth of literacy among Seraiki-speakers is far worse than in the more prosperous central and northern belts, is reflected in a lower average for the Punjab. Punjab's urban figures are particularly impressive, implying that the high level of urbanization may have brought positive consequences for health and education. Surprisingly, despite Karachi's dominance of urban Sindh, urban Punjab performs better than urban Sindh.

17.4.2 The Issues

Much of the research that has been undertaken on regional or inter-district disparities lacks an analysis of the *reasons* for the differences between areas and regions. Some researchers have not been interested in looking at the issues behind the numbers, while others have tried to shy away from what are heated and controversial political issues. In this section, we present some of the explanations that have been offered for why imbalances exist in the first place, why they either continue to exist or are exacerbated, and how the differences over time can be decreased.

Soon after the independence of East Pakistan, a paper was published in 1974 by Naved Hamid and Akmal Hussain,[26] which examined the extent of regional inequality in what remained of Pakistan. For the authors, capitalist development was 'almost always accompanied by increasing income inequalities in every field and Pakistan's experience shows that of these, regional disparities are potentially the most explosive'.[27] Using Gunnar Myrdal's theory of 'Circular Cumulative Causation' as an adequate explanatory tool, the authors agree that 'once inequalities are created, the play of market forces normally tends to increase rather than decrease the inequalities between regions. If market forces were allowed to operate, industrial production, commerce, banking, insurance, shipping, etc., would cluster in certain localities and regions, leaving the rest of the country in the state of backwardness'[28] (see Appendix 17.3 for a more extensive explanation). The basic premise of the thesis presented by Naved Hamid and Akmal Hussain is that once

Table 17.8
Percentage of population within provinces and development levels

	Top quartile	Second quartile	Third quartile	Bottom quartile	Total
Punjab	18	37	27	18	100
Karachi	100	0	0	0	100
Rest of Sindh	21	0	43	36	100
NWFP	27	7	18	48	100
Baluchistan	9	0	0	91	100

Source: Zaidi, S. Akbar, 'The Economic Bases in the National Question in Pakistan: An Indication', in Zaidi, S. Akbar, *Regional Imbalances and the National Question in Pakistan*, Vanguard, Lahore, 1991, p. 126.

Table 17.9
Literacy in Pakistan, 1972, 1981 (%)

	Total			Urban			Rural		
	Both sexes	Male	Female	Both sexes	Male	Female	Both sexes	Male	Female
Pakistan									
1981	23.3	31.8	13.7	43.4	51.5	33.7	14.8	23.1	5.5
1972	21.7	30.2	11.6	41.5	49.9	30.9	14.3	22.6	4.7
NWFP									
1981	14.3	22.7	4.9	32.1	42.8	18.8	10.9	18.7	2.5
1972	14.5	23.1	4.7	33.7	44.7	19.9	11.0	19.0	2.2
Punjab									
1981	24.5	33.5	14.4	43.1	51.5	33.2	17.3	26.4	7.4
1972	20.7	29.1	10.7	38.9	47.8	28.0	14.7	22.9	5.2
Rest of Sindh									
1981	21.0	30.0	10.0	–	–	–	12.7	20.8	3.4
1972	22.5	32.6	10.0	–	–	–	17.6	27.5	5.8
Baluchistan									
1981	8.2	12.5	2.9	27.9	37.7	14.3	4.4	7.3	0.8
1972	10.1	14.8	4.2	32.3	42.4	19.2	5.6	9.2	1.2
Karachi									
1981	55.0	60.0	48.8	–	–	–	–	–	–
1972	51.2	55.8	45.0	–	–	–	–	–	–

Source: Zaidi, S. Akbar, 'The Economic Bases in the National Question in Pakistan: An Indication', in Zaidi, S. Akbar, *Regional Imbalances and the National Question in Pakistan,* Vanguard, Lahore, 1991, p. 116.

Table 17.10
Regional differences in human development indicators, 1991

	Literacy rates		Net primary school enrolment rates		Infant mortality rate (per thousand)
	Male (%)	Female (%)	Male (%)	Female (%)	
Punjab					
Urban	62.9	36.8	81.1	78.5	89
Rural North	44.6	13.6	70.8	52.9	111
Rural South	34.5	8.9	61.0	32.2	147
Sindh					
Urban	61.5	41.3	63.3	63.3	92
Rural	43.2	6.6	51.5	24.1	143
NWFP					
Uban	53.8	20.9	81.3	53.5	154
Rural	43.9	5.4	72.2	36.9	128
Baluchistan					
Urban	52.0	16.5	44.9	34.0	201
Rural	29.1	3.2	47.3	19.8	149
All Pakistan					119

Notes: Literacy rates are for population 15 years of age and older. Net primary school enrolment refers to grades 1–5, ages 6–10. Infant mortality rates are deaths in the 0–1 age bracket per thousand live births (average for the 1980–90 period).

Source: Behrman, J.R., 'Pakistan: Human Resource Development and Economic Growth into the Next Century', unpublished mimeo, 8 May 1995.

regional inequalities emerge, whether due to historical accidents, such as a city developing as a port, or to a region being particularly productive in one or many agricultural commodities, or to government efforts, *it is very likely that inequalities will increase.*

Shahid Kardar offers similar views and gives a number of explanations as to why regional economic disparities have existed in Pakistan in the past.

a) The differences in the growth rates of different regions are primarily because of the differences in the level of development of the different factors of production, level of technology, capital intensity, the productivity of the capital structure, and the degree of complementarity offered by the social environment in which the productive forces are required to operate.

b) The economic disparities are partly the outcome of the pattern of public investment undertaken by the British for their own political and economic interests as colonizers.

c) Regional differences can be narrowed and spatial imbalances corrected by the transfer of resources from the centre by setting up public sector projects in backward areas, through a credit policy for industry locating in backward regions, through other investment in physical and social infrastructure or by indirectly making private investment cheaper in the relatively backward areas. The policy measures introduced, however, to bring about balanced regional growth have been ineffective in arresting the increasing disparities in the income of different provinces. Per capita plan outlays did not reflect the professed desire to achieve regional balanced development. Consequently, even the savings of less well-off regions got invested in the relatively industrialized regions, given the advantages of external economies and the resultant high returns.

d) Development of different regions has proceeded in a lopsided manner – the distribution of industrial growth, in particular, is horribly skewed. Consequently, one of the main advantages of industrialization, the potential for creating backward and forward linkages, was lost. Most industrial licences were issued and credit was provided to the industries that were locating in the provided developed area – which had skilled labour and provided specialized and auxiliary inter-industrial linkages and engineering and repair and maintenance workshops.

3) Private investment demonstrated its natural tendency to flow into the already developed areas, as such a move ensured higher marginal returns.

f) The poorer areas have shown smaller credit absorptive capacity because of the low level of infrastructural development.

g) Financial assistance from the centre has not, by operating as a balancing factor, helped in neutralizing the differences that existed in development potential for historical reasons. Regional disparities cannot be removed by simply making financial resources available.[29]

A third study that has examined the process of regional/provincial imbalances over time using a political economy approach, while accepting the earlier positions of Naved Hamid and Akmal Hussain, and of Shahid Kardar, argues that much of their analysis was useful for the earlier phases of capitalist development in Pakistan. It maintains that, towards the end of the 1980s and especially now, in the 1990s, 'the development of productive forces has brought together, rather than disintegrated, the people of Pakistan ... and what we are seeing for the first time, is the birth of the *Pakistani Nation*'.[30] This view holds that:

> There has been a very marked trend of the coming together of the various regions of Pakistan. A greater integration, even of 'culture', the loaded term that it is, has been observed. While capitalist development acts as a force which results in fissiparous tendencies, recent trends in Pakistan suggest that there has been a process of integration, and assimilation. After the initial distancing when capitalism is in its earlier phases [as argued by Naved Hamid and Akmal Hussain], with relatively more advanced capitalism, the demand by newly emergent regional (nationalist) groups is directed towards gaining more spoils from the centre. [Hence] their nature to use their special position as regionalists to acquire accommodation at the centre. This has been the pattern observed in Pakistan over the last few years.[31]

While differences in economic and social development will continue to exist, and possibly worsen in a capitalist economy like Pakistan, it is important to understand why they exist in the first place and how some sort of balance through political and policy initiative can be maintained. Many of the earlier chapters of this book – especially those on agriculture and industry – explain how inequalities emerged, some for historical and accidental reasons, others through conscious government policy interventions. For example, it is improbable to assume that the Green Revolution in agriculture could have taken place anywhere else but in the central region of the Punjab; Baluchistan, Sindh, the NWFP, and much of the rest of the Punjab were not suited to the highly water-dependent technology of the agricultural package. Karachi developed as Pakistan's leading industrial and commercial city mainly because it was a port, and was the capital of Pakistan for many years. The provincial capitals have developed far in excess of the rest of their provinces because they are the largest cities, have some industry and trade, and have the presence of a huge government machine. District headquarters have similar advantages. Moreover, despite the government's attempts to promote underdeveloped and backward regions by giving them tax breaks and other incentives, private enterprise will not shift there as these places lack skilled labour, infrastructure, and a business 'culture'.

This section has dealt with an emotional and politically sensitive issue. Given Pakistan's history, some area or group of people has always felt discriminated against. Many of these groups have been organized and militant and have been able to express their resentment and concern; others have had to live with discrimination without being in a position to voice their protest. It is inevitable that regional imbalances will continue to exist in Pakistan. Nevertheless, it is likely that greater integration, rather than disintegration, will occur over the next few decades. This theme is explored further in the last part of this book. For more indicators of regional and provincial differentiation, see Tables 17.13 and 17.14 and the next section.

17.5 Poverty

A long-run definition of the causal and structural mechanisms that produce and perpetuate poverty would include the following:

> Discrimination across various dividing lines, the distribution of political and economic power in the country, the distribution of income earned

Table 17.11
Survey of poverty estimates

		Poverty line	1963/4	1969/70	1971/2	1978/9	1984/5	1987/8
Naseem (1977)	(1959/60 Rs)/capita							
Rural		250	43	36	19			
		300	61	60	58			
Urban		300	55	35	25			
		375	70	59	63			
Alauddin (1975)	(1959/60 Rs)/capita							
Rural		250	57	36	42			
		300	67	61	65			
Urban		300	50	30	42			
		375	71	60	62			
Naseem (1977)	% of 2,100 cals RDA							
		95	72	68	74			
		92	54	46	55			
		90	45	36	43			
Mujahid (1978)	% of 2,100 cals RDA							
Rural		250	27	35				
		300	40	48				
Urban		300	36	29				
		375	52	46				
Irfan and Amjad (1984)	(1979/80 Rs)/capita							
Rural		109	41	55		41		
		95	32	43		29		
Kruijk and Leeuwen	(1978/80 Rs)/HH							
Rural		700		73		51		
Urban		700		50		30		
Malik (1988)	(1984/85 Rs)/capita							
Rural		159	37	44		29	24	
		172	43	51		35	29	
Urban		185	40	34		24	19	
		207	49	43		31	26	
Ahmed and Allison (1990)	(1979 Rs)/capita							
Rural		100				25	20	
Urban		110				20	16	
Malik (1991)	2,550 cals RDA							
Rural							21	16
Urban							11	7

Source: Kemal, A.R. and Moazam Mahmood, 'Poverty and Policy in Pakistan', in Banuri, Tariq (ed.), *Just Adjustment: Protecting the Vulnerable and Promoting Growth*, UNICEF, Islamabad, 1992, p. 51.

from physical and human capital, possible biases towards one of these in market returns, and the contribution of government policy towards the aggravation or amelioration of such biases. By calling into question the underlying socio-economic structure, this perspective helps identify policies and actions to decrease the level of poverty.[32]

The somewhat more conventional approach to defining poverty is 'the number of individuals or households (a head-count) below a poverty line drawn arbitrarily or on the basis of nutritional requirements or other basic needs'.[33] Usually such indicators are constituted on the basis of anthropometric surveys of calorie intake, but such surveys do not take place in Pakistan. The method adopted in Pakistan is to 'designate as the poverty line the estimated rupee value of a food basket which will deliver the Recommended Daily Allowance (RDA) for an adult equivalent in Pakistan (2,550 calories). Poverty is then defined as the proportion of the population that falls below this poverty line.'[34]

Table 17.11 shows various estimates of poverty in Pakistan since the early 1960s. There is some disagreement over the extent of poverty in Ayub Khan's Decade of Development in the 1960s, but there is a clear consensus that after the 1960s there has been a consistent decline in poverty. Rural poverty in the 1960s is believed to have existed due to the impact of the Green Revolution and mechanization, which led to the eviction of tenants, at least in the short term. For the 1970s and 1980s, there is complete unaminity that both urban and rural poverty have decreased.

Sohail Malik in a recent paper has argued that 'there was an increase in poverty during the 1960s, but (according to almost all studies) a decline in poverty ever since about 1970'.[35] Other analysis has confirmed that this decline continued throughout the 1980s. Poverty is said to have fallen 'rapidly and unambiguously between 1984–85 and 1987–88. This favourable trend may or may not have continued into the early nineties ... but at the very least one can say that (a) the rate of poverty reduction fell in the late eighties and (b) poverty did not rise significantly.'[36] However, recent work by Asad Sayeed and Aisha Ghaus,[37] Shahrukh Rafi Khan,[38] and A.R. Kemal[39] has shown quite conclusively that *poverty has returned to Pakistan* in the 1990s. This is essentially the outcome of the structural adjustment programme imposed by the IMF and World Bank since 1988 (see Chapter 15).

A more interesting finding regarding poverty, income distribution, and concentration can be gauged from Table 17.12. A strong belief still persists that in the 1950s and 1960s the process of economic development caused substantial income inequality. However, Table 17.12 shows that the income distribution improved during the 1960s with the Gini coefficient falling from 0.36 in 1963/4 to 0.33 in 1970/1. This fall was more marked for the rural population, although income inequality also decreased in urban areas. The share of the lowest quartile of the population also increased in this period and, quite against conventional wisdom, that of the highest quartile fell quite considerably. More surprising still is the rise in inequality in the 1970s, when a 'people's government' was in power.

17.5.1 Who Are the Poor and Where Do They Live?

Some of the salient features of poverty in Pakistan can be summarized as follows:

1 Rural areas have an unambiguously higher rate of poverty than urban areas for a wide range of poverty lines.[40] Table 17.13 shows that the percentage of the population living in poverty in rural areas is twice that of urban areas.

2 As Table 17.14 shows, in 1991 rural Punjab had the highest head-count ratio (i.e. percentage of people considered poor) with 35.4 per cent. Sindh came next, with rural NWFP having the lowest number of poor.[41]

3 North Punjab has a smaller incidence of poverty than Sindh, which is better off than southern Punjab.[42]

4 Across the country as a whole, head-count ratios have fallen from 46 per cent in 1984/5, to 37.4 per cent in 1987/8, and to 34 per cent in 1990/1; between 1984/5 and 1987/8, the head-count ratio fell by 18.6 per cent, while it fell by 9.1 per cent between 1987/8 and 1990/1.[43]

5 The gender structure of income is significantly linked to poverty, but household size and dependency ratios are not. The poor have significantly smaller family size than the middle and upper income categories, a somewhat surprising result; the dependency ratio for the poor, in both urban and rural areas, is the lowest.[44]

Table 17.12
Income distribution in Pakistan, 1963–1988

Year	Gini coefficient			HH income share	
	Total	Rural	Urban	Lowest 20%	Highest 20%
1963/4	0.355	0.348	0.368	–	–
1966/7	0.351	0.314	0.388	6.4	45.3
1968/9	0.358	0.293	0.370	7.6	43.4
1969/70	0.330	0.295	0.361	8.2	42.0
1970/1	0.326	0.273	0.359	8.0	41.8
1971/2	0.344	0.309	0.381	8.4	41.5
1979	0.375	0.319	0.380	7.9	43.0
1984/5	0.428	0.345	0.379	7.4	45.0
1985/6	0.355	0.330	0.354	7.3	45.0
1986/7	0.346	0.312	0.357	7.6	44.0
1987/8	0.348	0.307	0.366	7.9	43.6

Source: Kemal, A.R. and Moazam Mahmood, 'Poverty and Policy in Pakistan', in Banuri, Tariq (ed.), *Just Adjustment: Protecting the Vulnerable and Promoting Growth*, UNICEF, Islamabad, 1992, p. 52.

Table 17.13
Distribution of the poor by province and residence

	Percentage of people living in poverty				1991 index of concentration
	1985	1985	1988	1991	
Residence					
Urban	10	11.1	8.7	9.8	57
Rural	20	21.1	19.6	20.6	119
Province					
Baluchistan		27.5	9.3	7.1	41
Urban	19	17.0	4.4	4.5	26
Rural	31	28.5	10.0	7.7	45
NWFP		9.6	15.5	20.2	117
Urban	8	7.5	12.4	14.3	83
Rural	10	9.0	16.0	21.4	124
Punjab		19.0	19.9	19.0	110
Urban	13	12.8	11.9	11.4	66
Rural	21	21.3	22.6	21.9	127
Sindh		15.3	9.5	12.3	71
Urban	6	7.0	3.1	6.7	39
Rural	21	22.2	14.6	17.6	102
Overall		18.3	16.6	17.2	100

Source: Government of Pakistan, Planning Commission, *Pakistan Country Paper: World Summit for Social Development*, 1995, p. 37.

6 The poor have the lowest earners per household; female-headed households, or households reliant on women's income, are likely to fall into poverty. The poor have a much higher proportion of female-headed households; this poverty is due to gender discrimination, the male–female income ratio being 17 in rural areas and 16 per cent in urban areas.[45]

7 In the rural areas, the poor are predominantly sharecroppers. They own the least land, are the smallest landlords, and have not shifted to modern forms of lease contracting.[46]

8 In the urban areas, the poor have a low share of income from manufacturing, and earn most of their income from construction.[47]

9 The poor earn only 29 per cent of their income from wage employment, compared to 38 and 32 per cent for the middle and upper income groups; the poor are also more dependent on gifts and remittances, making them more dependent on others.[48]

10 The rural poor spend 80 per cent of their budgets on the four essentials – food, rent, energy, and apparel – while the middle and upper income groups spend 74 and 66 per cent, respectively. Likewise, in urban areas, the poor spend 82 per cent on these items, compared to 76 per cent by the middle income group and 70 per cent by the upper income group. Both in relative and certainly in absolute terms, the poor have less to spend on other commodities, which include essentials like health and education.[49]

Table 17.14
Rural head-count ratios and nutrition levels, by province

	Punjab	Sindh	NWFP	Baluchistan
Rural head-count ratios				
PIHS 91	35.4	32.3	19.8	41.2
HIES 84/5	50.4	45.3	46.2	55.4
HIES 87/8	42.1	34.0	38.3	44.6
HIES 90/1	38.5	30.8	40.6	20.9
RIDS 86	33.4	36.3	31.2	50.5
Percentage of children nutritionally normal				
	48.2	36.3	32.7	27.2

PIHS = Pakistan Integrated Household Survey.
HIES = Household Income Expenditure Survey.
RIDS = Rural Integrated Development Survey.
Source: Gazdar, Haris, *et. al.*, 'A Profile of Poverty in Pakistan: Some Insights from Pakistan's Integrated Household Survey, 1991', unpublished mimeo, 1996.

One reason why there is regional variation in poverty is that poverty depends greatly on natural and infrastructure endowments, on the distribution of resources within a region, and on the structure of the economy. Institutional structures and arrangements, and regional policy variables, both in the private sector and due to public policy, also influence poverty.

In more general terms, the overall downward trend in poverty in the country, at least until the 1990s, is an impressive achievement, most of the credit for which goes to Pakistan's significant growth since the 1960s. Moreover, factors such as remittances from the Middle East and aid money being distributed across regions have helped in dealing with poverty. It is believed that 'poverty will continue to decline rapidly if growth continues, as long as there are no adverse distributional changes'.[50] It seems that the trickle-down approach does work for the alleviation of poverty, if not for development (see Table 17.15).

One must add one last point to the (so far) positive evidence that has emerged from the numerous poverty studies conducted on Pakistan. Until now, while poverty has been declining due to high growth, it is not clear that this trend will persist into the near future. Most studies have summarized results until about 1991. GDP growth rates in excess of 6 per cent in the 1980s have had a positive effect. However, with the imposition of the structural adjustment programme from 1988 onwards, GDP growth rates have varied and declined considerably. GDP grew by only 2.27 per cent in 1992/3, 3.8 per cent in 1993/4, and 4.7 per cent in 1994/5. Studies in different countries have shown that the structural adjustment programme has led to increasing income inequality and greater poverty.[51] Moreover, urban poverty has also increased, often sharply. Hence it is likely that the very positive record of a decline in poverty in Pakistan may become blemished. In ten years' time when an

Table 17.15
Trends in economic growth, poverty, and inequality, 1960s to the 1990s

	1960s	1970s	1980s	1990s
GDP growth rate	High	Low	High	Low
Trends in poverty				
Urban	Evidence	Decreasing	Decreasing	Tending
Rural	is	Decreasing	Decreasing	to increase
Overall	mixed	Decreasing	Decreasing	after 1988
Trends in inequality				
Urban	Increasing	Constant	Decreasing	Tending
Rural	Decreasing	Increasing	Decreasing	to increase
Overall	Decreasing	Increasing	Decreasing	after 1988

Source: Government of Pakistan, Planning Commission, *Pakistan Country Paper: World Summit for Social Development*,
1995, p. 37.

evaluation of the 1990s is being undertaken, it is possible that the results may be somewhat different from those of the past. Already, initial findings seem to confirm the fears that poverty has indeed returned to Pakistan in the 1990s in a big way.[52]

17.6 Summary and Further Reading

17.6.1 Summary

Some non-traditional social sectors have been evaluated in this chapter, starting with gender inequality. All statistics show that women fare far worse than men in an already underdeveloped social sector. This lack of development, which exists for historic reasons of patriarchy, class, and power, continues even as the twenty-first century approaches. However, development, no matter how conceived, cannot succeed unless there is equal participation by women. Women are, in many ways, the core of economic activity in the country, though their contribution is neither recorded nor lauded. While incentives and changes in policy at the margin may help in promoting economic and social sector development, unless the cultural, historical, political, and social issues of gender discrimination are addressed, it is unlikely that women's emancipation will take place.

Without basic infrastructure, countries will not progress. Whether it is energy, communications, roads, or ports, unless there is investment in these sectors, economic growth and development will be slow. Pakistan's record in infrastructure provision is as poor as it is in the social sector, and a great deal needs to be done to achieve progress.

While economic development must take place, it must take care not to deteriorate or degrade the natural environment. Although Pakistan consumes far fewer natural resources than most countries, and while Pakistan's record has not been particularly poor, the strains of growth and industrialization on the environment are beginning to tell. Environmental sustainability will have to be a key

component of economic growth in the future. Regional inequalities exist wherever there is economic growth. Pakistan's performance is probably no worse than that of most countries. However, after having lost more than half of the population in 1971, and with numerous political movements demanding regional or 'national' rights, the issue in Pakistan is particularly sensitive. Much of the data confirm the perception generally held, that Karachi and the other provincial capitals are far better developed than the rest of the country, with the province of Baluchistan being least developed. We have examined some of the causes of regional disparity in Pakistan and have argued that differences in economic and social development are likely to persist into the future.

Poverty, which diminished during the 1970s and 1980s, has now returned to Pakistan in the 1990s. Income inequality has also probably worsened. The high growth performance of the economy after 1977 acted as a palliative for poverty, and remittances from the Middle East helped in distributing income to different regions of the country. However, with lower growth, more poverty, higher inflation, and less expenditure by government on the social sectors, all following the structural adjustment programmes of 1988 and 1993, poverty has returned to Pakistan, and is likely to worsen in the years to come.

17.6.2 Further Reading

Given the diverse contents of this chapter, the Notes provide the most appropriate reading for the different sections. However, the World Bank's *Women in Pakistan: An Economic and Social Strategy*, Washington, 1989, is a useful text on the extent of gender inequality in the country. The paper by S. Akbar Zaidi, 'Gender Perspectives and Quality of Care in Underdeveloped Countries: Disease, Gender and Contextuality', *Social Science and Medicine*, vol. 43, no. 5, 1996, is a good summary of many of the issues concerning gender discrimination, and offers a radical critique of the most common arguments. Tariq Banuri's edited *Just Adjustment: Protecting the Vulnerable and Promoting Growth*, Oxford University Press, Karachi, 1998, is also a useful reference for many of the issues in the social sector. See also S. Akbar Zaidi's *The New Development Paradigm: Papers on Institutions, NGOs, Gender and Local Government*, Oxford University Press, Karachi, forthcoming 1999.

On the environment, by far the best volume is the IUCN's *Pakistan National Conservation Strategy*, Karachi, 1992, along with its ancillary volumes and documents. See also Arif Hasan's and Ameneh Azam Ali's *Environmental Repercussions of Development in Pakistan*, OPP-RTI, Karachi, 1993. The papers in *Regional Imbalances and the National Question in Pakistan*, Vanguard, Lahore, 1992, by S. Akbar Zaidi, still provide the best comparative analysis of issues of regional inequality. On poverty, excellent sources are the text edited by Tariq Banuri cited above; the paper by Asad Sayeed and Aisha Ghaus, 'Has Poverty Returned to Pakistan?', mimeo, Social Policy and Development Centre, Karachi, 1996; and Haris Gazdar's two unpublished manuscripts, 'Recent Trends in Poverty in Pakistan' and 'A Profile of Poverty in Pakistan: Some Insights from Pakistan's Integrated Household Survey 1991'.

Appendix 17.1

The gender trap

The following article examines the reasons why women are discriminated against and argues that most of the causes for gender discrimination are structural and deep-rooted. The article makes the point that marginal changes will be ineffective, and that in order to address and reverse gender discrimination, structural changes at the societal and economic level are essential.

There is little doubt that the position and status of women in almost all societies is far worse than that of men. Sexual and domestic violence, added to more subtle forms of oppression and deprivation, are especially prevalent in underdeveloped countries. Higher morbidity and mortality rates, poor health, low levels of education and literacy, and few opportunities for gainful employment are among those factors which restrict the development and fulfilment of the potential of women. By any yardstick, the position of women is far worse than that of men.

Much blame has been heaped on men, or patriarchy, for causing this system of inequality, and very little on the social, economic and political structures in which both men and women live and co-exist. While numerous researchers and scholars – almost all of them women – have identified the extent of gender inequality in the third world, and have made suggestions for redressing these inequalities, their well-meaning recommendations have been largely ineffective. And this is to be expected, because unless the material conditions and causes of gender inequality are evaluated and understood most attempts at reform will fail.

The evidence in support of the fact that women are discriminated against is extensive and indisputable. Numerous studies have shown that low levels of education and training, poor health and nutritional status, and lack of access to resources affect the quality of life for women. The allocation of resources at the household level also affects the nature and quality of women's health and their lives. At the same time, norms and customs such as female seclusion and the resulting lack of interaction with the outside world have also had a negative impact on the economic situation of women.

In addition, procreation with its consequences on the well-being of women, is considered in many underdeveloped societies to be a social activity influenced by cultural norms which encourage high fertility rates, a custom which no household desires unilaterally to break. High fertility, high rates of illiteracy, a low share of paid employment and a high percentage of women working at home for no pay seem to coexist together, all aggravating the situation.

Work on the economic and social status of women in South Asia has shown that 'the gender gap in the ownership and control of property is the single most critical contributor to the gender gap in economic well-being, social status and improvement' in countries where property rights are governed by laws usually influenced by religious mandate. In many countries, male domination has become culturally sanctioned and gender based subordination is reinforced by religious systems. This sort of thinking has become ingrained in the consciousness of both men and women and is viewed as a natural corollary of the biological differences between them. Moreover, concepts of gender roles, desirable behaviour and appropriate expectations are learnt from a very early age, so much so that gender becomes an integral part of a person's identity and gender roles are seen to lie at the centre of people's cultural and religious heritage. As a result, in many countries there is a 'culture against women' in which women are socialized to sacrifice their health, survival chances and life options.

However, all these factors which affect women, their health and quality of life need to be seen in a somewhat broader context. The lack of access to resources, which is said to affect the status of women more adversely, is highly dependent on one's social and economic position. For instance, nutritional deficiencies in women, which are significant in much of the third world, are highly skewed towards the poorer women in these countries. It would be difficult to argue that class differentiation does not determine disease and health patterns in any country, especially in underdeveloped countries where this differentiation is more acute. Rich women in even the poorest of underdeveloped countries do not face most of the problems highlighted by the research on gender and health. Not only are richer women better off by far in terms of most social indicators than their poorer sisters, but they are also far better off than poorer men. Within societies, one's position – whether male or female on the social and economic ladder – determines access to resources, and hence well-being. Moreover, across nations there is a great deal of evidence which suggests that countries with higher levels of economic development, industrialization and urbanization are more likely to experience greater gender equality. With increased economic growth there is a likelihood that gender equality will also increase.

There is no denying the fact that legal structures and rules discriminate against women and need to be changed. However, the political economy of legal systems ensures that archaic and discriminatory legal practices are maintained indefinitely. The economic and class composition of society protecting a particular configuration of property rights warrants a particular legal structure. More often than not, a change in those property rights structures creates changes in legal structures. As such, to expect that substantial legal reforms will take place in society without a transformation of social, economic, property and political rights is a little simplistic. Moreover, even when the laws do exist, social and economic structures intervene. For example, gender equality in the legal right to own property does not guarantee gender equality in actual ownership, nor does ownership guarantee control. Also, traditions and customs continue to disregard laws, with many discriminatory and illegal practices being sanctified by religion.

Such values and norms which create and justify gender bias against women are the least likely to undergo change via direct intervention. Ancient traditions and customs survive even major economic transformations and epochs, because they are so ingrained in the social and cultural fabric of society. To challenge and question what are often defined as religious guidelines is perceived as betrayal of one's religion, community and culture.

When gender inequality is caused by values, norms, customs and religion, the process of change is made even more difficult and complicated. If religion or custom are responsible for, say, the seclusion or exclusion of women from the public and hence economic domain, no attempt to increase women's involvement in the public sphere will end the resulting gender bias, unless the foundations of the discriminatory practices are uprooted. Within existing social, economic and property structures this will be unlikely.

The key argument being made here is that while gender inequalities are substantial, they are a symptom of a social and economic structure which produces or results in those inequalities. Hence, any attempt to improve the status of women without questioning, challenging or changing the existing structure will be ineffective.

Feminists and women's groups strive for strategies to reduce gender inequality. They demand more equality and greater control over their lives and devise opportunities and insist on policies that will improve their well-being and absolute and relative status. But why must these initiatives be restricted to women alone? Just as much as women want equality and greater control over their lives, so do men, of all classes. But just as poorer women suffer from greater lack of control over their lives, so do poorer men. Thus, if control is dependent on income, wealth, class or location in the social matrix, it is unlikely that this control will be achieved without addressing the material conditions which affect the extent of control.

Much of the well-meaning research on gender discrimination, and ways to address and reverse that discrimination, ignores the existence of classes or social and economic differentiation. It omits an analysis of power relations, power that is usually though not exclusively articulated through an individual's or group's position in the social and economic hierarchy. Not all women are equal and hence to speak about the problems of 'women' obfuscates the extensive differentiation between different classes of women who are affected differently by discrimination. Furthermore, the same structural differentiation in society affects men of the poorer classes equally. In fact there may be more similarities between men and women of similar social and economic backgrounds than between members of the same gender with significantly different social and economic positions. The dominant thinking addressing the issues of gender ignores the social and economic construct of differentiation, as well as the similarities between the two genders.

Women's rights and the struggle for greater equality and opportunities cannot take place outside the overall social and political matrix which constitutes that particular society and defines their position in it. There can be no denying the numerous examples of successful interventions that have resulted in greater equality for women at a micro and project level. But to effectively change the position of women in the economic and social matrix, and to increase and improve their status, what needs to be dealt with are the structures which cause the inequalities in the first place, be they economic or spiritual. Since men too are victims, though certainly to a lesser degree, of the structures of society, there is also a need to incorporate men and their role in changing the inequitable system which distributes resources inequitably.

Almost all evidence from studies related to health, education and economic development shows convincingly that women are the very central, if not the most critical, component of the equation. While the western developed countries have only recently discovered the role of women in development, little do they know that in underdeveloped countries women are never 'outside' development, for their very existence and survival and that of their family and often of the entire country depends on their being 'in' development. This is precisely why their role and position cannot be analysed and examined separately and in isolation, without reference to, and in conjunction with, men and the broader social structure in which they coexist.

Feminist groups and women's activists have focused exclusively on the role of women alone. Possibly, it is time to bring both men and the social structure within the realm of analysis and practice. This at least is a minimum condition for greater equality for all, women and men.

Source: Zaidi S. Akbar, *The Herald*, April 1996.

Appendix 17.2

Power play

While energy is a key prerequisite to development, how should the government proceed with a policy? An analysis:

The government's much publicized energy policy took a new turn on March 3, 1996 when the Economic Coordination Committee (ECC) of the cabinet set a 3,000 mw limit for private power projects, including projects that had already been issued Letters of Support (LOS). They decided that only those projects closing before the cumulative 3,000 mw limit would be implemented while others would have to cash their bank guarantees and drop out of the race. The move was a belated response to the fact that, getting carried away with its own enthusiasm, the government had issued far too many LOSs (aggregating up to 9,000 mw) and there was no way they could afford to buy energy from all of the companies concerned.

However, in the next meeting on April 10 the ECC decided to exempt several projects from this 3,000 mw limit and approved 12 more projects aggregating 2,600 mw.

Consolidated Electric Power Asia Ltd's (CEPA) 1,320 mw project (owned by the famous Gordon Wu of Hong Kong) was deferred to the ninth plan as were the Tractable and Spencer projects with a cumulative energy potential of 640 mw.

Alarmed by the enormous amounts of megawatts pouring into the lot of WAPDA and KESC, the Ministry of Water and Power subsequently made a presentation to the cabinet in which it came up with serious misgivings about the energy policy. The ministry is said to have stated that if the projects issued LOSs under the policy came through, it would have serious repercussions on the economy in general and WAPDA and KESC in particular. They stated that it could result in system over-capacity and that scheduled payments to the private power companies would threaten the liquidity position of both WAPDA and KESC. They also reportedly stated that the foreign exchange obligation could exceed the Pakistan government's anticipated foreign exchange earnings from the extra trade resulting from increased energy capacity. Moreover, the tariff to the consumer would average 6.5 rupees per unit compared with the present average of 2.5 rupees.

Independent experts and consultants fear that these misgivings may be well-founded. The Bhutto government's policy is likely to extract a high cost, and distortions in supply and demand will continue to make their presence felt over the next decade.

On the other hand, the government's energy policy has been hailed as successful by external sponsors including the World Bank, which has been steering the institutional arrangements for the financing of energy projects. Inside sources reveal that it was, in fact, the World Bank that forced the government to set the 3,000 mw ceiling for companies importing fuel and gas.

At this stage, when WAPDA and KESC are set to buy some 7,000 to 8,000 megawatts by the year 2000 at more than twice their own cost of production, the management of the energy policy leaves several questions unaddressed. Financial experts like Abid Naqvi state that it will bring in an investment of three billion dollars but there seem to be several issues on the flip side.

The energy policy's roots can be traced to the Strategic Plan of 1992 that called for the deregulation of WAPDA and KESC and the setting up of the National Electricity and Power Regulatory Authority (NEPRA) to regulate the privatization of energy. As a follow-up, a task force was set up and an energy policy formulated in 1994. This policy was based on the premise that power is an indicator of economic development and that it was imperative to invest in energy for the economy to grow. The task force assumed that there was a shortfall of up to 2,000 mws and that there was an annual growth of 9 per cent in consumer demand and planned accordingly. The task force concluded that it would not be possible for the public sector to make such huge investments and recommended private power generation. In a bid to ensure private sector investment, the government bent over backwards to oblige prospective investors. 'The energy policy gives back to back guarantees and practically insulates investment against everything short of a nuclear holocaust,' says Abid Naqvi. Comprising three parts – the Power Purchase Agreement, the Fuel Transportation Agreement and the Implementation Agreement – the policy lays down the terms and conditions for investors. The 'take or pay' contracts bind the utilities to buy power up to 60 per cent of the capacity of the projects. Setting equity–debt ratio at 20:80 and bulk tariff at 6.5 cents a unit, the rate of return is estimated to be as high as 18 per cent, among the highest anywhere. The government ensures fuel transportation and insulates profits against inflation and devaluation.

The policy was therefore a real hit in terms of the response it generated. Enter US secretary for energy, Hazel O'Leary and hundreds of MOUs [Memorandums of Understanding] poured into the country, with the government blowing the trumpet of its own success. At that time it was felt that because of the sovereign risk of factor, lenders would not be interested in Pakistan. Eventually after sifting and shortlisting, 34 Letters of Support were issued to different companies totalling 9,000 mw by the Pakistan Private Power and Infrastructure Board (PPPIB). Says one official in the ministry, 'The government issued so many LOSs on the assumption that only 25 per cent of them would come through. However, the success rate has been more than 50 per cent.' By the time the policy makers realized that they may have overstepped their own limits, it was already too late. Hence they staggered projects like CEPA, Ali Habib's Tractable and Byram Avari's Spencer to the ninth year plan. But practically speaking, that does not make much of a difference since the next plan is just two years away.

There are now serious apprehensions about the overcapacity that may result from hasty decision-making. 'In effect we will be paying for idle capacity,' says one expert. The apprehensions are on two counts. One, that by the year 2000 there will be 6,000 to 8,000 mw of additional capacity available whereas the demand growth, even if estimated at the extremely high estimate of 9 per cent, will not require more than 5,000 mw, assuming that there is an existing shortage of 2,000 mw. However, the growth of demand in the past two years has been stunted. According to Ministry of Water and Power estimates, growth in the years 1994–1995 was 4.5 per cent as opposed to the nearly 9 per cent projection on which the energy policy was based. The reasons for decrease in the demand in the last two years are manifold. The decrease in the cotton crop and the consequent slump in the textile sector, and the law and order breakdown in Karachi are cited as major factors. 'One cannot rule out the increase in tariff, massive breakdowns and the resulting tendency in industry to generate its own power as contributing factors,' says one consultant. In fact, according to one analysis by a consultants' group, it is attributed to 'an additional capacity of about 600 mw installed in industry in response to increases in tariff imposed by WAPDA and KESC and to increase the reliability of power supply'. Industrialists in Lahore maintain that last year's massive loadshedding of 10 hours a day has come down to a few hours because of the closure of a large number of industries, which they attribute to high tariffs.

Some experts, however, maintain that this problem will last only for a few years, until demand starts matching supply and the distribution system becomes more effective. 'I don't think that electricity will be coming out of our ears as has been projected, but in the long term, there will be no problem. I feel the question is not so much of overcapacity as of synchronizing the three processes – power generation, transmission and distribution,' says Abid Naqvi. However, the bulk rate of 6.5 cents per unit is set for the first 10 years including a premium of 0.25 cents for those projects which go on stream at the end of 1997, after which the tariffs are expected to taper down. WAPDA will be buying extremely expensive energy for some years that may be idle capacity at worst and at best capacity that WAPDA or KESC may not be able to distribute effectively.

The high tariff is the most controversial issue in the energy policy. All cost increases will be passed on to the consumer. Increase in fuel prices, devaluation of the rupee, inflation – all these factors will increase the tariff. According to one analysis, the tariff can go as high as 10 rupees a unit by the end of 1997. 'This is an investment for which our children will be paying through their noses,' says one consultant. And this prediction when tariffs are already high. One study estimates that the middle income family in Pakistan pays 6 per cent! Pakistan is also one of the few countries where the commercial and industrial sectors are charged more than the domestic sector. According to another study, an industrial plant requiring an annual energy of 5 mw, produces energy 20 to 40 per cent cheaper than the going rate of electricity by installing its own generator. High tariff rates will increase theft and private generation by industry. However, it is felt that the government may discourage the mushrooming of captive plants through imposing barriers and tariffs.

Meanwhile, according to the Ministry of Water and Power estimates, payment to the generators of electricity may increase to 60 per cent of WAPDA's revenues, leading to a liquidity crisis for the utility. WAPDA's own generation capacity, according to the ministry, will come down to 14 per cent by the year 2002. An independent expert substantiates

this fear: 'Under the 4.5 per cent demand growth scenario, which is not so remote a possibility, the WAPDA and KESC-owned oil and gas fired plants will have to be virtually closed down in the summer when the power generation from Tarbela and Mangla dams is at its peak. In the winter, when hydel capacity is not available, the plants will at best operate at 10 to 20 per cent of their capacity.'

The government, too, will have a heavy price to pay. Fuel import bills and foreign exchange remittances from profits will add up to a colossal figure. According to some estimates, the government may end up paying more than what the trade-generated foreign exchange brings in. The figures quoted range from three to four billion dollars. According to Zahid Zaheer, Secretary of the Overseas Investors Chamber of Commerce and Industry, 'Academics will tell you that increasing energy will increase productivity and export earnings etc. But to increase exports your goods have to be competitive. If you have to pay such high tariffs will it also be possible for you to have competitive goods in the international market?' he asks, arguing that for the plan to work there must be parallel investment in industry.

There are also accusations of unfair practices in dealing with different groups. Some, like the Uch power plant, were given the option of using cheap fuel. Others, like National Power, were given an additional bonus of equipment to generate 600 mw of energy. It is alleged that Enron was thrown out of the race because they did not have a local agent to offer commissions and that Liberty got the deal although they came into the race after the set time schedule. It is alleged that Liberty was also given the option of using high quality piped gas.

Although a lot of investment has been made on the generation side, no parallel investment has been made on the transportation of fuel. The World Bank has come up with a project to lease out railway tracks to investors to transport fuel but the railway infrastructure itself may not sustain the requirement of thousands of tons of fuel that will need to be transported, unless additional investments in infrastructure are made. 'If I were to make a forecast, the government will fail to deliver the oil to generators and end up paying penalties and this is all going to tell on the consumer,' says Zahid Zaheer.

Critics also have reservations on selling off the best and newest power plants by WAPDA. 'I don't agree with selling WAPDA's installed capacity because these could be used to lessen the burden on the consumer,' says one official. 'Selling installed capacity only to be buying back energy at a far greater rate just because it is efficient energy does not make economic sense,' says another. And the use of local fuel is nowhere on the scene. Others say that the hydel option is the best for a third world country. It is a renewable source of energy that is both several times cheaper and one of the cleanest options available. Also, there is no local expertise in the field of tyro-electric power. The energy policy is geared to the supply side but demand reduction and efficient use of energy could have a higher rate of return in the long term.

Perhaps the biggest gap in the energy policy's implementation has been the absence of a regulatory authority. This is a glaring slip. Although provided for in the

Strategic Plan which was a precursor to the private power policy, NEPRA remains to date a nonentity. The mandate stated in the NEPRA ordinance, promulgated in January 1995, is to regulate the granting of licences for generation, transmission and distribution, the determination of the tariffs and the setting of standards of enforcing safety specifications in environment and technology, etc. Today, one-and-a-half years down the road and with dozens of power projects about to materialize this ordinance has yet to be enforced.

'NEPRA would have applied the rule of least cost expansion for any increase in capacity. This rule aims to control costs by considering the location, capacity type and size technology and fuel type of the project,' says an expert. As things stand, no such controls seem to be in evidence, adding to the apprehension that the policy may cost more in the long run than it promises to deliver.

Source: Shah, Nafisa, *Newsline*, July 1996.

Steep Rise in Power Tariff Indicated

The cost to the final consumer of the electricity that would be bought at 6.65 US cents (Rs2.29 at the current official rate of exchange) a unit by WAPDA from the private power stations now being set up, would be around 10 US cents or Rs3.45, estimates a study prepared by a government department.

The almost doubling of the final cost of private power at the consumption stage is attributed mainly to the transmission and distribution expenses made heavier because of the long distances the networking systems have to cover, the study further said.

The main argument in favour of setting up private thermal power stations producing costly electricity is that the wheels of the country's economy would grind to a halt if by the year 2000 'we do not add at least 3000 mw of additional power generating capacity to the national grid'.

The proponents of power at any cost point out that even 10 cents a unit would look cheaper when considered against the cost of having the economy come to a standstill.

They further argue that with the addition of adequate generating capacity within a matter of a few years domestic economic activities would be accelerated enough to generate sufficient resources to more than pay for the high cost of private thermal power.

However, the official study points out that since only the domestic consumer gets subsidized electricity and the industrial and commercial consumers pay very high tariffs, the expectation that the additional generating capacity, whatever its cost to the end-consumer, would accelerate the domestic economic activity was misplaced.

The ever increasing cost of power to industrial and commercial consumers has already forced many of them to make arrangements for in-house generation, the study points out and says the relatively high cost of energy would also price Pakistan exports goods out of the world market.

In this connection, it notes that in most other countries the cost of energy to industrial and commercial consumers is much lower than that for the domestic consumer. This is not so because of any subsidy but because the cost of transmitting power in bulk to a single consumer is much less per unit than the cost for taking it to smaller domestic consumers each of whom has to have separate individual meters and there are millions of independent lines cascading from the thousands of transmitters tumbling off the national grid.

In India, too, industrial and commercial consumers pay less than what domestic consumers do on account of this very reason and that is why the cost of production of competing export goods in India is much less than in Pakistan.

The study maintains that providing high-cost private thermal electricity to domestic consumers at subsidized rates would put a very heavy burden on the budget and render unavailing the entire exercise of having the private sector quickly fill a crucial part of the widening gap between supply and demand of power.

The study observes that the government could not reverse this socially gratifying but economically very costly policy of charging high from industrial and commercial consumers and low from domestic consumers overnight to rationalize the national energy development programme.

The study advises the government to take a close look at the power tariff policies of other countries in a comparable development stage, especially those of Pakistan's closest competitors in the export markets, and start bringing about suitable changes at this juncture in its tenure when the elections are still two years away.

Meanwhile, it has been learnt on good authority that, contrary to the general belief, the actual average price WAPDA would be paying to private power producers for one unit of electricity over the projected 25 years of operation, would be much less than 6.65 cents (Rs2.29). In some cases like the Uch Power which would be operating on local gas of very low Btu, the average purchase price has been estimated to be about 4.50 cents a unit and for others, like the furnace oil fuelled Hub Power, it would be around 5 cents a unit.

'The credit for creating the impression that WAPDA would be paying as high as 6.65 cents a unit to attract international investment interest and actually lure many into launching their projects, goes to those who promoted the government's 1994 energy policy in the world market,' said the sponsor of a private power plant awaiting financial closure.

He, however, apprehended that WAPDA might exploit the impression and inflate the cost of power to the final consumer by at least 1.5 to 2 cents.

He also clarified the impression that the private sponsors would import their furnace oil directly on their own and said that according to the agreement all of them would buy their feed stock from the PSO [Pakistan State Oil] in rupees and collect their payment from WAPDA in rupees.

In his opinion a large part of the tariff the private power plants would charge from WAPDA would be spent in Pakistan and only a fraction of this, which he estimated to be no more than about 2 cents per unit, would get repatriated on an average.

Another sponsor said that under the agreement the government was obliged to arrange confessional loans for the investors like it did for the Hub Power from the Private Sector Energy

Development Fund (PSEDF) established by the World Bank.

He said while the PSEDF resources cost the government an interest rate of only 0.5 per cent these are lent onward by the NDFC at commercial rates amounting to as much as 17 per cent in rupee terms and 9 per cent in the repayment is indexed to the dollar.

However, some officials who are still opposed to this method of obliging the private power project sponsors believe that such a practice would only add to the budgetary burden of the government.

Source: *DAWN*, 25 April 1996.

Appendix 17.3

Capitalist development and regional inequalities

Naved Hamid and Akmal Hussain analyse the causes of regional inequalities under capitalist development.

Theoretical Framework

Within the framework of neo-classical economics the existence of regional inequalities is regarded as only a temporary phenomenon. It is argued that given perfect mobility of factors of production, a free market economy and profit seeking entrepreneurs, regional inequalities will be eliminated over time. The reasoning is as follows: as more and more capital and labour are employed in a particular region, a point will be reached beyond which it is assumed that diminishing returns will set in and the returns on factors of production will begin to decline. This will induce capital and labour to move out from the developed region, where the return (marginal product) has become low, to the backward region where it is still high. This process will continue until the marginal product of each factor of production becomes equal in all regions. Thus there can be no rich or poor regions in the long run.

However, in reality, regional inequalities have persisted in capitalist countries, both rich and poor. For example, in Brazil's north-east the average per capita income is one-third of the richer south. In Mexico, the per capita income in the richest state is twelve times that in the poorest one. Other underdeveloped countries like Egypt, Pakistan, Thailand, Indonesia, etc., have similar problems. Regional inequalities are, however, not limited to poor countries. For example, the south of the USA has always been poorer than other parts; in Italy the southern region is in a virtual state of stagnation and Australia, France, the UK, etc., are also faced with regional problems.

Myrdal's Thesis

Clearly, the market mechanism does not operate to eliminate regional inequalities, rather to the contrary, it tends to increase them. Marxist writers have been aware of this, and the proposition was first stated by Lenin as the 'Law of Uneven Capitalist Development'. However, one of the first Western economists to state this categorically was Gunnar Myrdal, who, in his theory of 'Circular Cumulative Causation', argued that once inequalities are created, the play of market forces normally tends to increase rather than decrease the inequalities between regions. If market forces were allowed to operate, industrial production, commerce, banking, insurance,

shipping, etc., would cluster in certain localities and regions, leaving the rest of the country in a state of backwardness.

The power of attraction of a centre today either has its origins in an initial advantage the area may have had or is a result of a historical accident. Once started, however, there is a systematic divergence in the levels of development between regions. Internal and external economies lower costs of production, relative to other regions, thus making the initiating region cumulatively more advantageous for further investment. The factors that would tend to cause cumulative divergence in the attractiveness of regions for future investment, and hence growing disparity in the regional growth rates, include growth of infrastructure, i.e. communications, banking facilities, public utilities (electricity, gas, water, etc.), trained manpower, technical know-how and maintenance facilities. Also, as most of the new investment is undertaken by existing industrialists and traders, they, for convenience of management and supervision, tend to locate it near their business. Finally, a government in an underdeveloped country plays an important role as it is normally the final authority for permission to set up industry, sanction of loans and grant of licences. Thus industry also tends to concentrate around the federal capital.

As the disparities between the regions widen, capital and labour flow from the backward to the relatively more developed region where returns are greater. Capital is transferred through banks which channelize the savings of people in backward areas as loans to capitalists in the developed region. Labour shifts to the more developed region looking for better employment opportunities. Not only does the outflow of capital reduce the future possibility of growth but there also develops an unfavourable age and sex composition of the population in the backward region (greater percentage of old men, children and non-working women) thus making it even less attractive for future industrial location. These have been defined by Myrdal as the 'backwash' effects of development.

It may be argued that as development proceeds its effects will permeate further into the economy. This process Myrdal defines as the 'spread effects' of expansion to other regions. However, he points out that ordinarily even in a rapidly developing country, many regions will be lagging behind, stagnating or even becoming poorer, and there will be more regions in the last two categories if market forces alone are left to decide the outcome. As an example, he cites the USA and Sweden which despite over a century of sustained development, reveal great regional disparities.

The Lewis Model

The Lewis model of a dual economy can also be used to show that interaction between modern and backward sectors of the economy will ultimately eliminate regional inequalities as the development diffuses. It may be argued that once the surplus labour of the stagnant sector has been absorbed by the developed sector, real wages in both sectors will rise. This will induce investment in labour-saving technology in both sectors and consequently increase productivity and growth.

In reality, however, the model does not work, as it is based on two critical assumptions which are invalid in underdeveloped countries. Firstly, it assumes that capitalists in the developed sector plough back most of their profit so that the process of absorbing surplus labour from the backward sector continues until the excess labour is eliminated. This assumption does not hold in underdeveloped countries because of the absence of a capitalist class which is prepared to invest its profits in industry rather than dissipate it in luxury consumption.

Secondly, the model assumes the capitalists will continue to expand production irrespective of any demand problem. In actual fact, there will be a shortage of effective demand because the section of society demanding luxury consumer goods in an underdeveloped country is small. The shortage of effective demand is especially important, since the model assumes that the bourgeoisie (from which demand for consumer goods comes in the first place) does not spend much on consumption.

The reason why the model ignores the problem of expanding output is that it assumes perfect competition where the individual producer sells all that he produces. However, in underdeveloped countries, monopolies have come into existence in the early stages of development with the result that capitalists tend to restrict production for the domestic market. Given the difficulties of exporting manufactures in the present framework, the process of industrialization tends to slow down so that surplus labour may never be entirely absorbed from the backward region. Hence even the Lewis model of dual economies cannot be used to argue that the market mechanism will eliminate regional inequalities over time.

Source: Hamid, Naved and Akmal Hussain, 'Regional Inequalities and Capitalist Development: Pakistan's Experience', in Zaidi, S. Akbar (ed.), *Regional Imbalances and the National Question in Pakistan*, Vanguard, Lahore, 1992, pp. 2–6.

Notes

1. World Bank, *Women in Pakistan: An Economic and Social Strategy*, Washington, 1989, p. (iii).
2. Cornia, Giovanni, 'Accelerating Human Development in Pakistan', in Banuri, Tariq (ed.), *Just Adjustment: Protecting the Vulnerable and Promoting Growth*, UNICEF, Islamabad, 1992, p. 101.
3. World Bank, op. cit., 1989, p. (xiv).
4. These observations are extracted from World Bank, op. cit., 1989; World Bank, *World Development Report 1995*, Oxford University Press, New York, 1995; and UNDP, *Human Development Report 1995*, Oxford University Press, New York, 1995.
5. See also Zaidi, S. Akbar, 'Gender Perspectives and Quality of Care in Underdeveloped Countries: Disease, Gender and Contextuality', *Social Science and Medicine*, vol. 43, no. 5, 1996.
6. Ibid.
7. World Bank, op. cit., 1989.
8. Ibid., p. 41
9. Ibid.
10. Ibid., p. 48.
11. *Economic Review*, Karachi, July 1994 and August 1994.
12. World Bank, op. cit., 1995.
13. This section makes extensive use of IUCN, *The Pakistan National Conservation Strategy*, Karachi, 1992, and Hasan, Arif and Ameneh Azam Ali, *Environmental Repercussions of Development in Pakistan*, OPP-RTI, Karachi, 1993.
14. World Bank, op. cit., 1995, p. 170.
15. IUCN, op. cit., 1992, p. 10.
16. Ibid., p. 21.
17. Hasan Arif and Ameneh Azam Ali, op. cit., 1993, p. 47.
18. Ibid.
19. This section makes extensive use of Zaidi, S. Akbar (ed.), *Regional Imbalances and the National Question in Pakistan*, Vanguard, Lahore, 1992.
20. See Zaidi, S. Akbar, 'Sindhi vs Mohajir: Contradiction, Conflict, Compromise', in Zaidi, S. Akbar, op. cit., 1992.
21. For articles that provide a somewhat more detailed and lengthy historical analysis, see Zaidi, S. Akbar, op. cit., 1992, especially chapters 3 and 12.
22. Pasha, Hafiz A., *et al.*, 'The Changing Profile of Regional Development in Pakistan', *Pakistan Journal of Applied Economics*, vol. 9, no. 1, 1990, p. 16.
23. Ibid.
24. Ibid., p. 17.
25. Unfortunately no similar table exists for 1980.
26. Hamid, Naved and Akmal Hussain, 'Regional Inequalities and Capitalist Development: Pakistan's Experience', in Zaidi, S. Akbar, op. cit., 1992.
27. Ibid., p. 1.
28. Ibid., p. 3.
29. Kardar, Shahid, 'Polarization in the Regions and Prospects for Integration', in Zaidi, S. Akbar, op. cit., 1992, pp. 320–1.
30. Preface, in Zaidi, S. Akbar, op. cit., 1992, p. (i).
31. Ibid.
32. Kemal, A.R. and Moazam Mahmood, 'Poverty and Policy in Pakistan', in Banuri, Tariq, op. cit., 1992, p. 49.
33. Ibid., p. 50.
34. Ibid., p. 51.
35. Gazdar, Haris, *et al.*, 'Recent Trends in Poverty in Pakistan', mimeo, 1996(a), p. 21.
36. Ibid.
37. Sayeed, Asad and Aisha Ghaus, 'Has Poverty Returned to Pakistan?', mimeo, Social Policy and Development Centre, Karachi, 1996.
38. Khan, Shahrukh Rafi, 'Do IMF and World Bank Policies Work?', Sustainable Development Policy Institute,

Monograph No. 6, Islamabad, 1997.

39. Kemal, A.R., 'Structural Adjustment, Employment, Income Distribution, and Poverty', *Pakistan Development Review*, vol. 33, no. 4, 1995.

40. Gazdar, Haris, *et al.*, 'A Profile of Poverty in Pakistan: Some Insights from Pakistan's Integrated Household Survey 1991', mimeo, 1996(b), p. 8.

41. Ibid., p. 10.

42. Ibid., p. 16.

43. Gazdar, Haris, *et al.* op. cit., 1996(a), p. 16.

44. Kemal, A.R. and Moazam Mahmood, op. cit., 1992, pp. 55–6.

45. Ibid., p. 56.

46. Ibid., p. 58.

47. Ibid.

48. Ibid.

49. Ibid.

50. Gazdar, Haris, *et al.*, op. cit., 1996(a), p. 21.

51. Zaidi, S. Akbar, 'The Structural Adjustment Programme and Pakistan: External Influences or Internal Acquiescence?', *Pakistan Journal of Applied Economics*, vol. 10, no. 102, 1994.

52. See Kemal, A.R., op. cit., 1995; Sayeed, Asad and Aisha Ghaus, op. cit., 1996; and Khan, Shahrukh Rafi, op. cit., 1997.

18 Institutional Issues in the Social Sector

The cliché-ridden New World Order is said to have had its beginnings in the mid-1980s following Michael Gorbachev's *perestroika* in the Soviet Union, finding its crystallization with the fall of the Berlin Wall in 1989. We are told that this is the triumph of the West and the End of History; the New Age is one of the free man and woman, unencumbered by the state; and freedom of choice and action are now set to dominate economic and political thinking.[1] This is the era where the neo-liberal synthesis has found its expression in economics and politics. Market-friendliness, privatization, deregulation, devolution and democracy are now the key clichés that form the mix (and fix) for societies which were hitherto deviant from the norm adhered to in the West. With the demise of the bipolar world, the unipolar world now sees itself as an elongated extension of the West to the non-West. The measuring-rod for success and achievement is now the ability to ape developed western countries in order to make development 'sustainable'.[2] Governance, democracy, and devolution form a critical union to make development sustainable, and are said to comprise the key prerequisites for progress.[3]

With the breakdown of the command economies of the former Soviet regime and its allies, devolution of control and power has been seen as a particular means for increasing participation, and hence, progress. Today, in matters of governance and government structures, huge centralized machineries that were deemed competent and capable of delivering on promises to their people have floundered. The new thinking has shifted away from the central and federal government's role in developing the economy and society, and has begun to incorporate the private sector and non-governmental organizations as important key actors in development strategies. Furthermore, the need for less bureaucracy, more efficient and timely delivery of services, and a closer and more direct access to the beneficiaries of development-related projects have also been important considerations in this shift in thinking and strategy.[4]

Not only has there been a move away from government control; there has also been a noticeable shift *within* government structures. Furthermore, the concept of government itself has changed. The control economies of eastern Europe, and the military governments in much of the Third World, have been replaced by some form of democratic regime. There is agreement now that strong centralized states are out of tune with the reality on the ground, and thus there has been a growing demand for more active participation, and hence, *devolution*. The controlling federal/central state has been forced to extend more powers to smaller units at the provincial, district, and local level, so as to enable these units to play an active role in providing welfare to the people. More autonomy has been granted to provincial and state governments, and local municipal government has also been expected to play an increasingly prominent role. While the world climate has been the critical factor in causing this shift of emphasis,[5] the economic constraints faced by many, if not most, underdeveloped countries have helped accentuate this shift.

Many Third World governments find themselves in dire financial straits and are forced to reduce public expenditure to cut the budget deficit, and to restructure their economies. The term 'structural adjustment' acts as a metaphor for the state of the economy in most underdeveloped countries.[6] Budget cuts – an essential ingredient of any structural adjustment programme – have meant that central/federal governments have had fewer funds to make available to lower echelons in the hierarchy. Thus, provincial and local governments that were dependent on the state have now had to become more disciplined financially, and have seen their grants and aid cut. It is this dual shift – a resource constraint faced by the federal government, and the belief that more participation and devolution of power and control leads to better, more effective, and sustainable development – that has brought local governments, the private sector, and non-governmental organizations into the foray of development planning.

Pakistan, too, has been influenced by these changes in thinking and perception taking place at a global level. While the structural adjustment programme, with its multifaceted emphasis on privatization, deregulation, and liberalization, has been accepted wholesale by different governments in Pakistan, often without enquiry about the possible repercussions (see Chapters 14 and 15), the institutional and governance issues have yet to be tackled – and for obvious reasons, we will argue.

Nevertheless, there is a growing debate about and awareness of issues related to the delivery and functioning of the social sector in Pakistan. There is a general belief that social development has been poor, not because facilities have been inadequate in number, but because organizational and managerial issues, and issues of delivery, have ensured poor progress. At present, there is growing recognition of a need for change in the way social development is delivered. Even official government documents have started paying lip-service to the need for administrative reforms: 'the effectiveness of planning and administration has progressively been eroded by the growing inability of government to effectively implement its policies'.[7] The government believes that it has not been able to make collective decisions in the past, a major reason for which is

> that all administrative, political and even scholarly attention has been focused on bureaucratic and centralized forms of collective decision making, with little attention towards representative decision making (as in the parliament, cooperative societies, district councils), and downright hostility towards participatory decision making arrangements. This needs to be reversed.[8]

Moreover, the government believes that 'effective reform of local government institutions has to be at the core of any development strategy aimed at the alleviation of poverty or the development of the social sectors'.[9]

This chapter will examine some of the more general issues that have recently been raised concerning attempts to improve the delivery and functioning of the social sector. In particular, the government's much publicized Social Action Programme (SAP) will be examined, as will some of the institutional components of SAP, such as governance, decentralization, and popular participation. This chapter differs from the earlier ones on the social sector in that it provides information and offers interpretation by other analysts of the institutional components, and then offers some collective comments on this new way of thinking.

The renewed commitment to the social sector is supposed to have 'transparent and accountable' government as an important cornerstone. 'This transparency will entail decentralization, better monitoring and accountability of public institutions and greater involvement and strengthening of civil society instruments, primarily NGOs [non-governmental organizations] and CBOs [community-based organizations].'[10]

18.1 The Social Action Programme (SAP)[11]

In response to the relative failure of the development of the social sector, compared to the somewhat buoyant economic growth in recent decades, the government of Pakistan, on the initiative of the World Bank, launched an extensive Social Action Programme to address the imbalances of the earlier years. In 1993/4, one year after a highly focused programme was initiated, funding for a three-year period was made available by a number of donors. The first phase of SAP, between 1993/4 and 1995/6, would cost about US$4 billion (development and recurrent costs). About $3 billion (76 per cent) is expected to be contributed by the government of Pakistan, with the remainder being provided by donors.

In identifying the need to look at the social sector in a different way and to focus on existing problems with new alternative solutions, the World Bank has highlighted a number of weaknesses in basic social services in Pakistan. With regard to primary education, the World Bank has identified the following problems:

> objectives are unrealistic, resource requirements are inaccurately projected, and critical paths and monitorable indicators are unclear; too little emphasis on quality with insufficient budgeting for books; cultural requirements, such as schools close to home for girls, the need for female teachers and schools with toilets, are often overlooked; development budgets are released late, so implementation is also delayed; misplaced political influences especially regarding site selection of local schools; and, irregularities in construction.[12]

On these grounds, 'primary education is often inefficient, of poor quality and insensitive to local views on what should be taught and how'.[13]

The problems with primary health care are quite similar to those of primary education. Basic Health Units (BHUs) and other lower-tiered health facilities are considered to 'seldom work efficiently'. The problems are as follows:

> Most health facilities deliver poor quality basic care and do not reach most communities; poorly furnished, without medicines; non availability of staff especially at BHU level; a dearth of female trained health workers; inefficient structure of primary health care; duplicative and centralized structures; inadequate planning and budgeting; delay in release of funds and excessive staff turnover.

Table 18.1
Targeted development allocations by sector in the Social Action Programme (four provinces combined, Rs m)

Sector[a]	1992/3	1993/4	Cumulative	1994/5	Share (%)
Education	6,013	6,559	7,123	19,695	48
Health	1,982	2,679	3,071	7,732	19
Water supply and sanitation	3,777	4,941	5,229	13,947	33
Total	11,772	14,179	15,423	41,374	100

[a] Excluding population welfare and nutrition, for which the allocations are small.
Source: Iqbal, Mohd Asif and M. Ahmed, 'A Review of the Social Action Programme', in *Provincial Governments and the Social Sectors*, mimeo, Social Policy and Development Centre, Karachi, 1995, p. 43.

Table 18.2
Extent of achievement of targeted allocations to SAP sectors, 1992/3 to 1994/5[a] (Rs m)

	Targeted allocation	Budget allocation	% achievement
Education	19,695	9,438	48
Health	7,732	4,210	54
Water supply and sanitation	13,947	8,790	63
Total	41,374	22,438	54

[a] Cumulative.
Source: Iqbal, Mohd Asif and M. Ahmed, 'A Review of the Social Action Programme', in *Provincial Governments and the Social Sectors*, mimeo, Social Policy and Development Centre, Karachi, 1995, p. 43.

In the primary health sector, as in much of the social sector, 'as communities are too little involved in the design or delivery of such services, their preferences are not adequately considered. Thus, many local health facilities are underused or abandoned, because they fail to meet users' needs.'[14]

Rural water supply and sanitation (RWSS) are the two other areas focused on by the Social Action Programme. The main problems in rural water supply are that less than half of the population has access to water, and for areas that do receive water, the quality is also not particularly good, indeed it is often below a minimum acceptable standard. Problems of availability of sanitation are even worse. The World Bank feels that:

> RWSS systems would be more effective and more affordable if they involved community-based approaches using simpler and less costly technology that could be operated and maintained at the local level, with communities covering the costs of operation and maintenance ... Communities and users have been too little involved in the design, operation, and management of RWSS systems, with the result that they feel little ownership and so contribute little.[15]

It is in response to these systemic, conceptual, and structural problems that the Social Action Programme has been launched. The SAP is supposed to take an "umbrella" approach to improving basic social services in Pakistan because the main problems are not sector-specific but endemic – common across all services and areas of the country'.[16] These endemic problems result in the social services being operated inefficiently. All four SAP components – primary education, primary health care, rural water supply, and sanitation – suffer from the following:

i)   Poor planning and budgeting;
ii) Bureaucratic delays in the release of budgeted funds to line departments and executing agencies;

iii) Lack of trained staff to meet rapidly expanding needs, made worse by recruitment bans imposed by the Government on all programmes to promote fiscal discipline, without exemptions for priority needs;
iv) Absenteeism and excessive or improper transfers of staff – managers as well as front-line workers, including teachers and health workers;
v)   Inadequate and unreliable supplies of key inputs (including books, medicines, and contraceptives) needed to maintain service quality;
vi) Locating schools and health units within communities with too little attention to the location of most potential users;
vii) Faulty construction;
viii) Excessively centralized management of dispersed front-line services, which could be more effectively run through decentralized systems with flatter 'organizational pyramids';
ix) Weak monitoring and bureaucratic obstacles to mid-course correction (particularly in the rigid application of the government's procedures for modifying projects).[17]

With these systemic problems pervasive in the social sector and in the four areas that constitute the Social Action Programme, in order to achieve any success in the programme, the World Bank feels that it is essential to make the following improvements:

1   Implementation needs to be strengthened by improving planning, budgeting, and operational efficiency.

2   The design of services should focus on quality and access, with particular emphasis on women and girls.

3   There is a need to improve on the level of effort in projects, on government funding, and on community responsibility.

4   There has to be an improvement in political will.

The key elements of the SAP framework are as follows:

i)   A decentralized structure, to clarify responsibilities for implementation of programmes in each of the four social services, province by province;
ii) Performance-based annual agreements, with detailed operational plans and measurable targets, to determine funding;
iii) Mechanisms for continuing policy dialogue, coordination and monitoring which reach from front-line ministries and departments through to the highest levels of Government; and
iv) A Participatory Development Programme to encourage community participation and experimentation through non-governmental organizations (NGOs) and related private institutions.[18]

Table 18.3
Social Action Programme targets for 1987/8, with comparisons with Indonesia, Philippines, and Thailand

Human resource indicator	Pakistan 1997/8 SAP targets	Early 1990s values for		
		Indonesia	Philippines	Thailand
Primary school enrolment rates (% of age group)				
Total	87.7	117	110	88
Female	81.6	114	110	88
Male	95.4	119	109	89
Ratio of girls' enrolment to total enrolment	45	48	49	49
Adult literacy (%)	53	84	90	94
Female	40	77	90	92
Male	66	91	90	96
Health				
Life expectancy at birth (years)	63.5	62.0	64.6	68.7
Female	63.3	63.8	66.5	71.3
Male	62.6	59	63	67
One-year-olds immunized (%)	90	92	92	86
Rural access to safe water (%)	70.5	43	79	72
Rural access to sanitation (%)	31.5	36	63	72
Population				
Growth rate (%)	2.7	2.2	2.7	2.4
Contraceptive prevalence rate (%)	27.9	50	40	66
Population coverage (%)	80	80	75	70

Source: Behrman, J.R., 'Pakistan: Human Resource Development and Economic Growth in the Next Century', mimeo,
8 May 1995.

In addition, there is much greater emphasis on community participation, due to the belief that this will ensure that 'services would be better used, better managed, and better maintained. Communities would feel a greater sense of "ownership" and would be more likely to contribute to their costs. In addition, popular political support for government programmes would be more likely to grow, thus enhancing government commitments to investments in social services.'[19] These broad outlines encompass all four sectors of the Social Action Programme. The specific reforms to which the government committed itself in each sector and in each province for 1993/4 are given in Appendix 18.1.

An evaluation of the Social Action Programme by the World Bank, two years into its three-year duration, argues that 'considerable progress has been achieved under the SAP, but the achievements are fragile and are not yet institutionalized'.[20] The report states that SAP has made 'substantial progress' at policy reforms to improve quality and delivery of services, and has undertaken a number of the specific measures proposed originally (see Appendix 18.1). One of these measures is the increased involvement of the community in social services, with more supervisory control over staff attendance at schools and health units. While the World Bank has been a little cautious in its enthusiasm over the Social Action Programme, the government of Pakistan has claimed the SAP to be a great success. It argues that the 'legacy of SAP has facilitated a relative shift in emphasis from training as a stand alone intervention to training as a programme approach. Moreover, SAP has instituted the concept of

accountability through the site verification process ... which is once again an essential ingredient of institutional reform.'[21] And finally, the government of Pakistan feels that 'the role of SAP in ensuring effective development in the social sectors *has been phenomenal*'.[22] Although it is too early to evaluate the Social Action Programme (for at the time of writing, it is still in progress), the more conceptual issues and requirements of the SAP – good governance, decentralization, local-level and community participation, and non-governmental organizations – are discussed in the following sections; see also Appendix 18.2.

18.2   Governance, Decentralization, and Local-Level Delivery[23]

One of the key concepts to emerge in the present world climate is that of governance, a term applied particularly to underdeveloped countries.[24] While it is not the objective of this section to examine the epistemological, philosophical, or political genesis of this concept, some comments on the concept will be useful to our discussion.[25]

Governance has been described as 'an act or manner of governing, of exercising control or authority over actions of subjects, a system of regulations'[26] and 'reflects a judgement on the quality of government'. 'It refers to a certain system of politics and how this functions in relation to public administration and law. Governance has also been used to focus specifically on development. Governance, in this context, means the manner in which power is exercised in the management of a country's economic and social resources for development.'[27] Among the earlier public statements on good governance is the 1989 World Bank report on Africa, where the concept included the following features: 'an efficient public service; an independent judicial system and legal framework to enforce contracts; the accountable administration of public funds; ... respect for the law and human rights at all levels of government; a pluralistic institutional structure, and a free press'.[28] In later works, a clearer idea of the World Bank's understanding of the concept emerges, where good governance is synonymous with sound development management.[29]

M. Halfani and his associates, in their work on the implications of governance for urban research in developing countries, state that governance is distinct from government and 'refers to the relationship between civil society and the state, between rulers and the ruled, the state and society, the government and the governed'.[30] According to Tariq Banuri, the crisis of governance 'refers to an excessive degree of centralization, overburdening, and rigidity of the government machinery; the absence of local participation which can provide the requisite attention to detail; the deterioration in the professionalism, competence and integrity of public functionaries; and the weakening of judicial and quasi-judicial institutions'.[31] While it is clear even from this insufficient selection of definitions that 'the meaning of governance depends on who is looking at the term and what he/she is looking for',[32] there does seem to be a core body of concern and focus. However, given the ambiguity and ambivalence in the use of the term, good governance has also been used by pro-marketeers, wherever found expedient, to mean *minimum* government.

In a sense, the term reflects within it almost all facets of civil society and government, and the relationship between the two. Economic development needs to be examined with its social and cultural consequences. Governance also encompasses the relationship between participation and development by governments. Furthermore, community participation, the role of women, sustainable development, and economic effects on the environment and consequently on the population all form some part of the concept of governance. It is a huge term used to capture a large number of ideas about political, social, and economic development. Not only is governance about how governments function, but it is a multi-relational concept of society as a whole. One cannot argue that governments *per se* are inefficient and corrupt, and have no respect for the law – though this is true in most underdeveloped countries – without examining the links with the nature of society in which government functions. We need to examine the level and structure of economic development and of society, the historical and cultural traditions of particular societies, and the influence of the government on civil society, before any concept of governance emerges. Furthermore, particular perceived facets of good governance, such as community participation, need not be 'good' or beneficial in all societies, regardless of specific social structures.[33] Essentially then, even if there is

some general consensus about what constitutes (good) governance, these rules need not be universally applicable. With these remarks on what constitutes the still evolving concept of governance, we examine the role that the government has played in development in Pakistan.

18.2.1 Government and Development in Pakistan[34]

While there may be differences of opinion about what constitutes the concept of governance – good or bad – there would be little disagreement over our claim that governance has been noticeably poor in Pakistan. On this single count alone, most conceptualizers of the term 'governance' would agree. Public participation, or democracy, must surely be one of the central tenets of any definition of good governance. Pakistan's political leaders have carefully done away with this feature altogether.

Twenty-five of Pakistan's fifty years have been ruled formally by three military dictators at different junctures of its history. From 1947 to 1985, only one free and fair general election was held, and even then, Zulfiqar Ali Bhutto's democracy (1972) would hardly be termed a model of good governance. 1985 saw a military dictator hold a form of general election, where individuals rather than political parties were given the right to participate. Ironically, though, the three-year period (1985–8) with Mohammad Khan Junejo as prime minister, despite the domination and control of General Zia-ul-Haq as president, can be considered to have provided better government and governance than the (truly?) democratic regimes of Z.A. Bhutto, Benazir Bhutto, and Nawaz Sharif. Nevertheless, on the whole, the lack of popular participation in Pakistan would suggest that the system of governance has been quite poor.

With regard to the social sector and social development, it is generally believed that the main obstacle to the achievement of comprehensive development in Pakistan has been the crisis of governance. Giovanni Cornia defines this as the crisis

> of the government's ability to design and implement policies, particularly policies which require targeting, selection or judgement. Such crisis manifests itself in the fact that over the years the GOP [government of Pakistan] has become excessively centralized; that participatory institutions have eroded, and are virtually non-existent today; that the hostility towards participatory institutions and local-level democracy has led to the gradual erosion of the self-confidence, the skills and the system of grass-root institutions needed for organizing collective action; that the breakdown in professional standards, lax supervision and growing corruption of large sections of the civil service (including those dealing with education, tax administration, law and order) and arbitrary procedures are causing a severe crisis of legitimacy of government institutions which are no longer perceived as acting in the public interest.[35]

Having identified the problem, Cornia argues further that it is imperative that reform of the state apparatus take place, even though such a reform will be 'painful and difficult', but there is urgent need for greater 'participation of civil society in the design and execution of social sector activities'.[36] What this requires is that *institutional reform* take place, so that basic functions of the state 'such as public security, fair judicial recourse, enforcement of contracts, and so on, are actually being fulfilled'.[37]

Along with institutional reform to bring about some semblance of good governance, advocates of this line of thinking also believe that better delivery of social services requires decentralization: the hold and role of the central government should be weakened, while the role of lower tiers of government and other participants in the social sector matrix should be increased.[38] Asad Sayeed argues that the centralization of the delivery mechanism is among the most serious impediments to the provision of adequate social services. As an illustration of the excessive extent of centralization, he cites the example of the rural water supply schemes (RWSS) and argues that:

> in RWSS the provincial Public Health and Engineering Departments (PHEDs) are responsible for not only the development of water supply schemes but they also perform the function of O & M [operation and maintenance] and revenue collection. Originally established for the provision of urban water supply schemes, the PHEDs have approached the problem of rural water supply and management from the standpoint of urban needs with the consequent urban bias in technology. Institutionally local government and its related departments (such as the LGRDD) [Local Government and Rural Development Department] are designated to provide for RWSS. But because of the weak financial and technical base of local government, this role has de facto been handed over to the PHEDs. With little interest in the collection of revenues (as their budget is not affected by recovering revenues) monitoring of projects is weak. The RWSS case illustrates that in spite of the mandate given to local government, its weak financial and technical base renders it incapable of performing these tasks. Similarly, in other social sectors also, according to the Local Government Ordinance of 1979, local bodies have the mandate to undertake development and O & M work for social sectors, but for the above reasons they have, by and large, abdicated this responsibility to provincial governments.[39]

Giovanni Cornia believes that to break the hold of the federal/central governments, decentralization should take place not just at the provincial level, but beyond, at the district and local/union level. His rationale for decentralization is that

> the greater closeness of public administration to the problems of society allows for faster and more relevant and efficient decisions concerning local needs. In addition, decentralization allows for more genuine democratic control from the beneficiaries of the services (through school boards, parent commissions, user associations, etc.): such informal bodies should provide support to teachers and health workers, oversee the attendance to and quality of services, decide on the siting of new facilities, provide additional resources, etc.[40]

The third key requirement for better governance, along with institutional reform and decentralization, is community participation and democratic control.

> The case for a far greater reliance on the communities, their local representative bodies and the NGOs in Pakistan is a strong one. Greater reliance on community participation and social mobilization in the design, delivery and monitoring of social activities ensures in the first instance, a greater relevance of these programmes to the actual needs of the population, and a greater internalization of their benefits by the poor and unreached. In addition, community-based programmes generally employ less unnecessarily skill-intensive approaches and ensure greater overall efficiency. Community participation also facilitates the mobilization of additional cash resources and of other resources in kind such as labour and locally available material which have a low opportunity cost but intrinsic productive value. And, finally, the active involvement of the community enhances the sense of self reliance and responsibility of people and their ability to take care of their lives.[41]

18.3 NGOs and Community Participation[42]

There are about 8,500 registered non-governmental organizations (NGOs) in Pakistan, and an unaccounted larger number of unregistered organizations. Of those that are registered, 70 per cent are registered under the voluntary Social Welfare Act, while the remainder are registered under the Societies Registration Act, the Trust Act, the Companies Act, or the Charitable Endowment Act. Not surprisingly, given greater population densities and proximities, most NGOs are urban based with different focuses of locational and operative interest. Each NGO has its own particular philosophy, priority, focus, area, and manner of interaction with its client population. Despite the very large number of NGOs in different regions in Pakistan, most NGOs being highly localized – in fact, this is one of the key elements that distinguishes NGO activity from other types of intervention. There are fewer than a dozen NGOs that have a national coverage. Approximately 70 per cent of the registered NGOs are in the Punjab, probably because of the higher level of urbanization in that province.

There are essentially three types or categories of NGO working in Pakistan. These are as follows:

1 Welfare oriented, which provide social services mainly to the poor and underprivileged.

2 Grassroots development organizations, which work with specific targeted communities for the development and economic and social uplift of the area or people.

3 Women's NGOs, which specifically target and focus on issues related to the economic and social status of women. Activities of these NGOs are not restricted to the delivery of social services alone, and research, information, dissemination, legal advice and advocacy, and other development issues are also on their agenda.

In the 1940s and 1950s, NGOs were mainly charitable and philanthropic organizations, but since the 1970s, and especially in the 1980s, NGOs have 'stepped into welfare oriented roles as the state system increasingly failed to deliver. After the seventies [the] shift has been towards development community based initiatives.'[43] Most NGOs receive financial support from community contributions, local donors and often receive funds from the government through the Social Welfare Departments of the provincial governments. Increasingly though, funding from international donors has become a major component of funds for NGOs.

Most NGOs in Pakistan belong to the first category listed above, i.e. they are welfare oriented. They are usually operative at the level of neighbourhoods and 'are involved in the provision of civic amenities such as basic health, education, library facilities, vocational training, youth programmes, credits, income-generating activities, etc. Education and social community services are priority areas of NGO activities'.[44] Development-oriented grassroots organizations with specific and focused objectives, such as rural development, provision of urban water supply and sanitation, have emerged over the last fifteen years or so, as have NGOs with a specific women's focus. A study in 1990 identified the following issues faced by the NGO sector in Pakistan:

i) uneven quality of service;

ii) limited attention to developing the indigenous capacity of the people;

iii) weak structures and means to become self-sustaining;

iv) social welfare orientation;

v) vague and limited objectives specific to immediate problems;

vi) inability to conceptualize for long term objectives;

vii) non-professional in outlook resulting in incompetent management of accounts, planning and budgeting;

viii) top-heavy structures, lacking in mid-level cadre of professionals or trained support staff. Shortage of staff was a major problem identified by NGOs;

ix) almost all operate with limited budgets relying usually on community contribution or local donors;

x) absence of capacity to expand or absorb additional funds

xi) no systematic monitoring of activities by themselves or government;

xii) weak coordination between NGOs; largely operating in an isolated manner.[45]

Community development based on the principles of community participation is seen as a key component of an alternative strategy for social sector development. This view rests on the central premise that local communities are the best protectors of their own interests and hence should play a more active role in their own development. Tariq Banuri and Moazzam Mahmood put the theoretical argument as follows:

> Define a community on the basis of relative spatial proximity, like a village or an urban *abadi*. This very largely also defines the community in terms of common requirements for social services, like education, health, housing, water, sanitation, roads, energy needs, and the environment. It also defines the community in terms of basic classes, and therefore employment and income needs. If the community has a set of common social service requirements, then the community's perception of the problem is the highest. If its perception of the problem is the highest, then the community's solution to the problem will be the most relevant and useful under any given set of constraints. And the community's response to the problem will also be the fastest.[46]

Having defined the community as the principal agent of change, the two authors maintain that the role of the community then becomes one of deciding 'what services to demand under a given set of constraints; it establishes a clear responsibility with the community, and gives the system an endogenous dynamic which is not immediately obvious to traditional development strategy'.[47]

Community participation along with NGO-oriented activity now forms a critical component of the new conventional wisdom of development. As Asad Sayeed argues:

> It is now acknowledged across the board that monitoring the efficiency of delivery at the grass roots as well as several other mediatory tasks can be best performed by non-governmental organizations (NGOs). NGOs can articulate the beneficiaries' needs to project authorities, provide information about the scheme to communities, organize community based organizations to maximize their gains from schemes, deliver services to less accessible populations and serve as intermediaries to other NGOs. Government, on the other hand, can also learn from alternative development strategies pursued by NGOs.[48]

However, while there has been a growing consensus around the belief that NGOs, as an alternative 'development paradigm', offer an answer to state failure, NGO failure too has now begun to concern academics and practitioners, and the NGO sector, rather than being promoted wholesale, needs to be critically evaluated[49] (see also Appendices 18.3 and 18.4 for concerns raised about community participation and NGO activity). In the next section of this chapter, we try to examine in more detail some of the issues raised so far.

18.4 Issues of Interpretation and Implementation in the Social Sector

It seems difficult to disagree with the emphasis of the government of Pakistan on the Social Action Programme. SAP seems to be the right solution for lingering problems, with its focus on the most basic sectors and on decentralization, better governance, and community participation. Indeed, one might expect quite remarkable results, given new structures and delivery mechanisms. However, this section raises a number of issues that require us to evaluate all such initiatives in a critical and ongoing manner.

In an excellent paper, Hafiz Pasha[50] raises some of the most damning and critical questions that face the Social Action Programme. The first question is 'given high budget deficits, can governments, particularly the provincial governments (who are primarily responsible in Pakistan for delivery of social services) afford the downstream recurring expenditure liabilities arising from the accelerated development programme under SAP?'[51] This is especially pertinent for the education and health sectors, where there are high operations and maintenance costs. In primary education, for example, for every rupee spent on the construction of schools, there is a subsequent increase annually in the recurring liabilities due to teachers' salaries, books, etc., of about one-fifth, or 20 paisa. Hafiz Pasha adds that 'while the provincial governments may have access to additional development funds through the Social Action Programme, there exists no such provision for financing the higher recurring costs given the strong economic arguments against achieving high levels of direct cost recovery in basic education and health'.[52]

The second key question asked by Hafiz Pasha is 'will the present public institutions in the country be able to handle such an accelerated expansion of facilities proposed by SAP?'[53]

A study conducted by the Social Policy Development Centre has revealed that, if the Social Action Programme contains only a development, i.e. capital cost, component including the construction of new facilities, 'the impact on the fiscal status of the provincial governments tends to be *significantly negative*'.[54] For every 100 rupees invested through SAP, the deterioration in the budgetary position of the four provincial governments will be 8 per cent, or 8 rupees. Thus, the Rs9 billion annually spent on SAP for the first three years of the programme will worsen the financial position of the provincial governments by about Rs2 billion annually, imposing a severe financial strain on provincial government budgets. Clearly, provincial governments will have to deal

with this situation, and the likely response will be 'either that the provincial governments will scale down their commitment to the Social Action Programme in the absence of revenues to cover the higher recurring expenditure or that the annual allocations of operating budgets to the social sectors will not rise in proportion to the expansion in facilities'.[55] Hence, there will either be a substantial slowdown in the rate of acceleration in investment in the social sectors, or key ratios, such as teacher/student and doctor/bed, will decline. Hafiz Pasha argues that

> when this foreign aided initiative comes to an end there is likely to be a major curtailment in recurring expenditure on the social sectors in the absence of a continuing source of funding. Provincial governments are likely then to be left with newly hired doctors, teachers, etc., who they cannot pay for. Therefore, all this strategy achieves is to temporarily postpone the problem.[56]

Hence, no matter how useful a strategy the Social Action Programme may be, financial and institutional constraints faced by the provincial governments may leave the government with yet another failure in its attempts to deal with the growing crisis in the social sector. This crisis is likely to emerge once SAP comes to an end unless more foreign aid funds are received. As countless examples all across the world have demonstrated, once the aid givers decide to curtail or terminate aid, many projects and programmes are not sustainable. However, this is something that will be determined in the near future. In the meantime, let us continue with our review of the Social Action Programme.

Mohammad Asif Iqbal and N. Ahmed, in another very interesting evaluation of the Social Action Programme, also have some important misgivings.[57] Their findings are as follows:

1 The Social Action Programme envisages a threefold increase in development allocations by the provincial governments to the basic social sectors. This is an *overly ambitious* programme, especially given the financial and budgetary constraints faced by both provincial and federal governments.

2 There are *recurring financial liabilities* of SAP due to downstream requirements, which provincial governments will have to deal with in the future.

3 There is *lack of local participation*; local participation is 'necessary in programmes like SAP because effective demand for investment can be better identified by lower tiers of government with greater knowledge of local needs and programmes. Community participation is also necessary in the delivery mechanisms which can create a sense of ownership and raise the willingness to pay among the people. For this purpose, NGOs have not yet been adequately involved.'[58]

4 In some cases, provinces have failed to utilize even the released funds for SAP. This *non-utilization of funds* has been due to bureaucratic delays in project approvals.

5 The *monitoring and evaluation* requirement of SAP projects has been slow and inadequate.

Initial evaluations of the Social Action Programme, especially those based on its financial and budgetary aspects, have been rather critical. Although it is too early to reach final conclusions, most observations about SAP are not very flattering (see Appendix 18.2). Asad Sayeed has argued that 'it is unfortunate that the greater policy emphasis on the social sectors has occurred at a juncture when the fiscal crisis in Pakistan has assumed serious proportions'.[59] Hence, he suggests that 'in a resource constrained scenario, the only manner in which improvements in these [SAP] indicators can be achieved is by enhancing the efficiency of delivery mechanisms through appropriate policy and institutional reforms'.[60] Let us then examine the institutional issues of implementation and delivery, first regarding the Social Action Programme, and then in more general terms.

Asad Sayeed, having suggested that institutional reform may be the only manner in which progress is possible, himself provides an analysis of why this, too, is unlikely. He writes:

> Over the last decade it has become increasingly obvious that public representatives at the federal and provincial levels prefer to keep delivery mechanisms centralized so that they can derive political mileage from being involved in delivering new schemes. In an environment where federal and provincial level politics has been reduced to the delivery of a school, a hospital or a road to the constituency, persistence with centralized mechanisms is inevitable.[61]

He adds that 'it is also commonplace to observe that one reason for inadequate site and personnel selection as well as excessive emphasis on development expenditure is because of the prevalence of rent-seeking and patronage for politicians',[62] a finding confirmed in subsequent field work and investigation (see Appendix 18.2).

The Social Action Programme, with its emphasis on decentralization, community participation, and NGO involvement, is not the first of its kind to include such components. The 1978 'Health For All by the year 2000' strategy, endorsed by almost all underdeveloped countries, also required these ingredients.[63] Many of the issues pertinent to primary health care are equally important to the Social Action Programme in Pakistan today. Appendix 18.3 explains how and why community participation and NGO-led development strategies do not always work. Appendix 18.4 provides an intriguing look at the NGO sector in Pakistan, indicating that what would have been a useful channel for development has now become a racket for making money and offering patronage.[64]

Conventional wisdom and liberal politics (which, incidentally, are closely related) offer decentralization, local-level delivery, and community participation as yet another panacea for solving the problems of countries like Pakistan. While these strategies may have worked in some countries, Pakistan seems to be faced with specific concerns. Probably the most important recent and current issue regarding decentralization in Pakistan is the non-existence of elected local government. The elected urban and rural local bodies were dismissed and dissolved by the respective provincial governments, in 1991 in the NWFP, in 1992 in Sindh, and in the Punjab in 1993. Irrespective of when and if elections are held for local government, it is clear that a critical tier of democracy and government has been missing. That higher tiers of government feel threatened by local government, which resulted in the latter's dismissal, is testimony to the potential vibrancy, power, and effectiveness of local government. Had the lowest tier of government been a mere appendage to higher levels of government, it would probably not have been dismissed in the first place, or elections would have been held without controversy, much earlier.[65]

Adherents of the decentralization and community participation argument almost always overlook issues of political, social, and economic power and differentiation. It is not possible to conceive of communities without a degree of hierarchy, although conventional wisdom consciously and repeatedly does exactly this. Patronage and power are equally present in all their manifestations at the 'local' level as at the higher level, and the platitudes offered by proponents of participation seem rather hackneyed.

We conclude this chapter with some extracts from a paper by Jean Dreze and Haris Gazdar, based on their research in Uttar Pradesh in India. The similarities between Pakistan and one province of 130 million people in India merely exemplify the fact that many of the problems faced by underdeveloped countries are quite similar. They write:

> given the current political links between the schooling establishment and the rural élite, formal decentralization cannot be expected to achieve very much unless it goes hand in hand with more active political mobilization of disadvantaged groups.[66]

> Privileged groups (usually high caste landlords) have exercised tight control on local government institutions, and use them to their private advantage at the expense of public needs.[67]

> Decentralization was perceived as a problematic issue from the very start. Those familiar with rural inequalities warned that devolution of political power might well result in the enhanced tyranny of dominant élite groups. As a matter of fact, it soon became clear that political power at the village level remained with the propertied classes. Contrary to common expectations based on an idealized view of harmonious village coexistence, the introduction of new elected bodies led to exacerbated tensions in the early years.[68]

> This system of patronage-based governance is not simply a localized phenomenon, it has corrupted political institutions at all levels. Leading political parties have played a critical role in the development of this perverted system of governance. In these circumstances, it would

be naive to expect state action to promote social opportunities on a wide basis, or the electoral process to act as a sound instrument of accountability.[69]

And finally,

> In the present political climate, it would be naive to expect the government to initiate major reorientation of development priorities on its own, or on the basis of bland expert advice.[70]

What this large array of quotes from the paper by Jean Dreze and Haris Gazdar highlights is the reality that decentralization, community participation, local government, etc. are terms and concepts which, rather than being promoted and endorsed enthusiastically, need to be seen in light of relations of power, patronage, class, and gender. While there are certainly numerous benefits from promoting development along the lines that many academics and developmentalists suggest, caution and open-mindedness are essential.

18.5 Summary and Further Reading

18.5.1 Summary

Having examined in Chapters 16 and 17 the factual position and the salient issues in a large group of areas which make up the social sector, we have looked in this chapter at the overall institutional issues and issues of governance and delivery. We have examined how, due to the failure of conventional top-down approaches to development, usually led by the state, new approaches have been evolved and implemented.

The focus has now moved towards participation, devolution, and NGOs. New ways of thinking have been ostensibly designed for Pakistan under the Social Action Programme, focusing on a handful of sectors, but promising new delivery mechanisms. Although large amounts of money have been spent on the Social Action Programme, analysis suggests that once foreign funding ceases, so will the programme. Moreover, the programme seems to be imposing high financial costs on both federal and provincial governments. The community participation spirit and the 'new way' of delivery are also lacking.

Much of this chapter has examined, in some detail, the alternative development paradigm – governance, decentralization, NGOs, local government, etc. We find that there is far more hype and rhetoric than substance and reality to many of the claims made by and about this so-called alternative paradigm. By ignoring issues of class, gender, and power, much of what constitutes the philosophy of the new thinking is mere wishful thinking. While decentralization,

delegation, and more local government are possibly a better mechanism for delivering development, enthusiasm needs to be tempered with some caution, and should take cognizance of the contradictions existing even at the local level.

18.5.2 Further Reading

On the Social Action Programme, the following references are essential: World Bank, *Towards a Social Action Programme for Pakistan: Impediments to Progress and Options for Reform*, Report No. 9619-Pak, 1991; World Bank, *Staff Appraisal Report: Social Action Program Project*, Report No. 12588-Pak, 1994. For a critique of the Social Action Programme, see: Sayeed, Asad, 'Social Sector Development and the Social Summit', mimeo, Social Policy and Development Centre, Karachi 1996; Pasha, Hafiz, 'Is the Social Action Programme Financially Sustainable?', *Provincial Governments and the Social Sectors*, Social Policy and Development Centre, Karachi, 1995; other articles in *Provincial Governments and the Social Sectors*, Social Policy and Development Centre, Karachi, 1995; and *Review of the Social Action Programs*, Social Policy and Development Centre, Karachi, 1995.

On institutional issues, local government, decentralization, etc., see Banuri, Tariq (ed.), *Just Adjustment: Protecting the Vulnerable and Promoting Growth*, Oxford University Press, Karachi, 1998; 1992; Zaidi, S. Akbar, 'Planning in the Health Sector: For Whom, by Whom', *Social Science and Medicine*, vol. 39, no. 9, 1994; Zaidi, S. Akbar, 'Urban Local Government in Pakistan: Expecting Too Much from Too Little?', *Economic and Political Weekly*, vol. 31, no. 44, 1996; Zaidi, S. Akbar, 'An Evaluation of Community Participation and NGO Capability in the Rural Water Supply Sector', mimeo, Social Policy and Development Centre, Karachi, 1996; Zaidi, S. Akbar, 'Urban Local Governance in Pakistan', in Islam, Nazrul and M.M. Khan (eds.), *Urban Governance in Bangladesh and Pakistan*, Centre for Urban Studies, University of Dhaka, Dhaka, 1997; Zaidi, S. Akbar, 'Poverty, Politics, Institutions: The Case of Karachi', *Economic and Political Weekly*, vol. 32, no. 51, 1997; Zaidi, S. Akbar, 'Karachi: Prospects for the Future', in Khuhro, Hameeda (ed.), *Karachi: Megacity of Our Times*, Oxford University Press, Karachi, 1997; Zaidi, S. Akbar, 'NGO Failure and the Need to Bring Back the State', *Journal of International Development*, forthcoming, 1999; Zaidi, S. Akbar, *The New Development Paradigm: Papers on Institutions, NGOs, Gender and Local Government*, Oxford University Press, Karachi, forthcoming 1999; McCarney, Patricia, L. (ed.), *Cities and Governance: New Directions in Latin America, Asia and Africa*, Centre for Urban and Community Studies, University of Toronto, 1996; McCarney, Patricia, L. (ed.), *The Changing Nature of Local Government in Developing Countries*, Centre for Urban and Community Studies, University of Toronto, 1996; and Jean Dreze and Haris Gazdar, 'Uttar Pradesh: The Burden of Inesha', mimeo, 1996.

Appendix 18.1

The composition and targets of Social Action Programmes

Here we present the main ingredients of the Social Action Programme.

Primary education programmes will:

- improve the functioning and utilization of existing schools through such measures as filling vacant teacher posts, reducing absenteeism and sharply restricting staff transfers; establishing a separate management structure for primary education; strengthening management information systems; and, through PDP [Participatory Development Programmes] and other efforts, promote community and parental involvement.
- improve the quality of education, by expanding teacher training and increasing expenditure on non-salary recurrent costs from its present low base to supply more items like books;
- improve access to education, particularly in rural areas, by building more schools and siting them according to need based on population criteria;
- increase girls' enrollments (and particularly their retention rates) by recruiting and training more female teachers and either instituting co-education or providing more girls' schools;
- expand primary education systems as fast as is practical, increase Government support, and encourage greater community participation in education [see Table 1].

Primary health care programmes will:

- improve the efficiency and utilization of basic health care by strengthening management units and planning capability, by rationalizing the structure of different levels of health care, and by linking programs now run vertically, such as those for communicable disease control, more effectively with basic services;
- improve programme design by paying more attention to 'quality' inputs such as medicines (improving logistics and increasing expenditures); by giving more priority to communicable disease control including immunizations; and by including more family planning in basic health care;
- increase access to health care by constructing more basic facilities in those areas still lacking them (particularly in the more remote areas) and by consulting users more in the design and delivery of services;
- increase women's access to health care by recruiting and training more female medical staff at various levels of service;
- increase Government expenditure on and promote community participation in health care [see Table 2].

Population programmes will:

- improve the operation and utilization of existing services through better planning, management, and logistics and through decentralization of more activities to the provinces;
- sharply expand access to family planning and improve quality of services, particularly by instituting government-sponsored, community-based outreach programmes in

Table 1 Primary education

Strategy	Targets	Means
Emphasis on girls' education especially in rural areas.	Increase participation rate from 69% to 88% by the end of Eighth Plan.	Creation of new seats of 5.5 million students.
Provision of facilities to shelterless schools.	Ratio of girls enrolment to rise from 35% to 45% by 1998.	Opening of new primary/mosque schools.
Improvement in school environment.	Female literacy rate to rise from 25% to 40% by 1998.	Additional classrooms in existing primary schools.
Teachers' training.		Appointment of additional female primary teachers.
Emphasis on recruitment of female teachers.		Improvement in service conditions/ appropriate posting and transfer policy.
Govt's commitment to buy land for girls' schools if community cannot provide it free of cost.		Incentives for female teachers in shape of higher allowances.
Introduction of co-education.		Extensive Teachers' Training Programme.
New curricular development for quality education.		

Table 2 Primary health care

Strategy	Targets	Means
Consolidation and improvement of primary health care services (PHC).	Immunization coverage to increase from 80% to 90% by 1998.	Extended EPI and CDD Programme and in the Prime Minister's prog. of 33,000 VHWs.
Complementary utilization of PHC to deliver family planning facilities.	ORS distribution to rise from 13.5% million to 23.5 million.	Training of 58,000 TBAs.
Enhance community involvement.	TBAs training to rise from 60 to 16,425 by 1998.	Increase female staff in BHUs and RHCs.
Provide remedy for under-staffing and under-utilization of BHUs and RHCs.	BHUs/RHCs would be upgraded and made fully functional.	Establishment of 616 urban health centres.

rural areas and by helping train health workers in the health departments in clinical as well as non-clinical methods of contraception;

- encourage interest in family planning through information and education programmes to increase public understanding of contraception and its links to maternal and child health;
- increase government expenditures as fast as practical and encourage community participation (for both men and women) [see Table 3].

The RWSS programmes will:

- improve performance and utilization of local RWSS systems and ease financial dependence on the Government and on donors by: improving planning and management of Government agencies; by encouraging the involvement of communities; and by promoting

community responsibility, particularly for operation and maintenance;

- improve quality and expand access, especially for women, through greater reliance on community-based approaches.
- improve rural sanitation by increasing the share of RWSS budgets devoted to sanitation and promoting community-based approaches, using appropriate, maintainable and affordable technology [see Table 4].

Source: World Bank, *Staff Appraisal Report: Social Action Program Project*, Report No. 12588-Pak, 1994, pp. 21–2 and Government of Pakistan, Planning Commission, *Social Action Programme, Report to the Pakistan Consortium, 1995–96*, Islamabad, 1995, pp. 2–3.

Table 3 Population programme

Strategy	Targets	Means
Unequivocal political support.	Reduce growth rate from 3% to 2.7% by 1998.	Implementation of accelerated family planning programme, especially in rural areas with highest-level commitment.
Strong and bold Information, Education and Community (IEC) system.	Extension of Population services to entire urban areas and 70% rural areas, by 1998.	Use of all public sector health outlets for delivery of family planning services.
Improve service delivery network.		
Crash training programme.	Increase in Contraceptive Prevalence Rate (CPR) from 14% to 28%.	Active training programme including PM's prog. of 33,000 VHWs.
Linkage between Population Welfare and Health Departments at provincial level.	Raise user level from existing 3.8 million to 7 million.	Involvement of NGOs.
		Appointment of married village-based female planning workers.
		Establishment of additional 200 family welfare centres, 120 mobile service units, and 100 reproductive health service centres.

Table 4 RWSS

Strategy	Targets	Means
Adoption of policy framework of Strategic Investment Plan.	Increase in rural water supply coverage from 46% to 70%.	Increased involvement of local govt, local councils, rural support programme, NGOs, and communities.
Community-based approach for identification, planning, and implementation of RWSS schemes.	Increase in rural sanitation from 13.5% to 31.5%.	Co-ordination among PHED and LG&RD departments.
Adoption of affordable and least-cost design and appropriate technology.	Serve additional 27 million population for water supply and 9 million for sanitation during 8th Plan.	
Willingness of the people, to pay for RWSS services.		

Appendix 18.2

Is the Social Action Programme working? Observations from a field survey

The following extracts are based on a field survey conducted by S. Akbar Zaidi and Aly Ercelawn in Mardan and Mianwali districts, in May 1996, for a study to investigate how the Social Action Programme was working. The study, which was ongoing at the time of writing, was commissioned by the Social Policy and Development Centre, Karachi.

The Impact of the Politicization of SAP

The field survey revealed that the Social Action Programme had become highly politicized, and the main beneficiaries of SAP were current members of the ruling party in the national and provincial assemblies. While on the one hand the survey revealed that much of the SAP agenda and SAP implementation was unfulfilled, with very few concrete measures taken, it became clear that in future the mechanisms through which SAP will be implemented will prove to be a powerful vehicle for patronage, and eventual implementation will be highly selective.

There seemed to be considerable overlap between SAP and non-SAP delivery, and in many cases it was difficult to distinguish between different programmes. The People's Works Programme, the MNA and MPA programmes, and the 'normal' annual development schemes of the provincial government were often intermingled with some of the Social Action Programme schemes. At times, even the implementing agency or district department itself could not clearly distinguish under which programme a certain scheme had been started or planned.

The role of the Social Action Board was also not clear. The Board was constituted by sitting members of parliament of the ruling party, and a Chairman nominated by the Federal Government. It seemed that (in one case at least) the Chairman of the SAB felt that all developmental roles in the district – including roads and electricity, which do not form part of SAP – were part of the Social Action Programme. The role of the SABs, to themselves and to others in the district, is quite unclear.

It was reported in the course of the field work that, due to a great deal of pressure applied at the provincial and federal level, the attitude of the bureaucracy towards SAP, SABs and elected representatives was changing. Originally, there was a great deal of resentment by the bureaucracy when it felt that elected representatives would have a greater role to play in the delivery of certain social services. There has been some recent change in the stance of the bureaucracy regarding delivery. The bureaucracy, in some cases, is now seen to be working with the SABs and elected representatives.

Due to the politicization of SAP and the patronage mechanism being evolved, it is likely that stark inter-district disparities may emerge. Not only are areas where the local elected representative of the ruling party or the SABs are based being given clear preferences for proposed projects, but simultaneously, there is also a preference in giving employment in SAP-related facilities to individuals of the area of the ruling party. This process of politicization and patronage implies that the people who live in areas where the opposition parties have been elected will be denied SAP-funded facilities. If SAP becomes the main or only delivery mechanism of social sector development, this deprivation can have serious implications.

NGO and CBO Participation

Probably the most clear finding of the field survey was the conspicuous absence of any popular or public participation. Not only were there no Village Health or Education Committees, there was no evidence of any sort that NGOs had been consulted or considered when policy and programmes were being framed, at either the district or provincial levels. The methods adopted for delivery were the same old bureaucratic methods, some of which have been held responsible for the poor performance of the social sectors in the first place.

Not only were NGOs not involved, there was also a lack of awareness of their presence in the district. Either they did not exist at all – a small possibility – or they had no contact at all with SAP-related elected and non-elected members.

In one case (in Thatta district, which was visited subsequently), an NGO had tried to get funds for some of its projects which were SAP-approved, but on each of the numerous visits, they were told by the Project Director of the SAB that they had to get approval from their MNA, the Chairman of SAB. The transaction costs in such an endeavour were quite considerable. Not only are there hindrances in the manner in which NGOs are to access SAP-funds, and through which mechanism, there was also a substantial lack of awareness about SAP amongst the NGOs. Even the better functioning, well-established local NGOs, did not know how they should access SAP funds.

This report is based upon visits to rural primary schools and Basic Health Units, Social Action Boards, and district offices for primary education and health. Discussions with local beneficiaries were also undertaken by the team.

Findings

The initial impression is that SAP has generated very limited formal local-level participation in implementation and monitoring. Careful field work will therefore be even more essential to probe into the barriers to equitable formal participation, and the degree to which informal participation of potential beneficiaries has promoted equitable and efficient implementation of sectoral programmes.

In the absence of effective political reforms, SAP appears to be viewed by local élites as a conduit for local income generation through construction and supply contracts, and through additional employment. SAP funding through ruling-party MNAs and MPAs appears to have a very selective impact upon broadening community participation in the formulation and implementation of SAP. Only appropriate field work can indicate the pros and cons of the new electoral politics *vis-à-vis* the traditional bureaucratic delivery systems.

Employment generation appears to be a major objective of those implementing SAP. One major issue is whether this objective has become an obstacle to the short-term and sectoral effectiveness of SAP investments, but may yet provide other long-term social benefits such as the synergistic effects of increased female participation in the formal labour force. If this is the case, it is worth examining the potential gains of an alternative SAP that places less emphasis upon construction of new facilities.

SAP appears to guarantee some local employment in return for donation of land. The landowner is entitled to one or more school jobs, varying with the level of the school. It appears doubtful that this is generally the most cost-effective means of obtaining land, and it is unlikely to promote equity in the choice of locations – villages with relatively well-off landowners will be naturally preferred over more egalitarian and poorer villages. In the schools visited, the donation of land also did not appear to have engendered an enduring sense of ownership among the community which could mobilize resources for maintenance and other supplies.

There was no evidence of NGO involvement in SAP. This is particularly disturbing in view of the evident absence of support for school maintenance by local communities. As an extreme, one female primary school had no floor mats whatsoever, and teachers complained that locals used the grounds as a latrine during the night.

Official records substantially overstate both actual attendance through new schools, as well as increased quality of schooling through additional school supplies. In one extreme case, the female primary school has had no students whatsoever for many months, despite postings of teachers. Neighbours reported that a fair number of students came when the school was constructed, but dropped out or went or returned to nearby older schools, after the teachers stopped regular attendance.

Physical targets of additional school places through new schools or additional rooms are not always accompanied by corresponding additional financial allocations for increasing teachers and supplies. Salary arrears of one or more years were reported by school staff. It is unclear whether postings were actually in excess of sanctioned posts or, more ominously, the reported arrears are an indirect extraction of bribes for employment. Another, more interesting possibility is that the education department is using SAP to influence priorities *vis-à-vis* other departments.

Inappropriate sites for new schools are one reason for low enrollments: catchment areas can frequently overlap.

Alternatives to increase the cost-effectiveness of primary education do not seem to have been seriously discussed with communities. There was no indication of plans to convert male schools into mixed-gender primary schools through replacement of male by female teachers, to add second-shifts for females in male primary schools, or to add rooms and teachers to existing female primary and middle schools.

Basic Health Units appear to be popular whenever there is an adequate supply of medicines, which are supplied at nominal charges. Since the well-off continue with the time-honoured pattern of hijacking resources meant for the poor, increased provision of supplies in remoter areas may only result in higher levels of subsidy to the well-off. It is also worth examining the circumstances under which élites may become satiated or disinterested and may therefore permit a substantial redirection of resources towards the poor.

SAP's emphasis upon primary education and primary health care may have led to unintended adverse effects upon the poor. Tertiary facilities have become overcrowded, possibly leading to less use and a drop in the quality of care. Increased use of more expensive, private facilities could impose undesirable tradeoffs of reduced food and nutritional intakes among the poor.

Appendix 18.3

Community participation and NGOs: some experiences from the health sector

Community participation seems to be such an obvious choice as a vehicle for development-related projects. Why, then, does it fail? Here are some reasons.

On the face of it, community participation seems like a desirable component to any development policy and there is a growing belief that as long as the 'community' is involved, development will be somewhat better and more effective. However, numerous experiences have shown that the imposition of community participation on health structures has had disastrous consequences on the health programme and on the welfare of the affected people. The 1978 Alma Ata Declaration of Health for All by the year 2000 which emphasizes primary health care, also makes a universal declaration for community participation which forms a cornerstone of providing health for all. Both WHO and UNICEF, and now the World Bank, have consciously, and often aggressively, highlighted the need for the participation of communities. This over-enthusiasm, often in disregard to specific cultural, social and political conditions, has in many cases caused the participatory approach to fail.

Lynn Morgan in her study on primary health care [PHC] in Costa Rica, one of the world's success stories in PHC, argues that 'Costa Rica's experience with community participation in health exemplifies the complexities and social contradictions that emerge when a small, economically dependent country feels the need to adopt externally-sanctioned models when structuring rural health services.' She argues that 'participation was a concept introduced by the US and promoted by foreign aid agencies to promote a western democratic political ideology' and the international agencies 'justified community participation in health more because they wanted to reinforce the symbolic identification of 'health' with 'democracy' than because they knew that community participation would improve health'. WHO and other international agencies made community participation a pivotal strategy 'because it satisfied politico-ideological needs. The international agencies needed a cooperative non-confrontative approach to address issues of poverty and inequitable distribution of wealth.' The community participation component in Costa Rica's rural health programme lasted a mere four years, as officials quickly realized how the objective had failed and let the successful rural health programme continue without any forced participation, which, in the first instance, had been included only on the insistence of international organizations following Alma Ata in the period 1978–82. Interestingly, Morgan argues that the international organizations themselves, discouraged by the results of the exercise of participation, withdrew their insistence, but she argues, 'Costa Rica's willingness to comply with international mandates suggests that the government would have continued to support community participation if the agencies had continued to deem it necessary.'

The case of the Dominican Republic is somewhat similar where a primary health care programme was also short lived, as its development and dissolution formed part of US foreign policy. Whitford argues that 'the Dominican institutionalization of primary health care succeeded in meeting political needs, even as it failed to raise health levels'. Its broader purpose was to counter 'Castro-communist' policies and not necessarily one of attacking morbidity and mortality. As US foreign policy particularly favoured the Dominican Republic, substantial assistance in the health sector came from USAID, the World Bank, the Inter American Development Bank, as well as other health and development agencies. The result of the imposition of the primary health care scheme was that since it was a foreign model, it resulted in intensifying class, status and regional differences. Whitford believes that the model for the Dominican primary health care system should 'have been created in response to host country needs, abilities, and capabilities; it should not have come from a lender-country formula'. In the case of Nepal, where also due to the thinking of the international agencies, Judith Justice has found that the primary health care approach was 'accommodated' in the health care system, and the results were far from positive.

Also in Nepal, Linda Stone's work has shown how the focus on community participation 'appears to be an attempt to promote the western cultural values of equality and self-reliance (values not shared by the local population), while ignoring alternative values and perceptions of how development might work in rural, non-Western societies of developing countries'. In Nepal and other south and south-east Asian countries, primary health programmes have been ineffective 'because they were designed to meet the needs of various health bureaucracies rather than the needs of local villagers'. Antonio Ugalde has also reached similar conclusions where he has shown how the concept of community participation in Latin America is based on the needs, demands, insistence, and direction, of international organizations.

Other than the problems with the imposition of community participation in primary health care on the insistence of donors, there are numerous other problems within local hierarchies which frequently subvert any possible gains to be made by participation.

Community participation has been seen as a means of control and manipulation of the people, the supposed beneficiaries of the process of participation, by politicians, bureaucrats and technocrats. Cultural concepts within communities and of those who locally implement primary health care and participation have been seen to make such programmes dysfunctional. Urban trained professional workers who are requested (or forced) to work in rural primary health care settings are unable and/or unwilling to work in a system which they are neither trained for, and nor particularly like; their training has made them competent to work in urban hospital settings, not in the community. Conflict is seen to emerge within and around community projects when the local social structure impinges on the proper functioning of (democratic) community participating. Additionally, government bureaucrats are faced with a two-edged sword regarding community participation in development related schemes: if a scheme works due to 'self-help' or on the community's combined effort, government is relieved of providing these services and can concentrate on a different set of priorities; however, if schemes continue to work and more self-reliance, political consciousness and 'empowerment' takes place, and people begin to get collectivized and demand better facilities, further pressure is put on the government to deliver. Similarly, the failure of community projects would mean to some members of government, that the people are still dependent on government and cannot manage without it; the government would, however, have to cope with increased demands on its resources.

Non-governmental Organizations (NGOs)

The recent mushrooming of all sorts of voluntary agencies and NGOs – one observer counted 700 'missionaries of progress' and 50 donor agencies in Khatmandu in 1986, including a maritime agency which was 'of the opinion that landlocked Nepal ought to own a cargo vessel moored across India, in Calcutta' – has reinforced the view that community participation is the key to progress and development. It is readily believed, especially by those working for and involved with NGOs, that the solutions to the problems of the poor in the Third World rest in the arms of these NGOs. Strong claims have been made on behalf of NGOs, claims which range from those that suggest that NGOs are the truest forms of democracy, to those that they are responsible for a new development vision.

While numerous local voluntary groups and NGOs have proven effective in their attempts to improve the well-being of their reference group, many, especially those who have had to depend on foreign donors making often considerable contributions to the cause of their choice, have had to compromise to rules and concepts which are unworkable and/or alien to the perceived beneficiaries' needs. Some NGOs have been set up by organizations like the Ford Foundation and USAID and this has resulted in a relationship of severe dependence of local NGOs on external agencies.

One observer has argued that NGOs in some countries have been taken over by the élite: 'Expensive conferences are arranged all over the world on NGOs. Young men and women who look good and talk good are now seen in five star lobbies talking participation with donors. Lengthy consulting reports at highly inflated rates are prepared for NGOs by NGOs. The upper class has shown its alacrity yet again. They are taking full advantage of the new and generous opportunity being offered by the NGO.' Those NGOs which are dependent on foreign funding often have to provide reports which continue to prolong their own existence. Since many foreign donors are not particularly familiar with local conditions, progress reports are often 'fudged' and fabricated to justify further funding. Bratton argues that 'since all African NGOs rely heavily on donated funds, NGO leaders must cultivate more productive relations with the organizations and individuals who provide their resources'. With growing amounts of international aid and assistance being channelled through NGOs, the blossoming of the voluntary sector is bound to continue. And as its role and presence grows, its interests will get further entrenched.

Source: Zaidi, S. Akbar, 'Planning in the Health Sector: For Whom, by Whom?', *Social Science and Medicine*, vol. 39, no. 9, 1994, pp. 1389–91.

Appendix 18.4

NGOs for the élite

Abdus Samad takes a rather critical look at NGO culture in Pakistan:

The Pakistani élite has been a wonderful survivor in Pakistan. It has adapted itself to changing incentives very well. No matter what government is in power or what the new thinking of the expatriate expert, you can be sure that members of our élite will be drawn to money, funding and power as honeybees are to honey. This class has, through our brief history, shown itself to be very agile in discovering the latest trend for acquiring fame and fortune. The middle classes that attempt to ape the élite, unfortunately, are always a little late in catching the trend and arrive largely after the élite has moved on. Or perhaps the élite moves on when the lesser classes arrive.

In the fifties, the civil service was the only game in town. It was the only way for any young man to achieve distinction, power and moderate wealth in the newly formed country. Young men from the élite would obtain the best of grooming and education at home and coast into the academy. All they had to do was look good, talk good and rule. No burden of serving the people was placed on them. The government was there to serve them and not the other way around.

By the late sixties, the lower classes had caught on and their young men, driven by ambition, and by the dint of effort, began to compete for the civil service. Local institutions, that groomed the élite, became accessible to all and the relatively poor and less privileged began to flock to them. The distinction between the ruler and the ruled was being eroded.

This was an easy matter to deal with. The upper classes simply abandoned those institutions and started to send their children abroad. The result was fortunate for the upper classes in two respects. First, the polish added on by Oxbridge and the like, maintained the distinction between the high born and the low born. Second, this distinction could be further sharpened by allowing the domestic institutions to fall into a state of rapid decline since the élite needed them no longer.

However, the onslaught of the lower classes for some form of power sharing or democratization could be resisted no longer. Succumbing to this, Bhutto, in 1973, proceeded to reform the civil service in a manner that ended the éliteness of the club forever. The lower classes invaded the club in large numbers.

The élite responded by abandoning the civil service. It is interesting to observe that the socio-economic background, the education, as well as the extent of polish, of the average recruit changed dramatically during this period. The élite having abandoned the system allowed it again to deteriorate rapidly.

However, an alternative had to be found for the polished and educated young men of the élite. Fortunately, the multinationals saw the opportunity as well as the tremendous economic advantage of exploiting the powerbase of the élite and its princes. Thus, in the mid-seventies, we saw that the élite children were employed by multinational companies. Interestingly enough, the very same individuals who had been preparing almost their entire life for the big civil service exam, suddenly forgo the exam and start beating a path to the door of the BCCIs, Citibanks, Banks of America, ICIs etc. The multinational, in turn, hires them, treats them in a manner that is in keeping with their stature. Of course, these foreign firms exploited the contact base, élite position in society, as well as the better education, of their new hirees from the élite classes for their own advantage in Pakistan. Consequently, we see unprecedented growth of these firms and their profits in Pakistan during the seventies and eighties.

Meanwhile, during the roaring eighties, a new trend started setting in. The deterioration of the civil service and the public sector had reached an advanced stage. Public sector personnel became both corrupt and incompetent. The government became virtually paralysed and had only one unabashed aim – to confer rents and benefits on the élite. The truly well-connected élite could safely use the government institutions to his own advantage. The result: a) rent-seeking which earlier was in its infant stages now is a growth industry, and b) white collar crime is now in fashion. Distributor/agents of foreign companies specialise in selling any and all equipment to the government at highly inflated prices. Individuals from the élite classes now turn to obtaining loans from the nationalized financial institutions with every intention of not returning them. Scams such as finance companies and the cooperatives are run with impunity and with absolutely no fear of retribution.

Unfortunately, the roaring eighties came to an end. BCCI was caught out. The phenomenal pace of growth of the multinational firm could not be maintained forever. Petrodollars were gone and the bipolar world had made its way into history books. The government had borrowed too much and was being forced by international agencies to curb its spendthrift ways. This meant that multinational jobs were relatively scarce now, bank loans were more difficult to obtain, and selling worthless equipment to the government at inflated prices was now more difficult.

As luck would have it, an opportunity again presented itself to the élite. Donor agencies and the development-oriented 'thinkers' (henceforth DOT) had long relied on the government for the development miracle. Frustrated with the dismal performance over the years, they were seeking an alternative approach but one that would still limit the role of the private sector (for the private sector and the DOT are mutually hostile). The new approach that they thought up was based on the notion of 'participation' where citizens were only to be consulted in decision-making. Of course having consulted with the people, the government would continue to spend money on behalf of the people awarding the contracts to its favorites.

The modes of participation remained to be determined. Since the average DOT is suspicious of the private sector and profit, he dreamed up the nearest equivalent to the government – a non-profit organization – as his basic unit for this participation. As the DOT desired, the NGO, like the government, is responsible to no one. So long as funding is available, the NGO can continue to do as it pleases with absolutely no regard to private or social productivity.

Pleased with this line of reasoning, the donor agencies encouraged rapid growth of the NGOs. Funding was easy and the educated upper classes cashed in. The living rooms of almost every house in Gulberg, Defence and the Fs and Gs [F and G sectors] of Islamabad were quickly converted to NGOs. Once a donor is convinced, there is no looking back. An NGO is born. Its health and growth is determined only by the glibness of its parent.

The decade of the NGOs is here. Expensive conferences are arranged all over the world on NGOs. Young men and women who look good and talk good are now seen in five star hotel lobbies talking participation with donors. Lengthy consulting reports at highly inflated rates are prepared on NGOs by NGOs. The upper classes have shown their alacrity yet again. They are taking full advantage of the new and generous opportunity being offered by the NGO. Like before, the bill for this high living by means of the NGOs will be paid for by the people of Pakistan when the loans of the donors, financing these organizations, are called.

To me the only remaining question of interest is: After the NGOs what will be the next goose that lays the golden eggs for the élite?

Source: *The News*, Karachi, 18 July 1993.

Notes

1. See, for example, Zaidi, S. Akbar, 'The Structural Adjustment Programme and Pakistan: External Influence or Internal Acquiesence?', *Pakistan Journal of Applied Economics*, vol. X, nos. 1 and 2, 1994(a); Zaidi, S. Akbar, 'Planning in the Health Sector: For Whom, by Whom?', *Social Science and Medicine*, vol. 39, no. 9, 1994(b); Zaman, Arshad, 'Sustainable Development, Poverty and Policy Adjustments: Linkages and Levers for Change', mimeo, International Institute for Sustainable Development, Canada, 1993; Banuri, Tariq, *Economic Liberalization: No Panacea*, Clarendon Press, Oxford, 1991; Banuri, Tariq (ed.), *Just Adjustment: Protecting the Vulnerable and Promoting Growth*, UNICEF, Islamabad, 1992(a).

2. Zaman, Arshad, op. cit., 1993.

3. Leftwich, A., 'Governance, Democracy and Development in the Third World', *Third World Quarterly*, vol. 14, no. 3, 1993.

4. Zaidi, S. Akbar, op. cit., 1994(b); Zaidi, S. Akbar, 'Urban Local Government in Pakistan: Expecting Too Much from Too Little?' *Economic and Political Weekly*, vol. 31, no. 44, 1996(a); Zaidi, S. Akbar, 'An Evaluation of Community Participation and NGO Capability in the Rural Water Supply Sector', mimeo, Social Policy and Development Centre, Karachi, 1996(b); Zaidi, S. Akbar, 'Urban Local Governance in Pakistan', in Islam, Nazrul and M.M. Khan (eds.), *Urban Governance in Bangladesh and Pakistan*, Centre for Urban Studies, University of Dhaka, Dhaka, 1997(a); Zaidi, S. Akbar, 'Poverty, Politics, Institutions: The Case of Karachi', *Economic and Political Weekly*, vol. 32, no. 51, 1997(b); Zaidi, S. Akbar, 'Karachi: Prospects for the Future', in Khuhro, Hameeda (ed.), *Karachi: Megacity of Our Times*, Oxford University Press, Karachi 1997(c); Zaidi, S. Akbar, 'NGO Failure and the Need to Bring Back the State', unpublished paper, 1997(d); Zaidi, S. Akbar, *The New Development Paradigm: Papers on Institutions, NGOs, Gender and Local Government*, Oxford University Press, Karachi, forthcoming 1999.

5. Zaidi, S. Akbar, op. cit., 1994(b); Zaman, Arshad, op. cit., 1993.

6. Zaidi, S. Akbar, op. cit., 1994(a); Zaidi, S. Akbar, op. cit., 1994(b).

7. Government of Pakistan, Planning Commission, *Eighth Five Year Plan (1993–8): Approach Paper*, Islamabad, 1991(a), p. 9.

8. Ibid., p. 11.

9. Ibid., p. 8.

10. Sayeed, Asad, 'Social Sector Development and the Social Summit', mimeo, Social Policy and Development Centre, Karachi, 1996, p. 1.

11. For an extensive understanding of what the Social Action Programme constitutes, see the following: World Bank, *Towards a Social Action Program for Pakistan: Impediments to Progress and Options for Reform*, Report No. 9619-Pak, 1991; World Bank, *Pakistan: Poverty Assessment*, Report No. 14397-Pak, 1995; Government of Pakistan, Planning Commission, *Social Action Programme (SAP) 1992–95*, Islamabad, 1992(a); Government of Pakistan, Planning Commission, *Memorandum for the Pakistan Consortium, 1992–93*, Islamabad, 1992(b); Government of Pakistan, Planning Commission, *Social Action Programme, Report to the Pakistan Consortium, 1995–96*, Islamabad, 1995. See especially World Bank, *Staff Appraisal Report: Social Action Program Project*, Report No. 12588-Pak, 1994.

12. World Bank, op. cit., 1994.

13. Ibid., p. 3.

14. Ibid., p. 4.

15. Ibid., p. 5; see also on the rural water supply sector, Zaidi, S. Akbar, op. cit., 1996(b).

16. World Bank, op. cit., 1994, p. 6.

17. Ibid., pp. 6–7.

18. Ibid., p. 13.

19. Ibid., p. (vi).

20. World Bank, op. cit., 1995, p. 27, emphasis added.

21. Government of Pakistan, op. cit., 1995, p. 20.

22. Ibid., emphasis added.

23. This section makes use of Zaidi, S. Akbar, op. cit., 1996(a); Zaidi, S. Akbar, op. cit., 1997(a); McCarney, Patricia, L. (ed.), *Cities and Governance: New Directions in Latin America, Asia and Africa*, Centre for Urban and Community Studies, University of Toronto, 1996(a); and McCarney, Patricia, L. (ed.), *The Changing Nature of Local Government in Developing Countries*, Centre for Urban and Community Studies, University of Toronto, 1996(b).

24. See, Leftwich, A., op. cit., 1993, and Zaidi, S. Akbar, op. cit., 1997(a).

25. For an excellent summary and critique of governance, see Leftwich, op. cit. 1993.

26. Khan, M.M., 'Governance: A Conceptual Framework', mimeo, Global Urban Research Initiative, Centre for Urban Studies, Department of Geography, University of Dhaka, Dhaka, Bangladesh, not dated, p. 1.

27. Ibid.

28. Leftwich, A., op. cit., 1993, p. 610.

29. World Bank, *Governance and Development*, Washington, 1992.

30. Halfani, M., *et al.*, 'Towards an Understanding of Governance: The Emergence of an Idea and its Implications for Urban Research in Developing Countries', mimeo, 1994, p. 4, subsequently published in McCarney, Patricia, L., op. cit., 1996(b).

31. Banuri, Tariq, 'Just Adjustment: Protecting the Vulnerable and Promoting Growth', *Pakistan Development Review*, vol. 31, no. 4, 1992(a), pp. 685–6.

32. Khan, M.M., op. cit., p. 1.

33. Zaidi, S. Akbar, op. cit., 1994(b); Zaidi, S. Akbar, op. cit., 1997(b); and Zaidi, S. Akbar, op. cit., 1997(d).

34. See also the references in nn. 1, 4.

35. Cornia, Giovanni, 'Accelerating Human Development in Pakistan', in Banuri, Tariq (ed.), *Just Adjustment: Protecting the Vulnerable and Promoting Growth*, UNICEF, Islamabad, 1992(b), p. 105.

36. Ibid.

37. Ibid.

38. See also the references in nn. 1, 4.

39. Sayeed, Asad, op. cit., 1996, pp. 13–14; see also Zaidi, S. Akbar, op. cit., 1996(b).

40. Cornia, Giovanni, op. cit., 1992, p. 106.

41. Ibid.

42. This section makes extensive use of Mumtaz, Khawar, 'NGOs in Pakistan: An Overview', in Banuri, Tariq, op. cit. 1992(b). However, for a critique of NGO activities, see Zaidi, S. Akbar, op. cit., 1997(d), and Zaidi, S. Akbar, op. cit., forthcoming 1999.

43. Ibid., p. 129.

44. Ibid.

45. Ibid., p. 134–5.

46. Banuri, Tariq and Moazam Mahmood, 'Learning from Failure', in, Banuri, Tariq, op. cit., 1992(b), pp. 117–18.
47. Ibid., p. 118.
48. Sayeed, Asad, op. cit., 1996, p. 19.
49. See Zaidi, S. Akbar, op. cit., 1996(b), Zaidi, S. Akbar, op. cit., 1997(d), and Zaidi, S. Akbar, op. cit., forthcoming 1999.
50. Pasha, Hafiz A., 'Is the Social Action Programme Financially Sustainable?', in Policy and Development Centre, *Provincial Governments and the Social Sectors*, Karachi, 1995.
51. Ibid., p. 35.
52. Ibid.
53. Ibid., p. 36.
54. Ibid., p. 37, emphasis added.
55. Ibid., p. 38.
56. Ibid.
57. Iqbal, Mohd Asif and N. Ahmed, 'A Review of the Social Action Programme', in Social Policy and Development Centre, op. cit., 1995.
58. Ibid., p. 45.
59. Sayeed, Asad, op. cit., 1996, p. 6.
60. Ibid.
61. Ibid., p. 14.
62. Ibid., p. 17.
63. See Zaidi, S. Akbar, op. cit., 1994(b).
64. See also Zaidi, S. Akbar, op. cit., 1996(b), and Zaidi, S. Akbar, op. cit., 1997(d).
65. See also Zaidi, S. Akbar, op. cit., 1996(a); Zaidi, S. Akbar, op. cit., 1997(a); and Zaidi, S. Akbar, op. cit., 1997(b).
66. Dreze, Jean and Haris Gazdar, 'Uttar Pradesh: The Burden of Inesha', mimeo, 1996, p. 47.
67. Ibid., p. 67.
68. Ibid.
69. Ibid., p. 71.
70. Ibid., p. 84.

Part 6

Political Economics

This last chapter tries to tie the numerous threads running through this book into one, showing how economics and politics entwine. The argument presented in Chapter 19 is that a middle class is emerging on the political horizon of Pakistan, after having established itself as a formidable economic entity. We may just be seeing the beginning of a middle-class 'order' in Pakistan, but a lot still needs to be done to ensure that this order is orderly. Currently, the dozens of crises and fault lines seen in the structure of the economy and society emphasize the fact that the old order may have been lost for ever. What is going to replace it is still somewhat debatable in this era of visible transition. The last chapter of the book is in lieu of a conclusion, and highlights current political and economic issues in the country, with one eye on future directions.

19 Political Economics: Class, State, Power, and Transition

In the year leading up to the celebrations for the fiftieth anniversary of Pakistan's independence, the one word that has been most audible is 'crisis'. And not just one crisis, but a large number of crises or fault lines in our society, polity, and economy. There has been a bombardment of mainly newspaper articles, which have articulated the presence of a crisis of the economy, of governance, of the judiciary, of government, and so on. The general perception among the newspaper-reading élite of Pakistan is that the country has, in a sense, lost its way. Even after fifty years, the perception goes, we have not been able to address central issues in our society, and the belief is that rather than heading towards progress, the country is unravelling, becoming more like Somalia than South Korea. This chapter will argue that, while numerous structural problems exist in the different layers that constitute Pakistan, what we are seeing is a manifestation of the particular form of transition through which Pakistan is going.

It is clear that the economic, political, and social structure that had existed until quite recently, the 'old order', is in an advanced stage of decay; hence the mayhem that exists. Although it is very evident that a new social and political order is emerging, what direction it will take seems less easy to predict. Crises emerge at such junctures, where the old order and the new come into conflict. In Pakistan it seems that, while the old order is lost for good, its replacement, in terms of political alignments, social values and movements, methods of governing and governance, codes of ethics and conduct, etc., is not yet well defined. It is probably this vacuum which best articulates the extent and nature of the many crises that currently exist.

This is, clearly, a difficult chapter to formulate, as it will be subject to a large number of opinions which interpret the same facts in very different ways. It tries to interpret all the economic and other issues discussed in the previous eighteen chapters in terms of politics. Moreover, while historical trends can be discerned relatively easily, the current imbroglio is not easy to understand, especially when one is part of it. With these words of caution and warning, let us begin to assess how the economic processes in Pakistan's five decades have influenced politics, the state, classes, and society, and also how all of them have, in turn, affected each other and the economy.

An examination of the different chapters of this book will inform the reader about the massive changes that have taken place in different sectors of the economy over the last fifty years. These changes came about due to alliances between different political and economic élites, and their relationship to the more permanent institutions of the state. A number of important economic and political turning points in the last fifty years have affected the nature of class formation that has taken place in the country, and this in turn has had repercussions for the political settlement and on the nature of politics.

19.1 Civilian Bureaucracy and Industrialization: 1947–1958

In the early years soon after Pakistan came into being, the state was run by a small group of bureaucrats who were essentially responsible for bringing about policies to ensure the survival of the country at a time when the odds were clearly stacked against it. With seven million migrants, a political system that was greatly dependent on that devised by the British to preserve and extend their role as a colonial power, and without much industry to speak of, the first few years were such that the civil service seemed to be the only institution organized and modern enough to run the country. In terms of political entities, there were a large number of big landowners, mostly feudals, and an equal number of sardars and tribal leaders. Since there was no industry, there was no class of individuals related to the industrialization process. Essentially, bureaucrats dominated the political scene in Pakistan for the first few years, with a collection of land owning politicians, nawabs and sardars comprising the core political equation.

Mercantile capitalists soon emerged as an economic group and, after making unprecedented gains from the Korean War bonanza, consolidated their economic position. Many traders who had made money in the early 1950s began to invest their profits in industry, and emerged as the main industrialists of the 1960s. The industrialization process that took place in Pakistan in the mid and late 1950s was ably nursed through by the bureaucracy, which played perhaps the key role in establishing industrial units in the country. State-owned institutions like PICIC and PIDC were fundamental in encouraging the development of industry in key sectors. Moreover, a trade policy that had a formative influence on industry was also actively pursued, so that a particular type of industrialization process could take root. The conventional wisdom at the time, of import substituting industrialization, seems to have been carefully thought through by the institutions of government and bureaucracy, and acted as an impetus to the nature and direction of industrialization.

The first decade after independence, hence, seems to be one where bureaucracy-led and assisted industrialization took place. The bureaucracy seemed to be the leading unequal partner in any political settlement that existed between the key players, and determined the outcome of policy and its application. Industry was the junior partner in this formation, and other political groups, many of which were nascent at that time, had little role to play in the political economy of the country. While the landlords and nawabs may have had some political clout, clearly economic policy was not focused towards increasing or improving their economic well-being. The growth rates in agriculture, for example, were dismal in the first decade, emphasizing the belief of the bureaucracy that the way to develop was through industrialization, even at the cost of agriculture and the rural areas, where almost 80 per cent of the population lived. Since much of the bureaucracy was composed of urban migrants from India, it had little knowledge of or interest in agriculture, and felt that manufacturing should receive far greater state patronage.

Industrialists, while gaining economic clout through very high profits made in the early years, were never a political force and depended greatly on the benevolence of the licence-raj of the civil servants. Political wrangling between different actors of the landowning class also did not allow those politicians to emerge as a strong and united political force. With disarray in the ranks of the political groups that existed, the military stepped in to restore law and order and to continue and escalate the bureaucratic capitalism that had emerged in the 1950s.

19.2 Civil and Military Bureaucratic Capitalism: 1958–1971

The military emerged as the stabilizing shell under which industrialization, with the help of the bureaucracy and the emerging industrialists, could develop further. The very high growth rates in the economy and in large-scale manufacturing would not have been possible without a central command, and the only institution capable of providing that sense of order at the time was the military.

Although there is debate about the reasons for the land reform of 1959, whether it was undertaken to break the hold of the bickering political landowning class, or to provide an impetus to the process of capitalist agricultural development, the consequences of the reform were that both outcomes took place. The hold of the large landowners was indeed dented, but more importantly, the reforms and the numerous other interventions that took place in the agricultural sector brought about nothing less than a revolution in agricultural production and social relations of production, and in fact altered the face of Pakistan once and for all. Shahid Javed Burki has argued that, towards the late 1950s, landlords were again emerging on the political horizon, and Ayub Khan's shifting of power from Karachi to Lahore and Rawalpindi resulted in more representation for indigenous and rural Pakistan, which is one reason why agriculture gained prominence throughout the decade.[1]

Industrialization, which began in the late 1950s, was not in itself sufficient to lead to economic growth and development,

unless there was a change in the rest of the economy as well. Industrialization required consumers, and consumers could emerge only if there was a class of individuals who had purchasing power in excess of their subsistence wages. With 75–80 per cent of the population in a rural economy where agriculture was the only mainstay, and that too an agriculture with a declining output each year, it is unlikely that the consumer boom of the 1960s, and hence the phenomenal growth in agriculture, could have taken place, unless agriculture had developed and unless rural areas and semi-urban areas had become more than just crop-producing areas. Without an agricultural revolution, the industrial revolution in Pakistan could not have taken place. This symbiosis between industry and agriculture was critical to any development or growth plan for the economy.

If the development of agriculture following the land reform of 1959 was indeed a thought-out process and policy of the military-civil bureaucracy-industrialist nexus, it shows the deep political and economic insight of the main policy makers of the time. If it was a matter of accident, then this is one of the many fortuitous moments in Pakistan's history which have changed its destiny on numerous occasions.

The 1960s witnessed the emergence and consolidation of many political groups and economic classes. In agriculture, the hold of the large landowners may not have been broken, but it was certainly shaken enough to allow other economic categories to emerge. Many of the large landowners had the foresight to read the writing on the wall, and accepted the Green Revolution technology package introduced by the government. Although this was an élite farmer strategy, given the high costs associated with the purchase of tractors, the sinking of tubewells, and other ingredients of the package, state subsidization gave the middle farmers, too, the opportunity to adopt this technology. This was the essence of the Green Revolution: the middle and kulak farmers, along with many other farmers at both ends of the spectrum, emerged as capitalist farmers, soon to become a dominant economic and political force, in agriculture and in the country.

In the rural areas, alongside this emerging capitalist farmer we also see the genesis of the small-scale manufacturers, and the skilled and technical workers, the growth of an ancillary service sector in order to service the new economy, and a disenfranchised, landless agricultural wage-labour class. To some extent, the political ambitions of the newly emerging agricultural capitalists were accommodated in the Basic Democracy Scheme of Ayub Khan, but without giving them any real political power. This was perhaps the beginning of the apprenticeship of this class of rural politicians, which was to emerge, especially in the Punjab, in the 1970s and was to stamp its mark on the political economy of the country. The military and civilian bureaucrats under Ayub 'had forged a strong political alliance with a number of middle class urban and rural groups', which helped in fostering economic development and political participation. Moreover, the Basic Democracies[2] system 'not only gave a voice to the middle class peasantry of Punjab and the NWFP, but also converted Pakistan's powerful civil bureaucracy from an apparatus for maintaining law and order into a remarkable vehicle for promoting development'.[3]

On the industrial side, with excessive profits in industry and an industrial class protected by government policies, we see a great consolidation of the economic power of this class. Interestingly, despite emerging excessive wealth, the industrial capitalist class did not emerge as a *political* class in terms of seeking political office. Its relationship was that of a partner with the bureaucracy, through which it sought economic gain and wealth. It did not need to seek political power in a more overt manner, as perhaps the large landlords did, since they had no other sense of identity except the desire to rule the country. While the military governed in the 1960s, it was not involved then in the economic process, as it was to become involved in the period under General Zia ul Haq.

Hence the political nature of the regime, or the political settlement in the Decade of Development, was one where the military and the bureaucracy governed Pakistan, assisted by allies in the industrial and agricultural sectors. Economic power lay essentially with industrialists, but with the capitalist agriculturists swiftly emerging to stake their claim. Moreover, this period also saw the rise of an aspiring, but small, educated middle class that wanted to impart a vision on the political scene, but which lacked the economic power to do so. In Zulfiqar Ali Bhutto, it found a leader on whom it could pin its hopes of fulfilling a social and socialist agenda.

19.3 A Shift in Emphasis: 1971–1977

Zulfiqar Ali Bhutto emerged from the numerous contradictions of the Decade of Development. His constituency, which varied at different times of his political career, shows how all those social groups and classes which had not been direct beneficiaries in either political or economic terms rallied behind Bhutto. Hence, other than the large industrialists, the military, and the bureaucracy, Bhutto at different times reflected the aspirations of all classes.

In the beginning, leading up to the general elections of 1970, and in the first two years of his rule, organized labour, peasants, middle farmers, the urban and rural middle class, and the educated professional urban middle class all supported Bhutto's left-leaning economic policies. The bureaucracy and industrialists were the key 'enemies' of the new social programme of the early 1970s, while the discredited military, although not such a direct target as the other two, was marginalized and sidelined. The large landowning lobby, too, suffered the anger of the establishment, and the 1972 land reforms were meant to break their (dormant though aspiring) political ambitions.

However, the political settlement that emerged in the early years of the Bhutto regime soon changed, and the same classes which had been targeted, regained their prominence. The 1972 land reforms did not really break the hold of the large landowners and were more a showpiece political ploy, despite the avowed political programme of the Pakistan People's Party. Having abused and insulted the 'feudal' landowners, Bhutto brought them back into his fold. The educated left-leaning urban middle class was in disfavour in the Bhutto ranks, although Bhutto persisted with much of his social reform agenda. With massive nationalization, the bureaucracy was back in favour and began to consolidate its hold over the means of production. The military, too, found favour when Bhutto had to quell the armed rebellion in Baluchistan. Hence, the political groups which had been discredited in the early Bhutto period re-emerged as Bhutto needed their assistance, and were ready to take revenge for the show trials of the earlier period.

The industrialists, however, were never welcomed back. The nationalization of banks broke the critical link between finance and industrial capital, and much of the capital held by industrialists fled overseas. While this class of industrialist was discriminated against and hounded out, not just from the economy, but also from the country, Bhutto's reforms helped to consolidate the small-scale manufacturing process started by the Green Revolution. Small-scale industry and the informal sector became the backbone of industry, replacing the twenty-two families of Ayub's era. This urban middle class, which consolidated itself under Bhutto, eventually allied itself with other sections of the urban middle class, backed by the bureaucracy and probably the military, and was instrumental in removing Bhutto in 1977. Thus, the beneficiaries of Bhutto's economic programme led the movement to remove him from power, just as the results of Ayub Khan's programme caused his (Ayub's) downfall.

Hence, between 1947 and 1977 the following picture of Pakistan's political economy emerges. Large-scale economic development had taken place, in both urban and rural areas, giving rise to a middle class that was still young and economically prosperous, but was essentially non-existent in political terms. Industrialists, having made great inroads and extraordinary economic gains in the first twenty-five years, were nowhere on the scene, even in economic terms, in 1970; many had lost their fortunes, while others had fled the country. The 'feudals' had increasingly been losing economic power as mechanization took hold in agriculture, and as capitalist agriculture began to dominate production. Those large landowners who could see the changes taking place and were able to adapt managed to survive financially, while others were forced to sell or rent out their land to the aggressive middle farmers. As a political entity, however, especially under a democratic order, the large landowners did control a number of seats, particularly in Sindh, southern Punjab and parts of Baluchistan, where tribal lords held power. The civilian and military bureaucrats were the only political grouping which, despite a small period in quarantine, continued their influence on the political structure of the country. The heyday of the civil and military bureaucracy, however, was still to come.

19.4 A Military State and the Middle Classes: 1977–1988

The takeover by General Zia ul Haq crystallized the hegemony of the civil and military bureaucracy, not just on the political map of Pakistan, where they had existed previously, but also, for the first time, in the generation and distribution of economic resources and wealth. With political and administrative roles and interests, the civil and military bureaucracy emerged as a key and entrenched entity in the economy. It established and consolidated its role in economics and politics throughout the Zia period, going from strength to strength.

Despite the pro-private sector penchant of Zia's regime, much of the industry nationalized under Bhutto was not returned to the original owners because it permitted the bureaucracy to continue to play an important role in the economy. The bureaucracy emerged as a critical ally for Zia, and he had no need to undermine their role by distancing them from key areas of economic control and power. The role of the military also changed compared to when it was first in power under Ayub. Earlier, the military had played primarily an administrative role, but under Zia it became more and more visible in the economic sector as well. Many lucrative positions in the huge public sector were made available to retired and serving military personnel, and it became far easier for private companies to curry favour and make economic progress if they had close ties with members of the military establishment. Military personnel were invited to serve on the boards of companies to assist in negotiating the controls and regulations involved in investment decisions. This networking paid great dividends both for industrialists and the private sector, and for individuals from the military. From the Zia period right up to today, the personal wealth of a very large number of military personnel has grown in a way that could not have originated from their official salaries. Today, many large businesses and enterprises are owned by retired military officials and they have joined the ranks of the industrialists, thanks to the links established under the rule of General Zia.[4]

The windfall gain that resulted from the Soviet invasion of Afghanistan, in the form of substantial aid to the (military) government and to the military directly, was also an important conduit for making personal fortunes. There is extensive evidence of corruption, smuggling, and the emergence of a drug and arms mafia and economy due to the fallout from the Soviet invasion of Afghanistan. It resulted in many civil and military bureaucrats making huge sums of money, even through legitimate channels, as opportunities to amass wealth were widespread. In an economy of defence, with the bogey of Soviet expansionism used to acquire more arms and more aid, military personnel used contracts of different types to further their personal fortunes. Moreover, the armed forces also emerged as a collective economic institution, where the different welfare foundations of the army, navy, and air force became more involved in economic activities and even in direct economic production. In economic terms and by amassing huge fortunes, the military was a major beneficiary of the rule of General Zia ul Haq. The image of soldiers fighting to defend the motherland changed to one of serving military generals who were acting as corporate bosses, soldiering over tonnes of sugar, cement, and steel.

The nationalization of banks by Bhutto and the emergence of the small-scale manufacturing and services sector in the early 1970s broke the hold of the big industrialists, and permitted a new class of small industrialists to emerge. However, the real impetus to this middle class came as a consequence of the Gulf boom in the late 1970s and early 1980s.

In the period 1977–87, more than $20 billion was remitted into Pakistan by workers overseas through official channels. This figure ignores the large amounts which came in through unofficial means, which suggests that twice as much as the official figure may have been remitted to Pakistan. Jonathan Addleton,[5] in his excellent book on Gulf migration, has argued that this was the main reason why General Zia was able to have an essentially trouble-free decade. If the Soviet invasion of Afghanistan prolonged Zia's political career, the Gulf boom resulted in unheard-of prosperity in most of the far-flung regions of Pakistan. While the amount remitted was itself very large, the geographical and locational dispersion of migrants, and hence remittances, was probably more important. Because this money was sent to numerous urban, peri-urban, and rural settlements of the country, it gave rise to economic development which was not concentrated in the more traditional regions of Karachi and central Punjab. The remittance economy permitted millions of individuals in thousands of villages to improve their standard of living by a considerable margin. It also gave rise to previously unskilled workers becoming shopkeepers, setting up small-scale industrial units, becoming transporters, etc. It allowed them considerable upward mobility and resulted in the broadening and strengthening of the middle class that had begun to emerge in the previous decade.

On the economic front, it was essentially Gulf remittances, money amassed though the massive black economy, and high growth rates that gave rise to the economic consolidation of the middle class, both urban and rural. On the political front, it was the reintroduction of the Local Bodies elections that led to the political emergence, and possibly even consolidation, of the middle class, both urban and rural. Given the intrinsic connection between politics and economics in Pakistan, it is not surprising that each reinforced the other.

Since 'real' elections to the provincial and national assemblies were not held under Zia until at least 1985 (and how 'real' they were is a moot point), most of the traditional political entities did not take the first Local Bodies elections seriously. Also, because severe restrictions were imposed by General Zia's government on participation, many stalwarts were excluded. This allowed those with some means, essentially the emerging middle class, to contest elections, perhaps for the first time. They were able to enter politics because room had been created by the absence of the richer, more influential, traditional political actors. Local government seemed to work well under military dictators, and under Zia it seemed to work rather better, because of the relative importance given to this tier of government by the large developmental funds channelled through it. Urban and rural councillors were the only elected representatives of the regime, and were responsible and accountable, given their limitations, to the needs and demands of the electorate.

Elections were held in 1979, 1983, and 1987, which allowed the same sections of the economic middle class to emerge as members of the political classes. General elections in 1985 even allowed some of the members to contest and win elections at the national level, when parliamentary elections on a non-party basis were held.[6]

The main beneficiaries of the Zia regime were, then, members of the urban and rural middle classes, and members of the civil and, particularly, military bureaucracy. The large industrialists of the Ayub era also returned to Pakistan, although the nature of the entrepreneur under Zia was considerably different from that under Ayub. Rather than twenty-two families dominating Pakistan, there were perhaps a few hundred or a thousand under Zia. The industrialists under Ayub may have been richer than those under Zia, but there was probably less concentration at the top under Zia than under Ayub. However, despite this emergence of the middle class and of the new entrepreneur under Zia, political power was clearly retained in the hands of the military with a subservient bureaucracy alongside. Large landowners, too, had made a comeback under Zia, hovering around the political establishment and being allowed some room in the 1985 elections. Nevertheless, the power of the military was endorsed by the summary end to Mohammad Khan Junejo's tenure as Prime Minister in May 1988. The somewhat unique concept of a praetorian democracy worked rather well for many months, but once elements of the democratic forces began to impinge upon the terrain of the military, the military demonstrated that it was well in control.

The death of General Zia ul Haq is still shrouded in mystery, and if it was not an accident, as many believe, his murder may have been an outcome of the struggle over the future course of Pakistan among members of the ruling clique, almost exclusively the military. The political process following the General's death, with the army remaining calm and allowing the electioneering process to take place, may suggest that members of the ruling establishment were responding to the developments that had taken place under General Zia and wanted to take them further. If this is indeed the case, then it seems that yet again, the contradictory results of certain policies undermined the ruler of the time. Under Ayub it was inequitable and uneven development that set forth socialist rhetoric; under Bhutto, the small-scale urban petit-bourgeois elements undermined his government; and under Zia, the middle class and its representatives, who owed a great deal to Zia in the first place, may have become more politically ambitious and assertive. Nevertheless, the period after Zia marks the first real demonstration and formal consolidation of the middle classes on Pakistan's economic and political map.

19.5 The Rise and Rise of the Middle Classes: 1988 Onwards

The most obvious and noticeable phenomenon on the political, economic and social scene in Pakistan today, one which is linked closely with historical trends, is the buoyant and vibrant middle-class revolution rampant in all parts of the country. From as far north as Skardu and Gilgit, through the plains of the Punjab and Sindh, to the coast of Karachi and the Mekran, a major transformation is redefining existing cultural, political, social, and economic identities and relationships (see also Appendix 19.1).

Probably the most significant symbol of the rise of a relatively well-to-do middle class is the excessive consumerism prevalent almost everywhere in Pakistan. It is not just large urban conglomerations which exhibit new consumer trends; the smaller rural and semi-urban towns in Sindh, Punjab, and the NWFP reveal the demands of a new breed of consumer. With transport more accessible and communications of all sorts improved, the further reaches of the country are being brought into the net of Pakistan's particular breed of private sector capitalism.

The middle-class revolution under way in Pakistan has taken place side by side with the failure of governance. The middle class has recognized this failure by the government to deliver on its promises and has found its own solutions in the private sector. The most noticeable failure of the government has been its inability to cope with, and thus provide for, the growing need for social services. Here, one of the biggest industries in recent years has been the private education and health markets. The growth in private sector social services emphasizes the vibrancy of the middle class, which has built institutions of varying quality for its growing clientele. Demand and the market, rather than the state and its political agenda, have determined these trends. In addition, the failure to provide protection for life and property, one of the major responsibilities of the state, has given rise to a protection industry that fulfils the needs of this class.

Capitalist development, with the private sector playing an aggressive role, seems to be the norm for the economic development taking place over the last decade. While this gives rise to some of the trends identified above, it also causes severe inequities in the nature of development. This is more marked when the role of the state begins to diminish. There are obvious beneficiaries of capitalist development, but at the same time a huge section of the population does not yet have access to the fruits of this development, which increases disparities, both across class and across region. In some ways, the middle class seems to be self-absorbed, and in its prosperity is ignoring the repercussions its own growth has on the less privileged classes. If growth and prosperity exclude sections of the population, with the state being sidelined the potential for social strife increases. In such situations, the most likely outcome will be the renewed perception of the military as peace maker. For with the dismantling of the state, and the loss of credibility among politicians, the military is likely to be perceived as the only institution that survives all crises and as the saviour of society.

The ongoing middle-class revolution does seem to have an economic agenda, but because this class has not fully consolidated its hold on power, it has as yet an unevolved philosophy and ideology. One of the features of this development has been a move away from regionalism and nationalism, towards a more articulate Pakistani identity. The middle class, which was earlier vociferous about its claim to 'national' rights in Sindh and the NWFP, has evolved into an entity that is fully entrenched in the economic, social, and political package called Pakistan. It sees its interest closely aligned to Islamabad, and the demands for autonomy and secession have given way to increased access to the centre. What sort of cultural and social values, other than greed, this identity espouses is still uncertain. Its stand on religion is ambivalent, although there has been a noticeable shift away from official Islam.

So what do these general tendencies and trends regarding the process of economic development reveal about political choices? Does the presence of a vibrant middle class imply the election of a political leadership whose policies favour this class?

19.6 Concretizing the Thesis: The 1997 Elections and Reform of the Economy

After the death of General Zia ul Haq in 1988, when Nawaz Sharif emerged on the political scene as an independent entity, he was first seen as a spokesman for the upwardly mobile, indigenous urban middle class, essentially of the Punjab. Many observers believed that the Punjab was the only province at that time which had a large and identifiable middle class, and that once the wave of pro-Benazir sentiment died down after her triumphant return to the Punjab in 1986, Nawaz Sharif would emerge as the true leader of the province, and possibly of the country. The 1990 elections may have been the first reflection of the fact that a new Pakistan was emerging; that a new type of economic and political class had finally matured, and had found at least one national leader.[7]

Although Pakistan's politics has been one of coups, intrigue, betrayal, and deceit, the thesis that a new Pakistan was emerging was given further credence by the extraordinary victory of the Pakistan Muslim League and Nawaz Sharif in the elections of February 1997. The political moment for Pakistan's urban middle class, rich peasantry, industrialists, traders, professionals, and so-called economically forward-looking or progressive forces, had probably arrived.

The political economy of the Nawaz Sharif regime – the fact that he represents the urban middle class, industrialists, traders, etc. – could not have been better crystallized than by the economic reforms package announced in the last week of March 1997, a few weeks after he assumed power. If ever politics reflected economics and vice versa, this was the moment.

In the economic reforms package, a huge reduction in personal income tax rates was announced, the largest beneficiaries being those who, not surprisingly, earn the largest amount of income. There are only 800,000 registered taxpayers in the country in the first place, and even among these the benefits are unevenly distributed, with the higher salaried individuals gaining the most. Banks and public and private limited companies had their corporate income tax rates reduced by 8 per cent, with private companies getting the biggest break. This economic group is considered to be the real economic backbone of the Pakistan Muslim League, and here, perhaps, the link between economics and politics is closest and most organic. Traders are an equally important category for Nawaz Sharif, and they too have received a huge boost from the reduction in import duty from a maximum of 65 per cent to 45 per cent. Moreover, the rationalization of tax slabs will also simplify things and help traders. With a cut in tariffs, prices of imported commodities should fall markedly, and this should benefit distributors, transporters, and traders.

A reduction in the general sales tax from a maximum of 18 to 12.5 per cent should also boost trade, consumption, and industry. More importantly, this measure favourably affects the urban middle-class consumer, as it does all other consumers. However, Nawaz Sharif's most vociferous, organized, and volatile supporters, the urban consumers, will also gain from the cut in the import tariff.

These economic signals help partially to explain the thesis presented above about the emergence of a new class, composed of traders, middlemen, transporters, and a host of other entities, which emerged partially through the local bodies process of the 1980s, and is now maturing. Nevertheless, there are also numerous contradictions in the formation of groups, and in their existence with each other. This is not a harmonious class, and it contains a multitude of currents. Even the economic reforms package had its share of contradictions.

The large single fall in import duties does not bode well for the Pakistani industrialist, pampered and nurtured by state protection behind huge tariff walls. The contradiction between the traders and the industrialists is apparent in this struggle over protection. However, a fall in tariffs has been inevitable for a number of years, and industry had been forewarned, especially with the emergence of the World Trade Organization. Not even the most ardent of nationalist industrialists could have resisted that inevitability.

Pakistan's middle-class revolution has been in progress for some time now, but still has to concretize itself. However, the repeal of the eighth amendment and the removal of the extra-parliamentary powers of the President were perhaps indicative of change. Besides, while the Pakistani middle-class capitalist revolution may be far more advanced and progressive than the feudal system, it is not possible to romanticize about Pakistan's middle class. Perhaps because of culture or military dictatorships, or because it cannot decide on its own identity, it is an evolving, immature, crude, greedy, selfish, narrow-minded middle class, whose only pursuit is self-interest. The type of democracy and governance that exists in Pakistan (which Pakistan's liberal and westernized élite abhors, for it fails to understand how these forms evolved in the first place), and to which this class belongs and subscribes, is not part of any imaginary or ideal form of society, but is very much a reflection of social, cultural, and historical processes specific to Pakistan. Good or bad, Pakistan's democracy and governance represent who we are, and how we function. To expect things to be very much different is mere wishful thinking.

The economic reforms package and the evolving economic and social programme of the present government reflects, at times, the naiveté of our middle class. This is a largely self-made class, which has worked hard, but has also learnt how to succeed in Pakistan the hard way. Its success rests on its ability to be more street smart than academically wise. It has arrived here without much formal education and does not really grasp the importance of social development. Although it is beginning to see the benefits of this type of development, it still has a long way to go. Hence the absence of any social programme from the Muslim League's current economic agenda. This class does not realize adequately, for it has never gone through this process itself, that success in the modern age is predicated upon human capital formation. When it finds the need to do so, it will have to act accordingly.

Many commentators have held the belief that Nawaz Sharif and his party represent the interests of an anti-feudal Pakistan, as compared to Benazir Bhutto, who is supposed to draw her strength from the 'feudals'. This view then argues that Nawaz Sharif should have imposed a large tax on the 'feudals', by taxing agriculture. It is true that the so-called feudals are essentially large landlords and did tend to support Benazir Bhutto's government. However, increasingly rich and prosperous, if not also large, landlords come from non-feudal sections of society, and are comprised of military personnel, bureaucrats, and middle and rich farmers. The tax on agriculture is not a tax on the non-existent feudals, but a tax on the constituency which supports Nawaz Sharif. Hence the delay in this direction.

For the first time, the middle class in Pakistan finds itself in a position to consolidate and extend its hold on economic and political power. Pakistan's middle class is, however, still immature and evolving, and although it has won the struggle over whatever constituted the 'old order', it has not yet captured power in the real sense. Some signs suggest that it has begun that process – see Appendix 19.1 for an interesting interpretation of the changes that are believed to be taking place in Pakistan.

19.7 The Collapse of the State

There is a very obvious and growing disillusionment with the state and its institutions. The general feeling is that the state has failed to deliver on basic issues, that it can no longer govern, administer justice, provide essential and basic social services, or collect taxes, and its only function seems to be coercive, with institutions of law and order increasingly turned not towards protecting the life and property of citizens, but against the people of Pakistan. Corruption is noticeably rampant, and affects all institutions of the state, not even sparing Zakaat committees, or the religious establishment. The decline of state authority and credibility is obvious, and one wonders whether there is any real state or government in Pakistan at all.

While much of the new liberal agenda believes in a small state and argues for public institutions to play a decreasing role in the affairs of society (see Chapter 18), in Pakistan government has played a primary role in economic and social development, and deserves credit where it is due. Even

Gustav Papanek, the author of ideas such as the 'social utility of greed', concedes that government has played a key role in Pakistan's development. He writes of the 1960s:

> Government played an important positive role in protecting infant industries and thereby making rapid industrialisation possible in Pakistan despite the shortage or virtual absence of experienced industrialists, industrial labour, professional and technical personnel, infrastructure, experienced bankers, and so on. It subsequently provided heavy subsidies to industries to export to the world market, a difficult challenge at first. Government also played a crucial role in the Green Revolution by guaranteeing the price of some agricultural products and heavily subsidising some inputs. And it carried out a labour intensive public works programme that was effective for several years in creating rural infrastructure and providing jobs in the agricultural off season. Finally it developed the physical and institutional infrastructure essential for economic functioning and development.[8]

As we have argued in the Introduction to this book and elsewhere, the much cited success story of East Asia would not have been possible without active and persistent state intervention. While Pakistan was not able to adapt to the nature of the state to the needs of society, the East Asian countries perhaps did a more consistent job of keeping the state well equipped to deal with the changing realities.

This, perhaps, is the key crisis of the state in Pakistan. It is probable that the reason why the state and its institutions are in such disarray is that, as we have emphasized above, society has been transformed quite radically in Pakistan over the last few decades, and the state has not been able to understand or keep up with the nature of those changes. The crisis in Pakistan exists due to the mismatch of the state with the needs, demands, and aspirations of the new Pakistan. While the 'old order' is now redundant for much of Pakistan, its persistence in the realm of state and its institutions results in the many crises that are so visible. The key political struggle of the emerging economic and political classes in Pakistan will have to concern itself with who rules the state, but more importantly, what is to be the nature of the state which reflects the new and emerging society. Unless this issue is resolved, and for as long as it is contested, we are more than likely to be involved in an endless stream of crises – see Appendix 19.2 for an evaluation of the nature of Pakistan's crisis of governance and of the state.

19.8 Summary and Further Reading

19.8.1 Summary

The key argument made in this chapter is that Pakistan has now emerged as an economy dominated, at least in number, by a middle class, which is now trying to consolidate its hold on political power. We do not subscribe to the view that 'feudals' hold power, an economic category which this book has argued, at different times, is incorrect. Large landowners do wield political clout in areas that they dominate, but as a consolidated political category they have diminishing political representation and strength. Traders, small and large industrialists, transporters, educated and semi-educated urban dwellers, capitalist farmers, and small-scale manufacturers dominate the economy, and are now trying to cash in on their economic strength for political power. Even sections of the petit-bourgeoisie and lower middle classes, who have little economic power, in the sense that they do not own assets, are now important holders of political power, most noticeably in Karachi and in other towns in Sindh. The political equation has, not surprisingly, changed from one where large landowners held sway, to one where they are now for the most part marginal, replaced by middle-level industrialists and other elements of the service sector, in urban and rural society.

This realignment of the political settlement does not detract from the perception that the military still holds formidable power over the institutions of state. This is more marked in its coercive functioning. However, the nature of the military has changed considerably from its glory days under General Zia-ul-Haq. Depending upon the nature of political forces and their economic strength, the balance which has been shifting away from the military may continue to do so. Whether Pakistan will emerge as a modern developing capitalist state, with some real demonstration of democratic processes, remains to be seen.

19.8.2 Further Reading

There are some excellent books which are essential to understanding the nature of and relationship between politics and economics in Pakistan. Shahid Javed Burki's *Pakistan: A Nation in the Making*, Westview Press, Boulder, 1986, is particularly recommended, although see also Zaidi, S. Akbar, 'How the Bourgeoisie Views Pakistan', *Economic and Political Weekly*, vol. 23, no. 48, 1988, for a critique of the book. Shahid Javed Burki's *Pakistan Under Bhutto, 1971–77*, Macmillan, London, 1980, is also recommended. Khalid bin Sayeed's *Pakistan: The Formative Phase, 1857–1948*, Oxford University Press, Karachi, 1978, and *Politics in Pakistan: The Nature and Direction of Change*, Praeger, New York, 1980, are very good. See also Gardezi, Hasan and Jamil Rashid (eds.), *Pakistan: The Roots of Dictatorship*, Zed Press, London, 1983; Ziring, Lawrence, *The Ayub Khan Era: Politics in Pakistan, 1958–1969*, Syracuse University Press, 1971; Kochanek, Stanley, *Interest Groups and Development*, Vanguard, Lahore, 1984; Jalal, Ayesha, *The State of Martial Rule: The Origins of Pakistan's Political Economy of Defence*, Cambridge University Press, Cambridge, 1991; Addleton, Jonathan, *Undermining the Centre: Gulf Migration and Pakistan*, Oxford University Press, Karachi, 1992; Khan, Mahmood Hasan, *Underdevelopment and Agrarian Structure in Pakistan*, Vanguard, Lahore, 1986; Noman, Omar, *The Political Economy of Pakistan*, KPI, London, 1988; Papanek, Gustav, *Pakistan's Development: Social Goals and Private Incentives*, Harvard University Press, Cambridge, Mass., 1967; Waseem, Mohammad, *Politics and the State in Pakistan*, Progressive Publishers, Lahore, 1989; and Zaidi, S. Akbar, *Regional Imbalances and the National Question in Pakistan*, Vanguard, Lahore, 1992.

Appendix 19.1

Radio as a social metaphor

This article interprets the form and content of the new FM radio stations opened in Pakistan and argues that they act as a mirror of the nature of Pakistani society.

The extraordinary revolution that has taken place in Pakistani society is best captured by the form and content of the new FM radio stations operating in the cities of Islamabad, Lahore and Karachi. The music played, the dialogue and language used by the DJs, the conversation between callers and show hosts, and the entire package and style of FM 100 is an accurate manifestation of a new generation of Pakistanis that is coming of age. The style of the radio station is lively and upbeat, youthful and optimistic, reflecting the new, particularly urban, indigenous middle class culture which has increasingly come to dominate this nation.

Most of what is played in the three cities on FM 100 is a new Pakistani music which now influences the lifestyles of many young urbanites. It is modern in style and critically dependent on the use of modern instruments and technology. The harmonium and tabla have been replaced by electric keyboards and guitars, and harmony by noise. While the FM radio stations play much more of this kind of music – a clear reflection of the social and cultural changes that have taken place in the country – the airwaves are not restricted solely to new Pakistani music. Just as Pakistani society is hybrid and constitutes a large part of the old with the new, so is the repertoire of FM 100.

Despite the waves of modernization sweeping Pakistani society, numerous traditions and older forms and values continue to persist. FM 100 reflects this eclectic composition in its choice of music, with a good dose of ghazals and the music of yesteryear thrown in. Just as in our society, where the old and the new compete for social space, on the radio, too, tradition and modernity vie for air time.

If the newly westernized indigenous cultural and social norms of the country are reflected in the new Pakistani music played on FM 100, the radio stations also imitate the process of globalization and internationalization so integral to present day Pakistan. Each day, FM 100 dishes out a large dose of current western music for its Pakistani listeners, with a weekly spot for the latest from the US top 20 hit list. What is most interesting, however, is the fact that even when Pakistani society was dominated by the westernized élite a couple of decades ago, western English music played on the radio was restricted to only half an hour each day. But now, with Pakistan an active part of the global market and of the westernized world – and despite the fact that the westernized élite no longer governs – the amount of western music on the airwaves has increased. However, the major difference is that now this English music runs far deeper roots into urban middle class society than ever before, whereas in the past it was restricted to a very small section of the westernized élite.

No matter how modern Pakistan may become, however, it is highly improbable that religion will cease to play a role in the lives of this nation. FM 100 recognises this social reality, and new Pakistani music or the latest music from the US suddenly comes to a halt at the time of prayer. Then, the moazzin's call is beamed out to the faithful, followed by a *naat* and *qawwali*. Just as Pakistan balances its modernity with religion, so does the new radio station. Moreover, the fact that FM 100 is permitted to air the music it does, despite the protestations of the religious lobby which considers such music and its connotations vulgar, is possibly the best indication of the social and political reality in Pakistan today where global and modern forces have marginalised religion and religious forces in the public arena. Had a dominant or even effective religious sentiment existed in Pakistani society, FM 100 could not have played the music it does.

If the music played on FM 100 is one symbol for what constitutes contemporary Pakistan, the nature and content of the dialogue and language used by the DJs is another. The puritanism and tradition of the old order has been lost to a new language which forms part of urban middle class culture. The Urdu that the urban middle classes spoke up to a generation ago contained few words from the English language. Today, it is unlikely that this class can speak a single sentence without a smattering of English. As the isolationism of the past has given way to a global or western order, colloquial Urdu too has lost much of its pristineness. Interestingly, the earlier impact of Bollywood on Urdu seems to have been replaced in the very recent past by a bombardment of English words on the Pakistani language. The DJs on FM 100 articulate this phenomenon perfectly as is best demonstrated by the following instructions to their listeners: *aap apna* face soap *say* wash *kar key* towel *say* dry *kar lain.*

Courtship, affection, flirtation, or even plain interest in the opposite sex takes on a very different form in South Asian society compared to the West. Salman Rushdie, in his *Midnight's Children*, demonstrates this brilliantly in a scene where two lovers in Bombay drink tea from the same glass at a *khoka*, with the dark red lipstick of the woman firmly glued to the glass for her companion to savour. There is a unique South Asianness in such forms of flirtation and love which, surprisingly, is also observable in FM 100's live phone-ins. The flirtation on air between the mostly female callers and male DJs seems to be the sole purpose of the phone-ins. Just as a glass of tea shared between a man and a woman in a novel symbolises physical and sexual attraction and communication, the drooling and cooing young girls with their *hai Allah! Aap*

ki awaaz to bohat hi achi hai does the same on FM 100. The sexual innuendoes in such conversations are clearly observable.

Despite the movement towards a modern society, one aspect of the old which continues to persist is that of the extended family. Listening to FM 100 confirms this aspect of Pakistani society. The phone-in on air, on its own, is a good mirror of many features of Pakistani society. A lone caller is seldom heard, and one often hears the DJ talking to the entire family of the caller. It happens very matter of factly with the telephone being handed from the female to another, from daughter to mother and sister to cousin. If the family is considered to be an extension of one's self in South Asian society, the phone-ins on air mirror this social reality.

Pakistani society has yet to acquire the curtness and brusqueness of the modern world, and the deference for the old order continues. This too is reflected in the mannerisms of the DJs and show hosts. Despite being in great pain over the belligerence and persistence of some callers, they are unable to slam the phone down and continue to tolerate each and every caller until they have spoken to their heart's content. The callers are almost invariably female and hail mainly from middle class localities in the city. Some conversations take place totally in English, an English which itself makes interesting listening. Most callers, however, speak Urdish, increasingly the lingua franca of this urban middle class.

For any astute listener, FM 100 presents the best caricature of contemporary Pakistani society in all its forms. After a few days of listening one can get a fairly accurate picture of modern urban middle class Pakistan. This relationship between what we hear and what we are, is not simply unilinear. Rather, it is a dialectical relationship where the airwaves play a critical role in determining social and cultural history. If entertainment and awareness about the world around us is one of the more positive attributes of FM 100, alienation from one's own culture and context may be its biggest failing. Questions-for-cash on FM 100 stations, for example, ask listeners to name the team which currently heads the US NBA championship, or to give the names of all the members of Bon Jovi or Salt n Pepa, two American bands. This is utterly absurd, to say the least. These competitions on air seem to be the strangest and most unreal aspect of a package which, for the most part, gives a fairly decent reflection of the Pakistan urban middle class scene. However, what at present seems to be a distortion may yet turn out to be the harbinger of a new, thoroughly Americanised order some years from now. But if our own economic and political alignments with Washington today are any indication, one may not have long to go before what at present sound like the most absurd questions, become culturally very contextual and relevant.

FM 100, in its own way, represents deep rooted changes that have taken place in Pakistani society and culture, a transformation that has found expression in numerous ways. Contrary to what most intellectuals argue, Pakistan is a vibrant and dynamic capitalist country and the perception that a feudal order still holds sway over a large section of the population is utterly fictitious. Ours is no longer an 'agricultural' or rural society, and agriculture's contribution to GDP is now less than that of the industrial or service sectors.

In fact, today agriculture contributes only half the share contributed by the services sector.

Over the last two decades, there has also been a large scale migration from the rural areas to towns and cities, with urban culture now dominating almost the entire country. Ours is a thoroughly consumerist society, and we have acquired what many would call the worst attributes of the western capitalist nations without imbibing the more positive social, political and cultural mores which are part of the bourgeois order.

In the age of openness and globalization, Pakistani society is now also more internationalized and westernized than it has ever been in the past. Through instant access of the media, news, information and values are immediately communicated to us from different parts of the world. The isolationism of the past has been broken, probably for ever, by the integrating forces of the new world disorder. With the collapse of the Soviet Empire, at least for the moment, only one economic, social and political system determines the history of humankind. Ironically, in an age that supposedly offers unprecedented freedom and choice, the choices available for the evolution of society seem to be restricted to only one.

Internally, the social and economic fabric of the country has also undergone an unprecedented metamorphosis in the last two decades. The westernized English speaking élite has been replaced by a more indigenous élite whose mother-tongue is most likely to be Punjabi or Pushto but is increasingly speaking a great deal of Urdish. The bureaucracy, military and business classes are now more often of lower middle and middle income origins. Never before has there been as much social mobility –both upwards and downwards – as has been witnessed over the last two decades. The English speaking élite would probably be the first to bear witness to this development, clearly demonstrated by its own loss of exclusive privilege and power.

In a nutshell, then, Pakistan is a modern, dynamic, capitalist country where a dominant indigenous, badly westernized urban middle class rules. Gone are the days of the feudal and of big landlords with their endless hours of leisure. As a result, tradition as expressed in social graces and in music has also been lost. Possibly the best reflection of this extensive change is the new sound on the airwaves. Indeed, FM 100 may be a better mirror of our society than we first imagined.

Source: Zaidi, S. Akbar, *The Herald*, Annual, January 1996.

Appendix 19.2

Crisis of governance

There is a growing consensus in Pakistan that the state and its institutions are teetering on the brink of a collapse. There seems to be agreement that the country is faced with numerous crises or fault lines, ranging from a crisis of the economy to a crisis of governance, incorporating crises of the judiciary and of development. The general prognosis seems to be that, unless some action is taken in the immediate future, these fault lines will grow into gaping holes, into which this country and society will collapse.

Indeed, there is no denying the fact that in Pakistan, the government does not really govern efficiently or effectively, the judiciary is not as just as one would want it to be, the police is often unscrupulous in its workings, and most institutions of the state and of government do not deliver the basic goods and services for which these institutions were established in the first place. Individuals and groups from different social and economic backgrounds would all agree with the statement that there has been large-scale institutional collapse in Pakistan. However, since the reasons for this collapse have not been fully understood, the so-called remedies advocated lose all semblance of efficacy and cause further frustration to those who are concerned and want change. In order to be able to change the existing world, one needs to understand it first.

The reasons for the institutional collapse in Pakistan are, at one level, fairly simple. Most of the state institutions in Pakistan, of government, of governance, of administration, and of control, are obsolete in the present social and economic reality that is Pakistan. Simply because these institutions have not been able (or allowed) to evolve in tune with the dramatic changes that have taken place in Pakistan over the last three decades, they are becoming, or as most would suggest are already, dysfunctional. Although not a surprising conclusion, this simple fact is often overlooked in the zeal to reform.

Many years ago, when the structures and systems of general administration, law and order, revenue collection and expenditure were put in place, Pakistan's social and economic structure was very different from what it has evolved into today. In the 1950s and 1960s, Pakistan's economy was principally agricultural and rural, with large landowners (many of whom were probably 'feudal') ruling the roost, in terms of both economic and political power. The deputy commissioners in the districts were lord and master of their often huge terrains, usually in cohorts with the large landlords and other influentials in the district. There was very little mobility in rural areas, both geographically and socially. Few roads existed and there was little opportunity or justification to travel outside one's immediate environs. Local ties of culture, kinship and economic exchange dominated this world. In addition, literacy levels were low and infrastructure and opportunities little developed. Even basic amenities which we now take for granted, like the telephone or electricity, were considered to be a luxury, not just in rural areas, but even in many large towns as well. The level and nature of development and hence of culture, all across Pakistan, was rural, if not feudal. Needless to say, this has now all changed.

Today there are few pockets in Pakistan which can be considered to be remote or isolated, with economic and communication links not only integrating the whole country internally, but integrating far-flung areas with the rest of the world. Moreover, the share of urban population, which was only 17 per cent in 1951, is estimated to be at least 40 per cent today, and by 2010 the majority of Pakistanis will be living in cities.

Literacy and education, still low by international standards, have grown markedly over the last three decades and have even spread to many remote rural areas. Mobility and migration from rural to urban areas and to other countries has become a part of Pakistani society and culture, and remittances, both international and domestic, now contribute a large share to the economy. Agriculture provides less than a quarter to GDP, with the service sector now providing more than half of the total.

One can continue to cite numerous examples that amplify the extent and nature of change in Pakistan over the last three or four decades. The focus of all these changes put together represents a new Pakistan, with a vibrant urban sector, a growing and aggressive urban and rural middle class, and a more modern economic order integrated into the wider world market. This changing economic and social structure in Pakistan has come into conflict with the old institutional set-up, and hence explains the reasons for the institutional collapse.

The old order of governance was structured upon a highly centralised system of governance, perhaps best epitomised by Pakistan's 'One Unit'. In the late 1960s, the status of the provinces was restored, but today, given the nature of diverse developments, many of the functions of not just the federal government, but also government at the provinces, seem quite redundant in the new Pakistan. With eight cities with a population of over one million and with over a hundred districts, the extent and nature of centralisation at the federal and provincial level seems at odds with the requirements and ability to address the most essential of issues, most of which are of a specifically local nature. Sanitation, sewerage, water, health and education, to name a few, are local issues which are inconsequential to the administrators in Islamabad. These concerns would be far better addressed by effective, autonomous and elected municipal and district governments than by officials in the national or provincial capitals. Institutions, wherever they happen to be, exist because they serve certain interests and work effectively, fulfilling the requirements of particular political and economic interest groups and classes. To say that Pakistan's institutions are inappropriate in the current social and economic context ignores the fact that, no matter how out-moded, these institutions are in place because a powerful section of society benefits from their continued unreformed existence.

The institutions in Pakistan serve the interests of those with money, influence, power and connections. We all know how easy it is to bribe any government functionary (if you have the money) to get almost any job done in this country; equally, if you can drop the right names (if you have the right connections and are well networked into the power system) all doors will open to you, overriding all possible institutional rules and constraints. Institutional norms for this group of people in the country have more or less become redundant. However, the demand for change and for institutional reform has come, not surprisingly, not from those who supersede or benefit from the system, but from those who increasingly suffer it.

There are at least three key players in the new Pakistani society which have been championing institutional reform in Pakistan. First, there is the educated, often westernised, élite, which has lost its foothold in power as it has been sidelined by a more indigenous Pakistani middle class. This élite, which ruled the country in the 1950s and 1960s through jobs and linkages with the military and bureaucracy, no longer sends its children to these services, and as the composition of the bureaucracies has changed, the links with this élite have withered away. They now send their children to get MBA degrees so that they end up in multinationals, or in their own businesses, or even in the development business. Many are probably still part of the economic power nexus, but politically this class has been effectively disenfranchised. This group has been the most vocal demanding institutional reform, asking for good governance, by writing in newspapers and by holding seminars and discussions, because it has been the most affected by the new changes, which have resulted in their loss of political power and control.

The second vocal group is that of the urban middle and lower middle classes who, perhaps, suffer the most at the hands of the old order of governance in the country. Whether it is law and order or the courts, or the relationship with the police, or even the provision and delivery of basic urban services, unlike the élite, this urban group cannot buy its way out, and hence, suffers the worst form of misgovernance. It is this group which has the most to gain from institutional reform, a process in which it wants to play a key role. Demands for more decentralisation and devolution for more effective municipal government with control over local revenue and expenditure, are becoming part of the political programmes of this growing section in society. Unlike the élite, many of whom see good governance and institutional reform as an academic exercise, the urban middle and lower middle classes see these reforms as essential means to improve their chances of survival.

With the increased role of international donors in Pakistan's economic and social administration, this third group has also been pushing for a new and diversified agenda of institutional reform. For donors like the IMF and the World Bank, only such reform can guarantee that the loans taken in the past can actually be serviced. The old order, which does not pay its taxes and believes that corruption is an additional perk which comes with public office, is a serious constraint to the perception of a modern Pakistan which both the IMF and World Bank are propagating. Their desire to see their loans returned explains their enthusiasm for public sector reform.

The old social, cultural, economic and institutional order has been based upon patronage, kinship and a personalised way of doing things. While the economic and social structure of Pakistan has become more modern compared to what it was in the past, institutional reforms have not taken place in accordance with those changes. Since there is a large economic and political group which benefits from the status quo, it will not voluntarily give up its privileged position. As the westernised élites and the international donors continue to hold their seminars and propagate the virtues of good governance, the likely motor of change and institutional reform will be the growing urban middle classes, as has been the case in contemporary history.

Dozens of countries, from Brazil to the Philippines, have rewritten their constitutions and undergone far-reaching institutional reforms, with more decentralisation, devolution and enhanced powers to local governments. Broad-based alliances, between academics, intellectuals, NGOs, and the urban middle and lower middle classes have been the motor of that change. If we desire institutional reform in Pakistan, similar alliances and linkages with political entities will need to be established and fortified. Institutional reform will not take place without the active participation of those who have the most to gain from a new institutional order in the country.

Source: Zaidi, S. Akbar, 'Crisis of Governance', *Economic and Political Weekly*, vol. 33, no. 11, 1998.

Notes

1. Burki, Shahid Javed, *Pakistan: A Nation in the Making*, Westview Press, Boulder, 1986, p. 112.
2. Ibid.
3. Ibid., p. 54.
4. In a list of Pakistani dollar billionaires and millionaires published by the *Wall Street Journal*, of the top seventeen names on that list, eight were either retired military officers or sons of retired military generals, seven of whom made their fortunes during the Zia years (*The News*, Karachi, 18 July 1997). Moreover, General Fazle Haq, a close contemporary of General Zia and Governor of the NWFP during much of the Zia Martial Law, was considered to be one of the richest serving military personnel in the world.
5. Addleton, Jonathan, *Undermining the Centre: Gulf Migration and Pakistan*, Oxford University Press, Karachi, 1992.
6. In 1985, of the 240 Punjab MPAs, 124 were sitting Councillors; of the eleven metropolitan/municipal corporations of Punjab and Sindh, at one time or another, mayors of ten have been either MNAs or MPAs, in the elections held in 1993, it was estimated that more than 70 per cent of members of the Punjab and National Assemblies started their political careers from local bodies. See *The News* on Friday, Special Report on Local Bodies, 30 September 1994.
7. The extent of the changes on the political and economic scene can best be gauged by the two very different slogans of the 1970 and 1993 elections. Zulfiqar Ali Bhutto's *roti, kapra aur makaan* was replaced by the more urban and middle-class *bijli, pani, amn amaan* in 1993, showing how much the Pakistani electorate and the economic and political situation had changed.
8. Papanek, Gustav, 'Alternative Development Strategies', in Nasim, Anjum (ed.), *Financing Pakistan's Development in the 1990s*, Oxford University Press, Karachi, 1992, p. 45.

Bibliography

Adams, John and Sabiha Iqbal, *Exports, Politics and Economic Development in Pakistan*, Vanguard, Lahore, 1987.

Addleton, Jonathan, *Undermining the Centre: The Gulf Migration and Pakistan*, Oxford University Press, Karachi, 1992.

Aftab, Khalid and Eric Rahim, 'The Emergence of a Small Scale Engineering Sector: The Case of Tubewell Production in the Pakistan Punjab', *Journal of Development Studies*, vol. 23, no. 1, 1986.

Ahmad, Muzaffar and Robert Laporte, *Public Enterprise in Pakistan: The Hidden Crisis in Economic Development*, Westview Press, Boulder, 1989.

Ahmed, Meekal, 'Productivity, Prices and Relative Income Shares in Pakistan's Large Scale Manufacturing Sector, 1958–70, unpublished D.Phil dissertation, University of Oxford, 1980.

Ahmed, Viqar and Rashid Amjad, *The Management of Pakistan's Economy, 1947–82*, Oxford University Press, Karachi, 1984.

Alavi, Hamza 'India: The Transition to Colonial Capitalism', in Hamza Alavi, *et al.*, *Capitalism and Colonial Production*, Croom Helm, London, 1982.

Alavi, Hamza, 'The Rural Élite and Agricultural Development in Pakistan', in Ali, Karamat (ed.), *Pakistan: The Political Economy of Rural Development*, Vanguard, Lahore, 1986.

Alavi, Hamza, *et al.*, *Capitalism and Colonial Production*, Croom Helm, London, 1982.

Ali, Imran, *The Punjab Under Imperialism, 1885–1947*, Oxford University Press, Delhi, 1989.

Ali, Karamat (ed.), *Pakistan: The Political Economy of Rural Development*, Vanguard, Lahore, 1986.

Alvi, Imtiaz, *The Informal Sector in Urban Economy: Low Income Housing in Lahore*, Oxford University Press, Karachi, 1997.

Amjad, Rashid, *Private Industrial Investment in Pakistan, 1960–1970*, Cambridge University Press, Cambridge, 1982.

Amjad, Rashid, 'Industrial Concentration and Economic Power in Pakistan', in Gardezi, H. and J. Rashid (eds.), *Pakistan: The Unstable State*, Zed Press, London, 1983.

Amjad, Rashid, 'The Employment Challenges for Pakistan in the 1990s', in Nasim, Anjum (ed.), *Financing Pakistan's Development in the 1990s*, Oxford University Press, Karachi, 1992.

Applied Economics Research Centre, *Impact of Tractors on Agricultural Production in Pakistan*, Research Report No. 20, Karachi, 1982.

Applied Economics Research Centre, *An Analysis of Provincial Finances in Pakistan*, Research Report No. 55, Karachi, 1986.

Applied Economics Research Centre, *Local Government Finances and Administration in Pakistan* (in two volumes), Research Report No. 72, Karachi, 1990.

Applied Economics Research Centre, *Resource Mobilization and Institutional Capacity* (in seven volumes), Research Report No. 85, Karachi, 1991.

Applied Economics Research Centre, *Resource Mobilization by Federal Government*, Research Report No. 91, Karachi, 1992.

Applied Economics Research Centre, *Resource Mobilization by Provincial and Local Governments in Pakistan*, Research Report No. 93, Karachi, 1992.

Applied Economics Research Centre, *Metropolitan Resource Generation Study*, Research Report No. 97, Karachi, 1993.

Arrow, Kenneth and M.J. Boskins (eds.), *The Economics of Public Debt*, Macmillan, London, 1988.

Asian Development Bank, *Strategies for Economic Growth and Development. The Bank's Role in Pakistan*, Manila, 1985.

Asian Development Report, *Pakistan Urban Sector Profile 1993*, Manila, 1993.

Banerji, D., 'Social and Cultural Foundations of Health Services Systems', *Economic and Political Weekly*, vol. 9, 1974.

Banuri, Tariq, 'Just Adjustment: Protecting the Vulnerable and Promoting Growth', *Pakistan Development Review*, vol. 31, no. 4, 1992.

Banuri, Tariq (ed.), *Economic Liberalization: No Panacea*, Clarendon Press, Oxford, 1992.

Banuri, Tariq (ed.), *Just Adjustment: Protecting the Vulnerable and Promoting Growth*, UNICEF, Islamabad, 1992.

Banuri, Tariq and Moazam Mahmood, 'Learning From Failure', in Banuri, Tariq, (ed.), *Just Adjustment: Protecting the Vulnerable and Promoting Growth*, UNICEF, Islamabad, 1992.

Banuri, Tariq and Juliet Schor, *Financial Openness and National Autonomy*, Oxford University Press, New York 1992.

Banuri, Tariq, *et al.*, 'Human Resource Development', in Banuri, Tariq (ed.), *Just Adjustment: Protecting the Vulnerable and Promoting Growth*, Oxford University Press, Karachi, 1998.

Behrman, J.R., 'Pakistan: Human Resource Development and Economic Growth into the Next Century', mimeo, 1995.

Belokrenitsky, Vyacheslav, *Capitalism in Pakistan: A History of Socioeconomic Development*, Patriot Publishers, New Delhi, 1991.

Blinder, A.S. and Robert Solow, *The Economics of Public Finance*, Brookings Institute, Washington, 1974.

Boskins, M.J., 'Concepts and Measures of Federal Deficits and Debt and their Impact on Economic Activity', in Arrow, Kenneth and M.J. Boskins (eds.), *The Economics of Public Debt*, Macmillan, London, 1988.

Buiter, Willem, *Principles of Budgetary and Financial Policy*, Harvester, Brighton, 1990.

Burki, Shahid Javed, 'The Development of Pakistan's Agriculture: An Interdisciplinary Explanation', in Stevens, Robert D., *et al.*, (eds.), *Rural Development in Bangladesh and Pakistan*, University Press of Hawaii, Honolulu, 1976.

Burki, Shahid Javed, *Pakistan Under Bhutto, 1971–77*, Macmillan, London, 1980.

Burki, Shahid Javed, 'A Historical Perspective on Development' in Burki, Shahid Javed and Robert Laporte, *Pakistan's Development Priorities: Choices for the Future*, Oxford

University Press, Karachi, 1984.

Burki, Shahid Javed, *Pakistan: A Nation in the Making*, Westview Press, Boulder, 1986.

Burki, Shahid Javed and Robert Laporte, *Pakistan's Development Priorities: Choices for the Future*, Oxford University Press, Karachi, 1984.

Cheema, Ali, 'Pakistan's Textile Policy and Trade Performance: 1972–1990', mimeo, Sidney Sussex College, Cambridge, 1995.

Cornia, Giovanni, 'Accelerating Human Development in Pakistan', in Banuri, Tariq (ed.), *Just Adjustment: Protecting the Vulnerable and Promoting Growth*, UNICEF, Islamabad, 1992.

de Tray, D., 'Comments', in Thomas, V., *et al.*, *Restructuring Economies in Distress*, Oxford University Press, New York, 1991.

Dreze, Jean and Haris Gazdar, 'Uttar Pradesh: The Burden of Inesha', mimeo, 1996.

Easterly, W. and K. Schmidt-Hebbel, 'The Macroeconomics of Public Sector Deficits: A Synthesis', World Bank Working Paper No. 775, Washington, 1992.

Easterly, W. and K. Schmidt-Hebbel, 'Fiscal Deficits and Macroeconomic Performance in Developing Countries', *World Bank Research Observer*, vol. 8, no. 2, 1993.

Eisner, Robert, 'Budget Deficits: Rhetoric and Reality', *Journal of Economic Perspectives*, vol. 3, no. 2, 1989.

Eisner, Robert, 'Sense and Nonsense about Budget Deficits', *Harvard Business Review*, May–June 1993.

Eisner, Robert and P.J. Piepper, 'Deficits, Monetary Policy and Real Economic Activity', in Arrow, Kenneth and M.J. Boskins (eds.), *The Economics of Public Debt*, Macmillan, London, 1988.

Faruqee, Rashid, 'Pakistan's Agricultural Sector: Is 3 to 4 per cent Annual Growth Sustainable?', World Bank Policy Research Working Paper No. 1407, Washington, 1995.

Ferreira, F., 'The World Bank and the Study of Stabilization and Structural Adjustment in LDCs', DEP No. 41, Development Economics Research Programme, STICERD, London School of Economics.

Gardezi, Hasan and Jamil Rashid (eds.), *Pakistan: The Roots of Dictatorship*, Zed Press, London, 1983.

Gazdar, Haris, *et al.*, 'A Profile of Poverty in Pakistan: Some Insights from Pakistan's Integrated Household Survey 1991', mimeo, 1996.

Gazdar, Haris, *et al.*, 'Recent Trends in Poverty in Pakistan', mimeo, 1996.

Ghaus, Aisha, 'Local Government Finances: Efficiency, Equity and Optimality', unpublished, Ph.D dissertation, University of Leeds, 1994.

Ghaus, Aisha and Mohammad Asif Iqbal, 'Resource Mobilization by Provincial Governments', *The News on Friday*, 25 August 1996.

Government of Pakistan, Agricultural Census Organization, *Pakistan Census of Agriculture, 1972*, Islamabad, 1976.

Government of Pakistan, Agricultural Census Organization, *Pakistan Census of Agriculture, 1980*, Islamabad, 1983.

Government of Pakistan, National Taxation Reforms Commission, *Final Report*, Islamabad, 1986.

Government of Pakistan, Ministry of Food and Agriculture,

Report of the National Commission on Agriculture, Islamabad, 1988.

Government of Pakistan, Planning Commission, *Eighth Five Year Plan (1993–8): Approach Paper*, Islamabad, 1991.

Government of Pakistan, Planning Commission, *Memorandum for the Pakistan Consortium, 1992–93*, Islamabad, 1992.

Government of Pakistan, Planning Commission, *Social Action Programme (SAP) 1992–95*, Islamabad, 1992.

Government of Pakistan, Planning Commission, *Pakistan Country Paper: World Summit for Social Development*, 1995.

Government of Pakistan, Planning Commission, *Social Action Programme, Report to the Pakistan Consortium, 1995–96*, Islamabad, 1995.

Government of Pakistan, *Pakistan Economic Survey*, various issues, Islamabad.

Gotsch, Carl H., 'Tractor Mechanization and Rural Development in Pakistan', in Ali, Karamat (ed.), *Pakistan: The Political Economy of Rural Development*, Vanguard, Lahore, 1986.

Habib, Irfan, *The Agrarian System of Mughal India*, Asia Publishing House, London, 1963.

Habib, Irfan, 'Potentialities of Capitalist Development in Mughal India', *Journal of Economic History*, vol. 29, no. 1, 1969.

Habib, Irfan, *Essays in Indian History: Towards a Marxist Perspective*, Tulika Publishers, New Delhi, 1995.

Halfani, M., *et al.*, 'Towards an Understanding of Governance: The Emergence of an Idea and its Implications for Urban Research in Developing Countries', mimeo, 1994.

Hamid, Naved and Akmal Hussain, 'Regional Inequalities and Capitalist Development: Pakistan's Experience', in Zaidi, S. Akbar (ed.), *Regional Imbalances and the National Question in Pakistan*, Vanguard, Lahore, 1992.

Haque, Nadeemul and Peter Montiel, 'The Macroeconomics of Public Sector Deficits: The Case of Pakistan', World Bank Working Paper No. 673, Washington, 1991.

Haque, Nadeemul and Shahid Kardar, 'The Development of Financial Markets in Pakistan', mimeo, 1993.

Hasan, Arif, *Seven Reports on Housing*, OPP-RTI, Karachi, 1992.

Hasan, Arif, 'The Unresolved Conflict', *DAWN*, Magazine, 13 March 1992.

Hasan, Arif and Ameneh Azam Ali, *Environmental Repercussions of Development in Pakistan*, OPP-RTI, Karachi, 1993.

Helleiner, G.K. *et al.*, 'IMF Adjustment Policies and Approaches and the Needs of Children, *World Development*, vol. 19, no. 12, 1991.

Hoeven, R. Van der, 'Adjustment with a Human Face: Still Relevant or Overtaken by Events?', *World Development*, vol. 19, no. 12, 1991.

Hughes, Alan and Ajit Singh, 'The World Economic Showdown and the Asian and Latin American Economies: A Comparative Analysis of Economic Structure, Policy and Performance', in Banuri, Tariq (ed.), *Economic Liberalization: No Panacea*, Clarendon Press, Oxford, 1992.

Hussain, Akmal, 'Technical Change and Social Polarization in Rural Punjab', in Ali, Karamat (ed.), *Pakistan: The Political Economy of Rural Development*, Vanguard, Lahore, 1986.

Hussain, Akmal, 'Land Reforms in Pakistan', in Hussain,

Akmal, *Strategic Issues in Pakistan's Economic Policy*, Progressive Publishers, Lahore, 1988.

Hussain, Akmal, *Strategic Issues in Pakistan's Economic Policy*, Progressive Publishers, Lahore, 1988.

Ihori, I., 'Debt Burden and Intergeneration Equity', in Arrow, Kenneth and M.J. Boskins (eds.), *The Economics of Public Debt*, Macmillan, London, 1988.

Institute of Developing Economies, *The Study on Japanese Cooperation in Industrial Policy for Developing Economies: Pakistan*, Tokyo, 1994.

Institute of Development Studies, 'The Political Analysis of Markets', *IDS Bulletin*, vol. 24, no. 3, 1993.

Iqbal, Mohammad Asif and N. Ahmed, 'A Review of the Social Action Programme,' in Social Policy and Development Centre, *Provincial Governments and the Social Sectors*, Karachi, 1995.

Islam, Nazrul and M.M. Khan (eds.), *Urban Governance in Bangladesh and Pakistan*, Centre for Urban Studies, University of Dhaka, Dhaka, 1997.

IUCN, *The Pakistan National Conservation Strategy*, Karachi, 1992.

Jalal, Ayesha, *The State of Martial Rule: The Origins of Pakistan's Political Economy of Defence*, Cambridge University Press, Cambridge, 1991.

Karachi Chamber of Commerce and Industry (KCCI), *Proceedings of the Seminar on Reducing Fiscal Deficit – Key to Salvage Economy*, Karachi, 1994.

Kardar, Shahid, 'Polarization in the Regions and Prospects for Integration', in Zaidi, S. Akbar (ed.), *Regional Imbalances and the National Question in Pakistan*, Vanguard, Lahore, 1992.

Kemal, A.R., 'An Analysis of Industrial Efficiency in Pakistan: 1959–60 to 1969–70', unpublished Ph.D dissertation, University of Manchester, 1978.

Kemal, A.R., 'Structural Adjustment, Employment, Income Distribution, and Poverty', *Pakistan Development Review*, vol. 33, no. 4, 1995.

Kemal, A.R. and Moazam Mahmood, 'Poverty and Policy in Pakistan', in Banuri, Tariq (ed.), *Just Adjustment: Protecting the Vulnerable and Promoting Growth*, UNICEF, Islamabad, 1992.

Khan, Mahmood Hasan, *Underdevelopment and Agrarian Structure in Pakistan*, Westview Press, Boulder, 1981.

Khan, Mahmood Hasan, *Lectures on Agrarian Transformation in Pakistan*, PIDE, Islamabad, 1985.

Khan, Mahmood Hasan, 'Classes and Agrarian Transition in Pakistan', in Karamat, Ali (ed.), *Pakistan: The Political Economy of Rural Development*, Vanguard, Lahore, 1986.

Khan, M.M., 'Governance: A Conceptual Framework', mimeo, Global Urban Research Initiative, Centre for Urban Studies, Department of Geography, University of Dhaka, Dhaka, Bangladesh, not dated.

Khan, Mohsin S., 'The Macroeconomic Effects of Fund-Supported Adjustment Programmes', *IMF Staff Papers*, vol. 37, no. 2, June 1990.

Khan, Mohsin S., 'Comments', in Thomas, V., *et al.*, *Restructuring Economies in Distress*, Oxford University Press, New York, 1991.

Khan, Shahrukh Rafi, 'Do IMF and World Bank Policies Work?', Sustainable Development Policy Institute, Monograph No. 6, Islamabad, 1997.

Khuhro, Hameeda (ed.), *Karachi: Megacity of Our Times*, Oxford University Press, Karachi, 1997.

Kochanek, Stanley, *Interest Groups and Development*, Vanguard, Lahore, 1984.

Leftwich, A., 'Governance, Democracy and Development in the Third World', *Third World Quarterly*, vol. 14, no. 3, 1993.

Lewis, Stephen, *Economic Policy and Industrial Growth in Pakistan*, George Allen and Unwin, London, 1969.

Lewis, Stephen, *Pakistan: Industrialization and Trade Policies*, George Allen and Unwin, London, 1970.

McCarney, Patricia, L. (ed.), *Cities and Governance: New Directions in Latin America, Asia and Africa*, Centre for Urban and Community Studies, University of Toronto, 1996.

McCarney, Patricia, L. (ed.), *The Changing Nature of Local Government in Developing Countries*, Centre for Urban and Community Studies, University of Toronto, 1996.

McCleary, William, 'Pakistan: Structural Adjustment and Economic Growth', in Thomas, V., *et al.*, *Restructuring Economies in Distress*, Oxford University Press, New York, 1991.

McEachern, Doug, 'Capitalism and Colonial Production: An Introduction', in Alavi, Hamza, *et al.*, *Capitalism and Colonial Production*, Croom Helm, London, 1982.

Mahmood, Moazam, 'The Pattern of Adoption of Green Revolution Technology and its Effect on Landholdings in the Punjab', in Karamat, Ali (ed.), *Pakistan: The Political Economy of Rural Development*, Vanguard, Lahore, 1986.

Marx, Karl, *On Colonialism*, Foreign Language Publishing House, Moscow, 1960.

Mehar, A.K., 'A Forecasting Model of Public Finance: An Experience from the Pakistani Economy', unpublished M.Phil thesis, Applied Economics Research Centre, Karachi, 1992.

Meenai, S.A., *Money and Banking in Pakistan*, Oxford University Press, Karachi, 1984.

Mumtaz, Khawar, 'NGOs in Pakistan: An Overview', in Banuri, Tariq (ed.), *Just Adjustment: Protecting the Vulnerable and Promoting Growth*, UNICEF, Islamabad, 1992.

Nabi, Ijaz, *Entrepreneurs and Markets in Early Industrialization: A Case Study From Pakistan*, International Center for Economic Growth, San Francisco, 1988.

Nabi, Ijaz and Naved Hamid, 'The Aid Partnership in Pakistan', in Lele, M. and Ijaz Nabi, *Transition in Development: The Role of Aid and Commercial Flows*, ICEG, San Francisco, 1991, p. 53.

Nadvi, Khalid, *Employment Creation in Urban Micro-Enterprises in the Manufacturing Sector in Pakistan*, ILO/ARTEP, Bangkok, 1990.

Naqvi, S.N.H. and A.R. Kemal, 'The Privatization of the Public Industrial Enterprise in Pakistan', *Pakistan Development Review*, vol. 30, no. 2, 1991.

Naqvi, S.N.H. and Khwaja Sarmad, *Pakistan's Economy Through the Seventies*, PIDE, Islamabad, 1984.

Naqvi, S.N.H. and Khwaja Sarmad, *External Shocks and Domestic Adjustment: Pakistan's Case 1970-1990*, General Monograph No. 1, University Grants Commission, Islamabad, 1993.

Nasim, Anjum (ed.), *Financing Pakistan's Development in the 1990s*, Oxford University Press, Karachi, 1992.

Nasim, Anjum and Asya Akhlaque, 'Agriculture Taxation and Subsidies', in Nasim, Anjum (ed.), *Financing Pakistan's Development in the 1990s*, Oxford University Press, Karachi, 1992.

National Development Finance Corporation, *Research Report*, Financial Liberalisation Series, Karachi, 1993.

National Institute of Population Studies, *Pakistan Demography and Health Survey 1990/1991*, Islamabad, 1992.

Noman, Akbar, 'Industrialization in Pakistan: An Assessment and an Agenda', paper presented at the Seventh Annual General Meeting of the Pakistan Society of Development Economics, Islamabad, 1991.

Noman, Omar, *The Political Economy of Pakistan: 1947–85*, KPI, London, 1988.

Papanek, Gustav, *Pakistan's Development: Social Goals and Private Incentives*, Harvard University Press, Cambridge, Mass., 1967.

Pasha, Hafiz A., 'Is the Social Action Programme Financially Sustainable?', Social Policy and Development Centre, *Provincial Governments and the Social Sectors*, Karachi, 1995.

Pasha, Hafiz A., 'Political Economy of Tax Reforms: The Pakistan Experience', *Pakistan Journal of Applied Economics*, vol. 11, nos. 1 and 2, 1995.

Pasha, Hafiz A. and Mohammad Akbar, 'IMF Conditionalities and Structural Adjustments in Public Finances', *Pakistan Economic and Social Review*, 1993.

Pasha, Hafiz A. and M. Asif Iqbal, 'Taxation Reforms in Pakistan', *Pakistan Journal of Applied Economics*, vol. 10, nos. 1 and 2, 1994.

Pasha, Hafiz A., *et al.*, 'The Changing Profile of Regional Development in Pakistan', *Pakistan Journal of Applied Economics*, vol. 9, no. 1, 1990.

Patnaik, Prabhat, 'International Capital and National Economic Policy: A Critique of India's Reforms', *Economic and Political Weekly*, vol. 29, no. 12, 1994.

Patnaik, Prabhat and C.P. Chandrasekhar, 'Indian Economy Under "Structural Adjustment"', *Economic and Political Weekly*, vol. 30, no. 47, 1995.

Platteau, J.-Ph., 'Formalization and Privatization of Land Rights in Sub-Saharan Africa: A Critique of Current Orthodoxies and Structural Adjustment Programmes', DEP No. 34, Development Economics Research Programme, STICERD, London School of Economics, 1992.

Reed, David, *Structural Adjustment and the Environment*, Westview Press, Boulder, 1992.

Riazuddin, Riaz, 'An Evaluation of Trade Policy', *Pakistan Journal of Applied Economics*, vol. 10, nos. 1 and 2, 1994.

Sakr, Khalid, 'Developments of Private Investment in Pakistan', IMF Working Paper, 1993.

Salop, J., 'Reducing Poverty: Spreading the Word', *Finance and Development*, December 1992.

Sanderatne, Nirmal, 'Landowners and Land Reforms in Pakistan', in Karamat, Ali (ed.), *Pakistan: The Political Economy of Rural Development*, Vanguard, Lahore, 1986.

Sayeed, Asad, 'Political Alignments, the State and Industrial Policy in Pakistan: A Comparison of Performance in the 1960s and 1980s', unpublished Ph.D dissertation, University of Cambridge, 1995.

Sayeed, Asad, 'Social Sector Development and the Social Summit', mimeo, Social Policy and Development Centre, Karachi, 1996.

Sayeed, Asad and Aisha Ghaus, 'Has Poverty Returned to Pakistan?', mimeo, Social Policy and Development Centre, Karachi, 1996.

Sayeed, Khalid bin, *Pakistan: The Formative Phase, 1857–1948*, Oxford University Press, Karachi, 1978.

Sayeed, Khalid bin, *Politics in Pakistan: The Nature and Direction of Change*, Praeger, New York, 1980.

Senses, F., 'Turkey's Stabilization and Structural Adjustment Programme in Retrospect and Prospect', *The Developing Economies*, vol. 29, no. 3, 1991.

Social Policy and Development Centre, *User Charges in Education*, Karachi, 1994.

Social Policy and Development Centre, *Provincial Governments and the Social Sectors*, Karachi, 1995.

State Bank of Pakistan, *History of the State Bank of Pakistan, 1948–60*, Karachi, 1992.

State Bank of Pakistan, *History of the State Bank of Pakistan, 1961–77*, Karachi, 1994.

State Bank of Pakistan, *Rural Financial Market Studies: Phase 1*, Karachi, 1994.

Stevens, Robert D., *et al.*, (eds.), *Rural Development in Bangladesh and Pakistan*, University Press of Hawaii, Honolulu, 1976.

Stewart, Francis, 'The Many Faces of Adjustment', *World Development*, vol. 19, no. 12, 1991.

Thomas, V., *et al.*, *Restructuring Economies in Distress*, Oxford University Press, New York, 1991.

Tobin, James, *Asset Accumulation and Economic Activity*, Blackwell, Oxford, 1980.

Tobin, James, *Policies for Prosperity: Essays in a Keynesian Mode*, Wheatsheaf, Brighton, England, 1987.

Tybout, J.R., 'Industrial Performance: Some Stylized Facts', in Thomas, V., *et al.*, *Restructuring Economies in Distress*, Oxford University Press, New York, 1991.

UNDP, *Human Development Report*, various years, Oxford University Press, New York, 1995.

UNIDO, *Pakistan: Towards Industrialization and Revitalization*, Blackwell, Oxford, 1990.

Veltmeyer, V., 'Liberalization and Structural Adjustment in Latin America: In Search of an Alternative', *Economic and Political Weekly*, vol. 28, no. 39, 1993.

Waseem, Mohammad, *Politics and the State in Pakistan*, Progressive Publishers, Lahore, 1989.

Weiss, Anita, *Culture, Class and Development in Pakistan: The Emergence of an Indigenous Bourgeoisie in Punjab*, Vanguard, Lahore, 1991.

White, L., *Industrial Concentration and Economic Power in Pakistan*, Princeton University Press, Princeton, 1974.

World Bank, *Pakistan: Health Sector Report*, Washington, 1983.

World Bank, *Pakistan: Growth Through Adjustment*, Report No. 7118-Pak, Washington, 1988.

World Bank, *Women in Pakistan: An Economic and Social Strategy*, Washington, 1989.

World Bank, *Towards a Social Action Program for Pakistan:*

Impediments to Progress and Options for Reform, Report No. 9619-Pak, Washington, 1991.

World Bank, *Changes in Trade and Domestic Taxation for Reform of the Incentive Regime and Fiscal Adjustment*, Report No. 9828-Pak, Washington, 1992.

World Bank, *Governance and Development*, Washington, 1992.

World Bank, *Pakistan: Country Economic Memorandum FY931*, Report No. 11590-Pak, Washington, 1993.

World Bank, *Staff Appraisal Report: Social Action Program Project*, Report No. 12588-Pak, 1994.

World Bank, *Pakistan: Poverty Assessment*, Report No. 14397-Pak, 1995.

World Bank, *Pakistan: Rural Finance for Growth and Poverty Alleviation*, Washington, 1995.

World Bank, *Staff Appraisal Report: Pakistan Population Welfare Program Project*, Report No. 13611-Pak, 1995.

World Bank, *World Development Report*, various years, Oxford University Press, Washington.

Zaidi, S. Akbar, 'How the Bourgeoisie Views Pakistan', *Economic and Political Weekly*, vol. 23, no. 48, 1988.

Zaidi, S. Akbar, *The Political Economy of Health Care in Pakistan*, Vanguard, Lahore, 1988.

Zaidi, S. Akbar, 'Effective Local Level Delivery of Human Resources: Development Related Programmes – The Case of Pakistan', mimeo, UNESCAP, Bangkok, 1991.

Zaidi, S. Akbar, 'Sindhi vs Mohajir: Contradiction, Conflict, Compromise', *Economic and Political Weekly*, vol. 26, no. 28, 1991.

Zaidi, S. Akbar (ed.), *Regional Imbalances and the National Question in Pakistan*, Vanguard, Lahore, 1992.

Zaidi, S. Akbar, 'The Roots of the Crisis', *The Herald*, Karachi, August 1992.

Zaidi, S. Akbar, 'A Study on Making Optimal Use of Municipal Budgets to Finance Child Development (Pakistan)', mimeo, UNICEF, Karachi, 1994.

Zaidi, S. Akbar, 'Pakistan's Economy in Deep Crises', *Economic and Political Weekly*, vol. 29, no. 28, 1994.

Zaidi, S. Akbar, 'Planning in the Health Sector: For Whom, by Whom?', *Social Science and Medicine*, vol. 39, no. 9, 1994.

Zaidi, S. Akbar, 'The Structural Adjustment Programme and Pakistan: External Influence or Internal Acquiescence?', *Pakistan Journal of Applied Economics*, vol. 10, nos. 1 and 2, 1994.

Zaidi, S. Akbar, 'Locating the Budget Deficit in Context: The Case of Pakistan', *Pakistan Journal of Applied Economics*, vol. 11, nos. 1 and 2, 1995.

Zaidi, S. Akbar, 'An Evaluation of Community Participation and NGO Capability in the Rural Water Supply Sector', mimeo, Social Policy and Development Centre, Karachi, 1996.

Zaidi, S. Akbar, 'Gender Perspectives and Quality of Care in Underdeveloped Countries: Disease, Gender and Contextuality', *Social Science and Medicine*, vol. 43, no. 5, 1996.

Zaidi, S. Akbar, 'Urban Local Government in Pakistan: Expecting Too Much from Too Little?', *Economic and Political Weekly*, vol. 31, no. 44, 1996.

Zaidi, S. Akbar, 'Karachi: Prospects for the Future', in Khuhro, Hameeda (ed.), *Karachi: Megacity of Our Times*, Oxford University Press, Karachi, 1997.

Zaidi, S. Akbar, 'NGO Failure and the Need to Bring Back the State', in Zaidi, S. Akbar, *The New Development Paradigm: Papers on Institutions, NGOs, Gender and Local Government*, Oxford University Press, Karachi, forthcoming, 1999.

Zaidi, S. Akbar, 'Poverty, Politics, Institutions: The Case of Karachi', *Economic and Political Weekly*, vol. 32, no. 51, 1997.

Zaidi, S. Akbar, 'Urban Local Governance in Pakistan', in Islam, Nazrul and M.M. Khan (eds.), *Urban Governance in Bangladesh and Pakistan*, Centre for Urban Studies, University of Dhaka, Dhaka, 1997.

Zaidi, S. Akbar, 'Crisis of Governance', *Economic and Political Weekly*, vol. 33, no. 11, 1998.

Zaidi, S. Akbar, *The New Development Paradigm: Papers on Institutions, NGOs, Gender and Local Government*, Oxford University Press, Karachi, forthcoming, 1999.

Zaman, Arshad, 'Sustainable Development, Poverty and Policy Adjustments: Linkages and Levers of Change', mimeo, International Institute of Sustainable Development, 1993.

Zaman, Arshad, 'The Government's Present Agreement with the IMF: Misgovernment or Folly?', *Pakistan Journal of Applied Economics*, vol. 11, nos. 1 and 2, 1995.

Ziring, Lawrence, *The Ayub Khan Era: Politics in Pakistan, 1958–1969*, Syracuse University Press, 1971.

Zuckerman, E., 'The Social Cost of Adjustment', in Thomas, V., *et al.*, *Restructuring Economies in Distress*, Oxford University Press, New York, 1991.

Index

Index entries are arranged in word-by-word order. Page numbers given in bold refer to subject matter in boxes while those given in italics refer to appendices.